Asia's New Regionalism

Ellen L. Frost

LYNNE
RIENNER
PUBLISHERS

BOULDER
LONDON

Published in the United States of America in 2008 by
Lynne Rienner Publishers, Inc.
1800 30th Street, Boulder, Colorado 80301
www.rienner.com

and in the United Kingdom by
Lynne Rienner Publishers, Inc.
3 Henrietta Street, Covent Garden, London WC2E 8LU

Library of Congress Cataloging-in-Publication Data
Frost, Ellen L.
   Asia's new regionalism / Ellen L. Frost.
     p. cm.
   Includes bibliographical references and index.
   ISBN 978-1-58826-554-8 (hardcover : alk. paper)
   ISBN 978-1-58826-579-1 (pbk. : alk. paper)
   1. Regionalism—Asia. 2. Asian cooperation. 3. Asia—Economic
integration. 4. Globalization—Economic aspects—Asia. 5. Asia—Economic
conditions—1945– 6. Asia—Politics and government—1945– I. Title.
HC412.F74 2008
337.1'5—dc22

                                           2007031851

British Cataloguing in Publication Data
A Cataloguing in Publication record for this book
is available from the British Library.

Printed and bound in the United States of America

∞ The paper used in this publication meets the requirements
of the American National Standard for Permanence of
Paper for Printed Library Materials Z39.48-1992.

5 4 3 2 1

Contents

Preface

I wrote this book in the spirit of adventure. I wanted to take one aspect of a vitally important subject—essentially, Asia's future as a region and its contribution to world order—and make it interesting to both experts and generalists.

The goals of this book are to describe, explain, measure, evaluate, and convey the significance of contemporary Asian regionalism. I began by shaking up the topic, so to speak, to see what fell out. I plunged into research on Asia from a variety of intellectual disciplines, including history, geography, political science, economics, sociology, security studies, travel books, and literature. For comparative perspective, I dipped into studies of European and North American integration and their role in world order. I cannot say that I did full justice to existing scholarship, because doing so would occupy several lifetimes. Nevertheless, I believe that my interdisciplinary approach, especially my focus on maritime issues, uncovered interesting linkages and paradoxes overlooked by most other analysts.

"Imagination labors best in distant fields," said Mark Twain wryly, poking fun at "experts" who pretend to know a lot but are completely wrong. Despite the great distance that separates me from Asian fields, I believe that I have captured some essential truths about Asian integration that conventional assessments overlook. I hope that this book motivates others to travel around Asia and test my conclusions more rigorously. Even if those conclusions prove to be faulty, I like to think that my errors will stimulate experts to bridge the disciplinary divide, broaden their geographic vision, explore new ideas, and open new avenues of field work.

I did not, however, write this book only for experts. Policymakers and opinion leaders in the United States and elsewhere need to learn more about Asia. The apparent budding of Asian integration and China's role within it should interest not only foreign policy experts but also all those who seek to understand history and world affairs. But as anyone who specializes in Asian affairs will confirm, even Westerners with some understanding of international affairs tend to treat Asia as an inaccessible and exotic domain, an intellectual conversation-stopper. Although Asia is on a different trajectory from Europe, it is not beyond comprehension. I hope that my book encourages Western readers to learn more about this important region.

Some Asian readers may question the judgments I have reached and the Western perspectives I undoubtedly bring to bear on them. I fully respect cultural, linguistic, and historical differences and have studied several of them in some depth. Sensitivity to such factors and awareness of one's own assumptions and mental structure ought to be in the toolkit of every social scientist. I tried hard to understand how Asians view the prospect of closer integration, not just how it appears through North American eyes. I strongly hope that what I have to say about it is relevant and useful to them.

Any summary evaluation of the Asian integration movement risks diverting attention from the multiple complexities of the region. Each country is different. Each leader is different. Each bilateral relationship is different. China, Japan, South Korea, Australia, and New Zealand are all members of what I call Asia Major, but each is unique. Even the five founders of the Association of Southeast Asian Nations (the ASEAN 5), presented as a core actor throughout much of this book, do not constitute a hub but a cluster. As of 2007, for example, Thailand was under interim military rule, the Philippines was suffering from yet another political crisis, and Malaysia's former prime minister Mahathir was bitterly bombarding his successor. Fragile, far-flung, democratic Indonesia and rock-ribbed, compact, authoritarian Singapore made odd bedfellows as Southeast Asia's most stable leaders, and in 2007 even those two were sparring over trade in sand (for concrete), an extradition treaty, a security agreement, and various environmental issues.

*   *   *

I am profoundly grateful to the Smith Richardson Foundation for its generous support of this book and to its program officer, Allan Song. My sponsoring institution was the Peter G. Peterson Institute for International Economics, where I am a visiting fellow. C. Fred Bergsten, the institute's energetic and creative director, has long experience in the field of Asian and transpacific economic integration. For me he is a mentor and stimulating critic.

I also owe thanks to the US-Indonesia Society, which funded my expenses during a very useful four-day visit to Indonesia. The Institute for Southeast Asian Studies in Singapore invited me to chair a session at their 2005 conference on Asia's regional outlook, where I made many useful contacts. The Atlantic Council of the United States helped me fill an important gap by inviting me to participate in a series of high-level conversations in Taipei. During my visits to Japan and Australia, I received excellent support from US embassy and consulate staff.

I acknowledge with pleasure all the individuals who helped me along the way. Richard Ellings of the National Bureau of Asian Research got me started by inviting me to write a chapter on economic integration for *Strategic Asia 2003–04*. Banning Garrett introduced me to the Smith Richardson Foundation and encouraged me to apply for a grant. T. J. Pempel, a pioneering expert on East Asian regionalism, welcomed me into the field, alerted me to his relevant writings, and offered help at several key moments.

Readers who waded through an early manuscript pointed out omissions and structural flaws and offered helpful ideas on how to fix them. They included I. M. Destler, Gary Clyde Hufbauer, Jacob Kirkegaard, Bronson Percival, Teresita Schaffer, and Amy Searight. I owe special thanks to Phillip Saunders of the National Defense University's Institute for National Strategic Studies, who not only caught errors and brought related research to my attention, but also wrote a long commentary that helped me focus and tighten my analysis. His knowledge, carefully reasoned insights, thorough research, and thoughtful perspectives added substance to my thinking and continue to set a high standard.

Two anonymous reviewers wrote long, constructive appraisals of a subsequent draft and suggested a number of improvements. Peter Katzenstein reviewed my bibliography and kindly shared the manuscript of his book *A World of Regions* well before it was published. William Grimes gave me helpful guidance on financial integration initiatives. At the Peterson Institute for International Economics, Evan Gill walked me through the mysteries of computerized graphics, and Gary Clyde Hufbauer and Jisun Kim shared their data on the overlapping coverage of Asian trade agreements. In Hawaii, Leif Rosenberger and his assistant, Major Miemie Byrd, set up very useful interviews at the US Pacific Command in Honolulu. Richard Baker and Lieutenant Colonel Frederick Anthony did the same at the East-West Center and the Asia-Pacific Center for Security Studies, respectively.

In Asia, many people commented helpfully on my then inchoate ideas. Hadi Soesastro organized a stimulating group discussion at the Centre for Strategic and International Studies in Jakarta. Umar Hadi kindly arranged a fruitful meeting with Indonesian foreign minister Hassan Wirajuda. I also owe thanks to Ali Alatas, Mohamed Ariff, Barry Desker, Ralf Emmers, Evelyn Goh, Tatik Hafidz, Kenichi Ito, Tommy Koh, Naoko Munakata, John Ravenhill, Dennis Rumley, Takashi Shiraishi, Soemadi D. M. Brotodiningrat, the late Noordin Sopiee, R. M. Sunardi, M. Supperamaniam, Augustine Tan, Jusuf Wanandi, Wang Gungwu, Yeo Lay Hwee, Zakaria Ahmad, and Zhang Yunling, all of whom deepened my understanding of Asian regionalism from various non-US perspectives. In Brussels, Willem van der Geest of the European Institute for Asian Studies and Alex Berkofsky of the European

Policy Center summarized various European perspectives, shared their own views, and directed me to several useful publications.

My husband, Bill Pedersen, plowed through not one but two versions of the entire manuscript. His lawyerly eye, structural editing, and detailed comments led me to clarify and tighten my argument, omit vague or inaccurate wording, and bring into sharper focus what I was trying to say. I am very grateful for his help as well as for his unflagging support during the three years I spent on this project.

Working with Lynne Rienner Publishers was a pleasure. Marilyn Grobschmidt guided me through the initial stages of the project with professionalism and grace. Shena Redmond and Dorothy Brandt corrected my numerous errors and put the manuscript into publishable form. Their enthusiasm about the book inspired me to do my best.

I fear, however, that my reach may have exceeded my grasp. Any remaining errors, creative or harebrained, are entirely mine.

—Ellen L. Frost

1

Asia's New Momentum

Something significant is pulsing through Asia. Not for centuries has that region been so fluid, so open, so cosmopolitan. Never has communication been so inexpensive and widely available, nor transport so rapid and efficient. Cross-border business—old and new, legal and illegal—flourishes. Newly laid roads connect megacities with spanking new suburbs and chockablock shanties. Integrated production networks span far-flung manufacturing hubs. Sleepy ports lined with tumbledown warehouses are waking up, and airlines offer a starburst of new routes. City and local governments are setting up new offices to handle record numbers of tourists and entrepreneurs. Environmental, health, and human rights groups are forming information networks and patchy cross-border coalitions. Sensing new prey, transnational criminal gangs have stepped up their activity.

Nowhere is this regional pulse more palpable than in what I call Maritime Asia, the vast sweep of coastline and water connecting central and southern India, Southeast Asia, China, the Korean peninsula, Japan, Australia, and New Zealand. In maritime communities, integration is spontaneous and tangible. A visitor to Asia's major ports and coastal communities is likely to jostle against people from all over the region: a Malaysian official, an Indian engineer, a Chinese tourist, a Japanese banker, a Filipino bar hostess, a Korean professor, and an Indonesian businessman, perhaps. Most of them carry cellular telephones equipped with the latest devices and talk on them frequently—often in English, the region's lingua franca. The visitor's day might include a dim sum lunch, a stroll along a waterfront packed with cargo ships, a shopping trip to a mall packed with Asian products, a sushi dinner, and a Bollywood film. Westerners, no longer stared at, are lost in the crowd.

This quickening to life is highly uneven. In Asia's remote rice paddies and dry plains, in the highlands and hill country, in the more distant islands of the archipelagos, in countless villages and small towns, lies a slow-moving, more

1

isolated, less cosmopolitan Asia. Foreign visitors are rare. Nevertheless, in local markets one might find "Hello Kitty" dolls, American T-shirts made in China, and pirated CDs featuring a Korean pop singer.[1] The sons of the wealthiest families in Cambodia ride Honda motorcycles imported from Vietnam and wear trendy clothes copied from Japanese fashions. A customer in Sri Lanka was amused to spot a can labeled "Mongolian Seafood," because Mongolia is landlocked; the contents were processed in Malaysia.[2]

Meanwhile, Asian government officials are promoting a different version of integration. Motivated primarily by reasons of state, members of the ten-nation Association of Southeast Asian Nations (ASEAN 10) are the drivers of this new movement. They have spun a series of concentric organizational circles dedicated to closer integration and what they call "community building." This activity is the chief expression of Asia's new regionalism.

The innermost circle is ASEAN itself. Founded in 1967 by Indonesia, Malaysia, the Philippines, Singapore, and Thailand, ASEAN was originally designed as an anticommunist organization. Since then it has transformed itself into a cooperative grouping with numerous committees and working groups. In addition to the original ASEAN 5, it now includes Brunei, Cambodia, Laos, Myanmar (Burma),[3] and Vietnam. ASEAN leaders have pledged themselves to an ASEAN Community resting on three pillars: economic, security, and sociocultural.[4]

The next circle is ASEAN + 3—ASEAN plus Japan, China, and South Korea (but not Taiwan or Hong Kong). This grouping periodically heralds the formation of an East Asian Community as a long-term goal. Meanwhile, India knocks, welcomed by some but judged by others to have shown up too soon or to be unwelcome for political reasons. India, Australia, and New Zealand are members of a wider circle, the East Asian Summit grouping, first convened in December 2005 and meeting annually thereafter. Movement within these circles bends and shapes itself around various gaps and roadblocks but continues on, however slowly.

The bureaucratic process fleshing out this so-called community building generates literally hundreds of meetings a year. ASEAN + 3 alone has spawned some four dozen committees and working groups. The ASEAN secretariat has established a unit dedicated to ASEAN + 3 to coordinate it all. ASEAN has also established "dialogue partner" relationships with India, Australia, New Zealand, and Russia, among others, and each of these links creates its own cascade of meetings. In a parallel but separate series of meetings known as Track 2, Asian intellectuals, business leaders, journalists, and other elites flock to conferences and workshops to discuss the advantages and modalities of integration.[5] Some participants are genuinely independent, but others, handpicked by suspicious governments, echo the policies of their rulers or remain silent.

ASEAN is at the forefront of this activity. A core paradox of Asia's new regionalism is that leaders of four or five Southeast Asian nations, acting in the name of ASEAN and with the acquiescence of ASEAN's other members, control the basic tone, scope, speed, and direction of the integration movement. ASEAN is more accurately described as a cluster or grouping than as a coherent political organization. Compared to China, Japan, and India, ASEAN is extremely weak, but its very weakness makes it the least distrusted. Under its roof some very creative diplomacy is taking place.

◼ Rhetoric or Reality?

Does all this buzz and hum add up to the first rumblings of genuine political integration? Are we witnessing a defining moment in history when the vision of a regional community begins to crystallize into sustainable, institutionalized cooperation? Or is the new regionalism just rhetoric, trumpeted by political leaders to hide tense and prickly politics and warmed-over historical disputes?

The momentum of Asian regionalism is real and irreversible, say its partisans. Although integration will remain loose and largely informal for the indefinite future, the political will to create a meaningful community of some kind now exists. What Westerners dismiss as a "talk shop" is laying a foundation for progressively closer ties.[6] Moreover, Asian integration contributes to peace, prosperity, and progress. There has been no armed conflict between members of ASEAN since its formation in 1967;[7] community building will extend this zone of peace. The integration movement engages a rising China and exerts collective pressure on both Japan and China to handle their quarrels with restraint. Efforts to deepen market integration may produce tariff adjustments that favor Asians over non-Asians, but that is no worse than the North American Free Trade Agreement (NAFTA) or the European Union (EU). Asians need a robust US presence and have no intention of expelling the United States from Asia. The combination of the US market and US security guarantees are so important to Asians that Americans will remain fully engaged, whether or not Washington has a seat at the table. Asian integration is therefore both real and a good thing.

Not so, reply the skeptics. Asian regionalism and community building are mostly talk. Too many divisions roil the region, and nationalism is on the rise. Japan has difficulty getting along with China and South Korea. Distances, both cultural and geographic, are too great. Integration is not sustainable unless it relies on enforceable rules with timetables and penalties, but these are unlikely to be adopted without wide-open escape clauses. Besides, Asian interests are global, not narrowly regional. Asians are trading, investing, and bonding not only with each other but also with their counterparts around the world. Any "community" that excludes the United States, a giant market and by far the most powerful military power in Asia, will not serve Asians well. Asians need the United States as a benign balancer. India is eager to take part in Asian integration but has such a long way to go that it will be decades, if ever, before New Delhi can play a major balancing role. China practices "integration diplomacy" but does not take the vision of integration as anything more than an opportunity to win friends, reduce US influence, and overshadow Japan. Asian integration is nowhere in sight, but if it were, it would not be a good thing.

So who is right? The two sides may be talking past each other because they are talking about different things. Doing justice to both sides in this somewhat airless debate requires both objective analysis and intuitive understanding.

The Asian integration movement is an experiment reflecting far-reaching political and economic shifts. It is partly a natural outgrowth of globalization and partly an artificial construct reflecting conscious strategic judgments in key Asian capitals. On the surface it is all about Asian harmony, and it muffles numerous bilateral tensions with cottony rhetoric and backroom mediation. But it also shelters a trilogy of dramas—the resurgence of China, Asian reactions, and the future role of the United States. How Asia's new regionalism evolves will thus have huge bearing on regional stability and prosperity and may well have implications for the way the rest of the world governs itself.

■ Why Asia Matters

Why does it matter how Asians design their bonds with each other and what they achieve?

The simplest answer is that any major new trend in Asia is worth knowing about, because Asia is relevant to just about any challenge that a concerned citizen of the twenty-first century can dream up. Asia matters because of its size, population, economic dynamism, demand for energy, the presence of a rising power, residual military threats, the struggle for democracy, and a variety of nontraditional threats ranging from separatist movements, religious agitation, and criminal activity to environmental pollution and disease.

First, Asia is big. Flying from Tokyo to Jakarta takes most of a working day; from Madrid, a similar flight over Europe would land the traveler in Kazakhstan. The world's largest landmass contains the world's highest mountains and largest cities.[8] Four of the world's seven largest islands lie just off the coast.[9]

Second, Asia is home to half the world's population. It houses more than a billion Chinese and Indians each and contains more than half of the world's population between the ages of fifteen and twenty-four. It has more Muslims than all Middle Eastern countries combined. Its languages and cultures are rich and highly diverse. Demographically, Asia has it all: youth bulges, graying populations, high birthrates, low birthrates, and bride shortages.

Third, Asia is economically dynamic. Alone among world regions, it features growth rates that approach and occasionally exceed double digits. Most governments have embraced privatization, free enterprise, and openness to trade and investment. Jobs are being created faster than they are disappearing. Highly globalized, Asia now boasts world-class manufacturing hubs, research facilities, financial centers, and transportation networks. It has accumulated two-thirds of the world's foreign exchange reserves; China's hoard alone is in the neighborhood of $1 trillion. Not counting Japan, East Asia's real per capita annual income quadrupled in the last forty years or so to more than $7,000. Although some areas remain very poor, tens of millions of people have been lifted out of absolute poverty. Hundreds of millions enjoy middle-class status or higher.

This growth has turned Asia into a hub of global commerce, especially seaborne trade. The region is dotted with large ports and awash with sea lanes. About 90 percent of world trade moves by ship, of which about 70 percent is in containers; Singapore and Hong Kong are the world's busiest cargo and container handling ports, respectively. Some 55,000–60,000 commercial vessels traverse the strategically vital Strait of Malacca each year. They carry more than a third of the world's shipping trade and half of its crude oil shipments, including about 70 percent of Japan's oil. Asia is also the most important source of global electronics exports, which fuel productivity and efficiency and link people everywhere through information and communication devices.

Fourth, feeding Asia's boom requires large supplies of energy. Asia's hunger for energy, particularly in the transport sector, has already heated up the world's oil and gas markets. It is estimated that fueling growth in China and other rapidly growing Asian countries in the next fifteen to twenty years will require an additional volume of oil equivalent to the current output of the entire Persian Gulf.[10]

Fifth, a new power—China—is arising in Asia, altering the regional and global order. The rise of Germany and subsequently Japan led to two world wars; the expansion of the Soviet Union created the Cold War. The current challenge for the rest of the world, especially the United States, is to overturn this precedent and accommodate China's legitimate interests. The challenge for China is to exercise its growing power in a way that promotes prosperity and peace.

Sixth, Asia is brimming with demands for democracy, or at least for more open, accountable, and participatory forms of government. Four countries previously dominated by military strongmen—Taiwan, South Korea, the Philippines, and Indonesia—are now democracies. (Thailand has reverted to military rule, but democracy there had been corrupted and the junta is pledging a return to civilian government.) Even undemocratic nations pay lip service to democracy. But democracy requires a supportive institutional framework, and institutions in much of Asia are weak. Asian democracy faces a strong challenge from China's economic success.

Seventh, Asia houses several military threats to regional and global security. Before and during the Cold War, the region rippled with communist-backed insurgencies. Within living memory, the United States has fought three major wars in Asia and still maintains a larger, long-term military presence there than anywhere else.

From a US perspective, the strategic outlook is favorable. Japan, South Korea, Thailand, the Philippines, and Australia are US allies, Taiwan is under US military protection, and Singapore and India have significantly deepened their military ties with Washington. Relations with China are occasionally tense but normally businesslike and frequently constructive.

Two relics of the Cold War remain. The grimacing totalitarian state that calls itself the Democratic People's Republic of Korea has tested a nuclear weapon and brandishes the specter of a future nuclear attack. Meanwhile, China refuses to rule out the use of force in its unbending insistence that Taiwan is part of one China. China has deployed hundreds of missiles facing Taiwan.

Finally, a variety of nontraditional dangers threaten domestic, regional, and global security. Many of them are not unique to Asia, but Asia's size, dynamism, and connectedness with the rest of the world make them important to others. Separatist movements, sometimes fueled by a radical-fundamentalist version of Islam, unsettle parts of the Philippines, Thailand, Myanmar, and, until recently, Indonesia. Criminals and terrorists have taken advantage of local conflicts, corruption, and other weaknesses in governance to set up cells that operate across borders and sea lanes.

World health officials are warning that diseases originating in Asia, such as avian flu, could give rise to the next global pandemic. Environmental damage includes deforestation, depletion of scarce marine and mineral resources, loss of biodiversity, inadequate sanitation and waste disposal, severe air and water pollution, and the consequences of climate change.[11] These pressures compound the devastation of Asia's frequent natural disasters and intensify calls for humanitarian aid from abroad.

In short, what happens in Asia has bearing on almost every major challenge of our time. No serious global problem can be solved without some degree of cooperation between Asians and everybody else.

■ Asian Regionalism and Progress in History

Asia's new regionalism and its political avatar, the Asian integration movement, may have implications for the way the world governs itself. Could a well-designed outcome set a good example for other regions and contribute meaningfully to a peaceful, prosperous, just, and stable world order?

People who believe that history has a purpose, that it reveals a hidden plan of nature or a design of God, might well embrace Asia's new regionalism as a major step on the road to world peace and freedom. The eighteenth-century philosopher Immanuel Kant argued that after endless devastation and upheaval, nations would eventually exhaust themselves and enter into a "federation of peoples" in which every nation would have security and rights.[12] Sooner or later, he predicted, the spirit of trade would dominate the spirit of war.[13] But for this to happen, people must be free to hold public discussions based on reason and to make decisions for themselves.[14] In today's Asia, the spirit of trade is flourishing and political freedom has been gaining ground in all but a handful of countries. The Asian integration movement cannot take credit for this trend, but declarations issued on its behalf increasingly echo the trend.

A modern-day Kantian of sorts is Robert Wright, author of *Non-Zero: The Logic of Human Destiny.* Like Kant, whom he cites repeatedly, Wright believes that war contains the seeds of its own demise. Drawing a parallel with the evolution of organic life, he argues that as interdependence expands, social complexity grows and competition fosters integration. Information keeps parts of the whole organism in touch with each other as they collectively resist destruction. Armed with information, people will increasingly turn toward "non-zero-sum" solutions to common problems—that is, cooperative solutions from which one person's gains need not spell another person's loss. This trend enhances the prospects of peaceful coexistence and may even nurture human goodness.[15] To borrow his framework, Asians are being "pulled" together for common gain in a linear historical process, not "pushed" by a common enemy.

Over time, such Kantians argue, cooperation tends to create shared norms, which foster further cooperation. Sociologist Amitai Etzioni argues that both "West" and "East" are contributing to a "new normative synthesis" that rests on a balance between autonomy (rights, liberty) and social order. He adds that social order is increasingly based on persuasion rather than coercion—a notion that ASEAN, at least, warmly embraces.[16]

Others have dreamed of a creative "fusion" of East and West. The word suggests melding diverse things together and releasing energy in the process. Former Singaporean diplomat Kishore Mahbubani foresaw a fusion of East Asian and Western cultures in the western Pacific.[17] Japanese journalist Yoichi Funabashi, in his *Asia Pacific Fusion,* published in 1995, predicted a fusion of civilizations and ideas rather than of cultures. Like Mahbubani and others, he rejected Samuel Huntington's notion of a clash of civilizations and looked forward to the blending of Asian work habits, respect for education, and social cohesion with Western achievements in democracy and market economics.[18]

The decline of high-level interest in the once vital Asia-Pacific Economic Cooperation (APEC) forum in the mid-1990s and the austere Western response to the Asian financial crisis of 1997–1998 sliced off the "Pacific" part of Funabashi's vision. The majority of Asian leaders turned away from the vision of an Asia-Pacific community in favor of Asia alone. (Some Asian members may be drifting back to APEC, but not at the expense of Asian community building.) Today the word *fusion* shows up not as a vision but as a tagline for music, art, fashion, and styles of cooking. Asian Fusion is a rock group.

■ A Fluid World: The Changing Context of Asian Regionalism

According to Henry Kissinger, world order is now "more fluid than it has been in centuries."[19] Asian leaders learned at their mother's knee that great powers mold and constrain their country's options, but in the post–Cold War period the signals received from these powers are weaker and less consistent. At the same time, several long-term, structural shifts are taking shape. This blend of fluidity and coagulation presents Asians with both opportunities and threats.

Opportunities

Today's Asians have more freedom to create their own destinies than at any time in recent history. Democratization of one kind or another has made widespread gains. The rigid overlay of Cold War rivalry has melted away. One superpower has disappeared and the other is distracted by problems elsewhere. The Sino-Soviet dispute is history. Marxist ideology is little more than a soggy crust. With a few isolated exceptions, local communist movements have petered out. In contrast to other developing regions, Asia displays a high degree of peace and stability. Of the countries surveyed in this book, only Myanmar is a failing state. All the others are stable or nearly so.[20]

Despite occasional gunboat incidents, and with the exception of the China-Taiwan problem, the peaceful settlement of disputes is now an established habit. No ASEAN member has gone to war with another since ASEAN's founding in 1967.[21] China has changed from an inward-looking, land-based, poor, relatively self-sufficient power into an outward-looking regional player with a large stake in the stability of the region. The Chinese government has redirected its quest for regional influence from exporting revolution to cultivating diplomatic ties and managing its rocketing economy.

Major bilateral points of tension are relatively calm. China and India have settled a large portion of their long-festering border disputes, and China and Russia have resolved them completely. Cross-strait relations lurch and lunge, but a military confrontation over Taiwan is clearly avoidable. The risk of large-scale conventional war on the Korean peninsula has faded, and the talks devoted to North Korea's nuclear program may yet succeed in reducing anxiety about Pyongyang's arsenal. Other multilateral approaches to security are also gaining ground; joint patrols, military training exercises, and military exchanges are becoming commonplace even among mutually suspicious neighbors.

The opening of China's economy has created enormous opportunities for its neighbors, particularly in China's coastal provinces and maritime regions. Most educated Asians believe that China's commitment to peaceful growth is irreversible. They reason that the political legitimacy of the Chinese Communist Party depends heavily on economic growth and thus on peaceful economic engagement with the outside world.

Regionwide stability has fostered market-oriented economic policies, unshackled entrepreneurship, and spurred record levels of intra-Asian trade and investment. Asian growth rates are the highest in the world. India has turned outward and is growing almost as rapidly as China. Japan's economy is finally on an upswing. In 2006, trade between Japan and China reached a record level for the eighth straight year. Cities are sprouting skyscrapers, and ports are adding capacity. Investor confidence is relatively high. Foreign exchange reserves are huge. Currencies are bobbing gently rather than plunging.

With some exceptions, Asian governments can claim legitimacy and plan for a reasonably stable future. Their officials are slowly building personal trust and engaging in direct communication to an unprecedented degree. They see the political and economic benefits that closer integration can deliver and the price to be paid for openly resisting the trend.

Threats and Challenges

Despite these encouraging developments, many Asian governments face compelling domestic challenges. They are still struggling to weld fractious ethnic and religious groups into viable nations, to consolidate power, and to preserve their autonomy. Their societies radiate extremes of wealth, privilege, and poverty. A radical, distorted version of Islam has begun infiltrating parts of Southeast Asia, inspiring a shadowy network of suicide bombers.

The financial systems of many Asian countries are vulnerable to the jolts of globalization. Global economic imbalances, driven by yawning US budget and current account deficits and dramatized by the US trade deficit with China, make investors jittery and occasionally trigger short-term plunges in Asian stock markets. Asian memories of the financial crisis of 1997–1998, which toppled many governments and left many Asian economies in tatters, are still fresh.

The regional and global environment is wobbly and unpredictable. The biggest current challenge to global and regional order is how to adapt to and peacefully incorporate China as a newly emerging great power. David Kang argues provocatively that Asia may be drifting back toward a China-centered hierarchy—a modern version of the tribute system. Others resist this notion.[22] Although Asia's future is debatable, there is no doubt that China is rapidly gaining influence.

China's resurgence in Asia provokes mixed reactions. Asians almost uniformly welcome China's booming economy and constructive diplomatic engagement. Many believe that economic growth will inevitably make China more democratic. But Beijing's growing military strength in the region, its secretive decisionmaking, its periodic flare-ups with Tokyo and Taipei, and widespread uncertainty about its long-term motives are all of concern. Asians are also watching to see how the Chinese government handles China's social problems, labor unrest, severe pollution, and the rise of nationalism.

The end of the Cold War dried up support for former Soviet clients, but it left standing two dangerous relics, both located on China's periphery: a standoff across the Taiwan Strait, brought to an occasional simmer by brinksmanship on both sides, and a divided Korean peninsula. China refuses to rule out the use of force in settling the Taiwan issue, and certain Taiwanese leaders seem determined to push for independence. Five governments—China, Russia, Japan, South Korea, and the United States—have worked hard to persuade Pyongyang to abandon its nuclear weapons program, but enforcement will be problematic at best.

The security of energy supplies has become an urgent priority. Governments clash over where one country's share of the ocean floor and its resources ends and another's begins. Fanned by hoped-for discoveries of oil and gas, seabed territorial disputes fester in the South China and East China Seas, the Kurile Islands, and other locations.

A challenge of a different sort is the gradual emergence of Japan as a "normal" country—that is, an active strategic player in the region. Both the Japanese government and the Japanese public reacted with alarm and anger to the 1998 flight of a North Korean missile over Japanese territory, the successful test of a nuclear weapon in 2006, and Pyongyang's refusal to account for Japanese citizens kidnapped and taken to North Korea decades ago. Japan has gradually extended its strategic reach and is taking more responsibility for countering threats to its own defense. The Japanese are participating in a US-led missile defense program.

Handling the United States is a perpetual puzzle for Asians, who are never entirely sure about US commitments. The notion that US priorities lie elsewhere arose during the Cold War and more recently during the Asian financial crisis. Washington's passive response to the crisis drove Asian leaders to rely more on their own efforts, of which the integration movement is one.

Many other challenges loom. The combination of democratic self-expression and weak democratic institutions makes it difficult to restrain rising nationalism. Episodes such as border clashes and the flight of asylum seekers cause tense standoffs—as has happened, for example, between Myanmar and Thailand and between Thailand and Malaysia. Crime is a regionwide problem; pirates, illegal traffickers, smugglers, and other criminals gravitate to areas where the rule of law is weak, undermining the legitimacy of national governments.

Finally, Asia is susceptible to natural disasters. The killer wave of December 2004 destroyed lives and livelihoods from Aceh to Thailand and Sri Lanka. Since then, Indonesia has been hit with several other catastrophes. Typhoons, floods, earthquakes, volcanoes, mudslides, and other calamities are all too common in the region. Poor planning, widespread pollution, and destruction of endangered resources compound these tragedies. The threat of pandemic disease frightens the whole world.

In this new global and regional context, *integration* and *community building* should be understood as code words. They symbolize Asian leaders' search for autonomy, self-reliance, growth, security, and influence without the conditions and rules imposed by a foreign power or global institutions. These leaders look to the integration movement for opportunities to cope more successfully with shared domestic challenges—and thus to strengthen their national sovereignty, not to share it. This search is at the core of Asia's new regionalism.

Basic Differences Between European and Asian Regionalism

Is Asian regionalism, then, on a different historical trajectory? I think so, and so do the architects of Asian integration. But to paraphrase Karl Marx, a specter is haunting Asia watchers—the specter of European integration. Europe often comes up in conversations about Asian integration, as if the creation of the EU were the only relevant standard for Asia. If that were true, this book would be short and merciless. On a Europe-centered scale of 1 to 10, where 10 signifies a single market, regionwide law and institutions, the free migration of labor, and a common foreign and security policy, the score would be roughly Europe: 8 and Asia: 0, on its way to 1.

Numerous Asian and European commentators assert flatly that EU-style integration cannot serve as a role model for Asia in any meaningful way.[23] Europeans seek political union based on pooled sovereignty, whereas Asians reject that goal. The desire to create a single market is a driving force behind European integration, whereas most Asian governments see the complete elimination of economic barriers as more of a threat than an opportunity. Europeans are debating a revised draft constitution, whereas Asians do not seem ready for anything more than watery declarations, unenforceable pledges, and "vision" statements. Europeans have achieved what looks like permanent peace within their own territory, whereas Asians live in a more insecure environment.

Europe cannot and should not be considered a model for Asia for several additional reasons.[24] First, Europe is not nearly as diverse as Asia. It inherits a single Judeo-Christian tradition. Its few major languages are derived from Latin or Germanic roots. Until recently, Europe was racially homogeneous. Asia, by contrast, is pebbled with diversity. Three great cultural and religious waves—Hindu-Buddhist, Chinese, and Islamic—mingled there, flowed into local cultures, and transformed local religions. Asia's printed languages appear as ideographs, scripts, and alphabets. Its spoken languages are mutually unintelligible, even within the same country and sometimes in the same locality.[25]

Second, geography sets Europe apart from Asia and works against Asian integration. Europeans enjoy a moderate climate, free from both the freezing winds of the steppe and the sticky heat of the tropics. Its core is a small, contiguous landmass where distances are short. The bodies of water that separate the continent from Great Britain and Ireland and from southern Scandinavia are small. By contrast, Asia is huge, spanning not only the central and eastern tranche of the great Eurasian landmass but also masses of water many times the size of the Mediterranean or the North Sea. Takeshi Hamashita notes that maritime Asia is "far larger, at least as complex, and more diverse than the Mediterranean."[26]

Third, Europe and Asia have evolved from vastly different legal traditions. Europeans imbibed the notion of civil law from the Roman Empire, which established certain boundaries between public and private domains. Socrates, the Bible, certain aspects of medieval philosophy, and particularly the Renaissance and the Enlightenment emphasized the importance of the individual. Europeans emphasize the rule of law as a means of limiting the power of rulers and protecting the rights of citizens.

Asians, by contrast, typically assign a higher priority to family and group solidarity and social stability than to the rights of the individual. Compared to Europeans, they have fewer defenses against arbitrary government. Whereas Europe relies on formal institutions founded on predictability, transparency, enforceable rules, and the rule of law, Asia does not. In fact, Asians make a point of *not* creating institutions of that kind. Some skeptics dismiss the integration movement on this ground alone.

Fourth, Europeans and Asians hold different views of national sovereignty because they are at different points in their history. European boundaries have been largely settled ever since the Treaty of Westphalia (1648); Germany and Italy crystallized as sovereign nation-states in the nineteenth century. The European Community (now the European Union) has watered down national sovereignty and erased many of the barriers between domestic and foreign affairs, creating what statesman and author Robert Cooper calls "a highly developed system for mutual interference in each other's domestic affairs, right down to beer and sausages."[27]

In Asia, national sovereignty is too new and fragile to surrender. In many former colonies, national boundaries were not established until after World War II. Even nominally independent nations, like China and Thailand, had suffered a wartime loss of sovereignty. Once rid of the colonial powers, Asian leaders faced the challenge of setting up viable governments without external interference. In some countries, this challenge is compelling and overshadows almost everything else.

Fifth, the economic history of the two regions followed trajectories too different and too numerous to relate here. European city-states gradually merged with princely domains to form larger identities, where capitalism flourished, but nothing like that happened in Asia. China was the hub of the tribute system, which had no counterpart in Europe. Asians did not experience the Industrial Revolution and the accompanying revolution in science, and during the colonial era they had few opportunities to industrialize. What European powers and imperial Japan wanted from Asia were not rival products but raw materials and markets for their own industrial goods.

Sixth, maritime integration in Asia is proceeding far more rapidly than land-based integration, whereas the formation of a single market in Europe began with land-based industries (coal and steel) and proceeded from there. Inland transport links in Europe are strong and extensive; maritime linkages are important but not as central to integration as they are in Asia. Not counting the Hanseatic League, the distinction between Maritime Asia and Asia Major (see Chapter 2) has no real counterpart in Europe.

Finally, modern European integration sprang up from the bones and ashes of centuries of war between France and Germany. Two large powers located side by side at the heart of the continent had exhausted themselves in mutual killing. The central imperative was to embed the Germans in the heart of the new Europe in such a way that France and Germany would never go to war against one another again. Franco-German reconciliation is the bedrock of European integration.

The two neighboring great powers of East Asia—China and Japan—are separated by water as well as by history. They fought one war in 1894–1895 and another, more devastating, war from 1937 to 1945. But after the war, the two countries took separate paths. Japan, an island nation, lived through a far-reaching and all-controlling US occupation and ended up with a right-of-center democratic government, while China erupted in civil war and emerged as a left-wing totalitarian state. Politically, they are farther apart than were France and Germany after World War II.

Because of these and other basic differences, the European experience cannot serve as a model for Asia. Nevertheless, selected aspects of European integration are now more relevant to Asia's future design than at any time to date. They are examined in Chapter 10 of this book.

■ Regionalization, Regionalism, Integration, and Community Building

The framework that I use to weigh and evaluate Asian integration from these broad perspectives relies mainly on two organizing concepts: regionalization and regionalism. In Asia, these forces overlap but do not geographically coincide. Each is a key feature of what Peter Katzenstein has labeled "a world of regions"[28] and each contributes to closer integration in Asia, albeit unevenly and in different ways. Regionalization and regionalism manifest themselves as spontaneous integration and the government-driven integration movement (or community building), respectively. Governments seek a form of regionalism that both takes advantage of and protects them from the economic and social forces that fuel regionalization. Part 1 of this book is devoted to regionalization and Part 2 to regionalism.

Regionalization, defined here as the creation or realignment of transactions and attitudes along regional lines, is a manifestation of globalization.[29] Globalization is "intrinsic to the Asian integration story," proclaimed Singapore's education minister in 2006. Describing an "arc of prosperity" stretching from India east, he added that this region is both the biggest beneficiary of and contributor to globalization.[30]

Regionalization is driven, brokered, and carried out primarily by private individuals acting on their own.[31] Real-life integration requires people— employees of multinational corporations, small-scale traders, representatives of civil society organizations, and many others. "Spontaneous" is a better way to describe this form of integration than "bottom-up," because many of the people who embody it—from corporate executives and tourists to criminal bosses—possess powerful connections and a great deal of money. National and local governments and international institutions can create the framework for integration and pave the way, but none of them can make it happen.

Asia would not be becoming "regionalized" at such a breathtaking pace were it not for the recent and ongoing revolutions in information, telecommunications, and transportation technology. These breakthroughs are the core "propellers" of globalization. Together with the lowering of tariffs and other border-based barriers, they have enabled companies to adapt, customize, and rapidly deliver goods and services around the world. These same innovations have sped up travel and personal communication and made them much more affordable. They have also nourished criminal networks and other cross-border threats, which stimulate regionwide countermeasures.

Regionalization is a process; integration is its fruit. There are many varieties of integration. For an economist, the integration of *markets* requires the disappearance or substantial reduction of national barriers to market entry. It can be measured by flows of goods and capital; the convergence of prices, wages, and interest rates; and other indices. The integration of *technology* marks the spread of know-how and "best practices." The integration of *financial systems* refers to common and/or closely coordinated fiscal and monetary policies, leading to coordinated exchange rate policy, a unified bond market, a common currency unit or "basket," and eventually a single currency. The integration of *labor* permits a free flow of workers across national boundaries, regardless of their skill level. The integration of *society* features the disappearance of formal and informal barriers to social connections and the subsequent mingling of different groups. In today's Asia, the integration of markets and technology far outstrips other forms.

Regionalism connotes a political movement based on awareness of and loyalty to a region, combined with dedication to a regionwide agenda of some kind. It provides a way of filtering knowledge and grouping perspectives on the rest of the world. The suffix ("-ism") suggests a conscious set of related ideas or ideology capable of forming the basis of a political movement or an intellectual trend. It implies top-down, coordinated action on the part of governments based on some vision or set of ideas. Essentially political, it is driven by government fiat and stems from the actions of political authorities. Although it derives legitimacy from a collective vision of a more integrated community, it is planned and executed for reasons of state.

Asian intellectuals, policy experts, and a handful of top leaders engaged in dialogues about integration have provided the conceptual and intellectual foundations of Asian regionalism. Many if not most of them take regional integration as a core value. For them it is a goal in itself rather than an action-forcing tactic designed to achieve larger ends, such as global free trade or global institutions that are more responsive to Asia.

The most unusual—and, some would say, unnatural—feature of Asian regionalism is that it links Southeast Asia with three countries in Northeast Asia hitherto considered culturally and historically separate: China, Korea, and Japan. Another new but more superficial development is the inclusion of India, Australia, and New Zealand. In this constellation, Taiwan does not officially exist and Hong Kong is subsumed in China.

The most visible expression of Asian regionalism is the upsurge of free-trade agreements, more accurately described as preferential or discriminatory. Most of these are bilateral. In addition, China, South Korea, and Japan have negotiated wide-ranging agreements with ASEAN as a whole, and India, Australia, and New Zealand are engaged in the same process. These agreements symbolize closer political ties as well as economic opportunity.

The initial report of the East Asia Vision Group of 2001 listed among its recommendations the "promotion of regional identity and consciousness." In other documents, this notion is clothed inelegantly as "*we*-ness." But among Asian leaders, *community building* is the most commonly used description of the Asian integration movement. Community building is a safe term because it resonates with cultural ideals, permits a wide variety of interpretations, and promises nothing specific. It implies that a true community is somewhere off in the future.

A community is a body of persons or nations having a common history or common social, economic, and political interests.[32] Community building is the process of melding disparate national and subnational individuals and groups into an effective, legitimate, sustainable, self-aware, and coherent community. A community may imply common rights and duties.[33] Its focus is not necessarily geographic; for example, some leaders talk about "the community of democracies."

Among Asians, *community* has a looser meaning than *integration* and tends to convey the sense of "big family" rather than pooled sovereignty. It suggests that people coexist peacefully and cooperate with each other according to common sense, courtesy, and habit. Members of a community rely on informal compromise, not formal rules and adjudication, to settle differences. The emerging Asian "community" combines geography and norms, but its exact membership is undecided.

This book delves into the two major outgrowths of regionalization and regionalism visible in today's Asia: spontaneous integration and the government-driven integration movement, respectively. Spontaneous integration knits the economies and societies of this huge region closer together; the government-driven integration movement establishes political space within which competing powers, divergent interests, and diplomatic realignments can be accommodated. These forces find expression in what I call Maritime Asia, the water-bound world of coastal zones and ports, and Asia Major, a grouping of nation-states.

The distinction between spontaneous and government-driven integration is not absolute. The behavior of governments variously maximizes, channels, and limits what private individuals can do. Conversely, the Asia-wide wash of money, technology, and people is one of the factors driving governments to cooperate. Most of them have taken steps that make it easier to trade, invest, and travel throughout the region, but some drag their feet.

Another reason why spontaneous and government-driven integration cannot be neatly separated is that some governments have close ties to production networks and own controlling or minority shares in large companies. Local officials as well as national policies influence the choices that spontaneous "integrators" make; they may compete with each other to make their locality attractive to investors and tourists, or they may undermine integration initiatives because they rake off a share of the profits from local monopolies or because they have some other vested interest in the status quo.

Despite the substantial overlap between public policies and private behavior, there are at least five analytical reasons for seeking to understand spontaneous integration on its own terms. First, the integration initiatives issuing from government office buildings, important as they are from a strategic perspective, are slow-moving and superficial compared to what is happening in the private sector. Government officials and politicians have limited freedom of action. Second, private capital flows and other resources available in the private sector dwarf corresponding provisions of government budgets. They are responsible for most of Asia's development.

Third, the private sector is the mainspring of technology. The airplanes that fly government officials to meetings on integration and the computers and telephones that enable them to continue their discussions are produced by the private sector. Fourth, spontaneous integration extends to criminal and terrorist networks. The reach and sophistication of some of these networks threatens the entire region. Finally, spontaneous integration influences government behavior profoundly. The surge of intraregional flows of trade, investment, capital, people, and threats is a powerful catalyst prompting governments to act. Along with conventional military threats and other security challenges, these flows are the raw material of strategy.

The overarching theme of this book is that Asian integration reflects the momentum and recoil of these two forces: spontaneous integration in Maritime Asia, a manifestation of regionalization fueled by market forces, economic opportunity, social and ethnic ties, and the ease of communication and travel; and the government-driven quest for closer integration in Asia Major, a form of regionalism pushed as much by a quest for security and national autonomy as by economic interdependence and a desire for efficiency. Asian integration can be thought of as a blend of complementarity, overlap, and mismatch between the integrating "pull" of a Maritime Asia and the wobbly and uneven "push" of the governments of Asia Major. The contrast between this pull and push infuses the rest of this book.

◼ Preview and Key Questions

This book is about Asia's future as a region in a globalizing world. I examine both regionalization and regionalism, identify the obstacles that they face, comment on their interaction, and derive implications for US and Asian policies toward the region.

Chapter 2 sets the stage by asking, "What is 'Asia'?" It draws on geography and history to justify remapping our understanding of this label. It develops the two core concepts of Maritime Asia as the locus of regionalization and Asia Major as the invention and broadest expression of regionalism.

The three chapters that constitute Part 1 of this book are devoted to regionalization. Chapter 3 traces Maritime Asia's historical legacy. Chapter 4 traces the technologies that propel the resurgence of spontaneous integration in Maritime Asia, and Chapter 5 profiles the individuals who carry it out.

The four chapters in Part 2 shift the focus to regionalism. I focus on the group of nations that I call Asia Major and analyze the policy-driven integration movement designed and promoted (but also ignored or resisted) by national governments. Chapter 6 analyzes the catalysts and motivations of the movement, Chapter 7 surveys its architecture, and Chapters 8 and 9 selectively identify initiatives, tools, and results in the fields of trade, finance, foreign policy, and security.

Part 3 draws together some judgments about the future of Asia's new regionalism. Chapter 10 sizes up the promise of integration and measures the readiness of Asian participants against various yardsticks. Chapter 11 surveys obstacles and potential threats. Chapter 12 sets forth overall judgments and derives selected policy implications for Asian governments and for the United States.

Questions tumble out. Since spontaneous integration in Maritime Asia overlaps but does not coincide with the government-driven Asian integration movement, is Asia's new regionalism a sustainable and successful strategy for creating wealth? For coping with globalization? For overcoming security threats and promoting stability? For adapting to a resurgent China? For promoting basic human rights, good governance, and the rule of law? For contributing to world order? Finally, what US actions would most effectively serve America's wide-ranging interests in Asia while accommodating legitimate Asian goals?

▪ Notes

1. For a vivid description of contrasts like these, see Buruma, *God's Dust*.
2. *Far Eastern Economic Review*, July 8, 2004, p. 53.
3. Henceforth called Myanmar, as the country is now known throughout Asia.
4. "Charting East Asia's Milestones," keynote address by Prime Minister Badawi at the Second East Asia Forum, December 7, 2004, *The Star Online*.
5. For a description and appraisal of the Track 2 process, see Paul Evans, "Between Regionalism and Regionalization: Policy Networks and the Nascent East Asian Institutional Identity," in Pempel, *Remapping East Asia*, pp. 195–215.
6. For an argument along these lines, see Milner, "Region, Security, and the Return of History."
7. Vietnam and Cambodia were not members of ASEAN during the conflicts of the late 1970s.
8. Starting from east of the Ural Mountains, the Asian landmass spans 17.4 million square miles, compared to Africa's 11.7 million. The world's largest city is Shanghai; more than half the world's megacities (cities with populations of more than 10 million) are in Asia.
9. They are New Guinea (2), Borneo (3), Sumatra (6), and Honshu, Japan (7).
10. Mikkal E. Herberg, "Asia's Energy Insecurity: Cooperation or Conflict?" in Tellis and Wills, *Strategic Asia 2004–05*, p. 343.

11. Asian Development Bank, *Technical Assistance for the Formulation of the Pacific Region Environmental Strategy,* p. 1.

12. Immanuel Kant, "Idea for a Universal History with a Cosmopolitan Intent," in Kant, *Perpetual Peace and Other Essays,* p. 34.

13. Immanuel Kant, "To Perpetual Peace: A Philosophical Sketch," in Kant, *Perpetual Peace and Other Essays,* p. 125.

14. Immanuel Kant, "An Answer to the Question: 'What Is Enlightenment?'" in Kant, *Perpetual Peace and Other Essays,* pp. 42, 45.

15. Wright, *Non-Zero,* esp. p. 250.

16. Etzioni, *From Empire to Community,* pp. 20, 215.

17. Mahbubani, *Can Asians Think?* pp. 130–131.

18. Funabashi, *Asia Pacific Fusion,* pp. 9–10.

19. Henry A. Kissinger, "A Global Order in Flux," *Washington Post,* July 9, 2004.

20. *Foreign Policy* and the Fund for Peace, "The Failed States Index," pp. 50–58. Indonesia—inaccurately, in my view—and Laos are listed as "in danger."

21. When Vietnam invaded Cambodia in late 1978, neither country was a member of ASEAN.

22. Kang, "Getting Asia Wrong," esp. pp. 66–70. Amitav Acharya argues vigorously against this idea in "Will Asia's Past Be Its Future?"

23. For an example of recent discussions, see Berkofsky, "Comparing EU and Asian Integration Processes."

24. For a longer and more nuanced comparison, see Katzenstein, *A World of Regions,* chap. 3.

25. See the description of a marketplace in China's Fujian province in Howard W. French, "Uniting China to Speak Mandarin, the One Official Language: Easier Said than Done," *New York Times,* July 10, 2005, p. 4.

26. Takeshi Hamashita, "The Intra-regional System in East Asia in Modern Times," in Katzenstein and Shiraishi, *Network Power,* pp. 115, 135. In *Guns, Germs, and Steel,* Jared Diamond argues that Europe's deeply indented coastlines, numerous inlets, and mountain barriers stimulated competition among political entities, whereas China's uniform administration contributed to the technological standstill imposed by Chinese rulers.

27. Cooper, *The Breaking of Nations,* p. 27.

28. Katzenstein, *A World of Regions.*

29. Gennady Chufrin, "Regionalism in East Asia," in Chufrin, *East Asia: Between Regionalism and Globalism.*

30. Speech by Tharman Shanmugaratnam at the Sixteenth Asian Corporate Conference, Mumbai, India, March 20, 2006, available at http://economictimes.indiatimes.com/articleshow/1456005.cms.

31. T. J. Pempel, "Introduction," in Pempel, *Remapping East Asia,* p. 6.

32. Definitions are adapted from *Webster's New Collegiate Dictionary* (Springfield, MA: G. & C. Merriam, 1981).

33. Robin Ramcharan, "ASEAN and Non-interference: A Principle Maintained," *Contemporary Southeast Asia* 22, no. 1 (April 2000): 75, quoted and discussed in Elliott, "ASEAN and Environmental Cooperation," pp. 31–32.

2

Remapping Asia

The way that we conceive of the world's continents and regions shapes our understanding of them. Maps and their labels reflect our political assumptions, influence the way we sort out facts, color our priorities, and mold our actions. A world centered on the North Pole or Australia looks different from a world with the United States in the middle. To flip through a collection of old maps is like viewing world history in motion. It is as if a huge continent depicted on the page of our atlas stirs itself, shakes itself gently, and settles back into new contours.

To know whether what we call *Asia* is beginning to coalesce into an integrated region, we need to identify these new contours and decide what Asia is, or at least which of several possible Asias we are talking about. Few regions are geographically self-evident. Some bear names that are accurate in political terms but not in other ways, or vice versa. Their boundaries at any given time are reflections of history, political will, leadership priorities, economic ties, sociological trends, the movement of ideas, and perceptions of collective identity.[1]

Remapping can help comb out this tangled landscape. It means redesigning the spatial structures through which we filter and organize our knowledge of a region. Remapping does not erase political boundaries but rather superimposes other spatial perspectives. The content of any given map varies according to what the cartographer wants to emphasize.

Scholars applying remapping to East Asia have pointed to emerging "webs of interconnectedness," ranging from transnational investment to civil action groups.[2] This book adopts this framework and extends it westward to include India. It traces two Asias. One Asia needs little remapping because it is constructed from the familiar mosaic of nation-states—a political construct I call Asia Major. The national units that constitute the core membership of Asia Major are fixed and clearly drawn. The other Asia—the one I call Maritime Asia—is a sweep of coastal zones, deltas, and ocean-accessible villages, towns, and cities. It is where most Asians live and work.

21

An observer from Mars who knew nothing of national boundaries would conclude that Maritime Asia is far more vital and dynamic than interior regions. Seen at night from a satellite, Maritime Asia shows up as pinpoints and strands of light that gleam in major cities and along seas, harbors, and major waterways. The National Aeronautics and Space Agency (NASA) confirms that cities tend to grow along coastlines and that most of Asia's outline would still be visible from space even without an underlying map.[3]

A few dark patches interrupt these strings of illumination. Lights glimmer feebly on the shores of Myanmar and not at all in North Korea. Poverty and corruption hamper maritime activity in Bangladesh and Cambodia, and local rebellions still hold back northern Sri Lanka, northeast India, the southern Philippines, and extreme western and eastern parts of the Indonesian archipelago.

This chapter delves into remapping in order to offer an alternative to an exclusive preoccupation with national boundaries. As historian Jeremy Black observes in his book *Maps and History,* the modern emphasis on boundary lines "places a misleading weight on the edges rather than the centers of units."[4] By highlighting spontaneous cross-border flows of goods, services, capital, technology, knowledge, ideas, cultures, and people, remapping can correct this misleading emphasis. These flows account for much of Asia's success. Remapping helps identify the obstacles clogging natural flow fields.

Remapping can also alter the perception of foreign policy interests, economic priorities, and national security strategy in a context of rapid change. The way people see and think about a place influences the way they act. During the Cold War, for example, wall-sized maps in the Pentagon featured a modestly sized United States at the center, flanked by two huge, Mercator-enlarged Soviet Unions bearing down on it. Understanding the history and geography of Asian integration from different spatial perspectives could help governments channel the political drive toward integration in directions best suited to the region.

This chapter begins the process of remapping by scanning Asia's physical geography in order to pry the reader's imagination loose from national borders. (Later chapters hammer it back again.) To justify the invention of new labels, it lists old ones that have fallen out of use. It shows that over the centuries, notions of Asia rolled steadily eastward and are now centered primarily in China and Japan. It then makes the case for "recentering" Asia by tugging it westward so that it once again includes India. Finally, it elaborates on Asia Major and Maritime Asia, the dual subjects of this book, as valid regions.

■ Defining "Asia"

Defining Asia's boundaries appears simple at first. Surely, one would think, Asia is that part of the Eurasian landmass that is left over when European and

Mediterranean portions of it are sawed off. But this is a negative definition: Asia is not Europe. Moreover, authorities do not all agree on where this sawed-off line is. According to the National Geographic Society, a commonly accepted division between Asia and Europe runs along the Ural Mountains and down the Ural River, across the Caspian Sea, and along the Caucasus Mountains and the Black Sea to the Bosporus and the Dardanelles. Despite similarities of local culture and climate, the Suez Canal and the Red Sea separate Asia from Africa.[5] But this is arbitrary. If geographers used the same continent-defining criterion that they have applied to Africa and other continents, there would be no Europe or Asia—just Eurasia, stretching from Korea to the western tip of Spain.[6]

Half a century ago, University of Chicago geographer Norton Ginsburg used the term *Asian Asia* to describe the Asia that rims the southern and eastern margins of the continent. This is the Asia that contains great cultures and dense centers of population living within 750 miles (1200 kilometers) of the sea. Ginsburg included India but excluded the Russian Far East and Central Asia because they were oriented more toward the Russian heartland than toward the rest of Asia. He also left out "southwest Asia," a former crossroad between "Asian Asia" and the West, because he believed that the cultures and economies there were too different from those found elsewhere in Asia. He was ambivalent about Pakistan and Afghanistan but conceded that they could be excluded from Asian Asia.[7] My notion of Maritime Asia tracks quite closely with Ginsburg's concept.

Water is a marked feature of Asia's profile. Asia rims the world's largest and third-largest oceans, the Pacific and the Indian. Its eastern edge peters out into the "commons" somewhere in the western Pacific Ocean. Asia is fed by three of the world's longest rivers—the Yangtze and the Huang Ho (Yellow River) in China and the Mekong, which runs from China through or along Laos, Thailand, Cambodia, and Vietnam.[8] The Strait of Malacca and the Strait of Sunda, through which Herman Melville's fictitious *Pequod* sailed in search of Moby Dick, are located there.[9]

These waterways nourished some of the region's earliest civilizations and continue to connect its people today. Historian Takeshi Hamashita uses the term *Maritime Asia* to describe "a series of seas connected by straits." This series includes not only the Indian and Pacific Oceans but also the seas of Okhotsk and Japan, the East China and South China Seas, the Java Sea, the Banda Sea, the Coral Sea, and several others. He believes that we must study Asian regional history as the history of Asian seas.[10] Donald Emmerson notes that early maps of Southeast Asia featured "whales and mermaids, waves and ships" but that modern observers underestimate or ignore the centrality of the region's maritime nature.[11] The influence of the sea on everything from climate and environment to settlement, culture, and communications is stronger there than anywhere else in the world.[12]

Pasting the name Asia on a vast, bulky mass of plains, mountains, penin-sulas, islands, rivers, straits, and seas stretching from the Urals to New Guinea is unsatisfying. How can we carve it up into meaningful subregions? Physical geography gives us only partial answers. South Asia would appear to be dis-tinct because it is rimmed by mountains on the north and the ocean on the south. But Indian history and civilization are historically linked with the rest of Asia, especially Southeast Asia but also China.

Earlier geographers turned to climate and agricultural practices and came up with terms like *Monsoon Asia*, as opposed to the *Eurasia* of the northern lowlands.[13] But these indicators fall short of the mark. Climate, for example, does not explain why Southeast Asia is considered a region; no single descrip-tion encompasses the semiarid scrublands of central Myanmar and the rain-forests of central Borneo. Buddhist Thailand arguably has more in common with Sri Lanka than with the Christian/Muslim Philippines. Agricultural prac-tices are likewise misleading; southern China and eastern India share with much of Southeast Asia a pattern of alternating paddy-field cultivation with the burning of fields.[14] Historian and sinologist Karl Wittfogel ascribed China's then totalitarian system to what he called "Oriental despotism," a sys-tem derived from total control over the management of water, but this notion no longer corresponds to reality (if it ever did).[15]

Then there is Russia, not normally thought of as an Asian country. Indeed, the Kremlin has mostly resisted that label except when it is politically conven-ient to wave it. But the conventional line dividing Europe from Asia consigns everything east of the Urals to Asia. If Kazakhstan and India are Asian, Russia's eastern stretches—revealingly called the Russian Far East—are Asian, too.

Finally, where does Australia fit? During the last Ice Age, Australia and New Guinea were a single landmass. The fauna is still similar. But today the western half of New Guinea, peopled by Melanesians, is part of Indonesia, an Asian country. Air links to and from the eastern half, Papua New Guinea, typ-ically go through Australia, a non-Asian country that exercises considerable influence there and in the islands of Oceania as well. Former Australian for-eign minister Gareth Evans once attended a meeting armed with a map that placed Australia at the heart of the East Asian hemisphere. Predictably, his Malaysian counterpart would have none of it.[16]

■ The Vagaries of Labels

The labels that appear on maps of Asia are mirrors of history. The collision of expanding knowledge and shifting power has sent whole subregions to the dustbin. Whatever happened, for instance, to "Independent Tartary" and "Farther India"? As the British established direct or indirect rule over the Indian subcontinent, names like Hindoostan fell into disuse. The Dutch East

Indies or East Indies disappeared, replaced by Indonesia. When the United States withdrew from Vietnam, Indochina began a slow fall into history.

Some labels lie in hiding, ready to resurface when the timing is right. A pathetically large number of statelets popped up after World War I, issuing their own stamps before sinking back into occupation and dependence. Central Asia virtually disappeared during the decades of Soviet rule, only to struggle up again after the fall of communism freed this region from Moscow's grip. Presumably the Eurasian counterpart to Central Europe, Central Asia is oddly named because it does not occupy the center of Asia unless one chops off Southeast Asia. Central Eurasian Landmass or Asia Medior (my invention) would be more accurate.

China still calls itself the Middle Kingdom, but the United Kingdom claims centrality as well: despite the eclipse of the British Empire, Greenwich is still the imagined center of the world from which exact time is calculated and points east and west are measured. But the Anglocentric term *Far East* has become mildly absurd (far from what?) and *Near East* has likewise fallen out of use. *The Orient* is about as rare as *the Occident*.

Linguistic confusion is another problem. Most of the major labels describing Asia in international usage are derived from Western languages, highly distorted transliterations, or colonial convenience. The Pacific Ocean, for example, owes its name to Balboa and is derived from the Latin word for peace *(pax)*. The term *Silk Road* was not coined until 1877—by a German.[17] The word *Indochina* roped Laos and Cambodia together with Vietnam because all three were French colonial possessions. But in historical and cultural terms, Cambodia and Laos are closer to Thailand than to Vietnam.

Although water knows no boundaries, Western cartographers have mentally segmented Asian seas into separate bodies of water and named them after the corresponding littoral state: the Indian Ocean, the South China Sea, the East China Sea, the Gulf of Thailand, the Sea of Japan, and so on. This habit subtly colors today's territorial disputes over offshore resources. In some cases, neighboring states reject this cartographic imperialism and adopt their own labels; Koreans, for instance, refer to the Sea of Japan as the East Sea. In Europe, by contrast, the various seas are generally not named for countries.[18]

Abandoning Western names in favor of labels invented by Asians cannot solve the problem of arbitrary names because few such Asia-wide labels exist. Throughout most of their history the peoples of East Asia rarely adopted a regional perspective.[19] The traditional Japanese term *sangoku* (three countries or three civilizations) referred only to Japan, China, and India. Indian conceptions of the region were mingled with religion and did not coalesce into a workable scheme.

Some labels took China as their point of reference. Others referred to the weather or to wealth. For the Chinese, China was *zhong guo*, the Middle Kingdom or Middle Country, the center of the civilized world. The character for *middle* is still part of Beijing's contemporary name for China. Taipei uses a different label for Taiwan but retains the character for *middle* as well.

Viewed from the Chinese capital, concentric circles historically defined the various categories of lesser civilizations and barbarians. The first encompassed territories within the Chinese cultural orbit that lay to the east and south. Tributary states such as Japan, Korea, Vietnam, Siam, Burma, and the Ryukyu Islands were all autonomous political identities, but their rulers formally acknowledged the Chinese ruler as emperor under heaven and China as the center of world order as they knew it. The second circle included Inner Asia to the north and west, the source of many invasions. The outermost circle described the "outer barbarians" *(waiyi)*, including most of Southeast Asia, South Asia, and Europe. Today's Chinese use the term *Western Regions* to describe western and central Asia, the Caucasus, and parts of South Asia.[20]

When viewed from China, Japan was (and still is) *zhi bun* in Chinese—the origin of the sun, the land east of China. The Japanese obligingly adopted both the name and the image of a rising sun (*Nippon* or *Nihon* in Japanese). Like other places in Asia, Japan's territory was not precisely defined. Over the centuries, the outer boundaries of Japan shifted up and down the long chain of islands stretching from Sakhalin in the north toward the Philippines in the south.[21]

Further to the south, Malay traders, who like others timed their voyages up and down the coasts of Asia in accordance with seasonal monsoons, called their region "the land below the winds." Indians, Arabs, and later Europeans came from "above the winds."[22] Another source of names was the wealth associated with trade. Centuries before Columbus, the Spice Islands attracted Indian and Arab traders. Looking for gold and eager to supply pepper and other products to the lucrative Roman market, they called this region the Land of Gold (a label subsequently applied to other regions as well).[23]

In sum, conventional geography does not yield a single, generally agreed upon definition of *Asia*. Fortunately, that open-endedness serves the purpose of this book because it allows room for both the fluid composition of Maritime Asia and the deliberately flexible identity of Asia Major.

■ Recentering Asia

Over the centuries, Western notions of Asia slowly rolled eastward. When Saint Paul told the Corinthians about his sufferings in the "province of Asia," he was referring to Anatolia, in what we now call Asia Minor (Turkey). Modern scholars link the term *Asia* to the kingdom of Assuwa in Anatolia or the city of Assos near Troy.[24] The European division of the world into Europe, Asia, and "Libya" (Africa) evolved in the ninth to fifth century B.C. After western Anatolia was incorporated into the Persian Empire in the sixth century B.C., geographers extended the term eastward and began calling Asia a continent, along with Europe and Africa. Asia meant the lands east of the Nile and later east of the Don River at the eastern end of the Black Sea. Aristotle believed that inhabitants of Asia possessed intelligence and skill but lacked spirit.[25]

Centuries later, after Marco Polo returned to Venice from his travels, Europeans stretched their notion of Asia farther east. The great voyages of exploration of the fifteenth and sixteenth centuries challenged European cartographers to design new horizons. They also ignited a great race to trade, conquer, and exploit. Images of Asia's fabulous wealth inspired John Milton to rhapsodize that "the gorgeous East with richest hand / Showrs on her kings Barbaric Pearl and Gold."[26] Like Milton, John Keats saw Asia as feminine, the daughter of the earth-mother goddess Tellus, a spiritual landscape of "palm-shaded temples, and high rival fanes [temples] / By Oxus or in Ganges' sacred isles."[27] Asia was rich, spiritual, and passive, a ripe target for merchants and missionaries.

As reports filtered back to the West, "India" acquired near-mythic dimensions and greatly expanded in size. A map of India drawn up in 1570, for example, included not only all of modern-day South Asia but East and Southeast Asia as well.[28] The Asian art collection of Hapsburg emperor Rudolph II (1552–1612) contained items from Japan and China as well as India but was known as *Indienische Sachen* (Indian things).[29] Since cultural boundaries featured prominently in maps of that era, the notion of an enormous "India" radiating cultural influences to distant places was not as outlandish as it seems.

As the Mogul Empire slowly decayed, Britain's East India Company consolidated its rule, political boundaries replaced cultural ones, and India shrank again to something like the form we know today (minus Pakistan and Bangladesh). The name *Indonesia* and the residual terms *East Indies* and *Indochina* are vivid reminders of the once-pervasive role of India in greater Asia.

In the tumultuous twentieth century, the names assigned to the regions of Asia shifted in response to the two world wars, the end of colonialism, the rise and fall of the Soviet Union, ideological struggles, and the Cold War. *East* and *West* took on new meaning. The West was the NATO alliance plus Japan, and the East was the area subjected to communist dictatorship, from Prague to Peking. Just as Austria's Prince Metternich had declared that "Asia begins at the Landstrasse" (the road leading east from Vienna), so postwar German chancellor Konrad Adenauer was said to mutter "Asia" whenever he crossed the Elbe into Prussia.[30] After the fall of the Soviet Union, citizens of what used to be called Eastern Europe shook themselves free from Moscow and now prefer the designation Central Europe.

In the second half of the twentieth century, the notion of Asia rolled too far east. Asia became strongly identified with East Asia, at least in Western minds. Maps and organization charts alike grouped India with the Middle East. This mental equation crystallized in part because Japan, and subsequently China, earned starring roles in the global economy and in part because India retreated into economic autarky. Now that India has turned outward again and sought closer ties with its Asian neighbors, it has regained a place corresponding more closely to its long cultural and historical footprint in the region.

In addition to tugging "Asia" back from its extreme eastern edge, China should be nudged somewhat southward. Our mental maps currently assign China to Northeast Asia, presumably because of its Confucian heritage and the present location of its capital. But China also overlaps substantially with parts of Southeast Asia. Guangdong, Hong Kong, and Hainan Island are on roughly the same latitude as Vietnam and Myanmar. They are also closer to Manila and Hanoi than they are to Beijing. Much of China's wealth and population is clustered in southern regions. Moreover, many of China's richest civilizations and societies arose along great rivers or in areas not far from the sea. When it comes to contemporary integration, these southern and maritime characteristics of China's geography should be kept in mind.

Southeast and Central Asia

Not until World War II did the term *Southeast Asia* come into common use, when military strategists used it to designate Mountbatten's theater of command.[31] After the war, Southeast Asia became a fixed strategic entity. Although the US-backed Southeast Asia Treaty Organization (SEATO) did not last, Asian-only arrangements reinforced Southeast Asia's new identity. In 1961, the Malay leader Tunku Abdul Rahman took the lead in establishing the Association of Southeast Asia, consisting of Malaya, Thailand, and the Philippines.

In 1967, Southeast Asia acquired wider geopolitical meaning when five nations—Indonesia, Malaysia, the Philippines, Singapore, and Thailand—cobbled together the Association of Southeast Asian Nations. This group of governments, called in this book the ASEAN 5, deliberately set out to nurture a sense of regional identity as well as establish a regional organization. They did so both to counteract the threat of communism and to dispel the Western notion that they were nothing but dominoes in a Cold War struggle. They also saw regionalism as a way of strengthening nation building, promoting autonomy, avoiding war among themselves, and protecting national interests.[32]

"Central Asia," virtually erased by the Soviet occupation, rose again in the 1990s. Central Asian countries have assumed new prominence because of the conflict in Afghanistan, the establishment of US bases in the region, and the abundance of energy—a strategic currency of enormous importance to China's future. Taking advantage of US preoccupation with antiterrorism and mindful of cross-border support for Uighur insurgents in Xinjiang, China organized the so-called Shanghai Cooperation Organization. This group, which includes Russia, Kazakhstan, Kyrgyzstan, Tajikistan, and Uzbekistan as members and India, Iran, Mongolia, and Pakistan as observers, has begun cooperating on antiterrorist operations and expanding economic cooperation. It also called for the removal of foreign (read: US) troops from the area.

Labels pasted on Asia continue to reflect changing perceptions and priorities. *Emerging Asia* appears as the term du jour in working papers issued by the International Monetary Fund (IMF) and other institutions. This term encompasses India but excludes Japan. In IMF parlance, the "Asia region" includes Australia and New Zealand as well as India.[33] East Asia is taking on a new identity altogether. Australia is not ethnically and culturally "Asian," but it has become so deeply enmeshed in Asia Major that Canberra sought and gained an invitation to the East Asian Summit. New Zealand did likewise. To smooth over this odd bump, Asian leaders now say that East Asia is a political construct, not a geographic entity.[34] Exactly.

■ Maps and Grand Strategy: The Mahan-Mackinder Debate

Remapping has always reflected strategic opportunities and concerns, but in the last century and a half, gateways to Asia have taken on vivid strategic importance. The opening of Japan (1854) and the Suez Canal (1869) offered new and convenient gateways to the riches of Asia from the east and the west. By then European minds had grasped the Eurasian landmass as a whole. Portions of Asia that lay closer to Europe came to be known as the Near East and farther realms as the Far East. Only at the end of the nineteenth century did the term *Middle East* come into being to describe the area around the Persian Gulf. Today's Middle East has spread out and seems to mean all Arabic-speaking countries plus Israel and Iran, while Near East and Far East have sunk into disuse.

As in the great age of exploration, maps of the nineteenth century had a strategic character. The question was not only what the world looked like in physical ways but also what those maps revealed about the way to acquire and exercise power and identify threats.

For Oxford geographer and strategist Halford Mackinder, control of the land was the central pivot of "geopolitics," a word he invented. At stake was the mastery of the "World-Island" of Europe and Asia. For much of recorded history, sprawling, land-based empires were centers of power. The Persians, Alexander the Great, the Romans, the Huns, and the Mongols, to name a few, had swept over the land in waves, creating vast dominions of hybrid governance and culture. Mackinder predicted a struggle between the land-based, authoritarian empires of the "Heartland" and the maritime, commercial powers of the West. Russia's strategic railways were snaking toward the Ottoman Empire, he argued, and there was nothing that battleships could do about it. The battle zones would be the "Inner (or Marginal) Crescent"—the lands stretching from Eastern Europe and Central Asia through the Middle East and the Himalayas to East Asia. In the "Outer (or Insular) Crescent" were Africa, the Americas, and Southeast Asia.[35]

Pitted against Mackinder was military theorist Alfred Thayer Mahan, who stressed sea power as a key to world leadership. While land-based empires in Asia and elsewhere had concentrated their forces against threats from the interior, Westerners had completed the circumnavigation of the globe, built the clipper ships, invented steam navigation, and revolutionized naval warfare. By building better and faster ships, Western countries had conquered much of the world and were pushing up the three largest rivers in Asia: the Yellow River, the Yangtze, and the Mekong.

Great Britain in particular had ridden the waves to global dominion. Mahan and others saw the value of a strong navy not only to attack an enemy but also to impose an economic blockade or to use the threat of force to influence political developments onshore. In language remarkably similar to descriptions of present-day globalization, Mahan believed that navies knit nations together into a global system unprecedented in size, activity, and sensitivity.[36] The Mahan-Mackinder debate is still required reading in the education of US military officers.

◼ Inventing Asia Major and Maritime Asia

If defining "Asia" is so open-ended, how can it be called a region? Political scientist Peter Katzenstein looks at contemporary regions in international perspective and observes that they are hybrid and porous, not closed blocs. Regions are open to and shaped by global forces, ties to other countries and regions, the evolution of the international state system, and the power of the United States.[37]

In their book *The Myth of Continents,* geographer Martin Lewis and historian Kären Wigen develop the notion of remapping as a blend of physical geography and human interaction. Stressing the diminishing importance of distance, they see discontinuous "regions" taking a variety of spatial forms, not necessarily contiguous blocs. Regions are sprawling and complex, shaded by borderlands and etched by multiple corridors and crossing points. They reflect historical processes, interaction with others, and assemblages of ideas, practices, and social institutions. They contain not only dominant populations and postcolonial nation-states as we know them, but also vast diasporas, cultural archipelagos, and populations whose religion, language, and material culture endow them with various mixed or "matrix" identities. These hybrid zones exist in their own right.[38]

Inspired by this multidisciplinary approach to regions, I have invented two ways of defining Asia, captured in two different mental maps. One is geographically vague but vibrant. It is organized on the basis of networks and flows of all kinds—commercial, financial, intellectual, social, and cultural. It includes southern and coastal India. The other one is more precise, clearly showing national boundaries. Stretching well beyond East Asia, it includes the ten members of ASEAN, plus China, Japan, South Korea, India, Australia, and New Zealand. It may be stretched even farther in years to come.

Maritime Asia

In policy circles, the word *maritime* usually refers to the peninsular and insular nations of Southeast Asia, as opposed to those on the mainland. A contemporary atlas, for instance, puts Thailand in Mainland Southeast Asia and Malaysia in Maritime Southeast Asia even though the two share a long peninsula.[39] In this book, however, Maritime Asia is not defined by nation-state boundaries at all. It is the timeless sweep of coastal communities, port cities and towns, and inland trading nodes clustered along ocean-destined rivers not far from the sea. Maritime Asia is where at least 60 to 70 percent of Asians live.

Today's Maritime Asia splays out farther than its precolonial parent. At its northeastern and southeastern tips are maritime Russia and coastal Australia, its modern-day wings. On its western flank, Maritime Asia once more embraces southern and coastal India, its prodigal son. India's physical infrastructure is rickety and decrepit, but its urban and maritime zones are rejoining their old community. In the middle is coastal China, still a magnet for trade but no longer earthbound.

Taiwan, once a haven for bandits and now a world-class font of advanced technology, has been a full member of Maritime Asia for some time. So has Australia. Not only does Australia attract large numbers of Asian immigrants and students; it also sends a higher proportion of its exports to Asia than any Asian country. A lucky visitor to the port city of Fremantle in remote southwestern Australia might catch a glimpse of a fully rigged "tall ship" slipping gracefully through the sea. Such a sight is a breathtaking symbol of Maritime Asia's history. But the visitor is more likely to find a huge ship ready for a load of iron ore, flying a Chinese flag and marked "Shanghai." Near the dock is an indoor hodgepodge of food stalls brimming with Chinese, Korean, Japanese, and Indian dishes as well as fish and chips. Such was this author's good fortune in 2006.

In the far northeast, Maritime Asia draws in Russia's energy-rich maritime provinces. Although the Russian and Japanese governments still main-

Bangkok
Tianjin
Inchon
Busan
Nagoya
Qingdao
Tokyo
Yokohama
Shanghai
Kitakyushu
Ningpo
Xiamen
Shenzhen
Taipei
Guangzhou
Kaohsiung
Hong Kong
Kolkata
Mumbai
Chennai
Bangkok
Laem Chabang
Manila
Ho Chi Minh City
Colombo
Port Klang
Medan/Belawan
Kuala Lumpur
Singapore
Tanjung Pelepas
Jakarta/Tanjung Priok

Yellow
Yangtze
Mekong

PACIFIC
OCEAN

INDIAN
OCEAN

Port Hedland
Dampier
Brisbane
Perth/Fremantle
Sydney
Melbourne

Maritime Asia

tain a tense standoff over four disputed islands, "ships of peace" carrying local officials between Japan's northernmost island of Hokkaido and Russia's Sakhalin region for the last twenty-five years are now open to ordinary citizens as well.[40] A planned 850-kilometer gas pipeline will link the two zones by 2008, if politics do not intrude.[41] Limited visa-free travel arrangements between Hokkaido and the disputed islands were established in 1992 and are open to all in summertime.[42]

The rest of Maritime Asia's contours are uneven. Vietnam, fiercely independent of China for more than a millennium, has recently earned a place in the region's China-tilted manufacturing network. But maritime North Korea and Myanmar slipped out of the orbit of Maritime Asia into isolation. Laos is landlocked, and Cambodia, mired in misrule and corruption, is only beginning to recover from genocide. To the east, maritime frontiers are still unsettled.

Water is the lifeline of Maritime Asia. Jeffrey Sachs and two of his colleagues have presented strong evidence linking economic growth to coastal economies. They found that the regions within the United States, Western Europe, and temperate-zone East Asia that lie within roughly 60 miles (100 kilometers) of the coast account for only 5 percent of the world's inhabited land but at least 37 percent of the world's gross national product (GNP—measured in terms of purchasing power parity). Nearly all landlocked countries are poor (e.g., Laos). Coastal regions and regions linked to coasts by ocean-navigable waterways are "strongly favored in development in comparison to the hinterlands"—a point made more than two centuries ago by Adam Smith.[43]

Robert Scalapino and others describe the lands constituting portions of Maritime Asia as "natural economic territories." Some such territories have existed for centuries, while others are recent creations. Trade between southern China, Hong Kong, Taiwan, and northern parts of insular Southeast Asia has flourished off and on for centuries, while the growth triangle connecting Singapore with Johor (Malaysia) and Riau (Indonesia) is relatively new.

Another concept in common use is *gateways*. Gateways typically sit astride major trading routes and tend to be more highly developed than their neighboring territories or host states. Their inhabitants often possess strong entrepreneurial habits and extensive overseas links. They are highly dependent on trade and are catalysts for subregional economic interaction. Geographer Saul Cohen lists Singapore, Hong Kong, and Taiwan as existing gateways and adds Guam, southwest Australia, the Russian Far East, and the Hong Kong/Shenzhen/coastal Guangdong/Fujian area as new ones.[44]

The concept of Maritime Asia is quite similar to what the US Department of Defense calls the "East Asian littoral." A quadrennial report published in 2001 defined this term as "the region stretching from south of Japan through Australia and into the Bay of Bengal."[45] Operational concepts adopted by the US Navy divide the East Asian littoral into "seaward" and "landward" portions.[46]

34

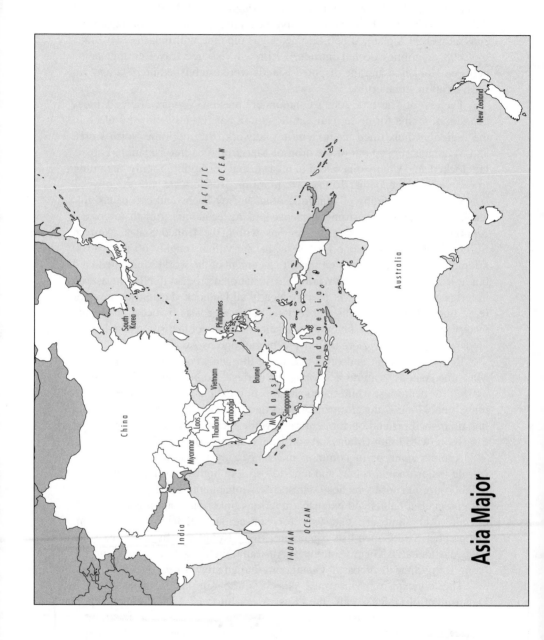

Asia Major

Cities also qualify for remapping. Leading coastal cities dominate both East Asia and India, but on conventional maps they show up as mere dots. Thomas Rohlen has sketched an imaginary map depicting the dozen key metropolitan areas in East Asia as mountains (of activity), while relatively tranquil interior areas would be shown as flat lowlands. Rohlen comments that this "transactional" topography is almost the perfect inverse of the region's actual plains and mountains.[47]

Asia Major

The second mental map reverts to the more familiar world of nation-states. I call it Asia Major.[48] (As noted above, the obsolescent term Asia Minor refers to modern-day Turkey.)[49] Asia Major is a political construct. It is the locus of planned integration driven by national governments. It encompasses the entire territory of nation-states, not just maritime zones. Its core is ASEAN + 3, with India, Australia and New Zealand joining in to make ASEAN + 6. (Taiwan has a de facto presence but is officially excluded.) The governments of these countries have met annually since 2005. The leaders of Asia Major stress that the community that they anticipate could sooner or later admit other nations.

■ Conclusion

Leaders of Asia's new regionalism are sometimes ridiculed for the vagueness with which they define their envisaged "community." Just who is in this community, and who is not? Who counts as truly "Asian?" Who will be invited next? Since Asians disagree, the drafters of Asia-wide communiqués and declarations deliberately leave the answers open-ended.

As this chapter has shown, however, such political evasion can be justified. Asia is an especially porous region that can be defined in different ways for different purposes. Its boundaries have always been subject to interpretation and imagination. Today, informed by remapping and by an appreciation of history, our notion of Asian integration should be recentered to include India and stretched southeastward to include Australia and New Zealand. Since Maritime Asia is older, more persistent, and more dynamic than Asia Major, it is the focus of the next three chapters.

■ Notes

1. See the discussion of defining regions in T. J. Pempel, "Introduction," in Pempel, *Remapping East Asia*, p. 4.
    2. Ibid., p. 2.

3. See http://visibleearth.nasa.gov/view_rec.php?id=1438. NASA's comments are global; I have adapted them to Asia.

4. Black, *Maps and History*, p. 195.

5. *National Geographic Atlas of the World*, 4th ed. (Washington, DC: National Geographic Society, 1975).

6. Robert Bartlett, "Off to a Good Start," review of Jacques Le Goff's *The Birth of Europe*, in *New York Review of Books*, June 9, 2005, p. 43.

7. Norton Ginsburg, "Geography, the Physical Basis," in Matthew, *Asia in the Modern World*.

8. This book uses China's *pinyin* system of phonetics except in the rare cases where a place name or historical period is well known in the West in the older Wade-Giles system, as is the case here.

9. Herman Melville, *Moby Dick* (1851; repr. New York: Modern Library, 1982), pp. 549–550. Melville wrote that the land bordering the Strait of Sunda seemed to guard the riches of Asia from the "all-grasping western world."

10. Takeshi Hamashita, "The Intra-Regional System in East Asia in Modern Times," in Katzenstein and Shiraishi, *Network Power*, p. 115.

11. Emmerson, "The Case for a Maritime Perspective on Southeast Asia," p. 139.

12. Chia Lin Sien and Martin Perry, "Introduction," in Chia, *Southeast Asia Transformed*, p. 4.

13. See the discussion in Charles A. Fisher, "The Maritime Fringe of East Asia," in East and Spate, *The Changing Map of Asia*.

14. Lewis and Wigen, *The Myth of Continents*, pp. 185–188.

15. Wittfogel, *Oriental Despotism*.

16. Murray Hiebert, "Wizard of Oz: Australia's Evans Redraws the Map of Asia," *Far Eastern Economic Review*, August 17, 1995, p. 26.

17. According to Frances Wood of the British Library, the term *die Seidenstrasse*, the Silk Road, was invented by German explorer and geographer Baron Ferdinand von Richthofen. Wood, *The Silk Road*, p. 9.

18. An exception is the North Sea, which was known for a while as the German Sea.

19. Rozman, *The East Asian Region*, p. 6.

20. Zhang Xiaodong, "Geopolitical Changes in the Western Regions," in *Heartland: Eurasian Review of Geopolitics* 1 (2000): 31.

21. Tessa Morris-Suzuki, "Thinking 'Japan': Frontiers and Minorities in Modern Japan," *International House of Japan Bulletin* 24, no. 1 (Spring 2004): 3.

22. Reid, *Charting the Shape of Early Modern Southeast Asia*.

23. Shaffer, *Maritime Southeast Asia to 1500*, p. 2.

24. Martin Bernal, *Black Athena: The Afroasiatic Roots of Classical Civilization*, vol. 2 (New Brunswick, NJ: Rutgers University Press, 1991), p. 191, cited in Lewis and Wigen, *The Myth of Continents*, footnote 11.

25. Macfie, *Orientalism*, p. 14.

26. John Milton, "Paradise Lost," in Scott Elledge, ed., *Paradise Lost* (New York: W. W. Norton, 1975), p. 29.

27. John Keats, "Hyperion" (1884), in Douglas Bush, ed., *John Keats: Selected Poems and Letters* (Boston: Houghton Mifflin, 1959), p. 170.

28. Lewis and Wigen, *The Myth of Continents*, p. 159.

29. Lach, *A Century of Wonder*, p. 29.

30. Buruma and Margalit, *Occidentalism*, p. 52.

31. Lewis and Wigen, *The Myth of Continents*, p. 172. Mountbatten's command included Sri Lanka but excluded the Philippines.

32. Acharya, "Imagined Proximities," pp. 55–76.

33. Cowen et al., "Financial Integration in Asia," p. 4.

34. See, for example, Goh, "Towards an East Asian Renaissance," p. 12.

35. Halford Mackinder, *Democratic Ideas and Reality* (London: Henry Holt, 1919). Cited in Douglas E. Streusand, "Geopolitics Versus Globalization," in Tangredi, *Globalization and Maritime Power,* p. 42.

36. Alfred Thayer Mahan, *The Influence of Sea Power Upon History 1660–1783* (Boston: Little Brown, 1890). Quoted in Sam J. Tangredi, "Globalization and Sea Power," in Tangredi, *Globalization and Maritime Power*, p. 3.

37. Katzenstein, *A World of Regions*, pp. 13–19.

38. Lewis and Wigen, *The Myth of Continents*, pp. 2–3, 151–157, 187–188, 200; Pempel, *Remapping East Asia*; Katzenstein, *A World of Regions*, pp. 13–19.

39. *Compact World Atlas* (London: DK Publishing, 2001).

40. Alexei Sukhorukov, "Russia, Japan United Town Residents Conclude Meet at Sapporo," ITAR-TASS World Service, June 26, 2006.

41. "Japan, Russia to Build Sakhalin-Aomori Gas Pipeline," *Dow Jones Emerging Markets Report*, Dow Jones Newswires, June 12, 2006.

42. Leonid Vinogradov, "South Kuriles, Hokkaido Open Summer Seas of Visa-Free Trips," ITAR-TASS World Service, May 19, 2006.

43. Gallup and Sachs, "Geography and Economic Growth," pp. 8–11. I am grateful to J. David Richardson for bringing this paper to my attention.

44. Cohen, "Geopolitics in the New World Era," pp. 60–66, table 3.5.

45. Department of Defense, *Quadrennial Defense Review Report,* p. 2.

46. The Navy defines the seaward portion as "that area from the open ocean to the shore which must be controlled to support operations onshore." The landward portion is "the area inland from the shore over which friendly forces can be supported and defended directly from the sea." Department of the Navy, *Naval Operations Concept*, p. 9.

47. Rohlen, "Cosmopolitan Cities and Nation States," p. 9.

48. *Asia Major* is also the name of a scholarly journal. Founded in Germany in 1923, *Asia Major* was revived in the United Kingdom but was forced to close in 1975. Revived at Princeton in 1988, it later moved to Taiwan's Academia Sinica and now focuses exclusively on China.

49. The territories lying between Asia Minor and Asia Major might be called "Asia Medior," as in "Mediterranean."

PART 1

Maritime Asia Resurgent

3

The Legacy
of Maritime Asia

Two great chains of trade and travel lacing through Asia date back
to ancient times. In the Book of Exodus, the Lord directs Moses to mix "fra-
grant cinnamon," a product of Sri Lanka, with other spices to make holy oil
for anointing.[1] Chinese silks have been found in Roman tombs. During the
reign of Marcus Aurelius, trade officials in Alexandria imposed a duty on pepper imported from India's Malabar Coast.[2]

Both routes linked the eastern Mediterranean with China. One was the
branched vein of highways known collectively as the Silk Road. The other
route carried goods and travelers by sea. It ran along coasts and great waterways, dipping south to Africa's east coast and linking a string of maritime
cities. Unlike the Silk Road, maritime trade and transport never stopped flowing, but locally imposed restrictions, two centuries of colonialism, and two
world wars broke up the essential unity of the region's coastal communities.

This ancient maritime complex, reinvigorated by modern technology and
new frontiers, is the locus of the spontaneous integration now manifest in
much of Asia. The coastal communities, ports, and other ocean-linked trading
nodes of what I call Maritime Asia are powering most of Asia's dynamic economic growth. They also contribute substantially to its strategic value and
potential power as a region.

This chapter looks briefly at the history of the Silk Road and then turns to
Maritime Asia. These were not the only routes linking Asian societies, of course.
Numerous kingdoms and empires, some of which broadly coincide with the
nation-states of Asia Major, were in regular contact with each other. Travelers
could be found everywhere: emissaries engaged in the Chinese tribute system,
private traders, monks, missionaries, adventurers, warriors, and others. As Nayan
Chanda points out, people like these were the ones who shaped globalization.[3]

Maritime connections were more extensive and more relevant to today's
integration movement than the Silk Road, the Chinese tribute system, or other
precedents. Unlike either the Silk Road's checkered past or the formalized rituals of the tribute system, Maritime Asia's history illustrates the continuity,

complementarity, vitality, and natural connectedness of this region. It suggests that the maritime aspects of the Asian integration movement may reflect an enduring regional equilibrium.

The Silk Road

Of the two great trading routes of Asia, the Silk Road enjoys the more colorful reputation. Who could fail to thrill to "those long caravans that cross the plain / With dauntless feet and sound of silver bells?"[4] Camel caravans trudging through wind-swept deserts and harsh mountain passes stopped at Bokhara, Samarkand, Kashgar, Dunhuang, and many lesser-known crossways. They carried colorful brocades, flowered ceramics, and gleaming gems. Resins, aromatic woods, spices, ginger, medicinal herbs, precious stones, and other treasures and novelties of the known world were also in demand.

After the collapse of the Roman Empire, the great caravans dwindled to an uneven trickle. Trading routes were ravaged by brigands and frequently closed. Ironically, the Silk Road was reopened and safeguarded by the Mongols, despite their blood-curdling reputation. Mongol leaders introduced or promoted remarkably modern commercial practices. The administration of Genghis Khan's grandson Khubilai (Khublai) guaranteed property rights, reduced taxes, improved roads, established bankruptcy laws, and greatly expanded the use of paper money.[5] Describing the international trading economy from the mid-thirteenth to the mid-fourteenth century, historian Janet Abu-Lughod wrote that "goods were transferred, prices set, exchange rates agreed upon, contracts entered into, credit—on funds or on goods located elsewhere—extended, partnerships formed, and, obviously, records kept and agreements honored."[6]

These new procedures smoothed the way for goods, cultural artifacts, ideas, and styles to be shuttled across vast distances. Well into the Ming Dynasty (1368–1644), for example, Persian cobalt traveled to Chinese kilns to color the famous Ming blue porcelain. But these routes gradually broke up again as the descendants of Genghis Khan were assimilated into different civilizations, converted to different religions, and drawn into war against one another. In the nineteenth century, rival rulers of key parts of the Silk Road became pawns in the "Great Game" between England and Russia.

Maritime Routes and Realms

The Unifying Power of the Ocean

Oceans divide people, but they also define and unite them. The great French historian Fernand Braudel named a whole cultural region after a body of water, the Mediterranean.[7] Travel writer Jan Morris wrote that one element made a unity of British colonies from Vancouver to India, Hong Kong, and New Zealand: the sea.[8] Former Indian diplomat Sudhir Devare views seas as natural integrators and cites the "strategic homogeneity" of the whole maritime region stretching from India to Southeast Asia to China.[9]

Nowhere is this unifying and naming power of the sea more manifest than in the history of Asia. The Indian Ocean, the Bay of Bengal, the East China Sea, the South China Sea, the Banda Sea, and major straits and river deltas in between were the watery arms of a great Asia-wide system. The sea defined and bound its parts. The Chinese name for Southeast Asia was *nan yang*—(the region of) the southern oceans. Two contemporary scholars assert that the maritime character of Southeast Asia is its "first and primary unifying feature."[10] Historian Anthony Reid argues that in past centuries Southeast Asia was "manifestly better integrated" by the warm and calm South China Sea than were Europe, the Levant, and North Africa by the Mediterranean.[11] The late maritime historian Ashin Das Gupta discerned a creative power at work in the Indian Ocean. He went so far as to say that it was not that the continental state upheld port cities, but rather that the Indian Ocean itself created them.[12]

People who live along the coast look outward toward the sea but also toward each other. Communities bordering the sea tend to develop links. Residents often buy the same foreign goods and discuss the same ideas. Their cultures are cosmopolitan. Races and nationalities vary widely, mingling more easily and freely than they do in more isolated communities. Not only goods and money but also people, ideas, technology, religion, art, literature, music, and other aspects of the human experience travel along coastal routes and ocean-accessible waterways.[13]

Claiming greater knowledge and sophistication and enjoying higher incomes, residents of maritime communities and ocean-accessible cities frequently look down on inland inhabitants. Naturally enterprising, they find ways of getting around restrictions that violate their cosmopolitan and tolerant habits. Venice, for example, resisted a sixteenth-century campaign against the Jews and maintained control of the press despite strong pressure from Rome.[14] Similarly, coastal residents often defied or ignored directives from the great inland kingdoms of Asia.

Until the age of steam navigation, travel by ship was slow and often dangerous. Not for centuries did traders and other travelers stray far from the coast. Sudden storms could blow them into unknown waters; the great fourteenth-century Muslim traveler Ibn Battuta described just such an episode near Sumatra. "We then betook ourselves to repentance and prayer to Almighty God, with all our hearts," he wrote, "and, in addition to this, the merchants made many vows."[15]

Maritime historian Samuel Eliot Morison wrote that ships returning to Boston from Canton would first catch the northeast monsoon down the South China Sea. Encountering "fantastic islands, baffling winds, and treacherous currents" as they passed Borneo, ships that struck a reef would attract hundreds of Malay *proas* (praus, small vessels) manned by fierce pirates. Once free of the dangerous Sunda Strait, also plagued by Malay pirates, the ships would pick up the southeast wind across the Indian Ocean to Madagascar, the Cape of Good Hope, and home.[16]

Traveling to and around Asia by water depended on the wind. Asia experiences a seasonal reversal of winds and rains (the "monsoon effect") stronger than that found anywhere else. Voyages were timed in accordance with the monsoon, which confined sailors and merchants to long stays in port. These lengthy sojourns facilitated the spread of technology, culture, and religion and frequently led to intermarriage.

The Maritime Trading System

In contrast to the Silk Road, maritime routes adapted to or bypassed political interference and flourished virtually without interruption. If skirmishes closed a port or if a river delta silted up, ship captains found new routes.

Sea-based trade stretched from the eastern Mediterranean down the Red Sea and the Persian Gulf to Yemen and eastern Africa, coastal India, Sri Lanka, the northern edge of the Bay of Bengal, Sumatra, Java, the southern Philippines, and southern China, and from there to northern China, Korea, and Japan. As knowledge of navigation grew and the technology of sailing vessels improved, trading vessels struck out for open water and crossed the Indian Ocean and the South China Sea.

In this maritime system, the great civilizations of Asia rippled and overlapped. There was neither a single hegemon nor a single "golden age." Local rulers launched wars over land but did not succeed in controlling the oceans on any significant scale. Although Muslims gradually came to dominate major sea routes, blocking direct access to India from Europe, no single political authority dominated Asia's precolonial maritime trade with any consistency. The great powers of the day were land-based empires: China was a land-based power, India was centered in the Gangetic plain for most of its history, and the rice kingdoms of Java looked not to the sea but inward.

As kingdoms rose and fell, ownership of major shipping fleets fluctuated. In the seventh century, Persian merchant ships led navigation to and from China, but by the ninth century, Arab traders had largely supplanted them. In the tenth and eleventh centuries, new maritime powers such as the Cholas of India and the Burmese at Pagan arose and eclipsed their rivals. By the twelfth century, huge Chinese junks had nosed other ships aside. The success of each group of ship owners and merchants stimulated the others to compete.

In the fifteenth century, the expansion of Gujurati commerce and the rise of western Javanese shipping swelled the sea routes. The spread of Islam, which had arrived in coastal Southeast Asia by sea, spelled the decline of the Hindu-Buddhist kingdom of Majapahit in east Java. It also boosted demand for voyages to Mecca. The end of the fifteenth century saw the first trickle of seaborne explorers from the West. In the early seventeenth century, Aceh was a thriving power and still retains the mixed cultures and cuisines of a former trading center.

Except for general location at key points such as the Strait of Malacca, there was little continuity in the exact location of prosperous port towns. The town of Masulipatam, for example, had once been the principal trade depot of India's Coromandel Coast, linking the Golconda kingdom with the outside world. But by 1800, it was a "small, ramshackle place, with a crumbling fort, a newly rebuilt English church and a graveyard."[17] Wherever they were, maritime cities would contain a customs house, a shipyard, and a place to do business. Neighboring villages supplied food and manpower for voyages.

What defined a thriving maritime city was its ability to offer tradable goods. Much depended on the quality of the goods and whether the city's port facilities were capable of handling the flow of commodities between east and west. In Gujurat, home of many of the great Indian merchant shipping families, ascendancy passed from Broach to Cambay, Surat, and eventually Bombay (Mumbai). In the Bay of Bengal, Thai ports formed connections between the China Sea and networks to the west.[18] This mingling branched out unevenly; it largely bypassed Cambodia and Vietnam, for example.

In major port cities of the Indian Ocean and South China Sea, merchants enjoyed considerable autonomy. Each of the major trading groups was allowed to have a local manager who took care of the community's needs without interference from local authorities. Merchants also banded together in associations for protection and the promotion of mutual interests. Unlike the Hanseatic League in Europe, however, these merchant societies did not share a common body of law and custom.

Merchants, sailors, and other travelers moved freely among maritime cities and often resettled in one of them. In the eighteenth century, Chinese sojourners migrated to Java as merchants, to Borneo and the Malay sultanates as miners, and as merchants to Thailand. Penang, on the Strait of Malacca, attracted Chinese, Thai, Burmese, Javanese, and Sumatran merchants and sailors, among others.[19]

Naval power deployed to defend these cities was cross-cultural and rudimentary. It consisted mainly of oar-driven galleys whose inadequacy became pitifully apparent after Portuguese and Dutch warships arrived. Cannons were loaded on board in the fifteenth century. In Southeast Asia, it was customary for rulers to counter a naval attack by employing Gujurati, Malay, or Chinese vessels and their crew.[20]

▦ Magnets, Magnates, and Marauders

China

China was a powerful magnet for traders. Chinese silks were prized everywhere. Chinese porcelain and earthenware influenced ceramics throughout the known world. Tea from China spread through monastic communities to Japan, Central Asia, Siberia, Tibet, and the Middle East before seeping into Europe as a luxury item in the seventeenth century. The Chinese government did its best to control trade, but at various times the tribute system served as little more than a formal and ceremonial overlay supplementing extensive private trade.

China's relations with maritime Southeast Asia were based primarily on trade. China never played an important political role there. But China's contacts with its neighbors on the mainland included not only trade but also the spread of Buddhism, involvement in local conflicts, and periodic warfare to secure its frontiers.[21]

During the Ming Dynasty (1368–1644), China drew inward. Trade was restricted to tributary states, and the consumption of foreign goods was discouraged or forbidden. In 1394, for example, ordinary Chinese were prohibited from using foreign perfumes and other foreign goods.[22] The famous fifteenth-century voyages of the Chinese Muslim admiral Zheng He, who plowed the seas with armadas of up to 300 vessels and 30,000 men, reached Hormuz, Aden, and the east coast of Africa as well as Southeast Asia. But the goals of Ming emperor Yung-lo were not to conquer territory or establish beachheads for commercial expansion but rather to assert China's presence in the Indian Ocean, encourage Indian Ocean states to come to China to trade, and discipline Chinese merchants engaging in piracy. In the 1420s, Ming rulers turned inward and these voyages ceased.[23] As the government turned its attention to meeting the Mongol threat from the north and subduing unruly "barbarians" in the west, the imperial capital moved from Nanking to Peking, which was not a commercial city. Not until 1567 did the Ming government finally revoke its prohibition on maritime trade.

After Manchu invaders seized power in China in 1644, the Ming loyalist Koxinga (Zheng Chenggong) fled to Taiwan and continued to resist the alien dynasty. From there he launched attacks on China. In some coastal communities, particularly Fujian and Guangdong, Chinese authorities forcibly moved entire populations ten miles (16 kilometers) inland, not so much to protect them from attack as to thwart any effort by Taiwan-based Ming loyalists to cultivate local support.[24]

For a while, Taiwan was a free-trade entrepôt of sorts. Before the arrival of the Dutch, Chinese and Japanese traders evaded various restrictions by doing business in Taiwan. Even after the Dutch East India Company was established in the area, Taiwanese were in a position to capitalize on the company's unique foothold in Japan. Koxinga took Taiwan from the Dutch in 1662 but died shortly thereafter. In 1683, Taiwan was incorporated into China and almost immediately lost its value as a handy place to conduct maritime trade.[25] As the Chinese navy continued to fall into disuse, pirates operating from Japan and Taiwan repeatedly raided China's southern and eastern coastline. Thenceforth Chinese merchants confined themselves to Malacca and points east. Even in the nineteenth century, when the importance of maritime power was glaringly obvious, the Chinese government failed to appreciate the importance of a navy and was thrown on the defensive as seaborne Westerners demanded one concession after another.

Thus, in Wang Gungwu's wonderful prose, China remained "earthbound"; the great "seaward sweep" of Chinese sojourners settling elsewhere in Asia did not begin until the nineteenth century.[26] Despite Zheng He's achievements, China never became a maritime power, and its leaders consistently underestimated the threat from the sea. Confucian officials could not understand why Western governments would subordinate statecraft to the dictates of mere merchants and glorify trade as a national goal. For them, trade was an instrument of statecraft, not something of value for its own sake.

By the time Chinese authorities finally recognized the need for a muscular navy, in the mid–nineteenth century, the Qing Dynasty was decaying and statecraft was tottering. The once-mighty Chinese empire, sapped by revolts and corruption, lapsed into a semicolonial coma. When funds for the navy were finally appropriated, they were diverted to the construction of a summer palace for the empress dowager. Watching all this, the Meiji government in Japan modernized and expanded its military forces, declared war on China, and won a decisive victory in 1895. China's "century of humiliation" was at its midpoint.

India

India was literally central to the precolonial trading network. It was a huge, U-shaped anchor of trade—"on the way to everywhere," as one scholar put it.[27] Indian, Chinese, Malay, Arab, and (eventually) Western merchants took advantage of India's central location, and Indian merchants were active throughout the entire trading system. Indian merchants were the first outsiders to seek out Southeast Asia's wealth.[28] In an early example of what we now call the export of services, several thousand men from India traveled with the ships and took care of all their commercial needs while in port. When the Indian merchant fleet dwindled and disappeared, the men of this service sector accommodated themselves to shipowners of other nationalities.[29]

Indians were avid traders. For centuries, Indian ships from both western and eastern ports crisscrossed the ocean. They were familiar with the Strait of

Malacca and docked regularly in Vietnamese, Burmese, and Chinese ports. They knew their way to the islands of present-day Indonesia. Their contacts with the Srivijaya and Majapahit in Sumatra and Java are well documented. They docked at the Kra peninsula in southern Thailand, where Indian goods would be carried across the narrow slice of land on their way to China. They may have visited Korea.

Like China, India was a rich source of religion and culture for the rest of Asia. In the first few centuries of the Christian era, monks and scholars from India carried Hinduism and Buddhism into China and Southeast Asia, where they blended with and enriched the civilizations of their converts. Anyone who wanders through the great temple complexes of Asia sees carvings and inscriptions reflecting India's influence. Panoramic battle scenes from the *Ramayana* enliven the walls of Cambodia's Angkor Wat. Vivid scenes from the life of the Buddha ring Indonesia's great temple-mountain complex, Borobodur. Monks from China, Japan, and elsewhere made pilgrimages to India to visit holy sites associated with the life of Buddha. Traveling by foot, horse, camel, and elephant, the revered Chinese Buddhist monk Hsuan Tsang (Xuan Zang) crossed more than 4,800 miles (8,000 kilometers) of forbidding territory to seek the original classics of Buddhist thought from its source in India.[30]

Indian notions of cosmology and universal kingship found ready supporters throughout much of Southeast Asia. What is sometimes called the "Indianization" of Southeast Asia was actually the blending of certain Hindu ideas with indigenous cultures. O. W. Wolters highlighted one of those ideas, the concept of *mandalas* (circles of kings), to describe the overlapping kingdoms and diffuse political power characteristic of early Southeast Asia.[31] To bolster their legitimacy, Hindu-Buddhist rulers in Southeast Asia sometimes claimed descent from an Indian prince and commissioned great temples in honor of Shiva and Vishnu. Indian influence lasted from the fourth century A.D. until as late as the fifteenth century.

Indians had greater cultural and religious influence on Southeast Asia (except Vietnam) than the Chinese did. Why and how crossing the ocean became a Hindu taboo in a country that boasts well over 4,000 miles (7,000 kilometers) of coastline is both a mystery and a historical disaster.[32]

Japan

Japan was the far northeastern peg of the maritime trading system. Until the Ming Dynasty (1368–1644), the Japanese traded almost continuously with China and Korea, sharing and adapting cultural and religious influences. At the same time, Japanese brigands carried out repeated raids on Korea and China. One reason why the Mongols tried to conquer Japan in the thirteenth century was that they wanted to suppress these maritime incursions.[33]

Legal trade among Japan, China, and Korea was strictly controlled. Under the Chinese tribute system, Japanese traders were licensed, regulated, and assigned to specific ports. A treaty signed in 1443 governed trade between Japan and Korea for a century and a half, designating three ports for Koreans and limiting the number of Japanese traders. The Japanese military leader Hideyoshi brought peaceful trade to an end by invading Korea at the end of the sixteenth century. By the sixteenth and seventeenth centuries, Japanese settlers seeking better opportunities had made their way to the Philippines, Siam (Thailand), Cambodia, Annan (Vietnam) and elsewhere in Asia.

In 1600, forces loyal to Ieyasu Tokugawa, Hideyoshi's successor, won a decisive battle and unified Japan. The new shogunate gradually closed off the country. After 1625 or so until the arrival of Commodore Perry in 1854, the Japanese government attempted to wall off Japanese traders based in the home islands from participation in external trade. In 1635, it forbade foreign voyages, leaving trade in the control of resident foreign traders.

Tokugawa Japan was never completely closed. Although Japanese authorities refused to take part in the China-centered trading system as a tributary state and declined either to send or receive state-to-state trade missions, they tolerated an unofficial Chinese trading community in Nagasaki. Trade relations with Korea were delegated to the lord of Tsushima, who maintained an outpost in Pusan; imports from Korea sometimes exceeded those entering Nagasaki. Satsuma, in the south, seized Okinawa in 1609 and profited from the Ryukyu Islands' status as a tributary to China.[34] Trade with the West, however, was largely closed off, because Westerners sought to convert Japanese to Christianity and thus posed a political threat to Tokugawa rule. Even so, Tokugawa authorities kept a tiny window open to the Dutch at Nagasaki and permitted a small group of scholars to pursue "Western learning" (*orangaku,* literally Holland studies).[35]

Both before and after the Tokugawa victory, groups of Japanese and other pirates used Taiwan and other islands as staging areas to engage in smuggling and launch attacks on the Chinese coast. Raw silk and other textile goods from China were particularly prized. Even after the Ming government relaxed its restrictions on trade, Japan remained off-limits to Chinese traders and vice versa. Seizing an opportunity to make a profit, the Portuguese stepped in as middlemen.[36] Only in the Tokugawa period were Sino-Japanese commercial relations reestablished. Japanese forces conquered Okinawa in 1609 but permitted the kingdom to retain nominal independence so that the Ryukyus could continue to trade officially with China as a tributary state.

After the opening of Japan in 1854, and particularly after the Meiji Restoration of 1868, Japan rejoined the maritime Asian trading system. Numerous Japanese consulates were established throughout Asia, beginning with Manila (1888). After Japan wrested Taiwan from China in 1895, Japanese traders turned south and began eyeing what would become a coveted prize in the 1930s—Southeast Asia's natural resources. Manchuria and Korea were also attractive commercial targets.

Japanese investors were among the first to establish operations in Asia. In the latter part of the nineteenth century, they financed railroads and other transportation networks, especially in Manchuria and Korea, and began investing in mines. Trading companies moved into China to capture exports of raw cotton, soybeans, and other products. By 1914, Mitsui had set up some forty-six branches in Asia, mostly in China. Shipping and financial services were also priority sectors for Japanese investors.[37]

Southeast Asia

Long known as a source of the rarest and finest spices, Southeast Asia also produced aromatic woods and resins, textiles, dyestuffs, rice, and other products. Evidence of trade with India dates back at least 2,000 years. In later centuries, traders from the Ryukyu Islands introduced Southeast Asian wares to Japan, China, and Korea. The Malays were great seafarers and soon spread out on their own.

The maritime history of a region as diverse as Southeast Asia is too complex to summarize here,[38] but the rise and fall of three prominent kingdoms underscore the importance of trade and maritime power. Prospering centuries before the rise of Singapore and Hong Kong, the three were Majapahit, Srivijaya, and Malacca.

Majapahit. The kingdom of Majapahit in eastern Java, which reached a pinnacle in the fourteenth century, was an inland hub but also a thriving trade center. Its rulers claimed authority over vassal states in Sumatra, the Malay Peninsula, Kalimantan, and eastern Indonesia as well as ritual hegemony in the southern Philippines and New Guinea.[39] Majapahit kings also maintained relationships with the kingdoms of mainland Southeast Asia and sent tributary missions to China. Scholars believe that trade connections rather than religious authority probably linked Majapahit's diverse territories.[40] Historical records confirm that despite Majapahit's relatively remote location, traders from China, India, Cambodia, Vietnam, Thailand, and elsewhere gathered in Bubat, the kingdom's twin-city trading center.

Ironically, the very growth and development of the international spice trade that had boosted Majapahit's position ultimately undermined it. The trade was so profitable that it spread beyond the authorities' control, fostering new ports and coastal communities whose traders had no intention of submitting to the king's regulations. As a further signal of independence, Java's coastal communities defied Majapahit's Hindu-Buddhist kings and converted to Islam.[41]

The arrival of Islam in Southeast Asia from the ninth century on strongly influenced the maritime history of the region. Islam arrived not by the sword but in the minds and souls of seaborne traders. After taking root in the port cities of Southeast Asia, the new religion soon spread along the coasts. Starting from northern Sumatra, it took hold most firmly in the areas most important to trade: the Sumatran coast bordering the Strait of Malacca, the Malay peninsula, the north coast of Java, Brunei, Sulu (in the southern Philippines), and Maluku (Indonesia's Spice Islands).[42] Muslim traders dominated the sea routes between Asia and Europe for the five centuries following the introduction and adoption of Islam in the region.

Since Islam assigns a higher status to the merchant than does any other major religion, arriving merchants possessed status as well as wealth and were often able to marry into local ruling families. Adopting the new religion went along with this intermingling. In the process of assimilation and synthesis, "Arab Islam" was transformed into South Asian and Southeast Asian Islam and was modified by local patterns of politics, law, and society.[43] Reflecting the tolerant and cosmopolitan culture of the maritime region, its converts eschewed fanaticism, the seclusion of women, and more extreme versions of the faith.

Not surprisingly, religion and power politics became entangled. Islam helped cement political alliances among those defying non-Muslim authority, as in the case of Majapahit. Islamic ties also made it easier for smaller communities to enter into the trading system.[44] In regions where a Muslim ruler battled a non-Muslim one, military power decided the religious fate of the population, but the victor's ambition was rarely if ever to spread the teaching of the Prophet.

Srivijaya. Srivijaya, which spanned the seventh to the fourteenth centuries, was an early ancestor of Malacca and Singapore and a clear example of the importance of maritime power as a source of wealth.[45] The exact location of its capital is unknown and may have shifted several times. Srivijaya controlled the strategically vital Strait of Malacca and both of its two adjacent coasts—eastern Sumatra and the west coast of the Malay peninsula. It became a key entrepôt, an intermediary center of trade and transshipment, straddling trade with India and Persia to the west and China to the east. Its rulers succeeded in establishing a tributary relationship with China, which earned them the right to trade with China and guaranteed Chinese protection.[46] Srivijaya began to decline in the twelfth century, when the rise of Chinese shipping undermined both Malay competitors and the leverage of Malay authorities. Military expeditions from Thailand and Java over the next two centuries completed its fall.

Malacca. On the eve of the arrival of the Portuguese and the Dutch, around the turn of the sixteenth century, residual landlocked kingdoms with highly developed cultures were still vying for territory even if maritime trade contributed a greater share of wealth. But as shipping technology advanced, maritime centers flourished. The successor to Srivijaya was Malacca

(Melaka). Malacca was an upstart, founded only in the early years of the fifteenth century. Located midway along a vital strait and initially sponsored and protected by Chinese fleets, Malacca quickly became a major hub.

"Whoever is Lord of Malacca has his hand on the throat of Venice," declared the Portuguese envoy Tomé Pires shortly after Portugal conquered the city in 1511. Cambay, a Portuguese trade enclave in India, "could not live" if it were cut off from Malacca.[47] Although Pires was deliberately making a case for Portuguese control of Malacca and the Indonesian archipelago, he was not far wrong.[48] Malacca in the east and Cambay and Calicut on India's west coast (in Gujurat and Kerala, respectively) were links in a single maritime chain. Like Srivijaya before it, Malacca was a thriving commercial center and point of transshipment. Its power derived from control of the key strait linking trade between the east and the west. Chinese, Japanese, Okinawans, Gujuratis, Indian merchant groups from Burma, and Southeast Asians from as far as the Philippines mingled with Persians and Arabs.

Malacca's decline began when the Portuguese conquered the city and continued when it was passed to the Dutch in 1641. An English traveler reported in 1699 that in Malacca the "Moors" sold goods from Bengal, the Indian city of Surat (just north of today's Mumbai), and the Coromandel Coast in southeast India, while the Chinese sold "Tea, Sugar-candy, and other Sweetmeats."[49] If it is true that the Chinese sold only tea and candy, the city had sunk low indeed.

The British acquired Malacca in 1795, but its successor, Singapore, was almost 200 miles (322 kilometers) down the coast. Founded by Thomas Stamford Raffles in 1819 and ceded to the British by the sultan of Johor in 1824, Singapore soon became an exporter of tin and rubber as well as a naval base. But by that time, control of the Strait of Malacca was already divided—and remains so today.

■ The Colonial Era

In the late 1490s, Vasco da Gama blazed the way from Europe to Asia around the Cape of Good Hope. Lured by the fabled wealth of the Indies, others soon followed. The Western colonial presence in Asia, which began on a large scale with the Portuguese conquest of Malacca in 1511, lasted four and a half centuries.

The first groups to arrive in Asia were mostly ragtag adventurers and buccaneers, but merchants soon banded together to finance more voyages. Mouthwatering profits awaited them. In 1603 alone, ships carrying a million pounds of pepper arrived in London; their investors reaped a whopping 170 percent profit on each of the first eight voyages.[50] Rival European governments soon recognized what was at stake and organized state-supported trading companies. The Portuguese and the Dutch came first, closely followed by the British and somewhat later by the French.

Western warship technology was superior to anything Asians had ever seen. Westerners used it to battle not only the natives but also each other. They armed their allies, replacing swords with cannons. Between them they compiled an appalling record of betrayal, bloodshed, and plunder.[51] Their behavior toward native peoples was equally unscrupulous in the early years. In India, Burma, and elsewhere, the French and the British engaged in elaborate games of intrigue. Playing local rulers against each other, Europeans tricked and fought their way into the interior.

Asian rulers were slow to realize the full extent of the threat from these seaborne barbarians. Before the thirteenth century, Europeans were mere upstarts compared to the great civilizations of China and the Middle East,[52] but several centuries later a remarkable reversal occurred. In most Asian capitals, curiosity—"one of the permanent and certain characteristics of a vigorous mind," as Samuel Johnson put it—somehow died and traditions froze. The belief that moral superiority would triumph over Western greed was to prove disastrous. The Qing emperor Kang Xi told a pesky British envoy that China already had everything it needed. With the exception of two remarkable Thai kings, no Southeast Asian ruler fully realized what he was up against when Western powers began knocking.[53]

After the first and second Opium Wars (1840–1842 and 1856–1860), Westerners essentially controlled China's trade and customs. Trade with Asia was popular at home; trade symbolized peace, prosperity, and civilization. Tennyson looked into the future and "saw the heavens fill with commerce / argosies of magic sails."[54] The Dutch and the French established corresponding monopolies of power in their respective colonies. Americans were also in the game, demanding equal access to markets and trading widely in the region. It was said that young men from Salem were likely to see Canton before they visited Boston.

Western traders needed local partners. Initially, indigenous traders found that inviting European and US participation sometimes worked to their advantage because it stimulated competition and drove up prices. For their part, Westerners needed local partners to handle complex business arrangements in their own language. In some places, these partnerships persisted. The sea captains of Boston, for example, worked closely with Hong merchants. One of them, Houqua, was described by a Boston Brahmin as a "perfect gentleman"; his name was a household word in Boston merchants' families.[55]

Western traders did not so much invent new routes and patterns of exchange as move in on old ones. Once they established a foothold, the various colonial merchant groups and their Asian partners typically adopted a triangular trading pattern. The strategy of the Dutch East India Company, for example, revolved around Indian textiles and raw silk, Indonesian spices, and Japanese silver. Dutch investment in India produced textiles that were sold to buy Indonesian spices, and what was not sent home became the basis for the further expansion of trade. Indian textiles and raw silk constituted about half of Japanese purchases from the Dutch, who alone were formally allowed to maintain a presence in Japan after the closing of the country. It was highly advantageous for the Dutch to convert Japanese silver into Taiwanese gold, which in turn funded further investments in Indian textiles. In 1612, a future Dutch governor of the East Indies described India's Coromandel Coast as "the left arm of the Moluccas" (Indonesia's Molukus or Spice Islands), because without the textiles that came from there, the textile-spices-silver trade triangle could not flourish.[56]

The Regional Impact of Colonialism

As colonial rule became more forceful and exclusive, at least seven profound changes broke upon the entire region. First, the imperial powers divided up most of Asia into spheres of influence, took control of trade and customs, and restricted access to inland waterways. These moves severed the great unity of the Indian Ocean trading system. This process was gradual; not until well after the arrival of the Portuguese did the western and eastern halves of the Indian Ocean become functionally separate.[57] Over time, trade within empires nudged out trade among them. Sharply discriminatory trade practices arose late in the game; Britain's imperial tariff preferences, first introduced in 1898, took on real significance only in the wake of the Great Depression, when global free trade broke down and Europe prepared for war.

Wherever they could, colonial authorities imposed direct or indirect rule and pacified, bought off, or otherwise neutralized most of the remaining "independent" governments. Within these territories or zones, Westerners controlled trade and set up separate courts. They encouraged trade within the empire and sometimes erected new barriers between contiguous states ruled by different colonial powers.

Second, the Western powers consolidated a number of loose entities into larger groupings and demarcated them clearly. Before the colonial era, India did not exist as such. What is now Indonesia was ruled by a number of local kingdoms. Several other countries began their national existence as colonial groupings or acquired their current boundaries as a consequence of great-power rivalry. For example, when Burmese rulers tried to reaffirm their paramount position in what they regarded as frontier zones to the west, they clashed with British interests. When they invaded Bengal in the 1820s, the British launched what became a staged conquest of Burma, culminating in the capture of Mandalay in 1886 and the consolidation of Myanmar as we know it today.

Meanwhile, French forces invaded Vietnam in the 1850s and Cambodia in the 1860s, creating a new state—Laos—along the way. Thailand was a buffer state between French and British interests and maneuvered accordingly. Further to the south and east, the three British bases of Singapore, Penang, and Malacca constituted the Straits Settlements. Before the British arrived, the northern states of the Malay peninsula had maintained vassal relationships with Thai kings, while the Islamic southern states had ties to the sultanates of what is today's Indonesia. The Philippines came into being as a fixed entity only when it succumbed to Spain.

As the scramble for Asia intensified and rival colonial empires jostled for control of frontier areas, dividing up previously uncharted areas became vitally important. Western cartographers soon hardened anything that still remained fluid into black lines on a map. Asian rulers were unaccustomed to and unprepared for such precise notions. In their world, as Benedict Anderson puts it, "sovereignties faded imperceptibly into one another." They failed to grasp the modern conception of sovereignty, which in Anderson's words is "fully, flatly, and evenly operative over each square centimeter of a legally demarcated territory."[58] Writing about British expansion, historian Milton Osborne calls this failure "an almost textbook instance of the clash between alien and Southeast Asian values."[59]

Third, in the nineteenth century, Japan joined the colonial game, annexing Taiwan in 1895 and Korea in 1910. After Germany was defeated in World War I, Japan took over German colonial possessions and privileges. Many leaders from Korea and Taiwan studied in Japan and spoke Japanese, and many of the commercial ties established in that era persist to this day. Japan's Greater East Asia Co-Prosperity Sphere was a colonial scheme.

Fourth, Western and Japanese colonialists created the physical foundations of modern Asia's place in the world trading system. They transformed many of Asia's small-scale subsistence farms into large-scale plantations producing cash crops for the world market. Vast tracts of forest and jungle were cleared without regard to preserving the natural environment. Asia became a global supplier of rubber, tin, rice, palm oil, coffee, tea, and sugar on a large scale. By the 1930s, Southeast Asia produced 85 percent of the world's rubber and 65 percent of the world's tin.[60]

The development of these commodities expanded trade significantly and had a huge impact on world markets. Tea was one of the earliest commodities to be traded on a world basis, aside from spices. The Chinese tea monopoly prompted the British to experiment in Assam with growing tea, which grew into a major Indian export industry. Whoever returned to London with the first chests of fine tea from China and India stood to earn a great deal of money. When these ships began making direct runs to China in the 1730s, prices in the British Isles and the American colonies dropped so low, as one observer put it, that "the *meanest* labouring Man could compass the Purchase of it."[61] A century later, the tea trade helped spur the invention and design of the clipper ships.

Whenever the colonial powers consolidated their rule, their determination to develop large-scale commodity exports sparked the development of roads and railroads connecting remote parts of the interior with the coast (and sometimes with each other). In Malaysia, for example, almost all communication took place by water until the last decades of the nineteenth century; roads and railways were built to carry tin and rubber to the coast.[62] Banking and communications facilities sprouted up along these routes, but transport between interior regions remained rudimentary.

Starting from fragile trading posts and "factories," early colonizers built or expanded large numbers of ports and exercised substantial extraterritorial jurisdiction within them. As new ports arose, many older ports and their associated merchant groups fell into decline. Wealth and power drifted from the cultural capitals of the interior—such as Mandalay, Jogjakarta, and Delhi—to the mercantile world of the coast even more rapidly than before. Among the new ports built or expanded by colonial powers were Bombay (Mumbai), Madras (Chennai), Calcutta (Kolkata), Chittagong, Rangoon (Yangon), Penang, Singapore, and Batavia (Jakarta). Asia thus became more interconnected and irreversibly bound up with world markets.

Fifth, colonial rulers hardened social distinctions as well as boundaries. In some cases they sharpened ethnic, religious, class, and caste divisions by choosing one group over another in the administration of government or in military service. These groups became a privileged class, with secure jobs and higher incomes than others. They learned the colonial power's language and were educated in Western ways. They often adopted the lifestyle of their conquerors.

Colonial subjects were taught to look toward and up to their Western or Japanese rulers. Missionaries and educators established Christian schools and did their best to convert Asians to the form of Christianity that they practiced at home. Children living on one side of the Strait of Malacca were taught to speak Dutch, while those on the other side learned English. On the eastern side of the Gulf of Thailand, Cambodians and Vietnamese learned French. Koreans were forced to learn Japanese and to imbibe Japanese culture.

Sixth, the development of large-scale mining, agriculture, and shipping altered the character of the migration of labor. In the nineteenth and early twentieth centuries, Europeans and Japanese recruited Asian laborers to clear jungles, drain swamps, lay transport lines, and dig mines. If local workers were unwilling or unable to meet the demand, workers were imported from China or India. Western and Japanese companies recruited labor from within their colonial region; the British shipping companies, for example, recruited sailors from Bombay and Bengal and carpenters, cooks, and launderers from Singapore.[63] The introduction of steam navigation created skilled jobs for Europeans and consigned Asians to lower positions.

Finally, the colonial era created and buffeted Asian self-images in ways that both fostered and hindered a sense of community. Colonialism created the very idea of "Asia," displacing the China-centered mental map long internalized by tributary states. But this Asia was largely a foreign creation. It stressed East-West differences and thereby bestowed an imagined unity on the "East."

The Western cultural movement known as Orientalism is an extreme example. Derived from a Latin word meaning "rising" and signifying the East, Orientalism first focused its gaze on an imaginary Egypt and then moved eastward, just as "Asia" did. The prisms through which this group of Orientalists filtered what they saw in Asia often reflected the fantasies and fashions of the day. Rather than search for common traits, they emphasized the differences, ascribing a sensuous, irrational, and despotic character to the "East."[64] Viewing the same tendency toward distortion from a twentieth-century perspective, French expert François Godement remarked, "The words 'Asia' and 'the East' are loaded terms from a fantasy seemingly woven from a Baudelaire poem, a melody by Ravel, a short story by Somerset Maugham, and a James Ivory film."[65]

Westerners came to instruct and "enlighten" Asians, with motives and results that seem offensive today. For France, the goal of the *mission civilisatrice* was to bring dark-skinned people into the orbit of French culture and civilization. Thomas MacAulay believed passionately that British authorities in India needed to form "a class of persons, Indian in blood and color, but English in taste, in opinions, in morals, and in intellect."[66] What attitudes like this did to cultural pride and individual self-respect can easily be imagined.

Many Orientalists, however, approached Asia with respect. Some adapted to their new environment with enthusiasm, married local women, and never returned home.[67] Others pioneered the field of Asian studies. At a time when the great empires of Asia were bowing to Western guns, they fostered scholarship and research on Asian languages, art, literature, religion, philosophy, flora and fauna, and history.[68] William Jones, Ernest Fenollosa, Thomas Stamford Raffles, Emile Guimet, Max Müller, and many others recorded, safeguarded, and collected much that would have been lost or underrated by Asians themselves. The College of Fort William in Calcutta, for example, founded in 1800 by Governor General Lord Wellesley in collaboration with the Asiatic Society of Bengal, helped to revive the study of Sanskrit and other ancient Indian languages, added vernacular languages to the curriculum, and planted the seeds of the Bengal Renaissance movement, an ancestor of the Congress Party.[69]

Colonial powers taught Western languages to the educated elite, enabling people from different ethnic backgrounds to communicate with each other. Today, English is the regionwide lingua franca. The new rulers introduced notions of universal rights, freedom, justice, and equality, which later served to rally Asians to the cause of anti-imperialism. They drove Asian intellectuals like the Chinese scholar Yen Fu to search for the sources of Western "wealth and power" and to adapt them to Asian cultures, a process that is still under way today.[70]

■ Asian Responses

For Asians, the idea of *Asia* as a collective label was inseparable from the corresponding idea of "the West." As an imagined locus of shared identity and common purpose, Asia was an antidote to the sense of weakness and humiliation bred by foreign occupation and control. Japan's victory over Russia in 1905 stimulated pan-Asianism and anticolonialism because it demonstrated that an Asian country could defeat a "white" country.

Most reformers stuck to their own country, but a few argued that if Asians could only unite, they could shake off the colonial yoke. At the core of their thinking was the notion of moral superiority, or at least a distinctive set of moral virtues. The West might have superior weapons, but Asians had superior values. Western technology and wealth hid a profound moral weakness. Asians were spiritual, devoted to the communal good, whereas Westerners were materialistic, grasping at individual rights. Since Asians were morally superior, there was no need to emphasize such "Western" ideas as individual rights and the rule of law.

In a book published in 1904, for example, the Japanese pan-Asianist Okakura Kakuzo coined the phrase "Asia is One." "The common thought-inheritance of every Asiatic race," he wrote, was the "broad expanse of love for the Ultimate and Universal." Westerners, by contrast, were bogged down in "the Particular," fixated by the means, not the end, of life.[71]

For Sun Yat-sen, Asia represented "benevolence, justice, and morality," which he called the Rule of Right. Westerners, by contrast, relied on the Rule of Might.[72] Visiting China in 1924, the Indian poet and philosopher Rabindranath Tagore hailed the dawning of a "new age" in the East. "No people in Asia can be wholly given to materialism," he said, adding approvingly, "You are not individualists in China."[73]

As international tensions mounted in the 1920s and 1930s, this conviction of moral superiority slid easily into racism. To rationalize their military aggression, Japanese leaders drew on race to promote the virtues of the Greater East Asia Co-Prosperity Sphere. They also played an anticolonialist card, joining with Asian nationalists to throw off the colonial yoke. This took some doing, since Japan had colonized Korea and Taiwan and set up a puppet kingdom in Manchukuo (Manchuria), but Japan's message attracted a number of nationalist leaders. Meanwhile, the Communist International (Comintern), run from Moscow, championed anticolonialism but trumpeted off-key concepts like the "Asiatic mode of production."

After the War in the Pacific (as Asians call their half of World War II), the Asia debate entered an up-and-down phase. Japan concentrated narrowly on healing its bomb-blasted economy, newly independent governments struggled to extinguish local insurgencies, and the Maoist regime in China preached revolution and class struggle. The notion that "Asia is One" sank into irrelevance. But when Japan and the "four tigers" (South Korea, Taiwan, Singapore, and Hong Kong) chalked up one economic gain after another, the notion of an "East Asian Miracle" (as a World Bank report called it) caught the world's attention. In the wake of the Asian financial crisis, the idea of a unique and successful "Asian" model fell out of favor once again.

■ Conclusion

The legacy of Maritime Asia features some traits that leaders of the integration movement might usefully ponder. First, traders and others overcame distance and diversity and turned them into assets. Both the Silk Road and the great maritime trading routes connected the economies and cultures of vastly different regions. The free movement of goods and people was the norm; the main obstacle was the weather.

Second, like other seagoing communities, Maritime Asia was open, diverse, tolerant, and cosmopolitan. Residents and travelers shared knowledge, innovations, religion, and ideas as well as goods.

Third, a well-developed maritime infrastructure and attractiveness to traders were keys to wealth and power. Adequate ports, up-to-date shipping technology, and the absence of burdensome restrictions characterized a successful maritime hub, reduced transport costs, and enriched those who controlled it.

Fourth, merchants in major maritime cities enjoyed considerable local autonomy. They developed numerous means of conducting long-distance business largely on their own, including long-distant banking and letters of credit.

Fifth, although China's tributary system defined the formal architecture, unofficial trade flourished. As long as tribute rituals were observed, China did not interfere with either the independence of tributary states or their ability to trade with each other.

Finally, restrictions on trade, such as embargoes, discriminatory taxes, and exorbitant tariffs, prompted merchants to find ways of circumventing them and to make money in the process. The closure of Tokugawa Japan encouraged smuggling, as did the prior clampdown by Ming authorities. Forbidding trade simply gave Ryukyu Islanders, the Portuguese, and others a chance to serve as middlemen. When authorities banned the sale of certain goods, merchants made profits in the black market. When they imposed price controls, sellers sought other markets even if forbidden to do so.

Like the cultures of other maritime regions, Maritime Asia's culture was cosmopolitan and adaptable. The region inherits a rich legacy of trading networks, long-distance banking and credit mechanisms, the free movement of persons, and a certain degree of local autonomy.

The colonial powers divided up Maritime Asia, hardening old boundaries and creating new and artificial ones. The boundaries of many of today's Asian nation-states rarely conform to natural social, ethnic, or geographic divisions. Colonial rulers also crystallized social structures, established cartels and monopolies, and created a new class of elites oriented to the metropolis instead of to their neighbors. The wash of trade, culture, and labor passed through profit-seeking Western and Japanese hands. But the physical infrastructure, technology, education systems, and ideas built or imported by the colonial powers connected Asians as never before.

Following colonial-era partition came a string of calamities: the Sino-Japanese War, the Russo-Japanese War, World War I, Japan's military expansion, the Great Depression, World War II, the anticolonial struggle, local communist insurgencies, the Cold War, the Vietnam War, the ravages of Maoist dictatorship in China, the genocide in Cambodia, and wars of national liberation in Southeast Asia, to name only the major ones.

Once Asian leaders shook off these traumas, they clung tightly to borders that were often artificial. Their economic policies also worked against the revival of Maritime Asia. Many governments embraced protectionism, central planning, socialist ownership schemes, and a quest for autarky. Only in the last two decades of the twentieth century, as globalization blazed up and the Cold War spluttered out, did the natural flow and equilibrium of Maritime Asia revive in modern form.

The next two chapters survey the current state of Maritime Asia as the primary locus of regionalization. Part 2 examines the other half of the integration story—the behavior of governments and the search for Asia Major.

■ Notes

1. Exodus 30:23.

2. Rosengarten, *The Book of Spices*, p. 339.

3. Chanda, *Bound Together*.

4. From James Elroy Flecker, "The Golden Journey to Samarkand," quoted in Wood, *The Silk Road*, p. 9.

5. See Weatherford, *Genghis Khan and the Making of the Modern World*, esp. pp. 200–206.

6. Abu-Lughod, *Before European Hegemony*, p. 8.

7. Braudel, *The Mediterranean and the Mediterranean World in the Age of Philip II*. These volumes appeared in French in 1949 and in a revised edition in 1966.

8. Morris, *The Spectacle of Empire*, p. 41.

9. Devare, *India and Southeast Asia*, chap. 3.

10. Chia Lin Sien and Martin Perry, "Introduction," in Chia, *Southeast Asia Transformed,* p. 4.

11. Reid, *Southeast Asia in the Age of Commerce,* vol 1, p. xiv.

12. Das Gupta, *The World of the Indian Ocean Merchant,* pp. 37–38.

13. Wolters, *History, Culture, and Region,* p. 46. Wolters argued that these traits are characteristic of seagoing communities generally.

14. Wills, *Venice: Lion City,* pp. 188–190, 343–344.

15. Ibn Battuta, *Ibn Battuta in the Near East, Asia, and Africa,* p. 221.

16. Morison, *The Maritime History of Massachusetts,* pp. 67–68.

17. Dalrymple, *White Mughals,* p. 347.

18. Ashin Das Gupta, "India and the Indian Ocean, c. 1500–1800: The Story," in Das Gupta, *The World of the Indian Ocean Merchant,* p. 49.

19. McPherson, *The Indian Ocean,* p. 239.

20. Reid, *Southeast Asia in the Age of Commerce,* vol. 1, p. 128.

21. Percival, *The Dragon Looks South,* chap. 3, 4.

22. Mungello, *The Great Encounter of China and the West,* p. 3.

23. Das Gupta, *The World of the Indian Ocean Merchant,* pp. 61–62.

24. Wang, *The Chinese Overseas,* p. 32.

25. Rubinstein, *Taiwan: A New History,* pp. 85–86. Phillip C. Saunders suggests that in those circumstances, separation from a dominant continental power was a commercial advantage. The rise and subsequent decline of traders from the Ryukyu Islands supports this idea.

26. Wang, *The Chinese Overseas,* passim.

27. Abu-Lughod, *Before European Hegemony,* chap. 8.

28. Paul Wheatley, *The Golden Khersonese* (Kuala Lumpur: University of Malaya Press, 1961; Westport, CT: Greenwood Press, 1973, p. 184), quoted in Shaffer, *Maritime Southeast Asia to 1500,* p. 2.

29. Das Gupta, *The World of the Indian Ocean Merchant,* pp. 25–26.

30. For a near-recreation of this journey in our time, see Bernstein, *Ultimate Journey.*

31. Wolters, *History, Culture, and Region,* chap. 2.

32. Devare, *India and Southeast Asia,* pp. 90–91.

33. Kawazoe, "Japan and East Asia," p. 397.

34. Jansen, *China in the Tokugawa World,* chap. 1, 2.

35. For a scholarly survey of these interactions, see Toby, *State and Diplomacy in Early Modern Japan.*

36. Elisonas, "The Inseparable Trinity," p. 261.

37. Katzenstein and Shiraishi, *Network Power.*

38. Two useful, short introductions are Shaffer, *Maritime Southeast Asia to 1500*; and Osborne, *Southeast Asia.*

39. Tarling, *Cambridge History of Southeast Asia,* p. 218.

40. Ricklefs, *A History of Modern Indonesia,* p. 19.

41. Tarling, *Cambridge History of Southeast Asia,* pp. 226–227.

42. Ricklefs, *A History of Modern Indonesia,* p. 8.

43. Esposito, *Islam in Asia,* p. 15.

44. Ruthven, *Historical Atlas of Islam,* pp. 106–107.

45. An authoritative survey of what little is known about Srivijaya can be found in Wolters, *Early Indonesian Commerce.*

46. Osborne, *Southeast Asia,* pp. 27–30.

47. Taken from Armando Cortesao, ed., *The Suma Oriental of Tomé Pires* (1944), and quoted in Yapp, *The Travellers' Dictionary of Quotation,* p. 629.

48. Pires sought in vain to meet with the Chinese emperor, was imprisoned in Canton, and died there, after urging the Portuguese king to attack China. Wisely, the Portuguese established a trading settlement at Macao instead.

49. William Dampier, *Voyages and Description* (1699), quoted in Yapp, *The Travellers' Dictionary of Quotation*, p. 629.

50. Wolpert, *A New History of India*, p. 142.

51. For a picturesque description of the link between early English buccaneers and the East India Company, see Ferguson, *Empire*.

52. For details, see Abu-Lughod, *Before European Hegemony;* and Jones, Frost, and White, *Coming Full Circle*, chap. 2.

53. The prescient Thai rulers were King Mongkut, parodied in *The King and I*, and his son, King Chulalongkorn. See Osborne, *Southeast Asia*, chap. 5.

54. Alfred Lord Tennyson, "Locksley Hall," in Bartlett, *Bartlett's Familiar Quotations*, p. 548b. An argosy is a kind of ship, typically a large merchant ship.

55. Morison, *The Maritime History of Massachusetts*, p. 65.

56. Prakash, "European Corporate Enterprises," pp. 166–168.

57. Das Gupta, *The World of the Indian Ocean Merchant*, pp. 51–52.

58. Anderson, *Imagined Communities*, p. 19.

59. Osborne, *Southeast Asia*, p. 64.

60. Maidment and Mackerras, *Culture and Society in the Asia-Pacific*, p. 20, table 2.1.

61. Duncan Forbes (1744), quoted in Macfarlane and Macfarlane, *The Empire of Tea*, p. 70.

62. For a concise description of this transformation, see Osborne, *Southeast Asia*, chap. 6.

63. McPherson, *The Indian Ocean*, p. 237.

64. The most famous book on the subject is Said, *Orientalism*, a passionate critique. For two of many rebuttals, see Robert Irwin, *Dangerous Knowledge*, and Christopher de Bellaigue, "Where Edward Said Was Wrong," *Times on Line*, http://tls.timesonline.co.uk, reproduced in *Arts and Letters Daily*, www.aldaily.com.

65. Godement, preface to *The New Asian Renaissance*.

66. Thomas B. Mac Aulay, "Minute on Education," in De Bary et al., *Sources of Indian Tradition*, p. 49.

67. For examples drawn from India, see Dalrymple, *White Mughals*.

68. Irwin's *Dangerous Knowledge* profiles these Orientalists, explicitly rebutting Edward Said's *Orientalism*.

69. An excellent source on this subject is Kopf, *British Orientalism and the Bengal Renaissance*.

70. Schwartz, *In Search of Wealth and Power.* Yen Fu was a nineteenth-century Chinese intellectual who translated and studied Western works in order to identify ways of thought that could help overcome China's weakness. Schwartz admired his effort but was troubled by his focus on state power and his corresponding neglect of the worth of the individual.

71. Quoted in "Pan-Asianism," http://en.wikipedia.org/wiki/Pan-Asianism, p. 1. The Bengali artist Abanindranath Tagore, brother of the famous poet and philosopher Rabindranath Tagore, applied the notion that "Asia is One" to the world of art.

72. "Sun Yat-sen's Speech on Pan-Asianism," http://en.wikipedia.org/wiki/Sun_Yat_Sen%27s_speech_on_Pan-Asianism, p. 3.

73. Rabindranath Tagore, "Talks in China," in Chakravarty, *The Tagore Reader*, pp. 209–210.

4

The Great Revival

Linked by the ocean and invigorated by the spindrift of trade and culture, Maritime Asia is shaking off the divisions of the past two centuries. While national government officials inch their way around prickly barriers to closer cooperation, private citizens from Asia's new middle class are trading, investing, traveling, studying, and talking with each other in record numbers.

After briefly contrasting the revival of Maritime Asia with prospects for the Silk Road, this chapter describes the technologies propelling spontaneous integration in Maritime Asia and their effect on the changing economic geography of the region as a whole. It highlights the growth of urban areas and the rise of maritime China as a manufacturing and final-assembly hub for the region. The next chapter profiles the people who are spearheading, taking advantage of, or otherwise reacting to these opportunities.

◼ The Revival of Maritime Asia

It is a truth universally acknowledged that if people are given a chance to make money by doing business with each other without being arrested or killed, they will do so. Many of them will even travel to other countries in pursuit of a better life. Throughout two millennia, Asians never stopped trading, investing, traveling, and migrating. Their connections were often interrupted but most of them survived, at least tenuously.

Today, Maritime Asia is flourishing again. Despite serious problems, such as rising inequality, residual poverty, crime, corruption, and spotty governance, most of it is stable and open for business. It is both globalized and internationalized.[1] The sleepy coastal town of Hoi An in Vietnam has suddenly sprouted some 200 clothing factories. The once-backward Chinese port city of Wenzhou on the East China Sea, officially labeled an Open Coastal City, now hums with the production of shoes, pharmaceuticals, clothes, sporting goods, optics, kitchen appliances, and other wares.[2] Strong majorities in those countries, and solid majorities in most of the region except Japan, are optimistic about their prospects in the near-term future as well as about their children's future life.[3] A mobile phone, a small truck, a little cash, and a good idea can open doors to opportunity.

The Silk Road

The Silk Road, by contrast, is unlikely to recapture its prior status as a commercial route despite brave attempts to revive it. Its cultures are rich and unique, but it is difficult to imagine what would move along it except energy and tourists. As a general rule, cargoes move far more cheaply by sea and by air than by land. Nearly 100 percent of China's exports to Europe travel by sea. Moreover, the Silk Road's western wing is mired in the pitiless politics of the Middle East, where whole stretches of territory are pockmarked by instability.

These awkward facts fail to deter governments from dreaming up glossy political schemes. China is touting a Eurasian Continental Bridge, alternatively dubbed the New Silk Road. Stretching more than 6,800 miles (11,000 kilometers) between China and Europe, the route would supposedly inspire new or revived commercial hubs along the way, including a border trade zone in the westernmost point of the Sinkiang Uighur Autonomous Region.[4] The planned chain of rail and air links would avoid excessive reliance on maritime transport and thereby reduce China's current dependence on the US Navy to maintain the security of the sea-lanes. Such ties would also strengthen bonds with Central Asia (Asia Medior, as I call it). Implementing the New Silk Road plan, however, would require negotiating agreements with several dozen Asian and European governments, all of which have their own ideas about tariffs, fees, customs procedures, and health and safety standards.

Question: When is a camel not a camel? Answer: When customs officials in Turkmenistan declare that camels are trucks and demand $150 for each. Such was the experience of a Turkish photographer who traveled by camel caravan across the ancient route.[5] The more frequent the border crossings, the greater the opportunity for customs officials and gun-toting border guards to shake down travelers and demand bribes. Corrupt officials also plague ports lining the maritime route, but ship captains do not have to stop at every one. They can also swerve around war zones and embargoed destinations. That is a big reason why Maritime Asia, not the Silk Road, is the chief engine of raising Asia's wealth and power.

■ Technological "Propellers"

Stunning breakthroughs in technology have spurred the rapid expansion of communications, shipping, and aviation. These advances make it possible for

Asians to do business and otherwise connect with each other at record speed and in record numbers. They are the "propellers" driving the revival of Maritime Asia, the web of production networks, the construction of new roads, and the sky-scraping cities that reflect and enhance Asia's new wealth.

Communications

World-class communications technology has not changed the essentially cosmopolitan character of the region but rather propelled it into a fast-forward mode. New lines of communication are racing across long distances, bouncing up to space and back again. The number of Asians connected to the Internet has been growing faster than anywhere else in the world. Tens of millions get connected every year. E-commerce is exploding. Mobile telephones are popular throughout the region; in Thailand, for example, mobile telephones outnumber landline telephones by four to one.

According to the website Internet World Stats, Asians account for about a third of the world's Internet usage. Hong Kong, Singapore, Japan, South Korea, and Taiwan are among the countries with the world's highest Internet penetration. Almost 50 million people in ASEAN countries are plugged in, along with an estimated 111 million in China, 86 million in Japan, 34 million in South Korea, and 50 million in India. English is the language most commonly used on the Web, but three of the next six are Chinese, Japanese, and Korean.[6]

Transmission lines are thickest in Maritime Asia, especially in coastal or near-coastal cities. The Seoul metropolitan area, for example, accounts for nearly three-quarters of Korea's overseas telephone traffic.[7] Almost 70 percent of the population in Hong Kong and Singapore uses the Internet, matching the level of use in Japan and South Korea (and the United States). Taiwan has actively promoted broadband and Internet access and has achieved the world's best wireless Internet penetration. Sixty percent of Taiwanese are Internet users. Poorer regions, however, lack the telephone lines and bandwidth necessary for Internet access and are finding themselves on the wrong side of the digital divide. Even dynamic China and resurgent India have a long way to go because of their huge rural and poor population; as of 2007 it was estimated that fewer than 10 percent of Chinese and 5 percent of Indians use the Internet.

The revolution in communications greatly facilitates integration, but in the wrong hands it also serves repression and crime. Authoritarian governments have learned to monitor the content of the Internet, censor undesirable political messages, and track down rebellious users. Terrorists and criminals use high-technology communications to operate across borders. Victims of repression and crime fighters use the same technology to fight back.

On balance, computers, mobile telephones, and other advanced electronic devices have greatly enriched Maritime Asia. They have speeded up communication within the long-distance ethnic business networks for which

Maritime Asia is known. They have helped streamline the operations and on-time logistics of vertically integrated shipping companies. They have stimulated entrepreneurs in interior and border regions to raise productivity and seek new export markets. They have brought pop music and films to young Asian audiences, creating a huge new business. They have added a whole new range of high-value products to the composition of cargoes coming in and out of port. The products enriching Maritime Asian merchants are no longer silks and spices but modems and monitors.

Shipping

Improvements in ship design, materials, and propulsion have always helped one set of traders or conquerors in Asia to edge out, defeat, or impress another. But in the twentieth century, the world's major shipping companies revolutionized ocean trade by replacing bulk cargo with truck-compatible standardized containers.[8] This revolution in shipping technology is as dramatic as the invention of the jet engine or the Internet. In the last thirty-five years or so, it has slashed the cost of shipping by two-thirds.[9]

An estimated 90 percent of the world's trade is still carried by sea, including about 90 percent of traded oil. About 70 percent of non-oil trade moves in containers. Close to 20 million containers make over 200 million trips per year. About a quarter of those containers are manufactured in China.

The boom in container shipping has spurred the shipping industry to unprecedented levels of productivity. The key advantage of containers is that goods can be sealed, transported by rail or truck, loaded onto a ship, and unloaded onto a railway car or truck almost seamlessly. Containerization has transformed both the design of commercial vehicles and the layout and development of ports. Containers also deter theft and enhance security because they are locked with tamper-resistant seals and can be scanned for dangerous contents in a matter of seconds.[10]

Containerization has created an incentive to build bigger and bigger ships. In 1958, the largest container vessel had a capacity of fifty-eight twenty-foot equivalent units (TEUs), the standardized global unit of measurement. Today's largest ships can carry over 6,000 TEUs, and designers are planning ships capable of carrying 13,000 TEUs. Even some passenger ships are the size of small towns.

No region of the world has felt the effect of containerization more than Maritime Asia. Ranked according to TEUs of container traffic actually handled, the world's top six ports are in Maritime Asia: Hong Kong, Singapore, Pusan, Shanghai, Kaohsiung, and Shenzhen. (US ports Los Angeles and Long Beach were ranked seventh and thirteenth, respectively.)[11] One of the world's biggest shipping companies is Taiwan-based Evergreen Marine Corporation, which operates 150 vessels, including 100 container ships, and serves eighty countries.

Once ramshackle and riotous, major ports have ballooned into huge and gleaming marvels of dockside logistics. Tumbledown houses and bars that once sheltered armies of unskilled dockworkers have been turned into parking lots fenced by sky-high cranes. Smaller shipping companies unable to pay for the shift to containers have gone out of business. Ports like South Korea's Pusan and Malaysia's Port Kalang have adapted to the new pattern and flourished as a consequence; rubber from Sabah, for example, is now shipped from Port Kalang instead of from Singapore. Darwin, Australia's northernmost city, is now linked by rail to urban and industrial centers and is becoming a trade gateway to Asia.[12]

India's business leaders are racing to catch up. India's infrastructure is dilapidated, but corruption and local political squabbles hamper improvements. India's ports handle only a little more than 5 percent of global shipping trade.[13] In 2004, India's dozen or so container ports handled 4.4 million TEUs compared with 70 million in China.[14] Despite these handicaps, India's annual container traffic has been growing at least at double digits since the 1990s and may now be increasing by a fifth annually. This boom makes India one of the fastest-growing container traffic markets in the world. In 2005 alone, Evergreen Marine Corporation opened five new offices in India, bringing the total to eleven.[15] The government's drive to privatize port concessions has met resistance from unions but has steadily proceeded, attracting worldwide interest, including from Dubai (blocked in 2006 from a similar transaction in the United States).[16] Major funding for port expansion is also coming from Japan.

Seeking to strengthen maritime links with the rest of Asia, local officials and business groups hope to upgrade their ports to regional shipping hubs. Colombo, a centrally located stopping point in precolonial times, already has a deepwater port and has secured a loan from the Asian Development Bank (ADB) to increase its efficiency. Okinawa also has substantial capacity but is stymied by Japan's cargo-preference regulations and other political barriers. Other ports have further to go. One candidate is Guwahati, capital of far northeastern Assam state, located on the Brahmaputra River. On India's southern tip, the government of Kerala plans to build a deepwater container terminal in Vizhinjam.[17] Shippers in General Santos City, in Mindanao, want to put their port on the global maritime map.[18] These may all be pipe dreams, but they illustrate the direction in which local authorities and business groups believe competition is headed.

At least two problems loom. The first is that container ships are getting so big that fewer and fewer facilities can handle them. The Panama Canal is becoming clogged. Tankers carrying crude oil have also grown likewise and now require depths of 68 to 70 feet, beyond the capacity of both the Suez Canal and the Panama Canal.[19] Centuries-old ports are sinking into irrelevance. The second problem is a reflection of the huge trade imbalance between Asia and the United States. For every three full westbound containers leaving

Singapore, for example, only two full eastbound ones arrive.[20] Empty containers mean higher costs for shipping companies.

Aviation

"Aviation changed all that," wrote Somerset Maugham in a preface to his Malayan stories. By "all that" he meant the world of slow-moving travel and communication, in which a British colonial officer at a hill station in Borneo would wait six weeks or more for a copy of the *Times of London*.[21] Although Asia's record in aviation is not as stellar as its shipping record, six of the world's thirty busiest airports are in Asia, and the number is growing.[22]

Asia's new wealth swells and multiplies urban hubs, attracts more airline passengers, and boosts demand for airborne cargo. Japan's National Institute for Land and Infrastructure Management calculates that the number of air routes within East Asia more than doubled between 1985 and 2000, from 54 to 117.[23] According to the International Air Transport Association (IATA), carriers based in the Asia Pacific added 42 percent to their capacity from 2001 to 2007.[24] In 2005 the IATA predicted that between 2005 and 2009, passenger traffic within the Asia region would grow at a faster rate than almost any other intraregional or transregional route in the world: 6.8 percent, compared with 5.8 percent for transpacific traffic.[25] The aviation industry already employs more than 1 million Asian workers.

Not only business executives but also tourists, students, and other non-business travelers are crowding into Asian skyways. This trend is closely linked with urbanization: according to aviation experts, the propensity to fly increases when more than 50 percent of the population resides in urban areas.[26] Air travel in Asia is soaring so rapidly that airports have trouble keeping up with it. Singapore, Kuala Lumpur, and Hong Kong have opened high-technology airports, and Seoul and Bangkok plan to follow suit.

China is the predictable magnet for aviation. On average, some 10,000 people travel between China and Japan every *day*. At least 700 flights connect the two countries every week. Airplanes lift off from runways in China at the rate of almost a million a year, four times that of India. Passenger traffic is growing at double-digit rates. According to a Shanghai official, Shanghai's Pudong International Airport alone will handle 80 million passengers a year by 2010, compared to the estimated 135 million handled by all Chinese airports in 2005.[27]

The sheer volume of goods produced in China has prompted other air-cargo hubs to compete for dominant positions in China's Shanghai, Guangzhou Baiyan, and Shenzhen airports.[28] Meanwhile, China's own aviation industry is steadily adding flights to other countries from Chengdu, Kunming, and other interior cities as well as from coastal hubs.

Flagship Asian airlines advertise lovely young stewardesses offering pleasing smiles and efficient personal service. But low-cost, no-frills carriers are beginning to make inroads. In 2005, for example, the privately owned, Indonesia-based budget carrier Awair (now Indonesia AirAsia) offered one-way flights between Singapore and Jakarta for a jaw-dropping S$19.99 (US$13) to promote "connectivity," according to its spokespeople. In mid-2006, Malaysia's US-style AirAsia website offered "Midweek Madness" flights from Jakarta to Kuala Lumpur for 450,000 Indonesian rupiahs—about US$49. In 2007 travelers finding themselves in Kota Kinabalu, East Malaysia, could get to Shenzhen, China's huge manufacturing hub near Hong Kong, for about US$15.

Cargo flights are booming as well. Not surprisingly, Asia's airborne cargo hubs are the same as Asia's shipping hubs. Between 1985 and 1995, Asian airports increased their share of the world's international air cargo from 30 percent to 42 percent.[29] The International Air Transport Association's prediction for 2005–2009 projected an 8.5 percent growth rate for Asian cargo flights compared to 6.0 percent for transpacific flights.[30] According to the Boeing World Air Cargo Forecast, Asia will lead the world's air-cargo markets in average annual growth rates through 2023. The domestic China market for air-cargo services will grow by 10.6 percent and intra-Asian markets by 8.5 percent.

Despite the boom in air travel, air routes in Asia are still heavily regulated. The market for direct flights between smaller cities in Asia is huge but underdeveloped. Partly in response to the 2007 "open skies" agreement between the United States and the EU, the Japanese government plans to announce an Asian Gateway Plan. Its goal is to stimulate competition and lower ticket prices by granting foreign airlines access to local airports, including Japan's main domestic airport (Haneda). Japanese officials hope that ASEAN, India, South Korea, and China will follow suit. According to the Centre for Asia-Pacific Aviation, opening up local and regional airports in Japan, China, and South Korea alone would spur incremental growth of 300 million passengers.[31]

Roads and Railroads

Although the colonial powers built many roads and railroads, distances in Maritime Asia are so great that most people and goods travel to other countries by airplane or ship. As recently as the 1970s, the ADB described inland transport as an "appendage" of international sea and air transport.[32]

"Good roads are really the most pressing need of Japan," remarked the intrepid traveler Isabella Bird tartly in 1878, after spending days on horseback. It would be far better, she added, for the government to build roads through the interior instead of "indulging in expensive western vanities."[33] Today, Japan has gone to the opposite extreme, and roads in South Korea and increasingly in China are generally excellent. But Southeast Asia and India have a long way to go. A handful of showcase highways snake across the region, but other roads are poor—and security is often a problem. The great travel writer Norman Lewis grumbled that the security of roads under the Mongols was much superior to that of twentieth-century Burma.[34]

Even in secure regions, roads are often poorly maintained and trucks are ancient. In India, it costs more to transport Australian wheat from south to north than it does to ship it from Australia in the first place. In Southeast Asia, the only modernized cross-border land route carrying a significant volume of passengers and freight is the short corridor between Singapore and Malaysia.

The new prevalence of container shipping may be changing this picture. Owners of container-hauling trucks are staking out both ends of logistically seamless transportation routes. Refrigerated trucks are coming into use. One bold company, the Dutch mail and logistics services provider TNT, is challenging the notion that land-based transport is too expensive. In 2005 it announced plans for an integrated road network across Singapore, Malaysia, and Thailand that will link more than 120 cities. The company also intends to add Cambodia, Vietnam, and China.[35]

Road building in Asia opens up opportunities for foreign donors and lenders to get political credit in the competition for regional influence. It is one of China's favorite tools. Cross-border road transport has leaped into a high-priority position at both the United Nations Economic and Social Commission for Asia and the Pacific (UNESCAP) and the ADB. UNESCAP is working with governments to identify investment needs for an Asian Highway Network. The ADB's East-West Corridor project is repairing and upgrading a number of roads connecting Thailand, Laos, and Vietnam,[36] and there are plans, on paper at least, for a highway extension across Thailand to the coast of Myanmar on the Andaman Sea. One enthusiast has already reported that he can now have breakfast in Hue (Vietnam), lunch in Savannakhet (Laos), and dinner in Khon Khaen (eastern Thailand).[37]

Feeder roads to Maritime Asia's new ports and megacities are publicly financed, but they respond to private-sector needs and function as arteries of market-driven integration. Without roads and railroads connecting ports and airports with the interior, shipping lines and airlines would have fewer loads. Superhighways linking southern China with other parts of Asia make sense. But in promoting highways linking remote interior regions, political authorities are responding to domestic pressures. They are hoping for a "field of dreams": build the roads and business will come. These roads should attract local investment and relieve poverty, which are worthy causes in themselves. But it is hard to see how east-west land links can attract significant foreign investment or fit into the greater maritime trading system. The market is just too small.

A look at the map provides examples. About half of the ADB's imagined Southern Economic Corridor, linking Bangkok with southern Vietnam, would pass through Cambodia, which is still in a sorry state. An extension of the Yunnan-Bangkok route through the Malay peninsula to Singapore, also planned, would be expensive to build compared with sea routes and would pass through an area of southern Thailand now scarred by conflict. The ADB's two North-South Economic Corridors, linking China's Yunnan province with Bangkok and Haiphong (Vietnam), are more likely to stimulate commerce.

Much useful work remains to be done to improve cross-border land transport. Whose gauge should prevail on a cross-border railroad track? Who decides on uniform safety standards for trucks? What health restrictions are appropriate? Compromises are in order. Issues to be resolved include hardware and software standards, cross-border fees, and safety and environmental considerations.[38] Engineers and negotiators can begin solving these problems if governments give them some leeway.

■ The New Economic Landscape

Thanks in part to breakthroughs in information technology, shipping, and aviation, the landscape of Maritime Asia brims with integrated production networks, export processing zones, "growth triangles," container ports, and other market-inspired inventions. Tokyo is a financial and technology hub. China's Pearl River and Yangtze River deltas have become manufacturing giants. Hong Kong, Singapore, and Shanghai are both shipping and financial centers. Singapore, Hong Kong, and increasingly India are services exporters. Coastal Vietnam is picking up new manufacturing business. Raw materials, agricultural products, minerals, and energy fill ships and tankers in Australia and Indonesia. Financial houses in Tokyo, Hong Kong, Shanghai, Singapore, and Mumbai keep nighttime hours to synchronize transactions with New York and London.

At "sub-hubs" in Malaysia, Thailand, South Korea, and Taiwan, factories spew forth parts for production networks. Growth triangles (not always triangular) connect labor-surplus areas with capital and technology in a duty-free business environment. Probably the most successful is the Singapore-Johor-Riau triangle, which links Indonesia and Malaysia with Singapore. Other major growth experiments, such as the Tumen River Area Development project, the Greater Mekong Subregion Economic Cooperation program, the Indonesia-Malaysia-Thailand Growth Triangle, and the Brunei-Indonesia-Malaysia-Philippines East Asian Growth Area, are either less successful or still at an early stage in their development. India is setting up a number of special economic zones, but key decisions must still pass through multiple government offices.[39] Many countries have set up export processing zones; the Philippines alone has more than twenty.[40]

Production Networks

Defined broadly, production networks are sets of interfirm and intrafirm relationships through which a leading company organizes the entire range of its business activities. These include research and development, the definition and design of products and services, supplies, manufacturing and assembly, distribution, sales, and support. They encompass subcontractors, suppliers, services providers, and others.[41] Their customers are global. The network's "flagship" controls resources and decisionmaking but also provides for the sharing and creation of knowledge.[42]

"How big is East Asian production sharing? The answer is *very big!*" reported two World Bank economists in 2003.[43] Companies engaging in networked production and their partners are powerful integrators. Their resources dwarf those of the public sector. Their actions are knitting Asia's enormously diverse regions together in ways that governments cannot master.

The exact structure and composition of these newer production networks varies considerably. Many factors influence the choice of location, including local labor (wages and skills), the investment climate (regulatory stability, taxation, and local incentives), physical infrastructure, the proximity of customers, the activities of competitors, and the economics of transportation.

Typically, supplies of parts and components from Southeast Asia, Japan, and South Korea go to factories in China, where more parts and components are added and final assembly is completed. The product then leaves China by container ship, bound for customers in North America, Europe, and (increasingly) other destinations in Asia.

Cities, Megacities, and Peri-urban Zones

Within the sweep of land and sea that bounds today's Maritime Asia lies a string of cities—some old, some new. Their size, peripheral expansion, and relative weight are changing rapidly. Increasingly connected by land, sea, air, and telecommunications, these urban areas are the new nodes of spontaneous integration. Capital cities have always attracted elites, but cutting-edge cultural and intellectual trendsetters now cluster in Asia's largest coastal cities and ports.[44] The new jobs that coastal cities offer draw rural migrants in huge numbers. For example, the population of Inchon, a major port in South Korea, swelled from 1.4 million in 1985 to over 2.6 million in 2007.[45]

Cities in Asia have been becoming larger and more crowded for decades, particularly in rapidly industrializing countries of East Asia. By one count, fourteen of the world's thirty largest urban agglomerations are in Asia.[46] Roughly 130 cities house more than a million residents. About 140,000 people migrate to cities or peripheries of cities every day.[47] According to UNESCAP, the population of East Asian urban centers has surged by more than 250 percent since 1970 and is expected to continue at the same rate. This means that there will be an *additional* 500 million people living in East Asian urban areas by 2025.

In China, at least 40–50 million farmers have lost some or all of their land to development projects, and as many as 150 million rural residents have drifted to urban areas in search of work. This influx has swelled China's urban population from 18 percent in 1978 to well over 40 percent. According to a 2005 United Nations report, this "floating population" is expected to reach 200 million by 2020.[48]

In India, urbanization has been less rapid but substantial. According to the Indian census data, the urban population grew by 36 percent in the 1980s and 31 percent in the 1990s, while the rural population grew by 20 and 18 percent, respectively.[49] India contains twenty cities with a population of 1 million or more. A highway now links India's "big three" maritime cities—Mumbai, Chennai, and Kolkata—with New Delhi.

In the last decade or two, the centuries-old wash of maritime cities has jelled lumpily into a dozen or so megacities, complete with modern port facilities, sprawling peripheries, and a rising middle class. About a dozen of these megacities dominate everything from finance to fashion. They are closely linked by air and sea and increasingly by highways. Capital cities located apart from this thickening chain of nodes, such as New Delhi and Phnom Penh, now resemble isolated dots in a relatively empty quarter of a scatter diagram. Even Beijing seems too far north.

These cities account for 80 to 90 percent of East Asia's international business activities. Although greater New Delhi attracts considerable foreign investment, India's two major coastal hubs (Mumbai and Chennai) are more vibrant business capitals. Asian cities used to be ringed by rice paddies and fields. No longer. The wave of incoming manufacturing investment has pushed out farms and replaced them with hastily erected, haphazard development areas on the outskirts of urban areas. Land in such peri-urban zones, as they are now called, serves a variety of uses and extends as far as 93 miles (150 kilometers) from core cities. These patchworks typically sprawl over several administrative jurisdictions, giving rise to local conflicts and political disputes. Companies seeking space for large-scale manufacturing typically end up there. In East Asia, such zones are expected to absorb about 200 million people by 2025, or about 40 percent of greater-urban population growth.[50]

The Flowering of Maritime China

Ever since the victory of the Chinese Communist Party in 1949, Chinese leaders have striven to overcome China's humiliating weakness and restore what they see as China's rightful place in the world. In the late 1970s, Deng

Xiaoping and his allies concluded that opening up the Chinese economy to foreign trade and investment would be the fastest way for China to acquire technology and management skills and thus to increase the nation's wealth. Abandoning collectivization and the more extreme forms of socialism, they restored private agricultural incentives and blessed the creation of private wealth. In the first stage (1978–1984), they encouraged or acquiesced in the establishment of township and village enterprises and permitted the free sale of agricultural goods at market prices. They also pushed through China's first law on joint ventures, introduced Special Economic Zones that welcomed foreign investors, and opened up fourteen coastal cities.

A second wave of reforms, spearheaded by Zhao Ziyang and enacted in 1984, focused on urban areas and further liberated maritime China. Tapping the supply of labor, these reforms included the opening of more coastal cities and three coastal delta regions, as well as the decentralization of harbor management and foreign trade. In 1987, Zhao and Deng launched the Coastal Development Strategy, which further decentralized control of foreign trade, added Hainan Island as a Special Economic Zone, and threw open the entire coast to foreign direct investment. Following shortly thereafter were the opening of twenty-eight "harbor cities" on the Yangzi River as well as Shanghai's Pudong New District. By 1995, the State Council had approved not only the original fourteen open coastal cities but also a whopping 260 coastal areas (cities and counties), plus a handful of open river-valley cities, open border-region areas, and open provincial capitals.[51]

These moves stood Maoism on its head. After 1949, the Chinese government had channeled industrial development to inland regions to establish a more equitable regional balance and to establish a less vulnerable industrial base in the event of war.[52] If Deng's reforms had been limited to remote interior areas rather than maritime zones, they would not have stimulated China-centered production networks and thus would not have contributed to China's economic modernization—Deng's number-one goal. Since coastal areas have a competitive advantage, restoring a large and lucrative slice of Maritime Asia to business-as-usual yielded spectacular results.

Ever since Chinese leaders began opening their economy to trade and investment in the late 1980s and early 1990s, an estimated 85–90 percent of new foreign investment in China has been flowing into coastal regions, ports, and ocean-accessible cities. Nine of the ten provinces and province-level municipalities receiving the most foreign investment are maritime, and the tenth (Hubei) spans the Yangtze.[53] Economist Thomas Rawski calculated that in 2005, the combined ratio of trade to domestic production in twelve coastal jurisdictions was 95.5 percent, compared to 13 percent in western China; in Shanghai and Guangdong the ratios were 176.2 and 174.5 percent, respectively.[54] By 2003 some 280 of the world's 500 largest companies had set up shop in China's Pearl River delta, which encompasses such dynamic cities as Guangzhou, Shenzhen, and Dongguan. The region accounts for an overwhelming share of all foreign direct investment into China and about a third of China's exports. As of 2003 more than 40 percent of the world's light fixtures, for example, were made there.[55]

According to official Chinese statistics, Jiangsu, located just north of Shanghai, is typically the number-one target of new incoming foreign direct investment, followed by other coastal provinces and municipalities—Zhejiang, Fujian, Shandong, Guangdong, and Liaoning provinces, plus Shanghai, Beijing, and Tianjin (the port of Beijing).[56] Robert Ash, who has studied investment in China in detail, sees in this lopsided concentration "the creation of growing economic integration through the forging of increasingly close transnational investment and, by implication, foreign trade links."[57]

Predictably, inland provinces are lobbying the leadership for access to maritime wealth. In a process known as the "four borrows," they began hitching their development wagons to Maritime Asia by investing in harbors, gaining access to berths, and promoting their products. The four borrows were "borrow ships to go out to sea; borrow borders to go out of the border; borrow stages to perform operas (promote business in other provinces); and borrow hens to lay eggs (establish companies in Special Economic Zones)."[58] This creative variant of "remapping"—essentially creating a coastal outpost and maintaining it from an inland base—only underscores the primacy of maritime regions.

China's new maritime orientation fuels rising national income but also speeds up the spiraling income gap that burns holes in the social fabric. Although workers migrating to coastal regions send remittances to their families in the countryside, per capita income in coastal provinces and administrative districts is consistently higher than that of inland regions. President Hu Jintao has openly acknowledged this problem and has repeatedly vowed to redress it. But despite strong government-backed incentives, central and western China receives little foreign investment. The Chinese government has invested heavily in improvements in inland transportation, but regions deep in the interior are simply too far from the sea.

As wages rise in maritime China, some companies are moving inland, but many others are adding capacity elsewhere in Asia, especially in labor-intensive industries like apparel. Japanese companies, unwilling to place all their bets on China, have adopted what they call a "China + 1" policy with respect to new investment. Vietnam is receiving much of this investment, followed by India and Indonesia.

■ Conclusion

Thanks in part to technology, Maritime Asia has revived and surpassed its historical role after centuries of conquest and division. Its contours now extend from coastal India to the Russian Far East and coastal Australia. Taiwan, once a backwater, is a star. China, blessed with a coastline that spans Northeast and Southeast Asia, is already a maritime power in a commercial and geopolitical sense and is striving to catch up as a naval power.

The application of new technology does not just happen. Governments try their best to develop it or to attract it; business executives prefer to own it. No matter how it is developed, it is carried—literally—on container ships, in airplanes, on roads, along telephone lines, in computers, and from satellites. Each of these modes of transmission depends on technology invented wholly or in large part in the private sector. Each application of that technology represents a decision by some individual. These people are real or would-be "spontaneous integrators," the individuals who bring about regionalization. They are the people on whose success governments want to build. It is to them that the book now turns.

■ Notes

1. The distinction between globalization and internationalization is summarized in Katzenstein, *A World of Regions*, pp. 13–19.

2. Stephen Glain, "A Tale of Two Chinas," *Smithsonian*, May 2006, pp. 40–49. The contrast is with Shenyang, located inland north of Beijing, a former industrial hub that has fallen on hard times. In 1984, the Chinese government designated Wenzhou and thirteen others, not including Shenyang, as "open coastal cities" featuring various tax breaks. See Fung, Lau, and Lee, *U.S. Direct Investment in China*, p. 28.

3. Pew Research Center for the People and the Press, "What the World Thinks in 2002," Pew Global Attitudes Project, 2002, pp. 22–24, available at http://pewglobal .org/reports/pdf/165.pdf. For a more recent poll with similar findings, I consulted "Chinese and Vietnamese Most Hopeful for 2006, Australians and New Zealanders Not So Upbeat," Morgan Poll Finding No. 3954, Royal Morgan International in conjunction with Gallup International, March 15, 2006. The question was, "As far as you're concerned, do you think next year will be better or worse than this year?" The reference year was 2006.

4. Fu Jing, "Re-Building the Ancient Silk Road," *China Daily*, September 1, 2004, available at www2.chinadaily.com.cn:80/english/doc/2004-09/01/content_370519 .htm. Sent by Paul S. Giarra.

5. Hugh Pope, "The Millenium—Trade and Commerce: A Route Reborn," *Wall Street Journal*, January 11, 1999, p. R.49.

6. All statistics in this paragraph are taken from www.internetworldstats.com. At least until recently, most telecommunication was routed through the United States.

7. Rohlen, "Cosmopolitan Cities and Nation States," p. 9.

8. For a history of the development of containers, see Levinson, *The Box*.

9. Shuo Ma, vice-president of the World Maritime University, in remarks to the 2004 Asia Pacific Maritime Summit, as reported in Jinks, "Containerised Trade Imbalance," p. 2.

10. Wikipedia, "Containerization," available at http://en.wikipedia.org.

11. World Port Ranking 2003, available at www.infoplease.com/ipa/A0104779. html.

12. "Vision of Northern Gateway Takes Shape," *Today International* (Sydney), December 19, 2003, p. 19.

13. "Time to Beef Up Port Infrastructure," *Businessline* (Chennai), April 14, 2001, p. 1.

14. Khozem Merchant, "The Shift from Socialism Has 'Passed Us By,'" Special Report: Indian Infrastructure, *Financial Times*, April 24, 2006, p. 5.

15. "Evergreen Enhances Presence in India," press release, October 3, 2005, available at www.evergreen-marine.com.

16. It could be argued that the United Arab Emirates has become an extension of Maritime Asia, like Australia and New Zealand.

17. "Kerala Govt's Dream Project," *Businessline* (Chennai), July 28, 2003, p. 1.

18. "GenSan Shippers Step Up Drive on Competitiveness," *Business World* (Manila), May 20, 2003, p. 1.

19. Nincic, "Sea Lane Security," p. 150. See also Robert Wright, "Ship of Trade Drags New Challenges in Its Wake," and "Size Is Not Everything," both in "FT World Ports," Special Report, *Financial Times*, May 23, 2005, pp. 1, 6.

20. Jinks, "Containerised Trade Imbalance," p. 2.

21. Quoted in Anthony Burgess's introduction to Maugham, *Maugham's Malaysian Stories,* p. xviii.

22. In 2005, they were Tokyo/Haneda, Beijing, Hong Kong, Bangkok, Singapore, and Tokyo/Narita; see "World's 30 Busiest Airports by Passengers and Cargo, 2005," available at www.infoplease.com/ipa/A0004547.html. In 2006, Jakarta replaced Bangkok.

23. Cited in Greenwood, "Thinking Regionally and Acting Nationally," p. 5.

24. "IATA More Optimistic for 2007," press release 31, September 17, 2007, available at http://www.iata.org/pressroom/pr/2007-17-09-02.

25. "Five Year Forecast Shows Rapid Growth in Asia and Central Europe: 2005–2009 Forecast Summary," October 31, 2005, available at www.iata.org/pressroom/economics_facts/stats-2005-10-31-03.htm. The IATA uses the term "Within Asia Pacific," with "Asia Pacific" defined as all countries from Pakistan east (including Pakistan) plus Afghanistan, Turkmenistan, Uzbekistan, and Kazakhstan.

26. Mathews, "Regional Flights May Be Ticket to Success," p. 415.

27. "Lessons from Shanghai," *India Today*, April 24, 2006, p. 1.

28. James Ott, "Future Cargo Hubs," *Aviation Week and Space Technology,* November 15, 2004, p. 66.

29. Rimmer, "The Asia-Pacific Rim's Transport and Telecommunications Systems," table 4.

30. Jinks, "Containerised Trade Imbalance," p. 2.

31. Mariko Sanchanta, "Tokyo Plans for Asian Open Skies," *Financial Times*, March 31–April 1, 2007, p. 5.

32. Asian Development Bank. *Southeast Asian Regional Transport Survey,* 5 vols. Singapore: Asian Development Bank, 1972–1973. Quoted in Rimmer, "The Spatial Impact of Innovations," p. 287.

33. Bird, *Unbeaten Tracks,* p. 107.

34. Lewis, *Golden Earth.* Lewis traveled throughout Burma in the early 1950s.

35. "Asia Deliveries Faster and Cheaper by Road, Claims TNT," *Air Cargo Asia-Pacific News*, December 5, 2005, available at www.aircargo-ap.com.au/ac/ac-news-dec05.htm.

36. Information on the East-West Corridor project is available at www.adb.org. It is part of the Greater Mekong Subregion development project.

37. Tran Dinh Thanh Lam, "Trans-Asian Highway Already Bringing Benefits," *Imaging Our Mekong,* April 22, 2006, www.newsmekong.org.

38. John Moon and R. Alexander Roehri, "Infrastructure Networks to Extend Regional Production Networks to Inland Sites in Asia," in Asian Development Bank, *Asian Economic Cooperation and Integration*, pp. 320–321.

39. Singh, "Indian Special Economic Zones and Bilateralism in Asia," p. 2.

40. Landingin and Wadley, "Export Processing Zones and Growth Triangle Development," table 1.

41. This definition is adapted from a summary contained in Eisuke Sakakibara and Sharon Yamakawa, "Market-Driven Regional Integration in East Asia," paper presented to the G-20 Workshop on Regional Economic Integration in a Global Framework, September 22–23, 2004, pp. 4–5.

42. Dieter Ernst, "Searching for a New Role in East Asian Regionalization," in Katzenstein and Shiraishi, *Beyond Japan*, p. 165.

43. Ng and Yeats, "Major Trade Trends in East Asia," p. 55. Italics in original.

44. Rohlen, "Cosmopolitan Cities and Nation States," p. 9.

45. *UN World Urbanization Prospects,* http://esa.un.org/unup.

46. Estimated as of April 2007. The fourteen are Tokyo, Seoul, Mumbai, Delhi, Shanghai, Osaka, Calcutta, Manila, Jakarta, Canton, Beijing, Shenzhen, Bangkok, and Wuhan. "Agglomerations" include a central city and neighboring communities linked to it. See www.citypopulation.de.

47. UNESCAP, *Municipal Land Management in Asia.*

48. United Nations, *China Human Development Report 2005*, available at www.undp.org.cn/modules.php?op=modload&name=News&file=article&topic=40&s id=228.

49. "Rural-Urban Distribution of Population," *eCensusIndia*, www.censusindia.net /results/eci14_page2.html.

50. Webster, "On the Edge," pp. 5–6.

51. Dali Yang, *Beyond Beijing: Liberalization and the Regions in China* (New York: Routledge, 1997), p. 31; Ding Lu and Zhimin Tang, *State Intervention and Business in China* (Cheltenam, UK: Edward Elgar, 1997), pp. 42–43, cited in Zweig, *Internationalizing China*, p. 59, table 2.2.

52. Mao Zedong, "On the Ten Great Relationships," in Stuart Schram, ed., *Chairman Mao Talks to the People: Talks and Letters, 1956–1971* (New York: Pantheon, 1975), cited in Zweig, *Internationalizing China*, p. 53. Industrialization in China's interior is discussed at length in Naughton, "The Third Front."

53. Fung, Lau, and Lee, *U.S. Direct Investment in China,* p. 47, table 4.2.

54. Personal communication from Thomas G. Rawski, University of Pittsburgh. See also Keller and Rawski, *China's Rise,* table 2.2, p. 20. The trade ratio is exports plus imports divided by total gross domestic product. Anything over 100 means that the subject locality is trading more than it is producing.

55. Rana Foroohar, "Do the Math," *Newsweek*, October 20, 2003, p. E22.

56. Adapted from data available at www.fdi.gov.cn.

57. Robert Ash, "China's Regional Economies and the Asian Region," in Shambaugh, *Power Shift*, p. 110. Other investment data come from Ash's tables 15 and 18.

58. Zweig, *Internationalizing China*, p. 68, footnote 71.

5

Individuals as Spontaneous Integrators

Private citizens are driving the revival and reintegration of Maritime Asia. Taking advantage of globalization and new technology, they are thickening its urban clusters and multiplying its corridors and gateways. They are doing so with or without the cooperation of their governments—and sometimes despite them.

Political scientist T. J. Pempel calls the people engaging in spontaneous integration the "key spinners of the web of cooperation (and occasionally conflict)."[1] Just so: the words *spin* and *spontaneous* are related. This chapter is about the spinners or "integrators," as I sometimes call them. I look first at pioneers and managers of Asian production networks. I then turn to five other categories of individual integrators: conceptual, values-based, unintentional, unwilling, and unwanted.

■ Architects of Production Networks

The "spinners" of production networks and their local partners are the commercial pioneers of Asian economic integration. Their on-the-ground initiatives have been much more important than preferential trade agreements, many of which are riddled with loopholes and years away from full implementation.

Executives engaged in multinational production networks take thousands of high-skilled Asian and Western managers out of their homeland and assign them to production spots in countries with inadequate or mismatched indigenous labor skills.[2] These networked producers are more natural integrators than traders because they bring people from different cultural backgrounds into sustained face-to-face contact at the worksite. Engineers possessing technology and know-how must not only transfer and license this knowledge to others but also adapt, teach, maintain, and continuously upgrade their skills. Executives in parent companies must monitor this process and, if they are smart, learn from it. Regionwide business and banking associations are also spinners of integration because they share information, devise collective positions and strategies, and press for the removal of obstacles to cross-border trade and investment. Mayors and other local authorities compete for investment and serve as brokers. They make suitable local arrangements and act as go-betweens with higher authorities.

Japanese Pioneers

Modern, seamless, high-technology production networks as we know them today sprang from Japanese industrialists. Their outstanding achievements in high-quality, just-in-time manufacturing and their long-term strategic perspective served them well in Asia. The role of Japanese businessmen in initiating Asian market integration recalls what Jacques Servan-Schreiber said in the 1960s about Americans. Observing that US companies ignored national barriers and invested all over Europe, he wrote, "It is American-style management that is, in its own special way, unifying Europe."[3]

Japanese companies pioneered the trend toward networked production in response to the sharp hike in the value of the yen, engineered by the Group of Seven (G-7) in 1985.[4] Firms manufacturing textiles and many other products lost their competitiveness and set up shop in Southeast Asia. Higher oil prices, mounting wages, and growing environmental awareness in Japan pushed energy-hungry industries like aluminum smelting offshore. Automobile companies proved particularly adept at distributing the production of parts and integrating final assembly. Demand for energy, raw materials, and food boosted long-standing investment in the oil and gas sectors, agribusiness, and mining.

Dennis Tachiki reports that the most active Japanese investment corridors still stretch from Tokyo through coastal China to Hong Kong and from Thailand to Indonesia and the Philippines.[5] These are the two central arteries of Maritime Asia.

Overseas Chinese Investors

In most Asian countries, ethnic Chinese constitute 5 percent or less of the population but account for a significant proportion of national wealth. The five richest Indonesians, for example, are ethnic Chinese, as are a majority of the country's forty richest people.[6] Most of this wealth comes from business activities generated by family-owned companies.

Ethnic Chinese business owners and entrepreneurs living or sojourning outside of China were among the first to feed China's economic boom. Until the mid-1990s, they accounted for an estimated 70 to 80 percent of foreign direct investment in China.[7] (Much of their investment came from or through Hong Kong.) Business networks headed by family-owned overseas Chinese firms are renowned for using *guanxi* (connections) to identify promising investment opportunities and to forge coalitions capable of winning over—or working around—Chinese authorities.[8]

This impressive record has given rise to two assumptions concerning the role of overseas Chinese business networks in Asian integration. The first is that Chinese are inherently more successful, entrepreneurial, dynamic, and market-oriented than other Asians and that they will therefore reap most of the economic benefits of integration.

Those who believe that Chinese living overseas are inherently more successful point to long-standing social and cultural factors, such as a "Confucian" work ethic, a strong sense of family, and self-discipline. But sociologists report that there is no single "market culture" monopolized by Chinese.[9] Before the arrival of the Europeans, Maritime Asia's most active and successful traders were Southeast Asians, Arabs, and Indians, not Chinese. Moreover, many of the 20 million or so Chinese emigrants or Asians of Chinese descent living outside of China are still poor.[10]

The second assumption is that Chinese business networks are so loyal to family, clan, and lineage (and perhaps to Chinese ethnicity more generally) that they will continue to plough large amounts of capital into China even if China's growth prospects dim. This perception is also open to challenge. Young Chinese entrepreneurs favor a diverse investment portfolio. Often educated in the West and comfortable in English, they feel no overriding loyalty to family and clan. They say that profits in China are not what they once were. They also believe that Chinese authorities are quite capable of confiscating wealth without adequate compensation. They are therefore pushing their companies to seek higher returns in the global marketplace.

Ironically, other Asians are moving into China just as Chinese business networks are diversifying. Non-Chinese investors from South Korea, Japan, Malaysia, Singapore, and India are investing in China in record numbers. According to Chinese statistics, Asian investors account for roughly two-thirds of China's incoming investment (including Hong Kong).[11] Examining data on foreign direct investment in China's Jiangsu province in 2002, China expert Robert Ash reported that companies based in Hong Kong and Taiwan led the way with $4 billion and $2.5 billion, respectively. Japanese, ASEAN, and Korean companies followed at $1.7 billion, $1.3 billion, and $900 million, respectively. US companies were also in the game, investing $1.5 billion in Jiangsu alone that year. Another $4.5 billion came from companies of unknown nationality registered in the Cayman Islands or the British Virgin Islands, some of which are based in Europe and North America.[12]

In short, overseas Chinese business owners and entrepreneurs have contributed heavily to China-centered integration by creating extensive regional networks. But ethnic claims are becoming weaker and their role as a catalyst of ethnically based Asian integration is diminishing.

■ Values-Based, Religious, and Cultural Integrators

Values-Based Integrators

Promoters of Asian values. Confucian values such as order, mutual obligation, ethical behavior, and observance of correct family relationships still have considerable influence in East Asia.[13] The "Asian values" championed by Singapore's Lee Kuan Yew and Malaysia's Mahathir bin Mohamad in the 1990s evoked a Confucian-flavored Asian identity compatible with but different from that of the West.[14]

Paradoxically, the concept of Asian values would not exist without the West because it presumes the existence of, and reacts to, "Western values." Whereas Western liberalism cherishes the value of the individual and upholds unfettered individual rights (the reasoning goes), Asians assign a higher value to family, group, and community. Westerners rely more on law and Asians on trust. Western-style democracy is not suitable for Asia; economic development requires discipline and must therefore precede full-scale political and individual liberty.

Reactions to the notion of Asian values were mixed. When polled in 1993–1994, Asian elites tended to agree that Asians valued loyalty to the family and the community over individual rights. Majorities in most (but not all) countries preferred consensus-based decisionmaking and nonbinding commitments over majority voting and legal procedures.[15] Some Asian intellectuals went along with these basic values, but those supporting a transition to more democratic governance did not warm to what they saw as a justification of authoritarian government.

Moreover, Mahathir's "East Asian Community" implicitly sidelined India along with the two "Western" countries in the region, Australia and New Zealand. Indians were too preoccupied with Pakistan and too wedded to autarkic policies to care that they were left out, and Australia's prime minister was feuding with Mahathir at the time. Japan was included, but as an industrial democracy and close ally of the United States, it was caught in the middle and demurred. China was diplomatic but basically uninterested.

The Asian values crusade ran aground on two sandbars. First, the financial crisis of 1997–1998 knocked a big hole in the Asian values thesis and took the wind out of the "East Asian Miracle," the "Asian Century," and other slogans of the day. Critics argued that excessive reliance on trust, the lack of transparency, the absence of hardheaded economic analysis, and weak legal and supervisory mechanisms contributed substantially to the sudden collapse of investor confidence.

Second, growing enthusiasm for democracy in the region trumped what appeared to be a rationale for authoritarian rule. Singapore and (to a lesser extent) Malaysia still limit political freedoms, thwart opposition leaders, and exercise selective information control.[16] Military leaders in Thailand carried out a bloodless coup in 2006, and the Myanmar regime cracked down on demonstrators in September 2007. But none of the leaders of these four countries justify their actions in the name of Asian values.[17]

China's surging economy has given rise to two new trends related to values. First, there is talk of a Beijing Consensus, loosely understood as a combination of market-based economic policy, state supervision, and authoritarian or quasi-authoritarian rule. The choice of this label is intended to signal a contrast with the Washington Consensus, a term coined in 1989 by economist John Williamson to describe ten specific policies recommended for crisis-ridden economies in Latin America. To Williamson's dismay, the term is now misrepresented as unrestrained market fundamentalism.[18] But no matter what term is used, the contrast between China's (and Vietnam's) strong economic record and the feeble economic performance of some of the democracies in the region works against the idea that political and economic liberalization must go hand in hand.

Confucianism has recently resurfaced as a tool of Chinese diplomacy. Reviled as "feudal" during China's Cultural Revolution, Confucius now occupies an honored place in the constellation of historical figures displayed in China's national wax museum. Selected Confucian values such as ethical behavior, respect for education, social harmony, and loyalty to family and group have some appeal in societies undergoing rapid change, especially in Northeast Asia. The Chinese government has set up Confucius institutes in more than thirty countries around the world, including the United States, and plans to establish many more. Some are freestanding and some are lodged within universities, but all promote the study of Chinese language and culture.[19] In short, the Asian values debate may resurface in a Sinocentric form.

China's success subtly flavors economic debates as well. Western capitalism operates within a framework of laws and regulations governing competition, insider trading, disclosure, and many other forms of economic behavior. But champions of an "Asian way" seem to regard Western-style capitalism as unrestrained and thus unsuitable for Asia. Unfettered free markets produce lopsided results and occasional exploitation, they argue; capitalism is an engine of growth, but it requires checks and balances on the part of the state.

In a different vein, former deputy prime minister Anwar Ibrahim of Malaysia calls for an Asian Renaissance that embraces democracy in a Kantian spirit but draws on Asian cultures.[20] Speaking to a 2006 conference on the revival of Buddhist cultural links, Singapore's foreign minister used "Asian Renaissance" to describe what he sees as a "tremendous burst of creative adaptation" in Asia combining Buddhist values with Islamic and Western religious influences.[21]

Defining *Asian-ness* is an ongoing theme in Asian intellectual circles. Amitav Acharya and others argue that a new set of Asian norms, values, and institutions is emerging from the reality of interdependence. It is conservative in the sense of slow-moving and consensus-based, but it is based neither on traditional notions of hierarchy nor on realpolitik. It blends modern Westphalian notions of sovereignty, equality, and noninterference with evolving techniques of dealing peacefully with changes in power relationships.[22] Acharya sees Asia's future in these terms, not as a throwback to warmed-over traditions.[23] He and other so-called constructivists believe that those norms are compatible with the Western world order. Indeed, the West itself is evolving.

The notion of Asian norms and values is more prevalent in elite circles and the urban middle class than in the population at large and is thus easy to dismiss. But as Nietzsche's *Zarathustra* intoned, "Not around the inventors of new noises but around the inventors of new values does the world revolve."[24] So far *Asian-ness* is mostly noise. But as a set of values, an open and tolerant form of Asian identity appears to be gaining ground, especially in Maritime Asia.

Environmentalists. In December 2004, a powerful earthquake thundered below the sea near the western tip of Sumatra, belching up a monster tidal wave (tsunami) that ravaged a semicircle of maritime communities rimming the Bay of Bengal. The disaster elicited a four-navy emergency relief operation and prompted regional authorities to join forces in an intensified early-warning system.

Some of the damage could have been avoided if humans had not systematically destroyed one of the most effective shields against the power of the ocean—mangrove forests. Developers have slashed an estimated 35 to 50 percent of these wooded barriers to make way for shrimp farms, tourist resorts, and suburban development.[25] In Indonesia, for example, fully 70 percent of mangrove areas had been cut down or damaged.[26]

Environmental destruction and pollution compound natural disasters, ignore man-made boundaries, and impose the unwanted integration of shared misery. They challenge the cherished Asian principle of nonintervention and undermine the sanctity of national autonomy as it has been pursued to date. In recent years, for example, land-clearing fires in Sumatra's Riau province have polluted the air in Malaysia, Singapore, and Thailand. China's planned dams on the Mekong River and its tributaries jeopardize downstream livelihoods in Laos, Thailand, and Cambodia, not to mention an ecosystem containing an estimated eighty rare or endangered animals and fish.

Maritime Asia is particularly vulnerable to cross-border environmental problems. As many as 1 billion Asians depend on fish as their primary source of protein, but fishing stocks are dwindling and coastal shellfish are often unsafe. The shipping boom has boosted the number of oil spills. Inefficiently powered factories clustered within reach of the sea or near ocean-accessible rivers spit forth sulphur dioxide and nitrogen dioxide as well as industrial waste, threatening livelihoods in neighboring countries.[27]

Because of the large size and rapid growth of the Chinese economy, China is the largest source of cross-border pollution. According to one count, in the years 1993–2003, more than 2,350 oil spills occurred off China's coast alone, averaging one spill every 4.6 days.[28] Some of this oil washes up on other people's shores. China's mushrooming coal-fired plants spew filthy air into South Korea, Japan, and beyond.[29] In 1998, the widespread flooding of the Yangtze caused China to ban most logging. Since then, however, China has imported ever-larger amounts of timber, some of which is illegally harvested in Indonesia and Myanmar.

Environmentalists with regionwide awareness of these problems and who seek bilateral, subregional, or regional solutions are protective integrators. They are few in number and almost always highly educated. Many have traveled to Western countries and speak fluent English. They believe strongly in cross-border cooperation. They know that solving cross-border environmental problems means changing the way people in different countries behave, sharing information, and enforcing common standards.

The intellectuals and statesmen who contributed to the East Asia Vision Group Report of 2001 asserted that environmental problems provided "strong incentives for collective environmental cooperation." They called on governments to establish a regional environmental body with a dispute settlement mechanism and a regional environmental database. They also encouraged environmental education in schools, the development of environmental networks linking community programs at the grassroots level, and various other regionwide measures.[30]

The World Wide Fund for Nature and other international environmental organizations publicize regionwide environmental problems, sponsor many worthwhile projects, and put pressure on governments to join forces and take stronger action. But their commitment to the global environmental movement is carried out mainly by elites, and their offices are mainly in cities. Foreign funding erodes their credibility, and job-hungry local populations resist being told what to do by people with perceived links to the West. Despite these drawbacks, they are active network builders and consciousness raisers and have had some effect on governments and development institutions.

The other end of the spectrum teems with homegrown, locally funded environmental groups. Most of these are local, single-issue, ragtag organizations operating on a shoestring budget and acting largely alone. By one count,

Thailand and South Korea host about 200 each and Japan a whopping 4,500.[31] Many local groups have risen in protest against a specific project, such as a dam. Some rail against the depletion of life-sustaining resources in their community or abroad, such as fish or tropical timber. The Japan Tropical Forest Action Network, for example, has had some success in persuading Japanese companies to reduce their imports of tropical timber. Some are antinuclear, especially in Japan. Meanwhile, the regionalization of civil society networks and grassroots groups in Asia is growing.[32] Frameworks for environmental cooperation in East Asia are plentiful—more abundant, in fact, that in other issue areas, such as drug control.[33] For example, more than twenty regional and national NGOs from eleven Asian countries have teamed up to promote sustainable agriculture and rural development.[34] In Southeast Asia, environmentalists persuaded ASEAN to adopt several regional environmental programs as early as the 1980s, and they continue to press for enforcement of various agreements. In Northeast Asia, clean-air groups have formed a coalition.

Although respect for the natural environment for its own sake is still a relatively low priority in most of Asia, leaders in both the public and the private sector are beginning to pay serious attention to pollution because of its high economic cost. The threat of global climate change in particular is beginning to attract notice. Scientists predict that typhoons in Asia will become more severe and that rainfall will come in a cycle of severe bursts and dry spells. They also fear that warmer climates and rising sea levels will intensify the spread of disease and threaten the very existence of coastal zones and islands.[35]

Insurance companies are making it known that they may raise premiums to cover these risks. In 2004, the Asian Business Council, a group of chief executive officers from some of the biggest companies operating in Asia, received an expert briefing on the subject for the first time.[36] Like their counterparts elsewhere, Asian companies are now joining with financial brokers to create cap-and-trade schemes to cope with carbon emissions.

Executives and managers of companies that produce goods for regional and global markets are more connected than most environmental activists and have far more resources to deal with pollution. They are would-be integrators only in the sense of seeking regional business opportunities. But they are increasingly aware of the cost of pollution, and they bring financial resources, energy-efficient production methods, and environmentally friendly technologies to the table.

Democracy and human rights activists. Groups upholding and promoting universal norms of human rights and democracy face steep challenges in Asia. Regional human rights regimes are in effect in Europe, the Americas, and even Africa, but Asians lack a common framework. In many parts of Asia, democracy creaks and stumbles. In some countries, elections are manipulated by vested interests, to the detriment of political opponents and the public interest. Some regimes claiming to represent "the people" have been captured by old elites. Many ooze with corruption. As yet, there is neither a common standard nor a shared vision of "Asia whole and free."

Nevertheless, democracy and human rights have made considerable headway in Asia. Although research is imperfect, there appears to be a positive two-way relationship between democracy and globalization, and Asia is highly globalized.[37] One dictatorship after another has tumbled, eased its grip, or relinquished control. Voices using or misusing "Asian values" to justify authoritarianism have fallen silent, at least for now. The governments of Japan, India, Taiwan, and Indonesia all highlight democracy in their public diplomacy. Even undemocratic governments pay lip service to democracy and mumble assent (at least when it suits their interests) to watery statements on human rights.

Organized champions of human rights and democracy can be found in every country but are particularly strong in three of the original founders of ASEAN—Indonesia, the Philippines, and Thailand. In 2004 parliamentarians from these three countries plus Malaysia and Singapore formed the ASEAN Inter-Parliamentary Myanmar Caucus. Their priorities include placing and keeping Myanmar on the agenda of the UN Security Council, applying pressure to secure the release of dissident leader Aung San Suu Kyi, and promoting other democratic reforms.[38] What is equally noteworthy is that top officials from Indonesia and Malaysia publicly criticized the Myanmar regime even before the 2007 crackdown. (Myanmar is discussed further in Chapter 9.)

The declaration of the 2003 ASEAN summit, known as Bali Concord II, named "democracy" as a stated goal of the ASEAN Security Community. Overcoming resistance from Myanmar and reservations from others, ASEAN heads of state agreed in 2007 to establish a human rights commission, although how such a body will function is not yet clear.

Access to information technology and the use of computers are among the most vital tools of democracy and human rights integrators.[39] Thanks to this technology, networked groups can be in daily contact with each other, their supporters, the media, and international human rights organizations like Amnesty International's Human Rights Watch/Asia and Freedom House. As one Jakarta-based reformer told me, "We first learned about human rights abuses in East Timor from Amnesty International in New York."

Religious Integrators

Islam. Are Muslims integrators? Two kinds of Islamic integration are visible in Maritime Asia. One links radical-fundamentalist Muslims who increasingly identify themselves with the *umma* (community) and support or carry out violent activities, and the other connects moderate Muslims trying to counter the radicals' rising influence.

The region inherits a moderate version of Islam and shelters many progressive Islamic thinkers, especially in the cosmopolitan cities of Maritime Asia. These Muslims believe that Islam values the intrinsic humanity in all peoples and that it is therefore compatible with the notion of universal human rights, including basic rights of women.[40] They support political and social rights, including the rights of women, but argue that such rights are more likely to be legitimate and sustainable if they are developed within a religious and cultural Islamic tradition. They argue that for historical reasons Islam in Southeast Asia is an instrument of modernity and debunk the idea that it is antidemocratic.[41] Excessive repression in much of the Muslim world, they say, has frozen intellectual inquiry and held back technological achievements.[42]

But moderate, reform-minded Muslims face at least three challenges. The first is strong opposition from conservative rural leaders. Globalization has shaken the foundation of traditional authority and introduced pop culture, more relaxed sexual mores, and a greater voice for women, setting off a backlash. The second is the rise of radical-fundamentalist groups, which attract jobless, frustrated, and humiliated young men. Taking advantage of rising Muslim self-awareness and conservative rural prejudices, Islamist fighters from the Middle East and Pakistan have joined forces with local discontents and burrowed into certain communities, where they plan attacks and pursue twisted dreams of a new dominion of Islam, purged of infidels.

The third challenge is financial dependence on the Middle East, the main source of fundamentalist Islam to date. Many Muslim schools in Asia receive funds, books, and teacher training from Middle Eastern sources, because national and local governments have no funds to support them. Some of these schools teach neither science nor English.

As members of a worldwide community, Asian Muslims are sympathetic to the Palestinians and critical of US support for Israel. The US war in Iraq has strengthened these feelings and created the perception that Americans are anti-Muslim. One result is a stronger sense of common identity among Southeast Asian Muslims. This process of Muslim (re)integration is uneven, however. In China, Muslim minorities maintain separate identities. Uighur separatists in Xinjiang receive support from groups in Pakistan and Central Asia, but they have little or no direct contact with Muslims in Southeast Asia. Ties between China's Yunnan province and Muslims in northern Thailand appear to be getting weaker, not stronger.[43]

Islamic thinking colors the perceived legitimacy of domestic political actions and shapes the way decisions are presented, but it has never been a unified force. Until recently it has not been a major factor in the formulation of national interest,[44] but that may be changing as Muslims continue to assert their identity and strengthen their cross-border ties. Governments are attempting to steer this process in constructive directions. In November 2006, for example, a group called the Center for Moderate Muslims in the Philippines hosted a meeting of Islamist teachers from ASEAN at which delegates agreed to draw up a plan for ASEAN members to develop their own regional standard for teaching and spreading Islam.[45] In June 2007, a former president of Indonesia chaired an international conference specifically affirming the reality of the Holocaust—thus rebutting a Holocaust-denying meeting sponsored by the president of Iran that received wide publicity in the West.

Buddhism. Buddhism is a living force in Asia. Unlike Islam, Buddhism has no equivalent of a sharia-based legal system and does not seek to replace national governments. Its two great branches are Mahayana and Theravada. Mahayana (literally, great wheel) Buddhism is found in "Sinicized" East Asia—Japan, Korea, parts of China and Vietnam, and (in a different and complex form) Tibet and Mongolia. The Dalai Lama is its most revered figure. The Zen and Pure Land sects are offshoots of Mahayana Buddhism. Theravada (literally, the way of the elders) Buddhism predominates in Southeast Asia—Sri Lanka, Thailand, Myanmar, Cambodia, Laos, and parts of Vietnam.

Buddhism entered China primarily by land during the Han Dynasty (206 B.C.–A.D. 220). The earliest evidence of Buddhism at the court of a prince, who also practiced Taoism, dates from A.D. 65, but the long process of absorbing Buddhism into Chinese culture did not begin until the third century.[46] During the Tang Dynasty (A.D. 618–907), Buddhism had acquired such political strength that Tang rulers engaged in a selective revival of Confucianism to control it. Under the Mongols, Buddhism enjoyed a renaissance.[47]

Buddhist organizations maintain extensive contacts with each other. The Nichiren sect, which originated in Japan, actively promulgates its teaching in Asia and maintains an active network. It was once linked to a Japanese political party, but the link was formally severed. Buddhists are active in the interfaith movement.

New Delhi has used the fact that Buddhism originated in India to strengthen its ties with East Asia and to offset China's influence in a constructive way. Backed by India's most important friend in the region, Singapore, and also supported by Japan, India plans to restore and expand Nalanda University in Bihar. Nalanda is an ancient Buddhist center of learning that dates from at least the fifth century A.D. (The famous Chinese monk Xuan Zang visited there in the seventh century.) The idea is to establish an international university near the Nalanda site, with centers of excellence in science, religion, and the humanities. A conference, "Reviving Buddhist Cultural Links," held in November 2006, attracted over 200 scholars, officials, and Buddhist monks and nuns from all over Asia. The Indian government subsequently presented the Nalanda initiative to the second East Asian Summit, held in the Philippines in January 2007, where heads of state formally welcomed it.[48]

Christianity.   Christianity still flourishes in the Philippines and South Korea and is practiced here and there in China, Taiwan, Indonesia, Japan, Vietnam, India, and Singapore. In recent years, evangelical sects have been gaining converts. The work of Christian missionaries affects the health and education of millions of Asians. In some parts of Asia, Christians face persecution or local hostility, especially when their religion is associated with ethnicity and when sudden migration upsets the local political balance (as in Indonesia's Moluku Islands). A few have been accused of violence against rival sects as well as non-Christians.

By nature, Christians are a more potent political force than Buddhists because they are very much "in the world." Not only do they try actively to spread their religion, but they are also quick to bring examples of persecution to the attention of Christian organizations in the West, including the so-called Christian Right in the United States. Although no one knows for sure, China may have 50 million or more closet Christians in addition to those officially recognized and tolerated by the state. Ever mindful of history and wary of threats to their power, Chinese leaders may recall that the leader of the disastrous Taiping Rebellion of the 1860s claimed to be the younger brother of Jesus.

Cultural Integrators

Youthful audiences all over Asia thrill to Korean pop songs, Bollywood films, Japanese anime (cartoon animation), and other forms of pop culture, paying no attention to nationality. Indeed, as entertainers adapt to regionwide audiences, pop culture is increasingly interactive. Not only Korean women but also women from Japan, Taiwan, China, and Vietnam swoon over Bae Yong-joon, star of the Korean soap opera *Winter Sonata*.[49] Actors from different countries are even appearing in the same films. Such entertainment gives young Asians something in common. But chances are that this cultural wash is shallow and transient, with no political spillover effect. As yet there is little or no real "we" feeling among the young, except perhaps among Asian students at overseas universities.

At the other end of the cultural spectrum, high culture such as classical music, dance, and theater tend to be national in the way they are presented and described. Gamelan music is Indonesian, Peking opera is Chinese, Noh drama is Japanese, and so on. Such performances are attracting regionwide audiences, but their drawing power in Asia (and elsewhere) is limited to elites. There is no reason to expect Thais, Vietnamese, or Indians to appreciate gamelan music, Peking opera, or Noh drama any more than anyone else in the world. Besides, the goals of artists and cultural authorities alike are the preservation of diversity and mutual enrichment, not the integration of cultures.

It is good that Asians are being exposed to each other's cultures. The richness and diversity of Asian cultures of all kinds are regional assets. But on the whole, even interactive pop culture contributes only superficially to integration, and high culture not at all.

Unintentional Integrators

The New Middle Class

Until the middle of the twentieth century, Chinese, Indian, and other "sojourners" in Asia lived away from home for years at a time. They sired offspring who became the ancestors of today's overseas minorities. They waited for the chance to return home, perhaps only to die. Some never left.[50]

Thanks to the technology described in the previous chapter, sojourners no longer feel cut off from their original homes and compelled to adapt to an alien culture. Chinese breadwinners, nicknamed "astronauts" in Hong Kong, leave their families at home and travel to and from the city on business.[51] They and their counterparts from other parts of the region are the traveling tip of a broadly homogenous middle class that increasingly defines and unites Maritime Asia.

Members of this new class are what Kwame Appiah calls "rooted cosmopolitans"—rooted in their country and culture of origin but sophisticated and open to new influences. They live in urban or peri-urban areas, usually on or near the coast. They have similar tastes, habits of consumption, and lifestyles. They get regionwide news and commentary from Asia News Network, an organization of daily newspapers covering regional events, or from online sources like Asia Times and numerous blogs.[52] Their affinity stems not from culture or civilization but from their engagement with the global economy and their entry into new middle classes.

Japanese scholar Takashi Shiraishi, who has looked at Asia's new middle classes in detail, argues that in Japan, South Korea, coastal China, and the wealthier countries of Southeast Asia, members of these classes are the main consumers in a regional market that indirectly creates new forms of identification. They may or may not be united or influential within their own societies, but they all have a "middle-class consciousness" derived from market networks and global cultural and financial flows. Along with states and markets, Shiraishi believes that these groups are laying the foundations for regional integration and regional identification.[53]

Members of the new middle classes pursue an increasingly similar lifestyle. Their jobs, income, education, linguistic ability, food preferences, shopping habits, and material aspirations have more in common than the lifestyles of their parents' generation. Television has popularized a US-inspired but increasingly hybrid image of the good life: Shiraishi's list includes "a suburban house, a car, a TV set, a refrigerator, a washing machine, and well-known brands of packaged food, clothing, and cosmetics."[53] Multinational corporations target middle-class consumers of these products on a regional basis.

The lifestyle and consumption patterns of India's huge urban middle class increasingly resemble those of their East Asian counterparts. Middle-class Indians are prospering despite their country's stifling bureaucracy. Author and former Procter & Gamble India executive Gurcharan Das cites the case of a young man named Shashi Kumar. Overcoming his low-caste rural background, Kumar now lives in a nice apartment with a mortgage, drives a good car, and sends his daughter to private school.[54] Whether or not Indians continue on this path depends on the extent to which national and local authorities reform archaic regulations and institutions and dismantle barriers to the global economy. In the first decade of the twenty-first century, a regional identity linking Indians with East Asians seems remote, but markets have a funny way of changing people's outlook.

Tourists

Except for certain remote centers of high civilization, most tourist destinations in Asia are coastal or urban. As Asian incomes rise and transportation improves, enthusiastic travel executives in Maritime Asia are rushing to accommodate visitors. Western tourists will continue to come, but Asians are a new growth market. According to the World Tourism Organization, intraregional tourist travel in Asia will grow considerably faster than long-haul travel, reaching 265 million arrivals by 2020 compared to 152 million in 1995. Most of this traffic will fan out to cities and maritime regions.[55]

Predictably, the resurgence of China profoundly influences this trend. In 1995, only 4.5 million Chinese tourists traveled overseas. Ten years later, that number had rocketed to 31 million and continues to climb sharply. The World Tourism Organization estimates that the volume of Chinese travelers is expected to hit 50 million by 2010 and 100 million by 2020, making China the world's fourth largest source of outbound tourists. By comparison, 17 million Japanese traveled abroad in 2004.

The Chinese are big spenders. Young, career-oriented Chinese, nicknamed the "Billion Boomer" generation, drop large amounts of money when they travel. According to industry sources, Chinese tourists spend 80 percent more than Japanese and in Thailand, at least, almost 15 percent more than Europeans.[56] Hotel and resort owners are scrambling to adjust to the new wave. Along with miso soup, a guest perusing the breakfast buffet at a luxury hotel is likely to find congee, a rice pudding popular with Chinese.

For Chinese, travel to Taiwan is restricted to those going for business or to visit relatives, but they can go to Hong Kong and Macao relatively easily. Each year Hong Kong receives almost twice as many visitors from China as its entire population.[57] In the 1990s, the Chinese government granted "approved destination status" in return for extended visas for group tours to Thailand, Singapore, Malaysia, the Philippines, South Korea, Australia, and New Zealand. Between 2000 and 2003, Japan, Indonesia, Vietnam, Cambodia, Brunei, Sri Lanka, and India joined the list. A majority of European countries came on board in 2004 (but not the United States).

In addition to the Chinese, tourists from Japan, South Korea, Taiwan, Hong Kong, and Singapore are flocking to popular sites throughout Maritime Asia. Like most other Asian tourists, they buy package tours, stay in big hotels, and stop in several countries; but individual travel is also growing at double-digit rates. Pop culture attracts a growing number of Asians to Korea and Japan. For instance, there are tours to the filming locations of Korean soap operas. Fashion, high-technology gadgets, popular recording artists, manga (comic books), and anime draw rising numbers of Asian visitors to Japan.

Buoyed by Indonesia's recovery, the leisure cruise industry is on an upswing. A glossy ASEAN cruise directory, published for the first time in 2006, lists twenty-two ports in six nations. Travel agents are billing Southeast Asia as the "Caribbean of the East."[58] In 1999 the chairman of the Singapore-Johor-Riau Growth Triangle's Maritime Tourism Sub-Working Group dubbed the region "Aseanarean" (ASEAN + area + n) because it adds a "nautical twist" and "complements the Mediterranean and the Caribbean."[59]

Charter flights are surging as well. Australian ski enthusiasts are escaping from their summer to Japan's winter, renting or buying ski lodges in Hokkaido. Flights to Asia's best golf resorts are popular with Japanese, Singaporeans, and others.

Not surprisingly, Indian tourist authorities are actively trawling for tourists from East and Southeast Asia. A joint India-ASEAN working group is in place. Tour packages and the exchange of tourism experts are under way. The problem is that, except for luxury hotels, India's tourist infrastructure is not up to world standards.

Maritime Asia hosts an unknown but surely predominant percentage of these cross-border tourists. Many ancient treasures—such as Cambodia's Angkor Wat, Laos's Luang Prabang, China's tombs and cave sculptures, and the temples of eastern Java—are located in the interior. But it is a safe bet that most tourists spend considerable time and money in the cities, on the beaches, and among the islands of Maritime Asia.

Migrant Laborers

Job seekers gravitate to Maritime Asia because that is where the fastest growth is taking place. Others stumble in because they are being displaced or deprived of their traditional livelihood. Large numbers in both categories are spilling across borders. Some are young and ambitious; others are desperate. For the first time in history, a majority of these job seekers are women.

The flow of job seekers in Maritime Asia tracks the changing location of money and jobs. Thousands of unskilled laborers are on the move. Malaysia and Singapore are magnets for migrant labor from Indonesia, the Philippines, and the former Indochina. Construction workers from south India are a common sight. The Filipino maid is an established fixture of upper-class households in Singapore, Hong Kong, and Taiwan.

Many job seekers are exploited. Extreme poverty and lack of opportunity in Myanmar have pushed an estimated 600,000 migrant workers over the border into Thailand, two-thirds of the total number of migrant workers registered there. Despite miserable wages, they pay agent fees and taxes to Thais, and the Myanmar government reportedly takes 10 percent of their overseas earnings.[60]

It is hard to find reliable statistics on transnational job seekers because much of the migration that occurs is either unreported or short-term and seasonal. What seems clear from official records is that the tide of undocumented and contract laborers is rising. Until the Malaysian government cracked down on undocumented migrant workers in 2005, Indonesians surged into Malaysia at levels second only to Mexicans entering the United States. A 1997 United Nations publication documented the rise in contract labor migration from the Philippines, Indonesia, and (to a lesser extent) Thailand and a parallel rise in importance of Asian destinations.[61]

Migrant laborers are big business. Receiving countries in Asia depend on them just as the United States depends on Mexicans and Central Americans. Countries of origin depend on them because of their remittances. According to the World Bank, remittances from Asian workers doubled after 2000, reaching $75 billion in 2005, almost half the world's total. Some 30–45 percent of global remittances flow between developing countries.[62] The figure is almost certainly higher for Maritime Asia.

Since China's economy is booming, one would not expect to see much labor migrating from China. But young and ambitious Chinese job seekers face intense competition in China. Many are apparently moving to Southeast Asia, legally or illegally, in growing numbers. Equipped with a fairly high level of education and entrepreneurial experience, they use *guanxi* (connections) to pinpoint opportunities. Many flock to poor and unregulated environments. For example, it is common knowledge that Chinese are entering northern Thailand from Yunnan as "tourists," only to stay on illegally.[63] Similarly, Chinese entrepreneurs are finding opportunities in Laos and Cambodia, where corruption is widespread and regulations can be ignored or manipulated.[64] Ethnic Chinese populations in Singapore, Malaysia, and Indonesia are also targets of opportunity.

Can migrant laborers really be called integrators? Those who work abroad send remittances to their families. They experience life in another country and another culture. They learn rudiments of another language. Those who employ them have a cross-cultural experience. But on the whole, their most durable impact on Asian integration is that they force governments to talk about what to do about them.

Seafarers

More than a third of the world's 1.2 million seafarers are Asian.[65] The boom in containerized shipping and stepped-up activity in Asia is creating a shortage of marine officers and skilled seafarers. According to the Baltic and International Maritime Council (BIMCO) and the International Shipping Federation, the center of gravity of the labor market for seafarers has continued to shift from Western Europe, Japan, and North America to the rest of East Asia and the Indian subcontinent.

Seafarers are thrown together, spending weeks and months at sea. Cruise ships can have crews from as many as twenty countries. English is often the common language. Filipinos are in demand because they speak English; according to Philippine authorities, almost a quarter of a million Filipinos were deployed at sea in December 2005—a 9.3 percent increase over 2004. But seafarers from China, India, Myanmar, and Vietnam are entering the market at lower salary levels.

Students

Students studying abroad are "spontaneous integrators" by nature. Their motives, of course, have nothing to do with some vision of Asian integration. Two-thirds of the Indonesians studying in Australia say that they do so simply because overseas education programs are better than what they can get at home.[66] But studying abroad has spawned a new class of young Asians with experience in other Asian cultures and long-lasting personal ties with people in other parts of their region.

Asians are hungry for education. About 2 million students worldwide are studying abroad, and half of them come from Asia. Asians continue to study in the United States (where the total number of foreign students exceeds half a million). But the number of Asians studying abroad but closer to home is shooting up at a faster rate.

The destination of Asia-bound foreign students has changed in one big respect: China. Only two decades ago, China hosted only 8,000 foreign students (not counting students from Hong Kong, Taiwan, and Macau). In 2005, China took in about 86,000 full-time foreign students, of whom more than

60,000 came from other parts of Asia. (If all foreign students are included, the number reached almost 111,000, but the proportions are roughly the same: about three quarters came from Asia.)[67] South Koreans were some 35,000 strong, more than double the number from Japan.[68] Two reasons besides proximity may explain this bulge: South Korean universities are wickedly hard to get into, and fluency in Chinese is considered to be a career asset in Korea (and elsewhere).

The number of students in China from Southeast Asia has also surged. Vietnamese students have increased sixfold. Tighter visa restrictions in the post–September 11 United States have helped steer Indonesian students to China; in the 2003–2004 academic year, the number of Indonesian students receiving visas to study in China jumped by 51 percent, while the number of student visas for Indonesians entering the United States plunged from 6,250 in 2000 to 1,333.[69]

What happens when these foreign students in China return home? To assume that all of these students radiate a desire for closer integration between China and the rest of Asia would be absurd. On the other hand, studying in any foreign country increases understanding and awareness of that country's perspectives; that is a major purpose of educational exchange. Some of the students returning home from China enter government service, where their insights and language skills are presumably brought to bear on their government's policies on issues like Taiwan. According to official statistics, some thirty former foreign students in China are now cabinet ministers, and several dozen more have served as diplomats in China. More than 120 are senior faculty members at universities.[70]

Despite China's new status, Japan still gets high scores. Japan's foreign student population has tripled in the last fifteen years to more than 120,000. Of that total, some 80,000 come from China and another 15,000 from South Korea.[71] These students bring home a more nuanced understanding of a country that is still a major power in the region.

Many other students seek an English-language environment. Reasonable fluency in English is still a sine qua non for international business, diplomacy, engineering, and other careers. Australia, New Zealand, and Singapore continue to attract students for that reason. About 80 percent of Australia's more than 100,000 foreign students are Asian. Singapore receives over 50,000 foreign students, also preponderantly Asian, and hopes to double that number by 2010.[72] Fee-paying students in New Zealand are on the rise; some Asian mothers take their sons to New Zealand for a year so that they can learn English in particularly safe surroundings. By comparison, about 58 percent of foreign students studying in the United States in the 2005–2006 academic year came from Asia. The United States attracted more than 76,000 students from India (the number-one source of foreign students), more than 62,000 from China (the number-two source), almost 59,000 from South Korea, and almost 28,000 from Taiwan.[73]

Unwilling and Unwanted Integrators

Refugees

Refugees are unwilling integrators. They are also unwanted. Unable to gain redress from injustice or threatened by political violence and repression, they stagger across borders or crowd into boats. Few Asian governments have either the will to take them in or the resources to care for them. They create political problems with neighbors and strain the resources of the host country.

The first large-scale waves of refugees in Maritime Asia were Vietnamese "boat people" fleeing from war and repression. They took to the water in leaky and overcrowded boats, helpless victims in the face of storms and natural prey for pirates. But even boat people who are rescued face problems. In a notorious incident in 2001, the *Tampa,* a Norwegian cargo ship, rescued 438 people, mostly from Afghanistan, but the Australian government refused to let the ship dock. The refugees were eventually forced onto a warship and taken into Australia's island possessions and neighboring small states.

What to do with people rescued at sea is still a problem for shipowners and captains. Under international law, passing ships are required to rescue people who are in distress or danger. What happens next is the problem. The ship must often sit at anchor and waste large amounts of money while political authorities and humanitarian organizations fight and the refugees languish.[74] International law prohibits receiving authorities from sending refugees rescued at sea back to their homes if their life and freedom are threatened. These authorities are not obligated, however, to take in refugees in the first place. In 1978, the office of the United Nations High Commissioner for Refugees (UNHCR) worked out an agreement in which coastal states would accept refugees if other states (mostly Western) would relocate them within ninety days. The deadline was never met and the effort lapsed. Refugees have fled from the violence-prone southern Philippines to Sabah, in East Malaysia. Others are Bugis from southern Sulawesi and Javanese, fleeing East Timor in 1999, and East Timorese themselves. Grim conditions in Myanmar have given rise to huge numbers of refugees. In 1992, some 300,000 Muslims from Myanmar fled to Bangladesh. Some 125,000 refugees from Myanmar are living in camps in northern Thailand monitored by UNHCR. The 2007 crackdown on public demonstrations adds political refugees to this displaced population.

Refugees create touchy bilateral problems. For one government to grant asylum to refugees amounts to a political condemnation of the other government. Recent cases have pitted Indonesia against Australia and Malaysia against Thailand. The real nightmare would be massive emigration from China in the wake of civil war or economic collapse, a highly unlikely scenario for which no government is prepared. A more likely nightmare would be a sudden implosion in North Korea that could launch waves of refugees in all directions.

Like everyone else, refugees are more connected and more mobile than at any time in history. They are a living reminder that repression and civil war in one country imposes tangible costs on governments in the region. They are an integrating force in the sense that they force governments to focus on them, but in most cases they get little help from that source.

Criminals, Terrorists . . . and Viruses

Like others in the region, criminals and terrorists take advantage of globalization and technological breakthroughs. Maritime Asia has always bred skullduggery and thievery of every kind, but the scale and reach of cross-border criminal activity has grown. The combination of new wealth, weakly guarded maritime borders, and inadequate or corrupt policing encourages cross-border terrorists, smugglers, traffickers, money launderers, and fly-by-night swindlers of every stripe. Many of them are members of integrated criminal networks.

Chinese triads and Japanese *yakuza* (gangsters) now rub up against Korean, Vietnamese, and other Chinese gangs and a hugely wealthy, Mafia-like Russian network of criminal entrepreneurs. At one extreme, aggressive Chinese criminals have muscled into Japan's bars and brothels. At the other, minority peoples in remote frontier territories cash in on their location. In northern Myanmar, for instance, Thai farmers complain that the Wa tribesmen protect Chinese boats going downriver to Thailand but attack Thai boats going the other way. All these activities are well known to local authorities. Indeed, the governments of Myanmar and North Korea are believed to engage directly in criminal activity to prop up their regimes.

Criminal gangs armed with high-technology weapons and detection devices are quick to take advantage of Maritime Asia's increasingly porous borders. Some feed demand for drugs and prostitutes in the rest of Asia, North America, and Europe. Unscrupulous "agents" extract money from Indonesian women who end up being exploited in low-end jobs in Singapore or Malaysia. According to the United Nations Children's Fund (UNICEF), some 70,000 Indonesian children have been sold as sex commodities in other Asian countries and Australia.[75]

Other criminal gangs prey on endangered species and resources. Traditional Chinese medicine and cuisine feeds a demand for wild animals as delicacies and alleged aphrodisiacs; trafficking in wild animals is particularly intense in the border area between China and Vietnam.[76] Smugglers take advantage of discriminatory tariffs and price controls to make a profit. Terrorists financed by criminal activity cross borders to receive training and join cells in Indonesia, the southern Philippines, and elsewhere. All benefit from weak coastal and maritime policing.

Pervasive crime works against growth and undermines the legitimacy of presiding governments. Crime quashes tourism, distorts trade, arms terrorists, plunders the environment, and makes investment riskier and more expensive. Regions infested with crime stand no chance of developing the thriving markets and grassroots-level support on which successful integration depends. One of the conditions associated with Northeast Asia's thus-far failed experiment with regionalism in the Tumen River delta is the "criminalization" of borders.[77]

Crime also promotes the spread of AIDS. Cross-border organized crime largely controls the sex trade. Criminal networks do not allow trafficked women to register with their governments and sometimes confiscate their passports. Many women who were promised a job in the hotel, restaurant, or entertainment business in another Asian country end up in the sex industry. As of 1995, Japan alone provided employment for an estimated 150,000 foreign sex workers, most of them Thais and Filipinos. A 1996 study tracking the movement of Thai women to Japan, Taiwan, and Australia revealed that networks link the sex industry of several nations.[78]

Like environmental pollution, viruses do not carry passports, and they cross borders with impunity. A 2004 report on AIDS in Asia, published by the United Nations, documented a rise in HIV infection among drug injectors and sex workers in many Asian countries. A number of NGOs hold conferences and share information with their counterparts across borders to prevent or cope with AIDS.

The outbreak of the Severe Acute Respiratory Syndrome (SARS) in 2002–2003 started in China and spread to Vietnam, Singapore, and as far away as Canada. It sickened thousands of people and killed several hundred, including doctors and nurses. The disease temporarily froze travel and dried up investment, causing an estimated loss in the region of $50 billion. The crisis exposed secrecy and cover-ups in China, revealed a lack of coordination, and highlighted other weaknesses of governance.

Authorities confronted the next threatened pandemic somewhat more effectively. In 2005, the threat of a human-to-human outbreak of virulent avian flu mobilized international, regional, and grassroots health groups and health care workers. This time around, governments cooperated more swiftly and effectively across borders. Poultry suspected of infection were slaughtered in many parts of the region. Even so, Indonesia and Vietnam recorded several dozen deaths each, and the crisis is not over.

Serious disease is an obstacle to integration. Like criminals, viruses raise the risk of investment and undermine development. They are more naturally "integrated" than the national efforts underway to fight them. And the more integrated they are, the weaker the economic foundation for spontaneous integration.

■ Conclusion

Linked by high-speed communication and transport and taking advantage of maritime geography, a wide variety of spontaneous cross-border contacts are bubbling up in Maritime Asia. Executives of production networks and a converging middle class are in the forefront of this trend, but tourists, students, migrant workers, and a variety of other people are following in their wake.

In the Middle East and the former Soviet Union, religious groups and ethnic factions often slide into conflict once the heavy lid of dictatorship is lifted. Not so in most of Asia, even in former dictatorships—at least not recently and not on a major scale. Since Asia's history of warfare reveals that Asians are not inherently more peaceful than anybody else, what makes the difference?

I would argue that Maritime Asia is prospering not only because the global and regional environment has improved, but also because unlocking the capacity of urban and maritime individuals and groups contributes substantially to wealth and power. Asian entrepreneurs benefit from a flexible and tolerant culture, sophisticated economic and financial tools, widely dispersed ethnic groups accustomed to facilitating long-distance business transactions, and respect for scientific and technical education. These gifts make it easier for Asians living in urban and maritime regions to develop a common lifestyle and to adapt creatively to globalization. If given free rein, the groups that embody the legacy of Maritime Asia spin distance and diversity into assets and opportunities to an even greater degree.

Some governments, however, place obstacles in the way of these individuals and groups, either because they do not recognize their potential or because they see them as a threat. Conscious identification with Maritime Asia is weak or nonexistent. Regulatory convergence and other measures that would facilitate commercial and social integration are in their infancy. Pop culture and same-brand washing machines are thin glue. If Asian integration is a good thing, and if regionwide problems such as crime, pollution, and disease are to be tackled in a meaningful way, Asian governments must be involved. Are these governments facilitators, procrastinators, adversaries, or all three? Part 2 turns the spotlight on them.

■ Notes

1. Pempel, *Remapping East Asia,* p. 12. Pempel's phrase refers to East Asia only.
2. Graeme Hugo, "International Migration in Southeast Asia Since World War II," in Ananta and Arifin, *International Migration in Southeast Asia,* pp. 52–53.
3. Servan-Schreiber, *The American Challenge,* p. 8.
4. For a definitive account, see Yoichi Funabashi, *Managing the Dollar: From the Plaza to the Louvre* (Washington, DC: Institute for International Economics, 1988).

5. Dennis Tachiki, "Between Foreign Direct Investment and Regionalism," in Pempel, *Remapping East Asia*, p. 167, fig. 6.1.

6. *Forbes* magazine, cited in "More Reactions to Lee Kuan Yew's Remarks," SEAPSNet, September 29, 2006, www.siiaonline.org.

7. Constance Lever-Tracy, David Ip, and Noel Tracy, *The Chinese Diaspora and Mainland China* (New York: Macmillan, 1996). Cited in Zweig, *Internationalizing China*, p. 13.

8. Zweig's *Internationalizing China* illustrates the relationships between local officials and foreign investors at many points in the text. A different and highly public example of the dynamic between central and local authorities comes from Malaysia. Johor state officials are reportedly resisting Singapore's participation in an economic zone in southern Johor, causing Prime Minister Lee Hsien Loong to complain about "mixed signals" from Malaysia. This is by no means an unusual conflict. See "Singapore-Malaysia Bilateral Issues Crop Up Again Over 'Mixed Signals,'" SEAPSNet, December 8, 2006, www.siiaonline.org.

9. For a variety of examples, see Hefner, *Market Cultures*.

10. Jamie Mackie, "Business Success Among Southeast Asian Chinese," in Hefner, *Market Cultures,* p. 129. Mackie takes a skeptical view of the idea that Southeast Asian Chinese are "more strongly predisposed than others to accept markets and market outcomes," p. 130.

11. Trade and investment statistics issued by the Chinese government are available in English at www.fdi.gov.cn.

12. Robert Ash, "China's Regional Economies and the Asian Region," in Shambaugh, *Power Shift*, appendix 3. Many companies registered in the Virgin Islands are reportedly Taiwanese.

13. Rozman, *The East Asian Region*, p. 32. See also Tu, *Confucian Traditions.*

14. See Zakaria, "A Conversation with Lee Kuan Yew," and Mahbubani, *Can Asians Think?*

15. Hitchcock, *Asian Values and the United States,* p. 39. For the results of a subsequent questionnaire, see Hitchcock, *Factors Affecting East Asian Views of the United States.*

16. For a wide-ranging and detailed critique of these practices, see Rodan, *Transparency and Authoritarian Rule.*

17. A recent exception is a book called *The Dignity of the State,* written by a Japanese mathematician, which asserts that liberal democracy is unsuited to Asia because it emphasizes reason rather than "deep emotion."

18. John Williamson, "A Short History of the Washington Consensus." Paper presented to the conference "From the Washington Consensus Towards a New Global Governance," Barcelona, September 24–25, 2004. Available at www.peterson institute.org.

19. "Chinese Language and Culture Renaissance in the Name of Confucius," July 7, 2006, http://www.asianews.it/view.php?1-en&art=6642, p. 1. In "Sources and Limits of Chinese 'Soft Power,'" p. 18, Gill and Huang counted thirty-two institutes in twenty-three countries as of late 2005. The explanation for the different numbers may be that some "institutes" are lodged within a university.

20. Anwar Ibrahim develops these themes in *The Asian Renaissance.* See also his personal website, www.anwaribrahim.com.

21. Yeo, "The Asian Renaissance," p. 2.

22. Acharya, "Will Asia's Past Be Its Future?"

23. Ibid.

24. Friedrich Nietzsche, *Thus Spoke Zarathustra,* cited in Schwarcz, *The Chinese Enlightenment*, p. 11.

25. Marilyn Smith, "The Right Way to Rebuild Asia's Coastal Barrier," *Science and Development Network*, January 12, 2006, www.scidev.net.

26. "Vanishing Skyline, Vanishing Forest and Vanishing Mangroves," SEAPSNet, July 21, 2006, www.siiaonline.org.

27. Elliott, "ASEAN and Environmental Cooperation," pp. 32–35.

28. Cao Desheng, "Increased Shipping Brings Oil Pollution," *China Daily*, July 6, 2005, www2.chinadaily.com.cn/english/doc/2005-07/06/content_457481.htm, p. 1.

29. Andrew Batson, "China's Choke-Hold Over Asia," *Far Eastern Economic Review*, July 8, 2004, pp. 29–33.

30. East Asia Vision Group, "Towards an East Asian Community," par. 70–82.

31. For more details, see Lee and So, *Asia's Environmental Movements*; and Hillstrom and Hillstrom, *Asia: A Continental Overview*.

32. Elliott, "ASEAN and Environmental Cooperation," p. 47.

33. Keiichi Tsunekawa, "Why So Many Maps There?" in Pempel, ed., *Remapping East Asia*, p. 144.

34. The group is called the Asian NGO Coalition for Agrarian Reform and Rural Development (ANGOC). See www.angoc.ngo.ph/profile.html, p. 1.

35. "Climate Change—Impact on Asia," SEAPSNet, February 23, 2007, www.siiaonline.org.

36. Victor Mallet, "Weather Upsets on the Way, Climate Expert Warns CEOs," *Financial Times*, November 19, 2004, p. 7.

37. For an example of recent research, see Eichengreen, "Globalization and Democracy."

38. For details, see www.aseanmp.org. See also www.burmaguide.net, which outlines a number of prodemocracy initiatives.

39. Chetan Kumar, "Transnational Networks and Campaigns for Democracy," in Florini, *The Third Force,* p. 140.

40. Norani Othman, "Grounding Human Rights Arguments in Non-Western Culture: Shari'a and the Citizenship Rights of Women in a Modern Islamic State," in Bauer and Bell, *The East Asian Challenge for Human Rights*, chap. 7.

41. Anwar, "The Modernity of Southeast Asian Islam," p. 2.

42. Anwar, "Asian Renaissance and the Reconstruction of Civilization."

43. Jean Berlie, "Cross-Border Links Between Muslims in Yunnan and Northern Thailand: Identity and Economic Networks," in Evans, Hutton, and Eng, *Where China Meets Southeast Asia,* p. 233.

44. James Piscatori, "Asian Islam: International Linkages and Their Impact on International Relations," in Esposito, *Islam in Asia*, p. 238. This book is out of date but contains many useful insights.

45. "Islam in Southeast Asia: Towards an ASEAN Understanding?" SEAPSNet, November 27, 2006, www.siiaonline.org.

46. For a concise and thoughtful history of the spread of Buddhism in China, see Wright, *Buddhism in Chinese History.*

47. Wales, *The Indianization of China,* p. 127.

48. Kalinga Seneviratne, "Singapore to Help Revive Ancient Indian University," Inter Press Service, New Delhi, November 20, 2006; Raja Mohan and J. P. Yadav, "Nalanda Opens Window for Bihar to Look East," posted online November 4, 2006; "The Asian Renaissance," speech by George Yeo, minister for foreign affairs, at the Nalanda Buddhist Symposium, November 13, 2006. My thanks to C. Raja Mohan of *The Indian Express* for sending these to me.

49. Anna Fifield, "South Korea's Soppy Soaps Win Hearts Across Asia," *Financial Times*, December 14, 2004, p. 7.

50. For a short, eloquent history of Chinese "sojourners," see Wang, *The Chinese Overseas.*

51. Wang, *The Chinese Overseas*, p. 105.

52. Kurlantzick, *Pax Asia-Pacifica,* p. 10.

53. Takashi Shiraishi, "The Third Wave: Southeast Asia and Middle-Class Formation in the Making of a Region," in Katzenstein and Shiraishi, *Beyond Japan,* pp. 237–245, 267–271.

54. Gurcharan Das, "The India Model," *Foreign Affairs* 85, no. 4 (2006): 15.

55. Adapted from www.world-tourism.org/market_research/facts/market_trends.htm.

56. Howard W. French, "Chinese Globe-Trotters: The Next Big Wave," *International Herald Tribune,* May 17, 2006, p. 1; "Chinese Tourists Coming, Ready or Not!" *CLSA Special Report,* September 2005; and Marwaan Macan-Markar, "Chinese Boost for Asian Tourism," October 30, 2004, www.atimes.com/atimes/printN.html, p. 2.

57. Joyce Hor-Chung Lau, "Drawn by Vibrant City, Mainlanders Reshape Hong Kong," *New York Times,* June 24, 2007, p. 3.

58. Susan Carey, "Cruise Industry Turns to Southeast Asia," *Wall Street Journal,* December 2, 1991, p. A7.

59. "Pushing Marine Tourism," *Travel Trade Gazette Asia* (Singapore), December 3, 1999, p. 1.

60. "Helping Myanmar's Suffering Masses," SEAPSNet, October 6, 2006, www.siiaonline.org.

61. Hugo, "Migration in Southeast Asia Since World War II," pp. 44–45.

62. Cited in Montes and Wagle, "Why Asia Needs to Trade Smarter," pp. 46–47.

63. I am grateful to Richard Cronin of the Henry L. Stimson Center in Washington, DC, for this information.

64. David Fullbrook, "Chinese Migrants and the Power of *Guanxi,*" www.atimes.com/atimes/Southeast_Asia/FG30Ae04.html.

65. International Labour Organization, www.ilo.org.

66. IDP Education Australia and Australia Education International, cited in Monfries, *Different Societies, Shared Futures,* table 8.4.

67. The larger numbers, derived from the Chinese Ministry of Education, appear in Gill and Huang, "Sources and Limits of Chinese 'Soft Power,'" p. 18. I am guessing that the smaller numbers do not include part-time or short-term students.

68. Chen Yinghui, director of the international students division of China's Ministry of Education, reported in "China Expects Influx of Foreign Students," *China Daily,* September 29, 2004, www.chinadaily.com.cn/english/doc/2004-09/29/content_378812.htm.

69. Data from the Chinese Ministry of Education, the Institute of International Education, and the *New York Times,* cited and summarized in Gill and Huang, "Sources and Limits of Chinese 'Soft Power,'" pp. 18–19.

70. Gill and Huang, "Sources and Limits of Chinese 'Soft Power,'" p. 19.

71. "Foreign Students in Japan (1991–2005)," http://web-japan.org/stat/stats/16EDU61.html.

72. Damien Duhamel, "Can Singapore Become the Boston of Asia?" *Singapore Business Review,* November 2004, pp. 40–42.

73. Institute of International Education, "Open Doors 2006," www.iie.org.

74. Kathleen Newland, "Troubled Waters: Rescue of Asylum Seekers and Refugees at Sea," Migration Policy Institute, January 1, 2003, www.migrationinformation.org/Feature/print.cfm?ID=80.

75. Devi Asmarani, "Indonesia's Shameful Export," *The Straits Times,* June 8,

2004, reproduced in *YaleGlobal Online*, July 27, 2004, http://yaleglobal.yale.edu/display.article?id=4043.

76. Su Yongge, "Ecology Without Borders," in Evans, Hutton, and Eng, *Where China Meets Southeast Asia,* p. 64.

77. Rozman, *Northeast Asia's Stunted Regionalism,* pp. 116–117; passim.

78. A. Sherry, M. Lee, and M. Vatikiotis, "For Lust or Money," *Far Eastern Economic Review,* December 14, 1995, pp. 22–23, cited in Hugo, "International Migration in Southeast Asia Since World War II," p. 61.

PART 2

Designing Asia Major

6

Sources of the Asian Integration Movement

This chapter turns from the flowing, spontaneous integration that is washing through Maritime Asia to the other half of the integration story— the halting, top-down integration movement driven by governments.

The entities that these governments are nudging together bear little resemblance to the contours of Maritime Asia. They are planted on brindled parcels of land stretching far into the interior, pegged at the edges by black-line boundaries inherited from history. In the driver's seat of the journey toward closer integration and community building is not China but fewer than half a dozen Southeast Asian governments.

This narrative has bumped into governments before. As noted in Chapter 3, in prior centuries, Chinese and Japanese governments occasionally clamped down severely on trade and travel. Colonial governments carved up much of Asia and eventually went to war. Modern-day governments regulate trade, collect tariffs, regulate investment, and garner loans for ports, airports, and roads. They have a monopoly on security and defense and sole responsibility for coping with crime and terrorism. But in previous chapters, I skirted the role of governments as much as possible. I did so because I wanted to explore what ordinary people are doing spontaneously before I described the policy grid that governments are imposing on them.

Spontaneous integrators can only go so far, however. The businesspeople, ship captains, tourists, urban consumers, and others who pump new life into Maritime Asia need to be able to go through customs quickly, travel safely, start a new business without endless regulatory roadblocks, conduct cross-border financial transactions efficiently, take out valid insurance policies, and do a hundred other things. They need modern roads, ports, and airports and reliable supplies of electricity. All that requires help from governments.

Today's governments are not passive facilitators of spontaneous integration. Indeed, they put the brakes on it as often as they promote it. They have their own agendas. They care about managing domestic tensions, making their countries more competitive and less vulnerable to external shocks, warding off foreign pressure, and staying in power, among other things. They support (or go along with) closer integration and community building to enhance rather than limit their sovereignty and to cope with common threats. Helping emerging cross-border communities within Maritime Asia get closer and even richer is not on their list of priorities. The more visionary among them are groping instead for what I call Asia Major.

◼ The Vision

Ideas matter. As I argued in Chapter 2, *Asia* is an idea. (So are *France* and the *United States*.) Benedict Anderson observes that nationalism requires a conception of an "imagined community," which he describes as a sense of "deep, horizontal comradeship" stretching far beyond face-to-face proximity.[1] The construction of Asian regionalism requires the same mental and emotional construction; ASEAN, ASEAN + 3, and Asia Major (ASEAN + 6) are all imagined communities.

In the late 1990s, the governments of ASEAN + 3 handpicked a group of leading intellectuals and statesmen and charged them with developing a "vision" of Asian integration. This became the East Asia Vision Group, chaired by former South Korean foreign minister Han Sung-Joo and consisting of two nongovernmental representatives from each of the thirteen countries. In a landmark report in 2001, "Towards an East Asian Community," the Vision Group and stressed the constructive and outward-looking nature of the community-building effort: "We, the people of East Asia, aspire to create *an East Asian community of peace, prosperity, and progress* based on the full development of all peoples in the region. Concurrent with this vision is the goal that the future East Asian community will make a positive contribution to the rest of the world."[2]

Offering more than seventy proposals, the report envisaged East Asia as a "bona fide regional community." It emphasized economic interdependence as a catalyst and endorsed ideas like cooperative security and good governance, but it did not otherwise define the content of the proposed community. It also omitted any reference to supranational institutions.[3] A group of officials known as the East Asian Study Group subsequently narrowed down the list of recommendations and ranked the remainder in terms of priority. Those accepted by consensus form the basis of the various committees, study groups, and workshops.

◼ Why Integration?

At first sight, the Asian integration initiative looks like too many diplomats chasing too few gains. Economists have repeatedly shown that global or transpacific liberalization would reap far more welfare benefits for Asians than a slurry of narrow, exclusive, inconsistent intra-Asian arrangements.[4] Intra-Asian trade has expanded enormously, but much of it consists of parts and components for final products destined for European and North American markets.[5]

The case for integration on security grounds seems even shakier. In a region where military power matters a lot, hard-core security arrangements and the stability that they engender still center on the United States' crazy-quilt cluster of bilateral alliances and military cooperation agreements, especially since the attacks of September 11, 2001. No other country can offer region-wide security. Moreover, this would-be community is riddled with rivalries. Asian governments no longer declare war on each other, but tensions crackle periodically.

Why, then, have East Asian governments supported—or reluctantly gone along with—summitry and community building in the name of long-term integration? And what drove the two major powers flanking East Asia—India and Australia—to seek membership in or closer association with Asia Major, a political construct symbolized by the East Asian Summit process? In other words, what do governments want—and why?

■ Historical Roots of the Integration Movement

Seen in historical perspective, the Asian integration movement is the latest response to the dilemma that has been gnawing at Asian leaders ever since the nineteenth century: how to adopt and adapt Western technology and methods so as to catch up with the West without losing Asian identity and legitimacy. Just as Western travelers once imagined "Asia," so a group of former government officials and policy-attuned intellectuals are striving to invent an "Asia" of their own. But unlike the Asia imagined by Western explorers, theirs is a vision of nation-states. Their efforts reflect a strategy of maneuver in a world still dominated by larger powers.

Many Asian governments gained or regained their sovereignty quite recently. The Philippines, a self-governing colony since 1935, attained full independence on July 4, 1946. India became independent in 1947 and Indonesia and Burma in 1948. The victory of the Chinese Communist Party in 1949 and Vietnam's expulsion of the French in the mid-1950s rolled back the last vestiges of foreign incursions. Thailand, alone among the nations of Southeast Asia, has never been governed by colonial powers.

Pleas for Asian unity accompanied the struggle for independence. As early as 1945, Ho Chi Minh called for a "pan-Asian Community" combining India with Southeast Asia but omitting China, Japan, and Korea. In the following year General Aung San of Burma advocated a Southeast Asian entity that would later join forces with India and China. Jawaharlal Nehru envisaged an anticolonialist, nonaligned, pan-Asian solidarity movement with India, China, and Indonesia at its core.[6] But China shattered Nehru's dream of Asian unity by attacking India in 1962 and aligning itself with Pakistan.

Meanwhile, war swept the Korean peninsula. National governments were preoccupied with postwar recovery and some were fending off communist movements. They thought little about integration except when the transition away from colonial rule suggested consolidating smaller units into a larger nation. This was the case in Malaysia. The Federation of Malaya, uniting British-ruled Malay states on the peninsula, became independent in 1957. In 1963, Tunku Abdul Rahman united the Federation of Malaya with Singapore and the eastern states of Sabah and Sarawak, forming the new country of Malaysia. Two years later Singapore left the federation and became independent.

In the mid-1960s, communist forces in the former French Indochina gained strength, and China's Cultural Revolution erupted into fury and mayhem. After Sukarno's fall, five Southeast Asian governments with friendly ties to the United States saw advantages in banding together in a loose anticommunist grouping. They did so formally by creating the Association of Southeast Asian Nations in 1967. The ASEAN 5, as they are sometimes called (and are called in this book), were Indonesia, Malaysia, the Philippines, Singapore, and Thailand. To the extent that they can reach agreement, they have the strongest influence on the agenda of the integration movement.

■ Catalysts

At least five catalysts ignited the current form of the Asian integration movement. In roughly chronological order, they are (1) growing interdependence triggered by the rise of production networks; (2) regionalism in Europe and the Americas; (3) the loss of momentum in APEC and the World Trade Organization (WTO); (4) the Asian financial crisis; and (5) the transformation and resurgence of China.

The Rise of Production Networks

The mushrooming of regionwide production networks described in Chapter 4 created an expanding web of interdependence. From 1985 to 1995, over half the growth in exports from ASEAN + 3 and Taiwan came from sales within their region.[7] Interdependence was an explicit factor in then Malaysian prime minister Mahathir's mind when he called for an East Asian Economic Group (later Caucus) in the late 1980s and early 1990s. Mahathir's hostility to what he called the "West," his chip-on-the-shoulder leadership style, and his racist generalizations triggered public criticism of his proposed group from the

United States and private objections from others. His proposed caucus, nick-named the "Caucus without Caucasians," bristled and died, but the underlying conditions that he was describing intensified. Ministerial declarations endorsing closer integration and community building regularly cite economic interdependence as a major rationale.

Regionalism in Europe and the Americas

The drive toward closer Asian integration would not have acquired a sense of urgency had it not been for the sudden burst of regionalism elsewhere in the world. The current phase of the Asian integration movement began defensively, as a reaction to these new clusters.[8] The main examples were the deepening of the European single market in 1992 and the subsequent widening of the EU; the creation of NAFTA, concluded in 1992 and ratified in 1993; the US-backed proposal for a Free Trade Area of the Americas (FTAA), launched at the same time; and the inauguration of the Southern Common Market (Mercosur) among several major South American countries.

This barrage of regionalism aroused fears that Asia would be excluded from a world of preferential trading blocs. ASEAN's support for intra-ASEAN and transpacific free trade and its shift away from import substitution policies toward market-opening measures must be seen in this context. India's "Look East" policy, which sought to hitch India's creaky economy to East Asia's dynamic wagon, also made its appearance at this time.

Loss of Momentum in APEC and the WTO

Seen from Asia, the flowering of the APEC forum in the early 1990s served several purposes at once. It was a regional organization that included Asians. Its membership brought together Americans, Chinese, Japanese, and other real or potential rivals and gave them space for useful conversations on the side. By calling its members "economies" rather than states and by excluding security, APEC was able to include Taiwan and Hong Kong. It eschewed protectionist blocs and championed regional and global free trade. Heads of state attending the first APEC summit in Seattle in 1993 pledged themselves to "free and open trade and investment" in the Asia-Pacific area. In the following year, they nailed this vision to a deadline— 2010 for developed countries and 2020 for everybody else. The future looked promising.

But APEC gradually lost altitude, in part because a voluntary, sector-by-sector liberalization plan yielded a meager harvest, especially from Japan, and in part because APEC proved to be irrelevant to the financial crisis. As a consequence, the governments most committed to APEC lost interest. US president Bill Clinton, who had lent his personal and visible support to APEC, abandoned it in favor of more pressing political needs. President Suharto of Indonesia, a key supporter, was forced out of office.

Meanwhile, the WTO's Uruguay Round of trade negotiations, which ended in 1993, improved market access for rich countries' exports but failed to lower barriers to poor countries' exports to the same degree. The subsequent round, dubbed the Doha Development Round, was supposed to rectify this perceived imbalance, but doubts about its prospects appeared from the start. The WTO ministerial meeting held in Seattle in 1999 ended in failure. By then, Japan and South Korea, longtime supporters of multilateralism, had initiated what would become an avalanche of bilateral trade agreements under the heading of closer regional integration, and China was devising a free-trade agreement with ASEAN. Low expectations for the Doha Round continue to motivate the negotiation of such agreements, which are discussed more fully in Chapter 8.

The Asian Financial Crisis

The fourth catalyst was the financial crisis of 1997–1998. The crisis flattened several Asian economies, especially Indonesia, tarnished the Asian Miracle, and drove several heads of state out of office. The hardship that swept the region during the crisis left a lingering sense of disillusionment with the United States and the IMF.

ASEAN leaders were dismayed by Washington's failure to offer assistance to Thailand following the collapse of the baht in July 1997, which started the financial fireball rolling. Japan and Australia participated in the IMF's loan packages for the most affected countries, but Washington did not. Asians contrasted this passivity with US assistance to Mexico after the collapse of the peso in 1994–1995. In Asian eyes, the United States claimed to be a regional leader but did not act like one. The memory of an unresponsive America persists to this day.

This perceived US tilt away from Asia can be laid at the door of the Clinton White House, which was then negotiating with Congress on replenishing US funding for the soft loan window of the World Bank. Many members of Congress had reacted irritably to the Mexican deal and had tried to block it. This experience convinced the White House not to try something similar for Thailand and to concentrate instead on gaining passage of the World Bank package. This outcome also satisfied proponents of the so-called moral hazard argument, who claim that the likelihood of a US-backed bailout encourages reckless economic policies.

In Asia, the end result was the widespread perception among government officials and opinion leaders that US authorities could not be counted on in a financial crisis. Compounding this perception was the fact the US-backed IMF conditions associated with financial rescue packages were widely believed to be too severe, especially in Indonesia. The number of Indonesians living in absolute poverty temporarily doubled, to a quarter of the population. Since the US Treasury Department exerts a strong influence on IMF policy, the United States came to be associated with widespread suffering and harsh austerity measures. When Japan proposed an Asian Monetary Fund, the United States was among those who vetoed it, on the grounds that it would undercut the IMF and permit wayward governments to postpone reforms.

The financial crisis taught Asian governments several lessons. Above all, it demonstrated that capital flight could overwhelm national governments and sweep out their leaders. Whereas Western authorities believed that market forces enhance discipline and efficiency, shaken Asian officials saw them as a threat, at least in the absence of strong domestic institutions.

The crisis illustrated vividly that Asian economies are linked not only by trade and investment but also by shared vulnerability to sudden, panic-driven capital movements ("contagion"). The catastrophe began in Thailand, slowly spread to Indonesia, and then infected Malaysia, the Philippines, and South Korea. Malaysia defied the IMF, restricted capital flows for a year, and recovered, but its financial system was arguably in stronger shape to begin with. The others were forced to endure both painful domestic reforms and a regionwide slowdown in growth of demand for their exports.

Another lesson was that Asians could not count on outside assistance. The crisis underlined the need for getting domestic economies in order and avoiding major risks. It also spurred discussions on closer precrisis coordination. On the eve of the crisis, Asian financial reserves, if mobilized, would have been large enough to meet the crisis-induced need for liquidity.[9] If the United States would not help rescue plummeting currencies, Asians would. When the proposed Asian Monetary Fund ran aground, ASEAN + 3 finance ministers turned to currency swap agreements (discussed in Chapter 8).

The Resurgence of China

The giant chugging sound of China's economic growth provided another powerful catalyst. Of the various changes in the Asian strategic landscape, none stands out more forcefully than the resurgence of China as a commercial powerhouse and magnet for investment. In the 1960s and 1970s, Japan and the so-called Asian Tigers (South Korea, Taiwan, Hong Kong, and Singapore) also experienced explosive growth. But no single nation besides China has ever opened its economy and gained significant international economic weight as quickly as China has,[10] and none had a noteworthy military force at the time.

China's share of global trade has grown tenfold since economic reforms began to take effect in the early 1980s, but it was not until the mid-to-late 1990s that the full force of China's transformation became evident. Accession to the WTO committed Beijing to a degree of liberalization exceeding that required of other developing countries admitted earlier, especially India.[11] In 2000, China's share of world trade was still only about 4 percent, but China has accounted for about 12 percent of the growth of world trade since then.

In 2004, China overtook Japan to become the world's third largest trading economy, and in 2006 trade reached a ratio of 65 percent of China's gross domestic product (GDP). (The equivalent ratios for Japan and the United States are approximately 22–23 percent.) In 2006–2007, China's foreign exchange reserves reached almost $1 trillion and its current account surplus exceeded $100 billion, or 7 percent of GDP.

Foreign direct investment (FDI) in China has grown even more rapidly than trade. In 1990, foreigners invested about $4 billion. In 2003, temporarily China surpassed the United States as the world's number-one investment target. In 2004, China attracted $60 billion in FDI, compared to $4 billion for India and $1 billion for Russia.[12] (In 2005, the level dropped to $53 billion, the world's third largest amount for that year.) China has lured more investment than all developing countries combined. Outward investment has just begun but is growing rapidly; according to Chinese authorities, in 2005, Chinese companies invested an estimated $7 billion abroad.

China's economic transformation stimulates other Asian governments to redouble their search for closer cooperation with China for at least four reasons. First, Asian companies want to increase their share of China's huge market and find a profitable niche in regionwide, China-centric production networks. Second, Asian governments have been greatly reassured by China's postcrisis behavior but still harbor a certain degree of wariness. They calculate that enmeshing China in a plethora of agreements and committees encourages peaceful and cooperative behavior. Third, they believe that contributing to China's economic growth through regional engagement bolsters stability and raises the likelihood of eventual democratization there. Finally, embracing China makes it more likely that the United States, Japan, and India will pay more attention to the region and cooperate on even more attractive terms.

■ Motivations of Individual Actors

The ASEAN 5: Strength in Numbers

Generalizing about ASEAN is hazardous because it is not a coherent organization. Its ten members vary enormously, and each government has different priorities. Just one example, Indonesia, is profiled separately below. There is a tacit understanding that, with the partial exception of Vietnam, the poorer members of ASEAN are neither ready for nor equipped to deal with closer integration of any kind except as recipients of technical and educational assistance from the others. Nevertheless, ASEAN, led by the ASEAN 5, has managed to hold itself together enough to remain in the "driver's seat" of the integration movement, a metaphor routinely assigned to it in numerous declarations.

The most basic goals of all ASEAN governments are consolidating nation building, recapturing or strengthening domestic political legitimacy, fostering economic growth, ensuring peace and stability in the region, acquiring a stronger international voice in global institutions, and—particularly important, given the resurgence of China—preventing the domination of the region by a single outside power.

As individual countries, the ten members of ASEAN do not command much influence. But they represent a population of almost 560 million and a combined GDP heading toward a trillion dollars. The effort to knit ASEAN economies more closely together through trade, investment, and finance is intended to lend corresponding geopolitical weight and identity to its participants. By forging a larger group, creating an open regional market, and strengthening ASEAN's voice in world forums, leaders of the ASEAN 5 believe that ASEAN will be in a better position to demand greater market access for its products and to pursue other interests. By inviting in all of the major powers, they believe they will be able to engage in a constructive balancing act and prevent any one of these major powers from controlling them.

Among the ASEAN 5, there is broad support for the notion that closer economic integration with the global economy and with stronger economies elsewhere in Asia can help achieve these goals. But all except Singapore add the proviso that certain "sensitive" sectors should be shielded for a while longer. Both among and within these governments there are considerable differences of opinion on whether and how to pursue other forms of integration, and at what speed.

ASEAN leaders hope that forging preferential trade agreements with China, South Korea, Japan, and India will further stimulate trade and investment. They believe—in some cases erroneously—that they are competing with China for investment. New rumbles from an emerging India are injecting even more incentives for boosting efficiency and competitiveness. President Yudhoyono of Indonesia summed up the challenge when he attended his first ASEAN summit, in 2004. "Our main challenge today is to deepen our economic integration," he said. "Why? Two words: India and China."[13] Singapore, at least, seems confident. "By hitching ASEAN to these two powerful steeds," argued Singaporean leader Goh Chok Tong, "we can fly together to greater prosperity."[14]

For these reasons, leaders of the ASEAN 5 believe that they have no choice but to hasten ASEAN integration and to integrate their markets with larger economies in the region. Doing so will make it easier for enterprises headquartered in ASEAN countries to join regionwide production networks, expand their exports, and make their home economies more attractive to foreign partners. The logic of security also works in favor of closer integration. Gratefully or grudgingly, the leaders of ASEAN 5 recognize that the United States serves as a security arbiter and guarantor of regional peace and stability. They believe that conventional military threats such as foreign invasions and frontal military assault are unlikely. The real danger is the prospect of domination by a single outside power. Such a tilt in the "balance of influence," as they call it, would take the form of subtle but grinding pressure rather than military occupation, but it could stifle an independent foreign policy and subordinate local economic goals to the priorities of the hegemon. ASEAN members are careful not to specify who such a power might be, but China obviously comes to mind.

Rather than ganging up against a potential hegemon, the strategy of ASEAN leaders is to invite all regional players in. The Asian integration movement offers ASEAN governments a way to ensure that the various powers are in the room together, so to speak, where ASEAN strategists can watch them. Such a strategy minimizes the danger of domination by a single outside power, because ASEAN governments can team up with China, engage India, and hedge their bets by cultivating closer security ties with the United States, Japan, and Australia—all at the same time.

Another danger is the possibility of military conflict in the Taiwan Strait and the Korean peninsula. At a minimum, war in that region would roil the entire Asian economy, dry up investment, and freeze the economic growth on which Southeast Asian governments depend for legitimacy. There is little or nothing that ASEAN leaders can do to resolve the status of Taiwan or to quell North Korea's contrived nuclear spasms. All they can do is offer a diplomatic space for discussion in the hope that the peaceful resolution of disputes in their region sets a good example for others.

Indonesia: Recapturing Diplomatic Leadership and Reaping Economic Gains

Indonesia was once the anchor of ASEAN, a champion of APEC, an oil exporter, and an influential voice in the region. Then the Asian financial crisis hit. All of a sudden Indonesia was no longer a stable anchor but a rickety tower of "crony capitalism," corruption, unwise exchange-rate policies, real estate speculation, and other structural weaknesses. "We do not blame globalization," said an aide to then President Wahid, the successor of Presidents Suharto and Habibie. "This happened because we were unprepared for globalization."[15]

After two disappointing presidencies, Indonesia's new democracy is gaining ground and the country is on the move again. President Susilo Bambang Yudhoyono has adopted a high diplomatic profile. He visited Myanmar and offered to share lessons from Indonesia's transition to democracy. He went to

Saudi Arabia and, using the "we" language of the Islamic community, implicitly called for political reform and open intellectual exchange. He hosted the president of Iran and affirmed Iran's right to peaceful nuclear energy. He visited both Koreas and offered to help resolve the conflict over nuclear weapons. Indonesia was elected to both the revamped United Nations Human Rights Council and the UN Security Council. Jakarta's political challenge in the Asian integration movement is to exercise forward-looking leadership without stirring up resentment from smaller neighbors.

Compared with wealthier ASEAN countries, Indonesians have neither found nor created a competitive niche in response to the surge of investment in China.[16] The president and his advisers know that they must deliver a strong economic performance to ease pent-up dissatisfaction. Economic integration presents opportunities for growth and may help overcome resistance from groups opposed to more open trade and investment.

Cambodia, Laos, and Vietnam

The three nations once known as "Indochina" are far weaker than their huge neighbor, China. For them, Asian regionalism is a component of what Evelyn Goh calls a "coping strategy."[17] It tames China's preponderance, gives them access to a wider audience, and enables them to invoke such norms as noninterference and the peaceful settlement of disputes. In addition, they gain access to China's market, Chinese- and Japanese-funded infrastructure projects, and aid to regional development projects. Of the three countries, Vietnam is already enjoying a boom in regional trade and investment and no longer deserves to be grouped with the other two.

China: Maintaining Regional Stability While Expanding Influence

Before the Asian financial crisis of 1997–1998, China was a wary and suspicious outsider, preferring to deal bilaterally with other Asian governments. Just before the crisis, China had conducted provocative missile tests near Taiwan and seized a reef in the South China Sea. Those actions provoked a strongly critical reaction from other Asians and contributed to a broad strategic reappraisal by the Chinese leadership. That review resulted in an emphasis on a peaceful regional environment to support Beijing's number-one priority, economic modernization. This assessment included, or was at least consistent with, a more supportive approach to Asian integration.[18] The Asian financial crisis was a timely diplomatic windfall because it offered Beijing a highly visible opportunity to put this "good neighbor" policy into action.

Today's Chinese leaders have a huge stake in regional peace and stability. As politicians, they know that the legitimacy of continued one-party rule in

China depends almost entirely on satisfying rising economic expectations and hence on economic growth. As nationalists, they have harnessed their drive for prestige to economic engagement in Asia as well as in the global economy. They know that without a peaceful and stable neighborhood, they will be unable to become an even stronger economic power. As strategists, they realize that without national wealth, they will be unable to modernize their military forces. As economic realists, they are well aware that foreign-affiliated firms are responsible for more than half of China's total exports. As reformers, they are under pressure to carry out their ambitious pledges in the WTO without provoking either a backlash at home or even more protectionism abroad than they face already.

Chinese policymakers calibrate their policy toward the Asian integration movement with their relationships with the United States and Japan. Whether or not they are enthusiastic about the Asian integration movement per se, they have seized its diplomatic opportunities and sought to leverage them in a regional and global context. Chinese diplomats attend all ASEAN + 3 meetings and study groups and participate tactfully and constructively.

Conscious of Asian fears and concerns, China's leaders have made special efforts to reassure their neighbors. They now speak of China's "peaceful development" rather than "peaceful rise." Trade is an especially useful diplomatic tool. The very offer of a free-trade area with ASEAN appeared both generous and symbolic of China's new status as a power in Asia. Similarly, on China's western flank, the Shanghai Cooperative Organization meets a security need (cooperation against terrorists), but it also paints an image of Chinese leadership and opens the door to economic cooperation in a region courted by the United States.[19] Forging closer economic ties is a strand of Chinese diplomacy toward Russia and India as well, along with the resolution of most border disputes.

Thanks to Beijing's intransigence, Taiwan is not permitted to attend formal meetings devoted to Asian integration and is officially invisible.[20] Decades from now, this will seem absurd. Taiwan belongs in Asia Major and is a shadow member. More than 10 percent of China's imports come from Taiwan, and investment across the Taiwan Strait has grown exponentially, especially in the all-important information technology sector. Taiwanese experts estimate that roughly 70 percent of Taiwan's FDI goes to the mainland, including all but the high end of its electronics industry.[21] Despite culture and proximity, Fujian receives only about one-tenth of Taiwanese investment, while Jiangsu has absorbed almost 40 percent. As many as 1 million Taiwanese, almost 5 percent of the population, live and work on the mainland.

Nevertheless, the governments on both sides of the Taiwan Strait maintain stiff-necked, formulaic resistance to closer integration. China insists that Taiwan formally reiterate the "one-China principle" as a precondition for talks, while Taiwan restricts technology transfer, prohibits Taiwanese banks from opening branches on the mainland, and budges only rarely on several transportation issues important to Beijing (such as the sequence of permitting direct cargo flights versus direct passenger flights). A China-Taiwan investment treaty and a cross-strait free-trade agreement would make sense, but for political and symbolic reasons the Taiwanese government is pinning its hopes on a free-trade agreement with the United States despite its dubious economic value.[22] Ironically, the Kuomintang (National People's Party), once headed by Chiang Kai-shek and scorned on the mainland as a "running dog of American imperialism," favors closer relations with China and is thus Beijing's favorite.

Good relations with ASEAN are in China's interest, but other motives include minimizing the US role in high-level regional diplomacy, keeping Taiwan in the "domestic affairs" closet, and subtly marginalizing Japan. So far, they are evidently succeeding on all three fronts. On the question of Taiwan, other governments have largely gone along with China's demands. Apart from meetings on financial integration, Beijing has nudged Tokyo to the sidelines—a task made easier by Japan's own barriers to effective leadership.

Japan: Preserving Influence While Coping with China

Japan's goals with respect to Asian integration are both political and economic. Tokyo's first goal was reactive. Like their ASEAN counterparts, the Japanese perceived a drift toward regionalism elsewhere in the world. They were dismayed when the United States barred them from NAFTA and particularly upset when US government officials used their exclusion as an argument in NAFTA's favor.[23]

Rivalry with China constitutes a second motive. Anecdotal evidence suggests that China wields more influence than Japan does over the pace, shape, and direction of regional community building.[24] Japanese policymakers seek ways of coping with China's influential combination of a burgeoning economy and diplomatic finesse in order to retain a level of influence commensurate with Japan's wealth and power. Japanese leaders want to avoid being left out of the integration game, because they do not want Beijing to monopolize regional leadership via ASEAN + 3. They are watching China's military modernization carefully and prefer to be engaged with China as much as possible.

Like other Asian countries, Japan is strongly dependent on trade with China. In 2006, China (not including Hong Kong) became Japan's number-one trade partner. In any given year Japan's trade with China is roughly as important as its trade with the United States. It exceeds Japan's trade with ASEAN and is about forty times greater than Japan's trade with India.

A third advantage of the Asian integration movement is that it gives Tokyo diplomatic space. The US-Japan alliance is the bedrock of Japan's security, and bilateral relations remain close. But the Japanese have concerns of their own, such as learning the fate of Japanese abducted by North Koreans decades ago, and they want to handle the balance of influence between China and the United States their own way. ASEAN + 3 gives them a forum where they can participate without Americans in the room.

A fourth motive is economic. The slow recovery that began in 2002 is primarily investment-led, not export-led, but the growth of exports contributes to it. Asian customers offer an opportunity. Accordingly, Japan's Ministry of Economy, Trade, and Industry (METI) favors a broad trade agreement with ASEAN that would encompass agriculture as well as investment and services.

Japanese are reluctant to present themselves as leaders or as representatives of a new "Asian identity." The idea of an "Asian values" movement led by the Japanese died with the Greater East Asia Co-Prosperity Sphere, but history seems to fade slowly in Japan's neighborhood. Japan is also somewhat suspect because it is richer than its neighbors and closely allied to the United States. Many Japanese identify Japan in political terms as a member of the West, not as an extension of the Asian mainland.

These diplomatic handicaps might be overcome were it not for Japan's near paralysis at home. Its potential contribution has been hobbled by domestic politics, sputtering economic growth, and bureaucratic tangles. Japan is clearly a leader in finance but not in trade. Unfortunately for Japanese diplomacy, Tokyo is unable to match the scope of China's trade offers when it comes to agriculture. Although Japan imports a wide variety of agricultural products, its agricultural lobby fights diehard battles against imports that compete with domestic products. Moreover, Japan still resists expanding the number of immigrants, even skilled ones such as nurses from the Philippines. Although Tokyo is still the largest single donor, its foreign aid has been pruned back.

Until his term ended in 2006, Japan's talented but eccentric prime minister Junichi Koizumi outraged Chinese and Koreans by making repeated visits to a shrine where war criminals share pride of place with ordinary soldiers. The government that followed avoided the shrine but angered Asians and non-Asians alike by disparaging the credibility of women recruited by the Japanese army and used as sex slaves in World War II, most of whom came from Korea. The Fukuda government, which took office in the fall of 2007, is likely to avoid these unnecessary provocations.

Tokyo has attempted to regain good will and improve Japan's image by devising a broader set of measures and calling them "economic partnership agreements" (EPAs). Offering such agreements partially offsets recent cutbacks in foreign aid and puts a positive face on recent extensions of Japan's military and strategic reach. As of 2007, an EPA with ASEAN was negotiated but not implemented. Japanese officials make the case that EPAs go further than traditional preferential trade agreements because they provide for technical assistance and other forms of cooperation, but skeptics observe that their provisions are not enforceable.

Given Sino-Japanese rivalry, and tensions with South Korea, an obvious tactical move for the Japanese government is a closer relationship with India, which Tokyo is now seeking; India is now the biggest recipient of Japanese aid.[25] Beyond that, Japanese officials are divided about which Asian forum deserves the most diplomatic support. To generalize, the Finance Ministry and the Bank of Japan support the ASEAN + 3 process because serious and substantive progress on financial issues is taking place in that forum. But on issues other than finance, METI and the Foreign Ministry are said to be losing enthusiasm for the ASEAN + 3 process and prefer the East Asian Summit grouping. The inclusion of Australia, New Zealand, and India softens and dilutes China's otherwise powerful influence and permits diverse coalitions in a constructive setting. Accordingly, Japan has proposed a trade agreement among all sixteen countries, which it calls the Comprehensive Economic Partnership in East Asia. Tokyo may also be shifting back to supporting APEC, in part because that venue includes its key ally, the United States, as well as Taiwan and Hong Kong.

Although Japan's influence within the Asian integration movement adds up to less than the sum of its assets, Japan still retains considerable strategic advantages in Asia. Its large and modern economy and its extensive corporate and financial networks wield considerable influence. Japan is a leader in environmental technology, energy efficiency, health care, and many other fields. Japan dominates the Asian Development Bank and has taken the lead on other financial integration initiatives as well. With these tools Japan actively courts ASEAN.[26]

Many Asians are scrambling to learn Chinese, but Japan's influence extends to fashion, food, cars, video games, and animation. Software developed by the entertainment industry—nicknamed "Japan's Gross National Cool" by Japanese pundits—earns as much money as America's Walt Disney Studios. Moreover, Japan's defense ties with the United States, its strategic awareness, and the emerging reach of its slowly growing military power guarantee a prominent place at the strategic table.

South Korea: Slowly Uniting the Peninsula While Avoiding Difficult Choices

South Koreans are in a solid diplomatic position in Asia. They have world-class technology, a global economic presence, extensive investment throughout Asia Major, and a strong military force. They were victims rather than perpetrators of colonial aggression and evoke little or no distrust (except in Japan). Their country is large and wealthy enough to wield influence but small enough to avoid looking like a threat.

South Korea's primary goals are presiding over the slow and peaceful unification of the peninsula and avoiding the need to choose between China and

Japan or between North Korea and the United States. Seoul's balancing act plays out more visibly in the Six-Party Talks than at meetings of ASEAN + 3. ASEAN is equipped to handle disputes in the South China Sea but not on the Korean peninsula.

Sandwiched between two large powers, South Korean leaders have a strong stake in fostering close ties elsewhere in Asia and have taken advantage of the Asian integration movement to do so. As fellow sufferers during the Asian financial crisis, they support the Chiang Mai Initiative even though the swap funds available in a future crisis would add up to only a tiny percentage of their exports. They favor expanding trade and investment because they help create jobs in South Korea's crowded, competitive, and volatile society.

The South Korean government paints itself as a "balancer" between China and Japan and thus as a natural leader of the Asian integration movement. There is a presidential adviser for Asian regionalism, who has a large staff. Jeju Island, a conference center and resort, is being developed and promoted as a center for promoting regional peace.

Even though neither ASEAN + 3 nor the East Asian Summit (EAS) contributes much to Seoul's primary goals, South Korea is an active member of both. Seoul enjoys warm relations with Beijing but supports the inclusion of India in the EAS and other forums to balance China and Japan.

India: Playing Catch-Up

After winning independence in 1947, Nehru's India embraced socialism and economic autarky. Decades of inward-looking and protectionist policies reduced India's economic role in the regional and global economy to a level lower than it was at the time of independence. This combination ran counter to India's long commercial involvement with the rest of Maritime Asia and sent India into economic self-exile for almost half a century.

India's severe balance of payments crisis in 1990–1991 prompted a wave of economic reforms under the able stewardship of then finance minister Manmohan Singh. These included fiscal consolidation and limited tax reform, removal of controls on industrial investment, reduction of import tariffs and other barriers, the opening of the energy and telecommunications sector to foreign investment, and other investor-friendly changes in the regulatory mix. The "Look East" policy came into being at that time.

Since then, privatization and market-oriented reforms have blown fresh air into India's dusty economy. Certain regulatory powers have devolved to the states, not because New Delhi decided to bestow them but because certain forward-looking state governments simply took them. Southern states (and cities) like Karnataka (Bangalore) and Andra Pradesh (Hyderabad) began a process of competitive reform in order to attract investment and entice entrepreneurial members of the enormous Indian diaspora to return.

India has a long way to go before it catches up with the ASEAN 5, let alone China. India emerged from the last round of multilateral trade negotiations with tariff levels higher than any developing country, and it has resisted further liberalization in literally hundreds of product areas. Excessive regulation multiplies opportunities for corruption. Much of India's northern belt remains mired in outdated ideology and low levels of education. Hindu supremacists tarnish India's reputation. Coalition politics leaves many would-be reforms submerged or heavily waterlogged. Anticapitalist attitudes are in retreat but linger on; debates at some Indian universities are still punctuated by Marxist rhetoric. India's physical infrastructure is decrepit. It takes less time for grain shipments to travel from Australia to southern India than from southern to northern India.[27] Its regulatory inertia calls to mind Dickens's Office of Circumlocution.

The Indian government hopes that closer engagement with East Asia will not only ease some of these problems but also help them escape from their unpromising neighborhood. Apart from China, India's nearest neighbors are poor, strife-torn, or near-failing states—Pakistan, Afghanistan, Bangladesh, Myanmar, and Sri Lanka. The South Asian Association for Regional Cooperation (SAARC) has produced few results. On occasion, tensions with Pakistan have been such that India boycotted the meetings.[28]

Expanding trade and investment ties with the rest of Asia is a high priority for the Indian government. New Delhi keenly supports virtually any Asian integration initiative that would bring India closer to the rest of the region and participates actively in the EAS. A government-supported Indian research institution promotes the economic integration of what it calls JACIK (Japan, ASEAN, China, India, and Korea).[29] JACIK is the East Asian Summit minus Australia and New Zealand.

Latching on to East Asia's dynamic growth is one way for India to compete with Chinese diplomacy, gain new sources of energy, tap the Indian diaspora, and stimulate reform and domestic competition, especially in coastal cities and outward-looking southern states. For both economic and strategic reasons, New Delhi cannot afford to remain excluded from the fast-growing thicket of geopolitical trade relationships in the rest of Asia. Indians have entered the "free-trade" scramble partly because they are unwilling to cede leadership to Beijing even in a field where they have little to offer in the near term.

The Look East policy has already reaped blessings. By the end of the 1990s, about 17 percent of India's exports were going to non-SAARC Asia compared with 10 percent in 1988–1990. Similarly, India's imports from non-SAARC Asia reached 18.5 percent in 1998–2000, up from 12 percent in 1988–1990.[30] China is already India's number-one source of imports and number-two customer.

In 2001, Singapore persuaded a skeptical ASEAN to hold an ASEAN + 1 summit meeting with India and to launch follow-on ASEAN-India economic studies and dialogue. Trade between India and ASEAN is about five times higher than it was in the early 1990s and is shooting up as much as 30 percent a year. About two-thirds of this trade is with Singapore and Malaysia. Indian officials calculate that closer economic links with Myanmar and Thailand will help develop India's impoverished and unstable northeast. The large numbers of Indian merchants and traders in Southeast Asia should prove helpful in forging informal commercial ties. Although India's trade with ASEAN is only about one-third of its trade with China, the gap is narrowing.[31]

In contrast to its commercial frailties, India is a regional military power. It fields a powerful military force, including a blue-water navy and nuclear weapons. The Indian navy was one of only three in the region that the US Navy judged capable of delivering rapid relief to victims of the December 2004 tsunami. Although India's two biggest potential threats are land-based (Pakistan and China), in the last decade the navy's share of the defense budget has steadily increased.

Like everyone else, Indians keep an eye on the Chinese. Despite the thaw in Sino-Indian relations in recent years, they remain wary of China's growing power and influence and assess both Asian regionalism and the US-China relationship from that angle.[32] Unlike other Asians, fully half of Indians see China's growing economic power as a bad thing.[33]

India also shares with the rest of Asia concern about smuggling, piracy, terrorism, and other forms of crime. Its military forces engage in many bilateral military exercises. For instance, the Indian navy is cooperating with others to crack down on smuggling in and around the Andaman Islands. Indians may not be part of Southeast Asia's core security calculus, but they wield considerable capability when it comes to nontraditional security threats.

At least twice before, during the 1930s and the 1950s, the Indian government tried to portray itself as a leader of a united Asia. Indian leaders are well aware of the failure of these initiatives as well as the country's major weaknesses. New Delhi will have to deliver more extensive reforms and open its market more substantially before its economic and political influence in the rest of Asia matches its security profile.

Australia: "Golden Shrimp on the Barbie"

As cultural heirs of the Western tradition and longtime supporters of global trade negotiations, Australians took a long time to align their policies with Asia as a region. The debate between these two orientations dates back to the nineteenth century, arose again before and after World War II, and became a political issue in the 1990s.[34] During the Asian financial crisis of 1997–1998, Australia was one of two countries to contribute to all three IMF rescue packages. (The other was Japan.) Since then, Canberra has shifted decisively toward closer engagement with Asian regionalism.

Australia has profited enormously from the expansion of regional trade and especially from China's surging growth. Australia now sends a higher proportion of its exports to East Asia than any Asian country—more than half of its exports of goods and about a third of its exports of services. Seven of its top ten export markets are in Asia. Its imports of goods too reflect heavy dependence on East Asia. Although both incoming and outgoing investment are still skewed in favor of the United States and the European Union, more than twice as many arriving settlers come from East Asia as from those two regions.[35] These reasons alone would have driven Australia to seek membership in the first East Asian Summit.

Demand from China has pushed prices of Australian exports of energy and raw materials to record-high levels. From 2003 to 2006, shares of BHP Billiton, the world's largest mining company, more than tripled; as of mid-2006, exports to China had risen 10 percent over the previous year and accounted for nearly 17 percent of total revenue.[36] Exports of nonfarm commodities in the first quarter of 2006 were up 37 percent over the same period a year earlier. Australians are flashing their new wealth by snapping up yachts, prize racehorses, luxury homes, Lamborghinis, designer clothing, and paintings from Sotheby's in record numbers.[37]

India is also awakening Australia's interest, but on a much lower level. Australia's merchandise exports to India tripled from $2 billion in 2001–2002 to $6 billion in 2004–2005, but the number of Australian companies exporting to India is less than half of the number of those exporting to China. As of 2004, Australian companies had invested only about $1.4 billion in India, making Australia only the eighth largest investor. Nevertheless, Canberra and New Delhi share a mutual interest in persuading the governments of ASEAN + 3 to include them in emerging regional architecture.

Australia is a major US ally and takes an active part in regional security exercises and dialogues. It plays a significant security role in the islands of Oceania and the South Pacific. Together with the United Kingdom, New Zealand, Malaysia, and Singapore, it is a member of the Five Power Defence Arrangements (FPDA). Activities under this rubric have permitted Canberra to develop closer ties with the two Asian members than would be possible bilaterally.

Most Australian officials and intellectuals have a less guarded view of China than defense experts in Washington. "Being wary of authoritarian China while engaging with emerging China is a dualism we can live with," remarks China expert Ross Terrill.[38] Australians argue publicly and strenuously against any future "containment policy" toward China on the part of the United States.[39] Canberra does not speculate on what would happen in the event of war in the Taiwan Strait, but if Taiwan provokes the conflict and appeals for US military support, Australia would not automatically come to the rescue.

The Australian government attaches great importance to both APEC, of which it was a cofounder, and the EAS, of which it is a full member, and participates actively in both. After a lengthy debate, in 2005, the Australians signed the Treaty of Amity and Cooperation, a prerequisite for membership in the EAS. Like others, however, Australians have doubts about the effectiveness of the EAS. And when it comes to trade, they negotiate bilaterally but remain staunch supporters of the WTO.

Australia pays special attention to Indonesia, its large Muslim neighbor. Bilateral relations have been fractious in the past. From 1999 to 2002, Australians led a multinational UN force that intervened to stop the fighting in East Timor. Many Indonesians resented this role. Since then, the bilateral relationship has improved considerably, but almost one in three Australians still sees Indonesia as a threat.[40] In November 2006, the two governments signed a framework agreement on security cooperation. Covering such fields as counterterrorism, maritime security, and emergency response, it commits each of the signatories "not in any manner" to support or participate in activities that threaten the stability, sovereignty, or territorial integrity of the other.[41] Officials in Canberra hope that economic integration and other aspects of community building will reinforce moderate elements in Indonesia's polity and contribute to stability there.

Russia: Playing Its Energy Card

The Russian government wants to be invited to the East Asian Summit and to gain official recognition as a regional power in Asia. The Kremlin's proffered ticket for admission reads "oil and gas." Asia's soaring energy needs guarantee a strategic role for Russia. Pipeline diplomacy has already pitted China against Japan as each has competed for Russia's energy resources.

Russia will have a hard time gaining acceptance as an Asian power. An Asian official remarked that Russia "waves the flag" in the weeks leading up to the EAS but devotes little time and attention to Asia the rest of the year. For centuries the Kremlin has looked westward, stressing its European identity. A 1998 poll found that 70 percent of respondents believe that Russian culture is "Western" and only 17 percent "Eastern."[42] Despite Russia's long eastern coastline, the government does not present Russia as an "Asian" country except when there is a political reason to do so. One such reason was the formation of APEC. Russia managed to join APEC in 1998 even though former president Mikhail Gorbachev's vision of Vladivostok as a window on Asia had long since receded and the Pacific Fleet was no longer potent.

Russia has no intention of being marginalized in the competition for regional influence. Relations between China and Russia are quite good, but a certain degree of strategic rivalry is only natural. Like the United States, Russia is distracted by problems elsewhere: Chechnya, Ukraine, US plans to deploy a missile shield in eastern Europe, the evolving situation in Iran, and others.

Conclusion

The catalysts and motives that drove Asians to pursue closer integration are structural and irreversible in the foreseeable future. The spontaneous integration in Maritime Asia described earlier in this book creates an additional need for governments to work more closely together. Although the motivations of each government differ, there is enough convergence to keep the integration movement inching forward.

But who will lead the movement? No single government, it seems. A paradox of the Asian integration movement is that a handful of Southeast Asian governments, acting in the name of ASEAN, have managed to turn their collective weakness into a diplomatic advantage. They remain in the driver's seat partly because their giant neighbors do not fear them, and partly because none of the larger countries wants to cede leadership to any of the others.

ASEAN is a cluster rather than a coherent organization, but the meetings and agreements with which it draws in other governments convey a stamp of regional approval. ASEAN has become an object of competitive courtship, and integration is the theme song. ASEAN's leaders have corralled their bumptious suitors together, who grumble but do not dare drop out. Careful maneuvering has helped to ensure that such competition does not split the integration movement even when the suitors are quarreling. The overlapping structures within which these various dramas are played out are the subject of the next chapter.

Notes

1. Anderson, *Imagined Communities,* pp. 5–7; passim.

2. East Asia Vision Group, "Towards an East Asian Community," p. 6. Italics in original.

3. Paul Evans, "Between Regionalism and Regionalization: Policy Networks and the Nascent East Asian Identity," in Pempel, *Remapping East Asia,* p. 207.

4. See Scollay and Gilbert, *New Regional Trading Arrangements in the Asia Pacific?* pp. 57–58, 149; Dean DeRosa, "Gravity Model Calculations of the Trade Impacts of U.S. Free Trade Agreements," and John Gilbert, "CGE Simulation of US Bilateral Free Trade Agreements," papers prepared for the Conference on Free Trade Agreements and US Trade Policy, Peterson Institute for International Economics, Washington, DC, May 7–8, 2003, p. 35. Schott and Goodrich demonstrate the benefits of transpacific trade liberalization for South Korea in "Economic Integration in Northeast Asia," table 7.1.

5. Lincoln makes this argument forcefully in *East Asian Economic Regionalism.*

6. Devare, *India and Southeast Asia,* pp. 16–18.

7. Ravenhill, "Trade Developments in East Asia," p. 3.

8. Naoko Munakata calls this "the counter-regionalism factor" in "Whither East Asian Economic Integration?" Brookings Working Paper, June 2002, p. 2, accessed in 2003 at www.brook.edu/fp/cnaps/papers/2002_munakata.pdf. See also Munakata,

Transforming East Asia, pp. 27–29. Jeffrey J. Schott of the Peterson Institute for International Economics calls the new trend "'me, too' regionalism."

9. This point is discussed in Pempel, "Firebreak."

10. For a contrary view, see Anderson, "China's True Growth." Anderson argues that China is little different from its neighbors in terms of size, speed and importance and that India is a "'Stealth' Tiger," p. 14.

11. Daniel H. Rosen, "China and the World Trade Organization: An Economic Balance Sheet," International Economics Policy Briefs 99-6, Washington, DC, Institute for International Economics, June 1999.

12. Hufbauer, Wong, and Sheth, *US-China Trade Disputes,* p. 12. For other investment data, see UNCTAD, *World Investment Report 2005.*

13. Jane Perlez, "Southeast Asia Urged to Form Economic Bloc," *New York Times,* November 29, 2004, p. A6.

14. Keynote address at the launch of the CEO Circle, quoted in "How ASEAN Can Regain Its Shine," SEAPSNet, April 8, 2005, www.siiaonline.org.

15. Interview with Andi Mallagangreng, Jakarta, 1999.

16. Ravenhill, "Is China an Economic Threat to ASEAN?"

17. Goh, *Developing the Mekong,* pp. 19, 58.

18. See Shambaugh, "China Engages Asia."

19. Matthew Oresman, "The SCO: A New Hope or to the Graveyard of Acronyms?" *Pacnet,* No. 21, Pacific Forum CSIS, May 22, 2003, pacforum@hawaii.rr.com.

20. Interviews in Taiwan in December 2005.

21. Interview with economists at the Taiwan Institute of Economic Research, Taipei, December 2005.

22. Lardy and Rosen point out the weaknesses of such an agreement in *Prospects for a US-Taiwan Free Trade Agreement.*

23. See Noboru Hatakeyama, "Short History of Japan's Movement to FTAs," *Journal of Japanese Trade and Industry* (November–December 2002): 24.

24. Eric Heginbotham and Richard J. Samuels, "Japan," in Ellings, Friedberg, and Wills, *Strategic Asia 2002–03,* p. 109.

25. Jo Johnson and David Pilling, "India and Japan Seek to Rekindle an Element of Passion in Their Relationship," *Financial Times,* December 14, 2006, p. 4.

26. See the essays in Japan Center for International Exchange, *ASEAN-Japan Cooperation.*

27. During a trip to India in November 2002, I encountered this assertion repeatedly, but I have been unable to document it.

28. As of 2006, the members of SAARC are Bangladesh, Bhutan, India, Maldives, Nepal, Pakistan, and Sri Lanka.

29. Kumar, *Towards an Asian Economic Community,* and various other publications of the Research and Information System for Developing Countries, www.ris.org.in.

30. Srinivasan and Tendulkar, *Reintegrating India with the World Economy,* p. 56, table 2.17.

31. Walter Andersen, "India's Strategic Shift," in United States–Indonesia Society, "Rising India," p. 4.

32. See Garver, "The China-India-U.S. Triangle."

33. Pew Global Attitudes Project, "Publics of Asian Powers Hold Negative Views of One Another," p. 15.

34. Cotton, "Australia and Asian Institutions," pp. 1–8.

35. Lloyd, "Australia's Economic Diplomacy in Asia," p. 2, table 1. Data are from 2001–2002.

36. Wayne Arnold, "As Demand for Copper Soars, BHP Posts a Record," *New York Times*, August 24, 2006, p. C4.

37. Jason Gale, "A Golden Shrimp on the Barbie," *International Herald Tribune,* May 17, 2006, p. 19.

38. Terrill, *Riding the Wave*, p. 37.

39. When US secretary of state Condoleezza Rice visited Australia in March 2006, I happened to be there. Rice strenuously denied that Washington was pursuing "containment" of China, but some Australians did not appear to find her assertions convincing.

40. Louise Williams, "How a Little Boy Stirs Up Big Trouble with the Neighbors," *Sydney Morning Herald*, June 25, 2005, reprinted in Monfries, *Different Societies, Shared Futures*, pp. 84–86.

41. "Agreement Between the Republic of Indonesia and Australia," Article 2.3.

42. Rozman, *Northeast Asia's Stunted Regionalism*, p. 157.

7

The Architecture
of Regional Integration

"If Nature had been comfortable," remarked Oscar Wilde, "mankind would never have invented architecture."[1] Assessing Asia's regional architecture requires an understanding of the uncomfortable state of nature that has motivated its creation. In Asia, the strategic outlook is fluid and uncertain. Despite flourishing economic ties, the region is composed of fiercely independent nation-states with a history of rivalry and war. Two of them, China and India, are rising powers, while Japan is slowly broadening its military reach. Their competition for influence has direct bearing on the design of regional architecture.

In these circumstances, what kind of regional architecture is possible? From a traditional balance-of-power perspective, one might expect that weaker powers would form a coalition against stronger ones. From a liberal-internationalist perspective, one might look for a nascent collective security organization. Neither of these scenarios is remotely in sight. Far from uniting against China and India, small and medium-sized Asian states are seeking closer ties with them. At the same time, these weaker states are hedging their bets by maintaining or strengthening their military ties with the United States. As for a collective security organization, there is neither an "Asian NATO" nor any chance of establishing one.

Ever since the mid-1990s, Asian leaders have turned to organization building to construct their version of a regional order. The organizations they have created are a pastiche of history, commercial ties, political compromises, shared security challenges, strategic rivalry, and public relations. This combination has produced a model appropriate to Asia's unique anatomy and fluid environment. The membership of Asian organizations laps outward and recedes, depending on political circumstances and diplomatic opportunities.

At least two questions are in order. First, in what ways does this new architecture serve the needs of its members? Second, does it undermine or complement the existing global order?

◼ Circles Within Circles

Asia-wide organizations have proliferated so rapidly that casual observers get lost in alphabet soup. Most have sprouted subcommittees and working groups. The ASEAN secretariat currently juggles an average of nine or ten meetings a week.

The use of the plus sign, the geopolitical equivalent of et al., signifies an open-ended definition of "East Asia" and widens diplomatic opportunities. India is + 1; Australia and New Zealand are + 2. The numbers are awkward and a bit confusing. (Quiz: ASEAN + 3 + 1 + 2 = how many countries? Answer: 16.) Some have suggested that it is time for governments to abandon this exercise in arithmetic in favor of a single name. Asian Economic Community is too narrow. The East Asian Community, discussed later in this chapter, exists as a vision, but squeezing in India, Australia, and New Zealand is awkward. My candidate is Asia Major.

As illustrated in Figure 7.1, the structure of government-driven Asian integration can be thought of as a set of concentric circles (not counting the Six-Party Talks on North Korea, which are not part of the integration movement). ASEAN is at the core of the new structures. The next circle is ASEAN plus China, Japan, and South Korea (the "+ 3" countries). The proposed East Asian Community is still a vision but is presumed to center on ASEAN + 3. At the first-ever East Asian Summit in 2005, ASEAN welcomed Australia and New Zealand as representatives of Asia Major's southeastern flank and sidled over just enough to make room for a rising India, forming ASEAN + 6. In the waiting room is energy-rich Russia, representing Maritime Asia's northern frontier.

Farther to the east—of Asia, that is—is APEC. Seven out of the ten ASEAN members are also "member economies" of APEC, as are Hong Kong and Taiwan ("Chinese Taipei" in APEC-speak). Separately, the Shanghai Cooperation Organization (SCO) links China with four of the "-stans" plus Russia, with India and others as observers.

ASEAN

ASEAN comprises the architectural core of the Asian integration movement. It consists of the original five founders—Indonesia, Malaysia, the Philippines, Singapore, and Thailand (the ASEAN 5)—plus Brunei and the so-called CLMV countries (Cambodia, Laos, Myanmar, and Vietnam).

As a group, ASEAN commands few resources compared to its hefty northern neighbors. The GDP of its population of roughly half a billion people is less than $2 trillion (Japan's GDP is about $4.2 trillion), and its collective military strength is modest and uncoordinated. Hobbled by rigid insistence on national sovereignty and the extreme diversity of its members, ASEAN limps rather than strides.

Figure 7.1 The Structure of Asian Regionalism

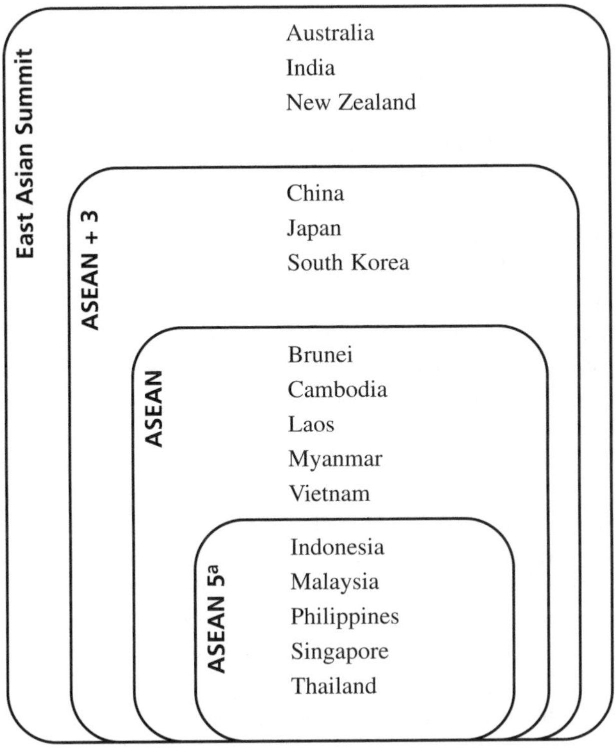

East Asian Summit
- Australia
- India
- New Zealand

ASEAN + 3
- China
- Japan
- South Korea

ASEAN
- Brunei
- Cambodia
- Laos
- Myanmar
- Vietnam

ASEAN 5ᵃ
- Indonesia
- Malaysia
- Philippines
- Singapore
- Thailand

Note: a. Indicates the five founders of ASEAN.

ASEAN was founded in 1967, when war in Indochina was raging. The ASEAN 5 wanted to checkmate the spread of communism, bolster national sovereignty, and ensure that the numerous bilateral conflicts in their region were resolved peacefully. "The truth is that politics attended ASEAN at its birth," says Ali Alatas, a former Indonesian foreign minister and leading statesman.[2] ASEAN remains a strongly political and normative organization.

ASEAN members have endorsed the vision of an ASEAN community resting on three pillars: an economic community, a security community, and a socio-cultural community. The word *community* has a history. For many years, Asian leaders rejected it because it suggested the European Community's model of shared sovereignty. In the early 1990s, for instance, when US leadership of the APEC forum was cresting, the word ran into stiff Chinese resistance for precisely this reason.[3] When Prime Minister Mahathir proposed an East Asian entity in the early 1990s, it was to be a "group" and later a "caucus." By the end of the 1990s, however, when Europe had become the

European Union and regionalism in Asian had gathered momentum, the word *community*—sometimes written with a capital *C*—finally prevailed, but it is strictly a long-term goal and does not imply the sharing of sovereignty.[4]

Closer economic integration is a major component of ASEAN's Vision 2020, a study commissioned and endorsed by ASEAN governments. It calls for comprehensive integration within the confines of ASEAN's guiding principles, which include equality, mutual respect, and noninterference. Meeting in Bali in 2003, ASEAN leaders endorsed the vision and issued a declaration known as ASEAN Concord II, or Bali Concord II.[5] The declaration reaffirmed the vision of an ASEAN Economic Community and the action plans and roadmaps associated with it. The proposed community builds on agreements in such areas as trade, customs, investment, services, tourism, telecommunications, crime, air transport, and energy.[6] An agreed priority is liberalizing trade in services, especially tourism and air travel.[7] In August 2006, ASEAN trade ministers agreed to accelerate to 2015 (from 2020) the deadline for implementation of the economic pillar.

Trade is the core of this pillar. In 1992, the year when Europe reached a new stage in the creation of a single market and renamed itself the European Union, ASEAN launched the so-called ASEAN Free Trade Area (AFTA). Thanks to AFTA, tariffs on unprotected products have fallen to less than 3 percent and are supposed to fall to zero by 2010 (2015 for CLMV countries). But AFTA permits three kinds of exclusions: "temporary," "sensitive" agricultural products, and "general." Many so-called sensitive sectors will be either protected during a long phase-in period or exempted altogether. Although freer trade in agriculture would raise rural incomes and create jobs in food processing, intra-ASEAN tariffs on agricultural products remain high.

ASEAN's core principles of security cooperation are set forth in a non-binding declaration called the Treaty of Amity and Cooperation (TAC), signed by ASEAN members in 1976. The principles enshrined in the TAC read like the nation-state equivalent of the Convention on Human Rights. They are: mutual respect for the independence, sovereignty, equality, territorial integrity, and national identity of all nations; the right of every state to lead its national existence free from external interference, subversion, or coercion; noninterference in the internal affairs of one another; settlement of differences or disputes by peaceful means; renunciation of the threat or use of force; and effective cooperation among themselves. There are separate rules of procedure and provisions for dispute settlement but no enforcement provisions. ASEAN governments have also negotiated a number of bilateral agreements in the security field.

Despite these promising steps, ASEAN's military authorities harbor a great deal of mutual mistrust. All ASEAN members except Singapore hesitate to engage in serious, combat-related joint military exercises with each other and resist collective security initiatives. Even when they are willing to engage with each other, they prefer to feel their way toward closer cooperation in twos and threes. Most of them greatly prefer bilateral exercises with the United States. As often as not, it is US military officers who encourage joint activities. In May 2006, ASEAN defense ministers met for the first time. (Myanmar did not attend the meeting.) Pledging to bring security cooperation to a "higher plane," ministers briefed each other and exchanged views.

Representatives from ASEAN countries participate in more than 400 meetings a year in various Asian locales or at ASEAN's large, modern secretariat building in Jakarta. Although many observers dismiss this blizzard of meetings, these gatherings foster personal relationships, strategic dialogue, and nuanced maneuvering. All ten members are usually represented, even when the issue at hand does not pertain to all of them. Chinese diplomats, for example, were reportedly surprised to find all ten ASEAN members represented at talks on territorial disputes in the South China Sea.

In reality, ASEAN is led, cajoled, and enticed into accepting integration initiatives proposed by some or all of the five founders because the remaining members have vastly different political anatomies. Brunei is a small, oil-rich state ruled by one family, whose economy depends overwhelmingly on exports of oil, natural gas, and petroleum products. Despite public declarations of solidarity, three and arguably four members of ASEAN—Cambodia, Laos, Myanmar, and Vietnam, the CLMV group—are poor and politically retrograde states that exercise a braking effect on integration initiatives.

Cambodia's corrupt and repressive government still harbors men who are implicated in genocide.[8] Myanmar is ruled by military dictators who have cold-shouldered ASEAN's attempt to promote political reform. The governments of Laos and Vietnam still take direction from aging cadres heading warmed-over communist parties. Vietnam is picking up spillover manufacturing work from China and experiencing an investment boom, but its political system has a long way to go before it can shrug off the CLMV label. None of these smaller and weaker members is either interested in or prepared for deeper integration on a regionwide basis. ASEAN has agreed on a broad set of measures to try to narrow the development gap but lacks the resources to follow Europe's example of "structural funds" to support the development of poorer members.[9] In short, it is more realistic to think of ASEAN as 10 minus 1 (Brunei) minus 4 (CLMV), leaving the original ASEAN 5 as the shepherds of Asian integration. The process of engaging the + 3 countries, especially China, has given ASEAN a new sense of momentum. Despite its relatively weak standing and lack of real unity, ASEAN has become the focus of a complex web of courtships. The major suitors are Japan, China, India, and Australia. Eyeing each other as rivals as well as partners, they both seek and offer well-publicized bilateral summit meetings, preferential trade agreements, pledges to settle disputes peacefully, and recognized geopolitical standing in the region.

Like most organizations, ASEAN responds to challenges and shocks. Stimulated by the formation of APEC in 1989, ASEAN leaders agreed to intensify the implementation of AFTA, but the pace remained slow. The devastating financial crisis of 1997–1998 spurred ASEAN negotiators to advance to 2003 the deadline for implementation of certain AFTA-mandated tariff cuts. (Poorer members were exempted.)

A shock of a different sort came from a 2005 study by a respected US consulting firm. Commissioned by ASEAN economic ministers, the report explicitly warned that in the new global environment ASEAN members were losing competitiveness. The clear implication was that ASEAN's sluggish, consensus-based style of decisionmaking, known as the ASEAN Way, cannot keep up with the rapid pace of economic change and should be reformed.[10] Former secretaries-general of ASEAN added that ASEAN was not a sufficiently credible organization because of its weak record in enforcement and implementation, lack of a monitoring system, and failure to establish a binding dispute settlement mechanism. For example, only about 30 percent of ASEAN agreements are implemented.[11]

Stung by these observations, ASEAN leaders gave a newly constituted Eminent Persons Group a mandate to devise a set of reforms, embodied in a formal document known as the ASEAN Charter. The Charter gives ASEAN a legal identity and consolidates its institutional existence. It strengthens the ASEAN secretariat, streamlines decisionmaking, provides for permanent representatives posted to Jakarta, and puts in place a system of compliance monitoring and compulsory dispute settlement. "If you have norms, you have to have consequences," says one high-ranking ASEAN official, but punitive consequences are not likely in an ASEAN context.

The ASEAN Inter-Parliamentary Assembly

The ASEAN Inter-Parliamentary Assembly, formerly called the ASEAN Inter-Parliamentary Organization, was initiated by Indonesia and founded in 1977 by the ASEAN 5. It consists of over 300 members from eight ASEAN parliaments. (Brunei and Myanmar have no parliament and are called Special Observers.) As democracy has gained ground, some delegations have become quite feisty. For example, they have publicly called on their executive authorities to press more forcefully for Aung San Suu Kyi's release from house arrest. They also conduct numerous dialogues with parliamentarians from non-ASEAN countries.

The ASEAN Regional Forum

Preferring to look outward rather than inward, the ASEAN 5 have been careful to maintain or establish some form of bilateral defense relationship with the United States. At the same time, they have actively engaged other outside powers in a security dialogue among foreign ministers known as the ASEAN Regional Forum (ARF). ASEAN has consistently endorsed the ARF as "the main forum for regional security dialogue, with ASEAN as the primary driving force."[12]

The ARF is the only regionwide gathering that resembles a security institution. But it is too big: as of 2007, there were twenty-seven members.[13] In addition to ASEAN members, participants in ARF meetings include the + 3 countries (China, Japan, and South Korea) as well as the United States, Canada, the European Union, Australia, New Zealand, India, Pakistan, Russia, Mongolia, North Korea, Papua New Guinea, and East Timor (but not Taiwan). The first working session of the ARF was held in 1993.

As an institution comprising so many members and led by foreign ministries, the ARF risks being sidelined.[14] Consistent with the so-called ASEAN Way, which emphasizes consensus and respects the principles of equality and noninterference, the ARF consumes large amounts of time before even simple decisions can be reached and implemented. Similarly, it has skirted formal, substantive discussions of actual conflicts. China refuses to allow Taiwan either to attend the ARF or to be the subject of debate. North Korea's nuclear program is never on the agenda. Other governments invoke the principle of noninterference to veto discussion of the various insurgencies and border clashes in their countries. In 2005, for example, Thailand threatened to boycott the ARF if Malaysia or anyone else insisted on discussing the violence and alleged mistreatment of Muslims in southern Thailand that caused some to flee to Malaysia.

Other topics that might entail a surrender of sovereignty are taboo as well. In 2005, Singapore's defense minister proposed ARF-sponsored joint maritime security drills, but the idea was spurned.[15] Competing energy claims and territorial conflicts in the East China Sea, the South China Sea, and the Spratly Islands are mostly off-limits.

The ARF has adopted a statement entitled "Concept and Principles of Preventive Diplomacy" but has limited itself to authorizing studies and meetings on the subject. China strongly opposes adding conflict resolution to the agenda.[16] Humanitarian interventions of the sort that NATO carried out in Kosovo are out of the question.[17] The result is that the ARF cannot begin to supply what NATO provides: legitimacy with respect to the use of force (when the UN Security Council is deadlocked), the sharing of knowledge and intelligence, joint education and training, scenario planning, and procedures for command and control.

Nevertheless, the ARF has value. Few issues of substance are discussed in any depth during the formal meetings, but useful bilateral exchanges take place on the sidelines. In formal sessions, members have discussed such issues as search-and-rescue at sea, peacekeeping, disaster relief, confidence-building measures, and preventive diplomacy. The ARF endorsed a disaster relief exercise, proposed by the Philippines, Australia, and the United States, with participation from the US Pacific Command, the Red Cross, and various UN organizations. The ARF also supports workshops and seminars on maritime security, antipiracy activities, traffic in small arms, export licensing, and other topics of regionwide interest.

Even on military issues there is some progress. Members submit prior notification of military maneuvers. Publication of the ARF's *Annual Security Outlook* nudges governments to reveal more about their defense posture and inaugurate confidence-building measures. There has been some discussion of missile defense. A new nonproliferation track, supported by China, is promising. Certain military topics, such as rules of engagement, are difficult to discuss in a military setting and easier to broach in an ARF setting.

The ten-page "Chairman's Statement" issued at the conclusion of the ARF's thirteenth annual meeting in 2006 was longer and more detailed than usual. Contrary to its usual pattern, it contained statements supported by "most ministers" (on North Korea's test-firing of missiles) or "some ministers" (on the "disproportionate, indiscriminate, and excessive use of force" in the Middle East, a reference to Israel and Lebanon). All ministers called for a cease-fire in the Middle East, expressed concern about conditions in Myanmar, and put themselves on record in other ways as well. But they reaffirmed the "basic principles" of decisionmaking by consensus and noninterference, which are code words for confining the ARF to a safe diplomatic corner.

ASEAN leaders attach more importance to the ARF than its tangible results would justify. They even call it ASEAN's "contribution to world peace."[18] It is the only regional security forum that brings together all major powers of the world. Unlike most others, it was launched by developing countries.[19] ASEAN controls the agenda and stamps its meetings with its own nonconfrontational style. The late Michael Leifer commented that to question whether the ARF can actually solve conflicts is a "category mistake"; its goal is simply to improve the climate so that problems can be managed more easily.[20] But unless the ARF sheds its consensual skin and confronts at least some of the "hard" issues threatening the region, it will remain marginal.[21]

Two meetings combining government officials and private experts have recently sprung up beside the ARF. The so-called Shangri-La Dialogue, named for its hotel venue in Singapore and organized by the London-based International Institute for Strategic Studies, brings defense ministers together with a range of experts. Not to be outdone, China now hosts the annual Boao Forum for Asia, modeled loosely on the World Economic Forum meetings in Davos, Switzerland. Held on Hainan Island, the gathering brings together high-level government officials, businesspeople, and scholars to discuss Asia-related issues concerning economics, society, and the environment. The 2006 meeting attracted over 800 people.

The ARF bears a partial resemblance to the Conference on Security and Cooperation in Europe (CSCE), established during the Cold War by the United

States, the Soviet Union, and their respective allies. In the early 1970s, members of the CSCE met for more than two years and agreed on the Helsinki Final Act, signed in 1975. The act's Declaration on Principles Guiding Relations Between Participating States is remarkably similar to those enshrined in the TAC. The act also linked commitments on politico-military, economic, environmental, and human rights issues. For example, the human rights "basket" was linked to the security "basket," and each legitimized the other. This might be a useful model for the ARF.

ASEAN + 3

ASEAN + 3 consists of the ten members of ASEAN plus China, Japan, and South Korea. This group coalesced informally in preparation for the first Asia-Europe Meeting in 1996 and began to take on institutional characteristics in the wake of the Asian financial crisis. It holds regular meetings of committees and working groups and fosters external studies in networked think tanks. Within ASEAN + 3, trade and financial arrangements have proliferated, but thus far they are mostly bilateral. (Chapter 8 delves further into this topic.)

The communiqué of practically every high-level ASEAN + 3 meeting announces some new agreement. If measured in terms of conventional power politics, this whorl of accords is a paradox. China, South Korea, and Japan are the powerhouses of Asia, but they vie with each other for good standing, like a trio of burly suitors. The object of their courtship—accepted in official documents as the "major driving force" of the whole East Asian Community project—is ASEAN.

Like APEC, ASEAN + 3 has branched out into nontraditional security fields such as antiterrorism and maritime safety. Unlike APEC, ASEAN + 3 has also ventured into the field of traditional security, at least on paper. All three of the + 3 countries have signed the Treaty of Amity and Cooperation. In 2002 ASEAN members floated a nonbinding Declaration on the Conduct of Parties in the South China Sea, to which all three + 3 countries claim to subscribe. All have pledged more transparency in defense spending.

The architecture of ASEAN + 3 trade agreements differs from the circles-within-circles pattern. On the surface it resembles a hub-and-spoke model with ASEAN as the hub. But the active members of ASEAN, the ASEAN 5, are a delicately balanced and often fractious cluster, not a hub. The CLMV members are mostly observers. The + 3 countries, however, can legitimately be described as spokes in this cluster-and-spokes arrangement.

The East Asian Community

As described in Chapter 6, the sweeping design of the East Asian Community (with a capital *C*) was the work of the East Asia Vision Group. Various official statements name the ASEAN + 3 process as the "main vehicle for the eventual establishment of an East Asian Community."[22] Although some governments want to limit membership to ASEAN + 3, future membership in the Community has been left open.

Like ASEAN itself, the Community is designed to rest on three pillars: economic, security, and sociocultural. The commercial pillar of this self-proclaimed community-in-process is currently the thickest. Many member governments have negotiated, or are in the process of negotiating or studying, a web of mostly bilateral trade agreements. (A number of trade agreements have also been signed with countries outside the region.) A system of currency swap arrangements is in place. In addition, governments have signed a wide variety of loose accords covering such topics as cultural and educational exchange, tourism, and environmental protection.

The security pillar centers on the TAC. Signature of the TAC is one of the criteria for membership in the East Asian Summit, described below. Since the treaty is not binding, signing it symbolizes good faith and peaceful intentions rather than anything resembling an alliance. Indeed, ASEAN has made it clear that signature of the treaty does not override other security obligations. In addition to Australia and the + 3 countries, other non-ASEAN signatories include India, Pakistan, New Zealand, Russia, France, and several smaller states.

The East Asian Summit

"One Vision, One Identity, One Community," read the banners decking the main streets of Kuala Lumpur in December 2005. The slogan was the theme of the eleventh ASEAN summit. The banners stayed up during the more unusual gathering that followed on its heels—the first-ever East Asian Summit, spearheaded by ASEAN and attended by sixteen heads of state.[23] Joining ASEAN were the + 3 East Asian countries (Japan, China, and South Korea) as well as the + 2 (Australia and New Zealand) and + 1 (India) countries—but not the United States.[24]

At the close of the meeting, the heads of state issued a declaration establishing the EAS as an annual forum for dialogue and legitimizing its associated community-building efforts as an "integral part of the evolving regional architecture." The EAS can thus be seen as Asia Major's official, political, sovereignty-minded, land-based counterpart to Maritime Asia. Made up of nation-states, it includes India, the western anchor of Maritime Asia, and Australia, Maritime Asia's historically recent addition. Hosted by ASEAN, its leaders are supposed to meet immediately after the annual ASEAN summit.

The idea of an East Asian summit was a brainchild of Malaysia's prickly former prime minister, Mahathir Mohamad, but he favored restricting it to ASEAN + 3. In the late 1980s and early 1990s, Mahathir proposed an East Asian Group (later renamed the East Asian Caucus) that would have included

Japan but excluded Australia. Early versions of his proposal aroused serious concerns in the United States and elsewhere. Mindful of this controversial legacy and departing decisively from Mahathir's clenched-fist rhetoric, leaders at the 2005 summit pledged that the EAS would be an "open, inclusive, transparent, and outward-looking forum in which we strive to strengthen global norms and universally recognized values."[25]

What the EAS community would achieve and who would be invited to join it had been subjects of months of wrangling. Japan, Singapore, and Indonesia opted for extending the membership beyond ASEAN + 3, while China, Malaysia, and Thailand resisted the idea. China had no appetite for an organization that would include India, a strategic rival, and Australia, a US ally.

In the end, advocates of wider inclusion won the day. ASEAN members papered over their differences and informally settled on three criteria: invitees to the inaugural summit meeting had to be "dialogue partners" of ASEAN, they had to have significant economic involvement in the region, and they had to sign the TAC. Russia signed the TAC but is not a major player (except for energy), whereas the United States is a huge player but refused to sign the TAC. Hence, neither was invited. India, Australia, and New Zealand, however, satisfied the conditions and were invited, bringing the total membership of the EAS to sixteen.

Nobody was fully satisfied with the outcome. Even the victors in the membership struggle expressed private doubts about the value of the EAS. China was on the losing side; even its offer to host the second EAS was rejected in favor of an ASEAN country. Once these setbacks occurred, the Chinese began to lose interest in the EAS. Although the final text declared that the EAS "could play a significant role in community building," Beijing stressed its supplementary role. At China's insistence, the declaration did not proclaim an "East Asian Community."[26] Instead, the chairman's statement summarizing the EAS recognized an undefined "East Asian community" (with a small c) as a long-term goal. ASEAN + 3 is clearly China's preferred forum. Depending on what happens in APEC and the ASEAN Regional Forum, China's attitude may well doom the EAS as a forum for meaningful dialogue and action.

Similarly, Malaysians groaned but went along with the group's decision to include Australia and New Zealand as ad hoc partners of convenience. Predictably, Mahathir was disappointed. "I think [Asian integration] will not happen soon," he grumbled. Revealing once again that his concept of East Asia is implicitly nonwhite and non-"Western" rather than political, he added, "Once you start talking about Australia and New Zealand, it is no longer East Asian."[27] Senior minister Goh Chok Tong of Singapore begged to differ. A champion of the EAS grouping, Goh was and is quite explicit on what East Asia now means. Rejecting "narrow notions of physical geography," he considers India, Australia, and New Zealand to be part of East Asia. "A region is what we define it to be in terms of real political, economic, social and other connections," he adds.[28] To adopt the language of Chapter 2, East Asia has been remapped.

Prior to the meeting, observers wondered whether ASEAN would remain in charge. The EAS declaration answered that question by specifying that ASEAN countries would host all future meetings of the EAS, thus retaining the power of the chair. At the conclusion of their own summit two days earlier, ASEAN leaders had specified that the EAS should be "a top-down forum for leaders," that is, a grouping that would not create a new bureaucracy. Thus, ASEAN appears to have a firm grip on a very nebulous process. This outcome satisfies one of ASEAN's key interests. As one writer indelicately put it, "[ASEAN] has to ensure that it is the stuffing in the vast sandwich being created by the accelerating economic engagement between the biggest economies of the region—Japan, China, India, and South Korea."[29]

Another question was whether and how the enhanced cooperation advocated by the EAS would dovetail with the work being carried out in literally dozens of existing committees and working groups in which EAS members participate. The 2005 summit declaration declared that "the EAS and ASEAN + 3 process should move on parallel tracks without overlapping and complement each other as well as other regional processes." How this will work in practice remains to be seen. At both the first and the second summits, EAS members ducked the question, settling for a broader EAS membership but a looser and less operational process. The only explicit goal is an annual summit. Nevertheless, after the first summit, Malaysia convened several EAS-wide meetings at the working level, and there are other signs that ASEAN + 6 may take on an organizational identity.

The second EAS meeting, hosted by the Philippines, took place in January 2007. This time preparations went smoothly. Heads of state issued a declaration on energy security, endorsed Japan's proposal for an Economic Research Institute for ASEAN and East Asia, "welcomed" India's initiative to revive Nalanda University, expressed "grave concern" over North Korea's nuclear weapons test, underscored the value of "open and spontaneous leaders-led discussions," and confirmed the view that the EAS "complements other existing regional mechanisms, including the ASEAN dialogue process, the ASEAN + 3 process, the ARF, and APEC."[30] ASEAN was described as "the driving force," working closely with other participants.

■ Central Asia

Meanwhile, Central Asia is tapping into the integration movement. (As suggested in Chapter 2, I would dub this region Asia Medior, befitting its location between Asia Minor and Asia Major.) In the mid-1990s, Beijing reached agreement with Kazakhstan, Kyrgyzstan, and Tajikistan on the delineation of its 4,340-mile (7,000-kilometer) border. China's actions were in line with its wider quest for a peaceful regional environment in order to concentrate on economic modernization. Beijing is also keenly interested in the region's energy resources and hopes to reduce its dependence on maritime routes. Like ASEAN, smaller nations find strength in numbers and benefit from constructive engagement with China.

To promote further confidence-building measures, these four nations plus Russia, historically the dominant military power in the region, formed what was then known as the Shanghai Five. The first meeting took place in 1996. Renamed the Shanghai Cooperation Organization (SCO) in 2001, and with Uzbekistan as a new member, the group took on new significance after the terrorist attacks on the United States on September 11 of that year. In 2004–2005, India, Pakistan, Iran, and Mongolia joined as observers. The primary emphasis of the SCO is a joint struggle against terrorism, separatism, and extremism. The SCO also serves as an "interfacing mechanism" that allows Moscow and Beijing to make trade-offs and coordinate policies.[31] Its emphasis on noninterference and consensus-based decisionmaking mirrors the ASEAN Way.

In 2005, the SCO urged NATO and US forces to set a timetable for withdrawing their troops from Uzbekistan and Kyrgyzstan. It has also conducted joint military exercises. But the SCO is not an anti-American grouping. Just as ASEAN has pursued a "hedging" strategy to avoid undue Chinese influence, so most of the smaller nations have continued to cooperate with the United States and NATO to avoid Sino-Russian hegemony.[32] These governments also welcomed a formal "dialogue" relationship between the SCO and Japan, which China resisted but could not openly oppose.

Like ASEAN + 3, the SCO has adopted a platform of economic cooperation both for its own sake and to promote political and security interests. In this area, China has a clear advantage over Russia. At the 2004 meeting of SCO heads of government, Chinese premier Wen Jiabao hailed the decision to put economic cooperation on the main track as the meeting's "biggest result."[33] Some 120 projects spanning trade, energy, telecommunications, transport, and infrastructure have been chosen for action. The June 2006 summit established a Moscow-based business council and an association of banks tasked with preparing a joint investment program. The Chinese government is pushing for a free-trade agreement and pursuing various energy projects. India, which is seeking to upgrade its status from observer to full member, also favors a strong economic agenda. But Russia and several smaller states remain cool to Chinese initiatives and prefer cooperative manufacturing and high-technology projects to commercial competition.[34]

There is talk of an SCO-ASEAN agreement to establish some sort of cooperative framework, or at least closer dialogue with the rest of Asia. Apart from China, however, SCO members have adapted poorly to globalization. The revival of significant nonenergy trade along the Silk Road looks unlikely, and the "-stans" lack access to the major oceans. The undertone of Sino-Russian rivalry, conflicting priorities, and poor governance in several SCO members stunt the group's potential as a locus for regional and subregional integration. To the extent that the SCO eases China's near-paranoia about energy supplies, it will alter Beijing's attitude toward the rest of Asia and the United States, but it does not yet qualify as an architectural wing of Asia Major.

■ The Role of Advisers

The Track 2 Process

The East Asia Vision Group set forth concepts, vocabulary, ideas, and projected fields of community building. Much of the subsequent staff work comes from scholars, intellectuals, independent policy analysts, and other experts not directly employed by governments. The so-called Track 2 process refers to an institutionalized network of such "conceptual integrators," who meet regularly and advise their governments on a variety of cooperative initiatives. ("Track 1" refers to government officials.) These individuals envisage a grouping of nation-states with their own norms and identities—diverse but loosely integrated, "Asianized" but cosmopolitan, open to the world but less dependent on foreign help. Their tenets are engagement and dialogue rather than containment and isolation. Their mode is adaptation, and their currency is influence.

Some Track 2 organizations span the Pacific. Two of the more active are the Pacific Economic Cooperation Council (PECC) and the Council for Security Cooperation in the Asia Pacific (CSCAP). Member committees from the United States are part of both PECC and CSCAP. PECC is a tripartite organization bringing together government officials, business leaders, and academic experts. A long-standing champion of APEC, PECC can claim credit for elevating the status of the organization to the head of state level in 1993 and actively promotes transpacific free trade. PECC is the only NGO with official observer status at APEC meetings.

CSCAP has done serious work on piracy and crime and continues to offer advice on human trafficking, terrorism, and the smuggling of nuclear material. At the 1996 meeting of the ASEAN Regional Forum, for example, ministers agreed that drug trafficking and other cross-border crimes "could constitute threats to the security of the region" and agreed to consider them as a group. CSCAP promptly set up a working group on the subject that identified eight types of crime and offered recommendations to governments.[35] New committees have been formed on energy and maritime security.

Although Asian members of Track 2 groups hold meetings and publish frequently, they have no hallmark journal. The Chinese journal *New Tide*, founded in 1919, and its Japanese predecessor, founded in 1904, promoted enlightenment ideas backed by a circle of reform-minded students and intellectuals. Besides resurrecting ideas promoted by earlier Chinese and Japanese reformers, they translated a number of Western articles and debated them earnestly.[36] To my knowledge, there is no privately published journal—titled, perhaps, *New Asia*—reaching Asia-wide audiences and promoting closer integration in the name of progress and reform.

A partial exception is the *New Asia Monitor*. Funded by Japan's Sasakawa Foundation, it actively promotes the cause of an "Asian Economic Community," the India-ASEAN economic partnership, and other initiatives. Predictably, perhaps, it is located not in ASEAN + 3 territory but in India, where it was initiated by a government-backed research institution.[37]

The most common criticism of the Track 2 process is that it is all talk and no action. But it is in the nature of intellectuals to talk rather than act, since they lack access to the levers of power. It is the governments that have failed to act. With the partial exception of Suharto, Mahathir, and various Singaporean leaders, no senior Asian politician has invested much political capital in implementing the products of Track 2 ruminations. Despite this record, Canadian participant Paul Evans observes that "in the scribblings and imaginings of a handful of cosmopolitan Asian intellectuals and political leaders are the seeds of a deeper East Asian regionalism."[38]

An Asian OECD?

In 2002–2003, a number of research institutions in ASEAN + 3 joined together to form the Network of East Asian Think-Tanks (NEAT). The NEAT holds annual meetings and has spawned a rich web of contacts, study groups, working groups, conference papers, and reports. Analysts at regional institutions such as Singapore's Institute of Southeast Asian Studies, Malaysia's Institute of Strategic and International Studies, and Indonesia's Centre for Strategic and International Studies take part in these discussions and churn out articles and books on various aspects of integration. But the headquarters of the NEAT ended up in a research institution associated with the Chinese Foreign Ministry instead of the somewhat more independent Chinese Academy of Social Sciences. For that reason, Asians who favor genuinely independent research concluded that the NEAT had been compromised.

An alternative initiative is loosely modeled on the Paris-based Organization for Economic Cooperation and Development (OECD). The OECD conducts in-depth economic research not only on trade and investment but also on a variety of domestically sensitive issues, such as labor and immigration. It has fostered a common approach to such issues as export controls, tied aid, and money laundering. It also provides an unpublicized forum for exploring emerging issues and deciding on basic principles to guide agreement before those issues are ready to be formally negotiated. The idea of trade rules on services, for example, was hatched there.

In January 2007, heads of state from EAS countries endorsed the establishment of an institution named the Economic Research Institute for ASEAN and East Asia (ERIA). The largest donor, Japan, has pledged $100 million toward this project. According to a Japanese official, ERIA will carry out research and analyses on both ASEAN and regional economic integration. Topics will extend beyond trade liberalization to include such issues as energy, the environment, and industrial cooperation. Whereas NEAT is merely a network, ERIA is projected to evolve into a real institution of sorts.[39] Inaugural conferences in various Asian capitals began in late 2007.

Five features of ERIA are worth noting. First, it is supposed to provide a credible and independent "roof" under which in-depth economic studies, seminars, and consultations can proceed without political interference. Hadi Soesastro of Indonesia's Centre for Strategic and International Studies and others have long advocated an "East Asian OECD," an independent economic research institution staffed by individual experts selected on a competitive basis.[40] Second, once ERIA comes into being, it will be the first major institutional structure erected in the name of all sixteen members of the EAS, including India, Australia, and New Zealand. Just as the summit process inaugurated in 2005 was called "East Asian," so ERIA will probably retain that title. Third, the proposed ERIA is supported and initially funded by Japan. Sino-Japanese rivalry strikes again: the reader will remember that ASEAN + 3's NEAT is headquartered in Beijing. Fourth, and true to form, ERIA caters somewhat to ASEAN. The secretariat will be located in an ASEAN country and ASEAN integration is called "the key" to regional integration. Finally, although the ERIA will be patterned somewhat on the OECD, a major difference is that the OECD is a club of industrialized democracies. Its members are described as "sharing the principles of the market economy, pluralist democracy, and respect for human rights." Japan and South Korea are OECD members, but China has not yet been admitted. ERIA, by contrast, will be inclusive.

The Asian Development Bank

The Manila-based Asian Development Bank is part of the World Bank Group. Although representatives from Europe and North America sit on its board, it is known as a "Japanese" bank. Japan is one of the largest shareholders, and the president of the ADB has always been Japanese. Eight of the twelve members of the board of directors come from the Asia-Pacific and the rest from other parts of the globe.

The ADB actively promotes regional and subregional integration. ADB president Haruhiko Kuroda was an original proponent of the aborted Asian

Monetary Fund. In 2005, he created an Office for Regional Economic Integration and chose Masahiro Kawai, an advocate of regional monetary union, to head it. (Kawai has since returned to Tokyo but continues to promote integration from there.) The ADB's Asia Regional Integration Center maintains a database of "integration indicators," such as intraregional trade share, share of foreign investment, and many others. Champions within the ADB exude vision and optimism. "Needless to say, there is a long way to go," comments the ADB's Yoshihiro Iwasaki. "But the question is no longer whether the region should integrate, but rather when, how quickly, and in what areas."[41]

Acting as a self-described catalyst, the ADB provides funding, technical assistance, and institutional capacity building. It actively supports regional financial initiatives such as the Chiang Mai Initiative and the development of an Asian bond market. It adopted a Regional Cooperation Policy in 1994 and updated it in 2006 to put more emphasis on transportation and other links connecting various parts of the region; expanded trade and investment; the development of financial systems and macroeconomic and fiscal stability; and improved environmental, health, and social conditions. Its economists produce numerous publications in support of regional integration.[42] No other regional bank plays such an active role in fostering integration.

◼ Conclusion

Centuries ago, Muslim architects in Persia faced the challenge of fitting a dome on top of a square and distributing its weight. They borrowed from the Byzantine Empire what English speakers now call a "squinch" (derived from an Old French word meaning "out of the corner") and turned it into an architectural gem. Squinches are among the most interesting and unusual features of old mosques.

In Asia, the underlying "square," so to speak, is Asia's diverse array of nation-states, each with its rigidly defined borders. The "dome" is integration—both the market-driven reality of spontaneous commercial and cultural integration in Maritime Asia and the political and strategic imperative of closer economic, political, and security integration in Asia Major. The architects of Asian integration need squinches to fit these two dimensions of integration together.

But the architecture of government-driven integration in Asia Major bears more resemblance to a rambling Victorian mansion than an elegant mosque. It is a hodgepodge that contains substantial overlap and duplication. It has a surplus of clubrooms and banquet halls but many of its passages go nowhere. Contrary to good architectural principles, many of its other spaces are not functional. It would not pass building inspection.

Before dismissing that structure, however, the reader should reflect on the forces that gave rise to it. First, the paucity of tangible results stems from fragile governments and weak domestic institutions in a number of key countries, not from the proliferation of meetings. Second, the jumbled structure of the new architecture corresponds nicely to the strategic context from which it springs. The numerous conference rooms both allow for and help tame the many bilateral rivalries that characterize the region. There are no trap doors, no ghosts, no risk of fire, and no madwomen in the attic.

The institutions with which this architecture tends to be compared, the European Union and NATO, were designed to link politically like-minded and culturally similar nations in an era when the global order was highly structured. The Cold War defined alliances and alignments, and much of Asia was locked into those alignments by colonial rule or its aftermath. Today, by contrast, the strategic context is highly fluid. The flexible and open-ended nature of Asian organizations makes room for the wide variety of political issues facing Asian governments, the strategic ambiguity associated with the resurgence of China, and the entry of India and Australia.

The circles-within-circles design allows for both diplomatic flexibility and functional cooperation on an ad hoc basis. Its ASEAN 5–centered cluster-and-spokes construction captures the web of north-south and west-south trade agreements among the members of Asia Major. Whereas ASEAN + 3 is the chosen clubhouse for financial discussions, small clusters of twos and threes are the preferred setting for discussions of security cooperation. This flexibility is broadly similar to what Europeans call "variable geometry"—the notion that not every country needs to take part in every policy initiative. Singapore's Goh Chok Tong, an architect of the East Asian Summit, uses this phrase to refer to Asian integration.

In a globalizing world, Asia's new architecture can be neither self-contained nor self-sufficient. Shoring up the whole structure is a sturdy combination of US military alliances, support from the Asian Development Bank, and membership in transpacific and global institutions. But skeptics should admit that Asians are doing a reasonably good job of taking care of themselves. Their new architecture sounds unnecessarily complex and expensive to maintain, but it is cheaper than huge defense budgets and definitely preferable to war.

■ Notes

1. Ralph Keyes, ed., *The Wit and Wisdom of Oscar Wilde* (New York: Gramercy Books, 1996), p. 104.

2. Quoted in "Overview," in the ASEAN secretariat's background paper on the ASEAN Regional Forum, www.aseansec.org/328.htm.

3. Funabashi, *Asia Pacific Fusion*, p. 1.

4. "Creating the East Asia Free Trade Area (EAFTA)," speech by Noboru Hatakeyama, chairman and chief executive officer of the Japanese Economic Foundation, Seoul, October 27, 2005. Hatakeyama believes that if Asian governments do not plan on sharing sovereignty and if they maintain highly divergent political values, the East Asian "Community" cannot come into being and should change its name. See www.jef.or.jp/en_act/act_speech_topics.asp?cd=52&num=1.

5. ASEAN, "Declaration of ASEAN Concord II."

6. For a useful summary, see ASEAN, *Vientiane Action Programme*, annex 2.

7. "Joint Media Statement of the Thirty-Seventh ASEAN Economic Ministers' (AEM) Meeting," Vientiane, September 28, 2005, www.aseansec.org/17780.htm.

8. For evidence of a new crackdown, see Seth Mydans, "Cambodian Leader Cracks Down in Bid to Solidify Power," *New York Times,* January 9, 2006, p. A3.

9. ASEAN, *Vientiane Action Programme*, annex 4.

10. Hadi Soesastro of Indonesia makes the case for a "new ASEAN way," in "Accelerating ASEAN Economic Integration: Moving Beyond AFTA," Economics Working Paper Series, Center for Strategic and International Studies, Jakarta, March 2005, available at www.csis.or.id/papers/wpe091.

11. Koh, Woon, Tan, and Wei, "The ASEAN Charter," p. 2.

12. ASEAN, "Declaration of ASEAN Concord II," p. 9, art. A.8.

13. Bangladesh was admitted in 2006 and Sri Lanka in 2007.

14. Desker, "The Worth of the ASEAN Regional Forum," p. 1.

15. "ARF Should Think About Joint Security Drills at Sea," SEAPSNet, March 4, 2005, www.siiaonline.org.

16. It was the Chinese representative who succeeded in watering down "conflict resolution mechanisms" as a proposed agenda item to "elaboration of approaches to conflict." See Rosemary Foot, "The Present and Future of the ARF: China's Role and Attitude," in Khoo, *The Future of the ARF*, p. 261. Once the Chinese realized that they could exercise some control over the agenda, their confidence in the ARF improved.

17. Dewi Fortuna Anwar, "Human Security," in Alagappa, *Asian Security Order*, p. 561.

18. ASEAN, *ASEAN Regional Forum: Documents Series 1994–2004,* p. iii.

19. S. R. Nathan, "Opening Address," in Khoo, *The Future of the ARF,* p. 9.

20. Leifer, *The ASEAN Regional Forum,* p. 59.

21. Alan Dupont, "The Future of the ARF: An Australian Perspective," in Khoo, *The Future of the ARF,* p. 43.

22. "Chairman's Statement of the 8th ASEAN + 3 Summit," Vientiane, Laos, 2004, in ASEAN, *ASEAN + 3 Documents Series 1999–2004,* p. 204, art. 11.

23. I use the term "first-ever" because I am not counting gatherings of puppet governments set up under Japan's Greater East Asia Co-Prosperity Sphere.

24. Russia attended as a "guest" of the Malaysian government, and its interest in attending future summits will be considered based on the criteria established by ASEAN.

25. Kuala Lumpur Declaration on the East Asian Summit, Kuala Lumpur, December 14, 2005, available at www.aseansec.org.

26. Wu, "East Asia: Building a Community," p. 7.

27. "Interview with Jeremy Hurwitz," *Far Eastern Economic Review* 169, no. 2 (March 2006): 54.

28. Goh Chok Tong, "Towards an East Asian Renaissance," pp. 12–13.

29. Ravi Velloor, "ASEAN in Driver's Seat of East Asia Summit," *The Straits Times*, December 15, 2005.

30. "Chairman's Statement of [*sic*] the Second East Asia Summit," Cebu, Philippines, January 15, 2007, available at www.12thaseansummit.org/ph/inntertemplate3.asp?category=docs&docid=36.

31. Yu Bin, "Central Asia Between Competition and Cooperation," *Foreign Policy in Focus*, December 4, 2006, p. 4, available at www.fpif.org/fpiftxt/3754.

32. For discussions of hedging, see Goh, "Understanding 'Hedging' in Asia-Pacific Security," and Medeiros, "Strategic Hedging."

33. Frank Ching, "China Girds for Wider Influence in Asia," *Yale Global Online*, http://yaleglobal.yale.edu/display.article?id=3736.

34. "The Shanghai Cooperation Organisation: Internal Contradictions," *IISS Strategic Comments* 12, no. 6 (July 2006): 1–2.

35. Dupont, *East Asia Imperiled*, pp. 176–178.

36. Schwarcz, *The Chinese Enlightenment*, p. 31.

37. *The New Asia Monitor*, www.newasiaforum.org/newasiamonitor.htm.

38. Paul Evans, "Between Regionalism and Regionalization," in Pempel, *Remapping East Asia*, p. 215.

39. Personal correspondence with the author, September 12, 2006.

40. Hadi Soesastro, "Building an East Asian Economic Community," in Zhang, *East Asian Cooperation*, pp. 28–29.

41. Yoshihiro Iwasaki, "What's Next as ASEAN + 3 Integrates?" *Japan Times Online*, January 1, 2005, www.japantimes.co.jp/cgi-bin/getarticle.p.15?eo20040512al.htm.

42. Information is available from the ADB's website, www.adb.org. See also Asian Development Bank, *Asian Economic Cooperation and Integration*.

8

Trade, Finance, and the Politics of Regionalism

Commercial and financial diplomacy is a key currency of Asia's new regionalism. Asian diplomats continue to negotiate trade and financial agreements in the name of bilateral and regional economic growth and financial stability. These pacts are also designed to shore up domestic economies, advance the foreign policy interests of each signatory, and enhance regional security.

The 2001 East Asia Vision Group's report listed as a guiding principle the notion that economic cooperation would serve as the catalyst for a "bona fide regional community" in which collective efforts are devoted to avoiding conflict and managing tensions as well as promoting prosperity.[1] Commercial and financial diplomacy symbolizes peaceful intent, sets up opportunities for rivals to score points, and serves as a proxy for various forms of Asian identity. Depending on what form it takes, it embeds a resurgent China in a web of agreements and extends, diffuses, or dilutes Chinese influence. This chapter expands on these themes.

But analyzing government-to-government economic initiatives alone runs into a contradiction. How does this form of regionalism square with the regionalization of Maritime Asia, which occupies only a fraction of the land ruled by national governments but where trade and financial interaction is most intense? Not very well. Most of Maritime Asia's commercial activity is propelled by the private sector operating across borders. There are exceptions, of course; airlines, broadcasting, banks, and the nuclear power industry are often partially or wholly owned by the state. But even state-owned entities propped up by state subsidies are beginning to establish branches abroad in order to compete, and some are being privatized and sold to foreign takeovers. As economists like to say, nations don't compete against nations; companies compete against companies, even if they are subject to some degree of state control. Like Americans in the 1980s, Asians might well ask (ungrammatically), "Who is us?"

Asia's new regionalism, however, reflects the way national governments see the world. Governments control national territory, and international transactions are chalked up in the ledgers of nation-states. To say, for example, that "China exports $X billion" or that a product is "made in China" is misleading, because those exporters may be headquartered elsewhere and because the exports contain imported parts. But the political reality is that exports—and the size of associated foreign exchange reserves—contribute to Asian governments' power, prestige, and legitimacy.

■ The Proliferation of Preferential Trade Agreements

The global trading system established in the aftermath of World War II is founded on the so-called most-favored-nation principle, which holds that the lowering of trade barriers to one country must be extended on a nondiscriminatory basis to all. Over time, however, the trading system has splintered into an unprecedented number of discriminatory agreements. The total number of active preferential trade agreements (PTAs) reported to the General Agreement on Tariffs and Trade (GATT) or its successor, the WTO, spiraled from two dozen or so in the late 1980s to more than 200 in 2007.[2] Asian trade agreements account for much of this growth.

Asian governments rely on many trade-related devices to limit their vulnerability to globalization, such as protection of weak sectors, restrictions on foreign investment, free-trade zones, and many others. Preferential trade agreements belong in this category. Numbering several dozen, they cover almost every feasible intra-Asian combination except—significantly—those connecting China, Japan, and South Korea. (Taiwan and North Korea are excluded from this scramble.) Singapore has concluded or is negotiating the greatest number in Asia Major: its current or would-be partners include Australia, India, Japan, Korea, New Zealand, Brunei, China, and its fellow ASEAN members.

Asians have also negotiated PTAs with a number of trading partners outside the region. South Korea, for example, has negotiated trade agreements with Mexico, Chile, Canada, Mercosur, the EU, the European Free Trade Area (Switzerland, Iceland, Liechtenstein, and Norway), and the United States.

As is the case with Asian regionalism more generally, ASEAN is the political hub of regional trade agreements. Even though ASEAN is a piebald cluster of mostly small economies, virtually all the major powers have negotiated or are negotiating PTAs of sorts with ASEAN as a whole. Chinese, Korean, and Japanese officials look south toward ASEAN and its individual members and west toward India, but not toward each other. The result is an ASEAN-centered cluster-and-spoke pattern of trade agreements rather than one centered solely on China. This outcome mirrors the paradox of ASEAN leadership of Asian regionalism in general.

ASEAN members prefer to negotiate collectively because they fear that individual ASEAN countries negotiating on their own will be at a disadvantage. (Again, Singapore is a partial exception.) Some Southeast Asians go so far as to argue that economic integration should begin within ASEAN and only subsequently spread outward. That way ASEAN would have market power.

Despite this brave talk, there are few signs of growing economic integration within ASEAN. Except for Singapore, Southeast Asian economies are similar and protectionism remains strong. Trade and investment among ASEAN members are expanding relatively slowly. In sharp contrast to intra-European trade, intra-ASEAN trade has rarely accounted for more than one-fifth of the trade of member states.[3] Trade among the ASEAN 5 plus Brunei exceeded 30 percent of total trade in 1962, but it sank to the 20 percent range and stayed there through most of the 1990s.[4] In 2006 the figure for intra-ASEAN trade as a whole was only about 23 percent, reflecting no significant growth.[5] The real growth in trade and investment is occurring between leading members of ASEAN and individual + 3 countries, especially China.

The proposed China-ASEAN PTA builds on this growth. In terms of market size, it is by far the most ambitious of the ASEAN-wide PTAs. As of 2007 ASEAN's combined GDP exceeds $850 billion and China's is about $2.5 trillion. Their combined populations approach 2 billion people. Unlike Japan, China includes agriculture in its PTAs. Like other agreements, however, this one may be less than it seems, at least for now.

As a goodwill gesture, China has already eliminated tariffs on a number of agricultural products. Nevertheless, ASEAN farmers report numerous non-tariff barriers. Thai farmers complain, for example, that a year after the 2003 China-Thailand PTA was signed, they recorded a deficit in sixty-three fruit and vegetable product areas covered by the agreement compared to only two the year before.[6] Moreover, full implementation of the agreement is several years away, and the final text will likely omit a fair and transparent dispute settlement mechanism.

The large and growing number of preferential trade pacts has raised concerns that the global trading system is degenerating into a tangle of complex, inconsistent, and often unenforceable agreements. That system is already in trouble; global negotiations have stumbled over rock-hard differences, and domestic political support for further globalization is weak.

Asians are not to blame for this situation; indeed, they are followers rather than leaders of the trend toward discriminatory agreements. But critics of preferential agreements argue that since Asians in particular benefit enormously from transpacific and global trade, they should adjust their trade priorities accordingly. They should also abandon—or at least standardize and liberalize—the intra-Asian PTAs negotiated or under negotiation thus far (collectively nicknamed the "noodle bowl"). But the politics of Asian regionalism dictate otherwise.

PTAs and Global Rules

From a trade policy perspective, most trade agreements negotiated between and among Asian countries are sorry things. Computerized information, lower transport costs, and improved supply chain management do far more to stimulate trade than bilateral or subregional FTAs. Although PTAs are supposed to create more trade than they divert, they often shield protectionism. The governments of Asia Major claim to support free trade, but devils lurk in the details of what they actually negotiate. Seeking a respite from incessant globalization, they have discovered that PTAs can work to their advantage.

All Asian PTAs lower average tariffs considerably, but most exempt or maintain high peaks of protection for "sensitive" goods and services. They exclude most nontariff barriers, and they lag behind in protecting intellectual property rights and establishing binding enforcement procedures. Most will not take full effect for years.

In addition, many such pacts set up a bewildering variety of rules that complicate business decisions and raise transaction costs. Particularly cumbersome are inconsistent rules of origin, which determine how much of a given product must be produced in a given country in order to qualify as a product of that country. The higher the percentage, the less free trade is permitted. In sectors where tariffs are low, most companies choose to pay the tariff rather than spend time and resources documenting their compliance with rules of origin. Within ASEAN, for example, the rules are so complex that AFTA's preferential tariffs are applied to less than 10 percent of exports.[7]

Although these agreements threaten to displace suppliers from nonmember countries, they are not subject to formal challenge because of the way WTO rules are written. These rules allow for the establishment of so-called free-trade areas between two or more countries under certain conditions.[8] If the parties to the agreement are developed countries, the rules require that a free-trade area should encompass "substantially all" trade. The word *substantially* is open to different interpretations; some governments make the highly disputed claim that it can exclude agriculture. But the prevailing view is that "substantially all" means 90 percent (but by value or by volume?). Another condition is that a free-trade area must be implemented within a "reasonable" period of time, understood to be ten years at most. A third is that such areas should create more trade than they divert.

These conditions originally applied to all countries. But a subsequent provision, known as the Enabling Clause, exempts agreements negotiated between or among developing countries. The rules also specify that if a trade agreement is negotiated between a developing country or countries and a developed country (Japan, Australia, and New Zealand are currently Asia

Major's only designees), the developing-country partner is not obliged to reciprocate. This exception legitimizes the nonreciprocal nature of the Generalized System of Preferences adopted by most developed countries. It is aimed at opening markets for poorer countries while giving them a breathing spell, but it also permits governments to postpone market-based reforms and shield vested interests from competition.[9]

Like PTAs elsewhere in the world, intra-Asian PTAs are exclusive and do not embody what trade experts call "open regionalism." There is no consensus on the exact meaning of this term, but it implies permitting outsiders to sign up to the terms of a trade agreement on a reciprocal basis: If you let me join your trade club, I'll lower my trade barriers to the same level as yours and meet your other conditions as well. For some, the choice of closed, preferential agreements over open regionalism is a missed opportunity.[10]

Drawbacks of Asian PTAs

The new web of PTAs will arguably prevent major backsliding toward protectionism, but it seems unlikely that they will contribute much more to Asia's future wealth.

There are at least four grounds for this prediction that go beyond the shortfalls and loopholes described above. First, the boom in intraregional trade and the realignment of trade pursuant to production networks took place before most of these agreements were negotiated. The two major agreements freeing up trade in telecommunications goods and services were initiated, partially drafted, and pushed by the private sector.

Second, since tariffs on imports in nonprotected sectors are already fairly low, most obstacles to trade consist of nontariff barriers such as subsidies, cartels, inefficient and duplicative customs procedures, and excessive regulation. Corruption and weak governance compound these problems. PTAs do not address these so-called structural barriers to market access.

Since central governments cannot always control local officials, the real villains are not necessarily hypocrisy and knowingly false promises but rather the inability of the central governments to fully determine what goes on at the local level. The governments of China and India are still struggling to establish free trade *within* their own economies. The competition for investment spurs some Asian governments to permit foreign investors to import what they need, but local impediments such as taxes, license requirements, special fees, and corruption may cancel out that advantage.

Third, in the unlikely event that intra-Asian PTAs created a single Asian common market, the economic benefits of such an arrangement for Asians would be small compared to free trade on a global or transpacific level.[11] Economists have used various models to predict the potential economic benefits of bilateral and regionwide PTAs. Their results vary according to methods and assumptions used. But their general conclusion is that no Asia-wide PTA can match the benefits of transpacific or global free trade because of the size of the US market.[12]

Masahiro Kawai, formerly of the Asian Development Bank, modifies this conclusion. Comparing various intra-Asian agreements with liberalization within APEC, he finds that an ASEAN + 3 PTA that included agriculture would benefit ASEAN and South Korea more than liberalization at the APEC level. He also estimates that an ASEAN + 3 PTA would have only a small impact on US exports.[13] Others argue that such estimates brush aside the need to modernize the agricultural sector and underestimate the dynamic effects of a pan-Asian PTA over time, including changes in the pattern of trade-related investment.

A political obstacle also looms. Without corresponding transpacific and global liberalization, diverting trade away from US-based exporters would invite legitimate criticism from the United States and sour the climate for further market opening in what is a much larger market. The US manufacturing sector is already alert to this possibility.[14]

Finally, Asian PTAs do not "ratchet up" WTO agreements. A common rationale for regional and bilateral trade agreements is that it is easier for a smaller number of countries to agree to liberalize trade above and beyond existing WTO levels ("WTO-plus") than it is for all members of the WTO. Such agreements then give those left out of them a strong incentive to match or exceed the standards set by new PTAs in subsequent WTO negotiations. But most Asian PTAs do not exceed WTO standards, and thus far they have nothing to break the impasse in global liberalization talks. Only a path-breaking PTA on a grand scale (discussed later in this chapter) would have such an effect.

Moreover, the emphasis on bilateral and regional PTAs soaks up time and attention that might otherwise be devoted to bringing about a successful conclusion to the WTO's Doha Round. Thus far, Asian governments have not lobbied forcefully in Geneva either individually or as a group, in part because of their widely different short-run interests, in part because they feel powerless, and in part because the Asian integration movement takes priority.

As of late 2007, it appeared that the Doha Round was likely to end in modest results at best and a papered-over failure at worst. Asians did not get the market access that they wanted from the Uruguay Round, which ended in 1993, but they cannot deny that the steady lowering of global barriers to trade and investment over the years is a major cause of their new wealth. They also benefit from the WTO's mandatory dispute settlement provisions, which are almost entirely lacking in their own agreements.

Why, then, do Asian PTAs continue to be negotiated, one after the other?

■ Sources and Motivations of Asian PTAs

The forces that drive the proliferation of trade agreements are a variant of what motivates Asia's new regionalism as a whole. They include the geopolitical nature of PTAs, protection against globalization, regionalization (real or perceived), reactions to PTAs elsewhere, diplomatic rivalry, and the resurgence of China.

PTAs as Geopolitical Expressions

Trade agreements are political instruments. Every government's trade policy contains an element of statecraft, but in Asia this ingredient is predominant. PTAs have assumed a role akin to that of security agreements in former years, serving as an expression of political and security ties as well as a harbinger of trade and investment. They are a safe and benign form of competition for influence in Southeast Asia and in the region more generally. They signal changes in the balance of influence and symbolize new political alignments. They are a surrogate of sorts for a code of conduct, implicitly guaranteeing peaceful behavior. Security treaties and military alliances are out; PTAs are in.

Shields Against Globalization

Most Asian governments are highly exposed to economic globalization. Except for Singapore, developing countries in Asia have become even more dependent on trade than they were before the Asian financial crisis. (And Singapore's very existence depends on trade.) During the 1990s, China's trade as a ratio to GDP rose from 32 to 49 percent, Indonesia's from 49 to 74 percent, Malaysia's from 147 to over 214 percent, South Korea's from 59 to 84 percent, and India's from 17 to 29 percent. Trade-dependent countries now have a huge stake in the economic health of their neighbors. This forces governments to think more strategically about regional economic policy and to pay more attention than ever before to the competitive aspects of their own and other's domestic policies.[15]

Governments with heavily protected sectors view PTAs as a tool to manage globalization on their own terms and to shield them from excessive external pressure. PTAs encourage gradual domestic reform without committing the signatories to excessively painful changes. Since they typically lack enforceable rules, they permit governments to cling to both sovereignty and flexibility. Since most of them permit large carve-outs and set up long phase-in periods, they serve to limit and postpone trade liberalization while ostensibly promoting integration.

Regionalization

As described in Part 1, regionalization is largely confined to maritime regions and ocean-accessible cities. Even the Asian financial crisis had very diverse effects within each economy. But the regional maritime boom shows up as a set of national statistics. Economic interdependence among East Asian nations was Mahathir's primary justification for the East Asian Economic Group, which he proposed in the late 1970s and early 1980s. Like Mahathir, proponents of the Asian integration movement point to rising economic interdependence within the region as a justification for more PTAs.

Reaction to PTAs Elsewhere in the World

Pressure for regional and bilateral trade agreements began building in the late 1980s but did not produce results until after the financial crisis of 1997–1998. At that point, APEC had lost high-level support and momentum, and China was preoccupied with negotiating entry into the WTO. Inspiration came from Mexico, which signed an "interim" (pre-PTA) trade agreement with the European Union in 1997. At about the same time, Mexico's commerce and industry minister proposed the idea of a PTA with Japan. In 1998, South Korean president Kim Dae Jung visited Japan and proposed new efforts to overcome long-standing antagonism. The idea of a Japan-Korea PTA grew out of this initiative, but talks soon stalled. Thus it was that odd couple Japan and South Korea, both longtime multilateralists, began separately to explore various other bilateral options. Meanwhile, Singapore and New Zealand agreed to begin PTA negotiations. The trickle that these various governments opened up became a torrent.[16]

Just as Asian regionalism can be thought of as a reaction to regionalism in Europe and the Americas, so Asian PTAs are in part a reaction to trade agreements negotiated by others. As recently as 2002, only five of the top thirty economies of the world were not members of functioning preferential trade agreements, and they were all Asian (Japan, China, South Korea, Taiwan, and Hong Kong).[17] Asians moved quickly to fill this gap. As of 2007, the governments of Asia Major had concluded or were negotiating more trade and "economic partnership" agreements between or among two or more countries than any other region.

Rivalry

Beijing, initially preoccupied with entry into the WTO, caught on fast. In November 2000, after Japan and South Korea began to explore bilateral options, China floated to ASEAN the idea of a comprehensive ASEAN-China free trade agreement. In 2002, the two sides announced a framework heralding such an agreement within ten years and stipulating that talks toward that end proceed "expeditiously." Not wanting to be left out, South Korea and Japan also launched negotiations with ASEAN. So have Australia and New Zealand, which are negotiating jointly.[18]

PTAs stimulate commercial rivalry for at least two reasons. First, governments seeking to attract more business to their countries want to sign more PTAs than their neighbor. If Thailand, say, has concluded more bilateral PTAs than any other country in the region, Bangkok will presumably become a sub-regional hub of trade and investment. This logic stimulates still more proposed PTAs.

Second, new trade agreements threaten to displace the exports of nonsignatories. The PTA concluded between South Korea and the United States in 2007 has not yet been approved by Congress, but it has already had a ripple effect in Tokyo because certain Korean exports will enter the United States duty-free, threatening comparable Japanese exports. In response, Tokyo has sought to revive talks on a proposed PTA between Japan and South Korea, but Koreans have reportedly turned a cold shoulder. A PTA between Japan and the United States would probably interest the Japanese government. Compared to China's alleged currency manipulation, subsidies, and violations of intellectual property rights, Japan's trade practices look good, but Japanese restrictions on agricultural imports and the ongoing imbalance in automotive trade would be likely deal-breakers.

Quite apart from commercial reasons, the race to conclude PTAs also reflects political rivalry. The diplomatic success of China's trade offers forces Japan to keep pace. Unable for domestic political reasons to expand agricultural imports in "sensitive" sectors such as rice, Tokyo has concluded or is negotiating wide-ranging economic partnership agreements with Singapore, Malaysia, the Philippines, and Thailand and has proposed something similar for ASEAN as a whole. Japanese officials are also engaging in joint studies with Australia and India. In 2006, Japan proposed a Comprehensive Economic Partnership in East Asia, which includes a PTA among all sixteen members of the East Asian Summit.

Japanese reluctance to liberalize trade in agriculture puts Tokyo at a disadvantage vis-à-vis Beijing. Negotiations to establish the ASEAN-Japan PTA bogged down at first, in part because Japan initially signaled an intention to exempt over 500 products. Although such products amount to only 1 percent of Japan-ASEAN trade, Japan's negotiating stance came across as stingy and unworthy of a rich country. Although an agreement was finally cobbled together, Japan lost the chance to reap good publicity and goodwill. ASEAN trade officials calculate that bilateral pacts with Japan may offer them a better deal, since bilateral arrangements typically offer deeper tariff cuts.[19]

Korea also pays a diplomatic price for its reluctance to liberalize agricultural trade. Thailand refused to sign the Korea-ASEAN agreement because Korea excluded rice and some 200 other agricultural products. Even the hard-nosed United States had to give in on rice; it is excluded from the Korea-US PTA.

Officials in New Delhi, mindful of China's diplomatic gains, want to step up engagement with the rest of Asia for both security and economic reasons. In 1997, India led the establishment of the Bay of Bengal Initiative for Multi-Sectoral Technical and Economic Cooperation (BIMSTEC), consisting of Bangladesh, Bhutan, India, Myanmar, Nepal, Sri Lanka, and Thailand. A PTA is on BIMSTEC's agenda, but expectations are low. Of more significance is the framework agreement between India and ASEAN, which envisages an India-ASEAN PTA by 2013.

Separately, the Indian government negotiated a PTA with Thailand and an economic cooperation agreement with Singapore, and agreements with Indonesia and Malaysia are under negotiation. Preliminary discussions on some form of bilateral economic agreement with Japan, South Korea, and China have also taken place, and an agreement with Australia is under study.

India's strengths include business processing, information technology, biotechnology, pharmaceuticals, petrochemicals, education, and medical services. The Tata Group and a handful of other large conglomerates, already well established abroad, are now building more production networks of their own, and other companies are investing actively in Asia. English-speaking technicians and engineers are abundant. But India maintains the highest levels of protection of any major developing country. Instead of embracing free trade and promoting domestic adjustment, Indian negotiators insist on so many exceptions that the Look East initiative is viewed with considerable skepticism in Asian trade circles.

Such skepticism is well grounded. Thanks to pressure from small Indian manufacturers and farmers, Indian negotiators blasted the proposed India-ASEAN free-trade agreement with so much protectionist buckshot that negotiations broke down in mid-2006. They began the talks by placing more than 1,400 items on the exclusion list, including major commodities like tea, pepper, and palm oil. This collection accounts for 44 percent of ASEAN's exports to India. After the list was narrowed to 854 items, ASEAN found itself pushing for a "mere" 400.[20]

Despite this record, India's trade and investment links with the rest of Asia Major are clearly growing stronger. India's trade with these countries rose from $8 billion in 1990 to $67.6 billion in 2005 and by 2007 was approaching 30 percent of India's combined exports and imports.[21] Since 2002, India's trade with developing countries in Asia has exceeded trade with the EU. Starting from a very low base, bilateral trade between China and India is in the neighborhood of $20 billion and is growing rapidly. From 2002 to 2004, India's imports from Australia nearly tripled.[22] India's $700 billion economy, growing at 7–9 percent a year, also attracts investors from Asia. Although it is easy to ridicule India's record, the economy is growing and India's economic ties with East Asia are growing closer every day.

Coping with the Resurgence of China

Other Asian countries have matched or exceeded China's rapid rate of growth. But none has possessed China's combination of huge size, low wages, openness to foreign investment, and determination to become wealthy. The Chinese economy is now far more open to trade and investment than the Japanese and Korean economies were at comparable stages of development.[23] China's share of Asia's trade with the rest of the world has risen to almost 40 percent, surpassing Japan's.

Asian PTAs serve three purposes related to the resurgence of China. First, Asian businesspeople, many of whom are ethnic Chinese with ties to China, do not want to miss out on an opportunity to sell more goods and services to a huge and growing market. Their governments do not want to be left out of the new political alignment that these agreements signify. In sectors where their companies are competitive, bilateral PTAs may well offer them more market access than the WTO's Doha Round is likely to do. Conversely, bilateral PTAs permit long-term protection for uncompetitive sectors threatened by globalization.

Second, since China's future political evolution and long-term intentions in Asia are still unclear, other Asian governments want to enmesh Beijing in as many agreements as possible. Doing so, they believe, raises the price for aggressive behavior. Third, other Asians are keen to negotiate PTAs with each other to avoid becoming even more China-centered than they already are. This leads to the question of just what their new trade relationship with China actually is.

■ The Impact of China's New Role

China's resurgence has rippled through the entire world of manufacturing, but nowhere more forcefully than in Asia. China's role as a production hub has brought about long-term changes in regional trade and investment flows. It has also fostered two related perceptions: first, that economic regionalization justifies the priority assigned to Asian PTAs; and second, that the rest of Asia is much more dependent on China than vice versa.

Both are open to question.

Changes in Trade and Investment Flows

China's exports have soared, but so have its imports. Although the world sees China as a giant export machine, imports into China nearly tripled over five years, from $225 billion in 2000 to $660 billion in 2005. Imports as a ratio of GDP skyrocketed from 4 percent in 1978 to 30 percent in 2005—two and three times larger than the ratio in the United States and Japan, respectively.

China-based companies have become the third largest exporter of electronics products (up from tenth in 2000) but also the second largest importer (up from seventh in 2000). Imported parts and components account for over

50 percent of China's exports and in some manufacturing sectors perhaps as much as 75 percent. It is a sign of the times that almost all of the production of Taiwan's electronics industry has moved to the mainland.

National trade statistics disguise the high degree of intra-industry trade and trade among different divisions of the same company. An estimated 60–70 percent of Chinese exports are sold by foreign firms or by partnerships between foreign firms and Chinese entities. Honda's automobile production in China, for example, uses 120 companies, but only seventeen are Chinese companies; the rest are either joint ventures or subsidiaries.[24]

China's manufactured imports from ASEAN countries and the rest of Asia are typically concentrated in three product areas: parts for office machines, electronic microcircuits, and parts for telecommunications equipment. Demonstrating the intra-industry nature of production networks, China's top *exports* to the rest of East Asia also include parts for office equipment and telecommunications equipment, along with toys and footwear.[25]

Although ASEAN continues to supply China with energy and agricultural raw materials, a growing share of the ASEAN 5's (and increasingly Vietnam's) exports to China consists of manufactured products. Between 1990 and 2004, ASEAN's share of China's imports of manufactures jumped from 31 percent to almost 56 percent. It is marked by increasing specialization and reliance on a relatively small number of product categories. This growing but highly uneven interdependence reflects China's move toward higher value-added production.

Access to China's market also attracts investors. The investment climate in many ASEAN countries needs improvement, but in 2005, foreign direct investment in ASEAN reached a record $38 billion. China, with more than twice the population, attracted about $60 billion in 2004 and $53 billion in 2005.[26] An unknown but surely substantial portion of the money flowing into ASEAN is tied to China-centered production networks.

From a Southeast Asian perspective, the good news is that ASEAN countries are selling more manufactured products to China and attracting more investors. The bad news is that those same countries have lost market share to China in major third-country markets. According to research on postcrisis trade patterns conducted by John Ravenhill of Australian National University, in only one sector/country combination (electrical machinery in Japan) did both the value of imports from ASEAN into US and Japanese markets and ASEAN's share in the total imports of those two countries increase. And in only one additional sector (telecommunications equipment) did the value of imports from ASEAN increase in both markets (even though ASEAN lost market share to China). Ravenhill concludes, however, that to a considerable extent, ASEAN's increased exports to China have offset the losses to China in third-country markets.[27]

Regionalization: Real or Perceived?

Champions of Asia's new regionalism argue that economic interdependence among Asian nations is rising faster than integration with the global economy, and therefore that Asian-only trade pacts are justified. In the last quarter of the twentieth century, East Asia's share of global exports expanded more than threefold to almost 20 percent, but intraregional trade expanded by more than sixfold, more than in any other region.[28] For Asia Major as a whole, the percentage of intraregional trade exceeds trade within NAFTA (the United States, Canada, and Mexico) and begins to approach that within the European Union, as shown in Figure 8.1.

Using a slightly different base, IMF economists calculate that intraregional trade flows as a share of total exports among the major nations in Asia rose from 44 percent in 1985–1991 to 52 percent during 1999–2004. Growth in the rate of such trade spiked most sharply in South Korea and Taiwan, followed by Japan, Singapore, and the Philippines.

Two other indices of market integration—intraregional trade intensity and trade complementarity—have risen likewise.[29] Domestic markets are opening up as growth continues at a steady pace. Intraregional investment is climbing, led by companies from wealthier Asian countries. Even in India, outgoing investment in 2006 almost caught up with what came in.[30] Thanks to the dynamism of Maritime Asia and the gradual lowering of barriers, the globalized sectors of ASEAN 5 economies are partially integrated with those of the + 3 countries.

Nevertheless, the effort to justify Asian PTAs as a reflection of rising economic integration is shaky. Asia's intraregional trade has indeed risen rapidly, but so has integration with the global economy.[31] Roughly half of Asia's trade is with the rest of the world, and Asia has held that share since the early 1990s.[32] Trade openness, defined as the ratio of goods and services trade to GDP, is higher in Asia than in almost any other region. Such openness has stimulated a shift in trade and production patterns, not changes in final demand.

The soaring increase in what is seen as intraregional economic integration in Asia is caused primarily by China-centered production networks, whose output flows to Western consumers.[33] China has actually become *more* dependent on North American and European markets. It follows that other Asians also depend heavily on global markets, albeit indirectly. According to a World Bank study, the dependence of "emerging Asia" on markets in Japan, the EU, and the United States has not diminished very much, if at all.[34]

The near-total liberalization of trade in information and telecommunications technology and products accounts for a large portion of Asia's intraregional trade. Parts and components make up the fastest-growing product cate-

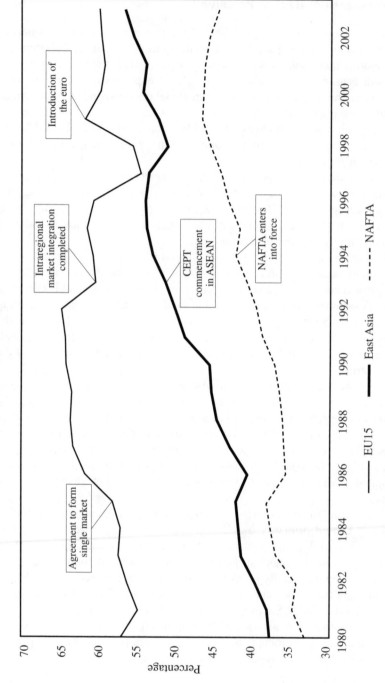

Figure 8.1 Intraregional Trade in Asia Major

Source: METI, derived from data supplied by the IMF and the Board of Foreign Trade, Taiwan.
Note: East Asia includes Japan, China, Korea, Hong Kong, Taiwan, ASEAN, Australia, New Zealand, and India.

gory of traded goods. They account for roughly a quarter of both Asian exports and imports, as opposed to 16–18 percent ten years earlier. Japan is the source for about a third of all regional exports of components for assembly; another 50 percent comes from Taiwan, the Philippines, and South Korea.[35] Today, such components typically end up in China, which also manufactures parts and components, for final assembly. Thanks to production networks, Asia's share of world exports of parts and components is somewhat higher than its share of overall world exports.[36]

Finally, Asia Major's intraregional trade statistics are stoked by China's hunger for energy and raw materials. Trade data disguise the soaring price of commodities like oil and mineral products like iron ore. Australia, a key supplier, figures prominently in this calculus.

In short, the supposed economic regionalization of Asia Major is actually somewhat skewed. It is centered on China-based production networks, concentrated in electronics and telecommunications parts and components, and inflated by the high price of energy and raw materials.

Asymmetrical Dependence?

Asian officials worry that their countries depend much more heavily on the Chinese market than the Chinese do on them. This asymmetrical dependence gives China a strategic advantage in Asia, or so the argument goes. But is this one-way dependence real? It is true that China has become the first or second largest trading partner of almost every country in the region. Economists Francis Ng and Alexander Yeats of the World Bank calculated that from 1985 to 2001, China accounted for the largest or second largest increase in export market share for eleven out of thirteen East Asian countries. From 1995 to 2001, those exports grew at the average annual rate of 11.5 percent, compared to 3.8 percent for world trade as a whole.[37] In 1985, only about a quarter of China's imports came from the rest of Asia (excluding Japan), but by 2001, that total reached 50 percent. From 1995 to 2004, China's share in ASEAN and Japanese exports more than doubled; in the 1990s, the value of ASEAN exports to China quadrupled. Meanwhile, Australia is enjoying a boom in exports of energy, minerals, and raw materials to China.

Many governments in the region now believe that the US market is less important than the Chinese market. Bilateral trade statistics would seem to prove them right. But this is a mistaken perception, because for many products China is only a stopping point rather than a final destination. China sends about a quarter of its exports to the United States, twice as many as it sells to Japan. As China turned toward the United States, the share of its exports destined for the rest of Asia (excluding Japan) dropped from 35 percent to 30 percent.[38]

What these trends suggest is that dependence is a two-way street. China's leaders rely on foreign trade and investment as engines of economic growth.

Chinese authorities promote economic openness and market-oriented reforms not only because trade and investment accelerate the growth of wealth and national power, but also because rising prosperity is the single most important guarantor of the government's perceived legitimacy. That prosperity depends on stability in the region.

In short, asymmetrical dependence is an only partially accurate description. Although individual countries may be more dependent on China than China is on them, China depends heavily on Asian countries as a group for imports and on North American and European markets for both imports and exports. China also depends heavily on foreign capital flows to sustain its current level of growth.

China's real leverage lies less in asymmetrical dependence than in the vast size of its market and the opportunities it offers to all. This combination gives the Chinese considerable leverage that does not need to be exercised explicitly. Only in cases of great importance to Beijing, such as moves affecting the status of Taiwan and Japan's bid to join the United Nations Security Council, does the Chinese government scold or lobby other Asian governments, as it did when Singapore permitted a visit from a former leader of Taiwan. The only major exception to this pattern was China's harsh and public reaction to former prime minister Koizumi's periodic visits to the Yasukuni Shrine. Despite these harangues, China's trade with Japan has steadily risen since the start of the millennium.

■ Prospects for New Trade Architecture

A Single PTA for Asia Major?

The Asian Development Bank and many others are urging Asian governments to harmonize if not standardize the clutch of preferential trade agreements and to bring them into closer conformity with WTO principles. Economist Richard Baldwin points to the Pan-European Cumulation System of 1997, which "multilateralized" intra-European PTAs and imposed common rules of origin. Baldwin believes that the WTO could develop protocols to involve nations excluded from this pact, including those in Asia.[39]

In August 2006, Japan took a step in the direction of a single agreement by formally proposing a Comprehensive Economic Partnership in East Asia (CEPEA), encompassing all sixteen of the current members of Asia Major (ASEAN + 3 and Australia, New Zealand, and India). The CEPEA would exclude agriculture but include rules of origin, services, investment, intellectual property, and other topics not covered in PTAs. (Not surprisingly, it would not contain mandatory dispute settlement and enforcement procedures.) ASEAN secretary-general Ong Keng Yong suggested a target date of 2020 for full implementation, to coincide with the original target date for full implementation of the ASEAN Economic Community (now advanced to 2015). "It can be done," proclaimed Ong. In a breathtaking understatement he added, "All you need is to get all the governments to sign on a piece of paper."[40]

How such an agreement would reconcile the various "noodles" is not clear, and reactions to the Japanese proposal were mixed. By now the reader should be able to predict how various governments line up on Japan's proposal. Singapore, India, and Australia support Japan's general idea, while China, South Korea, and Malaysia are cool.

This debate over CEPEA or a single PTA, or both, for Asia Major is really a proxy for deciding on the identity of a more closely integrated region. That decision in turn determines how concentrated or diluted China's influence will be. Which countries should constitute the proposed trade community? Should it be ASEAN + 3, ASEAN + 3 + 1 (India), or ASEAN + 6 (Asia Major)? Does being "ethnically European" rule out membership, as Mahathir still believes?[41] In the case of finance, where Japan enjoys an implicit leadership position, action is centered in ASEAN + 3, but in the trade world these questions are deliberately left open.

A Free Trade Area of the Asia Pacific?

The possibility of a single, Asia-wide PTA of some kind prompts a search for something to balance or absorb it. Global liberalization is clearly "first-best." But in light of the disappointing results of the WTO's Doha Round thus far and talk of a single PTA for Asians only, a proposed Free Trade Area of the Asia Pacific (FTAAP) has attracted new interest from US policymakers and the transpacific business community. President Bush himself presented the idea to the 2006 APEC summit. Heads of state agreed that free trade across the Pacific was an important long-term goal and agreed to study the idea "as a long-term prospect."

C. Fred Bergsten, director of the Peterson Institute for International Economics[42] and Chairman of APEC's original Eminent Persons Group, argues that APEC members should not merely study the FTAAP idea but should actually launch negotiations to establish it. Bergsten makes five main arguments.

First, an FTAAP would revitalize APEC and thereby ensure that any intra-Asian trade bloc would be firmly nested in a larger transpacific framework, where the interests of the United States and other nonmembers would be protected. Second, since global free trade talks have faltered, a decision to negotiate such an agreement would put pressure on the European Union, India, and Brazil, to modify their negotiating positions in the current Doha Round so that a successful conclusion can be reached. If they do not do so, they could face significant discrimination in the future. A similar dynamic succeeded, he observes, after Uruguay Round talks broke down in 1990, when the United States turned to NAFTA and APEC.

Third, if the current round collapses, an FTAAP would at least guarantee progress toward free trade in half of the world's economy. Liberalization could then be offered to nonmembers on a fully reciprocal basis.[43] Fourth, an FTAAP would group together all current and future FTAs in the Asia-Pacific region, eliminating or at least harmonizing the tariff preferences and conflicting rules of origin that are proliferating in the region. Politically, an FTAAP would reduce the risk that Asian governments would feel they had to choose between China and the United States. Finally, Asians would gain far more from an FTAAP than from any arrangement confined only to Asia.[44] Even a PTA encompassing the current sixteen members of Asia Major would not match the economic gains of a transpacific agreement.

Given US-China tensions, could an FTAAP be successfully concluded? Probably not, at least not in the near term, because of US-China bilateral trade friction.[45] Even the 2007 US-South Korea PTA was extremely difficult to negotiate and included major compromises that might not be acceptable in a US-China context. But as this book has argued, the Asian integration movement demonstrates that process is as important as substance. An FTAAP would symbolize the reawakening of US interest in the Asia-Pacific region. A slow-moving negotiation centered on an FTAAP should therefore be welcomed by Asians seeking alternatives to Chinese influence, however unlikely it is that an FTAAP could ever be successfully concluded and approved by Congress.

Advocating negotiations while suspecting that any resulting agreement might not be approved by Congress could be labeled "un-American." Don't Americans always intend to follow through on their commitments? And aren't practical results more important than "talk shops" and endless negotiations? These are serious questions. But dealing successfully with the Asian integration movement and engaging in the competition for regional influence requires a certain amount of patience, cultural adaptation, and recognition of the importance of process for its own sake.

■ Financial Initiatives

As expressions of Asia's new regionalism, finance and trade occupy separate worlds. Although exchange rates have a strong influence on trade, the two cultures are very different.

Current moves toward closer financial integration are a direct result of the financial crisis of 1997–1998. Nothing demonstrated the vulnerability of Asian governments more vividly than the massive outflows of capital triggered initially by the collapse of Thailand's currency and the hardship that ensued. The crisis mobilized and crystallized ASEAN + 3, gave rise to a series of currency swap agreements, and transformed closer financial integration into a mandate.

The Asian Monetary Fund (AMF), proposed by Japan in 1997, was seen as an alternative to dependence on the IMF and hence as a means of escaping from the IMF's ability to impose conditions designed to bring about needed policy reforms ("conditionality"). But as mentioned in Chapter 6, the United States, supported by the rest of the G-7, certain borrower governments, and China, shot it down. The G-7 governments believed that the AMF would encourage Asian governments to postpone reform and pursue reckless policies in the expectation that they would be bailed out. (This is the so-called moral hazard argument.) Asian governments whose financial systems were in relatively good shape worried that weaker conditionality, implicit in the AMF, would sap investor confidence in their currencies. China had political reasons for opposing an initiative that it could not match and that was already reaping goodwill for its rival. Some saw the Japanese proposal in political terms as an effort to create a yen bloc, but this was not a major element in the debate.

The 2001 report of the East Asia Vision Group argued that greater financial integration, including regional financing arrangements and exchange rate coordination, would enhance financial stability and economic efficiency and minimize vulnerability to future financial shocks associated with globalization.[46] ASEAN + 3 finance ministers routinely endorse closer integration as a means to promote these goals.[47] Implicit in these declarations is the notion that a stronger collective voice would help their governments resist potentially destabilizing conditions imposed by the IMF.

Left to their own devices, banks and other sources of credit would follow market forces. But Asian governments want to preserve their influence over financial institutions for a variety of reasons that have nothing to do with efficiency. State control enables them to mobilize capital for social development, direct resources to state-owned enterprises, and (in some cases) skim off profits.

Unlike the market in traded goods, the market in financial instruments is nowhere near the point where governments feel a need to catch up with it. Asian financial markets are small, fragmented, somewhat closed, not fully transparent, and oriented to the US dollar rather than to each other.

Many Asian governments have also built up huge foreign currency reserves as a defense against future speculative attack. As of 2006, for example, Thailand's and South Korea's reserves exceeded 30 percent of GDP, Malaysia's reached nearly 60 percent, and Singapore topped them all at 100 percent.[48] China's reserves alone approach $1 trillion. Most Asian governments have also adopted more flexible currency regimes that make them less vulnerable to a future crisis.

T. J. Pempel compares Asian integration to a steeplechase and notes that much depends on the agreed location of the finish line. Like many others, he

observes that agreement on the desirability of financial and monetary cooperation is not matched by implementation of the necessary steps to bring it
about, such as monitoring and surveillance mechanisms. Nevertheless, discussions of financial integration within ASEAN + 3 have yielded more tangible
results than many other integration initiatives, and Pempel believes that financial arrangements could acquire even more of a regionally integrated character than they have to date.[49] This is all the more remarkable because there is
no ASEAN + 3 PTA and little likelihood of one in the foreseeable future.

There are at least five reasons why ASEAN + 3's financial negotiators
have not only produced tangible results but also achieved a greater degree of
institutionalization than the multitude of PTAs would suggest.

First, the massive loss of investor confidence that triggered and spread the
1997–1998 financial crisis demanded remedial action. The crisis shocked
Asian governments into the twin realizations that they could not depend on the
United States and that they needed to do more to help themselves. Second,
financial negotiators are technocrats who operate in a secretive and exclusive
sphere. They are relatively immune from day-to-day political interference, if
only because few politicians understand what they do. Their activities are not
seen as politically sensitive. When it comes to actions affecting major banks,
of course, their freedom of maneuver is constrained, but they usually operate
out of the limelight.

Third, and by the same token, ASEAN + 3 discussions have been relatively free of the tensions and bickering between China and Japan that have stalled
progress on other fronts. Japan, which retains a competitive advantage in
finance, sees an opportunity to move out from under China's shadow and to
exert leadership without undue interference from Beijing. Chinese leaders evidently believe that both the substance of financial integration and the appearance of cooperating with Japan on a constructive initiative promote China's
long-term interests, as indeed they do. The major financial hubs in Asia are
Tokyo, Hong Kong, and Singapore, but Shanghai is capitalizing on its ties
with Hong Kong to regain its position as China's most important domestic
financial center. In 2006, Goldman Sachs became the first global financial
group to place its Asia-based head of investment banking in China.[50]

Fourth, despite their widely differing motivations and experiences,
ASEAN + 3 governments have found it in their interest to design financial integration initiatives that provide a limited haven from the demands imposed by
international financial institutions without undermining their credit standing.[51]
This time around, they face no opposition from the United States or the IMF.

Finally, in many parts of Asia, financial markets are still weak and slow-
moving, and negotiators share an interest in improving their health. Mergers,
acquisitions, and the deregulation of financial services are taking place, but
financial disclosure requirements, risk assessment capability, coordination of
fiscal and monetary policies, and other prerequisites of true financial integra-

tion are a long way off. Too many banks are under the thumb of political authorities and local elites and are forced to finance nonviable enterprises and speculative real estate deals. Regulations governing portfolio investment and financial aspects of foreign direct investment differ in each country and are often unnecessarily burdensome. Residual capital controls, the lack of transparency, overstretched banks, and the lack of alternative credit mechanisms also help explain why financial markets and institutions are weak and why financial integration has a long way to go.[52]

The Chiang Mai Initiative

The most concrete achievement of ASEAN + 3 as a group is the so-called Chiang Mai Initiative (CMI). At a meeting of ASEAN + 3 finance ministers in Chiang Mai, Thailand, in May 2000, ministers agreed to set up an expanded ASEAN swap arrangement involving ASEAN as a whole as well as a network of bilateral swap and repurchase agreement facilities among the ASEAN + 3 countries.

Once existing commitments are put in place, the sum of all swap arrangements will exceed $80 billion. No single country will have access to this sum. For countries with large economies, such as South Korea, available funds will be small. But Thailand, for instance, will have access to about four times as much as its IMF quota.[53] Use of these funds would not displace the IMF, since only 20 percent (originally 10 percent) of available funds can be used without IMF approval.

For larger countries, the swap agreements negotiated thus far are inadequate compared to potential need. But they are a psychological life preserver, and psychology mitigates market volatility. Although fixed exchange rates have largely disappeared and investors have become more confident, most governments practice "managed floats."

Plans are afoot to pool the various bilateral swap agreements into a single multilateral agreement, with earmarking. Each country would continue to manage its own reserves, however. How this combination would work is still being discussed.

The CMI also commits ministers to facilitate the exchange of consistent and timely data and information and to set up a system of economic and financial monitoring and surveillance.[54] Because of lingering sensitivities about national sovereignty and noninterference, this process is known officially as the Economic Review and Policy Dialogue Forum.

The Asian Bond Market Initiative

Taking diplomatic advantage of the depth and sophistication of Japan's financial sector, Japan's Ministry of Finance and the Asian Development Bank are taking the lead in the attempted creation of a regional bond market. Both METI and the Foreign Ministry support this proposal, lending unusual cohesion to the Japanese position.[55] Equally remarkable, considering that the proposal comes from Japan, China supports it as well. In 2003, central bankers from eleven East Asian countries announced the establishment of a $1 billion Asian Bond Fund.

The idea behind the Asian Bond Market Initiative (ABMI) is to mobilize Asia's considerable domestic savings and make them available for domestic investment without channeling them through foreign markets. Other goals include making more credit instruments available to small and medium enterprises, ending excessive reliance on bank borrowing, reducing dependence on the US dollar, and preventing the financial mismatch that caused the July 1997 collapse of the Thai baht to balloon into a regional crisis (short-term borrowing in foreign currency to finance long-term lending in domestic currencies). Related goals include broadening the investor base, reducing foreign exchange risks, and strengthening the credit ratings of the issuers by enhancing the capability of local bond rating agencies.

The ABMI entails two distinct projects: a medium-term drive to develop and strengthen domestic local-currency bond markets and a long-term effort to create regional markets. Bonds would be issued in local currencies (and eventually in a basket of Asian currencies) by multilateral development banks, foreign government agencies, and Asia-based multinational corporations.[56] To assist other governments in financial matters, Tokyo has established a Japan Financial Technical Assistance program.[57]

An Asian Currency Basket

Another idea under consideration in ASEAN + 3 and the Asian Development Bank is an Asian Currency Unit (ACU), or currency basket. The former term is a misnomer because it calls to mind the European Currency Unit, a predecessor of the euro, which is not at all what Asians have in mind in the short and medium term. The idea is to establish a common basket of currencies as a peg for individual exchange rates. China has already announced that it has pegged its currency to a basket instead of to the dollar, but the exact content and weight of the basket are unclear.

Economist John Williamson of the Peterson Institute for International Economics argues that the ASEAN 5, the + 3 countries, Hong Kong, and Taiwan might benefit from a common basket. For example, a common basket would preserve the stability of intra-Asian trading relationships even if third-country exchange rates changed.[58] China, however, reportedly resists the idea of adding Taiwan's currency to a common basket, proving once again that even finance is not immune from politics. Thus far, ASEAN + 3 governments have merely agreed to study the potential utility of regional currency "units" (plural, reflecting some resistance to the ACU idea). At this point, the exercise is mainly academic. All that is happening so far is ad hoc coordination on currency management.

Reforms such as full disclosure, transparency, surveillance, and other features of a credible supervisory and regulatory infrastructure will take years. Without them, realization of the ABMI and the ACU proposals could pose competitiveness and systemic risk concerns for US and global financial markets.[59] But the roadmap is clear. The effort to promote financial integration already helps encourage "best practices" in the financial sector and the sharing of information. In the language of this book, anything that facilitates efficient cross-border financial transactions in Asia Major will speed up the resurgence of Maritime Asia, which is where almost all the capital is generated or ends up.

■ Conclusion

Economic regionalism in Asia Major is not just about economics. Indeed, companies engaged in multilateral production networks have a far greater impact on regional economic integration than FTAs, and financial integration is still at a very early stage. The real significance of the various initiatives described in this chapter is political.

Trade agreements and financial initiatives are altering the political geography of Asia in at least four ways. First, both sets of accords are forging new links between two quite different subregions: Northeast Asia and Southeast Asia. Trade and investment are flowing most rapidly along this north-south axis. By contrast, north-north trade agreements languish as heavily bracketed drafts, and south-south agreements are shallow and slow-moving.

Second, trade agreements are slowly knitting together various US allies and partners and connecting them more closely with governments lacking formal security ties with the United States. China, initially wary of multilateral dealings, has become a skilled practitioner of commercial diplomacy, outpacing Japan. India, Japan, Australia, and New Zealand have entered the competition for PTAs while retaining or strengthening their bonds with Washington. ASEAN is a diplomatic hub of this activity, but actual trade flows respond to China-centered production networks and China's hunger for energy and raw materials.

Third, trade agreements have a spillover effect. China's courtship of ASEAN inspired a bouquet of PTAs from rivals. The PTA between the United States and South Korea, concluded in 2007, may also set a chain reaction in motion. Unwilling to be left out, Japan is seeking to revive its own PTA negotiations with South Korea. Meanwhile, Japan's leading business organization has called for a new "economic partnership agreement" with Washington.[60]

Japan does not oppose the proposed FTAAP but has apparently gone along with the move to consign it to the category of "long-term goal," thus implicitly acquiescing in "Asia first" as a negotiating priority.

Fourth, financial negotiations have legitimized and strengthened the role of ASEAN + 3 as the core of Asian regionalism. What started as the Chiang Mai Initiative has become institutionalized (in the "soft," nonenforceable meaning of that term). Unlike Asian PTAs, Asian financial initiatives in their current form do not undermine the global system. Nowhere does the "Vision" statement declare that regional trade and financial integration must surpass integration with the rest of the world in order for the envisaged East Asian Economic Community to justify its name. But it often seems that champions of Asian regionalism want to make that case.

No rational Asian trade minister could look at Asia's role in transpacific and global trade and conclude that Asia would benefit from a self-contained trade arrangement. Indeed, proposals for a PTA linking Asia Major and excluding the United States are couched in terms that envisage liberalization with the rest of the world as well. The problem is sequencing. Emphasizing "Asia first" rather than a more global perspective, these advocates downgrade the WTO and consign transpacific agreements to a later date.

One could argue that Asian governments should promote a free market within ASEAN, within Asia Major, within APEC, and in the WTO all at the same time. But negotiating resources are limited. More to the point, the "Asia first" option has the most political appeal for Asians. Overcoming this tilt will take concerted effort on the part of non-Asian powers, particularly the United States.

■ Notes

1. East Asia Vision Group, "Towards an East Asian Community," esp. par. 21–53.

2. Martin Wolf, "A Korean-American Strand Enters Trade's Spaghetti Bowl," *Financial Times*, April 4, 2007, p. 11.

3. Michael Yahuda, "The Evolving Asian Order," in Shambaugh, *Power Shift*, p. 350.

4. Frankel, *Regional Trading Blocs*, p. 22, table 2.1.

5. Thomas Fuller, "Southeast Asia Group Seeks to Accelerate a Trade Zone," *New York Times*, August 23, 2006, p. C5. The ASEAN secretariat issues annual data.

6. Goh Sui Noi, "ASEAN States Chase the Chinese Investment Dollar," *The Straits Times*, November 2, 2006, http://taiwansecurity.org/ST/2006/ST-021106.htm.

7. Alan Beattie, "Trading Ritual and Reality: How Global Business Reduces the Need for Bilateral Pacts," *Financial Times*, September 19, 2007, p. 11.

8. Regional free trade agreements and customs unions are the subject of Article XXIV of the General Agreement on Tariffs and Trade and Article V of the General Agreement on Trade in Services. The texts are available on the WTO's website, www.wto.org.

9. For a more complete discussion, see Patterson, "Rethinking the WTO's Enabling Clause."

10. Australian economists Ross Garnaut and David Vines propose "Open Trade Areas" in their paper "Regional Free Trade Areas: Sorting Out the Tangled Spaghetti." See also Holmes and Falconer, *Open Regionalism?*

11. Edward J. Lincoln develops this argument in some detail in *East Asian Economic Regionalism.*

12. Scollay and Gilbert, *New Regional Trading Arrangements in the Asia Pacific?* pp. 57–58.

13. Kawai, "Trade and Investment Cooperation and Integration in East Asia," in Asian Development Bank, *Asian Economic Cooperation and Integration,* pp. 182–183.

14. Ernest H. Preeg of the Manufacturers Alliance/MAPI makes the argument that an intra-Asian PTA would inflict significant damage on US exports to Asia, three-quarters of which are manufactured goods. See, for example, www.mapi.net/html/prelease .cfm?release_id=2054.

15. Frost, "Implications of Regional Economic Integration," pp. 403–404.

16. For a detailed history of this progression, see Munakata, *Transforming East Asia,* chap. 6, esp. pp. 106–112.

17. T. J. Pempel and S. Urata, "Japan: A New Move Toward Bilateral Trade Arrangements," in V. K. Aggarwal and S. Urata, eds., *Bilateral Trade Agreements in the Asia-Pacific: Origins, Evolution, and Implications* (London: Routledge Curzon, 2006), pp. 75–94, cited in Pempel, "The Race to Connect East Asia," p. 248.

18. Because of the Australia–New Zealand Closer Economic Relations Trade Agreement, the two countries are negotiating jointly with ASEAN as + 2, but each has also concluded separate trade agreements.

19. "The Slow Progress of Japan's Economic Partnership Agreement with Indonesia, Philippines, and ASEAN," SEAPSNet, December 5, 2006, www.siiaonline.org.

20. Ibid., p. 1. India subsequently offered to reduce the tariffs on palm oil from 90 to 60 percent, on tea from 100 to 50 percent, and on pepper from 70 to 50 percent. See Asher, "India's Rising Role in Asia," p. 32.

21. Singh, "India's 'Look East' Policy," p. 1.

22. Asher, "India's Rising Role in Asia," pp. 13–15.

23. In a landmark study of foreign investment in China, MIT professor Yasheng Huang asked why domestic firms cannot supply more of China's needs. His answer is that domestic firms face significant constraints, notably the persistence of political favors bestowed on state-owned enterprises and lingering internal barriers to domestic commerce. See Huang, *Selling China.*

24. *Financial Times,* April 17, 2006, p. 16.

25. Ravenhill, "Trade Developments in East Asia Since the Financial Crisis," table 5.

26. Thomas Fuller, "Southeast Asia Group Seeks to Accelerate a Trade Zone," *New York Times*, August 23, 2006, p. C5.

27. Ravenhill, "Trade Developments in East Asia Since the Financial Crisis," pp. 9–11.

28. Ng and Yeats, "Major Trade Trends in East Asia," pp. 2–3. These numbers exclude Japan but include Hong Kong, Taiwan, and Mongolia.

29. The trade intensity index measures the ratio of a bloc's share of intrabloc trade to the bloc's share in world trade. The trade complementarity index measures how well the export performance of one country or group meets the import needs of another country or group. For example, if no good exported by one country is imported by another, the complementarity index is zero.

30. Dealogic, cited in graph form in Tucker and Leahy, "On the March: How Corporate India Is Finding the Confidence to Go Global."

31. For a comprehensive review of East Asia's relationships within itself and with the world, see Lincoln, *East Asian Economic Regionalism.* Lincoln presents extensive data to support his conclusion that the region is more closely integrated with the rest of the world than within itself.

32. China Strategic Advisory, courtesy of Daniel Rosen. "Asia" is defined here as ASEAN + 3 plus Taiwan and Hong Kong.

33. See, for example, Lincoln, *East Asian Economic Regionalism*, pp. 71, 113.

34. Zebregs, "Intraregional Trade in Emerging Asia," p. 18. "Emerging Asia" includes China, Hong Kong, India, South Korea, the ASEAN 5, and Taiwan.

35. Ng and Yeats, "Major Trade Trends in East Asia," pp. 56–57.

36. Gaulier, Lemoine, and Unlal-Kesenci, "China's Emergence and the Reorganisation of Trade Flows in Asia," p. 12, and figs. 1, 2.

37. Ng and Yeats, "Major Trade Trends in East Asia," tables 6.1, 6.2.

38. Ibid., pp. 10–14.

39. Baldwin discusses this idea in "Multilateralising Regionalism."

40. "A Pan-Asian Free Trade Deal in the Making?" SEAPSNet, August 11, 2006, www.siiaonline.org.

41. Mahathir, "Let Asians Build Their Own Future Regionalism," pp. 14–15.

42. In September 2006, the Institute for International Economics was renamed the Peter G. Peterson Institute for International Economics.

43. C. Fred Bergsten, "The Free Trade Area of the Asia Pacific Is the Next Step Forward for APEC (and for the World Trading System)." This paper and other Bergsten commentaries are available at www.petersoninstitute.org. For more on APEC's original commitment to "free and open trade in the Asia Pacific," see Eminent Persons Group, *Implementing the APEC Vision*, esp. pp. 58–59.

44. Scollay, "Preliminary Assessment of the FTAAP Proposal," chart titled "Economic Effects."

45. For a concise summary of US-China trade tensions, see Hufbauer, Wong, and Sheth, *US-China Trade Disputes.*

46. East Asia Vision Group, "Towards an East Asian Community," par. 27–33, 44–53.

47. See, for example, "Joint Media Statement of the Eight ASEAN Economic Ministers and the Ministers of People's Republic of China, Japan, and Republic of Korea," Vientiane, Laos, September 29, 2005.

48. Grimes, "East Asian Financial Regionalism," p. 15.

49. Pempel, "The Race to Connect East Asia," pp. 249–251.

50. Francesco Guerrera, "Goldman Places Asia Head in China," *Financial Times*, May 27, 2005, p. 16.

51. Ibid., pp. 18–20.

52. Cowen et al., "Financial Integration in Asia," p. 5 ff.

53. Ibid., p. 7.

54. Henning, *East Asian Financial Cooperation*, chap. 3.

55. Interview with Yoshihiro Otsuji, deputy director, General, Economic and Industrial Policy Bureau, Ministry of the Economy, Trade, and Industry (METI), Tokyo, May 18, 2006. METI is interested in encouraging small and medium enterprises by facilitating the securitization of bonds and thereby reducing excessive reliance on banks.

56. See, for example, the keynote address given by a Japanese Finance Ministry official to a high-level ASEAN + 3 seminar on the Asian Bond Market Initiative, at www.mof.go.jp/english/if/hls20030301b.htm.

57. Oral presentation by Shigeki Kimura, director, Research Division, International Bureau, Ministry of Finance, to a Japan Chair Forum on the Asian Bond Markets Initiative, Center for Strategic and International Affairs, Washington, DC, September 14, 2005.

58. Williamson, "A Currency Basket for East Asia."

59. Personal e-mail from Karen Shaw Petrou, co-founder and Managing Partner of Federal Financial Analytics, Inc., September 15, 2006.

60. "Bush, Abe Seek Deeper Economic Ties, Industry Seeks Bilateral Deal," *Inside U.S. Trade* 24, no. 47 (2007): p. 7.

9

Foreign Policy and Security Cooperation

This chapter surveys two noneconomic aspects of Asia's new regionalism: foreign policy and security cooperation (including energy). Like the previous chapter, it assesses the changes both inspiring and wrought by the integration movement. Taken together, the two chapters demonstrate that economic and security concerns in Asia Major overlap substantially (but not entirely). They also demonstrate why Asians perceive China's resurgence as far more of an opportunity than a threat.

■ Foreign Policy

Hot Economics, Chilly Politics?

Amused by the apparent contradiction between booming trade and investment and frosty political relations, political wags have coined the phrase "hot economics, chilly politics." As a working hypothesis to describe the integration movement, this phrase contains much truth. But it suggests that economics and political-security factors are pulling in different directions: economics works in favor of integration and foreign policy considerations work against it. A related hypothesis is that, despite closer economic integration, cooperation in conventional security, nontraditional security, and foreign policy is moribund to a more or less equal extent.

Asian governments are intensifying economic engagement with China, but they are hedging their bets by strengthening their military ties with the United States. Observing this trend, some Asian policy experts are not convinced that economic and security initiatives should march forward in tandem. They argue that governments should stick to an economic agenda and postpone further security initiatives until markets become more integrated and mutual trust more solidly established.[1]

In my view, however, the supposed contrast between economic and security goals and interests is not clear-cut. Asian leaders see strong connections between economic growth, political stability, military modernization, national sovereignty, and regional order. Establishing an economic climate that provides jobs for young men who might otherwise be tempted to join extremist movements is a security imperative. Just as economic cooperation in Asia contributes to a more stable security climate, so security cooperation contributes to a safe and peaceful environment, without which trade and investment would not grow.

Although there are vast differences between trade officials and business-people on the one hand and military officers and security experts on the other, behavior and priorities in the two fields are quite similar. They both feature some degree of mutual mistrust; an emphasis on process and dialogue; limited, nonenforceable agreements, usually between pairs of countries; vaguely worded regional declarations; voluntary resolution of some disputes and deliberate neglect of others; preservation of good relations with the United States; India's debut as an Asian partner; thinly veiled Sino-Japanese rivalry; and accommodation of China's resistance to anything that smacks of US containment or recognition of Taiwan.

Moreover, traditional security, nontraditional security, and foreign policy are quite different. Common nontraditional security challenges, such as energy, piracy, illegal trafficking, disease, and pollution, have important economic implications. They also undermine national sovereignty and threaten political stability. These threats are on the rise in Asia as well as in the rest of the world. Efforts to counter them do not fit the "hot economics, chilly politics" model, as I attempt to show.

Is Distance Destiny? Proximity to China

China's impact on the foreign policies of the other nations in the region is similarly complex. In the world of commerce, proximity to large markets is an advantage. China-oriented trading hubs located just beyond Beijing's administrative reach, notably Hong Kong, Macao, and Taiwan, have prospered. But when it comes to foreign policy, governments in mainland Southeast Asia do not have the luxury of forgetting about their giant neighbor. An elephant in one's living room presents a greater challenge than an elephant seen through binoculars, especially if merely by flapping its ears it knocks over your grandmother's tea set.

This proximity-is-destiny thesis has limits, however. Vietnam confronted China for centuries and maintained its autonomy. China's neighbor Thailand is very accommodating toward China, but Thailand owes its national survival to a policy of accommodating everybody. Myanmar has largely slipped into China's orbit, but it has few choices. Ethnic Chinese in mainland Southeast

Asia identify themselves more closely with China than those located further to the south, but Beijing appears to have no intention of mobilizing them against their governments, as it was accused of doing almost half a century ago.

Farther away from China, attitudes seem to vary according to domestic politics and historical memories. According to opinion polls, fully a third of Indonesians, mindful of China's support for communist-inspired disturbances in the 1960s, register little or no confidence in China's leadership, and a majority holds "mainly negative" views of China's military buildup. A majority of Indians, however, register "mainly positive views" of that buildup.[2] Singapore, a mainly Chinese city, welcomes China's resurgence but has been the most ardent champion of adding India to the integration mix. South Koreans have tilted away from the United States and toward China; nevertheless, sandwiched as they are between China and Japan, they have also reached out to New Delhi. In short, distance from major power conveys more freedom of choice, but many other factors influence how governments exercise that freedom. With the exception of very few issues (notably the status of Taiwan), and with due attention to avoiding any initiative that smacks of anti-Chinese "containment," China's neighbors have plenty of room to maneuver. And they are geniuses at maneuvering.

North Korea and Myanmar

Most governments in Asia are regional activists or at least engaged observers. They think of themselves as members of a region and participate in regional diplomacy. But there are two exceptions: Myanmar and North Korea. Both of these regimes pose serious challenges for the rest of Asia and thus offer a means of measuring the effectiveness of the Asian integration movement with respect to foreign policy. North Korea is heavily armed and has the potential to destabilize the region or even trigger a war; Myanmar represses dissidents and minorities, engages in illegal trafficking, and is an embarrassment to ASEAN and a threat to the rest of the region.

Asian responses to North Korea and Myanmar are roughly divided between governments in northern and southern parts of the region, respectively. China, Japan, and South Korea are members of the Six-Party Talks on North Korea. Southeast Asians, excluded from the six-party process, have devoted far more time and attention to pressing for change in Myanmar. Far from contributing to regionwide integration, these two challenges have revealed the limitations of the integration process.

North Korea. The Six-Party Talks, which bring together North and South Korea, China, Japan, the United States, and Russia, fall outside the scope of this book because they are subregional and transpacific in composition rather than pan-Asian. Nevertheless, they have regionwide significance for the integration movement, especially if they become institu-tionalized.

When ASEAN was established in 1967, North Korea was seen as one part of a larger communist threat. Indonesia had just emerged from a bloody communist-led uprising. Communists were making gains in Vietnam, Laos, and Cambodia. China was in the throes of the Cultural Revolution, and its foreign policy preached revolution and anti-imperialism. Beijing formally embraced North Korean dictator Kim Il Sung and dismissed the rulers of South Korea and Japan as lackeys of the United States.

In subsequent decades, the North Korean problem lost much of its region-wide significance and shrank back into a relatively isolated case. It still posed an overwhelming threat to South Korea (and by extension to the United States and Japan), but the wave of communism had been confined and China was in the process of turning outward. For Southeast Asians, North Korea was more of an oddity than a threat.

Since the 1990s, developments in Pyongyang have once again acquired a regional flavor. Pyongyang's nuclear weapons program menaces Japan and perhaps the United States and Australia, and its 1998 missile test over Japanese territory prompted Tokyo to sign up for the US missile defense pro-gram. Former prime minister Abe and many of his colleagues support chang-ing the constitution to give Japan more military options, which raises hackles in Beijing and Seoul. That impetus gained strength when North Korea tested a nuclear bomb in October 2006. But the goal of Pyongyang's stilted bombast seems to be bargaining clout rather than war. Meanwhile, Pyongyang is open-ing its clamshell just enough to allow fenced-off investment zones, to which advocates of South Korea's "sunshine policy" have responded with enthusi-asm, putting another strain on Seoul's relations with Tokyo.

To generalize crudely, North Korea represents a conflict between nuclear proliferation, which other Asians oppose, and noninterference, which other Asians support. But virtually all the governments of the region support the Six-Party Talks because the prospect of nuclear weapons in the hands of a secretive, anti-American, totalitarian dictatorship is frightening. Moreover, South Korean investment in Southeast Asia and India is extensive; any shock on the Korean peninsula that temporarily froze or diverted South Korean busi-ness activity would have repercussions elsewhere. Failure to contain a crisis could also trigger military action on the part of the United States, which other Asians would consider extremely destabilizing. Even if such retaliation were limited to "surgical" strikes, North Korea would surely respond in kind. Thus, there should be ample incentive for a pan-Asian foreign policy initiative aimed at securing lasting peace on the Korean peninsula.

Reality dictates otherwise, however. Containing North Korea's nuclear weapons program is monopolized by the governments that constitute the Six-Party Talks: the + 3 countries (China, Japan, and South Korea) and

North Korea, plus the United States and Russia. Most other governments in Asia Major have neither the economic leverage nor the military resources to be invited in. Australia has both but is not seen as a major player that far north; Canberra has enough to cope with in the island region of the southern Pacific and in Southeast Asia. Indonesia's president Yudhoyono has offered his good offices, but so far no one in the six-party process wants to broaden the circle.

Nevertheless, a process that includes a few selected Southeast Asians might prove useful. Indonesia's offer to help mediate tensions on the Korean peninsula only seems odd if one disregards the large investment that South Korean companies have in Indonesia and the diplomatic skills and initiatives of Indonesia's current president. The United States would have to be involved in parallel, of course, but under which "roof" and through which process could be decided diplomatically. To avoid creating a new institution, diplomats could set up a subgroup within the ARF framework.

Myanmar. During the 1970s and 1980s, when ASEAN was smaller and less diverse than it is now, members of ASEAN often took a common position on international issues. Occasionally they still do. But Myanmar poses an especially difficult challenge to ASEAN governments. ASEAN leaders favor engagement but have trouble agreeing on more specific measures. The other governments of Asia Major are even more divided.[3]

Myanmar is a patchwork nation. It boasted a flourishing Buddhist empire in the twelfth and thirteenth centuries, but even then rulers in its upland capital city, Pagan, exercised no real authority in the Chin, Kachin, or Shan hills. Even lower Burma was considered alien.[4] In the nineteenth century, the British overthrew the monarchy, uprooted the existing social order, hammered down the borders that we know today, and pacified the country. Burma was occupied by the Japanese during World War II and became independent in 1948.

The end of colonial rule witnessed a resurgence of centuries-old tensions between the dominant Burman people and ethnic minorities and hill peoples fighting against repression and seeking more autonomy. In 1962, a group of military officers led by General Ne Win overthrew the democratically elected government. Faced with ethnic revolts and a communist insurgency supported by China until the 1970s, the government had its hands full merely keeping the country together, and the leadership's "Burmese Way to Socialism" was an economic failure. Another military coup took place in 1988.

This history helps to explain the military regime's near-fanatical insistence on national unity and sovereignty. Even as they fire on demonstrators and arrest monks, as they did in 2007, military authorities see themselves as representatives of the only institution capable of preventing the country from disintegrating and falling victim to aggressive foreigners. At the same time, they have proven to be both inept and highly corrupt.

Establishing democracy and building legitimate civilian institutions runs counter to the self-interest of the rulers. To keep themselves in power, Burmese leaders have compiled one of the contemporary world's worst human rights records, especially in minority areas. To augment the country's meager revenues they have relied directly or indirectly on drug trafficking, smuggling, money laundering, and other illegal activities. In 2006, they abruptly moved the administrative capital from the maritime city of Yangon (Rangoon) to Pyinmana, now called Nay Pyi Taw (or in some spellings Naypitaw). The new capital is a relatively remote crossing point 250 miles (400 kilometers) north of Yangon in the central part of the country.

Nobel prizewinner and political activist Aung San Suu Kyi, daughter of a famous general who led the fight against Japan in the latter part of World War II, threatens everything the military regime stands for. Founder of the National League for Democracy, she has relentlessly promoted democratic reform. Since the early 1990s, she has spent more than a decade in jail or under house arrest. To her worldwide admirers she is a courageous symbol of freedom; her less ardent supporters decry her house arrest but wish that she and her party would be a bit more open to political compromise.

Myanmar did not join ASEAN until 1997 but has sent a representative to virtually every available pan-Asian and interregional forum since then. These include not only ASEAN + 3, the ASEAN Regional Forum, and the Asia-Europe Meeting (ASEM), but also BIMSTEC, the Greater Mekong Subregion Development Program, the Indian-backed Ganga-Mekong Cooperation Program, and the Thai-sponsored Ayeyawady-Chao Phraya-Mekong Economic Strategy group.[5] Burmese officials now pay lip service to regional cooperation even as they limit foreign access and discourage foreign influence.

ASEAN members admitted Myanmar to full membership partly because Myanmar falls geographically within Southeast Asia and they saw no alternative, and partly because they hoped that regional engagement and expanding trade would soften the regime's brass fist. Thus far, the gamble has failed. Myanmar's military regime went along with Bali Concord II and other expressions of support for democracy, believing (correctly) that the principles of national sovereignty and noninterference would protect it. In 2007, the regime extended for another year the house arrest of Aung San Suu Kyi. According to one report, Myanmar's official newspaper declared that she will "never" be released until she abandons her policies, and even if she is, "the release will bring no changes."[6] Meanwhile, demands for more autonomy on the part of Myanmar's ethnic minorities and street demonstrations in Myanmar's major cities continue to be met with violence. Reports written by UN envoys have branded the regime's practices as unacceptable violations of inherent human rights.

The human rights situation in Myanmar poses ASEAN's most acute political and diplomatic dilemma. It is an embarrassment to the rest of ASEAN and an obstacle to closer integration. "We can't become [the] ASEAN Community that we have envisaged ourselves to be," said Indonesian foreign minister Hassan Wirayuda in 2006, "until and unless the promotion and protection of human rights is pervasive in our region."[7]

China and India have far more influence in Myanmar than all of ASEAN combined, but for reasons described below, neither is prepared to help. Neither is Russia, which is supplying arms and a small nuclear research center. The governments of Laos, Cambodia, and Vietnam are too weak and unsympathetic to political intervention to be of much help. That leaves the problem sitting squarely in the lap of the ASEAN 5.

Myanmar was in line to assume the rotating chairmanship of ASEAN's Standing Committee in 2005 and thus to become ASEAN's public face, but strenuous diplomatic efforts behind the scenes persuaded the regime to pass up its turn. Since then Myanmar has entertained some visitors from the rest of ASEAN but has rebuffed official visitors desiring to speak with Aung San Suu Kyi, including the foreign ministers of Malaysia and the Philippines. Rejection of Malaysia's foreign minister was particularly galling, since the 2005 ASEAN summit had agreed on his visit. As is typically the case in ASEAN gatherings, Myanmar's representatives displayed an accommodating and nonconfrontational attitude and then returned home to business as usual. The regime evidently prefers to deal with the United Nations rather than with ASEAN and permitted a UN envoy to speak with Aung San Suu Kyi in 2003 and again in 2006.

Neighboring Thailand has generally avoided expressing public concern about the current regime. Thailand is Myanmar's largest trading partner, accounting for more than a third of its trade and the bulk of its trade with ASEAN. Since the end of the 1980s, Thai companies have invested well over $1 billion in Myanmar. Thailand's flawed democracy and the military coup of 2006 disqualify it for human rights leadership. In 2006, Thailand's new military leader was the first ASEAN head of state to visit the government of Myanmar in its new capital.

Thailand's nonconfrontational stance is understandable. Thailand has a history of border clashes with Myanmar. It already houses some 160,000 refugees in nine camps, and more are expected to arrive.[8] Bangkok has long complained that large supplies of drugs are entering the country from Myanmar. In 2001, fighting in Shan territory spilled over into Thailand, resulting in a serious border clash and many fatalities. From Bangkok's perspective, any move that destabilizes the current regime could produce more turmoil.

Energy is also a factor in the Thai calculus. Thailand has joined China and India in a quest for exclusive energy exploration and production rights in the Bay of Bengal. The two countries have opened free-trade zones on the border. During then prime minister Thaksin's visit in 2006, the governments agreed to resume the timber trade despite well-known environmental risks and concerns about the rights of minorities. Bangkok is also providing funds for road construction, infrastructure development, and dams. A large but unknown share of the necessary equipment will come from Thailand. South Korea is also providing assistance in this area.

Indonesia, located far away from Myanmar, is taking a different approach from neighboring Thailand. Indonesia's president Yudhoyono, a military man with credibility in the eyes of Burmese generals, strongly supports democracy and has made that clear to Myanmar's leaders. Jakarta's approach is neither to publicize human rights abuses nor to press for access to Aung San Suu Kyi but to offer to share, if asked, lessons learned from Indonesia's experience with political transition and economic reform.[9] Indonesia hopes that this active but restrained approach will yield better results and "demystify" rigid and outdated concepts of absolute national sovereignty and noninterference.[10]

Besides ASEAN, China and India are actively pursuing engagement with Myanmar, but for reasons having nothing to do with human rights. Both governments have their eyes on Myanmar's strategic location as well as its natural gas, which together with minerals, timber, and fisheries constitutes the country's most desirable resource.

Beijing exercises far more influence on Myanmar than India, especially in the northern part of the country. In the period 1997–2007 more than a million Chinese are believed to have moved to Myanmar.[11] China is proposing a Chinese-built road connecting Myanmar with southern China. In 2005, China offered to invest in such a pipeline and the two governments signed a memorandum launching the idea. An oil pipeline through Myanmar to southern China would short-circuit Beijing's reliance on long, US-patrolled sea routes from the Persian Gulf. (Whether the pipeline will ever be completed and be cost-effective are different questions.) China has also courted the regime with foreign aid and commercial diplomacy, including free-trade zones on the border and other privileges.

Not wanting to be outdone, and keeping a watchful eye on China, India has also pursued a policy of active engagement with the regime. In addition to energy, India hopes that Myanmar will clean out border areas harboring armed rebels operating in India's extreme northeast, where fighting has claimed thousands of lives. In 2006, India's president visited Myanmar and signed three memorandums of understanding, one of which pertains to the transport of natural gas to northeast India. All three chiefs of the military services have visited the country, and the commander of the Indian navy has offered to transfer three airplanes to Myanmar at "friendship prices." New Delhi describes Myanmar as its "gateway to ASEAN."[12]

If a common approach to Myanmar is a test of foreign policy integration—and admittedly it is a difficult one—Asia Major and ASEAN + 3 each deserve something close to a zero. Members of ASEAN, by contrast, have achieved a broad consensus on engaging with Burma, signaling displeasure at the regime's record, and backing Indonesia's efforts, but their specific interests and approaches differ considerably.

One obvious possibility would be to suspend Myanmar's membership in ASEAN, just as Greece was suspended from the Council of Europe during the period of dictatorship. But ASEAN leaders reject that option as counterproductive. They veto sanctions for similar reasons. Sanctions imposed by the United States and others are widely judged to be a failure. Not only do they fail to change the regime's behavior; they also feed anti-Western paranoia, impoverish the poor, and provide new opportunities for criminal behavior. It may well be that when something so basic as the survival of a regime and the unity of the country are perceived to be at stake, outside powers can only watch and wait while encouraging private contacts.

Forging a common policy toward Myanmar is difficult because several competing forces are in play. These include respect for Myanmar's national sovereignty, competition for energy resources, and efforts to establish support for basic human rights as a component of ASEAN's emerging institutional identity. Each government reacts to this mix in its own way. China and India court the regime, Malaysia tries to engage in dialogue about a possible roadmap, and Indonesia gently offers lessons on the transition away from dictatorship. Most other governments look the other way.

What hampers a common approach to Myanmar also precludes common positions and joint actions on Iran's nuclear program, Sudan's ethnic massacres, and other problems. Even the most ardent conceptual integrators do not envisage a common Asian foreign policy. Europe, the world's only example of in-depth integration, is still struggling to speak with a united foreign policy voice. A common Asian foreign policy can wait, perhaps forever.

■ Security Cooperation

Another test of incipient Asian integration is security cooperation. Is an "Asian security community" a distant dream, or is security cooperation among Asians actually increasing from near-zero to a meaningful level?

The timing is right to promote security cooperation because the state of conventional security in Asia is generally peaceful. Since the Cold War is over, governments are no longer forced to take sides. Rhetoric in North Korea, China, and Taiwan occasionally bursts into stridency, but it is beaded with ritualized phrases and falls far short of declarations of war. No Asian government faces a serious threat of invasion. No leader today could rally public support by cooking up a crisis and invading a neighbor. Gone are the days when a dictator like Indonesia's Sukarno could wave the flag of *konfrontasi* and hurl threats at "neocolonialist" Malaysia, newly established across the Strait of Malacca, as he did from 1963 to his downfall in 1966. Peaceful coexistence has seeped thoroughly into the body politic.

The real security challenge comes from within. Many Asian nations either harbor armed insurgencies or have pacified them only recently. For them, "nation building" is still a difficult challenge. According to the International Institute for Strategic Studies, 11,000 people in Aceh, Indonesia, lost their lives in the separatist conflict that raged from 1989 to 2005; another 24,000 people have died in the southern Philippines since conflict erupted there in 1968; 30,000 have lost their lives in West Papua, Indonesia, since 1965; and 24,000 people have died in India's northeastern regions in various conflicts dating back to 1956. In 2006, violence in southern Thailand drove Muslim refugees into Malaysia. China faces an armed Uighur separatist movement in its westernmost regions. Sporadic fighting continues in parts of Myanmar, Sri Lanka, and scattered small localities elsewhere.[13]

New and ongoing conflicts have prompted some thinking about establishing an ASEAN peacekeeping force as an arm of the proposed ASEAN Security Community. Such a force would supplement ASEAN's stated commitment to preventive diplomacy and the nonviolent resolution of disputes. Indonesia has floated the idea at various ASEAN meetings, but it is judged to be premature.

Insurgent movements are often located in remote areas or in regions where a distinct local culture clashes with the dominant one. But other nontraditional threats are concentrated in or take advantage of maritime zones. Armed smugglers ply the seas carrying women, children, and drugs. The waters connecting Indonesia with the southern Philippines are maritime transit routes for terrorists planning bombing attacks. Tourist hotels have already been hit; beachfront resorts sporting bikini-clad foreign women could be at risk. Hub ports and commercially vital sea lanes would also make headline-grabbing targets.

No single government can overcome the threat of terrorist attacks alone, but each wants to retain sovereign control. Thanks in part to terrorist attacks on revenue-earning tourist destinations and in part to pressure from the United States, ASEAN adopted a declaration that envisages a framework of joint countermeasures to fight terrorism. Since 2001 the governments of the ASEAN 5 have launched several cooperative activities to fight both terrorism and crime. Supported by a staff unit at the ASEAN secretariat, Southeast Asia now features the Center on Transnational Crimes in the Philippines, the Center for Law Enforcement Cooperation in Jakarta, the Law Enforcement Academy in Bangkok, and the Southeast Asia Regional Center for Counterterrorism in Kuala Lumpur. Although prickly issues like extradition are typically worked out bilaterally (if at all), joint training and exchanges of personnel and information are becoming routine.

Maritime Security and the Rise of Piracy

Pirates have always plagued Asian waters, but in recent years the wealth accruing to Maritime Asia has stimulated a growing number of incidents of piracy and other maritime crimes, especially in Southeast Asia. To track these incidents, the International Maritime Bureau, an arm of the International Chamber of Commerce, set up a reporting center in Kuala Lumpur. The center reported that during the period from January to June 2004, the number of worldwide piracy attacks shot up to 234 incidents, a 37 percent increase over the same period in the previous year. Sixty-four of those took place in the waters off Indonesia and another fifteen in the Strait of Malacca. Attacks also occurred near the island of Bintam, a forty-five-minute ferry ride from Singapore and the locus of considerable investment.[14]

The pirates in question are a far cry from the kris-armed ruffians of yore and use equipment that Blackbeard never dreamed of. They travel in high-speed boats, rely on sophisticated navigation systems, and wield automatic weapons, grenades, and even antitank missiles. They have money and frequently use it to bribe coastal police forces, which are not well armed and often easily corruptible.

The Strait of Malacca is a tempting target zone for such pirates, just as it would be for terrorists. Its many coves and narrow shape—it is about 600 miles (960 kilometers) long and less than 1.7 miles (2.8 kilometers) wide at its narrowest point—have beckoned criminals for centuries. Just as globalization and technology have greatly stimulated legal trade today, so they have boosted the capability of pirates and smugglers to step up the pace of crime.

The attacks of September 11, 2001, raised concerns that terrorists or their criminal allies could take advantage of lax security to transport weapons of mass destruction. In one incident, ten armed men seized an Indonesian chemical tanker and reportedly steered it for an hour through the Strait of Malacca before departing with equipment and technical documents.[15]

Another locus of piracy is the Bay of Bengal, especially the waters off India and Bangladesh. The International Maritime Bureau has labeled this area "piracy-prone" as well. In 2006, a pact called the Regional Cooperation Agreement on Combating Piracy and Armed Robbery Against Ships in Asia (ReCAAP) came into force. The signatories include not only ASEAN + 3 but also India, Bangladesh, and Sri Lanka. ReCAAP commits signatories to do what they can to prevent and suppress piracy and robbery at sea, subject to national laws, resources, and capabilities; to cooperate with others; and to settle disputes peacefully. The agreement established the ReCAAP Information Sharing Centre in Singapore whose mission is to promote close cooperation among the contracting parties.[16] Mely Caballero-Anthony notes that ReCAAP is "the first government-to-government agreement to enhance the security of regional waters beyond Southeast Asia."[17]

Eyes in the Sky

Most efforts to fight piracy involve governments acting alone or in strictly limited cooperative operations. As early as 1999, Japan reacted to attacks on Japanese-flag vessels in Southeast Asian waters and on the high seas by proposing the establishment of a regional coast guard, but the proposal went nowhere. In 2004, the commander in chief of the US Pacific Command floated the idea of a Regional Maritime Security Initiative. His proposal was misinterpreted, deliberately or not, as a signal that the US wanted to dispatch naval vessels to patrol the Strait of Malacca. Indonesia and Malaysia dismissed the idea as unwarranted interference in their sovereign affairs, but the admiral's remarks prompted them to announce that they would henceforth intensify and coordinate joint naval patrols on their own.

In the winter of 2004–2005, Lloyd's of London declared the Strait of Malacca a "war risk area" and raised insurance rates for ships transiting the strait. This move shocked the major shipping companies and spurred the three littoral governments—Indonesia, Malaysia, and Singapore—to work harder at putting aside their differences.

One result was the "Eyes in the Sky" initiative, the main goals of which are to improve the safety of navigation and to prevent and suppress criminal activity. On September 13, 2005, the first plane dedicated to joint, coordinated patrols in the Strait of Malacca took off from an air base near Kuala Lumpur. These planes are the airborne complement to naval patrols launched by the three littoral nations in 2004. The initial launch featured a flotilla of seventeen warships and a ceremony attended by top military officials.

What makes the Eyes in the Sky unusual is that it forces shoulder-to-shoulder teamwork in a security context. Despite long-standing secretiveness and suspicion among the three participants, team members must share information and reveal closely guarded capabilities. Each patrol aircraft is supposed to have one military officer from each of the three countries. (The half-serious joke is that two of them are so busy sizing up the military capabilities of the third that they have no interest in looking down at the water.) The number of such truly joint flights is not clear, but even single-nation sorties are coordinated among the three. Suspicious activity is immediately reported to authorities in each country and to a joint fleet of patrol boats.

The sticking point is hot pursuit. Each plane is allowed to fly over the territorial waters of the other participants but must remain at least three miles (4.8 kilometers) offshore. Chasing suspected criminals into the national territory of a country that is not one's own requires the permission of local officials, who presumably check with higher authorities. This requirement greatly reduces the chances of immediate capture. To deal more effectively with this problem from the water, naval and coast guard vessels are moving from coordinated patrols to joint patrols with mixed crews.

Another drawback is the choice of means. According to US military experts, a combination of ground-based radars and improved domestic surveillance and law enforcement would be a more effective way of detecting and suppressing piracy than airborne activity.[18] Such radars are beginning to be installed, but improving surveillance and law enforcement will take time.

Meanwhile, participants in the so-called Five Power Defence Arrangements (FPDA) are broadening their agenda to include antipiracy activity. The FPDA groups the United Kingdom, Australia, and New Zealand with Singapore and Malaysia. This combination wields much more capability than the Eyes in the Sky initiative has mustered so far.

Eyes in the Sky is still in its infancy. Meeting for the second time in the fall of 2006, thirty-one members of the International Maritime Organization (IMO) hailed the initiative, together with the IMO's companion project, the Marine Electronic Highway. Only days earlier, however, an expert group reported that the combined resources of the three littoral states are not sufficient to carry out these tasks. Worse still, on the eve of the meeting, Malaysian border police fired at an Indonesian fishing boat (for allegedly trespassing), wounding two crew members and creating a diplomatic incident.

Nevertheless, putting aside their earlier insistence on protecting the strait itself, the three littoral governments agreed at the meeting to accept outside help on a voluntary basis. They are listing specific steps that governments whose vessels use the strait can take to contribute.[19] They have also signed a memorandum of understanding with the International Maritime Organization to establish a regional Marine Electronic Highway on the Indonesian island of Batam. Vessels traveling in the shipping lane will have equipment on board that will enable their officers to notify authorities about security threats.

The number of actual and attempted attacks in Southeast Asia has fallen steadily since 2003–2004. The tsunami of December 2004 destroyed a number of pirate vessels, which contributed to the sharp drop in attacks reported in 2005. The peaceful settlement of the conflict in Aceh, brokered in 2005, also helped substantially. Incidents of piracy in Indonesian waters fell from their 2003 peak of 121 to 50 in 2006. Those in the Strait of Malacca declined from their 2004 peak of 38 to 11 in 2006.[20] Noting these improvements, Lloyd's of London lowered its premium for vessels transiting the strait.

Other Initiatives

ASEAN has approved a Plan of Action to Combat Transnational Crime that covers drug trafficking, human trafficking, piracy at sea, arms smuggling, money laundering, terrorism, international economic crime, and cybercrime.[21] ASEAN members take part in numerous meetings and training exercises in these areas with the other members or near-members of Asia Major as well as with the United States. But extradition agreements are largely lacking.

ASEAN + 3 has also focused on transnational crime. Senior officials meet yearly both as a group and in separate meetings between ASEAN officials and representatives from individual + 3 countries. Australia, the European Union, and others also consult within an ASEAN + 3 framework. In 2006, ASEAN + 3 adopted a Work Plan on Cooperation to Combat Transnational Crime.

The attacks of September 11, 2001, gave rise to a thicket of new security initiatives, justified in the name of "human security" and centered on the struggle against terrorism. As part of the Bush administration's so-called war on terror, US negotiators initiated a work program on maritime trade and port security known as Secure Trade in the APEC Region (STAR). APEC's Transportation Working Group has participated in a simulation exercise focused on sea lane disruption. Leaders have pledged stricter measures to prevent attacks on airplanes using man-portable air defense systems (MANPADS).

The governments of Asia Major meet regularly on other maritime issues as well. The demand for better working conditions at sea has spurred negotiation of a new Consolidated Maritime Labor Convention.[22] Ports are another topic. To ensure consistency in the management of ports, improve training, exchange information, and establish standard enforcement and detention procedures, a number of Asia-Pacific authorities established a Memorandum of Understanding on Port State Control known as the Tokyo MOU. Among its eighteen members are eleven of the sixteen members of Asia Major and all of its core members minus India. An organization representing Indian Ocean ports has observer status.[23]

■ The Role of the United States

All of the previously described security measures undertaken by Asian governments take place in a regional theater dominated by the US military presence. The United States maintains significant forces in the region, including the Seventh Fleet, a Marine division, and an Air Force fighter wing. Almost 100,000 US military personnel are stationed in Asia, of whom about 40,000 are in Japan and 37,000 in South Korea.

In 2003 the Defense Department announced that it was planning to restructure, redeploy, and partially withdraw some of these forces with the aim of improving mobility, flexibility, and the ability to react quickly to crises. Instead of massive force levels designed for conventional warfare, the plan features small, jointly operated bases and other military facilities strung out across the world, nicknamed "lily pads." The plan calls for partial troop reductions in South Korea and Japan and enhanced military cooperation with other nations, including Singapore, Indonesia, Malaysia, and India. This major realignment, the first since the Korean War of 1950–1953, requires host-nation consent and is still being negotiated. Full implementation will take many years.

The network of US alliances in Asia, previously described as "hub and spokes," has evolved into a set of customized and flexible bilateral arrangements. The US Pacific Command works closely with military personnel from a number of Asian countries to stage joint exercises and foster cooperative approaches to piracy, crime, terrorism, pollution, and other threats. The Navy's hospital ship *Mercy* went back to Southeast Asia after conducting emergency relief operations in the wake of the 2004 tsunami.

US officials have gone to great lengths to reassure Asian governments that the realignment of forces does not signal retrenchment or a lower level of commitment. The Honolulu-based Pacific Command has also tried to express US priorities in language more consistent with Asian priorities than "homeland security." For example, US Navy and Coast Guard officers use the phrase "maritime border control" rather than the "war against terror," even though the operational challenge (enhanced port security) is substantially the same. Similarly, they speak of "maritime domain awareness" and "global maritime partnership" rather than the Pentagon's original notion of a multinational "1,000-ship navy," which seems too militaristic and US-centered for Asian sensibilities.[24]

The ability to provide education and training to non-US military officers is a major incentive for strengthening military ties with the United States. The Seventh Fleet maintains an extensive web of joint exercises—well over 300 a year. The value of these exercises to non-US participants lies in observation of US military methods and professional standards, participation in simulated crisis response, and access to real-time information. In addition, America's International Military Education and Training program brings together military personnel and civil servants from mutually suspicious governments, offers them professional, high-level instruction, and gives them plenty of opportunities to mingle.

These US military initiatives have the effect of fostering closer cooperation among Asians. Far from pursuing a divide-and-conquer strategy, as suspicious Asians occasionally allege, US officers encourage joint efforts. For example, Cobra Gold, an annual military exercise with Thailand inaugurated in the early 1980s, now includes Japan, Singapore, and Indonesia in field and computer-simulated operations. To bolster its legitimacy and quell suspicions of US motives, Cobra Gold's stated mission now encompasses improved multilateral support for UN-sanctioned peace operations in the region. More than a dozen countries, including China and India, are observers.

■ Coping with Energy and Environmental Threats

The Search for Energy Security

The governments of Asia Major have a huge stake in energy security, defined here as an adequate and reliable supply of energy that can be safely transported and freely purchased at a reasonably affordable price. Except for Brunei and Indonesia, Asian nations are partially, heavily, or overwhelmingly dependent on imported energy. By most estimates, by 2025 the extra demand for oil on the part of "developing Asia" (excluding Japan) will require the equivalent of another Persian Gulf. But Asia's skyrocketing demand for energy is a relatively neglected item on the agenda of the Asian integration movement.

Energy is not an integrating "propeller" of the sort described in Chapter 4. In fact, it is divisive. Projected growth in demand for energy, particularly oil, has ignited a strategic scramble and revived long-slumbering territorial claims. In the East China and South China Seas, maritime border disputes that would otherwise be obscure have heated up as governments try to monopolize suspected oil and gas deposits below the ocean floor. Precedents exist for settling these disputes legally or through mediation, but it is doubtful that sufficient political will can be found.

Inland routes and pipelines exist and more are under construction, but most of Asia's traded energy arrives by sea. The coastline of Maritime Asia is studded with offloading facilities, refineries, and pipeline terminals. China meets most of its mushrooming demand from non-Asian sources. As of 2006, only about 14 percent of China's oil imports came from Asia, compared with 23 percent from Africa and a whopping 56 percent from the Middle East.

China is already the world's second largest oil consumer and the third largest importer of oil. Although the United States consumes three times as much oil as China and imports twice as much, the growth of China's demand for energy has been especially rapid. In the last decade, China has accounted for 30 to 40 percent of new demand growth and about the same increase in tanker traffic. Although electricity can come from several sources, the transport sector demands oil. Commercial demand is mounting. In the next decade, private cars in China are projected to multiply from 10 million to 90–110 million. By 2020, China will likely import 70 percent or more of its total oil needs, up from about 40 percent in 2006.

China's worst-case scenario is that if Beijing is perceived to have provoked a war in the Taiwan Strait, the United States would both intervene militarily and initiate an energy embargo against China, dragooning the rest of Asia to take part in it.[25] Mistrustful of market mechanisms, Chinese state-controlled or state-influenced companies are busy acquiring equity or joint ownership of upstream oil facilities. About 15 percent of China's oil imports are derived from such sources. By way of comparison, about 40 percent of US oil imports come from facilities owned or controlled by US companies. Ironically, only a small percentage of the oil that China is trying to lock up actually reaches China; the rest enters world markets.

On the one hand, China's mercantilist approach to oil supplies breeds cozy relations with some very unattractive governments. China is the biggest investor in Africa and supports some of the world's most atrocious regimes.

On the other hand, Chinese investment has brought energy from these sources into world markets, which frees up other supplies that the Chinese would otherwise have bought.

Even if China's economy cools down, China will have a large stake in open and secure sea lanes now patrolled by the United States. According to interviews, this role splits Chinese energy experts into two camps: those who see the United States as a benign hegemon, and those who see it as a potential threat.[26] In the latter camp are Chinese naval officers and military analysts who seek to justify higher budget outlays for the Chinese navy by citing America's supposed ability to choke off China's oil supplies. But a US naval blockade is not a feasible military option. A US naval force watching an oil tanker approaching the Strait of Malacca would be unable to tell who owned the oil, who owned the tanker, and where it was headed. A close-in blockade of China would run into a formidable barrage of missiles, incurring unacceptable risks and costs.[27] The only option would be the use of submarines in an all-out war, which no responsible policymaker seriously envisages.

Nevertheless, China's "hawks" will not be easily convinced. The political hysteria in the US Congress that caused the Chinese National Offshore Oil Corporation (CNOOC) to withdraw its bid for Unocal—whose assets are mainly in Southeast Asia, not the United States—sent an unfortunate signal and only reinforced China's near-paranoid approach to its oil needs.

China's quest for oil and gas also draws in India, whose demand for energy is mounting rapidly. India's net imports of crude oil and petroleum products have doubled since the mid-1990s. In 2007, India drew 90 percent of its gas from domestic sources, but consumption is projected to quadruple by 2025.

Publicly, the Indian government has called for cooperation. "It took the Europeans centuries of war to come up with the idea of the European coal and steel community," said then minister of petroleum Mani Shankar Aiyar in 2005. "India and China don't have to go through fratricide in order to arrive at the conclusion that it is better to cooperate on energy security."[28] Privately (and to a limited extent publicly), however, Indian officials say they have no choice but to compete for energy.

A vocal champion of democracy, New Delhi keeps mum on the subject when dealing with Myanmar and Iran. India has negotiated an agreement in principle for a pipeline that would bring Myanmar's natural gas reserves to India via Bangladesh. India is keenly interested in a pipeline from Iran and has cultivated Iran's leaders. Investing in such a large deal, however, would trigger sanctions under US law. It was reported—but publicly denied by US officials—that the Bush administration tied the US-India agreement on civilian nuclear technology to India's support for the US position on Iran's nuclear program in the International Atomic Energy Agency and the UN Security Council.[29]

Japanese leaders have thought systematically about energy supplies since the mid-nineteenth century. Japan leads the world in energy efficiency. Measured in terms of energy consumed per unit of output, Japan's energy efficiency is four and a half times greater than America's and more than ten times greater than China's. Thanks to a declining population and the fact that Japanese companies moved energy-intensive industries offshore some time ago, Japan's demand for oil is projected to be relatively flat.

Lacking energy resources of its own, Japan has taken impressive strides toward diversifying its sources of energy. Nevertheless, Japan is still vitally dependent on Middle East oil arriving through the Strait of Malacca. Its hopes for major deals in Russia and Iran are in peril. Japan has proposed several initiatives designed to enhance regional energy security and has the financial resources and technical expertise to back them up, but thus far other Asians have lacked the political will to respond collectively.

At the second East Asian Summit, held in Cebu, Philippines, in January 2007, heads of state adopted the Cebu Declaration on East Asian Energy Security. The declaration recognized shared challenges and endorsed a cooperative, market-based approach to energy, including conservation, regional infrastructure development, alternative fuels, environmental performance, research and development, and other energy-related initiatives "through existing ASEAN mechanisms and in close consultations among EAS participants."[30] Whether the will exists to implement these pledges on a cooperative basis remains to be seen.

Environmental Threats

Many Asian countries have reasonably good environmental laws on the books, but with few exceptions enforcement ranges from spotty to nonexistent. High-level officials recognize the threat posed by severe pollution and global warming but lack the resources to combat them. National budgets and growth statistics do not adequately reflect the long-term cost of environmental damage.

Analysts traditionally divide environmental problems into areas of purely domestic concern, such as local air and water pollution or unsafe waste disposal, and areas of regional or global concern, such as transboundary pollution, depletion of common resources, damage to the ozone layer, and changes in the atmosphere that lead to global warming.

Asia today presents problems of both types. Local pollution in China (and to a lesser extent elsewhere) stands at levels of health risk that would never be tolerated in Europe or the United States. Indeed, many analysts believe that environmental degradation presents one of the biggest potential obstacles to continued economic growth in China. Only recently has the Chinese government begun calculating the huge costs that pollution inflicts on public health and economic development. Although top Chinese officials have acknowledged the need for environmental protection, local authorities still suppress groups protesting against severe environmental degradation.

Environmental protection in China is now a regional challenge. Pollution from China can be detected in the atmosphere of all of China's neighbors. Chinese dams on the Mekong River threaten to damage downstream fisheries and other resources. China is not alone: forest burning in Indonesia now causes crisis levels of air pollution in other countries on an almost annual basis. Indonesia in turn complains that Singaporean companies are damaging its coastal environment. Depletion of fishing stocks and destruction of coral reefs are also serious problems.

Another threat comes from the huge number of ships and tankers that pollute narrow waterways and harbors, especially the 600-odd ships that transit the Strait of Malacca every day. Indonesia and Malaysia are reportedly pushing for a user tax, but imposing such a tax on vessels transiting an international waterway is likely to run counter to international law. Thus far, only Japan has contributed to environmental cleanup, and Tokyo is considering supporting some kind of a fee.

In Asia as elsewhere, global warming is rapidly overtaking other threats in scope, policy significance, and public concern. If present trends continue, Asia will become the largest single source of greenhouse gas emissions within a very few years. Unless current trends are checked, Asia will suffer more than almost any other region in the world because of its high maritime profile and characteristic storm systems. In a few decades, the coastal areas that make up Maritime Asia's identity and provide most of Asia's new wealth run the risk of becoming partially submerged, and some islands could disappear altogether.

■ Conclusion

Of the topics examined in this chapter and the previous one (trade, finance, foreign policy, and security, including energy), community building in the financial field continues to yield the most tangible and constructive results, and cooperation in foreign policy and energy the least.

Security cooperation, in my view, is edging toward the middle of the cooperative spectrum. Most analysts rank security as the most difficult arena for cooperation. The NATO standard—an attack against one is an attack against all—is out of the question, but this yardstick is not very relevant; full-scale conventional war between states is unlikely. It is in the field of nontraditional security that Asians should be judged. Asian governments have taken important steps toward detecting and cracking down on maritime crime and terrorism, but they have not done nearly enough. The lack of progress on regional energy security is particularly disturbing.

But however feeble intra-Asian security cooperation appears to be at present, and however much both traditional and nontraditional security depends on US forces, fledgling security cooperation should not be dismissed. Cooperation is growing, especially bilaterally, especially in Southeast Asia, and especially in nontraditional areas of security, where governments have common fears and interests. The Eyes in the Sky initiative in and over the Strait of Malacca, despite its obvious inadequacies, is an example of what governments can do once they decide to devote real resources to tackling a serious common problem.

Asian governments are unwilling to describe these emerging arrangements as nascent "security communities" for at least two reasons. One is mutual mistrust. The second is the fear that new security arrangements would be perceived as anti-Chinese. In 2007, Japan and Australia signed a pact pledging closer maritime security cooperation, which aroused fears in some circles that the two powers were initiating a policy of containment against China.

The challenges and threats facing Asian governments are real, and they know it. Joint, coordinated efforts to deal with regionwide, nontraditional problems such as crime, terrorism, pollution, and disease are beginning to produce results because they do not significantly threaten national autonomy. In fact, they arguably strengthen it because they address threats to the domestic legitimacy and stability of national governments. The new Consortium of Non-Traditional Security Studies in Asia, comprising more than a dozen Asian research institutions, provides an avenue for intra-Asian discussion and, "where possible," policy recommendations.[31]

There is zero chance of a regional collective security agreement with firm and specific obligations, but I would argue that any such agreement would not suit today's realities. The struggle between communist powers and the free world is long gone. Since Asian governments face very different security problems, joint police and military operations involving only two or three countries on a subregional basis are quite appropriate, particularly in light of the US role.

The examples described in this chapter and in the previous chapter on trade and finance demonstrate that political and strategic considerations weigh heavily in *all* fields of the government-driven integration movement. "Fundamentally," argues Evelyn Goh, "regionalism in East Asia, including Southeast Asia, stems from the security concerns of key regional states."[32] All Asian governments desire economic growth and financial stability, but how they pursue those goals owes as much to noneconomic calculations as to anything gleaned from an economics textbook or inspired by the logic of the marketplace. This is the major difference between government officials and the spontaneous integrators of Maritime Asia described in Part 1 and accounts in large part for their partially mismatched agendas.

All governments without exception recognize the strong connection between regional stability, territorial integrity, economic growth, and political legitimacy. That is why all support continued economic development, even if they find it hard to clear away the obstacles. All acknowledge that their economies are interconnected and that the health of one affects the health of all. All believe that economic engagement with China will improve the chances for China's domestic stability and peaceful evolution; indeed, Chinese leaders themselves may well share this conviction, whatever else may be going on in their minds. All seem to respect the territorial integrity of their neighbors, not out of kindness but out of a recognition that war would dry up investment. None has any reason to provoke a regionwide crisis, to threaten anyone too explicitly, or to push a local quarrel beyond a certain tipping point.

The concept of "security" in Asia appears to be changing appropriately, albeit very slowly. It is moving from conventional war-fighting capability directed at or protecting against attacks from nation-states to a combination of unconventional warfare, nontraditional security, and measures to enhance economic growth and financial stability. "Security versus economics" still applies, but "security *and* economics" is becoming more accurate. Asian regionalism plays to this emerging reality.

Paradoxically, although Asians' economic and security interests often mesh, economic and political ties vary inversely. ASEAN has more or less institutionalized cooperation and the peaceful settlement of disputes, but economic integration among ASEAN members remains stuck at a fairly low level. By contrast, ASEAN's economic ties with China, Japan, and South Korea are burgeoning, but ASEAN's political and strategic bonds with its powerful neighbors are in their infancy. The governments of the + 3 countries and Taiwan, who have the most to gain from closer economic integration, frequently bare their teeth, but businesspeople trade and invest with enthusiasm, creating significant economic interdependence.

Another paradox is that the most dangerous disputes are in Northeast Asia, but the mechanisms and institutions best equipped to handle disputes are in Southeast Asia.[33] This contrast suggests that, over time, deepening north-south ties in Asia could broaden diplomatic opportunities and reap security benefits. Such benefits are more likely to result from carefully targeted, bilateral, or subregional arrangements than from more comprehensive initiatives.

What is still missing in Asian community building is a common set of *political* values. Asian governments exemplify every category of governance known to the modern world. They range from democracy to dictatorship, from transparency to secrecy, from efficiency to near-paralysis, from dedication to the public good to outright exploitation, and everything in between. Observance of basic human rights varies likewise. The same is true of Asia Major as a whole. Until these gaps are significantly narrowed, a true East Asian Community is beyond reach.

■ Notes

1. A prominent and well-respected member of this camp is former Indonesian foreign minister Ali Alatas, an architect of APEC, who shared these views with me in March 2006.

2. Pew Global Attitudes Project, "Publics of Asian Powers Hold Negative Views of One Another," p. 4; and "China's Economic Growth Considered Positive But Not Its Increasing Military Power," available at http://www.pipa.org/OnlineReports/China /China_Mar05/China_Mar05_rpt.pdf.

3. In deference to the wishes of dissident leader Aung San Suu Kyi, the US government and other opponents of the current regime refuse to accept the name Myanmar.

4. Lieberman, *Strange Parallels: Southeast Asia in Global Context,* p. 112. Lieberman's book contains a lengthy analysis of the possible reason for Pagan's decline.

5. Haacke, *Myanmar's Foreign Policy*, pp. 21–22. Ayeyawady is better known by its Western spelling, Irawaddy.

6. Agence France-Presse, cited in "Finding Energy to Resist International Pressure," SEAPSNet, July 7, 2006, www.siiaonline.org.

7. "The Long and Difficult Search for Human Rights in ASEAN," SEAPSNet, December 29, 2008, www.siiaonline.org.

8. "Thailand Steels Itself for More Refugees as Myanmar 'Melts Down,'" SEAPSNet, September 28, 2007, www.siiaonline.org.

9. Personal interview with former Indonesian foreign minister Ali Alatas, Jakarta, March 2006.

10. Personal interview with Indonesian foreign minister Hassan Wirajuda, Jakarta, March 2006.

11. "ASEAN Dilemmas—Too Many Bilaterals, Too Little Unity?" SEAPSNet, July 7, 2007, www.siiaonline.org.

12. Singh, "India's 'Look East' Policy," p. 1.

13. International Institute for Strategic Studies, "The 2007 Chart of Conflict."

14. David Boey, "Jump in Piracy Attacks off Bintan," *The Straits Times*, July 24, 2005, accessed from YaleGlobal Online, http://yaleglobal.yale.edu/display.article?id =2153, pp. 1–2. See also "Piracy and Maritime Terror in Southeast Asia: Dire Straits," *Strategic Comments*, International Institute for Strategic Studies, August 2004, pp. 1–4.

15. Luft and Korin, "Terrorism Goes to Sea," p. 67.

16. "Regional Cooperation Agreement on Combating Piracy and Armed Robbery Against Ships in Asia," available at www.mofa.go.jp.

17. Caballero-Anthony, "Nontraditional Security and Multilateralism," p. 7. Caballero-Anthony is secretary general of the Consortium on Non-Traditional Security Threats in Asia.

18. Interview at the Pacific Command, Honolulu, Hawaii, January 29, 2007. The Pacific Command is the headquarters of all US forces in the Pacific and the Indian Ocean.

19. "Malacca Strait Security Talks Are Underway," SEAPSNet, September 22, 2006, www.siiaonline.org.

20. ICC International Maritime Bureau, *Piracy and Armed Robbery,* table 1.

21. Details can be found at www.aseansec.org/13844.htm.

22. See www.ilo.org/public/english/bureau/inf/event/maritime/index.htm. The convention was adopted at the Maritime Session of the International Labour Conference, February 7–23, 2006.

23. See www.tokyo-mou.org/geninfor.htm.

24. Interview at the headquarters of the US Pacific Command, Honolulu, January 29, 2007.

25. Zha, "China's Energy Security," pp. 179–189.

26. MacDonald et al., *Energy Futures in Asia,* p. 29.

27. Panelists at a December 2006 conference, "China's Energy Strategy," held at the Naval War College in Newport, RI, spelled out these conclusions in detail.

28. Edward Luce and John Ridding, "Indian Vision Puts Warmer Cross-Border Relations in the Pipeline," *Financial Times*, January 20, 2005, p. 2.

29. Aziz Haniffa, "Why Aiyar Lost the Petroleum Ministry," *Rediff India Abroad,* April 25, 2006, http://us.rediff.com/money/2006/apr/25aziz.htm?q=tp&file=.htm.

30. The full text of the declaration is at www.mofa.go/jp/region/asia-paci/eas/energy0701.html.

31. See the Consortium's vision statement, available at www.rsis-ntsasia.org/vision.htm.

32. Goh, *Developing the Mekong*, p. 12.

33. Stanley Foundation, "New Power Dynamics in Southeast Asia," pp. 2–3.

PART 3
Sizing Up the Asian Integration Movement

10

Assessing the Promise of Integration

Previous chapters explored what the Asian integration movement has achieved so far. This chapter looks forward and poses three questions. First, Asian regionalism is still at an early phase. The world has changed since it first took root. It has served useful purposes to date, but is it a good idea for the future? Second, to the extent that closer integration is desirable, what conditions must be in place to ensure that it is legitimate and sustainable? Third, are these conditions in place in Asia Major?

■ Is Asian Integration a Good Idea?

The Asian integration movement is in transition. ASEAN is in the process of acquiring a stronger institutional identity. Japan and China are attempting to ease the tensions of the Koizumi era but remain divided over many issues, clouding the prospects for progress in ASEAN + 3. No one is quite satisfied with the compromise-ridden creation of the East Asian Summit. The global trading system appears stalled. Now is a good time to revisit a basic question: would a genuinely integrated community be good for Asians—and for the United States?

If designed well, closer integration could help Asians adapt to the competitive pressures of the global economy while stimulating domestic demand and raising standards of living. It could improve Asia's financial markets by encouraging best practices, channeling Asia's mountain of savings into local credit markets, reducing dependence on banks, and facilitating cross-border financial transactions while avoiding the capital flight that ravaged much of Asia in the late 1990s. If properly nested within the global trading system, it could further liberalize trade, resulting in more jobs and a more efficient allocation of resources.

In addition, a more integrated Asia would lay down a stable regional cornerstone in the changing architecture of world order and give Asians a stronger and legitimate political voice in global organizations. It could embed a rising China and India, along with Japan, in a web of commitments and channel their energies into constructive rivalry and regional responsibility. It could encourage democratic, honest, and accountable governments. It could reduce energy insecurity by cooperating on energy projects and setting up a regional energy-sharing scheme. It could foster Asia's rich tradition of cultural interaction and nurture regional centers of excellence in education and technology. It could permit more effective Asian responses to common problems, such as crime, terrorism, pollution, resource scarcity, destabilizing migration, and disease. To the extent that Asians cooperate more effectively with each other in pursuit of regional stability, growth, and engagement with the global economy, they are likely to cooperate more effectively with others.

If designed badly, Asian integration would achieve none of these things. Forcing the integrating impulse into unproductive and unrealistic channels would dampen or even stifle Asia's surging prosperity and vibrant self-expression. Setting up a trade bloc that diverts more trade than it creates would violate other countries' rights, perpetuate vested interests, and distort growth. Widespread discrimination against imports from nonmembers would trigger a backlash and undermine the WTO. Creating common financial instruments or even a common currency without the reporting, monitoring, and surveillance required by a modern financial system would lead to failure. Platitudes, too many meetings, and the absence of tangible results would frustrate expectations and tarnish Asian reputations in the rest of the world.

Discouraging cooperation with the United States in the name of Asian solidarity would strain relations with the region's most important provider of security, technology, and markets. In such circumstances America's friends and allies might find themselves under mounting pressure to choose which way to lean, toward the United States or toward the Asian mainland (read: China). Asians would be better off without integration of that kind.

Why Go Further?

Thus far, the "process regionalism" that characterizes Asia Major is all that most governments seem to want. Why spend time, energy, and political capital going any further? There are four reasons.

First, the integration movement keeps security cooperation moving forward, particularly with respect to China. At present, there appears to be a growing divergence between Asian economic interests, which are closely linked to China, and Asia's security needs, which are largely met by the United

States. Whether or not these trends blend into a constructive division of labor based on complementary interests depends enormously on how China evolves in the next decade.

The integration movement engages Chinese officials and provides opportunities to build long-term personal relationships between Chinese and other Asians, which is important everywhere but particularly in Asia. This process gives other Asians a window into what is happening in China and arguably helps lower long-standing Chinese walls of secrecy. What China gains in return is a peaceful neighborhood in which to concentrate on economic modernization and increase its influence.

The integration movement also contributes to security cooperation among non-Chinese Asians, many of whom do not get along well (Singaporeans and Malaysians, for instance). When it comes to protecting something as vital as the Strait of Malacca, Asians resist an obtrusive US role and insist on handling the job themselves. The integration movement helps them train their guns on criminals and terrorists instead of on each other.

Second, the Asian integration movement helps prevent a gradual schism between nations bordering the western rim of the Pacific and those on the mainland. Separating those governments that currently qualify for deeper integration from those that don't would draw a line down the Sea of Japan through the East China Sea, the Taiwan Strait, and the South China Sea, creating two camps. Roughly speaking, countries east of this line are wealthier, more democratic, and/or more closely tied to the United States than mainland countries to the west, which include China and its weaker neighbors. Such polarization would inevitably raise Chinese fears of encirclement and stoke further tensions between China and the United States and—assuming the continuation of a robust US-Japan alliance—between China and Japan as well.

Third, closer integration would extend the advantages of complementarity between Japan, South Korea, and China on the one hand and Southeast Asia and India on the other. Many Southeast Asian political authorities like to say that ASEAN economic integration is the key to regionwide integration, but this does not make sense. Complementarity is more important, and ASEAN's economies are too much alike. The effort to nurture ASEAN integration has fostered significant cooperation and some degree of trade liberalization, but more than a decade of negotiations has still not brought the ASEAN Free Trade Area into being. Intra-ASEAN trade in 2005 was a mere $165 billion, compared to about $3 trillion within the proposed FTAAP.[1] North-south commercial ties, by contrast, are already extensive and are deepening daily. The elimination of most tariffs in just one sector—telecommunications services and equipment—has prompted a regionwide division of labor and given rise to unprecedented levels of trade and investment. Imagine what freeing up other important sectors would do.

Finally, Asians still lack a voice in international institutions commensurate with their wealth, population, location, and contributions to the rest of the world. Efforts to give them more votes or more seats run into trouble from incumbents. Moving toward a common market and developing greater regional identity would help Asians prevail over this resistance, thus giving them the chance to wield more global influence.

■ Prerequisites for Sustainable and Legitimate Integration

Scholars have identified various political, economic, and security criteria for sustainable integration. None to my knowledge has named a minimum level of GDP or per capita income as a requirement, and none has emphasized geography. Their conclusions are fairly consistent, as a survey of integration in Northeast Asia and other regions of the world reveals.

Northeast Asia

In a powerfully argued study, sociologist Gilbert Rozman has analyzed why an integration project centered on the Tumen River area and spanning Northeast China, Eastern Siberia, North and South Korea, and the west coast of Japan remains "stunted" despite considerable local enthusiasm. Drawing on what he observed while living in the region as well as what he read, he lays great stress on globalization as a precondition for successful regionalism.

Rozman defines the appropriate standards for successful regionalism as: (1) *rapidly increasing economic ties* backed by a joint strategy of economic integration; (2) *growing political ties* nurtured by summits and organizations that set goals for collective actions, regionally and globally, that have a good chance of implementation; (3) *advancing social integration* through labor migration, business networks, and a common agenda on outstanding problems; (4) *shared consciousness of regional identity* enhanced by awareness of shared culture in the face of globalization; and (5) *a widening security agenda* to resolve tensions and ensure stability.[2]

Rozman goes on to argue that regionalism requires some combination of five conditions in order to succeed. The first is national strategies for modernization that allow for openness, decentralization, a division of labor, and a diminished role for borders. The second is national identities that accept neighbors as partners and cultivate trust. The third is acceptance of an evolving balance of regional power by the United States. The fourth is progress in bilateral relations so that territorial and other disputes can be set aside while ties are expanded. The fifth is a vision of regionalism that elites and public opinion alike find persuasive.[3]

Western Hemisphere

In 1994, Jeffrey J. Schott and Gary Clyde Hufbauer of the Institute for International Economics examined the prospects for economic integration in the Western Hemisphere and came up with the notion of "readiness indicators."[4] These are macroeconomic and microeconomic variables that taken together portray each country's economic conditions. They include price stability, budget discipline, national savings, external debt, currency stability, market-oriented policies, and reliance on protectionist trade taxes (tariffs and other fees) for government revenue. In 2001, Schott added an indicator, "policy sustainability," on the sensible assumption that support for economic reforms will depend on whether the average worker receives tangible benefits and has a voice in the political process.[5]

Readiness indicators do not measure readiness for integration as such but rather the readiness of a given country to open its market to foreign competition and compete in the global economy. They are intended as a tool of self-examination as governments contemplate closer economic integration. They do not factor in the state of the physical infrastructure, which is highly relevant to the future of Maritime Asia. Nevertheless, readiness indicators point the way toward a common agenda for governments seeking closer integration. They link domestic macroeconomic performance, normally the domain of central bankers and finance ministers, with a highly political regional movement.

Europe

As argued in Chapter 1, Europe differs from Asia in fundamental ways. But certain aspects of the European experience can teach Asia some lessons, both positive and negative. Indeed, Asian policymakers and intellectuals no longer reject the European model in its entirety.

Examining possible European lessons for Asia, Craig Parsons and J. David Richardson suggest that sustainable integration requires legitimacy, market integration, political bargains between integration's winners and losers and between business and government, and a top-down effort to achieve integration.[6] Analyzing prospects for integration in North America, Robert Pastor also draws a number of lessons from Europe. One is a clear declaration of goals. Another is a limit on the number of supranational institutions; Europe established too many, he writes, and NAFTA too few. Several others suggest the need for distributing funds from richer countries to poorer ones to reduce income and employment disparities among nations and regions and thus to ease pressures to emigrate. Among the negative lessons from Europe are growing inequality within "successful" poor countries and the fact that more than half of the regional aid funds flow to rich countries.[7]

A key long-term lesson from Europe is that cooperation in specific, tangible areas of mutual benefit builds communication and trust and helps to manage change in regional power relationships, thus contributing substantially to regional peace, prosperity, and security. Citing gains of this kind in Europe, the European Commission now asserts that the European Union provides an "interesting model" for Asia.[8] Slowly, grudgingly, and awkwardly, with occasional bursts of triumph, Europe has managed to create a common structure and at least some common identity while managing conflict and preserving diversity. The European Union should be seen not only, and perhaps not even primarily, as a pioneer in integration but rather as a living expression of managing differences and fragmentation in the context of economic interdependence, converging political values, and shared security goals. This grand experiment is profoundly relevant to the future of Asian integration.

Judged by these various standards, Asian integration in the form of ASEAN + 3 has taken promising baby steps but has a lot of growing up to do, and Asia Major is not yet born. The two most important prerequisites for closer, legitimate, and sustainable integration—and hence for the future of Asia as a region—that I derive from these regional comparisons are good governance and economic reform. What follows is a rudimentary effort to apply these yardsticks to Asia.

◼ Good Governance

Political Stability

Political stability is an obvious condition of sustainable integration. Why would any government tie its future to a group of leaders who cannot deliver on their promises and who may not be in office next week?

According to an index of "failing states" constructed by *Foreign Policy* magazine and the Fund for Peace, stability in Asia varies widely. A failing state is defined as one in which the government does not have effective control of its territory, is not perceived as legitimate by a significant portion of its population, does not provide domestic security or basic public services to its citizens, and lacks a monopoly on the use of force.[9] Quantitatively ranked indicators range from refugees and demographic pressures to public services, factionalized elites, and foreign intervention. Five "states of failure" descend from "most stable" to "critical."

According to this index, only Japan, Australia, New Zealand, Mongolia, and South Korea are "most stable" or "stable," while all the others are "borderline" or below. Myanmar is "critical" and Laos and Indonesia are "in danger." Taiwan and Singapore were omitted but are presumably "stable" and "most stable," respectively.

Participatory Governance

People are more likely to support or at least tolerate closer integration if they can express their political views without fear of arrest and if they and their children have both enough to live on and the chance to make more. By my rough count, eleven of the sixteen countries included in this book—the ASEAN 5, Brunei, Japan, South Korea, India, Australia, and New Zealand—have some claim to this mantle, as do Taiwan and Indonesia. But two of the ASEAN 5 are shaky: Thailand is under temporary military rule, and the Philippines seems to be in perpetual political turmoil. The CLMV countries do not qualify at all, which is consistent with the way they behave and are treated in integration-related forums.

According to Freedom House rankings, Australia, India, Indonesia, Japan, New Zealand, South Korea, and Taiwan are "free," and Thailand, Malaysia, Singapore, and the Philippines are "partly free."[10] China ranks with Brunei and the CLMV countries as "not free."[11]

The secluded nature of official meetings on Asian integration provides an opportunity to address common problems away from the public eye. In the trust-building phase, such seclusion is helpful. Sooner or later, however, these bodies will come under pressure to build in more accountability, transparency, and access on the part of the private sector and NGOs. Otherwise their decisions will lack legitimacy.

Public participation has another advantage: civic activists and nongovernment groups bring knowledge to the table. Responsible environmental groups, for example, collect scientific data and disseminate "best practices." Unfortunately, failed politicians and dissidents sometimes take refuge in existing NGOs or form their own to retain influence or escape prosecution. Since the transparency and accountability of these NGOs may be poor or nonexistent, rules need to be designed to distinguish between qualified and unqualified participants in the decisionmaking process.

■ Economic Reform

Integration that goes beyond production networks and gated industrial zones requires governments to get the basics right—and then let competition flourish. Healthy societies need a framework of enforceable laws and regulations governing the basic operation of the free market and a safety net for those who lose their livelihoods. They depend on government to invest in long-term assets like education, advanced technology, and transportation systems. Governments should concentrate on these priorities, not on propping up heavily subsidized companies and banks. Once a reasonable framework is in place, they should let Asians compete and rely on a

fair and transparent tax system to reap and distribute the benefits of competition.

Easier said than done? Of course. Economic reform sounds easy when we
wish it on other people, but it is difficult to carry out at home. Nevertheless,
readiness for sustainable integration depends on sustained progress toward
these goals. How does Asia score?

Macroeconomic Indicators

In 2006, a team of economists at the International Monetary Fund applied to
Asia the European Union's Maastricht Criteria, used to assess qualification for
a monetary union. Their aim was to assess prospects for Asian integration.
Criteria for compliance cover the inflation rate, interest rates, the fiscal bal-
ance, and gross debt. The team chose to look at ASEAN (minus Laos and
Myanmar), the + 3 countries, India, Australia, New Zealand, and Hong Kong.
It reported that no combination of countries met all the Maastricht Criteria and
most missed at least two out of the four.[12]

Readers will protest that I have set up Europe as the standard after specifically disavowing that idea. It is true that not even the most visionary champions of Asian integration advocate a monetary union in the foreseeable future.
Nevertheless, the Maastricht thresholds say something useful about convergence and identify weaknesses that must be tackled in the future.

The work of Schott and Hufbauer yields similar lessons. Although most
Asian countries score reasonably well in price and currency stability and
many have accrued substantial national savings, wide gaps exist in two of
Schott's readiness indicators—market-oriented policies and protectionist
trade taxes. Leaders of the integration movement must either try harder to
narrow these gaps or informally establish a second track so that certain countries do not have to conform to the standards applicable to all the other members. Although no one will officially endorse two-track integration, giving the
CLMV countries more time to meet various ASEAN goals accomplishes the
latter task.

Openness to Globalization

Asian countries that have adjusted successfully to globalization are the most
prepared for closer integration in Asia. Highly globalized Singapore fits readily into both regional and global integration (and will do its best to make sure
that there is no serious conflict). At the other extreme, Cambodia, Laos,
Myanmar, and North Korea are relatively unglobalized.

The Globalization Index, compiled by *Foreign Policy* magazine in collaboration with A. T. Kearney, measures a large number of variables: economic
integration, personal contact, technological "connectivity," and political

engagement.[13] According to the 2007 rankings, Singapore retained its number-one spot, but no other country in Asia Major made the top ten. Australia weighed in at number thirteen, followed by New Zealand, Malaysia, Japan, South Korea, the Philippines, Vietnam, and Thailand, in that order. In the next tier were China, Indonesia and India, respectively.

When it comes to economic globalization, which combines incoming and outgoing trade and investment, Singapore remained in the top spot. In the trade category, Vietnam made the top ten for the first time. Taiwan and Australia ranked high on trade but considerably lower on investment. Indonesia was trading more but still attracted relatively little investment. India was gaining ground but started from a very low base.

Countries may be highly globalized in economic terms but far less so in terms of personal contact, technology ties, and political engagement (measured in terms of international organizations, UN peacekeeping, treaties, and amounts of governmental transfers and receipts). China is a good example: highly ranked in terms of trade, investment, and UN peacekeeping, it drops precipitously when other yardsticks are applied.

The Globalization Index demonstrates the influence of size and access to maritime resources. Given two countries with roughly comparable per capita incomes, the smaller one tends to be more globalized than the larger one. China and India are dual economies with vast unglobalized interior regions. Smaller, maritime, and peninsula nations like South Korea, Singapore, and Malaysia are more open to globalization.

The Globalization Index also confirms that there is a gap between the richer, democratic nations of the Pacific Rim and the countries on the Asian mainland. By contrast, the original twelve nations of the pre-expansion European Union are clustered near the top. This suggests once again that the economies of Asian countries are too diverse to form a common market in the near term and that adjustment to globalization is a key to future integration.

Ease of Doing Business and Conducting Trade

The International Finance Corporation (IFC), an arm of the World Bank Group that is oriented toward the private sector, publishes an index that ranks countries according to the ease of doing business.[14] Categories include starting a business, dealing with licenses, employing workers, and similar factors. Singapore, New Zealand, Hong Kong, Australia, Japan, Thailand, South Korea, and Malaysia get high marks here, followed by Taiwan. Farther down on the list are China and Vietnam. The Philippines, India, Indonesia, Cambodia, and Laos are lower still. (Myanmar and North Korea were not ranked.)

The IFC also ranks countries according to the procedural requirements for exporting and importing a standardized cargo of goods. The index surveys the entire process, from the initial contract to final delivery and every step in between. These steps include the number of documents required, the time necessary to complete the transaction, and the cost to export and import per container. As a region, East Asia does quite well, but once again individual countries vary. Singapore, Hong Kong, and China are almost off the scale. Australia and Malaysia do extremely well, Vietnam and even Cambodia do reasonably well, India is catching up, and the Philippines and Laos lag behind.

◾ Conclusion

Whether or not Asian regionalism is a good idea in the future depends on how it is designed. In my judgment, the good will outweigh the bad, but we will have to wait a long time to see. Judged by the three basic criteria highlighted in this chapter—good governance, economic reform, and mutual trust—not many countries will qualify for sustainable, legitimate, in-depth integration in the next fifteen to twenty years.

The most promising candidates for such integration are Japan, South Korea, Taiwan, Singapore, Australia, and New Zealand. These countries form an ocean-facing rim or arc that skips over the Philippines (unless Manila's political and economic record improves). Among the least prepared are the CLMV countries and India.

China's maritime provinces are highly integrated with the regional and global economy, but the country as a whole shows only limited signs of readiness for wider integration. Economic reform has surged through the country, but political and civil rights are still suppressed. New laws protecting civil society groups are being drafted and passed, but no one in their right mind would rely on the courts for protection. Emerging from decades of autarky, the Chinese are still catching up with their new, modern selves. Shaking off both the humiliation of the past and the madness of Maoism, they are proud of their achievements. Rapid growth appears to compensate for the absence of freedom.

Given the history of the last two centuries, it is remarkable that the "Asia" envisaged by the leaders of the contemporary Asian integration movement is as cooperative, outward-looking, cosmopolitan, and technology-oriented as it is. The statesmen and intellectuals of Asia Major have at last found a version of Asia that works. In their eyes, Asian norms and values, however they are defined, are appropriate for Asia and worthy of sharing with others, but they provide neither an excuse for failure nor proof of superiority. This attitude alone may be more important in the long run than any quantitative achievement.

To answer a question posed in Chapter 1, we are not yet witnessing a defining moment in history when the vision of integration crystallizes into hard-edged reality. Nevertheless, the political *process* of Asian integration has value, not primarily because it contributes to economic growth but because it provides some degree of reassurance in an uncertain environment. That fact remains central to understanding the current form of Asia's new regionalism and helps to explain its persistence.

Skeptics who have been waiting for a more peppery view of Asian regionalism will greet the next chapter with relief. It demonstrates why meaningful integration among the nation-states of Asia Major remains a distant vision despite both the appeal of regionalism and Maritime Asia's integrating pull.

▦ Notes

1. Peterson Institute for International Economics.
2. Rozman, *Northeast Asia's Stunted Regionalism*, p. 6 (italics in original).
3. Ibid., p. 16.
4. See Hufbauer and Schott, *Western Hemisphere Economic Integration.*
5. Schott, *Prospects for Free Trade in the Americas,* p. 17 ff.
6. Parsons and Richardson, "Lessons for Asia?" pp. 885–907.
7. Pastor, *Towards a North American Community,* chap. 3.
8. Delegation of the European Commission to the USA, "EU Relations with China and Southeast Asia," *EU Focus*, EU Special Advertising Supplement in *Foreign Policy* 162, September–October 2007, p. 1.
9. *Foreign Policy* and the Fund for Peace, "The Failed States Index," p. 52.
10. For a critique of the weakness of democracy in Singapore and Malaysia, see Rodan, *Transparency and Authoritarian Rule in Southeast Asia.*
11. "Table of Independent Countries: Comparative Measures of Freedom," available at www.freedomhouse.org.
12. Cowen et al., "Financial Integration in Asia," pp. 54–55.
13. *Foreign Policy* and Kearney, "The Globalization Index." Explanation of the various categories is available at www.atkearney.com.
14. Data for this and the following paragraph can be found at the International Finance Corporation's website established for this purpose, www.doingbusiness.org.

11

Current Obstacles and Potential Threats

Observers of Asia's new regionalism are quick to point out the gap between rhetoric and reality. Tangible results of the government-driven Asian integration movement have come in droplets rather than cascades. Even if governments come closer to meeting the prerequisites for successful and legitimate integration listed in Chapter 10, they face many hurdles. This chapter lists the many obstacles that tether the vision of "community building" and thwart regionalist hopes. It also surveys external threats that could blight the promise of the integration movement or kill it altogether but that are outside their control.

■ Geography, Culture, and History

Diversity

The landscape of Asia Major presents some of the greatest variations of wealth, geography, climate, race, religion, and culture on the planet. Unlike the Arab world, Latin America, and to some extent Europe, Asia lacks a common language, a common religion, and a shared classical culture. The region contains four of the five major religions, a panorama of racial types and ethnic groups, and literally thousands of local languages. Australia and New Zealand add their own mixtures.

Standards of living vary widely. According to the UN's Human Development Index, which measures life expectancy, literacy, and standard of living, the countries of Asia Major that enjoy "high human development" are Australia, Japan, New Zealand, Singapore, South Korea, and Brunei, in that order. Malaysia is near the top of the category called "medium human development," followed at some distance by Thailand and China. On the lower end of that spectrum are Vietnam, Indonesia, India, Myanmar, Cambodia, and Laos.[1]

When the colonial powers planted their flags and divided up their posses-sions, they imposed different regulatory and legal traditions as well as differ-ent languages and varieties of education. Memories of colonial rule linger and can sometimes summon a sense of solidarity, but for practical purposes the colonial legacy still divides them.

Contemporary political diversity is equally marked. Governments range from dictatorships to democracies and everything in between. The composi-tion of elites and domestic interest groups varies according to ethnicity, histo-ry, landholding, form of government, and other factors. In some areas, the combination of local politics and violence in the Middle East appears to be fostering a stronger sense of Muslim identity, creating a de facto divide between governments that are sensitive to Muslim opinion and those that can afford to ignore it.

Artificial Boundaries

Few countries in Asia Major other than Australia and New Zealand can be said to have "natural" political boundaries on all sides—that is, borders that are his-torically constant or correspond to the distribution of ethnic groups, or both. As recently as the late nineteenth and early twentieth century, for instance, the area comprising the ten members of today's ASEAN was dotted with about forty principalities. It was not until the latter phase of the colonial era (and sometimes later) that boundaries hardened into the barriers that prevail today.

For better or worse, Asians are stuck with their current boundaries, artifi-cial as they are. Any effort to redraw them would open a Pandora's box of secessionist claims and unstable clusters.

Artificial boundaries inhibit integration in at least two ways. First, they foster local unrest by fanning irredentist claims, arousing suspicion that the left-behind minority is loyal to another country, and providing safe havens for cross-border insurgents. This agitation forces leaders trying to consolidate national unity to insist on absolute national sovereignty as a higher priority than cooperation with others. Second, according to research conducted by a team of economists, artificial boundaries hamper economic development.[2] They hinder trade and investment prospects and reduce the chances that disaf-fected communities can be "bought off" by higher growth.

■ Reactions to Globalization

Globalization and Vulnerability

Most governments in Asia are highly exposed to globalization. This exposure works both for and against integration. On the one hand, globalization is partly responsible for Asia's new wealth and underlines the need for more open-ness. On the other hand, Asian governments find globalization unsettling and threatening. Underneath butter-smooth ministerial declarations pledging clos-er integration lie the hard realities of holding national societies together at a time of rapid change.

Just when Asian economies seemed to be adapting most successfully to globalization, the financial crisis hit. The devastation that followed taught Asian leaders that rapid capital movements could hammer their currencies, topple their governments, and undermine their hard-won national autonomy.

Many Asian governments are still attempting to consolidate nation building, fortify their rule over unruly populations, tame criminal activity, and legitimize central power. Sudden shifts in the pattern of trade and invest-ment can impoverish industries not nimble enough to anticipate and adapt to them. Uneven surges of wealth widen the income gap between maritime and interior regions and between urban and rural areas. They may also enrich minorities and elites whose interests differ from those of the ruling party— or threaten groups whose support is essential to that party's continued rule. Faced with such challenges, national leaders often take a go-slow approach to the integration movement and favor only those aspects of it that do not threaten them.

National Sovereignty and the Doctrine of Noninterference

When the colonial powers left the scene, fledgling governments clung to their newly won boundaries so tightly that the doctrine of national sover-eignty and noninterference became a mantra. Threats from Chinese- and Soviet-backed communist movements on the one hand and the US Central Intelligence Agency on the other were quite real at the time. Many govern-ments are still struggling to consolidate their power and autonomy. In the name of national sovereignty and noninterference, they continue to reject anything that smacks of formal and enforceable decisionmaking or penal-ties for noncompliance.

The principles of national sovereignty and noninterference mean more than simply doing nothing that might trouble a neighboring government. On some occasions they work against what Chapter 5 called "values-based inte-grators," such as environmentalists and human rights activists. For example, in the mid-1990s, governments or government-affiliated groups disrupted conferences organized by NGOs in Manila, Bangkok, and Kuala Lumpur because Indonesia's Sukarno regime objected to them.[3] At China's request, several Asian governments have also banned Falun Gong and vetoed requests from Buddhist and human rights groups to permit visits from the Dalai Lama.

■ Regional Politics

Mutual Suspicion

Mutual suspicion is pervasive in Asia. The most important reason why the envisaged East Asian Security Community lags so far behind other integration initiatives is that military authorities are ashamed to reveal their weaknesses to their neighbors. Singapore is the most open, in large part because the custodians of Singapore's military arsenal have much less to be embarrassed about.

Another reason why governments find it hard to share information on defense planning and military capability is that the military arsenals of at least some of these countries are targeted at each other.[4] Moreover, some programs and purchases are hidden. In some countries, white papers, posture statements, and published military budgets omit off-budget activities because political and military officers do not want to reveal them. In Indonesia, this practice conceals the role of military forces in the private economy. In China, it hides additional military and quasi-military expenditures. Chinese procurement of foreign weapons, for example, is an off-budget activity. Joint military exercises, the publication of more detailed military budgets, and other confidence-building measures are increasing, but there is a long way to go.

Competing and unresolved border claims constitute another source of suspicion. Major land-based disputes have been settled, but a number of others remain. Most involve ownership of small islands (the Paracels, the Spratlys, and the Senkaku Islands) and/or jurisdiction over areas of the East China Sea and the South China Sea believed to harbor undersea oil and gas. Despite its trumpeted good-neighbor policies, China has made few compromises on maritime disputes. According to Taylor Fravel, China has settled fourteen out of sixteen land border disputes but only two out of eight maritime border disputes.[5]

Conflicting claims in the Spratly Islands and the East China Sea have been put on the back burner for now, but rival gunboats patrol the area. Malaysia's decision to grant a concession to Royal Dutch Shell in a disputed block of the Sulawesi Sea ignited a dangerous standoff between the Malaysian and Indonesian navies. The Indonesian navy has also been capturing and detaining Thai fishermen using deep-sea trawls to scoop up massive and valuable catches around Indonesia's Riaui Islands. One admiral has reportedly threatened to "sink their boats" and "shoot them on the spot according to standard procedures."[6]

Most governments restrict investment in certain industries or from certain countries on security grounds. In 2006, in an example highly relevant to the integration of Maritime Asia, the Indian cabinet denied security clearance to three Chinese firms attempting to bid for container terminal projects at newly privatized port facilities in Mumbai and Chennai.[7] The companies included the operator of a similar terminal in Pakistan, whose government is still suspected of supporting or providing sanctuary for insurgents in Kashmir. No doubt ministers also remembered that during the Cold War China was aligned with Pakistan in opposition to the Soviet Union and India.

Sino-Japanese Tensions

When former Japanese prime minister Koizumi was in office, Chinese and Koreans lashed out at his visits to Yasukuni Shrine and at certain Japanese textbooks that whitewash Japan's wartime record. The vehemently anti-Japanese demonstrations at soccer matches in China shocked the Japanese public and lowered China's popularity among Japanese. According to the Pew Global Attitudes Survey, roughly seven in ten Japanese express an unfavorable view of China, and about the same number of Chinese say the same about Japan.[8] The incessant clang of criticism from China and South Korea has also fed a small but semiviolent right-wing backlash in Japan. The homes of many prominent individuals who criticized Koizumi's visits to the Yasukuni Shrine are under police protection.

Rancor between China and Japan reached such an alarming level that it drew unprecedented public comment from ASEAN leaders. Speaking in May 2006, Prime Minister Abdullah bin Badawi of Malaysia cited tensions between Japan and China and warned that "the situation had worsened" with respect to an East Asian community. Singaporean leader Lee Kuan Yew agreed, adding that such friction "will slow down the process of integration." Both leaders mentioned friction between South Korea and Japan in a similar vein. Lee urged all three feuding governments to promote cooperative approaches to energy and to stop competing with each other in energy negotiations with Russia. Less surprisingly, South Korea's minister of commerce also called on Japanese leaders to stop visiting the Yasukuni Shrine and "take responsibility for its past conduct" in order to help lay the foundation of the East Asian community.[9]

As described in Chapter 1, Franco-German reconciliation is the bedrock of European integration. Neither the misery suffered during the 1930s and 1940s nor the appeal of an "(East) Asian community" has melted the underlying frost between China and Japan. The initial thaw in Sino-Japanese tensions initiated by former Prime Minister Abe helped ease relations between the two giants, but historically inaccurate and insensitive comments about wartime "comfort women" stoked the cycle of criticism and hardened attitudes all over again.

Prime Minister Fukuda, who took office in 2007, opposed the Yasukuni visits and is likely to improve relations with China. But the two countries have a long way to go before they achieve a historical reconciliation of the sort that binds postwar Germany and France, and no towering statesmen are in sight.[10] In fairness, other nationalities in Asia also find it difficult to get along—

notably Chinese and Malays but also Thais and Cambodians and many other pairs. In this category, the Asian integration movement gets a low score.

The ASEAN Way

The "ASEAN Way," a style of decisionmaking that emphasizes lengthy dialogue, harmony, and consensus, is often listed as an obstacle to integration. It rests on the notion that all ten members of ASEAN are equal and that each needs to agree to everything. Discussion can drag on endlessly and often does. In July 2006, the chairman of the Eminent Persons Group, which drafted the ASEAN Charter, said publicly that consensus-style decisionmaking "has more negative than positive attributes" for integration and that it needed to be changed.[11] The new ASEAN Charter provides for streamlined decisionmaking, but it is too early to say how these reforms will work in practice.

The ASEAN Way prevails not only in ASEAN but also in ASEAN + 3 and the East Asian Summit process (where it is known as the Asian Way). The reluctance of national governments to further institutionalize the process of Asian integration contributes to the lack of substance. Governments now retain virtually all decisionmaking in their own offices. Until now, there have been no "permanent representatives" to ASEAN as there are to the United Nations. This means that delegates fly in for meetings in Jakarta or elsewhere and then fly home again. The new ASEAN Charter rectifies this shortcoming, but ASEAN governments are likely to retain a firm grip on both the agenda and the process.

The CLMV Countries and the Integration Gap

Inclusion of the CLMV countries (Cambodia, Laos, Myanmar, and Vietnam) makes the current size and composition of the proposed Asian community problematic. The most natural pan-Asian grouping in terms of complementarity and mutual benefit is not ASEAN by itself but rather the original ASEAN 5 founders (Indonesia, Malaysia, the Philippines, Singapore, and Thailand) and the + 3 countries (China, Japan, and South Korea) as the core, joined by Australia, New Zealand, and, once further reforms are in place, India.

The CLMV countries drag down the integration movement, and Myanmar hurts its reputation. It is good for CLMV representatives to be exposed to modern governance, market-oriented economies, and outward-looking policies. That is why they were admitted to ASEAN in the first place. But expanding ASEAN to include the CLMV countries as full members rather than candidate members or observers works against integration.

A rising tide lifts all boats, but Vietnam has only recently started to float. Its economy is flourishing, but its government is still nominally communist and its institutions are weak. The other three are still stranded on the beach. Cambodia's GDP is less than 5 percent of neighboring Thailand's. Its per capita income in 2006 was less than $500, compared to more than $31,000 in Singapore.[12] These disparities are far greater than the gap between, say, Germany and Portugal, or France and Romania. The promise of future membership in the European Union has induced a wide range of democratic and market-oriented reforms in poorer European countries, lubricated by funding from Brussels, but no such mixture of demands and incentives is available to Asians, at least not yet.

In reality, Asian integration is a two-track process, but no one wants to admit that officially. When decisions are taken, it is understood that CLMV countries will take a pass because they are unprepared to participate in the integration movement in a meaningful way. They are moving so slowly that an "integration gap" is widening between them on the one hand and the ASEAN 5, the + 3 countries, Australia, and New Zealand on the other. The more that officials from richer Asian countries make excuses for the poorer ones and prolong the timetable for reform, the more this gap will grow.

The Taiwan Problem

Taiwan is a thriving democracy whose economy has become closely enmeshed with that of China. It is a shadow member of Asia Major, but its pariah diplomatic status defies reality. Thanks to Chinese pressure, Taiwan is officially excluded from the Asian integration movement and thus cannot make political contributions commensurate with its economic standing. Taiwan is a "member economy" of APEC but not a member of ASEAN + 3 or the EAS. Thanks to Chinese pressure, Asian governments prohibit direct commercial flights to Taiwan, ban high-level trips, refuse to allow the Dalai Lama to visit, and conform in other ways to Beijing's will.

Anyone who studies China's modern history understands the depth of Chinese emotions on the subject. Every loyal Chinese has been taught to believe that restoring Taiwan to China will put an end to almost 170 years of humiliation and restore China's rightful status in the world. Other Asian governments should be able to find ways of respecting Chinese feelings and supporting the one-China policy while showing a little more collective courage, but few want to brave a public tongue-lashing from Beijing (as feisty Singapore has done).

■ Problems of Governance

Absence of Strong Leadership

Several remarkable leaders have wielded power and influence in postwar Asia, but none has labored so tirelessly in support of integration as Jean Monnet and Robert Schuman did in Europe. Among public figures, the most forceful and consistent advocate of Asian integration is Haruhiko Kuroda, president of the Asian Development Bank, but his domain is financial and economic only. Former prime ministers Lee Kuan Yew and Goh Chok Tong of Singapore, Malaysia's Mahathir bin Mohamad, and South Korea's Kim Dae Jung all took steps to foster closer integration, but they are no longer heads of state.

Today there are no government leaders who both champion Asian integration and wield regional influence. Prime ministers heading many of the democratic and quasi-democratic Asian governments cling to slender parliamentary majorities or rely on fractious coalition partners. Regardless of what they may think, they lack the strength and legitimacy to face down political resistance from those with a vested interest in restricting integration.

Bureaucratic Politics and Inertia

Like governments everywhere, Asian governments often become hamstrung by turf fights and bureaucratic infighting. Who gets to attend a particular meeting—the defense minister or the foreign minister, or both? Who decides on trade concessions in agriculture—the trade ministry, or the agricultural ministry and the agricultural lobby? What happens if an industry protected by one ministry is challenged by the actions of another? The form, intensity, and outcome of these time-consuming internal struggles vary with each country.

In no Asian government that I am aware of is there a high-ranking "czar" in the prime minister's office or in a similarly influential position tasked with resolving bureaucratic conflicts in favor of regional integration. Japan's former prime minister Koizumi created high-level positions to push through selected high-priority goals such as structural economic reform, but he restricted his leadership initiatives to domestic issues. Amy Searight has observed that bureaucratic segmentation and rivalry, combined with the absence of high-level leadership, are allowed to "fester and disrupt a coherent Japanese diplomatic voice" in discussions of regional architecture.[13] Japan is particularly egregious in this respect, but it is not alone.

Protectionism and Vested Interests

Cartels, monopolies, state-owned or state-controlled enterprises, and hothouse industries protected by high tariffs hinder economic integration. Some were established by the colonial powers, others resulted from postwar experiments in socialism, and still others arose in priority sectors identified by national governments committed to guiding the economy toward development. They are usually inefficient and rely on politicians to sustain them. Even state-owned companies that have competed successfully in the global marketplace do not want to see a competitor in their own home market. Political elites often profit handsomely from their stake in these entities. In consequence, many bilateral PTAs in the region are riddled with exceptions.

Nonenforcement of Agreements

The implementation of agreements and the settlement of disputes in the region are highly uneven. Agreements to carry out some integration initiative or cooperative program are often signed by governments but not enforced. There is little or no way for private persons to compel enforcement, and none for other Asian governments other than diplomatic pressure. In countries where legal and quasi-legal institutions are weak or overburdened, political influence peddling is common.

Lack of Transparency and Absence of Public Participation

Closer integration requires a certain degree of trust and information sharing. But many, if not most, governments in Asia inherit a tradition of secrecy. Most governments lack a structured advisory process requiring agencies to publish draft regulations and solicit comments so that all interested parties have a chance to influence the outcome. Interest groups most directly affected by a pending government decision bend regulators' ears as they do everywhere, but there is no mechanism that grants appropriate political weight to the spontaneous integrators from the private sector described in Chapter 5. Those opposed to closer integration have more access to power than those who support it. Only Singapore and Japan appear to have systematic bargaining mechanisms engaging those who benefit from closer integration and those who do not.

Secretiveness characterizes the private sector as well. Corporate data are becoming more transparent, but practices like the payment of bribes are still concealed. Companies are not required to disclose the impact of their activities on the environment. In many countries, reliable data from the banking sector are still either unavailable or closely guarded. These habits hamper even rudimentary financial integration.

■ Corruption

Corruption works against integration because it erodes the trust, confidence, and sense of well-being on which sustainable integration must ultimately rest. Corruption misallocates wealth to unproductive use and prevents ordinary people from witnessing and participating in the benefits of closer integration.

Even though investors participate in corruption, they dislike the uncertainty that it entails. In Asia, bribes paid to local police, customs agents, and coast guard officials facilitate organized crime and the pilfering of endangered resources.

According to Transparency International's 2007 Corruption Perception Index, no ASEAN country except Singapore scores higher than a 5.1 (Malaysia); 10 is best. The others range from 3.3 (Thailand) to 2.5 (the Philippines), 2.0 (Cambodia), 2.3 (Indonesia), and a dismal 1.4 (Myanmar). By comparison, China and India are tied at 3.5.[14] Ordinary citizens in these countries consider corruption a fact of life and doubt that it will diminish. Only in Indonesia is there expectation of improvement, thanks to repeated pledges from Indonesia's president, retired general Susilo Bambang Yudhoyono.[15]

Weak Public Support for Integration

Governments have done little to raise public awareness of the benefits of integration. Asia suffers from what came to be known in Europe as the "democratic deficit." Except for Singapore, national leaders have done little or nothing to prepare the public for closer integration. ASEAN parliamentarians meet from time to time, but they have little to say about the substance and mechanics of closer integration. Sooner or later, the Asian integration movement will need a certain amount of legitimacy to succeed, but no government seems prepared to invest its political capital in such a far-off vision.

Lack of Skills and Information

Doing business in a globalized market economy requires both skills and information. But respect for market principles, entrepreneurial skills, and technical expertise in areas like risk assessment and accounting are often limited or absent. Inadequate banking supervision, high rates of nonperforming loans, and reluctance to divulge information complicate the prospects for financial coordination, let alone full-scale integration.

■ Potential Threats

Social scientists like to speak of "independent variables" and "dependent variables." Asian integration is a dependent variable. Its future is not secure. One can imagine any number of crises and historical surprises that could throw it off course, split it into hostile camps, or (conceivably) accelerate it. The most important variables are the evolution of China and the future of the US-China relationship. Others include the China-Japan relationship, a North Korean nuclear incident, the evolution of India, the future of global trade and growth, and "wild cards" such as a devastating pandemic.

China

The main independent variable that could sustain, shrink, or shatter Asian integration is the evolution of China.[16] China has never solved the problem of the peaceful transfer of power and thus has not yet established a truly stable and predictable political system. No one knows who will be the next to govern China until half a dozen aging men walk out on a stage. A major social upheaval and the collapse of the Chinese economy are nightmare scenarios for Asians. A nationalist backlash in China could trigger aggressive behavior elsewhere in Asia. One of the cornerstones of the integration movement is the widely shared conviction that including and engaging China will encourage cooperative behavior. If that strategy fails, the integration movement will stall or flounder.

The US-China Relationship

What happens inside China will strongly influence the US-China relationship, which suffuses everything in the region and is thus a related independent variable. A war in the Taiwan Strait would spell temporary disaster for the rest of Asia. Depending on how it started, Asians could find themselves paralyzed and polarized, especially if Washington called for a trade embargo. In almost any scenario, Japan would be under enormous pressure. Conversely, if the Chinese political system softens into mild authoritarianism, combined with more participatory governance and respect for basic human rights, occasional tension between Beijing and Washington would not threaten the region's peaceful evolution.

China's participation in the Asian integration movement since the financial crisis has matched Beijing's stated goal of regional peace and growth-friendly stability.[17] Authorities in China and Taiwan are exercising restraint, and territorial claims in the South China Sea have been put on hold. Except for Myanmar, the noxious regimes that Beijing is cultivating for the sake of imagined energy security lie outside Asia. China is cooperating with regional and US-backed initiatives to thwart terrorists and criminals. On the negative side, political freedoms have been trimmed, tensions in the East China Sea still crackle, China's future goals in the region are still unclear, and the secrecy still veiling the full extent of China's defense spending is not reassuring.

Rivalry Between Japan and China

Japan and China are engaged in a subtle but intense struggle for influence in the rest of Asia, with China trumping Japan on trade and Japan leading China on finance. China is trying with some success to marginalize Japan, but Japan's financial strength, technological know-how, and modern military forces still carry weight. On balance, Japan's influence adds up to less than the sum of its assets, and China's adds up to more.

The integration movement is a moving vehicle. Its speed drops to a crawl whenever the two strongest passengers do not work cooperatively to move it along. Significant progress toward Asia-wide integration depends heavily on whether Japan's prime minster and his colleagues can restrain more extreme members of the right wing, improve relations with China and South Korea, and accept more farm goods from the rest of Asia. For their part, Beijing and Seoul must find a manageable way to cultivate healthy patriotism, provide a good education and jobs for their young people, and engage North Korea without alienating Japan.

Political Polarization

US commitment to the spread of democracy has inspired proposals to create a "Concert of Democracies," or something similar.[18] This idea appeals to those who look at Asia from a human rights perspective. There is every reason to pursue cooperation and dialogue among democratic countries, as the United States, Japan, Australia, and (to some extent) India do. But going further than that runs into the sticky question of which Asian countries would qualify. Any State Department officer charged with drafting reports for Congress can testify that lists create unnecessary diplomatic problems. But the real reason why even an unofficial union of democracies is not a good idea is that such a policy framework would implicitly create two divergent camps and thus undermine the stability of the region.

A formal grouping that explicitly promotes democracy and takes coordinated action based on democratic values would likely be seen in China as an expression of containment and an "us against them" reversion to Cold War thinking. Such a perception could raise the risk of armed clashes in the Taiwan Strait, the waters surrounding disputed areas of the seabed, or maritime choke points along sea lines of communication. Instead of encouraging the evolution of participatory governance in China, the Chinese Communist Party might choose to whip up nationalist sentiment and tighten the screws of one-party rule. No leaders in Beijing would believe that the United States was motivated by idealism; instead, they would see a plot to extend US hegemony. Advocates of democracy and human rights who live in countries ruled by repressive governments would face yet another allegation that they are serving the interests of foreigners.

Polarization would put pressure on smaller nations to act or not act in a way that favors one camp over the other, reducing their autonomy and depriving them of the benefits of friendship with both. Those located on China's border would feel compelled to lean toward Beijing. Tension between the two camps would set back or preclude joint efforts to deal with emerging threats and dampen regionwide trade and investment. Integration in Maritime Asia, the engine of Asia's growing wealth, would stall. All this would be just the opposite of what Asian governments are trying to achieve.

A North Korean Nuclear Incident

North Korea is the most secretive regime in the world, its people are highly disciplined, and its few treasures are closely guarded. It is likely that the Kim Jong Il regime conducted a nuclear weapons test in 2006 not only to gain prestige but also to ward off a possible US attack.

It seems unlikely that having labored so hard to acquire nuclear weapons, North Korea will readily transfer them to others. Nevertheless, the North Korean government is strapped for cash and engages in many illicit activities. The sale of plutonium to, say, Hamas or Al-Qaida operatives cannot be ruled out. Such a transaction would trigger extreme reactions from the United States and Japan and perhaps even from China.

The Evolution of India

India is a strategic counterweight to China. New Delhi tracks and seeks to moderate Chinese influence, although all parties publicly deny this obvious reality. Domestic politics in India, relations with Pakistan and China, and willingness to further liberalize trade and investment will determine whether or not India's membership in Asia Major acquires flesh and bones. If India drops out, however, the integration movement would still roll on but would suffer a loss. India has many commercial assets, including an extensive coastline, a huge and literate middle class, a free press with sophisticated economic reporting, trained economists, advanced technology, excellent research institutes, a globally accessible popular culture (films and food in particular), widespread fluency in English, and a vast diaspora of relatively wealthy and well-educated Indians abroad. New Delhi's Look East policy connects these assets with the rest of Asia.

The cultural adaptability of Indians to East Asian ways is an intangible variable. Indians started the "dialogue" process with ASEAN somewhat later than the others and have not yet built extensive personal networks. The outspoken, logical, and somewhat argumentative nature of Indian discourse runs counter to the prevailing East Asian style.[19] Diplomats and business leaders tend to be fluent in English and are often educated in the United States or the United Kingdom. "An Indian businessman can have dinner with a European or US businessman and have five things in common to talk about," says the head of Merrill Lynch's investment banking service in Mumbai. "He can't do that in East Asia."[20]

Global Trade and Growth

Asian integration depends in part on vigorous economic growth in Japan, China, the United States, and the European Union. Individuals and companies will invest in Asian production networks on a large scale only if they have cash to invest and if potential demand in major global markets justifies those investments. That was the pattern throughout much of the 1990s. A global shock associated with the falling dollar and the current overhang of large external imbalances could send Asia reeling.

Smaller setbacks are also possible. In the 1980s, Japan, not China, was the rising giant. But Japan succumbed to a decade of stagnation that ended only in 2002. Its challenges include caring for an aging population, halting deflation, coping with high public debt, boosting productivity and innovation, and opening up protected sectors to competition. China's challenges are more daunting. A major economic setback there is unlikely but cannot be ruled out.

Another variable is the outcome of the WTO's Doha Round of trade talks. If the talks end in failure or with minimal results, as appears likely, and if the US Congress will not grant the president renewed "trade promotion authority," open trade and global growth could go into reverse. In such a case, unemployment would rise and incomes would stagnate, making it difficult for Asian governments to retain the legitimacy they need to pursue integration.

Wild Cards: Unexpected Disasters

In many parts of Asia the risk of an environmental or health disaster looms large. Misuse of natural resources can trigger a catastrophe. Polluted and overcrowded megacities and peri-urban zones are cradles of disease. No one can rule out the eruption of a pandemic such as a human-to-human version of avian flu, a life-threatening environmental disaster, or a lethal terrorist attack. If the damage is contained quickly, economic integration will not be significantly affected. If not, business travel and tourism will shrivel and investment will be postponed. In a worst-case scenario, millions will die. Meanwhile, climate change continues apace, threatening the very existence of Maritime Asia.

■ Conclusion

Some obstacles, such as distance, diversity, and artificial boundaries, cannot be altered, but others, such as mutual mistrust and Sino-Japanese tensions, could soften over time as new habits and norms take hold. Most of the obstacles and threats listed in this chapter are barriers not only to closer integration but also to development. They suggest that government-driven integration among the nation-states of Asia Major is far more difficult to achieve than integration in Maritime Asia.

■ Notes

1. North Korea and Taiwan were not ranked. The list is available at www
.undp.org.

2. This theme is developed in Alesina, Easterly, and Matuszeski, "Artificial States."

3. Kraft, "Human Rights in Southeast Asia," p. 11.

4. Michael Yahuda, *The International Politics of the Asia Pacific,* 2nd ed. (London: Routledge Curzon, 2004), p. 229, cited in Pempel, "The Race to Connect East Asia," p. 243.

5. Fravel, "China's Management of Territorial Disputes," p. 1.

6. "Thai Fishermen Dominate RI Waters," *Jakarta Post,* January 3, 2006, summarized as "Fishing Rights as a Source of Conflict," Singapore Institute of International Affairs, www.siiaonline.org.

7. Saritha Rai, "As Foreign Investment Rises, India Addresses Security Concerns," *New York Times,* August 24, 2006, p. C4.

8. Pew Global Attitudes Project, "Publics of Asian Powers Hold Negative Views of One Another," p. 1.

9. "Japan the Weakest Link in East Asian Regionalism?" SEAPSNet, May 26, 2006, www.siiaonline.org.

10. For a skeptical Asian reaction to the notion of an integrated East Asian community, see Lee, "East Asian Community and the United States," pp. 29–32.

11. "All Eyes on ASEAN Meetings in Kuala Lumpur," SEAPSNet, July 25, 2006, www.siiaonline.org.

12. *CIA World Factbook,* available at www.cia.gov.

13. Searight, "Process and the Art of Diplomacy," p. 7.

14. "TI 2007 Corruption Perceptions Index," available at www.transparency.org.

15. According to a survey conducted by Transparency International, 81 percent of Indonesians polled in 2005 expected that corruption would decrease in the next three years. By contrast, respondents in India and the Philippines were extremely pessimistic.

16. See the four "Illustrative Asian Economic Scenarios" in Sokolsky, Rabasa, and Neu, *The Role of Southeast Asia in U.S. Strategy Toward China,* pp. 81–84.

17. For positive and negative China scenarios and suggestions for US policy, see Krawitz, "China's Trade Opening."

18. Ivo Daalder and James Lindsay, "Democracies of the World, Unite!" *The American Interest*, January/February 2007, available at www.the-american-interest .com/ai2/article.cfm?Id=220&MId=7.

19. Sen, *The Argumentative Indian,* chap. 1.

20. Tucker and Leahy, "On the March."

12

Looking to the Future

In previous chapters of this book, I described and analyzed two quite different forces shaping Asia's future as a region. One is regionalization, the spontaneous integration pulsing through Maritime Asia and fueled largely by economic globalization and technology. The other is regionalism, expressed as the government-driven integration movement, whose member governments seek to both profit from and temper the forces of globalization as they strive to enhance their autonomy and security. In this chapter, I bring these two forces together and suggest some implications for Asian policymakers. I also offer selected policy recommendations for a key player—the United States.

Thus far I have not devoted much space to the US role in Asia because I wanted to focus on what Asians are doing. This was an artificial device. No other power defines and shapes the regional and global order to the same degree as the United States. The US military presence in Asia, especially the Seventh Fleet, is widely appreciated. The 1960s-era riots protesting the renewal of US security treaties are largely absent today. The US market, US investors, US technology, and the US dollar are overwhelmingly important to Asians. US reactions to the Asian integration movement—and the resurgence of China in particular—will have strong bearing on the future of Asian regionalism.

■ Suggested Course Corrections

I argued in Part 1 that we are now witnessing the spontaneous resurgence and reintegration of Maritime Asia, a centuries-old locus of Asian wealth and power. The "spinners" or "integrators" of Maritime Asia are private individuals clustered along major bodies of water. Taking advantage of globalization, new technology, regional peace and stability, and China's rocketing economy, they form a newly wealthy and highly cosmopolitan middle class. Integration in Maritime Asia exceeds integration with or within any other major region except Europe.

By contrast, Asia's new regionalism centers on the land-based Asian integration movement, which aims at strengthening and stabilizing a group of nation-states. Its agenda overlaps with but does not fully correspond to the needs of individual integrators in coastal zones or ocean-accessible cities. It devotes insufficient attention to the overlap between land and sea and thus understates the richness and unifying pull of Asia's maritime legacies, livelihoods, and resources.

It follows that the Asian integration movement should build on the region's most dynamic shared asset—Maritime Asia. Recognizing the unifying power of the ocean, the governments of Asia Major should explicitly build Maritime Asia into their vision of integration and devise corresponding roadmaps and action plans. Residents of Maritime Asia are natural integrators and will connect with each other if their governments "go with the flow" and remove the barriers to their interaction.

Thinking this way will not come easily. Locked in a nation-state mindset and still preoccupied with consolidating national unity within their unwieldy territories, Asian governments have not focused on Maritime Asia as such. They are slow to recognize, let alone correct, the partial mismatch between what is transpiring in official meeting rooms and scholarly conference halls on the one hand and what is happening on the street, in ports and airports, and on computers and mobile phones on the other. All but the most specialized maps and statistical handbooks focus on the land, leaving the seas blue and blank.

Selected maritime initiatives are in place (for instance, to improve maritime security and simplify port procedures), but they are limited in number and lack both a regionally endorsed "vision" and high-level political momentum. Individual governments promote maritime free-trade zones and other special arrangements in their own territory, but to my knowledge no one in power has acknowledged that Maritime Asia has a cross-border identity of its own and that its resurgence serves both integration and development.

The need to narrow large and growing income gaps between coastal and interior zones and between urban and rural populations might argue against a stronger emphasis on Maritime Asia. But evidence from China and elsewhere demonstrates that opening up opportunities in maritime regions does far more than just "trickle down." Such moves stimulate competition from and among interior regions and trigger pressure for reform, competition, a modern infrastructure, and a more equitable distribution of wealth. The more national income that is generated, the more governments will be able to help remote regions tap into their nation's rising wealth. Conversely, there is little or no evidence that focusing development resources in commercially unviable regions will set a larger process of national growth in motion.

Critics might also respond that a stronger emphasis on Maritime Asia is unfair to countries whose maritime resources are limited. Only in Singapore does the maritime zone coincide with the national territory. At the other extreme, Laos is landlocked (but has access to a major ocean-flowing river). All the other countries in Asia Major enjoy direct access to the sea. They have a dual identity—maritime and interior. China is a land-based power but increasingly a maritime power. Japan, South Korea, Thailand, Indonesia, Malaysia, and the Philippines all contain dynamic, cosmopolitan coastal zones and interior communities less connected to the globalized world. India is saddled with a rickety infrastructure, high tariffs, restrictions on investment, and regulatory overkill but is recovering its maritime legacy. Two countries belonging geographically to Maritime Asia are self-isolated (Myanmar and North Korea), and a third is unable to take full advantage of its coastline (Cambodia). Delaying the reintegration of Maritime Asia will not help them; inability to participate more fully in the resurgence of Maritime Asia is a symptom of poor governance and an unappealing investment climate and should not be used as an excuse to hold back others.

A more concentrated focus on Maritime Asia by no means excludes other ways to promote healthy regional initiatives. I suggest that Asian leaders seeking to deepen and strengthen integration should join forces with their private sector counterparts and with representatives from civil society organizations to focus on six challenges in particular. They are the migration of labor, energy and the environment, the integration gap, trade, decisionmaking, and the construction of a regional identity.

The Migration of Labor

The free or nearly free migration of labor is a legacy of Maritime Asia. In a perfectly integrated market, workers would be able to move as freely as capital. Only in the European Union has this vision taken hold; elsewhere, governments generally welcome skilled workers but restrict the flow of semiskilled and unskilled laborers. In Asia Major, Indonesia, the Philippines, and India are the largest exporters of labor, and Singapore and Malaysia are the largest importers.

Although professional and skilled workers in Asia can migrate more freely than semiskilled and unskilled ones, there is no regionwide system. Mutual recognition of skills and qualifications is in its infancy. Unskilled and semiskilled workers seeking cross-border work face high barriers to full-time entry and often migrate illegally. Although Maritime Asia is booming, central authorities place numerous barriers against the long-term employment of foreign workers. Visas issued to migrant workers are limited in number and sometimes confined to particular seasons, depending on the nature of the employment. Illegal foreign workers are subject to deportations, as happened to as many as 800,000 of them in Malaysia in 2005.[1] Japan suppresses immigration despite its aging population and shortage of manual laborers and makes it difficult for those who do enter to obtain citizenship. In all countries, criminal gangs prey on immigrants seeking jobs, especially women.

Commenting on what it would take to create a genuine Asian Economic Community, two Asia-based officials of the United Nations Development Programme list "the need to devise a regional agreement on the temporary movement of labor across borders."[2] Two other experts suggest that there is no escape from market forces: if unskilled workers cannot come in the front door, they will come in at the side or at the back. They urge the governments of labor-receiving countries to think about international labor migration "more pragmatically and more in economic terms."[3] The president of the ADB has made the same suggestion to ASEAN.

A few governments have moved in this direction. The government of the Philippines, for one, has factored remittances into its economic plans and taken steps to protect Filipino workers abroad. The government of Singapore has incorporated the demand for foreign labor into its overall economic plan and adjusted its immigration policies accordingly. A handful of bilateral agreements exist. These are exceptions, however.

Neither the "Vision" statement nor subsequent declarations endorse the free movement of workers as a long-term goal. Communiqués and other vision statements call for higher safety standards and better education and training, but they are silent on the freedom to work in a country of one's choice. Instead, the emphasis is on human resources—training, enhanced productivity, social protection, and the like. This thrust is certainly necessary, but it is not sufficient.

Policies on the migration of semiskilled and unskilled labor are mostly ad hoc and uncoordinated. There are no enforceable Asia-wide employment standards and no meaningful moves to integrate the market for unskilled and semiskilled labor. No high-level leader wants to spend political capital talking about an enforceable regional agreement on the migration and mutual protection of laborers. Nevertheless, Asian governments should put more effort into devising a coordinated approach to the flow of unskilled and semiskilled workers. Such an initiative should include a common registration scheme and agreed procedures to protect workers, expanded quotas, training, and a crackdown on illicit job hawkers and traffickers.

Energy and the Environment

Most governments in Asia Major have not taken adequate steps to cope with the combination of Asia's surging demand for energy and current distortions in the energy market. Nor have they adequately addressed the substantial overlap between patterns of energy consumption and environmental degradation.

This failure has many dimensions. Perceived vulnerability to energy disruptions creates strategic dependence, intensifies maritime border disputes, and stimulates efforts to lock up supplies. Reliance on dirty coal creates enormous health and environmental problems. Pell-mell industrial development and the proliferation of cars foul the air and the water. Global warming threatens the very existence of low-lying maritime communities.

Energy.   Major proposals to enhance Asian energy security include emergency-sharing stockpile arrangements, stepped-up efforts to resolve energy-related maritime border disputes in the East China and South China Seas, fewer restrictions on foreign investment in Russia's eastern regions, jointly funded measures to improve the efficiency of energy consumption, investment in alternative fuels, hybrid cars, completion of various pipelines and construction of new ones, and various foreign policy measures, including an end to US efforts to stop the construction of new pipelines from Iran. Indonesia, Malaysia, the Philippines, Thailand, and Vietnam have all expressed an interest in developing nuclear energy.

APEC's Energy Working Group has focused extensively on regional energy security. APEC energy ministers have endorsed two sensible initiatives. One is the Asia Pacific Energy Research Centre to monitor supply-and-demand trends. The other is the Energy Security Initiative, which is charged with developing plans to deal with supply disruptions. ASEAN + 3 have also debated energy issues, but with few tangible results.

Since demand for energy in Northeast Asia is particularly intense, a subregional organization might be appropriate. One idea is a Northeast Asian Energy Community based on the European-inspired Energy Charter Treaty or something similar.[4] Another is a Northeast Asian Energy Cooperation Council, a private-sector organization that would act as a broker to facilitate energy development.[5]

Environmental protection.   Improved environmental protection is a mandate, not a luxury. After years of arguing that protecting the environment was a luxury that only rich countries could afford, Asian leaders now take environmental issues seriously. Global and regional environmental programs include application of clean coal technology via the Kyoto Protocol's Clean Development Mechanism, funds to halt slash-and-burn agricultural practices, measures to protect fish stocks, and many others. Enforcement, however, remains limp and uneven.

Dangers stemming from environmental pollution and global warming call for a stronger and more enforceable commitment to environmental protection as part of the Asian integration movement. Governments need to strengthen and standardize efforts to collect statistics on health and pollution, apply objective policy analysis to set up control systems, and then implement and enforce those controls through honest and effective administrative and legal systems. All these capabilities are needed for economic development as well.

Leaders of the Asian integration movement should therefore consider the following joint environmental and energy agenda. First, taking better care of the environment calls for national budgets that accurately reflect the costs of pollution and the loss of natural resources such as forests. There is room for a centralized effort to devise accounting systems that would be consistent from nation to nation to quantify these impacts. Either APEC or the new ERIA could help here.

Second, energy efficiency can provide both dramatic economic benefits and a brake on the growth of greenhouse gas emissions. Since energy efficiency depends heavily on accurate prices, it is also completely consistent with economic modernization. Although actual efforts to achieve energy efficiency will inevitably have a national focus, a coordinated regional effort to summarize existing proposals, identify the options, and recommend the most promising approaches in order of priority would be entirely appropriate. Japan, a world leader in energy conservation, has floated proposals of this kind.

Third, coping with the emission of greenhouse gases and its effect on the climate and weather requires far more vigorous efforts. In 2005, Australia, the United States, China, Japan, South Korea, and India, which together account for 50 percent of greenhouse gas emissions, established the Asia-Pacific Partnership on Clean Development and Climate to develop future carbon-free energy sources. Initiatives stemming from this group could be incorporated into the agenda of the Asian integration movement.

Finally, improving environmental governance calls for urgent, high-level attention. Any system for global carbon control (as well as control of more conventional pollutants) will need the capacity to translate limits on emission into national regulatory systems designed to achieve the overall goal. Ideally, these should be "cap and trade" regulatory systems that work by creating a market in pollution rights. However, the legal and governance systems of many Asian countries may not be developed enough to support such a sophisticated approach. There is a real need for regional work on the design of future carbon control and other pollution control mechanisms adapted to local circumstances and capabilities.

All of these energy and environmental initiatives should be developed in consultation with private companies as well as civil society groups, depending on the relevance of their expertise and the legitimacy of their concerns.

Narrowing the Integration Gap

Richer members of Asia Major need to intensify collective, behind-the-scenes pressure on the retrograde and self-serving governments of Cambodia, Laos, and Myanmar, which perpetuate poverty and pose problems for their neighbors. Engagement with the rest of ASEAN has not changed their nature. Since "sticks" in the form of trade sanctions enrich black marketeers and hurt poor people, it may be time for a larger and more imaginative package of "carrots." Such an approach would not rule out narrowly targeted financial sanctions aimed at individual dictators and their cohorts, such as those imposed on Myanmar in the wake of the bloody 2007 crackdown.

Richer governments should study the experience of Europe's Structural Funds and consider something comparable, suitably adapted to Asian conditions. These governments need to mobilize significant new resources and transfer them directly, if possible, to poor people and communities, preferably through nonprofit organizations. Their focus should be small enterprise development and technical aid to local government officials, small businesses, and nonprofit groups in such fields as accounting, finance, budgetary procedures, evaluation, personnel management, and antibribery systems. Such incremental steps would encourage both job creation and more honest, accountable, and participatory governance. Japan, South Korea, Singapore, Australia, and New Zealand all have much to contribute in these areas.

To symbolize the inclusion of Cambodia, Laos, Myanmar, and Vietnam in Maritime Asia, heads of state in the richer Asian countries should announce a forward-looking, coordinated maritime initiative to modernize CLMV ports and maritime infrastructure. Their vision should include feeder roads and rail links, container-capable and refrigerated trucks, and financial services such as long-distance credit, insurance, and risk assessment. The ADB already funds many of these projects and has the technical expertise to back up a high-level political commitment. Additional funds should be channeled to small businesses, civil society groups, and other nongovernment recipients in interior regions so that remote communities can tap into their countries' maritime assets.

Safeguarding major rivers provide one way to narrow the integration gap. Both the ADB and ASEAN governments, especially Thailand, need to work more closely with China to modify plans to erect more dams on the upper Mekong. Failure to keep the Mekong healthy and flowing in the right seasonal patterns and depths poses a severe risk to downstream livelihoods and environmental diversity. Although the governments of the affected countries have challenged China's plans, they are thinking about following China's example and developing hydropower for themselves. These competing priorities call for a high degree of coordinated planning and leverage.[6]

Alternatives to Preferential Trade Agreements

Asian governments could and should do something about the flood of half-baked PTAs, discussed at length in Chapter 8. They have already signaled that they want to be on good terms with everyone and that they don't want to be left out of the game of commercial diplomacy. Enough is enough.

Five alternative measures would facilitate integration while preserving or enhancing national sovereignty. First, Asian governments could turn the "noodle bowl" into clear soup by standardizing PTAs to the greatest extent possible. They could also add services and investment, improve the protection of intellectual property, and bring dispute settlement into closer conformity with WTO procedures. Gradually adding teeth to Japanese-sponsored "economic partnership agreements" would be one way to accomplish these goals. Second, they could take further unilateral steps to liberalize trade and investment without waiting for "concessions" from trading partners. Third, they could improve the transparency and viability of financial institutions and establish credible risk assessment agencies. Fourth, they could do more to facilitate movement in and out of ports, such as streamlining customs procedures and security checks. Finally, they could improve and expand the collection and dissemination of all relevant maritime data, not just terrorist movements and criminal activity.

Intraregional trade is not an alternative to ongoing engagement with the transpacific and global economy and global institutions and should not be seen as such. Talk of integrating ASEAN first, ASEAN + 3 next, followed by ASEAN + 6 after that, and the transpacific and global trading communities in the distant future makes little sense and could cause serious medium-term distortions. There is every reason for Asians to remove barriers among themselves, but parallel efforts should be devoted to liberalizing global and transpacific markets and supporting the institutions that sustain them, notably the WTO and APEC.

Encouraging Local Decisionmaking

Governments cannot and should not wrestle with transnational challenges alone. ASEAN is in the process of opening the door to wider participation in its decisionmaking procedures. But all governments, not just those of ASEAN members, need to listen to and work in close partnership with those most able to construct healthy and outward-looking communities. Such people are close at hand. They are business and financial leaders, civil society activists, labor representatives, port directors, educators, tourist and travel agents, mayors, and others.

Local autonomy for merchant groups is a historical legacy of Maritime Asia. Asian governments should consider devolving more autonomy to local authorities and establishing a structured advisory process for cross-border business groups, merchant associations, and qualified civil society organizations. Governments should draw more systematically on the advice of national and cross-border business organizations before they set priorities. They should dismantle out-of-date regulations and delegate some of their remaining authority to local officials, who would be required to consult formally with affected groups.

Such reforms could further stimulate competitive liberalization among regional port authorities and local officials eager to capture expanding business. Even the retrograde governments of the CLMV countries could permit greater local participation in Maritime Asia without feeling threatened. Cities and provinces located in the interior of all countries would soon demand policy changes and improvements to gain access to comparable economic opportunities, contributing to a virtuous circle. This is what happened in China, and there is every reason to expect that the process would repeat itself elsewhere.

Construction of a Regional Identity

Educated Southeast Asians have had the existence of ASEAN drummed into their heads for a long time, but the intensity of self-defined regional identity among the general population varies considerably. In 2005, according to the Asian Barometer, the percentage of Southeast Asians who named "Asian" as the transnational group they identified with was quite high, except for Indonesians (39 percent). Figures ranged from nearly 60 percent in landlocked Laos to over 90 percent in Cambodia and Myanmar. The latter figures suggest that assertions of Asian identity may have something to do with bad government at home. (Poles living under Soviet domination overwhelmingly identified themselves as "European," partly because they genuinely felt European and partly because they wanted to make a political statement.)

Regional identity is much weaker in Japan, South Korea, China, and India than in Southeast Asia. In response to the same question ("Do you identify with any transnational group?"), 42 percent of respondents in Japan, 21 percent in India, and only 6 percent in China chose "Asian."[7] State officials and opinion leaders in those countries do not think primarily in regional terms. Australians do not identify themselves with "Asians," but awareness of the region is quite high.

The Japanese are important global players but still display traces of what they call an "island-country mentality." They are ambivalent about developing Asia, identifying themselves more readily with Western democracies. The great majority supports the US-Japan alliance as a hedge against North Korea and potentially China. In none of these countries is there a serious effort to cultivate regional identity in public speeches or in schools.

Self-perceptions can change, but they usually change slowly. Strengthening regional awareness and identity as cornerstones of Asian integration, and adding a maritime perspective, will require governments to launch an educational campaign lasting for many years.

Policy Implications for the United States

Pay Attention and Listen

Despite the changing balance of influence, most high-level US officials devote little serious attention to the Asian integration movement. US engagement with Asian regionalism chugs along at a working level, but high-level appointees have little time to think about Asia. They are preoccupied with more immediate challenges, notably the war in Iraq and violence elsewhere in the Middle East, the development of nuclear weapons in North Korea and Iran, and the struggle against terrorist groups.

Many officials responsible for US policy toward Asia see the integration movement as merely a "talk shop." This attitude is characteristic. Americans are practical and pragmatic in nature: They are impatient with process and dialogue. They want results. They see challenges in Asia that Asian governments are not addressing effectively. US officials therefore favor "functional" integration—that is, specific initiatives that yield tangible achievements. They believe that new architectural structures should be considered on the basis of what gaps they fill and what value they add.[8] Many Asians agree with them and bemoan the high degree of overlap and duplication characteristic of the architecture of Asian integration. But for many Asian governments, the very process of integration is a goal in itself.

The huge cost of the Iraq war has a spillover effect on US foreign policy in Asia because it severely constrains the availability of US diplomatic tools. It is forcing civilian agencies to absorb budget cuts, trim travel expenses, and postpone the staffing and implementation of initiatives that would help restore America's image, such as more grants for education and research. Although the United States is still a magnet for students and job seekers, fewer educational and travel opportunities are available to Asians compared to the first few decades after World War II. After September 11, it became more difficult for Asians to get a visa.

Late in the day, the Bush administration tried to counter the impression that the United States was neglecting Asia. Speaking in Singapore in June 2007, US defense secretary Robert Gates explicitly rebutted such a perception, saying, "We are an Asian power with significant and long-term political, economic, and security interests." Although he named the United States as a "Pacific nation" from its very inception, the greater part of his speech was devoted to the Middle East and Central Asia.[9]

Compounding the impression of high-level US neglect is the widely shared opinion that the Bush administration overreacted to September 11, harped incessantly on antiterrorism and "homeland security," engaged in tin-ear moralizing instead of listening, hammered on North Korea's nuclear weapons programs while downplaying Asians' other security concerns, and limited its leadership initiatives to its own narrow interests.[10] Reporting on the 2003 APEC Leaders' Meeting, for example, Japanese journalist Yoichi Funabashi reported that "when Bush doggedly pursued his anti-terror agenda … Asian leaders let out a collective groan."[11]

Since then the Bush administration has toned down its emphasis on terrorism in Asia. But by focusing so heavily on its own security needs while refusing to sign ASEAN's Treaty of Amity and Cooperation (TAC), Washington has largely excluded itself from the delicate dance of integration politics. If this trend continues, nothing drastic will happen, but the US voice will be slowly drained of influence.

Don't Overreact to the Exclusion of the United States

Some Americans worry because the United States is excluded from various pan-Asian organizations. They should not be concerned.

As a general rule, the US approach to regional integration since World War II has been and remains cautiously benign, provided that such movements are (1) not designed to undermine global and regional institutions of which the United States is a member, such as the WTO, the IMF, and APEC; (2) not intended as an alternative to security ties between the United States and a US ally (in this case, Japan, South Korea, Thailand, the Philippines, or Australia); (3) not dominated by a power unfriendly to the United States (this would be a concern if a future Chinese government were strongly anti-American and if pro-US governments were marginalized); (4) consistent with market-oriented trade and investment policies, with a goal of creating more trade and investment rather than diverting them; and (5) accompanied by compensation for lost US exports, if any.[12] This last condition is premature, but the others look likely to be satisfied, at least to a substantial degree.

In Asia Major, the United States starts from a position of strength. It is the least distrusted country in the region, which is actually saying a lot. It is still an indispensable security arbiter. Even after planned restructuring and redeployment, US naval and air power in Asia will remain overwhelming. Asians still rely on the United States to maintain open sea lanes and provide overall stability in the region and will do so for the foreseeable future. Aid programs are modest but respectable and beginning to grow again. Diplomatic relations with most of the governments of the region are good, and social links are extensive. The United States attracts tens of thousands of Asians seeking better economic and educational opportunities. No other country wields such a combination or is likely to do so soon.

In addition, the United States has extensive trade, investment, and financial ties with individual Asian countries. The US market, along with markets in Europe and Japan, is indispensable as a final destination for products manufactured in Asia. US investors bring capital, technology, and expertise to the region. For those reasons, there is virtually no possibility of a closed trade bloc or Fortress Asia. (Fortress Europe also failed to materialize.) Singapore, Australia, and Japan would never approve it, and they have clout. China presumably wants a lower US profile in Asia but would not risk antagonizing either the United States or its fellow Asians over regional trade arrangements when more important bilateral issues are at stake.

All signs point toward a form of Asian regionalism that will be broadly compatible with US interests. No government in the region wants to alienate Washington. "America need not be a part of each and every aspect of the emerging East Asian construct," says Singapore's Goh Chok Tong. "But it cannot and should not be excluded from East Asia."[13] This is the majority view.

Re-Engage with ASEAN

It is always difficult to persuade a US president to travel overseas, especially to a place as far from Washington as Southeast Asia, when nothing very tangible will be announced. Secretaries of state who get bogged down in the Middle East do not have time to go to Southeast Asia either. But there is no substitute for the personal relationships and political visibility associated with high-level visits and meetings.

In 2007 President Bush agreed to mark the fortieth anniversary of ASEAN's founding by participating in a US-ASEAN summit. This was a breakthrough, but then he decided not to attend after all. This cancellation, combined with the absence of US secretary of state Condoleezza Rice at the 2005 and 2007 meetings of the ASEAN Regional Forum, left Southeast Asians feeling slighted. Thus far, summit-level discussions have been limited to the seven members of ASEAN that are also members of APEC. This reluctance to engage with ASEAN leaders as a group stems in large part from US fears that a summit would legitimize the regime in Myanmar. This is a case of the tail wagging the dog.

The Bush administration's trade, energy, and health initiatives toward Southeast Asia are technically solid but lack resources and high-level political visibility. The Enterprise for ASEAN Initiative, for instance, offered bilateral PTAs to individual ASEAN members only. (Singapore quickly accepted the invitation and became the first to conclude an agreement.) The subsequent

ASEAN-US Enhanced Partnership promised cooperation in a range of activities, but budget outlays to bring most of these initiatives to fruition are insufficient. On the positive side, in 2006 the Office of the US Trade Representative and trade officials from ASEAN member governments negotiated a US-ASEAN Trade and Investment Framework Agreement (TIFA).[14] A TIFA is normally a prerequisite for a PTA with the United States, so this step was well received in Southeast Asian capitals.

The most direct way for the United States to re-engage with ASEAN would be to sign the TAC, with appropriate caveats of the sort negotiated by Australia (summarized in Chapter 7). Since the TAC is only a statement of principles and contains no binding provisions, eventual Senate approval should not be beyond reach.

US policies in the Middle East have direct impact on ASEAN, especially the ASEAN 5. The Bush administration's disastrous war in Iraq, combined with its perceived bias toward Israel, increasingly disturb ASEAN Muslims. The number of Malaysians identifying themselves as "Muslim first, Malaysian second" is growing, and the same may be true in Indonesia and the southern Philippines. This trend is of great concern to governments that are still struggling to manage ethnic and religious tensions. Forced to accommodate Islamic parties and groups, political leaders have less room to maneuver at home. Mounting political awareness among Asian Muslims also raises a risk that the political fault line separating Muslim from non-Muslim countries will become more marked.[15] Most ASEAN leaders do not voice these concerns because they have more immediate interests to discuss with Washington. But rightly or wrongly, they blame US policy in the Middle East for inflaming Muslim opinion.

Finally, since the new Asian Charter commits ASEAN governments to sending permanent representatives to ASEAN's headquarters in Jakarta, the United States should strongly consider following suit. The planned establishment of a US ambassador for ASEAN affairs is a step in the right direction.[16]

Get Used to a Resurgent China—and Make Room for It

US policymakers do not want to see the integration movement become a tool of Chinese foreign policy. (Neither do other Asians.) Some Americans believe that China seeks to establish regional domination, undermine US influence, reduce the US military presence in Asia, and regain possession of Taiwan, by force if necessary.

China has clearly gained ground in the regional balance of influence, capitalizing on its economic growth and reassuring its Asian neighbors about its peaceful intentions. Unlike Washington, Beijing has projected a sympathetic and listening attitude and offers aid and trade deals without appearing to demand anything in return. As Chinese influence waxes, US influence is still strong but is in relative decline.

There is little or nothing that the United States can or should do to halt this trend. The resurgence of China means that some adjustment is inevitable, and the balance of influence in Asia between China and the United States is by no means zero-sum. Beijing's diplomatic initiatives are generally constructive, and Sino-American cooperation in the UN Security Council and in some functional areas is solid. Experts note that Chinese leaders seem determined to minimize conflicts with the United States and that they see little to gain from an anti-American strategy.[17]

The two most important variables influencing Asia's future are China's domestic evolution and the US-China relationship, and they are related.[18] China's embrace of market capitalism and its implicit rejection of Maoism are reassuring and probably irreversible. But its leaders face massive and destabilizing domestic problems, and their long-term goals in Asia are unknown. It would be naïve to think that China's prosperity rules out the chance that China will go to war, especially when it comes to Taiwan. But other things being equal, a wealthier, more open, and more secure China means more people with a stake in regional peace and stability and fewer people succumbing to anti-American paranoia.

Military strategists have a duty to plan for all possible scenarios, including war. Devising worst-case scenarios is part of their job. But "China hawks" employed by the US government should not be allowed to make public statements that exaggerate China's military might and depart from the nuanced policy articulated by then deputy secretary of state Robert Zoellick and followed ever since.[19] Even data on military spending should be kept in perspective. A rising power whose leaders inherited a peasant army is surely going to spend more on defense, boost salaries and pensions, conduct more sophisticated exercises, and modernize its weaponry, especially in a world where military power buys influence. As self-described "realist" Robert Ross observes, security trends in the region justify US confidence. The challenge for Washington is to shape future US foreign and security policy in such a way that other countries welcome US power rather than fear it.[20] This includes contributing to a regional environment in which China finds reasons to cooperate with the United States rather than to feel threatened. A confrontational attitude toward China reduces the likelihood that this challenge can be successfully met.

US officials and politicians should realize that encouraging China to become a "responsible stakeholder" (in Zoellick's words) means not only sharing global and regional responsibilities. It also means recognizing China's legitimate national interests and remaining open to possible modifications of regional and world order. The present order is not synonymous with narrow US interests, but it looks that way to others. If China is supposed to be "responsible," it has a right to help decide what kind of system it is expected to be responsible about.

Finally, Americans should break their shortsighted habit of alternately demonizing and applauding China's leaders. Instead, they should approach China with the caution and respect due to a great civilization that has emerged from war, domestic turmoil, and humiliation to become both a major commercial actor and a rapidly emerging regional power.

Revitalize APEC

APEC is too big and its political space is too thin. But in the competition for influence, it is a constructive strategic counterweight to ASEAN + 3 and a natural complement to the Asian integration movement. For Asians, APEC is a way of getting constructive US attention.

APEC has much to offer. It mobilizes business groups and utilizes their expertise. Its transpacific membership is more inclusive and the scope of its market is much bigger than intra-Asian trade groupings. Important nontrade initiatives develop there as well. APEC's committees and working groups continue to devise agreed measures to improve customs procedures, cope with disasters and accidents at sea, combat crime, protect and improve health, promote energy cooperation and research on alternative energy, prevent terrorist attacks through improved port security, and address a variety of other challenges. This work is directly relevant to Asia's needs.

The second Bush administration began paying more attention to APEC and doubled APEC-related expenditures. But US officials still do not have sufficient budgetary resources to fund travel and implement agreed-on initiatives. Antiterrorism and security measures still absorb the biggest share of the relevant agencies' budget categories. There is not enough high-level US engagement with APEC between annual summits.

Although the commitment to free and open transpacific trade and investment by 2010 (2020 for developing countries) is dead, the proposed FTAAP could restore APEC's role as a stimulus for free trade in half of the world and a driver of competitive liberalization in the other half. That is not to say that an FTAAP is either likely or possible. But echoing a lesson learned from Asian regionalism, I would say that the *process* of beginning to negotiate an FTAAP is valuable in itself.

■ Conclusion

"Elsewhere is a negative mirror," remarks the fictitious Marco Polo to the elderly Genghis Khan in Italo Calvino's *Invisible Cities*.[21] Analysts from Europe and North America run the risk of viewing Asia through their own historical prisms and concluding that they must "catch up" with Western standards in some linear-historical sense. But in Asia, we are witnessing something unique.

In a region where many national boundaries are artificial and political cohesion is gossamer-thin, most Asian governments are still trying to cobble together stable and viable nations. They are maneuvering in a regional environment in which their basic security—defined broadly to include domestic and regional stability, national autonomy, and enough economic growth to guarantee their legitimacy—is not guaranteed. Continuation of the US military presence responds to some but not all of their needs. Balance-of-power thinking based on assessments of military capability is still relevant to the Taiwan Strait and the Korean peninsula, but even there it is not sufficient. Elsewhere it is less relevant because most of the threats facing Asian governments are nontraditional and diffuse, and some are mainly economic.

Asian governments seek a form of regionalism that both manages and takes advantage of market forces while enhancing their national sovereignty and their ability to cope with the challenges of governance. As they see it, selective cooperation shelters them from the worst extremes of globalization and gives them breathing space to cope with shared problems. Governments of smaller and weaker states particularly value regionalism because it helps them avoid being dominated by larger powers.

Although Asia's new regionalism may strike rational minds as a "regional delusion,"[22] the calculations that justify participation in the integration movement correspond to the circumstances in which Asians find themselves. The small group of leaders, bureaucrats, and intellectuals who favor accelerating closer Asian integration lack both an agreed end-goal and an enforceable mandate, but that is the way most governments want it. Sovereignty is still precious and no government is ready to cede it to others. At the same time, absolute national sovereignty is beginning to wear thin as an excuse for resisting change when other countries' interests are affected. The integration movement enshrines national sovereignty, but it also blurs and demystifies it. In extreme cases, such as the 2007 crackdown in Myanmar, Asian governments have spoken out publicly, both individually and through ASEAN.

The integration movement redefines *Asia* in a positive and open-ended way and remains open to the rest of the world. Its flexible nature offers a "roof" under which the management of great-power relations can be legitimized and steered. Its very fluidity functions like a shock absorber. It tamps down territorial disputes and economic clashes and provides diplomatic space to resolve or postpone them.

Rejecting a coalition of smaller powers against a rising one, leaders of the integration movement seek to absorb a rising power in a fabric of peaceful norms and commitments and thus avoid a costly arms race. Their efforts help prevent a polarizing schism between democracies on the rim of Asia and China on the mainland. The prospect of closer integration stimulates trade-liberalizing agreements, infrastructure projects, and financial coordination, however feeble these measures may be. In the long run, more robust economic growth, combined with the vision of an Asia-wide community, may offer separatists and fundamentalists an attractive alternative to radical movements. All of these aspects of the integration movement are "public goods" that contribute to prosperity and stability in Asia, the United States, and the rest of the world.

Asia's new regionalism is far less successful as a mechanism for creating and distributing wealth, jobs, and technology. Its limited achievements are riddled with holes and excuses. It skirts some important issues, moves with the speed of an inchworm, relies far more on talk than on action, and thus falls far short of its potential. Too many regionwide threats remain to be tackled more decisively and collectively, including crime, terrorism, disease, and environmental pollution. For all these reasons, Asia still adds up to little more than the sum of its parts.

The keys to sustainable integration, economic development, and successful adaptation to globalization are good governance, economic reform, and enough mutual trust to permit some form of security cooperation. Many Asian governments have a long way to go before they get the basics right. Nevertheless, unless some new crisis intervenes, a lumbering momentum toward closer integration seems irreversible.

Is there a better way to design Asia's future? The path to greater wealth and power, the historical goals of the Asian integration movement, winds partly through the global economy and partly through the cities, coastal communities, and ocean-bound rivers of Maritime Asia. Building on Maritime Asia's rich legacy might lead to new forms of local autonomy and cross-border governance, such as a limited, modern-day Asian equivalent of the Hanseatic League or a maritime version of an "Asian Renaissance." Pursuing such long-range visions would mean thinking holistically about the interaction of land and sea and realigning the agenda of the integration movement more closely with Asia's maritime potential.

In the end, the future of Asian regionalism depends on answers to three sets of questions. First, to what extent will China's surging economy and increasingly outward-looking society soften and open up its authoritarian political system? How will this evolution affect US-China relations, the US military presence, and the US-Japan alliance? My guess is that the Chinese Communist Party will stay in power but that it will continue to move toward "authoritarian capitalism."[23] This prospect challenges the Western model of market-oriented democracy and runs counter to certain basic Western values but it poses no inherent threat to vital Western interests.

Second, will Asia's diverse political values converge and nurture a true community in Asia Major, redrawing the world's political maps? Will Asian governments become capable of—and willing to—promote closer integration in both Maritime Asia and Asia Major, or will they quietly abandon such approaches? Alternatively, will Asia drift apart along democratic and non-democratic lines, giving rise to a rim-based league of Asian democracies that challenges and implicitly resists growing Chinese power on the mainland?

My guess is that Asia will neither unite into an Asian bloc nor remain as fragmented as it is today. Although Asian governments will mostly resist my vision of a fully restored Maritime Asia, they will slowly lower trade and investment barriers and improve maritime and security cooperation. Under the heading of community building, Asian governments will select regional initiatives that preserve or enhance their sovereignty and security. They will rely on flexible bilateral, national, and subnational arrangements based on shared norms and legitimized by an open-ended regional framework. An Asian common market and an Asian security community, however, lie far off in the future and may never be realized. Modes of governance will converge slightly as repressive regimes edge toward authoritarian capitalism and democracies remain democratic or nearly so, but it will be a long time before shared political values can form the basis of a true community. In the meantime, the flexible, open nature of Asia's new regionalism will accommodate China's peaceful development while allowing plenty of room for the United States to compete for influence.

Finally, will US policymakers ever be able to shift their attention from the Middle East and pay more sustained attention to what is going on in the other half of the world? If they do, will they employ their assets wisely and contribute to the common good?

The changing balance of influence in Asia calls for high-level US engagement, a better balance between US military and nonmilitary tools, more understanding of Asian needs, more recognition of the benefits of closer integration, more acceptance of China's new status, more willingness to grant legitimacy to ASEAN and to trust ASEAN leaders' ability to handle tensions and crises, continuing partnership with Japan and other allies and friends, more public diplomacy and educational exchanges, and less zero-sum thinking. The United States has neglected or downgraded regional, transpacific, and global institutions and needs to do more to support them. Just showing up and listening is important; active encouragement and respect for others' needs and interests are more valuable at this stage than long lists of US-designed projects that lack political visibility.

Asia's new regionalism amounts to more than a marriage of convenience but considerably less than a marriage of the heart. Political values remain so far apart that Asia is far from becoming a true community, an "Asia Whole and Free." For many Asian leaders, nation building and political stability need to be consolidated first. For some, the Asian integration movement is a long-term strategy; for others, it is merely a tactic serving diplomatic goals; and for still others, it is something to be tolerated and occasionally blocked.

Nevertheless, Asian governments cannot afford *not* to pursue integration because the consequences of not doing so are too risky. The alternative—

doing nothing—would be destabilizing and would leave smaller Asian countries at the mercy of unrestrained rivalry among the regional powers. The implicit rift between the rim democracies and China would grow wider, putting pressure on other governments to take sides. Such a division would likely stimulate an arms race, stoke Chinese and Japanese nationalism, and reduce the prospects for stability.

Americans should therefore encourage Asian regionalism, not merely tolerate it or fear it. They do not have to join the East Asian Summit group in order to protect their interests and participate in meaningful dialogues and decisions about Asia's future. But they do have to send more encouraging signals. If they approach Asia in a constructive spirit and with a listening ear, Asians will welcome their presence—not at every table, but definitely under their roof.

▪ Notes

1. Jake Lloyd-Smith, "Malaysia Moves on Illegal Workers," *Financial Times,* February 1, 2005, p. 6.

2. Montes and Wagle, "Why Asia Needs to Trade Smarter," p. 46.

3. Pan-Long Tsai and Ching-Lung Tsay, "Foreign Direct Investment and International Labour Migration in Economic Development: Indonesia, Malaysia, Philippines, and Thailand," in Ananta and Arifin, *International Migration in Southeast Asia,* p. 131, figs. 4.2–4.5.

4. A. F. M. Maniruzzaman, "It Is Time for Asia to Co-operate on Energy Supplies," *Financial Times,* November 14, 2005, p. 17.

5. Kessler, "Energy Cooperation in Northeast Asia," p. 14 ff.

6. Evelyn Goh suggests that downstream governments could offer to allow their territory to be used for regional links in exchange for detailed information on Chinese water development schemes and adherence to requirements stemming from social and environmental impact assessments. She adds that this may be unrealistic, however. See Goh, *Developing the Mekong,* p. 56.

7. The figure for China is not strictly comparable because it appears in a separate poll among urban residents taken a year earlier. See Inoguchi et al., *Values and Life Styles,* question 16-1, p. 335; and Inoguchi et al., *Human Beliefs and Values,* question 17-1, p. 455.

8. See, for example, "U.S. Views on Asia Regional Integration," remarks by US senior official Michael Michalak, Tokyo, January 25, 2006, http://tokyo.usembassy.gov /e/p/tp-20060206-06.html.

9. Mark Mazzetti, "Gates, in Fresh Tone for U.S., Offers to Work with China's Military to 'Build Trust Over Time,'" *New York Times,* June 2, 2007, p. A6. The text of his speech referred to the United States as a "Pacific nation," not an "Asian power." The text is available at www.defenselink.mil/speeches/speech.aspx?speechid=1160.

10. Mahbubani argues that self-serving US behavior began at the end of the Cold War. See *Beyond the Age of Innocence,* chap. 2.

11. Funabashi, "The Power of Ideas," p. 2.

12. For a brief survey of US attitudes since World War II, see Frost, "Strategic Engagement or Benign Neglect?"

13. Goh, "Towards an East Asian Renaissance," p. 12.

14. Fact sheets and complete texts of these agreements are available at www. whitehouse.gov.

15. Goh, *Betwixt and Between*, p. 6.

16. A similar option already exists for APEC.

17. For more on China's policies in Asia, see Shambaugh, "China Engages Asia"; Sutter, *China's Rise in Asia;* and Keller and Rawski, *China's Rise and the Balance of Influence in Asia.* Writing from a Chinese perspective, the influential intellectual Wang Jisi reports that the Chinese government is worried about US power but has concluded that it shares many common interests with Washington and that it would be both counterproductive and foolhardy to challenge US dominance. Wang, "America in Asia," pp. 4–5.

18. Shirk, *China: Fragile Superpower,* chap. 9.

19. Zoellick, "Whither China: From Membership to Responsibility?"

20. Ross, "A Realist Policy for Managing US-China Competition," p. 11.

21. Italo Calvino, *Invisible Cities,* translated by William Weaver (New York: Harvest Books, 1972), p. 29.

22. Jones and Smith, *ASEAN and East Asian International Relations.* The subtitle is *Regional Delusion.*

23. For a discussion of this challenge, see Azar Gat, "The Return of Authoritarian Great Powers," *Foreign Affairs* 86, no. 4 (July–August 2007): 59–69.

Acronyms and
Regional Definitions

ABMI	Asian Bond Market Initiative
ACU	Asian Currency Unit
ADB	Asian Development Bank
AFTA	ASEAN Free Trade Area
AMF	Asian Monetary Fund
APEC	Asia-Pacific Economic Cooperation forum
ARF	ASEAN Regional Forum
ASEAN	Association of Southeast Asian Nations (Brunei Darussalam, Cambodia, Indonesia, Laos, Malaysia, Myanmar [Burma], the Philippines, Singapore, Thailand, and Vietnam)
ASEAN + 3	ASEAN plus China, Japan, and South Korea
ASEAN + 6	ASEAN + 3 plus Australia, New Zealand, and India
ASEAN 5	Indonesia, Malaysia, the Philippines, Singapore, and Thailand
ASEM	Asia-Europe Meeting
Asia Major	ASEAN, China, South Korea, Japan, India, Australia, and New Zealand (ASEAN + 6) and, unofficially, Taiwan
BIMSTEC	Bay of Bengal Initiative for Multi-Sectoral Technical and Economic Cooperation
CEPEA	Comprehensive Economic Partnership in East Asia, proposed by Japan
CEPT	Common Effective Preferential Tariff (ASEAN)
CLMV	Cambodia, Laos, Myanmar, and Vietnam
CMI	Chiang Mai Initiative, a set of currency swap agreements
COMECON	Council for Mutual Economic Assistance
CSCAP	Council for Security Cooperation in the Asia Pacific
CSCE	Conference on Security and Cooperation in Europe (later renamed OSCE)

EAS	East Asian Summit; the members of this grouping are ASEAN + 6
East Asia	(1) ASEAN + 3 plus Taiwan, Hong Kong, and Macao; (2) a political construct, loosely defined as ASEAN + 6 but possibly open to other members
EPA	economic partnership agreement
ERIA	Economic Research Institute for ASEAN and East Asia
EU	European Union
FDI	foreign direct investment
FPDA	Five Power Defence Arrangements; members are Singapore, Malaysia, Australia, New Zealand, and the United Kingdom
FTA	free trade agreement
FTAA	Free Trade Area of the Americas
FTAAP	Free Trade Area of the Asia Pacific
GATT	General Agreement on Tariffs and Trade
GDP	gross domestic product
GNP	gross national product
IATA	International Air Transport Association
IFC	International Finance Corporation, part of the World Bank Group
IMF	International Monetary Fund
IMO	International Maritime Organization
JACIK	Japan, ASEAN, China, India, and Korea (ASEAN + 3 plus India)
Maritime Asia	Coastal zones, ocean-accessible cities and towns, and adjacent waterways, from southern and coastal India eastward to Japan, Indonesia, and coastal Australia and New Zealand
METI	Ministry of Economy, Trade, and Industry (Japan)
MOU	Memorandum of Understanding
NAFTA	North American Free Trade Agreement
NEAT	Network of East Asian Think-Tanks
NGO	nongovernmental organization
Northeast Asia	China, Japan, Korea, Taiwan, Hong Kong, and Macao; not Mongolia
OECD	Organization for Economic Cooperation and Development (Paris)
OSCE	Organization for Security and Cooperation in Europe
PECC	Pacific Economic Cooperation Council
PTA	preferential trade agreement
ReCAAP	Regional Cooperation Agreement on Combating Piracy and Armed Robbery Against Ships in Asia
SAARC	South Asian Association for Regional Cooperation

SCO	Shanghai Cooperation Organization
SEATO	Southeast Asia Treaty Organization
Southeast Asia	The ten members of ASEAN plus East Timor
TAC	Treaty of Amity and Cooperation
TEU	twenty-foot equivalent unit, the standard unit of measurement of containers
TIFA	Trade and Investment Framework Agreement
Track 2	A structured set of discussions consisting of intellectuals, business leaders, and other nongovernment elites, established to advise governments
TSD	Trilateral Security Dialogue, held by Australia, Japan, and the United States; inaugurated in 2006
UNESCAP	United Nations Economic and Social Commission for Asia and the Pacific
UNHCR	UN High Commissioner for Refugees
WTO	World Trade Organization

Bibliography

Abramowitz, Morton, and Stephen Bosworth. *Chasing the Sun: Rethinking East Asian Policy.* New York: Century Foundation Press, 2006.

Abu-Lughod, Janet. *Before European Hegemony: The World System A.D. 1250–1350.* New York: Oxford University Press, 1989.

Acharya, Amitav. *Constructing a Security Community in Southeast Asia.* London: Routledge, 2001.

———. "Imagined Proximities: The Making and Unmaking of Southeast Asia as a Region." *Southeast Asian Journal of Social Science* 27, no. 1 (1999): 55–76.

———. "Will Asia's Past Be Its Future?" *International Security* 28, no. 3 (Winter 2003–2004): 149–164.

Aggarwal, Vinod K., and Edward Fogarty, eds. *EU Trade Strategies: Regionalism and Globalization.* Basingstoke, UK: Palgrave Macmillan, 2004.

Aggarwal, Vinod K., and Min Gyo Koo. "Shifting Ground: Is It Finally Time?" *Global Asia* 1, no. 1 (September 2006): 28–41.

Alagappa, Muthiah, ed. *Asian Security Order: Instrumental and Normative Features.* Stanford: Stanford University Press, 2003.

Alesina, Alberto, William Easterly, and Janina Matuszeski. "Artificial States." NBER Working Paper 12328, National Bureau of Economic Research, Cambridge, MA, June 2006.

Ananta, Aris, and Evi Nurvidya Arifin, eds. *International Migration in Southeast Asia.* Singapore: Institute of Southeast Asian Studies, 2004.

Anderson, Benedict. *Imagined Communities.* London: Verso, 1983.

Anderson, Jonathan. "China's True Growth: No Myth or Miracle." *Far Eastern Economic Review* 169, no. 7 (2006): 9–16.

Anwar Ibrahim. *The Asian Renaissance.* Singapore: Times Books International, 1997.

———. "Asian Renaissance and the Reconstruction of Civilization." Speech presented at University Loyola Heights, Quezon City, Philippines, May 2, 1996. Available at http://ikdasar.tripon.com/anwar/96-09.htm.

———. "The Modernity of Southeast Asian Islam." Lecture presented at St. Antony's College, Oxford University, May 3, 2005. Available at www.malaysia-today.net/columns/minda/index.htm.

Appiah, Kwame Anthony. *The Ethics of Identity.* Princeton: Princeton University Press, 2005.

Arjomand, S. A. "The Emergence of Islamic Political Ideologies." In J. Beckford and T. Luckman, eds., *The Changing Face of Religion*. London: Sage, 1989.

ASEAN. *ASEAN Regional Forum: Documents Series 1994–2004*. Jakarta: ASEAN Secretariat, 2005.

———. *ASEAN Statistical Pocketbook*. Jakarta: ASEAN Secretariat, 2005.

———. "Declaration of ASEAN Concord II (Bali Concord II)." In *ASEAN Knowledge Kit*. Jakarta: ASEAN Secretariat, June 2005.

———. *Text of the Treaty of Amity and Cooperation in Southeast Asia and Related Information*. Jakarta: ASEAN Secretariat, March 2005.

———. *Vientiane Action Programme (VAP), 2004–2010*. Jakarta: Association of Southeast Asian Nations, undated.

Asher, Mukul G. "India's Rising Role in Asia." RIS Discussion Paper No. 121. New Delhi: Research and Information System for Developing Countries (RIS), 2007. Available at www.ris.org.in.

Asian Development Bank. *Asian Development Outlook 2006*. Available at www.adb.org.

———. *Asian Economic Cooperation and Integration: Progress, Prospects, and Challenges*. Manila: Asian Development Bank, 2005.

———. *Technical Assistance for the Formulation of the Pacific Region Environmental Strategy, 2004–2008*. TAR: REG 35479. Manila, June, 2002.

Asian Development Bank, Japan Bank for International Cooperation, and the World Bank. *Connecting East Asia: A New Framework for Infrastructure*. Washington, DC: World Bank, 2005.

Asian Development Bank and the UN Environment Programme. *The Greater Mekong Subregion Atlas of the Environment*. Manila: Asian Development Bank, 2004.

Asia Pacific Agenda Project. *Toward East Asian Community Building*. Tokyo: Japan Center for International Exchange, 2004.

Baker, Richard W., and Charles E. Morrison, eds. *Asia Pacific Security Outlook 2005*. Tokyo: Japan Center for International Exchange, 2005.

Baldwin, Richard E. "The Causes of Regionalism." *World Economy* 20, no. 7 (1997): 865–888.

———. "Multilateralising Regionalism." Revision of the 2006 World Economy Annual Lecture, Nottingham, June 22, 2006. Manuscript, October 2, 2006.

Bartlett, John. *Bartlett's Familiar Quotations*. Boston: Little Brown, 1955.

Bauer, Joanne R., and Daniel A. Bell, eds. *The East Asian Challenge for Human Rights*. Cambridge: Cambridge University Press, 1999.

Bentley, Jerry H., Renate Bridenthal, and Kären Wigen. *Seascapes: Maritime Histories, Littoral Cultures, and Transoceanic Exchanges*. Honolulu: University of Hawaii Press, 2007.

Bergsten, C. Fred. "Embedding Pacific Asia in the Asia Pacific: The Global Impact of an East Asian Community." Speech presented at the Japan National Press Club, Tokyo, September 2, 2005. Available at www.petersoninstitute.org.

———. "The Free Trade Area of the Asia Pacific Is the Next Step Forward for APEC (and for the World Trading System)." November 2006. Available at www.petersoninstitute.org.

———. "Reviving the Asian Monetary Fund." *Institute for International Economics Policy Brief* 98-8. Washington, DC: Institute for International Economics, 1998.

Berkofsky, Axel. "Comparing EU and Asian Integration Processes—Is the EU a Role Model for Asia?" EPC Issue Paper No. 23. Brussels: European Policy Centre, January 2005.

Bernstein, Richard. *Ultimate Journey*. New York: Alfred A. Knopf, 2001.

Beyer, P. *Religion and Globalisation*. London: Sage, 1994.

Bird, Isabella. *Unbeaten Tracks in Japan.* Boston: Beacon Press, 1984.

Black, Jeremy. *Maps and History: Constructing Images of the Past.* New Haven: Yale University Press, 1997.

Blank, Stephen J. *Natural Allies? Regional Security in Asia and Prospects for Indo-American Strategic Cooperation.* Carlisle, PA: Strategic Studies Institute, 2005.

Braudel, Fernand. *Civilization and Capitalism, 15th–18th Century,* 3 vols. Translated by Sian Reynolds. New York: Harper & Row, 1984.

———. *The Mediterranean and the Mediterranean World in the Age of Philip II.* 2 vols. New York: Harper & Row, 1972–1973.

Brown, Peter. *The Rise of Western Christendom.* Malden, MA: Blackwell, 2003.

Buruma, Ian. *God's Dust: A Modern Asian Journey.* New York: Farrar, Straus & Giroux, 1989.

Buruma, Ian, and Avishai Margalit. *Occidentalism: The West in the Eyes of Its Enemies.* New York: Penguin Press, 2004.

Caballero-Anthony, Mely. "Nontraditional Security and Multilateralism in Asia: Reshaping the Contours of Regional Security Architecture?" *Policy Analysis Brief.* Muscatine, IA: Stanley Foundation, June 2007.

Center for Strategic and International Studies and Institute for International Economics. *China: The Balance Sheet.* New York: PublicAffairs/Perseus Book Group, 2006.

Chace, James. *Acheson.* Cambridge: Harvard University Press, 1998.

Chakravarty, Amiya, ed. *The Tagore Reader.* Boston: Beacon Press, 1961.

Chanda, Nayan. *Bound Together: How Traders, Preachers, Adventurers and Warriors Shaped Globalization.* New Haven: Yale University Press, 2007.

———. "When Asia Was One." *Global Asia* 1, no. 1 (September 2006): 60–68.

Chaudhuri, K. N. *Trade and Civilisation in the Indian Ocean: An Economic History from the Rise of Islam to 1750.* Cambridge: Cambridge University Press, 1985.

Chellaney, Brahma. "Forestalling Strategic Conflict in Asia." *Far Eastern Economic Review* 169, no. 9 (November 2006): 29–33.

Chia Lin Sien, ed. *Southeast Asia Transformed: A Geography of Change.* Singapore: Institute of Southeast Asian Studies, 2003.

Chicago Council on Global Affairs, in partnership with the Asia Society. *The United States and the Rise of China and India: Results of a 2006 Multination Survey of Public Opinion.* Chicago: Chicago Council on Global Affairs, 2006.

Chirathivat, Sutiphand, et al., eds. *Asia-Europe on the Eve of the 21st Century.* Bangkok: Centre for European Studies at Chulalongkorn University; Singapore: Institute of Southeast Asian Studies, 2001.

Chufrin, Gennady. *East Asia: Between Regionalism and Globalism.* Singapore: Institute of Southeast Asian Studies, 2006.

Cohen, Saul B. "Geopolitics in the New World Era: A New Perspective on an Old Discipline." In George J. Demko and William B. Wood, eds. *Reordering the World: Geopolitical Perspectives on the 21st Century.* Boulder, CO: Westview Press, 1999.

Cohen, Stephen Philip. *India: Emerging Power.* Washington, DC: Brookings Institution Press, 2001.

Commission of the European Communities. "Towards a Future Maritime Policy for the Union: A European Vision for the Oceans and Seas." Outline of a Green Paper on a Future EU Maritime Policy, COM(2006)275, June 7, 2006, http://ec.europa.eu/maritimeaffairs.

Cooper, Robert. *The Breaking of Nations: Order and Chaos in the Twenty-First Century.* London: Atlantic Books, 2003.

Cossa, Ralph A. "East Asia Community-Building: Time for the United States to Get on

Board." *Policy Analysis Brief.* Muscatine, IA: Stanley Foundation, September 2007.

———. "The Emerging East Asian Community: Should Washington Be Concerned?" Honolulu: Pacific Forum CSIS, 2005.

Cotton, James. "Australia and Asian Institutions: Bilateral Preferences, Multilateral Gains." Manuscript, n.d.

Coulter, Daniel Y. "Globalization of Maritime Commerce: The Rise of Hub Ports." In Sam J. Tangredi, ed., *Globalization and Maritime Power.* Washington, DC: National Defense University Press, 2002.

Council for Security Cooperation in the Asia Pacific (CSCAP). "The Practice of the Law of the Sea in the Asia Pacific." CSCAP Memorandum No. 6, n.d. Available at www.cscap.org.

———. "The Weakest Link? Seaborne Trade and the Maritime Regime in the Asia Pacific." CSCAP Memorandum No. 8, April 2004. Available at www.cscap.org.

Cowen, David, Ranil Salgado, Hemant Shah, Leslie Teo, and Alessandro Zanello. "Financial Integration in Asia: Recent Developments and Next Steps." IMF Working Paper WP/06/196, August 2006.

Curtis, Gerald. "The US in East Asia: Not Architecture, but Action." *Global Asia* 2, no. 2 (Fall 2007). Available at http://globalasia.org.

Dalrymple, William. *White Mughals: Love and Betrayal in Eighteenth-Century India.* London: Penguin Books, 2002.

Das Gupta, Ashin. *The World of the Indian Ocean Merchant, 1500–1800.* Compiled by Uma Das Gupta. New Delhi: Oxford University Press, 2001.

De Bary, William Theodore, ed., with Stephen Hay and I. H. Qureshi. *Sources of Indian Tradition,* vol. 2. New York: Columbia University Press, 1958.

Demko, George J., and William B. Wood, eds. *Reordering the World: Geopolitical Perspectives on the 21st Century.* Boulder, CO: Westview Press, 1999.

Department of Defense. *Quadrennial Defense Review Report,* September 30, 2001, www.defenselink.mil/pubs/qdr2001.pdf.

Department of Foreign Affairs and Trade, Government of Australia. *Trade 2006.* Canberra: Department of Foreign Affairs and Trade, 2006.

Department of the Navy. *Naval Operations Concept.* Washington, DC: Department of the Navy, 2006.

Desker, Barry. "The Worth of the ASEAN Regional Forum." *ISN Security Watch,* July 31, 2006. Available at www.isn.ethz.ch/news/sw/details.cfm?ID=16439.

Devare, Sudhir. *India and Southeast Asia: Towards Security Convergence.* Singapore: Institute of Southeast Asian Studies, 2006.

Diamond, Jared. *Guns, Germs, and Steel.* New York: W. W. Norton, 1997.

Dibb, Paul. *Towards a New Balance of Power in Asia,* Adelphi Paper 295. London: International Institute for Strategic Studies, 1995.

Dupont, Alan. *East Asia Imperiled: Transnational Challenges to Security.* Cambridge: Cambridge University Press, 2001.

East, W. Gordon, and O. H. K. Spate, eds. *The Changing Map of Asia: A Political Geography.* London: Pan Macmillan, 1999.

East Asia Vision Group. "Towards an East Asian Community," 2001. Available at www.aseansec.org.

Eberstadt, Nicholas. "Power and Population in Asia." *Policy Review* 123 (February 2004). Available at www.policyreview.org/feb04/eberstadt_print.html.

Eichengreen, Barry. "Globalization and Democracy." NBER Working Paper No. 12450. Cambridge, MA: National Bureau of Economic Research, August 2006.

Elisonas, Jurgis. "The Inseparable Trinity: Japan's Relations with China and Korea." In

John Whitney Hall, ed., *The Cambridge History of Japan.* Cambridge: Cambridge University Press, 1991.

Ellings, Richard J., and Aaron L. Friedberg, with Michael Wills, eds. *Strategic Asia 2002–03: Asian Aftershocks.* Seattle: National Bureau of Asian Research, 2002.

———, eds. *Strategic Asia 2003–04: Fragility and Crisis.* Seattle: National Bureau of Asian Research, 2003.

Elliott, Lorraine. "ASEAN and Environmental Cooperation: Norms, Interest and Identity." *Pacific Review* 16, no. 1 (2003): 29–52.

Eminent Persons Group. *Implementing the APEC Vision.* Third Report of the Eminent Persons Group. Singapore: APEC Secretariat, August 1995.

Emmerson, Donald K. "The Case for a Maritime Perspective on Southeast Asia." *Journal of Southeast Asian Studies* 11, no. 1 (March 1980): 139–145.

Encarnation, Dennis. *Japanese Multinationals in Asia.* New York: Oxford University Press, 1999.

Esposito, John L., ed. *Islam in Asia.* New York: Oxford University Press, 1987.

Etzioni, Amitai. *From Empire to Community.* New York: Palgrave Macmillan, 2004.

Evans, Grant, Christopher Hutton, and Kuah Khun Eng, eds. *Where China Meets Southeast Asia: Social and Cultural Change in the Border Regions.* Singapore: Institute of Southeast Asian Studies, 2000.

Ferguson, Niall. *Empire: The Rise and Demise of the British World Order and the Lessons for Global Power.* New York: Basic Books, 2003.

Fisher, Charles A. *The Changing Map of Asia: A Political Geography.* London: Methuen, 1971.

Florini, Ann M., ed. *The Third Force: The Rise of Transnational Civil Society.* Tokyo: Japan Center for International Affairs; Washington, DC: Carnegie Endowment for International Peace, 2000.

Foreign Policy and the Fund for Peace. "The Failed States Index." *Foreign Policy* 154 (2006): 49–58.

Foreign Policy and A. T. Kearney. "The Globalization Index." *Foreign Policy* 163 (2007): 68–76.

Frankel, Francine R., and Harry Harding, eds. *The India-China Relationship: What the United States Needs to Know.* New York: Columbia University Press; Washington, DC: Woodrow Wilson Center Press, 2004.

Frankel, Jeffrey A. *Regional Trading Blocs in the World Economic System.* Washington, DC: Institute for International Economics, 1997.

Fravel, M. Taylor. "China's Management of Territorial Disputes: Comparing the Settlement of Land and Maritime Conflicts." Presentation to the China Security Perspectives Series. Washington, DC: Institute for National Strategic Studies and the National War College, 2006. Personal communication.

Frost, Ellen L. "Globalization and National Security: A Strategic Agenda." In Richard L. Kugler and Ellen L. Frost, eds., *The Global Century: Globalization and National Security.* 2 vols. Washington, DC: National Defense University, 2001.

———. "Implications of Regional Economic Integration." In Richard J. Ellings and Aaron L. Friedberg with Michael Wills, eds. *Strategic Asia 2003–04: Fragility and Crisis.* Seattle: National Bureau of Asian Research, 2003.

———. "Promise or Threat? China's Commercial Diplomacy in Asia." Chapter 5 in William W. Keller and Thomas G. Rawski, eds., *China's Rise and the Balance of Influence in Asia.* Pittsburgh: University of Pittsburgh Press, 2007.

———. "Re-Engaging with Southeast Asia." *PacNet* No. 37. Honolulu: Pacific Forum CSIS, July 26, 2006.

———. "Strategic Engagement or Benign Neglect? Current and Future U.S. Policy

Responses to East Asian Regionalism." Paper presented to the Conference on East Asian Regionalism and Its Impact, Beijing, China, October 21–22, 2004.

Funabashi, Yoichi. *Asia Pacific Fusion: Japan's Role in APEC.* Washington, DC: Institute for International Economics, 1995.

———. "The Power of Ideas: The US Is Losing Its Edge." *Global Asia* 2, no. 2 (Fall 2007). Available at http://globalasia.org.

Fung, K. C., Lawrence J. Lau, and Joseph S. Lee. *U.S. Direct Investment in China.* Washington, DC: American Enterprise Institute Press, 2004.

Gallup, John Luke, and Jeffrey Sachs with Andrew D. Mellinger. "Geography and Economic Growth." Paper prepared for the Annual Bank Conference on Development Economics, Washington, DC, April 20–21, 1998.

Garnaut, Ross, and David Vines. "Regional Free Trade Areas: Sorting Out the Tangled Spaghetti." Paper presented at the Peter G. Peterson Institute for International Economics, April 6, 2007.

Garver, John W. "The China-India-U.S. Triangle: Strategic Relations in the Post–Cold War Era." Published as *NBR Analysis* 13, no. 5 (October 2002), National Bureau of Asian Research, Seattle.

Gaulier, Guillaume, Françoise Lemoine, and Deniz Unlal-Kesenci. "China's Emergence and the Reorganisation of Trade Flows in Asia." Working Paper No. 2006-05. Paris: Centre d'Études Prospectives et d'Informations Internationales, March 2006.

Ghosh, Swati R. *East Asian Finance.* Washington, DC: World Bank, 2006.

Gill, Bates, and Yanzhong Huang. "Sources and Limits of Chinese 'Soft Power.'" *Survival* 48, no. 2 (Summer 2006): 17–34.

Gill, Indermit, and Homi Kharan. *An East Asian Renaissance.* Washington, DC: World Bank, 2007.

Godement, François. *The New Asian Renaissance: From Colonialism to the Post–Cold War.* Translated by Elizabeth J. Parcell. London: Routledge, 1997.

Goh, Evelyn, ed. *Betwixt and Between: Southeast Asian Strategic Relations with the U.S. and China.* Singapore: Institute of Defense and Strategic Studies, 2005.

———. *Developing the Mekong: Regionalism and Regional Security in China–Southeast Asian Relations.* Adelphi Paper 387. London: International Institute for Strategic Studies, 2007.

———. *Meeting the China Challenge: The U.S. in Southeast Asian Regional Security Strategies.* Washington, DC: East-West Center, 2005.

———. "Understanding 'Hedging' in Asia-Pacific Security." *PacNet* No. 43. Honolulu: Pacific Forum CSIS, August 31, 2006.

Goh Chok Tong. "Towards an East Asian Renaissance." Speech presented at the opening session of the Fourth Asia-Pacific Roundtable, Singapore, February 6, 2006. Available at http://app.sprinter.gov.sg/data/pr/20060206999.htm.

Goodwin-Gill, Guy S. "Refugees and Responsibility in the Twenty-First Century." *Pacific Rim Law and Policy Journal* 12, no. 1 (January 2003): 23–47.

Government of Australia. "Agreement Between the Republic of Indonesia and Australia on the Framework for Security Cooperation." Obtained from the Embassy of Australia, Washington, DC, November 13, 2006.

Greenwood, C. Lawrence. "Thinking Regionally and Acting Nationally." Speech presented at the Conference on East Asia's New State of Economic Integration, Singapore Institute of International Affairs, June 26, 2006.

Grimes, William. "East Asian Financial Regionalism, in Support of the Global Financial Architecture? The Political Economy of Regional Nesting." *Journal of East Asian Studies* 6, no. 3 (September–December 2006): 353–380.

Haacke, Jurgen. *Myanmar's Foreign Policy: Domestic Influences and International Implications.* Adelphi Paper 381. London: Institute of International Strategic Studies, 2006.

Haass, Richard. *The Opportunity.* New York: PublicAffairs Books, 2005.

Hamilton-Hart, Natasha. "The Regionalization of Southeast Asian Business: Transnational Networks in National Contexts." In T. J. Pempel, ed., *Remapping East Asia: The Construction of a Region.* Ithaca, NY: Cornell University Press, 2005.

Hansen, Valerie. *The Open Empire: A History of China to 1600.* New York: W. W. Norton, 2000.

Hardoy, Jorge E., Diana Maitlin, and David Satterthwaite. *Environment Problems in an Urbanizing World: Finding Solutions for Cities in Africa, Asia, and Latin America.* London: Earthscan, 2001.

Hatakeyama, Noboru. "Japan's New Regional Trade Policy." Speech presented at the Peterson Institute for International Economics, Washington, DC, March 13, 2002. Printed handout.

Hatch, Walter, and Kozo Yamamura. *Asia in Japan's Embrace: Building a Regional Production Alliance.* Cambridge: Cambridge University Press, 1996.

Hathaway, Robert M., and Wilson Lee, eds. *George W. Bush and East Asia.* Washington, DC: Woodrow Wilson International Center for Scholars, 2005.

Hefner, Robert W., ed. *Market Cultures: Society and Values in the New Asian Capitalisms.* Singapore: Institute of Southeast Asian Studies, 1998.

Hemmer, Christopher, and Peter J. Katzenstein. "Why Is There No NATO in Asia? Collective Identity, Regionalism, and the Origins of Multilateralism." *International Organization* 56, no. 3 (2002): 575–607.

Henning, C. Randall. *East Asian Financial Cooperation.* Policy Analysis 68. Washington, DC: Institute for International Economics, 2002.

———. "Regional Arrangements and the International Monetary Fund." In Edwin M. Truman, ed., *Reforming the IMF for the 21st Century.* Washington, DC: Institute for International Economics, 2006.

———. "Regional Economic Integration and Institution Building." Paper presented to the G-20 Workshop on Regional Economic Integration in a Global Framework, Beijing, September 22–23, 2004.

Herberg, Mikkal. "Asia's Energy Insecurity: Cooperation or Conflict?" In Ashley J. Tellis and Michael Wills, eds., *Strategic Asia 2004–05: Confronting Terrorism in the Pursuit of Power.* Seattle: National Bureau of Asian Research, 2004.

Higgott, Richard, and Richard Stubbs. "Competing Conceptions of Economic Regionalism: APEC Versus EAEC in the Asia Pacific." *Review of International Political Economy* 2, no. 3 (1995): 516–535.

Hillstrom, Kevin, and Laurie Collier Hillstrom. *Asia: A Continental Overview of Environmental Issues.* Santa Barbara, CA: ABC-CLIO, 2003.

Hitchcock, David I. *Asian Values and the United States: How Much Conflict?* Washington, DC: Center for Strategic and International Studies, 1994.

———. *Factors Affecting East Asian Views of the United States.* Washington, DC: Center for Strategic and International Studies, 1997.

Holmes, Frank, and Crawford Falconer. *Open Regionalism? NAFTA, CER and a Pacific Basin Initiative.* Wellington, NZ: Institute of Policy Studies, 1992.

Huang, Yasheng. *Selling China: Foreign Direct Investment During the Reform Era.* Cambridge: Cambridge University Press, 2003.

Hufbauer, Gary Clyde, and Jeffrey J. Schott. *Western Hemisphere Economic Integration.* Washington, DC: Institute for International Economics, 1994.

Hufbauer, Gary Clyde, Yee Wong, and Ketki Sheth. *US-China Trade Disputes: Rising Tide, Rising Stakes.* Washington, DC: Institute for International Economics, 2006.

Hugo, Graeme. "International Migration in Southeast Asia Since World War II." In Aris Ananta and Evi Nurvidya Arifin, eds., *International Migration in Southeast Asia.* Singapore: Institute of Southeast Asian Studies, 2004.

Ibn Battuta. *Ibn Battuta in the Near East, Asia, and Africa, 1325–1354.* Edited and translated by Samuel Lee. Mineola, NY: Dover Publications, 2004.

ICC International Maritime Bureau. *Piracy and Armed Robbery Against Ships: Annual Report, 1 January–31 December 2006.* London: ICC, January 2007.

Inoguchi, Takashi, Miguel Basáñez, Akihiko Tanaka, and Timur Dadabaev, eds. *Values and Life Styles in Urban Asia.* Tokyo: University of Tokyo, 2005.

Inoguchi, Takashi, Akihiko Tanaka, Shigeto Sonoda, and Timur Dadabaev, eds. *Human Beliefs and Values in Striding Asia.* Tokyo: Asahi Shoten, 2006.

Institute of Defence and Strategic Studies. *Contending Perspectives: Southeast Asian and American Views of a Rising China.* Singapore: Institute of Defence and Strategic Studies, 2005.

Institute of Southeast Asian Studies. *Developing ASEAN-China Relations: Realities and Prospects.* Singapore: Institute of Southeast Asian Studies, 2004.

International Institute for Strategic Studies (IISS). "Piracy and Maritime Terror in Southeast Asia: Dire Straits." *Strategic Comments* 10, no. 6 (August 2004): 1–4.

———. "The 2007 Chart of Conflict." Published as an insert to *The Military Balance 2007.* London: IISS.

International Labour Organization. "The Global Seafarer: Mixed Fortunes Mirror Global Trends." Maritime Session of the International Labour Conference, 2006. Available at www.ilo.org.

Irwin, Robert. *Dangerous Knowledge: Orientalism and Its Discontents.* New York: Overlook Press, 2006.

Jacquet, Pierre. "Regional Economic Integration: The European Model." Paper presented to the Korea Institute for International Economic Policy, October 9, 2001.

Jansen, Marius B. *China in the Tokugawa World.* Cambridge: Harvard University Press, 1992.

Japan Center for International Exchange. *ASEAN-Japan Cooperation: A Foundation for East Asian Community.* Tokyo: Japan Center for International Exchange, 2003.

Jinks, Beth. "Containerised Trade Imbalance Set to Worsen." *Business Times,* March 25, 2004. In Yale Global Online, http://yaleglobal.yale.edu/display.article?id =3583.

Jones, David Martin, and M. L. R. Smith. *ASEAN and East Asian International Relations.* Northampton, MA: Edward Elgar, 2007.

Jones, Eric, Lionel Frost, and Colin White. *Coming Full Circle: An Economic History of the Pacific Rim.* Boulder, CO: Westview Press, 1993.

Kalicki, Jan H., and David L. Goldwyn. *Energy and Security: Toward a New Foreign Policy Strategy.* Washington, DC: Woodrow Wilson Center Press; Baltimore: Johns Hopkins University Press, 2005.

Kallard, Anne, and Gerard Persoon, eds. *Environmental Movements in Asia.* Richmond, VA: Curzon, 1998.

Kang, David C. "Getting Asia Wrong: The Need for New Analytical Frameworks." *International Security* 27, no. 4 (Spring 2003): 57–85.

Kant, Immanuel. *Perpetual Peace and Other Essays.* Translated by Ted Humphrey. Indianapolis: Hackett, 1983.

Katzenstein, Peter. *Asian Regionalism.* Ithaca, NY: Cornell University East Asia Program, 2000.

———. "Hierarchy, Balancing, and Empirical Puzzles in Asian International Relations." *International Security* 27, no. 4 (Summer 2003–2004): 165–180.

———. *A World of Regions: Asia and Europe in the American Imperium.* Ithaca, NY: Cornell University Press, 2005.

Katzenstein, Peter, and Nobuo Okawara. "Japan, Asia-Pacific Security, and the Case for Analytical Eclecticism." *International Security* 26, no. 3 (Winter 2001–2002): 153–185.

Katzenstein, Peter, and Takashi Shiraishi, eds. *Beyond Japan.* Ithaca, NY: Cornell University Press, 2006.

———. *Network Power: Japan and Asia.* Ithaca, NY: Cornell University Press, 1997.

Kawazoe, Shoji. "Japan and East Asia." In John Whitney Hall, ed., *The Cambridge History of Japan.* Cambridge: Cambridge University Press, 1991.

Keller, William, and Thomas G. Rawski, eds., *China's Rise and the Balance of Influence in Asia.* Pittsburgh: University of Pittsburgh Press, 2007.

Kessler, Carol. "Energy Cooperation in NE Asia." Paper presented to the Shanghai Forum, Shanghai, China, May 25–27, 2007.

Keyes, C. F., L. Kendall, and H. Hardacre. *Asian Visions of Authority, Religion, and the Modern States of East and Southeast Asia.* Honolulu: University of Hawaii Press, 1994.

Khoo How San, ed. *The Future of the ARF.* Singapore: Institute of Defence and Strategic Studies, 1999.

Kitamura, Toshiaki. "Japan's New Deal for Asia." *Far Eastern Economic Review* 169, no. 7 (September 2006): 41–44.

Koh, Tommy, Walter Woon, Andrew Tan, and Chan Sze-wei. "The ASEAN Charter," *PacNet* no. 33A. Honolulu: Pacific Forum CSIS, 2007.

Kopf, David. *British Orientalism and the Bengal Renaissance: The Dynamics of Indian Modernization, 1773–1835.* Berkeley: University of California Press, 1969.

Kraft, Joseph S. "Human Rights in Southeast Asia: The Search for Regional Norms." Working Paper No. 4. Washington, DC: East-West Center, July 2005.

Krause, Joachim. *The OSCE and Co-operative Security in Europe: Lessons for Asia.* IDSS Monograph No. 6. Singapore: Institute for Defence and Strategic Studies, 2003.

Krauss, Ellis S., and T. J. Pempel, eds. *Beyond Bilateralism: The U.S.-Japan Relationship in the New Asia-Pacific.* Ithaca, NY: Cornell University Press, 2004.

Krawitz, Howard M. "China's Trade Opening: Implications for Regional Stability." *Strategic Forum.* No. 193. Washington, DC: National Defense University, August 2002.

Krumm, Kathie, and Homi Khanas, eds. *East Asia Integrates: A Trade Policy Agenda for Shared Growth.* Washington, DC: World Bank, 2003.

Kumar, Nagesh, ed. *Towards an Asian Economic Community: Vision of a New Asia.* New Delhi: Research and Information System for Developing Countries; Singapore: Institute of Southeast Asian Studies, 2004.

Kurlantzick, Joshua. *Pax Asia-Pacifica: Asia's Emerging Identity and Implications for US Policy.* Joint Report by Pacific Council on International Policy and the USC Center on Public Diplomacy, April 2007.

Kwan, C. H. *Yen Bloc: Toward Economic Integration in Asia.* Washington, DC: Brookings Institution Press, 2001.

Lach, Donald F. *A Century of Wonder.* Vol. 2 of *Asia in the Making of Europe.* Chicago: University of Chicago Press, 1970.

Landingin, Nathaniel, and David Wadley. "Export Processing Zones and Growth Triangle Development: The Case of the BIMP-EAGA, Southeast Asia." *Journal of International Development* 17, no. 1 (January 2005): 67–96.

Lardy, Nicholas R., and Daniel H. Rosen. *Prospects for a US-Taiwan Free Trade Agreement*. Policy Analysis 73. Washington, DC: Institute for International Economics, 2004.

Le Billon, Philippe. *Fueling War: Natural Resources and Armed Conflict*. Adelphi Paper 373. London: International Institute for Strategic Studies, 2005.

Lee, Chung Min. "East Asian Community and the United States: A Contrarian Perspective." In "The Emerging East Asian Community: Should Washington Be Concerned?" *Issues and Insights*. Honolulu: Pacific Forum CSIS, 2005.

Lee, Yok-shiu, and Alvin Y. So, eds. *Asia's Environmental Movements: Comparative Perspectives*. Armonk, NY: M. E. Sharpe, 1999.

Leifer, Michael. *The ASEAN Regional Forum: Extending ASEAN's Model of Regional Security*. Adelphi Paper 302. London: IISS, 1996.

Leonard, Jane Kate. *Wei Yuan and China's Rediscovery of the Maritime World*. Cambridge: Harvard University Press, 1984.

Levinson, Marc. *The Box: How the Shipping Container Made the World Smaller and the World Economy Bigger*. Princeton: Princeton University Press, 2006.

Lewis, Martin W., and Kären E. Wigen. *The Myth of Continents*. Berkeley: University of California Press, 1997.

Lewis, Norman. *Golden Earth: Travels in Burma*. London: Eland Books, 1983.

Lieberman, Victor. *Strange Parallels: Southeast Asia in Global Context, c. 800–1830*, vol. 1. Cambridge: Cambridge University Press, 2003.

Lieberthal, Kenneth, and Mikkal Herberg. "China's Search for Energy Security: Implications for U.S. Policy." *NBR Analysis* 17, no. 1 (April 2006): 1–42. National Bureau of Asian Research, Seattle.

Lincoln, Edward J. *East Asian Economic Regionalism*. Washington, DC: Council on Foreign Relations; Brookings Institution, 2004.

Liu, Guoli, ed. *Chinese Foreign Policy in Transition*. New York: Aldine de Gruyter, 2004.

Liu, Xinru. *Ancient India and Ancient China: Trade and Religious Exchanges, A.D. 1–600*. Cambridge: Oxford University Press, 1988.

Lloyd, P. J. "Australia's Economic Diplomacy in Asia." *Melbourne Asia Policy Papers*, No. 3. Melbourne: University of Melbourne, July 2003.

Luft, Gail, and Anne Korin. "Terrorism Goes to Sea." *Foreign Affairs* 83, no. 6 (November–December 2004): 61–71.

MacDonald, Juli A., Amy Donahue, and Bethany Danyluk. *Energy Futures in Asia*. Prepared for the director, Net Assessment, Office of the Secretary of Defense, Contract DASW01-02-D-0011, 2004.

Macfarlane, Alan, and Iris Macfarlane. *The Empire of Tea*. Woodstock, NY: Overlook Press, 2003.

Macfie, A. L. *Orientalism*. London: Pearson Education, 2002.

Mahathir, Mohamad. "Let Asians Build Their Own Future Regionalism." *Global Asia* 1, no. 1 (2006): 13–15.

Mahbubani, Kishore. *Beyond the Age of Innocence*. New York: Public Affairs, 2005.

———. *Can Asians Think?* Singapore: Times Books International, 1998.

———. "Wake Up, Washington: The US Risks Losing Asia." *Global Asia* 2, no. 2 (Fall 2007). Available at http://globalasia.org.

Maidment, Richard, and Colin Mackerras. *Culture and Society in the Asia-Pacific*. London: Routledge, 1998.

Mansfield, Edward D., and Brian M. Pollins, eds. *Economic Interdependence and International Conflict*. Ann Arbor: University of Michigan Press, 2003.

Mastanduno, Michael. "Incomplete Hegemony: The United States and Security Order in Asia." In Muthiah Alagappa, ed., *Asian Security Order: Instrumental and Normative Features.* Stanford: Stanford University Press, 2003.

Mathews, Neelam. "Regional Flights May Be Ticket to Success for Asian Discounters." *Aviation Week and Space Technology* 158, no. 2 (2003): 415.

Matthew, Helen G., ed. *Asia in the Modern World.* New York: Mentor Books, 1963.

Maugham, Somerset. *Maugham's Malaysian Stories.* Edited by Anthony Burgess. Singapore: Mandarin Paperbacks, 1994.

McKay, Julie M., Maria Oliva Armengol, and Georges Pineau, eds. *Regional Economic Integration in a Global Framework.* Papers from a G-20 Workshop, European Central Bank and the People's Bank of China, 2004.

McKendrick, D., R. F. Doner, and S. Haggard. *From Silicon Valley to Singapore: Location and Competitive Advantage in the Hard Disk Drive Industry.* Stanford: Stanford University Press, 2000.

McPherson, Kenneth. *The Indian Ocean: A History of People and the Sea.* New Delhi: Oxford University Press, 1998.

Medeiros, Evan S. "Strategic Hedging and the Future of Asia-Pacific Stability." *Washington Quarterly* 29, no. 1 (2005–2006): 145–167.

Merchang, Khozem. "Aggressive Bidding for Port Assets Is Driven by Pace of Growth." FT Special Report on Indian Infrastructure. *Financial Times,* April 24, 2006, p. 2.

Milner, Anthony. "Region, Security, and the Return of History." The Raffles Lecture Series. Singapore: Institute of Southeast Asian Studies, 2003.

Monfries, John, ed. *Different Societies, Shared Futures: Australia, Indonesia, and the Region.* Singapore: Institute of Southeast Asian Studies, 2006.

Montes, Manuel F., and Swarnim Wagle. "Why Asia Needs to Trade Smarter." *Far Eastern Economic Review* 169, no. 5 (June 2006): 45–48.

Morison, Samuel Eliot. *The Maritime History of Massachusetts.* Cambridge: Riverside Press, 1923.

Morris, Jan. *The Spectacle of Empire.* London: Faber & Faber, 1982.

Morrison, Charles E., and Eduardo Pedrosa, eds. *An APEC Trade Agenda: The Political Economy of a Free Trade Area of the Asia-Pacific.* Singapore: Institute for Southeast Asian Studies, 2007.

Mote, F. W. *Imperial China, 900–1800.* Cambridge: Harvard University Press, 1999.

Mukherjee, Rudrangshu, and Lakshmi Subramanian, eds. *Politics and Trade in the Indian Ocean.* New Delhi: Oxford University Press, 1998.

Munakata, Naoko. *Transforming East Asia: The Evolution of Regional Economic Integration.* Washington, DC: Brookings Institution, 2006.

Mungello, D. E. *The Great Encounter of China and the West, 1500–1800.* Lanham, MD: Rowman & Littlefield, 1999.

Naquin, Susan, and Evelyn S. Rawski. *Chinese Society in the 18th Century.* New Haven: Yale University Press, 1987.

Nathan, John. *Unbound Japan.* Boston: Houghton Mifflin, 2004.

Naughton, Barry. "The Third Front: Defence Industrialization in the Chinese Interior." *China Quarterly* 115 (September 1988): 351–386.

Ng, Francis, and Alexander Yeats. "Major Trade Trends in East Asia." Policy Research Working Paper 3084. Washington, DC: World Bank, June 2003.

Nincic, Donna J. "Sea Lane Security and U.S. Maritime Trade: Chokepoints as Scarce Resources." In Sam J. Tangredi, ed., *Globalization and Maritime Power.* Washington, DC: National Defense University Press, 2002.

Osborne, Milton. *Southeast Asia: An Introductory History.* 8th ed. Crows Nest, NSW, Australia: Allen & Unwin, 2000.

Parsons, Craig, and J. David Richardson. "Lessons for Asia? European Experiences—in American Perspective—in Legitimizing Market Integration." *Journal of Asian Economics* 14, no. 6 (January 2004): 885–907.

Pastor, Robert. *Towards a North American Community.* Washington, DC: Institute for International Economics, 2001.

Patrick, Hugh. "Japan's Official Development Assistance to, and FDI in, Southeast Asian Countries." Paper presented to a workshop sponsored by the Bureau of Intelligence and Research, Department of State, Washington, DC, March 20, 2006.

Patterson, Eliza. "Rethinking the WTO's Enabling Clause." *Journal of World Investment and Trade* 6, no. 5 (October 2005): 731–749.

Pempel, T. J. "Firebreak: East Asia Institutionalizes Its Finances." Paper prepared for the conference "Institutionalizing Northeast Asia: Making the Impossible Possible?" United Nations University and Aoyama Gakuin University, September 20–22, 2005.

———, ed. *The Politics of the Asian Economic Crisis.* Ithaca, NY: Cornell University Press, 1999.

———. "The Race to Connect East Asia: An Unending Steeplechase." *Asian Economic Policy Review* 1 (December 2006): 239–254.

———, ed. *Remapping East Asia: The Construction of a Region.* Ithaca, NY: Cornell University Press, 2005.

Percival, Bronson. *The Dragon Looks South.* Westport, CT: Praeger Security International, 2007.

Permal, Sumathy. "Indonesia's Efforts in Combating Piracy and Armed Robbery in the Straits of Malacca." Maritime Institute of Malaysia, May 2006. Available at www.mima.gov.my.

Pew Global Attitudes Project. "Publics of Asian Powers Hold Negative Views of One Another." September 21, 2006. Available at www.pewglobal.org.

Poon, Jessie P. H. "Trade Networks in Southeast Asia and Emerging Patterns." In Chia Lin Sien, ed., *Southeast Asia Transformed.* Singapore: Institute of Southeast Asian Studies, 2003.

Prakash, Om. "European Corporate Enterprises and the Politics of Trade in India, 1600–1800." In Rudrangshu Mukherjee and Lakshmi Subramanian, eds., *Politics and Trade in the Indian Ocean.* New Delhi: Oxford University Press, 1998.

Prestowitz, Clyde. "The Purpose of American Power in Asia." *Global Asia* 2, no. 2 (Fall 2007). Available at http://globalasia.org.

Rangnekar, Sharif D., and Manish Sharma. "India's Split Personality." *Far Eastern Economic Review* 169, no. 1 (2006): 18–21.

Ravenhill, John. *APEC and the Construction of Pacific Rim Regionalism.* Cambridge: Cambridge University Press, 2001.

———. "Is China an Economic Threat to ASEAN?" In William W. Keller and Thomas G. Rawski, eds., *China's Rise and the Balance of Influence in Asia.* Pittsburgh: University of Pittsburgh Press, 2007.

———. "Is China an Economic Threat to Southeast Asia?" *Asian Survey* 46, no. 5 (2006): 653–674.

———. "Trade Developments in East Asia Since the Financial Crisis." Paper prepared for "East Asia—A Decade After the Crisis," sponsored by Australian National University and University of California, Berkeley, July 21–22, 2006.

Ravi, Srilata, Mario Rutten, and Beng-Lan Goh. *Asia in Europe, Europe in Asia.* Singapore: Institute of Southeast Asian Studies, 2004.

Reid, Anthony. *Charting the Shape of Early Modern Southeast Asia.* Chiang Mai, Thailand: Silkworm Books, 1999.

———. *Southeast Asia in the Age of Commerce, 1450–1680.* 2 vols. New Haven: Yale University Press, 1988, 1993.

———. "Studying Southeast Asia in a Globalized World." *Taiwan Journal of Southeast Asian Studies* 1, no. 2 (October 2004).

Research and Information System for Developing Countries. *India-ASEAN Partnership in an Era of Globalization: Reflections by Eminent Persons.* Singapore: Institute of Southeast Asian Studies, 2004.

Ricklefs, M. C. *A History of Modern Indonesia Since c. 1300.* 2nd ed. Stanford: Stanford University Press, 1993.

Rimmer, Peter J. "The Asia-Pacific Rim's Transport and Telecommunications Systems: Spatial Structure and Corporate Control Since the Mid-1980s." *GeoJournal* 48, no. 1 (May 1999): 43–65.

———. "The Spatial Impact of Innovations in International Sea and Air Transport Since 1960." In Chia Lin Sien, ed., *Southeast Asia Transformed.* Singapore: Institute of Southeast Asian Studies, 2003.

Robinson, Thomas W. "Asia-Pacific Security Relations: Changes Ahead." In Richard L. Kugler and Ellen L. Frost, eds., *The Global Century: Globalization and National Security.* 2 vols. Washington, DC: National Defense University, 2001.

Rodan, Garry. *Transparency and Authoritarian Rule in Southeast Asia: Singapore and Malaysia.* London: Routledge, 2005.

Rohlen, Thomas P. "Cosmopolitan Cities and Nation States: Open Economics, Urban Dynamics, and Government in East Asia." Working Paper, Shorenstein Asia-Pacific Research Center, Stanford University, February 2002.

Rosengarten, Frederic, Jr. *The Book of Spices.* New York: Pyramid Books, 1973.

Ross, Robert. "A Realist Policy for Managing US-China Competition." *Policy Analysis Brief.* Muscatine, IA: Stanley Foundation, November 2005.

"Roundtable on Asia-Pacific Regional Security Cooperation." Institute for National Strategic Studies, National Defense University, Washington, DC, November 3, 2006.

Roy, Tirthankar. *The Economic History of India, 1857–1947.* Oxford: Oxford University Press, 2006.

Rozman, Gilbert, ed. *The East Asian Region.* Princeton: Princeton University Press, 1991.

———. *Northeast Asia's Stunted Regionalism.* Cambridge: Cambridge University Press, 2004.

Rubinstein, Murray A., ed. *Taiwan: A New History.* Armonk, NY: M. E. Sharpe, 1999.

Ruthven, Malise, with Azim Nanji. *Historical Atlas of Islam.* Cambridge: Harvard University Press, 2004.

Ryan, John. "APEC's Regional Approach to Energy Security." In Jan H. Kalicki and David L. Goldwyn, eds., *Energy and Security: Toward a New Foreign Policy Strategy.* Washington, DC: Woodrow Wilson Center Press; Baltimore: Johns Hopkins University Press, 2005.

Said, Edward W. *Orientalism.* New York: Vintage Books, 1979.

Sakakibara, Eisuke, and Sharon Yamakawa. "Market-Driven Regional Integration in East Asia." Paper presented to G-20 Workshop, September 22–23, 2004. Edited by Julie McKay, Maria Olivia Armengol, and Georges Pineau. Available at www.ecb.int/pub/pdf/other/regionaleconintegrationglobalframework2005en.pdf.

Saunders, Phillip C. *China's Global Activism: Strategy, Drivers, and Tools.* Institute for National Strategic Studies, Occasional Paper 4. Washington, DC: National Defense University Press, October 2006.

———. "The United States and East Asia After Iraq." *Survival* 49, no. 1 (Spring 2007): 141–151.

Schott, Jeffrey J. *Prospects for Free Trade in the Americas.* Washington, DC: Institute for International Economics, 2001.

Schott, Jeffrey J., and Ben Goodrich. "Economic Integration in Northeast Asia." Paper presented to the 2001 KIEP/KEI/CKS Conference on the Challenges of Reconciliation and Reform in Korea, Los Angeles, California, October 24–26, 2001. Available at www.petersoninstitute.org.

Schwarcz, Vera. *The Chinese Enlightenment.* Berkeley: University of California Press, 1986.

Schwartz, Benjamin. *In Search of Wealth and Power: Yen Fu and the West.* Cambridge: Harvard University Press, 1964.

Scollay, Robert. "Preliminary Assessment of the FTAAP Proposal." Presentation to the PECC Trade Forum and ASCC Joint Meeting, Jeju, Korea, May 2005. Available at www.apec.org.au/docs/koreapapers2/SX-RS-Slides.pdf#search=%22Robert%20Scollay9622.

Scollay, Robert, and John P. Gilbert. *New Regional Trading Arrangements in the Asia Pacific?* Washington, DC: Institute for International Economics, 2001.

Searight, Amy. "Process and the Art of Diplomacy in Asian Multilateralism: The United States, Japan, and China Compared." Discussion paper prepared for the conference "Open Political-Economic Systems: Globalization and Institutional Change," sponsored by Waseda University and Renmin University, Beijing, China, December 21–22, 2005.

Sen, Amartya. *The Argumentative Indian.* New York: Farrar, Straus & Giroux, 2005.

Sen, Rahul. *Free Trade Agreements in Southeast Asia.* Singapore: Institute of Southeast Asian Studies, 2004.

Servan-Schreiber, Jean-Jacques. *The American Challenge.* New York: Atheneum, 1968.

Severino, Rodolfo C. *Southeast Asia in Search of an ASEAN Community.* Singapore: Institute of Southeast Asian Studies, 2006.

———. "Towards an ASEAN Security Community." *Trends in Southeast Asia Series,* No. 8. Singapore: Institute of Southeast Asian Studies, 2004. Available at www.iseas.edu.sg/82004.pdf.

Shaffer, Lynda Norene. *Maritime Southeast Asia to 1500.* Armonk, NY: M. E. Sharpe, 1996.

Shambaugh, David. "China Engages Asia: Reshaping the Regional Order." *International Security* 29, no. 3 (2004–2005): 64–99.

———, ed. *Power Shift: China and Asia's New Dynamics.* Berkeley: University of California Press, 2005.

Shirk, Susan L. *China: Fragile Superpower.* Oxford: Oxford University Press, 2007.

Singh, Aparna Shivpuri. "Indian Special Economic Zones and Bilateralism in Asia." *Global Evian Trade Update,* No. 3. Lausanne: Evian Group, 2006.

Singh, Manmohan. "India's 'Look East' Policy Seeks to Deepen Economic Integration with Asia." *New Asia Monitor* 4, no. 2 (April 2007): 1.

Slaughter, Anne-Marie. *A New World Order.* Princeton: Princeton University Press, 2004.

Sokolsky, Richard, Angel Rabasa, and C. R. Neu. *The Role of Southeast Asia in U.S. Strategy Toward China.* Santa Monica, CA: RAND, 2000.

Spence, Jonathan D., and John E. Wills Jr. *From Ming to Ch'ing: Conquest, Region, and Continuity in Seventeenth Century China.* New Haven: Yale University Press, 1979.

Srinivasan, T. N., and Suresh D. Tendulkar. *Reintegrating India with the World Economy.* Washington, DC: Institute for International Economics, 2003.

Stanley Foundation. "New Power Dynamics in Southeast Asia: Issues for US Policymakers." *Policy Dialogue Brief* (October 2006).

Starr, S. Frederick, ed. *Xinjiang: China's Muslim Borderland.* Armonk, NY: M. E. Sharpe, 2004.

Stokes, Bruce. "Seoul Brothers." *National Journal* 38, no. 48 (December 2, 2006): 33–38.

Suryadinata, Leo, ed. *Southeast Asia's Chinese Businesses in an Era of Globalization.* Singapore: Institute of Southeast Asian Studies, 2006.

Sutter, Robert G. *China's Rise in Asia: Promises and Perils.* Lanham, MD: Rowman & Littlefield, 2005.

Tanaka, Hitoshi. 2007. "East Asia Community Building: Toward an 'East Asia Security Forum.'" *East Asia Insights* 2, no. 2 (April 2007): 1–6.

Tangredi, Sam J., ed. *Globalization and Maritime Power.* Washington, DC: National Defense University Press, 2002.

Tarling, Nicholas, ed. *Cambridge History of Southeast Asia,* vol. 1. Cambridge: Cambridge University Press, 1999.

Tellis, Ashley J., and Michael Wills, eds. *Strategic Asia 2004–05: Confronting Terrorism in the Pursuit of Power.* Seattle: National Bureau of Asian Research, 2004.

———. *Strategic Asia 2005–06: Military Modernization in an Era of Uncertainty.* Seattle: National Bureau of Asian Research, 2005.

———. *Strategic Asia 2006–07: Trade, Interdependence, and Security.* Seattle: National Bureau of Asian Research, 2006.

Terrill, Ross. *Riding the Wave: The Rise of China and Options for Australian Policy.* Barton, ACT, Australia: Australian Strategic Policy Institute, March 2006.

Thapur, Romila. *Early India: From the Origins to AD 1300.* Berkeley: University of California Press, 2002.

Toby, Ronald P. *State and Diplomacy in Early Modern Japan: Asia in the Development of the Tokugawa Bakufu.* Stanford: Stanford University Press, 1992.

Tu Wei-Ming, ed. *Confucian Traditions in East Asian Modernity.* Cambridge: Harvard University Press, 1996.

Tucker, Sandeep, and Joe Leahy. "On the March: How Corporate India Is Finding the Confidence to Go Global." *Financial Times,* October 4, 2006, p. 13.

UNCTAD (United Nations Committee on Trade and Development). *World Investment Report 2005.* New York: UNCTAD, 2005.

UNESCAP (United Nations Economic and Social Commission for Asia and the Pacific). *Municipal Land Management in Asia: A Comparative Study.* Bangkok: UNESCAP, 2001.

United Nations Environment Programme. *Global Environmental Outlook 2000.* London: Earthscan, 2000.

United States–Indonesia Society. "Rising India: A Win-Win for All?" Summary of remarks by Walter Andersen, Dewi Anwar Foruna, and Satu Limaye, Washington, DC, February 21, 2006.

Wales, H. G. Quaritch. *The Indianization of China and of Southeast Asia.* London: Bernard Quaritch, 1967.

Wang Gungwu. *The Chinese Overseas: From Earthbound China to the Quest for Autonomy.* Cambridge: Harvard University Press, 2000.

Wang Jisi. "America in Asia: How Much Does China Care?" *Global Asia* 2, no. 2 (Fall 2007). Available at http://globalasia.org.

———. "China's Search for Stability with America." *Foreign Affairs* 84, no. 5 (2005): 39–48.

Weatherford, Jack. *Genghis Khan and the Making of the Modern World.* New York: Three Rivers Press, 2004.

Webster, Douglas. "On the Edge: Shaping the Future of Peri-urban East Asia." Working Paper, Shorenstein Asia-Pacific Research Center, Stanford University, May 2002.

Wessels, Wolfgang. "An Ever Closer Fusion? A Dynamic Macropolitical View on Integration Processes." *Journal of Common Market Studies* 35, no. 2 (June 1997): 267–299.

Williamson, John. "A Currency Basket for East Asia, Not Just China." *Policy Briefs in International Economics,* No. PB05-1. Washington, DC: Institute for International Economics, August 2005.

Wills, Garry. *Venice: Lion City.* New York: Simon & Schuster, 2001.

Wills, John E., Jr. "Maritime Asia 1500–1800: The Interactive Emergence of European Domination." *American Historical Review* 98, no. 1 (February 1993).

Wittfogel, Karl. *Oriental Despotism.* New Haven: Yale University Press, 1963.

Wolf, Martin, *Why Globalization Works.* New Haven, CT: Yale University Press, 2004.

Wolpert, Stanley. *A New History of India.* New York: Oxford University Press, 1977.

Wolters, O. W. *Early Indonesian Commerce: A Study in the Origins of Srivijaya.* Ithaca, NY: Cornell University Press, 1967.

———. *History, Culture, and Region in Southeast Asian Perspectives.* Ithaca, NY: Southeast Asia Program Publications in cooperation with the Institute of Southeast Asian Studies, 1999.

Wood, Frances. *The Silk Road: Two Thousand Years in the Heart of Asia.* Berkeley: University of California Press, 2002.

Wright, Arthur F. *Buddhism in Chinese History.* Stanford: Stanford University Press; London: Oxford University Press, 1979.

Wright, Robert. *Non-Zero: The Logic of Human Destiny.* New York: Vintage Books, 2000.

Wu, Xinbo. "East Asia: Building a Community in the 21st Century." Paper presented to a conference sponsored by the Stanley Foundation and the Center for Strategic and International Studies, "The Future Institutional Architecture of Asia," St. Michaels, MD, November 15–17, 2006.

Wyatt, David K. *A Short History of Thailand.* New Haven: Yale University Press, 2003. First published in 1982.

Yapp, Peter, ed. *The Travellers' Dictionary of Quotation.* London: Routledge & Kegan Paul, 1983.

Yeo, George. "The Asian Renaissance." Speech presented at the Nalanda Buddhist Symposium "Reviving Buddhist Cultural Links," New Delhi, November 13, 2006. Available at http://app.sprinter.gov.sg/data/pr/20061113987.htm.

Zakaria, Fareed. "A Conversation with Lee Kuan Yew." *Foreign Affairs* 73, no. 2 (March–April 1994): 109–127.

Zebregs, Harm. "Intraregional Trade in Emerging Asia." IMF Policy Discussion Paper PDP/04/1. Washington, DC: International Monetary Fund, 2004.

Zha Daojiong. "China's Energy Security: Domestic and International Issues." *Survival* 48, no. 1 (Spring 2006): 179–189.

Zhang Yunling, ed. *East Asian Cooperation: Searching for an Integrated Approach.* Beijing: World Affairs Press, 2004.

———. "Emerging New East Asian Regionalism." Asian Voices Seminar Series transcript. Washington, DC: Sasakawa Peace Foundation USA, December 7, 2004.

Zheng Bijian. "China's 'Peaceful Rise' to Great-Power Status." *Foreign Affairs* 84, no. 5 (September–October 2005): 18–24.

Zhou Hong. "The Political Economy of Subregional Economic Cooperation in East Asia." *The Japanese Economy* 32, no. 2 (2004): 53–64.

Zoellick, Robert. "Whither China: From Membership to Responsibility?" Speech presented to the National Council on U.S.-China Relations, New York, September 21, 2006.

Zweig, David. *Internationalizing China: Domestic Interests and Global Linkages.* Ithaca, NY: Cornell University Press, 2002.

Index

275

About the Book

As the political drive to establish closer ties among Asian governments continues to gain momentum, there has been much debate about the realities of Asian regionalism. Does the community-building activity add up to
nothing more than talk, or does it signal the birth of "Asia Major"? What are
the obstacles to closer integration? And is the integration movement actually a
positive trend for the region, for external actors, and for world order? Sifting
rhetoric from fact and drawing on a rich variety of perspectives, Ellen Frost
offers a nuanced analysis of the historical, political, economic, and strategic
issues at stake.

A central theme in *Asia's New Regionalism* is the contrast between integration driven by national governments for political and security reasons and
spontaneous integration in maritime regions fueled by the resurgence of
centuries-old ethnic, cultural, and economic ties. Frost's lively exploration of
these sometimes mismatched dynamics also highlights critical implications for
policies both in the region and in the United States.

Ellen L. Frost is visiting fellow at the Peterson Institute for International
Economics and adjunct research fellow at the National Defense University.
She is author of *For Richer, For Poorer: The New U.S.-Japan Relationship*
and *Transatlantic Trade: A Strategic Agenda*.

Days	Itinerary	Visits
6	**Revelstoke – Lake Louise** 228km/142mi	Roger ... Rocky ... Emerald Lake★★★ *(p 62)* Yoho Valley★★ *(p 61)* Kicking Horse Pass *(p 61)*
7	**Lake Louise excursions** 81km/50mi	Lake Louise★★★ *(p 60)* Mt. Whitehorn★ *(p 61)* Moraine Lake★★★ *(p 60)*
8	**Lake Louise – Jasper** 233km/145mi	Rocky Mountain Parks★★★ *(p 55)* Icefields Parkway★★★ *(p 62)*
9	**Jasper excursions** 167km/104mi	Jasper National Park★★★ *(p 65)* Mt. Edith Cavell★★ *(p 65)* Maligne Valley★★★ *(p 66)*
10	**Jasper – Prince George** 376km/234mi	Yellowhead Highway ★★ *(p 67)* Mt. Robson Provincial Park ★★ *(p 67)* Mt. Robson★★★ *(p 67)*
11	**Prince George – New Hazelton** 446km/277mi	'Ksan *(p 70)*
12	**New Hazelton – Prince Rupert** 295km/183mi	Skeena Valley★★ *(p 68)* (described in opposite direction)
13	**Prince Rupert – Port Hardy** by ferry	Inside Passage★★ *(p 46)*
14	**Port Hardy – Tofino** 542km/337mi	Vancouver Island★★★: from Parksville to Pacific Rim★★ *(p 82)*
15	**Tofino – Victoria** 320km/198mi	Pacific Rim National Park★★ *(p 83)*
16-17		Victoria★★★ *(p 83)*
18	**Victoria – Vancouver** by ferry	Butchart Gardens★★★ *(p 87)*

2 **Northern British Columbia and the Yukon** – *Round-trip of 5,185km/ 3,222mi (not including ferry) from Edmonton. Time: 17 days.* This tour combines the wild beauty of the Yukon with the adventure of driving the Alaska Highway, and the misty and romantic Inside Passage cruise down the West Coast.

1-2		Edmonton★★ *(p 112)*
3	**Edmonton – Fort St. John** 665km/413mi	Alaska Highway★★ *(p 37)*
4	**Fort St. John – Fort Nelson** 416km/258mi	Alaska Highway★★ *(p 37)*

From Fort Nelson, travellers can make an optional 1-day excursion to Nahanni National Park★★★ (p 307).

5	**Fort Nelson – Watson Lake** 546km/339mi	Alaska Highway★★ *(p 38)*
6	**Watson Lake – Whitehorse** 455km/283mi	Alaska Highway★★ *(p 39)*
7		Whitehorse★ *(p 89)*
8	**Whitehorse – Dawson City** 540km/336mi	Yukon Circuit★★ *(p 93)* Klondike Highway *(p 93)*
9		Dawson City★★ *(p 41)*

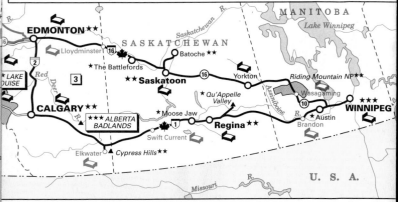

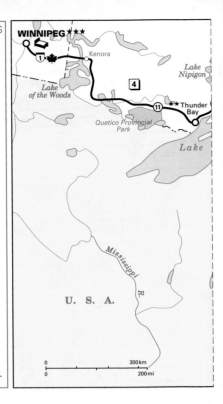

	DISTANCES FROM MAJOR US CITIES

San Francisco to Vancouver
1,537km/955mi

Seattle to Vancouver
230km/143mi

Spokane to Calgary
711km/442mi

Duluth to Winnipeg
637km/396mi

Minneapolis to Winnipeg
730km/454mi

Chicago to Winnipeg
1,419km/882mi

Chicago to Toronto
801km/498mi

Detroit to Toronto
373km/232mi

Pittsburgh to Niagara Falls
388km/241mi

Washington DC to Niagara Falls
660km/410mi

New York to Niagara Falls
658km/409mi

New York to Ottawa
747km/464mi

New York to Montreal
608km/378mi

Boston to Montreal
512km/318mi

Boston to Saint John NB
570km/354mi

Boston to Yarmouth NS
386km/240mi not including ferry.

Days	Itinerary	Visits
10	**Dawson City – Haines Junction** 744km/462mi	Yukon Circuit★★ *(p 94)* Top of the World Highway★★ *(p 94)* Alaska Highway★★ Kluane Lake★★ *(p 95)*
11	**Haines Junction – Whitehorse** 161km/100mi	Kluane National Park★★ *(p 96)*
12-13	**Whitehorse – Prince Rupert** 180km/112mi and ferry	Klondike Highway to Skagway★★ *(p 91)* Skagway★ *(p 92)* Inside Passage (US)

From Prince Rupert, travellers can take the ferry through the Inside Passage★★ (p 35) to Seattle, arriving Day 15, or optional 3-day excursion to Queen Charlotte Islands★★ (p 51).

14-16	**Prince Rupert – Jasper** *(see Days 12, 11, 10 of Tour 1)*	
17	**Jasper – Edmonton** 361km/224mi	

3 **Prairies** – *Round-trip of 3,371km/2,095mi from Winnipeg. Time: 17 days.* This tour enables visitors to discover some of the fascination of the Prairies—grand vistas, wheat fields, ranches and cowboys. The oil-rich Alberta cities of Calgary and Edmonton are visited as well as the interesting city of Winnipeg.

1-2		Winnipeg★★★ *(p 123)*
3	**Winnipeg – Wasagaming** 265km/165mi	Riding Mountain National Park★★ *(p 120)*
4	**Wasagaming – Yorkton** 230km/143mi	Yorkton *(p 128)*
5	**Yorkton – Saskatoon** 331km/205mi	Saskatoon★ *(p 121)*
6	176km/109mi	Excursion to Batoche★★ *(p 122)*
7	**Saskatoon – Lloydminster** 276km/171mi	The Battlefords★ *(p 105)*
8-9	**Lloydminster – Edmonton** 248km/154mi	Edmonton★★ *(p 112)*

Optional 5-day excursion, 1,034km/642mi, can be made to the Rockies: Edmonton–Jasper 339km/210mi; Jasper–Lake Louise see Days 9, 8, 7 of Tour 1; Lake Louise–Calgary 214km/133mi.

Days	Itinerary	Visits
10-11	**Edmonton – Calgary** 297km/185mi	Calgary★★ *(p 106)*
12	**Calgary – Elkwater** 432km/268mi	Alberta Badlands★★★ *(p 103)*
13	**Elkwater – Swift Current** 227km/141mi	Cypress Hills★★ *(p 110)*
14	**Swift Current – Regina** 243km/151mi	Moose Jaw★ *(p 117)*
15		Regina★★ *(p 118)*
16	**Regina – Brandon** 423km/263mi	Qu' Appelle Valley★ *(p 120)*
17	**Brandon – Winnipeg** 211km/131mi	Austin★ *(p 105)*

4 **Northern Ontario** – *Trip of 2,271km/1,411mi from Ottawa to Winnipeg. Time: 10 days.*
On this tour visitors can experience the wild, untouched beauty of the Canadian
Shield country with its rocks, trees and lovely lakes. The drive around Lake Superior
is particularly attractive.

1-2		Ottawa★★★ *(p 154)*
3	**Ottawa – North Bay** 363km/226mi	North Bay★ *(p 152)*
4	**North Bay – Sault Ste Marie** 427km/265mi	Sudbury★★ *(p 169)*
5		Sault Ste. Marie★★ *(p 167)*
6	**Sault Ste Marie – Thunder Bay** 705km/438mi	Lake Superior Drive★★ *(p 168)* North Shore Lake Superior★★ *(p 171)* (described in other direction)
7		Thunder Bay★★ *(p 170)*
8	**Thunder Bay – Kenora** 569km/353mi	Kakabeka Falls★★ *(p 171)*
9-10	**Kenora – Winnipeg** 207km/129mi	Winnipeg★★★ *(p 123)*

5 Southern Ontario – *Round-trip of 1,737km/1,079mi from Niagara Falls. Time: 18 days.* This tour combines the vibrant city of Toronto with the magnificent falls on the Niagara River, the highly cultivated southern Ontario, some Canadian Shield country and the nation's capital of Ottawa.

Days	Itinerary	Visits
1-2	60km/37mi	Niagara Falls★★★ *(p 148)* Niagara Parkway (north)★★ *(p 149)*
3	**Niagara Falls – Toronto** 147km/91mi	Hamilton★ *(p 141)*
4-7		Toronto★★★ *(p 172)*
8	**Toronto – Kingston** 269km/167mi	Oshawa★★ *(p 153)*
9		Kingston and The Thousand Islands★★ *(p 143)*
10	**Kingston – Ottawa** 201km/125mi	Upper Canada Village★★★ *(p 191)*
11-12		Ottawa★★★ *(p 154)*
13	**Ottawa – Gravenhurst** 406km/252mi	Gravenhurst★ *(p 141)*
14	**Gravenhurst – Midland** 56km/35mi	Orillia★ *(p 152)* Ste.-Marie among the Hurons★★ *(p 138)* Midland★ *(p 138)*
15		Penetanguishene★ *(p 139)* Georgian Bay★★ *(p 138)*
16	**Midland – Goderich** 249km/155mi	Wasaga Beach★ *(p 139)* Blue Mountains *(p 140)* Goderich★ *(p 140)*
17	**Goderich – London** 140km/87mi	Stratford★ *(p 168)* London★ *(p 147)*

Optional 2-day excursion, 482km/300mi, can be made to Windsor★ (p 192) and Point Pelee National Park★★ (p 165); overnight stop at Leamington.

18	**London – Niagara Falls** 209km/130mi	Brantford★ *(p 137)*

6 Quebec – *Round-trip of 2,359km/1,466ml (not including ferries) from Montreal. Time: 17 days.* This tour combines the charm of Quebec City, the ancient capital, with the impressive fjord on the Saguenay; the beautiful Gaspé peninsula culminating in the scenic wonder of Percé; and the modern vibrant city of Montreal.

1-3		Montreal★★★ *(p 211)*
4	**Montreal – Quebec City** 277km/172mi	Trois-Rivières★★ *(p 233)*
5-6		Quebec City★★★ *(p 223)*
7	**Quebec City – Île aux Coudres** 107km/67mi and ferry	Beaupré Coast★★ *(p 229)* Charlevoix Coast★★★ *(p 202)* Île aux Coudres★★ *(p 202)*

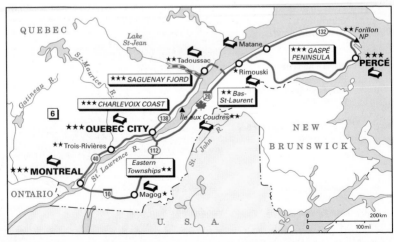

Days	Itinerary	Visits
8	**Île aux Coudres – Tadoussac** 104km/65mi and ferry	Charlevoix Coast★★★ *(p 202)* Tadoussac★★ *(p 232)*
9		Whale-Watching Cruise★★ *(p 232)* or Cruise on the Saguenay Fjord★★★ *(p 233)*
10	**Tadoussac – Matane** 204km/127mi (ferry Les Escoumins – Trois-Pistoles)	Gaspé Peninsula★★★ *(p 206)* Métis Gardens★★ *(p 206)* Matane *(p 206)*
11	**Matane – Percé** 404km/251mi	Forillon National Park★★ *(p 207)* Gaspé★ *(p 207)*
12-13		Percé★★★ *(p 207)*
14	**Percé – Rimouski** 466km/290mi	Gaspé Peninsula★★★ *(p 206)* South Coast *(p 207)* Rimouski★ *(p 202)*
15	**Rimouski – Quebec City** 312km/194mi	Bas-St.-Laurent★★ *(p 200)* (described in opposite direction)
16	**Quebec City – Magog** 275km/171mi	Eastern Townships★★ *(p 204)* Magog★ *(p 204)*
17	**Magog – Montreal** 210km/130mi	Richelieu Valley★★ *(p 230)*

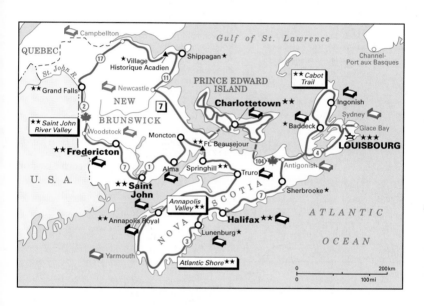

7 Maritime Provinces – *Round-trip of 4,235km/2,632mi (not including ferries) from Halifax. Time: 22 days.* This tour of the three Maritime provinces is an interesting blend of seascapes, rocky headlands, sandy beaches and the high tides of the Bay of Fundy with historical highlights such as the French fortress of Louisbourg, Halifax and its citadel, the Acadian country and the important port of Saint John.

Days	Itinerary	Visits
1-2		Halifax★★ *(p 271)*
3	**Halifax – Antigonish** 261km/162mi	Sherbrooke★ *(p 276)*
4	**Antigonish – Sydney** 212km/132mi	Louisbourg Fortress★★★ *(p 275)*
5	**Sydney – Ingonish** 127km/79mi	Glace Bay (Miners' Museum★★) *(p 270)* Cabot Trail★★ *(p 266)* (described in opposite direction) Ingonish *(p 269)*
6	**Ingonish – Baddeck** 233km/145mi	Cabot Trail★★ *(p 266)* Cape Breton Highlands National Park★★ *(p 268)* Chéticamp *(p 267)* Baddeck★ *(p 267)*
7	**Baddeck – Charlottetown** 263km/163mi and ferry	Prince Edward Island *(p 278)* Charlottetown★★ *(p 279)*
8-9-10	800km/500mi (maximum)	Prince Edward Island Scenic Drives *(pp 280-282)*

Days	Itinerary	Visits
11	**Charlottetown – Newcastle** 259km/161mi and ferry	
12	**Newcastle – Campbellton** 301km/187mi	Shippagan★ *(p 256)* Village Historique Acadien★ *(p 256)*
13	**Campbellton – Woodstock** 311km/193mi	Saint John River Valley★★ *(p 254)* (described in opposite direction) Grand Falls★★ *(p 255)* Hartland★ *(p 255)*
14	**Woodstock – Fredericton** 101km/63mi	Kings Landing★★ *(p 254)*
15	**Fredericton – Saint John** 109km/68mi	Fredericton★★ *(p 246)*
16		Saint John★★ *(p 252)*
17	**Saint John – Alma** 143km/89mi	Fundy National Park★★ *(p 248)*
18	**Alma – Truro** 254km/158mi	Hopewell Cape★★ *(p 249)* Moncton *(p 249)* Fort Beausejour★★ *(p 245)* Springhill★★ *(p 277)*
19	**Truro – Annapolis Royal** 243km/151mi	Truro *(p 277)* Annapolis Valley★★ *(p 260)* (described in other direction)
20	**Annapolis Royal – Yarmouth** 131km/81mi	Annapolis Royal★★ *(p 259)* Port Royal Habitation★★ *(p 260)*
21	**Yarmouth – Lunenburg** 311km/193mi	Atlantic Shore★★ (described in opposite direction) Liverpool *(p 265)* Ovens Natural Park★ *(p 265)* Lunenburg★ *(p 264)*
22	**Lunenburg – Halifax** 176km/109mi	Atlantic Shore★★ *(p 263)* Peggy's Cove★★ *(p 263)*

8 **Newfoundland** – *Round-trip of 2,073km/1,288mi (not including ferries) from North Sydney, Nova Scotia. Time: 12 days.* This tour of Canada's most easterly province enables visitors to discover the scenic wonders of Gros Morne, the French island of St.-Pierre and the old port city of St. John's.

1	**North Sydney – Port aux Basques** by ferry *(it is advisable to spend the previous night in Sydney)*	
2	**Port aux Basques – Wiltondale** 305km/190mi	

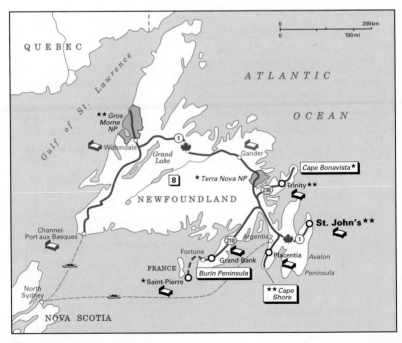

Days	Itinerary	Visits
3	191km/119mi	Gros Morne National Park★★ *(p 287)*
4	**Wiltondale – Gander** 356km/221mi	
5-6	**Gander – Trinity** 182km/113mi	Terra Nova National Park★ *(p 297)* Cape Bonavista★ *(p 298)* Trinity★★ *(p 297)*
7	**Trinity – Grand Bank** 333km/206mi	Burin Peninsula *(p 286)* Grand Bank *(p 286)*
8	**Grand Bank – St.-Pierre** by ferry from Fortune	St.-Pierre★ *(p 296)*
9-10	**St.-Pierre – St. John's** 362km/224mi	St. John's★★ *(p 291)*
11	**St. John's – Cape Shore** 175km/109mi	Placentia (Castle Hill★) *(p 286)* Cape St. Mary's★ *(p 287)*
12	**Cape Shore – North Sydney** by ferry from Argentia	

List of Maps

Introduction to Canada

Canada's Landscapes

Covering nearly 10 million sq km/3.9 million sq mi, Canada is the second largest country in the world in terms of physical size. It is exceeded only by Russia, whose landmass totals some 17 million sq km/6.6 million sq mi. Having shores on three oceans (Atlantic, Pacific and Arctic), Canada occupies most of the northern part of the North American continent. Yet its inhabitants, largely concentrated along the Canadian/US border, number only about 30 million—roughly the population of the state of California. The country is divided into ten provinces and two territories.

Spanning six time zones *(p 319)*, the country stretches from latitude 41°47'N at **Pelee Island** in Lake Erie (the same latitude as Rome, Italy) to 83°07'N at **Cape Columbia** on Ellesmere Island, a mere 800km/500mi from the North Pole. This north-south extension of about 4,600 km/2,900mi is countered only by its width. Canada covers more than 5,500km/3,400mi from **Cape Spear** in Newfoundland (longitude 52°37'W) to the **Yukon/Alaska** border (141°W). One of the most remarkable features is the immense bite cut out of the coastline by **Hudson Bay**, named for famed British explorer Henry Hudson. This enormous gulf or inland sea (637,000sq km/245,946sq mi) could be considered part of either the Atlantic or the Arctic Ocean. In common with the US, Canada shares another noteworthy feature—the **Great Lakes**, which together form the largest body of fresh water in the world. Finally, the country is characterized by its extremely mountainous western rim.

The Great Ice Ages – The physiographic regions described below have been extensively modified in more recent geological times by the advance and retreat of glacial ice. Four times during the past million years, the North American climate has become progressively colder. Snowfall became increasingly heavy in the north and was gradually compressed into ice. This ice began to flow south, reaching its maximum extent at the Ohio and Missouri River Valleys in the US before retreating. At peak coverage, 97 percent of Canada was submerged under ice up to 3km/2mi deep at the centre and 1.6km/1mi deep at the edges. Only the Cypress Hills and the Klondike region of the Yukon escaped this cover. The last Ice Age receded more than 10,000 years ago. A sheet of ice of such thickness exerts a great deal of pressure on the earth below. As the ice from each glacial advance retreated, hollows were scoured out of the land and filled with water, and mountain ranges were worn away and sculptured. Today about 2 percent of Canada is covered by glacial ice, mainly in the Arctic islands, but glaciers are found in the western mountains (Columbia Icefield and St. Elias Mountains).

THE GREAT NATURAL REGIONS

Physiographically, Canada has at its centre a massive upland known as the Canadian Shield, which forms the geological platform for the whole country. This upland is partially surrounded by areas of lowland that in turn are rimmed by mountain ranges on three of Canada's four sides; to the south the country lies open to the US. Only in parts of the north do these mountain rims flatten out to form a coastal plain. Seven major physiographic regions can be distinguished.

The Canadian Shield – This massive horseshoe-shaped region surrounding Hudson Bay encompasses nearly half of Canada's area. The terrain is formed of ancient, hard rocks of the **Precambrian** era (over 500 million years old) known for their great rigidity and strength. This strength and the region's shape are the origin of the name "Shield." The region is characterized by its innumerable lakes and rivers (Canada possesses as much as a quarter of the world's total supply of fresh water, largely concentrated in the Shield), by its rugged nature

Canadian Shield's Rocky Terrain

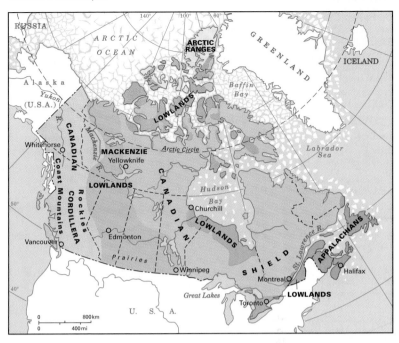

(a combination of rock and bog that makes much of the area inaccessible) and by its lack of agricultural soil. However, the region is also the source of much of the country's extensive mineral, forest and hydro-electric wealth.

Great Lakes/St. Lawrence Lowlands – Despite their comparatively small size, these lowlands, which extend south into one of the great industrial and agricultural belts of the continent, are home to over 50 percent of the country's inhabitants. They were created in **Paleozoic** times (200-500 million years ago) when great stretches of the region were flooded by the sea for long periods. During this flooding thousands of feet of sedimentary rock accumulated on top of the Shield, providing fertile soil that has made the region important for agriculture today. This factor, combined with a favourable climate and proximity to the US, has made these lowlands Canada's richest and most industrialized area as well as its most populous.

Prairies and Mackenzie Lowlands – The geologic history of these lowlands is similar to those of the Great Lakes/St. Lawrence region. Material eroded from the Shield and the marginal mountains (in particular, the Rockies) was first deposited in shallow seas. Subsequently swept by glaciers, the flat plains in the south consist of fertile soils ideal for wheat and general farming. The Mackenzie Lowlands begin north of a low divide between the Saskatchewan and Athabasca Rivers, and support little agriculture because of their northerly latitude. In places where the Mackenzie Plain joins the Shield, there are large natural basins partially filled with water. Indeed, the dividing line between these two regions is marked by a series of great lakes—Winnipeg, Athabasca, Great Slave, Great Bear and others.

Hudson Bay and Arctic Archipelago Lowlands – The northern counterpart of the Great Lakes/St. Lawrence region, these lowlands are widely scattered portions of a partially drowned plain of Paleozoic rock that once covered the northern part of the Shield. They slope gently away from the latter with little relief. Owing to its northerly latitude, severe climate and frozen soil, this area supports little except a vegetation of moss and lichens.

Appalachian Mountains – About 200 million years ago, these mountains, which stretch from Alabama in the US to Newfoundland, were the first to be folded on the edges of the continent. Since then, extensive erosion by ice, rivers and sea has reduced them to mere stumps of their former heights. Today the region is a series of generally flat to rounded uplands, with few sharp peaks rising to no more than 1,280m/4,200ft. Prince Edward Island, and the Annapolis, Restigouche and Saint John River Valleys are notable areas of plain where ancient glacial lakes have left fertile soil.

Canadian Cordillera – The Canadian Cordillera consists of five major parts (from east to west): the Rocky Mountains, the interior basins and plateaus, the Coast Mountains, the Inside Passage along the coast, and finally the outer system of islands. Covering the western quarter of the country, this great sweep of mountains is part of North America's long mountain systems known as the Western Cordillera.

The Canadian Cordillera is a relatively recent geological development. About 70 million years ago, enormous earth forces thrust these mountains up with a great deal of faulting, folding and volcanic activity. Since then, erosion and uplifting by glaciers, and partial drowning by sea have produced a deeply indented coast.

Arctic Ranges – These mountains in the extreme north of the country probably rose after the Appalachians. They consist of two fairly distinct parts: the rounded hills of the Parry Islands and the folded peaks of Ellesmere Island.

GEOGRAPHICAL FEATURES

Vegetation – The tree line crosses Canada in a rough diagonal from the Mackenzie Delta to Hudson Bay and the Atlantic. North of this line lies the **tundra**, a land of lichens, miniature flowering plants and stunted shrubs. South of this line, the **boreal forest** of black and white spruce, tamarack and other conifers gradually begins, becoming increasingly dense as it extends south. More deciduous trees are found until it becomes a **mixed forest**. But only in southern Ontario are the conifers of the north completely left behind and a true **deciduous forest** exists. In the Prairies, the trees almost completely disappear, making way for the flat former **grasslands** that are now highly cultivated. The mountain region of the West also has its own vegetation pattern, the trees thinning out as they approach the alpine tree line in the same way as they do in the north.

Wildlife – Canada's varied landscape hosts several species of animals typical of regional fauna. Vast forests provide habitat for **white-tailed deer**, **black-tailed deer** and **mule deer**, while **wapiti**, also known as the American elk, populate mountainous terrain and prairieland. Largest of the deer family is a distinctively Canadian animal, the **moose**, inhabiting the forests of Newfoundland west to British Columbia as do **woodland caribou**, another member of the deer family. Also distinct is the Canada **lynx** previously located throughout the country, but now surviving in the northern mainland and in Newfoundland. Rare in Canada is the **wolverine** (of the weasel family), found in sparse populations in the western and northern part of the country. The **grizzly bear** and particularly the **black bear** (*illustration p 320*) are common denizens of Canada's coniferous and deciduous forests. Trapped nearly to extinction, **beavers** now thrive across Canada, occupying the streams and ponds of forested regions. Once common to forest, prairies and tundra, **wolves** reside primarily in the northern wilderness.

Humpback Whale

Arthur C. Smith/Grant Hellman Photography

Mountain Goats

Populating Arctic coasts and islands are **polar bears** *(illustration p 110)* that feed on Canada's varied **seal** population, such as the grey, harp and hooded seals. Over 30 species of **whales** ply Canada's coastal waters, including the humpback and fin (off Newfoundland); the killer (or orca) and the grey (off British Columbia); and the beluga, blue, fin, and minke (St. Lawrence estuary). The Arctic tundra supports **muskoxen**, lemmings, white foxes and Arctic wolves as well as barren-ground caribou.

Wildlife of the prairies includes the **gopher**, **jackrabbit** and **grouse** in addition to **pronghorns** and **bison** (cattle family), known more commonly in North America as buffalo. Once numbering in the millions, bison were nearly extinct by 1885, hunted for their hides and meat. Wood Buffalo National Park protects a large population today.

Roaming the mountains of Western Canada are **mountain goats** and mountain sheep. Thinhorn or **Dall sheep** are found along Canada's Alaska Highway *(p 37)*, while **bighorn sheep** frequent British Columbia's southcentral ranges and the Canadian Rocky Mountains.

Canada's bird population ranges from waterfowl such as the Canada goose, Atlantic puffin and piping plover to the interior's peregrine falcon and rare whooping crane. The majestic **bald eagle** *(illustration p 90)* breeds in parts of northern and eastern Canada, but is confined largely to the coasts of north and central British Columbia. Although most species are migratory, over 400 species of birds have been documented as breeding in Canada.

Climate – Canada's climate is as varied and extreme as its geography. In a large area of the country, winter lasts longer than summer, yet the latter, when it comes, can be very hot. In the north, long hours of daylight cause prolific plant growth. The central provinces of Canada receive the most snow, far more than the Arctic, which in fact, receives the least precipitation of any region.

Fall Foliage

One major factor influencing climate is proximity to large bodies of water: chiefly, the Pacific and Atlantic Oceans, Hudson Bay, and the Great Lakes. Such expanses tend to make winters warmer and summers cooler. Regions distant from them are inclined, therefore, to have much colder winters and hotter summers. But terrain is also a factor. In the West the high Coast Mountains shield the interior of British Columbia and the Yukon from the mild and moist Pacific air, making their climate more extreme than their location would indicate. The Rockies intensify this trend, leaving the Prairies vulnerable to both Arctic winds and hot southern breezes.

Each regional introduction has a summary of climatic conditions with average summer temperatures and precipitation.

19

Time Line

Pre-Colonial Period

c. 20,000–15,000 BC	First migration of Asiatic peoples to North American continent.
c. AD 1000	Norse reach Newfoundland *(p 290)*.
1492	Christopher Columbus lands on San Salvador.
1497	**John Cabot** explores east coast of Canada.

New France

1534	**Jacques Cartier** claims Canada for France *(p 195)*.
1565	St. Augustine, Florida, the oldest city in the US, is founded by Spaniards.
1583	Sir Humphrey Gilbert claims Newfoundland for England.
1605	Samuel de **Champlain** establishes **Port Royal** *(p 260)*.
1610	Henry Hudson enters Hudson Bay.
1620	Pilgrims found Plymouth, Massachusetts.
1670	**Hudson's Bay Company** is formed *(p 23)*.
1713	Treaty of Utrecht is signed. France cedes Acadia to Britain.
1722	The **Six Nations Iroquois Confederacy** is formed.
1730s-1740s	La Vérendrye family explores Canadian West *(p 99)*.
1755	Acadians are deported from Nova Scotia *(p 240)*.
1756-1763	Seven Years' War.
1759	British defeat the French in QUEBEC CITY *(p 196)*.
1763	**Treaty of Paris** is signed. France cedes New France to Britain.

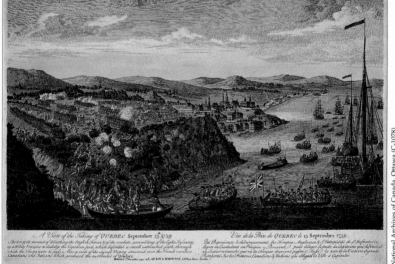

National Archives of Canada, Ottawa (C-1078)

Battle of the Plains of Abraham (1759)

British Regime

1775	War of Independence begins in American colonies.
1778	James Cook explores coast of British Columbia.
1783	American colonies gain independence from Britain. Loyalists migrate to Canada.
1791	**Constitutional Act** creates Upper Canada (Ontario) and Lower Canada (Quebec).
1793	Alexander Mackenzie crosses British Columbia to the West Coast.
1812-1814	War of 1812.
1837	Rebellions in Upper and Lower Canada *(pp 173 and 212)*.
1841	**Act of Union** creates the United Province of Canada.
1847	**Responsible government** system is implemented in Canada *(p 24)*.
1848	California Gold Rush begins.
1858-1861	British Columbia's gold rushes *(p 33)*.
1861-1865	American Civil War.

Canadian Confederation

1867	British North America Act establishes Canadian Confederation.
1869-1870	The Riel Rebellion occurs in Red River Valley.
1870	Canadian Confederation buys Hudson's Bay Company land; Manitoba is created *(p 99)*.
1872	**Dominion Lands Act** is passed *(p 100)*.
1874	NWMP (Royal Canadian Mounted Police) is established.

Courtesy Royal Canadian Mounted Police

Royal Canadian Mounted Police

1881-1885	The Canadian Pacific Railway is constructed *(p 24)*.
1885	The Northwest Rebellion occurs. Canada's **first national park** is created *(p 57)*.
1896	Gold is discovered in the Klondike *(p 33)*.
1914-1918	World War I.
1931	**Statute of Westminster** grants Canada control of external affairs.
1939-1945	World War II. Canada receives large numbers of European immigrants.
1942	Alaska Highway is completed *(p 37)*.

Contemporary Canada

1959	**St. Lawrence Seaway** is opened *(p 28)*.
1962	The Trans-Canada Highway is completed *(p 49)*.
1968	The Québécois Party is founded.
1982	The **Constitution Act** is passed. Quebec refuses to sign the new constitution.
1986	Nunavik *(p 222)* is created.
1987	**Meech Lake Accord** calls for special status for Quebec *(p 196)*.
1990	Manitoba and Newfoundland refuse to sign Meech Lake Accord. Quebec refuses to sign 1982 constitution. **Oka**, Quebec is site of armed conflict between Mohawks and Canadian government over native land claims.
1992	A national referendum to grant Quebec special status is defeated. Nunavut *(p 302)* is established.
1993	Negotiation of **North American Free Trade Agreement** (NAFTA) among Canada, Mexico and the US *(p 26)*.
1994	Approved by Canada, Mexico and the US, **NAFTA** takes effect Jan 1.
1995	Residents of Quebec vote by a narrow margin (50.6 percent to 49.4 percent) not to secede from the rest of Canada *(p 196)*.
1996	Canada's last census of the century is conducted in May. The country's population is projected to reach 30 million.

Historical Notes

The First North Americans – Man is not indigenous to North America. According to recent archaeological findings, prehistoric tribes from the mountains of Mongolia and the steppes of Siberia crossed to the continent some 15,000 to 20,000 years ago by a land bridge that once existed across the **Bering Strait**. They gradually moved south across the whole continent and into South America. Their descendants are the native Indian and Inuit peoples of Canada today, and they can be divided into six groups. The **Northwest Coast tribes** constituted a highly developed civilization, well known for its totem poles and other carved objects. Principal tribal groups are the Bella Coola, Coast Salish, Haida, Kwakiutl, Nootka (along the West Coast), Tlingit and Tsimshian (including the Gitksan). Also known as the Plateau culture (named after the Columbian Plateau region), the **Cordillera Indians** eked out an existence in the British Columbia interior as hunters and fishermen. The Athapaskan, Salishan and Kutenai language families represent this native culture. The **Plains Indians**—the Assiniboine, Blackfoot, Cree, Gros Ventre and Sarcee tribes—were nomadic buffalo hunters who lived in teepees and wore decorative clothing made of animal skins. The Beothuk, Cree, Dene, Montagnais and other **Sub-Arctic Indians** lived a nomadic existence hunting caribou and other animals. The Algonquin and the Iroquoian peoples formed the **Eastern Woodlands** culture of bellicose farmers who lived in fortified villages, growing corn and squash. Nomadic inhabitants of the most northerly regions, the **Inuit** traditionally lived in ice houses in winter, and in tents and sod houses during the summer. Using their highly developed navigational skills, they hunted seals and whales off the coast and caribou and waterfowl in the interior.

The Arrival of the Europeans – Long after the migrations of Asiatic peoples from the west, Europeans arrived on the shores of present-day Canada and proceeded to conquer the land and impose their own civilization. The Norse explored the coast of Labrador in the 10C and are believed to have founded the earliest known European settlement in North America around AD 1000 (*p 290*). Basque and English fishermen knew of the rich resources of the Grand Banks as early as the 15C.

However, the first permanent settlements began in the 17C. Within seven years of each other (1603-10), Frenchman **Samuel de Champlain**, and Englishmen Henry Hudson and John Guy claimed the riches of the continent for their respective kings. Their claims led to nearly two centuries of war among the empires of France and England and the native peoples for hegemony. The rivalry in North America revolved mainly around the lucrative fur trade. In 1713 the **Treaty of Utrecht** secured a temporary peace that lasted until the **Seven Years' War** (1756-63), in which France, Spain, Austria and Russia opposed Britain and Prussia. Before their final defeat by

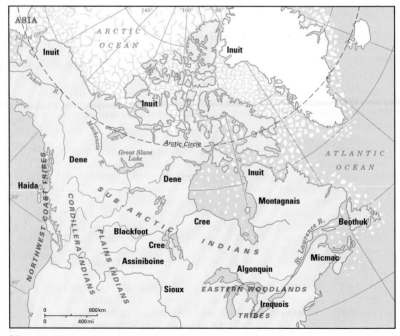

the British on the **Plains of Abraham** in 1759 *(p 196)*, the French not only established enduring settlements in the St. Lawrence Valley, but also explored half the continent, founding an empire known as **New France**, which, at its greatest extent, stretched from Hudson Bay to New Orleans (Louisiana) and from Newfoundland nearly to the Rockies. This empire thrived on the fur trade. However, England's **Hudson's Bay Company (HBC)**, founded in 1670, gained control of all the lands draining into the great bay and exercised a monopoly over that area, challenged only by Scottish merchants who established themselves in Montreal after the British conquest of France and formed the **North West Company** in 1783.

HBC Vancouver Store, Cordova Street (1887-93)

The Movement towards Confederation – In 1763, when the fall of New France was confirmed by the **Treaty of Paris**, the population of the future confederation of Canada was overwhelmingly French. A few settlements in Newfoundland and Halifax in Nova Scotia were the only English-speaking exceptions. This imbalance was not to endure. The aftermath of the American Revolution brought thousands of **Loyalists** to the remaining British colonies (Nova Scotia, Prince Edward Island and Lower Canada, later named Quebec) and led to the creation of two more colonies— New Brunswick and Upper Canada (later Ontario).

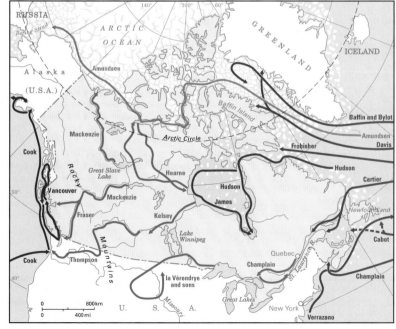

Lower Canada and Upper Canada were reunited by the British Parliament's **Act of Union** in 1841. This law was prompted by a report by then–governor general, Lord Durham, based on his investigation of the 1837 rebellions in which Americans had participated. In addition to recommending union, the report proposed **responsible government**, a system of majority party rule in the assembly (the British government did not formally implement this system until 1847), partly in the hope of reducing American influence.

Threats and incursions by Americans during the War of 1812, the Rebellions of 1837, the American Civil War and the Fenian Raids of 1866-1870 convinced the British government that more settlers were needed if their colonies were to survive. The policy of offering free land to potential settlers played a significant role in the development of Canada during the 19C and early 20C.

Fear of American takeover encouraged the small groups of British colonists to unite for common defence. Their actions helped to propel the British Parliament into ratifying the **British North America Act** of 1867, which provided for **Canadian Confederation**. The resulting new political entity, initially composed of four founding provinces—**Ontario**, **Quebec**, **New Brunswick** and **Nova Scotia**—adopted a parliamentary system of government and separation of federal and provincial powers. Even as confederation was negotiated, chief proponents John A. Macdonald and George-Étienne Cartier envisaged a dominion stretching from coast to coast. Between the eastern provinces and the small colony of British Columbia on the West Coast lay the immense, empty domain of the Hudson's Bay Company. Pressured by the British government, the company finally agreed in 1868 to relinquish its lands to the new Confederation for a cash settlement and rights to its posts and some land. As the new Dominion of Canada took possession, the Métis rebellion in the Red River Valley led to the creation of the fifth province, **Manitoba**, in 1870. Meanwhile, **British Columbia** began negotiations to become the sixth province, prompted by fear of an American takeover, and **Prince Edward Island** joined its sister maritime provinces in the Confederation in 1873. The Yukon Territory was created in 1898 and entered the Confederation in the same year.

Construction of the Canadian Pacific Railway – To encourage British Columbia to join Confederation in 1871, the province was promised a transcontinental rail link. After a few false starts, construction finally got underway in 1881. It was an immense and difficult project, the western mountain ranges alone posing a formidable barrier. Building the line over the steep grades of **Kicking Horse Pass**, for example, was one of the great achievements of railroad engineering. **Rogers Pass** and **Fraser Canyon** were only slightly lesser obstacles.

Serious problems beset the laying of track in the Canadian Shield country north of Lake Superior where, at one moment, tonnes of granite had to be blasted out and at the next, track lines would collapse into the muskeg. In the Prairies, however, all records for tracklaying were broken: in one day, a total of 10km/6mi were laid, a record never surpassed by manual labour. This progress was achieved under the dynamic management of **William Van Horne**, who later became president of the Canadian Pacific Railway Co. In only four years, the line was completed.

The Twentieth Century – Canada's purchase of land, controlled by the HBC opened the way for settlement of the West; the building of the transcontinental rail line provided the means. Thousands of immigrants poured into the region, necessitating the creation of two new provinces in 1905—**Saskatchewan** and **Alberta**. Soon afterwards, what was then much of the remaining Northwest Territories was redistributed to the other provinces.

Canada played a substantial role in both world wars, and finally achieved complete control of its external affairs in 1931 by the **Statute of Westminster**, a British law that clarified Canada's parliamentary powers. After World War II Canada's tenth province was added when the citizens of **Newfoundland** voted to join the Confederation in 1949. In the post-war years Canada found itself becoming a major industrial country, with an influx of immigrants who provided the skills and labour vital to economic growth.

The 1960s saw the beginnings of Quebec's **separatist movement**, resulting from cumulative grievances of French Canadians. The federal government accelerated efforts to accommodate Quebecers' demands, including broader educational funding and official recognition of the French language. In 1969 institutional bilingualism was established at the federal level by the Official Languages Act. Separatists were defeated at the provincial polls in 1973, but were victorious in 1976. In 1980 a move toward independence was rejected by the Quebec electorate, but the controversy continued.

In 1982, the British North American Act (1867) was renamed the Constitution Act, which repatriated the constitution from London. Quebec refused to sign the constitution, mainly since the agreement did not provide for transfer of legislative powers between federal and provincial governments. In 1987 the **Meech Lake Accord** *(p 196)* called for special status for Quebec. Federal and provincial ratification was not forthcoming by 1990, however. In 1992 a national referendum that would have granted special constitutional status to Quebec was defeated, but the movement toward independence gained support within Quebec. In the fall of 1995, secession from Canada was narrowly defeated by voters in the province by a margin of just over one percent.

Canada's native population continues to press for autonomy and land settlements. The defeated 1992 referendum included a provision for self-governing powers for native peoples. Earlier that year, however, Canadians had voted in favour of dividing the Northwest Territories to form a self-administered Inuit homeland called **Nunavut** *(map pp 3-4)* after a seven-year transitional period. A goal of the **Assembly of First Nations** (AFN), representing some 500,000 Indians of the country's nearly one-million native population, is constitutionally guaranteed rights of self-government. Multiculturalism is nothing new to Canada, a nation of wide ethnic and racial diversity. It remains to be seen, however, if the current socio-political upheaval and resulting introspection will fracture national unity or restore it.

Canada Today

Population – This immense country is inhabited by a relatively small number of people: about 30 million in 1996, compared to over 260 million in the US. The United Kingdom's total area of only 244,019sq km/94,216sq mi is home to some 57 million people. Canada's inhabitants are largely concentrated in a band about 160km/100mi wide immediately north of the Canadian/US border. The regional distribution is approximately British Columbia, Rockies, Yukon 12 percent; the Prairie provinces 18 percent; Ontario 37 percent; Quebec 25 percent; the Atlantic provinces 9 percent; Northwest Territories 0.2 percent. Although 62 percent of the population lives in Ontario and Quebec, mainly between QUEBEC CITY and WINDSOR, Canada is strongly characterized by regional distinctions.

Language and Culture – Canada is a land of immigrants. A population of 5 million in 1900 grew to 12 million by the end of World War II and to almost 26 million in 1988, thanks largely to immigration. Considered to be the **"founding" nations**, the British and the French are the largest populations (37 and 32 percent respectively). To reflect this composition, Canada is officially bilingual. The largest concentration of French-speaking people is in Quebec, but Francophones are found in every province. The federal government tries to provide services in both languages nationwide. There are significant numbers of Germans, Italians, Ukrainians, Dutch and Poles, especially in the Prairie provinces and, of native Indian and Inuit, resulting in an interesting mosaic of cultures across the country.

Government – Canada is a **federal state** with ten provinces. Each province has its own elected legislature controlling regional affairs. The central government in **Ottawa**—the federal capital—assumes responsibility for such matters as defence, foreign affairs, transportation, trade, commerce, money and banking, and criminal law. The federal government is also directly responsible for administering Canada's two territories, the Yukon and the Northwest Territories (which is only one territory despite its name), and for overseeing the affairs of state of the country's Indian and Inuit peoples.

Though officially part of the Commonwealth, Canada functions in actuality as an independent nation. The Canadian Head of State is the **British monarch**. Her authority is exercised by the **governor general**, who was at one time appointed by the monarch, but today is chosen by the elected respresentatives of the Canadian people. However, the governor general is little more than a figurehead as actual power lies in the hands of the Canadian **prime minister**, the leader of the majority party in Canadian **Parliament**. This latter institution consists of an elected legislature called the **House of Commons**, and an appointed **Senate**, members of which are chosen by the governing party. The prime minister rules through a cabinet drawn from the elected representatives (sometimes from members of the Senate also), and must submit his or her government for re-election after a maximum of five years, or if he or she is defeated in the House of Commons.

International Relations – After World War II, Canada was catapulted to global leadership as a founding country in the United Nations and as a member of the North Atlantic Treaty Organization (NATO). The country retains diplomatic missions in over 80 countries and has earned respect as an international peacekeeper. In addition, Canada is a regular participant in international conferences, including the yearly economic summit of the seven major industrialized democracies, known as the G7. Canada, Mexico and the US ratified and are implementing the **North American Free Trade Agreement** (NAFTA), a pact designed to increase trade and investment among the three countries largely by eliminating tariffs and other barriers. Both NAFTA, which became effective in 1994, and an earlier free-trade agreement between the US and the US have contributed to a sharp increase in Canadian exports in recent years.

Food and Drink – Food in Canada varies little from that in the US, but there are many regional specialities of interest. British Columbia is famous for its **seafood**, especially king crab and salmon. The country produces a variety of fruit, such as peaches, cherries, grapes, and its own wine in the Okanagan Valley in British Columbia and in the Eastern Townships of Quebec. In the Prairies the **beef** is excel-

Seafood Dinner

lent, along with fresh lake fish in the north, wild rice (a great delicacy collected by certain Indian tribes), berries of all types, and the heritage of many immigrant cultures—cabbage rolls, *pierogis* (dumplings), and borscht, for example. Southern Ontario is the great fruit and vegetable area of Canada and is also another wine-producing region.

Owing to its French heritage, Quebec has a fine culinary tradition. Many French restaurants, especially in MONTREAL and QUEBEC CITY, serve traditional French-Canadian cuisine—pork dishes, meat pie *(tourtière)*, soups, and a generous quantity of maple syrup. The Atlantic provinces are another great **seafood** region, especially oysters, lobster, scallops, and mussels. In Newfoundland **screech**, a heady dark rum, or one of the country's fine **beers** is popular with meals—Canadians are great beer drinkers. New Brunswick is famous for **fiddleheads**, the new shoots of ferns available fresh in May and June, and for **dulse**, an edible seaweed. **Moose meat** and fresh lake fish are available in the Northwest Territories, as is **Arctic char**, a delicacy similar to trout and salmon in taste.

"Few Englishmen are prepared to find it [Canada] what it is. Advancing quietly; old differences settling down, and being fast forgotten; public feeling and private enterprise alike in a sound and wholesome state; nothing of flush or fever in its system, but health and vigour throbbing in its steady pulse: it is full of hope and promise."

Charles Dickens, *American Notes*, 1842

Economy

The following is a very general account of economic activity in Canada. Additional information can be found in the regional introductions. The Canada Year Book *(published by Statistics Canada, Ottawa, Ontario K1A 0T6) is an excellent reference for readers seeking detailed information.*

Canada's great strength lies in the wealth of its natural resources such as forests, minerals, and energy fuels that contribute greatly to its economy. Mining and agriculture are part of the country's highly diversified economy, whereas energy is among the top-performing sectors, along with transportation and telecommunications. Canada has become an important trading nation. Its largest single export market is the US. Since the signing of the North American Free Trade Agreement *(p 26)*, Canada's exports to the US have grown rapidly.

Land of Forests – Forestry is of prime importance to Canada; trees in one form or another are among the country's most valuable assets. Over half the total land area is forested, and the forestry industry exists in every province. The industry is of great importance to British Columbia, which is best known for its sawn lumber, and to Quebec, a major producer of **newsprint**. Canada is the world's largest exporter of the latter commodity, supplying nearly a third of total world consumption.

Traditional Occupations – Despite Canada's tough climate and terrain, **agriculture** occupies an important position in the economy, making up 8 percent of the country's gross domestic product. Wheat has long been the leader in agricultural exports from the Prairie provinces, challenged in more recent years by canola, a new oilseed crop. Beef cattle are also raised in the Prairie provinces, whereas dairy products, poultry and hogs are more important in British Columbia, Ontario and Quebec. Potatoes, which have been a mainstay of the Maritime provinces, are of growing significance in the prairie lands. Apples, grapes and several hardy small fruits are harvested in the southernmost areas of the country.

Fishing and **trapping** were for centuries Canada's primary industries and today, Canada is still a leading exporter of fish in the world. The Atlantic Coast supplies the vast majority of this resource, although 15 percent of the value is provided by the rich Pacific salmon fishery. Canada is one of the largest suppliers of animal pelts in the world.

Inspecting Grain in Saskatchewan

Riches Beneath the Soil – Mining is an important activity in every region of Canada; it is the principal industry in the Northwest Territories and the Yukon. The country is a leading international producer of metals including nickel (Ontario, Manitoba), zinc (New Brunswick, Northwest Territories, Quebec, Ontario), molybdenum (British Columbia), uranium (Saskatchewan, Ontario), gold (Ontario, Quebec,

British Columbia, Northwest Territories) and lead (New Brunswick, British Columbia, Northwest Territories). Leading nonmetals are potash (Saskatchewan, New Brunswick) and asbestos (Quebec). Iron ore is produced in the Labrador Trough (Quebec and Newfoundland) and in Ontario.

Alberta is the leading province for **fossil fuels**. Its oil and gas production are greater in dollar value than all of Ontario's mines. Alberta possesses immense reserves awaiting exploitation in its Athabasca oil sands, and shares substantial coal reserves with British Columbia. Although fossil fuel production is almost entirely restricted to Western Canada at present, recent offshore oil developments, including the Hibernia project *(p 285)* on the continental shelf off Newfoundland, could change this restriction in the future.

Manufacturing – Canada's manufacturing industry, traditionally based on resource-processing (forest products, minerals, food and beverages, for example), has largely shifted into secondary manufacturing. A significant petrochemical industry exists in Alberta, Manitoba, Ontario and Quebec. Automobile and auto parts manufacturing is based in Ontario and Quebec; electrical and electronics industries are strong in those same two provinces. British Columbia is becoming a centre for telecommunications, pharmaceuticals and biotechnology. In Atlantic Canada commercial medicine, environmental industries and information technologies (the latter most notably in New Brunswick) complement traditional industries.

Transportation – Because of Canada's size, transportation has always been of prime importrance. Until about 1850 waterways commanded the country's economic growth. Fishing and timber industries and the fur trade all depended on water transport. Since then, wheat farming, mining and pulp and paper industries have grown largely dependent on rail transport. Even in these industries, movement of goods by water is not insignificant. The network of locks and canals known as the **St. Lawrence Seaway** was opened in 1959, a massive joint engineering achievement between Canada and the US. This 3,790km/2,350mi waterway through the St. Lawrence River and the Great Lakes significantly boosted Canada's economy: in particular, the country became an exporter of iron ore after the seaway facilitated exploitation of Labrador and Quebec's huge deposits. The road network has expanded since World War II with the completion of the Trans-Canada Highway and the opening of the great northern roads—the Alaska and the Dempster Highways. Aviation plays an important role, especially in the North. Airplanes are sometimes the only means of supplying mineral exploration teams there and may, in the future, be used to remove exploited resources.

Hydro-electric Giant – The abundance and power of Canada's water sources offer exceptional opportunities for generation of hydro-electricity. Almost two-thirds of the country's electricity comes from this source. Generating stations operate in every province except Prince Edward Island, and Quebec's massive **James Bay Hydro-electric Project** *(p 199)*, with a capacity of more than 12,000 megawatts, is one of the largest hydro-electric engineering projects in the world. In Labrador, a huge generating station is located on the Churchill River. Other examples are in British Columbia on the Peace and Columbia Rivers, in Quebec on the Manicouagan and Outardes Rivers combined, in both Ontario and Quebec on the St. Lawrence, in Saskatchewan on the South Saskatchewan, and in Manitoba on the Nelson.

The electricity produced powers industries involved in natural resource utilization such as smelting businesses and pulp mills. Plentiful and inexpensive hydro-electricity has attracted other industries such as the aluminum industry to Canada (British Columbia and Quebec). Canada's energy is transported via high-voltage power lines to southern Canada to heat Canadian homes. Canada's surplus electricity is exported to the US.

We welcome your assistance in the never-ending task of updating the texts and maps in this guide. Send us your comments and suggestions:

> Michelin Travel Publications
> Editorial Department
> PO Box 19001
> Greenville, South Carolina 29602-9001

Further Reading

Canada

A Concise History of Canadian Painting by Dennis Reid (*Oxford University Press, 1988*)

A Short History of Canada by Desmond Morton (*McClelland & Stewart, 1994*)

Canada: A Story of Challenge by J. M. S. Careless (*Stoddart Publishing Co. Ltd., 1991*)

Cycling Canada: Bicycle Touring Adventures in Canada by John M. Smith (*Bicycle Books Inc., 1995*)

British Columbia, Rockies, Yukon

Looking at Indian Art of the Northwest Coast by Hilary Stewart (*Douglas & McIntyre, 1995*)

The National Dream and the Last Spike by Pierre Berton (*McClelland & Stewart, 1994*)

The Streets Were Paved with Gold by Stan Cohen (*Pictorial Histories Publishing Co., 1995*)

Prairie Provinces

The Promised Land: Settling the West by Pierre Berton (*McClelland & Stewart, 1984*)

Who Has Seen the Wind? by W. O. Mitchell (*Bantam Books, 1989*)

Wilderness Man: The Strange Story of Grey Owl by Lovat Dickson (*General Publishing, 1991*)

Ontario

Rideau Waterway by Robert Legget (*University of Toronto Press, 1986*)

Roughing it in the Bush by Susannah Moodie (*McClelland & Stewart, 1992*)

Toronto: No Mean City by Eric Arthur (*University of Toronto Press, 1986*)

Quebec

Discover Montréal: An Architectural and Historical Guide by Joshua Wolfe & Cécile Grenier (*Libre Expression, 1991*)

Maria Chapdelaine by Louis Hémon (*General Publishing, 1992*)

Two Solitudes by Hugh Maclennan (*General Publishing, 1993*)

Atlantic Provinces

Anne of Green Gables by Lucy Maud Montgomery (*McGraw Hill Ryerson, 1968*)

Coastal Nova Scotia Outdoor Adventure Guide by Joanne Light (*Nimbus Publishing, 1993*)

Nature Trails of Prince Edward Island by J. Dan McAskill & Kate MacQuarrie (*Ragweed Press, 1996*)

Rocks Adrift: The Geology of Gros Morne National Park edited by Michael Burzynski & Anne Marceau (*Canada Communications Group Publishing, 1991*)

Saint-Pierre and Miquelon by William Rannie (*W. F. Rannie, 1977*)

Northwest Territories

Company of Adventurers by Peter C. Newmann (*Penguin Books, 1987*)

People of the Deer by Farley Mowat (*Seal Books, 1993*)

Sculpture of the Inuit by George Swinton (*McClelland & Stewart, 1993*)

The Snow Walker by Farley Mowat (*Seal Books, 1995*)

British Columbia,
Rockies, Yukon

Icefields Parkway/Travel Alberta

Known as the **Canadian Cordillera** *(p 18)*, this region consists of the province of British Columbia, part of the province of Alberta, and the Yukon Territory. Covering the extreme west, it stretches from the Pacific Ocean to the Rockies and from the Canadian/US border to the Beaufort Sea. The high snow-capped peaks, massive glaciers, rugged ranges, mighty rivers, wild streams and tranquil lakes of this land of beauty attract millions of tourists every year.

Geographical Notes

Mountainous Terrain – Contrary to the belief that all mountains between the Prairies and the Pacific Ocean are the Rockies, this famous mountain range is only one of many in the region. Starting in the west the **Coast Mountains** of British Columbia rise steeply out of the deeply indented and heavily forested Pacific Coast to over 3,000m/10,999ft. North of this chain in the Yukon are the high St. Elias Mountains, which peak with Mt. Logan at 5,959m/19,520ft, the highest point in Canada.

East of this coastal system lies an immense, elevated **plateau**. In the south, where it is nearly 300km/200mi wide, this plateau encompasses such diverse areas as the Cariboo ranch lands *(p 40)* and the irrigated Okanagan fruit-growing belt *(p 50)*. In the southeast the plateau ends at the **Columbia Mountains** where the Cariboo, Purcell, Monashee and Selkirk Ranges *(p 47)* are found. In the north the plateau changes to an area of rugged hills—the Skeena and Cassiar Ranges—before spreading out into the vast Yukon Plateau, a basin-like area of rolling uplands, encircled by high mountains and drained by the Yukon River and its tributaries. It is east of this interior plateau, across the Columbia Mountains and the Rocky

Mountain Trench, that the **Rockies** are reached. About 150km/94mi wide at most, the Canadian Rockies stretch from the 49th parallel to the Yukon/British Columbia boundary. Rugged, with numerous peaks over 3,000m/10,000ft, they are spotted with glaciers, especially in the area of the Columbia Icefield *(p 64)*. In the east the Rockies' front ranges rise abruptly above the foothills, giving the impression of a wall towering above the seemingly flat prairie lands of Alberta. At the Yukon/British Columbia boundary, the **Liard River**, a tributary of the Mackenzie River, carves a channel between the Rockies and the **Mackenzie Mountains**. North of the Mackenzies are the Richardson and British Mountains, stretching almost to the Beaufort Sea.

Climate – Tremendous variation marks the climate of this region, which extends from latitude 49° to north of the Arctic Circle (66.3°), and has coasts on two oceans—the warm Pacific and the icy Arctic. Elevations range from sea level to nearly 6,100m/20,000ft.
The climate of coastal British Columbia is influenced by the warm waters of the Pacific, the prevailing westerly winds and the high Coast Mountains. Winters are mild (0°–5°C/30°–40°F) and summers warm, though not hot (15°–24°C/60°–75°F). Rainfall can be low in protected areas, but among the heaviest in the

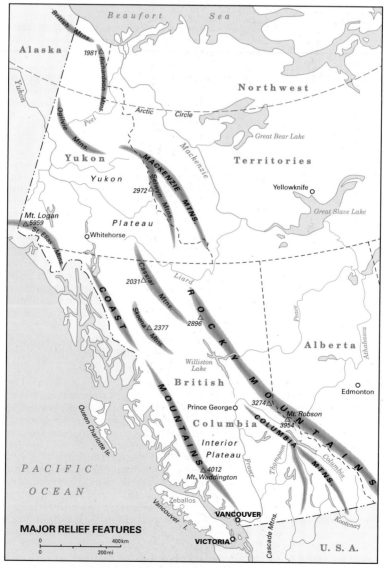

MAJOR RELIEF FEATURES

world in locations exposed to the full blast of winds off the Pacific (p 83). Similarly, cloud cover can be light in protected places and heavy in exposed areas. East of the Coast Mountains, one encounters a very different climatic regime with greater extremes of temperature and lower rainfall. Winters average –5°C/23°F and summers 22°C/72°F. Irrigation is needed in the OKANAGAN VALLEY to allow cultivation of its famous fruits, whereas the Selkirk Mountains have recorded the highest snowfall in Canada.

In the north the towering St. Elias Mountains cut the Yukon off from the moderating influences of the Pacific, but also from the high precipitation of the coast. Summers are pleasantly warm and dry (nearly 21°C/70°F and 230-436mm/ 9-17in of rain) with long hours of daylight (an average of 20 hours) during which the sun shines for a large percentage of the time. Winters, however, are dark and cold, though temperatures vary widely (DAWSON CITY –27°C/–16°F, WHITEHORSE –15°C/–5°F).

Historical Notes

The First Inhabitants – Native cultures of this region fall into three basic groups: the wealthy, artistic tribes of the Pacific Coast; the tribes of hunters and fishermen who inhabited the British Columbia interior (known as the Cordillera Indians); and the Athapaskan-speaking tribes of the Yukon, whose lives were spent following the caribou in the same way as the Indians of the Northwest Territories (p 30). The civilization created by the **Northwest Coast tribes** is unlike any other in North America. Before the Europeans arrived, they enjoyed, in a country rich in resources, a high standard of living—far above the subsistence living of tribes in other regions. Wood from giant **cedar trees** that proliferated along the coast, and **salmon** from the ocean were the basis of their livelihood.

Having leisure time to devote to art, they developed a creative expression unequalled on the continent north of Mexico. Tall tree trunks were carved with expressive forms and raised as **totem poles** before the houses of the chiefs. Carved with designs of birds, animals, humans and mythological creatures, these columns of cedar wood are not solely works of art. Each carving is a sign or crest of a family or clan, similar to coats-of-arms or heraldic emblems. Their purpose varied: sometimes they were functional, serving as house corner posts; sometimes decorative, serving as the entrance to a house (a hole was made at the bottom of the pole); other times they were memorials to dead relatives, or actually part of the grave. They represent an art form unique to the Northwest Coast Indians. The golden age of carving was 1850 to 1900, after the introduction of metal tools by Europeans. In recent years there has been a revival of the art as Indians seek to re-create their traditions. The same designs were woven onto blankets, and carved into masks, chests, ornaments and jewellery. The more of the latter a man possessed, the wealthier he was, and the higher he ranked in the tribe's social structure.

The arrival of Europeans disrupted tribal life on the Northwest Coast, in the interior and in the Yukon. Indians were encouraged to hunt for furs to satisfy the demands of the European market. In exchange they received firearms, alcohol and other imports, upon which many tribes became dependent, and their lifestyle altered. In the Yukon tribal life changed to a lesser degree because of the relative remoteness of the area. Along the Northwest Coast, perhaps because of the strength of the culture, many customs remain, however, and others are being revived ('Ksan p 70).

The Arrival of the Europeans – European discovery of the region occurred from two directions. Small ships explored the coast, while fur traders, seeking new supplies and transportation routes, approached the interior. Although **Francis Drake** may have sighted the coast of British Columbia during his around-the-world voyage of 1579, the area was not explored until the 18C. Spaniards journeyed northward from California, and Russians travelled southward from Alaska. Capt. **James Cook**, however, made the first recorded landing during his voyage of 1778, sailing up the coast of British Columbia. Landing on VANCOUVER ISLAND, he bought pelts from the Indians and sold them in China at great profit. News of this trade encouraged other Englishmen and Spaniards to visit the North Pacific. A clash was inevitable. The British forced the Spaniards—who later retreated entirely—to declare the coasts open to all traders. To reinforce its claims, the British government sent an expedition under the command of Capt. **George Vancouver**, who had been a midshipman on the Cook voyage, to map the coast. Between 1792 and 1794 Vancouver mapped practically the entire British Columbia coast.

Fur-Trading Empire – The first European to glimpse the Canadian Rockies had come and gone with little fanfare. **Anthony Henday** of the Hudson's Bay Company (HBC) sighted the mountain wall in 1754, about ten years after la Vérendrye's sons had viewed the range in Wyoming. Henday's report roused little interest at company headquarters. **Alexander Mackenzie** of the rival North West Company completed the last section of the first crossing of the continent north of Mexico in 1793, predating the **Lewis and Clark** expedition by 12 years. He climbed the Rockies by the Peace River, reaching the Pacific after a hazardous traverse of the British Columbia interior. Mackenzie had sought a route for transporting furs to the Pacific for shipment to Europe, rather than the long canoe journey to Montreal *(p 170)*.

Other "Nor'westers" sought alternative routes through the Rockies to the rich fur area west of the mountains. By following the Columbia and Kootenay Rivers, **David Thompson** explored the Howse and Athabasca Passes, the southeast corner of British Columbia, and northern Washington state between 1804 and 1811. Meanwhile **Simon Fraser** retraced Mackenzie's route in 1808 and descended the river that now bears Fraser's name.

While Fraser and Thompson were establishing posts and encouraging trade with Indians of the interior, an American fur-trading company created by **John Jacob Astor** founded a post at the mouth of the Columbia, beginning the American challenge to British ownership of the Oregon territory. In 1846 the rivalry was settled when the HBC (which merged in 1821 with its great competitor, the North West Company) was finally forced to accept the 49th parallel as the US frontier. The HBC moved its western headquarters from the Columbia River area to **Vancouver Island**, which was declared a crown colony in 1849 with Victoria as its capital. The rest of British Columbia (known as New Caledonia) remained the exclusive domain of the company, as did the Yukon, where the firm established itself after 1842. Thus, in 1858, British Columbia, the Rockies and the Yukon were predominantly a fur-trader's paradise—a state of affairs that was to change very quickly.

Gold – The discovery of gold in California in 1848 attracted countless people who hoped to make a fortune. Nine years later the gold was gone, but prospectors did not stop looking. Many entered New Caledonia to search. In 1858 the news spread like wild fire—there was gold in the sandbars of the lower Fraser River. The small settlement of **Victoria** (pop. 400) saw 20,000 people pass through en route to the gold fields.

Afraid the influx of Americans would lead to an American takeover (as had occurred in California), the governor of the island colony, **James Douglas**, stepped in quickly to assert British sovereignty. The mainland was rapidly declared a British colony and named British Columbia, with Douglas as first governor. Poor transportation routes made control of the new territory difficult. When rich gold strikes in the Cariboo brought even more people, Douglas planned construction of a wagon road—the famous **Cariboo Road**, built between 1862 and 1865, which helped ensure British control of the area.

Confederation and a Railway – The wealth from mining gold did not last long. The late 1860s saw economic disaster looming for the two western colonies (united in 1866; while in the east, the British colonies were discussing Confederation, which became a reality in 1867). US purchase of Alaska in 1867 again raised fears of an American takeover. Thus, negotiations concerning Hudson's Bay Company's domain were begun with the new Canada, located 3,200km/2,000mi away, and completed in 1871.

British Columbia entered the Confederation on the condition that, within ten years, a railway would be built to connect the province with the east. The birth pains of such a massive project nearly led to British Columbia's withdrawal from the Confederation; but the project, initiated in 1881, was completed in the remarkably short time of four years *(p 24)*. When the last spike was hammered in at Craigellachie in November 1885, and the transcontinental runs began the next year, the province was transformed. The railway brought tourists, settlers and capital to the impoverished region, and encouraged the search for mineral wealth and the utilization of natural resources that have made British Columbia what it is today.

"Ho for the Klondike" – When the Cariboo gold fields were exhausted, prospectors again moved north. Gold was found in the Omineca and Cassiar Mountains. Then prospectors entered the Yukon, which was declared a district of the Northwest Territories in 1895 by the Canadian government, again because of fear of American encroachment. A detachment of the **Mounted Police** *(p 111)* was dispatched to maintain law and order—a timely move. The long-hoped-for big strike was made in 1896 on a small creek renamed "Bonanza," which drained into the Klondike River, a tributary of the Yukon. When news of the find became common knowledge, what has been described as "one of the world's greatest economic explosions" occurred. Thousands of men and women set off from all corners of the globe to reach the Klondike by a variety of means *(p 41)*, an event dubbed the Klondike Stampede. In eight years $100 million worth of gold was shipped out, providing an enormous stimulus for this western frontier.

The Region Today

British Columbia/Rockies – In this century, especially since World War II, the growth of British Columbia has been spectacular. Discovery of gold in the Klondike spurred the search for minerals all over the Cordillera region, leading to the development of THE KOOTENAYS as the principal mining area for the extraction of **lead**, **zinc** and **silver**. Copper and molybdenum are mined extensively in the province, especially in the Highland Valley near Kamloops. Sulphur, peat moss and gypsum are also found. The Crowsnest Pass area of the Kootenays is rich in **coal**, which is exported mainly to Japan. At Kitimat there is a huge aluminum smelter (the bauxite, the principal source of aluminum, is imported), and asbestos is mined at Cassiar.

An international mining centre, the Greater Vancouver area serves as headquarters for major producers, equipment manufacturers and laboratories. Natural gas and oil are found in the Peace River area and farther north near Fort Nelson. They are transported south by pipeline where the oil is refined at Kamloops. British Columbia exports today about 95 percent of its minerals; metals and coal are shipped primarily to Asia. About 50 percent of its oil and gas is exported, principally to the US.

Construction of the **Panama Canal**, opened in 1915, greatly stimulated exploitation and export of the province's minerals by providing a cheap means of transport to Europe. British Columbia's products were thereby competitive, worth exploiting. Roads and railways were built to carry the minerals to smelters and ports. This transportation network stimulated growth of the **forestry** industry. About a quarter of the marketable timber in North America is found in the province. In the moist climate of its coast, trees grow to great size. Annual timber cut is about 74 million cu m/2.6 billion cu ft, making forestry British Columbia's prime industry.

Hydro-electricity has also boomed since World War II. Two vast projects—the W.A.C. Bennett Dam with generating stations on the Peace River, and Mica Dam with a station on the Columbia River—have capacities exceeding 2,000,000kW and 1,700,000kW respectively. Although British Columbia abounds with raw materials, it supports a large manufacturing industry. The province is also known for its rich coastal **fishing industry**: salmon, halibut, herring, clams, oysters and crab abound. Despite mountainous terrain and forest-covered slopes, **agriculture** thrives in some areas of the province. The lower Fraser Valley and VANCOUVER ISLAND are largely devoted to dairy cattle and crops; the Okanagan is famous for its tree fruits and wine industry; the Kootenays are also known for fruit; the great interior plateau called THE CARIBOO is cattle-raising country with large ranches, stampedes and rodeos; and the Peace River country east of the Rockies is British Columbia's chief grain-growing area.

Correspondingly, the **population** of British Columbia has increased from a little over 50,000 at the turn of the century to 3,282,000 today. The great majority of these inhabitants live in the southwest corner of the province, nearly half in the Vancouver metropolitan area.

The Yukon – This territory's development has not been as spectacular as British Columbia's. The golden years of the Klondike Stampede were followed by years of economic stagnation, with the population falling from 27,219 in 1901 (even greater at the height of the stampede) to 4,157 in 1921. World War II saw the construction of the Alaska Highway *(p 37)*, which has led to increased exploitation of the Territory's mineral wealth. Zinc, lead, silver, cadmium, copper, tungsten and gold are mined and transported south by road through the Coast Mountains to Skagway. Today the **population** is once again at the turn-of-the-century level of some 27,000. Well over half the residents live in the territorial capital of Whitehorse.

PRACTICAL INFORMATION

Getting There

By Air – International and domestic flights to Vancouver International Airport (15km/9mi south of downtown) ☎604-276-6101 via Air Canada ☎604-688-5515, or 800-776-3000 (US) and Canadian Airlines International ☎800-426-7000 (Canada/US) and other major carriers. Affiliated airlines offer connections to Prince Rupert, Victoria, and to Whitehorse (Yukon Territory) as well as to more remote regions: Air BC ☎604-688-5515 and Canadian Regional Airlines ☎800-665-1177 (Canada) or 800-553-0117 (US). Taxi to downtown Vancouver *($20-25)*. Airport **shuttle** Vancouver Airporter ☎604-244-9888 *($9)*. Airport Limousine Service ☎604-273-1331. Major car rental agencies *(p 315)* at the airport.

By Bus and Train – Greyhound **bus** service to BC and the Yukon (Whitehorse via Edmonton or Vancouver): ☎604-662-3222 (in Vancouver). Greyhound, Maverick Coach Lines ☎604-662-8051 and other bus companies serve Vancouver Island (consult the telephone directory). **VIA Rail** Canada: Skeena route from Vancouver to Prince Rupert connects Victoria to Courtenay and links Vancouver to Toronto ☎800-561-8630 (in BC), or ☎800-561-3949 (US). **BC Rail** services Whistler and Prince George from Vancouver ☎604-631-3500.

By Boat – BC Ferries operates 25 different routes connecting 42 ports of call on the coastline and many of the islands. BC Ferries, 1112 Fort St., Victoria, BC, V8V 4V2 ☎250-669-1211. For ferries from the US to British Columbia *p 82*.

General Information

Accommodations and Visitor Information – The government tourist office produces annually updated guides on accommodations, camping, fishing, skiing and vacations. The *BC Travel Guide* suggests driving tours and gives general travel tips. All publications and a map are available free of charge from: **Tourism British Columbia**, Parliament Buildings, Victoria, BC, V8V 1X4 ☎800-663-6000 (Canada/US).
The *Vacation Guide to Canada's Yukon,* which is updated annually, gives details on facilities and attractions, entertainment, adventure travel, outdoor activities and general travel tips. This publication and a road map are available free of charge from **Tourism Yukon**, PO Box 2703, Whitehorse, YT, Y1A 2C6 ☎403-667-5340.

Road Regulations – *(Driver's license and insurance requirements p 314.)* BC and Alberta have good paved roads. In winter certain precautions are necessary, especially when crossing Rogers Pass. Speed limits in BC, unless otherwise posted, are 80km/h (50mph), in Alberta 100km/h (60mph) in daylight and 90km/h (55mph) at night, and in the Yukon 90km/h (55mph). For road conditions in British Columbia ☎604-299-9000 (then press 7623). **Seat belt** use is mandatory. For listings of the **Canadian Automobile Assn. (CAA)**, consult the local telephone directory *(p 315)*.

Time Zones – Alberta and the BC Rockies region are on Mountain Standard Time. The rest of BC and the Yukon are on Pacific Standard Time. Daylight Saving Time is observed from the first Sunday in April to the last Sunday in October. The northeast corner of BC is on Mountain Standard Time year-round.

Taxes – In addition to the national 7% GST *(rebate information p 318)*, BC levies a 7% provincial sales tax, and an 8% accommodation tax (10% in some communities).

Liquor Laws – The legal drinking age is 19. Liquor is sold in government stores.

Provincial Holidays *(National Holidays p 319)*

BC Day	1st Monday in August
Discovery Day, Yukon	3rd Monday in August

Recreation – The rivers, mountains and many parks of this vast and sparsely populated region offer the outdoor enthusiast a variety of recreational activities: hiking, horseback riding, fishing, river rafting, canoeing and kayaking. Some guest ranches include several days on a trail into backcountry wilderness in their program.
Many **fishing** lodges arrange fly-in packages to remote lakes that attract anglers from around the world. Licenses are required for both saltwater and freshwater fishing, and can be obtained locally. The many navigable waterways, especially in the Shuswap Lake district, offer a host of water sports as well as houseboating. Marine adventures and cruises that include nature observation are popular along the coastline.

Whistler, north of Vancouver, is a popular ski resort with first-class accommodations and **winter sports** facilities, including glacier skiing from June through October *(p 81)*. The three ski resorts in the Rockies *(p 56)* offer a variety of winter activities. For information on recreation, contact Tourism British Columbia *(p 35)*.

Special Excursions – The **Rocky Mountaineer** journeys through some of the most spectacular mountain scenery in North America during a two-day trip from VANCOUVER to Jasper or Banff. The train travels in the daylight hours only; passengers spend the night in Kamloops. Eastbound, westbound and round-trip travel is possible *(departs from Vancouver May–Oct daily 8am; one-way $465/person May & Oct or $565/person Jun–Sept, double occupancy; add-on to Calgary $60; cost of lodgings in Kamloops included; reservations required; Rocky Mountaineer Railtours, 1150 Station St., Suite 130, Vancouver, BC, V6A 2X7* ☎*800-665-7245, Canada/US).*

Principal Festivals

Feb	**Sourdough Rendezvous** *(p 90)*	*Whitehorse, YT*
May	**Swiftsure Yacht Race Weekend**	*Victoria, BC*
Jun–Jul	**Stampede** *(p 40)*	*Williams Lake, BC*
Jun–Aug	**Festival of the Arts**	*Banff, AB*
Jul	**Sea Festival**	*Vancouver, BC*
	Peach Festival	*Penticton, BC*
Aug	**Air Show**	*Abbotsford, BC*
	Loggers' Sports Day	*Squamish, BC*
	Discovery Day *(p 42)*	*Dawson City, YT*
Aug–Sept	**Pacific National Exhibition**	*Vancouver, BC*
Sept	**Classic Boat Festival**	*Victoria, BC*
Sept–Oct	**Okanagan Wine Festival**	*Penticton, BC*

Starting October 1996 a new area code – 250 – became effective for all of British Columbia except the Greater Vancouver area and Whistler/Howe Sound region, which continue to have area code 604.

Skiing in Sunshine Village near Banff

ALASKA HIGHWAY★★

British Columbia, Yukon, Alaska
Map of Principal Sights p 2

This great road to the North, and adventure, passes through a land of mountains and lakes of rare beauty, largely untouched by mankind except for a scattering of small communities. Beginning at Dawson Creek in British Columbia, the highway parallels the Rocky Mountains, enters the Yukon along the valley of the Liard, touches the Cassiar and the Coast Mountains of British Columbia, and follows the St. Elias Mountains to enter Alaska, finally terminating in Fairbanks.

Historical Notes – To link Alaska and the Yukon with the road system farther south, the highway was constructed in 1942 by joint agreement between Canada and the US. When the Japanese bombed **Pearl Harbour** in 1941, landed in the Aleutian Islands, and threatened sea routes to Alaska, Americans feared an imminent invasion of mainland Alaska. A land route between the US and Alaska was considered essential. Thus, in only nine months, 2,451km/1,523mi of highway were built by the US Army Corps of Engineers. Traversing muskeg swamps, bridging wide rivers, climbing or avoiding mountain ranges, the road has become a legend in the annals of road construction. Upgraded after World War II and opened to civilian traffic, the highway is of major economic importance as a means of transporting the region's mineral wealth and the tourists who travel its length.

Practical Information

Driving the Highway – *(Driver's license and insurance requirements p 314.)* The Alaska Highway is either a paved or treated bituminous surface over most of its length. Travel on it is possible all months of the year. The period of thaw in spring can make driving conditions difficult some years, but highway advisories are broadcast promptly. Service stations able to perform repairs are situated at regular intervals; however, vehicles should be in good mechanical condition before starting out. The speed limit varies from 50km/h (30mph) to 90km/h (55mph); watch posted signs. Headlights should be kept on at all times. For the latest road conditions, contact the nearest tourist office *(p 35)*.
Distances are marked by kilometre posts and measured from Dawson Creek, BC. For example, Watson Lake is at KM 1,017/mi 632. **Historical miles** are measurements originally used in the 1940s by lodgings along the route. Although inaccurate now, these readings are traditionally employed by businesses as indicators of their location.

Accommodations and Visitor Information – A most helpful annually updated publication is *The Milepost*, which describes natural and historical sights, eating establishments and overnight accommodations mile by mile. This book may be purchased from Vernon Publications, Inc., 3000 Northup Way, Suite 200, Bellevue, WA 98004 ☎800-726-4707 (Canada/US).
Many tourists stay in campgrounds provided by the governments of the Yukon and British Columbia. There are, however, motels and other accommodations.

FROM DAWSON CREEK TO FORT NELSON *483km/300mi*

The Alaska Highway begins at **Dawson Creek** (pop. 10,981), BC, in the region of the Peace River. The rural nature of the area is immediately striking: green and gold patches of wheat, barley and other crops, neatly laid out in grid patterns. The descent into the river valley is lengthy and somewhat winding. At **Taylor**, which sits on a vast natural gas and oil field, the river is crossed. Gas processing plants can be seen along the highway and oil pipelines run beneath fields of crops all the way to **Fort St. John** (pop. 14,156).

★★ **Excursion to W.A.C. Bennett Dam** – *Allow 1 day. 234km/145mi round-trip. 11km/ 7mi north of Fort St. John, take Hwy. 29 to Hudson's Hope, then Dam Access Rd. Caution: steep, winding roads. Speed limits indicated for dangerous curves.* Except for the steep inclines of valley ascent and descent, this is a pleasant drive through lovely farmland with several breathtaking **views**★★ of the Peace River.
The road follows the river valley, climbing above it to permit exquisite **views**★ of the flat-topped hills and fertile fields. The little village of **Hudson's Hope** (pop. 985) was the site of one of Simon Fraser's trading posts and the place where Alexander Mackenzie began his portage around the Peace River Canyon on his epic trek to the West Coast. From the village the winding dam access road ascends into the mountains with views of snow-capped peaks ahead.

Built between 1963 and 1967, the enormous earth-filled dam wedges the upper end of the canyon, creating a reservoir, **Williston Lake**. Measuring 362km/225mi in length, the lake encompasses part of the valleys of the Parsnip and Finlay Rivers, which meet in the Rocky Mountain Trench and flow out eastward as the Peace River. The dam itself (183m/600ft high and 2km/1.25mi across) was constructed of glacial moraine deposited during the last Ice Age, 7km/4mi away from the old valley of the Peace River. In the post-glacial period the river cut a new channel, the aforementioned canyon. Material that blocked the river's course about 15,000 years ago was used to reblock it when the present dam was built. At present the project generates over 2,416,000kW of electricity—23 percent of the total electrical requirements for the province of British Columbia.

★ **G. M. Schrum Generating Station** – *Visit by guided tour (1hr) only, mid-May–mid-Oct daily 9am–6pm. Rest of the year Mon–Fri 8am–4pm (reservations required). Closed national holidays.* ✕ ♿ ☎250-783-5211. The tour begins at the **visitor centre**, which houses several interactive exhibits on electricity, waterwheels, magnets and motors. A film (*10min*) on the history of the site and building of the dam follows. Then visitors descend by bus to the powerhouse, 152m/500ft underground and hewn out of solid rock. At the manifold chamber, water surges from the turbines into the tailrace discharge tunnel. Explanatory diagrams are installed at each tour stop.

West Side Lookout – *3km/2mi across dam. Steep road.* This viewpoint affords good views of Williston Lake and the spillway. Part of the canyon of the Peace River is visible with the reservoir of the smaller Peace Canyon Dam downstream.

★ **Peace Canyon Dam** – *8km/5mi south of Hudson's Hope, on Hwy. 29. Visitor centre open mid-May–Labour Day daily 8am–4pm. Rest of the year Mon–Fri 8am–4pm. Closed national holidays.* ♿ ☎250-783-9943. Located 23km/14mi downstream, the Peace Canyon Dam reuses water from the larger W.A.C. Bennett Dam to generate additional electricity. The 200 tonne/220 ton turbine runners (or waterwheels) were manufactured in Russia and the generators in Japan. Visitors can view the powerhouse and the control room. The observation deck and walkway over the dam provide good **views**.

After the junction with Highway 29, the Alaska Highway passes through flat and heavily wooded country that gradually becomes more mountainous. there is a lovely **view**★ of the Rockies at KM 314/mi 195, across the Minaker River Valley.

These views continue through heavy forest until the road reaches **Fort Nelson** (pop. 3,804), a lumber centre and base for oil and gas exploration. The Liard Highway to Fort Simpson (Northwest Territories) via Fort Liard commences at this point, offering access to spectacular Nahanni National Park Reserve (*p 307*).

★★ FROM FORT NELSON TO WHITEHORSE   991km/616mi

After leaving Fort Nelson the highway turns west and offers many sweeping views of the mountains as the road traverses the end of the Rocky Mountains. The country is very open and during the initial part of the drive, the mountains are largely flat topped, more akin to the "mesa" mountains of the Southern Rockies in the US than to the pointed peaks of the Banff-Jasper area (*p 55*).

★ **Stone Mountain Provincial Park** – KM *627/mi 389. Open daily mid-May–Sept.* ⛺ ☎250-232-5460. A rocky and barren area resembling a stone quarry, this park is named for a mountain to the north of the highway. The mountains at this point are more rugged than previously. The highlight of the park is **Summit Lake**★, a lovely green-coloured stretch of water lying beside the highway.

After leaving the lake behind, the road passes through the rocky gorge of Macdonald Creek.

★★ **Muncho Lake Provincial Park** – KM *688/mi 427. Open daily mid-May–Sept.* ⛺ ☎250-232-5460. This park is one of the most beautiful parts of the drive. At first the road follows the valley of the Toad River, a wide, rocky and rather desolate area softened only by the pale green colour of the river. The vista widens ahead, and more mountains come into view, many snow-capped. Stone sheep can often be seen licking salt from the road bed. Reached after entering the park (*46km/29mi*), **Muncho Lake**★★ mirrors the surrounding folded mountains that rise over 2,000m/7,000ft. Its aquamarine colour is attributed to copper oxide.

At KM 788/mi 490 the **Liard River** is first glimpsed. Rising in the Yukon, this wild and turbulent river flows south into British Columbia and finally north again into the Northwest Territories to join the Mackenzie River. Its valley marks the northern limit of the Rocky Mountains. The highway follows the river for approximately 240km/150mi, providing some good views.

★ **Liard River Hot Springs Park** – KM *765/mi 478. Take side road on right to parking area; follow boardwalk. Open year-round. Changing rooms provided.* ⚠ ☎*250-232-5460.* This small park consists of large, hot sulphur pools (temperature averages 42°C/107°F) in natural surroundings, deep enough for swimming.

At KM 947/mi 588 the highway crosses the 60th parallel, entering the Yukon Territory. The exit from British Columbia is not yet final, however, as the highway crosses and recrosses the boundary several times. Travellers along this road are rewarded with fine views of the **Cassiar Mountains**.

Watson Lake – Pop. 912. KM *1,016/mi 632.* This transportation and communications centre for southern Yukon is famous for its collection of **signposts** (*illustration p 311*). In 1942 a homesick soldier, employed in the highway's construction, erected a sign with the name of his hometown and its direction. Tourists have kept up the tradition. Today some 17,000 signs from all over the continent and abroad line the highway through town.

From the south the **Stewart-Cassiar Highway** (Route 37) joins the Alaska Highway at KM 1,044/mi 649. Winding 800km/500mi through western British Columbia, this road provides an alternative route to the Yukon. After this junction the Alaska Highway begins to cross the Cassiar Mountains, with pretty views of snow-capped peaks on both sides of the road.

At KM 1,162/mi 722 a rise of land is traversed that marks the divide between two great river systems, the Mackenzie and the Yukon, which empty into the Beaufort and Bering Seas respectively.

Teslin Lake – KM *1,290/mi 802.* The name of this stretch of water means "long lake" in local Indian dialect. The highway crosses Nisutlin Bay and hugs the shore of this long narrow lake for about 48km/30mi. Frequently the mountains and lake are bordered by clusters of the Yukon's adopted emblem, the pinkish purple flower called **fireweed**, common throughout the Yukon and British Columbia. At the head of the lake, the road crosses the Teslin River by a high bridge, a remnant of the days when river steamers carried traffic in this area and needed clearance under bridges.

Teslin – Pop. 181. KM *1,294/mi 804.* This tiny town is the home of the **George Johnston Museum**, which contains native dress and artifacts (*open mid-May–Aug daily 9am–6pm; $2.50;* ♿ ☎*403-390-2550*). Featured are the black-and-white **photographs** by Johnston (1884-1972) of his fellow Tlingit (KLING-it) Indians during the early 1900s.

★ **Excursion to Atlin** – *At Jake's Corner,* KM *1,392/mi 865, take road south for 98km/ 61mi. This is a fairly isolated drive on unpaved road. Visitor centre (in the Atlin Museum, 1st & Trainor Sts.) open mid-May–mid-Sept daily 10am–6pm.* ☎*250-651-7522.* An old gold-mining town, the small community of Atlin in British Columbia has a pretty **site★** overlooking a beautiful lake of the same name, backed by majestic snow-covered peaks. From Warm Bay Road **Llewellyn Glacier** can be seen beyond Atlin Lake on a clear day.

★★ **Marsh Lake** – KM *1,428/mi 887.* Surrounded by mountains, this beautiful blue-green lake is really an arm of the much larger **Tagish Lake** to the south, and therefore part of the Yukon River system. Because of its proximity to WHITEHORSE, the lake is not as deserted as others passed on the highway; many houses can be seen along its edge. The road follows the lake for about 16km/10mi, with several lovely viewpoints. At the end of the lake, the road then crosses the Yukon River (*p 93*) at a dam.

At KM 1,445/mi 898 there is a good **view★** from above of the steep, white cliffs and clear green water of the fabled **Yukon River**, which rises only 24km/15mi from the Pacific Ocean and meanders nearly 3,200km/2,000mi, crossing the Arctic Circle before it finally jettisons its waters into the Bering Sea.

★ **Whitehorse** – KM *1,474/mi 916. Description p 89.*

★★ **From Whitehorse to Alaska Border (Alaska Highway)** – *491km/305mi. Description (in opposite direction) p 95.*

THE CARIBOO★

British Columbia

Map of Principal Sights p 2

The Cariboo is the name given to the region in the valley of the Fraser River north of the Thompson River. Part of the central plateau of British Columbia, this region is a vast rolling plain of low arid hills, lakes and sagebrush, bounded to the east by the Cariboo Mountains—from which the area gets its name—and to the west, by the Coast Mountains.

Historical Notes

The Cariboo Gold Rush – Opened by fur traders, the Cariboo first reached prominence with the Gold Rush of 1861, which led to the building of the Cariboo Road. Gold was first found in this area in 1859 by prospectors who had made their way from California to the lower Fraser and then north, following the gold trail. By 1862 large quantities were being extracted from the upper part of Williams Creek when **Billy Barker**, a Cornish sailor who had jumped ship at VICTORIA to try his luck, hit pay dirt in its lower reaches. Within 48 hours he had extracted $1,000 worth of gold. The area boomed and towns such as Barkerville (named for Billy), Camerontown and Richfield sprang up.

Ten years after the first discovery, no more gold could be found, and the towns of the Cariboo were almost deserted. In Williams Creek alone more than $50 Million worth of gold had been extracted. Barkerville was inhabited until 1958, when the provincial government transformed the site into a museum-town, carefully restoring it to its former splendour.

Cattle Country – Once the gold was gone, the miners left and farmers moved in. Today the main economic activity is cattle raising; some of the largest ranches in Canada are found in this region. The centre of the area is **Williams Lake** (pop. 10,385), which holds an annual stampede—considered the premier rodeo of the province—in the first week of July. Cowboys come from all over North America to vie for trophies. The largest stockyards of British Columbia are located in Williams Lake. A popular tourist area, the region is known for its sports fishing, game hunting, dude ranches and other traditional features of "Western" living, and for the restored Gold Rush town of **Barkerville**.

The Cariboo Road – To facilitate transportation to the boom towns of the gold discovery, the government of British Columbia (the province was created in 1858) decided to build a wagon road to Barkerville from the lower Fraser River near Yale, some 650km/403mi. Following the wild rocky canyon of the Fraser, the road, opened in 1864, was the remarkable engineering achievement of Royal Engineers from Britain, army engineers and private contractors. Over much of the route, solid rock had to be blasted. The old road has since been replaced by the Trans-Canada Highway, the Cariboo Highway (97) and Highway 26.

The **drive★** *(Hwy. 97 north, then Hwy. 26)* from Quesnel to Barkerville penetrates the Cariboo Mountains, passing **Cottonwood House** *(open May–Labour Day daily 8am–5pm; rest of Sept 10am–4pm; $2; ✗ ♿ ☎250-992-3997)*, one of the few remaining roadhouses on the old wagon road, and **Wells**, a mining community.

★★ BARKERVILLE HISTORIC TOWN *90km/56mi east of Quesnel by Hwy. 26.*

The old gold mining centre has a fine **site★** in the valley of Williams Creek, surrounded by mountains. The restored buildings of Barkerville include the stores, hotels, saloons and assay office of a mining community.

Visit – *Open May–Sept daily 8am–8pm. Rest of the year daily dawn–dusk. $5.50 ✗ ♿ ☎250-994-3332.* in the **visitor centre** the interesting video shows *(shown regularly in summer)* and displays on the town, the Gold Rush and methods of mining are a good introduction. Note the rather unusually shaped **St. Saviour's Anglican Church**, a structure of whipsawn timber and square nails. At the far end of the street is the Chinese section with its **Chinese Freemasons' Hall** (the Chinese followed the other gold rushers north from California, but tended to stay within their own community). **Billy Barker's claim** is marked, and the **Theatre Royal** stages typical Gold-Rush-era shows *(mid-May–Labour Day Sat–Thu 1 & 4pm; additional show 8pm Sat & Sun; $8; reservations required; ✗ ♿ ☎250-994-3232)*. Visitors can also pan for gold in the Eldorado Mine *($3.50)*.

A dramatized sketch of **Judge Baillie Begbie** is performed *(mid-Jun–Sept daily 11am, 1:45 & 3pm)* in the Richfield Courthouse *(1.6km/1mi walk up Williams Creek)*. Begbie was the famous Cariboo judge who enforced law and order in an unruly community.

DAWSON CITY★★

Yukon Territory
Pop. 972
Map of Principal Sights p 2
Tourist Office ☎403-993-5575

Set on a dramatic **site★** on the east bank of the wide Yukon at its confluence with the Klondike, this historic frontier town—the heart of the Gold Rush—is truly a delight. Remarkably like a Western movie set, the former destination of thousands of fortune seekers retains its unpaved streets, pedestrian boardwalks and false facades, which enhance the feeling of a bygone era.

Historical Notes

The Great Stampede – On August 16, 1896, **George Carmack** and his Indian brothers-in-law, Skookum Jim and Tagish Charlie, found gold on **Bonanza Creek** *(p 43)*, a tiny stream emptying into the bigger **Klondike River**, itself a tributary of the mighty Yukon. When news of their find reached the outside world, an estimated 100,000 people left their homes as far away as Australia to begin the long, arduous trek to Dawson City, the town that sprang up at the mouth of the Klondike. Stories of their travels are legion. Many never made it; of those who did, few made a fortune.

The Routes of '98 – There were several routes to Dawson City during the Gold Rush. The longest, yet easiest, was by sea to the mouth of the Yukon and then by riverboat the 2,092km/1,300mi upstream to the city of gold. But this passage was only for the rich. A few people tried an overland course from EDMONTON, Alberta, through almost impassable muskeg and bush, following more or less the present-day route of the ALASKA HIGHWAY. The majority, however, sailed up the Pacific Coast via the inside passage to Skagway *(p 92)* or Dyea, tiny way stations on the Alaska Panhandle, and trudged into the Yukon across the Coast Mountains.

Home of the Klondike– Soon after the discovery the whole area near Bonanza Creek was staked by prospectors. Instead of making a claim, a trader named **Joe Ladue** laid out a townsite on the level swampland at the mouth of the Klondike, amassing a fortune from his foresight. Lots were soon selling for as much as $5,000 a front foot on the main street. The heyday of Dawson was underway. Prices were skyhigh: eggs $1.00 each, nails $8.00 a pound; but everything was available, from the latest Paris fashions to the best wines and foods. At more saloons than one could visit in a night, drinks were normally paid for in gold dust.

Dawson had a unique feature: despite being the biggest and richest of all the mining boom towns, it was the most law-abiding. The North West Mounted Police maintained tight control. Everything was closed down on Sundays. No one carried a gun except the police. Offenders were given a "blue ticket" (i.e., run out of town).

Decline and Revival – The heyday was short-lived. By 1904 the rich **placer** fields were exhausted: $100 million in gold had been shipped out. Complicated machinery was needed to exploit any gold that remained. People left; the glamour departed. The age of the giant dredges began, and Dawson became a company town.

Dawson City c.1898

Yukon Archives/E.A. Hegg

Once the largest Canadian city (pop. 30,000) west of WINNIPEG, Dawson City maintained its preeminence until World War II when WHITEHORSE—connected to the outside world by road (Alaska Highway), rail and air—took over, growing as Dawson shrank. In 1953 Whitehorse was made the capital of the Yukon. With this blow and the end of commercial gold mining in 1966, Dawson might have become a ghost town were it not for the tourist boom that is reviving the city. People still make a living mining the creeks, but little gold is found in comparison to the $22 million discovered in 1900.

The year-round population of nearly 1,000 swells in summertime with the arrival of tourists and seasonal residents. Situated less than 300km/200mi south of the Arctic Circle on fertile soil untouched by the last Ice Age, Dawson enjoys hot summers with nearly 24 hours of daylight. Vegetables are cultivated in gardens, and flowers sprout through cracks along the streets. Many old buildings tell the story of a grandeur and wealth seen nowhere else so far north. Some sag sideways, however, because of permafrost. The Canadian government has embarked on a substantial restoration project that is returning the town to some of its former splendour.

Festivities – Two important dates for tourists in Dawson are: June 21 when the midnight sun barely dips down behind the Ogilvie Mountains, and the third weekend in August when the anniversary of **Discovery Day** is celebrated with a parade, raft races on the Klondike River and other activities.

Visiting Dawson City – Since Dawson's sights and tourist activities are numerous, it is best to first stop at the visitor centre *(Front and King Sts.; open mid-May–mid-Sept daily 8am–8pm;* & ☎*403-993-5566 or 403-993-5575)* for a schedule of events and guided tours as well as a map. Informative audiovisuals and displays are also in the centre. Sights that can be visited by guided tour only *(Jun–Aug twice daily; 1hr 30min; $3)* are indicated below by "*(guided tour)*." Historic buildings not open to the public usually have a window display [indicated *(wd)* below] depicting the structure's history.

★★ DOWNTOWN   *2 days*

Laid out in a grid pattern, this town lies in the shadow of the huge hill known as the Midnight Dome *(p 43)*, easily visible from downtown. On its face is **Moosehide Slide**, a natural landslide—thought to be the result of an underground spring—which has been less of a threat to the community than floods and fires.

On **Front Street** (also called First Avenue) stands the **SS Keno**, a sternwheeler once used to transport silver, lead and zinc on the Stewart River from the mines in the Mayo district *(p 94)*. Built in Whitehorse in 1922, the steamer also made trips to Dawson. After its last voyage in 1960, it was permanently dry docked there. Because damage was extensive, the flood of 1979 led to the building of a sand-gravel dike along the riverbank where the steamers once docked. Next to the *Keno* is the former **Canadian Imperial Bank of Commerce**, a stately building with a pressed-tin facade made to imitate stone. The plaque on the exterior refers to its famous teller, Robert Service.

The former **British North American Bank** *(guided tour)*, with its handsome polished wood teller enclosure, occupies the corner of Queen Street and 2nd Avenue. The **assay office** contains a wide sampling of instruments used to weigh Klondike gold. South on 2nd Avenue is **Ruby's Place** *(wd)*, one of several restored town buildings. At Princess Street and 3rd, the renovated **Harrington's Store** *(open Jun–Labour Day daily 11am–5pm)*, built in 1900, contains the comprehensive photo exhibit, *Dawson As They Saw It*. Across the street is **Billy Bigg's** blacksmith shop *(wd)* and north on 3rd, note the **KTM Building** *(wd)*, which served as a warehouse for the Klondike Thawing Machine Co. in 1912.

Formerly a Carnegie Library, the Neoclassical **Masonic Temple** corners 4th and Queen, while diagonally across the street is **Diamond Tooth Gertie's** Gambling Hall. Named for a notorious female resident, this establishment boasts a legalized casino *(floor shows mid-May–mid-Sept nightly 8:30, 10:30, 12:30pm; $4.75;* ⚔ &*)*. Behind Gertie's is the colourful **Fire Hall**, which also contains city offices.

Back on 3rd Avenue are the **Dawson Daily News** (1898-1953) *(wd)*, and **Madame Tremblay's Store** *(wd)*, restored to its 1913 appearance. Opposite, a clapboard building with a squat tower houses the original 1900 **Post Office** *(open Jun–Labour Day daily noon–6pm)*, designed by Englishman **Thomas W. Fuller**, who served as Canada's chief architect for 15 years, influencing the country's federal architecture in particular. He also designed the Government House and the Old Territorial

Administration Building *(below)*. Across King Street stands a replica of the **Palace Grand Theatre★** *(guided tour)*, a distinctive pinewood structure with an elaborate false front. Built in 1899 by "Arizona Charlie" Meadows, the original theatre offered everything from opera to wild west shows. Draped with Old Glory and Union Jacks, the colourful two-tiered, U-shaped interior seats audiences in rows of padded "kitchen chairs." *Gaslight Follies*, turn-of-the-century vaudeville and melodrama, plays nightly except Tuesdays *(mid-May–mid-Sept 8pm; $13; for reservations ☎403-993-6217)*.

On Harper Street between 2nd and 3rd Avenues is a photographer's favourite: the delapidated **Old Guns and Ammunition Shop**, victim to permafrost action. One street over is aptly named Church Street, site of the clapboard **St. Paul's Anglican Church** built in 1902 with money collected from miners in the creeks.

Southward, double-porticoed **Government House**, where the Yukon's commissioner, or governor, lived in the early 1900s, overlooks Front Street. Designed by T. W. Fuller, the original residence had a more ornate exterior than the present structure, a replacement after a house fire in 1906. The house and grounds, once abundant with flowers, were the centre of Dawson's social life—host to afternoon teas, dinner receptions and summer garden parties. To the rear are the remains of **Fort Herchmer** *(grounds open to the public)*, a former North West Mounted Police barracks: married quarters, stables, jail and commanding officer's residence. The renovated St. Andrews **Presbyterian Manse** stands behind **St. Andrews Church**, at 4th Avenue.

ADDITIONAL SIGHTS

★ **Dawson City Museum** – *5th Ave. Open mid-May–early Sept daily 10am–6pm. Rest of the year by appointment. $3.50.* ✗ ☎*403-993-5291.* Dominating the upper section of 5th Avenue, the impressive Old Territorial Administration Building (1901, T. W. Fuller), in Neoclassical style, houses the museum. The South Gallery has exhibits and re-creations of Dawson's Gold Rush; the North Gallery features early-20C city life in Dawson City. Locomotives of the short-lived Klondike Mines Railway are on display in an outdoor shelter.

Robert Service Cabin – *8th Ave. at Hanson St.* Overlooking the town from the southeast is a small log cabin with moose antlers over the door—the residence from 1909 to 1912 of the "poet of the Yukon" (1874-1958). Here he wrote his only novel, *The Trail of '98* and his last Yukon verses, *Rhymes of a Rolling Stone.* Though he arrived in Dawson shortly after the Gold Rush, his poetry—*Songs of a Sourdough* in particular—vividly re-creates the atmosphere of the times. Outdoor **recitals** *(1hr)* of his poems are presented on the grounds *(mid-May–mid-Sept daily 10am & 3pm; $6;* ☎*403-993-5462).*

Jack London Interpretive Centre – *8th Ave. at Firth St.* The cabin of another writer who spent time in Dawson City during its heyday, American author **Jack London** (1876-1916), has been reconstructed on the property. His stories of the North, *Call of the Wild, White Fang* and *Burning Daylight* are among his best-known works. The adjacent centre *(open mid-May–mid-Sept daily 10am–6pm;* ☎*403-993-5575)* houses a photo exhibit of London's life in the Klondike and of the mid-1960s search for his original cabin, found in the vicinity of Henderson Creek, some 73km/45mi south of Dawson City. There are also **readings** *(30min)* of his works *(twice daily).*

EXCURSIONS

Midnight Dome – *9km/5mi by Dome Rd.—a steep, winding road.* So named because of the midnight sun visible here on June 21, this mountain rises 884m/2,900ft behind the townsite. From the summit the **view★★** is splendid, day or night. Below lies Dawson at the junction of the Yukon and Klondike Rivers—the Yukon weaving its way south to north, wide and muddy; the Klondike making a clear streak that is absorbed as it enters the Yukon. Even Bonanza Creek can be seen entering the Klondike. The devastation of the whole area caused by the dredges is evident. There are mountains in all directions; to the north, the Ogilvie Mountains are particularly impressive.

★★ **Bonanza Creek** – *4km/2.5mi by Klondike Hwy. from town to Bonanza Creek Rd. Unpaved road, maintained for 16km/10mi.* The road along Bonanza Creek winds through huge piles of **tailings**, or washed gravel refuse, left by the mining dredges. Large-scale mining activity still takes place here and throughout the Klondike today. The largest remnant of earlier mining equiment is **No. 4 dredge** *($3; tickets* *available from on-site visitor centre)* on Claim 17BD. (Claims of 152m/500ft were staked out and numbered in relation to the discovery claim: 17BD means 17 claims below, or downstream of, discovery; 7AD means 7 claims above discovery.) An enormous wooden-hulled, bucket-lined machine, the dredge consists of four basic parts *(shown in the exhibit panels)*: a barge for flotation; a series of steel buckets to excavate the gravel in front of the barge and to deliver it to the barge's housing; the housing itself where gravel was washed with water and the gold recovered; and a conveyor or stacker to disgorge barren gravel behind the barge, creating tailings.

Signs designate a claim provided by the Klondike Visitors Assn. for enterprising visitors who wish to **pan for gold** *(for details ☎403-993-5575)*.

A simple plaque marks the place where the Klondike Stampede began: **Discovery Claim** itself *(14.5km/9mi from junction with Klondike Hwy.)*. Farther on *(19km/12mi from junction)*, Eldorado Creek joins Bonanza. Some of the richest claims were located on Eldorado and the community at the junction, Grand Forks, was once a thriving place. Today nothing remains.

Bear Creek – *13km/8mi by Klondike Hwy. from town to Bear Creek Rd. Visit by guided tour (1hr 30min) only, mid-May–mid-Sept daily 2–5pm. $3. ☎403-993-9939.* Closed by the Yukon Consolidated Gold Co. in 1966, this sizeable compound was once a busy community of over 2,000 workers engaged in the maintenance of a fleet of dredges. The visit includes the cavernous machine shop and the orderly **gold room**, where each step in the refining process is clearly described. An archival film *(11min)* closes the tour.

FORT ST. JAMES★

British Columbia
Pop. 2,058
Map of Principal Sights p 2

In a lovely setting beside Stuart Lake, this town, 154km/96mi northwest of Prince George, is one of the oldest settlements in British Columbia. Simon Fraser founded a trading post here in 1806 that became the chief Hudson's Bay Company post in New Caledonia *(p 33)* after 1821. It remained in operation until 1971.

SIGHT

★ **Fort St. James National Historic Site** – ☞ *Beside lake in town. Open mid-May–Sept daily 9am–5pm. $4. ☎250-996-7191.* The park contains five restored Hudson's Bay Company buildings that date from 1884 to 1889. The **men's house**, trading store and officers' dwelling with their meticulously stored furnishings can be visited. Built off the ground, the **fish cache** with its displays of dried fish and pork and the dove-tailed log **general warehouse** with its fur store can also be seen. The visitor centre has displays on the fort's history.

> ■ Billy Miner, who gained notoriety as the robber of Canadian Pacific Railway's Transcontinental Express, took up residence in Canada in 1904. Known for his courtesy during a hold-up, the American bandit is believed to have originated the command, "Hands up!"

FRASER AND THOMPSON CANYONS★★

British Columbia
Map of Principal Sights p 2

Between the city of VANCOUVER and Shuswap Lake, the Trans-Canada Highway follows deep valleys, cut by two of the wildest rivers in the province, through the rocky Coast Mountains and the dry, hilly scrubland of central British Columbia.

Historical Notes – Alexander Mackenzie was the first European to see the Fraser River. On his epic journey to the Pacific in 1793, he followed its northern course. His partner in the North West Company, Simon Fraser, descended and reascended the river's entire length in 1808, traversing on foot along rock ledges and down ladders slung over rockfaces by the Indians. Fraser gave the river his name and that of David Thompson, geographer and another North Westerner, to its major tributary.

Too wild for a fur-trading route, the Fraser was little used until gold was discovered at **Hill's Bar** near Yale in 1858. Much of the metal was found in the ensuing rush, but the major strike occurred in the then-inaccessible Cariboo farther north. Above Yale the river was too turbulent for steamboat passage (a few boats were winched through Hell's Gate, but a permanent water route was impossible). To solve the dilemma, the Cariboo Road was built *(p 40)*, the section through the Fraser Canyon taking two years to construct.

The Fraser and Thompson Canyons were again selected in the 19C for another substantial transportation venture: the Canadian Pacific Railway. The 20C has seen this once near-impassable passage become a major artery—now traversed by a second railway and the Trans-Canada Highway.

★★ ① FRASER CANYON – From Hope to Lytton   *109km/68mi. Map p 50.*

★ **Hope** – Pop. 3,147. The mountains close in around this community as the valley narrows and swings northwards. The wildness and unpredictability of the region were well demonstrated by the **Hope Slide** of 1965. One January day an immense amount of rock from Johnson Peak *(21km/13mi east by Rte. 3)* slid into the valley, filling a lake and forcing its waters up the other side. Route 3 had to be rebuilt more than 45m/148ft above its original level.

Excursion to Manning Provincial Park – *26km/16mi east of Hope by Rte. 3.* After entering **Manning Provincial Park★** *(open year-round; hiking, horseback riding, bicycling, cross-country skiing; △ ✕ &)*, Route 3 traverses an area called **Rhododendron Flats**, where these wild plants flower in profusion in mid-June and crosses **Allison Pass** (1,341m/4,400ft). This park is one of only two places in Canada where visitors can drive to extensive subalpine meadows *(Mt. Revelstoke p 48)*. In the **visitor centre** *(68km/42mi from Hope, just east of Manning Park Lodge; open Jun–Sept daily 8:30am–4:30pm; rest of the year Mon–Fri 8:30am–4pm; & ☎250-840-8836)*, the three vegetation zones of the park are featured: the western slopes covered with the damp, dense growth of coastal British Columbia; the central area reflecting the transitional zone; and the eastern part with its dry and arid sagebrush country, so typical of the interior of the province.

After Hope, mountains close in abruptly and farmland is left behind. The river changes to a rushing torrent, and the road is often situated on high rocky ledges or lower, at river level.

★ **Yale** – Pop. 18. Surrounded by high and impressive cliffs, this tiny hamlet was once a town of 20,000. During the Gold Rush it was the terminus of river navigation and the beginning of the Cariboo Road.

Hill's Bar is located just to the south. To the north the most spectacular part of the **canyon★★** begins. The cliffs are sheer, the valley narrow, tunnels are frequent, and the river below seethes along, around and over rocks. Just after Spuzzum the road crosses the river and continues on the east side.

★ **Hell's Gate** – The canyon here is 180m/600ft deep, but the river, rushing past at 8m/25ft per second, is only 36m/120ft wide. The river was once wider, but during construction of the Canadian National Railway in 1914, a rockslide occurred, narrowing the gap. Thereafter, upstream passage was almost impossible for the salmon, their spawning grounds being the lakes and streams around Shuswap Lake. A sharp decline in the Pacific salmon fishing industry occurred until "fishways" were constructed between 1944 and 1946 to enable the salmon to bypass the turbulent water.

An **airtram** *(Apr–Oct daily 9am–5pm; $9; ✕ & ☎250-867-9277)* descends 150m/500ft to river level, where the canyon and the incredible speed of the water can be appreciated. There are displays on the salmon and the fishways as well as a film *(20min)*. The fishways are visible in the river, but because the water is murky, salmon are rarely seen except in September and October when the water's depth is lower.

Pacific Salmon

■ Every summer and autumn British Columbia's five salmon species—sockeye, pink, coho, chinook and chum—leave the ocean and swim far inland up the province's rivers and streams to spawn. In none are their numbers greater than in the Fraser River, where they travel as far as 48km/30mi a day. Soon after spawning, they die. Their offspring remain in fresh water for about two years before heading to the ocean, where they mature in two to five years. Then the epic return journey to their spawning grounds occurs.

After Hell's Gate the canyon becomes less dark and formidable, and there are more trees on its rocky slopes. From **Jackass Mountain** there is a fine **view★** of the canyon from high above the river, and at Cisco Creek two bridges can be seen as the railways switch sides.

Lytton – Pop. 335. This community regularly registers the highest temperatures in Canada. Rather than the green pine trees of the lower Fraser Canyon, the vegetation is more the sagebrush of central British Columbia. At this point the clear blue waters of the Thompson River surge into the muddy brown Fraser, making a streak visible for a short distance downstream.

★★ 2 THOMPSON CANYON – From Lytton to Shuswap Lake
230km/143mi. Map p 50.

The Trans-Canada Highway and the two railways leave the valley of the Fraser and turn east along the Thompson, passing through a dry, treeless and steep-sided **canyon★★**. The road winds and weaves along, making sharp bends. Just before Spences Bridge, where the road crosses the river, the remains of a great landslide that occurred in 1905 can be seen.

Then the river **valley★** gradually widens into a semidesert area where scrub vegetation and sagebrush predominate. Occasionally there is some cultivation of the terraces above the river, but only for irrigation. The remains of one such attempt can be seen 17km/11mi after Cache Creek at a place once called **Walhachin** ("abundance of the earth"). Between 1907 and 1914 a group of young British aristocrats built irrigation flumes to carry water to their fields, and for a while, the area flourished. World War I ended the experiment, as most of the men left to fight and were killed. Odd bits of flume and withered apple trees are all that remain.

Just before Savona the Thompson expands to form **Kamloops Lake**. From the Trans-Canada Highway there are some pleasant **views★** of this blue lake set in rocky arid hills. Again irrigation is bringing some of the land under cultivation. The highway bypasses the industrial city of **Kamloops** (pop. 67,057) and follows the south branch of the Thompson to its headwaters in **Shuswap Lake**. Here the country changes from dry barrenness to verdant green with sparkling waters. Many salmon spawn in this region after their long swim up the turbulent Fraser and Thompson Rivers.

INSIDE PASSAGE★★

British Columbia
Map of Principal Sights p 2

This protected inland waterway, the result of past glaciation, cuts between the wildly indented northwest coast and the myriad islands that stretch from Puget Sound in Washington state to Skagway, Alaska—a total distance of 1,696km/1,060 statute mi. The portion of the route served by Canadian ferries extends from Port Hardy on the northern tip of VANCOUVER ISLAND to Prince Rupert (507km/ 314mi), on the northwest coast of British Columbia, ushering visitors into a world of lush, tranquil beauty.

VISIT

Cruise – *Departs Port Hardy late May–late Sept every other day 7:30am, arrives Prince Rupert 10:30pm (even-numbered days Jun, Jul & Sept; odd-numbered days Aug). Weekly service rest of the year. Reservations required. One-way $100 plus vehicle charge. Check-in 1hr before sailing.* ✗ &. *BC Ferries, 1112 Fort St, Victoria, BC, V8V 4V2* ☎*250-386-3431.* From Port Hardy the ferry crosses the open sea at Queen Charlotte Strait, then enters the sheltered waters of Fitz Hugh Sound. The remainder of this voyage through the narrow, spectacular Inside Passage offers close-up **views★★**, weather permitting, of islands to the west and the fjord-slashed coast of western British Columbia to the east. The low, mountainous terrain, densely forested in spruce and hemlock, drops steeply into the sea. Virtually uninhabited, the area retains only one substantial community, the town of Bella Bella (pop. 1,104), home to the native Heiltsuk. Several abandoned cannery communities are passed during the cruise.

Eagles and sea birds, as well as such marine mammals as seals, dolphins, orca and humpback whales may be sighted during spring and fall migration. The highlight of the voyage comes near its northern end as the ferry enters the 40km/25mi **Grenville Channel★★**. At its narrowest the channel measures only 549m/1,800ft across, with a maximum depth of 377m/1,236ft.

THE KOOTENAYS★

A major tributary of the Columbia, the Kootenay River winds through the south-east corner of British Columbia—an area of mountains, beautiful lakes and lush valleys—giving the region its name. Rising in the Rockies, the Kootenay traverses its own national park *(p 68)*, misses the headwaters of the Columbia by just over a kilometre at Canal Flats, flows south into the US, loops and returns to Canada to form Kootenay Lake, and finally joins the Columbia at Castlegar.

At the south end of the lake, the valley around **Creston** (pop. 4,205) is full of grain-fields, orchards and other fruit-bearing plants. The **Crowsnest Pass** region has some of the largest soft-coal deposits in North America. Farther west, copper, lead, zinc and silver are mined and processed in the huge smelter at **Trail** (pop. 7,919).

Historical Notes – The first settlers came to the region in 1864 when gold nuggets were found in the valley of the Wild Horse River, a tributary of the Kootenay. At the junction of these rivers, a certain John Galbraith set up a ferry service, and the settlement that developed took the name Galbraith's Ferry. From New Westminister, the former capital of British Columbia, a road was pushed through the mountains to the site by a young English engineer, **Edgar Dewdney**. To this day the road (Route 3) bears his name. After the gold dwindled, settlers increas-ingly turned to farming and ranching. Land disputes with the Kootenay Indians resulted. A detachment of the North West Mounted Police was sent under the command of the famed Mountie **Sam Steele** (1849-1919). He restored peace and order to the settlement, which changed its name to Fort Steele to honour him and to mark the first posting of police west of the Rockies.

SIGHT

★**Fort Steele Heritage Town** – *16km/10mi northeast of Cranbrook by Rte. 95. Open Jun–Aug daily 9:30am–10pm. Rest of the year daily 9:30am–dusk. $4.25.* ✗ ⅙ ☎*250-426-6923.* This former centre of a mining boom that brought prosperity to the Kootenays has a fine **site**★ at the foot of the Rockies. The townsite has been re-created to represent a typical Kootenay community at the turn of the century. The town of Fort Steele flourished in the early 1890s. Its death knell sounded when the railway over Crowsnest Pass bypassed the town, going instead to Cranbrook. In 1961 the provincial government began restoration of the practically deserted townsite. Today Fort Steele lives again.

Among the many restored buildings, the **museum**, set in an old hotel, is the most interesting, with excellent displays on the history of the region. The North West Mounted Police barracks can also be visited. Live entertainment is provided in the **Wildhorse Theatre** *(Jul–Aug Sat–Thu 2 & 8pm; $6.50;* ☎*250-426-5682).* An old steam locomotive offers rides *(20min; $4)* and there are stagecoach tours of the site. Overlooking the Kootenay River stands a large wooden waterwheel, once used to haul water out of the mines.

MONASHEES AND SELKIRKS★★

Part of the Columbia Mountain System, the Monashee and Selkirk Ranges are located in southeastern British Columbia between the central plateau and the Rockies. Starting as rolling hills in the west, they soon develop sharp ridges, deep valleys and pyramid peaks—the results of heavy glaciation, especially in the Selkirks of Glacier National Park where several valley glaciers still exist. The Trans-Canada Highway crosses the two ranges by an often spectacular route through Eagle and Rogers Passes.

FROM SICAMOUS TO GOLDEN
Allow 6hrs. 219km/136mi by Trans-Canada Hwy.

★**Eagle Pass** – *71km/44mi from Sicamous to Revelstoke.* This pass through the Monashee Mountains (*Monashee* is a Gaelic word meaning "mountain of peace") was discovered by **Walter Moberly** in 1865. According to popular legend Moberly fired his gun at an eagle's nest and watched the birds fly away up a valley. Following them, he discovered the pass, henceforth known as Eagle Pass, which eventually became the chosen route for the Canadian Pacific Railway as well as the Trans-Canada Highway.

From the small town of **Sicamous** (pop. 2,501), set on the narrows between Shuswap and Mara Lakes, the Trans-Canada begins to climb the valley of the Eagle River. After 26km/16mi the highway reaches **Craigellachie**. On November 7, 1885, the last spike of the Canadian Pacific Railway, linking east and west, was driven here *(note the plaque erected beside the railway tracks off the road on the right)*. Craigellachie is Gaelic and refers to the rallying point of the Grant clan in Scotland, a symbol well known to the Banffshire-born directors of the railway.

The highway rises more steeply and the valley narrows before the road reaches **Three Valley Gap★** *(47km/29mi)*, occupying a lovely **site★** beside Three Valley Lake, edged with sheer cliffs. Soon afterwards the road arrives at the top of the pass *(55km/34mi)*, and then begins a steep descent to the Columbia in the valley of Tonakwatla Creek.

★★ **Revelstoke** – Pop. 7,729. Set on the east bank of the Columbia River at its junction with the Illecillewaet, this small community has a picturesque **site★** surrounded by mountains—the Selkirks to the east, the Monashees to the west. Named for **Lord Revelstoke**, head of the London banking firm of Barings, which financed completion of the Canadian Pacific Railway in 1885, the town has become a summer-winter sports centre because of its proximity to **Mt. Revelstoke National Park** *(open year-round; hiking, fishing, skiing, cross-country skiing; ☎250-837-7500)*.
Just to the north the **Revelstoke Dam** can be seen rising 175m/574ft above the Columbia River. A visitor centre *(4km/2.5mi north by Rte. 23; open mid-Mar–mid-Jun daily 9am–5pm; late Jun–mid-Sept daily 8am–8pm; late Sept–Oct daily 9am–5pm; BC Hydro ☎604/837-6211)* features displays on its construction and a model of all Columbia River power projects.

★★ **Mt. Revelstoke Summit Parkway** – *27km/16mi of gravel road, unsuitable for trailers. Begins on Trans-Can Hwy. 1.6km/1mi east of Revelstoke turnoff. 45min ascent.* This road ascends the southwest face of Mt. Revelstoke in a series of switchbacks. After 5.6km/3.5mi there is a **viewpoint★** of the town of Revelstoke, spread out on the bank of the Columbia. The snow-capped twin peaks of Mt. Begbie dominate the Monashees, which backdrop the river. Just east of the town, the valley of Tonakwatla Creek is visible, cutting its way through the mountains.
At the summit the **view★★** extends to the north. The Columbia's steep-walled valley and the glaciated mountains of the Clachnacudainn Range, with their jagged peaks and bare slopes, can be seen. A short distance from the parking area, a lookout tower has displays identifying the visible peaks. The vegetation has completely changed. Instead of the red cedars, hemlocks and spruce of the lower slopes, there are only stunted and wind-pruned firs. Paths at the summit descend into the **alpine meadows**, where multicoloured wild flowers abound in summer: Indian paintbrush (red), lupines (blue), arnica (yellow) and valerian (white).

★★ **Rogers Pass** – ✪ *148km/92mi from Revelstoke to Golden.* After crossing the Rockies by Kicking Horse Pass *(p 61)*, the Canadian Pacific Railway was supposed to follow the Columbia River loop *(map p 49)* because the Selkirks were considered an impenetrable barrier.

In 1881 however, a determined surveyor, **Albert Rogers**, followed the Illecillewaet River into these same mountains and discovered the pass named for him. The railroad was routed this way, achieving a savings of 240km/150mi.

Avalanches – From the beginning, incredibly high snowfall in the Selkirks (annual average 940cm/370in) and avalanches were obstacles to construction through the pass. Since the steep

Snow Shed Construction c.1903

Provincial Archives of Alberta (B6011)

slopes of the mountains had been worn smooth by previous slides, nothing blocked the path of new avalanches. Kilometres of snowsheds were constructed over the railway, but the yearly winter battle with the elements proved too costly

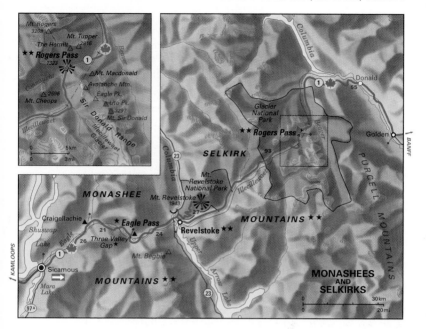

for the Canadian Pacific. To avoid the most hazardous area, the Connaught Tunnel was built through Mt. Macdonald in 1916. For the next 40 years, the Rogers Pass section remained untouched.

In 1959 however, after surveys were conducted, the decision was made to extend the Trans-Canada Highway through the pass, using the original railway road-bed. The highway was completed in 1962 when the section through the pass, the most expensive and challenging segment, was finished. To double the track under Mt. Macdonald, a second railway tunnel, the longest in North America (over 14km/9mi), was opened in 1988.

An elaborate defence system is in place. Concrete snowsheds deflect slides over the road, while rubble barriers divert and break up dangerous falls. Rangers stationed high in the mountains monitor snow pile-up; a howitzer is fired to trigger avalanches before they become too large.

★★ **From Rogers Pass to Golden** – *May be temporarily closed when avalanche control is underway. Winter travellers must follow instructions by park wardens.* The Trans-Canada Highway follows the high-walled valley of the Illecillewaet River into the Selkirks, and soon passes through snowsheds that provide winter protection for the road. After 48km/30mi the highway enters **Glacier National Park** *(open year-round; hiking, fishing, skiing, cross-country skiing; use fees vary, phone for schedule;* △ ☒ ☎250-837-7500). Ahead, the four pointed peaks of the **Sir Donald Range** are visible: *(left to right)* Avalanche Mountain, Eagle Peak, Uto Peak, and the great slanting slab of Mt. Sir Donald itself. To the north the steep pyramidal form of **Mt. Cheops** can be seen. To the south there are views of glaciers across the rocky and bounding Illecillewaet River.

The road swings around the Napoleon Spur of Mt. Cheops to reach the summit of the pass *(72km/45mi)*, where a double arch commemorates the completion of the highway in 1962. The **Rogers Pass Centre★** *(open Jun–Sept daily 8am–6pm; rest of the year daily 9am–5pm;* ☒ ☎250-837-7500) has displays, models and films that explain the history of the pass and the annual battle against avalanches. The **view★** includes the slide-scarred peaks of **Mt. Tupper** and **The Hermit** to the north; the Asulkan Ridge and snowfields, including the Illecillewaet Glacier, to the south; and the peaks of the Sir Donald Range and Mt. Cheops.

The road begins its steep descent between the bare slopes of Mt. Tupper and The Hermit to the north and the looming form of **Mt. Macdonald**. Passing through a series of reinforced concrete snowsheds, it swings into the valley of the Beaver River, a tributary of the Columbia, which separates the spiky Selkirks from the more rounded Purcell Mountains. Then the road leaves the park, crosses the Columbia at the town of Donald and follows the river south to **Golden** (pop. 3,721) in the Rocky Mountain Trench.

49

OKANAGAN VALLEY★★

British Columbia
Map of Principal Sights p 2

An important fruit-growing and wine-making region, this valley in south central British Columbia consists of a large lake (Okanagan), several smaller lakes, and the river of the same name (south of the US border, it is spelled Okanogan). Combined with lots of sunshine, intensive use of lake water for irrigation has made apple, peach, plum, grape, cherry, apricot and pear growing possible in this area of low rainfall, arid hills and sagebrush. Beautiful lakes with sandy beaches have made the valley a popular resort.

FROM OSOYOOS TO VERNON
Allow 6hrs. 177km/110mi by Rte. 97. Map below.

★ **Osoyoos** – Pop. 3,403. This community lies on narrows in the middle of **Osoyoos Lake**. It is surrounded by arid hills and semidesert country where sagebrush, greasewood and cactus thrive, in sharp contrast to the green orchards on the lakeshore. **Anarchist Mountain** *(6km/4mi east by Rte. 3)* provides a fine view★★ of the area.

★★ **Route 97 to Penticton** – Through orchards and past fruit stands, Route 97 follows the Okanagan River to **Oliver** (pop. 3,743). As the road approaches **Vaseux Lake★**, the scenery is impressive, with huge rocks and barren slopes. In contrast, the hills surrounding **Skaha Lake★★** are sandy, covered with sagebrush and small trees. They offset the blue waters of this lovely lake.

★★ **Okanagan Game Farm** – *8km/5mi south of Penticton. Open year-round daily 8am–dusk. $9. ✗ ⅙ ☎250-497-5405.* Overlooking Skaha Lake, this pleasant zoo is set among the low, rolling hills and scrub vegetation typical of the area. A circular drive *(5km/3mi)* enables visitors to view the animals from all parts of the world.

★ **Penticton** – Pop. 27,258. A corruption of a Salish Indian word meaning "a place to live forever," Penticton has a pleasant **site★** on narrows between Okanagan Lake and Skaha Lake, surrounded by rolling hills. It is a tourist resort with attrac-

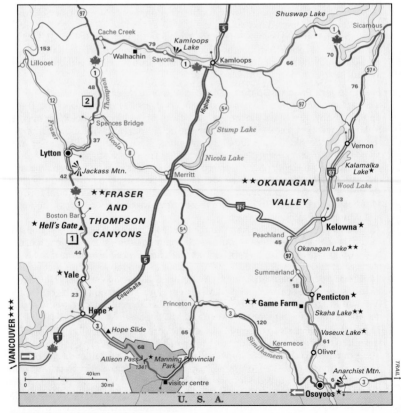

50

tive beaches and parks on both lakes. Beside Okanagan Lake lies the *SS Sicamous*, a sternwheeler once used on the lake *(open Jul–Aug daily 9am–9pm; rest of the year Mon–Fri 9am–3pm; $2; 250-492-0403).*

★★ **Route 97 to Kelowna** – After leaving Penticton Route 97 borders **Okanagan Lake★★**, offering lovely views. Near Summerland steep, white cliffs stand beside the lake. The road then passes through terraces of orchards and vineyards supported by irrigation. Note the lovely contrast between the blue of the lake, the green orchards, and the semidesert sagebrush, rock and dry-soil hills.

The road follows the bend of the lake where, according to local Indian legend, the monster **Ogopogo** lives. Like his name, Ogopogo is supposed to look the same viewed from either end, but the descriptions of him are as varied as the people who claim to have spotted him. After Peachland the road climbs up above the lake, leaving it temporarily to pass through the orchards before Kelowna.

★ **Kelowna** – Pop. 75,950. Route 97 crosses the narrows of Lake Okanagan to enter this town by a floating bridge, part of which can be raised to allow boats to pass. On this attractive **site★** the town was founded by **Father Pandosy**, an Oblate priest who established a mission in 1859 and encouraged the settlers who followed him to cultivate the land. Today Kelowna is the marketing centre for the Okanagan.

Route 97 to Vernon – After Kelowna the road skirts Wood Lake and winds along the eastern edge of **Kalamalka Lake★**, where the rolling hills, still rocky but greener than farther south, descend directly into the water. This change of terrain continues as the fruit-growing area is left behind. North of the town of Vernon (pop. 23,514), cattle raising predominates.

QUEEN CHARLOTTE ISLANDS★★

British Columbia
Pop. 5,316
Map of Principal Sights p 2

Separated from the northwest coast of British Columbia by the expansive Hecate Strait (50-130km/31-81mi), this remote archipelago comprises some 150 islands with a total landmass of approximately 10,126sq km/3,910sq mi. The two principal islands are Graham Island in the north, the largest and most populous; and, at the southern end, Moresby Island, which is predominantly a national park reserve. Essentially wilderness, the islands remain a habitat for a variety of marine mammals, sea birds and fish. The archipelago is renowned as the traditional homeland of the Haida, whose monumental totem poles are widely considered to represent the height of artistic expression among the **Northwest Coast cultures**.

Historical Notes

Haida Gwaii – The islands have long been known as Haida Gwaii, "Island of the Haida." Ethnically distinct from other Northwest Coast tribes, the Haida are believed to have inhabited this archipelago for over 7,000 years. Traditionally they were superb craftsmen, seafarers and fearless warriors given to plunder.

Canadian Museum of Civilization, photo #255

Haida Village, Skidegate (1878)

Their villages were richly adorned with massive **totem poles** carved in the distinctive Haida style. Employing strong ovoid lines and animal motifs, the poles served different ceremonial and social purposes: house poles flanked doorways of clan longhouses; mortuary poles contained remains of important deceased villagers; memorial poles commemorated chiefs; heraldic poles recorded myths associated with a clan; and potlatch poles were raised during ceremonial feasts. The Haida were divided into two clans, Raven and Eagle, which were then subdivided into families. Kinship was traced matrilineally (through the mother's line).

European Contact – In 1774 Spanish navigator Juan Perez Hernandez was the first European to sight these islands while on an expedition north from California. In the 1780s and 90s, other Europeans sailed the Northwest Coast, bartering with natives for treasured sea otter pelts. George Dixon, a British trading captain, named the islands for **Queen Charlotte**, wife of King George III.
European contact introduced the Haida to iron tools that facilitated their wood carving. Larger, more elaborate totem poles were erected (some extant today) and more dugout canoes produced, allowing the Haida to trade and raid farther south. By the end of the 19C, however, Haida civilization was in decline: European diseases had decimated the population, and "pagan" potlatches and totem carving were halted as a result of missionary influence. By the early 20C most of the traditional villages were abandoned as the Haida relocated to Graham Island.

The Islands Today – Though located only 55km/34mi south of the Alaska Panhandle, the islands enjoy a temperate climate, thanks to the moderating effects of the warm Kuroshio Current. High annual rainfall and fertile soil support forests of Sitka spruce, hemlock and cedar. The southern third of the archipelago is a national park reserve that contains a World Heritage Site *(p 55)*. Year-round residents inhabit six communities on Graham Island and one on Moresby. Logging, fishing and tourism are major industries. A resurgence of Haida art and traditions, begun in the late 1950s, is evident today. Wood and argillite carvers, as well as silk-screen artists, are at work on Graham Island.

Practical Information

Getting There – **Air** service to Sandspit from Vancouver is provided daily by Canadian Regional Airlines ☎604-637-5660; to Masset daily from Prince Rupert by Harbour Air ☎250-627-1341. Car rentals (Budget Rent-a-Car) available at both airports ☎800-577-3228. Limosine service: Eagle Cab ☎250-559-4461. BC Ferries offers year-round **ferry** service between Prince Rupert and Skidegate *(departs Prince Rupert 11am; arrives Skidegate 5:30pm; one-way 7hrs; $22.25/person plus $84.75/vehicle; reservations strongly suggested; for schedules and fares contact BC Ferries, 1112 Fort St., Victoria, BC, V8V 4V2 ☎250-669-1211).* Another ferry service connects Skidegate to Alliford Bay *(departs year-round daily; $8.50/vehicle, $3/passenger round-trip).*

Accommodations and Visitor Information – A guide ($3.95) about area history, attractions, parks, campsites and accommodations can be obtained from Observer Publishing Co., PO Box 205, Queen Charlotte, BC, V0T 1S0 ☎250-559-4680. B&Bs, full-service hotels, self-contained cottages and campgrounds offer a range of lodgings. For outfitters, kayaking tours and cruises contact Parks Canada, Box 37, Queen Charlotte, BC V0T 1S0 ☎250-559-8818 or Queen Charlotte Islands Chamber of Commerce, Box 38, Masset, BC, V0T 1M0.

GRAHAM ISLAND   *Map p 53*
Largest of the Queen Charlottes, Graham Island is by far the most populous, home to roughly 4,600 inhabitants. The majority of residents live in the small logging, fishing and administrative towns and Haida villages on the east side of the island. A continuation of the mainland's Yellowhead Highway, Highway 16 runs in a north–south direction along the east side of the island, between Queen Charlotte City and Masset.

Queen Charlotte City – Pop. 1,200. This small town functions as the administrative heart of the islands. Catering to tourists from the mainland, many of whom arrive by ferry at nearby **Skidegate** (SKID-eh-get) **Landing,** the community centre consists of a line of hostelries, restaurants, gift shops and related services scattered along Skidegate Inlet.

★ **Queen Charlotte Islands Museum** – *1km/.6mi from ferry landing. Open Jun–Aug Mon–Fri 10am–5pm, weekends 1–5pm. Oct–Apr Mon & Wed–Fri 10am–noon & 1–5pm, Sat 1–5pm. May & Sept Mon–Fri 10am–noon & 1–5pm, Sat 1–5pm. $2.50.* ☎250-559-4643. Natural history exhibits and native artifacts, including argillite carvings and totem poles, are displayed in this museum.

An adjacent shed *(open Mon–Fri 9am–4:30pm; Haida Gwaii Watchmen* ☎250-559-8225*)* houses the stunning **Loo Taas**, an ornate 15m/50ft hand-crafted dugout canoe produced in traditional Haida style for Expo '86 in Vancouver.

Nearby, a reproduction longhouse serves as the offices of the Haida Gwaii Watchmen *(p 54)*.

Skidegate – Pop. 469. *1.5 km/.9mi from ferry.* Facing Rooney Bay, this long-time Haida community, locally called "the Village," serves as a political and cultural centre of the present-day Haida Nation. The offices of the Skidegate Band Council are housed in an impressive reproduction of a cedar **longhouse,** painted with Haida motifs. Internationally known Haida artist **Bill Reid** (b. 1920) created the elaborate frontal **totem pole★★**.

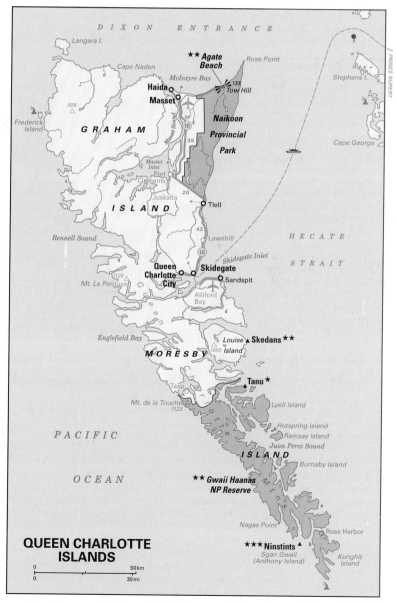

QUEEN CHARLOTTE ISLANDS

At the crossroads community of **Tlell**, the headquarters for Naikoon Provincial Park provides information on recreation and beach access *(open May–Sept daily 8am–5pm; ♿ ☎250-557-4390)*.

Masset – Pop. 1,476. Located on Masset Sound, near its entrance to the open waters of McIntyre Bay, this community is the islands' largest municipality, owing in part to the presence of the Canadian Forces station. The town attracts sports anglers and beachcombers interested in exploring the island's spectacular northern beaches.

Haida – Pop. 632. Adjacent to Masset, this town, also known as Old Massett, overlooks Masset Harbour. An important hub of Haida culture, the community boasts several totem poles erected in recent years. Note especially the one located in front of St. John's Anglican Church by acclaimed Haida artist **Robert Davidson**. The works of Haida artists are sold in several village craftshops, including one whose exterior is painted with Haida designs and fronted by a finely carved totem pole by Davidson's brother, **Reg Davidson**.

Naikoon Provincial Park – *9km/6mi east of Masset. Unpaved, but well-maintained beach access road. Open year-round. Park visitor centre in Tlell. Hiking, fishing, beachcombing. ⚠.* This 72,640ha/179,421 acre park encompasses the low-lying northeast corner of Graham Island, with broad beaches and dunes fronting both Hecate Strait (east) and Dixon Entrance (north). At **Agate Beach★★** *(25km/15mi from Masset; public parking and beach access available at campground)*, beachcombers congregate to search for the elusive stones that give the beach its name. To the north is a parking area for **Tow Hill** *(26km/16mi)*, a forested basalt outcropping that rises 133m/436ft above the beach. An easy trail *(round-trip 1hr)* leads to the summit, affording **views★** of the sweeping expanse of beach to the east and west. If weather permits, Alaska can be seen across the Dixon Entrance.

MORESBY ISLAND   *Map p 53*

Rimmed with inlets, fjords and smaller islands, the second largest island in the archipelago forms the bulk of the Gwaii Haanas National Park Reserve. The southern three-fifths of Moresby is encompassed by the park. The island's only town, **Sandspit**, traditionally a logging community, has become an access point for kayakers and cruise passengers beginning a tour of the reserve.

Moresby Island has been periodically logged since the mid-20C. Beginning in the mid-1970s, a ten-year conflict between logging interests on the one hand, and Haida and environmentalists on the other, ultimately resulted in the creation of the park reserve. Scars of clear-cutting are still visible.

Forming the backbone of the island, the forested slopes of the Queen Charlotte Mountains (maximum elevation about 1,000m/3,300ft) often drop directly into the sea. Abundant rainfall has nourished impressive **rain forests★★** of towering spruce and cedar, luxuriant ferns and mosses. Bald eagles are frequently sighted in this wilderness, as well as deer, otters and bears. Seals, sea lions, porpoises and orca whales can sometimes be seen. A variety of fish, including red snapper, salmon, halibut and cod, abound in island waters.

★★ Gwaii Haanas National Park Reserve – Deserving its Haida appellation, this wild and verdant 1,400sq km/541sq mi "Island of Wonder" nurtures a variety of wildlife and shelters the remains of a number of Haida villages. In 1988 the reserve was created to protect these natural and historical treasures.

Though many villages have reverted to forest, at several sites totem poles still stand and the remains of longhouses are clearly discernible. At several important sites, **Haida Gwaii Watchmen**, in residence at base camps during the summer, serve as caretakers and share their culture with visitors. *Limit of 12 visitors at base camps at any one time. Reservations required. User fees in effect in 1997. Contact the park office ☎250-559-8818.*

Access – *By sea or air only. Touring with an outfitter is strongly recommended since waters can be hazardous and weather is subject to sudden changes. For a list of licensed operators of kayaking and diving tours and cruises contact Gwaii Haanas, Box 37, Queen Charlotte, BC, V0T 1S0 ☎250-559-8818. Visitors are asked to register with Parks Canada or with the Haida Gwaii Watchmen office at Second Beach, Skidegate ☎250-559-8225.*

Cruise – *The following describes an outfitter cruise along the east and south coast of Moresby Island with disembarkation at sites described. Note: not all outfitters stop at these sites.* Situated on the east coast of Louise Island *(outside the national park* *reserve*), the remains of the village of **Skedans**★★ contain a few erect totem poles, the overgrown and decaying remains of toppled ones and the depressions of several longhouses. Located on the east coast of Tanu Island, the ancient site of **Tanu**★ also has the remains of fallen poles and longhouse depressions. Popular Hotspring Island offers three rock-lined natural **pools**★★ *(open for public bathing)* in a fine coastal setting.

Added to the World Heritage list in 1981, Sgan Gwaii (or Anthony Island) occupies a spectacular site at the edge of the Pacific. Believed to have been occupied for 1,500 years, celebrated **Ninstints**★★★ was one of the largest villages in the southern archipelago, with a population of 400. It faces a protected cove, and many of its totem poles have survived the effects of weathering. Today a score of poles are still upright, giving the visitor a rare taste of what Haida civilization was like in the 19C.

ROCKY MOUNTAIN PARKS★★★

Alberta, British Columbia
Map of Principal Sights p 2

Internationally renowned for its spectacular mountain scenery, this chain of four contiguous national parks is one of Canada's most popular natural attractions, beckoning some six million sightseers a year. These terrestial wonders, with their diverse topography, vegetation and wildlife, are the jewels of western Canada.
Modern parkways dissect the region's wide river valleys, and hiking trails crisscross the backcountry, allowing access to an awesomely rugged mountain world of soaring peaks, alpine lakes, waterfalls and glaciers.
The major parks in the Canadian Rockies are Banff, Jasper, Yoho and Kootenay National Parks and Mt. Robson Provincial Park. Situated next to each other in the southern part of the mountain range, they form one of the largest mountain parklands in the world, covering over 22,274sq km/8,600sq mi. The area contains other impressive provincial parks and reserves, notably **Mt. Assiniboine** *(between Banff and Kootenay; not accessible by road)*; and the **Kananaskis Country**, a preserve 90km/56mi southeast of Banff that includes three provincial parks. Waterton Lakes National Park *(p 89)* is situated apart from the other Rocky Mountain parks in the southwest corner of Alberta.

Geographical Notes

Canada's Rooftop – Frequently rising over 3,000m/10,000ft, the Canadian Rockies constitute the easternmost range of North America's **Western Cordillera** *(p 00)*. Beginning at the border with the US, the Canadian Rockies stretch roughly 1,550km/900mi through western Alberta and eastern British Columbia in a northwesterly direction. To the north these mountains are bounded by the broad plain of the Liard River; to the east by the Interior Plains; and to the west by the **Rocky Mountain Trench** *(map p 62)*, one of the longest continuous valleys in the world. The spine of the Rockies forms part of the **Continental Divide**.
Composed of sedimentary rock deposited by ancient seas some 1.5 billion years ago, the Rockies have a distinct layered appearance. They first began to uplift 120 to 70 million years ago because of the collision of tectonic plates. During the last Ice Age (75,000 to 11,000 years ago), glaciation carved the mountains into the terrain seen today: U-shaped valleys, glacially fed lakes, canyons, bowl-shaped cirques and hanging valleys with waterfalls and glaciers. Since the end of the Little Ice Age, or Cavell Advance, in 1870, the Rockies' glaciers have begun a significant retreat.

Fauna and Flora – Still largely wilderness, the Rockies are inhabited by a variety of animal and plant life. Even along roadways black bear, coyote, elk, moose, mule deer, mountain sheep, squirrels and chipmunks are often seen. More rarely, bighorn sheep and white-coated mountain goats may be sighted, and in more remote areas, grizzly bears and wolverines make an infrequent appearance.
Plant life varies greatly because of the drastic changes in elevation. Wildflowers are abundant throughout the vegetation zones. Their bloom follows the snowmelt up the mountainsides from late June through early August. Stands of Douglas fir, lodgepole pine, white spruce and quaking aspen often cover the valleys, gradually giving way to alpine fir, Lyall's larch and Engelmann spruce on the higher slopes. Just below the tree line lies a band of krummholz vegetation—trees dwarfed by the severe conditions. Above the tree line (normally 2,200m/7,200ft on south-facing slopes, lower on north-facing), only the low, ground-hugging vegetation of the alpine tundra survives: mosses, lichens, wildflowers and grasses.

Getting There

By Air – Flights daily on Canadian and US air carriers to Calgary International Airport (17km/11mi from downtown Calgary) ☎292-8418. Banff is 128km/79mi west of Calgary via Trans-Canada Highway and Jasper is 366km/227mi west of Edmonton via Hwy. 16. **Airport shuttle** from Calgary to the Banff/Lake Louise area: Brewster Tours ☎762-6767 *($33 and $38)* or Laidlaw Transportation ☎800-661-4946 (Canada/US) *($31)*. Car rentals (Avis, Hertz, Tilden and others) at Calgary Airport and in Banff.

By Bus and Train – Greyhound **bus** service from Calgary to Banff/Lake Louise area ☎265-9111. One-way fare $23.38. **VIA Rail** connects Jasper with Calgary, Edmonton and Vancouver ☎604-669-3050, or ☎800-561-3949 (US).

General Information

When to visit – The Rocky Mountain Parks are open year-round. The **summer season** is July to mid-September, peak season being July and August when daylight extends to 10pm. Visitors should be prepared for cold weather even in summer, since snowfall in August and September is not unusual. Throughout the **winter** most park roads are open. Parkways are regularly cleared, but snow tires are recommended from November to February.

Visitor Information – Each national park has a visitor centre, operated by Parks Canada, where schedules, pamphlets, maps and permits are available. A park pass *($8/day per vehicle, valid until noon the next day)* is required for entry to each national park (multiday and multipark passes available) and can be obtained from park visitor centres, entrance gates or campground kiosks. For information on Banff National Park, contact **Banff Visitor Centre**, 224 Banff Ave. in Banff ☎762-1550. At this location the Banff/Lake Louise Tourism Bureau ☎762-8421 provides information on area commercial facilities, services and activities. The **Lake Louise Visitor Centre** *(p 60)*, next to Samson Mall ☎522-3833 provides information on Banff National Park and on Lake Louise area facilities and activities. A visitor guide to the area, *Where*, features activities, lodging, dining, shopping and maps.

Accommodations – The Canadian Rockies are known for their **backcountry lodges**, generally accessible only by hiking, skiing or helicopter. These wilderness hostelries, most of them family-operated, range from rustic cabins to comfortable alpine chalets with fine food. Primitive cabins that rent for $8-24/night per person can be reserved through the Alpine Club of Canada, PO Box 2040, Canmore, AB, T0L 0M0 ☎678-3200. Numerous commercial campgrounds are located adjacent to the national parks. For information and reservations for campgrounds within the national parks, contact the individual park *(p 321)*. Hotels, resorts, motels, B&Bs, chalets and condominiums are available in the area. For information on lodging, contact the Banff/Lake Louise Tourism Bureau ☎762-8421.

Recreation – All four national parks offer **hiking, backpacking, bicycling, horseback riding, canoeing, fishing, swimming** (except Yoho) and **winter sports**. Banff and Jasper have facilities for **tennis** and **golf**; boat tours and canoe rental are also available; for details contact Parks Canada *(p 320)*.

The Banff Springs hotel boasts a 27-hole **golf** course. To reserve, contact the hotel ☎762-6801. Kananaskis Country Golf Course has two 18-hole courses; bookings should be made 60 days in advance ☎591-7272. Other area hotels offer golf. Outfitters specializing in **wilderness excursions** provide equipment, guides and transportation. Helicopter sightseeing excursions begin at $80. For more information contact the Banff/Lake Louise Tourism Bureau ☎762-8421.

The Banff/Lake Louise area offers **winter sports** from mid-November to mid-May including downhill skiing, heli-skiing, ice skating, dog sledding and cross-country skiing. There are three ski resorts: Lake Louise (☎800-258-7669, Canada/US); Sunshine Village (☎800-661-1676, Canada/US); Banff Mt. Norquay (☎762-4421). Amenities include mountain lodges, daycare, ski rentals and professional ski schools. Access is offered with the purchase of a tri-area lift pass ($140/3 days). There is a free shuttle bus between hotels in Banff and all three ski resorts.

The site of the 1988 Olympic nordic events has 70km/43mi of trails for the intermediate and advanced skier. Facilities include ski rentals, lessons and a day lodge. Canmore Nordic Centre, Box 1979, Canmore, AB, T0L 0M0 ☎678-2400.

Useful Numbers ☎

RCMP (Police)	762-2226
Alberta Motor Assn. (CAA affiliate)	762-2711
Park Weather Forecasts	762-2088
Trail Conditions (summer); **Avalanche Hazard** (winter)	762-1460

Historical Notes

From Wilderness to Watering Hole – Archaeological evidence indicates early nomads traversed this region 10,000 years ago. The Indians living here were overwhelmed, prior to European contact, by the **Stoney tribe**, who moved into the Rockies in the early 1700s. During the mid- to late 18C, the European **fur trade** burgeoned in the Rockies, and by the mid-19C, mountaineers and explorers had arrived.

By 1885 the **Canadian Pacific Railway** (CPR) line had crossed the Rockies and reached the West Coast. Recognizing the mountains' tourist potential, the CPR company convinced the government to establish "preserves"—the origin of the current parks. During the late 18C and early 19C, the railway company built a series of fine mountain chalets and hotels, a number of which are still in operation. By the 1920s all four Rocky Mountain national parks had been established. In 1985 the combined four parks were designated a World Heritage Site.

Lake Louise, Banff National Park

★★★ ① **BANFF NATIONAL PARK**   *Allow 2 days. Map p 63.*

Canada's first and most famous national park, Banff encompasses impressive peaks, scenic river valleys and the popular resort towns of Banff and Lake Louise. This preserve lies at the southeastern end of the chain of mountain parks.

Historical Notes – In the 1880s construction of the transcontinental railroad and discovery of natural hot springs on Sulphur Mountain elevated Banff to national prominence. The mineral springs were first noted by Sir James Hector in 1858, the first European to cross Kicking Horse Pass *(p 61)*, which became the rail route through the Rockies. In 1883 Siding 29 (sidings are switch tracks from the main track) was constructed near the hot springs. While prospecting for minerals, three rail workers discovered the springs and attempted to stake a claim. But the interests of the railroad magnates prevailed. Canadian Pacific president **George Stephen** felt the siding needed a romantic name, so he called it Banff after his native Banffshire, Scotland. The 26sq km/10sq mi Banff Hot Springs Reserve was established in 1885 by the government around Cave and Basin hot springs. In 1887 bathhouses were installed and a rail station built. The federal reserve was expanded to 673sq km/260sq mi and renamed Rocky Mountain Parks Reserve. In 1888 the CPR opened what was then the world's largest hotel, the **Banff Springs Hotel**. Built at the confluence of the Bow and Spray Rivers, this renowned "chateau" remains the dominant landmark.

Banff gradually became a social gathering place for wealthy travellers, who arrived by train. Not until 1915, after a bitter fight, were automobiles admitted to the park, a factor that made the area more accessible to the general public. The reserve was renamed Banff National Park in 1930. One of Canada's major resort areas today, Banff draws an international crowd.

★★ Banff Townsite and Area *Map below*

At the southeast end of the park system, this well-known resort town (pop. 5,688) on the Bow River sits at an elevation of 1,380m/4,534ft amid breathtaking mountains. Though bustling with visitors much of the year, the community maintains the charm of a small alpine town.

Tourists and residents alike celebrate artistic creations during the annual summer-long *(Jun–Aug)* **Banff Arts Festival**. A **visitor centre** *(224 Banff Ave; open mid-Jun– Labour Day daily 8am–8pm; early Sept–mid-Sept daily 8am–6pm; late Sept–May daily 9am–5pm; closed Dec 25; & ☎403-762-1550)* operated by Parks Canada provides information on park activities. *Information on commercial facilities and services is available at the centre.*

★ **Whyte Museum of the Canadian Rockies [A]** – *111 Bear St. Open mid-May–mid-Oct daily 10am–6pm. Rest of the year Tue–Sun 1–5pm (Thu 9pm). Closed national holidays. $3. & ☎403-762-2291.* Opened in 1968, this contemporary building houses a heritage gallery that traces the history of mountaineering and tourism in the Canadian Rockies, and art galleries featuring changing exhibits by regional and international artists. The museum sponsors tours of the on-site heritage homes *(summer Tue–Sun)*.

★ **Banff Park Museum [B]** – ☞ *93 Banff Ave. Open Jun–Labour Day daily 10am–6pm. Rest of the year daily 1–5pm. Closed Jan 1, Dec 25. $2.25. ☎403-762-1558.* Constructed in the trestle-like "railway pagoda" style of the turn of the century, this historic museum maintains its 1905 appearance, both inside and out. Glass cases display a variety of minerals and taxidermied animals of the Rocky Mountains. Among the collections is a series of prints by renowned contemporary wildlife artist **Robert Bateman**.

★ **Cascade Gardens [C]** – *At the south end of Banff Ave., across Bow River Bridge. Open daily year-round.* These terraced gardens, with their rock-lined pools and cascades, provide an excellent **view★** of **Cascade Mountain**, the 2,998m/9,836ft peak that towers above the north end of Banff Avenue. The stone Gothic Revival building at the centre of the grounds houses the park administration offices.

★ **Luxton Museum** – *1 Birch Ave., on the southeastern bank of the Bow River. Open Apr–Oct daily 9am–9pm. $5. & ☎403-762-2388.* A replica of a log fur-trading fort, this museum displays native artifacts and life-size dioramas depicting aspects of Plains Indian life. Formerly owned by the Glenbow Museum *(p 107)* of Calgary, the Luxton is now operated by the Buffalo Nations Cultural Society.

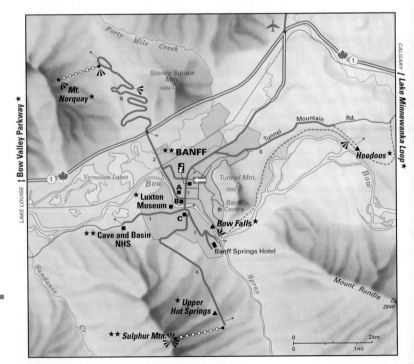

★ **Bow Falls** – At the foot of the Banff Springs Hotel, the Bow River tumbles over a wide, low lip, just before flowing into the Spray River.

★★ **Cave and Basin National Historic Site** – ☝ *Open Jun–Aug daily 9am–6pm. Rest of the year daily 9:30am–5pm. Closed Jan 1, Dec 25.* ✗ *(summer)* ⅙ ☎*403-762-1557.* The Canadian park system began at this site. The arched stone building, restored to its 1914 appearance, surrounds an open-air swimming pool *(not open for swimming)* of hot springs water (average temperatures 30–35°C/86–95°F). The complex includes the natural cave pool fed by a hot spring, and a museum tracing the more than 100-year history of the Canadian parks system.

★★ **Sulphur Mountain** – *3.5km/2.2mi from downtown. Access by gondola (8-10min ascent) Jan–mid-Nov daily, hours vary. $9.95.* ✗⅙ ☎*403-762-5438.* The 2,285m/7,500ft summit allows a 360° **panorama**★★★ of the Bow Valley, Banff and the turreted Banff Springs Hotel (east and north); the Spray Valley (southeast); Mt. Rundle and the more distant Fairholm Range and Lake Minnewanka (northeast); Mt. Norquay (north), and the Sundance Range (southwest). Bighorn sheep frequently browse along the trails here.

★ **Upper Hot Springs** – *3.5km/2.2mi from downtown. Open mid-Jun–mid-Sept daily 8am–11pm. Rest of the year Sun–Thu 10am–10pm, Fri–Sat 10am–11pm. $5.* ☎*403-762-1515.* Discovered a year after the Cave and Basin hot springs, the mineral waters (average temperature 38°C/100°F) now feed a large public pool.

★ **Hoodoos** – These naturally sculpted pillars of cemented rock and gravel can be viewed from a scenic nature trail above Bow River *(1km/.6mi; trailhead off Tunnel Mountain Rd.).*

★ **Lake Minnewanka Loop** – *Begins 4km/2.4mi from downtown.* Along this 16km/10mi drive, three lakes serve as natural water-sports playgrounds: Johnson; Two Jack; and Minnewanka, a dammed reservoir that is Banff Park's largest waterbody. Tour boats offer cruises down this lake to Devil's Gap *(depart mid-May–mid-Jun daily 10:30am, 12:30, 3 & 5pm; late Jun–Labour Day additional departure 7pm; rest of Sept daily 10:30am, 12:30 & 3pm; $22; Minnewanka Tours* ☎*403-762-3473).* Included on the drive is **Bankhead**, an abandoned early-20C coal-mining operation. An interpretive park trail explains the history of the site.

★ **Mt. Norquay** – *8km/5mi from downtown. Access by chair lift Dec–mid-Apr daily 9am–4pm. $33. Daily bus service from many Banff hotels.* ✗⅙ ☎*403-762-4421.* A well-graded switchback road climbs Stoney Squaw Mountain toward Mt. Norquay's chair lift, providing increasingly better **views** south and east over Bow Valley and of the townsite of Banff, backdropped by **Mt. Rundle**, which is shaped like a tilted writing desk.

★ **Bow Valley Parkway to Lake Louise (Highway 1A)**
48km/30mi. Begins 5.5km/3.5mi west of town. Map pp 62-63.
An alternative to the faster-paced Trans-Canada Highway, this scenic parkway was the original 1920s road connecting Banff and Lake Louise. Sightings of elk, deer, moose and coyote are not uncommon along the road. Curving through evergreen forests along the north bank of the Bow River, the route offers **views**★ of the Sawback Range to the northeast—in particular, crenellated Castle Mountain—and of the Great Divide peaks to the southwest. Frequent lookouts feature interpretation of regional geology, flora and fauna. At **Johnston Canyon**★★ *(17km/11mi)*, a paved, often cantilevered, pathway over the narrow limestone canyon leads to **lower falls**★★ *(about 1km/.6mi)* and **upper falls**★★ *(about 1.6km/1mi).* The Inkpots, a collection of cold springs, are located beyond the upper falls *(6km/4mi).*
At Castle Junction Highway 93 leads west from Bow Valley Parkway to Kootenay National Park (p 68).

★★★ **Lake Louise and Area**   *Map p 60*
Smaller and less congested than Banff, this townsite and its environs in the park's west-central section encompass massive, glaciated peaks and pristine lakes, most notably the legendary Lake Louise. Called "lake of little fishes" by the Stoney tribe, Lake Louise was first viewed by a non-native in 1882. Taken there by a Stoney guide, **Tom Wilson**, a packer for railway survey crews, named the waterbody Emerald Lake because of its brilliant blue-green colour. Two years later the lake was renamed for Queen Victoria's daughter, Princess Louise Caroline Alberta. By 1890 a small guest chalet had been built on the shore. By the early 1900s a road had been built to the lake, a larger chalet constructed, and guests

were flocking there. In 1925 the CPR completed the present hotel, **Château Lake Louise**, which rises elegantly by the lake.

Lake Louise Village – A small resort crossroads with several shops, hotels and visitor facilities, the village is located just off the Trans-Canada Highway. A park **visitor centre** *(open Jun 1–mid-Jun daily 8am–6pm; late Jun–Labour Day daily 8am–8pm; rest of the year hours vary; closed Jan 1, Dec 25 & 26; & ☎403-522-3833)* features excellent **displays** on the natural history of the area, including the Burgess Shale *(p 61)*, and provides information about drives, hikes and natural attractions.

★★★ **Lake Louise** – *4km/2.5mi from village.* Set in a hanging valley backdropped by the majestic mountains of the Continental Divide, this beautiful glacier-fed lake, with the stately chateau near its shore, remains one of the most visited and photographed sites in the Canadian Rockies.

Visible at the far end, the **Victoria Glacier** once stretched to the site of the chateau. The 2km/1.2mi long, .5km/.3mi wide tarn (maximum depth 75m/246ft) was created when this glacier retreated, leaving enough morainal debris to serve as a dam. The chateau is actually built on the moraine. Fed by glacial meltwater draining off the surrounding peaks, the lake (maximum temperature 4°C/40°F)

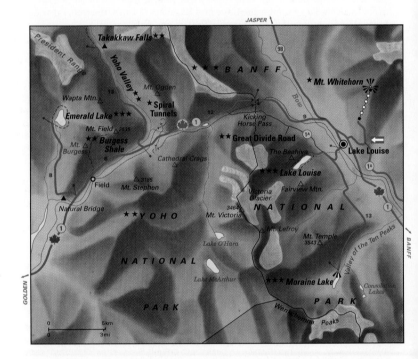

changes colour with light conditions and as the summer progresses. Known as glacial flour, fine powdery silt suspended in the water refracts the green rays of the spectrum and emits hues ranging from bluish-green to emerald.

The far end of the lake is dominated by **Mt. Victoria** (3,464m/11,362ft). To the left of Victoria stands the rocky face of **Fairview Mountain** (2,744m/9,000ft), and to the right of Victoria rises the distinctive rounded shape of **The Beehive**. A 3km/1.8mi trail circles the lake. Additional trails ascend into the backcountry. Two popular day hikes lead to teahouses: one at Lake Agnes *(3.5km/2.2mi from the lake)* and another at the Plain of Six Glaciers *(5.5km/3.3mi from the lake)*. *Details on hikes available at the chateau and at park visitor centres.*

★★★ **Moraine Lake** – *13km/8mi from village.* Smaller and less visited than Lake Louise, Moraine Lake nonetheless occupies a splendid **site**★★ below the sheer walls of the Wenkchemna peaks.

Moraine Lake Road climbs above Bow Valley, offering an impressive **view**★★, first of one of the park's highest peaks—ice-capped **Mt. Temple** (3,543m/11,621ft)—and then of the glaciated **Wenkchemna** or **Ten Peaks**. A short walk leads up the rock pile damming the north end of the lake, providing the best **view**★ of the surroundings.

The pile is believed to be the result of a rock slide from the adjacent pinnacle of rock called the Tower of Babel. Other trails lead around the lake and to nearby backcountry lakes and valleys.

★ **Mt. Whitehorn** – *Access by gondola (12min ascent) Jun–Sept daily 8am–8:15pm. $9.* ✗ ☎403-522-3555. From the top of the Friendly Giant gondola lift, a **panorama**★★ of Bow Valley is obtained, with the Wenkchemna peaks and Mt. Temple filling the horizon. To the west Lake Louise can be seen cupped below the Victoria Glacier.

★★ Great Divide Road (Highway 1A) *Map p 60*
14km/8mi from Lake Louise Village to western junction with Trans-Can Hwy.; access 3km/1.8km west of the village.

Weaving through subalpine stands of fir, spruce and pine, this highway parallels the southwest side of the Trans-Canada Highway. An arch across the road *(10km/ 6mi from the village)* marks **Kicking Horse Pass** (1,625m/5,330ft), a point on the Great Divide, as well as the boundary between Alberta and British Columbia and between Banff and Yoho National Parks. The name of the pass derives from an incident here that befell geologist **James Hector** of the Palliser Expedition (1857-1860). Accidentally kicked by his horse, he became unconscious and, mistaken for dead, was almost buried by his men.

★★ ② YOHO NATIONAL PARK *1/2 day not including Burgess Shale. Map p 60.*

Smallest and most compact of the parks, Yoho (a native word meaning "awe") is a place of raging rivers and waterfalls. The preserve enjoys international renown as the site of the Burgess Shale, decidedly one of the most important fossil beds ever discovered.

The Trans-Canada Highway cuts diagonally through the park. Situated in the centre of Yoho in the valley of the roaring Kicking Horse River, the small town of **Field** serves as a park hub. The **visitor centre** features displays and videotapes on the Burgess Shale and other park attractions *(open May–Sept daily 9am–5pm; rest of the year daily 9am–4pm;* ♿ ☎250-343-6783*).*

★ **Spiral Tunnels** – In the shape of an elongated figure eight, these tunnels allowed trains to make the treacherously steep, 4.5 percent descent down "The Big Hill" leading into the valley of the Kicking Horse River. A lookout about 9km/6mi beyond the northeast entrance to Yoho has interpretive signs tracing the history of the CPR's upper and lower tunnels. The opening of the lower tunnel in Mt. Ogden can be seen from this vantage point.

★★ **Yoho Valley** – *Access road of 13km/8mi with switchbacks; no trailers allowed.* Situated between Mt. Field and Mt. Ogden, lovely Yoho Valley is accessed by a climbing road that includes a lookout above the confluence of Yoho and Kicking Horse Rivers. Near the road's end Yoho Peak and Glacier can be seen straight ahead, with Takakkaw Falls to the right.

★★ **Takakkaw Falls** – One of the highest waterfalls on the continent, this torrent of meltwalter from the Daly Glacier cascades in two stages for a combined total of 254m/833ft to join the Yoho River. A short paved walk leads to the base of the falls, which are visible from the road.

★★ **Burgess Shale** – *Because of the fragile nature of the sites, the public can visit by guided hike only. 4km/2.5mi round-trip to Mt. Stephen's trilobite beds; 20km/12mi round-trip to Burgess Shale. Note: both are strenuous all-day hikes on steep trails. Jul-Sept by reservation only. Space is very limited. Contact the park in advance* ☎250-343-6783. *Instead of hiking, visitors may choose to view Burgess Shale exhibits at, for example, Field and Lake Louise visitor centres.* Located on **Mt. Field** (2,635m/8,6432ft), the Burgess Shale contains evidence of multicellular life found in the oceans 515 million years ago *(p 55)*. Because of its excellent fossil preservation, the Burgess Shale enjoys world renown among professional paleontologists and amateur enthusiasts and is considered the richest Cambrian site in the world.

In 1886 an employee of the Canadian Pacific Railway discovered rich trilobite beds on **Mt. Stephen** (3,185m/10,447ft). In 1909 American paleontologist **Charles Walcott** found unique fossils of soft-bodied animals on loose pieces of shale on Mt. Field. He later discovered a rich fossil-bearing shale layer higher up the slope and spent five summers quarrying this layer. The Royal Ontario Museum is currently conducting research on the Burgess Shale.

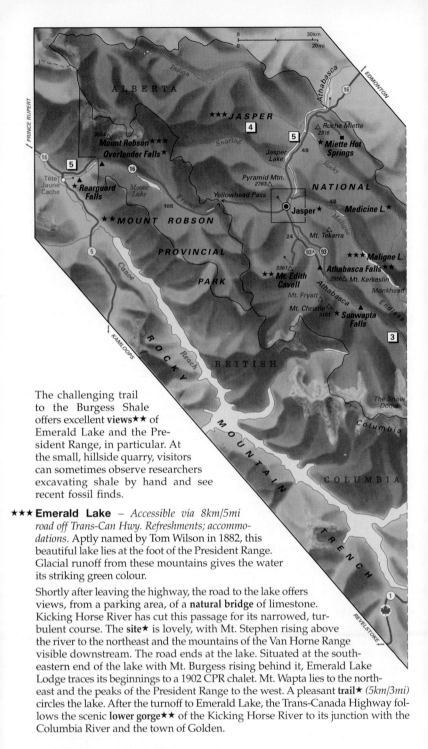

The challenging trail to the Burgess Shale offers excellent **views★★** of Emerald Lake and the President Range, in particular. At the small, hillside quarry, visitors can sometimes observe researchers excavating shale by hand and see recent fossil finds.

★★★ Emerald Lake – *Accessible via 8km/5mi road off Trans-Can Hwy. Refreshments; accommodations.* Aptly named by Tom Wilson in 1882, this beautiful lake lies at the foot of the President Range. Glacial runoff from these mountains gives the water its striking green colour.

Shortly after leaving the highway, the road to the lake offers views, from a parking area, of a **natural bridge** of limestone. Kicking Horse River has cut this passage for its narrowed, turbulent course. The **site★** is lovely, with Mt. Stephen rising above the river to the northeast and the mountains of the Van Horne Range visible downstream. The road ends at the lake. Situated at the southeastern end of the lake with Mt. Burgess rising behind it, Emerald Lake Lodge traces its beginnings to a 1902 CPR chalet. Mt. Wapta lies to the northeast and the peaks of the President Range to the west. A pleasant **trail★** *(5km/3mi)* circles the lake. After the turnoff to Emerald Lake, the Trans-Canada Highway follows the scenic **lower gorge★★** of the Kicking Horse River to its junction with the Columbia River and the town of Golden.

★★★ ③ ICEFIELDS PARKWAY
Allow 1 day. 233km/145mi (Trans-Can Hwy. junction to Jasper). Map above.

Designed expressly to dramatize the incredible landscape, this unequalled parkway (Highway 93) runs below the highest mountains in the Canadian Rockies. Following the valleys of five rivers, the road angles northwesterly along the eastern flank of the Continental Divide, connecting Banff and Jasper Parks. Glaciers, lakes and waterfalls are abundant along the route, as are interpretive lookouts that explain the natural and human history of the area. From its southern terminus the parkway quickly climbs, with fine views of the Waputik Range.

★ **Hector Lake** – *16km/10mi.* Named for James Hector *(p 61)*, the lake is set below the Waputik Range (south), Mt. Hector (east) and Bow Peak (north).

★★ **Crowfoot Glacier** – *33km/20mi.* After rounding Bow Peak the parkway reaches a viewpoint for this glacier spread across the lower rock plateaus of Crowfoot Mountain. Now in retreat, the glacier has lost some of the ice that made it resemble a crow's foot.

★★ **Bow Lake** – *37km/23mi.* Directly by the road, this lovely lake is best seen from the lookout leading to historic, red-roofed Num-ti-jah Lodge, visible on the north shore of the lake. The Bow Glacier hangs above the lake between Portal and St. Nicholas Peaks.

Passing through a green meadowland of birch and willow, the parkway reaches Bow Summit (2,069m/6,786ft), the highest pass on the route.

★★★ **Peyto Lake** – *40km/25mi to spur road; park in upper lot where short trail leads to a viewpoint.* The striking turquoise waters of this lake are fed by Peyto Glacier. Both lake and glacier are named for turn-of-the-century guide, Bill Peyto. **Mistaya Mountain** rises sheerly from the opposite side of the lake, with Peyto Peak on its left. The Mistaya River Valley stretches north beyond the lake.

The road descends to the valley and passes a series of lakes. At **Upper Waterfowl Lake** lookout *(56km/35mi),*

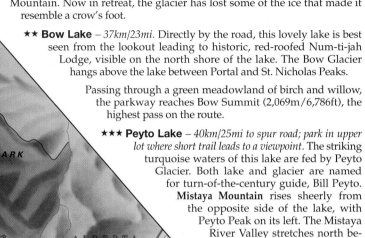

there is a fine **view★** of the formidable stone expanse of the Great Divide peaks, especially towering Howse Peak (3,290m/10,791ft) and pyramidal Mt. Chephren (3,307m/10,847ft).

★ **Mistaya Canyon** – *72km/45mi to spur road for parking; follow trail into valley for 400m/.3mi.* This narrow gorge, cut by the Mistaya River, is notable for its smooth, sculpted limestone walls.

Continuing northward, the parkway passes Mt. Murchison (3,337m/10,945ft), which rises to the east, and the steep cliffs of Mt. Wilson (3,261m/10,696ft), looming above the road. Both are part of the **Castle Mountain Syncline**, a downfold stratum that runs from Castle Mountain, outside Banff, to Mt. Kerkeslin, near Jasper. After the road descends into the valley of the North Saskatchewan River, a lookout *(76km/47mi; trail through trees)* affords a **view** of the Howse River Valley. David Thompson travelled this corridor in 1807 on his way to set up the first trading post west of the mountains, near present-day Invermere.

Very quickly the parkway reaches its junction with Highway 11—the David Thompson Highway *(restaurant, services)*. The parkway then runs below the massive cliffs of Mt. Wilson (to the east), with views first of Survey Peak and Mt. Erasmus to the west and then the layer-cake facade of **Mt. Amery**.

At 105km/65mi the road hugs the base of Cirrus Mountain, the sheer cliffs of which are known as the **Weeping Wall** because streams cascade down them. Soon thereafter the parkway rounds what is called the "big bend" and climbs quickly above the valley where a lookout allows a spectacular **view★★** of the North Saskatchewan Valley. A second, almost adjacent, lookout directly faces the filmy spray of **Bridal Veil Falls**.

★★ **Parker Ridge** – *118km/73mi.* This ridgetop affords a magnificent **view★★★** of glaciated backcountry, particularly the **Saskatchewan Glacier**, one of the major outlet glaciers of the Columbia Icefield *(below)*. A switchback trail *(2.4km/1.5mi)* ascends through dwarf, subalpine forest and then through treeless tundra *(roundtrip 1.5hrs)*, carpeted in summer with dwarf alpine flowers.

At 122km/76mi the parkway crosses Sunwapta Pass (2,035m/6,675ft) to enter Jasper National Park, with views ahead of Mt. Athabasca and other peaks surrounding the Columbia Icefield.

★★★ **Athabasca Glacier** – *127km/79mi.* This glacier is part of the vast **Columbia Icefield**, the largest subpolar icefield on the continent. The 325sq km/126sq mi Columbia lies along the Alberta/British Columbia boundary. The Athabasca and four other major outlet glaciers (Saskatchewan, Dome, Stutfield and Columbia), as well as smaller ones, flow off its eastern edge. Meltwater from these glaciers eventually feeds into three oceans: the Atlantic, Pacific and Arctic.

Situated along the high, remote tops of the Rockies at an altitude of over 3,000m/10,000ft, the icefield was apparently unknown until 1898, when a mountaineering expedition from Britain's Royal Geographical Society discovered and named it. From the parking lot of the Columbia Icefield Chalet, a **view★★★** encompasses the Athabasca, Kitchener and Dome Glaciers. Nearby, the Columbia Icefield Information Bureau serves as the southern **visitor centre** *(open mid-Jun–Labour Day daily 9am–6pm; rest of the year daily 9am–4pm;* & ☎*403-852-7030)* for Jasper National Park and functions as a small museum, with displays and an audio-visual presentation on glaciology.

Across the parkway is Sunwapta Lake, fed by the Athabasca Glacier. From the parking area a short trail ascends to the toe of the glacier. In recent decades the glacier has retreated dramatically. The progress of its recession is marked on signposts along the parking-lot access road and the trail.

★★ **SnoCoach Tours on the Glacier** – *Note: expect long waiting lines from 11am-2:30pm in Jul & Aug. Depart from Icefield Centre May–mid-Oct daily 9am–5pm. $21.50. Brewster Tours* ☎*403-762-6735.* These specially designed ultra-terrain vehicles travel a short distance onto the upper end of the Athabasca Glacier and allow passengers to get off to briefly experience the glacial surface.

★ **Sunwapta Falls** – *176km/109mi; 400m/.3mi spur road to parking.* The Sunwapta River circles a small island, plunges over a cliff, makes a sharp turn around an ancient glacial moraine, and enters a deep limestone canyon.

Soon after the falls, the parkway enters the valley of the mighty **Athabasca River** and follows it to Jasper. This impressive valley is dominated on the west by the distinctive off-centre pyramidal shape of **Mt. Christie** (3,103m/10,180ft) and the three pinnacles of the Mt. Fryatt massif (3,361m/11,024ft). To the northwest the distant snow-capped summit of Mt. Edith Cavell (*below*) slowly assumes prominence, while **Mt. Kerkeslin** (2,956m/9,696ft), the final peak of the Castle Mountain Syncline, towers over the parkway to the east.

★★**Athabasca Falls** – *199km/123mi; turn left on Rte 93A for 400m/.3mi.* The silt-laden waters of the Athabasca River roar over a lip of quartzite and down a canyon smoothed by the force of the rushing waters. Backdropping the cataract, Mt. Kerkeslin, slightly reddish from quartzite, has the same layering as the rock by the falls.

As the parkway approaches Jasper townsite, the Whistlers can be seen to the west. Straight ahead rises Pyramid Mountain, and to the east, the pinnacled peak of **Mt. Tekarra**. At dusk elk are frequently spotted grazing alongside the parkway near the Wapiti Campground.

★★★ ④ **JASPER NATIONAL PARK**   *Allow 2 days. Map p 62.*

The largest and northernmost of the four Rocky Mountain Parks, Jasper National Park covers 10,878sq km/4,200sq mi, most of which is remote wilderness. In addition to spectacular terrain, Jasper also offers frequent opportunities to view the varied wildlife.

★ **Jasper Townsite and Area**   *Map p 66*

This pleasant town sits in the valley of the Athabasca River near its confluence with the Miette River. Small and very beautiful lakes—**Pyramid**, **Patricia**, **Annette**, **Edith** and **Beauvert**, site of the well-known **Jasper Park Lodge**—surround the townsite. The peaks of nearby mountains are visible on the horizon, most notably Mt. Edith Cavell to the south and rugged **Pyramid Mountain** (2,763m/9,063ft) to the north from the townsite.

Historical Notes – In the early 19C area Indians saw increased European presence as fur traders used the Athabasca River and Pass as a route through the Rockies. In 1801 Jasper Hawes, a clerk for the North West Company, established a supply depot on Brule Lake, 35km/22mi north of the present townsite. The depot became known as "Jasper House," and ultimately gave the current townsite its name. In the 1860s the **Overlanders**, a party of 125 gold seekers, passed through the region on their way to the goldfields of the Cariboo Mountains (*p 40*). Except for mountaineers and trappers, the area had few inhabitants until the early 20C. In 1907 Jasper Forest Park, as it was then called, was created in anticipation of completion of the Grand Trunk Pacific Railway across the Yellowhead Pass. The townsite grew from a railroad construction camp set up in 1911. Situated at the junction of the Yellowhead Highway and the Icefields Parkway, Jasper is the focal point of activity for the park and contains a park **visitor centre** (*Connaught Dr. & Miette Ave.; open mid-Jun–Labour Day daily 8:30am–7pm; rest of the year daily 9am–5pm; closed Dec 25;* ☎403-852-6176).

★★**The Whistlers** – *Access by tramway (8min ascent) Apr–May daily 9am–5pm. Jun–Aug daily 7:30am–10pm. Sept-Oct daily 9am–5pm. $12.15.* ☎403-852-3093. The tramway ascends more than 900m/3,000ft to the terminal perched on the ridge of these 2,470m/8,102ft peaks named for the sound made by resident marmots. The **panorama★★★** from this elevation includes the townsite, the lake-dotted Athabasca Valley and the Colin Range to the northeast, and Mt. Yellowhead and the Victoria Cross Ranges to the northwest. If visibility permits, the great white pyramid of Mt. Robson (*p 67*) can be spotted beyond them.
A trail climbs an additional 180m/600ft to the treeless ridgetop (*round-trip 1.5hrs*), offering a **view** to the south of Mts. Edith Cavell and Kerkeslin.

★★**Mt. Edith Cavell** – *24km/15mi from townsite. Access via Icefields Pky. to junction with 93A, then Mt. Edith Cavell Rd.* Known as the queen of the range, this massif (3,368m/11,047ft) was named for an English nurse executed by the Germans in World War I for assisting Allied prisoners of war.
The narrow, twisting access road climbs steeply into the high country, paralleling the dramatic Astoria River Valley. By walking a short distance to **Cavell Lake** from the parking area for the Tonquin Valley Trail (*26km/17mi*), visitors can obtain a good **view** of the mountain. The lake's bright-green waters feed from the fast-receding, but lovely **Angel Glacier**, which is located on the mountain. At the end of the road (*2km/1.2mi drive*), the trailhead is reached for the Path of the Glacier Trail (*round-trip 40min*), which follows the toe of this ice river.

★★★ Maligne Valley

5hrs, including boat trip. 96km/60mi round-trip by Hwy. 16 and Maligne Lake Rd. Maps p 62 and at right.

This valley cradles a magnificent lake and canyon, both also named Maligne (Ma-LEEN), which can mean malignant or injurious in French. Despite its name, the valley is among the most beautiful in the Rockies.

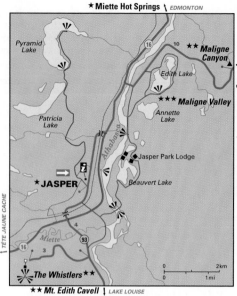

★★ **Maligne Canyon** – *7km/ 4mi from Rte. 93 junction.* The most spectacular of the Rocky Mountain gorges, this great slit carved in limestone reaches depths of 50m/164ft, while spanning widths of less than 3m/10ft in some places. A paved trail *(round-trip 30min)* follows the top of the canyon, descending with the drop of the Maligne River. Bridges crossing the canyon serve as viewpoints.

★ **Medicine Lake** – *22km/14mi.* The Colin Range to the north and the Maligne Range to the south hem in this lovely lake. From its highest levels during the snowmelt of early summer, the waterbody gradually shrinks as the season progresses, sometimes becoming only mud flats. Intriguingly the lake has no surface outlet, draining instead through sink holes in the limestone bedrock and resurfacing in the waters of the Maligne River. The road follows the edge of the lake for 8km/5mi with several advantageous viewpoints.

★★★ **Maligne Lake** – *For boat rentals, hiking trips, white-water rafting contact Maligne Tours ☎403-852-3370 or Maligne Lake Book Store in Jasper Park Lodge ☎403-852-4779.* At 23km/14mi long Maligne is the largest natural lake in the Rockies and one of the most spectacular.

In 1875 surveyor Henry MacLeod was the first European to see the lake, naming it "Sore-foot." The lake and the peaks that rise from it were initially explored in detail in 1908 by an expedition led by Mary Schaffer, a middle-aged widow from Philadelphia who spent her summers in the Rockies.

Spirit Island, Maligne Lake

The road ends at the northern shore of this glacial lake. As seen from the road, the twin peaks of **Mts. Unwin** (3,300m/10,824ft) and **Charlton** (3,260m/10,693ft) on the southwest side are most prominent. However these peaks and the others at the southern end can be appreciated only by boating down the lake.

★★★ **Boat Trip** – *Departs from chalet at Maligne Lake mid-May–mid-Oct daily 10am–5pm. Round-trip 1hr 30min. $29. ♿ Maligne Tours* ☎403-852-3370. As the boat proceeds down the lake, the water colour changes from green to deep turquoise because of the presence of suspended glacial silt. After passing Samson Narrows the boat stops so passengers can disembark near tiny **Spirit Island** to enjoy the **view★★★** of the half-dozen glaciated peaks framing the south end of the lake.

★★ ⑤ THE YELLOWHEAD HIGHWAY   *Map p 62*

Also designated Highway 16, this major thoroughfare runs east-west through Jasper and Mt. Robson Parks and continues westward to the Pacific at Prince Rupert *(p 69)*. The highway was named for a fair-haired Iroquois fur trader known as Tête Jaune ("yellow head") who, in the 1820s, set up a cache in the small town now named in his honour.

★★ From Jasper to Miette Hot Springs   *Allow 4hrs. 49km/31mi.*

Heading eastward from Jasper the highway enters, and then follows, the broad valley of the Athabasca River. The craggy pinnacles of the Colin Range are soon silhouetted against the eastern horizon.

For the remaining 40km/25mi, the highway offers breathtaking **views★★★** of the braided course of the river and the peaks surrounding it. The road passes between **Talbot Lake** (east) and **Jasper Lake**, which is backdropped by the **De Smet Range**. At the Disaster Point **animal lick★**, small pools on the east side of the road attract mountain sheep and the less frequently sighted white-coated mountain goats. The close proximity of the highway has led to animals being hit by cars; hence the point's name. From approximately this location on, the drive holds fine views of **Roche Miette** (2,316m/7,599ft).

★ **Miette Hot Springs** – *42km/26mi to junction with Miette Hot Springs Rd. Open mid-May–mid-Jun daily 10:30am–9pm. Late Jun–Labour Day daily 8:30am–10:30pm. Rest of Sept daily 10:30am–9pm. $4. ♿* ☎403-866-3939. A road winds 18km/11mi through a pleasant green gorge to the park's hot springs bathhouse. The springs are high in calcium and the hottest in the Canadian Rockies (maximum temperature 54°C/129°F). The natural **setting★★** for the springs, with mountains hovering close by, makes this the most spectacular location among all the mountain parks' bathhouses.

After this junction, the highway continues east another 7km/4mi to the east gate of Jasper National Park.

★ From Jasper to Rearguard Falls   *Allow 5hrs. 100km/62mi.*

West of Jasper, Highway 16 follows the narrowing valley of the Miette River. At **Yellowhead Pass**—the lowest pass on the Continental Divide, and also the boundary between British Columbia and Alberta—the road leaves Jasper National Park *(24km/15mi)* and enters Mt. Robson Provincial Park.

★★ **Mt. Robson Provincial Park** – *East boundary at 24km/15mi. Open year-round.* ⛺♿ ☎250-566-4325. Encompassing magnificent mountain terrain, this 217,200ha/536,484 acre park is named for its greatest attraction: 3,954m/12,972ft **Mt. Robson★★★**, the highest peak in the Canadian Rockies.

After entering the park Route 16 picks up the course of the Fraser River, skirting Yellowhead Lake and larger Moose Lake. At **Overlander Falls★** *(88km/55mi; accessible by trail, round-trip 30min)*, the blue-green Fraser River drops off a wide ledge, and then narrows as it enters a canyon. Just beyond the falls, the park **visitor centre**, backdropped by Mt. Robson, displays natural history exhibits on the area *(open mid-May–mid-Jun daily 8am–5pm; late Jun–Labour Day daily 8am–8pm; early Sept–mid-Oct daily 8am–5pm; ♿* ☎250-566-9174).

★ **Rearguard Falls** – *Allow 40min round-trip. 3.2km/2mi walk.* Part of a small provincial park by the same name, these wide, low falls on the Fraser River are particularly noted as a place where chinook salmon can be seen leaping upstream during the August spawning season. The salmon have made a 1,200km/744mi journey inland, from the Fraser outlet on the Pacific to this point.

The crossroads town of Tête Jaune Cache is 5km/3mi farther west.

★★ ⑥ KOOTENAY NATIONAL PARK *Map p 63*

This park was formed in 1920 as a result of the federal government's completion of the Banff-Windermere Highway (Route 93)—which would provide an important commercial link between southwestern Alberta and the Columbia Valley—in exchange for land bordering the road. Extending 8km/5mi from both sides of the highway, the strip of land became Canada's tenth national park.

From Castle Junction to Radium Hot Springs
Allow 3hrs. 105km/65mi by Rte. 93.

This picturesque **route★★** through Kootenay National Park leaves the Trans-Canada Highway at Castle Junction and climbs steeply to the summit of **Vermilion Pass** (1,650m/5,412ft). The pass marks the Great Divide and coincides with the borders of Banff and Kootenay National Parks and the provincial boundaries between Alberta and British Columbia.

★ **Marble Canyon** – *17km/11mi from junction.* The rushing waters of Tokumm Creek charge through this narrow limestone gorge on their way to meet the Vermilion River. The **visitor centre** *(open mid-Jun–Labour Day Sun–Thu 9am–4pm, Fri–Sat 8am–8pm; park fee $8/per vehicle; &)* for the park's north entrance is located here. Interpretive signs explain the geology of white-dolomite outcroppings, a natural bridge and other features along a trail *(1.6km/1mi, round-trip 30min)* that leads through the canyon.

Paint Pots – *20km/12mi from junction; trail of 1.2km/.7mi.* Of historic interest, this area contains pools of ochre clay first used as body paint and dyes by Indians, and later mined by Europeans. The three cold **mineral springs★** near the end of the trail were considered places of spiritual power by native tribes.

The highway follows the Vermilion River to its confluence with the Kootenay. At 89km/55mi a lookout provides a sweeping **view★** of the wide, wooded **Kootenay Valley** and the **Mitchell Range** flanking its west side. After topping Sinclair Pass (1,486m/4,874ft) the road follows Sinclair Creek's tumbling descent through **Sinclair Valley★**, passing between the precipitous red cliffs called the **Iron Gates**, because of the iron oxides that give them their colour.

★ **Radium Hot Springs** – *103km/64mi.* The waters of Radium Hot Springs (average temperature 47°C/117°F) feed the swimming pools in the park complex *(open year-round daily 9am–10:30pm; closed Dec 25; $4; ✕ summer ☎250-347-9485).* The mineral content of the springs is generally lower than that of other springs developed in the Rockies.

Immediately after the hot springs, the highway passes through the rocky cleft of **Sinclair Canyon★** before reaching the park's southern entrance gate. A park **visitor centre** *(open mid-Jun–Labour Day daily 9am–7pm; early–mid-Sept daily 9am–5pm; late Sept–mid-Oct weekends only 9am–5pm; ☎250-347-9505; winter ☎250-347-9551)* is located just inside the gate.

SKEENA VALLEY★★

British Columbia
Map of Principal Sights p 2

Cleaving the rugged Coast Mountains of northwest British Columbia, this verdant river valley holds the second largest river in the province. Rising in the Skeena Mountains of the interior, the 565km/350mi "river of mists" flows south to the town of New Hazelton, then southwest toward its confluence with Hecate Strait, following a massive channel cut by Ice Age glaciers. The valley is noted for its spectacular scenery and for the rich Tsimshian culture of the **Gitksan** tribe, which still inhabits the riverbanks.

Historical Notes

Ancestral Home – The Skeena River and its tributaries have been the territory of the Gitksan Indians for close to 10,000 years. Part of the native **Northwest Coast cultures** *(p 32)*, the Gitksan traditionally based their subsistence on salmon, berries and western red cedar used to construct longhouses and to carve elaborate totem poles *(p 32)*. Pole-raisings, as well as weddings, funerals and other important occasions, were accompanied by great feasts called **potlatches**.

European Contact – In the 19C European fur-trading posts, dominated by the Hudson's Bay Company, were established along the Skeena. The area was further opened to European settlement in the 1880s with the coming of sternwheelers to the Skeena. During the same period fishing and cannery operations, established near the mouth of the river, attracted Asians and more Europeans. In 1912 the Grand Trunk Pacific Railway was completed through the valley, an additional means of influx. Today the Yellowhead Highway follows the Skeena from east of Prince Rupert to New Hazelton.

Native Decline and Renewal – The Gitksan Indians were greatly affected by the arrival of Europeans. Several factors combined to decimate the aboriginal culture of the Northwest: old patterns of hunting and gathering were curtailed in favour of supplying furs to the new immigrants; missionary zeal and European misapprehensions about the potlatch led to its ban between 1884 and 1951; totem poles were destroyed; and the introduction of diseases such as smallpox significantly reduced the native population. The Gitksan, however, maintained their system of clans and of matrilineal descent. In the 1970s a renaissance of native culture began. Today their language, Tsimshian, is taught in reserve schools, and traditional

from photo by Otto Nelson, Denver Art Museum

Chilkat Blanket

crafts such as wood- and stone-carving have been revived. The technique of silk-screening, introduced in the past few decades, has allowed artists to develop innovative approaches to classic designs.

PRINCE RUPERT

Served by BC Ferries (see Inside Passage p 46). Situated on Kaien Island near the mouth of the Skeena, this maritime city (pop. 16,620) faces a scenic deep-water harbour dotted with islands. Canada's westernmost seaport, Prince Rupert was established in 1906 when its site was chosen as the terminus of the Grand Trunk Pacific. Located just south of the Alaska Panhandle, the town was expected to surpass VANCOUVER as Canada's major Pacific port. By 1922, however, Vancouver had secured that role. Today with its ice-free harbour, the city is a fishing and fish-processing centre as well as a coal, grain, pulp and lumber port. It also serves as the major urban hub for northwest British Columbia. Known as the "City of Rainbows," Prince Rupert receives an annual rainfall of 2564mm/100in. Fine reproductions of Tsimshian and Haida *(p 51)* **totem poles★** are scattered throughout the city.

The **Cow Bay** area has a pleasant dockside atmosphere, with a few cafes and shops. Removed to the Prince Rupert waterfront, the Grand Trunk Pacific Railway's small **Kwinitsa Station★** serves as a railroad museum, which traces the history of railroading in this region through artifacts and old photographs *(open mid-May–Labour Day daily 9am–noon & 1–5pm; contribution requested;* ☎250-624-5637).

★★ **Museum of Northern British Columbia** – *Open mid-May–Labour Day daily 9am–8pm (Sun 5pm); rest of the year daily 10am–5pm. Closed Jan 1, Dec 25 & 26. Contribution requested.* ⅂ ☎250-624-3207. This museum has a fine collection of native Northwest basketry, argillite and wood carvings, as well as a carving shed where craftsmen demonstrate their talents. The small museum displays selections from its holdings of over 8,000 artifacts.

★★ **FROM PRINCE RUPERT TO NEW HAZELTON**
Allow 5hrs, including visits. 300km/180mi by Rte. 16.

★★ **North Pacific Cannery Museum** – *22km/14mi east of Prince Rupert, southeast of Port Edward, 1889 Skeena Dr. Open May–Sept daily 10am–7pm. Rest of the year Wed–Sun 10am–4pm. Closed Jan 1, Dec 25 & Dec 26. $5.* ⅂ ☎250-628-3538. In the late 19C this fish cannery was one of more than 220 on the British Columbia coast.

Built in 1889 on an arm of the Skeena, the complex is the oldest surviving cannery village on the north coast. The picturesque village is still intact, as is the factory equipment, which has been out of operation since 1972. Fishing and canning methods are explained during the guided tours (*five times daily in summer, 45min*). A historical drama about Prince Rupert is included on selected tours.

East of Port Edward the road meets the Skeena River, paralleling it through its magnificent valley. The entire route provides excellent views of the broad, turbulent river and of the cloud-shrouded, snow-capped Coast Mountains rising to 2,000m/6,000ft above. In the town of **Terrace** (pop. 11,433) the **Heritage Park**, a collection of eight old log buildings moved here from outlying areas, depicts pioneer life in the region. The river waters around the town and around nearby Kitimat to the south (*52km/31mi*) provide excellent sportfishing for trout and salmon. After Terrace, where the valley widens briefly, the road winds through the Hazelton Mountains. East of Terrace (*12km/7mi*) at the village of **Usk**, a small cable ferry breasts the treacherous waters of the Skeena.

★★ **Tour of the Totems** – *Self-guided driving tour. Information about the native villages is available at the New Hazelton visitor centre on Rte. 16 (open May–Aug daily 9am–5pm;*

Sept daily 8am–3pm; ☎250-842-6071). Today the Gitksan still inhabit five ancient villages along the Skeena and its tributaries. Four of these villages have impressive stands of **totem poles★★★** that date from the late 19C. The weathered poles, devoid of paint, range in height from 5-9m/15-30ft.

Kitwanga – *Junction of Rte. 16 and Rte. 37 north, after crossing the Skeena River; then turn right on Bridge St.* Situated beside the Skeena River, a fine stand of about a dozen 19C totem poles graces a flat, grass-covered field against a backdrop of the impressive **Seven Sisters** Mountains (2,755m/9,039ft).

Kitwancool – *Rte. 37, 18km/11mi north of Kitwanga.* This village has the oldest existing stand of Gitksan totem poles, though several of its most venerable ones are now stored in a shed at the rear of the totem field for preservation. Active carving is still going on in this field.

Return to Rte. 16 and continue east.

Kitseguecla – *Rte. 16, 19km/12mi east of junction with Rte. 37.* The original totem poles in this village were destroyed by fire (1872) and by flood. New poles, however, now stand scattered throughout the village

Continue east to New Hazelton and turn left on Rte. 62.

'Ksan – *Rte. 62, 7km/4mi northwest of New Hazelton. Grounds open year-round. Tour buildings open early May–mid-Oct daily 9am–6pm. $6.* ☎250-842-5544. A complex of totem poles and longhouses re-created in the traditional style, this historical village museum provides an insight into the Gitksan culture. 'Ksan, the Gitksan name for the Skeena, is situated on the site of an ancient village near the confluence of the Skeena and Bulkley Rivers, with a magnificent view of Mt. Rocher Déboulé.

The village consists of seven major buildings: an exhibit hall featuring travelling displays and fine examples of Gitksan basketry, carving and weaving; a carving house and silkscreen workshop, where native artists from throughout the Northwest Coast work; a gift shop; and three longhouses where an extensive **native collection★★** of artifacts is used to explain the culture and lifestyle of these people. The acclaimed 'Ksan dancers perform in the summer (*mid-Jul–mid-Aug every Fri evening; $6; for schedule* ☎250-842-5544).

Kispiox – *19km/12mi north of 'Ksan on Kispiox Valley Rd.* Situated near the confluence of the Skeena and Kispiox Rivers, this large village boasts a dozen impressive totems in a field by the waters of the Kispiox.

VANCOUVER★★★

British Columbia
Metro Pop. 1,542,744
Map of Principal Sights p 2
Tourist Office ☎604-683-2000

Canada's third largest metropolis, this West Coast city has a magnificent **site★★★** on a peninsula protruding into the Strait of Georgia. Situated between Burrard Inlet—the most southerly of a series of deep fjords cut into the coast of British Columbia—and the delta of the Fraser River, the city covers 113sq km/44sq mi of the peninsula's western end. A protected deep-sea port, accessibility to the Pacific Ocean, and a virtually snow-free climate have contributed to Vancouver's prosperity and rapid growth.

The city is almost surrounded by mountains. To the north the Coast Mountains rise steeply, the most prominent peaks being **Hollyburn Mountain**, the twin summits of **The Lions**, **Grouse Mountain** with its ski slopes and **Mt. Seymour** to the east. To the west across the Strait of Georgia stand the mountains of Vancouver Island and to the southeast rises the Cascade Range, topped by the snow-clad peak of **Mt. Baker** in Washington state. Despite heavy snowfall that provides superb skiing conditions in these mountains, Vancouver itself rarely receives snow. Instead the city has a high rainfall compared with the rest of the country (1524mm/60in a year). Even in July and August, the sunniest months, a light rain and mist may shroud the mountains.

Historical Notes

Early History – The shores of the Strait of Georgia were the preserve of the Coast Salish Indians until 1791, when Spanish captain José Maria Narvaez was the first European to enter their waters. Surveying the coast for the British Navy, Capt. **George Vancouver** explored Burrard Inlet a year later. In 1808 Simon Fraser saw the area from the land side, at the end of his descent of the river bearing his name. Bypassed by the Fraser River gold rushers, the site aroused little interest until three Englishmen opened a brickworks in 1862 on land stretching over much of the present downtown. Having poured their life savings into what is today reputed to be the most densely populated square mile in Canada, they received the epithet "the three greenhorns." The 1860s saw the opening of sawmills on both sides of the inlet to process the area's rich timber. In 1867 John Deighton *(p 76)* opened a saloon for the mill workers. The community that developed around it became known as Gastown and was eventually named Granville in 1869, when a townsite was laid out by government surveyors.

The Coming of the Railway – The location of the terminus of the Canadian Pacific Railway was a long-standing controversy. When it was finally decided to route the railway down the Fraser Valley to Burrard Inlet, land prices skyrocketed at Port Moody, a tiny settlement at its head *(map p 80)*. The prices and lack of space

Vancouver

there caused **William Van Horne** in 1884 to extend the line farther down the inlet to the site of Granville. Overnight a town was born. At its official incorporation in 1886, the city was baptized Vancouver, Van Horne's choice. Almost immediately thereafter fire destroyed the community, but by 1887 it had recovered sufficiently to welcome the first trans-Canadian passenger train.

Vancouver Today – Vancouver has become the largest city in the province, with a metropolitan population of over 1.5 million; in Canada, only Toronto and Montreal have greater populations. The financial, commercial and industrial centre of British Columbia, Vancouver is also the province's major port—indeed, Canada's largest port. Bulk loads of grain and potash from the Prairies, and of lumber, logs, coal, sulphur and other minerals from interior British Columbia arrive by train and are exported chiefly to Japan and other countries bordering the Pacific Ocean. Vancouver is a centre for forestry and fishing as well. The city and its environs continue to be a popular tourist destination, particularly for cruise-ship passengers.

In 1986 Vancouver hosted the world exposition, **Expo '86**, as part of its centennial celebrations. The exposition site on the north and east shores of False Creek (*map p 74*) has been cleared for commercial and residential development.

In recent years Vancouver has added a variety of structures to its skyline, notably the turquoise-topped Cathedral Place, which mirrors its venerable neighbour, Chateau-styled **Hotel Vancouver** (1939); the swank 23-storey Waterfront Centre Hotel opposite Canada Place; the colosseum-shaped public library of controversial Library Square (Robson & Homer Streets) and, opposite it, the 1,800-seat Ford Centre for the Performing Arts. The glittering Price Waterhouse complex next door to Harbour Centre sports a domed atrium and garden. Overlooking False Creek, General Motors Place, a more intimate venue than its larger counterpart, BC Place Stadium, is the new home to Vancouver's ice hockey team, the *Canucks*.

★★★ STANLEY PARK   *Map p 74*

Vancouver's outstanding attraction, the 405ha/1000 acre park has a magnificent **site★★★** at the end of a peninsula that almost closes Burrard Inlet at **First Narrows.** Washed on three sides by the inlet waters, this densely forested expanse offers splendid views of the North Shore Mountains, the peaks of Vancouver Island, the city and the port.

In 1886 the month-old city of Vancouver asked the Canadian government for the peninsula, planning to convert the former military reserve into a public park. The idea of a woodland reserve was rather advanced at the time, primarily because Vancouver consisted of almost nothing except forest. Ottawa agreed, and Governor General **Lord Stanley** dedicated the park.

Today the park is well used by city dwellers and tourists alike. Especially on weekends joggers, skaters, amblers, dog-walkers (including professionals walking four to five dogs at once), stroller-pushers, camera-clickers and artists crowd the green spaces, beaches, recreational facilities and walkways.

Visiting the Park – The park is open daily year-round. To access the park by car, stay in the far right lane of Georgia St. and follow the overhead sign. Traffic within the park is routed counterclockwise one-way along the two-lane perimeter road (*see scenic drive below*), except for Pipeline Road near Beaver Lake. Coin-operated parking machines are located throughout the park for all spaces (*$1/2hrs or $2/all day*). Numerous walking trails crisscross the forested interior and a much-used 9km/5.5mi paved path known as the "sea wall" rims the shoreline. Facilities include cricket grounds, tennis courts, shuffleboard, picnic areas, children's playgrounds, and a swimming pool at Second Beach. Maps available at information kiosk. ☎604-257-8400. Horse-drawn carriage tours depart from the lower zoo parking lot (*May–mid-Oct daily 10am–4pm; $10/1hr; AAA Horse & Carriage Ltd. ☎604-681-5115*).

Scenic Drive – *About 1hr. 10km/6mi.* Circling the park in a counterclockwise direction, the drive begins and ends at Georgia Street. The route follows the edge of Coal Harbour, offering views of the yacht clubs, port and city as far as **Brockton Point**, with its fine **view** of the inlet and North Shore Mountains. Just before the point note the display of brightly painted **totem poles**, the work of the Northwest Coast Indians. The road continues to **Prospect Point** where ships, passing through First Narrows in and out of port, can be observed. Then the road turns inland, but paths lead to the sea wall near **Siwash Rock**, cut off from the rest of the peninsula.

Getting Around

By Public Transportation – Vancouver Regional Transit System operates an integrated network of rapid transit, ferries and buses. Hours of operation vary among the different services. **SkyTrain**, the city's rapid transit, services downtown, Burnaby, New Westminster and Surrey; *(daily 5:30–1am; every 2-5 min)*. **SeaBus**, passenger harbour ferries, operates between Vancouver and the North Shore *(Mon–Sat 6–12:30am, Sun 8am–11pm; every 15-30min)*. Adult fare during off-peak hours is $1.50; weekdays before 9:30am and from 3–6:30pm fares are based on zone boundaries. Fares are the same for all services; exact fare is required. FareSaver books of 10 tickets *($13.75)* and a DayPass *($4.50)* are available from ticket machines and outlets. Transfers are free for 90min of unlimited travel. **Bus** service connects SkyTrain and SeaBus at all stations. Buses operate 7 days/wk. A *Transit Guide* map *($1.50)* is sold at TicketMaster outlets and convenience stores. For route information and schedules ☎521-0400.

By Car – Use of public transportation or walking is strongly encouraged within the city as roads are often congested and street parking may be difficult to find. Metered and garage parking available. Car rentals: Avis ☎606-2847; Hertz ☎688-2411; Tilden ☎685-6111.

By Taxi – Advance Cabs ☎876-5555; Black Top Cabs ☎731-1111; Yellow Cabs ☎681-1111.

General Information

Accommodations and Visitor Information – For hotels/motels, contact Tourism Vancouver ☎683-2000. Reservation services: Beachside B&B Registry ☎922-7773; AAA B&B Ltd. ☎872-0938; Best Canadian B&B Network ☎738-7207. Vancouver Travel InfoCentre at Waterfront Centre (Plaza Level), 200 Burrard Street *(open mid-May–Labour Day daily 8am–6pm; rest of the year Mon–Fri 8:30am–5pm, Sat 9am–5pm)* or contact Tourism Vancouver, Waterfront Centre, Vancouver, BC, V6C 3L6 ☎683-2000.

Local Press – Daily: *The Vancouver Sun* and *The Province.* Monthly guide (free) to entertainment, shopping and restaurants: *Where.*

Entertainment – Consult arts and entertainment supplements in local newspapers (Thursday edition) for schedule of cultural events and addresses of principal theatres and concert halls. Ticketmaster ☎280-4444 (major credit cards accepted).

Sports – BC Lions Football Club: home games at BC Place Stadium; season Jun–Nov; schedules ☎583-7747. Vancouver Canadians (baseball): home games at Nat Bailey Stadium; season Apr–Sept; schedules ☎872-5232. Vancouver Canucks (ice hockey): home games at General Motors Place; season Oct–Apr; schedules ☎899-7400. Vancouver Grizzlies (NBA basketball): home games at General Motors Place; season Oct–Apr; schedules ☎899-4667. Tickets for all events are sold through the venues or through Ticketmaster ☎280-4400 (major credit cards accepted).

Useful Numbers ☎

Police ....911 (emergency) or	665-3321
BC Rail (North Vancouver), *1311 W. 1st St.*	984-5246
VIA Rail, *1150 Station St.*	669-3050
BC Ferries	669-1211
Greyhound Lines of Canada (bus), *150 Dunsmuir St.*	662-3222
Vancouver International Airport	276-6101
Canadian Automobile Assn., *999 W. Broadway*	268-5600
CAA Emergency Road Service (24hr)	293-2222
Shoppers Drug Mart (24hr pharmacy), *1125 Davie St.*	669-2424
Main Post Office, *349 W. Georgia St.*	662-5722
Road Conditions	660-9770
Weather (24hr)	664-9010

From **Ferguson Point** there are **views** of Third Beach; Point Grey Peninsula, where the University of British Columbia is situated; and the mountains on Vancouver Island. The road continues past Second Beach, various sports facilities (including a putting course and lawn-bowling green) and Lost Lagoon.

★★★ **Aquarium** – *Open Jul–Labour Day daily 9am–7pm. Rest of the year daily 10am–5:30pm (Dec 25 noon–5pm). $9.50 (Jul–Sept $11).* ⛫ 🅿 ☎604-268-9900. Home to more than 8,000 animals, this lauded aquarium is known for its extensive marine mammal centre featuring a variety of whales, seals and sea otters. Several galleries are devoted to ocean and freshwater fish native to British Columbia and exotic fish of the world. At its entrance there is a bronze sculpture of a killer whale by acclaimed Haida sculptor Bill Reid.

The aquarium was first to publicly exhibit **killer whales** (also known as orcas), distinguished by their black and white colouring and dorsal fin. Performing regularly for visitors in their 5 million litre/1.3 million gallon outdoor habitat, these large mammals demonstrate their amazing power, grace and intelligence.

A special feature of the Arctic Canada section is the **beluga whales**, seen through large viewing windows swimming underwater.

Indoors a highlight is the walk-in **Amazon Rain Forest** where crocodiles, anacondas, turtles, lizards and two-toed sloths live in a steamy environment, complete with suitable vegetation and a multitude of brightly coloured birds. Adjacent to the rain forest, tanks contain sharks, piranhas, electric and moray eels and other tropical creatures.

Near the aquarium is the **Children's Zoo and Miniature Railway** (*open May–Sept daily 11am–4pm; rest of the year weekends only 11am–4pm, weather permitting; $4.30;* 🍴⛫ ☎604-257-8531).

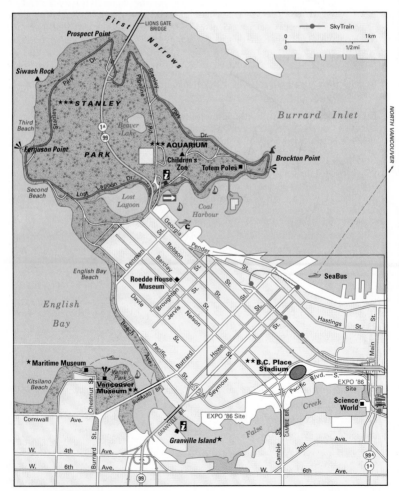

★★ DOWNTOWN   *5hrs. Map p 76.*

Positioned along Granville Street the commercial centre is closed to all traffic except buses for a six-block pedestrian thoroughfare known as **The Mall**. The major department stores and extensive underground shopping developments called the Pacific and Vancouver Centres are located here. At the northern end is Granville Square, a plaza with views of port activities at the wharves below. Steps lead to the attractively renovated rail station from which a passenger ferry service known as SeaBus crosses Burrard Inlet, offering good **views** of the harbour and city.

★★ **Canada Place** – Designed by architect Eberhard Zeidler, this gleaming white structure resembles a flotilla of sailing ships at anchor in Burrard Inlet. Constructed as the Canada Pavilion for Expo '86, the complex consists of a hotel, office tower and convention centre. Exhibition halls are enclosed by the "sails" of fibreglass yarn coated with teflon, tensioned to appear as though they are catching the ocean winds. Along with cruise ships that moor at its sides, Canada Place has transformed the waterfront.

★★ **Harbour Centre** – *Observation deck open Apr–Sept Sun–Thu 8:30am–10:30pm, Fri, Sat & holidays 8:30am–11:30pm. Rest of the year Sun–Thu 9am–9pm, Fri–Sat 9am–10pm. $7 (valid for same date return visit at night).* ✗ & 🅿 ☎604-689-0421. Visitors ascend this distinctive office building via exterior elevators to arrive at the circular observation deck (167m/553ft above ground) with its magnificent **panorama★★★** of the city, mountains, ocean and Fraser River delta.

★★ **Art Gallery** – *Open May–mid-Oct Mon–Fri 10am–6pm (Thu 9pm), Sat 10am–5pm, Sun noon–5pm. Rest of the year Wed–Fri 10am–6pm (Thu 9pm), Sat 10am–5pm, Sun noon–5pm. Closed Jan 1 & 2, Dec 25 & 26. $6 (Thu evenings contribution requested).* ✗ & ☎604-682-5621. Designed in 1907 by Francis Rattenbury, the Neoclassical building served as the city courthouse for 70 years. It was tastefully converted by Arthur Erickson so that galleries open off the central rotunda with its glass-topped dome, through which natural light enters.

A highlight is the collection of paintings and drawings by British Columbian **Emily Carr** (1871-1945), one of Canada's best-known and original artists. Her portrayals of West Coast landscapes and Indian villages are striking, as evidenced in such famous works on display as *Big Raven* (c.1931) and *Scorned as Timber, Beloved of the Sky* (c.1936). There are also changing exhibitions of regional, national and international interest from the permanent collection.

★★ **Robson Square** – Stretching from Nelson Street almost to Georgia Street, this complex was also designed by Arthur Erickson. Opened in 1979, the square helped transform the downtown area and now houses the offices of the provincial court. A 7-storey **law court building [A]** with a spectacular slanted-glass roof complements a series of terraced gardens with waterfalls and plants on top of offices *(between Smithe and Robson)*. A plaza under Robson Street contains outdoor cafes, a skating rink and a conference centre.

★★ **BC Place Stadium** – *For tour information* ☎604-669-2300. Resembling an enormous quilted marshmallow, this stadium is the largest air-supported domed amphitheatre in the world. Designed by Phillips Barratt, it opened in 1983. Inflated by huge fans the teflon and fibreglass roof is secured by steel cables. Containing heating elements to melt winter snow, the roof is self-cleaning with the aid of area rainfall and translucent enough so that artificial lighting is rarely required. The stadium seats up to 60,000 with no interior supports. A glass-enclosed concourse on the upper level offers a city **panorama**.

★ **Chinatown** – *Pender St. between Carrall St. and Gore Ave.* This colourful quarter is the centre of Vancouver's large Chinese community. Many restaurants and shops sell oriental foods and wares. The neighborhood is particularly lively during the Chinese New Year.

★ **Dr. Sun Yat-Sen Classical Chinese Garden** – *578 Carrall St. behind Chinese Cultural Centre on Pender St. Open May–mid-Jun daily 10am–6pm. Late Jun–Labour Day daily 10am–7:30pm. Early Sept–April daily 10am–4:30pm. Closed Jan 1 & Dec 25. $4.50.* & ☎604-689-7133. Modelled after classical gardens developed in the Chinese city of Suzhou during the Ming dynasty (14-17C), this garden is a small oasis of contemplative calm. Pine, bamboo and flowering plum trees grow amid sculpted rocks, water, arched bridges and covered walkways.

Next door to the garden is the equally serene Dr. Sun Yat-Sen Park, graced by a large, placid pond.

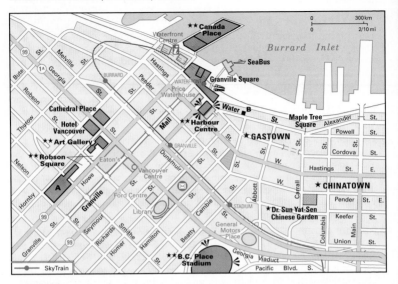

★ **Gastown** – This attractive area between Carrall and Richards Streets combines restored buildings of the late 19C with modern structures constructed to blend with their surroundings. Gastown has not always been chic. In the 1860s sawmill owners on Burrard Inlet had strict rules against consumption of alcohol on their premises. Thirsty mill employees had to walk 19km/12mi to New Westminster until an enterprising Englishman, John Deighton, arrived at the edge of mill property with a barrel of whisky. Nicknamed **Gassy Jack** because of his garrulousness, he enticed mill workers to build his saloon, rewarding them with whisky. Soon he had a lively trade and the resulting community took his name—Gassy's town or simply Gastown.

Over the years the character of the area has changed several times. Today its centre is **Maple Tree Square**, where a statue of Gassy Jack stands. **Water Street** is an attractive section with its gaslights and shops. On the corner of Cambie stands a **steam clock [B]**, powered by a steam engine. The mechanism actually works by gravity and the clock "hoots" out the hour, half hour and quarter hour.

★ **Harbour Tour [C]** – *Map p 74. Departs from Coal Harbour mid-Jun–late Sept Wed–Sun 11:45am & 1:45pm. Round-trip 1hr 30min. Commentary. Reservations required. $16.* ✗ ▣. *Harbour Ferries Ltd* ☎604-688-7246. This boat trip by paddlewheeler makes a pleasant excursion, enabling visitors to see Vancouver's busy port and offering fine views of the city and mountains.

Cathedral Place – This handsome glass and limestone high rise located opposite Hotel Vancouver is home to the small but fascinating **Sri-Lankan Gem Museum** *(ground floor, open year-round Mon–Sat 10am–5:30pm; closed national holidays; $3.50;* ᵭ☎604-662-7768). Emeralds, pearls, sapphires, jade, amethyst and topaz are among the many gems on display. The floor contains some 9,000 Brazilian agates and the coffered ceiling features 24-karat gold and enamel.

Off the courtyard is the Museum Building, which houses the **Canadian Craft Museum** *(open Jun–Aug Mon–Sat 10am–5pm, Sun noon–5pm; rest of the year Mon, Wed–Sat 10am–5pm, Sun noon–5pm; closed Jan 1 & Dec 25; $4;* ᵭ☎604-687-8266), a showcase for international as well as Canadian crafts. Furniture, textiles, jewellery and sculpture are displayed in changing exhibits in a large light-filled space on the ground floor. Note at the rear of the building the bevelled-glass doors (*Crystal Egress*, 1991), which are part of the permanent collection.

SIGHTS OUTSIDE DOWNTOWN

★★★ **UBC Museum of Anthropology** – *Map p 79. Open mid-May–early Sept daily 11am–5pm (Tue 9pm). Rest of the year Tue–Sun 11am–5pm (Tue 9pm). Closed Dec 25–26. $6.* ᵭ ▣ ☎604-822-3825. At the end of Point Grey Peninsula, the University of British Columbia has a large campus overlooking the Strait of Georgia and the mountains of Vancouver Island. Known for its site and for its research facilities in agriculture, forestry and oceanography, the university is also famous for its collection of Northwest Coast Indian art.

Opened in 1976 the **museum building★★**—the work of Arthur Erickson —is an architectural masterpiece. A glass and concrete structure, it admirably complements the site. Flanked by exhibits, a ramp leads down to the **Great Hall★★**. Glass walls rise 14m/45ft around the magnificent collection of Haida and Kwakwaka'wakw **totem poles** and other large wood carvings, many dating from mid-19C. The trees, sea, sky and mountains are visible through the glass walls, giving visitors the impression of seeing the poles in their original surroundings, not in a museum. The designs of the poles and Haida houses on the museum grounds were inspired by older carvings now decayed.

In contrast to the immense sculptures in the Great Hall, the carvings in the **Masterpiece Gallery** are tiny and intricate. Works in silver, gold, argillite, horn, bone, ivory, stone and wood bear the same designs in miniature as the monumental sculpture elsewhere.

One corner of the museum is devoted to **Raven and the First Men**, a massive modern carving in yellow cedar by Bill Reid *(p 53)*, symbolic of birth. A huge raven stands on a clam shell that is being pushed open by a series of small figures.

The remainder of the building is predominantly "visible storage" galleries, where the museum's worldwide collections from ancient times to the present are on display, catalogued by region and civilization. There are also galleries for changing exhibits.

★★ **Queen Elizabeth Park** – *Map p 79. West 33rd Ave. and Cambie St.* This beautiful park lies at the geographic centre and highest point (150m/500ft) of Vancouver. The road from the entrance climbs through an arboretum to the **Bloedel Floral Conservatory★**, a geodesic-domed structure of glass and aluminum *(open May–Sept Mon–Fri 9am–8pm, weekends & holidays 10am–9pm; rest of the year daily 10am–5pm; closed Dec 25; $3.10; & ℙ ☎604-872-5513)*. On the grounds near the fountain stands Henry Moore's monumental sculpture *Knife Edge, Two Piece*. Inside the conservatory are examples of tropical and desert vegetation, enlivened by a number of colourful birds. In clear weather there are extraordinary **views★★★** from the conservatory's plaza of the city and mountains by day and night, including the majestic snow-capped peak of Mt. Baker of the Cascades more than 110km/70mi away.

The other attraction of the park is the lovely **Sunken Gardens★★**. Paths weave among the flowers to a waterfall and a bridge, from which there are views of the gardens and city.

★★ **Vancouver Museum** – *Map p 74. In Vanier Park. Open year-round Tue–Sun 10am–5pm. Closed Dec 25. $5. ✗ & ℙ ☎604-736-4431.* Through permanent and rotating exhibits, this museum specializes in the history and art of Vancouver and Canada's native cultures. It also has a fine collection of Asian art and artifacts. Representing the creature that traditionally guards the harbour in Indian legend, a huge stainless steel **crab★**—the work of sculptor George Norris—dominates the front entrance in an ornamental pool. From the parking area there is an excellent **view★★** of the city and North Shore Mountains.

In the **Exploration and Settlement galleries**, Vancouver's past is traced from the first arrival of Europeans. A Hudson's Bay Company trading store has been re-created, along with steerage quarters on an immigrant ship. The birth of Vancouver as a lumber village is shown with its growth after the arrival of the "iron horse." A series of room reconstructions of the 1910 era illustrates the city's rapid development.

Changing exhibits draw on the museum's rich collection of artifacts of the **Northwest Coast tribes**, which show an extraordinary artistic finesse. Tiny woven baskets of cedar and bear grass, argillite carvings, shaman regalia, canoe-size feast bowls, and masks with two faces—the first, an animal, opening to reveal the second, a human, reflecting the union between these two lifeforms—are examples of the variety of items in the collection.

The buildings of the museum surround the distinctive conical dome of the **MacMillan Planetarium** *(open Jul–Sept 1 Sun–Thu 10am–10pm, Fri–Sat 10am–11pm; rest of the year Tue–Sun hours vary; $6.50; laser show $7.75; ✗ & ℙ ☎604-738-7827)*, which has become a Vancouver landmark since its opening in 1968. In the **Southam Observatory** visitors can look through the giant telescope at the sun, moon, planets and stars.

★ **Maritime Museum** – *Map p 74. In Vanier Park. Ferry to Granville Island departs from the museum wharf. Open Jun–Aug daily 10am–5pm. Rest of the year Tue–Sun 10am–5pm. Closed Dec 25. $5. & ℙ ☎604-257-8300.* Ship models and artifacts illustrate the maritime history of Vancouver and British Columbia. The highlight of the collection is the **St. Roch**★★, a Royal Canadian Mounted Police patrol ship, which navigated the Northwest Passage in both directions.

After Roald Amundsen's completion of the passage *(p 302)*, various countries sought control of the Arctic. To assert sovereignty over the northland, the Canadian government decided to send a ship through the passage. Under Capt. Henry Larsen, the *St. Roch* left Vancouver in June 1940 and, after being frozen in several times, reached Halifax in October 1942. In 1944 the return trip of 13,510km/7,295 nautical mi in ice-strewn waters took only 86 days. Not only was the *St. Roch* the first ship to navigate the passage both ways, but the first to complete the east-west voyage in one season. The 32m/104ft wooden vessel has been completely restored, with authentic items in all the cabins and can be boarded.

★ **Granville Island** – *Map p 74. Accessible by car from Granville Bridge & West 4th Ave. (follow signs to under the bridge), or by ferry from beside Vancouver Aquatic Centre on Beach Ave. or from Maritime Museum. Visitor centre, 1592 Johnson St., open year-round daily 8am–6pm.* ☎604-666-5784. This one-time industrial area under Granville Bridge has been renovated to house art galleries and studios, boutiques, restaurants, theatres and a hotel, in addition to some surviving industry. Visitors can observe artists as they craft jewellery, textiles, ceramics, glass and other wares in the numerous warehouse-sized workshops. The Emily Carr Institute of Art and Design is a dominant structure here, populating the island with students. The highlight is the **public market** *(open year-round daily 9am–6pm;* ☎604-689-8447) where stalls of fresh produce vie with products of Vancouver's many ethnic groups.

★ **VanDusen Botanical Garden [D]** – *Map p 79. On 37th Ave. at Oak St. Open Jun–mid-Aug daily 10am–9pm. Oct–Mar daily 10–4pm. Rest of the year hours vary. Closed Dec 25. $5.* ✗ ὁ 🅿 ☎604-257-8666. This 22ha/55 acre garden offers fine displays of plants in geographic as well as botanical arrangements. In addition to a rose garden, a magnolia garden and a rhododendron walk, there are sections devoted to vegetation of the Southern Hemispheric, Mediterranean and Sino-Himalayan areas.

★ **Vanterm [E]** – *Map p 79. At north end of Clark Dr.; take overpass to visitor parking lot. Public viewing centre open year-round Mon–Fri 9am–4pm.* 🅿 ☎604-666-0815. The enormous container-handling complex can be viewed from an observation lounge that overlooks the loading and unloading docks for ships, trucks and trains, against a backdrop of the North Shore Mountains.

★ **The North Shore** – *Map p 79.* The mountains descend quite precipitously towards Burrard Inlet on its north side, cut not only by deep fjords such as Indian Arm and Howe Sound, but by steep valleys or canyons of several small rivers and creeks—Capilano, Lynn and Seymour being the best known. Houses on the north shore are, for the most part, expensive and often cling to mountain slopes that permit good views of the inlet and city.

★ **Cypress Provincial Park** – *12km/7mi from downtown by Lions Gate Bridge and Hwy. 1/Rte. 99. Open year-round daily 7am–11pm. Hiking, picnicking, biking, skiing.* ✗ ὁ 🅿 ☎604-463-3515. *For trail maps contact BC Parks* ☎604-924-2200. This 3,000ha/7,400 acre expanse includes Hollyburn Ridge and Cypress Bowl, popular local ski areas. The access road leads through a forest of Douglas fir and western hemlock to Highview Lookout, which permits a breathtaking **view**★★★ of the Vancouver area. On clear days Mt. Baker adds its stunning snow-clad mass to the scene. At 1,300m/4,264ft above sea level, the ridgetops here abound with amabalis fir, mountain hemlock and yellow cypress, for which the park is named.

★ **Capilano Canyon** – *9km/6mi from downtown by Lions Gate Bridge and Capilano Rd.* This deep canyon can be appreciated by visiting the narrow pedestrian **suspension bridge**★ **[F]** 70m/230ft above the Capilano River *(open May–Oct daily 8:30am–dusk; rest of the year daily 9am–5pm; closed Dec 25; $6.95; May–Oct $7.45;* ✗ ὁ 🅿 ☎604-985-7474). Built in 1889 the bridge is 137m/450ft long and sways as visitors walk across it. On the opposite side is a pleasant glade of Douglas fir and western red cedar. The beauty of the entrance side has been marred by commercialization. Farther along Capilano Road, **Capilano River Regional Park** offers pleasant walks and views of the canyon from below. At the northern end of the park *(access from Nancy Greene Way)* are Cleveland Dam and Capilano Lake, a reservoir for the city of Vancouver. Across the lake there is a **view**★ of the double peak of the Lions.

★ **Grouse Mountain** – *13km/8mi from downtown by Lions Gate Bridge, Capilano Rd. and Nancy Greene Way. Tram operates year-round daily 9am–10pm. $14.95.* ✗ 🅿 ☎*604-984-0661.* The aerial tram rises to an elevation of 1,100m/3,700ft, offering, as it ascends, a splendid **view★★** of the city, and from the summit, a panorama embracing, on clear days, Vancouver Island, the Fraser delta and Burrard Inlet.

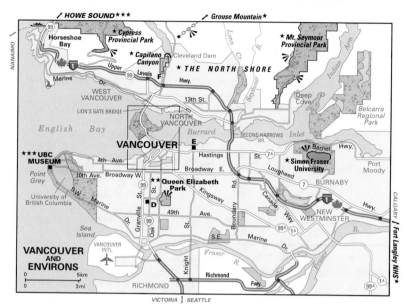

★ **Mt. Seymour Provincial Park** – *16km/10mi from downtown by Second Narrows Bridge; take the third exit (Mt. Seymour Parkway) and follow signs. Open year-round daily 7am–10pm. Hiking, horseback riding, mountain biking, skiing.* ✗ ♿ 🅿. *For trail maps contact park office* ☎*604-924-2200.* From the park entrance a road climbs steeply to Deep Cove Lookout *(8km/5mi; platform under repair)* from which there is a **view★★** to the east. The village of Deep Cove, Indian Arm and Simon Fraser University in Burnaby are visible in clear weather. From just below the ski centre *(13km/8mi)*, there is a **view★★** of the city and Vancouver Island on clear days. In the distance the peak of Mt. Baker in Washington state can usually be seen above the clouds. In winter visitors can reach the summit of Mt. Seymour by **chair lift** *(mid-Nov–mid-Apr Mon–Fri 10am–10pm, weekends 9am–10pm; $16, weekends $26;* ☎*604-986-2261).*

★ **Simon Fraser University** – *Map above. In Burnaby. Gaglardi Way. For guided tours* ☎*604-291-3224.* Located within the traffic-laden suburb of Burnaby, this architecturally famous, albeit controversial, university has a lovely isolated site on Burnaby Mountain, with **views** of the North Shore Mountains. The unique ensemble of interconnected buildings constructed along a tree-lined, partially covered pedestrian mall and around a large quadrangle with a pond was designed by Vancouver natives **Arthur Erickson** and **Geoffrey Massey**. The harmony of these somewhat harsh concrete structures derives from their design and construction as a unit. Erickson went on to design other interesting structures, among them the UBC Museum of Anthropology, Robson Square and the renovated Art Gallery, the Bank of Canada in Ottawa and Roy Thomson Hall in Toronto.

Since its opening in 1965, the university has gained a reputation as a progressive educational institution. It operates year-round on a trimester system, each term being independent so that students can study continuously or take only one or two terms a year.

Roedde House Museum – *Map p 74. 1415 Barclay St. (at Broughton St.). Visit by guided tour (30min) only, year-round Mon, Wed, Fri 2pm & 2nd and 4th Sun of each month 2pm. $2 (Sun $3, includes tea).* ♿ ☎*604-684-7040.* This Queen-Anne styled house with a characteristic polygonal tower was built in 1893 for Vancouver bookbinder Gustav Roedde. Its design is attributed to Francis Rattenbury, architect of Victoria's famed Empress Hotel *(p 84)*. Furnished to the period, six rooms on the ground floor of the 3-storey dwelling can be visited. On one side the house is bordered by a small Victorian garden with a gazebo and, on the other side, the intimate Barclay Heritage Square park.

Science World – *Map p 74. Quebec St. and Terminal Ave. Open Jul–Aug daily 10am–6pm. Rest of the year Mon-Fri 10am–5pm, weekends 10am–6pm. Closed Dec 25. $9.* ✗ ♿ 🅿 ☎*604-268-6363.* Situated on the Expo '86 site overlooking False Creek, this stimulating centre, opened in 1989, features interactive exhibits such as a plasma ball that demonstrates the properties of an electric current, and a cyclone chamber that re-creates nature's forces.

The centre includes an Omnimax theatre, where films are shown on a wrap-around, domed screen; the Music Machines Gallery, where visitors can operate a large synthesizer; and a children's problem-solving gallery.

EXCURSIONS *Map below*

★★★ **Howe Sound** – Extending some 48km/30mi into the Coast Mountains, this deep fjord provides some of the province's most dramatic coastal scenery.

Howe Sound can be admired by train, boat or car. A large steam engine that once pulled trains across Canada, the **Royal Hudson 2860**, makes regular trips to Squamish from the rail station in North Vancouver *(departs Jun–Sept Wed–Sun 9:30am; return by boat arriving Vancouver 4:30pm; round-trip 7hrs; commentary; reservations required; $58;* ✗ 🅿 ☎*604-688-7246).* The return trip is a spectacular voyage aboard the **MV Britannia**. The views of both sides of the fjord are excellent, as are those of Vancouver harbour, the point of disembarkation.

By car *(66km/41mi one-way, allow 3hrs),* travellers follow Route 99, a road built through virtually sheer cliffs, providing incredible **views★★★** of the mountains and the blue-green waters of the sound between **Horseshoe Bay**, a picturesque ferry port *(best viewed from Route 99 on return trip)* for Vancouver Island transit, and Squamish. Travellers may wish to continue 50km/31mi north of Squamish to the popular ski resort of Whistler, BC *(below).*

★★ **BC Museum of Mining** – *In Britannia Beach, 53km/33mi north of Vancouver. Open Jul–Aug daily 10am–4:30pm. May, Jun & Oct Wed–Sun 10am–4:30pm. $9.* ✗ ☎*604-688-8735.* Set in the Britannia mine, which was once the largest copper producer in the British Empire, this museum provides a fascinating introduction to mining. A video presentation *(20min)* traces the mine's history from discovery in 1888 to

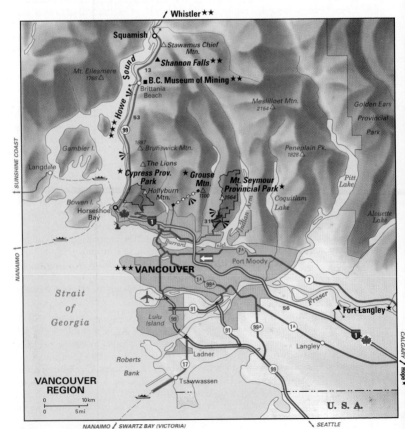

closure in 1974. Then follows a **guided tour** *(1hr 30min)* into one of the tunnels: visitors watch as mining equipment is demonstrated, and view the old gravity-fed mill. The mining house *(three levels)* has displays on mining in British Columbia, with particular emphasis on the Britannia mine.

★★ **Shannon Falls** – *60km/37mi.* These impressive falls cascade 335m/1,100ft over a cliff in pleasant surroundings.

As travellers approach the town of Squamish, the 700m/2,296ft granite monolith known as **Stawamus Chief** comes into view. Its sheer cliff face attracts rock-climbers from around the world.

Squamish – Pop. 10,157. *66km/41mi.* This lumber centre occupies a fine site at the foot of snow-capped peaks, including Mt. Garibaldi (2,678m/8,786ft).

★★ **Whistler** – Pop. 4,459. *117km/73mi north of Vancouver by Rte 99. Visitor centre in Whistler Conference Centre, open year-round daily 10am–4pm.* ☎604-932-2394. This well-planned resort community with its three alpine hamlets (Whistler Village, Village North and Upper Village) is dominated by two massive peaks, **Blackcomb Mountain** (2,284m/7,494ft) and **Whistler Mountain** (2,182/7,160ft), groomed for state-of-the-art skiing. Summer recreation is also plentiful: boating at nearby Alta Lake *(canoe rental $14/hr)*, fishing, horseback riding, tennis and golf. Hiking and biking trails abound *(map available from visitor centre or area hotels)*.

Nearby **Garibaldi Provincial Park**, a hike-in only park, offers additional trails of varying difficulty as well as campsites *(open year-round; parking area accessible by unpaved road from Whistler Village; park map available from Whistler visitor centre or contact BC Parks* ☎604-898-3678).

★ **Fort Langley National Historic Site** – ☞ *56km/35mi southeast of Vancouver by Trans-Can Hwy., Glover St. and Mavis Ave. or Rte. 7 and ferry. Open year-round daily 10am–4:30pm. Closed national holidays. $4.* ♿ ▣ ☎604-888-2822. The fort was one of a network of trading posts established by the Hudson's Bay Company in British Columbia in the early 19C. Fur trading was the predominant occupation, though a large farm was operated, and salmon were caught and packaged for trade.

Today the re-created buildings of the wooden-palisaded fort can be visited. The storehouse, the only structure original to the site, has a fine collection of **furs**★ and of the trading goods once exchanged for them. In the Big House, quarters of the resident Hudson's Bay Company officials can be seen. Costumed staff demonstrate smithery and barrel-making in the reconstructed blacksmith's shop and cooperage.

★ **From Vancouver to Hope** – *Map p 50. 141km/88mi east of Vancouver by Trans-Can Hwy.* The Trans-Canada Highway heads east from Vancouver along the wide valley of the Lower Fraser River, flanked by the Cascade Mountains—notably the pyramidal peak of Mt. Baker to the south and the Coast Ranges to the north. Rich black soil, deposited over eons, supports dairy cattle, hay fields and market gardens. The small town of **Hope**★ (pop. 3,147) serves as the gateway to the majestic Fraser and Thompson Canyons *(p 44)*.

VANCOUVER ISLAND★★★

British Columbia
Map of Principal Sights p 2

Covering an area of more than 32,000sq km/12,000sq mi, Vancouver Island is the largest of the islands off the Pacific Coast of North America. Mountains rise over 2,100m/7,000ft to form the central core. The west coast is deeply indented by inlets or fjords that almost dissect the island. The east coast slopes gradually, with wide beaches in the south and mountains farther north.

The climate is temperate throughout the island, but rainfall varies greatly: VICTORIA in the southeast receives 680mm/27in annually, whereas **Zeballos** *(map p 82)* on the west coast receives 6480mm/255in. This high rainfall supports dense forest growth. Not surprisingly, the island's major industry is logging: saw mills and pulp mills dot the island.

The population is concentrated mainly in the southeast corner around Victoria and along the shores of the Strait of Georgia.

Access – *Vancouver Island is served by 11 ferry services (map p 82).*

★★★ **Victoria** – *Description p 83.*

★★ FROM PARKSVILLE TO PACIFIC RIM

Allow 2hrs, 4.5hrs including visits. 154km/96mi by Rte. 4. Map below.

This winding route traverses the mountain backbone of the island through lovely scenery. Some parts are wild and untouched by mankind; other parts are the scene of great activity, particularly that of the logging industry.

★ **Englishman River Falls** – *From Parksville, take Rte. 4. After 5km/3mi, turn left and continue 8km/5mi.* This river tumbles over two sets of falls. The upper ones are narrow and deep, dropping into a gorge. A path bridges the river, following it to the lower falls *(round-trip 45min)* through a dense forest of tall trees, ferns and moss-covered rocks. The lower falls are twin jets dropping around a rock into a deep pool.

Route 4 leaves the plain behind and begins to enter the mountains.

★ **Little Qualicum Falls** – *26km/16mi from Parksville; turn right to parking area.* The Little Qualicum River descends over two sets of falls connected by a gorge. The lower falls are small, but the walk to the upper falls *(round-trip 30min)* through forest is pleasant, providing views of the canyon. The **upper falls★** are on two levels, with a pool between them.

Route 4 follows the south side of **Cameron Lake** with occasional views of it through the trees.

★★ **Cathedral Grove** – *35km/22mi from Parksville, part of MacMillan Provincial Park. Parking beside highway.* As the name suggests, Cathedral Grove contains some of the original tall trees of the island. Elsewhere Douglas firs have been cut for their wood, but fortunately this grove was preserved by the MacMillan Bloedel Paper Co. and donated to the province.

A walk *(45min)* under these giants is impressive, especially for those who have not seen the redwoods of California. Many of these firs rise to 60m/200ft or more. One is 3m/9.5ft in diameter and nearly 76m/250ft tall. The largest trees are 800 years old. Between them grow red cedar and hemlock trees.

Route 4 descends to the coast and bypasses **Port Alberni** (pop. 18,403), an important lumber centre that is situated at the head of Alberni Inlet. This arm of Barkley Sound reaches within 19km/12mi of the east coast of the island. The road then follows **Sproat Lake** with good views. Signs of logging activity are evident along the road, from cut areas to huge logging trucks. After leaving the lake Route 4 begins to climb Klitsa Mountain along the valley of the Taylor River.

After reaching the height of land, the road begins its winding descent to the Pacific along the Kennedy River, offering **views★** of snow-capped peaks. The

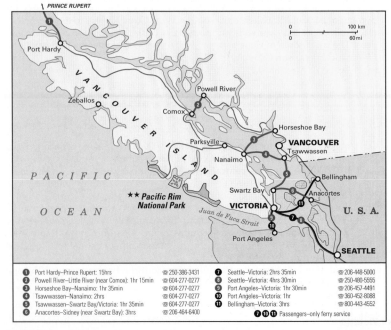

❶ Port Hardy–Prince Rupert: 15hrs	☎ 250-386-3431	❼ Seattle–Victoria: 2hrs 35min	☎ 206-448-5000
❷ Powell River–Little River (near Comox): 1hr 15min	☎ 604-277-0277	❽ Seattle–Victoria: 4hrs 30min	☎ 250-480-5555
❸ Horseshoe Bay–Nanaimo: 1hr 35min	☎ 604-277-0277	❾ Port Angeles–Victoria: 1hr 30min	☎ 206-457-4491
❹ Tsawwassen–Nanaimo: 2hrs	☎ 604-277-0277	❿ Port Angeles–Victoria: 1hr	☎ 360-452-8088
❺ Tsawwassen–Swartz Bay/Victoria: 1hr 35min	☎ 604-277-0277	⓫ Bellingham–Victoria: 3hrs	☎ 800-443-4552
❻ Anacortes–Sidney (near Swartz Bay): 3hrs	☎ 206-464-6400	❼ ❿ ⓫ Passengers–only ferry service	

river widens into **Kennedy Lake,** the largest stretch of fresh water on the island. The road follows the lake, alternately rising above it and dipping to water level. Pacific Rim National Park Reserve is reached near the junction with the Tofino-to-Ucluelet road.

★★ PACIFIC RIM NATIONAL PARK RESERVE

Open year-round. Hiking, fishing, canoeing, sailing, swimming. Park visitor centre open mid-Mar–mid-Oct daily 10am–4pm (extended summer hours vary). Parking $5/vehicle/day. Use fees in effect. △ ⚭ ♿ ☎ *250-726-4212 (summer) or 250-726-7721 (year-round).*

Situated on the rugged west coast of Vancouver Island, this reserve is a long, narrow strip of rocky islands and headlands, stretching intermittently for about 130km/80mi between Port Renfrew and Tofino. The park consists of the 77km/48mi **West Coast Trail** for backpackers between Port Renfrew and Bamfield *(each end is accessible by road; trail open mid-Apr–mid-Oct only; reservations & quota system in effect; use permit required;* ☎ *800-663-6000, Canada/US),* about 100 islands and rocky islets in Barkley Sound known as the **Broken Group Islands** *(cruise departs from Argyle St. dock in Alberni Jun–mid-Sept Mon, Wed & Fri 8am; additional cruise Jul–Labour Day Sun 8am; round-trip 10hrs, Sun 9hrs commentary; reservations required; $40, Sun $36;* ⚭ *; Alberni Marine Transportation* ☎ *250-723-8313)* and famous Long Beach.

★★ **Long Beach** – *Visitors can surf and swim. However the water is cold (10°C/50°F) and can be extremely dangerous due to changing tides and currents. For details contact the park visitor centre.* Pounded by the surf this 11km/7mi curve of sand and rock is backed by a dense rain forest and mountains rising to 1,200m/4,000ft. Offshore, sea lions bask on the rocks, and Pacific gray whales are often spotted. Numerous birds make the beach and forest their home, while many more visit seasonally.

The heavy rainfall and moderate temperatures of this coast have produced thick rain forests where Sitka spruce flourishes, and red cedar and hemlock grow. Breakers of the Pacific Ocean crash in, depositing huge drift logs over the beach one day and carrying them away the next. The power of these waves is immense; variation in sand level can be as great as 1.8m/6ft between winter and summer in one year. At low tide the beach is nearly 1km/.5mi wide, and tidal pools among the rocks brim with a variety of sea creatures.

There are several points of access to Long Beach. Paths weave through the high trees and mossy, fern-covered rain forest, offering views of the beach and ocean. From Combers Beach **sea lion rocks** can be seen offshore *(binoculars advisable).*

★★ **Radar Hill** – *22km/14mi from Ucluelet junction. Take road to left, ascending 1.6km/1mi to viewpoint.* From this point above the forest, a splendid **panorama**★★ of the area is obtained *(telescope available).* The mountains behind the park can be seen, as well as the wild and rocky coastline.

VICTORIA★★★

British Columbia
Pop. 71,228
Map of Principal Sights p 2
Tourist Office ☎ 250-953-2033

Facing the **Juan de Fuca Strait** and the **Olympic** and **Cascade Mountains** in Washington state, the capital of British Columbia occupies the southeast tip of Vancouver Island. Famous for its beautiful gardens, its elegance and gentility and its British traditions, the city contrasts with the rest of VANCOUVER ISLAND, which is largely untamed forest and rugged mountains pounded by raging seas. Canada's "gentlest" city, with its annual rainfall of 680mm/27in and large amount of sunshine, is a popular tourist destination. Author Stephen Leacock *(p 152)* wrote of it, "If I had known of this place before, I would have been born here."

Historical Notes – When it became clear that the location of their Pacific headquarters would be declared US territory, the Hudson's Bay Company built a trading post in 1843 on the site of present-day Victoria, naming the new post after the Queen of England. An important provisioning centre, the post grew in the 1850s and 60s during British Columbia's gold rushes *(p 33).* In 1849 the settlement was made the capital of the crown colony of Vancouver Island. When the island was united with the mainland, Victoria became the capital of British Columbia (except between 1866 and 1868, when New Westminster was the capital). A centre of gracious living, the city avoided industrial development when the Canadian Pacific Railway was terminated at Vancouver (trains cross to the island by ferry), which grew into a major commercial centre. Other than the Canadian Forces' Pacific Naval base in nearby **Esquimalt** (pop. 16,192), major employers for the Victoria area are the government and the tourism industry. The city's pleasant climate also has attracted a large retirement population.

★★ DOWNTOWN   *1 day. Map p 85.*

The city centre is situated along Government Street, which is the main shopping area, and around the James Bay section of the harbour where ferries from Port Angeles and Seattle dock. Intriguing little squares and alleys such as **Bastion Square** and Trounce Alley house elegant shops, restaurants and sidewalk cafes. Just north, vibrant **Market Square**, a collection of older renovated buildings, has shops around courtyard gardens.

To the south, located off Belleville Street, is Heritage Court. The narrow columns and arches on the ground floor of this group of striking modern buildings add a distinct Islamic flavour. The complex houses the provincial archives and the Royal British Columbia Museum. At the front stands the **Netherlands Carillon Tower [A]**, an open-sided 27m/88ft tower containing 62 bells given to the province by Canadians of Dutch origin (*concerts Jul & Aug ☎250-387-1616*).

★★★ Royal British Columbia Museum – *Open Jul–mid-Sept daily 9:30am–7pm. Rest of the year daily 10am–5:30pm. Closed Jan 1, Dec 25. $5.* ✗ ⅙ 🅿 ☎250-387-3701. One of the top museums in the world, this eminent institution has focused on the natural and human history of the province for over 100 years. Built in 1968, the museum is completing a new entrance hall to welcome its 850,000 annual visitors.

A selection of First Nations totem poles is on display there. At the north end an arcade called the **Glass House** contains a collection of totem poles from all over the province.

British Columbia's **natural history** is featured on the second floor. A series of spectacular **dioramas** of the coastal forest and seashore regions includes animal, bird and fish life. An unusual **Open Ocean** exhibit is based on William Beebe's deep-sea dive in 1930. Visitors follow his adventure through a succession of theatres, dioramas, observation platforms and models that portray life in the open seas (*30min; free timed ticket available from machine adjacent to exhibit*).

The third floor is devoted to British Columbia's **human history**. Starting with the province today, visitors walk backwards through time. Highlights are the reconstruction of a turn-of-the-century street, complete with shops, hotel, movie house and station; vivid re-creations of a sawmill, fish-packing plant, farmyard and mine, illustrating the development of industry; and, in the section on European discovery of the province, a reconstruction of part of George Vancouver's ship, *The Discovery*.

The **Native History Gallery**★★ contains an extensive collection of Indian art, arranged in striking dioramas. These exhibits depict the way of life prior to the arrival of Europeans and the changes after contact, such as smallpox epidemics, land settlement disputes and the banning of potlatch ceremonies. Note especially the totem poles, the reconstructed **big house** and furnishings that once belonged to a Kwa-gulth chief and the re-created **pit house**.

★ Parliament Buildings – On the south side of James Bay stands a long, squat stone building with a central dome, topped by a gilt statue of Capt. George Vancouver. Designed by **Francis Rattenbury** (1867-1935) and completed in 1898, "the buildings," as they are known, house the British Columbia legislature and government offices. Stationed in front of them is a bronze statue of Queen Victoria. A highly decorated arch beneath the dome marks the entrance (*open late May–Labour Day daily 9am–5pm; on weekends, visit by 30min guided tour only; rest of the year Mon–Fri 9am–4pm; closed national holidays;* ✗ ⅙ ☎250-387-3046). At dusk thousands of small lights outline the buildings' exterior, adding a romantic flair.

★ Empress Hotel – Also designed by Francis Rattenbury, and built by the Canadian Pacific Railway in 1908, this enormous turreted, ivy-covered hotel is a city landmark. For many years "tea at the Empress, " served in the **Palm Court**, was considered an essential part of gracious living. Still served at the hotel, tea is more a tourist attraction now than a facet of gracious living (*daily 12:30–5pm; $19.95; reservations suggested; no jeans, shorts or athletic wear;* ⅙ ☎250-384-8111). Be sure to see the clubby **Bengal Lounge** and the modern, airy Victoria Conference Centre with its outdoor fountain plaza.

Located within the hotel complex, on the Humboldt Street side, is **Miniature World [B]**, featuring a host of small-size re-creations ranging from the Battle of Waterloo to the Canadian Pacific Railway *(open Jun–mid-Sept daily 8:30am–9:30pm; rest of the year daily 9am–5pm; closed Dec 25; $6.75; & ☎250-385-9731).*

★ **Thunderbird Park [C]** – *Open daily year-round.* & ☎250-953-2033. This small park has a fine collection of original and replica totem poles and other Indian carvings. Many of the original works, on which these copies are based, were executed by Chief Mungo Martin, a famous carver. As each carving decays, it is copied and replaced *(carvers can sometimes be seen at work).*

Next to Thunderbird Park stands a clapboard dwelling, **Helmcken House [D]**, the original core of which was built in 1852 for Dr. John Helmcken and his wife *(open May–Sept daily 10am–5pm; rest of the year daily 11am–4pm; closed month of Jan & Dec 25, 26; $4; ☎250-361-0021).* Physician to the Hudson's Bay Company at Fort Victoria, Helmcken expanded the house in 1856 and again in 1884 to accommodate his growing family of seven children. His medical equipment is on display along with various house-
hold possessions.

★ **Maritime Museum** – *Open year-round daily 9:30am–4:30pm. Closed Dec 25. $5.* & ☎250-385-4222. A lighthouse beacon stands in front of the law court building that houses this museum. Inside there are model ships, marine paraphernalia and displays on Northwest Coast explorers. Of special interest are the *Tilikum,* a converted Indian dugout canoe that sailed from Victoria to England in the early 1900s, and the *Trekka,* a 6m/20ft sailing boat built in Victoria that sailed around the world from 1955 to 1959, the smallest boat ever to undertake such a voyage.

Crystal Garden – *Open mid-Jun–mid-Sept daily 8am–8pm. Rest of the year daily 9am–6pm. Closed first 2 weeks Jan & Dec 25. $6.50.* ✗ & ☎250-381-1213. The immense glass house was once the location of orchestral concerts, art exhibits and a large underglass sea-water swimming pool. Today it houses a tropical garden filled with exotic birds, monkeys and plants. Note the glassed-in emergence area in the walk-through butterfly room. Crystal Garden is also a pleasant place to have tea.

Undersea Gardens – *Open May–Sept daily 9am–9pm. Rest of the year daily 10am–5pm. Closed Dec 25. $6.75.* ☎250-382-5717. Situated in the inner harbour, this structure enables visitors to descend below the water's surface to see fish in aquariums. During the shows divers bring various species such as wolf eels and octopuses close to the glass walls for spectators to view.

★★ **SCENIC DRIVE**   *Allow 1hr. 13km/8mi. Map p 86.*

Leave from Thunderbird Park and take Douglas St.

This beautiful drive enables visitors to appreciate Victoria's grand site on the Strait of Juan de Fuca and the lovely gardens of the city's residents.

Skirting the large, flower-filled **Beacon Hill Park★**, the road passes a plaque **[1]** marking the initial kilometer of the nearly 8,000km/5,000mi **Trans-Canada Highway**, which stretches to St. John's, Newfoundland. *Turn left on Dallas Rd.* From Finlayson and Clover Points, there are fine **views★★** of the Olympic Mountains. *Continue to Hollywood Crescent. Turn right on Ross St. (at Robertson St.); Ross becomes Crescent Rd. Bear left at King George Terrace and ascend the hill.* The drive enters the community of **Oak Bay** (pop. 17,815), a wealthy suburb with large houses, beautiful gardens, pretty views and a very English population. Harling Point provides a good **view** of the rocky coastline and the houses perched along the coast. Directly below on the right, Gonzales Bay is visible and the Trial Islands can be seen offshore to the left. *Take Beach Dr.*

The drive continues around McNeill Bay with several more viewpoints. Bisected by the road, the Oak Bay golf course on Gonzales Point is one of the continent's most attractive courses with **views★★** of the sea *(weather permitting)*, the San Juan Islands and the snow-clad peaks of the Cascades, dominated by Mt. Baker.

The drive then passes through **Uplands Park★**, a pleasant section of Oak Bay with lovely homes and gardens. From **Cattle Point** there are views of the coast.

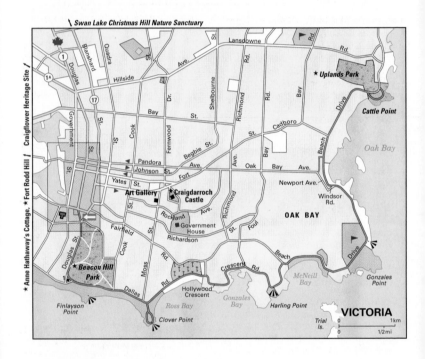

ADDITIONAL SIGHTS

★Craigdarroch Castle – *Map above. Open Jul–Aug daily 9am–7pm. Rest of the year daily 10am–4:30pm. Closed Jan 1, Dec 25 & 26. $6.* ▪ ☎250-592-5323. Built by Robert Dunsmuir, a Scot who made a fortune from coal, the huge stone mansion has towers, turrets and a carved carriage entrance. This former centre of Victoria's society (one Dunsmuir son became premier of the province and later lieutenant-governor) once stood amid 11ha/27 acres of gardens. Today the house is gradually being restored to its 1880s grandeur. Note the wood-panelled hall and massive oak staircase. A large dance hall is found on the fourth floor, and from the top of the tower *(accessible from dance hall)*, there is a good view of Victoria.

Art Gallery of Greater Victoria – *Map above. 1040 Moss St. Open year-round daily 10am–5pm. Closed Jan 1, Good Friday & Dec 25. $5.* ♿ ▪ ☎250-384-1531. Housed in a Victorian mansion (1890), to which several modern additions have been made, the gallery is home to the works of **Emily Carr** *(p 75)*, whose paintings are on permanent display. Shown in regularly changing exhibits is the gallery's collection of Asian art, the highlight of which is the Shinto Shrine (1899-1900), constructed of copper, Keiyaki wood and sandstone, in the small Japanese outdoor garden.

Swan Lake Christmas Hill Nature Sanctuary – *Map below. 3873 Swan Lake Rd. 8km/5mi north by Hwy. 17. Exit McKenzie Ave. Take first right onto Rainbow St. Follow the signs. Open year-round daily dawn–dusk. Visitor centre open year-round Mon–Fri 8:30am–4pm, weekends noon–4pm. Closed Jan 1, Dec 25 & 26.* & ⊡ ☎250-479-0211. This peaceful 45ha/110 acre preserve includes wetlands, fields and forest. Nature House, which serves as a visitor centre, features thought-provoking displays geared toward children and a small resource library. The lily pad-filled lake provides refuge for waterfowl and nesting birds. A 2.5km/1.5mi trail *(30min)* up Christmas Hill traverses sections of residential streets, but the summit affords a **panorama★** of Victoria and environs, including Elk Lake to the north.

★ **Fort Rodd Hill** – ☞ *Map below. 14km/9mi west by Rtes. 1, 1A and Ocean Blvd. Grounds open daily year-round. Buildings open Mar–Oct daily 10am–5:30pm. Rest of the year weekends only 10am–5:30pm. Closed Jan 1, Dec 25 & 26. $3.* & ⊡ ☎250-478-5849. Set in 18ha/44 acres of land at the southwest corner of Esquimalt harbour, the fort contains the remains of three coastal artillery-gun batteries and displays on-shore defences. Built to protect the approaches to the naval base at Esquimalt, the batteries were in operation until 1956. From beside Fisgard Lighthouse, there are fine **views★** of Juan de Fuca Strait, the Olympic Mountains and the naval base.

★ **Anne Hathaway's Cottage** – *Map below. In Esquimalt, 429 Lampson St., part of Olde England Inn complex. Open Jun–Sept daily 9am–7:30pm. Rest of the year daily 10am–4pm. $6.75.* ✗ ⊡ ☎250-388-4353. Covered with a thatched roof, this black and white half-timbered building is a replica of the Stratford (England) home of William Shakespeare's wife. Inside there are ten rooms with period furniture. Note especially the wooden panelling on the ground floor. An attractive "old world" English garden fronts the cottage. Adjacent to the house is a lane of quaint shops housed in half-timbered buildings reflective of the architecture of 16C England.

Craigflower Heritage Site – *Hwy. 1A (Craigflower Rd.) at Admirals Rd. Open Jul–Aug daily noon–4pm. Jun & Sept Mon, Thu–Sun noon–4pm. $4.50.* & ⊡ ☎250-383-4627. This Georgian clapboard house (1856) was constructed by Kenneth McKenzie, bailiff for Puget Sound Agricultural Co., the first organization to develop the island for farming. One of the earliest buildings in Victoria, the house boasts a handsome studded-oak front door. Most of the manor is original and contains period furnishings. Visitors may play the piano in the parlour and don period attire in a child's bedroom upstairs. The kitchen pantry is often stocked with the harvest from two vegetable gardens maintained on the premises.

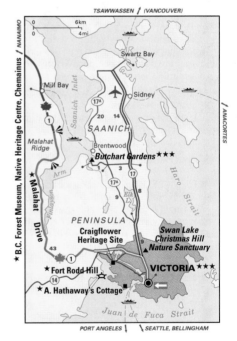

EXCURSIONS

★★★ **Butchart Gardens** – *Map above. 21km/13mi north by Rte. 17 and Keating X Rd. or by 17A. Open year-round daily at 9am. Closing times vary. $13.* ✗ & ⊡ ☎250-652-5256. Expanded to approximately 20ha/50 acres, these internationally famous gardens were started in 1904 by Jennie Butchart to beautify the quarry pit resulting from her husband's cement business. Still operated by the family, the grounds are maintained by a small army of gardeners in summer.

The floral showpiece is the beautiful **Sunken Garden★★★** *(illustration p 88)* with its green lawns, trees and exquisite flower arrangements that create a whirl of colour. The flowers change from season to season, but the effect is always striking. Set in a huge pit with ivy-covered sides, the garden is best viewed from above or from the rock island at its centre. Paths weave down into it through a rockery.

Sunken Garden in Butchart Gardens

The other gardens include the **Ross Fountain** with changing water displays in a rocky pool; the **Rose Garden★**, its rose-covered arbors full of blooms overhead and on both sides *(Jun–Sept)*; the dark, secluded **Japanese Garden★** with its lacquered bridges and wooden teahouses; and the formal **Italian Garden★** with statues and a star-shaped lily pond. On summer evenings the lighting of the gardens provides an entirely different perspective *(mid-Jun–mid-Sept)*. Fireworks are also displayed in summer *(Sat, Jul–Aug)*.

★ **Malahat Drive** – *Take Douglas St. north to Hwy. 1 (Trans-Can Hwy.). About 16km/ 10mi along the highway a marker signals the beginning of Malahat Drive.* This attractive stretch of road crosses Malahat Ridge with good **views★★** of Finlayson Arm, Saanich Inlet, the Gulf Islands and the mainland. On a clear day Mt. Baker *(p 71)* is visible through the trees.

Native Heritage Centre – *In Duncan, about 60km/37mi north by Hwy. 1. Open mid-May–mid-Oct daily 9:30am–5pm. Rest of the year daily 10am–4:30pm. $6.50.* ✗ ᴅ ☎*250-746-8119*. Enclosed by a high fence, the centre, located adjacent to a busy shopping mall, is a surprisingly tranquil setting of paved walkways and wooden buildings. A film *(23min)* on the history of the Cowichan people is shown in the theatre. The arts and crafts gallery features exquisite masks, cedar baskets, jewellery, Cowichan sweaters, and books on Indian culture *(for sale)*. The highlight is the large **carving shed** where native craftsmen apply traditional designs to tall red cedar poles, laid horizontally. Visitors are invited to try their carving skills.

★ **British Columbia Forest Museum** – *65km/40mi north by Hwy. 1, just after Duncan. Open daily May–Labour Day daily 9:30am–6pm. Early Sept–mid-Oct daily 10am–5pm. $7 ($5.50 after Labour Day).* ✗ ᴅ ☎*250-746-1251*. Covering 40ha/100 acres, this museum provides some background to the province's most important industry. Visitors can walk through a forest of Douglas fir trees, visit a log museum displaying the evolution of logging techniques, see a reconstructed logging camp and ride the narrow-gauge steam railway*(May–Labour Day)*.

Chemainus – *Pop. 562. 78km/48mi north by Hwy. 1. Visitor information* ☎*250-246-3944*. This small waterfront town has gained fame for 32 murals painted on the exteriors of its buildings. Resident Karl Schutz promoted the idea to revitalize the community's economy when the closing of the local lumber mill was imminent in the early 1980s. The mill has since reopened, but the artwork is the driving force of Chemainus' present prosperity, attracting reputedly some 400,000 visitors annually. Scenes from the town's past celebrate people, buildings and events. Especially fine are *Native Heritage* symbolizing the three tribes of the Coast Salish Nation and *Arrival of the 'Reindeer' in Horseshoe Bay*, featuring a native woman in a colorful robe as she watches a ship entering the bay.

WATERTON LAKES NATIONAL PARK★★

Alberta
Map of Principal Sights p 2

Situated in the province's southwest corner, this lovely preserve in the Canadian Rockies forms an International Peace Park with the larger Glacier National Park in Montana. Because its gently rolling hills (rarely over 1,200m/4,000ft) meet a vertical rock wall towering another 1,200m/4,000ft or more above the plains, the park has been described as the place "where the prairies meet the mountains." The underlying sediment of these mountains, which once were part of an inland sea, was thrust up and sculptured by erosion and glaciation into sharp peaks, narrow ridges and interlocked U-shaped valleys. Among them, the three Waterton Lakes lie in a deep glacial trough. Formerly a Blackfoot Indian stronghold, the mountains of Waterton were first visited by Thomas Blakiston of the Palliser Expedition, who explored the area in 1858 and named the lakes for an 18C English naturalist, **Charles Waterton**. Oil was discovered a few decades later, but never proved profitable. The area was designated a national park in 1895.

VISIT

➔ *Open year-round. Hiking, horseback riding, fishing, boating, golf, winter sports. $4/day.* △ ✕ ⴲ ☎403-859-2224.

Waterton Townsite – Built on delta materials deposited by Cameron Creek, the town has a lovely **site★★** near the point where Upper Lake narrows into the Bosporus Strait, which separates it from Middle Lake. Just south behind the townsite, the flat face of **Mt. Richards** can be distinguished. Beside it stands **Mt. Bertha**, marked by pale green streaks down the otherwise dark green surface. The streaks were caused by snowslides that swept trees down the mountainside. Across the lake rise **Vimy Peak** and **Vimy Ridge**. Upper Lake stretches south into Montana, separating the mountains of the Lewis and Clark range, which tower steeply above it. In summer **tour boats** make trips down the lake to the US ranger station at the southern end *(depart Jul–Aug daily 9, 10am, 1, 4, 7pm; mid-May–Jun & Sept departure times vary; round-trip 2hrs; commentary; $16; ✕ ⴲ ▣ Waterton Shoreline Cruises ☎403-859-2362).* Behind the townsite, **Cameron Falls** can be seen dropping over a layered cliff.

★★ **Cameron Lake** – *17km/11mi from townsite by Akamina Hwy.* Before reaching the lake the highway passes the site of the first oil well in western Canada. The lake itself is set immediately below the Continental Divide and, like Upper Waterton, it spans the international border. Dominating the view across the lake are, to the left, **Mt. Custer** and to the right, **Forum Peak**.

★ **Red Rock Canyon** – *19km/12mi from townsite; turn left at Blakiston Creek.* The drive to this small canyon offers good **views★** of the surrounding mountains. A **nature trail** follows the narrow canyon *(2km/1.2mi),* where characteristic colour is due to iron compounds in the rock that oxidized to form hematite.

★ **Buffalo Paddock** – *400m/.2mi from park entrance. Auto circuit 3km/2mi.* A small herd of buffalo occupies a large enclosure on a fine **site★** with Bellevue Mountain and Mt. Galway as a backdrop.

WHITEHORSE★

Yukon Territory
Pop. 17,925
Map of Principal Sights p 2
Tourist Office ☎403-667-5340

Situated on flat land on the west side of a big bend in the Yukon River, Whitehorse is the capital of the Yukon Territory and a regional service centre. Above it sharp cliffs rise to a plateau where the airport is located and across which the ALASKA HIGHWAY passes. On the river's east side, barren hills become mountains known as the Big Salmon Range.

Transport Town – The city owes its existence to the difficulty encountered by the Dawson City-bound Klondike Stampeders *(p 34),* in negotiating Miles Canyon and the Whitehorse Rapids (now tamed by a hydro-electric plant) on the Yukon River. A tramway was built to carry goods around these obstacles so that the boats could be piloted through with greater ease. The completion of the White Pass and Yukon Route Railroad in 1900, from Skagway *(p 92)* through the Coast Mountains, changed methods of transport in the area. The town soon bustled in summer with the transfer of passengers and goods from railway to riverboat, and from railway to overland stage in winter. The railway company's decision to end its line at Whitehorse (and not to continue to DAWSON CITY) resulted in the birth of the city. The presence of the railway and of a small airport were key factors when the decision to build the Alaska Highway *(p 37)* was made in 1942. Whitehorse became a major base for its construction, changing overnight at a time when Dawson City was declining in importance. Reflecting this change, the territorial capital was moved here in 1953. Today the city is a centre for tourism as well as communications in the Yukon. Proud of its part in the Klondike Stampede, the community stages a celebration every February called the **Sourdough Rendezvous** when people dress in the costumes of 1898 and race dog teams on the frozen Yukon River.

SIGHTS *1 day*

No longer a frontier town in appearance, Whitehorse retains, nevertheless, some historic structures, notably: the **old log church** on Elliott at Third, built in 1900; the **"skyscrapers"** on Lambert between Second and Third Avenues, built after World War II when there was a housing shortage, and still in use today; and

the log **railway station** on First Avenue at Main. In contrast is the modern steel and aluminum Yukon government **Administration Building** on Second Avenue, opened in 1976. Its light and airy interior, finished in wood, features an acrylic resin mural that looks like stained glass. The Yukon Permanent Art Collection installed here features contemporary art as well as traditional native costumes and artifacts.

Bald Eagle

★ **MacBride Museum** – *1st Ave. at Wood St. Open late May–Labour Day daily 10am–6pm. Rest of the year Tue–Thu noon–4pm. Closed national holidays. $3.50. ☎403-667-2709.* Situated in a log building (1967) built with a sod roof, this museum features Gold Rush memorabilia, Indian cultural objects and a splendid collection of old **photographs** of the men and women of the Yukon. A large number of preserved animals are displayed side by side, enabling the visitor to appreciate the relative size and characteristic markings of each, such as the differing antlers of moose, elk and caribou. Outside are relics of Yukon transport, examples of early machinery, Sam McGee's cabin and a government telegraph office c.1900.

★★ **SS Klondike** – *Second Ave. near Robert Campbell Bridge. Open mid-May–mid-Sept daily 9am–7pm. $3.25 .☎403-667-4511.* One of over 200 sternwheelers that once plied the waters of the Yukon between Whitehorse and Dawson City, this well-restored 1937 craft is the only remaining steamboat open to the public in the Territory.
Carrying passengers, ore and supplies, the vessel required 32 cords of wood to fuel the 40-hour, 700km/436mi downstream trip to Dawson. The return trip against the current took 96 hours and burned 112 cords of wood. Visitors can see the huge boiler, engine room and cargo space; from the wheelhouse, envision the captain's vantage point; and view the galley and first-class passenger accommodation, including the observation room and dining area with its elegant tablesettings.

Cross the river via Robert Campbell Bridge and stop to see the **fish ladder** at **Whitehorse Dam**, built to enable the chinook salmon to circumnavigate the dam and reach their spawning grounds upriver *(usually occurs in August)*. Interpretive panels and windows for viewing the fish as they "climb" the ladder are provided. These salmon are near the end of the longest-known chinook migration in the world—3,200km/2,000mi. The dam is best viewed from the fishway's observation deck.

★★ **Miles Canyon** – *9km/6mi south of Whitehorse via Canyon Rd.* Following the edge of Schwatka Lake, **Canyon Road** passes the *MV Schwatka* dock *(below)* and climbs above the canyon *(sharp curves and steep grades)* where there is a good **view★** from the lookout. Near the parking lot above Miles Canyon, another fine **view★** is possible. The river can be crossed by a footbridge for other clifftop views.

For more than 1km/.75mi, the Yukon River passes through a narrow gorge of sheer columnar basalt walls, grayish red in colour. Created by the shrinkage of volcanic lava upon cooling, these walls rise straight up, 9-12m/30-40ft above the river. Here the Yukon still flows through rapidly, swirling around Devil's Whirlpool. But construction of the power dam downstream has very much lessened the speed and navigational hazards the stampeders experienced.

Canyon **cruises** *(MV Schwatka departs Jun–mid-Sept daily 2pm; round-trip 2hrs; commentary; reservations required; $17; &Grayline Yukon* ☎*403-668-3225; take South Access Rd. towards centre of Whitehorse, turn right onto unpaved road immediately past railroad tracks)* afford good **views★** of the deep green waters of the Yukon and the steep canyon walls. The tremendous force of the river is better appreciated from the water level than from the viewpoints above. Interesting historical commentary is given.

Yukon Transportation Museum – *Alaska Hwy. near airport. Open mid-May–Labour Day daily 9am–6pm. Early–mid-Sept daily 9am–5pm. $3.50.* & ☎*403-668-4792.* Exhibits include archival photos of Yukon aviation and a replica of the 1920s mail carrier plane, *Queen of the Yukon.*

★★ EXCURSION TO SKAGWAY   1 day. Map p 92.

Note: Skagway is in Alaska. Canadian citizens need identification to enter the US. Other visitors need US visas, which are available from any US consulate, but not in Whitehorse.

An impressive trip in the Yukon is the traverse of the Coast Mountains to the Pacific tidewater at Skagway—terminus of the Klondike Highway—on the Alaska Panhandle. Tiny frontier towns, dramatic lake systems, barren flatlands, abandoned mines and coastal vistas season this outing with diversity, while summoning images of earlier sojourners struggling to reach the fields of gold.

Treacherous Trails – The majority of gold seekers en route to Dawson City *(p 41)* sailed up the Pacific Coast to Skagway or Dyea *(below)* and trudged into the Yukon across the Coast Mountains. From Skagway the trail followed the **White Pass**, a narrow and slippery climb of 879m/2,885ft. More than 3,000 horses were forced along this route in 1897. Most died before reaching the summit. Their remains were quickly trampled underfoot by the mass of humanity behind them. Dead Horse Trail, as it became known, was closed that same winter.

Stampeders who insisted on continuing turned to the more difficult **Chilkoot Pass**. Starting in Dyea, this route was 183m/600ft higher than the White Pass and much steeper—it climbed at an angle of 35° in places. Raw rock in summer, the pass became slick ice and snow in winter, and with temperatures of -50°C/-58°F, it was a nightmare to climb. Yet over the winter of 1897-98, 22,000 people scaled it, not just once but 30 to 40 times! The North West Mounted Police at the Canadian border insisted that anyone entering Canada have a year's supply of food and equipment because of shortages in the Territory. To carry this "ton" of goods over the pass, stampeders had to make numerous trips. Thus the Chilkoot was a stream of climbing humanity for the entire winter.

Today a hiking trail is maintained over the Chilkoot Pass. The adventurous can relive the stampeder experience by hiking the legendary **Chilkoot Trail**, which starts at the abandoned site of Skagway's former rival, **Dyea** *(15km/9mi north of Skagway by dirt road)* and ends at Bennett Lake. The arduous 54km/33mi trek can take up to five days and requires proper equipment *(for trail information and maps, contact the National Park Service in Skagway* ☎*907-983-2921).*

★★ **Klondike Highway to Skagway** – *180km/112mi by Alaska Hwy. and Klondike Hwy. (Rte. 2). About 3hrs; US border open year-round daily 24hrs; Canada Customs in Fraser open Apr-Oct daily 24hrs; Nov–Mar daily 8am–midnight.* ☎*403-821-4111 (Canada Customs) or 907-983-2325 (US Customs).* Adjoining the Alaska Highway south of Whitehorse, the Klondike Highway passes through forest and gradually enters the mountains, with views of snow-capped peaks ahead. At small, historic **Carcross** (pop. 183)—where the final rail was laid for the White Pass and Yukon Route—the scenery changes dramatically as the road follows the shores of **Tagish Lake**, **Windy Arm** and **Tutshi** (TOO-shy) **Lake**. The sight is striking: imposing mountains rise straight out of the blue waters of the lakes. After leaving Tutshi Lake the road begins the traverse of the White Pass with another change in scenery. The pass is desolate, almost lunar—treeless flatlands with lichen-covered rocks. The steep descent to Skagway on the coast permits views of the **Taiya Inlet** of the Lynn Canal far below.

★ **Skagway** – Pop. 692. The wide Pacific lying at its door, the historic little community, known as the "Gateway to the Klondike," occupies a lovely **site★** with snow-capped peaks as a backdrop. A port of call on the Inside Passage route *(p 46)*, this waterfront town, with its pervasive frontier flavour, attracts scores of visitors annually via road, rail and seaway.

Skagway was born with the Klondike Stampede. Until the first boatload of gold seekers docked in July of 1897, Capt. William Moore and his son were the only European settlers in the area, having arrived in 1888. Amid supplies, horses and equipment, tents and huts sprouted up everywhere. In three months the population swelled to roughly 20,000 and a grid pattern of streets sported saloons, casinos, dance halls and stores. Lawlessness was rife as the town became home to notorious characters such as **Soapy Smith**, a con artist *par excellence* who succeeded in divesting many greenhorn gold rushers of their money. In 1898 construction of the White Pass and Yukon Route Railroad *(below)* and a crackdown on crime helped stabilize the community.

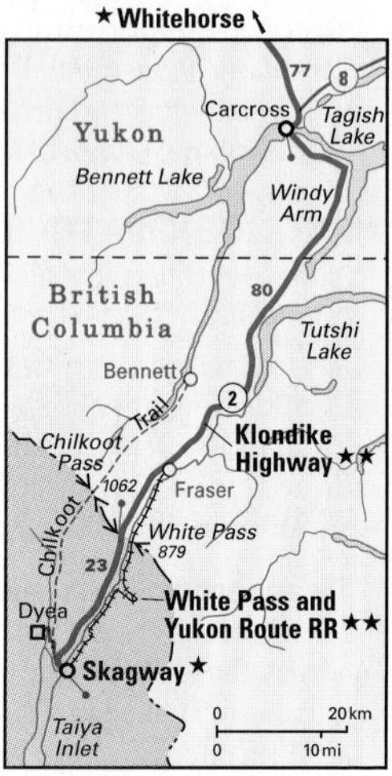

Northern terminus of the southeast ferry system, the small but busy port has received regular calls since 1963. The Klondike Highway from Skagway to Carcross was laid in 1978, and the railway restored in 1988.

The Town – *2.5hrs. Skagway visitor centre (new location in 1996) open mid-May–mid-Sept daily 8am–5pm.* ☎*907-983-2855.* Designated a historic district by the US National Park Service, the area along **Broadway** from First to Seventh Avenues contains several turn-of-the-century wooden structures housing hotels, saloons and shops restored to evoke the days of the Gold Rush.

The former railroad depot, a handsome 1898 building, serves as the Park Service **visitor centre** *(open mid-May–mid-Sept daily 8am–6pm; rest of the year Mon–Fri 8am–5pm; ♿☎907-983-2921)* and departure point for walking tours conducted by park rangers. Particularly noteworthy is the **Arctic Brotherhood Hall** *(Broadway between 2nd & 3rd Aves.)* with its fanciful driftwood facade. This building houses Skagway's **museum**, which features artifacts and documents from the town's colourful past *(open mid-May–Sept daily 9am–5pm; $2; ♿☎907-983-2420).*

★★ **White Pass and Yukon Route Railroad** – *Departs from 2nd & Spring Sts. mid-May–mid-Sept daily 8:45am & 1:15pm. Round-trip 3hrs. Commentary. $75. (Through-service to Whitehorse available; departs Skagway 12:40pm, transfer in Fraser, BC to motorcoach; arrives Whitehorse 6pm; $95 one way.) Reservations suggested. ♿ White Pass & Yukon Route* ☎*907-983-2217.* Conceived in 1898 as an alternative to the treacherous ascent of the White Pass and Chilkoot Trails, this narrow-gauge railroad stands as a testimony to the inventiveness and determination of the stampeder spirit. The route, which originally linked Skagway to Whitehorse, functioned commercially from 1900 to 1982. Operating solely as a tourist attraction since 1988, the refurbished railroad cars climb, in a mere 32km/20mi, to an elevation of 873m/2,865ft, providing **views★** of Skagway and the rugged peaks dominating the town. On-board commentary points out noteworthy features, such as waterfalls, bridges and remnants of the White Pass Trail. After reaching the summit at White Pass, the train concludes its thrilling 45km/28mi run at the Canadian station in Fraser, BC.

Before planning your trip to Canada be sure to consult:

- ***the Map of Principal Sights (pp 2-5);***
- ***the regional driving tours (pp 6-13).***

Covering a 483,450sq km/186,660sq mi triangle in Canada's northwest corner, the legendary Yukon conjures up images of raging rivers, snow-capped mountains, deserted valleys, long winters, the midnight sun and gold. An adventure to one of the truly faraway places of the globe, this scenic journey rewards travellers willing to traverse a relatively isolated frontier to witness nature's grandeur and mankind's diversions. The majestic Yukon River, a silent, but ever-present companion, dominates half the circuit.

The Mighty Yukon – One of the longest rivers in North America, this giant of the remote North—its Loucheux Indian name *Yu-kun-ah* means "great river"—traverses 3,185km/1,975mi of rugged territory. Originating in Tagish Lake on the Yukon/British Columbia boundary, the river flows northward through the Yukon Territory and Alaska to empty into the Bering Sea. The Teslin, Pelly, Stewart and White are its primary Canadian tributaries. Over the centuries this river's natural resources have sustained a native population, its wealth has lured fur traders and gold miners, its currents have transported scows and sternwheelers, and today its awesome beauty beckons adventurers from many countries.

Water Route to the Klondike – During the Gold Rush, thousands of stampeders travelling from Skagway ended their winter trek through Chilkoot Pass *(p 91)* at **Bennett Lake**, part of the lake system that forms the Yukon's headwaters. There, in the spring, they constructed boats to complete the journey via the Yukon and its tributaries to DAWSON CITY, a distance of some 800km/500mi. Hazards on the voyage, such as Miles Canyon *(p 91)* and Five Finger Rapids *(below)*, seemed minor after the traverse of the treacherous pass, but were harrowing in their own right. Reputedly, in the first few days of the mass exodus from Bennett Lake, 10 men drowned and 150 boats were wrecked in the rock-strewn rapids of Miles Canyon. Today thousands of people follow the route alongside the river, not to hunt for gold but to discover, as the Klondike Stampeders did, the beauty of that wild northland, and to experience what poet Robert Service called *The Spell of the Yukon:*

> *It's the great, big, broad land 'way up yonder,*
> *It's the forests where silence has lease,*
> *It's the beauty that thrills me with wonder,*
> *It's the stillness that fills me with peace.*

VISIT   *1 week, not including excursion to Skagway, Alaska.*
About 1,500km/930mi from Whitehorse via Klondike, Top of the World, Taylor and Alaska Hwys. Lengthy drive over stretches of gravel road. 4-wheel drive recommended. For road conditions, see p 37. In some sections, service facilities are few and infrequent. Prepare for emergencies with food, warm clothing and vehicle supplies. Be familiar with protection against weather and wild animals. The Milepost (p 37) is a useful reference for this trip.

★From Whitehorse to Dawson City
Allow 1 day. 540km/335mi by Klondike Hwy. (Rte. 2).

★ **Whitehorse** – *1 day. Description p 89.*

The **Klondike Highway** skirts Lake Laberge *(barely visible from the road)*, through which the Yukon River runs. At the end of the unpaved access road to the campground, there is a lovely **view** of this lake and the mountains beyond.
Passing through hilly and largely deserted country, the highway rejoins the river at **Carmacks** *(178km/110mi)*, named for the discoverer of Klondike gold *(p 41)*. After 196km/122mi, just beyond a bend in the Yukon, a series of small rock islands, varying in size, can be seen. These formations have divided the river into five fast-flowing channels, known as **Five Finger Rapids★**. A hazard to navigation even today, these rapids caused problems during the stampede; riverboats often had to be winched through the narrowest channel by cable. From the lookout *(panel exhibit)*, a good view of the rapids is afforded.
In the vicinity of Minto, about 2km/1mi past Minto Resorts, an unpaved road leads to the riverside *(1.6km/1mi)*. Here, amid the ruins of earlier log structures, a sign marks the Overland Trail, a wagon road built in 1902 and the winter mail route from WHITEHORSE to DAWSON CITY. The **view★** of the Yukon from the bank is grand.

Leaving the Yukon Valley the highway crosses the central plateau and bridges the Pelly and Stewart Rivers. At Pelly Crossing descriptive **panels** tell the history of the **Selkirk** people whose tradition it was to fish the area in spring, years prior to the coming of Europeans to the Yukon.

Note at Stewart Crossing Route 11 *(unpaved between Mayo and Keno)*, designated the **Silver Trail**, begins its 111km/69mi northeast traverse through Mayo (pop. 243)

Malak, Ottawa
Native Child with Fireweed

to Keno (pop. 36), a boom town in the 1920s when mining of the area's vast silver deposits was in its heyday *(p 42)*.

After Stewart Crossing the vast **Tintina Trench** runs parallel to the highway. From the designated lookout about 61km/38mi south of Dawson City, a good **view** of this valley can be obtained. Stretching through the Yukon and Alaska, the trench is another example of plate tectonics *(p 288)*.

There is a **viewpoint**, after 483km/300mi, of the valley of the Klondike River from above, with the Ogilvie Mountains to the

northeast. The road then follows the Klondike, but the river is not always visible because of the great mounds of tailings *(p 44)* left by mining dredges.

At 494km/307mi note that the **Dempster Highway** heads northward to Inuvik in the Mackenzie Delta *(p 306)* across the Ogilvie and Richardson Mountains. Named for Corporal Dempster of the North West Mounted Police, who pioneered the route by dogsled at the turn of the century, it is the only road in North America that crosses the Arctic Circle *(open all year except spring break-up and fall freeze-up when the Peel and Mackenzie River ferries do not operate)*.

The Klondike Highway crosses the Klondike River after 538km/334mi and enters Dawson City. The word *Klondike* is a Han Indian adaptation for "hammer water," suggestive of the posts hammered into the riverbed to make salmon traps.

★★ **Dawson City** – *2 days. Description p 41.*

From Dawson City to Whitehorse
945km/586mi by Top of the World (Rte. 9), Taylor (US-5) (both highways closed in winter), and Alaska Hwys. Allow 2-3 days. Caution: Reduced speeds necessary, usually 40–64km/h/25–40mph on winding and often unpaved road. Drive with headlights on. Canada and US Customs offices at border crossing for Rtes. 9 & 5 open mid-May–mid-Sept daily 9am–9pm (8am–8pm Alaska time). Alaska Hwy. border open year-round daily 24hrs. ☎403-862-7230 *(Canada Customs), 907-774-2252 (US Customs).*

★★ **Top of the World Highway** – *108km/67mi to Alaska border; road closed in winter. Entry only when US Customs open (see above).* Route 9 is called Top of the World Highway because most of its length is above the tree line, allowing magnificent **views★★★** in all directions. It leaves Dawson by the ferry *(continuous 24hr service May–Oct)* across the vast Yukon. At this point the river's waters are no longer the sparkling green colour of Miles Canyon *(p 91)*, but a light gray blue, resulting from the earth brought in by major tributaries—the Pelly, the White and the Stewart. For about 5km/3mi, the road climbs to a **viewpoint** at a bend in the road providing a different perspective of the city and rivers from that seen from Midnight Dome. After 14km/9mi there is another **viewpoint** of the Ogilvie Mountains, the Yukon Valley and, visible to the north, the Tintina Trench. From then on the road follows the ridgetops for 90km/50mi, winding up and down for some distance. Ever-changing vistas of mountains and valleys greet travellers on this route.

The Route in Alaska – *306km/190mi. At Alaskan border, set watches back 1hr.* Route 9 joins the Taylor Highway (US-5) after 23km/14mi *(services available at Boundary, Alaska)* and heads south along the valley of the Fortymile River. Shortly before the great Klondike discovery, gold was found here. In the creeks along the highway, evidence of mining remains today. **Chicken**, Alaska, *(food and fuel)* offers local colour and frontier history. Wanting to name their camp "ptarmigan" for a local bird, miners settled on "chicken" instead, it is said, because they could spell it! The community was home to Ann Hobbs, who chronicled her life as Chicken's teacher in the book, *Tisha*. The old mining camp, including the author's home, can be visited *(by 1hr guided tour only, mid-May–mid-Sept daily 1pm; $3.75; contact Chicken Creek Cafe, Airport Rd.)* At **Tetlin Junction** take the Alaska Highway south to the Canadian border *(set watches forward 1hr)*.

★★ **Alaska Highway** – *491km/305mi from Alaska border to Whitehorse. Along the highway, posts indicate the distance from Dawson Creek, BC, where the highway begins (p 00). Kilometres/miles in this section are shown in descending order to conform with these post readings.* North of the Canadian/US border, in the vicinity of Northway, Alaska, is the Tetlin National **Wildlife Refuge** *(open daily year-round)*, a 384,620ha/950,000 acre preserve of boreal forest, wetlands, lakes and glacial rivers. At KM 1982/mi 1229 the US Fish and Wildlife Service **visitor centre** *(open mid-May–mid-Sept daily 7am–7pm;* ☐ ☎*907-883-5312)* features exhibits of wildlife and flora indigenous to the Upper Tanana River Valley.

After crossing the Canadian/US border *(KM 1969/mi 1221)*, the highway *(caution: intermittent bumps)* passes through flat muskeg country and later bridges the White and then the Donjek Rivers, full of glacial silt. From the course of the latter *(KM 1810/mi 1125)*, there is a **view** of the Icefield Ranges of the **St. Elias Mountains**.

★★ **Kluane Lake** – Just before Burwash Landing *(KM 1759/mi 1093)*, the road approaches this vast lake, paralleling it for 64km/40mi and offering excellent **views**★★. The highest and largest lake in the Yukon, Kluane (kloo-ON-ee) is ringed by mountains and fed by glaciers, the factor in its incredibly beautiful colour. To the south

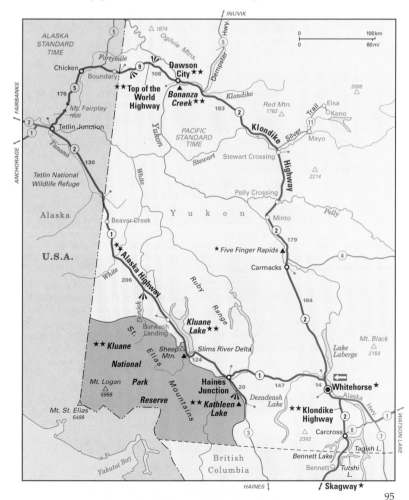

and west lie the **Kluane Ranges**, to the north and east the **Ruby Range**. All of them are reflected in the icy blue waters of this lake, the surface of which can change from a rippling mirror to a heaving mass of waves in a very short period.

In Burwash Landing (pop. 77), the **Kluane Museum of Natural History** *(open mid-May–mid-Sept daily 9am–9pm; $3;* ☎ *403-841-5561)* is housed in a six-sided log building. **Dioramas★** of native wildlife line the building's interior while a reconstructed mountain occupies the center, covered with preserved birds and animals of varying sizes. There is also a large relief map of the mountain ranges of Kluane National Park.

★★ **Kluane National Park Reserve** – ☞ *Park office in Haines Junction (below). Limited 4-wheel-drive vehicle access to park's interior (streams must be forded). Arrangements to visit interior must be made in advance with park authorities. Park open year-round. Hiking, rafting, fishing, cross-country skiing. Use fees in effect.* ⚠ & ☎403-634-7201. *Plane excursions: Glacier flights May–mid-Oct daily; $65–$200/person; reservations suggested; contact Sifton Air* ☎403-634-2916. *Trans-North Air offers charters by helicopter year-round; $600/hr plus fuel; for schedules & reservations* ☎403-634-2242. The scenic variety and beauty of this World Heritage Site (inscribed in 1980) are stunning. The park occupies the entire 22,000sq km/8,494sq mi southwest corner of the Yukon, including most of the St. Elias Mountains in Canada. From the Alaska Highway the rugged, snow-capped Kluane Ranges (as high as 2,500m/8,000ft) of these mountains can be seen. Behind them and largely invisible from the highway are the **Icefield Ranges**. Separated from the Kluanes by a narrow trough called the Duke Depression, these ranges contain the highest mountains in Canada, with many peaks exceeding 4,500m/15,000ft. Best known are **Mt. Logan** (5,959m/19,550ft) and **Mt. St. Elias** (5,489m/18,008ft). Mt. Logan is second in height only to **Mt. McKinley** (6,194m/20,320ft) in Alaska, the highest point on the continent. Forming the base of these peaks is an ice-covered plateau 2,500-3,000m/8,000-10,000ft high, from which many glaciers radiate.

At KM 1707/mi 1061 the Alaska Highway passes **Sheep Mountain** *(satellite visitor centre)*, a rocky and barren peak so named for the white Dall sheep sometimes seen on its slopes. The Alaska Highway crosses the large **Slims River Delta** *(KM 1707-2/mi 1061-58)*, its sandy streak of glacial silt from the Kaskawulsh Glacier penetrating the blue of Kluane Lake for some distance, until absorbed.

Haines Junction – Pop. 559. *KM 1635/mi1016. Kluane National Park Reserve visitor centre open mid-May–mid-Sept daily 8am–8pm.* & ☎403-634-1207. At the junction of the Alaska and Haines (Route 3) Highways, this community has a fine **site★** at the foot of the Auriol Range and is the location for Kluane National Park Reserve headquarters. The **visitor centre** provides information and registration services, and offers interpretive panels and a poetic audio-visual presentation of the park's diversity and grandeur *(25min)*.

Affording views of lovely **Kathleen Lake★★** as it parallels the park to the south, Haines Highway then crosses the Chilkat Pass before entering Alaska and reaching the town of Haines (pop. 1,151) on the Lynn Canal.

About 20km/12mi south of Haines Junction via Route 3, there is a lookout for a **view★★** of Kathleen Lake. At the park's only campground, visitors can drive to the edge of the lake with its shimmering blue waters. When untroubled by frequent winds, the lake's surface mirrors the imposing forms of King's Throne Mountain and Mt. Worthington, rising above.

Returning to Haines Junction, travellers can continue to Whitehorse (KM 1474/mi 916) on the Alaska Highway, with views of the Coast Mountains to the south most of the way. About 13km/8mi after the junction, there is a **view★** from the Alaska Highway *(weather permitting)* of two white pinnacles protruding above the Auriol and Kluane Ranges up the valley of the Dezadeash River: Mts. Hubbard and Kennedy of the Icefield Ranges.

Prairie Provinces

Southey, Saskatchewan/Malak, Ottawa

Alberta, Saskatchewan and Manitoba, known collectively as the Prairie provinces, are often declared flat and monotonous by visitors who drive the long 1,500km/930mi journey from Ontario to Banff. But few who spend time exploring this vast region of nearly 1,963,000 sq km/758,000sq mi come away with this impression. There is something awe-inspiring about the wide open spaces, extensively cultivated, yet sparsely populated (just over 4.6 million people). Despite the seemingly endless plain, there are variations. Rivers have cut deep valleys into the soft soil, and in some of these, **badlands**—the eery lunar landscape of another age—can be seen.

The countryside is an ever-changing rainbow of colours. Green in the spring, the wheat turns gold before harvest. Flax has a small blue or white flower, rapeseed a yellow one. Tall colourfully painted **grain elevators**—the "cathedrals of the plains"—rise beside the railway tracks. Above extends an infinite blue sky, dotted with puffy white clouds, sometimes black as a storm approaches. Prairie sunsets are a sight not to be missed, and nighttime skies are so full of stars, it is rarely dark.

Yet among ample evidence of man's handiwork, wildlife survives. Wild ducks, geese and other birds are frequently seen on prairie **sloughs** (small ponds), and ground squirrels (gophers) are a common sight along the roadside.

The people of this land represent an amazing mélange of ethnic groups and cultures, each maintaining its identity, perhaps because of the distances between communities. From afar, villages with their onion-domed churches rise like mirages from the wheat fields.

Geographical Notes

Diverse Region – The idea that the word prairie is synonymous with endless fields stretching to the horizon is a recent phenomenon. The word is, in fact, of French origin and means "meadow." It was given to the large area of natural

97

grassland that existed in the interior of the North American continent before the arrival of the Europeans. Characterized by its flatness and lack of trees, this grassland was an area where the buffalo, roaming in huge herds, were hunted by the various Plains Indians. Today little natural grassland survives, and in Canada the term "Prairies" now applies to the whole of the three provinces, despite the fact that this immense region is geographically quite diverse.

Semiarid Southwest – The southernmost part of Alberta and Saskatchewan is a relatively dry land of short grass. In 1857 a scientific expedition led by **John Palliser**, commissioned by the British government to study the possibilities for settlement in the Prairies, decided that the southwestern corner would never be productive agriculturally. Palliser did not foresee the widespread use of irrigation, which has brought much of the region into cultivation today, nor did he fully realize the nutritional value of the native grasses, which today provide adequate pasture for cattle. This region, especially the vicinity of CYPRESS HILLS, rates second in importance to British Columbia's Cariboo for cattle raising in Canada.

Wheat-Growing Crescent – To the north of the arid lands lies a crescent-shaped region of fertile soil, graced with more abundant rainfall. Once, the grass grew shoulder high, and few trees blocked the view of distant horizons over the flat plain. Today this is the wheat belt, the prairie of many people's imagination. Prim farm buildings dot the enormous fields of thriving crops, contributing to a general air of prosperity.

Aspen Parkland – North of the wheat belt is another roughly crescent-shaped region where trees grow in good soil and mixed farming flourishes. This is a region of rolling parkland, a transitional zone between the prairie and the forest of the north. It is in this region that the majority of the inhabitants of the three provinces live.

Boreal Forest and Tundra – Nearly half of the total area of the three provinces lies directly on the Precambrian rock of the Canadian Shield. This is a pristine, largely uninhabited land of lakes, trees and rocks. The few people who do call it home are involved either in the forestry industry or in mining. Along the shores of Hudson Bay in northern Manitoba, a small region of tundra thrives. Its treeless and forbidding winter landscape turns startlingly beautiful in summer.

Prairie "Steps" – Despite their reputation the Prairies are not actually flat. Apart from deep valleys cut by rivers, the Prairies rise gradually in three main levels or steps, from sea level at Hudson Bay to nearly 1,200m/4,000ft west of the Rockies. The first step ends with the **Manitoba Escarpment**, which rises to a maximum 831m/2,726ft. Encompassing the flattest lands, the second step ends with the **Missouri Coteau**, rising to a maximum 879m/2,883ft and visible from MOOSE JAW. The third step borders the Rockies. The Prairies are broken by numerous ranges of small hills in the north, in addition to these steps, and by the Cypress Hills in the south.

Climate – The Prairies experience a climate of extremes that varies from year to year, making average conditions difficult to gauge. Winter is generally long and cold; summer is short and hot. Precipitation is low (380-500mm/15-20in a year), frequently arriving in the form of blizzards in winter and violent thunderstorms in summer, often after periods of drought. Sunshine is plentiful, especially in July, the driest and hottest month of the year (mean maximum for CALGARY is 24°C/76°F, REGINA 27°C/81°F, WINNIPEG 27°C/80°F). In the southwest winter is alleviated by the chinook winds, which blow warm air from the Pacific through the Rockies. In a few hours temperatures can rise by as much as 28°C/82°F.

Historical Notes

Indians of the Plains – Once the only inhabitants of this region, the Assiniboine, Blackfoot, Cree, Gros Ventre and Sarcee Indians lived almost exclusively on buffalo. The animals were driven over cliffs or stampeded into pounds. Their meat was often dried and made into **pemmican**—a nutritious mixture of pounded meat, animal fat and sometimes saskatoon berries—which could be preserved for up to a year. Buffalo hides were used to make moccasins, leggings and tunics; the wool was left on to fashion robes for winter. Clothing was decorated with fringes and later, beads. Home was a **teepee**, a conical structure of poles (some almost 12m/40ft tall) covered with buffalo hides.

These nomadic tribes followed buffalo herds all summer, then dispersed in winter. Possessions were put on a **travois**, a structure of crossed poles pulled by a dog and later a horse (horses were in general use in the Canadian Plains by the mid-18C). In spring they reassembled to await the return of the buffalo and to celebrate the **sun dance** or medicine-lodge dance.

Existing rivalry and warfare among the tribes grew more lethal when fur traders began supplying guns. Since buffalo hunting was easier with guns, their use resulted in the gradual extinction of the great herds, which, in turn, destroyed the traditional life of the hunters. By the 1880s the herds were gone, and European settlers had arrived to cultivate and fence the once-open prairie. The Indians signed treaties and moved to reservations, but a sedentary life of farming did not come easily to the former nomadic hunters.

Fur Traders – The lucrative fur trade inspired the French to establish the first permanent settlements in mainland Canada in the 17C, and sent them farther into the continent in search of the elusive beaver. Eager to reduce the long journey by canoe between Ville-Marie (present-day MONTREAL) and Lake Superior, two traders, **Pierre Radisson** and **Sieur des Groseilliers**, proposed a quicker, cheaper way to transport furs to Europe via Hudson Bay, the huge waterway discovered by Henry Hudson in 1610. This scheme met with little interest in France, but "Radish and Gooseberry," as they became known, found a warmer reception at the English court of Charles II. The ketch *Nonsuch* was equipped and sailed to Hudson Bay in 1668, returning with a rich load of furs. In 1670 Charles II granted a royal charter to the "Governor and Company of Adventurers of England trading into Hudson's Bay." The **Hudson's Bay Company** (HBC), as it became known, held sole right to trade in the vast watershed that drains into the bay. Forts or factories were quickly established on its shores and trade thrived.

The first European to explore the interior of this large region was **Henry Kelsey** who travelled across northern Manitoba and Saskatchewan in the early 1690s. Threatened by Kelsey's contacts with the Indians, the **Sieur de la Vérendrye** established the first French trading posts on the plains in 1730. While travelling through Alberta in 1754, **Anthony Henday** of the HBC found the French so entrenched on the plains that he recommended the company abandon its policy of letting Indians bring their furs to the bay, and establish posts in the interior of the land. However, the fall of New France in 1759 *(p 196)* seemed to diminish the threat, and Henday's suggestion was not heeded.

Bitter rivalry developed among fur traders in the Prairies during the late 18C and the early 19C. The Scots quickly established themselves in Montreal and founded the North West Company, soon a ferocious competitor of the HBC. Rival posts sprang up along the Prairie rivers; every load of furs was grounds for contention. Competition finally ended in 1821 when the two companies merged; Hudson's Bay Company kept the upper hand.

The Métis and the Creation of Manitoba – A consequence of the fur trade was the creation of a new ethnic group, the Métis—offspring of Indian women and French *coureurs des bois* (and later of Scots and English traders). Though mainly French-speaking Roman Catholics, the Métis preserved the traditional lifestyle of their Indian forebears, hunting buffalo and making pemmican to sell to fur traders. The first threat to their lifestyle came with the arrival of settlers along the Red River in 1812 *(p 123)*. Conflict ensued since farms and fences could not share the prairie with wandering herds of buffalo and their hunters. In 1870 the situation escalated when the new Dominion of Canada decided to take over the vast lands of the Hudson's Bay Company. The Métis saw their traditional life disappearing with the arrival of more settlers and feared the loss of their language.

When Dominion surveyors began marking out long narrow strips of Métis land into neat squares, these people turned to 25-year-old **Louis Riel**. Soon after his return from Montreal, where he had completed his religious training, Riel declared the surveys illegal, since sovereignty had not yet been established, and set up his own provisional government to ensure the recognition of Métis rights in the new government. Although supported by his own people, Riel gained no sympathy from English Métis and other settlers, particularly many Ontarians of Irish origin who had recently moved to the area in anticipation of the Canadian sovereignty. After foiling a plot to assassinate him, Riel executed a boisterous adventurer from Ontario, **Thomas Scott**, an act that he was long to regret. Nevertheless his plea on behalf of his people was heard. In July 1870 the new province of Manitoba was created. Land was set aside for the Métis, and both

French and English settlers were given equal status. Riel was elected to Parliament several times, but was unable to take his seat in Ottawa because of anger in Ontario over Scott's death. Eventually Riel went into exile in the US, but resurfaced again 15 years later (p 122).

A Human Mosaic – Once the Hudson's Bay Company had ceded its immense territory to the government, treaties had to be negotiated with the residents of the region. Though established by 1877 the treaties proved unsuccessful as the Northwest Rebellion of 1885 showed (p 122). Some means of enforcing law and order was also required. In 1873 the **North West Mounted Police** force was created (pp 111 and 119). Third, land had to be distributed. The **Dominion Lands Act** of 1872 allowed prospective homesteaders to register for a quarter section (65ha/160 acres). Title was given after three years if a homestead had been built and a certain amount of the land cultivated. Settlers also had an option on an additional quarter section. Finally, a means of reaching the region and transporting produce to market was required. To solve this problem, construction of the **Canadian Pacific Railway** was begun in 1881. By the year of its completion (1885), the population of the Prairies was about 150,000; by 1914 it had reached 1.5 million.

The prospect of free land attracted inhabitants of an overcrowded Europe, especially those who lived in industrial cities, where factory hours were long and hard. The area also appealed to religious refugees who hoped to have the freedom to worship and live as they pleased. The Canadian government under **Sir Wilfrid Laurier** advertised all over the world: "Canada West—the last best west. Free homes for millions." Millions indeed came—from Ontario, the Maritimes (New Brunswick, Nova Scotia, Prince Edward Island), the US, Iceland, England, Scotland, Ireland, Germany, Austria, France, Scandinavia and Russia, especially the Ukraine. Mennonites, Hutterites and Doukhobors arrived from Russia, and Orthodox Christians from Eastern Europe. These immigrants were joined by Roman Catholics, Mormons, Jews and Protestants belonging to a variety of denominations. The provinces of **Alberta** and **Saskatchewan** were created in 1905. Since 1915 these peoples have been joined by those seeking refuge from political unrest in their homelands. They have made the Prairies a veritable mosaic of cultures. The **population** today stands at more than 4.6 million (Alberta 2,545,553; Saskatchewan 988,928; Manitoba 1,091,942).

Economy

King Wheat – Between 1876 and 1915, the land where the fur trade once reigned supreme suddenly developed a wheat economy. The region where giant bluestem and needle grass thrived and prairie flowers bloomed in millions vanished under the plough. Several factors contributed to the striking changes. In 1842 David Fife, a Scottish farmer living in Ontario, developed a strain of wheat that later proved ideal for cultivation on the prairies. Called **Red Fife** for its rich colour, it was resistant to rust and thrived in the drought-ridden, short summer season. It is the ancestor of all the strains used today. Another factor was the building of the Canadian Pacific Railway, which brought settlers to cultivate the land and provided transport for their produce to market.

Wheat did not always flourish in this region of changeable and unpredictable climate. Drought and hardships in the 1930s caused many farmers to abandon the land. Today farmers depend less on wheat than in the past. Barley, oats, rye, flax, rapeseed, mustard, buckwheat, peas, sunflowers and potatoes are all widely cultivated; nevertheless 50 percent of the land annually seeded to field crops is devoted to wheat. More than 22 million tonnes/25 million tons of wheat are produced in the western provinces every year, about three-quarters of which is exported.

Cattle Country – Although grain is by far the major economic staple of the Prairies, ranching is firmly established as a secondary industry. Canadian ranching began in British Columbia and spread into southern Alberta and Saskatchewan after the Indian treaties of the 1870s. The dry, short-grass country turned out to be fine pasture for cattle, and the chinook winds made winter grazing possible as they melted the snow, exposing the grass.

Slowly, as ranchers discovered that cattle would not run off with buffalo or be killed by winter or Indians, the number of ranches increased. By the turn of the century, cattle raising attained its present position as the second most important economic activity. To this day southern Alberta and Saskatchewan remain "cowboy country." Horseback riders among the herds are a common sight, and rodeos abound. The most popular cowboy event is the Calgary Stampede (p 107).

Riches Below the Earth – One of the first minerals exploited in the Prairies was coal, found in LETHBRIDGE, Alberta, in 1869. Later, coal was also mined near Estevan in Saskatchewan and at Canmore, Alberta. The giant zinc, cadmium and copper field at Flin Flon, Manitoba, was established in 1915. Today mining activity has spread across the border into Saskatchewan. Copper was discovered near Lynn Lake, Manitoba, and gold in the Lake Athabasca area of Saskatchewan.

In the 1880s Kootenay Brown found oil in the Waterton Lakes area of Alberta and sold it as machine grease. In 1914 oil was discovered in Turner Valley *(p 106)*, marking the beginning of Alberta's petroleum industry. The year 1947 saw the discovery of the Leduc oilfield *(p 112)*; subsequently numerous other small fields underlying Alberta were exploited. Alberta accounts for the vast majority of Canada's oil and natural gas production. Alberta's reserves are supplemented by the Athabasca oil sands in the northern part of the province, said to be the largest known hydrocarbon accumulation in the world.

Uranium was found in the late 1940s in the Beaverlodge area of Saskatchewan, north of Lake Athabasca, and in the 1960s, the giant nickel field of Thompson, Manitoba, came into production. The first potash was mined in 1951 near Esterhazy in Saskatchewan. This province's potash reserves are estimated at more than 25 percent of the world's total supply and, at current rates of consumption, enough to supply world needs for 2,000 years. Just as oil and natural gas underlie Alberta, potash underlies Saskatchewan in a wide arc roughly corresponding to the aspen parkland zone *(p 98)*. Saskatchewan also has sodium sulphate and oil in the Lloydminster, Swift Current and Estevan areas.

PRACTICAL INFORMATION
Getting There

By Air – Major domestic and international airlines such as Air Canada ☎403-298-9200 and Canadian Airlines International ☎800-426-7000 (Canada/US) service Calgary, Edmonton, Regina, Saskatoon and Winnipeg. Regional carriers offer connections to cities within the Prairie provinces: Calm Air ☎204-778-6471; Pro-Flight ☎306-569-6050; Canadian Regional Airlines ☎306-569-2307.

By Train – VIA Rail Canada has regularly scheduled transcontinental service to all three provinces. In Canada consult the telephone directory for nearest office; from the US ☎800-561-3949.

General Information

Accommodations and Visitor Information – The government tourist offices produce annually updated guides listing approved hotels, motels, B&B lodgings and cabins. Camping guides and discovery guides give detailed information on golf courses, outfitters, guest ranches and fishing camps. Winter vacation guides list ski areas, winter sports activities, hotels and ski lodges. These publications and maps are available free of charge from:

Alberta Tourism, 10155 102nd St., Edmonton, AB, T5J 4L6 ☎403-427-4321 or 800-661-8888 (Canada/US).

Travel Manitoba, Tourism Division, 155 Carlton St. 7th floor, Dept. RA6, Winnipeg, MB, R3C 3H8 ☎204-945-3777 or 800-665-0040 (Canada/US).

Tourism Saskatchewan, 500-1900 Albert St., Regina, SK, S4P 4L9 ☎306-787-2300 or 800-667-7191 (Canada/US).

Most major hotel chains have facilities in these provinces *(p 316)*. Independent hotels and B&B lodgings can be found along major routes. Farm vacations are offered in all three provinces, but Saskatchewan is especially popular. Alberta in particular boasts many guest ranches offering trail riding with overnight camping for the experienced or the novice rider, as well as families.

Road Regulations – *(Driver's license and insurance requirements p 314.)* All three provinces have good paved roads. Unless otherwise posted, speed limits are: Alberta: 100km/h (60mph) in daylight, 90km/h (55mph) at night. Manitoba: 90km/h (55mph). Saskatchewan: 100km/h (60mph). Use of seat belts is compulsory. For listings of the Canadian Automobile Assn. (CAA), consult the local telephone directory.

Time Zones – Alberta: Mountain Standard Time. Manitoba: Central Standard Time. Both observe Daylight Saving Time from the first Sunday in April to the last Sunday in October. Most of Saskatchewan is on Central Standard Time all year; thus it is the same as Alberta in summer, and as Manitoba in winter. Some border communities keep the same time as the neighbouring province all year.

Taxes – In addition to the national 7% GST *(rebate information p 318)*, Manitoba levies 7% and Saskatchewan 9% sales tax on all items. In Alberta there is a 5% hotel tax but no sales or restaurant tax. Manitoba offers a rebate of its provincial sales tax to non-residents; contact Retail Sales Tax Office, 101-401 York Ave., Winnipeg, MB, R3C 0P8 ☎204-945-5603.

Liquor Laws – The legal drinking age is 18 in Manitoba and Alberta, 19 in Saskatchewan. In all three provinces, liquor and wine can be purchased only in government stores. In isolated parts of the North where no government stores exist, grocery stores are licensed.

Provincial Holidays *(National Holidays p 319)*

Family Day *AB*	3rd Monday in February
Civic Holiday *MB and SK*	1st Monday in August

Recreation – The Prairies are especially prized by outdoor enthusiasts. **Water sports**—boating, sailing, canoeing, water skiing and swimming—are particularly popular because of the large number of lakes and river systems. Saskatchewan is famous for its **white-water rafting**, especially along the Churchill River.

The region is well endowed with national parks *(p 321)* and provincial parks, offering hiking trails and campsites in summer and cross-country skiing, snow-shoeing and snowmobiling in winter.

All three provinces offer good **fishing**, but northern Manitoba and Saskatchewan are particularly famous for their numerous fly-in lodges. Lac la Ronge in Saskatchewan is perhaps the best-known region for sport fishing. Fishermen and hunters must have a valid license, obtainable in most sporting goods stores. The *Anglers' Guide* and *Hunting and Trapping Guide* (available free of charge from provincial tourist offices) give valuable information such as hunting and fishing regulations, species and limits.

Special Excursions – The **Prairie Dog Central**, a turn-of-the-century steam train, makes weekly excursions from WINNIPEG northwest to Grosse Isle *(departs from St. James Station, 1661 Portage Ave., May–Sept Sun 11am & 3pm; round-trip 2hrs 30min; $13; Vintage Locomotive Society Inc. ☎204-832-5259)*.

Polar Bear watch excursions from Winnipeg are offered in CHURCHILL *(mid-Oct–mid-Nov; 6–9 days $1,700–3,000; 6–9 months advance reservation suggested; Natural Habitat Wildlife Adventures ☎303-449-3711 or 800-543-8917, Canada/US)*.

To relive the days of the Wild West, join a **covered wagon trek** and travel through the wide expanses of Saskatchewan. Experienced scouts take visitors from May to September on three- or six-day excursions that include campfire dinners. Contact Tourism Saskatchewan for details.

Principal Festivals

Feb	**Trappers' Festival**	*The Pas, MB*
	Festival du Voyageur *(p 126)*	*Saint-Boniface, MB*
	Winter Festival	*Prince Albert, SK*
Jun	**Provincial Exhibition of Manitoba**	*Brandon, MB*
	Western Canada Farm Progress Show	*Regina, SK*
	Red River Exhibition	*Winnipeg, MB*
Jul	**Folk Festival**	*Winnipeg, MB*
	Saskatoon Exhibition	*Saskatoon, SK*
	Manitoba Highland Gathering	*Selkirk, MB*
	Manitoba Threshermen's Reunion *(p 105)*	*Austin, MB*
	Calgary Exhibition and Stampede *(p 107)*	*Calgary, AB*
	Klondike Days *(p 113)*	*Edmonton, AB*
	Big Valley Jamboree	*Craven, SK*
Jul–Aug	**National Ukrainian Festival**	*Dauphin, MB*
	Pioneer Days	*Steinbach, MB*
	Buffalo Days	*Regina, SK*
Aug	**Whoop-up Days and Rodeo**	*Lethbridge, AB*
	Icelandic Festival	*Gimli, MB*
	York Boat Days (boat race)	*Norway House, MB*
	Folklorama *(p 124)*	*Winnipeg, MB*
	Folkfest	*Saskatoon, SK*
Nov–Dec	**Canadian Western Agribition**	*Regina, SK*

THE ALBERTA BADLANDS★★★

Alberta

Map of Principal Sights p 2

The meltwaters of the last continental glacier eroded a deep valley across southern Alberta, which today is occupied by the Red Deer River. In so doing they exposed rocks formed during the Cretaceous period (64-140 million years ago) and created the Alberta Badlands, a striking panorama of steep bluffs and fluted gullies. The area was a subtropical lowland inhabited by huge reptilian creatures known as dinosaurs. A number of these were fossilized and preserved to this day.

Haunt of the Dinosaurs – The word *dinosaur* is derived from Greek, meaning "terrible lizard," a reference to the predatory habits and great size of some of these creatures. In fact there were many types: some were small and most were plant eaters, but the biggest weighed as much as 27 tonnes/30 tons and grew to 24m/80ft in length. The **duckbilled dinosaur** walked on its hind feet, which were webbed for swimming, and sported a snout resembling a duck's bill, thus its name. The **horned dinosaur** walked on four feet and had horns—usually one over each eye and one on the nose. The **armoured dinosaur** was equipped with a row of bony plates on its back and spikes on its tail as a form of protection. All of these were herbivorous, slow moving and prey to the ferocious **carnivorous dinosaur** with its sharp claws and teeth, and muscular hind legs for running.

Dinosaur bones have been found on all continents, but this valley in Alberta is one of the richest in deposits. The first fossils discovered in 1884, along with the bones and several hundred complete skeletons unearthed since then, are on display in many world museums, including the Royal Ontario Museum *(p 185)* and the Canadian Museum of Nature *(p 161)*.

DINOSAUR TRAIL *2hrs. 51km/32mi circular drive. Map below.*

Connecting the sights of the Drumheller area, this loop on the plain above Red Deer River offers good views of the badlands.

★ **Drumheller** – *Pop. 6,277. Visitor Centre, 60 1st St. West. Open mid-May–Labour Day daily 9am–9pm. Rest of the year Mon–Fri 8:30am–4:30pm. Closed national holidays.* ☎403-823-2171. This former coal-mining town, 138km/86mi northeast of Calgary, lies amid the badlands of the Red Deer River as does Dinosaur Provincial Park *(p 104)*. Drumheller is surrounded by a fertile wheat-growing plain, unbroken except by occasional oil pumps known as "donkey heads" because they bob up and down continuously. Upon the approach to the town, the extensively eroded valley, nearly 120m/400ft deep and about 1.6km/1mi wide, comes as something of a surprise.

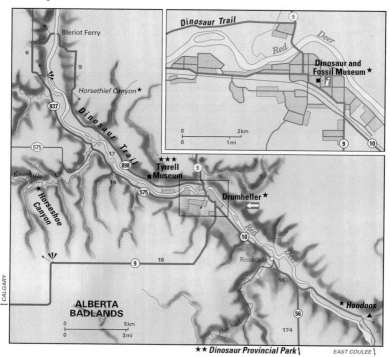

★ **Dinosaur and Fossil Museum** – *335 1st St. East. Open May–Jun daily 10am–5pm. Jul–Aug daily 10am–6pm. Sept–mid-Oct daily 10am–5pm. $2.* & ☎*403-823-2593.* Devoted to the region's geology, this museum features examples of dinosaur fossils. The most impressive is **Edmontosaurus**, a 9m/30ft long, 3.5m/11ft high duckbilled dinosaur with webbed feet and a strong tail for use when swimming.

★★★ **Tyrrell Museum of Palaeontology** – *6km/4mi northwest of Drumheller by Hwy. 838 (North Dinosaur Trail). Open year-round mid-May–Labour Day daily 9am–9pm. Rest of the year Tue–Sun 10am–5pm. Closed Dec 25. $6.50.* ⅟⅟ & ☎*403-823-7707.* This splendid museum, opened in 1985, is one of the largest in the world devoted to the study of life-forms from past geological periods. It has a fine setting in the badlands and blends well with its surroundings in a series of innovative structures designed by Douglas Craig of Calgary.

The highlight is the enormous **Dinosaur Hall**, where the major types of dinosaurs formerly inhabiting this area are re-created, some with original fossils, others with modern casting materials. The huge *Tyrannosaurus rex, Albertosaurus*, the armoured *Stegosaurus* and some smaller bird-like dinosaurs can be seen. One part of the hall represents the bottom of the ancient Bearpaw Sea, which covered the western Canadian interior 70 million years ago. Here, mosasaurs—large marine reptiles up to 15m/50ft long—can be viewed.

In the **palaeoconservatory** visitors can admire a large collection of plants descended from those the dinosaurs would have known. Some have changed little in 140 million years.

The museum's main theme is a "celebration of life," featuring displays, films and slide shows on such topics as the creation of the universe, evolutionary theories, diverse environments, the age of the dinosaurs and the mystery of their disappearance, mammals (including species now extinct), the ice ages and the evolution of *Homo sapiens*.

After passing the museum, Dinosaur Trail provides a good view of the badlands from **Horsethief Canyon★**, with its rounded, almost barren hills stretching to the river. The trail crosses the river by the **Bleriot cable ferry** and climbs to a fine **view★** of the valley. The green pastures beside the river provide an interesting contrast to the cactus-strewn bluffs and gullies immediately below.

ADDITIONAL SIGHTS

★ **Horseshoe Canyon** – *18km/11mi southwest of Drumheller by Rte. 9.* Paths leading through the hillocks to the river provide some of the best **views** of the badlands in the area.

★ **Hoodoos** – *16km/10mi southeast of Drumheller by Rte. 10.* These strange rock formations, which look like giant mushrooms, illustrate the work of erosion in the valley. Soft rock has been worn away, leaving harder pieces behind.

★★ **Dinosaur Provincial Park** – *174km/108mi southeast of Drumheller by Rte. 56 & Trans-Can Hwy. east to Brooks. Take Hwy. 873 for 10km/6mi, then right on Hwy. 544,*

Hoodoos

and left on Hwy. 551. Open daily year-round. Visitor centre open mid-May–Labour Day Mon–Thu 8:15am–4:30pm, Fri–Sat 8:15am–9pm, Sun 9am–4:30pm. Rest of the year Mon–Fri 8:15am–4:30pm. Closed national holidays. △ ⚔ 🕭 ☎403-378-4342. The park is set in the most spectacular part of the Red Deer River Valley and the richest fossil area. In 1979 UNESCO recognized its importance by placing it on the World Heritage List.

Immediately upon entrance to the park, an excellent **viewpoint**★★ overlooks nearly 3,000ha/7,000 acres of badlands cut by the Red Deer River. The road then descends to the valley.

A **circular drive**★ *(5km/3mi)* takes the visitor through this wild and desolate, almost lunar, landscape where little except sagebrush flourishes. At several points short walks can be taken to see dinosaur bones preserved where they were found. Explanatory panels offer details on the type of dinosaur and its size. Longer nature trails enable visitors to better appreciate this pristine terrain. Most of the park, however, is accessible only by special bus tours *(mid-May–Labour Day daily; 1hr 30min; $4.50)* or by conducted hikes *(contact visitor centre for details)*.

Tyrrell Museum Field Station – *1.6km/1mi from park entrance. Open mid-May–Labour Day daily 8:15am–9pm. Early Sept–mid-Oct Tue–Sun 8:15am–4:30pm (Fri & Sat 9pm). Rest of the year Mon–Fri 8:15am–4:30pm. $1.* ♿ ☎403-378-4342. Opened in 1987 this research satellite of the museum *(p 104)* is located within Dinosaur Provincial Park. The interpretation centre features habitat and fossil displays and an observation post for watching staff prepare fossils.

AUSTIN★

Manitoba
Map of Principal Sights p 3

Set in the centre of a rich agricultural region, this community, 123km/76mi west of Winnipeg, is renowned for its collection of operating vintage farm machinery.

SIGHT

★ **Manitoba Agricultural Museum** – *On Hwy. 34, 3km/2mi south of Trans-Can Hwy. Open May–Sept daily 9am–5pm. $3.* ♿ ☎204-637-2354. This museum has a splendid collection of "prairie giants"—steam tractors, threshing machines, and the cumbersome gasoline machines that replaced them in the early part of this century. Every year at the end of July, these machines are paraded and demonstrated in the Manitoba **Threshermen's Reunion and Stampede**. Drawing thousands of visitors from all over the continent, this festival features threshing, sheaf-tying and stooking contests, a stampede and steam engine races.

A **homesteaders' village** illustrates rural life at the end of the last century when the first giant steam engines were breaking the prairie sod and bringing it under cultivation. The village includes several log homes, a church and a school. The centennial building houses a large collection of pioneer artifacts.

THE BATTLEFORDS★

Saskatchewan
Pop. 18,457
Map of Principal Sights p 3
Tourist Office ☎306-445-6226

Surrounded by rolling country, the twin communities of **Battleford** and **North Battleford**, 138km/86mi northwest of SASKATOON, face each other across the valley of the North Saskatchewan River. North Battleford has a fine **site**★ overlooking the river.

Historical Notes – Fur traders established posts on the Battleford (south) side of the river in the 18C, but it was not until 1874 that the first settlers arrived. A North West Mounted Police post was established in 1876, and the settlement was chosen as the home of the government of the Northwest Territories. A bright future seemed assured. Then the Canadian Pacific Railway Co. decided to route its line through the southern plains, and in 1883 Battleford lost its status as capital when the government offices were moved to Pile O'Bones Creek (later REGINA). To add insult to injury, the settlement of Battleford was looted and burned by Poundmaker Crees during the Northwest Rebellion of 1885 *(p 122)* while the fearful inhabitants took refuge in the police fort. The death knell sounded in 1903 when the Canadian Northern Railway was built along the opposite side of the river, creating a new community, North Battleford, which grew as Battleford shrank. Today North Battleford, served by the Yellowhead Highway as well as the railway, is a distribution centre of no small importance.

SIGHTS

★ **Fort Battleford National Historic Site** – ⚑ *Central Ave., Battleford. Open mid-May–Jun daily 9am–5pm. Jul–Aug daily 9am–6pm. Sept–mid-Oct daily 9am–5pm. $3.* ♿ ☎*306-937-2621.* This North West Mounted Police post was the fifth established by the police in the Northwest Territories. Enlarged after the Northwest Rebellion, it was abandoned in 1924. Today restored, it provides insight into police life in the late 19C.

The **commanding officers' residence** suggests that police officers lived fairly comfortably. The **officers' quarters** house an office for the police. Just outside the palisade a former barracks has been converted into an **interpretation centre**, which provides a particularly good account of the 1885 rebellion.

★ **Western Development Museum** – *On Hwy. 16 at junction with Rte. 40 in North Battleford. Open mid-May–mid-Sept daily 8:30am–7pm. $4.50.* ✗ ☎*306-445-8033.* Devoted to agriculture, this branch of the Western Development Museum—one of four in the province (MOOSE JAW, SASKATOON, YORKTON)—displays a large collection of agricultural machinery and domestic artifacts used on farms in the 1920s. Outside, an interesting **heritage farm and village** of 1925 is set out with homes and churches reflecting the diverse origins of the peoples who settled this province. Note the Ukrainian Orthodox Church with its onion dome, and the thatched *dacha* displaying the handicrafts and household fittings of a pioneer Ukrainian home. Also featured are a general store, a police post and a railway station complete with a train.

CALGARY★★

Alberta
Pop. 710,677
Map of Principal Sights p 2
Tourist Office ☎403-263-8510

Set in the foothills of the snow-capped peaks of the Canadian Rockies, this thriving city lies at the confluence of the Bow and Elbow Rivers, two mountain torrents of clear blue water. Covering the largest land area of any city in Canada (420sq km/162sq mi), Calgary was Canada's fastest-growing, most prosperous metropolis in the early 1980s, mainly because of Alberta's vast oil wealth and the city's own importance as a transportation centre. Blessed with a pleasant climate (moderate rainfall, low humidity, lots of sunshine and a moderately cold winter, tempered by warm chinook winds), this tourist mecca is known for its internationally famous stampede and remembered fondly by millions around the world as host of the 1988 Winter Olympic Games.

Historical Notes

Origins – In 1875 a North West Mounted Police post was built on this site and named Fort Calgary by Col. James Macleod *(p 115)*, commander of the police in the Northwest, for his home in Scotland. The name is derived from what is most likely a Gaelic word meaning "Bay Farm."

A small community grew up around the post, which quickly developed in the 1880s when the Canadian Pacific Railway Co. decided to route its railway south through Calgary and the Kicking Horse Pass, rather than through EDMONTON and the Yellowhead Pass. This momentous decision resulted in a huge influx of settlers to the lush grazing lands of the region. The Dominion Lands Act *(p 100)* also encouraged the movement of cattle herds northward from the US. Canadians began to form their own herds in the area, and well-to-do Englishmen arrived from overseas to establish ranches.

Calgary rapidly became a marketing and meat-packing centre, gaining the nickname of Canada's Cowtown—a title it still has not relinquished, although cattle constitute a relatively minor part of its life today.

"Black Gold" – The discovery of oil in 1914 at Turner Valley, just southwest of Calgary, marked the birth of western Canada's petroleum industry. For about 30 years, this valley was the country's major oil producer. Then in 1947 a great discovery was made at Leduc *(p 112)*, and Calgary began a period of phenomenal growth. Although recent oil and gas discoveries have been closer to Edmonton, Calgary has predominated as the headquarters of the industry. According to recent statistics, Calgary is becoming one of the country's top financial centres, second only to Toronto in attracting corporate head offices.

"The Greatest Outdoor Show on Earth" – The **Calgary Stampede**, a grand ten-day event held in early July, attracts hundreds of thousands of spectators and competitors every year *(reservations recommended)*. The entire population dons western garb (boots, jeans and hats) and joins the festivities. There are flapjack breakfasts, street dances, and a huge parade in the city. Livestock shows and the famous **rodeo** and **chuckwagon races** are held in Stampede Park. Invented in Calgary the races recall the wagon races held by cowboys after a roundup. They are, without doubt, an exciting part of the stampede. *Details of all events can be obtained from the tourist office ☎800-661-1678 (Canada/US).*

DOWNTOWN   *1/2 day. Map below.*

Calgary's downtown has undergone a phenomenal transformation since World War II and continues to develop. In more recent years the Calgary Tower, surrounded by a host of attractive glass-fronted high rises, has been overshadowed by the sloping-top, brown marble headquarters of **Petro-Canada**. A pedestrian **mall** stretches four blocks along 8th Avenue. At the western end lie the big bank blocks: the reflecting glass Royal Bank Centre, the Scotia Centre and the black towers of the Toronto Dominion (TD) Square, all connected to one another and to The Bay and Eaton's department stores by second-floor pedestrian bridges.

Toronto Dominion Square boasts a fine indoor greenhouse featuring tropical plants called the **Devonian Gardens★** *(4th floor, access from Eaton's or, outside store hours, via elevator from TD Square entrance on mall; open year-round daily 9am–9pm; closed Dec 25; & ▯ ☎403-268-3888).* East of the mall the tiered, blue-reflecting glass structure of Calgary's **Municipal Building** rises around a 12-storey atrium. Across 2nd Street Southeast stands the **Centre for the Performing Arts**, an attractive series of brick buildings.

★★**Glenbow Museum** – *130 9th Ave. Southeast, in Convention Centre complex. Open mid-May–mid-Sept daily 9am–5pm. Rest of the year Tue–Sun 9am–5pm. Closed Jan 1, Dec 25–26. $5. & ☎403-268-4100.* Administered by the Glenbow-Alberta Institute, this museum contains displays from an outstanding **Plains Indians collection★★**. Note in particular the fine beadwork.

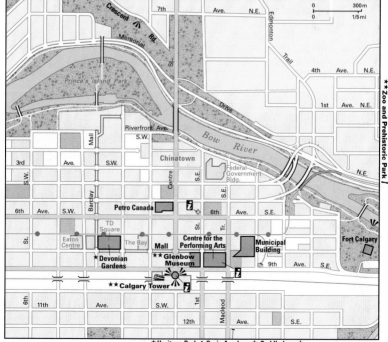

European settlement in the province is traced through exhibits focusing on the fur trade, the North West Mounted Police, missionaries, the Canadian Pacific Railway, the arrival of the first farmers, ranching, the discovery of oil and Alberta life in the 1920s and 30s.

Displays on weapons and arms, tracing their development from medieval times to recent years, are featured. In addition the museum mounts temporary exhibits of art and sculpture. A large acrylic and aluminum sculpture by James Houston, entitled **Aurora Borealis**, is the museum's focal point.

★★ **Calgary Tower** – *In Palliser Square, 101 9th Ave. Southwest. Observation deck open Jun–Sept daily 7:30am–midnight. Rest of the year daily 8:00am–11pm. $4.95.* ✕ ♿ 🅿 ☎*403-266-7171.* This 191m/626ft tower provides an excellent **view**★★ of the city and its site. To the west the snow-capped peaks of the Rockies rise above the rolling, arid foothills on which the city is built. Immediately below the tower the maze of railway lines attests to the city's importance as a transportation centre.

ADDITIONAL SIGHTS

★★ **Crescent Road Viewpoint** – *Map p 107.* Standing above the Bow River and Prince's Island Park, this crescent offers a fine view of the downtown buildings and, on clear days, the snow-capped Rockies to the west.

Fort Calgary – *Map p 107. 750 9th Ave. Southeast. Open May–mid-Oct daily 9am–5pm. $2.* ♿ 🅿 ☎*403-290-1875.* An interpretation centre on the site of the original North West Mounted Police post recounts the history of the city. The location of the post itself is indicated on the ground, and the house of the NWMP superintendent can be visited. Paths afford **views**★ of the Bow River, and a pedestrian bridge allows access to St. George's Island and the zoo.

★★ **Zoo and Prehistoric Park** – *1300 Zoo Rd. Northeast, on St. George's Island. Open year-round daily 9am; closing hours vary. $8.* ✕ ♿ 🅿 *(on St. George's Dr.)* ☎*403-232-9300.* Located on an island in the Bow River, this attractive zoo houses a wide variety of animals from all over the world and a tropical greenhouse filled with exotic plants, flowers, butterflies and birds. The **prehistoric park**★★ *(same hours as the zoo)* re-creates western Canada as it might have looked in the age of the dinosaurs between 225 and 65 million years ago. Life-size reproductions of these giant creatures stand among mountains, volcanoes, hoodoos and swampland, along with the vegetation that might have existed in their day.

★ **Grain Academy** – *South of downtown by Macleod Trail, in Roundup Centre, Stampede Park, 17th Ave. and 2nd St. Southeast. Open Apr–Sept Mon–Fri 10am–4pm, Sat noon–4pm. Rest of the year Mon–Fri 10am–4pm.* ♿ 🅿 ☎*403-263-4594.* This museum, Alberta's only grain interpretation centre, focuses on one of mankind's basic food sources. It presents a working model of a Prairie grain elevator, a model railway showing the movement of Prairie grain through the Rocky Mountains, and a film *(12min)* on the history of grain production in western Canada.

Saddledome, Calgary

The museum is located in Stampede Park near the distinctive 20,240-seat Olympic **Saddledome**★ *(illustration p 108)* constructed in 1983. The flowing saddle design of the stadium's roof echoes Calgary's cowboy past *(visit by 1hr guided tour only, year-round Mon–Fri; for hours* ☎*403-777-2177).*

★ **Heritage Park** – *16km/10mi southwest of downtown. Take Macleod Trail Southwest to 1900 Heritage Dr. Southwest. Open mid-May–Labour Day daily 9am–5pm. Early Sept–mid-Oct weekends only 9am–5pm. $16 (includes rides).* ✗ ⛿ ☎*403-259-1900.* Occupying a pleasant **site**★ in a recreation area overlooking Glenmore Reservoir, this park re-creates prairie life of a bygone era with a pioneer community and a reconstructed Hudson's Bay Company post. The turn-of-the-century town features a church, drugstore, bakery, general store, post office, newspaper office, pool hall, police post, houses and a station for a functioning steam train that gives tours of the site. Beside the tracks stands a working grain elevator, and on the outskirts of the town are farm buildings and a windmill. A replica of the *SS Moyie*, a stern-wheeler once used on Kootenay Lake, offers boat trips on the reservoir *(every 35min)* and memorable rides can be taken on the antique **midway**.

CARDSTON
Alberta
Pop. 3,480
Map of Principal Sights p 2

This small town, 25km/16mi north of the Montana (US) border, is an important Mormon centre. It was founded in 1887 by **Charles Ora Card**, a son-in-law of Brigham Young. Also known as the Church of Jesus Christ of the Latter Day Saints, the sect was established in 1830 by **Joseph Smith** at Fayette, New York. After his death most of his followers moved to Utah under the leadership of **Brigham Young**, establishing Salt Lake City in 1847.

SIGHT

Mormon Temple – *348 Third St. West. Visitor centre open May–Sept daily 9am–9pm.* ♿ ☎*403-653-1696.* This imposing white granite structure was completed in 1923 and is one of the few Mormon temples in Canada. The Mormon doctrine is based on the Bible, *The Book of Mormon* and Joseph Smith's writings. In Canada the church numbers about 135,000 and is largely concentrated in Alberta, Ontario and British Columbia.

CHURCHILL★★
Manitoba
Pop. 1,143
Map of Principal Sights p 3

On the shores of Hudson Bay, on the east side of the estuary of the wild and beautiful Churchill River, lies the little town of Churchill, Canada's most northerly deep-sea port. Situated north of the tree line, Churchill is bleak in winter, but during the summer months, a carpet of flowers covers the tundra, beluga whales abound in the blue waters of the bay, and myriad birds frequent the area. In autumn scavenging **polar bears**, a popular tourist attraction in and around the townsite, make their seasonal migration northward *(polar bear watch expeditions p 102)*. Because it experiences some of the world's most amazing spectacles of the Northern Lights *(p 300)*, the town has attracted much scientific interest.

Churchill also boasts an interesting history. A fur-trading post was founded at the mouth of the river in 1685 by the Hudson's Bay Company. Named for the governor of the company, **John Churchill**, later Duke of Marlborough, it remained an important fur-gathering and export centre until this century when wheat took over. A railway was built in 1931, and a grain elevator and port facilities shortly thereafter. The Hudson Bay and Strait are navigable only three months a year *(Aug–Oct)*. During this period trains arrive constantly and ships of many nations visit the townsite to take on grain.

Access – *Regularly scheduled flights from Winnipeg. Also accessible from Winnipeg by VIA Rail (summer daily Mon–Fri; winter Mon, Wed, Fri).*

SIGHTS

Town Centre Complex – Opened in 1976 the centre combines recreational and health facilities, a library, high school and business offices under one roof. This low-lying complex with its **views** of the bay displays interesting art work.

★★ **Eskimo Museum** – *Beside Roman Catholic Church. Open Jun–early Nov Mon 1–5pm, Tue–Sat 9am–noon & 1–5pm. Rest of the year Mon 1–4:30pm, Tue–Fri 10:30am–noon & 1–4:30pm. Contribution requested.* ☎*204-675-2030.* This museum houses a fine collection of Inuit carvings in stone, ivory and bone. Collected over 50 years by the Oblate fathers, these carvings depict various aspects of life. Many refer to Inuit legends and others to the arrival of the first airplanes or snowmobiles in the North. A recorded commentary describes some of the works.

Polar Bear

Steven Morello/Natural Habitat Adventures

★ **Prince of Wales Fort** – ☞ *Across Churchill River estuary from town. Access by boat depending on tides and weather conditions. Visit by guided tour (1hr) only, early Jul–Aug daily. Contact visitor centre* ☎*204-675-8863.* Built by the Hudson's Bay Company to protect its fur trade, this large stone fortress took 40 years (1731-71) to complete. The long-standing threat from the French was eliminated after the defeat of New France on the Plains of Abraham in 1759. Subsequently a group of Montreal traders, who later founded the North West Company, challenged the Hudson's Bay Company's monopoly. In 1782 a French fleet attacked the fort, then under the command of the explorer Samuel Hearne. Not knowing that England and France were again at war, Hearne surrendered without a shot being fired. Most of his garrison was inland preventing the Montreal traders from taking all the furs. The French commander, Comte de La Pérouse, blew up parts of the walls and set fire to the fort. Returned to the British soon afterwards, the fort was never again used by the HBC, which preferred to establish outposts farther upstream.

Visit – The boat trip to the fort is an excellent means of viewing the beluga whales that inhabit the estuary of the Churchill River in July and August.

The **visitor centre** *(open mid-May–mid-Nov daily 1–9pm; rest of the year Mon–Fri 8:30am–4:30pm; closed Jul 15;* ☎*204-675-8863)* offers videos, and a slide show on the **York Factory National Historic Site**, the remains of a major HBC trading post located 240km/149mi southeast of Churchill on Hudson Bay near the mouth of the Hayes River *(accessible only by canoe or charter plane; for information, contact the visitor centre).* In the fort itself, note the massive stone walls nearly 12m/40ft thick at their base and 5m/17ft high, and 40 huge cannon.

CYPRESS HILLS★★

Alberta-Saskatchewan
Map of Principal Sights p 3

Straddling the Alberta/Saskatchewan boundary, 70km/43mi north of the state of Montana, the plains give way to rolling, forested hills cut by numerous coulees, valleys, lakes and streams. These verdant hills rise prominently in the midst of otherwise unbroken, sunbaked, short-grass prairie. On their heights grow the tall, straight lodgepole pines favoured by Plains Indians for their teepees or lodges—thus the name. The trees were probably mistaken by early French voyageurs for the jack pines *(cyprès)* of eastern Canada. Although no such trees are in the vicinity, a bad translation further compounded the error, and the name Cypress Hills was born.

Historical Notes

Oasis in the Desert – In 1859 John Palliser camped in these hills during his tour of the western domains for the British government *(p 98)*. "A perfect oasis in the desert we have travelled," was his brief description. Later, settlers found the hills ideally suited for **ranching** and today much land is devoted to cattle raising.

Not only is the scenic beauty of the hills a surprise, but they also present unique geographical features. The highest elevations in Canada between Labrador and the Rockies, they rise to nearly 1,500m/5,000ft. A 200sq km/80sq mi area of their heights was untouched by the last Ice Age, which covered the rest of this vast area with ice more than 1km/.6mi deep. The hills form a divide between two great watersheds: Hudson Bay and the Gulf of Mexico. Streams flow south to the Missouri-Mississippi system and north to the South Saskatchewan River, Lake Winnipeg and Hudson Bay. The flora and fauna of the hills offer a remarkable diversity. Wildflowers and songbirds normally associated only with the Rockies flourish here, cactus grows on the dry south-facing slopes and orchids thrive beside quiet ponds.

The Cypress Hills Massacre – An event that occurred in these hills influenced the creation of that revered Canadian institution: the **Royal Canadian Mounted Police**. In the early 1870s several trading posts were established in the Cypress Hills by Americans from Montana. In exchange for furs, they illegally traded "fire water," an extremely potent and lethal brew. During the winter of 1872-73, Assiniboine Indians were camped close to two of these posts—Farwell's and Solomon's. They were joined by a party of Canadian and American wolf-hunters, whose entire stock of horses had been stolen by Cree raiders. Thinking the Assiniboines were the thieves, the "wolfers," fired up by a night's drinking, attacked the Indian camp, killing 36 people.

When news of this massacre reached Ottawa, Prime Minister Sir John A. Macdonald acted quickly. He created the **North West Mounted Police** (renamed the Royal Canadian Mounted Police in 1920) and dispatched them to the Northwest to stop such border incursions and end the illegal whisky trade. The perpetrators of the massacre were arrested but later acquitted for lack of evidence. However, the fact that white men had been arrested impressed the Indians with the impartiality of the new police force and helped establish its reputation.

Sitting Bull in Canada – In 1876 a force of Sioux warriors under their great chief, Sitting Bull, exterminated an American army detachment under Gen. **George Custer** on the Little Big Horn River in southern Montana. Fearing reprisals from the enraged Americans, Sitting Bull crossed into Canada with nearly 5,000 men. Inspector **James Walsh** of the North West Mounted Police was given the difficult task of trying to persuade the Sioux to return, in order to avoid war between the Sioux and their traditional enemies, the Cree and the Blackfoot, who inhabited the region. Riding into the sizeable Sioux encampment near Wood Mountain *(350km/217mi east of Fort Walsh)* with only four constables and two scouts, he informed Sitting Bull that he must obey Canadian law. Although this act of bravery won the respect of the chief, it was four years before Sitting Bull consented to returning to the US to live on a reservation.

SIGHTS

★★ **Cypress Hills Provincial Park** – *In Alberta, 65km/40mi southeast of Medicine Hat by Trans-Can Hwy. and Hwy. 41 south. Park office at Elkwater Lake. For road conditions check at park office* ☎403-893-3777. *Park open year-round. Visitor centre open mid-May–early Sept Mon–Thu 10am–4pm, Fri 1–9pm, weekends 10am–6pm.* ⌂ *(*☎*403-893-3782 after May 1 for reservations).* ✗ ᕟ ☎*403-893-3833.* This park encompasses the highest part of the Cypress Hills. From Elkwater Lake an interesting drive *(40km/25mi)* leads past **Horseshoe Canyon** to **Head of the Mountain**, which affords pleasant views of coulees and hills as far as the Sweet Grass Hills and Bear Paw Mountains of Montana. The drive proceeds to Reesor Lake and the park boundary. This road crosses the provincial boundary and continues to Fort Walsh, approximately 18km/11mi south.

★ **Fort Walsh** – ❀ *In Saskatchewan, 52km/32mi southwest of Maple Creek by Hwy. 271. Open mid-May–mid-Oct daily 9am–6pm. $3.* ✗ ᕟ ☎*306-662-3590.* Reached from Cypress Hills Provincial Park or by a pleasant drive from Maple Creek, this North West Mounted Police post, named for its builder, Inspector James Walsh, was constructed close to the site of the Cypress Hills Massacre. From 1878 to 1882 it served as the force's headquarters.

At the **visitor centre** displays and films provide a good introduction. The fort can be reached by foot or by park bus service. The white-washed log buildings include barracks, stables, a workshop and the commissioner's residence. At **Farwell's Trading Post★** *(2.5km/1.5mi south of the fort, access by park bus; visit by 30min guided tour only, mid-May–Labour Day; $1)*, visitors are shown around by costumed guides who depict historical figures of the trading post's past.

EDMONTON★★

Alberta
Pop. 616,741
Map of Principal Sights p 2
Tourist Office ☎403-496-8400

The capital of Alberta spans the deep valley of the North Saskatchewan River in the geographic midpoint of the province. This thriving metropolis is the heart of Canada's oil-refining and extraction industries. Located in a rich agricultural area, Edmonton is also a meat-processing and grain-handling centre as well as the major distribution hub for western Canada.

Historical Notes

From Fur Trade Post to Provincial Capital – By the end of the 18C, both the North West and Hudson's Bay Companies had erected fur-trading forts in the vicinity of present-day Edmonton. When the two merged in 1821, **Edmonton House** became the most important post in the West, serving not only Alberta but the territory west of the Rockies.

Settlement developed around the post, with goods arriving by York boat from York Factory *(p 110)* or overland from WINNIPEG by Red River cart. The growing community suffered a relapse when the Canadian Pacific Railway Co. decided to build its line through Calgary, but recovered when other rail lines were built at the end of the century. People poured in, especially during the Klondike Stampede of 1896-99 en route to DAWSON CITY, the beginning of Edmonton's development as a "gateway to the North." In 1905 the city became Alberta's capital; its strategic location between rich central farmland and northland resources was a major determinant.

Petroleum Centre – Edmonton might have remained a quiet administrative centre had it not been for **Leduc**, a small community located to the south. In February 1947 oil was found 1,771m/5,810ft below the ground, the first strike of what proved to be a 300-million-barrel bonanza. In 1948 the Redwater field was opened, followed by other discoveries. The city is the major service and distribution centre for the vast Athabasca oil sands to the north. The majority of Canada's oil reserves lie in Alberta, with the largest percentage of the province's producing oil wells concentrated in the Edmonton area.

Oil Pump near Leduc

Travel Alberta

Klondike Days – Every year in July Edmonton celebrates its role in the great **Klondike Stampede**. Bedecked in costumes of the Gay Nineties, inhabitants and visitors parade, eat flapjacks, dance in the streets, gamble at the casino, pan for gold at the Chilkoot Mine, compete in raft races on the river, and in general "whoop it up" for about ten days.

DOWNTOWN   *1/2 day. Map below.*

Edmonton's downtown is generally considered to be the vicinity of Sir Winston Churchill Square and Jasper Avenue. The square is surrounded by a collection of modern buildings including **City Hall**, the **Court House**, the Art Gallery *(below)*, the elegant glass and brick **Citadel Theatre [A]** with its three stages, the attractive **Centennial Library [B]**, and Edmonton Centre with its shops, restaurants and offices.

Two blocks south, the steel and glass structure of the Edmonton **Convention Centre** rises opposite Canada Place, which houses offices of the federal government.

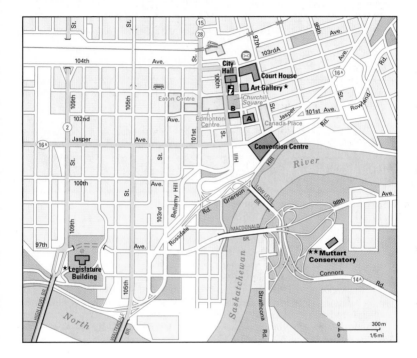

★ **Art Gallery** – *2 Sir Winston Churchill Square. Open year-round Mon–Wed 10:30am–5pm, Thu–Fri 10:30am–8pm, weekends 11am–5pm. Closed Jan 1 & Dec 25. $3.* ⚅ ☎*403-422-6223.* Constructed in 1969 this modern building, with its open central stairway, presents regularly changing and permanent exhibits. The development of Canadian art is traced by a selection of works from the gallery's collections.

★★ **Muttart Conservatory** – *9626 96A St. Open year-round Sun–Wed 11am–9pm, Thu–Sat 11am–6pm. Closed Dec 25. $4.25.* ✗⚅🅿☎*403-496-8755.* The four glass pyramids of this striking architectural ensemble provide a fine setting for displays of plants from three different climatic zones—tropical, temperate and arid. One pyramid is reserved as a showplace for changing displays of ornamental plants.

★ **Legislature Building** – *Legislature Centre. Visit by guided tour (45min) only, Mar–early May & Sept–Oct Mon–Fri 9am–4:30pm, weekends noon–5pm. Mid-May–Labour Day Mon–Fri 8:30am–5pm, weekends 9am–5pm. Nov–Feb Mon–Fri noon–4:30pm, Sun noon–5pm. Closed Jan 1, Good Friday & Dec 25.* ✗⚅🅿 ☎*403-427-7362.* Set in pleasant gardens overlooking the North Saskatchewan River, the yellow sandstone Alberta Legislature building (1912) occupies the original site of Fort Edmonton. The main entrance *(north side)* leads into an impressive hall from which a stairway ascends to the **legislative assembly**. The fifth floor of the dome presents an interesting display on Alberta history.

113

ADDITIONAL SIGHTS   *Map p 115*

★★ **Fort Edmonton Park** – *Open May–Sept daily 10am–6pm. $6.50.* ✗ ♿ 🅿 ☎*403-496-8787.* Set in the ravine of the North Saskatchewan River, this park re-creates the history of European settlement in Edmonton. Inside a high palisade the buildings of **Fort Edmonton**—the 1846 fur-trading post—have been reconstructed. Dominant is the Big House, a 4-storey residence with a third-floor balcony from which the chief factor, or governor of the fort, could survey his domain. Quarters of the other 130 inhabitants, such as clerks, artisans, labourers and servants, have been meticulously re-created. Also on view are trade and storage rooms, the forge, stable and boatshed, where York boats *(p 127)* are under construction (a completed one can be seen on the river), and the chapel built for Rev. **Robert Rundle**, the first missionary in Alberta, who spent the years 1840 to 1848 at Fort Edmonton.

Fort Edmonton Park

The **pre-railway village** contains a reconstruction of Jasper Avenue in 1885, notable for its width and boardwalks. Along the avenue stand stores selling furs, jewellery, drugs, and hardware, as well as the North West Mounted Police post, the Dominion Land Office, and the offices of the local newspaper. One original building, the McDougall Church, erected downtown in 1873, was moved to this site. Built by Rev. **George McDougall**, it was the first Protestant church in Alberta. The village gradually becomes **1905 Street**, which shows Edmonton at a time of great growth. A street car *(continuous service)* runs down the middle of the road lined with a penny arcade, Masonic Hall, two churches, a fire hall, civic centre and other structures.

Eventually "1905 Street" becomes **1920 Street**, which is currently under development. Commercial concerns such as a brickyard and greenhouse complex can be visited along with a Ukrainian bookstore and the train station *(continuous service)*.

West Edmonton Mall – *170th to 178th Sts., 87th to 90th Aves. Open year-round Mon–Fri 10am–9pm, Sat 10am–6pm, Sun noon–5pm. Closed Jan 1, Easter Sunday & Dec 25.* ✗ ♿ 🅿 ☎*403-444-5200.* Covering over 483,000sq m/5.2 million sq ft, this huge shopping centre is reputedly the largest in the world. It encloses an amusement park, full-size ice rink, waterpark, hotel and some 800 stores and restaurants.

★★ **Provincial Museum** – *12845 102nd Ave. Open mid-May–Labour Day Sun–Wed 9am–9pm, Thu–Sat 9am–5pm. Rest of the year Tue–Sun 9am–5pm. Closed Dec 24–25. $5.50.* ✗ ♿ 🅿 ☎*403-453-9100.* A showcase of Alberta's culture and human and natural history, this complex occupies an attractive **site**★ in a park overlooking the river beside the former residence of Alberta's lieutenant-governor.

On the ground floor are **dioramas**★ of the wildlife of the four great natural regions of the province—prairie, parkland, forest and mountain. The **Aboriginal Peoples Gallery**★★ *(under renovation until summer 1997)* details the life of the Plains Indians in western Canada. Displays encompass food, clothes (featuring exquisite beadwork), shelter, transportation, recreation and religion.

The second floor features displays on Alberta's geology and mineral wealth. Giant mammals and dinosaurs are exhibited in the Fossil Gallery. Educational displays on bird, mammal and insect life complete the exhibit. The **historical exhibits★** trace European settlement, with displays evoking life in the province in previous times.

★ **Edmonton Space and Science Centre** – *11211 142nd St. Open Jun–Labour Day daily 10am–10pm. Rest of the year Tue–Sun 10am–10pm. Closed Dec 25. $6.50.* 🍴 ♿ 🅿 ☎*403-451-3344.* Resembling a large space ship with its white steel cladding over a steel frame, the centre houses an IMAX theatre as well as a planetarium. Featured are exhibits on the planets, meteorites and space exploration.

Housed separately, an **observatory** offers a close-up view of the stars and planets *(weather permitting; Jun–Sept daily 1–5pm & 8pm–midnight; rest of the year Fri–Sat 8–11pm; Sun & holidays 1–4pm).*

EXCURSIONS

St. Albert – Pop. 42,146. *19km/12mi north by Rte. 2.* In 1861 a Roman Catholic mission was founded here on the banks of the Sturgeon River by Father **Albert Lacombe** (1827-1916). The simple log structure that served as his **chapel** still stands today and is the oldest building in Alberta *(St. Vital Ave., open mid-May–Labour Day daily 10am–6pm; rest of the year by appointment; contribution requested;* ♿ 🅿 ☎*403-459-2116).* The crypt of the modern-day church contains Father Lacombe's tomb and that of Bishop **Vital Grandin** (1829-1902), whose adjoining residence can also be visited.

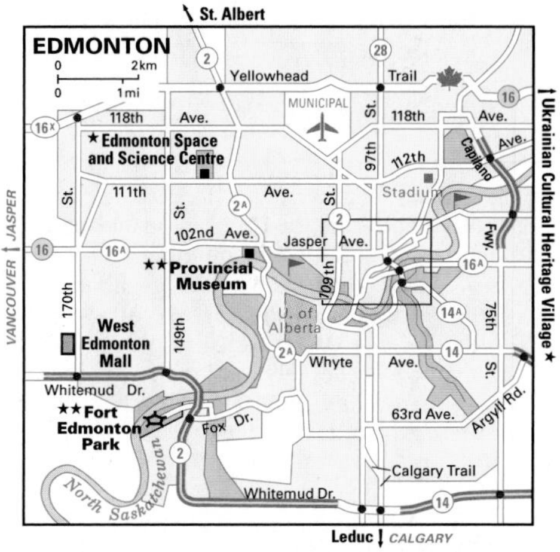

★ **Ukrainian Cultural Heritage Village** – *On Hwy. 16, about 50km/30mi east. Open mid-May–Labour Day daily 10am–6pm. Early Sept–mid-Oct daily 10am–4pm. $5.50.* 🍴 ♿ 🅿 ☎*403-662-3640.* This well-reconstructed village traces Ukrainian settlement in Alberta since the 1890s. Displays in the visitor centre provide insight into the mass migration of Ukrainian people to the Canadian Prairies. Homestead development—from early sod-covered dugout to white-washed dwelling—is explained in great detail by costumed interpreters. The village also includes a rural community and an early town, complete with a grain elevator, train station, provincial police post, domed churches and shops.

FORT MACLEOD★

Alberta

Pop. 3,112

Map of Principal Sights p 2

South of CALGARY (165km/102mi), this small town on the Oldman River was the site chosen for the first North West Mounted Police post in the West. In October 1874 a band of weary men arrived after a long and arduous trek from Manitoba. They had been quickly trained and dispatched to stop the illegal whisky trade and border incursions, such as the one leading to the Cypress Hills Massacre *(p 111).* Under the command of **Col. James Macleod**, they built permanent barracks on an island in the river.

Today Fort Macleod is a thriving agricultural community. Grain is grown with the aid of irrigation, and cattle are raised on the ranch land of nearby Porcupine Hills.

SIGHTS

★ **Fort Museum** – *On Hwy. 3, one block from centre of town. Open May–mid-Oct daily 9am–5pm. Jul–Aug daily 9am–8:30pm. Rest of the year Mon–Fri 9am–5pm. Closed Dec 24–Jan 2. $4.* ♿ ☎*403-553-4703.* This museum re-creates life in and around police posts during the early settlement of Alberta. Inside the wooden, palisaded walls stand a number of log structures. The **Kanouse House** with its sod roof is devoted to the early settlers of the region. The **Mounted Police Building** houses a model of the original fort and exhibits on the police. The Indian Artifacts Building contains a sizeable collection of native arts and crafts.

In summer students dressed in the police uniforms of 1878 (red jackets, black breeches, white pith helmets) perform a musical ride *(Jul–Aug daily)*.

★ **Head-Smashed-In Buffalo Jump** – *18km/11mi northwest by Hwy. 785 (Spring Point Rd.). Open mid-May–Labour Day daily 9am–8pm. Rest of the year daily 9am–5pm. Closed Jan 1, Easter Sunday, Dec 25. $5.50.* ✖ ☎403-553-2731. This buffalo jump has the most extensive deposits (9m/30ft deep) of any in North America. Its importance was recognized by UNESCO in 1981, when the site was inscribed on the World Heritage List.

For over 5,000 years buffalo were driven to their deaths over this cliff. The buffalo provided most of the necessities of life for the Indians—meat, hides for clothing and shelter, and bone for scrapers and needles. A visitor centre contains displays and films on buffalo-hunting cultures.

LETHBRIDGE★

Alberta
Pop. 60,974
Map of Principal Sights p 2
Tourist Office ☎403-320-1222

Located in southern Alberta, 216km/134mi southeast of CALGARY, this city overlooks a wide riverbed cut by the Oldman River. Constructed into the side of this riverbed are the striking buildings of the University of Lethbridge, and crossing it is the High Level Railway Bridge (about 1.5km/1mi long and 96m/314ft high). Lethbridge was founded in 1870, after coal deposits were discovered in the valley. Today the city is the centre of a productive agricultural region. Widespread irrigation and the relatively mild winters moderated by the warm chinook winds *(p 98)* have made the cultivation of grain and vegetables, especially canola and sugar beet, very profitable. Livestock are also raised here.

SIGHTS

★ **Nikka Yuko Japanese Garden** – *In Henderson Lake Park on Mayor Magrath Dr. Open Jun–Aug daily 9am–8pm. May & Sept daily 9am–5pm. $3.* ☎403-328-3511. The city built this garden in 1967 as a symbol of Japanese-Canadian amity (*Nikka Yuko* means "Japan-Canada friendship"). It is a wonderfully serene place where visitors can gain an appreciation for traditional Japanese landscape architecture. When Canada declared war on Japan in 1941, about 22,000 Japanese-Canadians living on the west coast were placed in internment camps in central British Columbia and Alberta, although in many cases they were Canadian citizens. About 6,000 of these Japanese-Canadians were resettled in Lethbridge, where they chose to stay after the war. Five types of formal landscapes are linked by meandering paths. At the centre lies a pavilion of Japanese cypress wood, laid out for a tea ceremony.

★ **Fort Whoop-up** – *In Indian Battle Park by river, access from Hwy. 3. Open May–Aug daily 10am–6pm. Rest of the year Tue–Fri 10am–4pm, Sun 1–4pm. $2.50.* ☎403-329-0444. In the deep riverbed of the Oldman River stands a replica of this once-notorious whisky trading post. Founded by Americans from Fort Benton, Montana, the post attracted Indians from far and wide to trade buffalo skins, furs, and indeed almost anything, for a particularly lethal brew bearing little resemblance to whisky (ingredients included chewing tobacco, red peppers, Jamaican ginger and black molasses, as well as alcohol).

Such illegal liquor forts, of which Whoop-up was the most important, sprang up all over southern Alberta and Saskatchewan in the early 1870s. The Canadian government formed the North West Mounted Police to counter this American encroachment of Canadian territory and to stop a trade that was demoralizing the Indians. In 1874 the force that arrived at the gates of Whoop-up found the premises vacated. The founding of Fort Macleod *(p 115)*, and later Fort Calgary *(p 106)*, effectively ended the illegal trade and brought law and order to the West. The reconstructed fort flies not "the Stars and Stripes" (the American flag) but the trading flag of the original Fort Benton company. Below it wooden buildings form a fortified enclosure. In the **visitor centre** a video presentation *(20min)* presents the history of the post in the context of the development of the Canadian West.

MOOSE JAW ★

Saskatchewan
Pop. 33,593
Map of Principal Sights p 3

Rising out of the flat wheat lands of southern Saskatchewan, 71km/44mi due west of REGINA, is the province's third largest city. Named for a sharp turn in the river that resembles a protruding moose jaw, this industrial centre, with flour mills, grain elevator and stock yards, is an important railway junction for agricultural produce of the area. The city is also involved in the refining of Saskatchewan's oil.

SIGHT

★ **Western Development Museum** – *At junction Trans-Can Hwy. and Hwy. 2. Open Apr–Dec daily 9am–6pm. Rest of the year Mon–Fri 9am–5:30pm. Closed Dec 25. $4.50.* ✗ ♿ ☎*306-693-5989.* One of four museums on Western development in the province (North Battleford, SASKATOON, YORKTON), this one is devoted to transportation in Saskatchewan. The water section has displays about the *Northcote,* a steamship used to take supplies up the South Saskatchewan River during the Northwest Rebellion, and on cable ferries, particularly that of the St.-Laurent *(p 123).* The land section features a Canadian Pacific locomotive, a reconstructed station and a 1934 Buick converted to run on rails and used as an inspection vehicle for 20 years. In addition there is an interesting collection of other automobiles. The air section presents several Canadian planes, including a 1927 Red Pheasant, and a gallery devoted to the British Commonwealth Air Training Plan.

PRINCE ALBERT NATIONAL PARK ★

Saskatchewan
Map of Principal Sights p 3

Located in the geographic centre of Saskatchewan, this large park consisting of wooded hills dotted with lakes and streams constitutes a fine example of Canada's southern boreal plains, an area where the aspen forest of the south mixes with the true boreal wilderness. Isolated pockets of grassland near the southern boundary support prairie animals—coyotes, badgers and ground squirrels. The northern forests are home to wolves, moose, elk, bears, beaver, otter, mink and a small herd of woodland caribou. In the extreme north white pelicans nest on Lavallée Lake.

Grey Owl – Famous for his writings and lectures on the fate of the beaver and the vanishing wilderness, this man posed as an Indian, dressing in buckskins and wearing his long hair in braids. He travelled throughout North America and Europe with a conservation message, even lecturing to the British monarch, George VI, in 1937. Trying to reestablish beaver colonies, he worked for Canada's national park service, first in Riding Mountain National Park *(p 120)* and then in Prince Albert. At his death in 1938, he was exposed as an Englishman, **Archie Belaney,** who had taken the Indian name *Wa-sha-Quon-Asin* ("the Grey Owl") about 1920. Though discovered to be an impostor, Grey Owl remains one of Canada's finest nature writers and among the first to preach the importance of the wilderness. His most famous books are *Tales of an Empty Cabin, Pilgrims of the Wild* and *Sajo and Her Beaver People.*

Access – *80km/50mi north of Prince Albert by Hwys. 2 and 264.*

VISIT

➔ *Open year-round. Hiking, canoeing, swimming, golf, tennis, winter sports. Accommodations in Waskesiu Lake. $3.50/day. Map available at visitor centre (open mid-May–Labour Day daily 8am–10pm; early Sept–mid-Oct daily 8am–5pm; rest of the year Mon–Sat 8am–4pm).* ⚠ ☎*306-663-5322.*

The **nature centre** *(open Jun–Labour Day daily 10am–5pm)* in Waskesiu (meaning "place of the elk") Lake provides an introduction to the park. The roads following both shores of Lake Waskesiu and **boat trips** on the lake in a paddlewheeler afford pleasant views *(depart Jul–mid-Sept daily 1, 3, 5 & 7pm; round-trip 1hr; $8; ♿ Neo-Watin Marine ☎306-663-5253).* Hiking trails and canoe routes crisscross the park. One interesting hike takes the visitor to the cabin and grave of Grey Owl *(15km/9mi).*

The ⚠ *symbol indicates that campgrounds can be found on the premises of the sight described.*

REGINA★★

Saskatchewan
Pop. 179,178
Map of Principal Sights p 3
Tourist Office ☎306-789-5099

Set in an extensive, fertile, wheat-growing plain and located on the main line of the Canadian Pacific Railway and the Trans-Canada Highway, this provincial capital has long been an important agricultural centre. Regina is the headquarters for the Saskatchewan Wheatpool, one of the largest grain cooperatives in the world.

Historical Notes

Pile O' Bones – Few cities have been established in less congenial surroundings—treeless plains stretching to the horizon; a scanty water supply from a sluggish creek; soil of gumbo clay, muddy in wet weather, dusty in dry. Nevertheless in the early 1880s, the Canadian Pacific Railway Co. decided to build its line across the southern plains, leaving the existing capital of the vast Northwest Territories at Battleford (*p 105*) high and dry. Determined to move the capital, the Dominion government, in collaboration with the railway company, chose a location where the future rail line would cross a creek long favoured by Indians and Métis for running buffalo into pounds to slaughter them. Testifying to their once great number, the remains of these animals had given this spot (as recorded by John Palliser, *p 98*) the Cree name, *Oskana*, translated as "pile o' bones." The choice was controversial, especially since the lieutenant-governor of the then Northwest Territories, Edgar Dewdney (*p 47*), owned land at that place. In August 1882 when the first train arrived, Princess Louise, wife of Canada's governor general, rechristened it Regina ("Queen" in Latin) after her mother, Queen Victoria.

Historic Court Case – After the defeat of the Northwest Rebellion in 1885 (*p 122*), the Métis leader, Louis Riel (*p 99*), was taken to Regina for trial. The court immediately became a centre of controversy. To Quebecers, Riel—a Catholic Métis who had studied for the priesthood in Montreal—was a patriot who had fought for the rights of his people. To Ontarians, he was a common rebel who had gone unpunished after murdering Thomas Scott during the Red River Rebellion (*p 99*). Defence counsel pleaded that Riel was insane: he had spent several years in asylums and had wished to set up a new Catholic state on the Saskatchewan River, with Bishop Bourget of Montreal as Pope. Riel himself rejected the plea and convinced the jury he was sane. But if sane, he was guilty: the verdict was death by hanging. Prime Minister Sir John A. Macdonald was inundated with petitions from both sides. The sentence was delayed while doctors studied Riel's mental health. The prime minister weighed the political consequences of hanging Riel and decided the sentence had to be carried out. Riel lost his life on November 16, 1885.

Every summer the MacKenzie Art Gallery is the setting for a dramatic reenactment of the **Trial of Louis Riel** based on actual court transcripts (*3475 Albert St.; Wed–Fri in Aug 8pm; tickets available at door or* ☎*306-522-4242*).

Queen City of the Plains – Regina became the capital of Saskatchewan when that province was created in 1905. As immigrants poured in from all parts of the world, the city burgeoned. Their enterprising spirit helped overcome the physical shortcomings of the city's site. To solve the water problems, Wascana Creek was dammed, creating an artificial lake. Trees were planted and carefully nourished, defying the notion of a treeless wilderness.

Though the city's development in the 20C has been precarious, Regina has experienced steady growth since World War II. The downtown core has been revitalized, and imposing buildings constructed. Today, from 80km/50mi distant, Regina rises above the flat, treeless prairie like a mirage, its quiet grace testifying to its epithet, "Queen City of the Plains."

DOWNTOWN   *1/2 day. Map p 119.*

★★ **Royal Saskatchewan Museum** – *College Ave. and Albert St. Open May–Labour Day daily 9am–8:30pm. Rest of the year daily 9am–4:30pm. Closed Dec 25. Contribution requested.* & 🅿 ☎*306-787-2815.* This long, low building of Tyndall stone housed one of the finest museums of natural history in Canada until a fire in 1990 destroyed the remarkable life sciences dioramas, highlight of the museum. Plans to re-create them are under way (*projected reopening of the Life Sciences Gallery is 1998*). Exhibits in the Earth Sciences Gallery feature dinosaurs (including a robotic *Tyrannosaurus rex*) and woolly mammoths, volcanoes and glaciers from the

118

province's geological beginnings to the appearance of mankind in Saskatchewan. The First Nations Gallery displays art and artifacts of the native cultures of the region. Especially noteworthy is the winter encampment, which features a bison-hide teepee.

★ **Legislative Building** – *2405 Legislative Dr. Visit by guided tour (30min) only, mid-May–Labour Day daily 8am–9pm. Rest of the year daily 8am–5pm. Closed Jan 1, Good Friday, Dec 25.* ✗ ♿ ⏏ ☎306-787-5358. Completed in 1912, this graceful building of Tyndall stone was built in the shape of a cross topped by a dome. It occupies a fine **site★** overlooking gardens and Wascana Lake.

The guided tour visits the legislative chamber, legislative library, the rotunda, and art galleries named after the rivers of the province.

★ **Wascana Centre** – *Picnicking, swimming, boating. Open mid-May–Labour Day daily 10am–7pm. Rest of the year Tue–Sat 10am–6pm, Sun 1–4pm.* ♿ ⏏ ☎306-522-3661. This 930ha/2,300 acre park is Regina's pride and joy. Formal gardens of beautiful flowers and trees surround the western part of the artificial Wascana Lake. **Willow Island** is a picnic site accessible by ferry *(ferry reservations required; mid-May–Labour Day Mon–Fri noon–4pm; $2)*.

Also in the park, which can be toured by car, are the provincial legislative building and the **Diefenbaker Homestead**, a three-room pioneer dwelling *(open mid-May–Labour Day daily 10am–7pm;* ♿ ⏏ ☎306-522-3661)*, home to John George Diefenbaker, Prime Minister of Canada from 1957 to 1963 *(p 121)*. This house was moved from its original site in Borden, Saskatchewan, where the Diefenbaker family homesteaded between 1905 and 1910.

East of Wascana Parkway the park is a bird sanctuary. Many species of waterfowl can be spotted, but by far the most common is the **Canada goose**. Some of these birds are year-round residents of the centre, benefiting from crops grown nearby. Visitors can also tour a waterfall display pond *(open mid-May–Labour Day daily)*.

ADDITIONAL SIGHTS

★ **Royal Canadian Mounted Police Training Academy** – *West of downtown by Dewdney Ave. Open Jun–mid-Sept daily 8am–6:45pm. Rest of the year daily 10am–4:45pm. Closed Dec 25. Guided tours vary, depending on the number of cadets and their activities.* ♿ ⏏ ☎306-780-5838. People who know nothing else about Canada have heard of the **Mounties**, the country's federal police force. Stories about them are legion, and many films have portrayed their ability to "always get their man." Created in 1873 as the **North West Mounted Police**, the force had to formulate as well as to preserve law and order in the Canadian West. Faced with problems such as the illegal sale of "fire water" to Canadian Indians by American traders, the police quickly established themselves as an effective force. They helped the various Indian tribes accept treaties and life on reservations, gave valuable aid to new settlers in the West, and enforced law and order during the Klondike Stampede *(p 34)*.

In 1920 they were united with the Dominion Police as the **Royal Canadian Mounted Police**. Today they enforce federal laws across Canada and act as the provincial police in all provinces and territories except Ontario and Quebec. They are famous for their **musical ride**, a collection of early cavalry drills performed on horseback and culminating in a rousing "charge." *Sunset Retreat Ceremony Jul & Aug Tue 7pm.*

★ **Museum** – *(same hours as academy)* This museum illustrates the history of the Mounties and recalls such famous incidents as Sitting Bull's years in Canada *(p 111)*, the Northwest Rebellion *(p 122)*, the Klondike Stampede and the voyage of the *St. Roch (p 78)*. Displays also explain the work of the force today.

EXCURSION

★ **Qu'Appelle Valley** – *Map p 3*. From Lake Diefenbaker to the Manitoba border, the Qu'Appelle (kap-PELL) Valley cuts a deep swath across the otherwise flat prairie. It was carved out 12,000 years ago by meltwaters from a retreating glacier that left a wide valley with only a small stream at its midst, surrounded by low, round-topped hills. As visitors approach the Qu'Appelle from any direction, the prairie seems endless, and then suddenly the road drops and a 2km/1.2mi wide stretch of verdant green comes into view. As much as 120m/400ft deep in places, with several sparkling lakes, the valley presents a complete contrast to the surrounding plains. The name derives from Indian lore. According to legend a brave in his canoe heard his name called. *Qu'appelle?* ("who calls?" in French) he shouted, but only an echo answered him. On returning home he found his sweetheart lifeless—she had called his name moments before dying.

★ **The Fishing Lakes** – *73km/45mi east of Regina by Trans-Can Hwy., northeast by Rte.10; 1/2 day*. The best way to appreciate the Qu'Appelle Valley is to drive alongside the river where it forms the Fishing Lakes—Pasqua, Echo, Mission and Katepwa. North of Lake Echo there is a particularly attractive stretch of road on Route 56 leading to **Echo Valley Provincial Park★** *(open year-round; visitor centre open mid-May–Labour Day, hours vary;* ⚠ ♿ ☎*306-332-3215).*

RIDING MOUNTAIN NATIONAL PARK★★
Manitoba
Map of Principal Sights p 3

Established in 1933 on the Manitoba plain, this lovely park is a rolling plateau of wooded slopes and lakes. Approached from the east and north, it rises 457m/1,500ft above the surrounding countryside (756m/2,480ft above sea level) and does indeed look like a mountain—or at least a hill.

Early fur traders named it "Riding" Mountain, the place where they exchanged canoes for horses to continue west. It is part of the **Manitoba Escarpment**, a jagged 1,600km/1,000mi ridge winding across North Dakota, Manitoba and Saskatchewan—a series of hills cut by many rivers, rather than a continuous ridge.

The park is also a crossroads where northern, western and eastern environments and habitats meet. High areas are covered with an evergreen forest of spruce, pine, fir and tamarack. Lower sections support a deciduous forest of hardwoods, shrubs, vines and ferns. In the west wildflowers thrive on meadows and grassland (July and August), forming some of the only true prairie left on the continent.

Access – *197km/122mi west of Winnipeg by Trans-Can Hwy., then 91km/56mi north of Brandon by Rte. 10.*

VISIT

☞ *Open year-round. Hiking, boating, tennis, golf, winter sports. Accommodations in Wasagamin. Map available at visitor centre. $3/day or $7/4 days per person.* ⚠ *(for reservations* ☎*800-707-8480 Canada/US).* 🍴♿ ☎*204-848-7275.* The **visitor centre★★** *(open mid-May–mid-Jun daily 9am–5pm; late Jun–Labour Day daily 9am–9pm; early Sept–mid-Oct daily 9am–5pm)* in Wasagaming features excellent displays on the park's geological history, the different habitats therein and the native wildlife. Visitors can view films on related subjects.

Near Lake Audy *(47km/29mi from Wasagaming)*, a herd of about 30 buffalo roams a large enclosure. From a viewpoint above the Audy plain, these animals can be seen in their true prairie environment. An exhibit explains how they nearly became extinct. Visitors can drive around the enclosure *(4km/2.5mi)*.

A good **view★** of the Manitoba Escarpment is obtained from Route 19 *(31km/19mi east of Wasagaming or 5km/3mi from park's east gate)*.

SASKATOON ★

Saskatchewan
Pop. 186,058
Map of Principal Sights p 3
Tourist Office ☎306-242-1206

Built on both sides of the South Saskatchewan River, this city, 259km/161mi northwest of REGINA, occupies a pleasant **site★** enhanced by wide, tree-lined streets as well as parkland beside the water (in particular, **Kiwanis Park** with its views of bridges and the University of Saskatchewan). The largest city in Saskatchewan, this manufacturing and distribution centre is set in a fertile wheat-growing area, amid the province's vast potash reserves. Surrounding prairie landscape is a little more rolling than around Regina, but is nonetheless dominated by the "heights" of **Mt. Blackstrap** (91m/300ft), an artificial ski hill rising south of the city (40km/25mi).

Historical Notes – Founded in 1883 by Methodists from Ontario, the city was to be the capital of a temperance colony. A leader of this venture, **John Lake**, selected the name *Saskatoon*, a small purplish berry native to the region. However the tee-totallers' paradise did not attract many settlers and two decades later, numbered only 113 souls. In 1908 the whole area quickly experienced a boom when colonists arrived by the new rail lines. German, Scandinavian, Ukrainian and British settlers transformed the city, and the early temperance ideals were laid to rest. Today the settlers are honoured once a year in July during **Pioneer Days**.

SIGHTS *1/2 day. Map p 122.*

★ **Mendel Art Gallery** – *950 Spadina Crescent East. Open mid-May–Labour Day daily 10am–9pm. Rest of the year daily noon–9pm. Closed Dec 25.* ♿ 🅿 ☎306-975-7610. This attractive modern gallery overlooking the river is named for **Fred Mendel**, a wealthy Saskatoon meat-packer of German origin who launched the idea of an art gallery and spent much of his time and money developing it.

The permanent collection includes works by the Group of Seven *(p 190)*, Emily Carr *(p 75)* and David Milne in the Canadian section, and Feininger, Chagall, Utrillo and Pissarro in the **European section**. The gallery displays travelling exhibits as well. There is also an attractive conservatory of exotic flowers and plants.

Ukrainian Museum – *910 Spadina Crescent East. Open mid-May–Labour Day Mon–Sat 10am–5pm, Sun 1–5pm. Rest of the year Tue–Sat 10am–5pm, Sun 1–5pm. Closed Jan 1 & 7, Good Friday, Dec 25. $2.* ♿ 🅿 ☎306-244-3800. This museum presents displays of traditional costumes, tapestries, pioneer tools, wood-inlaid objects, and other handicrafts illustrating the heritage of the people who have played such a large role in the settlement of the Prairies.

Boat Trip – *Map p 122. Departs from dock behind Mendel Art Gallery mid-May–Labour Day weekends 1–8pm on the hour (also Jun–Aug weekdays 1–4pm & 6–8pm on the hour). Round-trip 1hr. Commentary. $6.50.* ♿ 🅿 *Northcote River Cruises* ☎306-382-1166. This cruise on the South Saskatchewan River is a pleasant way to discover the scenic beauty of the area.

★ **John Diefenbaker Centre** – *On University of Saskatchewan campus, off Rte. 5. Open year-round Mon–Fri 9:30am–4:30pm, weekends 12:30–5pm. Closed Good Friday, Nov 11 & Christmas week.* ♿ 🅿 ☎306-966-8384. Upon his death in 1979, the former Canadian prime minister left his papers to the university. They have been assembled to form a veritable shrine to this man, a legend in his own time. A lawyer by training, well known for his defence of the "little man," Diefenbaker entered politics and became a strong proponent of Western Canadian ideas in the Conservative Party. Elected party leader in 1956, he served as prime minister from 1957 to 1963, remaining influential in federal politics until his death.

In addition to displays on his life and works, the centre features a replica of the office of the prime minister and the cabinet chamber as they existed in the Diefenbaker era.

★★ **Western Development Museum** – *In Prairieland Exhibition Grounds, 8km/5mi south of downtown by Rte. 11/16. Open year-round daily 9am–5pm. $4.50.* ✗ ♿ 🅿 ☎306-931-1910. The grand attraction of the Saskatoon branch of this museum (other branches in North Battleford, MOOSE JAW and YORKTON) is **Boomtown**, a faithful reconstruction of an entire street of 1910 vintage, complete with its Western Pioneer Bank, garage, stores, Chinese laundry, school, pool hall, theatre, hotel and railway station. The church, moved here in 1972, is the only original structure on the street. Several period automobiles and horse-drawn vehicles line the street.

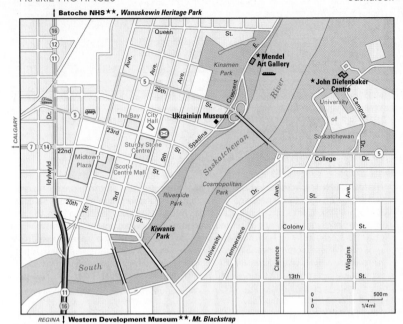

Separate halls house a large collection of automobiles and agricultural equipment, including steam tractors. The museum also features the Eaton collection of mechanized Christmas window displays.

Wanuskewin Heritage Park – *3km/2mi north of downtown by Hwy. 11. Open late May–early Sept daily 9am–9pm. Mid-Sept–Nov daily 9am–5pm. Dec–mid-May Wed–Sun 9am–5pm. $6. ✗ & ☐ ☎306-931-6767.* A series of archaeological sites on the banks of the South Saskatchewan River forms the basis of this testament to the survival of the Plains Indians. Translated from Cree as "seeking peace of mind," *Wanuskewin* was a meeting place and hunting ground for these nomadic Indians for more than 6,000 years until their removal to reserves in the 1870s.

Several trails in the 120ha/290 acre park link the prehistoric sites. Opened in 1992 a striking **visitor centre** features displays and demonstrations of native culture and allows observation of excavations and laboratory work.

EXCURSION

★★ **Batoche National Historic Site** – ☞ *88km/55mi northeast of Saskatoon by Rte. 11 to Rosthern, Rte. 312 east and Rte. 225 north. Grounds open daily year-round. Buildings open mid-May–Jun daily 9am–5pm. Jul–Aug daily 10am–6pm. Sept–Oct daily 9am–5pm. $3. ☎306-423-6227.* This quiet and beautiful spot on the banks of the South Saskatchewan River was the site of the final stand of the Métis in 1885.

The Northwest Rebellion – The seeds of the last armed conflict on Canadian soil were sown in Manitoba's Red River Valley early in the 19C when the Métis learned that land did not necessarily belong to those born and living on it. The uprising led to Louis Riel's provisional government of 1869, the formal creation of the province of Manitoba (1870) and the allocation of 567,000ha/1.4 million acres of land for Métis settlement (*p 99*).

Unfortunately the Métis, left leaderless when Riel was banished for five years, were prey to speculators who bought their land for a fraction of its worth. Many moved northwest to the valley of the South Saskatchewan River, hoping to lead traditional lives of buffalo hunting and to avoid survey groups and European settlers. The buffalo were nearly extinct, however, and the march of "progress" continued. Again the Métis found they had no right to land they farmed. The Dominion government consistently ignored their petitions. In 1884 they sent for Louis Riel.

Riel hoped to repeat his earlier victory at Red River. He allied the Métis with Cree Indians who were also discontent with changes in their lifestyle. An unfortunate incident resulting in the deaths of some members of the North West Mounted Police at **Duck Lake** destroyed all hope of a peaceful solution. In eastern Canada

122

there was outrage at the thought of police being killed by "lawless rebels," and a military force was quickly dispatched to the West under Maj-Gen. **Frederick Middleton**.

Restrained by Riel, the Métis—under their military leader, **Gabriel Dumont**, an experienced buffalo hunter—were unable to deter the advancing army by guerrilla tactics. Instead they made a stand at Batoche, which never could have succeeded against Middleton's overwhelming numbers. It was a heroic defence that lasted four days because of the strength of the Métis position. Afterwards Riel surrendered and was taken to Regina to stand trial for murder. He was found guilty and hanged *(p 118)*. Dumont fled to the US, though he was later pardoned for his part in the revolt and returned to Batoche. The struggle was not in vain, however, for in the wake of the rebellion, the Métis were offered the land title they had sought unsuccessfully for such a long time.

Visit – Today the site is a poignant tribute to the Métis. Little remains of the village except the tiny **church** dedicated to St. Anthony of Padua, the **rectory** with its bullet holes and a cemetery of Métis graves, including Dumont's burial place. The buildings have been restored to the period and house historic artifacts.

The **visitor centre** *(open mid-May–Jun daily 9am–5pm; Jul–Aug daily 10am–6pm; Sept–mid-Oct daily 9am–5pm; ✗ ☦ 🅿 ☎306-423-6227)* offers a moving audio-visual presentation on the rebellion and displays on Métis history and culture.

The return trip to Saskatoon can be made by the St.-Laurent cable ferry *(10km/6mi north of Batoche)*, past the small community of Duck Lake on Route 11, where the rebellion had its beginnings.

WINNIPEG★★★

Manitoba
Pop. 616,790
Map of Principal Sights p 3
Tourist Office ☎204-943-1970

Set on the banks of the Red and Assiniboine Rivers, the capital of Manitoba occupies the geographic heart of Canada and is often described as the place where "the West begins." Indeed, for over a century, it has been the traditional first stop for immigrants to the West. Not far to the east and north, the hilly and rocky tree-covered terrain of the Canadian Shield with its multitude of lakes gives way to the open fertile prairie with its endless horizons. This dramatic change clearly marks the division between east and west.

Named for the large and shallow lake to the north called *win-nipi* ("murky water") by the Cree, Winnipeg developed as the distribution and financial centre of the West. Although challenged by Vancouver and Alberta's cities in recent years, it retains a huge **commodity exchange** (the most important in Canada), vast stock and railway yards, a manufacturing industry and headquarters of the Hudson's Bay Company, so influential in the growth of the fur trade in the Prairies.

Historical Notes

The Red River Settlement – In the early 19C Thomas Douglas, Earl of Selkirk, obtained title from the Hudson's Bay Company to a large piece of land covering much of present-day southern Manitoba called **Assiniboia**. In 1811 he began resettling some of his poverty-stricken compatriots from the Scottish Highlands there in the Red River Valley. The success of this colony was slow in coming, mainly because of the Red River's tendency to flood, plagues of crop-eating grasshoppers and rivalry between the great fur-trading companies—the Hudson's Bay and the North West. The latter allied with the Métis, who had seen their traditional lifestyle gradually disrupted by settlers.

During the **Seven Oaks Massacre** of 1816, the Métis nearly succeeded in wiping out the colony: some 20 settlers were killed and the rest temporarily abandoned the settlement. Selkirk reestablished his colony, however, and it gradually grew in size as a commercial centre with brigades of Red River carts going to and from St. Paul, Minnesota and steamboats chugging along the Red River. The settlement's connections below the border made annexation by the US seem likely, but the Northwest Rebellion and the creation of Manitoba in 1870 prevented it.

Winnipeg Today – The community's future was assured when the Canadian Pacific Railway Co. chose the site as a major maintenance and repair centre and built a rail line through town. Floods of immigrants poured in by train. Winnipeg (the name was adopted at the time of the rebellion) not only assumed an outfitting role, but became a distribution centre for the entire Northwest. In the 19C the population consisted of Scots, Irish, English, French, Métis and Indians. During the 20C Germans, Eastern Europeans and especially Ukrainians joined their ranks. Winnipeg's skyline, dotted with spires, towers and domes of Catholic, Protestant and Orthodox churches, reflects this diversity. Every August the city's varied cultural background is celebrated in **Folklorama**, a festival held in pavilions throughout Winnipeg. The Folk Festival held in July is also a popular event.

Winnipeg is rich in cultural institutions—the Manitoba Theatre Centre, the Symphony Orchestra, the Manitoba Opera Company and, most famous of all, the Royal Winnipeg Ballet.

DOWNTOWN   *2 days. Map p 125.*

The intersection of **Portage Avenue** and **Main Street** has traditionally been considered the centre of Winnipeg. In a bygone era it was said these principal thoroughfares were wide enough for ten Red River carts to rush along side by side. Today this corner, long known as the windiest in Canada, is dominated by tall buildings, all connected underground by an attractive shopping area, **Winnipeg Square**. Extending for three blocks to the west, between Vaughan and Carlton Streets, is **Portage Place★**, a shopping and office complex with restaurants, three movie theatres and a giant-screen IMAX theatre.

Just south of the intersection at Portage and Main, in a small park below the Fort Garry Hotel, stands a stone gateway. It is all that remains of **Upper Fort Garry**, once the local headquarters of the Hudson's Bay Company. The present-day headquarters **[A]** rises a block away.

The **Forks**, 26ha/65 acres of riverfront property refurbished by the city, includes a **public market** housed within former stables, a National Historic Site and a waterside walkway.

North of the intersection lies the **Exchange District**, which has some remarkable examples of early-20C architecture (*walking tours daily Jul–Aug leaving from the Pantages Playhouse Theatre* ☎800-665-0204, *Canada/US*), and attractive boutiques and restaurants around the **Old Market Square** (*King, Albert and Bannatyne Sts.*). Close by is **Centennial Centre**, a complex enclosing a concert hall, theatre, museum and planetarium connected by terraced gardens. Just north is Winnipeg's **Chinatown**.

Another interesting quarter for shopping and dining is **Osborne Village**, south of the Assiniboine River between River and Stradbrook Avenues.

★★★ **Manitoba Museum of Man and Nature** – *190 Rupert Ave., across from City Hall. Open mid-May–Labour Day daily 10am–6pm. Rest of the year Tue–Fri 10am–4pm, weekends 10am–5pm. Closed Dec 25. $4.* ✗ ᴋ ₽ ☎204-956-2830. This excellent museum presents the history of human occupation in Manitoba by means of fascinating dioramas, displays and audio-visual presentations. It also portrays the great natural regions of the province.

On entering, the visitor is first struck by the magnificent diorama of a Métis rider, his spear poised, chasing several buffalo. The **Earth History Gallery** explains the geological creation of Manitoba. The mural by Daphne Odjig portrays the creation of the world according to Odawa Indian tradition.

The **Arctic/Sub-Arctic Gallery** is devoted to the northernmost part of the province. At its entrance stands an **inukshuk** (*illustration p 304*), a stone sculpture used as a navigational aid, campsite or hunting marker, or reminder of special occasions. Artifacts and photographs illustrate the dependence of the Inuit and Chipewyan Indians upon their environment; displays on Hudson Bay marine life and the phenomenon of the Northern Lights complete the exhibit.

In the **Boreal Forest Gallery** dioramas present the area's indigenous animals. One impressive "walk-through" diorama with a waterfall and cliffs depicts Cree Indians, one of whom is painting on a rock symbols that illustrate religious aspects of the hunt. Other displays feature life on the trapline and modern developments. A mural by Jackson Beardy depicts a world view of the Indians.

The **Grasslands Gallery** is devoted to the southern part of Manitoba. Insightful displays describe the Assiniboine Indians and first European settlers. There is an example of a **Red River cart**, the major means of pioneer transportation on the prairies: the axles never required greasing and the wheels were easily removed for river crossing. The gallery also has interesting displays on the diverse ethnic and religious groups of Manitoba's population.

The **Urban Gallery** captures a fall evening in Winnipeg in the 1920s. The wooden sidewalks, the railway station, shops, restaurant, rooming house, mission hall and theatre showing period movies have been frozen in time.

The highlight of the museum is the **Nonsuch★★★**, a replica of the ship that sailed from England to Hudson Bay in 1668 in search of furs. The successful enterprise led to the creation of the Hudson's Bay Company two years later *(p 99)*. Built for the company's tricentenary in 1970, the 15m/49ft ketch is anchored in a reconstructed 17C Thames River wharf. The wooden houses and the inn set around the harbour vividly re-create the scene.

A **planetarium** *(daily shows; $3.50)* and an innovative science centre, **Touch the Universe**, exploring sensory perception, *(same hours as museum; $3.50)* are located on the lower level.

★★ **Ukrainian Cultural Centre** – *184 Alexander Ave. East. Open year-round Tue–Sat 10am–4pm, Sun 2–5pm. Closed national holidays.* ▣ ☎*204-942-0218.* A visit to this centre, one of the largest of its kind outside the Ukraine, forms an interesting introduction to the history and culture of Manitoba's second largest ethnic group, whose influence on the province is very marked.

The **museum★★** *(5th floor)* features exquisite examples of Ukrainian traditional embroidery, wood carving, ceramics and beautifully painted *pysanky* ("Easter eggs"). The centre also houses an art gallery, library and archives.

★ **Art Gallery** – *300 Memorial Blvd. Open Jun–Aug daily 10am–5pm (Wed 9pm). Rest of the year Tue–Sun 11am–5pm (Wed 9pm). Closed Good Friday & Dec 25. $3.* ✕ & ☎*204-786-6641.* Designed by Winnipeger Gustavo Da Roza, this unusual wedge-shaped structure contains a beautiful art gallery. Shown in a constantly changing series of exhibits, the permanent collection is large and varied. The gallery is best known for its **Inuit art**, a selection of which is always exhibited, and for the Lord and Lady Gort Collection of Gothic and Renaissance panel paintings.

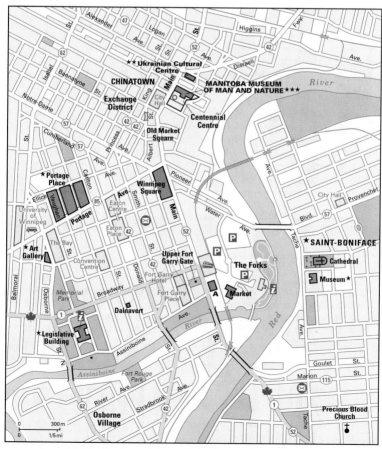

★ **Legislative Building** – *Broadway and Osborne St. North. Open year-round daily 8:30am–8pm. Closed Dec 25.* ✕ ㊤ 🄿 ☎*204-945-5813.* This harmonious Neoclassical building stands in an attractive park, close to the residence of Manitoba's lieutenant-governor. Completed in 1919 the Tyndall stone building forms an "H" with a dome at its centre. Above the dome stands the **Golden Boy**, cast by Charles Gardet, a bronze gold-plated statue clutching a sheaf of wheat in one hand and holding a torch aloft in the other to symbolize Manitoba's glowing future. Above the main entrance *(north side)*, a pediment depicts Canada's motto "From Sea to Sea"; at the centre is Manitoba, the keystone province (symbolized by a woman seated on a throne), joining east and west.

The main entrance hall opens onto a stairway flanked by two **bronze buffalo**, the provincial emblem. The guided tour enables visitors to view the horseshoe-shaped legislative **assembly chamber** and two reception rooms.

The statues around the building and in the park represent important figures in Manitoba history. Across Assiniboine Avenue stands a striking modern **monument** to Louis Riel *(p 99)* by Étienne Gaboury.

Dalnavert – *61 Carlton St. Visit by guided tour (1hr) only, Jun–Aug Tue–Thu & weekends 10am–5:30pm. Sept–Dec Tue–Thu & weekends noon–4:30pm. Jan–Feb weekends only noon–4:30pm. Mar–May Tue–Thu & weekends noon–4:30pm. $3.* 🄿 ☎*204-943-2835.* This large, brick Victorian house was built in 1895 by Sir Hugh John Macdonald, the only son of Sir John A. Macdonald, Canada's first prime minister. At the time of its construction, Dalnavert was equipped with numerous luxuries and state-of-the-art amenities, such as walk-in closets, electric lighting, indoor plumbing and central hot-water heating. Beautifully restored today, it reflects the life of this philanthropic politician (member of Parliament from 1891 to 1893, and premier of Manitoba from 1899 to 1900), who reserved part of his basement as a lodging for the homeless.

★ **Saint-Boniface** – In 1818 Fathers Provencher and Dumoulin arrived from Quebec to establish a Roman Catholic mission on the banks of the Red River. They were followed by other French Canadians who created, with the largely French-speaking Métis, a lively community. Saint-Boniface was incorporated into the City of Winnipeg in 1972, but it retains its distinctive French character. Every February a **Festival du Voyageur** is held, celebrating the early fur traders with ethnic food, dancing and outdoor activities.

★ **Museum** – *494 Ave. Taché. Open Jun–Sept Mon–Thu 9am–8pm, Fri 9am–5pm, Sat 10am–5pm, Sun 10am–8pm. Rest of the year Mon–Fri 9am–5pm. Closed Dec 25–Jan 1. $2.* ㊤ 🄿 ☎*204-237-4500.* This attractive frame structure of white oak was built for the Grey Nuns in 1846, making it the oldest building in Winnipeg. Inside are scenes portraying the work of this religious order and mementos of Saint-Boniface residents, in particular of Louis Riel.

Cathedral – Six churches have stood on this site since 1818. The fifth building was largely destroyed by fire in 1968, except for its white stone facade, which stands immediately in front of the new cathedral. Designed by Étienne Gaboury, the church features an attractive wooden interior. The **cemetery** contains the grave of Louis Riel.

Precious Blood Church – Also the work of Gaboury, the little brick and shingle church is built in the shape of an Indian teepee.

ADDITIONAL SIGHTS *Map p 127*

★ **The Mint** – *Trans-Can Hwy. at Hwy. 59. Open May–Labour Day Mon–Fri 10am–4pm. Closed national holidays. $2.* ㊤ 🄿 ☎*204-257-3359.* This branch of the Royal Canadian Mint is housed in a spectacular half-pyramid structure of rose-coloured reflecting glass. Inside, fountains and exotic plants surround a coin collection and displays on the history of coinage in Canada. The process of minting coins can be viewed.

Riel House – 👁 *330 River Rd., St. Vital. Visit by guided tour (30min) only, mid-May–Labour Day daily 10am–6pm. Contribution requested.* ㊤ 🄿 ☎*204-257-1783.* The tiny wooden house was built in 1881 by the Riel family who occupied it until 1968. Although Louis Riel *(p 99)* never actually lived in the house, his body lay in state there after his execution in November 1885. The residence has been meticulously restored to reflect the period immediately after his death. An interpretive display on the Riel family is presented outside.

Seven Oaks House – *115 Rupertsland Ave. East. Visit by guided tour (20min) only, late May–Labour Day daily 10am–5pm. $1.* 📶 ☎204-339-7429. This nine-room log structure was completed in 1853 by John Inkster, a wealthy merchant. It is believed to be the oldest remaining habitable house in Manitoba. It lies in the parish of West Kildonan, part of the original Selkirk settlement, and near the site of the Seven Oaks Massacre of 1816 *(p 123)*. Inkster's store and post office, both furnished with period pieces, stand beside the house.

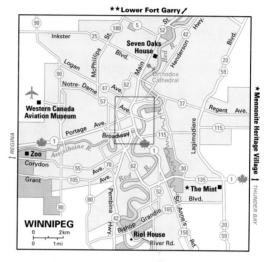

Zoo – *In Assiniboine Park. Open year-round daily 10am. Closing hours vary. $3.* 🍴♿📶 ☎204-986-6921. This large and pleasant zoo offers a **tropical house**, home to a variety of monkeys and birds, who thrive among the exotic plants.

Western Canada Aviation Museum – *At airport, Ellice and Ferry Rds . Open year-round Mon–Sat 10am–4pm, Sun 1–4pm. Closed national holidays. $3.* ♿📶 ☎204-786-5503. Over 20 aircraft are on display, ranging from early bush planes to jets. Others can be seen in the process of restoration.

EXCURSIONS

★★ Lower Fort Garry – 🚗 *32km/20mi north of Winnipeg by Hwys. 52 and 9.* This stone fort was built between 1830 and 1847 by the Hudson's Bay Company to replace district headquarters at Upper Fort Garry *(p 124)*, which was regularly subjected to flooding. An important company post until 1911, the fort received goods from the firm's warehouse at York Factory on Hudson Bay by means of **York boats**. These wooden-hulled boats were much larger and more unwieldy than canoes, but they could be sailed across lakes.

Visit – *Open mid-May–Labour Day daily 10am–6pm. $5.* 🍴♿📶 ☎204-785-6050. The visit begins at the **visitor centre**, where an audio-visual presentation *(20min)* forms a good introduction. Restored to reflect life in its mid-19C heyday, the fort itself is surrounded by stone walls. At its centre stands a large and gracious stone dwelling with high chimneys, built to house the offices and residence of the governor. Nearby, the trading store and warehouse display a wide range of goods; note in particular the **furloft** with its splendid collection of furs. On the grounds a York boat and a Red River cart are on display.

★ Mennonite Heritage Village – *In Steinbach, 61km/38mi southeast of Winnipeg by Trans-Can Hwy. and Hwy. 12.* This village presents the life of the first Mennonites who settled in Manitoba about 1874. Two groups of Mennonites exist in Canada: the Dutch-Germanic of Ontario and the Russian Mennonites of the West. Extreme pacifists who refuse to fight in any war, both are descended from the Protestant sect led by **Menno Simons**. Persecuted in 17C Europe, some fled to the US, some to Russia. Meeting persecution again, some of the Americans moved to Ontario and the Russians to Manitoba. The sect numbers approximately 100,000 in Canada—the majority live in Manitoba and Ontario *(p 000)*.

Visit – *Open daily May & Sept Mon–Sat 10am–5pm, Sun noon–5pm. Jun–Aug Mon–Sat 10am–7pm, Sun noon–7pm. Rest of the year Mon–Fri 10am–4pm.* 🍴♿📶 ☎204-326-9661. Of particular interest is the farmhouse built in characteristic style with the kitchen and stove in the centre (to heat all rooms) and a barn on one end. Other buildings include a church, school and windmill. A museum displays pioneer artifacts and a map of the various Mennonite migrations. The cafeteria serves Mennonite specialities.

Prairie Dog Central – *Steam train to Grosse Isle. Description p 102.*

Saskatchewan
Pop. 15,315
Map of Principal Sights p 3

This city, 187km/116mi northeast of REGINA on the Yellowhead Highway, was first settled by farmers from York County, Ontario. They were soon followed by a variety of other nationalities, especially Ukrainians. Today Yorkton is known as a manufacturing centre for agricultural equipment and for its stockyards.

SIGHT

Western Development Museum – *Hwy. 16 on west side of city. Open May–mid-Sept daily 9am–6pm. $4.50.* & ☎*306-783-8361.* The Yorkton branch of this museum (other branches in North Battleford, MOOSE JAW and SASKATOON) is devoted to the various ethnic groups found in Saskatchewan, in particular in the Yorkton area. There are interesting displays on the local Indians and the Métis, and dioramas of Ukrainian, German, Swedish, English and American pioneer homes. In addition there is a collection of antique steam and gas traction engines and a display on Saskatchewan inventions.

A Sampling of Canada's Collections of Native Culture and Art

Banff	Luxton Museum★ *(p 58)*
Calgary	Glenbow Museum★★ *(p 107)*
Churchill	Eskimo Museum★★ *(p 110)*
Edmonton	Provincial Museum★★ *(p 114)*
Fort Macleod	Head-Smashed-In Buffalo Jump★ *(p 116)*
Hull	Canadian Museum of Civilization★★★ *(p 209)*
'Ksan	Gitksan artifacts collection★★ *(p 70)*
Midland	Huron Indian Village★ *(p 139)*
Montreal	McCord Museum of Canadian History★★ *(p 218)*
Prince Rupert	Museum of Northern British Columbia★★ *(p 69)*
Queen Charlotte	Queen Charlotte Islands Museum★ *(p 53)*
St. John's	Newfoundland Museum★ *(p 293)*
Toronto	Royal Ontario Museum★★★ *(p 186)*
Vancouver	UBC Museum of Anthropology★★★ *(p 76)* Vancouver Museum★★ *(p 77)*
Victoria	Royal British Columbia Museum★★★ *(p 84)*
Winnipeg	Manitoba Museum of Man and Nature★★★ *(p 124)* Art Gallery★ *(p 125)*
Yellowknife	Prince of Wales Northern Heritage Centre★★ *(p 309)*

Ontario

CN Tower, Toronto/CN Tower Limited

anada's richest and most populous province (10,084,885 inhabitants), Ontario is the country's industrial, economic, political and cultural heartland. Stretching from the Great Lakes in the south to Hudson Bay in the north, the province encompasses a wide variety of scenery, the majority of its natural beauty spots being in or near water. Possessing nearly 200,000sq km/ 70,000sq mi of lakes, Ontario takes its name from the Iroquoian word meaning "shining waters."

Geographical Notes

A Land Shaped by Glaciers – When North America's last Ice Age receded about 10,000 years ago, it left the region that is now Ontario scarred and completely reshaped. Great holes gouged out of the earth had gradually filled with water and over much of the land, the geological core of the continent was revealed. The Precambrian rocks of this forested, lake-filled terrain known as the **Canadian Shield** *(p 16)* are still exposed over a large part of the province today. Only in the north and in the extreme south are they covered with sedimentary deposits that allow a landscape other than one of rock, water and rock-clinging trees, so typical of the Shield.

The Great Lakes – These vast expanses of fresh water are one of the most extraordinary legacies of the glaciers. **Lake Superior**, the largest, deepest and coldest of the lakes, was created before the ice ages by a fault in the Shield. The other four (Lakes **Huron**, **Michigan**, **Erie** and **Ontario**) were formed by erosion of the original sediment over millions of years. With each advance and retreat of the glaciers, their basins were reshaped. At one time they drained south to the Gulf of Mexico. Today their waters flow northeast down the St. Lawrence to the Atlantic. All but Lake Michigan border Ontario, giving the province a freshwater shoreline of 3,800km/2,360mi, which greatly affects its climate.

The North – The large region north of an imaginary line from the Ottawa River to GEORGIAN BAY via Lake Nipissing *(map p 132)* is referred to as "Northern Ontario." Sparsely populated except in areas of rich mineral deposits *(p 133)*, the land rarely rises above 460m/1500ft, other than a few higher rocky ridges near Lake Superior. Although a small number of farms exist in the clay belt between Lake Timiskaming and Cochrane, it is an unproductive region agriculturally. However, Northern Ontario does provide a large harvest of wood for the pulp and paper mills, and its many lakes have created a sportsman's paradise.

The South – The smaller region south of the Ottawa River–Georgian Bay dividing line is the most densely populated and industrialized part of Canada, especially the area at the western end of Lake Ontario, known as the **Golden Horseshoe**. Approximately a third of the region lies directly on the Canadian Shield. This section of the Shield cuts the rest of southern Ontario in two.

To the east lies a small agricultural triangle in the forks of the Ottawa and St. Lawrence Rivers. To the west are the fertile farmlands of the **Niagara Peninsula** and the region called Southwestern Ontario. Once, hardwood forests of maple, beech, walnut, elm and ash trees grew here. Today agriculture dominates Canada's most southerly and climatically favourable region.

Climate – The climate varies widely in this province. Northern Ontario experiences long, bright but cold winters, and sunny summers with hot days and cool nights. In the south the winters are less severe because of the moderating influence of the Great Lakes. The summers are also longer than in the north but much more humid, again due to the Great Lakes.

Average daily temperatures

	January		July	
	low	high	low	high
Ottawa	–15°C/5°F	–6°C/21°F	15°C/59°F	26°C/79°F
Toronto	–7°C/18°F	–1°C/30°F	17°C/63°F	27°C/81°F
Thunder Bay	–21°C/-6°F	–8°C/16°F	11°C/52°F	23°C/75°F
Windsor	–9°C/16°F	–1°C/30°F	17°C/63°F	28°C/82°F

Evenly distributed throughout the year in most regions, the amount of precipitation varies over the province (660-1016mm/26-40in) and includes 200-250cm/80-100in of snow in the north. July rainfall is about 100mm/4in in OTTAWA and 76mm/3in in TORONTO and THUNDER BAY. The number of frost-free days varies from 179 on the Point Pelee peninsula in the south to 60 on the shores of Hudson Bay.

Historical Notes

Before the Europeans – Northern Ontario was inhabited by Indians of the sub-Arctic culture whose subsistence lifestyle in a meagre environment was similar to that of the tribes in the Northwest Territories. The south, on the other hand, was the realm of Indians of the Algonquian and Iroquoian language groups commonly known as the **Eastern Woodlands culture** *(map p 22)*. These tribes generally lived a fairly sedentary life in organized villages around which fields of beans, corn and squash were cultivated. No crop rotation was practised; every ten or so years when the land was exhausted, the village was moved to a new site. Travelling by birchbark canoe in summer, and snowshoe and toboggan in winter, the men hunted and fished extensively, never staying away long from their palisaded villages.

Tribes lived in large rectangular huts made of a framework of poles covered with hides. These **longhouses** accommodated several families, each having their own fireplace and sleeping platform (some of the Algonquin tribes built circular, dome-shaped huts instead of longhouses). Minimal in summer, clothing consisted in winter of deerskin leggings, fur robes and moccasins.

Iroquoian society was matrilineal (descent was from the mother) and the women of these tribes wielded considerable power, selecting the male chiefs, for example. In contrast Algonquin society was patrilineal. Rich traditions of distinct religious and mythological beliefs and practices permeated both groups. To frighten away disease or other evils, the Iroquoian **False Face Society** performed dances in elaborate masks of wood and human hair.

Many of these tribes grew militant, owing in particular to their increasing dependency on European trade. Composed of five tribes (Mohawk, Onondaga, Seneca, Cayuga, Oneida), the **League of the Iroquois** warred repeatedly with the early French settlers, and defeated and dispersed the **Huron**, another Iroquoian group. Today little remains of the Eastern Woodlands Indians' former way of life.

Part of New France – The region that is now Ontario was crisscrossed by most of the 17C and 18C French explorers. First to visit was **Étienne Brûlé**, soon followed by **Champlain** himself, **Radisson** and **Groseilliers** in their search for a route to Hudson Bay, Marquette and Jolliet in their search for a river flowing west from Lake Superior, and **Sieur de La Salle** on his famous trip down the Mississippi. Fur trade was the main reason for exploration, and trading posts were set up all over the province. There were also two attempts at permanent settlement. In 1639 the **Jesuits** established a mission on the shores of Georgian Bay to convert the Huron to Christianity. Settlement lasted only until 1650 because of fierce attacks by the Iroquois who captured and martyred five of the Jesuit fathers. Then in the early 18C, farms were laid out on the shores of the Detroit River in Southwest Ontario. At the time of the fall of New France, about 400 people were living there.

At the same time, the **Hudson's Bay Company** was establishing itself in the province's northern section. In 1673 a post was founded at **Moosonee** on James Bay, which claims to be Ontario's oldest settlement. Despite these attempts at settlement, what is now Ontario was still very much the realm of Indians at the time of the American Revolution.

The Arrival of the Loyalists – When the American colonies revolted against British rule in 1775, many people refused to join the rebels. Called Loyalists (or "Tories," to use the American term) primarily because of their loyalty to King George III, they may have numbered as many as 1.25 million—a third of the population. When the American Revolution ended, Loyalists found themselves very unpopular; most were forced to leave their homes and flee for their lives.

An estimated 80,000 Loyalists settled in Canada—in Nova Scotia, New Brunswick, Prince Edward Island, the Eastern Townships of Quebec, the St. Lawrence Valley and the Niagara Peninsula. They also fled to England and the West Indies, but Canada was popular because they were promised free land. Among the Loyalists in Ontario were Indians of the **Six Nations Iroquois Confederacy** (the Tuscarora joined the five-nation Iroquois league in 1722) who, under their great chief **Joseph Brant** *(p 137)*, had fought for the British. The arrival of such a great number of people—one of the largest mass movements of the time—created, almost overnight, the province of Upper Canada (Lower Canada being present-day Quebec). In 1791 a separate administration was established in Niagara-on-the-Lake and later in Toronto. Although many more immigrants have settled in Ontario since that date, the influence of the descendants of these Loyalists is still strong in Ontario today.

Meanwhile, the waters and lakes of the province were alive with the brigades of fur traders of both Hudson's Bay and North West Companies. Indeed, the latter set up its great rendezvous point at Fort William on Lake Superior.

American Invasion – In 1812 the Americans, infuriated by British high-handedness on the open seas, declared war and invaded Canada, hoping to seize it quickly while the British were preoccupied fighting Napoleon in Europe. They were confident that the inhabitants would rush to join their standard. Instead they found the population of Upper Canada united in its dislike of the US, if not in its loyalty to Britain. The ensuing war was fought mainly in Upper Canada. Naval encounters occurred on the Great Lakes, during which Toronto was looted and burned. There was much fighting in the Niagara Peninsula where **Isaac Brock** and **Laura Secord** engraved their names in Canadian history; along the St. Lawrence, particularly at Crysler's Farm *(p 192)*; and in the province of Quebec at Chateauguay. Battles were often indecisive, but the Americans were kept out of Canada, and in Ontario at least, a sense of nationhood was born.

Toward Confederation – As a result of the war, the British government decided to encourage immigration to Upper Canada to bolster the population against further possible American attack. Free land was offered and, since economic distress in Britain was great, approximately 1.5 million people crossed the Atlantic from 1820 to 1840 to seek a better life in Ontario. Farms, villages and towns sprang up where previously there had been only bush. The face of the province was changed immeasurably.

131

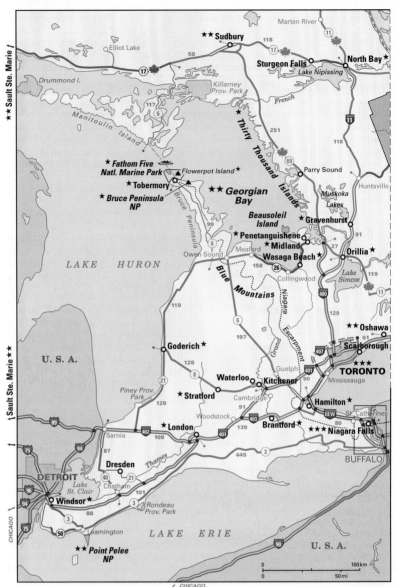

These new settlers brought not only their industry but also their political ideas. Fresh from a struggle to promote electoral reform in England, they found Canada backward. Real political power lay not with the elected assembly but with the governor and a council dominated by several well-connected groups known as the **Family Compact**. Opposition to this system was led by a fiery Scot, **William Lyon Mackenzie**, who eventually resorted to armed revolt in 1837. While the uprising was quickly suppressed by colonial authorities, it did persuade Britain to grant "responsible government"*(p 24)*. In 1841 Upper and Lower Canada were reunited as the Province of Canada in a kind of confederation with equal representation for each. This union led to a movement to unite all British colonies in North America, led by an Ontario politician, **John A. Macdonald** and his Quebec colleague, **George-Étienne Cartier**. When union *(Canadian Confederation p 24)* was achieved in 1867, Upper Canada officially took the name of Ontario.

Since Confederation, Ontario has grown enormously in population, attracting immigrants from all over the world. This large influx, added to the province's abundant natural resources and strategic location in relation to the rest of Canada and the US, led to Ontario's rapid industrial development and its preeminence in modern Canada.

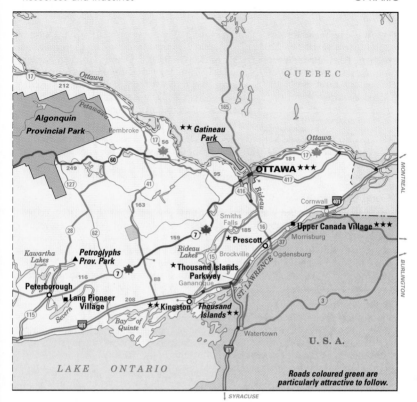

Roads coloured green are particularly attractive to follow.

Resources and Industries

Agriculture – Farming of various types has been practised in Ontario since earliest times, and it is still an important activity today. The southern part of the province boasts some of the richest soil in Canada as well as the province's longest frost-free season. Dairy farming is the predominant activity in the southeast corner, along the shores of Lake Ontario and in the Upper Thames Valley. Other livestock are raised in the Georgian Bay–Upper Grand River region. Soybean and field corn are the staple crops of the southwest, but crops such as sweet corn, tomatoes and other vegetables are also grown.

The section of the Niagara Peninsula on the shores of Lake Ontario sheltered by the Niagara Escarpment is Ontario's most important **fruit-growing** region. Not only are peaches, cherries, strawberries and grapes grown, but a **wine-making** industry thrives.

Mining – No other province is as rich in minerals as Ontario, one of the world's largest suppliers of nickel, and a major producer of gold, silver, platinum, urani-um, zinc, copper and a range of structural materials. The province is an important source of salt, gypsum and nepheline syenite. Ontario produces more nonfuel minerals for commercial use than any other Canadian province.

The vast majority of these minerals come from the Canadian Shield, which covers much of Ontario. The **Sudbury Igneous Complex** *(p 169)* is the largest single source of nickel in the world. Nickel from Sudbury accounts for 66 percent of Canada's total production, over 70 percent of which is exported to the US. Platinum, copper, cobalt, silver, gold, selenium, sulphur compounds and tellurium are also extracted from the ore.

In 1903 the great **silver** deposits of Cobalt were found during the building of a railway, followed by the discovery of **gold** in the Timmins-Kirkland Lake region. Gold was found at Red Lake to the west as well, and iron ore at Wawa, taken to SAULT STE. MARIE for smelting. During World War II, the iron ore deposits of Atikokan were developed, and a huge mining boom ensued in the wake of the war. In the 1950s, the vast **Manitouwadge** field of copper, zinc and silver deposits was exploited, and the uranium of Elliot Lake was tapped for the first time. In the 1960s, the Timmins-Kirkland Lake region was revived by zinc, copper, lead and

PRACTICAL INFORMATION

Getting There

By Air – Flights to Toronto's Pearson International Airport (25km/15mi west of downtown) ☎905-676-3506 are available via major domestic and international carriers. Air Canada ☎416-925-2311 or 800-776-3000 (US) and Canadian Airlines International ☎800-426-7000 (Canada/US) and their affiliates provide connections to regions throughout the province. Taxi to downtown *($30)*. Airport **shuttle**: Airport Express Aeroport ☎905-564-6333 *($11.45)* or Symcha Airbus ☎905-888-1122 *($45, door-to-door; 48hr advance reservation required)*. Major car rental agencies at the airport *(p 315)*.

By Bus and Train – Major **bus** lines are Voyageur Colonial ☎613-238-5900 and Greyhound ☎416-367-8747 (for local numbers consult the telephone directory). **VIA Rail** Canada links many cities within the province. In Canada consult the telephone directory for the nearest office; from the US ☎800-561-3949.

General Information

Accommodations and Visitor Information – The government tourist office produces annually updated regional guides that list accommodations, camping facilities, attractions and travel centres. The *Adventure Guide* and *Winter Guide* furnish recreational information for the province. All publications and a map are available free of charge from: **Ontario Travel**, Queen's Park, Toronto, ON, M7A 2E5 ☎800-668-2746 (Canada/US). For information on campground vacancies, spring blossoms and fall colours, or skiing conditions ☎416-314-0998.

Road Regulations – *(Driver's license and insurance requirements p 314.)* The province has good paved roads. Speed limits, unless otherwise posted, are 100km/h (60mph) on freeways, 90km/h (55mph) on the Trans-Canada routes, and 80km/h (50mph) on most highways. The speed limit in cities and towns is 50km/h (30mph). **Seat belt** use is mandatory. For listings of the **Canadian Automobile Assn. (CAA)**, consult the local telephone directory.

Time Zones – Most of Ontario is on Eastern Standard Time. Daylight Saving Time is observed from the first Sunday in April to the last Sunday in October. In the western third of the province (west of longitude 90) Central Standard Time applies.

Taxes – In addition to the national 7% GST *(rebate information p 318)*, Ontario levies an 8% provincial sales tax, a 10% alcoholic beverages tax and a 5% accommodation tax. Non-residents can request rebates of the provincial tax (a receipt must total $625 or more) from Retail Sales Tax, 2300 Yonge St., Toronto, ON, M4P 1H6 ☎416-487-1361.

Liquor Laws – The legal drinking age is 19. Liquor is sold in government stores.

Provincial Holiday *(National Holidays p 319)*

Civic Holiday .... 1st Monday in August

Recreation – An abundance of lakes and waterways offers the outdoor enthusiast a wide variety of **water sports**. Scenic routes to explore by boat are the Rideau Canal and lakes from Ottawa to Kingston, and the Trent-Severn system from Trenton to Georgian Bay via the Kawartha Lakes and Lake Simcoe. **Canoeing** is one of the most popular outdoor activities ranging from lake and river to white-water canoeing.

Many outfitters offer an array of excursions that include transportation, lodging, equipment and the service of experienced guides. The best-known regions are: **Algonquin Provincial Park** (☎705-633-5572), which has 1,600km/1,000mi of canoe routes and **Quetico Provincial Park** (☎807-597-2735), through which the Boundary Waters Fur Trade Canoe Route passes with 43 portages along 523km/325mi. For additional information contact the Canadian Recreational Canoeing Assn., 1029 Hyde Park Rd., Hyde Park, ON, N0M 1Z0 ☎519-473-2109.

Hiking is a favoured activity during the summer. The famous Bruce Trail follows the Niagara Escarpment for 692km/430mi across the southern part of the province *(map p 132)*. Hikers pass through wilderness on the Coastal Trail along the shores of Lake Superior in **Pukaskwa National Park** (☎807-229-0801).

Ontario is a fisherman's paradise particularly in the north, where many fly-in lodges arrange **fishing** expeditions. Non-residents must obtain a license available from local sporting good stores. For information on seasons, catch and possession limits contact the Ministry of Natural Resources, Information Centre, 900 Bay St., Toronto, ON, M7A 2C1 ☎ 416-314-1177.

In winter cross-country skiing and snowmobiling are prevalent recreational activities. Thunder Bay, Blue Mountain, Burrie and Searchmont are among the province's popular alpine ski centres.

For more information on outdoor activities contact Ontario Travel *(above)*.

Special Excursions– Several **white-water rafting** excursions, led by experienced guides, are available on the Ottawa River *(May–Sept; round-trip 4–6hrs; from $85, including equipment & meals; accommodations extra; reservations required; Wilderness Tours, Box 89, Beachburg, ON, K0J 1C0* ☎*613-646-2291).*

A fascinating all-day train trip, the **Polar Bear Express**, takes the traveller across terrain of giant forests, bushland and muskeg through the Arctic watershed to Moosonee on Hudson Bay. Arriving at midday, visitors have ample time to tour Ontario's oldest English settlement, founded by the Hudson's Bay Co. in 1673 on Moose Factory Island *(departs from Cochrane mid-Jun–Labour Day Sat–Thu 8:30am; returns to Cochrane 9:20pm; connecting bus service to Timmins; reservations required; round-trip $44; ⅹ ⅙; Ontario Northland* ☎*416-314-3750 or 705-472-4500).*

Luxury steamboat cruising, retracing routes of early explorers through inland waters, can be enjoyed aboard **MV Canadian Empress**. Cruises include shore visits to historic sites and to OTTAWA, MONTREAL, QUEBEC CITY and other cities. Trips of 5–7 days available *(depart from Kingston mid-May–mid-Oct; reservations required; ⅙; for rates and schedules, contact St. Lawrence Cruise Lines, Inc., 253 Ontario St., Kingston, ON, K7L 2Z4* ☎*613-549-8091.*

Principal Festivals

Feb	**Winterlude**	*Ottawa*
Mar	**Maple Syrup Festival**	*Elmira*
Apr–Nov	**Shaw Festival** (*p 151*)	*Niagara-on-the-Lake*
May	**Blossom Festival**	*Niagara Falls*
	Canadian Tulip Festival	*Ottawa*
May–Nov	**Stratford Festival** (*p 168*)	*Stratford*
Jun	**Metro International Caravan** (*p 175*)	*Toronto*
Jun–Jul	**International Freedom Festival** (*P 193*)	*Windsor*
Jul	**Great Rendezvous** (*p 170*)	*Thunder Bay*
	Molson Indy	*Toronto*
Jul–Aug	**Rockhound Gemboree**	*Bancroft*
	Glengarry Highland Games	*Maxville*
	Caribana (*p 175*)	*Toronto*
Aug	**Six Nations Native Pageant** (*p 137*)	*Brantford*
	Summerfolk	*Owen Sound*
Aug–Sept	**Canadian National Exhibition** (*p 175*)	*Toronto*
Sept	**Festival of Festivals**	*Toronto*
	Niagara Grape and Wine Festival	*St. Catharines*
Oct	**Oktoberfest** (*p 146*)	*Kitchener-Waterloo*
Nov	**Royal Agricultural Winter Fair**	*Toronto*
Nov–Jan	**Winter Festival of Lights**	*Niagara Falls*

Canada's 7% Goods and Services Tax (GST), effective since January 1991, replaced the federal sales tax. The GST is a personal consumption tax levied, for example, on groceries, vehicles, accommodation, and health, dental, financial and educational services. Non-residents are entitled to a rebate. For information, see p 318.

Unless stated otherwise, all prices quoted in this guide are in Canadian dollars and do not always include GST tax.

iron finds to replace the exploited gold. Most notable was the Kidd Creek copper-zinc-silver discovery. Recent gold discoveries at Detour Lake and Hemlo continue to demonstrate the wealth of the Shield.

Not all of Ontario's minerals are found in the Shield, however. Southwestern Ontario has produced a small amount of oil and gas since 1859. **Salt** is mined extensively at GODERICH and WINDSOR, and gypsum and a range of structural materials are found in sizable quantities. Mining is an essential base of Ontario's economy, reflected by the number of mining interests listed on the Toronto Stock Exchange.

Forestry, Fishing, Furs and Hydro-Electricity – These four resources significantly affect Ontario's economy. The province is still largely covered with forest, despite serious depletion in the last century. Today pulp, paper and sawn lumber are the main products, and Ontario ranks third after British Columbia and Quebec in the value of production. The province leads the rest of Canada in the value of fish taken from inland waters, thanks to the Great Lakes. Fur production, the province's oldest industry, is still carried on both by trapping and fur farms. The development of hydro power has accompanied the province's overall economic growth in this century, especially since Ontario has little oil or gas and no coal. The harnessing of the Niagara River, the St. Lawrence and other waters was essential for industrial development. Today Ontario ranks third after Quebec and British Columbia in hydro-electric output.

Manufacturing – Over half of Canada's total output of finished goods comes from Ontario. The province's largest industry, manufacturing has made Ontario Canada's industrial heart. Motor vehicles and parts rank first in production value, but also important are the production of telecommunications systems, aerospace and defence electronics equipment, electrical machinery, primary and fabricated metals, rubber, chemical goods and food products as well as printing and publishing. Most of these industries are concentrated in the Greater Toronto Area and along the Highway 401 corridor from Windsor to KINGSTON, which, when combined, represent Canada's largest marketing area. Other important industrial regions include Sarnia (petrochemicals), Niagara (auto parts), Sault Ste. Marie (steel and paper) and Ottawa-Carleton (telecommunications, computers).

Great Lakes/St. Lawrence Seaway System – Completed in 1959, this network of lakes, rivers, locks and canals extends 3,790km/2,350mi from the Atlantic Ocean to the western end of the Great Lakes. When combined, the St. Lawrence Seaway and the Great Lakes afford 15,325km/9,500mi of navigable waterways. Of the seaway's 15 locks between the St. Lawrence River and Lake Ontario, Canada operates and maintains 13, all of which are located within Ontario and Quebec; an additional lock at Sault Ste. Marie, closed for the past several years, is expected to reopen in 1997 for recreational traffic (*p 167*).

Cheap water transportation on this system has been of unparalleled importance to the development of Ontario. Iron ore, coal and grain are among the largest commodities shipped. Raw materials are transported to smelters and factories; finished products are moved to markets. Heaviest traffic is among the Upper Lakes; the four American locks at Sault Ste. Marie, though technically not part of the seaway, are some of the busiest in the entire system.

BRANTFORD★

Pop. 81,997
Map p 132
Tourist Office ☎519-751-9900

Named for Six Nations chief Joseph Brant, this manufacturing city is also famous as the family home of Alexander Graham Bell.

Historical Notes

A River Crossing – Brantford stands on what was once part of a grant of land in the valley of the Grand River given to the Six Nations Indians *(p 131)* in 1784 by the British government. Led by Chief Brant, these Indians fought on the British side in the American Revolution, and, like other Loyalists at the end of the war, were forced to flee the US. To show his personal gratitude to his Indian subjects, George III provided money for the construction of a chapel *(below)*. European settlers purchased land from the Indians in 1830, and the present city was founded, retaining the old name of the location—Brant's Ford, because the chief had crossed the river there. The Indian reserve still exists to the south, though much reduced in size. It is the scene every year of the **Six Nations Native Pageant** during which the Iroquois tribes commemorate their history and culture *(Aug)*.

Telephone City – In 1870 **Alexander Graham Bell** (1847-1922) moved with his parents to Ontario from Scotland. Soon afterwards he took a job as a teacher of the deaf in Boston, a profession he shared with his father. While trying to find a means of reproducing sounds visibly for his deaf pupils, he solved the problem by transmitting and receiving speech along an electrified wire. From this solution he developed the telephone, an idea he conceived in Brantford in 1874 while visiting his parents. He tested his invention in Boston the next year. The first "long distance" call was made from Brantford when Bell, in Paris, Ontario *(about 11km/7mi away)*, was able to hear his father's voice. The telephone's invention made Bell a fortune, enabling him to undertake research, in addition to his work for the deaf. Much of this research was carried out at his summer home in Baddeck, Nova Scotia *(p 267)*.

SIGHTS *3hrs*

★ **Bell Homestead** – *94 Tutela Heights Rd. From downtown, take Colborne St. West across Grand River, turn left on Mt. Pleasant St. and left again on Tutela Heights Rd. Open year-round Tue–Sun 9:30am–4:30pm. Closed Jan 1, Dec 25 & Tue after Mon holidays. $2.* ☎519-756-6220. This pleasant house with its covered veranda is furnished much as it would have been in Bell's day, with many original pieces. There is an interesting display on his life, inventions and research.

Next door stands a smaller clapboard structure moved to this spot from the centre of Brantford. Among other things it housed the first telephone business office in Canada. Inside there is an early telephone exchange and displays on the development of the telephone since Bell's day.

Museum of the Woodland Indian – *In Woodland Indian Cultural and Educational Centre, 184 Mohawk St. Open year-round Mon–Fri 8:30am–4pm, weekends 10am–5pm. Closed national holidays. $3.* ⊗ *(weekdays only)* ☎519-759-2650. This museum houses an interesting collection of artifacts depicting the way of life of the Eastern Woodlands Indians of which the Six Nations Indians are a part.

Nearby stands the the oldest Protestant church in Ontario, **Her Majesty's Chapel of the Mohawks** (it is of course "His" if the monarch is male), which was constructed with funds donated by the British Crown *(open Jul–mid-Oct daily 10am–6pm)*.

DRESDEN

Pop. 2,646
Map p 132

The country around this small manufacturing centre was first settled by black slaves who had escaped their masters in the US and fled to freedom in British North America.

One of these slaves was **Josiah Henson**, who arrived in Ontario with his family in 1830. With the aid of donations from Britain, Henson purchased land in the Dresden area, established a refuge for fugitives from slavery and founded a school to teach children skills their parents had never learned. Unable to write, Henson dictated the story of his life *(The Life of Josiah Henson–formerly a slave)*, which was subsequently published. This manuscript so impressed **Harriet Beecher Stowe** that she met him and used him as the model for her influential novel, *Uncle Tom's Cabin*.

SIGHT

★ **Uncle Tom's Cabin Historic Site** – *1.6km/1mile west off Hwy. 21. Open mid-May–mid-Oct Mon–Sat 11am–5pm, Sun 1–5pm. $3.25.* ⚐ ☎*519-683-2978.* This collection of wooden buildings includes Henson's house (Uncle Tom's Cabin), a simple church of the same era as the one in which he preached and a fugitive slave's house. In the museum there are such items as posters advertising slave sales, a ball and chain similar to those slaves were forced to wear to prevent escape, slave whips, handcuffs and clubs. A recorded commentary explains the exhibits and tells Henson's story. His grave is outside.

GEORGIAN BAY★★

Map p 132

Named for George IV of England, this immense bay is almost a lake in itself, cut off from the rest of Lake Huron by the Bruce Peninsula and Manitoulin Island. Most attractive sailing and boating country, it is a popular vacation spot; summer cottages line its shores and islands. More than a resort area, however, the region supports considerable light industry. Owen Sound, Collingwood, Midland, Port McNicoll and Parry Sound are fair-size ports with grain elevators.

Geographical Notes – Immortalized by the Group of Seven painters, the eastern and northern shorelines are wild and rocky with numerous indentations and thousands of islands. Some of these islands are mere slabs of rock with perhaps a few wind-swept pines or other hardy plants maintaining a precarious hold. The western, and part of the southern, shores form a section of the **Niagara Escarpment** with one gently rolling slope and one steep escarpment. This ridge of limestone crosses Ontario from Niagara Falls, mounts the Bruce Peninsula, submerges and then resurfaces to form Manitoulin and other islands, and ends in Wisconsin. A complete contrast to these rocky shores, the coast along the western side of the Midland Peninsula has long sandy stretches, especially in the region of Wasaga Beach. Located in the southeast corner of the bay are 59 islands that form Georgian Bay Islands National Park, established in 1929.

Historical Notes – Étienne Brûlé, one of Champlain's men, visited Georgian Bay in 1610. Fur traders and Jesuits soon followed, arriving via the 1,300km/800mi canoe route from Quebec. Eager to convert Huron Indians to Christianity, the Jesuits built a mission post called Sainte-Marie near the present site of Midland in 1639. At this time, the Huron were suffering frequent attacks from the Iroquois tribes to the south and, weakened as they were from the "white man's diseases," they were unable to resist the onslaught. Caught in the middle, several Jesuit fathers were killed after suffering incredible torture. The atrocities led to the abandonment of Sainte-Marie in 1649. After the Jesuits' return to Quebec, and the Huron's defeat, peace was restored until the early 19C when warfare erupted between the British and Americans over control of the Great Lakes. With peace, the present borders were established, and the region has seen no fighting since.

HISTORICAL SIGHTS

★ **Midland** – Pop. 13,865. This busy city on the bay is well known for its numerous historical and natural attractions.

★★ **Sainte-Marie among the Hurons** – *5km/3mi east on Hwy. 12. Open mid-May–mid-Oct daily 10am–5pm. $7.25.* ✕ ⚐ ☎*705-526-7838.* Consisting of 22 structures enclosed within a wooden palisade, the mission established by the Jesuits in 1639 and destroyed by them before their retreat in 1649, has been reconstructed.

An audio-visual presentation (*17min*) explains the mission's history and should be viewed before the rest of the visit. The chapel, forge, sawpit, carpentry shop, residences and native area are "peopled" by historical interpreters in 17C costume. The mission is divided into separate sections for the Jesuits, the lay workers (called *donnes*) and the Huron. A rectangular, bark-covered longhouse and a hospital where the Jesuits tended the sick have been constructed in the native section. In the **museum★★** slide shows illustrate Sainte-Marie in the context of its times. Topics such as 17C Europe, New France, the Jesuits and the Huron are explained in excellent displays.

Beside Sainte-Marie is the **Wye Marsh Wildlife Centre** (*open mid-May–Labour Day daily 10am–6pm, rest of the year daily 10am–4pm; $6;* ⚐ ☎*705-526-7809*) where nature trails, a boardwalk and an observation tower allow visitors to appreciate the life of a marsh. There are also slide and film shows, and a display hall.

★ **Martyrs' Shrine** – *5km/3mi east of Midland on Hwy. 12 near Wildlife Centre. Open mid-May–mid-Oct daily 8:30am–9pm. $2.* ✗ ♿ ☎ *705-526-3788.* This twin-spired stone church was built in 1926 as a memorial to the eight Jesuit martyrs of New France, who were declared saints in 1930. They were killed by the Iroquois between 1642 and 1649, the first five while they were missionaries at Sainte-Marie. On the front portico stand **statues** of Jean de Brébeuf and Gabriel Lalemant, the two Jesuits who were severely tortured before death. The church has a striking **interior** with wood panelling and a roof of sandalwood from British Columbia.

★ **Huron Indian Village** – *In Little Lake Park on King St. Open early Jan–Apr Mon–Sat 9am–5pm, Sun noon–5pm. May–Labour Day Mon–Sat 9am–5:30pm, Sun 10am–5:30pm. Rest of the year Mon–Sat 9am–5pm, Sun 10am–5pm. Closed Jan 1. $5.* ♿ ☎ *705-526-2844.* This village is a replica of a 16C Huron community. After viewing an introductory **film** *(15min),* visitors pass through the wooden palisade to examine examples of the long, rectangular, bark-covered frame houses in which the Huron lived communally. Animal skins, plants and herbs are hanging to dry. The medicine man's house, a sweat bath, storage pits and a canoe-making site can also be visited.

Beside the village, in the park is the **Huronia Museum** *(same hours as village),* which has an art gallery, a collection of Indian artifacts and pioneer displays.

★ **Penetanguishene** – *Pop. 6,643. 12km/8mi west of Midland by Rtes. 12 and 93.* The southern entrance to this town, which has a large French-speaking community, is guarded by two angels symbolizing the harmony between the English and French cultures.

★ **Discovery Harbour** – *93 Jury Dr. Open mid-May–mid-Oct daily 10am–5pm. $6.50.* ✗ ☎ *705-549-8064.* On a pleasant site above Penetang harbour stands this reconstruction of a British Naval dockyard and military garrison established here after the War of 1812.

An audio-visual presentation *(15min)* in the visitor centre presents the site's history. In the naval establishment, which existed from 1817 to 1834, costumed interpreters evoke the life of the commanding officer and his staff who worked in the naval storehouse and dockyard. At the wharf there are replicas of three 19C schooners. The military garrison was located here from 1828 to 1856. The original officers' quarters can be visited.

★ **Wasaga Beach** – *Pop. 6,224. Map p 132.* This popular resort is well known for its 14km/9mi stretch of white sand.

★ **Nancy Island Historic Site** – *In Wasaga Beach Provincial Park, Mosley St. off Hwy. 92. Open daily mid-May–mid-Jun weekends 10am–6pm. Late Jun–Labour Day daily 10am–6pm.* ♿ ☎ *705-429-2516.* The museum stands on a small island near the mouth of the Nottawasaga River. The island was created by silt collecting around the hull of a sunken schooner, the **Nancy.** During the War of 1812, the vessel was requisitioned by British forces to act as a supply ship for their military bases. After the American victory at the naval battle of Lake Erie, this British ship—the only one left on the Upper Lakes—was tracked down and sunk by the Americans while hiding in this spot on the Nottawasaga.

In 1927 her hull was recovered from the silt and is now displayed in the museum building with explanations of its history, and that of the War of 1812.

NATURAL SIGHTS

★ **Thirty Thousand Islands** – An excellent means of appreciating the natural beauty of Georgian Bay and its many islands is one of three boat cruises: from **Midland** town dock *(departs May–Oct daily 10:45am, 1:45, 4:30 & 7:15pm; round-trip 2hrs 30min; commentary; reservations required; $14;* ✗ ♿ *PMCL Boat Cruises* ☎*705-526-0161);* from Penetanguishene town dock *(departs late Jun–early Sept daily 2pm–7pm, less frequently in spring and fall; round-trip 3hrs; commentary; reservations required; $14;* ✗ *Argee Boat Cruises* ☎*705-549-7795);* and from **Parry Sound** town dock *(departs Jun–mid-Oct daily 2pm; additional departure Jul & Aug 10am; round-trip 3hrs; commentary; reservations required; $15.* ✗ ♿ *30,000 Island Cruise Lines* ☎*705-746-2311 or 800-506-2628, Canada/US).*

★ **Tobermory** – This tiny village is located at the tip of the Bruce Peninsula where the Niagara Escarpment becomes submerged and the waters of Georgian Bay meet those of Lake Huron. Tobermory provides hundreds of protected moorings around its double harbour known as Big Tub and Little Tub. The clear waters, underwater rock formations and number of old shipwrecks also attract divers.

The **MS Chi-Cheemaun** provides regular ferry service to Manitoulin Island *(departs mid-Jun–Labour Day daily 7, 11:20am, 3:40 & 8pm; mid-May–early Jun & early Sept–mid-Oct daily 8:50am & 1:30pm, additional departure Fri 7:55pm; one-way 1hr 30min; commentary; $23/car plus $10.50/adult; ✗ & Ontario Northland Marine Services ☎800-265-3163, Canada/US).*

★ **Bruce Peninsula National Park** – ☀ *Open daily year-round. Visitor centre on Little Tub harbour open Jul–Aug daily 9am–9pm.* △ & ☎519-596-2233. Established in 1987 this national park is known for its trails along the spectacular Niagara Escarpment. There is a 242-site campground at Cyprus Lake, 15km/9mi south of Tobermory *(for reservations ☎519-596-2263).*

★ **Fathom Five National Marine Park** – ☀ *Visitor centre on Little Tub harbour open Jul–Aug daily 9am–9pm.* ☎519-596-2233. This "underwater" preserve, Canada's first national marine park, encompasses 19 islands and the treacherous waters off Tobermory. The remains of 19 known wrecks of sail and steam vessels from mid-19C to 20C can be viewed close up with scuba-diving or snorkeling equipment, or from above by **glass-bottomed boat** *(departs May–mid-Oct daily; round-trip 1hr 45min; drop-off at Flowerpot Island possible; commentary; $12; ✗ & Blue Heron ☎519-596-2250; ✗ & Seaview III ☎519-596-2950; or & True North II ☎519-596-2600).*

Tiny **Flowerpot Island★**, the best known of the park islands, was at one time completely covered by the waters of Lake Huron. Caves high up on the cliffs and two rock pillars, known as the **flowerpots**, are evidence of the ancient water levels. These grey pillars have a dolomite base that has been eroded. They stand 7m/23ft and 11m/35ft high and can be closely approached by boat or on foot from the island. The tour boats circle the island, affording good views of the flowerpots.

Beausoleil Island – *Part of the Georgian Bay Islands National Park. Access by private boat or water taxi only from Honey Harbour (about 40km/25mi northeast of Midland via Rte. 12, Hwy. 69 and Rte. 5). $8/day use fee.* △ &. *Information & maps available at park office in Honey Harbour* ☎705-756-2415. There are walking trails, a picnic area and a visitor centre *(open late Jun–Labour Day daily 1–5pm)* on this island.

The Blue Mountains – *56km/35mi from Wasaga Beach to Meaford by Rte. 26.* This drive is pretty, with the waters of Georgian Bay on one side of the road and the Blue Mountains, the highest part of the Niagara Escarpment, on the other.

GODERICH★

Pop. 7,452
Map p 132

Built on a bluff above the point where the Maitland River joins **Lake Huron**, this town was founded in 1828 as the terminus of the Huron Road, a right-of-way built in the early 19C to encourage settlement. The town has wide, tree-lined streets that radiate like the spokes of a wheel from central, octagonal **Court House Square**. Goderich has a sizeable harbour and several industries, including rock-salt mining.

SIGHTS

Huron County Museum – *110 North St. Open May–Aug Mon–Sat 10am–4:30pm, Sun 1–4:30pm. Rest of the year closed Sat. Closed Easter & Dec 25–27. $3.* & ☎519-524-2686. All aspects of the region's history are depicted in this museum. Outside stands a stump puller used by pioneer farmers in clearing their land.

Huron Historic Gaol – *181 Victoria St. North. Open May–Sept daily 10am–4:30pm. $3.* ☎519-524-2686. This unusual 150-year-old octagonal stone structure housed the county jail *(gaol is British spelling)* until 1972. The governor's house, which was constructed in 1901, can also be visited.

"The Americans are our best friends whether we like it or not."

Robert Thompson, in the House of Commons, 1960s

GRAVENHURST★

Pop. 9,988
Map p 132

This attractive town with its tree-lined streets, elegant houses, and opera house (now a performing arts centre) on the main street lies at the southern end of the **Muskoka Lakes**, Ontario's most popular vacation region. Lake Joseph, Lake Rosseau and Lake Muskoka itself, on which Gravenhurst stands, are picturesque bodies of water with indented shorelines and numerous islands.

Historical Notes – Gravenhurst is the birthplace of Norman Bethune, surgeon, inventor, advocate of socialized medicine and a national hero in China. Born in Gravenhurst in 1890, the son of a Presbyterian minister, Bethune studied in Toronto. He then practised in Detroit, where he contracted tuberculosis. Confined to a sanitorium in Saranac Lake, he learned of a little-known method of treating tuberculosis by collapsing a lung and insisted that this operation be performed on him. The operation was successful. Between 1928 and 1936, he worked as a chest surgeon in MONTREAL but, disillusioned with the lack of interest in socialized medicine in Canada, he departed for Spain to fight on the Republican side in the civil war. There Bethune set up the first mobile blood-transfusion unit to treat soldiers where they fell. In 1938 he went to China and worked alongside the Chinese Communists fighting the Japanese. The surgeon organized a medical service for the Chinese army, but died of blood poisoning late in 1939. Fame in his own country stemmed from Bethune's status as a hero to the Chinese.

SIGHTS

★ **Bethune Memorial House** –*235 John St. Visit by guided tour (1hr) only, Jun–Oct daily 10am–noon & 1–5pm. Rest of the year Mon–Fri 10am–noon & 1–5pm. Closed national holidays in winter. $2.25.* ☎705-687-4261. The doctor's birthplace contains several rooms restored to their 1890s appearance, and an excellent **interpretive display** in three languages (English, French and Chinese) on his life and importance. A visitor centre offers an orientation video *(15min)*.

Steamship cruises from Gravenhurst's wharf aboard the **RMS Segwun** enable visitors to appreciate the beauty of the lakes and see some of the summer homes along their shores *(mid-Jun–mid-Oct daily cruises; round-trip 1hr to 7hrs; commentary; reservations required; $9.90-$47.50;* ※ *Muskoka Lakes Navigation* ☎705-687-6667).

HAMILTON★

Pop. 318,499
Maps pp 132 and 142
Tourist Office ☎905-546-2666

The city of Hamilton, "Canada's Pittsburgh," lies at the extreme western end of Lake Ontario. This city has a fine land-locked harbour bounded on the lake side by a sand bar. A canal has been cut through the bar to enable ships of the seaway to reach port with their loads of iron ore for Hamilton's huge steel mills. The sand bar is crossed by Burlington Skyway, part of the **Queen Elizabeth Way (QEW)**, which connects Toronto with Niagara Falls. Hamilton is set on the Niagara Escarpment, which swings around the end of Lake Ontario at this point, rising steeply to 76m/250ft in the city. Known locally as the "mountain," it provides pleasant parks and views.

SIGHTS

★ **City Centre** – Hamilton has a modern downtown area *(along Main St. between Bay and James Sts.)* with many attractive buildings, in particular City Hall; the Education Centre; the Art Gallery; and Hamilton Place, a cultural centre with two theatres. A few blocks west is **Hess Village★** *(junction Hess and George Sts.)*, a collection of attractive older homes now containing fashionable boutiques, restaurants and cafes.

Also in the vicinity is the **farmers' market** *(York Blvd.; open year-round Tue & Thu 7am–6pm, Fri 9am–6pm, Sat 6am–6pm;* ☎416-546-2096), one of Ontario's largest indoor markets selling the produce of the Niagara Peninsula, Canada's chief fruit-growing region.

★ **Art Gallery** – *Open year-round Wed–Sat 10am–5pm (Thu 9pm), Sun 1–5pm. Closed national holidays. Contribution requested.* ☎905-527-6610. This distinctive concrete structure stands across a plaza from City Hall. Its attractive interior is open and airy with wooden ceilings. Changing exhibits from its extensive permanent collection are displayed, as well as visiting shows.

Whitehern [A] – *Visit by guided tour (1hr) only, mid-Jun–Labour Day daily 11am–4pm. Rest of the year Tue–Sun 1–4pm. Closed Jan 1 & Dec 25. $2.50.* ☎905-546-2018. In small but pleasant gardens surrounded by Hamilton's city centre, this Georgian house was the residence of three generations of the McQuesten family until 1968. It reflects the life of a prosperous Ontario family between the years 1840 and 1960. The McQuestens, who arrived in Hamilton in the early 19C, were pioneers in the heavy industry that is now Hamilton's lifeblood. Involved in public life, they inspired such projects as the Royal Botanical Gardens and the Niagara Parkway. The house contains the original furnishings.

★ **Dundurn Castle** – *Visit by guided tour (1hr) only, Jun–Labour Day 10am–4pm. Rest of the year Tue–Sun noon–4pm. Closed Jan 1 & Dec 25. $5.* ☎905-546-2872. This grand stone house with its Neoclassical portico entry stands on a hill overlooking Hamilton Bay. A showplace of 19C privilege, it illustrates the wealth and power of the Family Compact *(p 173)*.

The residence was completed in 1835 by Sir Allan Napier MacNab—soldier, lawyer, politician and member of the Family Compact. In 1838 he was knighted by Queen Victoria for fighting against Mackenzie. From 1854 to 1856 MacNab served as prime minister of the Province of Canada.

The interior is elaborately furnished, though the contents are not original. Of particular interest is the basement, the domain of the army of servants needed to run a house of this magnitude in the mid-19C. (MacNab actually died in debt,

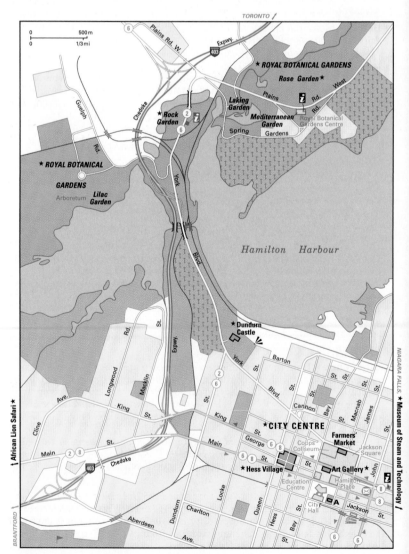

however.) The house is situated in Dundurn Park, which commands a good **view** of the bay and the city. A small military museum is situated in the grounds.

★ **Royal Botanical Gardens** – *Open year-round daily 9:30am–6pm. Closed Jan 1 & Dec 25. $6.* ✗ ☎905-527-1158. These gardens occupy 1,000ha/2,700 acres of land at the western tip of Lake Ontario. Much of this area is natural parkland with walking trails. Several featured gardens are worth visiting *(car required).*

At the Royal Botanical Gardens Centre, the **Mediterranean garden** can be visited. This conservatory houses vegetation from the five regions of the world that have this climate (the Mediterranean Rim, Southern Africa, Australia, California and Chile). Across the road the **rose garden**★ features magnificent displays *(Jun–Oct).* Nearby, the **Laking garden** abounds in irises and peonies *(May–Jun),* and herbaceous perennials *(May–Oct).* Farther afield, the **rock garden**★ is a whirl of colour in summer, with its flowering plants and shrubs set amid water and rocks. In the arboretum *(return along York Blvd. and turn right),* the **lilac garden** is especially lovely *(late May–early Jun).*

★ **Museum of Steam and Technology** – *900 Woodward Ave., just south of Queen Elizabeth Way (QEW). Visit by guided tour (1hr 30min) only, Jun–Labour Day daily 11am–4pm; rest of the year Tue–Sun noon–4pm. Closed Jan 1 & Dec 25. $2.50.* ☎905-546-4797. Hamilton's former water-pumping station, completed in 1859, now provides a rare example of 19C steam technology. Architecturally interesting with its arches and cast-iron Doric columns, the engine house contains two Gartshore steam-powered beam engines of 1859 in full working order. They once pumped as much as 5 million gallons of water a day, until they were replaced in 1910. The old boiler house has displays on the use of steam power and a working model of the beam engines.

EXCURSION

★ **African Lion Safari** – *32km/20mi northwest by Hwy. 8, right on Rte. 52N after Rockton and left on Safari Rd. Open Apr–Jun Mon–Fri 9am–4pm, weekends 9am–5pm. Jul–Aug daily 9am–5:30pm. Sept–Oct Mon–Fri 9am–4pm, weekends 9am–5pm. $14.50.* ✗ ☎519-623-2620. Visitors drive their own cars *(safari tram available at additional cost)* through various enclosures of African and North American free-roaming animals. One enclosure called the monkey jungle contains about 70 African baboons that will climb over your car and steal any removeable part they can.

KINGSTON AND **THE THOUSAND ISLANDS**★★

Map p 133

The city of Kingston lies on the north shore of Lake Ontario, at the point where the St. Lawrence River leaves the lake in a channel full of islands.

★★ **KINGSTON** Tourist Office ☎613-548-4415

This one-time capital (pop. 56,597) of the Province of Canada owes its political and economic development to its location at the junction of Lake Ontario and the St. Lawrence River. One of the main shipbuilding centres on the Great Lakes in the 19C, the former colonial stronghold is home to several military colleges.

Historical Notes – On the site of the present city in 1673, a French fur-trading post, called Cataraqui and Fort Frontenac at various times in its history, was established. Abandoned when New France fell, the area was later resettled by Loyalists, who called their community Kingston. The settlement soon became an important British naval base and dockyard, and a fort was built to protect it during the War of 1812. After the war Kingston's importance increased with the building of the Rideau Canal and of a stone fortress, Fort Henry. Having served as capital of the Province of Canada from 1841 to 1843, Kingston lost that honour, but remained a vital military centre.

Today the **Royal Military College** (Fort Frederick), the Canadian Army Staff College and the National Defence College are evidence of the military's continuing presence. Kingston is a pleasant city, with tree-lined streets, parks, and public buildings constructed of local limestone. Among these is the handsome **City Hall**★ in Confederation Park on the harbour, built as a potential home for parliament; the **Court House**★ with a small dome similar to that of City Hall; the **Cathedral of St. George**, which is reminiscent of Christopher Wren's London churches; the **Grant Hall** building of Queen's University; and some of the buildings of the Royal Military College.

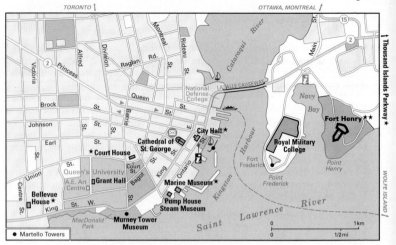

Sights *1/2 day.*

★ **Marine Museum of the Great Lakes** – *Open Apr–Dec daily 10am–5pm. Rest of the year Mon–Fri 10am–4pm. Closed Jan 1 & Dec 25. $3.75.* ᵴ ☎613-542-2261. Set in old shipbuilding works beside Lake Ontario, this museum has displays on sail and steam vessels that have plied the Great Lakes. An interesting shipbuilders' gallery explains various construction methods, and a special section is devoted to Kingston's shipbuilding days. There are audio-visual presentations and changing exhibits on various aspects of marine life.

Pump House Steam Museum – *Open Jun–Labour Day daily 10am–5pm. $3.75.* ᵴ ☎613-546-4696. Kingston's 1849 pumping station has been restored to pay tribute to Canada's steam age. Among the many machines and scale models are two enormous steam pumps once used in the pump house, restored as they were in 1897.

Murney Tower Museum – *Open mid-May–Labour Day daily 10am–5pm. $2.* ☎613-544-9925. This squat stone tower in a pleasant park beside the lake is one of Kingston's Martello towers, a National Historic Site. It is in good repair with fine stonework and vaulting. Inside, living quarters of the garrison have been re-created, and the gun platform with its 15kg/32lb cannon on a circular traverse can be seen.

★ **Bellevue House** – ☞ *Open Apr–May daily 10am–5pm. Jun–Labour Day daily 9am–6pm. Early Sept–Oct daily 10am–5pm. Closed Good Friday & Easter Monday. $2.50.* ᵴ ☎613-545-8666. Variously named the "Pekoe pagoda" and "Tea Caddy Castle," this somewhat exotic Italian-styled villa contrasts sharply with Kingston's more traditional stone buildings. When completed (c.1840), it caused quite a sensation and, for a short time (1848 to 1849), served as the residence of Canada's first prime minister.

A Scot by birth, **Sir John A. Macdonald** (1815-91) spent much of his youth in Kingston, and opened his first law office in the city in 1835. He went on to enter provincial politics, becoming one of the chief architects of Canadian Confederation in 1867. During his terms in office (1867-73, 1878-91), the building of the Canadian Pacific Railway was the realization of one of his dreams. The house is furnished to reflect Macdonald's time of residence. In the visitor centre there are exhibits and an introductory film *(8min)*.

★★ **Fort Henry** – *Open May–mid-Oct daily 10am–5pm. Rest of the year by appointment. $9.50.* ✗ ᵴ ☎613-542-7388. Completed in 1837 this large, exceedingly strong stone fortress is set on a peninsula above Lake Ontario. Its main defences face inland, expressly to guard the land approach to the naval dockyard at Point Frederick. The water approaches were covered by Martello towers built later. Having never been attacked, the fort eventually fell into decay. Restored in 1938, it is now best known for the **Fort Henry Guard**, a troop of specially trained students who re-create the life of the 19C British soldier, guide visitors around the restored quarters and storerooms, and perform military manoeuvres. In particular, the **commandant's parade** should not be missed *(daily)*.

★★ THE THOUSAND ISLANDS   Tourist Office ☎315-482-2520

As it leaves Lake Ontario, the St. Lawrence River is littered, for an 80km/50mi stretch, with about 1,000 islands (the exact number varies from 995 to 1,010, depending upon how many boulders are counted as islands!). Among the oldest and most popular vacation areas in northeastern North America, the islands with their sparkling waters and pink granite rocks attract Americans and Canadians. All of the islands are of Precambrian rock, the remnants of the **Frontenac Axis,** which links the Canadian Shield with the Adirondacks of New York state. The islands are large and lushly forested, small with a few ragged pine trees, or barren—mere boulders of rock worn smooth by retreating glaciers. The international border passes among them, leaving the greater number on the Canadian side.

Visit *Allow 1/2 day*

★★ **Boat Trip** – *Departs from Crawford Wharf in Kingston May–Oct daily; round-trip 3hrs; commentary; reservations suggested; $17; ✗ & Kingston 1000 Islands Cruises ☎613-549-5544. Also cruises from Gananoque (28km/17mi northeast of Kingston by Rte. 2) depart from customs dock mid-May–mid-Oct daily; round-trip 1hr & 3hrs; commentary; $11 & $16; ✗&; Gananoque Boat Lines ☎613-382-2146. Cruises from Ivy Lea (10km/6mi north of Gananoque by Hwy. 648) depart daily mid-May–mid-Oct; round-trip 1hr 30min; commentary; $12; & Ivy Lea Boat Tours ☎613-659-2293. From Rockport (7km/4mi northeast of Ivy Lea by Hwy. 648) cruises depart May–Oct daily 9am–5pm; round-trip 1hr; commentary; $10.50; ✗ & Rockport Boat Ltd. ☎613-659-3402.* This relaxing cruise through the maze of islands affords views of trees, rock and water interspersed at times with summer homes. These dwellings range from small shacks on rocky islets to the palaces of Millionaire's Row on Wellesley Island. The huge ships of the St. Lawrence Seaway, which follows the American coast, can be seen alongside private cruisers, yachts and canoes. A stop can be made at Heart Island to visit **Boldt Castle,** built by a German immigrant at great cost, but never finished *(in US, non-Americans must have identification to land).*

The Thousand Islands

★ **Thousand Islands Parkway** – *Begins 3km/1.8mi east of Gananoque at Interchange 648 (Hwy. 401); 37km/23mi to Interchange 685 (Hwy. 401), south of Brockville.* This scenic drive follows the shore of the St. Lawrence, offering many good views. The **Skydeck** *(open late Apr–mid-Jun Mon–Fri 8:30am–6pm, weekends 8:30am–7pm; late Jun–Labour Day daily 8:30am–8:30pm; early Sept–Oct Mon–Fri 8:30am–6pm, weekends 8:30am–7pm; $6.50; ✗ & ☎613-659-2335)* on Hill Island provides a fine **view★** of the islands and surrounding area *(take bridge to island, toll $2; do not enter US).*

At Mallorytown Landing the headquarters of the **St. Lawrence Islands National Park** can be visited *(open daily mid-May–Labour Day; for use fee, water taxi & boat rental information contact the park office; △ ᵴ ☎613-923-5261).* Beside the visitor centre, a hut encloses the remains of the wreck of an early 19C gun boat.

KITCHENER–WATERLOO
Pop. 239,463
Map p 132
Tourist Office ☎519-748-0800

Attractive, orderly and clean, these twin industrial cities in southern Ontario reflect their German heritage. The skills and industriousness of their immigrant founders created a diverse economy still evident today.

Historical Notes – At the beginning of the 19C, the first settlers here were Pennsylvania Dutch or **Mennonites**, a Protestant sect persecuted in Europe for its religious ideas and pacifism (members refused to serve in any army). Many emigrated to Pennsylvania in the 17C, but during the American Revolution, their pacifism again got them into trouble. Many moved with the Loyalists to Ontario, where they were granted land in the Kitchener area. Strict Mennonites live a simple, frugal life as farmers. They use no modern machinery, cars or telephones. They can sometimes be seen in the country to the north and west of Kitchener–Waterloo, driving along in horse-drawn buggies that display a fluorescent triangle on the back as a modern-day safety precaution. The men wear black suits and wide hats, the women ankle-length black dresses and small bonnets *(see also p 127).*

Other German-speaking people came to this area in the 19C, and the German influence remains strong. Every fall there is a nine-day **Oktoberfest** featuring German food and drink, oompah-pah bands and dancing. At the **farmers' market** *(entrance Market Sq. at Frederick & Duke Sts.; St. Jacobs Market: year-round Thu & Sat 7am–3pm, also Tue in summer; Kitchener Market: year-round Sat 5am–2pm),* German specialties are for sale. On Queen Street stands the **Centre in the Square**, which comprises a concert hall, studio theatre and art gallery.

SIGHTS

★★ **Seagram Museum** – *57 Erb St. West, Waterloo. Open May–Dec daily 10am–6pm. Rest of the year Tue–Sun 10am–6pm. Closed Jan 1, Dec 25 & 26.* ⅄ ᵴ ☎519-885-1857. This museum is devoted to the activities of the world's largest producer and marketer of distilled wines and spirits. Located on the site of the original Seagram distillery, the museum is housed in an old barrel warehouse with a modern extension. A series of fascinating displays covers the entire distilling process, augmented by short videos on key aspects.

Woodside National Historic Site – ⓥ *528 Wellington St. North, Kitchener. Open May–Dec daily 10am–5pm. Rest of the year by appointment. Closed Remembrance Day, Dec 25–26. $2.50.* ☎519-571-5684. This low-lying brick Victorian house stands in an attractive park. Built in 1853 it was for some years the boyhood home of **William Lyon Mackenzie King**, prime minister of Canada 1921-26, 1926-30, 1935-48. It has been restored to reflect the period of King's residence in the 1890s. In a theatre located in the basement, an audio-visual presentation *(14min)* provides an introduction, and there is an excellent **display** on King's life and association with Woodside. The influence of his grandfather, the rebel leader William Lyon Mackenzie, is of particular note.

Joseph Schneider Haus – *466 Queen St. South, Kitchener. Open mid-Feb–Apr Tue–Sat 10am–5pm, Sun 1–5pm. May–early Sept Mon–Sat 10am–5pm, Sun 1–5pm. Mid-Sept–mid-Dec Tue–Sat 10am–5pm, Sun 1–5pm. $1.75.* ☎519-742-7752. This Georgian frame house was built about 1820 by Kitchener's founder, Joseph Schneider. It is restored and furnished to the period of the mid-1850s. Special events and seasonal activities reflect the family's Mennonite roots.

Doon Heritage Crossroads – *About 3km/2mi from Hwy. 401; Exit 275; turn north. Open May–Aug daily 10am–4:30pm. Sept–Dec Mon–Fri 10am–4:30pm. $5.* ☎519-748-1914. Many authentic buildings have been removed to this site to depict a small rural Waterloo village c.1914. The visitor centre's orientation video *(8min)* incorporates vintage photographs from the sight's archival collection.

Throughout the village costumed interpreters demonstrate daily activities typical of rural life. The 2-storey frame house at the **Peter Martin Farm**, originally constructed c.1820, has been restored to its 1914 appearance and permits an overview of Mennonite family life.

LONDON★

Pop. 303,165
Map p 132
Tourist Office ☎519-661-5000

This major industrial centre serves Ontario's rich agricultural south. London is also the location of the University of Western Ontario.

In 1792 **John Graves Simcoe**, lieutenant-governor of Upper Canada (now Ontario), chose the present site of London as his capital. He considered the existing administrative centre, Niagara-on-the-Lake, too close to the American border. Simcoe named the site for the British capital and called the river on which it stood the Thames. However, approval of the choice of capital from higher authorities was never forthcoming, and York (TORONTO) received the honour instead. Today London is a pleasant city of tree-lined streets and attractive houses.

SIGHTS

★★ **Regional Art and Historical Museum** – *421 Ridout St. North. Open year-round Tue–Sun noon–5pm. Closed Dec 25.* ✕ ♿ ☎519-672-4580. Set in a park overlooking the river Thames, this spectacular museum is remarkable chiefly for its architecture. Designed by Toronto architect Raymond Moriyama, and opened in 1980, the structure of concrete barrel vaults covered by aluminum and baked enamel is unusual. Each vault contains skylights—Moriyama's answer to the problem of providing indirect natural lighting without damaging the art. The result is a series of airy and spacious galleries where changing exhibits are displayed. Selections from the permanent Canadian collection of 18C and 19C works are usually on view. The historical museum features exhibits on the city's past.

★ **Eldon House** – *481 Ridout St. North. Open year-round Tue–Sun noon–5pm. Closed Dec 25. $3.* ☎519-672-4580. Just north of a series of restored Georgian houses stands this large and elegant frame residence, completely surrounded by a veranda. Constructed in 1834 by John Harris, a retired Royal Navy captain, London's oldest house was for many years a centre of social and cultural activities in 19C southern Ontario.

Its furnishings reflect a refined way of life at a time when most pioneer settlers were living in log cabins. Owned by four generations of the Harris family, the house was donated to the City of London. The library and drawing room are particularly noteworthy.

EXCURSIONS

Fanshawe Pioneer Village – *In Fanshawe Park, 15km/9mi northeast. Open May–late Dec daily 10am–4:30 (reduced hours in fall). Closed national holidays. $5.* ✕ ☎519-457-1296. This reconstructed 19C community is part of a large park beside Fanshawe Lake, a reservoir constructed to control flooding by the river Thames.

The village contains several houses and shops, the Lochaber Presbyterian Church with a Gaelic bible, a fire hall, and an Orange Lodge—the social centre of the community. A Protestant fraternity founded in Ireland in 1795 and named for William III (of Orange), the **Orange Order** had considerable influence in the foundation of Ontario. Costumed guides lend life to the village.

Ska-Nah-Doht Iroquoian Village – *In Longwoods Road Conservation Area, 32km/20mi southwest by Hwy. 2. Open May–Labour Day daily 9am–4:30pm. Rest of the year Mon–Fri 9am–4:30pm. Closed national holidays. $6/car.* ♿ ☎519-264-2420. This village is a re-creation of the type inhabited by Iroquois in Ontario 800 to 1,000 years ago. These Indians cultivated the land, trapped animals and fished.

The village is surrounded by a stake palisade with a complicated entrance to make it easy to defend. Inside, daily life is depicted through displays and artifacts such as three longhouses where the families lived, a primitive sauna called a sweat lodge, drying racks for smoking meat, stretching racks for hides, storage pits and a fish trap. In the fields outside the palisade, corn, squash and tobacco crops are grown. The park visitor centre nearby has audio-visual programs and displays.

NIAGARA FALLS★★★

Map p 132
Tourist Office ☎905-356-6061

Roughly halfway along its course from Lake Erie to Lake Ontario, the Niagara River suddenly changes its level by plunging over an immense cliff, creating one of earth's great natural wonders. These famous falls are the most visited in the world, attracting more than 12 million people a year.

In the 19C Niagara was a hucksters' paradise where every conceivable ruse was employed to separate tourists from their money. The Province of Ontario and the State of New York stepped in, buying all the land on both sides of the river adjacent to the falls. Today beautiful parks full of flowers line the riverbank. Hucksterism still exists in the city of Niagara Falls (pop. 75,399), but visitors can enjoy the natural dignity of the falls without being bothered.

Geographical Notes

Two Cataracts – There are, in fact, two sets of falls separated by tiny Goat Island, which stands at their brink. The **American Falls** (so-called because it is on the US side of the river) is 300m/1,000ft wide and more than 50m/160ft high. The Canadian or **Horseshoe Falls** (named for its shape) is nearly 800m/2,600ft wide, about the same height, and contains 90 percent of the water allowed to flow down the river. It is the latter falls that people think of as Niagara.

Diverting the Waters – The river's water volume varies by hour and season. By means of canals, major power developments divert up to 75 percent of the water above the falls to generating stations downstream. Flow of water over the falls is reduced at night when additional electricity is needed to illuminate them. In

Niagara Falls

Malak, Ottawa

winter so much water is diverted that the falls partially freeze—a spectacular sight. Standing on the brink of the falls, watching the mighty rush of water, visitors should consider today's water diversion and try to imagine the cataract's appearance in 1678 when **Louis Hennepin** was the first European to view it. Hennepin heard such a mighty noise on Lake Ontario that he followed the river upstream to discover its source.

Erosion of the Falls – In geological terms the falls are not old. At the end of the last Ice Age, the waters of Lake Erie created an exit channel for themselves to old Lake Iroquois. The edge of the ancient lake was the present-day Niagara Escarpment, over which this new river plunged to the lake. The water's force immediately began to erode the underlying soft shale, causing the harder limestone to break off. A gorge was eventually created.

148

Today the waters of Lake Iroquois have receded to the present level of Lake Ontario, and the Niagara River has cut a gorge some 11km/7mi back from the edge of the escarpment at Queenston to the present position of the falls *(map p 151)*. In another 25,000 years or so, unless mankind intervenes, the gorge will extend back to Lake Erie, and the falls as we know them will practically cease to exist.

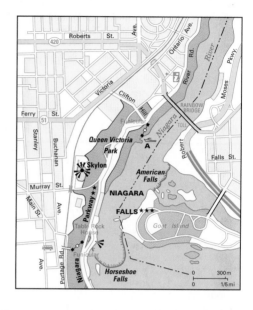

★★★ THE FALLS

The falls can be viewed from the riverbank level, from the water level at the bottom of the cataract and from the summit of various towers constructed especially for viewing purposes.

★★★ The Walk from Rainbow Bridge to Table Rock

About 1.6km/1mi. From Rainbow Bridge visitors can wander along the bank beside the river, passing **Queen Victoria Park** and its beautiful flowers *(especially lovely in April when the daffodils are in bloom)*. The American Falls are in view, and it is possible to stand on the brink of Horseshoe Falls at Table Rock. Watching the water cascade over the edge is an impressive experience. In Table Rock House, elevators descend to enable visitors to walk along **tunnels★** to see this immense curtain of falling water *(open mid-Jun–Labour Day daily 9am–11pm; rest of the year daily 9am–5pm, Sat & holidays 6pm; $5.50; ☎800-263-2558, Canada/US)*.

★★★ The Maid of the Mist [A]

– *Access from River Rd. Elevator & boat ride (weather permitting) mid–May–Jun Mon–Fri 9:45am–4:45pm, weekends 9:45am–5:45pm. Jul–Aug daily 9am–7:45pm. Sept–Oct 24 Mon–Fri 9:45am–4:45pm, weekends 9:45am–5:45pm. $9.55. ⚓& ☎905-358-0311.* This boat trip is exciting, memorable and wet *(visitors are equipped with raincoats and hoods)*. After passing the American Falls, the boat goes to the foot of the horseshoe cataract, the best spot to appreciate the mighty force of the water.

★★★ The View from Above

– Three towers in Niagara Falls provide a spectacular elevated **view★★★** of the cataract. The best view is from the **Skylon** *(Robinson St.; open Jan–Jun daily 9am–11pm; Jul–Aug daily 8am–midnight; Sept–Dec daily 9am–11pm; $6.95 ⚓& ☎905-356-2651)*, which looks like a miniature CN Tower *(p 175)* and is ascended by exterior elevators known as yellow bugs.

EXCURSIONS *Maps p 150 and p 151*

From the Falls to Niagara-on-the-Lake *5hrs with visits. 26km/16mi.*

Niagara Parkway (north)★★ follows the river to its junction with Lake Ontario. Maintained by the Niagara Parks Commission, the parkway has good viewpoints and attractive gardens. From the falls the parkway passes under Rainbow Bridge, through a pleasant residential area and past the Whirlpool Bridge.

★★ Great Gorge Adventure

– *4km/2.5mi. Open May–early Jun daily 9am–5pm (Sat 6pm). Mid-Jun–Labour Day daily 9am–8pm. Early Sept–Oct daily 9am–5pm (Sat 6pm). $4.75. ☎800-263-2558 (Canada/US).* An elevator descends to the bottom of the gorge. It is here that visitors can see some of the world's most hazardous water thundering, broiling and rising into huge **rapids★★**.

★★ The Whirlpool

– *5km/3mi.* A colourful Spanish aero car *(weather permitting, operates Mar–early Jun daily 10am–5pm, Sat 6pm; mid-Jun–Labour Day daily 9am–9pm; early Sept–Oct daily 10am–5pm, Sat 6pm; $5; ⚓ ☎800-263-2558, Canada/US)* crosses the gorge high above the river, with excellent **views★★** of the water as it swirls around the whirlpool and the rocky gorge. By driving another

149

1.5km/1mi, visitors reach the far side of the whirlpool. There is a **view★** from Thompson's Point scenic look.

★ **Niagara Glen** – *7.5km/4.7mi.* There is a view of the river from above. Trails lead to the water's edge *(15min to descend, 30min to ascend).*

★ **Niagara Parks Botanical Gardens [B]** – *9km/5.5mi. Open May–Oct daily 9am–8pm. Rest of the year daily 9am–5pm.* ✆ ☎*800-263-2558 (Canada/US).* Beautiful plantings of flowers, shrubs and trees are maintained by students of the Niagara Parks Commission School of Horticulture, which offers a three-year course. The **rose garden★** is particularly lovely in early June.

The industrial sector of Niagara is reached about 1.6km/1mi from the botanical gardens. Across the river on the US side, the immense **Robert Moses Generating Station** can be seen.

Farther on, still on the Canadian side, the **Sir Adam Beck Generating Station** is visible. These two large stations use water diverted from the river above the falls to generate electricity.

Just after the power stations, be sure to note the large **floral clock**.

★ **Queenston Heights** – ☞ *12km/8mi. Open daily year-round.* These heights are part of the Niagara Escarpment and were once the location of Niagara Falls. Today they have been made into a pleasant park that provides good views of the river *(open mid-May–Labour Day daily 9:30am–5pm;* ☎*905-468-4257).* At the centre of the park stands a monument to **Gen. Sir Isaac Brock**, the Canadian military hero of the War of 1812. The heights were captured by the Americans during the war. Brock was killed while leading the charge to recapture them. The heights were recaptured, and now Brock's statue overlooks them from the top of his monument.

★ **Queenston** – *14km/9mi.* This village at the foot of the escarpment has attractive houses and gardens.

Laura Secord Homestead – *Partition St. Visit by guided tour (20min) only, mid-May–Labour Day daily 10am–6pm. $1.* ☎*905-262-4851.* In 1813 Laura Secord set out from her home in enemy-held Queenston and walked 30km/19mi through the bush to warn the British of a surprise attack planned by the Americans. Forewarned, the British won a great victory at the subsequent Battle of Beaver Dams. Her rather plain house has been beautifully restored by the candy company named after this Canadian heroine. An interpretive display about Secord's life stands outside.

As visitors continue along the parkway, they can look back to see the statue of Brock at the summit of the escarpment. For the remainder of the drive to Niagara-on-the-Lake, there are several parks with picnic tables, and occasional fine views of the river. In summer, stalls selling the produce of the Niagara Peninsula line the route.

★★ **Niagara-on-the-Lake** – Pop. 12,945. Situated at the north end of the Niagara River where it joins Lake Ontario, this town resembles a picturesque English village. Settled by Loyalists, it was the first capital of Upper Canada. Burned to the ground by the Americans in 1813, it was rebuilt soon afterwards, and seems to have remained unchanged. The town is filled with tree-lined streets and gracious

19C houses with beautiful gardens. Pleasant shops, restaurants, teahouses, hotels and the **Niagara Apothecary**, an 1866 pharmacy *(open early May–mid-Sept daily noon–6pm; contribution requested; ☎905-468-3845)* line a wide, main thoroughfare, **Queen Street★**, with a clock tower at its centre. Niagara-on-the-Lake is also a cultural centre, home to the **Shaw Festival,** a season of theatre devoted to the works of the Irish playwright, **George Bernard Shaw** (1856-1950).

The main theatre, a brick structure with a beautiful wood interior, stands at the junction of Queen's Parade and Wellington Street. There are two other theatres in the town. *For details regarding performances (Apr–Oct Tue–Sun) contact the Box Office, PO Box 774, Niagara-on-the-Lake, ON, L0S 1J0 ☎905-468-2172 or 800-267-4759 (Canada/US).*

★ **Fort George** – ☞ *On River Rd. near the theatre. Open Apr–Oct daily 9:30am–5pm. Rest of the year by appointment. $4. &. ☎905-468-4257.* Built by the British in the 1790s, this fort played a key role in the War of 1812, being alternately captured by the Americans and recaptured by the British. Restored in the 1930s, it has grassy earthworks and a wooden palisade enclosing officers' quarters, a forge, powder magazine, guard house and three blockhouse barracks of 25cm/10in thick timbers housing military displays. Costumed staff demonstrate activities of the period.

★★ Welland Canal

From Niagara Falls, take Queen Elizabeth Way (QEW) to St. Catharines; exit at Glendale Ave. interchange, follow Glendale Ave. and cross the canal by the lift bridge; turn right or left on canal service road (Government Rd.).

From Niagara-on-the-Lake, take Niagara Stone Rd. (Rte. 55) to its end; turn left on the south service road, right on Coon Rd. to Glendale Ave.; turn right and cross the canal as above. The early explorers and fur traders portaged their canoes around the falls and rapids on the Niagara River, but navigation of any larger watercraft between Lakes Ontario and Erie was impossible until canals and locks were built in the 19C. The present canal, which is part of the St. Lawrence Seaway system, is 45km/28mi long, crossing the Niagara Peninsula between St. Catharines and Port Colborne. The canal's eight locks raise ships a total of 99m/326ft—the difference in the level between the two lakes.

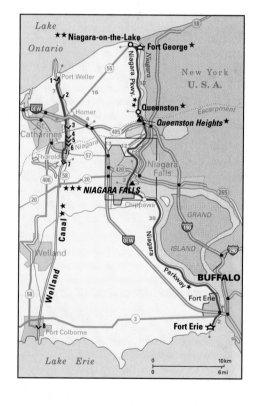

★★ **Drive Alongside Canal** – *About 14km/9mi from Lake Ontario to Thorold on Government Rd.* There are fine views of the huge ships on the seaway negotiating seven of the eight locks of this section. Just north of the lift bridge at Lock 3, the visitor centre *(open mid-May–Labour Day daily 9am–9pm; rest of the year daily 9am–5pm; closed Jan 1, Dec 25–26; ☎905-685-3711)* includes a convenient **viewing platform★** of the seaway. The times ships pass through the lock are posted and are fairly continuous *(it takes about half an hour for a ship to negotiate a lock).* Locks 4, 5 and 6 in Thorold raise ships over the Niagara Escarpment. They are twin-flight locks having two parallel sets of locks, so that one ship can be elevated as another comes down.

From the Falls to Fort Erie *1hr. 32km/20mi.*

Rushing along at 48km/h (30mph), Niagara River is impressive, revealing its **rapids★★** as it prepares to plunge over the cliff. **Niagara Parkway (south)★** crosses to **Dufferin Island**, where a pleasant park *(open May–Oct daily 9am–9pm; rest of the year daily 9am–5pm)* has hiking trails, streams and a swimming area. The parkway passes the large international control dam and gates that divert water along canals to the generating stations downstream. In complete contrast to its lower stretch, the river slowly becomes a broad, quietly flowing stream. There are some pleasant views of the US shore and Grand Island.

At the city of **Fort Erie** (pop. 26,006), the Peace Bridge crosses the river to the large American city of **Buffalo**. There are good **views★** of the Buffalo skyline.

Fort Erie – *Open May–early Jun daily 9:30am–4pm (Sat 6pm). Mid-Jun–Labour Day daily 9:30am–6pm. Early Sept–Sept 25 daily 9:30am–4pm (Sat 6pm). $4.* ✕ ☎800-263-2558 *(Canada/US).* A reconstruction of the third fort built on this site, the star-shaped stone stronghold is set at the mouth of Lake Erie. The first two forts were destroyed by storm and flood, the third by the Americans in 1814. Visitors enter by a drawbridge and can tour reconstructed officers' quarters, barracks, a guard house and powder magazine. Students in early 19C uniforms perform manoeuvres and serve as guides.

NORTH BAY★

Pop. 55,405
Map p 132
Tourist Office ☎705-472-8480

This resort centre on the shores of **Lake Nipissing** was located on the old canoe route to the West. The La Vase portage connected the waters of Trout Lake and the Ottawa and Mattawa Rivers with Lake Nipissing, the French River and Georgian Bay. Today these waters are used solely for recreational purposes. From the government dock on Main Street, there are **cruises** across Lake Nipissing and down the attractive French River, with several stops *(depart from Government Dock on Memorial Dr. mid-Jun–mid-Sept; round-trip 1hr 30min–5hrs; commentary; $7–19; ✕ ⓐ; for schedules contact the City of North Bay ☎705-474-0400 or 705-494-8167).*

North Bay is also the centre of a rich fur-trapping industry. Four times a year *(Dec, Feb, Mar, Jun)* beaver, marten, muskrat and other furs are auctioned at the Fur Harvesters' Auctions, which rank among the largest in the world *(for information ☎705-495-4688).*

SIGHT

Quints' Museum – *Beside tourist office on Hwy. 11/17. Visit by guided tour (20min) only, mid-May–Jun daily 9am–5pm. Jul–Aug daily 9am–7pm. Sept–mid-Oct daily 9am–5pm. $2.75.* ☎705-472-8480. On May 28, 1934 the **Dionne quintuplets** were born in this house. These five little girls quickly became the world's sweethearts. The museum displays "quint" memorabilia.

EXCURSION *Map p 132*

Sturgeon Falls – *37km/23mi west by Hwy. 17.* Just southwest of this community is the **Sturgeon River House Museum** *(open mid-May–Labour Day daily 10am–5pm; rest of the year Mon–Fri 10am–4pm; closed Jan 1, Remembrance Day, Dec 25–26; ✕ ⓐ ☎705-753-4716),* which tells the story of the fur-trapping industry. Exhibits include a Hudson's Bay Company trading post complete with equipment, pelts that can be touched and a wide range of traps.

ORILLIA★

Pop. 25,925
Map p 132

Set on the narrows between Lakes Simcoe and Couchiching, this small industrial centre and resort town has a reputation out of all proportion to its size. Orilla served as the model for "Mariposa" in *Sunshine Sketches of a Little Town* by famed humourist and author **Stephen Leacock** (1869-1944). Possibly the best known of Canada's literati, this political-science professor at McGill University spent his summers here, finding inspiration for some of his finest works.

SIGHT

★ **Stephen Leacock Museum** – *In Old Brewery Bay off Hwy. 12 Bypass. Open mid-Jun–Labour Day daily 10am–7pm. Rest of the year daily 10am–5pm (phone to confirm Jan–Feb hours). $5.* ✗ ♿ ☎*705-326-9357.* Set amid pleasant grounds overlooking Brewery Bay, this attractive house was designed and built by Leacock in 1928. The nonsensical, uproarious humour of this man, who stated he would rather have written *Alice in Wonderland* than the whole of the *Encyclopaedia Britannica,* pervades the house and the tour guides.

OSHAWA★★

Pop. 129,344
Map p 132
Tourist Office ☎905-728-1683

This industrial city on the north shore of Lake Ontario is one of the main centres of Canada's automobile industry. Its name has long been synonymous with industrialist and philanthropist, **Robert S. McLaughlin** (1871-1972).

SIGHTS *3hrs*

★★ **Parkwood Estate** – *270 Simcoe St. North, 2.5km/1.5mi north of Hwy. 401. Mansion: visit by guided tour (1hr) only, Jun–Labour Day Tue–Sun 10:30am–4pm. Rest of the year Tue–Fri & Sun 1:30–4pm. $5.* ✗ *(summer only)* ☎*905-433-4311.* This gracious, imposing residence was built by McLaughlin in 1917. Bequeathed by him to Oshawa General Hospital, the house is open to the public, maintained by the hospital as it was at his death.

Apprenticed in his father's carriage works, McLaughlin converted the manufacturing business into a motor company, and used an American engine in his famous **McLaughlin Buick**. In 1918 he sold the company to the General Motors Corp. of the US, but remained chairman of the Canadian division, whose main plant is in Oshawa.

A visit to Parkwood provides insight into the lifestyle of the immensely wealthy McLaughlin family. Beautifully and tastefully appointed, the house contains priceless antiques from all over the world. Every room has furnishings of the finest woods and fabrics representing the work of skilled craftsmen.

This gem of a house is set in some of the most beautiful **gardens** in the eastern half of Canada. Containing mature trees, manicured lawns and shrubbery, formal gardens, statuary and fountains, they are a delight to wander in. A visit is further enhanced by a stop at the pleasant **teahouse** *(light lunches, afternoon tea, Jun–Aug)* set beside a long pool with fountains.

★ **Canadian Automotive Museum** – *99 Simcoe St. South, about 1.5km/1mi north of Hwy. 401. Open year-round Mon–Fri 9am–5pm, weekends 10am–6pm. (Open Jan 1 noon–6pm). Closed Dec 25. $5.* ♿ ☎*905-576-1222.* The history of the automobile industry in Canada is explained by means of photographs, illustrations, models, and of course, by actual vehicles. Primarily from the 1898-1930 period, about 70 automobiles, in mint condition, are on display. Noteworthy among them are the 1903 Redpath Messenger built in TORONTO—the only remaining example of its type, the 1912 McLaughlin Buick, and the 1923 Rauch and Lang electric car.

Robert McLaughlin Gallery – *Civic Centre next to city hall. Open year-round Tue–Fri 10am–5pm (Thu 9pm), weekends noon–4pm.* ✗ ♿ ☎*905-576-3000.* Originally built in 1969 the expanded gallery designed by Arthur Erickson displays the works of the **Painters Eleven**, a group of artists who united in the 1950s to exhibit abstract art in Toronto. Changing exhibits feature contemporary Canadian art.

Cullen Gardens – *In Whitby, 5km/3mi north of Hwy. 401 by Hwy. 12 and Taunton Rd. Open Jul–Labour Day daily 9am–10pm. Mid-Apr–Jun & early Sept–mid-Nov daily 10am; closing hours vary. $9.95.* ✗ ♿ ☎*905-668-6606.* These attractive gardens combine flower beds, a rose garden, topiary, ponds and a stream with miniature reproductions of historic houses from all over Ontario.

The symbol ✗ *indicates that eating facilities can be found on the premises of the sight.*

OTTAWA★★★

Pop. 313,987
Map p 133
Tourist Office ☎613-237-5158 or 613-239-5000

Defying the stereotypical image of a capital city, this seat of national government lacks the imposing architecture, sweeping vistas and vast monuments of
other world capitals. The city's attraction is its charm, captured in such scenes
as joggers following the Rideau Canal in summer, briefcase-clutching civil servants skating to work on the frozen canal waters in winter, Sunday bicycle
brigades rounding a corner, or rows of colourful tulips adorning the many parks
and green expanses.

The city sits on the south bank of the **Ottawa River** at the point where it meets the
Rideau River from the south and the **Gatineau River** from the north. The capital is
due west of MONTREAL, about 160km/100mi upstream from the confluence of the
Ottawa and St. Lawrence Rivers. The Ottawa River marks the boundary between
the provinces of Ontario and Quebec, but the National Capital Region spans the
river, encompassing a large area in both provinces that includes the cities of
Ottawa and HULL.

Historical Notes

The First Settler – Although the region was known to the Outaouais Indians and
visited by French explorers, there was no settlement in the Ottawa area until 1800.
The first settler was **Philemon Wright**, an American who harnessed the **Chaudière**

Changing of the Guard, Parliament Buildings/Malak, Ottawa

Falls to power gristmills and sawmills on the Hull side of the river. He cut wood and floated the first raft of squared timber to Quebec in 1806, beginning what was to become a vast industry.

The Rideau Canal – The War of 1812 exposed the dangers of the St. Lawrence as a communications and supply route from MONTREAL for the military in Upper Canada. Ships were vulnerable to perilous rapids and gunfire from the US. After the war the **Duke of Wellington** sent men to Canada to look for a safer passage. The route selected followed the Ottawa, Rideau and Cataraqui Rivers and a series of lakes to reach the Royal Navy base at KINGSTON on Lake Ontario. Construction of the canals and locks necessary to make the route navigable was entrusted to **Lt.-Col. John By** of the Royal Engineers in 1826. The lieutenant-colonel established his base at the present site of Ottawa. Soon a thriving settlement developed known as Bytown. By 1832 the canal system was completed, but its cost was so great that By returned to England unemployed and penniless.

Lumbertown – The completion of canal construction did not signal the end of Bytown's boom. By the mid-1830s the community had become the centre of Ottawa Valley's squared-timber industry. Using the power of Chaudière Falls, as Philemon Wright had, residents built sawmills on the Bytown side of the Ottawa River. Splendid stands of red and white pine fell victim to the new industry. Over the century the industry concentrated more on exporting lumber to the US and less on floating timber to Quebec for export to England. Having never been used

militarily, the Rideau Canal blossomed briefly as a means of transporting the lumber south. Bytown became a rowdy centre for lumberjacks and rivermen skilled at negotiating the rapids (so skilled that the British government recruited them to negotiate the hazardous cataracts of the Nile in order to relieve Gen. Charles George Gordon at Khartoum in 1884).

Westminster within the Wilderness – The 1850s saw great rivalry among Montreal, Toronto, Kingston and Quebec, over which should be selected as the capital of the new united Canada. Contention was so intense that the government asked **Queen Victoria** to decide the issue. She chose Bytown, which had hastily changed its name to Ottawa as a more suitable appellation for a capital. The choice did not please everyone: "the nearest lumber village to the north pole" wrote Torontonian **Goldwin Smith**. But the American press discovered Ottawa's advantage—it eluded capture by the most courageous of invaders, because they would become lost in the woods trying to find it! Despite such quips, the parliament buildings were begun in 1859 and completed enough by 1867 to be used by representatives of the new Confederation, of which Ottawa was accepted as the capital—this time without demur.

Ottawa Today – A city of parks, pleasant driveways and bicycle paths, Ottawa is also a city of flowers, especially in May when thousands of tulips bloom—a gift from the Dutch whose queen spent the war years in Ottawa. It is a city that has capitalized on the the cause of its founding—the **Rideau Canal**. Flanked by tree-lined drives, this waterway is a recreational haven: canoeing, boating, jogging, strolling, biking in summer and skating and cross-country skiing in winter, when little "chalets,"set on the ice, offer food and skate rentals. The canal can be followed its entire 200km/125mi length to Lake Ontario through picturesque countryside with lovely lakes. Ottawa boasts other driveways that follow the Ottawa and Rideau Rivers *(p 163)*.

Although still a centre for forestry and for the rich agriculture to the south, Ottawa is chiefly a seat of government. Not here do "temples of finance" rule the skyline as in TORONTO and Montreal. Instead, high rises contain government departments and ministries, the most dominant being government-owned **Place du Portage** across the river in Hull.

Finally, Ottawa is a cultural centre, with a fine selection of museums and music, dance and drama at the **National Arts Centre**. The city is particularly lively in February during the winter festival titled **Winterlude**, in May for the **Canadian Tulip Festival**, and from late June to early July when **Canada Day** is celebrated in style on Parliament Hill.

★★ PARLIAMENT HILL AND AREA *Map p 157*

Parliament Hill, with its three Gothic-styled parliament buildings, dominates the northern side of **Confederation Square**, a triangular-shaped "island" that serves as the centrepiece for several of the capital's historic and cultural institutions. In the middle of the square stands the towering granite archway of the **National War Memorial [1]**, which was dedicated in 1939 by King George VI. Neighbouring the "Hill," as it is familiarly known, is **Château Laurier**, a distinguished hotel recognizable by its turrets and steeply pitched copper roofs. The government conference centre stands opposite and, bordering the southern tip of Confederation Square, is the National Arts Centre.

Historical Notes – The Hill was purchased in 1859 from the British military, which used it for barracks during the building of the canal. Construction began immediately on the parliament buildings. **East Block**, with its whimsical windowed tower that looks like a face, and **West Block**, both designed by Strent and Laver, were completed in 1865. The **Parliamentary Library**, begun in 1859 and designed by Thomas Fuller and Chilion Jones, was not finished until 1877. **Centre Block**, originally designed by Fuller and Jones, was reworked in 1863 by Fuller and Charles Baillairgé, and officially opened in 1866. In 1916 a disastrous fire destroyed the middle building, which was rebuilt in 1920. The **Peace Tower** at its centre was added in 1927 as a monument to Canadians killed since Confederation. Today Centre Block contains the Houses of Parliament—the Commons and the Senate. West and East Blocks contain the offices of senators and members of Parliament. Once, these buildings were sufficient to house not only Parliament, but the entire civil service.

Visiting Parliament Hill – No public parking is permitted on the Hill. Pay lots are available in the downtown area south of Wellington Street; metered parking is also provided there.

Since Parliament Hill's tourist activities are numerous during peak season *(mid-May to Labour Day)*, it is advisable to stop first at the large white tent **(Info-tent)** located between Centre Block and West Block for a schedule of the day's events. Information can also be obtained from the National Capital Commission's **visitor centre** at the corner of Wellington and Metcalfe Streets *(open mid-May–Labour Day daily 8:30am–9pm; rest of the year daily 9am–5pm; closed Jan 1, Dec 25–26; ☎613-239-5000)*.

Parliament Hill is "guarded" by the Mounties—members of the Royal Canadian Mounted Police, attired in their famous ceremonial uniforms of stetsons, red tunics, riding breeches, boots and spurs *(summer only)*. Regiments of Foot Guards wearing bearskin caps, scarlet tunics and blue trousers are also stationed on the Hill in summer. A **Changing of the Guard★★** is performed in summer *(Jul–Aug 10am)*, resembling the ceremony held outside Buckingham Palace and a seasonal **sound and light** show *(45min)* presents Canada's history *(nightly mid-May–early Sept; different hours for English & French productions; in case of rain show may be cancelled; ♿ ☎613-239-5000)*.

Sights 1 day

Approached from Wellington Street, Parliament "Hill" seems to belie its name. Canada's Parliament actually stands on a bluff overlooking the Ottawa River and must be viewed from that angle to appreciate its designation.

★★ **Ottawa River Boat Trip** – *Departs from Ottawa locks mid-May–mid-Oct daily 11am–7:30pm; cruise departs from Hull dock 30min earlier. Round-trip 1hr 30min. Commentary. $12. ✗ & Paul's Boat Lines* ☎613-225-6781. This is an excellent trip, especially at dusk, affording close-up views of Parliament Hill, the Rideau Falls and the houses along Sussex Drive overlooking the river, in particular the prime minister's residence. The sheer size and force of the Ottawa River are impressive.

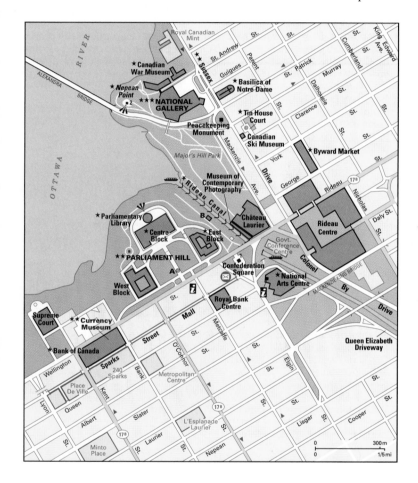

★ **Centre Block** – *Visit by guided tour (45min) only, year-round daily; phone for hours. Closed Jan 1, Jul 1 & Dec 25. ✗(courtyard, May–Sept) &* ☎613-992-4793. Tours enable visitors to enter the House of Commons, the Senate, a committee room and the **Parliamentary Library**★, the only part of the original structure to escape the 1916 fire. The wood-panelled library is modelled on the reading room of the British Museum. Separately, the Peace Tower can be ascended for a fine **view**★ of the sprawling capital *(may be closed for renovation)*. Parliamentary proceedings are open to the public if the House is in session. Each session begins with the **Speaker's Parade** through the Hall of Honour to the Commons.

★ **East Block** – *The interior can be visited by guided tour only. Tours might not be available; phone in advance. &* ☎613-239-5000. The interior of this mid-19C building has been restored to its 1872 appearance. Some of the offices have been authentically furnished to represent their occupants at the time: Prime Minister Sir John A. Macdonald; his Quebec colleague and fellow Father of Confederation, Sir George-Étienne Cartier; the governor general, Lord Dufferin; and the Privy Council.

The Grounds – In front of the parliament buildings is a low-lying fountain called the **Centennial Flame [A]** because of the natural gas always burning at its centre. Symbolizing the first 100 years of Confederation, it was lit at midnight on New Year's Eve, 1966. Around the flame the 12 shields of Canada's provinces and territories are displayed, with the date they entered Confederation.

The walk around Centre Block is pleasant, affording **views**★ of the river and of Hull *(p 209)*, which has rapidly changed from an industrial city to a federal government annex containing large office complexes. A notable collection of statues graces this walk, many of which are the work of well-known Quebec sculptor **Louis-Philippe Hébert** (1850-1917). Most commemorate Canadian prime ministers, with the exception of the Queen Victoria and Queen Elizabeth II statues.

At the back of Centre Block, the attractive exterior of the polygonal library looks like the chapter house of a Gothic cathedral.

★ **Rideau Canal** – ⏺ *Heritage Canal*. From Wellington Street visitors can descend into the small gorge where the Rideau Canal begins. Eight **locks**★ raise boats from the Ottawa River to the top of the cliff. There is also a **boat trip** on the canal *(departs from conference centre mid-May–mid-Oct daily from 10am–8:30pm; round-trip 1hr 15min; commentary; $12;* ♿ *Paul's Boat Lines* ☎613-225-6781)*.

Beside the locks stands the **Old Commissariat Building [B]**, completed by Colonel By in 1827 as a military supply depot and treasury. The historic edifice now houses the **Bytown Museum** *(open early Apr–early May Mon–Fri 10am–4pm; mid-May–mid-Oct Mon–Sat 10am–5pm, Sun 1–5pm; late Oct–Nov Mon–Fri 10am–4pm; Dec–Mar by appointment; $2.50;* ☎613-234-4570)* and a display on the canal builders.

Above the canal, and next to Château Laurier, is the **Museum of Contemporary Photography**, an affiliate of the National Gallery *(p 159)*, which features changing exhibits of works by Canadian photographers *(open May–mid Oct Fri–Tue 11am–5pm, Wed 4–8pm, Thu 11am–8pm; rest of the year Wed–Sun 11am–5pm, Thu til 8pm;* ☎613-990-8257)*. South of Wellington and facing the canal, the handsome **National Arts Centre**★ consists of interrelated concrete structures. Opened in 1969 the complex *(open year-round daily 8am–midnight;* ⚐ ♿ 🅿 ☎613-996-5051)* contains theatres and a charming cafe with an outdoor terrace *(summer only)* located beside the waterway. Across the canal stands the **Rideau Centre**, a hotel, convention and popular shopping complex.

Rideau Canal

Ontario Ministry of Tourism & Recreation

★ **Byward Market** – *Open Jan–Mar Tue–Sat 9:30am–5:30pm, Sun noon–5pm. Apr Tue–Sun 9:30am–5:30pm. May–mid-Oct daily 9:30am–5:30pm. Late Oct–Nov Tue–Sun 9:30am–5:30pm. Dec daily 9:30am–5:30pm. Closed Jan 1, Dec 25–26.* ☎613-244-4410. Stretching over several blocks, this colourful market *(indoors in winter)* has existed since 1846. From spring to fall there are stalls of flowers, fruit and vegetables. Year-round, people are also attracted to the neighbouring shops, cafes and restaurants.

★ **Tin House Court** – In this pleasant square with its stone houses and fountain, a strange object can be seen hanging on the wall of a building. It is the facade of a house built by Honore Foisy, a tinsmith. Foisy spent his time decorating the front of his home with sheet metal, making it look like wood or stone. When his house was destroyed, the facade was moved here to preserve this example of tinsmithing.

Around the corner from the court is the small **Canadian Ski Museum**, which chronicles the sport in North America from the 1800s to the present, with emphasis on Canada's skiers *(457A Sussex Dr., open May–Sept Tue–Sun 11am–4pm; rest of the year Tue–Sun noon–4pm; $1; ☎613-241-5832).*

★ **Basilica of Notre Dame** – *Open year-round Mon–Sat 7am–6pm, Sun 8am–6pm.* ♿ ☐ ☎*613-241-7496.* This church with its twin spires is a Roman Catholic cathedral built between 1841 and the 1880s. Note the gold-leaf statue of the Madonna and Child between the steeples. To the right of the basilica, there is a statue of Joseph-Eugene Guigues, the first bishop of Ottawa, who was responsible for the cathedral's completion.
The very fine **woodwork**★ of the interior was carved in mahogany by Philippe Parizeau. Around the sanctuary there are niches that contain statues of the prophets, patriarchs and apostles carved in wood by Louis-Philippe Hébert, though they have been painted to look like stone.

Peacekeeping Monument – Across the street, and adjacent to the basilica, is a prominent memorial to Canadians who have served as international peacekeepers. Entitled *The Reconciliation,* the monument, which was dedicated in 1992, features two male and one female bronze figures in military dress. They look toward a grove, the symbol of peace, their backs to the detritus of war lying between converging granite walls.

★ **Nepean Point** – Situated high above the river beside Alexandra Bridge, this point offers a splendid **view**★★ of Parliament Hill, Hull and the Gatineau Hills across the river. The statue is of **Samuel de Champlain [2]**, who sailed up the Ottawa River in 1613 and 1615.

Sparks Street Mall – South of Parliament Hill stretches this pleasant pedestrian mall with trees, seating and cafe tables between the shops. Note the **Royal Bank Centre**, and, at the opposite end of the mall, the attractive **Bank of Canada**★ designed by Arthur Erickson and opened in 1980. Set within a 12-storey court, this Neoclassical building is now flanked by two 12-storey towers of solar-tinted glass and oxidized copper. In the court are trees, shrubs, a pool and the Currency Museum *(p 161).*
Outside the east tower in a small park stands a bronze sculpture by Sorel Etrog entitled *Flight* (1966).

Supreme Court – *Visit by guided tour (30min) only, May–Aug Mon–Fri 9am–5pm, weekends 9am–noon & 1–5pm. Rest of the year Mon–Fri 9am–5pm. Reservations required.* ♿ ☎*613-995-5361.* Created in 1875, but not "supreme" until 1949 (when appeals to England's Judicial Committee of the Privy Council were abolished), Canada's Supreme Court occupies a building with green roofs overlooking the Ottawa River. The court itself consists of nine judges, five of whom constitute a quorum. Visitors can listen to the legal arguments if the court is in session, and visit two other court rooms.

★★★ THE MUSEUMS

As befitting a capital city, Ottawa has a number of fine museums, many of which are national museums and hence are large in size and comprehensive in scope. Several are concentrated within walking distance of one another within the city core. Others, such as the Aviation Museum and the Agriculture Museum, are on the outskirts of the city proper.

★★★ **National Gallery of Canada** – *Map p 157. 380 Sussex Dr. Open mid-May–mid-Sept daily 10am–6pm (Thu 8pm). Rest of the year Wed–Sun 10am–5pm (Thu 8pm). Closed Jan 1, Good Friday & Dec 25.* ✗ ♿ ☐ ☎*613-990-1985.* This magnificent glass, granite and concrete building (1988, Moshe Safdie), capped by prismatic glass "turrets" rises on the banks of the Ottawa River across from the Victorian Gothic parliament buildings. Its bold beauty, light and airy exhibit spaces and tranquil interior courtyards provide a unique setting for the remarkable national collections.

Canadian Art – *Second floor.* This collection is displayed in a series of galleries arranged to trace the development of Canadian art. Both the **garden court** with its colourful plantings and the restful **water court** add grace and beauty to the transition from gallery to gallery. In the centre is the reconstructed **chapel** of the Convent of Our Lady of the Sacred Heart (1888) with its decorative fan-vaulted ceiling, cast-iron columns and carved woodwork. Other highlights include the

Croscup Room murals, painted in Nova Scotia in the mid-19C; early Quebec religious art, including Paul Jourdain's gold gilt tabernacle and Plamondon's *Portrait of Sister Saint-Alphonse*; the works of Paul Kane and Cornelius Krieghoff; Lucius O'Brien's *Sunrise on the Saguenay*; a series of paintings by Tom Thomson and the Group of Seven (notably Thomson's *The Jack Pine,* Jackson's *The Red Maple,* Harris' *North Shore, Lake Superior* and the Group of Seven murals from the MacCallum-Jackman cottage on Georgian Bay). Emily Carr and David Milne are represented along with Marc-Aurèle Fortin, Jean-Paul Lemieux, Alfred Pellan *(On the Beach),* Goodridge Roberts, Guido Molinari and Claude Tousignant. Contemporary works by Paul-Émile Borduas, Harold Town, Jack Shadbolt, Michael Snow and Yves Gaucher are also featured.

Galleries devoted to Inuit art *(accessed from second-floor level)* feature contemporary sculpture, prints and drawings.

European and American Art – *Third floor.* In addition to its Canadian art, the National Gallery owns an impressive and comprehensive collection of European art. Among the highlights are Simone Martini's *St. Catherine of Alexandria,* Lucas Cranach the Elder's *Venus,* Bernard van Orley's *Virgin and Child,* Rembrandt's *The Toilet of Esther,* El Greco's *St. Francis and Brother Leo Meditating on Death,* Bernini's fine bust of *Pope Urban VIII* and Benjamin West's *Death of General Wolfe,* the original of this much-reproduced painting. Impressionists are well represented, as are such 20C masters as Fernand Léger *(The Mechanic),* Picasso and Gustav Klimt.

Sculpture on view in the Asian Galleries spans the third century AD to the present. The National Gallery's extensive collection of contemporary art is exhibited on both floors.

★★★ **Canadian Museum of Civilization (Quebec)** – *Description p 209.*

★★★ **National Aviation Museum** – *Map p 164. Rockcliffe Airport. Open May–Labour Day daily 9am–5pm (Thu 9pm). Rest of the year Tue–Sun 10am–5pm (Thu 9pm). Closed Dec 25. $5.* ✗ ⅃ ◨ ☎*613-993-2010.* This enormous triangular-shaped, high-tech building recalls the three-sided pattern of the numerous airfields built across the country during World War II, when Canada was known as the "Aerodrome for Democracy." Opened in 1988 the museum is devoted to the history of aviation from pioneer days to the present, with special emphasis on Canadian contributions.

A selection of old aviation films and videos accompanies the exhibits, presenting an interesting glimpse of the past. There is a replica of the *Silver Dart,* the first aircraft to fly in Canada *(p 267).* There are fighters and bombers used in both world wars: a Spad 7, a Sopwith Snipe, Hawker Hurricane, Supermarine Spitfire and a Lancaster Bomber. The beginnings of modern passenger service can be traced to the Boeing 247, the Lockheed 10A and the Douglas DC-3, examples of

Malak, Ottawa

National Gallery of Canada and Parliament Buildings

which are on view. Early "bush" float planes illustrate the importance of aviation in opening up Canada's vast northland. The **RCAF Hall of Tribute**, a memorial room adjacent to the entrance lobby, honours men and women of the Royal Canadian Air Force.

★★ **Canadian Museum of Nature** – *Map p 162. Open May–Labour Day daily 9:30am–5pm (Thu 8pm). Rest of the year daily 10am–5pm (Thu 8pm). Closed Dec 25. $4. ($2 Thu to 5pm; free 5–8pm).* ⚒ ♿ 🅿 ☎613-566-4700. In 1989 the museum took over the entire building at McLeod and Metcalfe Streets, which it formerly shared with the Canadian Museum of Civilization. The earth's geological history and the origin of life are the predominant topics of this comprehensive museum.

Interesting exhibits on the creation of oceans and continents, particularly North America, and an outstanding display on **dinosaurs**★★ with several complete reconstructions of skeletons, await visitors.

An interesting **Birds in Canada** gallery features life-like dioramas from all regions of the country. Note in particular the Canada geese, complete with sound effects. Also noteworthy are films and **dioramas**★★ of Canadian mammals, such as the muskox of the Northwest Territories, the pronghorn antelope of Saskatchewan, British Columbia's grizzly bear and the moose of New Brunswick.

Other galleries explore animal life in a more general way with displays on such topics as animal geography, animal behaviour and relationships with mankind. Finally, there is a large conservatory called the **Hall of Plant Life**.

★★ **Currency Museum** – *Map p 157. In Bank of Canada complex, 245 Sparks St. Open May–Labour Day Mon–Sat 10:30am–5pm, Sun 1–5pm. Rest of the year Tue–Sat 10:30am–5pm, Sun 1–5pm. Closed national holidays. $2 (free Tue).* ♿ ☎613-782-8914. This museum presents the history of money from early China, Greece, Rome, Byzantium, medieval and Renaissance Europe to its introduction and use in North America. The development of Canadian money is highlighted, with examples of wampum, the card money of New France, Hudson's Bay Company tokens, the first banknotes and decimal currency. The Bank of Canada's emergence is also depicted.

★★ **National Museum of Science and Technology** – *Map p 164. 1867 St. Laurent Blvd. Open May–Labour Day daily 9am–6pm (Fri 9pm). Rest of the year Tue–Sun daily 9am–5pm. Closed Dec 25. $6.* ⚒ ♿ 🅿 ☎613-991-3044. The flashing beacon of the old Cape North (Nova Scotia) lighthouse marks the museum's location. Visitors can tour the lighthouse *(visit by 30min guided tour only, mid-May–Labour Day daily 1pm)* and see outdoor exhibits such as an Atlas rocket and a steam locomotive.

Displays inside concentrate on transportation. The hall of **steam locomotives** is impressive because of the sheer size of the vehicles. Exhibits on early automobiles (1900-30) in Canada and ship models are also featured. Other sections of the museum are devoted to such themes as the development of printing, communications, computers, physics, astronomy and the exploration of space.

★ **Canadian War Museum** – *Map p 157. 330 Sussex Dr. Open May–mid-Oct daily 9:30am–5pm (Thu 8pm). Rest of the year Tue–Sun 9:30am–5pm (Thu 8pm). Closed Dec 25. $3.50 (free Thu 5–8pm).* ♿ 🅿 ☎613-776-8600. Exhibits on three floors trace the history of war in Canada and wars involving Canadians, from the strife between the French and Iroquois in the 17C to the Korean War. A life-size reconstruction of a World War I trench complete with sound effects, a diorama of the Normandy Landings in 1944, and a large armoured Mercedes Benz capable of reaching 170km/105mph and used by Adolf Hitler in the 1930s are featured. In addition, there are changing exhibitions on various military themes.

★ **Laurier House** – ⍟ *Map p 162. 335 Laurier Ave. East. Visit by guided tour (45 min) only, Apr–Sept Tue–Sat 9am–5pm, Sun 2–5pm. Rest of the year Tue–Sat 10am–5pm, Sun 2–5pm.* ☎613-992-8142. This yellow brick house with a veranda pays tribute to three Canadian prime ministers. In 1897 Canada's first French-speaking prime minister, **Sir Wilfrid Laurier**, in office from 1896 to 1911, moved into the house. After his death Lady Laurier willed the house to Canadian prime minister **William Lyon Mackenzie King**, grandson of the rebel William Lyon Mackenzie. King resided here until his death in 1950, bequeathing the house to the nation, along with his estate in the Gatineau Hills *(p 209)*.

The visit includes King's library, bedroom, dining room, two rooms containing Laurier memorabilia and a reconstruction of the study of **Lester Bowles Pearson**, 1957 Nobel Peace Prize winner and prime minister from 1963 to 1968. Pearson did not live in the house, but the photographs and cartoons in his study are fascinating.

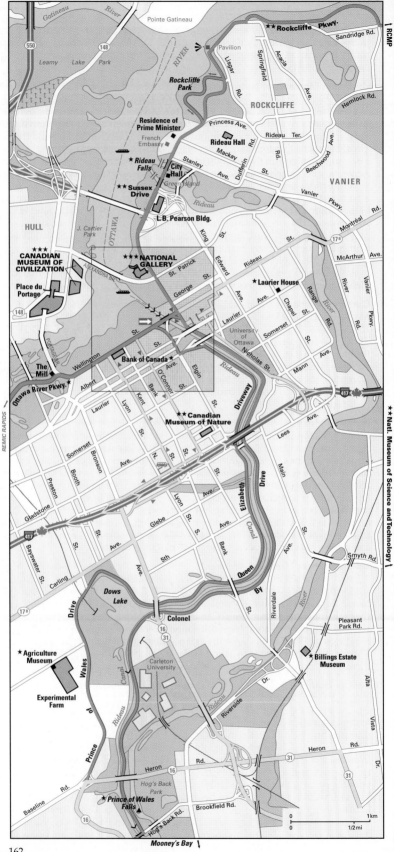

★★ RCMP

Gatineau River

Pointe Gatineau

550

148

Leamy Lake Park

★★ **Rockcliffe Pkwy.**

Sandridge Rd.

■ Pavilion

Lisgar

Springfield

Acacia Ave.

Rockcliffe Park

ROCKCLIFFE

Hemlock Rd.

Residence of Prime Minister ■

Princess Ave.

Rideau Ter.

French Embassy ■

Rideau Hall

Rd.

Dufferin

Mackay

Beechwood Ave.

★ *Rideau Falls*

Stanley Ave.

City Hall ■

Greenisland

Rideau

VANIER

★★ **Sussex Drive**

St.

Vanier

Ave.

Vanier Pkwy.

Montréal Rd.

L. B. Pearson Bldg. ■

King St.

17B

Edward Ave.

McArthur Ave.

HULL

J. Cartier Park

OTTAWA

★★★ **CANADIAN MUSEUM OF CIVILIZATION**

★★★ **NATIONAL GALLERY**

St. Patrick St.

Rideau St.

River

Vanier Pkwy.

Place du Portage

ALEXANDRA BR.

George St.

★ **Laurier House** ■

148

Laurier St.

St.

Somerset St.

Chapel

Range Rd.

★ **The Mill** ■

Wellington St.

Bank of Canada ★

University of Ottawa

Nicholas St.

Mann Ave.

Ottawa River Pkwy. ★

Albert St.

Kent

O'Connor

Bank

St.

Elgin

Ave.

St.

Rideau

Driveway

417

REMIC RAPIDS

Laurier Ave.

Lyon St.

St.

★★ **Canadian Museum of Nature**

St.

Lees Ave.

★★ Natl. Museum of Science and Technology

Somerset St.

Bronson

Ave.

Lyon St.

Ave.

Elizabeth

Drive

Preston

Booth St.

N. St.

Glebe Ave.

Bank St.

Ave.

Main St.

Smyth Rd.

Gladstone

St.

5th Ave.

Queen

By

Riverdale Ave.

River

Bayswater St.

417

17B

Carling Ave.

Dows Lake

Drive

Colonel

16

31

St.

Pleasant Park Rd.

★ **Agriculture Museum**

Wales

Rideau Canal

Carleton University

Riverside Dr.

◆ **Billings Estate Museum**

Alta Vista

Experimental Farm

Prince

of

Rideau

Riverside

Heron Rd.

31

Heron Dr.

Baseline Rd.

Heron Rd.

16

Hog's Back Park

Brookfield Rd.

0   1km
0 1/2mi

★ **Prince of Wales Falls** ▲

16

Hog's Back Rd.

Mooney's Bay ↓

162

★ **Agriculture Museum** – *Map p 162. Building 88, on grounds of Experimental Farm. Open Mar–Nov daily 9am–5pm. Museum closed rest of the year. Animal barns open year-round daily 10am–4pm. Closed Jan 1 & Dec 25. $3.* ✗ 🄿 ☎*613-991-3044.* This museum is housed in a barn dating from the 1920s. The machinery displayed, the techniques, even the smells, are evocative of farming in times past. The **Experimental Farm** is the headquarters of the Department of Agriculture. Its fine collection of dairy cattle *(in the basement)* and draught horses can be seen. There are also ornamental gardens and an arboretum. Visitors can take wagon rides *(Apr–Sept $2)* and sleigh rides *(Jan–mid-Mar $2)* on the premises.

★ **Billings Estate Museum** – *Map p 162. 2100 Cabot St. Open May–Oct Sun–Thu noon–5pm. Closed Thanksgiving weekend. $2.* 🄿 ☎*613-247-4830.* This attractive clapboard house with its dormer windows is one of Ottawa's oldest houses. Built in 1828 by Braddish Billings, the dwelling was inhabited by four generations of his family before becoming the property of the City of Ottawa in 1975. The rooms are full of artifacts, photographs and furniture relating to all four generations.

★★ DRIVES AROUND THE CAPITAL

Ottawa is well known for its lovely drives beside the river, along the canal and in the Gatineau Hills to the north.

★★ **Sussex Drive and Rockcliffe Parkway** – *Allow 1hr 30min. 8km/5mi from Confederation Square. Map p 162.* This drive along the river and through the prestigious residential area of Rockcliffe is a pleasant one. After passing the Basilica of Notre Dame and the Canadian War Museum, motorists will see on the right, immediately after the Macdonald-Cartier Bridge to Hull, a modern structure of darkened glass and concrete—the **Lester B. Pearson Building**, which houses the Department of Foreign Affairs and International Trade. The road then crosses the Rideau River to Green Island past **Ottawa City Hall**, which offers a pleasant **view**★ of the river from the top floor.

★ **Rideau Falls** – *Park beside the French Embassy.* On both sides of Green Island, the Rideau River drops over a sheer cliff into the Ottawa River. The falls are said to resemble a curtain, hence their name meaning "curtain" in French. The intensity of the flow depends on the time of year. The falls are best viewed in the spring, or in winter when they are frozen. To see the second set of falls, visitors can cross the first set by a bridge. There are good views of the Ottawa River and Hull.
Along Sussex Drive, the entrance to the official residence of Canadian prime ministers, **24 Sussex Drive**, is seen on the left. Hidden among the trees, the stone house overlooks the river and is best viewed from the water. Around the corner is the gate to **Rideau Hall**, official residence of the governor general *(p 25)*, guarded by military personnel. There are **walking tours** of the residence and grounds *(visit by 45min guided tour only, May–Sept daily 10am–4pm; rest of the year by appointment; ♿ ☎613-998-7113).*
The road then passes through **Rockcliffe Park** via a one-way route. On the return there are good views of the river. Farther on, however, there are excellent **views**★★ from a covered pavilion of Pointe Gatineau on the Quebec shore, of log booms in the river and of the Gatineau Hills in the distance. The steepled church in Pointe Gatineau is St. François de Sales, built in 1886.
Rockcliffe is an area of large stone houses, tree-lined streets and lovely gardens, occupied by senior civil servants and members of the diplomatic corps. The drive ends at **RCMP Rockcliffe**, where members of the famous **musical ride** and their horses are trained. When the troop is not on tour, the horses can be seen in training *(open Jun–Aug Mon–Fri 8:30am–11am & 1–3:30pm; rest of the year grounds only, same hours; occasional performances; follow signs to visitor parking outside administration building; ♿ 🄿 ☎613-993-3751).*

★ **Rideau Canal Driveways** – *Allow 1hr for both. Each drive is about 8km/5mi from Confederation Square. Map p 162.* These drives are especially picturesque in tulip time *(May).* In all seasons the canal is a centre for sports.
The **Queen Elizabeth Driveway** follows the canal's west bank; the **Colonel By Drive** parallels the east bank. The University of Ottawa is soon passed on the left. Later on, Carleton University will also be seen. At **Dows Lake** where the canal widens out, there are fine tulip displays in May and paddle boats can be rented. At this point the two driveways diverge, the Colonel By continuing along the canal, the Queen Elizabeth entering the Experimental Farm. From Colonel By Drive, there are views of Prince of Wales Falls and the Rideau Canal locks before the drive ends at Hog's Back Road.

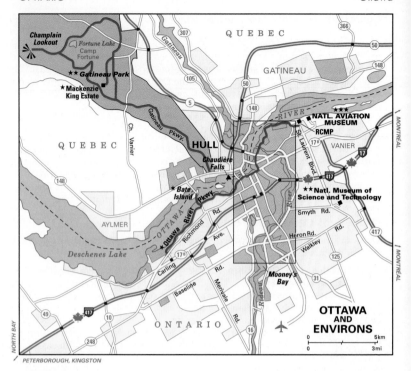

OTTAWA
AND
ENVIRONS

PETERBOROUGH, KINGSTON

★ **Prince of Wales Fall** – *Free parking in Hog's Back Park.* After leaving Mooney's Bay, the Rideau River drops over these falls and rushes through a small gorge. The result of a geological fault that exposed underlying formations and strata, the falls are particularly impressive in the spring thaw. The dam was built by Colonel By in 1829.
Mooney's Bay marks the end of the canal section of the Rideau Canal, after which the river is navigable. The Bay, with its beach and picnic grounds *(access from Riverside Dr.)*, is one of Ottawa's main recreational areas.

★ **Ottawa River Parkway** – *Allow 1hr. 11km/7mi from Confederation Square. Maps above and p 162.* Wellington Street passes the parliament buildings, the Bank of Canada and the Supreme Court, and becomes the parkway just south of Portage Bridge to Hull. Almost immediately, there are signs on the right to the **Mill**. Built in 1842 this old stone structure was once a sawmill and gristmill, standing near a log flume—a means by which timber could be floated downstream without being battered by the Chaudière Falls. The drive beside the Ottawa River is lovely, offering several lookout points for the Remic Rapids. The best view of these rapids is from **Bate Island★** *(take Champlain Bridge to Hull and exit for island).* The parkway continues, affording other good viewpoints.

★★ **Gatineau Park (Quebec)** – *Allow 3hrs. Circular drive of 55km/34mi from Confederation Square. Cross Portage Bridge to Hull, turn left on Rte. 148 for just over 2km/1.2mi, then turn right on the Gatineau Parkway. Map above. Description p 209.*

PETERBOROUGH

Pop. 68,371
Map p 133
Tourist Office ☎705-742-2201

This pleasant city is set on the Otonabee River where it widens into Little Lake, and on the Trent Canal, part of the Trent-Severn Waterway, which links Lake Ontario with Georgian Bay. At this point there are three locks on the canal, including the famous lift lock *(p 165)*. Boating, especially canoeing, is a popular activity in the region, particularly on the Kawartha Lakes to the north and, farther north, along the canoe routes in **Algonquin Park** *(map p 133)*, the impressive wilderness famous for having inspired the painter Tom Thomson. The Peterborough area is also known for its petroglyphic Indian relics.

SIGHTS

★ **Lift Lock** – ⚓ *In operation May–mid Jun daily 9am–4:30p. Late Jun–Labour Day daily 8am–8pm. Early Sept–mid-Oct daily 9am–4:30pm.* This hydraulic lift lock built in 1904 is one of only eight in the world. In two chambers mounted on large rams, recreational vessels are lowered and raised 20m/65ft. Visitors can watch the lock in action from the park beside it.

There are displays and audio-visual presentations on the construction and operation of the lock and the Trent-Severn Waterway in the **visitor centre** *(open Apr–mid-Jun daily 10am–5pm; late Jun–Labour Day daily 9am–6pm; early Sept–mid-Oct daily 10am–5pm; contribution requested;* ☎705-745-8389). Visitors who lack their own marine transportation can experience the lift lock by taking the **boat cruise** *(departs from Holiday Inn downtown; late May–mid-Oct daily 11am & 1:30pm; 2hrs; $15; commentary; reservations suggested; ✕ & Liftlock Cruises* ☎705-742-9912).

★ **Canadian Canoe Museum** – *Romaine St., one block north of junction of Monaghan and Lansdowne Sts. The museum is scheduled to open summer 1996. Phone for hours.* ☎705-748-9153. A former factory houses this fascinating array of over 600 canoes, kayaks and rowing craft of all types and construction. The fledgling museum incorporates the Kanawa International Collection of watercraft, which was formerly on view in Haliburton Highlands. Examples of boats of the various native cultures include West Coast dugouts, Inuit kayaks, a Kutenal canoe from central British Columbia and a Mandan Bull boat used by the Prairie Indians to cross rivers. Several finely crafted canoes made by immigrant artisans are displayed, along with paddles, models and related artifacts.

Ontario Ministry of Tourism & Recreation

Canoeing

EXCURSIONS *Map p 133*

Lang Pioneer Village – *16km/10mi southeast of Peterborough by Rte. 7 and Country Rd. 34. Open Jun–Labour Day Mon–Fri 11am–5pm, Sat 1–5pm, Sun noon–5pm. $6. &.* ☎705-295-6694. Set on 10ha/25 acres in a delightful rural setting, this 19C village contains reconstructed buildings and an original gristmill (1846), still in working order. The log cabin of David Fife *(p 100)*, famed for his hardy strain of wheat, has been moved here from its nearby place of construction. Costumed staff demonstrate daily chores and trades.

Petroglyphs Provincial Park – *55km/34mi northeast of Peterborough via Hwy. 28. Open mid-May–mid-Oct daily 10am–5pm. $6/car. & ☎705-877-2552.* The largest concentration of petroglyphs anywhere in Canada is protected in this park, located near Stony Lake. About 900 carvings of between 500-1,000 years of age can be seen.

POINT PELEE NATIONAL PARK★★

Map p 132

Situated on a pointed peninsula extending into **Lake Erie**, this park is one of the few places where the true deciduous forest of eastern North America still exists. Well known to ornithologists across the continent, the southernmost tip of the Canadian mainland possesses a unique plant and animal life, owing largely to its latitude of 42°N, the same as that of Rome.

The peninsula took its shape 10,000 years ago when wind and lake currents deposited sand on a ridge of glacial till under the waters of Lake Erie. Today the ridge is covered with as much as 60m/200ft of sand. The sand bar continues under the waters of the lake for some distance, creating a hazard for shipping. The sandspit is itself mantled with a lush forest of deciduous trees (there are few evergreens). White sassafras flourishes alongside hop trees, sumac, black walnut, sycamore, shagbark hickory, hackberry and red cedar. Beneath them, many species of plants thrive, including the prickly pear cactus with its yellow flower.

An Ornithologist's Paradise – For most people **birds** are Point Pelee's major attraction. Its location at the convergence of two major flyways, its extension into Lake Erie and its lack of cultivation have combined to foster large bird populations. Spring and fall migrations can be spectacular—as many as 100 species have been sighted in one day. Over 300 species have been recorded in the park, approximately 100 of them remaining to nest. September is the month of the southern migration for the **monarch butterfly**. Visitors can see trees covered with these beautiful insects.

Access – *About 10km/6mi from Leamington. Follow the ☞ signs.*

VISIT *Allow 1/2 day*

☞ *Open early Apr–mid-Apr daily 6am–10pm. Late Apr–mid-May daily 5am–10pm. Late May–Oct daily 6am–10pm. Rest of the year daily 8am–8pm. Hiking, fishing, canoeing, bicycling (bicycle & canoe rental), swimming, ski trails, skating. $3.25/day. ✗ ♿* ☎*519-322-2365. For recorded information on migration, weather conditions, events* ☎*519-322-2371.* Excellent flora and fauna displays await discovery in the **visitor centre★★** together with an interesting account of the peninsula's creation *(7km/4mi south of park entrance; open year-round daily 10am, May 8am; closing hours vary; ✗ ♿).* Films and a wide-screen slide presentation about the park *(20min)* are shown regularly. Be sure to view the day's recording in the visitor log of sighted species and buy a copy of *Checklist of Birds ($0.25)* to keep track of birds you see. From the visitor centre the Woodland Nature Trail *(2.75km/1.7mi)* begins *(trail guide $2).*

Transit to the tip of the peninsula departs from the visitor centre *(every 20min, Apr–Nov).* At the tip visitors can observe birds across the lake beginning their southern migration in the fall. From the peninsula's tip, paths lead in both directions along the park's 19km/11mi fine sandy beaches *(swimming prohibited at the tip; swimming beaches accessible from picnic areas).*

An 1840s house and barn are focal points of the DeLaurier Trail *(1km/.6mi),* along which panels and artifacts provide a brief history of the area's settlement.

Marshland between the sand bars can be toured by a **boardwalk★** *(1km/.6mi)* and two lookout towers provide good **panoramas★** of the marsh, where muskrats, turtles and fish as well as birds can be seen.

PRESCOTT★

Pop. 4,512
Map p 133

This small industrial town on the St. Lawrence is the only deep-water port between MONTREAL and Kingston. Originally settled by Loyalists, the community was the chosen location for a fort to protect ships from American attack during the War of 1812. It was also the site of the **Battle of the Windmill** in 1838 when rebel supporters of Mackenzie *(p 173)* and their American sympathizers were dislodged, only with difficulty, from a windmill on the riverbank.

Today an international bridge spans the river near the town, one of 13 bridges linking Ontario with the US.

SIGHT

★**Fort Wellington** – ☞ *On Hwy. 2, just east of town. Open mid-May–Sept daily 10am–5pm. Rest of the year by appointment. $2.25. ♿* ☎*613-925-2896.* Built by the British, this small earthen fort includes officers' quarters and a 3-storey stone **blockhouse**, restored to reflect its 1840s appearance. The third weekend in July, the fort becomes the annual setting of an historic **military pageant**. Performers are attired in British and American regimental uniforms of the period.

East of the fort *(1.5km/1mi),* between Highway 2 and the river, stands the **windmill** of battle fame. It features displays on the battle and offers a pleasant **view** of the river *(picnic tables).*

Sights described in this guide are rated:
★★★ *Worth the trip*
★★ *Worth a detour*
★ *Interesting*

SAULT STE. MARIE★★

Pop. 81,476
Map of Principal Sights p 4
Tourist Office ☎705-949-7152

Connected to Michigan's city of the same name by road and railway bridges, this Ontario city is an industrial centre with huge steelworks and a pulp mill. The "Soo," as it is commonly called, lies on the north side of **St. Mary's River**, the international boundary and waterway that connects Lakes Superior and Huron, forming an important link in the Great Lakes/St. Lawrence Seaway system *(p 136)*. The rapids in the river between the two cities were a gathering place from earliest times when Ojibwa Indians came to catch whitefish here. Étienne Brûlé visited the rapids in 1622, as did many of the great explorers of New France: Nicolet, Radisson, Groseilliers, Marquette, Jolliet, La Salle, the La Vérendrye family and others. In 1668 Pére Marquette established a mission beside them, calling it Sainte Marie du Sault (*sault* means "falls" in French). Gateway to the wild and uninhabited **Algoma** wilderness, Sault Ste. Marie today is also the headquarters of the Firebirds, the province's aerial fire fighters who control the spread of forest fires by such methods as waterbombing.

SIGHTS

★ **The Soo Locks** – To bypass the rapids the **North West Company** completed the first lock and canal in 1798 (destroyed during the War of 1812). Since then, locks of increasing size have been constructed and today, the enormous ships of the Great Lakes are able to bypass the rapids by four parallel locks on the American side of the river. These locks are one of the busiest sections of the entire seaway system, handling in excess of 8,000 lockages per year and an average of more than 73 million tonnes/80 million tons of cargo annually.

A new lock is under construction within the existing Canadian lock, which has been closed for a number of years; it will handle recreational vessels only. Projected reopening is scheduled for 1997-98. *Visitor centre, 1 Canal Dr., open Jun–mid-Oct daily 10am–5pm; rest of the year Mon–Fri 8:30am–4:30pm.* ☎705-941-6205.

At the base of Huron Street, there is a reconstruction of the **first lock [A]**. The vast lock system in the river can be appreciated by taking a **boat trip** *(departs from dock off Foster Dr. Jun–mid-Oct daily 10am–6pm; round-trip 2-3hrs; commentary; $16; ✕ & Lock Tours* ☎705-253-9850*)* that passes through one of the large American locks.

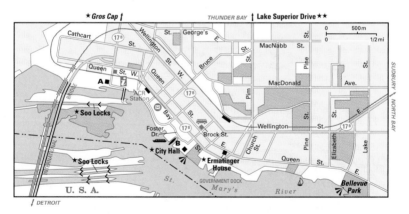

★ **City Hall** – At the base of Brock Street, Sault Ste. Marie has a pleasant riverfront area dominated by its attractive City Hall, built of copper-coloured reflecting glass. Nearby stands the permanently berthed **MS Norgoma [B]**, the last overnight passenger ship used on the Great Lakes *(docked next to Roberta Bondar Pavilion; open Jun–Aug daily 10am–8pm; $2.50;* ☎705-256-7447 or 705-942-2919*)*. On board the ship is a museum of Great Lakes history.

★ **Ermatinger House** – *Open mid-Apr–May Mon–Fri 10am–5pm. Jun–Sept daily 10am–5pm. Oct–Nov Mon–Fri 1–5pm. Dec by appointment. Contribution requested.* ☎705-759-5443. This attractive Georgian stone house was built in 1814 by Charles Oakes Ermatinger, a partner in the North West Company, and his Ojibway wife Charlotte. It has been restored to reflect the period when it stood almost alone in the region and received many eminent visitors.

167

Among the guests was **Paul Kane** (1810-71), who made several long canoe trips across Canada, sketching and making notes about the Indians of the Great Lakes, Plains and Pacific Coast regions. On his return to Toronto, he wrote *Wanderings of an Artist among the Indians of North America,* which was published in 1859. On the second floor there are interesting displays on the history of Sault Ste. Marie and of the Ermatinger family.

Bellevue Park – From this park on the river, there are fine **views★** of the ships using the locks and of the bridge to the US.

EXCURSIONS

★**Gros Cap** – *26km/16mi west by Hwy. 550.* From this headland there is a good view★ of Lake Superior and the beginning of the St. Mary's River.

Train Trip to Agawa Canyon – *183km/114mi. Departs from Bay St. depot Jun–mid-Oct daily 8am. Round-trip 9hrs. $46. Jan–Mar weekends only 8am. Round-trip 8hrs. $45. Commentary. Reservations suggested.* ✗ ⟨ *Algoma Central Railway Inc.* ☎*705-946-7300 or 800-242-9287 (Canada/US).* The train traverses some of the Algoma wilderness north of Sault Ste. Marie. At a stopover in Agawa Canyon *(2hrs, except in winter),* travellers can climb to a lookout for a fine **view★** of the canyon and the Agawa River. The trip is especially popular in late September for viewing the autumn colours.

★★**Lake Superior Drive** – *230km/143mi by Trans-Can Hwy. (Rte. 17) to Wawa. Map p 4.* This drive is ruggedly beautiful. The road cuts through some of the oldest rock formations in the world, the Canadian Shield. After Batchawana Bay the wild shore of Lake Superior is followed for a lengthy stretch, with views of headlands, coves, islands, rocks and high granite bluffs pounded by the waters of this, the deepest of the Great Lakes. The drive is especially fine around **Alona Bay★** *(viewpoint after 108km/67mi)* and **Agawa Bay★** *(viewpoint after 151km/94mi).* Lookouts have been built beside the road.

For 84km/52mi the road passes through **Lake Superior Provincial Park** *(open daily mid-May–mid-Oct; swimming, hiking; boat rental;* ⟨ ☎*705-856-2284),* a wilderness area of forested hills and cliffs rising straight out of the lake. The park is known for its Indian **pictographs**—primitive rock paintings often commemorating great events or relating to nature. After 153km/95mi a side road leads to a parking lot from which a rugged trail *(10min)* descends to the lake. A series of pictographs possibly several hundred years old can be found on **Agawa Rock★**, a sheer rock face rising out of the water. The **view★** of the lake is excellent.

STRATFORD★

Pop. 27,666
Map p 132
Tourist Office ☎519-273-3352

This community is home to the annual **Shakespeare Festival**, a major theatrical event of the English-speaking world that attracts people from all over North America. Though the focus is still Shakespearean, the festival offers a wide variety of drama and music.

The festival is said to have had its beginnings in 1830 when one William Sargint called his establishment on the Huron Road to Goderich the Shakespeare Inn. The community that grew up around the hostelry adopted the name of the birthplace of the famous English dramatist, and named the river the Avon. In 1952 local journalist **Tom Patterson** dreamed of creating a festival to celebrate the works of the town's namesake. From modest beginnings in a tent a year later, the festival has grown to its present seven-month season *(May–Nov)* in three theatres, drawing a yearly audience of nearly 500,000. *For performance schedule & reservations contact the Box Office, Stratford Festival, PO Box 520, Stratford, ON, N5A 6V2.* ☎*519-273-1600 or 800-567-1600 (Canada/US).*

VISIT *2hrs (not including performances)*

Festival Theatre – Reflecting the tent of its origin, this building resembling a circus "big top" contains an *apron* or thrust stage, surrounded by audience seating on three sides. This modern development of the Elizabethan stage used in Shakespeare's day was revolutionary in the 1950s (but much copied since) because no elaborate scenery could be used and no member of the audience was more than 20m/65ft from the stage.

The theatre is set at the edge of a pleasant park that stretches down to the river, dammed at this point to form **Victoria Lake**, the home of many swans. Before evening performances in the summer, the beautifully manicured lawns and the small island in the lake are covered with picnicking theatre-goers. At intermission the elegantly attired crowd wanders among the formal flower beds and over the lawns surrounding the theatre.

SUDBURY★★

Pop. 92,884
Map p 132
Tourist Office ☎800-465-6655 or 705-522-0104

Located on the largest single source of nickel in the world, Sudbury is the biggest and most important mining centre in Canada. Sudbury is also a principal centre of francophone culture in Ontario; about a quarter of the population of the region is **Franco-Ontarian. Laurentian University**, which serves the northeastern part of the province, is bilingual.

Historical Notes – The nickel-bearing rock strata are part of the **Sudbury Igneous Complex**, an approximately 60km/37mi long and 27km/17mi wide geological formation created by a meteorite impact or volcanic eruption millions of years ago. Geological opinion is divided on the issue. Whatever its origins, the area's wealth (platinum, copper, cobalt, silver and gold, in addition to nickel) was discovered in 1883 during the construction of the Canadian Pacific Railway. A blacksmith named **Thomas Flanagan** noticed a rust-coloured patch of rock while working with a crew in a recently blasted area just west of the present city.
Today the discovery is commemorated by a plaque *(on Hwy. 144 near the Murray Mine)*, and Sudbury claims the world's largest integrated nickel mining, smelting and refining complex. The **Super Stack**, an enormous smoke stack rising 380m/1,250ft above the surrounding countryside, tops the complex. In addition to its industrial importance, the Sudbury region is typical Canadian Shield country of beautiful lakes, rocks and trees. A number of lakes are encompassed within city limits, including **Lake Ramsey**, which has enough yellow pickerel (walleye) to supply local fishermen, and beaches just a short walk from the civic centre.

SIGHTS *1/2 day*

★★★ **Science North** – *About 1.5km/1mi south of Trans-Can Hwy. From Hwy. 69 by-pass, take Paris St. to Ramsey Lake Rd.* Perched on a rock outcropping on the shores of Lake Ramsey, this dramatic science centre was designed by Raymond Moriyama in association with local architects. A hexagonal exhibit building resembling a snowflake (to represent the glacial action that shaped Northern Ontario) is set over a cavern blasted out of the rock (to represent the probable creation of Sudbury Basin by a meteor). Exhibits emphasize first-hand experience with science and northern technology in a vivid way.

Visit – *Open May–mid-Jun daily 9am–5pm. Late Jun–Labour Day daily 9am–6pm. Early Sept–mid-Oct daily 9am–5pm. Late Oct–Apr daily 10am–4pm. Closed Jan 1, Dec 24–25. $8.50.* ✗ ♿ *☎705-522-3701.* Visitors enter a small reception building (also hexagonal in shape), and proceed to the centre proper via a **rock tunnel**. Raw rock is exposed as it is in the impressive **rock cavern** (9m/30ft high by 30m/100ft in diameter), where a 3-D film and laser show highlights geological history. Visitors then ascend to the exhibit floors via a spiral ramp that zigzags over the **Creighton Fault**, a geological fracture within the Canadian Shield, active over 2 billion years ago, that left a groove 4m/13ft deep at this point. Hanging over the fault is a 23m/72ft fin whale skeleton, weighing 1800kg/4,000lb, recovered from Anticosti Island. The glass walls of the ramp offer views of Lake Ramsey. Museum staff are on hand in the fitness centre, for example, where visitors can be tested for correct body weight, or in the Alex Baumann Human Performance Lab, where visitors can discover their fitness level. The small creatures area houses such insects as a "walking-stick" or the museum's pet porcupine, who grows his furry coat in summer when the building is air-conditioned and loses it in winter when his home is heated. State-of-the-art monitoring equipment can be viewed in the weather station, and science shows are presented regularly in the Discovery Theatre.

From the dock **boat tours** of the lake can be taken *(depart daily mid-May–early Oct; round-trip 1hr; commentary; reservations suggested; $9;* ✗ ♿ *Cortina Cruise Boat ☎705-522-3701).*

★★ **Big Nickel Mine** – *On Big Nickel Mine Dr., 5km/3mi west of Science North by Regent and Lorne Sts. Open May–mid-Jun daily 9am–5pm. Late Jun–Labour Day daily 9am–6pm. Early Sept–mid-Oct daily 9am–5pm. $8.50.* ✕ ♿ ☎705-522-3701 . Operated by Science North, this mine is one of a few authentic hard-rock mines open to the public in Ontario. Visitors descend 21m/70ft by a miners' cage to the underground "drifts" or tunnels where the mining process (drilling, blasting and other procedures) is explained and demonstrated. There is even a simulated blasting sequence.

Near the mine stands the **Big Nickel**, a replica of the 1951 Canadian commemorative five-cent piece. Long a Sudbury landmark, the replica is 9m/30ft high and 0.6m/2ft thick.

THUNDER BAY★★

Pop. 113,946
Map of Principal Sights p 00
Tourist Office ☎807-625-2149

Situated almost in the centre of Canada on the shores of Lake Superior, the city of Thunder Bay is an important port and the Canadian western extremity of the Great Lakes/St. Lawrence Seaway system. Its rail lines and roads transport a wide range of commodities—wheat from the Prairies being the most important—to docks for transfer to the huge ships of the seaway.

Historical Notes – This exchange of goods and transportation is not the result of the St. Lawrence Seaway's construction. For many years the area was the linchpin of the fur trade. Every summer brigades of canoes left the widespread posts of the North West Company in the northwest to transport a year's collection of furs to a trading post called Fort William. There these "wintering" partners (so named because they spent the winter in the wilds) met the Montreal partners who had made the long canoe trek through the Great Lakes with the trading goods their counterparts would need for the next year. Lasting about six weeks the "**rendezvous**" was a time of wild celebration, as well as serious discussion of trading policy and strategy against the rival Hudson's Bay Company, who took their furs to market by way of the great bay. When the two fur-trading companies merged in 1821, Fort William lost its position as the place of the great rendezvous, but remained a fur-trading post until late in the century. In 1970 the communities of **Fort William** and **Port Arthur** were amalgamated to create the city of Thunder Bay. The fort has been re-created as it was at its peak, and every year the rendezvous is re-enacted *(Jul)*.

The port's nine enormous grain terminals dominate the city skyline. Prairie grain arriving by rail is cleaned and stored in these terminals for transfer to the ships of the Greak Lakes fleet. Port facilities also include two terminals for coal, potash and other dry-bulk commodities, a malting plant, a bagging facility for specialty grains and a general cargo facility noted for its ship/rail heavy lift transfers.

SIGHTS

★ **The Waterfront** – To appreciate the impressive port, and the sheer size of the grain terminals and ships, view them from **Marina Park** *(end of Red River Rd., open daily year-round)*. The largest of these ships is 222m/728ft by 23m/75ft, capable of carrying up to a million bushels of grain—the yield of 20,650ha/51,000 acres of land. The breakwater protecting the harbour from the storms of Lake Superior can also be seen. Waves can reach 12m/40ft in height in autumn. In summer the lake is calmer, and sailboat races are held weekly within and outside of the breakwater.

★ **Viewpoints** – Thunder Bay is surrounded by the hills of the Canadian Shield. The city is hemmed in across the bay by a long peninsula that rears its head at the end to form a cape that is called **Sleeping Giant** because its resembles the prone figure of a man.

★ **Mt. McKay** – *At end of Mountain Rd. on Indian reserve.* This prominent flat-topped peak is the highest (488m/1,600ft) of the Norwester Chain. From a ledge 180m/600ft high, there is a fine **view** on clear days of the city, port and Sleeping Giant guarding the entrance to the harbour.

★ **Hillcrest Park** – *High St. between John St. Rd. and Red River Rd.* Located on a cliff above Port Arthur, this park provides a good **view** of the port, elevators, ore dock and, in the distance, Sleeping Giant and the islands that close the harbour mouth.

★★ **Old Fort William** – *16km/10mi south by Broadway Ave. Map below. Open Apr–mid-Oct daily 10am–5pm. $7.25.* ✗ ♿ ☎*807-577-6645.* Located on the Kaministikwia River, part of the trade route to the northwest, the fort of the great rendezvous has been superbly reconstructed. From the visitor centre, visitors can walk through the woods to the palisaded fort, which is almost a town. Inside the palisade, there is a large square of dovetailed log buildings, several raised above the ground on stilts (the river still floods). Some 50 structures represent all aspects of early-19C fur-trade society. Costumed guides help re-create fort life. The North West Company partners can be seen discussing business in the council house; the warehouses are full of furs and trading goods; and birchbark canoes, tinware and barrels are being crafted by hand. Other highlights include a farm, apothecary, Indian encampments, living quarters and a jail.

EXCURSIONS *Map below*

★★ **Kakabeka Falls** – *29km/18mi west by Trans-Can Hwy. (Rte. 17). Provincial park open year-round. Park open to vehicles mid-May–mid-Oct daily 8am–11pm. $6/car.* △ ♿ ☎*807-473-9231.* The Kaministikwia River plunges 39m/128ft over a cliff around a pinnacle of rock into a narrow gorge. A bridge crosses the river to enable visitors to view the falls from both sides. These falls were the first obstacle negotiated by the fur traders of the North West Company when leaving Fort William on their return trip to the northwest.

★★ **North Shore Lake Superior** – *211km/131mi to Schreiber by Trans-Can Hwy.* This route passes several interesting features northeast of Thunder Bay.

Terry Fox Monument and Scenic Lookout – *1km/.6mi east of Hodder Ave.* The fine bronze monument commemorates the heroic efforts of Terry Fox to raise money to fight cancer. Deprived of his right leg by the disease at age 18, he undertook a cross-Canada run in 1980, starting in Newfoundland. Two months later, he was forced to abandon his run close to this spot because of recurring cancer from which he died in 1981. The monument overlooks Lake Superior.

★ **Sleeping Giant Provincial Park** – *After 51km/32mi, take Rte. 587. Open daily mid-May–mid-Oct. Early Jan–Mar daily dawn–dusk. $6/vehicle.* △ ♿ ☎*807-977-2526.* Occupying most of the peninsula that has the Sleeping Giant at its end, this pleasant park features trails, high cliffs, fine **views**★ of Lake Superior and the remains of the village of Silver Islet. This community was formed in 1868 when a rich silver vein was discovered on the tiny islet offshore. The vertical vein yielded $300 million worth of ore before the shaft flooded at a depth of 400m/1,300ft.

Amethyst Mine – *After 56km/35mi, take East Loon Rd. for 8km/5mi. Open mid-May–Jun daily 10am–5pm. Jul–Labour Day daily 10am–7pm. Early Sept–mid-Oct daily 10am–5pm. $1.* ♿ ☎*807-622-6908.* Amethyst is found in many places along the north shore of Lake Superior. This open-pit mine is a rock hound's delight as pieces of the purple quartz can be collected *(charge of $1/lb.)*, or polished stones purchased.

★★ **Ouimet Canyon** – *After 76km/47mi, take road for 12km/8mi. Open mid-May–mid-Oct daily dawn–dusk.* ☎*807-977-2526.* This incredible canyon is quite a startling find in the country north of Lake Superior. Gashed out of the surface of the Canadian

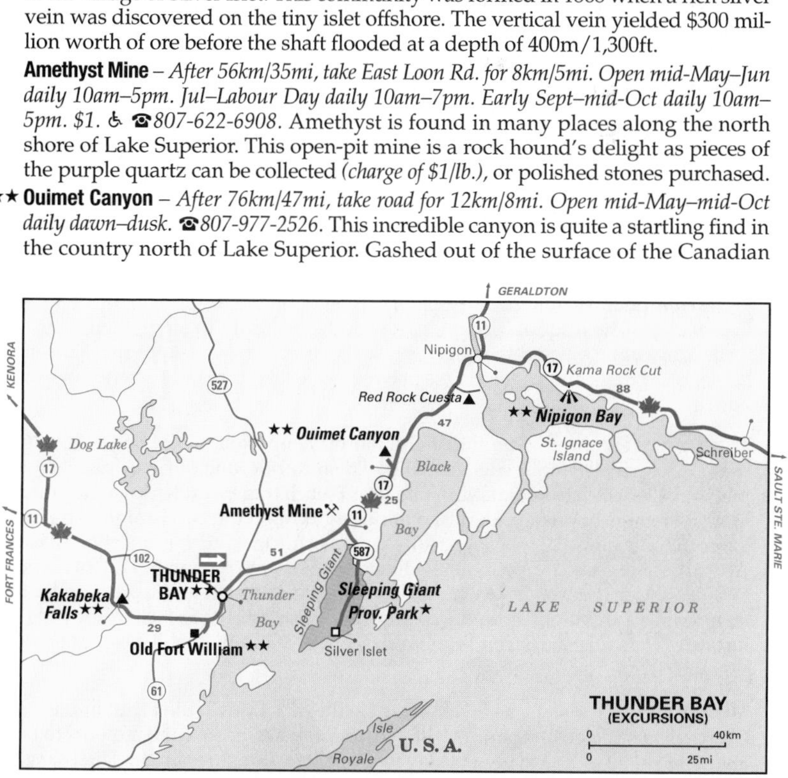

Shield during the last Ice Age, possibly along an existing fault line, the canyon is 100m/330ft deep, 150m/500ft across and more than 1.6km/1mi long. It is rocky and barren except for a few Arctic flowers that grow on its floor; the cold, sunless environment will support little else.

Just after the Red Rock turnoff on the Trans-Canada Highway, a cliff of layered limestone coloured red by hematite can be seen. Called the **Red Rock Cuesta**, this unusual geological formation is nearly 210m/690ft high and about 3km/2mi long.

★★ **Nipigon Bay** – *88km/55mi from Nipigon to Schreiber.* After crossing the Nipigon River, the Trans-Canada Highway runs along the shore of this bay, offering **views**★★ of rocky islands covered with conifers and rocks worn smooth by the action of Lake Superior.

The **view**★★ of Kama Bay through the Kama Rock Cut *(27km/17mi from Nipigon)* is particularly fine. The rock itself indicates the type of problems involved in the construction of this highway in 1960, the same encountered in the building of the Canadian Pacific Railway.

TORONTO★★★

Metro Pop. 2,275,771
Map of Principal Sights p 4
Tourist Office ☎416-203-2500

Dynamic, cosmopolitan, stimulating, Toronto is the heartbeat of Canada. Having surpassed MONTREAL in size in 1977, the country's largest city ranks ninth in North America. Toronto is the hub of the **Golden Horseshoe**, the 60km/100mi wide arc stretching from OSHAWA to HAMILTON where at least a quarter of Canada's manufacturing is based.

Sprawling over 600sq km/372sq mi in the southeast leg of the province, the metropolis is set on the broad north shore of **Lake Ontario**. Its fine harbour is almost landlocked by a chain of offshore islands *(p 176)* that provide the city with its major parkland. Flat beside the lake, the land rises noticeably about 5km/3mi inland at the old shoreline of prehistoric Lake Iroquois. The plain is intersected by a number of small rivers that have created a network of ravines. On the westside Toronto is bordered by the **Humber River** *(map p 189)* and to the east, the **Don River**. In the recent past the ravines and river valleys have largely been used for parks.

A forward-looking metropolis protective of its past, Toronto has restored its architectural treasures and preserved its history. Waves of immigrants have repeatedly integrated with the population, enhancing the city's cultural legacy. Toronto's size, heritage and diversity have much to offer: world-class exhibits, colourful neighbourhoods, lively markets, historic mansions, a vibrant harbourfront, wide-ranging cultural events and cuisine, and multiple recreational activities.

Historical Notes

"Toronto Passage" – In their search for food and trade, native inhabitants of the area had long used the rivers as a transportation system. Prior to 1600 the **Huron** and **Petun** peoples abandoned their north shorelands to the warring **Iroquois Confederacy**. The Iroquois occupied the vacated territory to strengthen their fur trade, only to be evicted themselves by French traders, to whom this "Toronto Passage" of trails and canoe routes between Lakes Huron and Ontario was well known.

The French Regime – The site of Toronto was important to the burgeoning fur trade. As early as 1615 it was visited by **Étienne Brûlé**, one of Champlain's men who travelled widely in Ontario. Years later French traders under royal command met native and English traders at a bartering post on the banks of the Humber River in the vicinity of what is now Toronto, a Huron word for "meeting place." Attempting to curb competition, the French began construction in 1720 of several forts around mammoth Lake Ontario. The remains of **Fort Rouillé** have been found in Toronto's Exhibition Grounds. To prevent British use, the French destroyed the fort in 1759 during the Seven Years' War, the war that signalled the end of French presence in the area.

Muddy York – The site was first ignored by the new British rulers, but in 1787, **Sir Guy Carleton**, the governor of British North America, made arrangements to buy land equivalent in size to present-day metropolitan Toronto from the **Mississaugas**, who had occupied it after the Iroquois. Loyalists fleeing the US had also settled along the lake; their demands for English law eventually led to the formation of Upper Canada (now Ontario) in 1791. Col. **John Graves Simcoe**, lieutenant-governor of the new territory, decided upon Toronto, despite its swamps, as the site for a temporary capital *(p 147)*, because of its fine harbour and distance from the American border. (The existing capital, Niagara-on-the-Lake, was considered too close to the enemy.) Baptized **York** after the victorious soldier-son of George III, the new outpost grew slowly, despite such grandiose projects as the building of **Yonge Street**. By the outbreak of the War of 1812, the unpaved streets of this swamp town gave the village the unfortunate sobriquet, "Muddy York."

In April 1813 the town was jolted by an American fleet that captured and set fire to the Legislature and other imposing buildings. In retaliation for this assault and the burning of Niagara-on-the-Lake, the British attacked and set fire to part of Washington, DC, the capital of the US, in 1814.

The Family Compact – After 1814 York grew as waves of immigrants from Britain came to Ontario in the wake of the Napoleonic Wars. A small group of wealthy, privileged men with strong British ties dominated the government of York—and the whole of Upper Canada. By appointing officials only from their ranks, they guarded their exclusive elite. New arrivals began to challenge the power of what was called "the Family Compact." An outspoken Scot named **William Lyon Mackenzie** (1795-1861) attacked the group in his newspaper, *The Colonial Advocate*. In 1828 he was elected to the legislative assembly, becoming leader of the radical wing of the Reform Party. Expelled by the compact, he was reelected and reexpelled five times. However, in 1835, he was elected the first mayor of the City of Toronto, newly incorporated in 1834 (the city's original name had fallen from favour as its namesake, the Duke of York, continued to lose in battle). Mackenzie then reassumed his seat in the legislature. The assembly was dissolved in 1836 by Gov. **Sir Francis Bond Head**, and subsequent elections brought the defeat of the Reform Party.

The Rebellions of 1837 – Gaining no satisfaction from the British Parliament, Mackenzie turned to armed rebellion in December 1837. When Toronto's garrison was away in Lower Canada, he gathered supporters at **Montgomery's Tavern** (which stood near the present intersection of Yonge Street and Eglinton Avenue) and marched towards the city. Loyal citizens hurriedly formed a defence, but quickly dispersed after a skirmish with Mackenzie's men. Unknown to them, Mackenzie's forces had also retreated. Reinforcements arrived under Col. Allan MacNab the following day, the revolt collapsed, and Mackenzie fled to the US. Although two of Mackenzie's men were publicly hanged, the revolt was effective in that British Parliament ultimately granted "responsible government" to the Canadian colonies. The united Province of Canada was created *(p 24)*, and Mackenzie was permitted to return in 1849.

Montreal was the site of another armed rebellion, also in 1837, against British rule *(p 212)*. Although it was crushed, the insurgence subsequently resulted in representative government for Quebec.

Toronto the Good – The revolt bred among Torontonians an enduring hatred of violence and a resulting support for government. By the end of the 19C, Toronto's reputation was one of Anglo-Saxon rectitude. As a major manufacturing centre, the city had become immensely wealthy. Prosperous financiers, industrialists and merchants were united in their desire to preserve Sunday as a day of rest and church-going, and in their belief that intemperance was a fundamental social problem. Toronto was nicknamed "The Good," but considered dull.

Toronto Today: The Urban Miracle – As late as 1941 Toronto was 80 percent Anglo-Saxon, but since World War II, this once-homogeneous city has opened its doors to immigrants from around the world. Today Italians, Germans, Ukrainians, Dutch, Poles, Scandinavians, Portuguese, East Indians, Chinese, West Indians and other nationalities have made their home here, giving Toronto a stimulating mix of indigenous and imported cultures. **Kensington Market** *(Kensington Ave., east of Spadina and north of Dundas)*, several adjacent streets containing outdoor and indoor vendors, is the realm of the Portuguese and East Indian communities *(best time to visit is Mon-Sat mornings)*. One of the largest Chinese districts in North America, **Chinatown** *(Dundas St. from Elizabeth to Spadina)* is also vibrant with street vendors, notably exotic-produce merchants. The Italian districts *(College St. and St. Clair Ave., west of Bathurst)* evoke the mother country. **Greektown** *(Danforth Ave.*

between Coxwell and Broadview; ● *Chester)* offers numerous cafes, specialty shops and fruit markets featuring Greek food. Particularly active between Spadina and John Streets, **Queen Street West** has become a colourful area of trendy bistros, unusual bookstores and young designer boutiques.

The last 30 years have seen the Toronto skyline transformed. Shining glass-fronted skyscrapers and "spacescraper" CN Tower overshadow the once-dominant **Royal York Hotel** and old **Bank of Commerce**. Rapid development has been highly controversial, however. Citizen-action groups formed to halt destruction of residential areas for proposed freeways and high rises. The city was the first in North America to adopt a tiered system of metropolitan government to solve problems caused by 19C municipal boundaries.

Toronto's port has suffered since the opening of the St. Lawrence Seaway when the era of containerization began. Cargo unloaded at ports such as HALIFAX and ST. JOHN'S on the East Coast is containerized, and shipped inland via rail, bypassing Toronto's waterways.

Cultural and Sports Centre – The centre of English-language culture in Canada, Toronto boasts the Toronto Symphony and the Mendelssohn Choir at Roy

Thomson Hall, concerts at Massey Hall, the National Ballet of Canada, the Toronto Dance Theatre, Harbourfront Centre's Premiere Dance Theatre, and the Canadian Opera Company at the O'Keefe Centre. The St. Lawrence Centre for the Arts, the Royal Alexandra, and the Elgin and Winter Garden Theatres stage traditional and popular drama. Every fall the city hosts a world film festival, and summer

Maple Leaf Ice Hockey Game

Graig Abel, Toronto

PRACTICAL INFORMATION .... Area Code 416

Getting Around

By Public Transportation – The Toronto Transit Commission (TTC) operates an extensive public transport system of buses, streetcars and subway. Hours of operation: Mon–Sat 6–1am, Sun 9–1am. Adult fare $2 one-way ($3.50 two-way ticket) for unlimited travel with no stopovers. Day Pass $6. Tokens 10 for $15. Exact fare required. Free transfers between buses & streetcars. System maps & timetables available free of charge. For route information ☎393-INFO.

By Car – Use of public transportation or walking is strongly encouraged within the city as streets are often congested and street parking may be difficult to find. Toronto has a strictly enforced tow-away policy. Motorists should park in designated **parking** areas; public, off-street parking facilities are located throughout the city. For parking fee information & free map ☎393-7275. Car rentals: Avis ☎777-AVIS; Hertz ☎620-9620; Tilden ☎922-2000.

By Taxi – Co-op ☎504-2667; Diamond ☎366-6868; Metro Cab ☎504-5757.

General Information

Accommodations and Visitor Information – For hotels/motels contact the Metropolitan Toronto Convention & Visitors Assn. ☎203-2500 or 800-363-1990 (Canada/US). For listing of major chains *(p 316)*. Reservation services: Accommodation Toronto ☎629-3800; Utell International ☎905-479-9794 or 800-448-8355 (Canada/US); Abodes of Choice B&B Assn. of Toronto ☎694-6491; B&B Homes of Toronto ☎363-6362; Downtown Toronto Assn. of B&B Guest Homes ☎368-1420. The visitor centre is located at Metropolitan Toronto Convention & Visitors Assn., 207 Queen's Quay West, Toronto, ON, M5J 1A7 *(open year-round Mon–Fri 8:30am–5pm).*

brings a variety of outdoor entertainment. Several annual events draw visitors: the **Canadian National Exhibition** *(at the Exhibition Grounds three weeks before Labour Day)*, reputedly the world's largest exhibition, now primarily of consumer goods; the **Metro International Caravan**, a festival of ethnic cultures *(late Jun, pavilions throughout the city, special buses)*; the **Dragon Boat Race Festival**, a Chinese celebration *(Jun)*, and **Caribana**, a West Indies festival of steel bands and floating nightclubs on the lake *(Aug)*. Spectators sports are plentiful: *Toronto Blue Jays* baseball, *Maple Leaf* ice hockey games, an annual canoeing and rowing regatta *(Jul 1)*, horse shows *(particularly the Royal Winter Fair)*, soccer and auto racing. *For details contact the Metropolitan Toronto Convention & Visitor Assn.* ☎416-203-2500.

★★ THE WATERFRONT *2 days. Maps pp 177 and 181.*

Built largely on land reclaimed in the mid-19C to mid-20C for the city's growing port installations, the area south of Front Street contains Toronto's foremost landmarks and its largest lakefront revitalization.

Crucial to the city's founding, the waterfront experienced growth and eventual decline of its maritime functions, now transferred to the commercial port east of Yonge Street. Lake shipping waned in the 1960s, and recession subsequently idled the harbourfront. Although scarred by the remains of defunct industries, the area underwent gradual revitalization beginning in the early 1970s. Over the following 20 years, land north of the expressway was selected as the site of two major building projects—the CN Tower and SkyDome.

Several quays were overhauled to house colourful shops, galleries, performance arenas, restaurants and sailing schools. Completion of an outdoor stage known as Molson Place in 1992 and construction of a 105,000sq ft expansion to the **convention centre** confirm the area's growing popularity. Neighbouring CN Tower to the southeast, the expansion is expected to be ready for use by mid-1997.

The grounds of both CN Tower and SkyDome can be reached on foot from Union Station by way of **Skywalk**, *a large glass-enclosed walkway containing eateries and souvenir shops.*

★★★ CN Tower – *Illustration p 129. Entrance at Front and John Sts.* ● *Union, then via Skywalk. Open May–Sept daily 10am–midnight. Rest of the year daily 10am–10pm. $12.* ✗ ♿ 🅿 ☎416-360-8500. The city's most prominent landmark, this concrete, rocket-like structure reaches 180 storeys (over 553m/1,815ft in height). Constructed at a cost of $52 million, the tower is the tallest free-standing structure in the world and a popular Toronto tourist attraction (1.4 million visitors a year).

Local Press – Daily: *The Toronto Star, The Toronto Sun*, and *The Globe and Mail*. Monthly guides (free) to entertainment, shopping, and restaurants: *Where, Now*.

Entertainment – Consult arts and entertainment supplements in local newspapers (Thursday edition) for schedule of cultural events and addresses of principal theatres and concert halls. Ticketmaster ☎870-8000 for concerts or 872-1111 for theatre & arts (major credit cards accepted).

Sports – Toronto Blue Jays (baseball): home games at SkyDome; season Apr–Oct; tickets ☎341-1111. Toronto Maple Leafs (ice hockey): home games at Maple Leaf Gardens; season Oct–Apr; schedules ☎977-1641, tickets ☎872-5000 (Ticketmaster). Toronto Argonauts (football): home games at SkyDome; season mid-Jun–Nov; schedules ☎341-5151, tickets ☎872-5000 (Ticketmaster). Toronto Raptors (NBA basketball): home games at SkyDome; season Nov–Apr; tickets ☎366-3865.

Useful Numbers   ☎

Police .... 911 (emergency) or	808-2222
Union Station (VIA Rail), *Front & Bay Sts.*	366-8411
Bus terminal, *610 Bay St.*	393-7911
Toronto (Pearson) International Airport	905-676-3506
Canadian Automobile Assn., *2 Carlton St.*	221-4300
CAA Emergency Road Service (24hr)	222-5222
Shoppers Drug Mart (24hr pharmacy) *various locations*	493-1220
Post Office Station A, *25 The Esplanade*	979-8822
Road Conditions	235-1110
Weather (24hr)	661-0123

Beginning in 1972, the tower was built over a four-year period by federally owned Canadian National (formerly Canadian National Railways) to provide telecommunications services. Topped by a powerful antenna, the tower serves FM radio and television stations *(telecommunications facilities not open to the public)* whose transmitters line the mast.

In only 58 seconds visitors are "beamed up" 346m/1,136ft (nearly the height of the Empire State Building) in an exterior glass-front elevator to **Skypod**, a circular steel "turban" seven storeys high. From its observation decks, **views★★** of the city and suburbs, the lake and shoreline are superb *(illuminated panels identify buildings and parks)*, providing a vivid aerial orientation to Toronto. One floor down, intrepid visitors can stand or sit on the **glass floor**, a small section of thick glass panels that permit an impressive view 342m/1,122ft straight down to the ground below.

Not for the faint-hearted is an ascent 33 storeys higher to the smaller observation gallery named **Space Deck**, a flying-saucer-shaped, windowed ring 447m/1,465ft above the ground, reached via an elevator inside the tower. The sweeping **views★★★** of the cityscape and Lake Ontario are spectacular. The feeling of height is reinforced by planes from nearby Toronto Island Airport flying below. If visibility is good, NIAGARA FALLS and Buffalo, 120km/75mi away, can be seen.

★★ SkyDome – ● *Union, then via Skywalk.* ✗ ♿ 🅿 ☎416-341-3663. *For tours* ☎416-341-2770. Dominating railway land next to CN Tower—one of the few central locations big enough to hold it—this huge, domed sports/entertainment complex is home to American League Baseball's *Toronto Blue Jays*. The multipurpose stadium hosts rock concerts, conventions and trade shows as well as sports. Designed by architect Roderick Robbie and engineer Michael Allen, SkyDome was built (1986-89) by a private consortium in partnership with local and provincial governments for over $570 million.

Projecting from the Front Street facade 5m/16ft above street level, Michael Snow's collection of 14 painted-fiberglass sculptures *(The Audience)* towers over arriving visitors. SkyDome boasts an 3ha/8 acre **retractable roof**, a 348-room hotel overlooking the playing field, a 150-seat cinema, several restaurants and underground parking for 575 vehicles. In the open-air mode, the four roof panels are stacked over the north end of the field. In 20 minutes the panels can be closed by pushing a button to activate a computer-controlled operation. Tall enough to accommodate a 31-storey building, the roof is 205m/674ft at its widest and rises to a height of 91m/299ft at its centre. The arena's flexible field (basketball, football, tennis, track or baseball configurations) and seating can be arranged for a crowd of 53,000 or an audience of 10,000.

★★ Harbourfront – *Access from York, Spadina and Bathurst Sts.;* ● *Union or Spadina, transfer to bus 77B or LRT York Quay; visitor centre at York Quay Centre* ☎416-973-3000. *For event schedule contact Box Office* ☎416-973-4000. Initiated in 1976, this colourful 40ha/100 acre development has transformed Toronto's previously neglected lakeshore into an attractive mix of marinas, outdoor cafes, antiques and crafts markets, modern hotels, sleek condominiums and pleasant miniparks. A focal point of the city's cultural life, especially in summer, Harbourfront is also the scene of year-round recreational, educational and commercial activities, commonplace in the renovated warehouses as well as out-of-doors.

The granddaddy of the waterfront warehouses, **Queen's Quay Terminal** (1927), with its imposing clock tower and rectangular solidity, was completely overhauled, perforated from top to bottom with wide bottle-green windows, and opened in 1983. Designed by Eberhard Zeidler, the refurbished terminal accommodates airy offices, plush living spaces, fashionable boutiques and eateries, the 450-seat Premiere Dance Theatre and, on the fifth floor, the Metro Toronto Convention and Visitors Assn. Nearby, **York Quay Centre** houses an art gallery, a craft studio and summer theatre. Fronting the **Power Plant [A]**, now a contemporary art gallery *(open year-round Tue–Sun noon–6pm; closed Jan 1 & Dec 25; $2;* ☎416-973-4949), the multipurpose **du Maurier Theatre Centre [B]**, with its glass-faceted foyer, evolved from a former 1920s ice house. **Molson Place [C]**, an open-air 1,750-seat concert facility, occupies the southwest corner of the quay. Sailing schools, nautical stores and restaurants are located at **Pier 4**, and the Marine Division of the Metro Police is based at John Quay.

★★ Toronto Islands – *Ferries (10-15min) depart from Queen's Quay to three points: Centre Island, Ward's Island and Hanlan's Point. Depart mid-May–Labour Day daily every 15min from 8am–12:45am. Rest of the year phone for hours. $3.* ♿ ☎416-392-8193. A popular retreat from the bustle of nearby downtown, these islands function as

Toronto's principal public parkland. Formed from the erosion of Scarborough Bluffs (*p 000*), this narrow landmass was a peninsula until 1853, when a violent storm severed it from the mainland, creating the present string of islands.

Extending 6km/3.7mi from end to end, the islands are graced with expansive lawns, age-old shade trees, sandy beaches, marinas and spectacular **views★★** of downtown Toronto. Attractions on **Centre Island** include restaurants, cafes, a beach (*on the Lake Ontario side*) and a delightful theme/amusement park for youngsters (*open mid-May–mid-Sept; ☎416-363-1112*). On foot or by bike (*motor vehicles prohibited on the islands*), visitors can explore the adjacent islands, particularly **Algonquin** and **Ward's Islands**, whose quaint roads lined with small, privately owned cottages lend a decidedly rural charm. Near the small airport located on the islands' western end is Hanlan's Point, renowned for its **views** of the city (*a trackless train operates continuously between Centre Island and Hanlan's Point*).

For visitors pressed for time, the hour-long **harbour cruise** offers a waterside perspective of the harbourfront and the islands. The return trip provides fine **views** of downtown (*departs from York St. late Apr–Jun & Sept–early Nov daily 10am–6pm every hour; Jul–Aug daily 10am–9pm every 30min; round-trip 1hr; commentary; $14.75;* 🅿 *Toronto Harbour Tours ☎416-869-1372*).

★ **Fort York** – *Access by Bathurst streetcar or by car: from Lakeshore Blvd. take Strachan just before Princes' Gate entrance to Exhibition Grounds, then right on Fleet St. and left on Garrison Rd. (under Gardiner Expressway). Open year-round Tue–Sun (phone for hours). Closed Jan 1, Good Friday, Dec 25–26. $5.* ✗ 🅿 *☎416-392-6907.* In stark contrast to the backdrop of Toronto's towering skyline stand the dwarfed remains of this historic garrison. Once strategically positioned on the lake's edge, Fort York was the primary guardian of Toronto's harbour.

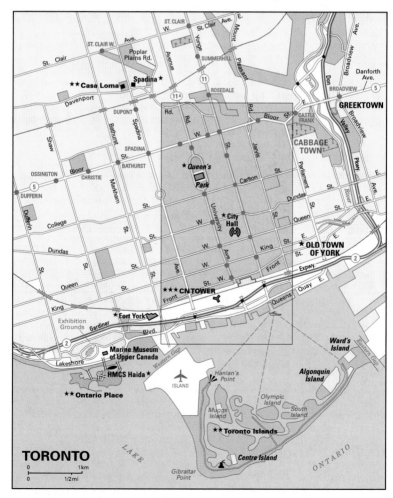

Constructed in 1793, the post was fortified 18 years later when Anglo-American relations soured. Devastated in 1813 during American capture, the fort was rebuilt by the British. As US threats subsided, its military importance diminished. A new fort was constructed to the west after 1841. Renovated for the city's centennial in 1934, this popular tourist attraction celebrated its 200th birthday in 1993.

The wooden blockhouses, powder magazines and barracks, completed in 1815, have been faithfully restored. The **officers' barracks** is furnished to show the lifestyle of senior officers of the period. Canada's military history is revisited in the junior officers' barracks, the only 20C building. Other exhibits include York in 1816 and an illuminated map of Toronto's changing lakeshore. Costumed staff conduct tours and perform demonstrations and, in summer, stage military manoeuvres (*Jul–Aug*).

Marine Museum of Upper Canada – *In Exhibition Grounds. Open year-round Tue–Sun (phone for hours). Closed Jan 1, Good Friday, Dec 25–26. $3.50.* ▣ ☎*416-392-1765.* Housed in barracks of the fort built in 1841, the museum is a tribute to Toronto's waterways and the Great Lakes. There are well-presented displays on navigational aids, shipwrights' tools, warships, whistles, underwater archaeology and other maritime themes.

The 25m/80ft steam tug *Ned Hanlan* stands restored outside the museum (*May–Oct*), one of the last to ply the Great Lakes.

★★ **Ontario Place** – *955 Lakeshore Blvd. West, access from Exhibition Grounds. Open mid-May–early Sept daily 10:30am–midnight. Some attractions close at dusk.* ✕ ▣ ☎*416-314-9900.* Like a space-age lunar base, this innovative, modular-piece leisure complex emerges from an extraordinary setting of lagoons, marinas and man-made islands on the lakefront bordering the Exhibition Grounds. The park's emphasis is on entertainment and leisure activities.

Metallic and fabric structures glorify the geometric shapes of modern technology, a trademark of architect **Eberhard Zeidler** (b.1926). The metal "pods" suspended above the lake enclose children's play areas and a theatre in which 3D films are shown. Resembling a giant golf ball, **Cinesphere** features IMAX films on a screen six storeys high. The **amphitheatre** is a 16,000-seat outdoor performance space used to stage a variety of musical productions. In the **waterplay area**, a series of wading pools full of water jets and games is a popular attraction.

At the large marina, Canadian **HMCS Haida★**, veteran of World War II and the Korean War, can be boarded (*open mid-May–Labour Day daily 10:30am–7pm; early Sept–mid-Oct weekends only 11am–5pm; $1.50;*☎*416-314-9775).*

★ **OLD TOWN OF YORK**   *2hrs. Map p 181.*

In 1793 Lieutenant-Governor Simcoe approved a surveyor's gridiron plan for York—ten city blocks bordered by present-day Front, George, Adelaide and Berkeley Streets. By 1813 Jarvis Street marked the west boundary. The block between Front and King Streets served as a public market.

Although not original to Simcoe's town, some remaining historic structures date from the first half of the 19C, including an active marketplace, the **South St. Lawrence Market** (*91-95 Front St. East at Jarvis St.,* ● *King; open year-round Tue–Thu 8am–6pm, Fri 8am–7pm, Sat 5am–5pm;* ✕ �& ☎*416-392-7219*), a cavernous brick building sheltering a 2-storey food hall. Especially lively on Saturday mornings when early-bird shoppers converge on countless fruit stands, bakeries, meat counters and delicatessens, the market encases the surviving portion of the **Second City Hall** (1845-99), built in 1844. The former second-floor council chamber houses the **Market Gallery** of the City of Toronto Archives, which presents rotating exhibits of historical documents and paraphernalia (*open Wed–Fri 10am–4pm, Sat 9am–4pm, Sun noon–4pm; closed Good Friday, Easter Monday & Dec 15;* & ☎*416-392-7604*). To the west, along Front Street, stands a handsome row of brick and stone 19C commercial buildings.

Directly across the street is **North St. Lawrence Market**, a bustling farmers' market (*open year-round Sat 5am–5pm;* ✕ & ☎*416-392-7219*) housed in a smaller building, where farm-fresh or prepared food is available. From the entrance there is a good view, to the west, of Toronto's **flatiron building**, the Gooderham (1892) on Wellington Street, against a backdrop of the towers of BCE Place (*p 180*).

Adjoining the market via a charming pedestrian mall is the Neoclassical **St. Lawrence Hall** (*King and Jarvis Sts.*), distinguished by its domed cupola. Former site of the city's market and social gatherings, this renovated mid-19C building houses various commercial enterprises.

Flatiron Building

Farther east is Toronto's **First Post Office**★ *(260 Adelaide St. East; open year-round Mon–Fri 9am–4pm, weekends 10am–4pm; closed national holidays;* ☎*416-865-1833)*, formerly York's fourth post office, opened in 1833. Re-created to the period, it operates again, with replicas of the original boxes and a reading room, complete with fireplace, where residents once read their mail. Costumed staff demonstrate quill-and-ink letter-writing.

★★ DOWNTOWN *2 days. Map p 181.*

Containing the city's formidable financial core, Toronto's downtown exudes a sense of momentum and prosperity, exemplified in its soaring skyscrapers and early-20C halls of commerce. Site of the country's leading banks, legal, insurance and brokerage firms, and the Toronto Stock Exchange, the area of King and Bay Streets constitutes Canada's "Wall Street."

By the 1840s growing commerce fostered creation of several banks. Warehouses and offices followed within the next 10 to 20 years. At the time of Confederation *(p 24)*, 11 financial institutions had head offices in Toronto, and another 9 had branches. The desire to appear forward-looking led to successive replacement of these mid-19C stalwarts with newer-styled buildings.

The skyscrapers are connected by an **underground city** of shops, eateries, banks and concourses—a welcome haven in inclement weather. Reputed to be the largest in the world, this subterranean complex extends eight blocks from Union Station and the Royal York Hotel to City Hall, Eaton Centre and on up to Dundas Street. The PATH network of walkways, clearly marked, covers10km/6mi.

One of the best-known and longest roads (1,896km/1,178mi) in Canada is **Yonge Street**, the city's east-west dividing line. Built by Simcoe in 1795 as a military route, this thoroughfare sports fancy boutiques, colourful flower stands, trendy restaurants, inviting bookstores and classy antique shops.

★★ Financial District ● *King or St. Andrew*

A stunning ebony-coloured ensemble covering an entire city block, the **Toronto-Dominion Centre**★★ was the first component of the current financial district. A fine example of International Style, the spartan black-glass towers, known locally as the T-D Centre, reflect the design of eminent 20C architect Mies van der Rohe, consultant for the project. Begun in 1964 the headquarters of the Toronto Dominion Bank consisted originally of three structures; today the towers number five. Fronting Bay Street, the Ernst & Young tower (1992) incorporates the former Art Deco Stock Exchange Building (1937) within its base. On view throughout the centre are works by contemporary artists, predominantly Canadian.

The downtown abounds in other skyscrapers by noted architects, among them, the adjacent **Royal Bank Plaza★ [D]** designed by Boris Zerafa. Completed in 1976 the 41-storey and 26-storey gold, reflecting-glass towers are linked by a 40m/130ft high glass-walled banking hall, entry point to the underground city. A suspended sculpture of 8,000 aluminum tubes, the work of renowned Venezuelan artist Jesus Rafael Soto, dominates the interior of the hall.

The tiered, aquaglass towers of **BCE Place**, designed by Spanish architect Santiago Calatrava, abut a lower central building bisected into matching office wings by an elaborate arched, aluminum **atrium★**. The southernmost tower is topped by a square telecommunications "cross." A 1990s newcomer to the financial district, the complex is the headquarters of Bell Canada Enterprises, and the new home of the **Hockey Hall of Fame★ [E]**, where the Stanley Cup is generally on display in the stately, domed lobby (1886) of the former Bank of Montreal building, which has been preserved and encased within BCE Place *(take the escalator to lower level; open mid-Jun–Labour Day Mon–Sat 9:30am–6pm, Sun 10am–6pm; rest of the year Mon–Fri 10am–5pm, Sat 9:30am–6pm, Sun 10:30am–5pm; closed Jan 1 & Dec 25; $8.75; & ☎416-360-7765).*

Four buildings (1931 to 1972) form **Commerce Court**, an office complex surrounding an outdoor courtyard of trees, benches and a central fountain. The dominant 57-storey stainless-steel tower, head office of the Canadian Imperial Bank of Commerce, was designed by famed architect I. M. Pei.

Opposite Commerce Court, the ruby-coloured **Scotia Plaza** (1988) by Boris Zerafa is a striking addition to Toronto's skyline. At street-level an "erector-set" canopy marks the entrance to the slender 68-storey building, distinguished by a V-shaped wedge in its summit.

First Canadian Place consists of a 72-storey white tower (1975) housing the Bank of Montreal and the 36-storey tower (1983) containing the **Toronto Stock Exchange [F]** *(open year-round Mon–Fri 9am–4pm; 45min presentation by reservation only; & ☎416-947-4676).* Richly coloured wall hangings adorn the white-marbled lobby at the King Street entrance. Connecting the towers is a three-level plaza with elegant shops and an attractive water wall. Under Adelaide Street, the PATH walkway leads to a grouping of shops known as the Lanes and another called the Plaza Shops, which extend to Sheraton Centre.

Designed by Boris Zerafa, the multi-faceted glass towers of **Sun Life Centre★** (1984) frame the east and west sides of University Avenue at King Street. Near the entrance to the 28-storey east tower, an outdoor sculpture by Sorel Etrog suggests a massive wheel-based tool.

★★ **Roy Thomson Hall** – *60 Simcoe St.* ● *St. Andrew. Visit by guided tour (45min) only, year-round Mon–Tue & Thu–Sat 12:30pm. $3. No tours Jan 1, Dec 25–Dec 30. Reservations suggested.* ✗ ☎416-593-4822. Resembling a large inverted bowl, this glass-sheathed concert hall, named for Canadian newspaper magnate Roy Thomson and designed by Arthur Erickson, dominates King and Simcoe Streets. Transparent at night when illuminated, the diamond-shaped exterior panels shimmer in daylight, their blue cast a reflection of the sky.

Opened in 1982, the home of the Toronto Symphony retains its architectural uniqueness and acoustical superiority. To insulate the performance area, a thick circular passageway with entry doors at intervals creates a "sound lock." Fabrics for the seats, carpet and ceiling decorations are designed to enhance acoustics. An illuminated double-ringed *oculus* forms the ceiling's centrepiece, while a shower of suspended metal "raindrops" lights the stage below. Woven, tubular hanging banners can be raised or lowered to achieve desired resonance.

On Front Street, south of Roy Thomson Hall, the concrete box-shaped **Canadian Broadcasting Centre** sports a red and white grid-patterned exterior, interrupted at intervals by glass geometric-shaped components. Illustrative of the Deconstructivist style, this 10-storey building was constructed in 1992 and designed by noted architect Philip Johnson.

★ **City Hall Area** ● *Osgoode or Queen*

City Hall★, with its crescent-shaped towers and mushroom-like council chamber, has been the symbol of Toronto since completion in 1965. Today, its former glamour somewhat diminished, the internationally acclaimed masterpiece by Finland's **Viljo Revell** remains a landmark nevertheless.

Unequal in height, the towers are clad in concrete on one side, windows on the other. They rise from a 2-storey podium, as does the "stem"of the mushroom, the only support for the council chamber at the summit. Spacious **Nathan Phillips**

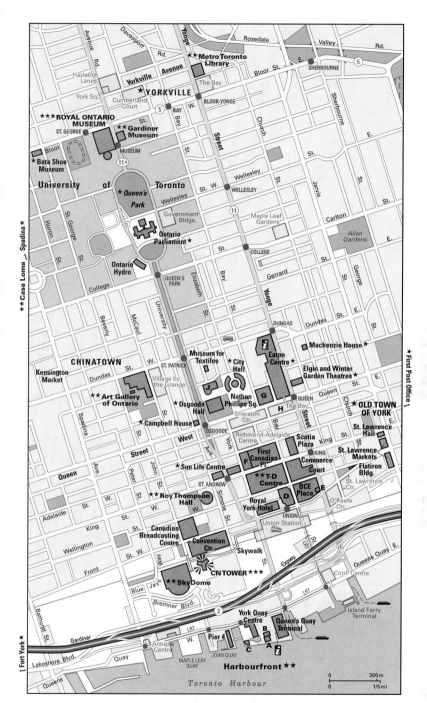

Square (named for a former mayor) with its wide, arch-covered reflecting pool attracts crowds of ice skaters in winter. Henry Moore's outdoor bronze sculpture, *The Archer*, was the precursor for the sizeable collection of his pieces in Toronto's Art Gallery of Ontario.

Occupying the east side of the square, **Old City Hall★ [G]**, designed by Toronto-born **Edward J. Lennox** (1855-1933), houses the provincial courts. Dominated by its clock tower, the massive Richardsonian Romanesque exterior of this previous home (1899-1965) of the city fathers conceals an ornate interior of patterned-tile floors and copper-painted capitals atop marble columns. Backing the grand iron staircase is a large stained-glass window with scenes symbolizing the city's growth.

Extending several blocks on Yonge Street between Queen and Dundas Streets is **Eaton Centre★** (● *Queen; open year-round Mon–Fri 10am–9pm, Sat 9:30am–6pm, Sun noon–5pm;* ✕ ⛊ 🄿 ☎*416-598-8700),* a five-level office/shopping complex with over 300 stores. Designed by Eberhard Zeidler the megastructure, with its trees, plants, fountains and natural lighting, was a novel approach to shopping mall construction when it opened in 1977.

Longtime retailer, the Hudson's Bay Company ("The Bay"), can be reached by a covered walkway across Queen Street.

The Thomson Gallery [H],*– 9th floor of The Bay department store at 176 Yonge St.* ● *Queen. Open year-round Mon–Sat 11am–5pm. Closed national holidays. $2.* ✕ ⛊ 🄿 ☎*416-861-4571.* A portion of the ninth floor of The Bay has been transformed into a showplace for Toronto businessman Ken Thomson's fine collection of Canadian art. The larger **20C gallery★** features important paintings by the **Group of Seven**, while works by 19C artists such as Cornelius Krieghoff are displayed in the adjacent gallery.

★ **Elgin and Winter Garden Theatres** – *189 Yonge St., opposite Eaton Centre north of Queen St.* ● *Queen. Visit by guided tour (1hr 30min) only, year-round Thu 5pm & Sat 11am. $4.* ✕ ☎*416-363-5353.* Reopened in 1989 after extensive restoration, this splendid structure houses one of the few remaining double-decker theatres in the world. Designed by Thomas Lamb, the 1,500-seat Elgin and 1,000-seat Winter Garden opened in 1913 and 1914 respectively as vaudeville, and later, silent film houses. The Winter Garden closed in 1928; the Elgin became a movie palace.

The plush amphitheatre of the Elgin, with its ornate box seats and gold-patterned ceiling, is reached through a gilded lobby of Corinthian pilasters and arched mirrors. A 7-storey marble staircase leads to the fanciful Winter Garden, with its unique ceiling of hanging beech boughs. Original *olios* ("hand-painted scenic drops") are on display.

★ **Mackenzie House** – *82 Bond St.* ● *Dundas. Visit by guided tour (30min) only, year-round Tue–Sun (phone for hours). Closed Jan 1, Good Friday, Dec 25–26. $3.50.* ☎*416-392-6915.* This 19C brick row house, with its four chimneys and single dormer, was the last home of William Lyon Mackenzie. Friends purchased the house in 1859 for the publisher-turned-politician, who resided there until his death. Rooms on the three floors have been restored to the 1850 period. In the kitchen visitors can sample baked goods based on 19C recipes and baked in the cast-iron oven. In the modern annex at the rear, a small display chronicles Mackenzie's life and times, and a replica of his **print shop** includes a hand-operated flatbed press on which his newspapers were printed *(demonstrations).*

★ **Osgoode Hall** – *130 Queen St. West.* ● *Osgoode. Quiet is necessary, since courts may be in session. Open year-round Mon–Fri 9am–5pm. Guided tours Jul–Aug Mon–Fri 1:15pm.* ☎*416-947-3300.* Home of the Supreme Court of Ontario and the Law Society of Upper Canada, this stately Neoclassical edifice graces expansive lawns west of Nathan Phillips Square. Erected in 1867 allegedly to keep cows out, an ornate cast-iron fence isolates the judicial bastion from the bustle of the city.

Begun in 1829 the hall consisted of only the east wing. Damaged by troops quartered there after Mackenzie's rebellion, the building was upgraded in 1844. The central pavilion and west wing were added, and the facade and interior were altered. Until as late as 1991, sporadic changes continued.

Enclosed by a rectangular stained-glass roof, the two-tiered arched interior courtyard induces admiration, as does the magnificent **Great Library**—said to be "perhaps the noblest room in Canada." Supported by rows of Corinthian columns, a 12m/40ft vaulted ceiling, richly adorned with intricate plaster work, crowns its interior.

North of Osgoode Hall stands the Metro Toronto **Court House [J]**, with its circular rotunda and walkway to Nathan Phillips Square.

★ **Campbell House** – *University Ave. at Queen St.* ● *Osgoode. Visit by guided tour (30min) only, year-round Mon–Fri (and weekends late May–mid-Oct); phone for hours. Closed Jan 1, Dec 25–26. $3.50.* ☎*416-597-0227.* Once belonging to **Sir William Campbell** (1758-1834), Chief Justice of Upper Canada from 1825 to 1829, the Georgian brick mansion was moved to this site in 1972 from its location in historic York. As it had been in the old town, the house is only a short walk from the city's courthouse. The restored rooms contain some fine period pieces and surviving portraits of the Campbell family. On the second floor, a model of York of 1825 can be seen. The property once belonged to the Canada Life Assurance Co., whose headquarters rises just behind Campbell House. A prominent landmark, the building is distinguished at night by its tower, the lights of which indicate the barometer reading.

★★ **Art Gallery of Ontario** – *317 Dundas St. West. ● St. Patrick. Open mid-May–mid-Oct Tue–Sun 10am-5:30pm (Wed 10pm). Rest of the year Wed–Sun 10am–5:30pm (Wed 10pm). $7.50 (free Wed 5–10pm).* ✗ ♿ ☎*416-979-6648.* Occupying nearly a city block, this low-rise, brick and concrete building with its distinctive metal tower retains the world's largest public collection of works by renowned British sculptor **Henry Moore** (1898-1986). The permanent collection ranges from 15C European paintings to international contemporary art, and includes Canadian art from 18C to the present. Tastefully incorporated into the complex is a historic 19C mansion, the Grange—original home of the Art Gallery of Ontario (AGO).

Established in 1900 as the Art Museum of Toronto, the gallery was permanently housed in the Grange by 1911. Adjacent quarters were constructed in 1918 and enlarged twice in less than 50 years. As its scope expanded, the publicly support-

Malak, Ottawa

Henry Moore Sculpture, Art Gallery of Toronto

ed institution underwent name changes. Modified in 1919, the Art Gallery of Toronto adopted its provincial status in 1966. After visiting Toronto to see his work in situ at the new City Hall, Moore announced, in 1968, his momentous gift to the gallery of over 150 of his works. He returned in 1974 to officially open the new sculpture centre named in his honour.

Extensively renovated with additions in 1977, and again, beginning 12 years later, the AGO now possesses a permanent collection of over 16,000 pieces. The new and renovated galleries, opened in 1993, increased exhibit space by 50 percent.

★★ **Henry Moore Sculpture Centre** – The centre owns over 1,000 of Moore's works, including 689 prints, 139 original plasters and bronzes and 74 drawings. Many were donated by the artist when he learned that the AGO intended to devote a gallery to him. Occupying a spacious room on the upper level, the centre was designed by the artist to use natural light from the glass-panelled roof. More than 20 massive forms—all plaster casts or original plasters for some of Moore's famous bronzes—electrify this spartan space. At night, the effect of artificial lighting, with its interplay of shadows on these sculpted shapes, is stunning. Selected smaller bronzes and miniature maquettes are on display in the entryway.

★★ **The Permanent Collection** – *Street level. Selections change regularly; not all of these works may be seen at one time.* Housed in galleries around Walker Court, the **European Collection** covers the Old Masters, Impressionism and early-20C movements. Highlights include works by Peter Brueghel the Younger, Rembrandt, Franz Hals,

Renoir, Degas, Monet, Sisley, Gauguin, Matisse, Picasso, Bonnard, Chagall and Dufy. Displayed in several galleries, the **Canadian Collection** features 18C to contemporary works. Early Quebec artists are represented along with Cornelius Krieghoff, Tom Thomson (*The West Wind*) and the Group of Seven, Emily Carr, David Milne and Paul Peel, to name a few.

Contemporary **Inuit art** on exhibit *(upper level)* dates from 1948 to the present. Carved in ivory, whalebone, gray stone or mottled greenstone, the sculpture (mostly miniatures) depicts native animals or Inuit people. Large fabric hangings of embroidery and felt, as well as prints (stonecuts and stencil on paper) complete the collection.

Contemporary art and 20C art are displayed in galleries on both levels.

★ **The Grange** – *Entrance through Art Gallery. Open mid-May–mid-Oct Tue–Sun noon–4pm (Wed 9pm). Rest of the year Wed–Sun noon–4pm (Wed 9pm).* This Georgian brick mansion (c.1817) once stood on a 41ha/100 acre site reaching from Queen to Bloor Streets. Socio-political life in Upper Canada during Family Compact days revolved around the residence of the Boulton family, Loyalists from New England who became leaders in the oligarchy.

Lawyer and politician **Henry John Boulton** (1790-1870) was largely responsible for four of the five expulsions of William Lyon Mackenzie from the legislature. In 1875 The Grange became the home of a well-known scholar, **Goldwin Smith**, Regius Professor of History at Oxford, who made it a centre of intellectual pursuits and progressive ideas. After Smith's death in 1911, his widow bequeathed the house to the Art Gallery of Toronto.

Restored to its mid-19C appearance in 1973, the mansion is meticulously furnished to give the aura of Family Compact days. Although few pieces are original to the home, much of the furniture is from the Georgian and Regency periods. All three floors are open to visitors. Of special interest is the beautiful, curved staircase in the entry hall. The basement contains kitchens typical of a 19C gentleman's house.

The residence faces lovely Grange Park, from which visitors can appreciate the mansion's gracious facade. The present entrance portico is a stone version of the original wooden one.

Museum for Textiles – *55 Centre Ave.* ● *St.Patrick. Open year-round Tue–Fri 11am–5pm (Wed 8pm), weekends noon–5pm. Closed national holidays. $5 (Wed 5–8pm by contribution).* ♿ 🅿 ☎416-599-5515. Occupying two floors of a high-rise hotel/condominium complex, the only Canadian museum devoted exclusively to the study, collection and display of textiles features traditional and contemporary works from around the world. The permanent collection of 7,000 pieces is presented alongside loaned works, on a rotating basis, in a series of temporary exhibits.

★ **QUEEN'S PARK**   *2hrs. Map p 181.*

Based on E. J. Lennox's landscape scheme of 1876, this oval-shaped park in the heart of Toronto is the setting for Ontario's Parliament and nearby government buildings. To the west and east sprawls the **University of Toronto**, Canada's largest institute of higher education, perhaps best known for its medical school where, in 1921, **Frederick Banting** and **Charles Best** succeeded in isolating insulin. To the south, the curved, mirrored, multistoried headquarters of **Ontario Hydro** (1975, Kenneth R. Cooper) rises above the surroundings. Inside, energy radiated by artificial lighting, equipment and people is stored in basement thermal reservoirs to be recirculated throughout the building, which has no furnace or heating plant.

★ **Ontario Parliament** – ● *Queen's Park. Open mid-May–Labour Day daily 9am–5pm. Rest of the year Mon–Fri 9am–5pm.* ✗ ♿ ☎416-325-7500. Dominating the south end of the park, the imposing sandstone **Legislative Building** typifies the solidity and mass of Richardsonian Romanesque architecture. Also called the Parliament Buildings, this seat of provincial government opened in 1893 after a controversial six-year, million dollar construction. The focus of the dispute, American-based architect **Richard Waite** (1846-1911), had awarded himself the project after serving as a judge in a fizzled design competition.

The ponderous exterior belies the interior's elegant beauty, particularly the white-marbled **west wing**, rebuilt after a fire in 1909, and the stately **legislative chamber** with its rich mahogany and sycamore. On view is the 200-year-old mace (*ground floor*), a ceremonial gold "club" mandatory at House proceedings. Taken by the Americans during their 1813 assault on York, it was returned years later by President F. D. Roosevelt.

★★★ ROYAL ONTARIO MUSEUM

Renowned for extensive research, this enormous museum consists of the H-shaped, five-floor main building at Avenue Road and Bloor Street —commonly referred to as the ROM—and the separately housed Gardiner Museum of Ceramic Art. Maintaining over 20 departments in art, archaeology and the natural sciences, the museum, known especially for its East Asian holdings, possesses a remarkable collection of six-million-plus artifacts and artworks from around the world.

In the early 1900s Toronto banker Sir Byron E. Walker campaigned to start a public museum. United in effort was archaeologist **Charles Trick Currelly**, whose world travels provided the first treasures for a collection. In 1912 the Ontario Legislature passed the ROM Act, and in 1914 the museum first opened as part of the University of Toronto. Independent by 1968, the ROM became a separate body under the provincial government. Officially reopened in 1982 after an ambitious four-year, $55 million expansion, the ROM remains one of the country's leading museums, attracting visitors and scholars worldwide.

Visit *Allow 1/2 day*

Main Building – *Open year-round Mon–Sat 10am–6pm (Tue 8pm), Sun 11am–6pm. Closed Jan 1 & Dec 25. $8. ⚒ ⚙ ☎416-586-8000. The ROM continues to open new galleries; some sections may be temporarily closed. The museum's floor plan, available at the information desk in the entrance rotunda or near the "Mankind Discovering" exhibit, is especially useful.*

Ground Floor – The grand entrance **rotunda** is vaulted, with an exquisite domed **ceiling** of golden mosaic *tessarae*—tiny squares of imported Venetian glass. The marble in the floor, with its radiant sun pattern, was extracted from an Ontario quarry. Before entering the galleries, note the two **totem poles** in the stairwells. Crafted of red cedar by the Nisgaas and Haida peoples of British Columbia in the second half of the 19C, the poles are so tall that their upper sections can be viewed from the second and third floors. The taller pole, 25m/81ft in height, depicts the family history of the chief who owned it.

The small centrepiece exhibit, **Mankind Discovering**, offers an excellent overview of the museum's research activities, illustrating through photos, documents, artifacts and equipment, the scientific process of artifact collecting.

The outstanding exhibit on this floor is the **Chinese collection★★★**, one of the largest and most important of its kind outside China. Spanning nearly 6,000 years, the exhibits range from the Shang dynasty 1523 BC (the Chinese Bronze Age) to the overthrow of the Qing or Manchu dynasty (1644-1911) and the setting up of the Republic in 1912. Artifacts were gathered mainly by **George Crofts**, a fur merchant who lived in Tientsin and, after his death in 1925, **William C. White**, Anglican Bishop of Honan. Assisted by Dr. Currelly, these men procured Chinese works of art when such pieces were little known to the Western world. Later in 1960, the museum acquired the coveted treasures of **Dr. James Menzies**, a missionary-scholar who lived in China for many years.

Royal Ontario Museum

Ming Tomb

The collection is noted for its clay **tomb figures**, small replicas of people and animals buried with the dead as their "servants," and dating from the 3C AD. The star attraction, however, is the **Ming Tomb**, the only complete example in the Western world. Within the archways, larger-than-life statues of animals and humans guard the "spirit way" to the tumulus, or mound, that marked the position of the subterranean chamber containing the coffin. This tomb is reportedly the burial place of Zu Dashou, a 17C general who served the last Ming emperors and lived into the Qing period.

A series of interconnected galleries is devoted to **Later Imperial China** (10-19C). Traditional room settings, a life-size Chinese courtyard and a moon gate re-create the life of the gentry during the Ming (1368-1644) and Qing dynasties. Ceramics pieces, including the ROM's famous Ming porcelain, are also on display.

Remarkable for its ink and colour clay wall paintings, the **Bishop White Gallery** simulates the interior of a Northern Chinese temple. Flanked by two Daoist frescoes from Shanxi province with a probable date of 1325, the largest painting —"The Paradise of Maitreya"—is Buddhist, c.1298. Life-size polychromed and gilded statues of *bodhisattvas* (those enlightened, compassionate individuals destined for Buddha status) of 12-14C stand in the centre.

Gems and minerals, some very large in size, can be seen off the Southwest Atrium.

Second Floor – Natural history exhibits occupy this floor, the highlight of which are the magnificent, reassembled **dinosaurs** in authentic settings. Many of these skeletons come from upper cretaceous rocks exposed in the badlands of the Red Deer River Valley in central Alberta, one of the richest collecting sites in the world. The glass atrium of the **Bird Gallery** is filled with Canadian geese, turkeys, owls, ducks, and an assortment of smaller birds, preserved in flight. A somewhat eery, sensory, sound and light experience is a walk through the **Bat Cave**, a lifelike reconstruction of the St. Clair Cave in Jamaica, complete with hundreds of hand-made bats.

Favourites from the ROM's possessions such as ceremonial headdresses, West African masks, Japanese ceramics, manuscripts and furniture are featured in **From the Collections**.

Third Floor – Interlinked galleries present a fascinating look at civilization around the Mediterranean basin in Egypt, the Classical World and the Near East. Opened in 1992 the **Ancient Egypt★** exhibit depicts **daily life** via tools, utensils, jewellery and miniature figures. The section on **religion** includes coffins, animal mummies and canopic jars, the remarkably preserved **Antjau mummy** and the upright **mummy case** of a female musician. A chronological survey from predynastic times to the Ptolemaic period is featured on the **history wall**. The **Punt wall reliefs★**, sculptural casts from the temple of Queen Hatshepsut (1503-1482 BC), illustrate her trade mission along the Nile. The exhibit on **Nubia**—a region south of the Sahara in present-day Lower Egypt and Northern Sudan whose early cultures date to 4500 BC—features pottery, glassware, arms and jewellery from 2000 BC to the 19C.

Classic forms of marble sculpture, gold coins, decorated amphora and a model of the Acropolis are displayed in the **Greeks and Etruscans Gallery** (1100-100 BC) while the **Islamic** section reproduces a life-size Middle East house and bazaar.

The **Samuel European Galleries★** are devoted to decorative arts from medieval times to the present. Note the elaborately carved coconut cups with their decorative silver mounts from the **Lee Collection**, exquisite medieval and Renaissance wares of gold and silver. In the **Arms and Armour** gallery, armaments from medieval chain mail to modern-day weaponry can be examined. Judaica, metalwork (1300 to the present), glass, and ceramics are given separate sections. **Costume and Textiles** is a well-organized exhibit featuring Victorian women's clothing. **Culture and Context** presents partial-room reconstructions, such as a Victorian parlour (1860-85). Art objects and furnishings from medieval times to the 20C are displayed in the South Wing, which was opened in 1994.

Lower Level – In the **Ontario Archaeology Gallery**, human-scale dioramas capture the life of the early Algonquin and Iroquoian peoples. Reproductions of limestone petroglyphs and a large mural of red-ochre rock paintings can also be seen.

The **Sigmund Samuel Canadiana Gallery** presents paintings and decorative arts from the late 17C to the early 20C, reflecting, for the most part, Canada's French and British cultural heritage. Note in particular the panelled room from the Bélanger House c.1820.

The **Discovery Gallery** (*2nd level below; open Jul–Aug Mon–Fri 11am–4pm, Tue 7:30pm, weekends 1–5pm; Sept–Dec Mon–Fri noon–5pm, weekends 1–5pm; Jan–Jun daily noon–5pm*) is a "hands-on" room where visitors can examine a dinosaur bone, inspect a Ming vase or don a medieval helmet, among other activities.

★★ **Gardiner Museum of Ceramic Art** – *111 Queen's Park across from ROM main building. Open year-round Tue–Sat 10am–5pm, Sun 11am–5pm. Closed Jan 1 & Dec 25. Admission included in ROM fee.* ✗ ♿ ☎416-586-8080. Located in a modern granite building, this museum, the project of collectors George and Helen Gardiner, features pottery and porcelain from a variety of countries and cultures.

The Pottery Gallery *(ground floor)* showcases **pre-Columbian** works from Mexico, and Central and South America dating from 2000 BC to about AD 1500—primarily figurines, vessels and bowls of Olmec, Toltec, Aztec and other cultures. The orange Mayan pottery and *plumbate* (fired with silica glaze) vases are especially noteworthy. Made in Italy in the 15C and 16C, **Italian maiolica** is colourful tin-glazed earthenware. Blues, greens and bright yellows dominate the exhibited pieces, mostly large plates with intricate designs and religious scenes. Tin-glazed earthenware made in England in the 17C became known as **delftware**, probably because of its similiarity to wares from the Dutch town of Delft. Note the chargers or large plates with an English monarch painted on each. A gallery for temporary exhibits is also housed on the ground floor.

The Porcelain Gallery *(2nd floor)* features **18C porcelains** of Du Paquier, Sèvres (characterized by bright yellows), the great English companies—Worcester, Derby, Chelsea—and others. Highlights are the Meissenware pieces, in particular, the large tea service (c.1745) in a fitted leather travel case, and the *commedia dell' arte* figures *(in the centre of the gallery)* crafted throughout Europe after this 16C form of improvised theatre spread from Italy. There is also an assemblage of tiny, exquisite scent bottles (1715-65) made primarily in England and in Germany.

ADDITIONAL SIGHTS *Maps pp 177 and 181*

★ **Bata Shoe Museum** – *327 Bloor St.* ● *St. George. Open year-round Tue–Sat 10am–5pm (Thu 8pm), Sun noon–5pm. $6.* ♿ ☎416-979-7799. Housed in a 5-storey building designed by renowned architect **Raymond Moriyama** to resemble a shoebox, this unique museum draws on its 10,000 piece collection to illustrate a 4,500-year history of mankind's footwear. Shoes in the permanent exhibit range from 3,550-year-old Theban funerary slippers and 1,500-year-old Anasazi sandals to singer Elton John's platform shoes. Changing exhibits are shown on two floors.

★ **Yorkville** – ● *Bay.* Once the hangout of drug addicts and dropouts, Yorkville today represents all that is chic in Toronto—and a remarkable transformation. Between Yonge Street and Avenue Road, **Yorkville Avenue** presents charming Victorian houses converted to expensive boutiques or trendy cafes sporting the latest architectural facades.

In York Square at the corner of Avenue Road and Yorkville Avenue, shops surround an interior brick courtyard where summer dining is *al fresco*. Behind the square, on University Avenue, lies posh Hazelton Lanes *(open during business hours)*, a labyrinthian shopping/office/condominium complex designed by Boris Zerafa (1978). On the other side of Yorkville Avenue, Cumberland Court is a rambling enclosure of old and new shops, eateries and offices, with a passageway to Cumberland Street.

★★ **Metro Toronto Library** – *789 Yonge St.* ● *Bloor-Yonge. Open May–mid-Oct Mon–Thu 10am–8pm, Fri–Sat 10am–5pm. Rest of the year Mon–Thu 10am–8pm, Fri–Sat 10am–5pm, Sun 1:30–5pm.* ♿ ☎416-393-7131. An architectural gem designed by Raymond Moriyama, this massive brick and glass building contains Canada's most extensive public library. The 5-storey structure, completed for $30 million in 1977, contains nearly 1.5 million volumes.

Rising from a wide, light-filled centre, the tiered balconies are bordered by solid undulating balustrades. Special baffles in the ceiling reduce sound to a minimum. The Gallery on the main floor regularly showcases materials, often rare, from the library's collections.

In a cozy corner on the fifth floor is a tiny room *(access from 4th floor)* brimming with the **Arthur Conan Doyle Collection**—famed Sherlock Holmes stories, Sherlockian criticism, Doyle's autobiography, historical novels, poetry and other writings. Worn Victorian furnishings complement mementos of the great detective's presence, felt chiefly in his pipes, a slipper and the inevitable deerstalker on the hat rack *(Sat 2–4pm & by appointment)*.

★★ **Casa Loma** – *2 hrs (including gardens). 1 Austin Terrace;* ● *Dupont, then climb steps. Open daily 10am–4pm. Closed Jan 1 & Dec 25. $8.* ✗ 🅿 ☎416-923-1171. This enormous sandstone castle, completed in 1914, was the lavish 98-room residence of prominent industrialist **Sir Henry Pellatt**. Maintained since 1937 by the Kiwanis Club, the medieval mansion is a popular tourist attraction.

Casa Loma's creator amassed a fortune from hydro-electric exploitation of Niagara Falls. Edward J. Lennox combined sketches of castles Pellatt drew as a youth during world travels to design a home to the owner's liking. Three years and $3.5 million later, the interior was still not finished; nevertheless, in 1914 the Pellatts moved in, staying less than 10 years. High upkeep plus a reversal in Sir Henry's enterprises led to his losing Casa Loma to the City of Toronto for back taxes.

The "house on the hill," as its Spanish name translates, stands on the crest of Davenport Ridge—the edge of glacial Lake Iroquois, which existed after the last Ice Age. Seven storeys in height, the castle boasts two towers—one open-aired, the other enclosed—which offer good views of the city; secret passageways; and a 244m/800ft underground tunnel to the magnificent **carriage house** and stables. The palatial residence includes 21 fireplaces, a **great hall** (22m/70ft ceiling), a marble-floor **conservatory**, an oak-panelled drawing room, and a **library** for 10,000 books. Especially well-appointed are the **Round Room★** with its exquisite Louis XV tapestry furnishings, the **Windsor Room** and **Lady Pellatt's suite**. Awash in conveniences uncommon to pre–World War I homes, the estate features an unfinished indoor swimming pool, 52 telephones, an elevator, a pipe organ and concealed steampipes.

★ **Spadina** – *285 Spadina Rd.* ● *Dupont, then climb steps. Visit by guided tour (45min) only, year-round Tue–Sun (phone for hours). Closed Jan 1, Good Friday, Dec 25–26. $5.* ⅅ ☎*416-392-6910.* Built on a former 32ha/80 acre hillside estate outside mid-19C Toronto, Spadina overlooks its remaining 2.5ha/6 acre grounds amid a fashionable residential district. The 50-room brick mansion was home to businessman **James Austin** and his heirs, who adapted the structure to prevailing architectural styles and family size.

In 1866 Austin acquired the estate, replacing the existing 1836 dwelling with a new Georgian-styled house. His successful grocery store business had enabled him to become a major shareholder in, and eventually head of (1874-97), the Consumers' Gas Co. He later founded Dominion Bank, incorporated 1869, serving as its first president. Austin's son added the spacious billiard room in 1898, and in 1907, added the terraces and porte-cochere. The third floor, with its hipped roof and pedimented dormers, was built in 1912.

Reflecting the grandeur of Victorian and Edwardian styles, the spacious **drawing room** with its matching striped seating, and the airy wicker-furnished **palm room** show the comforts the Austin family expected.

METRO SIGHTS   *Map p 189*

★★★ **Ontario Science Centre** – *1/2 day. 770 Don Mills Rd., 11km/7mi from downtown (22km/14mi by car via Don Valley Pkwy. to Eglinton Ave.);* ● *Don Mills or Eglinton bus E. Open year-round daily 10am–6pm. Closed Dec 25. $7.50.* ⅏ⅅ🅿 ☎*416-696-3127. Demonstrations and shows daily. For times and locations, check notice board at the bottom of escalator, level C.* Cascading down Don River ravine, this sizeable complex takes full advantage of its natural site. Raymond Moriyama designed a series of concrete and glass buildings on different levels connected by enclosed escalators. Opened in 1969 this popular attraction consists largely of interactive exhibits on science and technology.

Visitors learn, for example, by pushing buttons, rotating cranks, pedalling bicycles and turning wheels. Chemistry, printing, electricity and laser demonstrations, to name a few, provide another means of education.

The five levels are designated by letters, levels C, D and E being the exhibit/activity floors. Level C's **Earth/Food** section has a 5m/15ft high stack of grocery-filled shopping carts to illustrate "Food for a Year," while **Space** includes a rocket chair, hydroponics, supergravity and other exhibits. Highlights of level D are the new **Living Earth** exhibit, where visitors explore a limestone cave and experience a rain forest; the **Hall of Transportation** with its ascending model hot-air balloon, CA-3 powerboat and old-fashioned bicycles; the **Science Arcade** with humourous electricity demonstrations; and **Communications**, where visitors can participate in papermaking. The **Hall of Technology** features, among other displays, life-size and model cantilever bridges for observing the effects of strain, and most recently, an "Information Highway" exhibit where visitors can access the Internet.

★★★ **Metro Toronto Zoo** – *1/2 day. 35km/22mi from downtown.* ● *Kennedy, transfer to bus 86A. Open Apr–early May daily 9:30am–5:30pm. Mid-May–Labour Day daily 9am–7:30pm. Early Sept–Mar daily 9:30am–4:30pm. Closed Dec 25. $10.* ⅏ⅅ🅿 ☎*416-392-5900. A useful site map is available at the entrance gate. In summer it is* *recommended that visitors begin by boarding the narrated shuttle, the zoomobile (daily mid-May–Labour Day; $2.50), which provides an excellent overview of principal attractions. Disembark at the Serengeti station and continue the visit on foot.* Opened in 1974 this world-class zoological park features a remarkable variety of wildlife on 287ha/710 acres of tableland and forest. The 5,000 animals are divided into six "zoogeographic" regions: Africa, Australasia, Eurasia, the Americas, Indo-Malaya and Canada. Among the 550 species represented are numerous endangered or rare animals such as the Siberian tiger, the snow leopard, the Malayan tapir, the pygmy hippopotamus and the Indian rhinoceros. Designed by Raymond Moriyama, harmoniously integrated glass and wood pavilions provide shelter for animals unadapted to Canada's climate.

The popular **Africa Pavilion**, abundant with tropical vegetation and exotic birds, is home to lowland gorillas, mandrills and other primates. Nearby resides Canada's largest herd of African elephants. The smaller Indo-Malayan and the Americas pavilions should not be overlooked. The **Edge of Night** exhibit *(in the Australasia Pavilion)* provides a journey into a nocturnal world inhabited by seldom-seen species like the Tasmanian devil.

★★ **Black Creek Pioneer Village** – *2.5hrs. In North York, 29km/18mi northwest of downtown. 1000 Murray Ross Parkway.* ● *Yonge and Finch, transfer to Steeles bus 60. Open May–Dec daily 10am–5pm. Closed Dec 25. $7.50* ✗ 🅿 ☎*416-736-1733. Site plan is distributed at the entrance.* This 12ha/30 acre re-created farming community evokes the traditions and architecture of Ontario's rural past. Opened in 1960 the village comprises 40 buildings, including 5 from the original farm established between 1816 and 1832 by Pennsylvania-German settlers, and a collection of 19C structures moved to the site.

Upon exiting the modern structure housing the **orientation centre**, visitors enter mid-19C Ontario. Set among abundant greenery and dirt roads flanked by wooden sidewalks and split-rail fences, the ensemble exudes a bygone-era charm, marred only by the din of the nearby freeway and the sight of neighbouring high rises above the trees. The restored buildings are appointed with furnishings characteristic of the 1860s. Highlights include: the tinsmith shop; the **Stong farm**; the Half Way House, a spacious white inn with a two-tiered veranda; **Roblin's Mill**, a handsome 4-storey stone, water-powered gristmill; and the printing office, complete with a working flatbed press. Costumed guides demonstrate traditional 19C crafts and trades.

Scarborough – Canada's seventh largest city, this sprawling urban centre with its sizeable Asian population has seen rapid growth in the last 10 years. Named by Lieutenant-Governor Simcoe's wife, who kept a diary of their life in early York, it is known for picturesque cliffs along Lake Ontario, which reminded her of the town in Yorkshire, England.

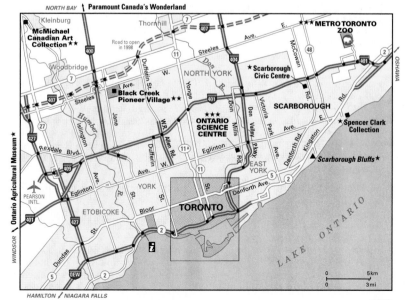

★ **Scarborough Civic Centre** – *35km/ 22mi from downtown Toronto. 150 Borough Dr., south of Hwy. 401 at McCowan Rd. Open year-round daily 8:30am–10pm. Closed Dec 25. Guided tours available.* ✗ ⟨ 🅿 ☎*416-396-7216.* One of the area's first civic show-places, the gleaming white concrete and glass complex, designed by Raymond Moriyama, was opened in 1973 by Queen Elizabeth II.

The interior is airy, filled with natural light from a central open shaft rising five storeys. Plant-bedecked balconies curve around in tiers that contain the office space. The council chamber is underground—the architect's solution to the necessity of constructing a large room without sacrificing structural lines.

Separating the centre from an adjacent shopping plaza is Albert Campbell Square. Located outdoors the square accommodates concerts and other activities in summer, and ice-skating in winter.

★ **Scarborough Bluffs** – Easily Toronto's most dramatic geographical feature, these buff-coloured cliffs, sprouting finger-like hoodoos *(p 00)*, protrude into Lake Ontario for about 16km/10mi along its shoreline. The focus of much interest from scientists around the world, the bluffs contain layers of fossil-rich sand and clay—a unique geological record in North America of the final stages of the great Ice Age.

The **Scarborough Bluffs Park** *(from Kingston Rd. South, turn left on Midland Ave., then immediate left onto Kelsonia and right onto Scarborough Crescent; at end, park on Drake Crescent; open daily year-round)* offers good **views★** of the high sand structures branching out from the cliffs, the vast lake and Bluffers Park below.

Bluffers Park – *Return to Kingston Rd. and travel east to Brimley Rd.; turn right and follow to the end. Open daily year-round.* The road descends the cliffs, emerging onto an artificial peninsula that has been constructed to protect the bluffs. This is a pleasant park on the lake with a marina.

★ **Spencer Clark Collection of Historic Architecture** – *On grounds of Guild Inn, 201 Guildwood Parkway off Kingston Rd. Open daily year-round.* ✗ ⟨ 🅿 ☎*416-261-3331.* This unusual sculpture park contains architectural features from about 60 demolished Toronto buildings. The collection was the idea of Rosa and Spencer Clark, who founded a haven for artists called "The Guild of All Arts" on this site in 1932. Among the most striking artifacts on view are the Corinthian columns and capitals of the Bank of Toronto (demolished 1966), which have been assembled to form a Greek theatre, and the white marble facade of the Imperial Bank of Canada (demolished 1972). Modern sculpture works, many by Guild members, adorn the grounds.

EXCURSIONS *Map p 189*

★ **Ontario Agricultural Museum** – *5km/3mi west of Milton. Exit Hwy. 401 at Hwy. 25. Travel north on Hwy. 25 to Campbellville Rd.; turn left. After 3km/1.9 mi, turn left onto Town Line. 144 Town Line Rd. Open late May–Sept daily 10am–5pm. $4.50.* ✗ ⟨ ☎*905-878-8151.* This collection of period homes, barns and museum buildings portrays the evolution of Ontario agriculture from early settlement to the 20C. Featured are vehicles of transport, agricultural equipment, farmsteads of different eras and displays on the province's agri-food industry. A crossroads community with a forge, harness shop, carriage works, shingle mill and a rare octagonal barn of the 1890s has been re-created.

Paramount Canada's Wonderland – *In Vaughan, 30km/19mi north by Hwy. 400 and Rutherford Rd. 9580 Jane St. GO TRANSIT from* ● *Yorkdale or York Mills* ☎*416-869-3200. Open mid-May–Labour Day daily 10am–10pm. Early Sept–mid-Oct weekends only 10am–8pm. $30.95.* ✗ ⟨ ☎*905-832-7000.* This theme park opened in 1981 and features areas such as International Street, Medieval Faire, Grande World Exposition of 1890 and Hanna Barbera Land. Visitors can climb a man-made mountain, enjoy the outdoor wave pool and experience a variety of rides and shows.

★★ **McMichael Canadian Art Collection** – *In Kleinburg, approximately 40km/25mi north. Hwy. 400 to Major Mackenzie Dr., then west about 6km/4mi to Islington Ave., then north 1km/.6mi. Special buses from Bay & Dundas Sts. and* ● *Yorkdale; Penetang-Midland Coach Lines* ☎*416-777-9510. Open mid-May–mid-Oct daily 10am–5pm. Rest of the year Tue–Sun 10am–4pm (Sun 5pm). Closed Dec 25. $7.* ✗ ⟨ ☎*905-893-0344.* Housed in square-hewn log buildings among the wooded hills of the Humber Valley, this gallery has the largest display in existence of paintings by the first truly Canadian school—the **Group of Seven**. The centre also owns a sizeable collection of contemporary Indian and Inuit art.

McMichael Canadian Art Collection 1966.16.76

Afternoon, Algonquin Park 1914, by Tom Thomson

Eight Canadian painters are credited with forging a uniquely Canadian art by painting, in a revolutionary way, the colours and landscapes of the country's wilds. Though pioneer **Tom Thomson** (1877-1917) died before the group was formed, his influence was substantial. The original members were **Lawren Harris**, **A. Y. Jackson**, **J. E. H. MacDonald**, **Franklin Carmichael**, **Arthur Lismer**, **Frederick Varley** and **Frank Johnston**. Johnston left after the first exhibition; **A. J. Casson** joined the group in 1926. The group officially disbanded in 1932, but some members formed the Canadian Group of Painters, which had much the same aims. In 1952 **Robert and Signe McMichael** bought land in rural Kleinburg, decorating their home with Group of Seven paintings. In 1965 they donated their famed collection and property to the province of Ontario. Subsequent gifts by such individuals as R.S. McLaughlin have enlarged the collection.

The ground level is largely devoted to the group's precursor, Tom Thomson; to A.Y. Jackson, "grand old man of Canadian art"; and to Lawren Harris, the "soul" of the group and a prime leader in Canadian art for decades. Examples by artists influenced by the seven, notably **Clarence Gagnon**, **Emily Carr**, and **David Milne,** are also displayed. On exhibit upstairs are fine works of contemporary Indian artists such as **Clifford Maracle**, **Norval Morrisseau**, **Daphne Odjig** and **Arthur Shilling**. There are excellent samples of **Inuit Art** as well, principally stone carvings and lithographs.

★★★ **Niagara Falls** – *1 day trip. 130km/81mi. Description p 148.*

★★ **Parkwood Estate** – *1/2 day trip. 61km/38mi. Description p 153.*

★ **Royal Botanical Gardens** – *1/2 day trip. 70km/44mi. Description p 143.*

UPPER CANADA VILLAGE★★★

Map p 133

Reflecting 1860s community life in Ontario, this 27ha/66 acre living museum is without equal in Canada, and is one of the finest restoration projects in North America. Lying in an area settled by Loyalists after the American Revolution, the village was created when plans were made to flood a large part of the St. Lawrence River Valley during the construction of the St. Lawrence Seaway and the control dam at Cornwall. Some of the older homes and buildings were moved to this site to preserve them.

Access – *11km/7mi east of Morrisburg off Hwy. 2 (Exit Hwy. 401 at Upper Canada Rd. Take Hwy. 2 east) in Crysler Farm Battlefield Park.*

VISIT *Allow 1/2 day*

Open mid-May–mid-Oct daily 9:30am–5pm. Horse-drawn transportation (free) on premises. $12. ✕ & ☎*613-543-3704.* The first impression upon entering the village is one of bustling activity. Visitors are transported at once to the 19C. Suitably attired "inhabitants" walk the streets or travel about by stagecoach or other 19C conveyance. They perform a variety of activities: cheese and bread making, quilting, cabinetmaking, printing and tinsmithing, in addition to farm chores. The progress in the life of the first settlers from pioneer shanties to substantial dwellings of brick and stone is excellently illustrated. Note in particular the elegant refinement of the **Robertson House**, the solid prosperity of the **farm**, and the evident wealth and luxury of **Crysler Hall** with its Greek Revival architecture. There are churches and schools, a village store, doctor's surgery and a tavern. An 1860s-style meal can be eaten at **Willard's Hotel**.

The **sawmill**, **woollen mill** (where woollen cloth was and is once again being produced) and flour mill operate on water power, and show the gradual trend toward industrialization evident in Ontario by 1867. Regular demonstrations are given for visitors. The flour mill has an 1865 steam engine.

Battlefield Monument – *Beside Upper Canada Village in the park.* This monument commemorates the Battle of Crysler Farm in 1813 when a small force of British and Canadian troops routed a much larger American force. It stands beside the St. Lawrence River with a fine **view** over the site of the farm now flooded by the seaway.

Quilting at Upper Canada Village

WINDSOR★

Pop. 191,435
Map p 132
Tourist Office ☎519-255-6530

The city of Windsor lies on the south side of the **Detroit River** opposite the American city of that name. A suspension bridge and tunnel connect both cities. Like Detroit, this industrial centre is a major automobile manufacturer and a port on the Great Lakes/St. Lawrence Seaway system.

Historical Notes – The Windsor/Detroit area was first settled by the French in the early 18C. In 1701 **Antoine de la Mothe Cadillac** built a post on the north side of the Detroit River that became the headquarters of the French fur trade in the Great Lakes/Mississippi River area. It was captured by the British in 1760. After the American Revolution, the fort and town were handed over to the Americans, and the Detroit River became the international border, except for a brief period during the War of 1812. The town of Sandwich developed on the Canadian side, but it was later engulfed by Windsor, founded in the early 1830s. In 1838 there were several invasions across the river by the American supporters of William Lyon Mackenzie, but since that time, relations between the two cities have been very cordial.

Every year an **International Freedom Festival** is celebrated *(Jun–Jul)* to include the national holidays of both countries: July 1st and 4th. Today Windsor is one of Canada's busiest points of entry.

SIGHTS

★ **Dieppe Gardens** – The outstanding attraction of this park, which stretches several blocks along the river west of the main thoroughfare *(Ouellette Ave.)*, is its **view**★★ of the Detroit skyline across the water. It is also a good vantage point from which to watch the huge ships of the seaway.

★ **Art Gallery of Windsor** – *In Devonshire Mall, 3100 Howard Ave. Open year-round Tue–Fri 10am–7pm, Sat 10am–5pm, Sun noon–5pm. Contribution requested.* ⬧ ☎*519-969-4494.* Featured on two levels are changing exhibits from the gallery's permanent collection of over 2,500 works of Canadian art dating from 1750 to the present, including paintings from the Group of Seven.

EXCURSIONS

★ **Fort Malden** – ☞ *In Amherstburg, 25km/15mi south via Rtes 2 and 18. Open May–Dec daily 10am–5pm. Rest of the year Mon–Fri 1–5pm, weekends 10am–5pm. Closed national holidays. $2.50.* ⬧ ☎*519-736-5416.* This fort, built by the British at the end of the 18C when they had abandoned Detroit to the Americans, occupies a fine **site**★ overlooking the seaway. Some ramparts remain, now grass-covered, and a barracks has been restored to its 1819 state. In the **visitor centre** a video *(6min)* explains the fort's role in the War of 1812 and the Rebellions of 1837. In the **interpretation centre** military displays include an example of Mackenzie's rebel flag.

Route 50 – *31km/19mi from Malden Centre to Kingsville.* This quiet road runs through long stretches of the flat farmland that borders Lake Erie, offering occasional vistas of the lake. It affords opportunities to view marshland birds and the colourful market gardens that grow a variety of fruit and vegetables.

Jack Miner's Bird Sanctuary – *In Kingsville, 2km/1.5mi north of town centre via Rte 29 (Division Rd.); then left on Road 3 West. Open year-round Mon–Sat 9am–5pm.* ⬧ ☎*519-733-4034.* Founded by conservationist **Jack Miner** (1865-1944), this sanctuary, one of the earliest in Canada, is a well-known stopping place for wildfowl on their seasonal migration. The best time to visit is late October and November when an estimated 40,000 geese and ducks land to feed. A small museum on the premises houses Miner memorabilia.

★★ **Point Pelee National Park** – *65km/40mi by Rtes. 3 and 33. Description p 165.*

Suggestions for further reading are given on p 29.

Quebec

Lower Town and Château Frontenac, Quebec City/Tourisme Québec

E ncompassing an area of 1,540,680sq km/594,860sq mi, or one-sixth of Canada's total landmass, this vast province is first and foremost the bastion of French-Canadian culture. More than 80 percent of its population of 6.9 million is Francophone, the survivors of an empire founded in the early 17C, which once covered half the continent. Very proud of this long tradition, the **Québécois** have maintained their own culture and lifestyle, creating a unique society in a North American milieu. About five percent of the province's population claims British origin and is concentrated largely on Montreal Island. About one percent claims native ancestry, primarily Indians as well as Métis and Inuit, who live in small settlements in the Great North. The remainder of Quebec's population hails from a wide variety of ethnic origins.

Geographical Notes

Regional Landscapes – Stretching almost 2,000km/1,240mi from the US border to Hudson Strait, Quebec is Canada's largest province. The extreme north is a forbidding land of treeless tundra underlain with permanently frozen ground that gradually turns to forest farther south. This forest covers most of the province, leaving only a sliver of arable land near the St. Lawrence River. The majority of Quebec's population is concentrated in the St. Lawrence Valley.

Three main physiographic regions can be distinguished in Quebec. The northern tundra and vast forested area lie on the **Canadian Shield** *(map p 17)*, a rocky expanse consisting of extensive plateaus interrupted by a few mountain massifs. In Quebec the Shield rises to heights of 1,166m/3,824ft at Mt. Raoul Blanchard in the Charlevoix region *(p 202)*, but otherwise presents a flat and monotonous surface, strewn with lakes. The extreme south of the province and the GASPÉ

PENINSULA, on the other hand, are part of the **Appalachian Mountains**. These chains reach heights of 972m/3,188ft in the EASTERN TOWNSHIPS and 1,288m/4,227ft in the Gaspé Peninsula *(p 206)*, and provide large sections of arable land, especially in the south. Lodged between these two regions, the **St. Lawrence Lowlands**, a triangular wedge graced with fertile soils and a moderate climate, support most of the province's agricultural production. Stretching some 1,197km/742mi in length, the **St. Lawrence River** issues from Lake Ontario and flows in a northeasterly direction along Ontario and through Quebec to the wide Gulf of St. Lawrence and into the Atlantic Ocean. Combined with the Great Lakes, this lengthy waterway reaches nearly 3,800km/2,400mi into the interior of the continent. Glacial recession created its riverbed some 10,000 years ago. Principal tributaries of the St. Lawrence are the Ottawa, Saguenay, Manicouagan, St. Maurice and Richelieu Rivers.

Climate – Quebec experiences a wide range of temperatures because of its location. Although bright and sunny, the winters can be bitterly cold, especially in the north. Snowfall can accumulate up to 150cm/5ft in much of the central interior. Following a short spring season, the southern regions of the province are suddenly plunged into summer, when hot weather and extremely humid conditions predominate. Summer departs slowly, and fall arrives with its beautiful colours. Sometimes, after all the leaves have dropped in late October or early November, summer returns briefly for a last fling. This "Indian summer" is another characteristic of Quebec's climate.

January temperatures in MONTREAL average –9°C/16°F, with an average of 254cm/8ft of snowfall for the entire winter season. Located farther north, Sept-Îles registers –10°C/14°F with 422cm/14ft of snow—the heaviest recorded snowfall in eastern Canada.

In July Montreal registers maximum means of 26°C/79°F, QUEBEC CITY 25°C/77°F and Sept-Îles 20°C/68°F. Temperatures in excess of 32°C/90°F are not uncommon, however, in the southern regions, and humidity frequently exceeds 80 percent. Total annual precipitation in the south varies from 750–1000mm/30–40in and is fairly evenly distributed throughout the year.

Historical Notes

Birth of New France – Before the arrival of Europeans, Quebec's territory was inhabited by Indians of the Eastern Woodlands culture, including Algonquins and Montagnais. During the 15C, Basque fishermen came to fish off the coast. A century later, during the era of European explorers, French navigator **Jacques Cartier** (1491-1557) set out across the Atlantic Ocean in search of riches and a route to the Orient. He landed on the GASPÉ PENINSULA in 1534 and claimed this new land for the King of France, François I. Although Cartier returned to the New World in 1535 and 1542, France did not establish a firm presence on the continent until 1608, when **Samuel de Champlain** left Port Royal in Acadia *(p 260)*, ascended the St. Lawrence, and founded Quebec City.

Soon after establishing his "Habitation" *(p 225)*, Champlain and his young colony suffered repeated attacks by Indians of the Iroquois nations. The **Iroquois Wars** continued until 1701, when the Montreal Peace Treaty established a temporary truce. The wars, combined with France's lack of interest in the colony, kept settlement to a minimum. The administration of New France consisted of an appointed governor responsible for conducting the colony's military and external affairs, and an intendant in charge of administrative and economic functions. The young colony was organized according to the feudal system that existed in France until the Revolution in 1789. A *seigneurie* or piece of land was granted to a **seigneur** or landowner who swore loyalty to the king. He in turn granted parts of his land to tenant farmers who paid him various dues. To provide as many people as possible with access to the river, the major means of transport, the land was divided into *rangs*—long thin strips that started at the river bank.

A Vast Empire – During the mid-17C the *coureurs des bois* (fur traders) and missionaries from New France explored wide areas of the continent. Champlain himself discovered the lake named after him, as well as the Ottawa River, Georgian Bay, Lake Simcoe and Lake Ontario. His followers, Étienne Brûlé, Jean Nicolet and Nicolas Perrot, reached Lake Superior. In the 1650s Pierre Radisson and the Sieur des Groseilliers travelled through the Great Lakes and north perhaps as far as Hudson Bay. They planned a quicker trade route to Europe via the bay that would avoid the long canoe/portage route back to Montreal. When France showed no interest in this scheme, Radisson and Groseillers turned to the British who eventually founded the Hudson's Bay Company.

The greatest explorers of them all were the **La Vérendrye family**. Pierre Gaultier de Varennes, Sieur de la Vérendrye, explored much of Manitoba and Saskatchewan between 1731 and 1738, setting up a series of trading posts. His sons François and Louis-Joseph explored even farther west, reaching the foot of the Rockies in present-day Montana in 1742, the first Europeans to behold this mountain range.

Anglo-French Wars – Part of a broader struggle in Europe and elsewhere, the conflict between France and England in North America centred on the profitable fur trade. Repeated assaults by the British led to the capture of Quebec City in 1629. The French regained control of the city three years later. The Treaty of Utrecht ushered in a period of peace that lasted until the Seven Years' War *(p 22)*. On September 13, 1759, British Gen. **James Wolfe** (1728-59) defeated French Gen. **Louis-Joseph de Montcalm** (1712-59) on the **Plains of Abraham** *(p 228)* in Quebec City, signaling the end of the French colony. After Montreal's surrender in September 1760, France capitulated. The colony was ceded to England in 1763 by the Treaty of Paris.

A British Colony – Faced with a Roman Catholic, French-speaking population, the new governor, **Sir Guy Carleton**, decided to recognize the rights of the Roman Catholic church, the seigneurial system and French civil law as a basis for government. These rights were enshrined in the **Quebec Act** of 1774.

During the American Revolution, the inhabitants of the 13 colonies tried unsuccessfully to persuade the French Canadians to join them. After the Revolution many Loyalists moved to the EASTERN TOWNSHIPS. In order to satisfy their demands for representation, the British government divided the colony into Upper and Lower Canada in 1791. Both colonies were granted elected assemblies, but their powers were strictly limited. Frustration over these limitations led to the **Rebellions of 1837** *(p 173)* in both colonies. The issue was further inflamed in Quebec because the governor and his council were British and the assembly French. Led by **Louis-Joseph Papineau** (1786-1871), the **Patriots** petitioned for the right of self-government. Rejection of their demands by the British government ultimately resulted in fighting that left 325 soldiers and rebels dead. The Patriots were defeated, but full representative government was eventually granted.

As a result of the Durham Report *(p 196)*, the Act of Union joined both colonies. Although the union was to usher in a period of political liberalism, frequent crises led the British Parliament to ratify the British North America Act in 1867, establishing **Canadian Confederation** *(p 24)*. Facing a progressive loss of rights, Quebec entered an era of nationalism that advocated greater autonomy for the province.

A Sovereign State? – During the 1960s, a climate of social, economic and political change, labelled the "Quiet Revolution," emerged in Quebec. Provincial powers grew and an increased nationalist ideology continued to dominate the political landscape. Spearheaded by the leader of the Parti québécois (1968), **René Lévesque** (1922-87), the issue of Quebec sovereignty became a hotly debated topic. In May 1980, however, Lévesque's party lost a referendum on Quebec sovereignty when 60 percent of Quebecers voted against separation. Two years later, still under Lévesque's leadership, Quebec refused to sign the Canadian Constitution *(p 25)*. When the Liberal government of Robert Bourassa took power in 1985, negotiations with the other Canadian provinces resumed. The **Meech Lake Accord** (April 30, 1987), which provided a special status for Quebec as a "distinct society," had to be ratified by the federal government and all ten provinces before June 23, 1990. The provinces failed to reach a consensus, and Quebec was left debating sovereignty, or adherence to the Canadian Constitution. In October 1992, a national referendum on, among other issues, Quebec's status as a distinct society was voted down by a majority of Canadians. However, the narrow defeat of Quebec sovereignty in a provincial referendum in 1995 (50.6 percent of Quebecers voted "no") indicates that the province's relationship to Canada will likely continue to dominate the political scene for some time.

Economy

Although over 70 percent of the gross domestic product stems from manufacturing and services, Quebec's economy relies on the province's abundant natural resources and on traditional activities such as fishing, trapping and agriculture. Since the opening of the **St. Lawrence Seaway** in 1959, linking the Atlantic Ocean to the Great Lakes, the economy of Quebec has been closely tied to that of the US. Over 50 percent of the province's manufactured goods are exported, 80 percent of which are bound for the US.

PRACTICAL INFORMATION

Getting There

By Air – International flights arrive at Montreal's Mirabel airport (55km/34mi north of downtown) ☎514-476-3010 and Quebec City's Jean-Lesage airport ☎418-640-2600. Domestic airlines (from US and within Canada) arrive at Montreal's Dorval airport (22km/14mi west of downtown) ☎514-633-3105. Air Canada ☎514-393-3333 or 800-776-3000 (US), Canadian Airlines International ☎800-426-7000 (Canada/US) and other affiliated carriers offer connections to many cities within Quebec. Major car rental agencies *(p 315)* at the airports.

By Bus and Train – Intercity **bus** service and connections to the regions of BAS-SAINT-LAURENT and GASPÉ PENINSULA are offered by **Autocars Orléans Express Inc.** ☎514-395-4000. **Amtrak** links MONTREAL and the US with daily connections from Washington DC via New York City. For information in the US ☎800-872-7245. VIA Rail train service is extensive within the province; ☎514-989-2626 (Canada); 800-561-3949 (US).

By Boat – The province has an extensive **ferry** boat system; for schedules contact Tourisme Québec *(below)*.

General Information

Accommodations and Visitor Information – The official government tourist office publishes annual summer and winter vacation brochures as well as regional guides that include points of interest, driving tours, hotels, activities, camping, etc. These publications and road maps can be obtained free of charge from: **Tourisme Québec**, CP 979, Montreal, PQ, H3C 2W3 ☎514-873-2015 or 800-363-7777 (Canada/US).

Major hotel chains can be found in urban areas. Small hotels and Bed & Breakfast lodgings offer quality accommodations at moderate prices throughout the province. **Farm holidays** may be especially appealing to families. For the guide *Gîtes du Passant ($13)*, listing facilities throughout the province, contact Fédération des Agricotours du Québec ☎514-252-3138.

Language – The official language of Quebec is French, spoken by 81% of the population. The second language is English. Quebeckers in urban areas tend to be bilingual. Tourist information is generally available in both languages. Telephone operators are bilingual.

Road Regulations – *(Driver's license and insurance requirements p 314.)* Quebec has a network of highways *(autoroutes)* and well-maintained secondary roads. Road signs are in French only. The speed limit on highways, unless otherwise posted, is 100km/h (60mph), on secondary roads 90km/h (55mph), and 50km/h (30mph) within city limits. Turning right on red is prohibited. **Seat belt** use is mandatory. **Canadian Automobile Assn. (CAA)**, Montreal ☎514-861-7111.

Time Zones – Quebec is on Eastern Standard Time, except the Magdalen Islands, which are on Atlantic Standard Time (one hour ahead of the rest of Quebec). Daylight Saving Time is observed from the first Sunday in April to the last Sunday in October.

Taxes – In addition to the national 7% GST *(rebate information p 318)*, Quebec levies a provincial sales tax of 6.5% for all goods and services. Non-residents can request rebates of the provincial tax from Revenue Canada, Visitor Rebate Program *(address p 319)* ☎800-668-4748 (Canada), 902-432-5608 (outside Canada).

Liquor Laws – The legal drinking age is 18. The sale of wine and liquor is regulated by the provincial government and sold in "Société des Alcools" stores. Beer and wine are also sold in grocery stores.

Provincial Holiday *(National Holidays p 319)*

Saint-Jean-Baptiste Day .... June 24

Recreation – Parks Canada operates three **national parks** in Quebec, which offer year-round activities such as hiking, backpacking, nature programs, biking, sailing, canoeing, fishing, camping and winter sports. For trail maps and brochures ☎418-648-4177, or in Quebec ☎800-463-6769; for camping reservations ☎418-890-6527, or in Quebec ☎800-665-6527.

A guide entitled *Découvrez votre vraie nature* (available in English) gives in-park accommodations, boat or ski equipment rentals, hunting and fishing information and other details for **provincial parks** and **wildlife reserves** and is obtainable free of charge from the Ministère de l'environnement et de la faune ☎418-643-3127.

Canoeing is practised on most of the rivers except those used for logging. **Kayaking** is popular in the northern regions of Saguenay and NUNAVIK, where camps have been set up. Ranch vacations that include **horseback riding** are prevalent in the EASTERN TOWNSHIPS, Gaspé Peninsula and Bas-Saint-Laurent regions. For further information on all outdoor activities contact Regroupement Loisir Québec ☎514-252-3000.

Major ski areas offering alpine and cross-country **skiing** are the Laurentians (Mt. Tremblant ☎819-425-8711), the Eastern Townships (Mt. Orford ☎819-843-6548) and the Quebec City region (Mt. Ste-Anne ☎418-827-4561). Abundant snowfall extends the ski season to mid-April. **Snowmobiling** is a popular outdoor activity. A network of well-marked trails crisscrosses the countryside interspersed with heated cabins and other accommodations. For a free copy of the *Trans-Quebec Snowmobile Trail Network Map* contact Tourisme Québec (*p 197*).

Many regions in Quebec are known for excellent **hunting** and **fishing**. Outfitters' lodges, easily reached by land or air, offer packages that include accommodations, transport to remote locations, equipment rental, permits and game registration. Above the 52nd parallel, non-residents are required to hire the services of an out-fitter. For regulations and seasons contact the Ministère de l' environnement et de la faune ☎418-643-3127. An annual publication on outfitters' lodges is available at tourist information kiosks or from Fédération des pourvoyeurs du Québec ☎418-527-5191. The rivers of the Gaspé Peninsula and ANTICOSTI ISLAND are well known for salmon fishing; central Quebec is known for its variety of fish species.

Special Excursions – Organized nature tours for canoeing, rafting, horseback riding, biking or hiking are offered through New World River Expeditions ☎819-242-7238. Activities such as rock climbing, dogsledding, canoeing and kayaking can be arrranged through CÉPAL ☎418-547-5728. For information on additional adventure travel, contact Tourisme Québec (*p 197*). Seal-watch excursions off MAGDALEN ISLANDS depart from HALIFAX, Nova Scotia (*p 243*).

Principal Festivals

mid-Feb	**Quebec Winter Carnival** (*p 223*)	*Quebec City*
	Carnaval-Souvenir	*Chicoutimi*
	Winterlude	*Hull*
mid-Mar	**Maple Sugar Festival**	*Saint-Georges*
Jun	**Grand Prix Molson**	*Montreal*
	International Jazz Festival	*Montreal*
Jul	**Festival Orford**	*Magog*
	World Folklore Festival	*Drummondville*
	International Summer Festival	*Quebec City*
	International Swim Marathon (*p 232*)	*Péribonka*
Aug	**Blueberry Festival**	*Mistassini*
	Hot Air Balloon Festival (*p 231*)	*Saint-Jean-sur-Richelieu*
	Montreal World Film Festival	*Montreal*
Sept	**Foliage Festival**	*Laurentides*
	Granby Song Festival	*Granby*

For in-depth information on the sights found in the province of Quebec, consult the Michelin Green Guide to Quebec, which highlights over 1,150 points of interest throughout the French-speaking province.

In addition, insightful essays trace Quebec's history, geography and artistic heritage, while detailed city and regional maps accompany various walking and driving tours.

— —— —— —— ———

Forest, Mines and Water Resources – Covering more than 1,550,000sq km/600,000sq mi, the province's extensive forest has been exploited for centuries. Quebec is the Canadian leader in production of **pulp and paper**, manufacturing about one-third of the country's total output, and about 15 percent of the world's supply of **newsprint**. The province supports some 60 processing mills located along the St. Lawrence, Ottawa, St. Maurice and Saguenay Rivers and in the EASTERN TOWNSHIPS.

Mining is concentrated in several regions lying on the Canadian Shield whose age-old rocks are a great source of mineral wealth. The Abitibi and Témiscamingue regions (Noranda, Matagami, Chibougamau) contain large deposits of **copper** as well as gold, silver, zinc, lead and nickel in smaller quantities. Copper is also found at Murdochville in the Gaspé Peninsula. Quebec is the world's largest exporter of asbestos, a fibrous silicate mineral found mainly in the Eastern Townships region *(p 204)*.

The province's industrialization has been closely linked to its abundant **hydro-electric resources**. The St. Lawrence, St. Maurice and Saguenay Rivers generate large amounts of electricity mainly for industrial use. The Manic-Outardes *(p 203)* project, located on the north shore of the St. Lawrence, produces in excess of 6,800 megawatts (1 megawatt=1 million watts). The enormous project on the La Grande River, which runs into James Bay, has a capacity of more than 15 million kilowatts. The low-cost energy generated from hydro-electric plants has spurred the province's electro-metallurgic industries. With smelters located at Beauharnois and Bécancour on the St. Lawrence, Shawinigan on the St. Maurice and Arvida on the Saguenay River, Quebec has become a major producer of **aluminum**.

Agriculture, Fishing and Trapping – These regionally based activities still form the traditional supports of the province's economy. Agriculture predominates in the southern regions of Quebec, in particular the island of Montreal, St. Lawrence Valley and Lake Saint-Jean area, which produce fruit, vegetables, beef and dairy products in sufficient quantities to supply the province's population. The major fishing centres are located on the Gaspé Peninsula, Magdalen Islands and Côte-Nord. Although trapping is no longer as important as it was during the settlement of the province, it is still practised in the northern areas.

For a listing of selected French terms used in this guide see p 235.

ANTICOSTI ISLAND★★

Map of Principal Sights p 5

Stretching more than 222km/138mi in length and 56km/35mi at its widest point, Anticosti Island is mantled with coniferous forests and crisscrossed by over 100 rivers teeming with Atlantic salmon and trout. Well known by deer hunters for the abundance of game, the island is also a pleasant vacation spot for nature lovers. French industrialist **Henri Menier**, who purchased Anticosti for the sum of $125,000 in 1895, transformed the island into his private paradise, constructing a sumptuous hunting lodge (destroyed by fire in 1953) and importing animals, in particular, white-tailed deer. In 1926 the island was sold for $6.5 million to the Anticosti Corporation. The Quebec government acquired Anticosti in 1974, and the majority of the island is now part of a reserve (4,575sq km/1,766sq mi).

Access – *Air service available through Inter-Canadian ☎418-962-8321 or Aviation Québec Labrador ☎ 418-962-7901. Boat service available through Relais Nordik Inc., from Rimouski ☎418-723-8787, Sept-Îles ☎418-968-4707 and Havre-Saint-Pierre ☎418-538-3533. A 4-wheel drive vehicle is indispensable on the island.*

VISIT *Allow minimum 2 days*

A tour of the island from **Port-Menier**, the island's only remaining permanent settlement, leads past such scenic wonders as Kalimazoo Falls and La Patate Cavern, **Vauréal Falls and Canyon★★**, with a 70m/230ft waterfall, and **Tour Bay★★**, renowned for its spectacular limestone cliffs that plummet dramatically into the sea. Located to the west of Port-Menier, Baie-Sainte-Claire provides an ideal setting for observing **white-tailed deer**, sometimes seen in herds of up to 100.

BAS-SAINT-LAURENT★★

Map below

Situated on the south shore of the St. Lawrence River, between QUEBEC CITY and the GASPÉ PENINSULA, this region is characterized by fertile plains, plateaus and, to the north, the foothills of the Appalachians. The peaceful, rural landscapes along the shore are divided into long, narrow strips of farmland, perpendicular to the river. To the north, the Laurentian Mountains plunge into the St. Lawrence, creating picturesque scenery.

Route 132 passes through the principal communities of this region, affording superb views of the St. Lawrence and of various islands dotting the river.

SIGHTS

★ **Lévis** – Pop. 39,452. *250km/155mi east of Montreal by Rte. 20 or Rte. 132. A ferry connects Lévis to Quebec City.* Located on the south shore of the St. Lawrence, opposite Quebec City, this important business centre is noted for its port and its wood-related industries. The city is also the birthplace and headquarters of the Desjardins cooperative savings and loan company *(Caisse populaire Desjardins)*. Founded in 1900 by journalist Alphonse Desjardins (1854-1920), this people's bank sought to bring economic independence to French Canadians.

At the corner of Avenue Mont-Marie and Rue Guenette, the white clapboard **Alphonse-Desjardins House★** (Maison Alphonse-Desjardins) presents a video *(15min)* and displays of artifacts *(open year-round Mon–Fri 10am–noon & 1–4:30pm, weekends & holidays noon–5pm; closed Dec 24–Jan 1.* ☎418-835-2090).

★ **Fort No. 1 National Historic Site** (Lieu historique national Fort-Numéro-Un-de-la-Pointe-de-Lévy) – ☞ *Open mid-May–mid-Jun Mon–Fri & Sun 9am–4pm. Mid-Jun–late Aug daily 10am–5pm. Late Aug–late Oct Mon–Sat by appointment & Sun noon–4pm. $2.50.*

☎418-835-5182. Forming an irregular pentagon, the fort (1865-72) stands atop Pointe-Lévis, the highest point on the south shore of the St. Lawrence. It is the sole vestige of three such forts built to protect Quebec City from possible American attack after the threat of the American Civil War, and from the Fenian Raids. The fort is composed of a series of massive earthen ramparts with a tall embankment protecting the casemates, ditches and vaulted tunnels leading to the *caponiers*—stone and brick structures armed with small cannon.

★ **National Historic Site of Grosse-Île** (Lieu historique national de Grosse-Île) – ☞ *Visit by guided tour only, May–Oct daily 8:30am–5:30pm.* ☎418-563-4009. *Several companies provide cruises to Grosse Île departing from Berthier-sur-Mer and Montmagny May–Oct. One-way 30min. Commentary. Reservations required. Guided visit & cruise $30–$45.* ✕ ▣ *Further information: Office du tourisme de la Côte-du-Sud* ☎418-248-9196. The ever-increasing number of European immigrants to Canada prompted the government to establish, in 1832,

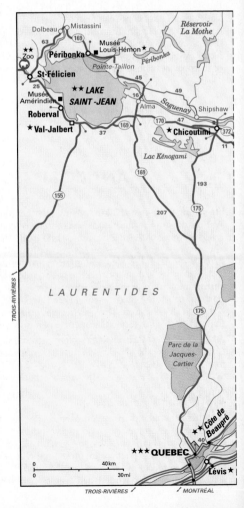

a quarantine station on Grosse Île, one of 21 islands making up the Île aux Grues archipelago. In the station's first year of operation, some 50,000 immigrants were examined in an effort to limit the spread of cholera into Canada. The western part of the island was known as the Hotel Sector. The Village Sector in the island's centre housed employees of the station and their families. To the east the Hospital Sector included 21 hospitals of which one is still standing. In 1990 Parks Canada opened the site to the public.

Route 132 continues through **L'Islet-sur-Mer**, a small maritime community known as the birthplace of famed Arctic explorer, Capt. Joseph-Elzéar Bernier (1852-1934), and through **Saint-Jean-Port-Joli★**, the craft and wood-carving capital of Quebec.

★ **La Pocatière** – Pop. 4,648. *60km/37mi from Montmagny.* Situated on a terrace above the coastal plain, this community is a leading centre for agricultural research. The **François Pilote Museum★** (Musée François-Pilote) illustrates rural life in the province at the turn of the century (*open May–Sept Mon–Sat 9am–noon & 1–5pm, Sun 1–5pm; $3;* ♿ ☎ *418-856-3145*). Collections focus on agriculture, the natural sciences and education.

Route 132 passes across a wide flood plain, affording expansive views of the Laurentian Mountains across the St. Lawrence. Perpendicular to the shoreline, eel-traps extend into the river. From the pleasant community of **Kamouraska★**, lines of stakes can be seen in the tidal flats. These traps divert fish and eels into enclosures where they can be netted.

★ **Rivière-du-Loup** – Pop. 14,017. *72km/45mi from La Pocatière.* Situated halfway between Quebec City and Gaspé Peninsula, this town has developed into a commercial and resort centre. A walk through the downtown leads past several buildings of interest, including the imposing Gothic Revival **St. Patrick's Church**

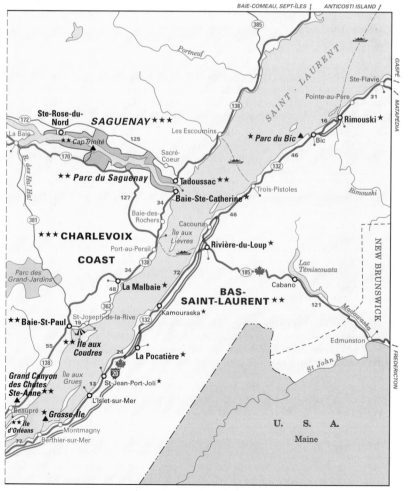

and Presbytery, surrounded by verandas, and the **Viatorian Clerics' Residence**. North of downtown, the Loup River drops over the cliff terrace in 38m/125ft high falls. Steps lead to a lookout providing an expansive view of the town and river.

★ **Bic Park (Parc du Bic)** – *81km/50mi from Rivière-du-Loup*. This 33sq km/13sq mi provincial conservation park, created in 1984, boasts a variety of flora, including both deciduous and boreal forests. The small town of **Bic** is known for its spectacular **setting★★** on the shores of the St. Lawrence.

★ **Rimouski** – Pop. 30,873. *25km/16mi from Bic Park*. Built along the banks of the St. Lawrence, this industrial city has developed in a semicircular pattern around the mouth of the Rimouski River and is now considered a major metropolis of eastern Quebec. Among sights of interest, note the **Lamontagne House★** (Maison Lamontagne), one of the few remaining examples of masonry half-timbering in North America *(open May–Jun 23 Mon–Fri 9:30am–4:30pm; Jun 24–Labour Day daily 10am–6pm; early Sept–Oct Mon–Fri 9:30am–4:30pm; $2; ☎418-722-4038)*.
Located 10km/6mi from town, the **Maritime Museum★** (Musée de la mer) at Pointe-au-Père displays hundreds of artifacts recovered from the wreck of the *Empress of Ireland*, nicknamed the "Titanic of the St. Lawrence" *(open mid-Jun–mid-Oct daily 9am–6pm; rest of the year by appointment; $4.75; ✗ ♿ ☎418-724-6214)*.

CHARLEVOIX COAST★★★

Map p 201

One of Quebec's loveliest, most varied regions, this rugged coast is best appreciated by following Routes 138 and 362, which weave up and down, affording magnificent clifftop or water-level views of forested hills, the pristine shore and mountains that sweep down into the mighty St. Lawrence. Named for Jesuit historian Pierre-François-Xavier de Charlevoix (1682-1781), this resort spot has long attracted and inspired painters, poets and writers.

SIGHTS

★★ **Grand Canyon of the St. Anne Falls (Grand Canyon des Chutes Sainte-Anne)** – *52km/32mi northeast of Quebec City. Open Jun 24–Labour Day daily 8am–6pm. Early Sept–Oct daily 9am–5pm. $6. ✗ ♿ ☎418-827-4057*. Pleasant paths lead to this steep and narrow waterfall, which drops a total of 74m/243ft over the edge of the Canadian Shield, creating a mass of shattered rocks and whirlpools at its base.

★★ **Baie-Saint-Paul** – *95km/59mi northeast of Quebec City*. Route 138 offers spectacular **views★★** on the descent to this celebrated artist haunt. Surrounded by rolling green hills, the charming community boasts more than a dozen art galleries and an **arts centre** that displays the work of local artists *(open year-round daily 9am–7pm; $3; ♿ ☎418-435-3681)*.
Departing by Route 362, visitors will find an overlook that provides another splendid **view★★** of the town, the St. Lawrence and the south shore.

★★ **Île aux Coudres** – *Access by ferry; departs year-round from Saint-Joseph-de-la-Rive (22km/14mi from Baie-Saint-Paul) daily 7am–11pm. One-way 15min. Société des traversiers du Québec ☎418-438-2743*. Named by Jacques Cartier in 1535 for its abundant hazel trees *(coudriers)*, this enchanting island, home to farmers, boat builders and fishermen, occupies a spectacular offshore **site** linked by ferry to the mainland. Each year, the island's inhabitants demonstrate their canoeing skills on the icy river at the Quebec Winter Carnival *(p 223)*.
A tour of the island *(21km/13mi)* by car or bicycle offers views of the north and south shores of the St. Lawrence. Remnants of a past age—beached schooners—dot the coast. The **Schooner Museum★** (Musée Les voitures d'eau) presents the region's maritime history *(open mid-May–mid-Jun weekends 9:30am–5pm; mid-Jun–mid-Sept daily 9am–6pm; mid-Sept–mid-Oct weekends 9:30am–5pm; $4; ♿ ☎418-438-2208)*. The **Île-aux-Coudres Mills★** (Moulins de l'Isle-aux-Coudres), both dating from the 19C, provide a rare chance to compare the mechanisms of a windmill and a water mill *(open Jun 24–Labour Day daily 9am–7pm; mid-May–Jun 23 & early Sept–mid-Oct daily 10am–5pm; $2.50; ♿ ☎418-438-2184)*. At La Baleine the **Maison Leclerc**, a simple stone dwelling, is among the oldest homes on the island.

★ **La Malbaie** – Pop. 3,968. *26km/16mi northeast of Île aux Coudres*. Occupying a beautiful **site★**, this resort community was named "Malle Baye" (bad bay) by Samuel de Champlain in 1608, when he discovered his anchored ships had run aground. After the British defeated the French *(p 196)*, Scottish soldiers renamed it Murray

Bay in honour of the colony's chief administrator. The picturesque **Manoir Richelieu** *(in Pointe-au-Pic)* is a grand reminder of the resort hotels that sprung up during the 19C.

★ **Baie-Sainte-Catherine** – Pop. 312. *74km/46mi northeast of La Malbaie.* Located at the mouth of the Saguenay River, this small community was settled in the 1820s. **Whale-watching cruises**★★ have become a popular attraction, just as in Tadoussac *(p 232)* across the fjord. Overlooking the mouth of the Saguenay in the **Saguenay-St. Lawrence Marine Park**, a lookout tower provides occasional glimpses of the large mammals frolicking in the water below *(open mid-Jun–Labour Day daily 9am–6pm; early Sept–mid-Oct Fri–Sun 9am–5pm; & ☎418-237-4348).*

CÔTE-NORD★

Map of Principal Sights p 5

The Côte-Nord, or North Shore of the St. Lawrence River extends from the mouth of the Saguenay River north to the Labrador border. This geographic entity is divided into three regions: the southernmost stretching from Tadoussac to Sept-Îles; the central North Shore from Sept–Îles to Havre-Saint-Pierre; and the northernmost region *(accessible only by boat or plane)*, encompassing the vast expanse of taiga and the villages between Havre-Saint-Pierre and Blanc-Sablon. Long known as an untamed wilderness of forests with occasional fishing villages, Côte-Nord underwent gradual industrialization with the development of **pulp mills** in the 1920s and 1930s and later, the discovery of rich **iron-ore** deposits. In the 1960s the region's enormous hydro-electric potential was harnessed, prompting another surge of economic growth. A drive along Route 138 leads through desolate stretches of pristine, rocky landscape, occasionally interrupted by developing towns and hydro-electric plants.

SIGHTS

Manic-Outardes Complex – *Manic-5 is located 210km/130mi north of Baie-Comeau (422km/262mi northeast of Quebec City) on Rte. 389.* Begun in 1959 the harnessing of the Manicouagan and Outardes Rivers took 20 years to complete. Today the seven plants strung along both rivers have a combined capacity of 6,821 megawatts (1 megawatt=1,000,000 watts). The first power plant of the complex to produce electricity was **Manic-2**★ *(visit by 1hr 30min guided tour only, mid-Jun–Labour Day daily 9am, 11am, 1pm & 3pm; ⚠ ✗& ☎418-294-3923).* The spectacular **Daniel Johnson Dam**★★ of **Manic-5**★★ is the largest arch-and-buttress dam in the world, measuring 214m/702ft in height and 1,314m/4,307ft in length *(visit by 1hr 30min guided tour only, mid-Jun–Labour Day daily 9am, 11am, 1:30pm & 3:30pm; & ☎418-294-3923).* Named for a former premier of Quebec, it was completed in 1968. During construction two semicircular lakes were united, creating the distinctive doughnut-shaped reservoir with a diameter of 65km/40mi.

On the Manic-5 tour, guides explain how electricity is produced and transmitted to consumers. A bus takes visitors to the base of the massive arches and then across the dam where good views of the reservoir and surrounding landscape are permitted.

★ **Sept-Îles** – Pop. 24,848. *640km/397mi northeast of Quebec City by Rte. 138.* Occupying a superb **site**★★ in a circular bay on the St. Lawrence, this dynamic city constitutes the administrative centre of the Côte-Nord. Sept-Îles' deep-water port enables ocean-bound vessels to transship coal and iron ore throughout the year. Stroll along the old wharf to enjoy views of the magnificent bays and the seven islands for which the city is named.

The reconstructed **Old Trading Post** (Le Vieux-Poste) pays tribute to the region's first inhabitants, the Montagnais *(open mid-Jun–mid-Aug daily 9am–5pm; $3.25; & ☎418-962-1456).* Offshore, the **Sept-Îles Regional Park**★ (Parc régional de l'Archipel des Sept-Îles) offers a good introduction to the history and natural beauty of the Côte-Nord.

The community of **Havre-Saint-Pierre** (pop. 3,344) marks the end of Route 138. The ferries for Anticosti Island *(p 199)* and the **Mingan Archipelago**★★, a national park reserve, depart from the wharf. The string of approximately 40 islands is renowned for its spectacular rock formations and unique flora and fauna. Havre-Saint-Pierre is also the departure point for the boat trip *(3 days)* to Blanc-Sablon, situated 1.5km/1mi from the Labrador border. *For more information, consult the Michelin Green Guide to Quebec.*

EASTERN TOWNSHIPS★★

Map below

A region of lush rolling hills named for its location east of MONTREAL, "the Townships" as they are generally called, occupy the southwest corner of the province along the US border. This area of deep valleys, tree-covered hills rising nearly 1,000m/3,280ft, and beautiful, sparkling lakes such as Brome, Memphrémagog, Magog and Massawipi, is a popular retreat for Montrealers, offering a variety of recreational activities.

The northeastern section, in particular the towns of **Asbestos** and **Thetford Mines**, is known for its asbestos production. Directly north of Asbestos lies the Bois-Francs (hard woods) area, named for the predominant maple tree. To the east, drained by the Chaudière River, the flat fertile farmland referred to as the **Beauce★** contains the greatest concentration of maple groves in Quebec. In spring, sugaring-off parties are a popular pastime.

After the American Revolution, land parcels along the border were granted to Loyalists fleeing the US. The towns and villages these first settlers established reflect their New England heritage. After 1850 increasing numbers of French-speaking people moved into the region, and today its population is predominantly Francophone.

SIGHTS

★ **Sherbrooke** – Pop. 76,429. *150km/93mi east of Montreal by Rtes. 10 and 112.* Straddling the confluence of the Saint-François and Magog Rivers, this industrial centre is the principal city of the townships. The **Museum of Fine Arts** (Musée des Beaux-Arts) exhibits a fine collection of Quebec art, focusing on the Eastern Townships *(open year-round Tue–Sun 1–5pm, Wed 9pm; $2;* & ☎*819-821-2115)*. Standing atop the Marquette Plateau, the imposing Gothic Revival **cathedral★** was designed in 1958 by Louis-Napoléon Audet, who also designed the basilica at Sainte-Anne-de-Beaupré *(p 230)*. From this vantage point the **view★** encompasses the entire city.

★ **Magog** – Pop. 14,034. *124km/74mi east of Montreal by Rte. 10.* This popular resort community enjoys a splendid **setting★** on the shores of Lake Memphrémagog, which stretches over 50km/31mi, crossing the border into Vermont. **Scenic cruises★** on this long and narrow lake afford splendid views of the snow-capped peaks of Mt. Orford, Sugar Loaf and Owl's Head *(depart from Quai Fédéral late Jun–Labour Day daily 9am–4pm; rest of Sept weekends 9am–4pm only; round-trip 1hr 45min; commentary; reservations suggested; $10.75;* ╳ & ☎*819-843-8068)*.

★ **Saint-Benoît-du-Lac Abbey** (Abbaye de Saint-Benoît-du-Lac)– *20km/12mi south of Magog by Rte. 112 west; follow signs. Open year-round daily 8–11am & 1–5pm.* & ☎*819-843-4080.* The pleasant drive to this Benedictine monastery offers lovely glimpses of the sparkling lake waters. Distinguished by its impressive bell tower, the complex was designed by Dom Paul Bellot (1876-1944), who is buried in the cemetery. The monks are famous for their Gregorian chant and for the cheese (L'Ermite and Mont-Saint-Benoît) they produce and sell on the premises.

★ **Mount Orford Park** – *116km/72mi east of Montreal by Rte. 10 (Exit 115) and Rte. 141. Open year-round. Visitor centre open mid-Jun–Labour Day daily 8:30am–4:30pm. Rest of the year Mon–Fri 8:30am–4:30pm. $3. sailing, swimming, hiking, golf.* ⌂ *(summer only)* ╳ & ☎*819-843-6233.* Created in 1938 this provincial park is dominated by Mt. Orford (881m/2,890ft), a well-known ski centre. Follow a short path around the television tower at the summit for a sweeping **panorama★★** north to the St. Lawrence Valley, west to the Monteregian Hills, south to Lake Memphrémagog and east to the Appalachians.

Orford Arts Centre (Centre d'Arts Orford) – *Open Apr–May & Sept–Oct daily 9am–5pm. Late Jun–Aug Mon–Tue 9am–5pm, Wed & Sun 10am–5pm, Thu–Sat 1–8pm.* ✗ ♿. *For information on concerts, workshops & exhibitions ☎819-843-3981.* Founded in 1951 the centre is renowned for its annual summer music festival *(Festival Orford)*. The great concert hall was formerly the Man and Music pavilion of Montreal's Expo '67.

Compton – Pop. 899. *172km/107mi east of Montreal by Rtes. 10, 143 and 147.* This quiet village is the birthplace of **Louis-Stephen Saint-Laurent** (1882-1973), Canada's 12th prime minister. An ardent Canadian nationalist, Saint-Laurent fought to establish a distinct Canadian identity during his years in office (1948-57).

★ **Louis-S. St.-Laurent National Historic Site** (Lieu historique national Louis-S. St-Laurent) – *Rue Principale. Open mid-May–mid-Oct daily 10am–5pm. $2.50.* ♿ ☎*819-835-5448.* The simple clapboard house, full of mementos of the Saint-Laurent family, has been restored to represent various periods of the prime minister's life. The adjoining general store, originally run by Saint-Laurent's father, is stocked with replicas of goods sold here at the turn of the century. A **multimedia biography** *(20min)* presents the highlights of Saint-Laurent's life and career.

Granby – Pop. 42,804. *80km/50mi southeast of Montreal by Rte. 10 (Exit 68) and Rtes. 139 and 112.* Set on the banks of the Yamaska River, this small industrial centre was settled by Loyalists in the early 19C. Today it is especially known for its **zoo★** one of the largest in Canada, featuring over 1,000 animals, including 225 species of mammals and birds *(Blvd. Bouchard; open mid-May–mid-Oct daily 10am–5pm; $15;* ✗ ♿ ☎*514-372-9113)*. Of particular interest is the reptile house, with over 350 reptiles displayed in a near-natural environment.

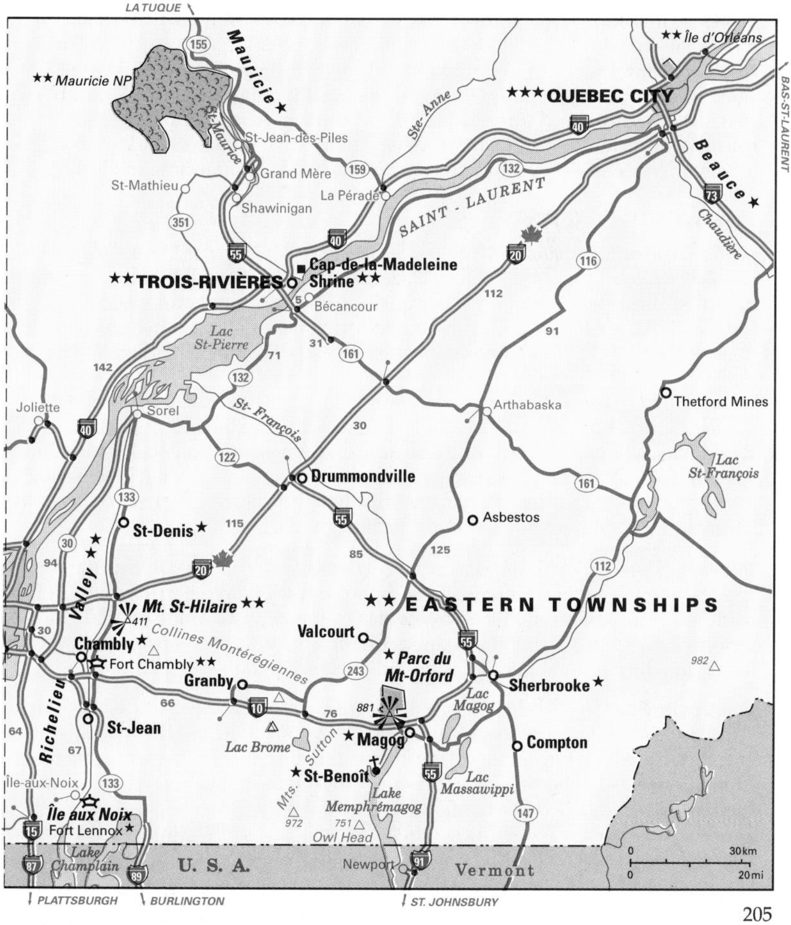

Valcourt – Pop. 2,284. *130km/81mi east of Montreal by Rte. 10 (Exit 90) and Rtes. 243 and 222.* Long a small agricultural community, Valcourt is today the centre of a thriving **snowmobile** industry, begun by one of its residents. Joseph-Armand Bombardier (1907-64) first developed a drive-wheel and track mechanism to power vehicles over snow in 1937. In 1959 he introduced the **Ski-Doo**, which went on to transform life in the north. Today J.-A. Bombardier Industries develops and sells snowmobiles all over the world.

★ **J.-Armand Bombardier Museum** (Musée J.-Armand Bombardier) – *1001 Ave J.-A. Bombardier. Open Jun 24–Labour Day daily 10am–5:30pm. Rest of the year Tue–Sun 10am–5pm. Closed Jan 1 & Dec 25–26. $5.* ☎514-532-5300. Divided into three sections, this fascinating museum highlights the life and work of Valcourt's native son. One section illustrates the Ski-Doo's assembly and usage; another section re-creates the garage where Bombardier worked as a mechanic and inventor.

Drummondville – Pop. 35,462. *110km/68mi east of Montreal by Rte. 20 (Exit 177).* Founded as a military outpost after the War of 1812, this community is today an important industrial centre for the garment industry.

★ **Québécois Village of Olden Times** (Village québécois d'antan) – *Rue Montplaisir, Exit 181 off Rte. 20. Open Jun 1–24 daily 9:30am–5pm. Jun 25–Labour Day daily 10am–6pm. Early Sept–early Oct weekends only 10am–6pm (ticket windows close 4pm). $9.* ☎819-478-1441. About 30 authentic buildings (church, school, tavern, forge, farm and homes) were relocated to this pleasant site to re-create life in the region during the 19C. Costumed interpreters explain the daily life of the former occupants.

GASPÉ PENINSULA★★★

Map of Principal Sights p 5

This peninsula extends along the southern shore of the St. Lawrence, advancing into the gulf of the same name. The interior is largely an impenetrable wilderness of mountains and forest, dominated by a continuation of the Appalachians—the mountains known as the **Chic-Chocs**, which rise to their highest peak at **Mt. Jacques Cartier** (1,288m/4,227ft). Tiny fishing villages dot the wild and rocky northern coast of the peninsula, culminating in the breathtaking beauty of Forillon and Percé. Agriculture and forestry are the primary industries along the southern coast. In addition to spectacular scenery that attracts visitors year-round, the region offers excellent cuisine and some of the best salmon fishing in Quebec.

THE NORTH COAST

★★ **Métis Gardens (Jardins de Métis)** – *350km/217mi southeast of Quebec City. Open Jun–Sept daily 8:30am–8pm. $6.* ☎418-775-2221. In 1918 Elsie Meighen Reford inherited this tract of land from her uncle, Sir George Stephen, president of the Canadian Pacific Railway Co. She transformed the estate into magnificent gardens. Since 1961 the property has been owned and maintained by the government of Quebec.

Over 1,000 varieties of flowers and ornamental plants, including many rare species, flourish in six distinct gardens that rank among the most beautiful in the world. Pleasant paths wind along a stream, revealing beautifully coloured plants, such as lilies, rhododendrons, azaleas, Asiatic gentians and Tibetan blue poppies. In the centre of the gardens stands the **Villa Reford**, an elegant mansion erected by Stephen. The first floor houses dining facilities and a craft shop.

Matane – Pop. 12,756. *55km/34mi east of Métis Gardens.* This small industrial centre is known for its salmon fishing and shrimp production. In the town centre, a **fish ladder**★ (passe migratoire) enables the fish to travel upstream from mid-June to October. The 44m/144ft channel passes through the lower level of an observation tower, in which several port holes provide a close-up look at the salmon.

★ **Gaspésie Park** – *103km/64mi east of Matane. Open year-round. Hiking, fishing, canoeing, cross-country skiing.* ☎418-763-3301. Created in 1937, this park encompasses 800sq km/309sq mi devoted to the conservation of plant and animal life indigenous to the province. It is the only place in Quebec where caribou, moose and white-tailed deer are known to co-exist.

The **Mt. Albert Sector** reflects vegetation characteristic of the northern tundra. In the **Lake Cascapédia Sector**, the ridges of the Chic-Chocs Mountains offer spectacular **views**★★ of the Appalachians. From the summit of Mt. Jacques Cartier, home to caribou and arctic-alpine flora, an expansive **view**★★ extends to the McGerrigle Mountains. The **nature centre** presents exhibits, films, lectures and slide shows *(open Jun–mid-Oct daily 8am–8pm;* ✗ ♿ ☎ *418-763-7811)*.

★★ **Scenic Route** – Past Gaspésie Park, Route 132 follows the contours of the coastline, up and over rocky cliffs, affording splendid views of hills, valleys, picturesque fishing villages and the ocean. Of particular interest are the impressive shale cliffs around **Mont-Saint-Pierre** and the expansive views of the gulf from the bustling fishing village of **Rivière-au-Renard**.

★★ **Forillon National Park** – ☞ *217km/135mi east of Gaspésie Park. Open year-round. $2.50.* △ ✗ ♿ ☎ *418-368-5505*. Located on the eastern tip of the peninsula, this 245sq km/95sq mi park includes limestone cliffs towering over the sea; mountains of spruce, fir, poplar and cedar; wildflower meadows; and sandy beaches tucked away in hidden coves. The visitor centre features displays and films on the park, as well as saltwater aquariums *(open early Jun–mid-Oct daily 9am–6pm;* ♿ ☎ *418-892-5572)*. A road leads to **Cape Bon Ami**, providing magnificent **views**★★ of the sea and the limestone cliffs. At **Cape Gaspé**★, a pleasant walk affords **views**★ of the Bay of Gaspé and Île Bonaventure. Nearby in the former fishing village of **Grande-Grave**★, several historic buildings have been restored.

★ **Gaspé** – Pop. 16,402. *42km/26mi south of Forillon National Park.* Occupying a pleasant site at the point where the York River empties into the Bay of Gaspé, this city is now the administrative and commercial centre of the peninsula. The **Museum of the Gaspé Peninsula**★ (Musée de la Gaspésie) *(open mid-May–Jun 23 Mon–Fri 9am–5pm, weekends noon–5pm; Jun 24–Labour Day daily 8:30am–8:30pm; early Sept–mid-Oct Mon–Fri 9am–5pm, weekends noon–5pm; rest of the year Mon–Fri 9am–noon & 1–5pm, weekends 1–5pm); $3.50;* ♿ ☎ *418-368-8600)*, dedicated to the preservation of Gaspesian culture and heritage, highlights historical events such as Jacques Cartier's discovery of the peninsula in 1534, the Micmac Indian population and regional geography. Completed in 1969 the **Cathedral of Christ the King**★ (Cathédrale du Christ-Roi) is distinguished by its unusual lines and a cedar exterior that blends harmoniously with the environment.

THE SOUTH COAST

★★★ **Percé** – Pop. 4,028. *76km/47mi south of Gaspé.* This bustling town was named for the massive offshore rock pierced *(percé)* by the sea. The landscape, a culmination of all the scenic beauty of the peninsula, is marked by reddish-gold limestone and shale rock, pushed and folded into a wonderful variety of cliffs, bays and hills. A tiny fishing village until the advent of tourism at the turn of the century, Percé now boasts some of the finest restaurants and tourist facilities on the peninsula.

★★ **Percé Rock** (Rocher Percé) – Once attached to the mainland, this mammoth rock wall is 438m/1,437ft long and 88m/289ft high. At one time the limestone block may have had up to four archways. One of them crumbled in 1845, leaving a detached

View of Percé Rock from Mt. Sainte-Anne

Sylvain Majeau/Tourisme Québec

slab called the Obelisk. Today only a 30m/94ft arch remains. The sculptured lime-stone rock is connected to **Mont Joli★★** by a sand bar, accessible at low tide.

★★★ **The Coast** – The shoreline along Route 132 offers spectacular **views★★** of the area. Just before entering Percé, a path leads up to **Cape Barré**, which affords a commanding view to the west of the the cliffs known as Trois-Sœurs (Three Sisters). South of Percé a promontory at **Côte Surprise** offers another superb view of the rock and the village.

Rising 320m/1,050ft above Percé, **Mt. Sainte-Anne** features extraordinary red-rock formations. Lookouts stationed along the way to the summit (*2hr trail*) provide increasingly expansive **views★★★** of Percé Rock, the village and the surrounding area. Following the top of the sheer cliff on the west side of Mt. Sainte-Anne, another trail provides views of the **Great Crevasse★**, a deep fissure in the red conglomerate rock.

★ **Île Bonaventure and Percé Rock Park** (Parc de l'Île-Bonaventure-et-du-Rocher-Percé) – *Open late May–Jun 24 daily 8:15am–4pm. Jun 25–Labour Day daily 8:15am–5pm. Early Sept–mid-Oct daily 9:15am–4pm.* ✗ ☎418-782-2240. In summer this flat-topped island is home to North America's largest **gannet** colony, with some 50,000 birds. These large, white sea birds nest in the crevices, cracks and ledges of the cliffs lining the island. A pleasant **boat trip** leads past Percé Rock and then around the island, affording superb views (*departs from Percé main wharf mid-May–mid-Oct daily 8am–5pm every 2hrs, Jul–Aug every hour; round-trip 1hr 30min; commentary; reservations suggested; $11; ⚲ Les Bateliers de Percé* ☎418-782-2974). In summer passengers can disembark on the island for a closer look at the birds and walk along the nature trails.

Bonaventure – Pop. 2,844. *131km/81mi southwest of Percé.* Founded in 1760 by Acadian settlers, this village is known for its salmon river and for its **Quebec Acadian Museum** (Musée acadien du Québec à Bonaventure), which illustrates the influence of these people on Quebec's culture (*open Jun 24–Labour Day daily 9am–8pm; rest of the year Mon–Fri 9am–noon & 1–5pm, weekends & holidays 1–5pm; $3.50;* ✗ ⚲ ☎418-534-4000).

Carleton – Pop. 2,749. *63km/39mi west of Bonaventure.* Nestled between the mountains and the sea, this community was founded by Acadians in the late 18C and has since become a choice summer resort. Carleton is dominated by **Mt. Saint-Joseph**, rising to 558m/1,830ft. From the summit, near a small stone shrine, the **panorama★★** encompasses Chaleur Bay from Bonaventure to the Miguasha Peninsula, and extends south to New Brunswick.

★ **Miguasha Park** – *24km/15mi west of Carleton. Open Jun–mid-Oct daily 9am–6pm.* ✗ ⚲ ☎418-794-2475. This national conservation park lies on an escarpment jutting out into Chaleur Bay, which contains fossils embedded in sedimentary rock since the Devonian Period (400 million years ago). Visitors are introduced to the world of fossils through exhibits at the interpretation centre, demonstrations in the laboratory and on-site observation of the cliff.

Battle of the Ristigouche National Historic Site (Lieu historique national Bataille-de-la Ristigouche) – ✈ *44km/27mi from Miguasha Park.* France's last attempt to save its North American colony from British domination during the Seven Years' War was thwarted in the estuary of the Ristigouche River in 1760. A **visitor centre** features exhibits and an animated film (*15min*) on the battle and displays the hull and anchor of the French warship *Le Machault*, which sank nearby (*open Mar–May by appointment; Jun–Labour Day daily 9am–5pm; early Sept–early Oct daily 9am–noon & 1–4:15pm; mid-Oct–Nov by appointment; $3;* ⚲ ☎418-788-5676).

Addresses, telephone numbers, opening hours and prices published in this guide are accurate at the time of publication.

We apologize for any inconveniences resulting from outdated information, and we welcome corrections and suggestions that may assist us in preparing the next edition.

HULL★

Pop. 60,707
Map of Principal Sights p 4

Facing OTTAWA across the wide waters of the Ottawa River, this bustling community was founded in 1800. Though Hull remains an important lumber, pulp and paper centre, today it functions primarily as an annex to the federal capital. The downtown area has witnessed a great deal of change, including the construction of two large federal government complexes and creation of a new campus for the University of Quebec.

SIGHTS 1 day

★★★ **Canadian Museum of Civilization** (Musée canadien des civilisations) – *Map p 162. 100 Rue Laurier. Open Jan–Apr Tue–Sun 9am–5pm (Thu 9pm). May–Jun daily 9am–6pm (Thu 9pm). Jul–Labour Day daily 9am–6pm (Thu–Fri 9pm). Early Sept–mid-Oct daily 9am–6pm (Thu 9pm). Rest of the year Tue–Sun 9am–5pm (Thu 9pm). $5 (free Sun 9am–noon).* ✗ & ☎819-776-7000. Inaugurated in 1989 this sizeable museum is dedicated to the history of Canada and to the art and traditions of native cultures and ethnic groups. The sweeping curves of the two large buildings designed by Douglas Cardinal evoke the emergence of the North American continent and its subsequent molding by wind, water and glaciers. The **Canadian Shield Wing** houses administrative offices and conservation laboratories, while the **Glacier Wing** provides 16,500sq m/33,792sq ft of exhibit halls.

In the **grand hall** six cultural regions of the Canadian Pacific Coast are illustrated through the wooden homes of village chieftains and majestic totem poles, rising to the ceiling. In the **Canada Hall** artifacts and reconstructed buildings re-create 1,000 years of Canadian heritage. The delightful **children's museum** encourages young people to explore the world, from a Mexican village to a Pakistani street. A costume room, puppet theatre, games section and art studio complete the exhibit. In the **CINÉPLUS Theatre** *($8)*, a 6-storey IMAX screen and an OMNIMAX dome provide unparalleled viewing opportunities for 295 spectators.

Canadian Museum of Civilization

★★ **Gatineau Park** – *Map p 164. Open daily year-round. Parkways closed from first snowfall until early May. Visitor centre open mid-May–Labour Day daily 9am–6pm. Rest of the year Mon–Fri 9:30am–4:30pm, weekends 9am–5pm. Beach access & skiing $6/day per car.* △ ✗ & ☎819-827-2020. Covering 356sq km/137sq mi, this enchanting place lies nestled between the valleys of the Ottawa and Gatineau Rivers. Formerly Algonquin and Iroquois territory, the land was designated a park in the 1930s with the assistance of **William Lyon Mackenzie King** *(p 161)*, tenth prime minister of Canada. Today the park encloses several federal government buildings. A scenic parkway winding its way through dense hardwood forests leads to **Champlain Lookout**, which offers a magnificent **panorama**★★ of the Ottawa Valley.

★ **Mackenzie King Estate (Domaine Mackenzie-King)** – *Open mid-May–mid-Jun Wed–Sun noon–5pm. Mid-Jun–mid-Oct daily noon–5pm.* ✗ & ☎613-239-5000. King willed his estate to Canada in 1950. His primary residence, **Moorside**, features exhibits and an audio-visual presentation *(15min)*, and houses a delightful tea room.

LAURENTIANS★★

Map p 204

Stretching along the north shore of the St. Lawrence, this range of low, rounded mountains rises to an altitude of 968m/3,175ft at **Mt. Tremblant**. Part of the Canadian Shield, the Laurentians (Laurentides in French), formed more than a billion years ago in the Precambrian era, are among the oldest mountains in the world. The area north of MONTREAL between Saint-Jérôme and Mt. Tremblant is especially noted for its string of resort towns that offer an attractive blend of recreational activities and fine cuisine. In winter alpine skiers have a choice of over 100 ski lifts and tows, while cross-country enthusiasts can explore a variety of lengthy trails. In summer water sports prevail on the innumerable lakes, and the surrounding hills cater to hikers, horseback riders and golfers. In the towns several renowned summer theatres open their doors to visitors.

Weaving through forest-clad hills, the drive along Route 117 from Saint-Jérôme to Saint-Jovite is particularly splendid in fall, when the mountains display a dazzling array of colours.

SIGHTS

★ **Sainte-Adèle** – Pop. 4,916. *68km/42mi north of Montreal by Rte. 15 and Rte. 117.* This resort community nestled around a small lake is popular with artists and writers. The **Séraphin Village Museum**★ (Musée village de Séraphin) comprises some 20 buildings re-creating the life of the first settlers in the area *(4km/2.5mi north of town; open mid-May–Jun 23 weekends only 10am–6pm; Jun 24–Labour Day daily 10am–6pm; early Sept–mid-Oct weekends only 10am–6pm; $8.75;* ✕ ☎514-229-4777). Inspired by Claude-Henri Grignon's 1933 work, *The Woman and the Miser*, several structures illustrate episodes in the life of Séraphin Poudrier, the novel's protagonist.

★ **Sainte-Agathe-des-Monts** – Pop. 5,452. *18km/11mi north of Sainte-Adèle by Rte. 117.* Set on the shores of the H-shaped **Sables Lake**★★, this lively town is the capital of the Laurentians region. A **scenic cruise** is recommended to discover the magnificent lake and the sumptuous homes lining its shores *(departs from dock at Rue Principale mid-May–late Oct daily 10:30, 11:30am & 1:30, 2:30, 3:30pm; round-trip 50min; commentary; $10; Les Croisières Alouette Inc.* ☎819-326-3656).

★ **Mt. Tremblant Park** – *About 140km/87mi north of Montreal. Open daily year-round. Park road sections closed in winter. Use fee.* ⚠ ♿ ☎819-688-2281. Dominating the long, narrow Lake Tremblant, Quebec's oldest provincial park abounds in lakes, waterfalls and hiking trails. This recreational wonderland is also home to rich and diverse fauna and a multitude of birds.

Laurentides – Pop. 2,336. *62km/38mi north of Montreal by Rte. 15, then east on Rte. 158.* This small industrial town is known as the birthplace of **Sir Wilfrid Laurier** (1841-1919), the first French-Canadian prime minister of Canada (1896-1911). The **National Historic Site** (Lieu historique national de Sir-Wilfrid-Laurier), a simple brick structure, stands on the place of Laurier's presumed birthplace *(open mid-May–Jun 23 Mon–Fri 9am–5pm; Jun 24–Labour Day Wed–Sun 10am–6pm; $2.50;* ☎514-439-3702). Next to it, a visitor centre exhibits displays on the influential role Laurier played in Canadian politics.

MAGDALEN ISLANDS★★

Pop. 14,397
Map of Principal Sights p 5
Tourist Office ☎418-986-2245

Located in the middle of the Gulf of St. Lawrence, this isolated, windswept outpost consists of eight islands and numerous islets connected by sandspits that form a hook-shaped mass about 72km/45mi long. The archipelago's most striking features are the spectacular rock formations, cut into the stone by the pounding sea. Contrasting with the red sandstone, expansive white beaches stretch to the blue sea.

Though discovered in 1534 by Jacques Cartier, the islands were not permanently inhabited until 1755, when they became a refuge for **Acadians** deported from Nova Scotia—the ancestors of many of the present population known as *Madelinots*. Supplemented by agriculture, logging and a growing tourism industry, fishing remains the primary economic activity of the archipelago. Today the islands offer a wealth of outdoor recreation, from sightseeing to swimming and hiking.

Access – *Car ferries from Souris, Prince Edward Island: Apr–mid-Jun & mid-Sept–late Sept daily (except Mon) 2pm; mid-Jun–early Jul & mid-Aug–Sept daily (except Tue) 2pm & 2am; Oct–Jan limited service; Feb-Mar no service; one-way $32/person, additional $61/car, 5hrs; reservations required; ℵ & Coopérative de Transport Maritime ☎902-687-2181. Flights from Montreal on Inter-Canadian ☎514-631-9802 and Air Alliance ☎514-422-2282. For information on guided tours, scenic cruises, restaurants and accommodations contact the tourist office in Cap-aux-Meules ☎418-986-2245.*

SIGHTS

★★ **Cap aux Meules Island** – The largest of the islands is also the archipelago's administrative and commercial centre. Cap-aux-Meules' highest point, **Butte du Vent**, affords extensive **views**★★ of the entire chain of islands. The western coast features some of the most dramatic **rock formations**★★ on the Magdalen Islands. The sea has carved the red sandstone into deep crevasses and defiant promontories, creating a spectacular landscape of crumbled arches and solitary columns of stone.

★ **Havre Aubert Island** – Marked by gentle, rolling hills, this southernmost island is the centre of the archipelago's cultural life. At the **Maritime Museum**★ (Musée de la Mer) displays of boats and navigational instruments aquaint visitors with the maritime history and culture of the Magdalen Islands *(open Jun 24–Aug 24 Mon–Fri 9am–6pm, weekends & holidays 10am–6pm; rest of the year Mon–Fri 9am–noon & 1–5pm, weekends & holidays 1–5pm; $3.50; & ☎418-937-5711).* The historic site of **La Grave**★ encompasses some 15 buildings, including stores, ironworks, *chaufauds* (sheds where cod was dried) and warehouses.

★ **Havre aux Maisons Island** – This elongated island has retained its rural charm and features some of the best examples of local domestic architecture, including the **baraque**, a small building designed to shelter hay. At **Dune du Sud**★ a fine beach and elaborate rock formations attract visitors.

On **Grande Entrée Island**★, coastal hiking trails afford spectacular **views**★★★ of jagged cliffs and jutting promontories, tidal pools and vast beaches, twisted trees and colourful wildflowers. The **Grande Échouerie Beach**★★ to the northeast is considered the archipelago's loveliest.

MONTREAL★★★

Metro Pop. 1,775,871
Map of Principal Sights p 5
Tourist Office ☎514-873-2015

Canada's second largest metropolis after Toronto *(p 172)* is located on a large island wedged into the mighty St. Lawrence River, some 1,000 miles from the Atlantic. Owing in part to its key geographical position, this cosmopolitan city has emerged as a leading industrial, commercial and financial centre.
Home to the world's largest Francophone population outside Paris, Montreal presents a unique combination of Old World cultures and North American modernity. A sizeable English-speaking community is particularly prominent in the business sector. The city offers visitors a wealth of cultural attractions and a diversity of urban settings, each with its distinctive ambience—from the charming cobblestone streets of Old Montreal to the landmark skyscrapers dominating the downtown cityscape.

Historical Notes

Early Exploration – While searching for riches and a route to the Orient in 1535, Jacques Cartier landed on the island of Montreal and visited the Mohawk village of **Hochelaga**. After founding Quebec City *(p 223)*, Samuel de Champlain sailed upriver and set foot on the nearby island of St. Helen *(p 221)* in 1611. However, European settlement of the area did not occur until the arrival, in 1642, of Paul de Chomedey, **Sieur de Maisonneuve** (1612-76), who is considered the founder of Montreal.

Under the French Regime – Early in the 17C, two superiors of the Sulpician order in France decided to found a mission on the island of Montreal, as part of an effort to revive Roman Catholicism in the aftermath of the Protestant Reformation. They chose Maisonneuve to sail across the Atlantic with some 40 companions and establish the mission of **Ville-Marie** (City of Mary).

Amid continued fighting between Iroquois inhabitants and the French settlers, Ville-Marie slowly developed into a commercial centre and was renamed Montreal in the early 18C. Seeking profit, the French set off across the Great Lakes to trap fur-bearing animals. The furs were highly prized in Europe, where they were transformed into luxurious apparel, and the trade boomed. By the time of the surrender of Montreal in 1760 *(p 196)*, the city had become a well-established, thriving community. After the British victory, most of the French nobility returned to France. A large number of Scots, attracted to the fur trade, and an influx of Loyalists from the US swelled the anglophone population.

From Rebellion to Confederation – The fur trade reached its heyday in the late 18C and early 19C, bringing great prosperity to Montreal. Two partnerships, the **North West Company** (based in Montreal) and the **Hudson's Bay Company**, established trading posts all over northern Canada and monopolized the market. By the time the companies merged in 1821, however, Montreal's dominance in the trade was in decline. Montreal was the centre of one of the **Rebellions of 1837** *(p 196)*, a political uprising against British rule, which, in Lower Canada, contested the power held by the Crown-appointed governor and his council. Led by Louis-Joseph Papineau, George-Étienne Cartier and other French Canadians, the **Patriots** engaged in several armed revolts against British troops. Although the insurgents were defeated, the British government subsequently decided to grant Quebec a representative government.

By the time of Confederation in 1867, Montreal stood at the forefront of railway development and claimed the world's largest grain port. Financial institutions sprouting along Rue Saint-Jacques promoted growth of the city and country and contributed to Montreal's dominance in Canada's financial sector until the 1970s.

Montreal Today – Following a period of slow growth after the Great Depression, Montreal experienced a revival in the 1950s and 60s, manifested in restoration projects throughout the city. Montreal has emerged as an international centre of commerce and culture. In addition to hosting such events as the 1967 World Fair (Expo '67), the 1976 Olympic Games and the 1980 International Floralies, the city features annual international festivals in jazz, film and comedy, attracting thousands of visitors. Internationally acclaimed artists regularly perform at Montreal's premier cultural complex, **Place des Arts★★**, home to the Montreal Symphony Orchestra, the Grands Ballets Canadiens and the Montreal Opera.

The city remains a major centre of francophone culture. Its numerous cafes and restaurants, especially along Saint-Denis and Crescent Streets, reflect Montrealers' *joie de vivre*. Visitors to this vibrant city will also enjoy the variety of shops and boutiques. In 1992 Montreal celebrated the 350th anniversary of its foundation.

In Montreal, the Sun Rises in the South – The St. Lawrence River generally flows in a west-to-east direction, and its banks are referred to as the north and south shores. At Montreal, however, the river takes a sudden turn northward. The streets parallel to the river are called east-west streets, although they actually run north-south, and the perpendicular streets are designated north-south, although they extend east-west.

Place Jacques-Cartier

Tourisme Québec

PRACTICAL INFORMATION .... Area Code 514

Getting Around

By Public Transportation – Société de Transport de la Communauté Urbaine de Montréal (STCUM) operates the city buses, and the **Metro** *(daily 5:30am–12:30 or 1:10am, depending on the line)*. Tickets are available individually *($1.75)*, or in books of six *($7.50)*; tourist passes also available. Metro lines are colour-coded and directions indicated refer to the station at the end of the line. Transfers to the bus system are free. For route information & schedules ☎288-6287.

By Car – Rental agencies include Avis ☎866-7906; Budget ☎866-7675; Hertz ☎842-8537; Tilden ☎878-2771.

By Taxi – La Salle ☎277-2552; Diamond ☎273-6331; Champlain ☎273-2435.

General Information

Accommodations and Visitor Information – For hotels/motels contact Tourisme Québec ☎873-2015; for a listing of major chains *p 316*. Reservation services: Hospitality Canada ☎393-1528; Montreal Reservations Centre ☎284-2277. Infotourist Office: 1001 Rue du Square-Dorchester, ● Peel *(open mid-Jun–Labour Day daily 8:30am–7:30pm; rest of the year daily 9am–6pm;* ☎873-2015*)*.

Local Press – English *The Gazette.* French *Le Journal de Montréal, Le devoir, La Presse* (daily).

Entertainment – For current schedules and for addreses of principal theatres and concert halls, consult the free tourist publications *Mirror* and *Hour* (English), *Montréal Scope* (bilingual) and *Voir* (French) or the arts and entertainment supplements in local newspapers (weekend editions). Tickets may be purchased from Admission ☎790-1245, Montreal Reservations Centre ☎284-2277 and Voyages Astral Inc. ☎866-1001 (most major credit cards accepted).

Sports – Montréal Canadiens (National Hockey League): home games at the Montreal Forum; season Oct–Jun; ☎932-2582. Montréal Expos (National League Baseball): home games at Olympic Stadium; season Apr–Sept; ☎846-39765.

Useful Numbers   ☎

Police	911
Central Station (VIA Rail), *895 Rue de la Gauchetière Ouest*	989-2626
Terminus Voyageur (Bus terminal), *505 Blvd. de Maisonneuve Est*	842-2281
Mirabel International Airport	476-3010
Canadian Automobile Assn., *1180 Drummond St.*	861-7575
Jean Coutu Drugstore (extended hours)	527-8827
Post Office, *1025 Rue Saint-Jacques Ouest*	846-5390
Road Conditions	873-4121
Weather (24hr)	283-4006

★★★ OLD MONTREAL (Vieux-Montréal)   *1 day. Map p 217.* ● *Place d'Armes.*

Bounded by the Old Port, Saint-Jacques, Berri and McGill Streets, Montreal's historic core was originally enclosed within imposing stone walls erected in the early 1700s. During the 19C the settlement expanded and Montrealers moved outside the fortifications. Warehouses and commercial buildings gradually replaced stone dwellings and gardens, and the area fell into decline. Interest in Old Montreal was revived in the 1960s: the surviving 18C homes were renovated, warehouses were transformed into apartment buildings, and restaurants and shops opened. Today Old Montreal is a pleasant area that caters mainly to tourists. Amphibious buses **(Amphi-bus)** tour part of Old Montreal *(map p 217)* before embarking on a cruise around Cité du Havre *(depart from Blvd. Saint-Laurent and Rue de la Commune May–Jun 23 daily noon–8pm every 2hrs; Jun 24–Labour Day daily 10am–midnight on the hour; early Sept–Oct daily noon–8pm every 2hrs; round-trip 1hr; commentary; reservations required; $18;* 🄿 *Amphi Tour Lté* ☎514-849-5181*)*.

★ **Place d'Armes** – Designed in the 17C by the Sulpician Dollier de Casson, this square long served as military drill grounds. A **monument★ [1]** (Louis-Philippe Hébert) in the centre honours the founder of Montreal, Sieur de Maisonneuve, who, according to legend, killed the local Indian chief on this site during a 1644 battle. The west side of this charming green space is dominated by the **Bank of Montreal★** (1847), one of the city's finest examples of the Neoclassical style.

213

Extending south, **Rue Saint-Jacques★**, the financial heart of Canada until the 1970s, is lined with elegant 19C and 20C edifices. Note in particular the Canadian Imperial Bank of Commerce *(no. 265)*, with its facade of fluted Corinthian columns, and the **Royal Bank of Canada★** *(no. 360)*, whose tower is a distinct feature of the city's skyline.

★★★ **Notre Dame Basilica** – *Open Jun 24–Labour Day daily 7am–8pm. Rest of the year 7am–6pm.* ♿ ☎514-842-2925. This twin-towered church rises on the south side of the Place d'Armes. Completed in 1829 under the supervision of James O'Donnell, the Gothic Revival basilica is especially renowned for its magnificent **interior**. The opulent decor, designed by Victor Bourgeau, features sculptures, wainscoting and giltwork typical of provincial religious architecture. The main nave, lined on both sides by deep-set double galleries, measures 68m/223ft long, 21m/69ft wide and 25m/82ft high. As visitors enter, eyes are drawn to the ensemble of white oak statues, part of the imposing **reredos** that stands out against the background's soft blue hues. The massive black walnut **pulpit★** is the work of Louis-Philippe Hébert. Behind the choir the Sacred Heart Chapel is dominated by an impressive **bronze reredos** representing mankind's difficult journey to heaven.

The **Old Sulpician Seminary★**, the oldest structure in the city, stands beside the basilica. Note the facade **clock**, installed in 1701, believed to be the oldest public timepiece in North America.

★★ **Place Jacques-Cartier** – *Illustration p 212.* Lined with outdoor cafes and flower parterres, this charming cobblestone square is lively all summer, especially in the evenings, when street musicians and acrobats entertain the crowds. Created in 1847 the square was named for the famous explorer who, according to tradition, docked his ship here in 1535. Marking the north end of the plaza, a **statue [2]** of Horatio Nelson (1809) commemorates the British general's victory at Trafalgar. Montreal's **City Hall★** (Hôtel de Ville), an imposing Second Empire building, stands across Rue Notre-Dame *(open year-round Mon–Fri 8:30am–4:30pm;* 🅿 ♿ ☎514-872-3355). Charles de Gaulle delivered his famous "Vive le Québec libre" speech in 1967 from the balcony overlooking the main entrance. The southern end of the square leads to **Rue Saint-Paul★★**, a charming street lined with lovely 19C buildings, and several warehouses transformed into shops and artists' studios. Along with Rue Notre-Dame, this narrow street is one of the oldest in Montreal.

★ **Old Port (Vieux-Port)** – Stretching along the St. Lawrence River, at the foot of Place Jacques-Cartier, the former port has been transformed into a pleasant waterfront park with bike and walking paths, a skating rink, exhibition spaces, an IMAX cinema and a flea market. Stroll along the wide boardwalk or take a **harbour cruise★** to enjoy scenic **views★** of the city and the majestic river *(departs from Quai de l'Horloge mid-May–mid-Oct daily 2:30pm; additional cruise mid-Jun–Labour Day daily at noon; round-trip 2hrs; commenˌ'ary; reservations required; $19.75;* ✗ ♿ ☎514-842-3871).

★★ **Jet Boat Trips on the Lachine Rapids** (Expéditions dans les rapides de Lachine) – *Departs from Quai de l'Horloge. Protective clothing provided. Warning: not for the faint-hearted. May–Sept daily 10am, noon, 2, 4 & 6pm. Round-trip 1hr30min. Commentary. Reservations required. $48.*♿ 🅿*Lachine Rapids Tours Ltd* ☎514-284-9607. On this wet and exciting voyage, passengers are whisked upriver in specially designed vessels that mount and descend the ferocious Lachine Rapids. The **views★★** of Montreal and the surrounding areas are spectacular.

★ **Château Ramezay** – *280 Rue Notre Dame Est. Open mid-Jun–mid-Sept daily 10am–6pm. Rest of the year Tue–Sun 10am–4:30pm. Closed Jan 1 & Dec 25. $5.* ♿ 🅿 ☎514-861-3708. Situated across from City Hall, this squat, fieldstone residence (1705) is a lovely example of early-18C domestic architecture. Constructed for Claude de Ramezay, 11th governor of Montreal during the French Regime, the building has undergone several renovations, yet remains relatively unchanged in appearance. It was acquired by the British government to serve as the official gubernatorial residence until 1849.

Restored and transformed into a **museum** in 1895, the interior presents Montreal's economic, political and social history. The highlight is the exquisite, hand-carved mahogany **panelling** produced in 1725 in Nantes, France.

★ **Sir George-Étienne Cartier National Historic Site** – ☞ *458 Rue Notre-Dame. Open mid-Feb–mid-May Wed–Sun 10am–5pm. Mid-May–Labour Day daily 10am–5pm. Early Sept–late Dec Wed–Sun 10am–5pm. $3.* ♿ ☎514-283-2282. This limestone, mansard-roofed structure, composed of two adjoining houses, was the home of **George-Étienne Cartier** (1814-73), one of the Fathers of Confederation. Displays trace his life and career as a lawyer, businessman and politician. Refurbished in the Victorian style, period rooms illustrate the lifestyle of 19C middle-class society.

★ **Rue Bonsecours** – This attractive street leading from Rue Notre-Dame to Rue Saint-Paul offers a charming perspective of the little Notre-Dame-de-Bon-Secours Chapel *(below)*. At no. 440 stands the **Papineau House** (Maison Papineau), a large grey edifice topped by a steeply pitched roof that is pierced by two rows of dormer windows. During an 1831 reconstruction, the original stone walls were covered in wood, sculpted and painted to resemble limestone. The building was home to six generations of the Papineau family, including Louis-Joseph, leader of the Patriots during the 1837 Rebellions *(p 212)*. The fieldstone walls, firebreaks, corner consoles, tall chimneys and pitched gables of the **Calvet House★** (Maison du Calvet) (1798), located at the corner of Rue Saint-Paul, are characteristic of a traditional 18C urban residence.

★ **Chapel of Our Lady of Perpetual Help** (Chapelle Notre-Dame-de-Bon-Secours) – *400 Rue Saint-Paul Est.* This small church, topped by a copper steeple, stands on the site of a wooden edifice commissioned by Marguerite Bourgeoys in 1657 and destroyed by fire in 1754. Facing the St. Lawrence, a 9m/30ft statue of the Virgin Mary crowns the rear of the church. Climb the observatory, accessible from the tower, to enjoy a **panorama★** of the river, Old Montreal and the Old Port.

Located in the basement, the **Marguerite Bourgeoys Museum** features a collection of dolls that re-creates the life of Bourgeoys (1620-1700), who came to Montreal with Maisonneuve in 1653 to found the Congregation of Our Lady *(open May–Nov Tue–Sat 9am–4:30pm, Sun 11:30am–4:30pm; rest of the year Tue–Fri 10:30am–2:30pm, Sat 10am–4:30pm, Sun 11:30am–4:30pm; closed national holidays; $2;* ☎*514-845-9991).* Bourgeoys was canonized in 1982.

Near the church, on Rue Saint-Paul, stands the **Bonsecours Market★** (Marché Bonsecours), a large Neoclassical stone structure crowned by a lofty dome. It served as the city hall from 1852 to 1878, housing municipal offices thereafter and today is leased for office space, temporary exhibits and other purposes.

★ **Place d'Youville** – Located south of Place d'Armes, this pleasant square is surrounded by grand edifices. Housed in a brick structure reflecting the Dutch Baroque architectural style, the **Montreal History Centre★** (Centre d'histoire de Montréal) presents the city's rich past through interactive displays, artifacts, animated mannequins and a slide show *(10min) (open late Jun–early May Tue–Sun 10am–5pm; mid-May–mid-Jun daily 9am–5pm; mid-Jun–Labour Day daily 10am–6pm; early Sept–mid-Dec Tue–Sun 10am–5pm; $4.50;* & ☎*514-872-3207).* To the east of the square stand the **Youville Stables** (Écuries), an ensemble of grey stone structures (1828) enclosing a lovely garden courtyard. Located in a former warehouse, the **Marc-Aurèle Fortin Museum★** *(118 Rue Saint-Pierre; open year-round Tue–Sun 11am–5pm; closed late Dec–Jan & Good Friday; $4;* & ☎*514-845-6108)* exhibits the works of this 20C Québécois artist. His subjects include regional flora and fauna and St. Lawrence River landscapes. Spanning the block between Saint-Pierre and Normand Streets, the **Grey Nuns Convent** (Hôpital général des Soeurs Grises) was erected in 1694 and extended in 1753 by Marie d'Youville, founder of the Grey Nuns order.

Callière Point (Pointe-à-Callière) – Maisonneuve established the settlement of Ville-Marie on this small triangle of land. A 10m/33ft **obelisk [3]** commemorates the occasion of his landing in May 1642. Opened in 1992, the **Montreal Museum of Archaeology and History★★** (Musée d'Archéologie et d'Histoire de Montréal), composed of a modern building, a crypt and an 1838 Neoclassical edifice, presents Montreal's fascinating history through permanent and temporary exhibits and a multimedia presentation *(open Jul–Aug Tue–Sun 10am–8pm; rest of the year Tue–Sun 10am–5pm, Wed 8pm; $7;* ⨯& ☎*514-872-9150).* Located under Place Royale, the crypt displays vestiges recovered during archaeological excavations.

★★ **DOWNTOWN**   *1 day. Map pp 216-217.* ● *Rue Peel.*

Bordered by Rue Saint-Jacques to the east, Rue Sherbrooke to the west, and Saint-Denis and Atwater Streets to the north and south, the city's commercial and cultural heart lies to the west of Old Montreal. The downtown developed into a prosperous and bustling quarter during the late 18C and 19C, and today features some of Montreal's most famous buildings and institutions. A walk along Sherbrooke, one of the most prestigious arteries in the city, reveals a lively retail sector alongside choice residences. Rue Sainte-Catherine is home to major department stores (Ogilvy, La Baie, Eaton Centre) and commercial centres, while Avenue McGill College is lined with the city's landmark 20C skyscrapers.

★ **Dorchester Square** – Formerly known as Dominion Square, this pleasant green space was renamed in 1988 in honour of Lord Dorchester, governor of British North America during the late 18C. Long considered the centre of the city, the square is surrounded by a group of remarkable buildings, including the imposing Renaissance Revival **Dominion Square Building★** (1929) and **The Windsor★**, an elegant hotel, with its mansard roof pierced by dormer and œil-de-bœuf windows. The **Sun Life Building★★**, an imposing Beaux-Arts edifice erected in 1913, dominates the north side of the square. Note the colossal colonnades adorning all four facades. Facing Dorchester Square is **Place du Canada**, a small green plaza bordered by more recent constructions. Of particular interest are the **Château-Champlain Hotel** (1967), marked by convex, half-moon windows and **1000 de la Gauchetière** (1992), Montreal's tallest skyscraper.

★★ **Mary Queen of the World Basilica-Cathedral** (Basilique-Cathédrale Marie-Reine-du-Monde) – *Main entrance on Blvd. René-Lévesque. Open year-round daily 7am–7:30pm (Sat 8:30pm).* ☏*514-866-1661.* Commissioned by Msgr. Ignace Bourget to reinforce the Catholic presence in a predominantly Protestant district, this monumental church is distinguished by large Greek columns, ornate decoration and a row of statues crowning the cornice. Designed by Victor Bourgeau and modelled after St. Peter's in Rome, the Baroque Revival edifice was consecrated in 1894. Inside is

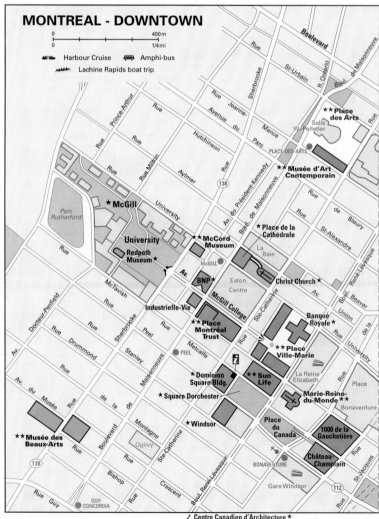

/ Centre Canadien d'Architecture ★

the magnificent gold-leaf **baldachin** (1900), a replica of the 16C ornamental canopy created by Bernini for St. Peter's Basilica. On the left side of the nave, a **mortuary chapel** (1933) decorated with beautiful mosaics contains the tombs of several archbishops and bishops as well as Msgr. Bourget's mausoleum.

★★ **Place Ville-Marie** – This 4-building complex ushered in the renaissance of the downtown area. Completed in the 1960s, it became the centrepiece of Montreal's underground city, an extensive network of spacious corridors connecting various hotels, office buildings, department stores, railway stations, cultural and conventions centres, as well as boutiques, cinemas and restaurants.

Dominating the complex is I. M. Pei's 42-storey **Banque Royale Tower★** (1962), a cruciform structure sheathed in aluminum. Along with the other three buildings, the Banque Royale encloses a concrete esplanade that affords an unparalleled **vista★** west to McGill University and Mt. Royal.

Extending from Place Ville-Marie to McGill University, **Avenue McGill College** is a veritable showplace for the city's post-Modern architecture. Completed in 1989, the enormous **Place Montréal Trust★★** *(no. 1500)* features a pastel blue, glass cylinder encased in a square base of rose marble and glass. Across the street *(no. 1981)* rise the sprawling, metallic-blue twin towers of the **National Bank of Paris (BNP)/ Laurentian Bank Towers★**. Designed in intricate geometric shapes, the towers were completed in 1981. The granite-clad **Industrial Life Tower** (Tour l'Industrielle Vie) *(no. 2000)* presents an elegant exterior enlivened by post-Modern ornamentation, such as the huge fanlight window.

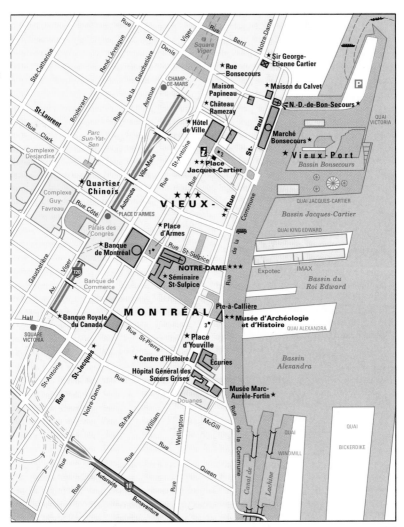

★ **Christ Church Cathedral** – *Entrance from Rue Sainte-Catherine between Rue University and Ave. Union. Open year-round daily 8am–6pm.* & ☎514-843-6577. Topped by a single, slender spire and distinguished by its triple portico, ornate gables and gargoyles, this handsome edifice (1859) exemplifies the Gothic Revival style. The ivy-covered church preserves a graceful interior, embellished by magnificent stained-glass windows and a beautifully carved stone **reredos**. The capitals of the arcaded nave are decorated with leaves representing trees indigenous to Canada.

Rising behind the church is a prominent landmark, the **Place de la Cathédrale★**, formerly the Coopérants Building. Designed to be viewed in tandem with the church, the copper-coloured edifice features colonnades, pointed entrances, arched windows and a pitched roof.

★★ **McCord Museum of Canadian History (Musée McCord d'Histoire canadienne)** – *690 Rue Sherbrooke Quest. Open year-round Tue–Fri 10am–6pm (Thu 9pm), weekends 10am–5pm. $5.* ✗ & ☎514-398-7100. One of Canada's foremost historical museums, the McCord was founded in 1921 and underwent extensive renovation in 1991. Holdings provide a fascinating insight into Canadian history, from the era of Indian settlement to the present day. In addition to more than 80,000 artifacts, the museum houses an outstanding compilation of over 700,000 photos that chronicle Canadian life in the 19C and 20C.

★ **McGill University** – *End of Ave. McGill College.* Set on the slopes of Mt. Royal, Canada's oldest university (1821) has witnessed much growth over the years and today claims an enrollment of some 30,000 students. The buildings gracing the 32ha/79 acre campus reflect a variety of architectural styles. Located on the campus and housed in a large structure designed in the style of an antique temple, the **Redpath Museum of Natural History★** (Musée d'histoire naturelle Redpath) displays vertebrate and invertebrate fossils, minerals, zoological artifacts, African art objects and Egyptian antiquities *(open Jun 24–Labour Day Mon–Thu 9am–5pm & Sun 1–5pm; rest of the year Mon–Fri 9am–5pm & Sun 1–5pm; closed national holidays;* ☎514-398-4086).

★★ **Montreal Museum of Fine Arts (Musée des Beaux-Arts de Montréal)** – *1380 Rue Sherbrooke Quest. Open year-round Tue–Sun 11am–6pm (Wed 9pm). $10.* ✗ & ☎514-285-2000. Ranked among Canada's finest museums, this 135-year-old institution boasts a permanent collection of over 25,000 objects ranging from Old Masters to contemporary Canadian art. The Beaux-Arts main edifice, known as the North Pavilion (1912), presents Canadian art on its three floors, while the South Pavilion (1991) displays masterpieces from all over the world. The buildings are linked by a series of underground galleries that exhibit Ancient, Asiatic and African art as well as **Islamic art**. Created by renowned architect **Moshe Safdie**, the new annex showcases travelling exhibits in five large vaulted galleries.

The North Pavilion's collection of **Canadian art**, ranging from the 18C to 1960, features paintings, sculpture and decorative arts. Of note are works by Paul Kane, Cornelius Krieghoff, J. W. Morrice, Suzor-Côté, the Group of Seven and modern artists Paul-Émile Borduas and Jean-Paul Riopelle. Of particular interest on the ground floor is the native American collection, including Inuit art. A fine collection of **prints and drawings**, including several by Albrecht Dürer, is found on this level.

The fourth floor of the South Pavilion is devoted to **European art** spanning the Middle Ages to the 19C, including works by Mantegna, Memling, El Greco, Rembrandt, Canaletto and Gainsborough. Displayed on the third level and the second underground level, the museum's rich collection of **20C Art** is represented by works by Picasso, Alexander Calder, Sam Francis, Betty Goodwin and others.

★ **Canadian Centre for Architecture (Centre Canadien d'Architecture)** – *1920 Rue Baile. Open Jun–Sept Tue–Sun 11am–6pm (Thu 8pm). Rest of the year Wed–Fri 11am–6pm (Thu 8pm) & weekends 11am–5pm. $5.* & 🅿 ☎514-939-7026. Designed by Peter Rose and Phyllis Lambert, the CCA (1989) is both an acclaimed museum and research facility and an original example of post-Modern architecture. Forming the core of the horseshoe-shaped building is **Shaughnessy House**, a Second Empire mansion built in 1874.

The main building's interior is embellished with limestone, black granite, maple panelling and aluminum fittings. Seven galleries display temporary exhibits on architectural themes. Also open to the public are the Shaughnessy House reception rooms and the delightful **conservatory** and **tea room**, which have been restored to their 19C splendour.

Across Boulevard René-Lévesque is an **architectural garden** by Melvin Charney, featuring an array of sculptures illustrating architectural elements such as pediments and columns.

★★ **Montreal Contemporary Art Museum (Musée d'art contemporarin de Montréal)** – *185 Rue Sainte-Catherine Ouest. Open year-round Tue–Sun 11am–6pm (Wed 9pm). $6.* ♨ ♿ 🅿 ☎*514-847-6212.* Housed in the most recent addition to the Place des Arts complex, this museum presents selections from the permanent collection of over 5,000 works of art, 60 percent of which is Quebec art. Emphasis is placed on post-1940 artists such as Paul-Émile Borduas, Alfred Pellan and Jean-Paul Riopelle. The rotating exhibits are supplemented by selections of contemporary art from all over the world.

★★ MT. ROYAL AND SURROUNDINGS *1/2 day*

Known to Montrealers as "the Mountain," Mt. Royal has become one of the city's most popular leisure spots. Rising abruptly from the otherwise flat plain, the 233m/764ft mountain forms part of the Monteregian Hills, a series of eight peaks located between the St. Lawrence and the Appalachians. The peaks are actually igneous plugs of magma that solidified before reaching the surface. To the west of Mt. Royal lies the former anglophone enclave of **Westmount**, one of the city's choicest residential areas. Gracing the hill's eastern flank is the town of **Outremont**, home to Montreal's Francophone bourgeoisie.

★★ **Mt. Royal Park (Parc du Mont-Royal)** – *Drive up Voie Camillien-Houde or Chemin Remembrance to the parking areas or climb on foot (20min) from Rue Peel at Ave. des Pins.* ● *Mont-Royal. Open year-round daily 6am–dusk.* ♨ ♿ 🅿 ☎*514-844-4928.* Opened to the public in 1876, the city's premier urban park was designed by American landscape architect **Frederick Law Olmsted**, creator of New York City's Central Park. Along with various plants and animals, the park has a lake, two lookout points, a chalet/visitor centre, an illuminated cross and numerous winding paths. In summer the park is lively with joggers; in winter horse-drawn sleds plow the snowy paths.

Viewpoints – The terrace fronting the **Chalet Lookout [A]** (Belvédère du Chalet) *(7min walk from parking area)* affords a splendid **view★★★** of the bustling downtown. Looming on the horizon, the Monteregian Hills dot the southern St. Lawrence shore. The walk around the summit leads to the **cross [B]**, a 36.6m/120ft metal structure, illuminated at night, that commemorates a wooden cross placed here by Maisonneuve *(p 211)*. From the popular **Camillien Houde Lookout** (Belvédère Camillien-Houde) *(accessible by vehicle on the Voie Camillien-Houde)*, the superb **view★★** of eastern Montreal is dominated by the Olympic Stadium *(p 220)*.

★★ **St. Joseph's Oratory (Oratoire Saint-Joseph)** – *Entrance on Chemin Queen Mary.* ● *Côte-des-Neiges. Open year-round daily 6am–9pm.* ♨ ♿ 🅿 ☎*514-733-8211.* Dominating the northern section of Montreal, this famed Roman Catholic shrine, set on the slope of Mt. Royal, is distinguished by its colossal dimensions and an octagonal, copper-clad dome.

A small chapel dedicated to the healing powers of St. Joseph was erected on this site in 1904 by Alfred Bessette, known as Brother André. Crowds of afflicted people came to pray with the friar. Leaving the chapel cured, they spread the lay brother's reputation as a healer. By the early 20C, a basilica was planned to receive the increasing number of visitors. Constructed under the supervision of the Benedictine monk and architect, **Dom Paul Bellot**, the monument was completed in 1967. Today over a million pilgrims visit the shrine annually.

In the immense, austere **interior**, note the carved bronze grilles executed by Roger Prévost, and the oak statues of the apostles and stone altar chiselled by Henri Charlier. From the wide terrace an excellent **view** of northern Montreal and the Laurentian Mountains can be obtained. Also contained within the edifice are a votive chapel, a 56-bell carillon and the **Brother André Museum** (Musée du Frère André), which displays a collection of photographs and mementos tracing the friar's life *(open year-round daily 10am–5pm; ☎514-733-8211)*. The **original chapel** (chapelle du Frère André) and Brother André's room are open to the public. Completed in 1960 the **Stations of the Cross★** are located in a pleasant hillside garden.

Boulevard Saint-Laurent – This bustling thoroughfare has traditionally divided the city into its predominantly Francophone eastern section and the Anglophone west. Today the boulevard attracts a diverse crowd to its shops, cafes, restaurants and "in" boutiques. Established in 1672 the artery long formed Montreal's principal passageway, hence its nickname "the Main." For centuries the Main has welcomed immigrants. During the 19C Chinese settled in the southern section, giving rise to a lively **Chinatown★** (Quartier chinois) *(at Rue de la Gauchetière)*. Jewish merchants arrived in the 1880s and moved into the northern section. Greeks moved to the area during the early 20C. More recent arrivals include Slavs, Portuguese and Latin Americans.

Hospitallers Museum (Musée des Hospitalières de l'Hôtel-Dieu de Montréal) – *201 Ave. des Pins Quest, entrance at Rue Saint-Urbain and Ave. du Parc. Open mid-Jun–mid-Oct Tue–Fri 10am–5pm, weekends 1–5pm. Rest of the year Wed–Sun 1–5pm. $5.* ☎514-849-2919. Housed in a former chaplain's residence (1925), this museum traces the history of the Hospitallers of St. Joseph (a religious order devoted to caring for the sick) and their presence in Montreal through documents, medical instruments and sacred art selected from the museum's permanent collection of over 7,000 artifacts. The viewing of temporary exhibits and a video *(15min, French only)* about the order's world role complete the visit.

★★★ OLYMPIC PARK AREA   *1 day*

This vast recreational area is situated in the eastern part of Montreal, which was known in the past as the city of **Maisonneuve**. Created by wealthy Francophone businessmen, the prosperous community launched a program of development during the late 19C, erecting grandiose mansions such as the Château Dufresne along its wide boulevards. The exorbitant cost drove Maisonneuve into bankruptcy, and the city was annexed to Montreal in 1918. Today, dominated by the striking silhouette of the Olympic Park, the area is home to Montreal's Botanical Garden and the 204ha/504 acre **Maisonneuve Park**.

★★ **Olympic Park** – *4141 Pierre-de-Coubertin Ave.* ● *Rue Viau. Information desk and ticket office at the base of the tower. Free shuttle service among the park, the Botanical Garden and the Biodome. Combination ticket for Biodome and Botanical Garden available ($14.75).* Constructed to accommodate the 1976 Olympic Games, this gigantic sports complex has become the symbol of Montreal's East End. The park includes a stadium, an aquatic centre, and a velodrome, which now houses the Biodôme *(below)*, a living museum of natural sciences. The **Olympic Village**—two striking 19-storey towers designed to lodge 11,000 athletes during the Games—now contains a residential and commercial complex.

Begun in 1973, the project soon encountered a series of technical difficulties, delaying construction of the stadium's roof and tower until 1987. Tremendously expensive ($1.2 billion), the complex became the city's most controversial public project. However, it has made a valiant effort to remain lucrative and has welcomed over 40 million visitors since 1976.

Stadium – *Visit by guided tour (30min) only, departing from the base of the tower, year-round daily 12:40 & 3:40pm. Closed mid-Jan–mid-Feb. $5.25.* ✗ ♿ ☐ ☎514-252-8687. Conceived by French architect Roger Taillibert, this immense concrete structure consists of 34 cantilevered ribs crowned by a structural ring and dominated by the world's tallest inclined tower. The building was originally designed to be covered by a retractable roof that could be hoisted into a niche at the summit of the tower by means of 26 cables and 46 winches anchored at the tower's base. Made of Kevlar—an ultra-thin synthetic fiber with the strength of steel—the roof has nevertheless been subject to deterioration. With a seating capacity of 55,147, the stadium hosts sporting events, rock concerts, opera and conventions. Hovering at a 45° angle above the stadium, the 175m/574ft **tower** can be ascended by a funicular elevator *(open Jun 22–Labour Day Mon noon–9pm, Tue–Thu 10am–9pm, Fri–Sun 10am–11pm; rest of the year Mon noon–6pm, Tue–Sun 10am–6pm; closed mid-Jan–mid-Feb; $7.25;* ✗ ♿ ☐ ☎514-252-8687). From the observation deck, the **panorama★★★** extends as far as 80km/50mi, weather permitting. Large skylights and windows afford breathtaking views of the stadium, downtown Montreal, the Laurentian Mountains and the Monteregian Hills. Located below the deck, an interactive interpretation centre presents exhibits on various aspects of the park.

★ **Biodôme** – *Open mid-Jun–Labour Day daily 9am–8pm. Rest of the year daily 9am–6pm. $9.50.* ✗ ♿ ☐ ☎514-868-3000. Opened in 1992, this innovative museum occupies a **building★** that was constructed as an Olympic cycling venue—the velodrome; its appearance resembles a cyclist's helmet. Re-created habitats, complete with climatic regulators, support plants and animals indigenous to four ecosystems: a tropical forest, the Laurentian forest, the St. Lawrence Marine and the polar region.

★★ **Montreal Botanical Garden [A]** – *4101 Rue Sherbrooke Est.* ● *Pie-IX. Open mid-Jun–Labour Day daily 9am–8pm. Rest of the year daily 9am–6pm. $8.75 (includes admission to the Insectarium).* ⌘ ㊊ 🄿 ☎*514-872-1400. A narrated train ride (30min) provides an overview of the garden.* Founded in 1931 this 75ha/185 acre botanical garden ranks among the world's finest horticultural facilities. Over 26,000 international plant species are exhibited in 10 greenhouses and 30 outdoor gardens.

The new **reception centre** (1995) leads to an introduction greenhouse for a preview of the plant kingdom. The **conservatories★** (serres d'exposition) present a wide range of tropical and semitropical plants alongside begonia, cacti and succulent plants. The Chinese Greenhouse, called the Jardin céleste, displays the superb **Wu Collection** of *penjing*, or "landscape in a pot." Opened in 1991 the **Chinese Garden★** (Jardin de Chine) is a replica of a typical Ming Dynasty (14-17C) garden from southern China, with pavilions, a rock mountain and waterfall. The combination of mountains and water is thought to provoke contemplation. The 2.5ha/6.2 acre **Japanese Garden** (Jardin japonais), designed in the traditional Oriental style, creates a peaceful atmosphere. The **Japanese pavilion** houses exhibit spaces, a tea library, Zen garden, a tea garden and a collection of **bonsai** *(on view seasonally)*. Other sections not to be missed include the **Rose Garden**, with over 10,000 specimens, the **Marsh and Bog Garden**, a re-created monastic garden, an Alpine garden, and an enclosure of toxic plants. Covering more than half of the total area, the **Arboretum** features over 10,000 tree specimens.

Near the Rose Garden, the **Montreal Insectarium★**, built in the shape of a giant bug, offers a wide selection of preserved and living insects from all over the world.

★★ **Château Dufresne – Montreal Museum of Decorative Arts (Musée des Arts Décoratifs de Montréal) [B]** – *Entrance on Blvd. Pie IX.* ● *Pie IX. Open year-round Wed–Sun 11am–5pm. $3.* ㊊ 🄿 ☎*514-259-2575.* Completed in 1918, this sumptuous Beaux-Arts mansion, commissioned by Marius and Oscar Dufresne, evokes the lifestyle of Montreal's moneyed class in the 1920s and 30s.

A total of 44 period rooms present a variety of styles, blending Gothic, Renaissance, Elizabethan and Louis XV and XVI influences. Note the beautiful mahogany panelling in the sitting room, the Moorish-style smoking room and the Hepplewhite furnishings in the dining room. Housed in the chateau since 1979, the **museum** displays an outstanding collection of decorative and industrial arts.

OTHER AREAS OF INTEREST *1/2 day*

★ **St. Helen's Island** – *Access by car on Jacques-Cartier or Concorde Bridge;* ● *Île Sainte-Hélène.* Located east of Montreal, this small island, discovered by Samuel de Champlain in 1611, was named for his wife, Hélène Boulé. Trans-formed into a pleasant park, it has become a popular weekend spot.

After purchasing the island in 1818, the British government erected a citadel, now known as the **Old Fort** (Vieux-Fort), on this strategic point *(open late Jun–Labour Day daily 10am–6pm; rest of the year Mon & Wed–Sun 10am–5pm; closed Jan 1 & Dec 25; military drills & Scottish dancing Jun 24–late Aug daily 11am, 1, 3:30 & 5pm;* ⌘ 🄿 ☎*514-861-6701).*

The island became federal government property after Confederation, and in the early 20C, it was annexed by the city. In 1967, along with Notre Dame Island, St. Helen's hosted the 1967 World Fair (Expo '67). Constructed to house the US pavilion, the **Biosphère★**, a geodesic dome designed by Buckmister Fuller, now contains Canada's first eco-watch centre *(open early Jun–Sept daily 10am–8pm; rest of the year Tue–Sun 9am–6pm; closed national holidays; $6.50;* ㊊ ☎*514-283-5000).* Hands-on exhibits and a multimedia presentation *(10min)* highlight the importance of water and the fragility of our natural environment.

The shaded woods and clearings are interspersed with fortress remnants. Located in the Old Fort is the **David M. Stewart Museum★**, which presents the history of European settlement in Quebec through displays of weapons, documents, maps and globes *(same hours as the Old Fort; $5;* ⌘ 🄿 ☎*514-861-6701).* Note the model of the city of Montreal as it appeared in 1760.

La Ronde, Montreal's major amusement park, occupies a pleasant site on the north end of the island *(open mid-May–Jun 22 daily 10am–10pm; Jun 23–Labour Day Mon–Thu & Sun 11am–11pm, Fri-Sat 11am–1am; $18.87;* ⌘ ㊊ 🄿 ☎*514-872-6222).*

The road skirting the island's western edge provides **views★** of Old Montreal, the port installations, and the **Cité du Havre** peninsula, which links the city to St. Helen's Island via the Concorde Bridge. **Habitat★** (Moshe Safdie), a futuristic, modular apartment complex built for Expo '67, dominates the peninsula.

★ **Notre Dame Island (Île Notre-Dame)** – *Access by car on Concordia Bridge or by free bus service from St. Helen's Island metro station.* This artificial island, created in 1959 and enlarged in 1967, contains a Formula 1 race track, a pleasant lake and beach, and a superb **floral garden** designed for the International Floralies of 1980 (*open daily year-round* ✗ ⚤ ☎514-872-4537). The Expo '67 French pavilion, formerly known as the Palais de la Civilisation, houses the **Montreal Casino**.

Sault-au-Récollet – *Located 12km/7mi north of Montreal by Sherbrooke Est (Rte. 138), Cartier and Rachel Sts. and Ave. Papineau. Gouin Blvd. is a one-way street east.* Set on rapids beside the Prairies River, Sault-au-Récollet is best known for its **Church of the Visitation of the Blessed Virgin Mary★** (Église de la Visitation-de-la-Bienheureuse-Vierge-Marie), the oldest religious structure on the island. The large nave and absence of lateral chapels illustrate the style of Récollet churches, which were popular in New France during the French Regime. The edifice boasts an elaborate **interior★★** fashioned by Louis-Amable Quévillon and his followers. Of particular interest are the turquoise and gold vault, adorned with diamond-shaped barrels; the sculpted decor in the chancel; and the magnificent **pulpit★**, one of the most beautiful pieces of liturgical furniture in Quebec.

NUNAVIK★★

Map of Principal Sights p 4

Officially recognized in 1988, after creation in 1986 by referendum, as the homeland of Quebec's **Inuit** population, the province's northernmost region offers the adventurous visitor a unique travel experience. Nunavik's spectacular expanses of rugged and pristine land, encompassing some 505,000sq km/194,980sq mi, appeal to travellers eager to explore one of the world's few remaining frontiers. Located on the **Ungava Peninsula**, this vast territory also encompasses numerous off-shore islands and part of the James Bay region to the west. A multitude of lakes and waterways drain east into Ungava Bay, or west into Hudson Bay. The lack of vegetation is characteristic of regions with harsh climates. In fact, most of the peninsula is under permafrost, reaching 275m/902ft in depth in Nunavik's northernmost areas.

The region's first inhabitants were hunters from Asia who crossed the Bering Strait some 9,000 years ago. Travelling in small family groups, the Inuit ancestors caught marine mammals along the coast and ventured inland to hunt musk ox, caribou and waterfowl. The arrival of Europeans in the 17C dramatically transformed the traditional nomadic lifestyle and led to the creation of permanent settlements.

Today the majority of the Inuit population inhabits 14 coastal villages and has access to schooling and professional training. Living in modern, prefabricated housing equipped with modern amenities, the Inuit have nevertheless maintained their traditional values and heritage.

Practical Information – The 14 villages lining Nunavik's eastern and western shores are accessible by airplane only. Contact Canadian Airlines International (☎514-847-2211), First Air (☎613-738-0200), Air Inuit (☎613-738-0200) or Air Creebec (☎819-825-8355) for schedules & flight information. It is best to visit the region through organized tours, offered by the official travel agency for Nunavik, the Fédération des coopératives du Nouveau-Québec (FCNQ ☎514-457-9371). FCNQ also provides information on the various accommodation possibilities. Several outfitters organize fishing, hunting, hiking, canoeing and nature observation trips (contact FCNQ for information).

VISIT

The largest among the 14 villages, **Kuujjuaq★** (pop. 1,405) is the seat of regional government offices. Located to the west, **Inukjuak** (pop. 1,044), serves as headquarters for the Avataq Cultural Institute, a non-profit organization devoted to the preservation and development of the Inuit heritage in Nunavik. The northeasternmost villages of **Kangiqsujuaq** (pop. 404) and **Salluit** (pop. 823) are especially remarkable for their spectacular **sites★★**, surrounded by rugged mountains and jagged cliffs. Located on the western shore, **Povungnituk** (pop. 1,091) has gained recognition as a centre for Inuit sculpture. The village's **museum★** features a collection of Inuit tools, objects and crafts. Situated just north of James Bay, **Kuujjuarapik** (pop. 605) is home to a sizeable number of Cree Indians and to most of Nunavik's non-native population.

QUEBEC CITY★★★

Pop. 167,517
Map of Principal Sights p 5
Tourist Office ☎418-651-2882

Built atop the Cape Diamant promontory jutting into the St. Lawrence River, Quebec's capital has delighted visitors for centuries. Throughout the years the city has retained its Old World charm, evident in the multitude of historic and religious monuments, fortifications and narrow cobblestone alleys. The distinctive French flavour is enhanced by fine restaurants, outdoor cafes and a lively nightlife. In 1985 the city became the first urban centre in North America to be inscribed on UNESCO's World Heritage List.

Historical Notes

Birthplace of New France – Long before Jacques Cartier's arrival in 1535, Indian hunters and fishermen inhabited the area of the village of Stadacona. Following a fruitless search for precious stones, Cartier soon abandoned the site, and interest in the area declined. Attempting to establish a fur-trading post, Samuel de Champlain set foot here in 1608 and constructed a rudimentary wooden fortress, known as the **Habitation**.

The first settlers arrived in Quebec during the 17C. Primarily craftsmen and merchants attracted to the profitable fur trade, they erected houses in the Lower Town *(p 225)*, which became the centre of commercial activity. Seeking protection offered by the fortifications, numerous religious institutions and colonial administration settled in the Upper Town.

18C and 19C – Quebec City's location atop the 98m/321ft high Cape Diamant promontory provided the colony with a naturally fortified area. Despite this strategic military location, the French city was repeatedly attacked—first by the Iroquois, then by the British. The escalating hostility between the small French colony and Britain culminated in the Battle of the Plains of Abraham *(p 228)*, which precipitated the British Conquest of 1759.

Following the Treaty of Paris in 1763, Quebec City became capital of the new British dominion, and quickly assumed a dominant position. Owing mainly to its busy port activities, the city maintained a competitive position with Montreal until the mid-19C. As the population shifted westward, Quebec City gradually lost its position as centre of production and trade in New France.

Quebec City Today – Since the turn of this century, most jobs have been related to public administration, defence and the service sector. The growth of the provincial government in the past 25 years has provided the capital city with renewed vitality. Throughout its turbulent history, the city has remained a bastion of French culture in North America. Although the Anglophone community accounted for more than half the population in 1861, Quebec City today claims less than 5 percent British residents, a factor that contributes to the city's distinctly Francophone character. The main metropolitan event is the famous winter **Carnival** *(illustration p 229)* in February, which attracts thousands of visitors.

★★★THE OLD CITY   *Map p 226*

The oldest part of the city is divided into Upper Town, set atop the massive Cape Diamant, and Lower Town, nestled between the rocky cliff and the St. Lawrence. It is best to visit the Old City on foot, in order to absorb the distinct character of the narrow, winding streets.

★★Upper Town (Haute-Ville)   *1/2 day*

The site of Samuel de Champlain's Fort Saint-Louis (1620), Upper Town was not developed until a group of wealthy merchants decided to increase settlement in the colony. Although a few houses appeared toward the end of the 17C, the area retained its administrative and religious vocation for over two centuries.

The handful of seigneurs and religious institutions who had established themselves on Cape Diamant, seeking protection from the military, refused to divide their land plots. It was only during the 19C that elegant residential neighbourhoods evolved along the Rues Saint-Louis, Sainte-Ursule and d'Auteuil, and Avenues Sainte-Geneviève and Saint-Denis. Today Upper Town still functions as the city's administrative centre.

★★ Place d'Armes and Vicinity – Bordered by prestigious buildings and restaurants, this pleasant square, once used for military drills and parades, forms the heart of Old Quebec, attracting throngs of visitors. It is dominated by the city's most prominent landmark, the **Château Frontenac★★** *(illustration p 194)*. A massive structure erected in 1893 in the Chateau style, this renowned hotel stands on the site of the former governor's residence. Next to the chateau the Governors' Garden features the **Wolfe-Montcalm Monument [1]** (1827), a joint memorial to the two enemies who died in combat and whose meeting resulted in the creation of the Canadian nation.

Located behind the chateau, **Dufferin Terrace★★★**, a wide wooden boardwalk, is perched 671m/2,200ft above the majestic St. Lawrence, offering breathtaking **views★★** of Lower Town and the river. A **monument [2]** to Samuel de Champlain, founder of New France, marks the northern end of the terrace. At the southern end, a flight of steps ascends to the **Governors' Walk★★** (Promenade des Gouverneurs) *(closed in winter)*, a spectacular boardwalk, precariously suspended along the steep cliff that leads from the terrace to National Battlefields Park *(p 228)*.

In the narrow **Rue du Trésor**, a quaint pedestrian street off Place d'Armes, artists exhibit sketches and engravings of typical city scenes.

★ **Fort Museum (Musée du Fort) [M¹]** – *10 Rue Sainte-Anne. Visit by guided tour (30min) only, Jan–Mar daily 11am–3pm (weekends 5pm). Apr–May daily 10am–5pm. Jun 24–Aug daily 10am–6pm. Sept–Oct daily 10am–5pm. Nov daily 11am–3pm (weekends 5pm) $5.50.* ☎418-692-1759. Housed in a castle-like structure, this museum features a sound and light presentation *(30min)* that traces the city's military and civil history.

★ **Old Post Office (Ancien bureau de poste) [A]** – *3 Rue Buade. Open year-round Mon–Fri 8am–6:45pm. Closed national holidays.* Erected in 1873, this large edifice presents an imposing facade adorned with Beaux-Arts embellishments. Inside, Parks Canada presents exhibits on the development of the country's historical and natural sites.

★ **Basilica-Cathedral of Our Lady of Quebec (Basilique-cathédrale Notre-Dame-de-Québec) [B]** – *Open year-round daily 7:30am–4:30pm.* ⑤ ☎418-694-0665. Originally consecrated in 1674, the cathedral was destroyed during the fighting between French and British forces in 1759. The church was reconstructed between 1768 and 1771 by Quebec's most prominent architects, the Baillairgé family. Jean Baillairgé rebuilt the south belfry with its two openwork drums surmounted by domes. François Baillairgé was responsible for the interior and designed the plans for the magnificent baldachin. His son, Thomas, designed the monumental Neoclassical facade in 1843. Although the structure was destroyed by fire in 1922, it was rebuilt to reflect its original appearance. Of note in the interior are the stained-glass windows, the baldachin and the Casavant organ.

The majestic **Quebec City Hall** (Hôtel de ville de Québec) dominates the Place de l'hôtel de ville across from the basilica. In the square stands a **monument [3]** to Elzéar Alexandre Taschereau, the first Canadian cardinal.

Located north of the basilica, Quebec City's **Latin Quarter★** is the oldest residential district in Upper Town. Narrow, crisscrossing streets add to the charm of the quarter, today inhabited mainly by students.

★★ **Quebec Seminary (Séminaire de Québec)** – *2 Côte de la Fabrique. Guided tours (2hrs) in summer; $3 (includes admission to Museum of French America)* ⑤ ☎418-692-2843. Founded in 1663 by Msgr. François de Laval to train priests for the colony, this institute of higher learning is the oldest in Canada. In 1852 the seminary was granted a university, Université Laval, which grew within the seminary walls until the Sainte-Foy campus opened in 1950.

The seminary comprises three sections arranged around an inner court. Note the sundial on the facade of the **Procure Wing**, completed in 1681. The highlights of the guided tour include the **Msgr. Olivier Briand Chapel★**, noteworthy for the fine wood panelling adorning its walls, and the **Congregational Chapel**, featuring a statue of the Virgin Mary crafted by Thomas Baillairgé.

Operated since 1995 as part of the Museum of Civilization *(p 227)*, the **Museum of French America★** (Musée de l'Amérique Française) **[M²]** presents France's historic, cultural and social heritage in North America *(9 Rue de l'Université; open Jun–Sept daily 10am–5:30pm; rest of the year Tue–Sun 10am–5pm; closed Jan 1 & Dec 25; $3;* ⑤ ☎418-692-2843*)*. The vast collections include some 180,000 rare books and journals. On display in the **François Ranvoyzé Pavilion★** (occupying the former outer chapel) is one of the most important collections of **relics★** outside St. Peter's in Rome.

★ **Augustine Monastery (Monastère de l'Hôtel-Dieu de Québec)** – *32 Rue Charlevoix.* Founded by Augustinian Nuns in the 1640s, this monastery is best known for its hospital, the Hôtel-Dieu, which still operates today. The **church**★*(same hours as museum, below)*, designed by Pierre Émond in 1800, features a Neoclassical facade adorned with a sculpted Ionic portal. Highlights of the interior, crafted by Thomas Baillairgé, include the high-altar **tabernacle**, the retable and the basket-handle wooden vault.

Opened in 1958, the **Augustine Museum★ [M³]** presents a collection of objects and artworks tracing the Augustinian Nuns' history and heritage *(open year-round Tue–Sat 9:30am–noon & 1:30–5pm, Sun 1:30–5pm; closed national holidays; & ☎418-692-2492)*. The museum includes one of the foremost collections of **paintings**★ dating back to the time of New France.

Rue Saint-Louis – This charming, bustling street is home to a variety of restaurants and boutiques. It also features some of the city's oldest architectural gems. The **Maillou House★ [C]** (Maison Maillou) (1736), located next the Château Frontenac, now houses the Quebec City Chamber of Commerce. The offices of the Consulate General of France occupy the adjacent house, the **Kent House [D]** (Maison Kent), dating from the 1830s. Standing at the corner of Rue Desjardins, the **Jacquet House★ [E]** (Maison Jacquet) was built in 1674. Reputedly the oldest house in Quebec City, it is occupied today by a restaurant specializing in traditional Quebec cuisine.

★★ **Ursuline Monastery (Monastère des Ursulines)** – *Rue Donnacona.* Founded in 1639 by Madame de la Peltrie and Marie Guyart (Mère Marie-de-l'Incarnation), the monastery is the oldest educational institution for young women in North America and is still in operation today. The **chapel** (1902) is particularly remarkable for its **interior decoration**★★ *(open year-round Tue–Sat 9:30am–noon & 1:30–4:40pm, Sun 12:30–5:10pm; ☎418-694-2523)*. Most of the ornaments were crafted between 1726 and 1736 under the supervision of Pierre-Noël Levasseur. Of particular interest are the wood sculptures of St. Augustine, St. Ursula and St. Joseph, the nuns' choir surmounted by a wooden vault, and the collection of paintings.

The **Ursuline Museum★★ [M⁴]** (Musée des Ursulines) occupies the former site of the house belonging to Madame de la Peltrie, the order's benefactress, in the 17C *(12 Rue Donnacona; open Jan–Mar Tue–Sat 1–4:30pm, Sun 12:30–5pm; Apr–Sept Tue–Sat 9:30am–noon & 1–4:30pm, Sun 12:30–5pm; Oct–Nov Tue–Sat 1–4:30pm, Sun 12:30–5pm; $3; ☎418-694-0694)*. Reflecting the occupations of the Ursuline Nuns, the collection features documents, furnishings, paintings, sculptures and numerous **embroideries**★ of rare beauty. The museum also contains altar frontals and ecclesiastic vestments of the 17C and 18C.

★ **Price Building** – *65 Rue Sainte-Anne.* This 16-storey Art Deco edifice, Quebec City's first skyscraper, was built in 1930 to accommodate the head office of Price Brothers, famed for introducing the pulp and paper industry to the Saguenay region *(p 231)*. Its copper roof blends well with the surrounding buildings.

★ **Holy Trinity Anglican Cathedral (Cathédrale anglicane de la Sainte-Trinité) [F]** – *31 Rue des Jardins.* Modelled after London's Church of St.-Martin-in-the-Fields, this edifice (1804) was the first Anglican cathedral built outside the British Isles. King George III provided the funding and sent English oak from the royal forests of Windsor for the pews. In summer, the courtyard is a gathering place for artists.

★★★ **Lower Town (Basse-Ville)** *1/2 day*
Access from Dufferin Terrace by funicular (cable car) (in service May–Oct daily 7:30am–11:30pm; rest of the year daily 7:30am–11pm; $1; ☎418-692-1132) or by the steep Frontenac stairway.

This narrow stretch of land dominated by Upper Town was the site of Champlain's "Habitation" *(p 223)*. The first settlers arrived here in the late 17C and established shops and residences around the fort and the market square, now known as Place Royale *(p 226)*. As commerce, shipbuilding and port activities increased, residents filled in parts of the shores, constructed numerous wharves and created new streets. By the 19C the area of Lower Town, the city's commercial centre, had doubled in size. As port activities declined in the 1860s, the neighbourhood lost its appeal and fell into decay. In 1970 the Quebec government began restoring the area.

Today restaurants, cafes and boutiques abound in the historic quarter of Place Royale. Lined with boutiques and art galleries, the pedestrian **Rue du Petit-**

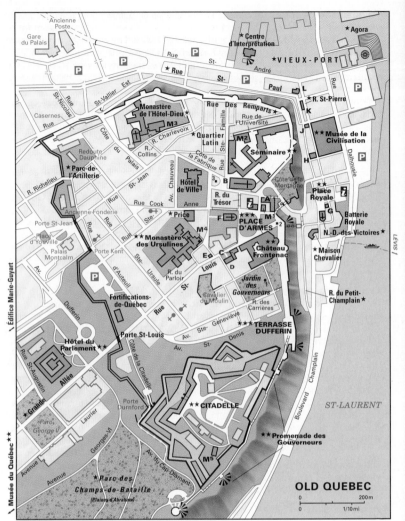

Champlain★ reflects the quarter's 18C appearance. Facing the Place de Paris, a **visitor centre** offers guided tours of the area *(215 Rue du Marché-Finlay; open Jun–Oct daily 10am–6pm;* ☎*418-643-6631).*

★ **Chevalier House (Maison Chevalier)** – *Corner of Rue du Marché-Champlain and Blvd. Champlain. Open early Jun–Sept daily 10am–6pm. Rest of the year by appointment.* ⛔ 🅿 ☎*418-643-2158.* This imposing stone structure, topped by a red roof and high chimneys, is composed of three separate buildings. The west wing was built in 1752 for a wealthy merchant, Jean-Baptiste Chevalier. Restored in 1956, the house now serves as part of the Museum of Civilization *(p 227)* and features exhibits on traditional Quebec architecture and furniture.

Royal Battery (Batterie Royale) – *At the end of Rue Sous-le-Fort and Rue Saint-Pierre. Open daily year-round.* ☎*418-643-6631.* Constructed in 1691 this thick, four-sided earthen rampart formed part of the fortifications of the city. It was destroyed during French-British fighting in 1759 and gradually buried. Archaeologists excavating the area unearthed it in 1972. It has been reconstructed and replicas of 18C cannon are positioned in the 11 embrasures.

★★ **Place Royale** – Today the heart of Lower Town, this charming cobblestone square was the hub of the city's economic activity until the mid-19C, when the port, and subsequently the area, fell into decline. Bordered by typical 18C stone houses, topped by steep roofs and chimneys, the square features a bronze bust of King Louis XIV as its centrepiece.

226

The 1656 **Fornel House [G]** (Maison Fornel) houses an **interpretation centre** featuring a permanent exhibit on Place Royale *(entrance on 25 Rue Saint-Pierre; open Jun–Sept daily 10am–6pm; rest of the year by appointment;* ✆ *☎418-643-6631)*. Highlights include a replica of a map of New France drawn in 1688, a scale model of a 17C house, and numerous artifacts uncovered during excavations in the square.

★ **Church of Our Lady of the Victories** (Église Notre-Dame-des-Victoires) – *Place Royale. Open mid-May–mid-Oct daily 9am–4:30pm. Rest of the year daily 9am–noon.* ☎418-692-1650. Completed in 1723, this stone edifice topped by a single spire stands on the site of Champlain's "Habitation" *(p 225)*. It was named in thanksgiving for two successful occasions when Quebec City resisted the sieges of the British. Inside, the magnificent **retable** represents the fortified city.

★★ **Museum of Civilization (Musée de la Civilisation)** – *85 Rue Dalhousie. Open Jun 24–Labour Day daily 10am–7pm. Rest of the year Tue–Sun 10am–5pm (Wed 9pm). $6.* ✗ & 🄿 ☎418-643-2158. Designed by Moshe Safdie, this acclaimed museum is housed in two stark, angular buildings crowned by copper roofs and a glass campanile. A monumental staircase links the buildings and leads to a terrace overlooking an inner court and the **Estèbe House** (Maison Estèbe), a 1752 stone structure, which was integrated into the museum. Inside the spacious entrance hall, note *La Débâcle* (Astri Reusch), a massive sculpture representing ice breaking up in spring.

The museum presents permanent and temporary thematic exhibits focusing on such topics as thought, language, natural resources, the human body and society. Among the permanent exhibits, **Objects of Civilization** highlights Quebec furnishings, tools and costumes. Covering over four centuries of Quebec history and culture, the **Memories** exhibit takes visitors on a thought-provoking journey through the past. Displayed artifacts illustrate a people's struggle to create a new life in a new land. The **Barque** is one of several 18C flat-bottomed boats uncovered during archaeological excavations on Place Royale.

★ **Rue Saint-Pierre** – During the 19C this busy thoroughfare emerged as the city's principal financial district. Among the noteworthy commercial buildings still lining the street are the **National Bank [H]** *(no. 71)*; the former **Molson Bank [J]** *(no. 105)*, now occupied by the Post Office; and the **Imperial Bank of Canada [K]** *(nos. 113-115)*. Dominating the corner of Rues Saint-Paul and Saint-Pierre, the **Canadian Bank of Commerce [L]** exemplifies the Beaux-Arts style.

The charming **Rue Saint-Paul★** is renowned for its antique shops and art galleries.

★ **Old Port (Vieux-Port)** – Located on the Louise Basin, the port played a major role in the development of Canada until the late 19C, when it fell into disrepair. Created by the federal government in the 1980s, the **Agora★** complex includes an amphitheatre, a wide boardwalk on the river and a marina. The Old Port of Quebec **interpretation centre★** is devoted to the port city's prominence during the 19C *(100 Rue Saint-André; open mid-May–Labour Day daily 10am–5pm; early Sept–late Oct daily noon–4pm; rest of the year by appointment; $2.50;* & 🄿 *☎418-648-3300)*. Exhibits on logging and shipbuilding and films on the port confirm the importance of these industries to Quebec's economy. The glassed-in terrace on the top floor serves as a fine **viewpoint** for Lower Town and the modern port.

★★ **FORTIFICATIONS**   *1/2 day. Map p 226.*

Much of the charm of Quebec City stems from the fact that it is the only walled-in city in Canada. Although fortification projects were undertaken during the French Regime, most of the existing walls, batteries and the citadel were erected by the British after the Conquest, and never used. **Lord Dufferin**, governor general of Canada between 1872 and 1878, initiated a beautification project that included refurbishing the fortified enceinte, rebuilding the gates to the city and clearing the ramparts.

★★ **Citadel** – *Entrance at end of Côte de la Citadelle. Visit by guided tour (1hr) only, mid-Mar–Jun daily 10am–3pm. Jul–Labour Day daily 9am–6pm. Early Sept–Oct daily 10am–3pm. $4.50. Changing of the guard mid-Jun–Labour Day daily 10am. The retreat Jul–Aug Tue, Thu & weekends 6pm.* & 🄿 *☎418-694-2815.* Some areas of the Citadel are off-limits as it is still a military base for the Royal 22e Régiment. Erected between 1820 and 1832, this massive fortress, enclosing 16ha/40 acres, is typical of star-shaped fortifications. Advanced works, or outworks, were devised to protect entrances and ramparts from enemy fire, while sloping earthworks forced the enemy to be exposed to cannon fire from the garrison. The enceinte was composed of bastions, linked together by curtains (straight walls) that protected the ditches. The guided tour leads past the renovated powder magazine, the old prison, and the governor general's residence to the Prince of Wales bastion. Occupying the old powder magazine, the **Museum of the Royal 22e Régiment [M⁵]** contains a collection of military objects from the 17C to the present.

Quebec Fortifications National Historic Site (Lieu historique national des Fortifications-de-Québec) – ✪ *100 Rue Saint-Louis. Open Apr–Oct daily 10am–5pm. $2.50.* ♿ ☎ *418-648-7016. Guided tours of the city wall available.* The **interpretation centre** presents the history of Quebec via the evolution of its defence systems. Near the centre *(to the right of the St. Louis Gate)*, lies the **powder magazine** (poudrière), built in 1810 on the Esplanade, a vast field used for military exercises between 1779 and 1783.

Visitors can stroll south along the ramparts over the **St. Louis Gate** (Porte Saint-Louis), and the Kent and St. John (Saint-Jean) Gates to Artillery Park. The fortifications afford panoramas of the city and surrounding areas.

★ **Artillery Park National Historic Site (Lieu historique national du Parc-de-l'Artillerie)** ✪ *Entrance at 2 Rue d'Auteuil near the St. John Gate. Open Apr–Oct daily 10am–5pm. Rest of the year by appointment only. $2.50.* ♿ ☎ *418-648-4205.* This huge site that includes barracks, a redoubt and an old foundry, commemorates three centuries of military, social and industrial life in Quebec City. Designed by Chaussegros de Léry in 1750, the barracks, housed in a structure 160m/525ft in length, contained armouries, stock rooms, a guard room and six prison cells. The redoubt (1748) is remarkable for its massive stone buttresses added to the original building after 1763. Inside, an **interpretation centre** features costumes, paintings and artifacts that offer insight into a soldier's life in the 18C and 19C. The old foundry contains a **scale model**★★ of Quebec City, produced between 1806 and 1808 by British engineers, that presents a stunning picture of the city as it appeared at the beginning of the 19C.

★ **Rue des Remparts** – Until approximately 1875, this street was a mere path that ran alongside the ramparts, connecting the various bastions and batteries. Today a pleasant stroll down the street allows visitors to recapture the atmosphere of the old fortified city.

OUTSIDE THE WALLS   *1/2 day*

★ **Grande Allée** – Departing from the St. Louis Gate and extending southward of Old Quebec, this wide avenue is to the city what the Champs-Élysées is to Paris. Lined with innumerable restaurants, bars, outdoor cafes, boutiques and offices, the bustling thoroughfare provides an elegant setting for the city's nightlife.

★★ **Parliament Building (Hôtel du Parlement)**– *Visit by guided tour (30min) only, Jun 24–Labour Day daily 9am–4:30pm. Early Sept–May Mon–Fri 9am–4:30pm.* ⍻ ♿ 🅿 ☎ *418-643-7239.* Overlooking the old city, this majestic edifice is the finest example of Second Empire architecture in Quebec City. Note the imposing **facade**, which presents a historic tableau wherein bronze figures commemorate the great names of Quebec history.

Inside, a grand staircase leads to the parliamentary chambers, which are accessed through finely chiselled doors. The Chamber of the National Assembly is used by Quebec's National Assembly, while the Chamber of the Legislative Assembly accommodates meetings of parliamentary committees and official receptions.

★ **National Battlefields Park (Parc des Champs-de-Bataille)** – *Map p 226. Open year-round.* Stretching 107ha/250 acres along a cliff overlooking the St. Lawrence, this park memorializes battles fought between the British and the French. A large section of the park occupies the former **Plains of Abraham**, where the French and British armies fought a major battle (1759) that eventually sealed the fate of the French colony. Both commanding generals, Wolfe and Montcalm, were mortally wounded during the short but decisive event. Located in the Quebec Museum *(below)*, the **interpretation centre** for the park presents the history of the Plains of Abraham *(open mid-May–Labour Day daily 10am–5:30pm; rest of the year Tue–Sun noon–5:30pm; $2;* ⍻ ♿ 🅿 ☎ *418-648-4071).*

★★ **Quebec Museum** (Musée du Québec)– *In National Battlefields Park. Entrance located between the two main buildings, on ground level. Open mid-May–Labour Day daily 10am–5:45pm (Wed 9:45pm). Rest of the year Tue–Sun 11am–5:45pm (Wed 8:45pm).*

Closed Jan 1 & Dec 25. $5. ✗ & 🅿 ☎*418-643-2150.* This remarkable 3-building complex provides an overview of Quebec art from the 18C to the present. Temporary and permanent exhibits drawn from a collection of over 22,000 works of art are organized throughout the modern Main Hall, the Beaux-Arts Gérard Morisset Pavilion and the Renaissance Revival Baillairgé Pavilion. Highlights include canvases by Charles Alexander Smith and Antoine Plamondon, sculptures by Alfred Laliberté and François Ranvoyzé's silver work.

Marie Guyart Building (Édifice Marie-Guyart)– *1037 Rue de la Chevrotière. Open mid-Jan–mid-Dec Mon–Fri 10am–4pm, weekends & holidays 1–5pm.* ✗ & 🅿 ☎*418-644-9841.* The Anima G observatory occupying the 31st floor of this administrative building provides a splendid **view**★★ of Old Quebec, the citadel and fortifications as well as the surrounding areas.

★ **Cartier-Brébeuf National Historic Site** – ⊙ *75 Rue de l'Espinay, 3km/2mi from St. John Gate by Côte d'Abraham, Rue de la Couronne, Drouin Bridge and 1re Ave. Open early Jan–late Feb weekends noon–4pm. Mid-May–Labour Day daily 10am–5pm. Early Sept–late Oct daily noon–4pm. Late Oct–Dec by appointment only. $2.50.* & 🅿 ☎*418-648-4038.* This park commemorates Jacques Cartier, who wintered on this spot in 1535-36, and Jean de Brébeuf, a Jesuit missionary. The **interpretation centre** features insightful displays that recall Cartier's second voyage to New France and his meetings with the Iroquois, as well as the Jesuit's first mission, established in 1626.

The highlight of the visit is a replica of **La Grande Hermine**★, the largest of Cartier's three vessels. Measuring less than 24m/80ft in length, the two-masted ship carried up to 60 men across the Atlantic.

Quebec Winter Carnival

EXCURSIONS

★★ **Beaupré Coast (Côte de Beaupré)** – *Map p 200.* Bordering the St. Lawrence, this narrow stretch of land extends from Quebec City to Cape Tourmente. Its name is attributed to an exclamation made by Cartier, who, noting the lush green meadowland, said *"Quel beau pré!"* ("What a fine meadow!"). A pleasant drive along Route 360 leads through a string of charming communities dating from the French Regime.

★★ **Montmorency Falls Park** (Parc de la Chute-Montmorency) – *10km/6mi east of Quebec City. Open year-round daily 8:30am–11pm.* ✗ & ☎*418-663-2877.* Before emptying into the St. Lawrence, the Montmorency River cascades over a cliff in spectacular falls 83m/272ft high (30m/98ft higher than Niagara Falls). In winter, the spray creates a great cone of ice that sometimes exceeds 30m/98ft in height. Elegant **Montmorency Manor** (1780) houses a restaurant and a **visitor centre**, which presents the area's heritage *(open year-round daily 9am–11pm;* ✗ & ☎*418-663-3330).* From the **upper lookout**, visitors can fully appreciate the height and force of the falls. The **lower lookout** affords the opportunity to approach the base of the falls *(rain gear is advised).* An **aerial tram** returns visitors to the upper level *(ascent $4.50).*

★★ **Sainte-Anne-de-Beaupré Shrine** – *In Sainte-Anne-de-Beaupré, 35km/22mi east of Quebec City. Open mid-Jun–mid-Sept daily 6:30am–9:30pm. Rest of the year daily 6:45am– 5pm.* ♿ ☎*418-827-3781.* Named for the patron saint of Quebec, this Roman Catholic shrine is visited by over a million and a half people yearly. An imposing, medieval-style basilica, consecrated in 1934, dominates the site. Divided into five naves separated by huge columns, the interior is lit by 200 **stained-glass windows**. Note also the glimmering **mosaics** adorning the barrel vault above the main nave. On the shrine's grounds are the memorial chapel and the Chapel of the Scala Sancta (Chapelle du Saint Escalier). Life-size representations of the Stations of the Cross (Chemin de la Croix) dot the hillside.

★★ **St. Joachim Church** (Église Saint-Joachim) – *In Saint-Joachim, 40km/25mi northeast of Quebec City. Open mid-May–mid-Oct daily 9am–5pm. Rest of the year by appointment.* The small church (1779) is best known for its magnificent **interior★★**, fashioned between 1815 and 1825 by François and Thomas Baillairgé. Of particular interest are the panelling, enhanced by gilded bas-reliefs, and the main altar, surrounded by majestic columns and free-standing sculptures of the Evangelists.

★★ **Île d'Orléans** – Pop. 6,938. *10km/6mi northeast of Quebec City. Map p 201.* This almond-shaped island wedged in the St. Lawrence was named Isle of Bacchus by Jacques Cartier in 1535, and renamed in 1536 to honour the son of King François I, the Duke of Orléans.

Route 368 runs along the 67km/41mi circumference, passing through six communities, each with its distinct flavour. Driving along the road, the visitor will discover splendid scenery and magnificent **views★★** of the St. Lawrence shoreline. The village of **Saint-Laurent★**, traditionally the island's maritime centre, still claims the island's only marina. In **Saint-Jean★**, the **Mauvide-Genest Manor★**, built in 1734, is considered the finest example of rural architecture under the French Regime *(visit by 20min guided tour only, late May–Aug daily 10am–5:30pm; early May & Sept–Oct by appointment; $3; ✗ ☎418-829-2630).* The manor now houses a restaurant and a museum featuring traditional Quebec furniture. The community of Sainte-Famille is best known for its tri-steepled **church★★** (1748), dating from the French Regime. In the Neoclassical interior, note the sculpted vault by Louis-David Bazile, student of Quévillon, and the tabernacle crafted by the Levasseur family. This elaborate edifice contrasts with the **old church★** in Saint-Pierre, remodelled in the 1830s by Thomas Baillairgé.

RICHELIEU VALLEY★★

Map p 205

Some 130km/81mi long, the majestic Richelieu River flows north from its source in Lake Champlain (New York) to join the St. Lawrence at Sorel. Champlain discovered the waterway in 1609, named later for **Cardinal Richelieu**, chief minister of Louis XIII. The river served as an invasion route and was heavily fortified during the French Regime. The forts at Chambly, Saint-Jean-sur-Richelieu, Lennox and Lacolle were built initially to protect Montreal against attacks by Iroquois, and later by British and American troops. The valley also played an important role in the Rebellions of 1837 (p 212), which resulted in several uprisings in Saint-Denis, Saint-Charles and Saint-Eustache. To facilitate transportation between the US and Quebec, an extensive canal system was built along the Richelieu in the mid-19C. The region remains one of the richest agricultural areas in the province. A popular weekend retreat for Montrealers, the valley attracts thousands of travellers and tourists every summer.

SIGHTS

★ **Chambly** – Pop. 15,893. *30km/19mi from Montreal by Rte. 10.* A residential suburb of Montreal, this community enjoys a beautiful site on the Richelieu. A pleasant walk along the river leads past the canal and Fort Chambly to **Rue Richelieu★**, lined with sumptuous 19C residences.

★★ **Fort Chambly National Historic Site** – ⚲ *Open Mar–mid-May Wed–Sun 10am–5pm. Mid-May–Jun 23 daily 9am–5pm. Jun 24–Sept Mon 1–6pm, Tue–Sun 10am–6pm (5pm in Sept). Oct–mid-Dec Wed–Sun 10am–5pm.* ♿ ☎*514-658-1585.* Located in a magnificent park on the Chambly Basin, this fort is the only remaining fortified complex in Quebec dating back to the French Regime. Erected between 1709 and 1711, the stone structure replaced an earlier wooden edifice constructed in 1665 by Jacques de Chambly.

The fort is laid out in a square with bastions at each corner. An **interpretation centre** features displays and dioramas on the history of the fort and a description of the restoration project. Located near the fort, the **Guard House** (Corps de Garde) (1814) exemplifies the Palladian style adopted by the military throughout the British colonies. Inside, displays illustrate the period of British occupation of the city (1760-1851). Built in 1820, the small fieldstone **St. Stephen's Church** served as the garrison's place of worship.

★★ **Mt. Saint-Hilaire Nature Centre (Centre de la nature du mont Saint-Hilaire)** – *23km/ 14mi north of Chambly. Open year-round daily 8am–1hr before dusk. Closed Jan 1 & Dec 25. $4. &* ☎*514-467-1755.* Rising abruptly above the valley, Mt. Saint-Hilaire (411m/1,348ft) is the most imposing of the Monteregian Hills. Several trails criss-cross the lush forests covering the mountain, and lead to the summit, which affords sweeping **views**★★ of the Richelieu Valley.

★ **Saint-Denis-sur-Richelieu** – *Pop. 1,038. 33km/20mi north of Nature Centre.* This agricultural community was the site of a Patriot victory in 1837. At the **Patriots' National House**★ displays and an audio-visual presentation *(23min)* explain *(in French only)* the background of the uprising and highlight the events leading to the Patriots' fight for freedom and democracy *(open May–Dec Tue–Sun 10am–6pm; closes at 5pm in May, Oct & Dec; $2.50; &* ☎*514-787-3623).*

Saint-Jean-sur-Richelieu – *Pop. 37,607. 40km/25mi southeast of Montreal by Rtes. 10 and 35.* Known today for its Hot Air Balloon Festival and renowned as a manu-facturing centre for pottery and ceramics, this industrial city once formed part of the chain of fortifications erected by the French along the Richelieu. The **Fort Saint-Jean Museum** contains a collection of weapons, uniforms and other military artifacts *(visit by 1hr guided tour only, late May–mid-Aug Tue–Sun 9:30am–4:30pm; $2;* ☎*514-358-6769).*

Île aux Noix – *48km/30mi south of Montreal by Rtes. 10 and 35 south, and Rte. 223.* This 85ha/210 acre island was fortified by the French in 1759 and captured by the British the following year. Having at various times served as a shipbuilding centre, a holiday resort and an internment centre, the island is now preserved as a national historic site.

★ **Fort Lennox** – 🐾 *Visit by guided tour (1hr) only, late May–Jun 24 Mon–Fri 9:30am–5pm, weekends10am–6pm. Jun 25–Labour Day Mon noon–6pm, Tue–Sun 10am–6pm. Holidays (Jun 24, Jul 1 & Labour Day) 10am–6pm.* ⚒& ☎*514-291-5700.* Erected in the 1820s, this bastion-type fortress occupies a pleasant **site**★ overlooking the Richelieu River. A wide moat surrounds the fort, which forms a five-pointed star with corners protected by bastions. The Neoclassical stone buildings have been restored to re-create life on a British army base in the mid-19C.

★★ **Safari Park** – *63km/39mi south of Montreal by Rtes. 15 and 202. Open mid-May–mid-Jun Mon–Fri 10am–4pm, weekends 10am–5pm. Late Jun–mid-Sept daily 10am–5pm. $16.67.* ⚒& ☎*514-247-2727 or 800-465-8724 (Canada, US).* Situated in an apple-growing region west of the Richelieu, this zoological park is renowned for its animals from all over the world that roam freely in large enclosures. Required to remain in their vehicles, visitors can follow the **Car Safari** *(4km/2.5mi)* along which they can take photographs, touch and feed the animals *(food can be purchased).* Highlights include the **Enchanted Forest**, a jungle walk, a theatre and a circus.

SAGUENAY FJORD REGION★★★

Map pp 200-201

Located at the southern tip of the Saguenay region, the immense, saucer-shaped Lake Saint-Jean empties into the Saguenay River. Measuring 155km/96mi in length, this river flows into the southernmost fjord in the world, the majestic Saguenay Fjord, which discharges its waters into the St. Lawrence.

Historical Notes – Fed by a number of rivers, including the Péribonka, Mistassini and Ashuapmushuan, Lake Saint-Jean is a small remnant of an original lake cre-ated over 10,000 years ago by the meltwaters of retreating glaciers. First called Piékouagami ("flat lake") by the Montagnais, Lake Saint-Jean was renamed for **Jean Dequen**, the first Frenchman to visit its shores in 1647. The area remained unsettled until the mid-19C when the first sawmills were built, and the rivers were harnessed for electricity. Hydro-electric power plants, pulp mills and aluminum smelters still line the shores of the lake and the Upper Saguenay.

Natural Attractions – Beyond Saint-Fulgence, the deep river channel was gouged in Precambrian rock by glaciers during the last Ice Age. Lined by rocky cliffs plunging into the water, the channel is 1,500m/4,920ft wide in places, having an average depth of 240m/787ft. The stark and untamed beauty of the river's southern section has attracted visitors for many years. Most choose to take a scenic river cruise *(below)*, but the fjord can also be enjoyed by exploring the villages nestled along its shores.

The spectacular, natural **Saguenay Park★★** has been created to preserve part of the shoreline *(open year-round; $7.50/vehicle;* △ ✗ & ☎418-272-2267). The region is famous for the landlocked salmon known as **ouananiche**, a favourite catch for sports fishermen; the wild **blueberries,** or *bleuets,* found on the north shore of the lake; and the famous nine-day **International Swim Marathon** held in July.

★★★ SAGUENAY FJORD

★★ Tadoussac – Pop. 832. *220km/136mi northeast of Quebec City by Rtes. 40 and 138.* This tiny community occupies a magnificent **site★★** at the mouth of the Saguenay on the cliffs and dunes lining the St. Lawrence. The resort town is popular as a place to see migrating whales.

In 1600 Pierre Chauvin built Canada's first trading post here, and Tadoussac became an important centre for the fur trade. Settlers moved into the area in the mid-19C, and the community developed into a lovely vacation spot. Today Tadoussac's principal attractions are whales that swim up the St. Lawrence to the mouth of the Saguenay for a few months each year.

The village is dominated by the red roofs of the **Hotel Tadoussac**, dating from 1941. Facing the hotel a boardwalk extends along the river, connecting a reconstruction of Chauvin's trading post and a tiny Indian chapel (1747). A short walk to the wharf affords fine views of the area.

★★ Whale-watching Cruises – *Depart from the Coast Guard pier at Tadoussac May–Oct daily 9:45am & 12:45pm (Jun 23–Labour Day additional cruises 2:45 & 4:15pm). Round-trip 3hrs. Commentary. Reservations suggested. $30.* ✗ & *Croisières Navimex Inc.* ☎418-237-4274 or 800-563-4643 (Canada, US). At Tadoussac, the St. Lawrence is more than 10km/6mi wide. Boats head for the centre of the river where whales surface to breathe and to dive in search of food. Spray erupting from their blowholes makes them easy to see. The most common species sighted on cruises are the **fin**, **minke** and **beluga** (white whales). Occasionally, a fortunate visitor may glimpse a **humpback** or even the huge **blue whale**.

★★ Scenic Cruises – *Depart from La Grève pier near the marina in Tadoussac or from Chicoutimi (below) mid-May–Jun & Sept–mid-Oct daily 9:30am & 1:30pm. Jul–Aug daily 9am, 1pm & 4:15pm. Round-trip 3hrs. Commentary. Reservations suggested. $34.25.* & *Croisières à la Baleine* ☎418-235-4585. A boat trip is the most spectacular way to discover the Saguenay Fjord. The longer cruises lead to Éternité Bay, a lovely cove dominated by twin cliffs, Cap Éternité and Cap Trinité. Rising some 518m/1,700ft over the fjord, **Cap Trinité★★** is renowned for the impressive statue of the Virgin Mary standing on a ledge 180m/590ft above the water.

Sainte-Rose-du-Nord – Pop. 408. *94km/58mi from Tadoussac.* Founded in 1838, this charming village occupies an exceptional **site★★** in a cove nestled between two rocky escarpments. The small **nature museum** contains a fascinating collection of nature's oddities *(open year-round daily 8:30am–9pm; $2.50;* ☎418-675-2348).

★ Chicoutimi – Pop. 62,670. *200km/124mi north of Quebec City by Rte 175.* Meaning "to the edge of deep waters" in the local Montagnais language, Chicoutimi sits on the banks of the Saguenay, at the point where it becomes a spectacular fjord. Site of an important fur-trading post in the mid-17C, the town is today the cultural and administrative centre of the Saguenay region.

★ Chicoutimi Pulp Mill (Pulperie de Chicoutimi) – *300 Rue Dubuc. Open year-round daily 9am–6pm.* This former pulp and paper mill (1896) was one of the most important industrial complexes in Quebec in the early 20C. The former workshop has been converted into an **interpretation centre** that features a fascinating audio-visual presentation on the mill and the lumber industry in general *(open mid-Jun–Labour Day daily 9am–6pm; $2.25;* ✗ & ☎418-698-3100).

★ Saguenay–Lac-Saint-Jean Museum (Musée du Saguenay–Lac-Saint-Jean) – *534 Rue Jacques-Cartier Est. Open Jun 24–Labour Day daily 8:30am–8pm. Rest of the year Mon–Fri 8:30am–noon & 1:30–5pm, weekends & holidays 1–5pm. $4.* & ☎418-545-9400.

This museum provides an insightful introduction to the Saguenay area. Exhibits focus on the Montagnais lifestyle, the first European settlers and the region's industrial development.

★★ **Scenic Cruises** – *Round-trip and one-way cruise/bus options. Depart from dock at foot of Rue Salaberry Jun–Sept daily 8:30am & 12:30pm. Commentary. Reservations required. $30. ✗ Croisières Marjolaine Inc.*☎*418-543-7630. For a description of cruise sights, see Tadoussac p 232.* On the return trip, the views of Ha! Ha! Bay and of Chicoutimi itself are equally magnificent.

★★ LAKE SAINT-JEAN

Péribonka – Pop. 635. *270km/167mi north of Quebec City by Rtes. 175 and 169.* After spending a few months in this charming community in 1912, the French author Louis Hémon (1880-1913) wrote his well-known novel, *Maria Chapdelaine, récit du Canada français.* Informative exhibits at the **Louis Hémon Museum★** (Musée Louis-Hémon) trace the life and work of the author *(open Jun–Sept daily 9am–5:30pm; rest of the year Mon–Fri 9am–4pm, Sun 1–5pm; $4.50; ⅋* ☎*418-374-2177).*

Saint-Félicien – Pop. 9,340. *67km/42mi west of Péribonka by Rte. 169.* Located on the western shore of the lake, this agricultural community is best known for its **zoo★★** *(6km/4mi on Blvd. du Jardin; open Jun–Sept daily 9am–5pm; $16; ✗ ⅋* ☎*418-679-0543).* A specially designed train takes visitors through the park, allowing them to admire a variety of animals roaming in natural surroundings. Of particular interest is the **Nature Trails Park★★**, inhabited by some 450 animals native to Canada.

Roberval – Pop. 11,628. *25km/15mi south by Rte 169.* Located on the southwestern shore of Lake Saint-Jean, this community is today an important service centre for the area. It is also the finish point of the annual International Swim Marathon.

Pointe-Bleue Amerindian Museum (Musée Amérindien de Pointe-Bleue) – *9km/6mi north of Roberval by Blvd. Saint-Joseph. Open mid-Jun–mid-Sept daily 9am–6pm. Rest of the year Mon–Fri 8am–noon & 1–4pm. $3. ⅋* ☎*418-275-4842.* Located in Mashteuiatsh, an Indian reserve created in 1856, this museum traces the history of the Montagnais and displays traditional tools and clothing. Note the poignant mural, *Hommage to the Montagnais or Twilight of a People* by André Michel.

★ **Val-Jalbert** – *9km/6mi south of Roberval by Rte. 169. Open mid-May–mid-Jun daily 9am–5pm. Mid-Jun–Labour Day daily 9am–7pm. Early Sept–mid-Oct daily 9am–5pm. $8.50. △ ✗ ⅋* ☎*418-275-3132.* Today a ghost town, Val-Jalbert was once the site of a thriving pulp mill. Built in 1902, the mill produced up to 50 tonnes/45 tons of pulp a day at the height of production in 1910. By the late 1920s, stiff competition led to the mill's closing, and the village gradually fell into ruins. Visitors can wander through the old residential sector that once contained over 80 residences and shops. Today many of these houses are in decay, creating an eerie atmosphere. The **Old Mill** (Vieux Moulin), standing on the Ouiatchouan River, now contains an exhibit on the mill's operation; a film *(20min)* shows the pulp-to-paper process. A steep stairway *(400 steps; cable car ascent $3.75)* leads to the top of an impressive waterfall on the Ouiatchouan River. From this vantage point, the **view★★** encompasses Lake Saint-Jean and the surrounding area.

TROIS-RIVIÈRES★★

Pop. 49,426
Map p 205
Tourist Office ☎819-375-1222

Capital of the Mauricie Region, this industrial centre is located on the north shore of the St. Lawrence River at the mouth of the Saint-Maurice. Just before joining the St. Lawrence, the Saint-Maurice branches around two islands, creating the three "rivers" for which the city is named.

Sent by Champlain, **Sieur de Laviolette** established a fur-trading post here in 1634. Home to many great explorers, including Pierre Radisson, Sieur des Groseilliers and Sieur de la Vérendrye, the city flourished. In the 1850s major logging companies began exploiting the surrounding forests, and a thriving pulp and paper industry took root in the area. By the 1930s Trois-Rivières was the world capital for the production of newsprint, a distinction it still holds to this day. This bustling city is also the location of a University of Quebec campus.

SIGHTS

★ **Rue des Ursulines** – This charming street is lined with some of the oldest structures of the city that survived a fire in 1908. Distinguished by a gracious dome and large wall sundial, the **Ursuline Monastery★** (Monastère des Ursulines) is the jewel of Trois-Rivières' old quarter. Inside, the **museum** features fine collections of ceramics, silver, books and furniture *(open May–Sept Tue–Fri 9am–5pm, weekends 1:30–5pm; Nov–Apr Wed–Sun 1:30–5pm; $2; ☎819-375-7922).* Other buildings of interest on this street include St. James' Church, erected in 1742 by the Récollet Brothers, and the Gannes and Hertel de la Fresnière Houses.

★ **Waterfront Park (Parc Portuaire)** – This attractive terrace affords superb **views** of the river and Laviolette Bridge, erected in 1967. At the eastern end of the park, a monument commemorates the Sieur de la Vérendrye, first European to reach the Rockies. At the **Pulp and Paper Industry Exhibition Centre** (Centre d'exposition sur l'industrie des pâtes et papiers) displays provide a fascinating introduction to the dominant industry of Trois-Rivières *(open Apr–May by appointment; Jun–Labour Day daily 9am–6pm; Sept Mon–Fri by appointment, weekends 11am–5pm; Oct by appointment; $2.50; ✗ ♿ ☎819-372-4633).*

★ **Scenic Cruise** – *Departs from dock at foot of Rue des Forges May–Sept daily 1pm & 8pm. Round-trip 2hrs. Commentary. Reservations suggested. $10. ✗ ♿ Croisières Jacques Cartier* ☎819-375-3000. This cruise offers an unequalled **view** of the port at Trois-Rivières and the pulp and paper installations. The shrine at Cap-de-la-Madeleine *(below)* is also visible.

EXCURSIONS   *Map p 205*

★★ **Cap-de-la-Madeleine Shrine** – *5km/3mi east of Trois-Rivières by Rtes. 40 and 755 (Exit 10). Open May–mid-Oct daily 8am–7pm. Rest of the year daily 8:30am–noon & 1–4pm. ♿. ☎819-374-2441.* This shrine attracts thousands of people annually. Two events are credited with its renown as a pilgrimage site.

In the mid-19C Father Luc Désilets decided his growing congregation needed a new church to replace the one built on this site in 1717. When unusually mild weather prevented the St. Lawrence from freezing, Désilets could not transport stones across the river for the church's construction. The Father vowed to preserve the existing church in exchange for a miracle. In March 1879, ice appeared on the river, remaining just long enough for parishioners to take the stones across. On the night of the new church's consecration in 1888, another miracle is said to have occurred when the eyes of a statue of the Virgin reportedly opened before three witnesses. Begun in 1955 to accommodate an even larger congregation, the present basilica replaced Désilets' church and was completed in 1964.

The imposing octagonal basilica is adorned with magnificent **stained-glass windows** designed in the medieval style by Dutch Oblate father Jan Tillemans. Set in attractive grounds beside the basilica, the original stone church now serves as a votive chapel. The miraculous statue stands above the altar. Winding their way through the park, the Stations of the Cross end before the replicas of the Crucifixion and the tomb of Jesus in Jerusalem.

★ **Mauricie Region** – Surrounding the valley of the Saint-Maurice River, this region ranks among the most industrialized in the province and the nation. Forestry operations began in the 1850s, and hydro-electric plants were erected in the late 19C. Hugging the river, which is still used to transport logs from the forests to the pulp mills, the drive along Route 155 affords fine **views★** of the Saint-Maurice and the rocky cliffs lining its sides. Located northwest of Grand-Mère, the **Mauricie National Park★★** offers a glorious landscape of dense forests interspersed with numerous lakes and rivers *(open year-round; visitor centres open mid-May–Labour Day daily 7am–10pm; rest of Sept–early Oct daily 9am–4:30pm, Fri 10pm; $2.50; hiking, bicycling, canoeing, swimming, fishing; △ ✗ ♿ ☎819-538-3232, or 819-536-2638 year-round).*

★★ **Saint-Maurice Ironworks National Historic Site** (Lieu historique national des Forges-du-Saint-Maurice) – *👁 13km/8mi from Trois-Rivières by Blvd. des Forges. Open May–Oct daily 9:30am–5pm. $3. ♿ ☎819-378-5116.* Established in 1729, these ironworks produced a variety of implements, including stoves, guns, ploughshares and dumbbells until 1883, when the iron ore and wood of the region were depleted. Only ruins remain, but the shapes of the original buildings are suggested by metal structures resembling scaffolding. At the **blast furnace** (haut fourneau), displays explain the smelting process. Beside the river a spring known as **Devil's Fountain** (Fontaine du Diable) emits natural gas.

French terms used in the text and on the maps in this guide:

anse	cove, bay	**monastère**	monastery
autoroute	highway	**mont**	mount
baie	bay	**montagne**	mountain
belvédère	viewpoint	**moulin**	mill
cap	cape	**musée**	museum
centrale hydro-électrique	hydro-electric power station	**Nord**	north
		Ouest	west
centre d'accueil	welcome centre	**palais de justice**	courthouse
centre d'interprétation	interpretation centre	**parc**	park
		phare	lighthouse
chute	waterfall	**place**	square
côte	shore, coast	**plage**	beach
croisière	cruise, boat trip	**pont**	bridge
Est	east	**rapides**	rapids
écluse	lock	**réserve faunique**	wildlife conservation area
église	church		
gare	train station	**rivière**	river
hôtel de ville	city hall	**rocher**	rock
île	island	**rue**	street
jardin	garden	**stationnement**	parking
lac	lake	**Sud**	south
maison	house	**téléphérique**	gondola
manoir	manor	**traversier**	ferry boat
métro	subway	**vallée**	valley
		ville	city, town

Tourisme Québec

Atlantic Provinces

Shag Harbour, Nova Scotia/Malak, Ottawa

B attered by the Atlantic Ocean on one side and washed by the calmer Gulf of St. Lawrence on the other, Canada's four Atlantic seacoast provinces (New Brunswick, Nova Scotia, Prince Edward Island and Newfoundland, including Labrador)—also known as Atlantic Canada—lie on the eastern side of the continent. The so-called Maritime provinces (New Brunswick, Nova Scotia and Prince Edward Island) together with Newfoundland, share the pervasive influence of the sea, which has molded, in great measure, their economic, political and cultural development.

Geographical Notes

Landscape – Parts of the region, notably northern New Brunswick and Cape Breton Island, are hilly, lying near the end of the **Appalachian Mountain** chain. In the western part of Newfoundland, the **Long Range Mountains** (average height 610m/2,000ft) are a continuation of this chain. A harsh, mountainous land, Labrador contrasts to Prince Edward Island with its stretches of flat lowland.

Barren and rocky by the sea while densely forested inland, the landmasses possess some fertile areas, however—the SAINT JOHN RIVER VALLEY, the ANNAPOLIS VALLEY and the whole of Prince Edward Island. Their long, deeply indented coastlines are ruggedly beautiful, studded with bays, inlets, cliffs and coves (Newfoundland alone has 9,660km/6,000mi of shoreline). Remarkable for its rapid tides, the **Bay of Fundy** produces the phenomenal tidal bore (*p 249*). The highest recorded tide in the world occurred at **Burncoat Head** (*map p 239*) on the Nova Scotia shore: a difference of 16.6m/54ft was measured between high and low tides.

Climate – The sea largely determines the climate of this region. Moving south down the Atlantic coast, the cold **Labrador Current** enters the Gulf of St. Lawrence by the Strait of Belle Isle. Because the region lies on the eastern side of an immense landmass, however, it receives air currents from the interior, since air masses generally move from west to east at these latitudes. Meeting warmer air currents off the continent, the cold waters of the Labrador Current can cause fogs throughout the year—less so in summer—along Newfoundland's and Nova Scotia's coasts especially.

Winters are stormy along the Atlantic but milder than inland. Coastal cities such as HALIFAX and ST. JOHN'S record a mean daily maximum in January of 0°C/32°F and 1°C/34°F respectively, whereas in northwestern New Brunswick extreme minimum temperatures of –34°C/–30°F are experienced.

Summers are cooler and less humid than in Ontario and Quebec at the same latitude. The coast is cooler than inland (Halifax 23°C/74°F, July mean daily maximum; Saint John 21°C/70°F) whereas extreme maximum temperatures in excess of 38°C/100°F have been recorded in northwestern New Brunswick.

In general, precipitation is evenly distributed throughout the year. Precipitation is greatest annually along the coasts of Newfoundland (St. John's 1,345mm/53in) and Nova Scotia (Halifax 1,372mm/54in) and least in Newfoundland's interior (Gander 1,016mm/40in) and northwestern New Brunswick (1,016mm/40in). The Great Northern Peninsula of Newfoundland is the driest region. Snow falls in all the provinces, but is heaviest in northwestern New Brunswick (254-305cm/8-10ft) and lightest along the coast (Halifax 163cm/5ft). Labrador experiences a more severe climate than other parts of the region with more extreme temperatures but less precipitation. Goose Bay registers a mean maximum of -14°C/7°F in January, and 21°C/70°F in July, with 737mm/29in of precipitation annually. With its sub-Arctic climate, northern Labrador is colder: winter mean temperatures, recorded at sea level, average -20°C/-4°F.

Population – More than two million people live in the Atlantic provinces, with Nova Scotia the most populous (899,942), followed by New Brunswick (723,900). Prince Edward Island has the lowest population (129,765). The majority of inhabitants claim origins in the British Isles (England, Scotland and Ireland). The most homogeneous of any province, Newfoundland sustains a population of 568,474 with 98 percent declaring English as their mother tongue. Yet there is a noticeable French-speaking minority in the region (largely Acadians), concentrated as follows: 1 percent in Newfoundland in the St. George's/Port au Port region; 4 percent in Nova Scotia; 17 percent in Prince Edward Island; and 34 percent in New Brunswick (mainly in the north and east). Nearly 30 percent of Nova Scotia's population is of Scottish origin, living mainly in Cape Breton Island and on the shores of Northumberland Strait; another 4 percent living on the south coast, west of Halifax, have German origins. The Micmac are the most populous of the Indians in Newfoundland, New Brunswick and Nova Scotia. Inuit and Montagnais-Naskapi Indians are found primarily in northern Labrador. The black population, which accounts for less than 1 percent of the region's inhabitants, is concentrated primarily in the towns of Nova Scotia and New Brunswick.

Historical Notes

Native Cultures – Before the arrival of Europeans, the Atlantic provinces were inhabited by Indians of the **Eastern Woodlands** culture *(map p 22)*: **Micmac** in New Brunswick, Nova Scotia and Prince Edward Island lived by hunting and fishing; **Maliseets** cultivated the land in southern New Brunswick like their Iroquoian brothers in Ontario *(p 131)*; and the **Beothuk** in Newfoundland also fished and hunted. As their ancestors had done, the latter painted themselves with red-powdered ochre, perhaps the origin of the term "redskins." The Beothuk's belief that all goods were held in common increased hostilities with the early European fishermen who frequently found their supplies missing. Mass murder and European diseases diminished these people greatly. The last known surviving Beothuk died in St. John's in 1829.

The First Europeans – Although he is credited as the first European arrival, **John Cabot** (1450-98)—an Italian navigator on a 1497 voyage of discovery for England's Henry VII—was not the first European to set foot in the region. One school of thought claims the Norse settled in Nova Scotia about AD 1000, but irrefutable evidence is lacking. Archaeological remains prove that the Norse settled on the Newfoundland coast at that time *(p 290)*. There is reason to believe the **Irish** reached the province's shore in the 6C, and it is possible that **Basques** fished the North Atlantic as early as the 14C. At Red Bay in Labrador, archaeologists have discovered the presence of a large 16C Basque whaling port. Cabot's

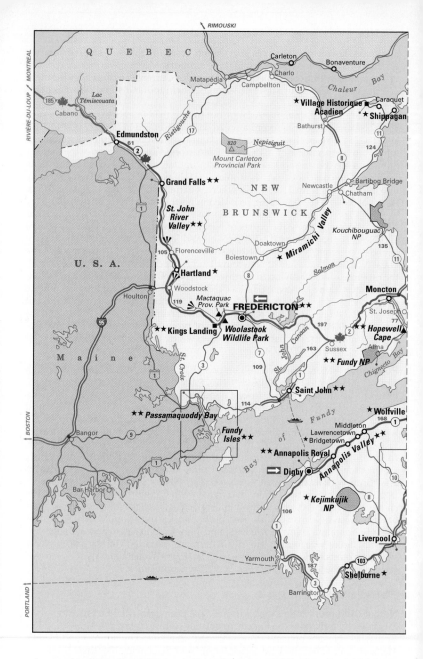

importance lies in his publicizing the region's rich fisheries. The Basques, English, French, Portuguese and Spanish came for the cod, especially abundant off Newfoundland's Grand Banks (*p 283*). Dried on racks on shore, the fish was light, almost indestructible, and easily transportable to a ready market in Europe.

Settlement was generally discouraged by the English West Country merchant owners of the fishing fleets, who feared competition from a resident population. Before the close of the 16C, English fishermen established small communities on Newfoundland's coasts, despite stiff anti-settlement laws.

In 1583 Newfoundland—the subject of great rivalry in Europe—was proclaimed the territory of Elizabeth I (*p 291*) at St. John's. Only the French attempted to wrest control of the region from the English. **Jacques Cartier** (*p 278*) had claimed Prince Edward Island for France in 1534, renaming it Île-St.-Jean, but serious attempts to colonize it were not forthcoming until the 18C. French efforts at settlement met with success in Nova Scotia, largely with the aid of the Micmac who taught them survival skills, when Sieur de Monts and Samuel de Champlain established **Port Royal** in 1605 (*p 260*).

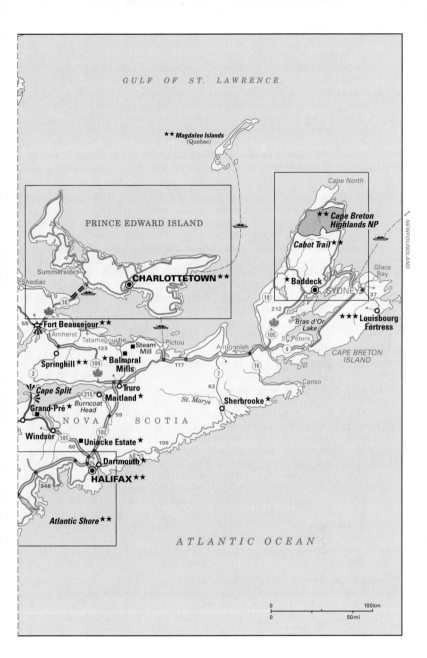

"New Scotland" – Port Royal fell to a force from Virginia in 1613 and, although the French reestablished it later, in the interim it was British. In 1621 James I granted present-day Nova Scotia, Prince Edward Island and New Brunswick to **Sir William Alexander** to establish a "New Scotland" there (both men were Scots)— hence the Latin name *Nova Scotia* used on the original charter. The settlements Alexander founded were short-lived, and in 1632 Charles I, who apparently did not share his father's desire for a New Scotland, returned the region to the French by the Treaty of St.-Germain-en-Laye. The future Nova Scotia had nonetheless been born—the coat of arms granted in 1621 is still the provincial emblem today.

"Acadie" – *Acadie* (Acadia) was what the French called a vague area covering much of Nova Scotia, Prince Edward Island, New Brunswick and Maine. The Acadians are descendants mainly of French colonists who came from western France to La Have and Port Royal between 1632 and 1651. As their numbers grew, settlements spread along the ANNAPOLIS VALLEY to Chignecto Bay *(p 245)*. Repeatedly attacked by expeditions from New England during the Anglo-French wars of the 17C, these settlements changed hands several times.

British Regime – The English Crown granted a few charters in the 17C for colonies on Newfoundland, but authority for local law and order, granted in 1634 by Charles I, belonged largely to the **fishing admiral**—master of the first British ship to enter a harbour, regardless if there were residents. Fear of French expansion prompted the British to create permanent settlements in Newfoundland. Only with a strong, stable base could Britain properly defend her Atlantic harbours from the French who attacked from their colony at **Placentia**, established in 1662. French claims to the region ended in 1713 when, by the Treaty of Utrecht, France retained only the small islands of **Saint-Pierre and Miquelon** *(p 296)* and ceded all of mainland Nova Scotia to the British. Port Royal, renamed Annapolis Royal, became its capital *(p 259)*.

Nova Scotia Again – The Treaty of Utrecht gave Acadians the choice of leaving British territory, or becoming British subjects. Taking an oath of allegiance to Britain would mean possibly having to bear arms against fellow Frenchmen. Leaving the area would deprive them of their rich farmlands. The Acadians maintained they were neutral, stating they would take the oath with exemption from military service. Initially the British governor agreed—his soldiers needed provisions that the Acadians supplied. In peaceful times the agreement may have lasted, but Anglo-French fighting in Europe was renewed and British rule in Nova Scotia was threatened by the building of Louisbourg *(p 275)*. Acadian sympathy for the French cause was undeniable, though it seems likely most Acadians were truly neutral. Then, in 1747, nearly 100 New England soldiers billeted in the village of Grand Pré were killed, as they slept, in a surprise attack by a French force from Quebec. Treachery among the Acadian inhabitants was suspected.

Acadian Deportation – Fear of future attacks hardened the British toward the Acadians, especially after 1749 when Halifax was founded with 2,500 English settlers *(p 271)* who could provision the army. In 1755 **Gov. Charles Lawrence** delivered his ultimatum—take an unqualified oath of allegiance or be removed from Nova Scotia. When the Acadians refused, Lawrence quickly issued the Deportation Order, with no reference to Britain. Over the next 8 years, 14,600 Acadians were forcibly deported. Others escaped to Quebec. Families were separated, some never to be reunited. Unwelcomed in the colonies, the Acadians were able to establish a new community only in Louisiana and, as **Cajuns**, survive to this day. Some escaped to Saint-Pierre and Miquelon. Others fled to Île-St.-Jean until 1758 when the island was captured by a British expedition under **Lord Rolo**, and later annexed by Nova Scotia. Left untouched was a small settlement in the Malpeque area, the origins of Prince Edward Island's French-speaking population today. When peace was restored between England and France in 1763, most exiles returned to Nova Scotia only to find their rich farmlands occupied by new English colonists. The Acadians settled mainly in New Brunswick, where their descendants live to this day.

Scots, Loyalists and Other Settlers – After Deportation the British offered free land to anyone willing to settle in Nova Scotia. New Englanders from the south, groups from the British Isles and from the German states along the Rhine, and the first wave of Scottish Highlanders accepted the offer. Dispossessed by big landowners who sought profit in sheep raising over tenant farming, the first 200 Scots who arrived in 1773 settled mainly in Cape Breton *(p 266)*, Pictou, Antigonish and on Prince Edward Island.

In 1775 when revolution erupted in the American colonies, it appeared Nova Scotia would join the other 13. Instead it became a receiving point for 30,000 Loyalists who fled the new US after the war. Their arrival transformed Nova Scotia. A separate administration was set up in 1784 and called New Brunswick for the German duchy of Braunschweig-Lüneburg, governed at that time by England's George III. Other Loyalists settled in Prince Edward Island, which was separated from Nova Scotia in 1769 and named in 1799 in honour of the father of Queen Victoria *(p 279)*.

Confederation – In September 1864, representatives of Nova Scotia, New Brunswick and Prince Edward Island met with a delegation from Canada (then only Ontario and Quebec) to discuss British union in North America. This historic conference *(p 279)* paved the way for Confederation in 1867. The island refused at first to join, but entered in 1873, pressured by Britain and threatened with impending bankruptcy from railway construction. Although its representatives attended the final conference in Quebec in October 1864, Newfoundland chose not to join, holding out until 1949 when it became Canada's tenth province.

Resources and Industries

The Atlantic provinces benefit from their vast forests as well as from other land resources. Magnificent scenery has made tourism a major economic factor, and the sea constitutes a rich resource on which the provinces have long depended.

Fishing Industry – Overtaken in value by manufacturing and mining, coastal fishing is still important to Newfoundland's economy. Cod has been the great catch as it has been since the 15C. (In Newfoundland cod is synonymous with "fish"; all other varieties such as herring, caplin or salmon are referred to by name.) Extending 500km/300mi from the coast, the submerged continental shelf known as the **Grand Banks** *(p 283)* has been one of the most extensive fish breeding grounds in the world. However, since the late 1980s there has been a marked decrease in cod stocks there, and in 1992, the Canadian government placed a two-year moratorium on cod fishing off the northeast coast of the island. The ban was subsequently extended to 1997 and widened to cover all waters, not only around Newfoundland, but also around all the Maritime provinces, excepting an area off the coast of southwest Nova Scotia. There are restrictions on redfish, plaice and other groundfish as well. Of late, there have been some signs that some of the fish stocks are recovering.

Maritime Fishing – Nova Scotia's commercial fishery ranks second in Canada behind British Columbia, while New Brunswick's share of the east coast fishing industry is 18 percent. Nova Scotia has an off shore fleet that fishes the Banks, but 70 percent of its fishermen are based inshore. The most valuable catch for the three Maritime provinces is **lobster**. Since the season is tightly controlled, saltwater pounds keep the catch year round to be sold fresh on the world market. Most of these pounds are located in New Brunswick, notably on Deer Island *(p 250)*. The province is also known for its sardines and Atlantic salmon, Prince Edward Island is famous for Malpeque **oysters**, and Nova Scotia for Digby **scallops**. Giant **bluefin tuna** are caught off the shores of all three provinces. In New Brunswick and in Nova Scotia, north of Dartmouth, **aquaculture** is a provincial-supported industry, concentrating on the cultivation of mussels, clams and oysters.

Sealing – The catching of seals for their skins and meat is as old as settlement in Newfoundland. In early winter adult seals leave their feeding grounds in the Arctic, floating south on ice floes carried by the Labrador Current to their birthing sites off northeast Newfoundland and in the Gulf of St. Lawrence. Here, mostly young adult harp and hooded seals are hunted by small-boat fishermen principally from Newfoundland and Quebec's MAGDALEN ISLANDS, for whom the harvest is a seasonal supplement to fishery income.

In 1987 Canada banned the killing of young seals (up to a year old) and the hunting of seals from large offshore vessels in response to international protests. In recent years the hunts have become controversial again. In 1996 the Canadian government sanctioned expanded harp seal quotas in an attempt to help revive the cod fishery, although, until 1996, quotas had never been reached in any year since 1987. Immature Atlantic cod are eaten by harp seals, but scientific opinion is divided as to whether their harvest will hasten the recovery of cod stocks.

Agriculture – Agriculture is important to the economies of the Maritimes, but it is the backbone of Prince Edward Island. While the island supports a wide range of farming, it is most famous for its **potatoes**. Together with New Brunswick, Prince Edward Island produces 86 percent of Canada's table exports (potatoes destined for consumption) and 80 percent of the country's seed exports.

The Saint John River Valley *(p 254)* and the Annapolis Valley *(p 260)* are the region's other great agricultural areas. Farms do exist in glacier-ravaged Newfoundland on **Avalon Peninsula** and in **Codroy Valley**, but they supply local markets only.

Forestry – Land not under cultivation in New Brunswick (85 percent) and Nova Scotia (77 percent) supports a sizeable forest industry. New Brunswick's **pulp**, **paper** and **lumber** industries have overtaken agriculture in domestic production. Previously dependent upon the fishing industry, Newfoundland's economy has diversified to include mining, and manufacture based on forest resources.

Mining and Energy – **Iron ore** has been mined in Newfoundland since the turn of the century. The Bell Island works in Conception Bay, now closed, were important enough to be attacked twice by German submarines. Today the mines of the **Labrador Trough** in western Labrador are the source of approximately 55 percent of Canada's iron ore products. Labrador City is the site of one of the world's largest open-pit mining, concentrate and pelletizing operations. Copper and gold are mined in Newfoundland.

Mining makes a sizeable contribution to New Brunswick's economy: in 1995 the value of production reached a billion dollars. One of the world's largest base metals (zinc, lead and copper) mines is located near Bathurst; a second mine is operating in the vicinity of Miramichi. Antimony is mined near FREDERICTON and two potash mines are situated near Sussex. **Coal** continues to be extracted at Minto-Chipman, where mining was first undertaken in 1639. In Nova Scotia coal, gypsum and salt are mined. Once a mainstay of the economy, Nova Scotia's coal industry slumped badly after World War II. Today, with renewed interest in coal as a fuel, several mines are operating again, producing some metallurgical coal for the steel industry, but primarily thermal coal for generating electricity.
New Brunswick's electric power resources are significant. The Saint John River has been harnessed in several locations, notably Mactaquac *(p 285)* and Beechwood. The Maritimes' only nuclear power station is located at Point Lepreau on the Bay of Fundy. Labrador's **hydro-electric** potential is enormous. Virtually all the power produced by the huge generating station at **Churchill Falls** goes to the province of Quebec. Technological advances are being applied to exploit the considerable **natural gas** and **oil** reserves off Newfoundland *(p 285)* and Labrador, where drifting icebergs have always posed a threat. Canada's first offshore oil production platform has been in operation since 1992 near Sable Island, 120 miles southeast of HALIFAX. Both New Brunswick and Nova Scotia realize the potential of the mighty Bay of Fundy tides; a pilot project has produced electricity at Annapolis Royal since 1983 *(p 259)*.

Manufacturing – The food sector dominates Atlantic Canada's manufacturing as a whole, fish processing being the largest industry. More than 300 companies engage in pharmaceutical and medical research, telecommunications and advanced technologies such as satellite remote sensing, environmental survival systems and ocean mapping. Manufacturing within the provinces is also diverse. Three tire-manufacturing facilities, an automobile assembly plant (Halifax), one steel plant (Sydney) and an aircraft engine plant (Halifax) are located in Nova Scotia. Oil refineries and shipbuilding/ship-repair facilities have been established at Halifax as well as at SAINT JOHN, New Brunswick. Newfoundland's large-scale manufacturing includes shipbuilding at Marystown *(p 286)*, oil refining at Come by Chance and paint manufacture in ST. JOHN'S. An international airport, road and rail links and the deepest ice-free ports in the country aid in transporting Atlantic Canada's products to domestic and overseas markets.

Recreation
For specific information on the activities below, contact the appropriate provincial tourism office: New Brunswick p 245, Nova Scotia p 258, Prince Edward Island p 278 and Newfoundland p 284.

Parks – All four provinces have excellent national and provincial parks with camping facilities and activities. Washed by the surprisingly warm waters of the Gulf of St. Lawrence *(p 280)*, Prince Edward Island National Park has lovely beaches. Miles of sand dunes are part of New Brunswick's **Kouchibouguac National Park**. Hiking trails abound in the province's Fundy National Park *(p 248)*, Mactaquac Provincial Park and Mt. Carleton Provincial Park, as they do in Nova Scotia's National Park in Cape Breton's Highlands *(p 268)* and Newfoundland's national parks *(pp 287 and 297)*.

Water Sports – With so much coastline the provinces offer unparalleled opportunities for swimming, boating and sailing. Water temperatures are surprisingly warm off Prince Edward Island's northern shores and New Brunswick's Northumberland Strait, in the vicinity of Shediac's Parlee Beach Provincial Park. Those who find Atlantic waters rough for boating may prefer huge Bras d'Or Lake in Cape Breton, or the beautiful Saint John River *(p 254)* where **houseboats** can be rented by the week. Canoeing is gaining popularity in this region: **Kejimkujik National Park** *(p 260)* has several routes, and there are sailing and canoeing opportunities in Newfoundland's lakes and rivers. **Sea kayaking** is offered along Nova Scotia's eastern shore, off Cape Breton in particular, and **river rafting** is available on the province's Medway River, or even the Fundy Tidal Bore. **Windsurfing** is practised on the bays and off the north shore beaches of Prince Edward Island, particularly Stanhope Beach, in the Eel River Bar of New Brunswick's Restigouche region and off the Acadian Peninsula.

Fishing – Trout and salmon fishing in Newfoundland and Labrador are probably unequalled elsewhere in eastern North America. A famous place to watch the salmon leap *(August)* is **Squires Memorial Park** near Deer Lake *(map p 283)*.

Especially noted for its Atlantic **salmon** are the Margaree Valley in Nova Scotia and the Miramichi and Restigouche Valleys of northern New Brunswick. **Fly fishing** is the only legal method for anglers to catch salmon in Nova Scotia. **Deep-sea fishing** is popular in the Maritimes, where boats can be chartered.

Whale Watching – Whales usually can be seen throughout the summer *(August and September, especially)* off the coasts of Newfoundland, New Brunswick and Nova Scotia. Cruises are available in Newfoundland in the vicinity of St. John's *(p 295)*, TERRA NOVA NATIONAL PARK, Trinity *(p 298)* and Twillingate. Deer Island, Grand Manan Island and St. Andrews are departure points for whale-watching voyages in New Brunswick. In Nova Scotia cruises depart from northern Cape Breton Island and from Digby Neck. Humpback, finback and minke are just some of the varieties of whales that can be seen. Tour boats attempt to get close to the mammals for a memorable sound and sight experience.

Bird Watching – There are many popular birding areas in the region, especially along the coasts. The bird population of **Grand Manan Island** *(p 251)* drew James Audubon to its shores to sketch its many species. In Nova Scotia, south of Liverpool, the **Seaside Adjunct** of Kejimkujik National Park protects a breeding grounds for piping plovers. Yarmouth harbours cormorants and black-backed gulls. The

Gannets at Cape St. Mary's Ecological Reserve

Bird Islands attract a variety of sea birds to its protected sanctuaries and McNab's Island in Halifax harbour provides a nesting site for osprey. Bald eagles can be seen in the Bras d'Or Lake area as well as in Cape Breton Highlands National Park. Of the 520 species found in Canada, 300 have been recorded in Newfoundland (and on Prince Edward Island as well). At its three famous sea bird colonies—**Cape St. Mary's**, **Witless Bay** and **Funk Island** *(map p 283)*—gannets, murres, kittiwake gulls, razorbilled auks, puffins, guillemots and dovekies can be observed. Bald eagles, and even occasionally a golden eagle, are sighted along the south coast.

Other Activities – **Adventure tours** on foot, by river boat or even **snowmobiles** (in Labrador) are offered by outfitters in the wilds of Newfoundland. Operating mainly out of HALIFAX, wilderness expeditions in Nova Scotia can include backpacking, photography and even cross-country skiing.
Helicopter tours depart Prince Edward Island in March for the ice fields of the Gulf of St. Lawrence where thousands of baby harp seals can be seen. Seal-watch excursions also depart Halifax, NS in February/March; contact Natural Habitat Wildlife Adventures, 2945 Center Green Court, Boulder, CO 80301 United States ☎303-449-3711 or 800-543-8917 *(Canada/US)*. Year-round flightseeing tours of Newfoundland and Labrador, some by **seaplane** or helicopter, originate mainly in St. John's. Both Prince Edward Island and New Brunswick contain some excellent golf courses.

Winter Sports – Downhill slopes and cross-country skiing trails are located in the northern part of Nova Scotia, notably Cape Breton Island. A number of snowmobile clubs have trails, accessible to the public, in the province's open fields and woods. Charlo bills itself as New Brunswick's cross-country ski capital. The province boasts some alpine ski centres as well. Skating on frozen ponds and lakes, and winter camping are popular in the region.

New Brunswick

Map pp 238-239

Bounded by the US on the west and Quebec to the north, New Brunswick is the Atlantic provinces' connection to the continental mainland. The province is linked to Nova Scotia by the Isthmus of Chignecto. Separated from Prince Edward Island by the Northumberland Strait, New Brunswick has relied on ferry service for access to the island in the past. The two provinces will soon be connected by a nearly 13km/8mi-long bridge, scheduled for completion in 1997 *(p 279)*.

Geographical Notes

Coastline and Interior – An extensive coastline faces Chaleur Bay in the north, the Gulf of St. Lawrence to the east and the Bay of Fundy in the south. Extending into the bay are the three **Fundy islands** of Deer, Campobello and Grand Manan *(p 000)*. The 73,436sq km/28,354sq mi interior consists of mountainous uplands reaching 820m/2,690ft in the northwest, central highlands of hills 610m/2,000ft above sea level, the nearly L-shaped SAINT JOHN RIVER VALLEY draining at the southern tidal shore, and a sloping plain extending east to Chaleur Bay.

The Saint John River – Named by Champlain and de Monts *(p 260)* in honour of Saint John, this largely tranquil, 673km/418mi river flows northeast from northern Maine along the US/New Brunswick border to empty into the Bay of Fundy. Between Edmundston and Grand Falls, rural villages intersperse the farmed river valley. Turbulent at Grand Falls gorge, the river cascades over 25m/76ft cataracts and 18m/59ft at Beechwood—both sites of hydro-electric dams. After the provincial capital of **Fredericton**, the river gradually broadens, traversing a picturesque valley of patchwork farmland. Fertile soil in its upper and lower regions sustains extensive cultivation, particularly the north's thriving **potato** industry. At the city of its namesake, the river is thrown back by the mighty Fundy tides in a slim gorge called **Reversing Falls** *(p 253)*. Fredericton and the major port city of **Saint John** are situated on the banks of this important waterway. Today the river carries little except pleasure boaters and sailing enthusiasts who find its wide expanses and deep waters a paradise, especially in the lower sections.

Historical Notes

Era of Wooden Ships – Pre-Loyalists and Loyalists established a great industry—the building of ships of timber cut from the region's forests, especially New Brunswick's. Beginning as mast making for British naval vessels, the industry grew, particularly at Saint John, which became one of the world's great shipbuilding centres by the mid-19C. Two brothers who opened a shipyard in Chatham were to become famous as founders of the **Cunard line**. Skilled craftsmen perfected clipper ships, schooners, brigs and barques for worldwide use as shipyards sprang up along the coasts of Nova Scotia and Prince Edward Island.
By Confederation in 1867, New Brunswick was well established and wealthy. In the latter half of the 19C, the province was the most prosperous in Canada. The prosperity did not last, however. By 1900 steam replaced sail power and steel hulls superseded wooden ones. Lack of foresight doomed the shipbuilding industry; only a few shipyards converted their operations to the newer technology. By World War I, wooden ships were no longer built, and the age of prominence was over.

Cultural Heritage – The social fabric of New Brunswick was woven over two centuries by a diverse population of Micmac and Maliseet Indians, New England Loyalists, Acadians, Scots, Irish, Germans, Danes and Dutch. Each group has left its imprint in the pioneer structures and celebrated traditions of rural communities and coastal villages throughout the province. Historic settlements such as **Kings Landing** *(p 254)*, MacDonald Farm Historic Park *(p 249)* and Acadian Historical Village *(p 256)* preserve the pioneer skills and crafts of the province's founders. The richness of place names, such as Kouchibouguac, Memramcook, Shediac and Richibucto, stems from original Indian designations. The Brayons' custom of flying the flag of their "republic," the Acadians' yearly "Blessing of the Fleet," Canada's largest Irish festival, an annual folk music celebration and a francophone festival featuring performers from France, Belgium and Louisiana illustrate the cultural variety of the province. Traditional feasts of seafood—particularly salmon, clams, oysters and lobster—or of earth's bounty ("corn boils," strawberry fests, "spud" days and even a brussel sprout festival) are staged from May through October. Generations have enjoyed hot Hodge Podge, a mix of new potatoes and vegetables in milk. Acadian potato and clam pie, a Loyalist dish of fish chowder, and buckwheat pancakes topped with maple syrup are old-time favourites.

244

PRACTICAL INFORMATION

Getting There

By Air – Air Canada and its affiliates provide direct air service to Saint John and Fredericton ☎902-429-7111; Air Nova has daily service from the US to Saint John and Moncton. Air Atlantic (an affiliate of Canadian Airlines International) has scheduled service to cities within the province and flights from the US ☎800-426-7000 (Canada/US).

By Train – **VIA Rail** services Moncton via Montreal, with connecting bus service to Saint John ☎902-857-9830.

By Boat – Government-operated ferries (free) provide service in the lower Saint John River area and to islands in the Bay of Fundy. Ferries connect the province with Nova Scotia, Quebec and Prince Edward Island. For information, contact Tourism New Brunswick (*below*).

General Information

Accommodations and Visitor Information – The official tourist office publishes an annual travel guide giving information on history, attractions and scheduled events. Government-inspected hotels and motels, Bed & Breakfast lodgings and country inns, farm vacations and campgrounds are also listed. For a free copy of the guide and a map, contact **Tourism New Brunswick**, PO Box 12345, Fredericton, NB, E3B 5C3 ☎800-561-0123 (Canada/US).

Language – New Brunswick is officially bilingual; approximately 35 percent of the population speaks French. All road signs are in English and French.

Road Regulations – (*Driver's license and insurance requirements p 314.*) The province has good paved roads. Speed limits, unless otherwise posted, are 80km/h (50mph) on provincial highways and 50km/h (30mph) in cities. **Seat belt** use is mandatory. **Canadian Automobile Assn. (CAA)** Saint John ☎506-634-1400.

Time Zone – New Brunswick is on Atlantic Standard Time. Daylight Saving Time is observed from the first Sunday in April to the last Sunday in October.

Taxes – The national GST of 7% (*rebate information p 318*) and a provincial sales tax of 11% (some items are exempt) are levied.

Liquor Laws – The legal drinking age is 19. Liquor is sold in government stores.

Provincial Holiday (*National Holidays p 319*)

New Brunswick Day .... 1st Monday in August

Recreation – *p 242.*

Principal Festivals

Jul	**Loyalist Days Festival** (*p 252*)	*Saint John*
	Lobster Festival	*Shediac*
Jul–Aug	**Foire Brayonne**	*Edmundston*
	Bon Ami Festival Get Together	*Dalhousie*
Aug	**Festival Acadien**	*Caraquet*
Sept	**Harvest Jazz and Blues Festival**	*Fredericton*

FORT BEAUSEJOUR★★

Map p 239

Overlooking the Cumberland Basin—an arm of Chignecto Bay—the Missiguash River Valley, and the Tantramar Marshes, this former French fort is exceptional for its impressive **panorama★★** of the surrounding country (*fog or rain may hamper visibility*). The scant remains of the mid-18C outpost testify to its turbulent history during the Anglo-French conflict in the New World.

Historical Notes – The fort stands on the Chignecto Isthmus, a narrow strip of land joining New Brunswick and Nova Scotia, which once marked the division between French and British lands. In 1672 the Acadians first settled in this area, which they called Beaubassin, reclaiming it from the sea by an extensive system of dikes. After the Treaty of Utrecht ceded mainland Nova Scotia to Britain in 1713, they found themselves in the middle of a border conflict. The British built Fort Lawrence on their side of the isthmus; the French built Fort Beausejour on

245

their side. Captured in 1755 by a British force under Col. Robert Monckton, the latter was renamed Fort Cumberland. The Acadians were the first to be removed from the land under the Deportation Order *(p 240)* of that same year. Strengthened by the British, the fort withstood an attack in 1776 by New England settlers sympathetic to the American Revolution. Although manned during the War of 1812, the outpost saw no further military action. In 1926 the fort, rechristened Fort Beausejour, was designated a National Historic Park.

Access – *At Aulac near Nova Scotia border, just off Trans-Can Hwy., Exit 550A.*

VISIT 1hr

☞ *Open Jun–mid-Oct daily 9am–5pm. $2.25.* ✗ ⚐ ☎506-536-0720. The **visitor centre** houses displays on the history of the fort, the Acadians and the region. Three restored underground casemates can be visited, and the earthworks are in good repair.

FREDERICTON★★

Pop. 46,466
Map p 238
Tourist Office ☎506-452-9500

Set on a bend in the placid Saint John River, opposite its junction with the Nashwaak River, this quiet city of elm-lined streets and elegant houses is the capital of New Brunswick. Largely because of the munificence of a locally raised benefactor, **Lord Beaverbrook**, the city is also the cultural centre of the province.

Historical Notes

From Fort to Capital – In 1692 the French governor of Acadie, Joseph Robineau de Villebon, constructed a fort at the mouth of the Nashwaak. Soon abandoned, the fort became an Acadian settlement called St. Anne's Point, which survived until the Seven Years' War. However, Fredericton's true beginning came, like Saint John's, with the arrival of the Loyalists *(p 252)* in 1783. Upon the formation of the province in 1784, the settlement they founded, complete with a college that is now the **University of New Brunswick**, was chosen as the capital. The more obvious choice, Saint John, was considered a less central site, vulnerable to sea attack. Named Fredericton after the second son of George III, the new capital soon became the social centre for the governor and the town's military garrison. Garden parties, gala dinners and visits from royalty were commonplace. In many ways, little has changed in this century. The vast majority of the population works for the provincial government or the university.

Lord Beaverbrook – Born William Maxwell Aitken in Ontario, and reared in Newcastle, New Brunswick, Lord Beaverbrook (1879-1964) was a successful businessman in Canada before leaving for England in 1910. After entering politics he was elevated to the peerage in 1917, adopting his title from a small New Brunswick town. Having established Beaverbrook Newspapers, he built a vast empire on London's Fleet Street. Influential in the government of **Winston Churchill**, he held several key cabinet posts during World War II. Although absent from the province most of his life, Beaverbrook never forgot New Brunswick. In addition to gifts to Newcastle, he financed, in whole or in part, an art gallery, a theatre and several university buildings in Fredericton.

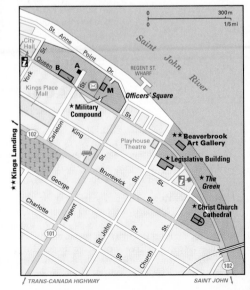

SIGHTS *3hrs*

Stretching along the southern bank of the Saint John River, the strip of parkland known as **The Green★** is one of Fredericton's most attractive landscapes. This grassy, tree-lined expanse provides a lovely setting for the city's historic buildings.

★★ **Beaverbrook Art Gallery** – *Open Jun–Aug Mon–Fri 9am–6pm, weekends 10am–5pm. Rest of the year Tue–Fri 9am–5pm, Sat 10am–5pm, Sun noon–5pm. Closed Dec 25. $3.* ☎506-458-8545. Designed and built by Lord Beaverbrook, the original structure was his gift to the people of New Brunswick. Opened in 1959 and expanded in 1983, the gallery is a major art centre of Atlantic Canada, featuring the donor's personally selected collection of British, European and Canadian art. At the gallery's entrance is Salvador Dali's huge surrealistic canvas, **Santiago el Grande**, depicting St. James on horseback being carried to heaven. Particularly strong in portraiture, the collection of **British art** is the most comprehensive in Canada. Paintings by Hogarth, Lawrence, Romney, Gainsborough and Reynolds are juxtaposed with striking works by Turner, Stanley Spencer, Augustus John and Graham Sutherland (*Portrait of Lord Beaverbrook*). An important collection of 18C and 19C English porcelain complements the artwork. Continental Europe is represented by paintings by Cranach, Botticelli, Delacroix, Tissot, Corneille de Lyon and Ribera. Fine European tapestries and furniture are arranged in period settings.The **Canadian Collection** features works by most of the country's best-known artists including Cornelius Krieghoff, Paul Kane, Emily Carr, David Milne and the Group of Seven.

★ **Legislative Building** – *Open Jun–late Aug daily 9:15am–8pm. Rest of the year Mon–Fri 9am–4pm. Closed national holidays.* ☎506-453-2527. Opposite the art gallery stands the stately Georgian seat of provincial government, with its classical dome and double-columned portico. Constructed of sandstone in 1880, this building replaced the old Province Hall, which was destroyed by fire.

Visitors are permitted to see the assembly chamber with its tiered balcony and to view **portraits** of Queen Charlotte and George III, replicas of paintings by Joshua Reynolds. The parliamentary library is reached by a striking wooden spiral staircase.

Legislative Building

Malak, Ottawa

★ **Christ Church Cathedral** *Open Jun–mid-Sept Mon–Sat 8am–8pm, Sun 1–8pm. Rest of the year Mon–Sat 8am–5:30pm, Sun 1–5:30pm.* ☎506-450-8500. This elegant stone church, distinguished by a copper-green spire and pointed arch windows, is surrounded by large, attractive Loyalist-built frame houses and tall shade trees. Completed in 1853 the church, modelled after the parish church of St. Mary in Snettisham, Norfolk, is an example of decorated Gothic Revival architecture. The interior is dominated by a hammer-beam wooden pointed **ceiling**. At the entrance to the south transept stands a cenotaph with a **marble effigy** of the Rt. Rev. John Medley, the first bishop of Fredericton.

★ **Military Compound** – *Changing of the guard daily in summer, weather permitting.* The central location of the former British military headquarters shows the importance of the infantry garrison in early Fredericton. (Today the country's major military training area—Canadian Armed Forces Base Gagetown—lies just to the southeast.) In 1869 shortly after Confederation, the British garrison vacated the quarters. Once stretching from Queen Street to the river between York and Regent streets, the compound retains few of its original buildings.

Now a pleasant park known as **Officers' Square**, the old parade ground is the site of the former **officers' quarters**, a 3-storey stone building with white arches, constructed in 1839 with additions in 1851. A few blocks to the west, the **Old Guard House [A]**, built in 1827, stands adjacent to the **soldiers' barracks [B]**, a stone building with red-painted wooden terraces. Both have been restored and furnished (*open mid-Jun–Labour Day daily 10am–6pm; rest of the year by appointment* ☎506-453-3747).

York-Sunbury Historical Society Museum [M] – *In Officers' Quarters. Open May–Labour Day Mon–Sat 10am–6pm (Mon & Fri 9pm), Sun noon–6pm. Early Sept–mid-Oct Mon–Fri 9am–5pm, Sat noon–4pm. Late Oct–Apr Mon, Wed & Fri 11am–3pm.* ☎506-455-6041. This museum provides a portrait of the Fredericton area from its settlement by the Indian population to the present. Exhibits on the Loyalists and the garrison are included, and a World War I trench has been reconstructed. The mounted Coleman frog, which weighed 19kg/42lbs, is on display.

EXCURSION

★★ **Kings Landing Historical Settlement** – *37km/23mi. Description p 254.*

FUNDY NATIONAL PARK★★

Map p 238

Extending 13km/8mi along the Bay of Fundy's steep seacliffs, this rolling parkland is cut by deep-cut rivers and streams in deep valleys. Created by 9m/29ft or higher tides, the vast tidal flats, explorable at low tide, contain a wealth of marine life. **Access** – *77km/48mi south of Moncton by Rte. 114.*

VISIT   1/2 day
❦ *Open year-round. Golf, boat rental, swimming, tennis, mountain biking, hiking. Visitor centre (east entrance) open mid-Jun–Labour Day daily 8am–9pm; early Sept–mid-Oct Mon–Fri 8:15am–4:30pm, weekends 10am–6pm; late Oct–early Jun Mon–Fri 8:15am–4:30pm. $3 entry fee.* △ ✕ ⚹ ☎506-887-6000. *Note: views described may be obscured by fog.*

Eastern Park Entrance – From the park gate there is a fine **view★** of the tranquil Upper Salmon River, the hills to the north, the small fishing village of Alma, Owl's Head and the bay. To appreciate the contrast, visit at both low and high tides.

Herring Cove – *11km/7mi from entrance.* At the end of the road, there is a good **view★** of the cove from above and a display on the tides. A path leads down to a cove that has tidal pools brimming with limpets, barnacles, sea anemones and other life at low tide.

★★ **Point Wolfe** – *10km/6mi from entrance.* The road crosses Point Wolfe River by a covered wooden bridge, below which is a small gorge forming the river's entry into Wolfe Cove. On this site a mill community once stood. To collect logs floated downstream from the north, a dam was constructed. Schooners loaded the sawn wood at wharves built in the coves. Today only the bridge and dam remain.
At the end of the road, a path leads to the cove, providing good **views★★** on the descent. At low tide the sand and rock pools are alive with sea creatures.

MIRAMICHI VALLEY★

Map p 238

The name Miramichi has long been associated with fine salmon fishing. A major spawning ground for Atlantic salmon, the river has two branches (the Southwest Miramichi and the Little Southwest Miramichi), which together traverse the province. The area is also lumber country; Newcastle (pop. 5,711) and Chatham (pop. 6,544), twin towns near the river's mouth, are known for their shipbuilding past. Joseph Cunard, founder of the famous shipping line, was born in Chatham.

SIGHTS

★ **Miramichi Salmon Museum** – *94km/58mi from Fredericton by Rte. 8 in Doaktown. Open Jun–Sept daily 9am–5pm. $4.* ☎506-365-4518. Overlooking a series of pools on the Miramichi River, this pleasant museum is devoted to the area's famed Atlantic salmon. Displays include boats, nets and fishing rods, migration routes and predators. The theatre features an audio-visual show on salmon fishing, and the small aquarium contains specimens of the fish.

Central New Brunswick Woodmen's Museum – *68km/42mi north of Fredericton by Rte. 8 in Boiestown. Open May–Sept daily 10am–5:30pm. $5.* ☎*506-369-7214.* Set in the geographical centre of the province, this museum presents life in a lumber camp. On display is a sawmill with its original equipment and a range of tools from axes to chain saws. The re-created bunkhouse and cookhouse evoke the flavour of camp life. A small train makes a tour of the site *(runs continuously; $1).*

MacDonald Farm Historic Park – *11km/8mi east of Chatham on Rte. 11 near Bartibog Bridge. Open Jun–Sept daily 9:30am–4:30pm. $2.25.* ☎*506-778-6085.* Overlooking the Miramichi estuary, this old stone farmhouse (1820) has been restored to the period when Alexander MacDonald and his family lived in it. Beside the river a "net" shed, complete with fishing gear, can be seen.

MONCTON

Pop. 57,010
Map p 238
Tourist Office ☎506-853-3590

Set on a bend of the Petitcodiac River, Moncton is famous for its tidal bore, which rushes up the river from the Bay of Fundy. Named after **Robert Monckton**, the British commander in the capture of Fort Beausejour *(p 245)*, the city is generally considered the capital of Acadie.

The first settlers in the area were German and Dutch families from Pennsylvania, but they were joined by Acadians when the latter were allowed to return to British territory after Deportation. Today one-third of the population is French-speaking, and the city boasts a French-language university, founded in 1963.

SIGHT

★ **Tidal Bore** – In the open ocean, the ebb and flow of the tide is barely noticeable, but in certain V-shaped bays or inlets, the tide enters the broad end and literally piles up as it moves up the bay. This buildup occurs in the Bay of Fundy, 77km/48mi wide at its mouth, narrowing and becoming shallower along its 233km/145mi length. Thus, the tide is squeezed as it travels the bay, a ripple increasing to a wave several feet high as it enters the rivers emptying into the bay. This wave is known as a "bore," a tidal wave of unusual height. At Moncton the bore varies from a few inches to nearly two feet. The highest bores occur when the earth, moon and sun are aligned.

Bore Park – *Off Main St. at the corner of King St. Bore schedules available from city hall; arrive 20min prior to view lowest level and return 2hrs later to see high tide.* The tidal bore and changing levels of the Petitcodiac River are best viewed from the park. A small stream at low tide, the river lies in the centre of a vast bed of red mud. At high tide the river widens to 1.6km/1mi, and the water level increases by 7m/23ft.

EXCURSIONS

★ **Acadian Odyssey Historic Site** – *20km/12.5mi southeast by Rte. 106 in St.-Joseph. Open Jun–mid-Oct daily 9am–5pm. $2.* & ☎*506-758-9783.* Located in the Lefebvre Building of the **College St.-Joseph**, the first Acadian institution of higher learning, the site chronicles the past struggles and present strength of this French-speaking culture.

Founded by Rev. Camille Lefebvre in 1864, the college trained Acadian leaders for nearly 100 years before its amalgamation with the Université de Moncton. The site of the first National Convention of Acadians in 1881, this small museum today features displays and audio-visual presentations, including those on the Memramcook Valley, one of the few regions in which Acadians maintained continuous settlement despite Deportation *(p 240)*.

★★ **Hopewell Cape** – *35km/22mi south of Moncton by Rte. 114. Directional signs en route. Morning light is best for photography. Note: Be sure to climb stairs at the posted time to avoid the 10m/32ft tides.* Near this little village (pop. 757) overlooking Shepody Bay is an interesting phenomenon known as **The Rocks**★★. Sculpted by tidal action, wind and frost, these red standstone formations, as high as 15m/50ft, stand on the beach, cut off from the cliffs. Tiny tree-covered islands at high tide, these shapes become "giant flowerpots" at low tide, their narrow bases widening to support balsam fir and dwarf black spruce at the top. Visitors can walk around them when the tide is out and look at crevices in the cliffs that, in time, will become new flowerpots.

PASSAMAQUODDY BAY/FUNDY ISLES★★

Map p 238

An inlet of the Bay of Fundy between Maine and New Brunswick, this body of water is dotted with islands and indented with harbours along its irregular shoreline, which includes the estuary of the **St. Croix River**. A popular resort, the area is also famous for its lobster and an edible seaweed known as **dulse**, a regional delicacy that is served in a variety of ways (p 251).

According to Indian legend, one day the Micmac hero-god **Glooscap** saw wolves about to attack a deer and a moose. Using his magical powers, he turned the animals into islands. In 1604 Samuel de Champlain chose the bay as the site of his first settlement and spent the winter with his followers on St. Croix Island (today in Maine) in the estuary of the river of the same name. However, the bleak conditions forced them to move the next year across the Bay of Fundy to Nova Scotia (p 260). Loyalists, arriving in 1783, settled the communities of St. Stephen, St. Andrews and St. George, and of Deer and Campobello islands. *Fog and cold weather occur even in summer, particularly on the islands.*

SIGHTS

★ **St. Andrews** – Pop. 1,652. Situated at the end of a peninsula that juts into the bay, this charming town is lined with tree-covered residential and commercial avenues. A resort centre for summer visitors who like tranquility, and boating in pleasant surroundings, the town supports the **Algonquin Hotel**, one of the foremost hostelries of the province.

Founded by Loyalists, St. Andrews became a prosperous mercantile and fishing town. In 1842 some of its century-old houses were floated intact across the estuary when the Webster-Ashburton Treaty declared the Canadian/US border to be the St. Croix River—and some Loyalists discovered they were on the "wrong" side of it. Among famous Canadians who have owned homes here is **William Van Horne**, president of Canadian Pacific Railway from 1888 to 1899 (p 72).

The town's quaint main thoroughfare, **Water Street**, mixes boutiques and cafes.

★ **HMSC Aquarium-Museum** – *At Brandy Cove. Open mid-May–Jun daily 10am–4:30pm. Jul–Aug daily 10am–6pm. Sept–Oct Mon–Tue noon–4:30pm, Wed–Sun 10am–4:30pm. $4.* ☎506-529-1202. This interesting little aquarium has fish tanks and displays on the marine ecosystems of the Bay of Fundy and neighbouring Atlantic waters. The star attraction, however, is a family of harbour seals, which perform all kinds of antics for visitors. Films are shown regularly in the theatre.

St. Andrews Blockhouse – ⊛ *On Joe's Point Rd. Open Jun–Labour Day daily 9am–8pm. Early–mid-Sept daily 9am–5pm.* ⅙ ☎506-529-4270. Constructed during the War of 1812, the square wooden structure stands guard over the harbour. Built to protect New Brunswick's western frontier from American invasion, it is the only blockhouse remaining of the original 14 erected. Inside, there are displays on the settlement of the town and on the blockhouse itself.

★ **Deer Island** – *Toll-free car ferry departs from Letete year-round daily 7am–6pm (Jun & Jul until 10pm) every 30min; additional departures spring and fall; one-way 20min. Dec 25 10am & 4pm only.* ☎506-466-7340. *From Eastport, Maine Jun–Sept daily 9:30am–7:30pm every hour (last departure Jun & Sept 6:30pm); one-way 15min; $8/car & driver, $2/passenger* ☎506-747-2159. *Ferry from Campobello Island, see p 251. Note: ferries operate on first-come, first-served basis. Lines form on weekends and at peak times.* Positioned so as to nearly enclose the bay, this

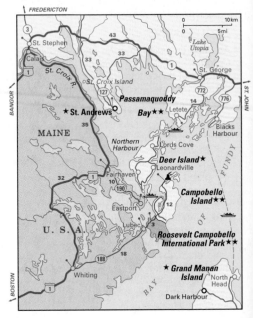

Fundy island is a quiet place, inhabited primarily by fishermen. The world's largest lobster pound is located on its western side. A pleasant **trip★** is the ferry ride to the island from Letete, among the smaller islands covered with birds. Swept by the tide in part of the narrow inlet of **Northern Harbour**, a corral where lobsters are kept year-round has been built with nets and fences. At the southern end of the island, a large whirlpool forms when the Fundy tides are running strong. Called "**Old Sow**" for the noise it makes, this vortex is visible from Deer Island Point or from the ferry to Campobello Island.

★★ **Campobello Island** – Pop. 1,317. *Car ferry departs from Deer Island Jun–Sept daily 9:15, 10:40am, 12:15, 1:40, 3:15, 4:40, 6:15pm (last departure Jun & Sept 4:40pm). One-way 45min. $11/car & driver, $2/passenger.* ☎*506/747-2159. Accessible by bridge from Lubec, Maine. Non-Americans need valid passport (p 312). See also Michelin Green Guide to New England.* Known as the "beloved island" of US President **Franklin D. Roosevelt** (1882-1945), the site is a summer resort for vacationing Americans. Sandy beaches, picturesque coves, headlands, lighthouses and an international park named in Roosevelt's honour attract numerous visitors annually.

First settled in the 1770s, Campobello was named for **William Campbell**, the governor of Nova Scotia, and for its beauty (*campo bello* means "beautiful pasture" in Italian). By the end of the 19C, it had become a retreat for wealthy Americans. In 1883 one-year-old FDR first visited the island. Thereafter he spent summers on Campobello with his parents and later with his wife, Eleanor. He taught his five children to appreciate nature, and took them fishing, boating and swimming—activities he had done as a child. Then, in 1921, FDR contracted polio and left the island for 12 years. In 1964 the Canadian and American governments jointly established the park to commemorate him.

★★ **Roosevelt Campobello International Park** – *Open late May–mid-Oct daily 10am–6pm.* ♿ ☎*506-752-2922.* Preserved as a memorial to FDR, the southern part of the island is natural parkland—forests, bogs, lakes, cliffs and beaches—crisscrossed by several lovely **drives★★**. Note the view of Passamaquoddy Bay from Friar's Head (*turn right at picnic area sign just south of visitor centre*), and of Herring Cove from Con Robinson's Point (*follow Glensevern Rd. East*). Built in the Dutch Colonial style, the red-shingled, green-roofed **cottage★** with 34 rooms belonged to FDR. Simply furnished, the rustic interior contains personal reminders of his childhood and years as president. The west side rooms, especially the living room, have pleasant views of Friar's Bay. Films on the life of Roosevelt are shown in the **visitor centre**. North of the visitor centre, **East Quoddy Head Lighthouse★** (*12km/7mi by Wilson's Beach and gravel road to the Point*) has a picturesque site overlooking Head Harbour Island.

★ **Grand Manan Island** – Pop. 791. *Car ferry departs Blacks Harbour Jun 30–Sept 4 daily 7:30, 9:30, 11:30am, 1:30, 3:30, 5:30pm (first departure 9:30am Sun). Rest of the year approximately three crossings daily. One-way 1hr 30min. $24.60/car, $8.20/passenger.* ✗ ☎*506-662-3724.* The largest of the Fundy islands, Grand Manan is noted for its rugged scenery that includes cliffs of 120m/400ft and picturesque harbours. A sizeable bird population inhabits the island; about 230 species have been sighted. On the island's rocky west coast, **Dark Harbour** is a processing centre for dulse, which grows on submerged rocks in the Bay of Fundy. Collected at low tide and dried in the sun, dulse has a salty, tangy flavour. Rich in iron and iodine, it can be added to soups and stews or eaten raw or toasted.

The **Michelin Green Guide to New England** spotlights the region's historical, cultural and natural attractions. Let Michelin's famous star-rating system direct you to a selection of over 1,000 attractions in the area.

Over 50 detailed city and regional maps are included to guide you through carefully designed walking and driving tours. The guide also contains maps of principal sights and regional driving tours, including itineraries for fall foliage viewing; practical information, such as helpful tips and useful addresses; and essays on New England's history, geography and artistic heritage.

SAINT JOHN★★

Pop. 74,969
Map p 238
Tourist Office ☎506-658-2990

The province's largest city, this industrial centre and major port is fondly called "fog city" because of the dense sea mists that roll in off the Bay of Fundy. Its rocky, hilly site at the mouth of the Saint John River at the junction with the bay has resulted in a city with few straight roads and many culs-de-sac.

Historical Notes

Part of Acadie – In 1604 Samuel de Champlain and the Sieur de Monts *(p 000)* landed briefly at the mouth of the river. Another Frenchman, **Charles de La Tour**, built a trading fort in 1630 on the site of present-day Saint John. In 1645 de Menou d'Aulnay *(p 259)*, his compatriot from Port Royal, destroyed the post. The ensuing trade rivalry among the French in Acadia was compounded by the Anglo-French struggles. Although the area was ceded by the 1763 Treaty of Paris to the English, who established their own post, Saint John records 1783 as the year of its inception.

The Loyalists Arrive – On May 18, 1783 some 4,000 Loyalists disembarked at the mouth of the river from their square-rigged ships. Overnight the tiny trading post became a boom town. Their wealth dissipated by the American Revolution, they possessed few pioneering skills needed to carve new lives out of the wilderness. However, they not only survived, but created a prosperous city of shipyards and social gatherings.Thriving on trade and shipbuilding, Saint John was known as the "Liverpool of America" during the 19C.

Decline and Renewal – From 1860 to 1880, however, Saint John began to decline: demand for wooden ships was decreasing; an international depression had set in by early 1874; and in 1877 more than half the city was destroyed by a great fire. During the 1880s the waterfront was modernized, a railway terminus established and by 1900, grain elevators completed. The port remained active, but not until the 1960s did the economy revive. Huge investment was made in pulp and paper, sugar and oil refining. A container shipping service was established and a deep-water terminal built for tankers.

Every July the city recalls its founding with a celebration known as **Loyalist Days**. Inhabitants dress in 18C costumes and re-enact the landing of 1783. Sidewalk breakfasts and a large parade complete the festival.

★★ DOWNTOWN   *1/2 day. Map p 253.*

Saint John's downtown has been revitalized, making it a pleasant area for visitors to explore on foot *(contact tourist office for designated walks)*.

★★ **Market Square Area** – Opened in 1983 the square contains an attractive shopping mall with a central atrium and several levels, a hotel, convention centre and the newly relocated New Brunswick Museum.

Incorporated into the complex, a row of late-19C warehouses fronts a pleasant plaza around the **market slip** where Loyalists landed in 1783. In summer there are outdoor cafes and concerts in the plaza.

On the plaza's south side stands an 1867 clapboard structure with gingerbread decoration, **Barbour's General Store [A]**, stocked with merchandise of the period *(open mid-May–early Jun daily 9am–6pm; mid-Jun–Labour Day daily 9am–7pm; early Sept–mid-Oct daily 9am–6pm; ☎506-658-2939)*. Over St. Patrick Street a pedestrian bridge links the square with the Canada Games **Aquatic Centre** and **City Hall [B]**, which has an observation gallery on the top floor *(open year-round Mon-Fri 8:30am–4:30pm)*. **Brunswick Square [C]** is a complex of shops, offices and hotel.

★ **New Brunswick Museum [M]** – *Open year-round Mon–Tue 9am–6pm, Wed–Fri 9am–9pm, Sat 10am–6pm, Sun noon–5pm. Closed Jan 1, Dec 24–26. $6.50. & ☎506-643-2300.* Devoted to the human, natural and artistic life of the province, this museum has excellent examples of Indian birchbark, quill and beadwork. European settlement is traced from contact with native inhabitants to the lumbering and ship-building industries of the 19C.

The gallery of natural science features displays of the province's animal life and geological specimens. There are exhibits of fine and decorative arts from New Brunswick and from other parts of Canada and the world.

Loyalist House [D] – *Open mid-May–Labour Day Mon–Fri 10am–5pm. Rest of the year by appointment. $2. & ☎506-652-3590.* One of the oldest structures in the city, this house was built in 1817 by David Merritt, a Loyalist who fled New York State in

252

1783. One of the few buildings to escape the fire of 1877, the house has a shingled exterior on two sides, and clapboard on the other. An expensive material at the time, clapboard was installed on only the north and east sides as weather protection. The plain exterior belies the elegant and spacious Georgian interior with its fine curved staircase and arches between rooms. Upon departure note the solid rock foundations on the Germain Street side. All of Saint John is built on such rock.

King Square Area – Generally considered the centre of Saint John, this square has trees, flowerbeds arranged in the form of the Union flag *(p 259)* and a 2-storey bandstand. In one corner stands the old **city market [E]**, where a variety of New Brunswick produce can be bought, including dulse *(p 250)*. On the other side of the square, the **Loyalist burial ground [F]** can be seen.

ADDITIONAL SIGHTS *1/2 day*

Fort Howe Lookout – *From Main St., take Metcalf St., then sharp right turn onto Magazine St.* From this wooden blockhouse *(not open)* on a rocky cliff above the surrounding hills, there is a **panorama★** of the docks, harbour, river and city.

★★ **Reversing Falls Rapids** – *To fully appreciate the rapids, visit at low tide, slack tide (below) and high tide. Contact tourist office for times of tides.* Where the Saint John River empties into the Bay of Fundy the tides are 8m/28ft high. At high tide when the bay water is more than 4m/14ft above river level, the water flows swiftly upstream. At low tide the bay is more than 4m/14ft below the level of the river, so the river rushes into it. As the tide rises, the rush of river water is gradually halted and the river becomes as calm as a mill pond (slack tide) before gradually being reversed in direction. This reversal of the river current is marked just before the river, narrowing and curving around a bend in a deep gorge, enters the bay. The narrow bend creates rapids and whirlpools whenever the current is great in either direction, a phenomenon known as "reversing falls rapids."

Reversing Falls Bridge Lookout [G] – *Parking at west end of bridge. Visitor centre open mid-May–mid-Jun daily 9am–6pm. Late Jun–mid-Oct daily 8am–8pm.* ✴ ☎506-658-2937. *Take steps to roof.* From this lookout fine **views★★** of the changing river current are afforded. Visitors unable to stay for the tidal cycle will enjoy the **film** ($1.25), which condenses the 24-hour event.

Falls View Park Lookout [H] – *Parking at end of Falls View Ave.* The **views★** of the rapids from the park are not as dramatic as those from the bridge.

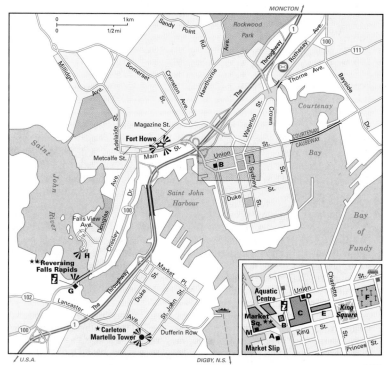

★ **Carleton Martello Tower** – ☞ *Open Jun–mid-Oct daily 9am–5pm. $2.25.* ☎*506-636-4011.* Built in 1813 as a defence for the city, this Martello tower *(p 274)* was used during the 19C and in both world wars. A 2-storey steel and concrete structure was added in World War II to house antiaircraft and fire-control headquarters for Saint John. Inside the tower there are displays on the history of the area. The tower stands above its surroundings, providing a **panorama★★** encompassing the harbour, the docks, rail yards, a breakwater that leads to Partridge Island, the bay, river and city.

■ None of the Martello towers constructed in British North America between 1796 and 1848 was ever attacked. Of the total 16 (Halifax 5, Kingston 6, Quebec City 4 and Saint John 1), 11 remain to this day.

SAINT JOHN RIVER VALLEY★★

Map p 238

In the south the valley of this wide and scenic river is rolling and rural, supporting some of the richest farmland in New Brunswick. Heading north, the river traverses hilly, almost mountainous forests, the source of the province's substantial lumber industry.

Settlements sprang up throughout the valley when some 4,000 Loyalists arrived in 1783 *(p 252)*. In the 19C numerous steamboats moved among these communities. Traffic took to the roads in the 1940s, but the valley remains the principal transportation route since the Trans-Canada Highway parallels it for much of its length in New Brunswick.

FROM FREDERICTON TO EDMUNDSTON   *Allow 1 day. 285km/177mi.*

★★ **Fredericton** – *Description p 246.*

> *Leave Fredericton on the Trans-Can Hwy. (Rte. 2).*

After traversing the provincial capital, the highway follows the river upstream to the Mactaquac Dam, New Brunswick's largest power project. The dam has created a reservoir, or headpond, about 105km/65mi long, affecting the valley as far as Woodstock.

On the north bank of the headpond lies **Mactaquac Provincial Park**, a haven for sports enthusiasts. The Trans-Canada Highway travels the south side of the pond with fine **views★** as the country becomes increasingly rural.

Woolastook Wildlife Park – *29km/18mi. Open mid-May–Jun daily 9am–5pm. Jul–mid-Aug daily 9am–9pm. Late Aug–Sept daily 9am–5pm. $5.75.* ✗ ☎*506-363-5410.* This is a pleasant park devoted to animals native to the Maritime provinces *(p 236)*. From the parking lot, there is a good **view★** of the Saint John River.

★★ **Kings Landing Historical Settlement** – *37km/23mi. Open Jun–mid-Oct daily 10am–5pm. $8.* ✗ ☎*506-363-5805.* This restored village has a beautiful **site★★** on the sloping banks of the Saint John, beside a creek that joins the river via a small cove. Typical of the Loyalist riverbank settlements where lumbering, farming and some shipbuilding were principal occupations, the village provides an authentic glimpse of life in the river valley from 1783 to 1900.

After the Revolutionary War the land on which the village stands was given to veterans of the King's American Dragoons. When the Mactaquac dam project flooded their original sites, the houses and other buildings were moved here.

Apart from the well-restored farms with their fields of crops, the village has a church, school, forge, store and a **theatre** with live entertainment *(ask for details at entrance)*. As they carry out routine chores, about 100 costumed interpreters explain aspects of 19C rural life.

Beside the mill stream is an operating water-powered **sawmill**. Activated by the large water wheel, a saw blade cuts through logs by moving along a wooden carriage. An example of a roadhouse of the period, the **Kings Head Inn** serves traditional refreshments. The commodious Morehouse residence stands near the elegant Ingraham house with its delightful garden overlooking the river.

Moored at the wharf (the "landing"), a half-size replica of a 19C **wood boat★** typifies vessels that transported lumber from sawmills and hay from farms to market.

Between Kings Landing and Woodstock, there are excellent **views★★** from the Trans-Canada Highway of the Saint John River traversing lovely rolling country of farms and forests.

After Woodstock, leave Trans-Can Hwy. and take Rte. 103 to Hartland.

★ **Hartland** – Pop. 890. Settled by Loyalists, this town in the centre of the potato-growing district is known for the longest **covered bridge★** in the world. Completed in 1901 and rebuilt in 1920, the 391m/1,282ft bridge crosses the Saint John River in seven spans. Until 1960 the Trans-Canada Highway was routed over it, but today it links Routes 103 and 105.

As in other provinces the first bridges built in New Brunswick were of wood, covered to protect the large timbers from weathering. These coverings could lengthen the lifespan of a bridge by 50 or 60 years.

Upon descending the hill on Route 103, note the good **view★** of the bridge, which resembles a barn-like tunnel. The woodwork construction can be appreciated only from the interior *(cars can be driven through; no trucks).*

Take Rte. 105 on the east bank to Florenceville and Trans-Can Hwy. to Grand Falls.

There are fine **views★** from the highway of the river and farms of the agricultural area north of Florenceville. The Saint John gradually approaches the Maine border and enters the more mountainous country of the north.

Leave Trans-Can Hwy. and enter Grand Falls.

★★ **Grand Falls** – Pop. 6,083. Built on a plateau above the river, this town is the centre of the potato belt. Here the Saint John changes suddenly and dramatically. The previous wide and tranquil river with gently sloping banks plunges over falls and, for about 1.6km/1mi, churns through a deep and narrow gorge. A power plant has diverted much of the water of the falls, but there are two good vantage points for the gorge.

Falls Park – *Accessible from Malabeam reception centre on Madawaska Rd. Open mid-May–mid-Oct daily 9am–9pm.* ✕ & ☎506-473-6013. This park offers a good **view★** of the gorge and the falls below the power plant.

★ **La Rochelle Centre** – *In Centennial Park. Accessible from Malabeam reception centre on Madawaska Rd. Open daily mid-May–Labour Day. $2.* ✕ & ☎506-473-6013. Stairs descend into the gorge, which has walls as high as 70m/230ft in places. At the bottom, there are some deep holes in the rock called wells, but it is the **gorge★★** that is impressive.

Return to Trans-Can Hwy.

After Grand Falls the Saint John becomes wide and placid again, marking the Canadian/US border. The towns and villages seen across it are in Maine.

Edmundston – Pop. 10,835. Situated at the junction of the Madawaska and Saint John Rivers, this industrial city, dominated by the twin-spired **Cathedral of the Immaculate Conception**, contrasts sharply with the rural landscape of the surrounding valley. Once called *Petit-Sault* ("little falls") to distinguish the rapids at the mouth of the Madawaska from those of Grand Falls, Edmundston was renamed in 1856 in honour of **Sir Edmund Head**, Lieutenant-Governor of New Brunswick (1848-54). The city's inhabitants are mainly French-speaking, although they claim Acadian, Quebecer, Indian, American, English and Irish origins.

> ■ Harvested from the riverbanks of the Saint John in spring, edible fiddlehead ferns, boiled and topped with butter and lemon, are a New Brunswick delicacy.

Republic of Madawaska – Long contested among Ontario, Quebec, New Brunswick and the US, the land south of Lake Témiscouata in Quebec and New Brunswick, and the area north of the Aroostook River in Maine were once collectively called Madawaska. When boundaries were finally fixed, New Brunswick was left with the city of Edmundston and a thumb-shaped stretch of land *(map p 238)*. The long-standing dispute forged a spirited independence among the Madawaskans, who created for themselves a legend, rather than a political entity—the Republic of Madawaska. Known as the Brayons because they crushed flax with a tool called a "brake," the Madawaskans have their own flag with an eagle and six stars (representing their different origins) and their own president, the mayor of Edmundston. The **Madawaska Museum** *(195 Herbert Blvd. at Trans-Can Hwy.; open Jun–Labour Day daily 8am–8pm; rest of the year Wed & Thu 7–10pm, Sun 1–5pm & by appointment; $1; ♿ ☎506-737-5282)* presents the history of this region.

SHIPPAGAN★

Pop. 2,760
Map p 238

This town on the Acadian peninsula has an important commercial fishing industry and peat-moss processing plants. A bridge leads to Lameque Island with its peat moss bogs. From there a ferry *(toll free)* crosses to Miscou Island, which has fine beaches on the Gulf of St. Lawrence.

SIGHT

★ **Aquarium and Marine Centre** – *Open May–Sept daily 10am–6pm. $5.35.* ✗ ♿ *☎506-336-3013.* Devoted to the marine life of the gulf, this pleasant museum features exhibits on the St. Lawrence River and New Brunswick's lakes and rivers. An audio-visual presentation *(20min)* explains the history of the fishing industry. In a series of aquariums and an outdoor seal pool, fish native to these waters are on view. Visitors can enter the cabin of a modern-day reconstructed trawler to see the mass of electronic devices used to find and catch fish.

VILLAGE HISTORIQUE ACADIEN★

Map p 238

This reconstructed village depicts the life of the Acadians from 1780 to 1890, a time of great hardship after Deportation *(p 240).*

Most of the gulf shore along New Brunswick is inhabited by Acadians still living traditional lives as farmers and fishermen. Each August nearby **Caraquet** (pop. 4,556) hosts an annual Acadian festival that is opened by a **blessing of the fleet**, symbolic of Christ's benediction to the fishermen of Galilee. As many as 60 fishing boats, decked with bunting, arrive from all over the province to be blessed by the bishop of Bathurst.

Access – *11km/7mi west of Caraquet by Rte. 11.*

VISIT *3hrs*

Open Jun–Sept daily 10am–6pm (5pm Sept). $8. ✗ *☎506-727-3467.* The village is entered through the **visitor centre** (centre d'accueil), where a **slide show** *(18min)* covering the entire history of the Acadians, provides a good introduction.

"Inhabited" by Acadians wearing traditional costumes, the village extends along a road nearly 1.6km/1mi long *(transport by horse and oxen-drawn carts provided).* Houses moved from various parts of the province have been furnished to represent the period. Only the wooden church is a copy of an original building.

Over the village flies the **flag of Acadie**, the French red, white and blue tricolour with a star symbolizing the Virgin Mary at the top left corner. The flag is often seen in Acadian regions of Nova Scotia and Prince Edward Island.

Acadian Flag

Extending north to south, Nova Scotia consists of Cape Breton Island, and a 565km/350mi long, fairly narrow peninsula, 130km/81mi at its widest. Linked to New Brunswick by the Isthmus of Chignecto, the province is surrounded by the Gulf of St. Lawrence, Atlantic Ocean, Northumberland Strait and Bay of Fundy, with 7,460km/4,625mi of serrated coastline. Proximity to the sea and natural harbours have defined its historical role as largely strategic. The provincial capital, HALIFAX, has long served as a military stronghold.

Geographical Notes

The Peninsula – The mainland is largely flat terrain, except for a rocky, indented eastern shore, and a forested interior (maximum elevation of 210m/689ft). **South Mountain** forms the northern border of this upland interior. Stretching from Cape Blomidon to the tip of Digby Neck, the **North Mountain** range parallels South Mountain for 190km/118mi along the Bay of Fundy shore. Sheltered between them is the heart of the province's apple industry, the fertile Annapolis and Cornwallis River Valleys. The cropped 300m/984ft **Cobequid Mountain** extends 120km/74mi over Cumberland County, which borders the Isthmus of Chignecto.

The Island – Northern Cape Breton Island is mostly a wooded plateau rising to 532m/1,745ft above sea level, a height that permits expansive views of the wildly beautiful, often mist-enshrouded, coastline. At the northern end is **Cape Breton Highlands National Park** with its celebrated route, the Cabot Trail *(p 266)*. Culminating in the Strait of Canso, the south is predominantly lowland. A vast inland sea 930sq km/359sq mi wide, **Bras d'Or Lake** nearly bisects the island.

Historical Notes

Seafaring Nation – Peopled with fishermen, sea merchants, privateers and boatbuilders, Nova Scotia's colourful past is interwoven with the sea. One great industry established by the Loyalists was **shipbuilding**. Blanketed by virgin forest, little of which remains today, the province used its rich timber resources to bring prosperity to its inhabitants, especially during the Napoleonic Wars (1803-15) when Britain's need for wooden ships and ship parts was great. Along the south coast, Nova Scotia's schooners became legend, as did the sailors who manned them—universally called **Bluenoses**, an American term of derision for people who could survive the region's cold climate. More than a few fortunes were made from privateering: the east coast's plentiful coves and inlets, particularly around Liverpool *(p 265)*, once concealed many an anchored pirate ship. Piracy diminished under threat of prosecution, and by 1900, the prominence of shipbuilding waned. Steam replaced sail power; steel hulls superseded wooden ones. Today wooden vessels are still crafted on a limited basis in the Lunenburg area.

Preserving the Past – Nova Scotia boasts more historic sites than any province in Canada except Quebec. In recent years the federal and provincial governments have played active roles in heritage preservation, as have countless local organizations and historical societies. Administered by the provincial museum system, the Nova Scotia Museum Complex, more than 20 historic sites, from heritage houses to restored mills, are open to the public.
Genealogy is popular here: local museums, schools and universities, genealogical societies, and churches have archival facilities for tracing one's roots. The migration of Nova Scotia's black population is chronicled in Dartmouth *(p 274)*, New England's planter immigrants in Kentville. Descendants of Dutch, English, French, German, Greek, Hungarian, Irish, Italian, Lebanese and Polish settlers diversify the population today.
Traditional dishes—Acadia's rappie pie, Cape Breton lamb, Scottish oat cakes and the "truly Nova Scotian" blueberry grunt—tempt visitors to partake of a **regional cookery** harking back to Samuel de Champlain's gourmandise. The gastronomy of his Order of Good Cheer *(p 260)* endures in the province's formalized food promotion entitled "Taste of Nova Scotia," offered by over 45 member dining establishments. Various cultural events and festivals preserve ancestral traditions, one of the largest being the International **Gathering of the Clans**, a tribute to the province's Scottish beginnings as *New Scotland (p 239)*. Acadian crafts and demonstrations of handiwork skills are featured in local shops and museums, particularly along the west coast of Cape Breton Island, while Gaelic wares abound along the east coast and on the mainland.

PRACTICAL INFORMATION

Getting There

By Air – Air Canada offers daily flights from the US and from Montreal and St. John's, Newfoundland to Halifax ☎902-429-7111, or 800-776-3000 (US). Its affiliate Air Nova provides connections within Atlantic Canada as does Air Atlantic, an affiliate of Canadian Airlines International (CAI). CAI provides daily service to Nova Scotia from the US and many Canadian cities ☎800-426-7000 (Canada/US).

By Bus and Train – Bus travel is offered by Acadian Lines ☎902-454-9321 or 902-454-9326. **VIA Rail** connects Nova Scotia through its transcontinental train service ☎902-857-9830 (Canada) or 800-561-3949 (US).

By Boat – Passenger & car ferry service connects Bar Harbor, Maine with Yarmouth *(departs mid-Jun–mid-Oct daily 8am; limited service in off-season; no service Nov–Apr; one-way 6hrs; reservations required; US$55/car, $41.50/passenger)* and Saint John, NB with Digby *(departs daily year-round; one-way 2hrs 45min; reservations required; US$50/car, $23/passenger)*. For ferry schedules & reservations contact Marine Atlantic ☎ 800-341-7981 *(Canada/US)*.
Yarmouth can also be reached by car ferry from Portland, Maine *(departs early May–late Oct on days scheduled 9pm; no service Nov–Apr; one-way 11hrs; reservations strongly suggested; US $80/car, $98 mid-Jun–mid-Sept, $58/passenger, $78 mid-Jun–mid-Sept; cabin extra $20–95; discount rates for some mid-week days)*. For schedules & reservations, contact Prince of Fundy Cruises ☎ 800-341-7540 (Canada/US).

General Information

Accommodations and Visitor Information – The official tourist office publishes a travel guide annually giving information on history, attractions and outdoor activities, scheduled events, accommodations, farm and country vacations as well as campgrounds. For a free copy of the guide and a map, contact **Tourism Nova Scotia**, PO Box 130, Halifax, NS, B3J 2M7. For information or hotel reservations contact ☎800-565-0000 (Canada/US).

Road Regulations – *(Driver's license and insurance requirements p 314.)* Nova Scotia has good paved roads; some interior roads are loose-surface. Speed limits, unless otherwise posted, are 100km/h (60mph) on the Trans-Canada Highway, 80km/h (50mph) on highways and 50km/h (30mph) in cities and towns. **Seat belt** use is mandatory. **Canadian Automobile Assn. (CAA)**, Halifax ☎902-443-5530.

Time Zone – Nova Scotia is on Atlantic Standard Time. Daylight Saving Time is observed from the first Sunday in April to the last Sunday in October.

Taxes – The national GST of 7% *(rebate information p 318)* applies. An 11% health services tax is also levied. To request a rebate non-residents should contact the Provincial Tax Commission, PO Box 755, Halifax, NS, B3J 2V4 ☎902-424-4411.

Liquor Laws – The legal drinking age is 19. Liquor is sold in government stores.

Recreation – *p 242.*

Principal Festivals

May–Jun	**Apple Blossom Festival**	*Annapolis Valley*
Jul	**Nova Scotia International Tattoo**	*Halifax*
	Metropolitan Scottish Festival and Highland Games	*Halifax*
	Antigonish Highland Games	*Antigonish*
	Gathering of the Clans and Fishermen's Regatta	*Pugwash*
Aug	**Natal Day**	*Province-wide*
	Nova Scotia Gaelic Mod	*St. Ann's*
	International Buskerfest	*Halifax*
Sept	**Nova Scotia Fisheries Exhibition &**	*Lunenburg*
	Fishermen's Reunion	
Oct	**Octoberfest**	*Lunenburg*

ANNAPOLIS ROYAL★★

Pop. 633
Map p 238
Tourist Office ☎902-532-5769

One of Canada's oldest settlements, Annapolis Royal has a pleasant **site★** overlooking the great basin of the Annapolis where it narrows into the river of the same name. Acadians reclaimed the marshland by building a dam across the river with flood gates to control the water level. Twice a day the Bay of Fundy tides rush in, reversing the river's flow. The quiet charm of this gracious town belies its turbulent past as site of French-English battles and Acadian struggles.

Historical Notes – The earliest settlement was a French colony at **Port Royal** *(p 260)* under nobleman, **Pierre du Gua, Sieur de Monts**, destroyed in 1613 by a force from Virginia. By 1635 the French governor, **Charles de Menou d'Aulnay**, had built a new Port Royal on the site of Annapolis Royal. Over the next century French settlement grew, forming the region called Acadia *(p 239)*. Port Royal suffered many raids by the New England colonies to the south. The predecessor of the present Fort Anne *(below)* was constructed by the French, but funds were insufficient to maintain it. In 1710 it fell to a New England expedition under Col. Francis Nicholson.

Renamed Annapolis Royal after England's **Queen Anne**, the fortified settlement became the provincial capital when the mainland was ceded to the British by the Treaty of Utrecht in 1713. Constantly threatened by surrounding Acadian settlements sympathetic to soldiers from Quebec or Louisbourg, it frequently withstood French attack. In 1749 the capital was relocated to Halifax where British military force was being strengthened. Annapolis Royal was relegated to an outpost, eventually losing detachments to Halifax. In 1854 the few troops remaining were removed to New Brunswick. Annapolis Royal had lost its importance.

Much of the area's history is evident today: de Monts' habitation has been reconstructed near Port Royal, Fort Anne has been partially re-created, and the older buildings along **Lower Saint George Street** have been renovated.

SIGHTS *1/2 day*

★ **Fort Anne National Historic Site** – ☜ *Open mid-May–mid-Oct daily 9am–6pm. Rest of the year Mon–Fri by appointment.* $2.25. ᴕ ☎902-532-2397. A peaceful expanse of green in the centre of town, this fort was once the most fought-over place in Canada, suffering 14 sieges during the Anglo-French wars. In 1917 Fort Anne became the first National Historic Park in Canada.

Existing earthworks were built by the French from 1702 to 1708 with later alterations by the British. In one of the bastions stands a stone **powder magazine** of the French period. From the earthworks there is a **view★** of the Annapolis Basin.

★ **Officers' Quarters** – A distinctive building with high chimneys and dormer windows stands in the centre of the fort. Built in 1797 by order of Prince Edward *(p 271)*, the quarters, now restored, house a **museum★**, which includes a display on the fort's military history.

Outside flies the flag of the Grand Union, a combination of the English cross of St. George, and the Scottish cross of St. Andrew. The Union Jack as we know it today did not come into existence until the union with Ireland in 1801, when the cross of St. Patrick was added.

★ **Historic Gardens** – *On Upper Saint George St. (Rte. 8) just south of Fort Anne. Open late-May–mid-Oct daily dawn–dusk.* $3.50. ᴕ ☎902-532-7018. Situated on a 4ha/10 acre site overlooking Allain's River, a tributary of the Annapolis, this series of theme gardens exemplifies the horticultural diversity of the region's past as well as recent gardening technology.

The Acadian Garden has a traditional cottage and a replica of the dike system *(p 262)*. Formal in style, the Governor's Garden is characteristic of early-18C landscape architecture when the English governor was based in Annapolis Royal. The Victorian Garden reveals a more natural setting, a trend that became fashionable in the 19C. The Rose Garden traces the development of this ever-popular species.

★ **Annapolis Tidal Generating Station** – *On the Causeway (Rte. 1). Visitor centre open mid-May–mid-Oct daily, phone for hours.* ᴕ ☎902-532-5454. North America's first tidal power project, this station uses a low head, straight-flow turbine generator to harness the enormous energy of the Bay of Fundy tides to produce electricity. The exhibit area upstairs in the visitor centre explains the project and its construction through models, photographs and a video presentation *(10min)*. A causeway over the dam affords views of tidal activity and of the generating station.

EXCURSIONS

★ **North Hills Museum** – *In Granville Ferry on road to Port Royal. Open Jun–mid-Oct Mon–Sat 9:30am–5:30pm, Sun 1–5:30pm.* ☎902-532-2168. Despite a series of modifications, this small wood-framed 18C house has retained a pioneer look. It provides a fitting setting for the predominantly 18C antique collection of a retired Toronto banker. Bequeathed to the province upon his death in 1974, the collection includes English furniture, ceramics, silver and Georgian glass.

★★ **Port Royal Habitation** – ☞ *10km/6mi from Annapolis Royal Causeway.* The *habitation* (French word for "dwelling") is a replica of Canada's first European settlement of any permanence. This collection of dark, weathered, fortified buildings joined around a central courtyard was designed in a style reminiscent of 16C French farms by **Samuel de Champlain**, captain and navigator of the expedition of Sieur de Monts. Granted permission by Henry IV of France to set up a colony and develop the fur trade, de Monts began his expedition to the New World in 1604. The first winter in Canada was spent on an island in the St. Croix River *(map p 250)* —a poor choice, as it was cut off from the fresh food of the mainland by the Bay of Fundy's storms and ice. The next year, the company moved to the Annapolis Basin where the habitation was reconstructed. Boredom and sickness prompted Champlain to form a social club wherein members alternated as grand master and organizers of gourmet feasts. In 1606 member Marc Lescarbot wrote the first play performed in Canada, the **Theatre of Neptune**. The **Order of Good Cheer,** as the club was called, proved successful. Crops were grown, and trade with the Indians was established. Just as the settlement seemed rooted, de Monts' trading rights were revoked in 1607, and the expedition returned to France. Destroyed in 1613 by English forces, the buildings were reconstructed in 1938 by the Canadian government, using Champlain's sketch and writings as guides.

Visit – *Open mid-May–mid-Oct daily 9am–6pm. $2.50.* ♿ ☎902-532-2898. Over the gateway entry hangs the **coat of arms** of France and Navarre, ruled by King Henry IV (French kings held the additional title of King of Navarre from 1589 until the French Revolution). A **well** with a shingled roof stands in the middle of the courtyard. Around it are the residences of the governor, priest and artisans. The kitchen, blacksmith's shop, community room where the Order met, and the chapel can be visited as can the storerooms, wine cellar and trading room where Indians brought their furs. All furnishings are meticulous reproductions of early-17C styles.

Each structure has a steeply pitched roof and, except for the storeroom, a field-stone chimney. A building technique known as **colombage**, the term used in France for log-filled wooden frame construction, was employed to form the walls. This construction can be appreciated only from the interior, since the exterior of the buildings is covered with lapped boarding. No nails or spikes join the timbers: they are mortised and tenoned and pinned together.

★ **Kejimkujik National Park** – ☞ *Rte. 8. From Annapolis Royal 48km/30mi to park entrance, near Maitland Bridge. Open year-round. $2.25/day. Visitor centre open Jun–Labour Day daily 8:30am–9pm; rest of the year daily 8:30am–4:30pm. Hiking, cycling, swimming, canoeing, cross-country skiing. Canoe & bicycle rental at Jakes Landing.* ⚠♿ ☎902-682-2772. Recreation and beauty await visitors to this 381sq km/147sq mi forest with its accessible lakes and plentiful wildlife. For centuries the park's waterways served the Micmac Indians as canoe routes and still afford peaceful passage through largely untouched wilderness.

The **Mill Falls** hiking trail leads through fern-filled woods along the amber **Mersey River** to its foamy rapids. The viewing tower *(on main park road, 10km/6mi from park entrance)* permits an elevated **view★** of lovely Kejimkujik Lake.

ANNAPOLIS VALLEY★★

Maps pp 238-239

Flowing 112km/70mi southwest to the sea, the Annapolis River widens into the **Annapolis Basin**, a tidal lake connected to the Bay of Fundy by a narrow outlet known as Digby Gut. The area commonly referred to as the Annapolis Valley includes other rivers and extends approximately 160km/100mi from Digby to Windsor on the Minas Basin.

Some of the earliest French colonists settled in this region, only to be deported by the British in 1755 *(p 240)*. The Acadians built dikes to reclaim the marshland for agricultural production. In addition, the valley is sheltered on both sides from heavy wind and fog by the North and South Mountains, a feature that has nurtured the valley's famed **apple orchards**. Today other fruits and crops are also grown in the fertile soil, while dairy cattle graze the meadows bordering the river.

FROM DIGBY TO WINDSOR   *2 days. 168km/104mi.*

Digby – Pop. 2,311. From this waterfront town, home of the famous scallop, ferries cross to New Brunswick. The harbour is often busy with fishing fleets. Local restaurants feature **Digby scallops** prepared in a variety of ways.

Take Hwy. 101 and then Rte. 1.

Highway 101 follows the shore of the Annapolis Basin with pleasant views until it turns inland at Deep Brook, where Route 1 continues along the shoreline.

★★ **Annapolis Royal** – *1/2 day. Description p 259.*

Remains of the old French dike system can be seen from the road. Route 1 crosses the river and continues through country that becomes more rural. Wide meadows line the riverbanks. At **Bridgetown★** elm-shaded streets contain fine houses, many built by Loyalists. **Lawrencetown** and **Middleton** are similarly graced with trees. Apple orchards line the hills, particularly between Kingston and Waterville, where fruit-selling stands and "U-pick" farms are common. This drive is especially lovely in apple blossom time *(late May or early June)*.

Continue 14km/9mi on Rte. 1 to junction with Rte. 358.

★★ **Excursion to Cape Split** – *28km/17mi north by Rte. 358.*

★ **Prescott House Museum** – *In Starr's Point, off Rte. 358, about 5km/3mi north of Rte. 1. Open Jun–mid-Oct Mon–Sat 9:30am–5:30pm, Sun 1–5:30pm.* ♿ ☎902-542-3984. This attractive whitewashed-brick house, set in lovely grounds, was built in the early 19C by **Charles Prescott**, legislator, successful merchant and acclaimed horticulturalist. On this estate Prescott experimented with new strains of wheat, planted nut trees, grapes and pear trees and introduced many varieties of cherries and apples. He gave away cuttings to valley farmers and is partly responsible for the development of the apple industry in this area.
The interior is attractively furnished with some original pieces. A pleasant **sun room** was added by Prescott's great-granddaughter. The **garden** is also worth visiting.

Return to Rte. 358 and continue north.

★★ **The Lookoff** – *Approximately 14km/9mi north of Starr's Point. Follow the signs on Rte. 358. Watch for paved pull-off with steel barricade.* Although there is no official marker for this site, one cannot pass by without stopping. The view★★ of Annapolis Valley is magnificent: a 180-degree sweep of patterned farmlands reaching toward the vast Minas Basin, interrupted only by the South Mountain in the distance. At least four counties are visible from this popular vantage point.

About 8km/5mi north of The Lookoff, as Route 358 descends into the tiny community of Scots Bay, there is a lovely **view★** of this bay, the Minas Channel and the Parrsboro Shore of Nova Scotia. At Little Cove boats can be seen resting on the channel bottom at low tide.

Cape Split – *Rte. 358 ends. Hiking trail 13km/8mi through woods to tip of cape.* This hook of forested land juts into the Bay of Fundy, edged by magnificent cliffs. Since the tides constantly ebb and flow, the bay's waters in the Minas Channel are muddied. From road's end there are **views** of the wide bay, the shoreline of the cape and the Parrsboro Shore.

Return via Rte. 358. After about 9km/6mi take the unpaved road on the left (Stewart Mountain Rd.). At junction turn left. Road terminates at provincial park. Follow signs. Hiking trails for Cape Blomidon shown on panel in visitor parking lot.

★ **Blomidon**– As the road leaves the woods and descends into flatlands, the first **view★** of the Minas Basin is grand. The patchwork farmlands of this rural coastland stretch to the cliffs of the basin. Bright red barns and 2-storey farmhouses dot the landscape, dominated by the reddish cliffs of Cape Blomidon. From the end of the picnic area, the **view★★** in both directions of the wide red beach (at low tide), and the stratified pinkish red cliffs, contrasted with the blue waters of the basin, are breathtaking.

At Blomidon junction, continue south via Pereau and Delhaven to Rte. 221.

About 2km/1.2mi south of the junction, there is a **view★** from the Pereaux Small Crafts Harbour of the hole in a rock formation known locally as **Paddys Island**, fully visible at low tide.

At the junction with Rte. 221, turn right to Canning for Rte. 358 back to Rte. 1.

★ **Wolfville** – Pop. 3,475. This charming town with shaded streets and heritage properties is home to Acadia University, founded 1838. Several mansions have been converted into wayside inns. Boutiques and eateries line the main thoroughfare, and during college sessions, the community is alive with scurrying students.

★ **Grand-Pré National Historic Park** – ✈ *Just north of Rte. 1, 4km/2.5mi east of Wolfville.* Inhabited between 1680 and 1755, the former Acadian village of Grand-Pré (French for "great meadow") has been transformed into a spacious park overlooking the flat dikelands the early settlers reclaimed. The well-maintained expanse of hedged lawns, flowerbeds and large shade trees serves as a permanent memorial to the Acadians.

Before Deportation *(p 240)*, Grand-Pré was the most important Acadian settlement in Nova Scotia, with about 200 farms along the edge of the Minas Basin. Residents who had moved here from Port Royal *(p 260)* realized the richness of the soil covered by the sea at high tide. They constructed a system of **dikes** to keep the sea out, while marsh water was allowed to escape through floodgates. The cultivated land soon supported crops, livestock and orchards. After Deportation, the farmlands were given to planters from New England, and later to Loyalists.

The American poet **Henry Wadsworth Longfellow** chose Grand-Pré as the setting for his poem, *Evangeline*. Published in 1847, the work describes a young couple's separation during Deportation and Evangeline's subsequent search throughout the eastern US for her lover Gabriel—only to find him dying. Symbolic of the tragedy of Deportation, the poem has become part of popular Acadian culture.

Visit – *Open mid-May–mid-Oct daily 9am–6pm.* ⚑ ☎*902-542-3631.* On the site of the first church of Grand-Pré stands a small **chapel** in a setting of maple, horse chestnut and willow trees. Completed in 1930, the chapel is constructed of local stone in a style reminiscent of churches in France. Inside, there are **displays** illustrating Acadian settlement, the British takeover, and the final deportation. A bronze **statue** of Evangeline by **Louis-Philippe Hébert** stands on the grounds.

Windsor – Pop. 3,625. Famous as the home of Thomas Haliburton, one of the foremost Nova Scotians of his day, the town is set at the confluence of the Avon and St. Croix Rivers. The Avon is sealed off from the Bay of Fundy by a causeway. A shipping point for lumber and gypsum mined nearby, the community was once the site of the 18C Acadian settlement of Piziquid, which was taken over by New Englanders after Deportation and renamed Windsor.

★ **Haliburton House** – *On Clifton Ave. Follow signs from causeway. Open Jun–mid-Oct Mon–Sat 9:30am–5:30pm, Sun 1–5:30pm. Contribution requested.* ⚑ ☎*902-798-2915.* At the end of a long, impressive drive stands this house, built in 1836 on the tree-covered estate of **Thomas Chandler Haliburton** (1796-1865), famous as the creator of **Sam Slick**, a fictitious Yankee peddler.

Judge, legislator, author and humorist of international renown, Haliburton started publishing stories in 1836 under the title, *The Clockmaker; or, The Sayings and Doings of Samuel Slick of Slickville*. Slick travelled all over Nova Scotia, making fun of its unenterprising inhabitants. Many of the epigrams he coined are still in use today: "six of one and half a dozen of the other," "an ounce of prevention is worth a pound of cure," "facts are stranger than fiction," "the early bird gets the worm," "as quick as a wink," and "jack of all trades and master of none" are among the most familiar.

The interior of the house with its spacious entry hall, elegant dining room and sitting room reflects the man.

Shand House Museum – *Avon St. Street parking prohibited. Upon entrance to Windsor, watch for signs to separate parking area. Uphill walk to house. Open Jun–mid-Oct Mon–Sat 9:30am–5:30pm, Sun 1–5:30pm.* ☎*902-798-8213.* The most imposing of the houses atop Ferry Hill overlooking the Avon River, this Victorian dwelling was completed in 1891. The staircase is of cherry, and several rooms have oak interiors. Furnishings are those of the original and only owners. Visitors can ascend the square tower.

Fort Edward – ✈ *Off King St. near causeway. Open mid Jun–end of Jun daily 11am–3pm. Jul–Labour Day daily 10am–4pm. Early Sept–end of Sept daily 11am–3pm. Contribution requested.* ☎*902-542-3631.* Possessing the oldest blockhouse in

Canada, this fort is situated on a hillock at the edge of town. Built in 1750 as a British stronghold in Acadian territory, it was later a point of departure for Acadians assembled for deportation.

From the grassy fortification, there are **views** of the tidal river, the causeway and Lake Pesaquid in the distance. Made of squared timbers, the dark wooden **blockhouse** is the only remaining building of the fort. The walls of its two storeys—the upper storey overhanging the lower—are pierced by square portholes for cannon and loopholes for musket fire. Inside, there are displays on the blockhouse defence system and the fort's history.

ATLANTIC SHORE**

Map pp 238-239

Nova Scotia's eastern shore is known for its rugged coastline, granite coves, sandy beaches, pretty fishing villages and attractive tree-lined towns with elegant houses built from shipbuilding or privateering fortunes. The entire coast from Canso to Yarmouth can be followed by road, but a greater concentration of quaint seaside communities is found south of Halifax.

FROM HALIFAX TO LIVERPOOL   *3 days. 348km/216mi. Map p 264.*

★★ **Halifax** – *2 days. Description p 271.*

> *Leave Halifax by Rte. 3. Turn left on Rte. 333.*

As the coast is approached, the landscape becomes wild, almost desolate. Huge boulders left by retreating glaciers, and stunted vegetation give the area a lunar appearance. *Fog is least common mid-July to October, but can occur any time.*

★★ **Peggy's Cove** – Immortalized by artists and photographers across Canada, this tiny village is unique among coastal communities, set as it is on a treeless outcropping of massive, deeply lined boulders. Its tranquil harbour with colourful boats, and fishing shacks built on stilts over the water is indeed picturesque.

Housing an operating post office *(mid-Jun–Oct)*, the **lighthouse** stands alone on a huge granite slab pounded by the Atlantic Ocean. *Sudden high waves and slippery boulders have resulted in personal tragedy. Use extreme caution when walking in this area.* Upon departing, note the **carvings** of village residents sculpted in the granite rock by William deGarthe (1907-83).

©Dick Dietrich

Peggy's Cove

The road follows the coast with views of the villages on **St. Margarets Bay**.

> *Rte. 333 joins Rte. 3 at Upper Tantallon; follow Rte. 3 until Rte. 329 turns off after Hubbards. Tour the peninsula and rejoin Rte. 3 just before Chester.*

★ **Chester** – Pop. 10,762. Perched on cliffs rising out of Mahone Bay, this charming town has beautiful elm and oak trees and traditional New England frame houses. Founded by New Englanders in 1759, the community is a popular summer residence of Americans and a favourite retirement spot for Canadians.

> *Take Rte. 12 north, 7km/4mi after Chester.*

★ **Ross Farm** – *24km/15mi one way. Open Jun–mid-Oct daily 9:30am–5:30pm. Jan–Mar weekends only 9:30am–4:30pm. $4.25.* ♿ ☎*902-689-2210.* Cleared from wilderness in 1816 by William Ross, this farm belonged to five generations of his family before acquisition by the Nova Scotia Museum Complex. Maintained as a living museum of 19C agrarian life, the farm features coopering, candle making, forging, sheep shearing and other demonstrations that vary with the season. There are displays of plows and harrows, buggies and other transport, including a well-stocked peddler's wagon. Horse-drawn wagon rides are available ($0.50).

Return to Rte. 3.

★ **Mahone Bay** – Pop. 1,096. Founded in 1754 by Capt. Ephraim Cook, the community was once a centre of piracy and privateering. Today this placid town is distinguished by three neighbouring churches lining the bay of the same name. Between 1756 and 1815 hundreds of small ships sailed from Nova Scotia ports to harass French, Spanish, Dutch and American vessels, from New

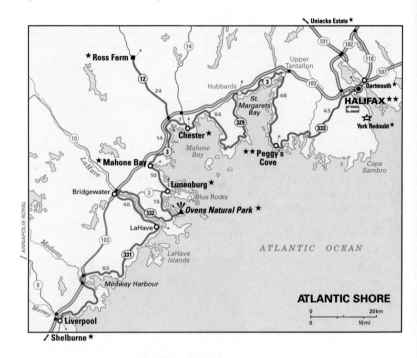

England to the Caribbean. These acts of piracy were carried out with royal blessing. After obtaining a license, a privateer owner could attack only enemy ships. All prizes had to be taken to Halifax where the Court of Vice Admiralty decided their legality. Despite these restrictions, profits were enormous and coastal communities prospered.

Upon approaching the town, there is a lovely **view**★ of the churches reflected in the water. Shops and restaurants, elegant frame houses and churches are set along tree-lined streets close to the bay.

Follow Rte. 3 south 10km/6mi.

★ **Lunenburg** – Pop. 2,781. Situated on a hilly peninsula with "front" and "back" harbours, picturesque Lunenburg is named for the northern German hometown (Lüneburg) of the first settlers who arrived in 1753. Colourful historic houses grace the grid-patterned streets rising from the waterfront.

Once a pirates' haven, the town was sacked by American privateers in 1782. Known for its former shipbuilding industry, Lunenburg was the construction site of many schooners that fished the "banks"(p 283), including the **Bluenose**, undefeated champion of the North American fishing fleet and winner of four international schooner races from 1921 to 1938. The **Bluenose II**, a replica of the original (p 273), was also constructed here in 1963 and offers seasonal **cruises** when in port (*departs from Fisheries Museum Jun–Sept daily 9:30am & 1pm; round-trip 2hrs; $20; & Bluenose II Preservation Trust* ☎902-634-1963 or 800-763-1963, Canada/US). Every August the popular **Fisheries Exhibition and Fishermen's Reunion** is celebrated in Lunenburg. Dory, yacht and schooner races, fish-filleting and scallop-shucking contests, parades and displays are featured.

★★ **Fisheries Museum** – *Lunenburg harbour. Open Jun–mid-Oct daily 9:30am–5:30pm. Rest of the year Mon–Fri 8:30am–4:30pm. $6.* ✗ ♿ ☎ *902-634-4794.* Housed in a former fish-processing plant on the waterfront, this 3-storey centre features a wide array of maritime displays. Exhibits range from the history of the Bluenose, and the illicit "rum-running" trade during Prohibition to the development of the banks fishery. A sailmaker's workshop and a 1920s fish company office have been re-created, and ship models, tools and navigational equipment are on display. A theatre *(regularly scheduled films)*, working dory shop and aquarium complete the museum.

Moored at the wharf, the **Theresa E. Connor**, one of the last saltbank schooners to fish the Grand Banks, can be boarded. Built in 1938, she has been refurbished to illustrate the era of dory fishing when small, two-manned boats (dories) would haul in fish using trawl lines. The fish were salted on board a schooner, aptly called a "saltbanker," which served as a supply and delivery base. Characteristic of craft that replaced dory schooners, the steel-hulled side trawler, **Cape Sable**, can also be boarded. Built in Holland in 1962, she hauled trawl nets off Lunenburg until 1982. A replica of a shucking house shelters equipment and mounted scallop shells.

> *Follow Rte. 3 and turn left on Rte. 332 for 15km/9mi. Turn left at Feltzen South and right on Ovens Rd.*

★ **Ovens Natural Park** – *Open May–Oct daily 9am–9pm. $3.* ✗ ♿ ☎ *902-766-4621.* The park has a lovely site, which offers **views**★ across Lunenburg Bay to Blue Rocks. A path along the cliff top leads to several sets of stairs by which visitors can descend to see the oven-like caves, cut into the cliffs by the action of the sea.

> *Continue on Rte. 332 and then left on Rte. 3.*

The road follows the wide and tranquil estuary of LaHave River. Boats can be seen along this stretch of water lined with frame houses and trees. The river is crossed at **Bridgewater** (pop. 7,248), a large, industrial town.

> *Turn left on Rte. 331.*

The road passes the town of **LaHave** itself, one of the earliest settlements in the province. Isaac de Razilly, Lieutenant-Governor of Acadie, built a fort here in 1632. The road continues along the coast with many pleasant views of the sea and fishing villages, especially in the vicinity of **Medway Harbour**.

Liverpool – Pop. 3,113. Founded in 1760 by New Englanders, Liverpool, like its great English namesake, is on the Mersey River. The privateering, fishing and ship repairing of the past have largely been supplanted by the modern industries of papermaking, fish processing and machine building.

★ **Perkins House Museum** – *On Main St. Open Jun–mid-Oct Mon–Sat 9:30am–5:30pm, Sun 1–5:30pm.* ☎ *902-354-4058.* This low-lying New England frame house, with odd-shaped corners and winding hidden stairs, was built in 1767 for Col. Simeon Perkins. A merchant and ship owner, Perkins moved to Nova Scotia from Cape Cod, assuming military, judicial and legislative roles beyond his business and family life. Surrounded by other elegant residences, the house is set in fine gardens among tall trees.

On display next door in the Queens County Museum is a copy of the colonel's diary, which captures life in a colonial town from 1766 to 1812.

EXCURSION TO SHELBURNE

★ **Shelburne** – Pop. 2,245. *64km/38mi south by Hwy. 103. Exit 25. Tourist bureau on Dock St.* ☎ *902-875-4547.* This small waterfront town was once one of the largest 18C cities in North America. Founded by Loyalists in 1783, the community's population swelled to an estimated 10,000 when additional British sympathizers sought sanctuary in Nova Scotia from the American Revolution. The expansion was short lived, however, since many settlers moved elsewhere.

Historic homes and commercial buildings line Dock Street, former hub of the town's bustling mercantile activity. Work continues at the barrel factory and in the **Dory Shop Museum**, a museum spotlighting the dory's historical importance and method of construction *(open mid-Jun–Aug daily 9:30am–5:30pm;* ☎ *902-875-3219).*

★ **Ross-Thomson House and Store Museum** – *Charlotte Lane. Open Jun–mid-Oct daily 9:30am–5:30pm.* ☎ *902-875-3219.* This 2-storey structure was in use by 1785 as a combination house, store and warehouse for items of international trade. Note the two roof shapes: gambrel and gable. Visitors can tour the well-stocked interior of the old store as well as the residence. Seasonal flower and herb gardens grace the front entrance.

BALMORAL MILLS★

Map p 239

Standing beside a stream in a pleasant valley, this fully operational **gristmill** was built in 1874. Although commercial use ceased in 1954, the mill has been completely restored.

VISIT *1hr*

10km/6mi southeast of Tatamagouche by Rte. 311. Grounds open year-round. Gristmill museum open Jun–mid-Oct Mon–Sat 9:30am–5:30pm, Sun 1–5:30pm. & ☎*902-657-3016.* When in operation *(a few hours daily)*, the mill is a hive of activity. Weighing over a tonne, the original millstones grind barley, oats, wheat and buckwheat into flour and meal *(for sale)*. The grain is moved from storey to storey by means of a series of buckets mounted on leather belts. Various milling processes are explained. Below the mill the revolving waterwheel can be seen.

EXCURSION

Sutherland Steam Mill Museum – *In Denmark, 10km/6mi northeast by Rte. 311, minor road and Rte. 326. Open Jun–mid-Oct Mon–Sat 9:30–5:30pm, Sun 1–5:30pm.* ☎*902-657-3365.* When Alexander Sutherland built this sawmill in 1894, steam was replacing water power as the most efficient means of cutting wood. He made sleighs, carriages and sleds; his brother and partner produced doors and windows for local houses. All machinery is in working order, and the mill "steams up" once a month *(phone ahead for schedule)*.

CABOT TRAIL★★

Map p 269

Named for explorer John Cabot, who is reputed to have landed at the northern tip of Cape Breton Island in 1497, this route is one of the most beautiful drives in eastern North America. Opened in 1936 the paved, two-lane highway makes a circle tour of the northern part of the island.

Initially traversing tranquil farmland, the trail then hugs the coast and winds up and down, providing scenic views of the immense Atlantic Ocean, craggy mountains, rocky inlets, magnificent headlands and dense forests. Some areas are reminiscent of the Scottish Highlands, ancestral home of many of the island's inhabitants. The east coast is especially rich in Gaelic culture. Derived from the language of the Celts in Ireland and the Scottish Highlands, Gaelic was the third most common European language spoken in Canada in the early 19C, and can still be heard here today.

Malak, Ottawa

Cabot Trail, Cape Breton Island

DRIVING TOUR *Allow 2 days*
Round-trip of 301km/187mi from Baddeck. The trail can be driven in either direction, but visitors may prefer clockwise travel for the security of hugging the mountainside during steep, curvy stretches.

★ Baddeck

Overlooking Baddeck Bay, this charming village is the starting point of the Cabot Trail. The popular resort town has a lovely **site★★** on the north shore of **Bras d'Or Lake**. This immense inland sea nearly cuts Cape Breton in two and is fed in the north by the Atlantic via two channels, the Great Bras d'Or and the Little Bras d'Or on either side of Boularderie Island. Bras d'Or Lake's resemblance to a Scottish loch has attracted many settlers of Scottish origin to its shores. Among them was **Alexander Graham Bell** (1847-1922), humanitarian, researcher and prolific inventor.

★★ Alexander Graham Bell National Historic Site – *On Hwy. 205 in Baddeck.* Bell's favourite shape, the tetrahedron, is used extensively in the design of this fascinating museum. Exhibits illustrate the genius of this remarkable man. A number of films and videos are shown during peak season.

In 1885 Bell first visited Baddeck, where he was to conduct much of his aeronautical work. Eventually he chose the location for his summer residence, naming his home, *Beinn Bhreagh*, "beautiful mountain" in Gaelic. His work as a teacher of the deaf led to the invention of the telephone, conceived in Brantford, Ontario *(p 137)*, in 1874, and tested in Boston the following year. The discovery brought him fame and the capital to continue other research. In Baddeck he built kites and heavier-than-air craft, using combinations of the tetrahedron shape—an almost perfect form because it is lightweight but strong. In 1907, with other pioneer aviators, he founded the Aerial Experiment Assn. and sponsored the first manned flight in Canada when the **Silver Dart** flew across Baddeck Bay in 1909. Before his death, he witnessed his hydrofoil craft reach the incredible speed (for 1919) of 114km/70mph on Bras d'Or Lake.

Visit – ⊙ *Open Jul–Aug daily 9am–8pm. Sept daily 9am–6pm. Rest of the year daily 9am–5pm. $3.50.* ♿ ☎*902-295-2069.* There are models of the telephone, the vacuum jacket (a forerunner of the iron lung), the surgical probe (a device used prior to the invention of the X ray), and Bell's kites. His project to prevent stranded sailors from dying of thirst at sea is on view—a model for converting fog to drinking water, using breath and salt water. A highlight is the superb **photograph collection**, oversized black-and-white prints of Bell's life and work. One wing of the museum is devoted to his hydrofoil, the HD-4. Both the original hull and a reconstruction of the entire craft are on exhibit.

From the museum's rooftop garden, there is a **view** of the wooded headland across Baddeck Bay. *Beinn Bhreagh (not open to the public),* Bell's Canadian estate, can be seen among the trees.

★ From Baddeck to Chéticamp *88km/55mi. Map p 269.*

The Cabot Trail follows the valley of the Middle River, passes the Lakes O'Law and joins the Margaree River's lush green **valley★** of meadows and abundant salmon pools, reputed to offer some of Canada's finest salmon fishing.

North East Margaree – Located in the heart of salmon-fishing country, the tiny rural community has a museum of note.

★ Margaree Salmon Museum – *Open mid-Jun–mid-Oct daily 9am–5pm. $1.* ♿ ☎*902-248-2848.* This pleasant little museum features a large collection of colourful fishing flies and rods—one actually 5.5m/18ft long, made in Scotland in 1880. Fishing tackle on display includes a sampling of illegal spears used by poachers. The life cycle of the Atlantic salmon is illustrated from birth to a full-grown adult's return trip upriver to reproduce. Unlike its Pacific cousin, the Atlantic salmon can make several such trips.

The Cabot Trail parallels the Margaree River northward, affording pastoral **views★** of the wide river valley and the town of East Margaree on the opposite side. The sudden vista of the wide expanse of the sea, after the road ascends out of farmland, is dramatic. Upon descent the **view★** of Margaree Harbour is lovely. The trail crosses the estuary of the Margaree River and heads north along the Acadian coast, with views of the Gulf of St. Lawrence.

Chéticamp – An enclave of Acadian culture, this fishing community sprawls along the coast opposite Chéticamp Island. A protected harbour and a large stone church dedicated to St. Peter distinguish the town. The Acadian tricolour flag *(p 256)* can be seen atop flagpoles scattered throughout the town. Locally made hand-hooked rugs are Chéticamp's claim to fame.

Acadian Museum – *Open May–Oct daily 7am–10pm. Contribution requested.* ✗ & ☎ *902-224-2170.* Operated by a cooperative of Acadian women, the museum and gift shop feature a large array of hooked mats, rugs and other crafted items. There are demonstrations of hooking, spinning, carding and weaving.The on-site dining room specializes in Acadian cooking.

From Chéticamp to Cape Smokey   *124km/77mi. Map p 269.*

★★ **Cape Breton Highlands National Park** – Spanning coast to coast across northern Cape Breton, this 950sq km/367sq mi wilderness park combines seashore and mountains. Hills ascend directly from the ocean to form a tableland more than 500m/1700ft high.

The west coast borders the relatively calm waters of the Gulf of St. Lawrence. On the eastern side, the Atlantic Ocean pounds the bare rocks with great force, yet there are several fine beaches throughout this preserve. Whales, and even bald eagles, can be found on either shore.

Inland, the park is heavily forested and boggy—the realm of moose, lynx and snowshoe hare. Several trails reach the interior *(details from park office)*, but the main attraction is the beautiful coastline.

Visit – ☞ *Open year-round. $3 entry fee. Hiking, picknicking, swimming.* △ *Information office (open mid-May–Jun daily 9am–5pm; Jul–Labour Day daily 8am–8pm; early Sept–mid-Oct daily 9am–5pm) at park entrances north of Chéticamp* ☎ *902-224-2306 and at Ingonish Beach* ☎ *902-285-2535 (summer only)* ☎ *902-285-2691 (year-round). There are many designated lookouts within the park along Cabot Trail.* From the park entrance at the Chéticamp River, Cabot Trail winds up Chéticamp Canyon to emerge on the coast and parallel the sea. Fine **views**★★ of the ocean and the road weaving up and down in the distance are afforded. From **Cap Rouge** lookout, there is an especially lovely **view**★★. The road gradually climbs French Mountain and heads inland across the plateau, the highest point on the highway.

After crossing several deep stream-lined valleys, the road descends to Mackenzie Mountain. Then, by a series of switchbacks, it reaches Pleasant Bay with outstanding **views**★★ on the descent. The **Lone Shieling**, a tiny hut of stone with rounded corners and a thatched roof *(about 6.5km/4mi from Pleasant Bay, then short walk)*, is a replica of a Scottish crofter's cottage, common in the Highlands and islands of Scotland. It was built to form a visible link between the adopted home of the Highland Scots who settled Cape Breton and their ancestral land.

Along its course Cabot Trail first climbs over North Mountain, descends steeply, allowing pretty **views**★, and then enters the valley of the North Aspy River, which it follows to the village of **Cape North**.

★★ **Excursion to Bay St. Lawrence** – *16km/10mi north.* This scenic drive rounds Aspy Bay with views of its long sandbar, and then heads inland across grassy hills spotted with pink rock to St. Lawrence Bay at the north end of Cape Breton Island. Before leaving the bay, the road passes Cabot Landing Beach, supposedly the first North American landfall of John Cabot *(p 298).* Whether visited by Cabot or not, it is a refreshing scene of a long beach backed by Sugarloaf Mountain.

At the end of the road is the tiny fishing village of **Bay St. Lawrence**★ built around a small lake with a narrow exit to the sea. Upon the approach to the village, a large white clapboard church (St. Margaret's) is prominent. From its grounds the **view**★ of the bay community is picturesque. The church's fine wooden interior has a ceiling shaped like the hull of a ship.

Upon leaving Bay St. Lawrence, turn right and continue 3km/1.8mi to Capstick.

Capstick – Less populous than Bay St. Lawrence, this hillside settlement consists of a few isolated houses on the grassy slopes above the seacliffs.

The dramatic **views**★ of the inlets through the scraggy pines are enhanced by the beauty of the water's colour.

Return to Cabot Trail. After South Harbour, take coast road.

Revealing fine **views**★ of Aspy Bay, its sand bar and the long Cape North peninsula, this coastal route is a pretty drive. The road turns south after White Point through the charming fishing villages of **New Haven** and **Neil Harbour**★, the latter with an artificial harbour beside a sandy bay.

Rejoin Cabot Trail.

This section of the trail is an especially splendid drive along the coast, particularly after **Black Brook Cove**. Worn, pink boulders stretch into the sea, while green forests cover the inlands. There are many little bays and coves, **Green Cove** being one of the loveliest. From Lakie's Head lookout the narrow peninsula of **Middle Head** and towering Cape Smokey can be identified, sometimes rising from a mist reminiscent of the Scottish Highlands.

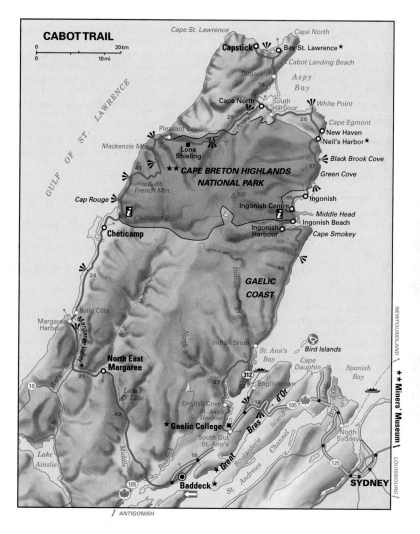

The Ingonishs – The relative solitude of the trail is left behind in the resort area of Ingonish Centre, Ingonish Beach, Ingonish Harbour, and other Ingonish desig-nations, popular for various forms of recreation *(fishing, boating, swimming, golf, tennis, and winter skiing)*. Many cruise ships stop over at the harbour.

The bay itself is cut into two parts—north and south—by Middle Head, the dra-matic setting of the **Keltic Lodge**, one of Canada's best known resort hotels. To the south, **Cape Smokey** rises 369m/1,210ft out of the sea. This headland is at times partially obscured by cloud, hence its name.

The Gaelic Coast   *Map above*

From Cape Smokey to Baddeck – *89km/55mi.* The trail climbs over Cape Smokey and then drops again, permitting several good **views★**. Descending the coast farther inland, the road passes through several fishing villages.

Offshore are the **Bird Islands**, a sanctuary where vast numbers of sea birds nest in summer. The trail rounds St. Ann's Harbour, offering lovely views after Goose Cove, but especially at South Gut St. Ann's.

269

★ **Gaelic College** – *In St. Ann's.* Founded in 1938 by Rev. A. W. R. MacKenzie, this school is the only one on the continent to teach the Gaelic language and Highland arts and crafts. Attracting youth from all over North America, the college offers courses in bagpipe music, clan law, Gaelic singing, Highland dancing and hand weaving of family and clan tartans. Students can often be seen performing Highland flings, sword dances and step dancing.

In August, a week-long **Gaelic Mod** is held when prizes are awarded to the best performers in each field *(for details, contact the college).*

Great Hall of the Clans – *On campus. Open daily mid-May–Jun Mon–Fri 9am–4pm. Jul–mid-Oct daily 8:30am–8pm. Late Oct–mid-Dec Mon–Fri 9am–4pm. $2.* & ☎902-295-3411. At the rear of the entrance is a room displaying Highlands pioneer crafts and memorabilia. Inside the large meeting hall, wall **exhibits** illustrate clan history and life. A variety of tartans and costumes are also on display. At one end of the hall stands a statue of Angus MacAskill (1825-63), the 236cm/ 7ft 9in tall,193kg/425lb "Cape Breton giant" who toured the US with the midget, Tom Thumb.

★ **Alternative Route** – *22km/14mi by Rte. 312 and Trans-Can Hwy.* This road enters St. Ann's Bay via a narrow spit of land that divides the bay from St. Ann's harbour. At the end of the spit, there is a ferry across the 270m/300yd outlet *(24hr/day every 5min; Feb–Apr no crossing due to ice; $0.50/car;* ☎902-929-2404).

EXCURSIONS

★ **Great Bras d'Or** – *Map p 269. 18km/11mi northeast along Trans-Can Hwy. from South Gut St. Ann's.* The road ascends Kelly's Mountain with a fine **view**★ from the lookout of the harbour, spit of land and the ferry. Crossing Cape Dauphin peninsula, it descends to the Great Bras d'Or. There are good **views**★ of this stretch of water, of the bridge that spans it, and, in the distance, of **Sydney** (pop. 26,063), Cape Breton's principal city and the site of eastern Canada's richest coalfields, which have fostered a sizeable steel industry.

★★ **Miners' Museum** – *Map p 269. In Glace Bay, 19km/12mi northeast of Sydney. Follow museum signs from town to Quarry Point.* Overlooking the vast Atlantic Ocean from its 6ha/15-acre site, this low-lying, geometric museum stands as a monument to Cape Breton's coal-mining history.

Sprawling Glace Bay—home of the museum—has been a mining town since 1720 when French soldiers from Louisbourg found coal in the cliffs at Port Morien to the southeast. The region is underlain with bituminous coal seams that dip seaward under the Atlantic. By the late 19C numerous coal mines were operating. When iron ore deposits were found in nearby Newfoundland *(p 241)*, a steel industry mushroomed in the vicinity of Sydney, using coal as coke in the refining process. Immigrants poured into the area in the 20C for mining jobs. By the early 1950s, use of oil and gas had reduced the demand for coal. Economic depression hit as the mines began to close. The federal government created the Cape Breton Development Corp., which operated the Glace Bay colliery until 1984, when coal mining in the area ceased.

Visit – *Open Jun–Labour Day daily 10am–6pm (Tue 7pm). Rest of the year Mon–Fri 9am–4pm. $3.25 plus $2.75 for guided mine tour. Protective clothing is provided.* ✗ & ☎902-849-4522. The museum has well-presented, colourful exhibits on coal formation and mining methods. Coal samples, equipment and transport are also on display. Films *(20-30min)* about Cape Breton's mining industry and labour history are shown in the theatre.

Retired miners conduct **mine tours** *(30min)*, interspersing commentary with tales from personal experience. Visitors walk down a sloping tunnel under the Atlantic Ocean to see the machinery and coal face of the Ocean Deeps Colliery. *Coal samples can be collected as souvenirs. Note: low mine ceilings may necessitate stooping for periods of time.*

Beside the museum building, a **miners' village** has been reconstructed. The mining company supplied employee housing and owned the only store. Transactions were based on credit secured against a miner's wages. After a week of work, a miner sometimes drew no pay, finding he owed for food, clothing and other necessities. In addition to a store, a miner's house of 1850-1900 has been re-created. The restaurant *(May–Labour Day)* serves home-cooked specialties such as "coal dust pie."

HALIFAX★★

Pop. 114,455
Map p 239
Tourist Office ☎902-421-8736

Situated on the east coast at about the mainland's midpoint, the capital of Nova Scotia overlooks one of the finest harbours in the world. The deep outer inlet of the Atlantic Ocean narrows into a protected inner harbour called the **Bedford Basin**. The foot-shaped peninsula upon which the city was built is dominated by a hill, topped with a star-shaped citadel. These two factors—a natural harbour and a man-made fortress—were the basis of the city's founding.

Historical Notes

Early History – Halifax came into being because of the existence of Louisbourg *(p 275)*. New Englanders had successfully captured the French fortress in 1745, only to see it later returned to France. Their anger prodded the British government to build a fortress as a counterweight to Louisbourg. In July 1749 the appointed governor of Nova Scotia, Col. **Edward Cornwallis**, and about 2,500 English settlers constructed a fortified settlement on the site of the present-day city.

From its inception Halifax was a military stronghold filled with soldiers from the fort and sailors from numerous naval vessels docked in the harbour. From the social gatherings of the nobility (officers in both services) to the presence of broth-els along the wharves, the military shaped the town. Indeed, even law was martial; citizens were deprived of control over their affairs for nearly 100 years, until Halifax achieved city status.

The Royal Princes – Forbidden by their father to remain in England, two scape-grace sons of **George III** made Halifax their home. The future **William IV** spent his 21st birthday in wild revels off the port. His brother **Edward**, Duke of Kent, and later the father of Queen Victoria, served as commander-in-chief in Halifax from 1794 to 1800. Spending a fortune on defences, he made Halifax a member of the famous quadrilateral of British defences, which included Gibraltar and Bermuda. A rigid disciplinarian, he had his men flogged or hanged for misdemeanours. He installed the first telegraph system in North America by which he could relay orders to his men from Annapolis Royal *(p 259)* or from his love nest on the Bedford Basin, where his mistress lived.

The Halifax Explosion – The city's history has not always been so colourful, but its prosperity has coincided with times of war, whereas peace has often brought economic depression. The Napoleonic Wars, the American Civil War, World Wars I and II saw great military activity in Halifax, great wealth —and great tragedy. During both world wars, the Bedford Basin was used as a convoy assembly point so ships could cross the Atlantic in the safety of numbers when German sub-marines were encountered. In December 1917 a Belgian relief ship, the **Imo**, had a fatal collision in the harbour with the **Mont Blanc**, a French munitions ship. The *Mont Blanc* was carrying a lethal combination of picric acid, guncotton, TNT and benzol. The explosion was the world's largest, until the atom bomb was dropped on Hiroshima in 1945. The entire north end of the city was wiped out; rail yards and docks were destroyed. Windows were shattered as far as Truro 100km/60mi away; the explosion was heard over 160km/100mi. Only the *Mont Blanc's* cannon (found in Albro Lake behind Dartmouth) and an anchor shaft (which landed more than 3km/2mi away) were left. Miraculously, the crew survived, having aban-doned ship in time. However, 1,400 people were killed outright, an estimated 600 died later, 199 were blinded and another 9,000 were injured. There are people in Halifax today who, injured for life as children, are still receiving compensation.

The City Today – Halifax is the largest city in the Atlantic provinces and the region's commercial and financial centre. Nova Scotia's administrative hub and an important centre for scientific research, Halifax is also a major commercial seaport and serves as the Atlantic base of the **Canadian Navy**. The 6.5km/4mi long outer habour inlet is lined with docks and piers where it narrows into the 5km/3mi long, 2.5km/1.5mi wide Bedford Basin. The port has two container terminals, a grain elevator, an automobile-handling facility and oil refineries for arriving tankers.

SIGHTS *2 days. Map p 272.*

★★ **Halifax Citadel** – Situated on a hill overlooking the city's commercial district, the citadel is the fourth of forts dating to 1749 to occupy this site, with its commanding views of the area. The present star-shaped masonry structure is a repository of Halifax's military history and tradition.

Begun in 1828 at the order of the Duke of Wellington, the bastioned fort was not completed until 1856. Although never attacked, the fortification served the British Army until 1906 and the Canadian military until after World War II.

Easily approached from downtown, or driven around via Citadel Road, the citadel's site offers views★ of the city, harbour, Dartmouth, George's Island, and the Angus McDonald suspension bridge. Note the attractive **clock tower★**, the symbol of Halifax. Completed in 1803, the original was ordered by Prince Edward with four faces and bells to ring out the hours. Restored in 1962, it remains a memento to the punctilious prince.

Surrounded by a dry defensive ditch, the fortification contains a large central parade ground where soldiers attired in 19C uniforms perform military drills (*mid-Jun–Labour Day daily*).

Visit – ✆ *Grounds open year-round. Citadel open mid-Jun–Aug daily 9am–6pm. Rest of the year grounds only, daily 9am–5pm. Closed Jan 1, Good Friday & Dec 25. $3 ($5 mid-Jun–Aug).* ✗ & 🅿 ☎*902-426-5080.* This sprawling complex houses an orientation centre, barracks, powder magazines, a small museum and numerous other exhibits. Visitors can walk on the ramparts, look at guns that served as the citadel's main defence and visit the outer ditches and ravelins. An audio-visual presentation *(50min),* **Tides of History★**, covers the history of Halifax and its defences.

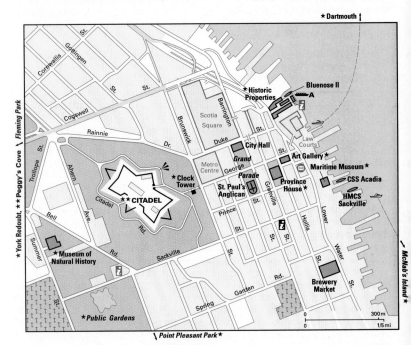

★ **Historic Properties and the Harbour** – Off Upper Water Street, the pedestrian area between Duke Street and the Cogswell interchange is commonly known as Historic Properties. Completely renovated, several 19C stone warehouses and wooden buildings house interesting shops, studios, restaurants and pubs, with outdoor seating overlooking the harbour.

From Historic Properties visitors can walk west through a series of restored buildings to the Granville Street Mall and Scotia Square. A **boardwalk** follows the harbourfront north around the Sheraton Hotel and south past the Law Courts and the terminus of the passenger ferry to Dartmouth *(p 274)* to the **brewery market**. A former brewery, the complex now houses several restaurants, shops and a farmers' market *(Sat 7am–1pm)* within its restored interior courtyards.

★★ **Harbour Cruise [A]** – *Departs from Cable Wharf Jun–Oct daily 10am–9pm. Round-trip 2hrs. Commentary. $16.* ✗ & 🅿 *Murphy's on the Water Tours* ☎*902-420-1015.* The *Haligonian III* cruise provides interesting commentary on the Halifax shipyards where 7,000 vessels were repaired during World War II; the naval dockyards with destroyers, preservers, submarines and other ships; the National Harbours Board terminal with its huge grain elevator; the container terminal where giant gantry cranes load odd-shaped ships specially constructed to carry containers; and other points of interest seen on the tour.

The cruise rounds Point Pleasant and enters the **North West Arm★**, a lovely stretch of water extending along the peninsula's west side and bordered by expensive homes and yacht clubs.

★ **Maritime Museum of the Atlantic** – *1675 Lower Water St. Open Jun–mid-Oct Mon–Sat 9:30am–5:30pm (Tue 8pm), Sun 1–5:30pm. Rest of the year Tue–Sat 9:30am–5pm (Tue 8pm), Sun 1–5pm. Closed Jan 1, Dec 24–26. $4.50.* ☎902-424-7490. Located on the waterfront with a view of Halifax harbour, this interesting museum presents a variety of small craft, ship models, photographs and displays on maritime history. Note the restored ship's **chandlery**, housed in an old warehouse where a range of mariner's equipment is exhibited. Sections are also devoted to the days of sail, the age of steam and naval history.

Outside the museum are two authentic vessels. Moored at the museum's wharf is the **CSS Acadia**, a steamship built in 1913 for the Canadian Hydrographic Service *(can be boarded Jun–mid-Oct)*. Berthed at Sackville Landing, adjacent to the museum, is the restored **HMCS Sackville**, a World War II corvette that served in the Battle of the Atlantic *(can be boarded Jun–Labour Day)*.

Berthed here seasonally is the **Bluenose II**, a replica of the schooner that held the International Fishermen's trophy 17 years, after capturing it in 1921. Constructed in 1963 as a goodwill ambassador for Nova Scotia, the *Bluenose II* offers **cruises** in Halifax harbour, when not visiting other ports *(departs from museum's wharf Jun–Sept daily 9:30am & 1pm; round-trip 2hrs; $20;* ☐ *Bluenose II Preservation Trust* ☎*902-634-1963 or 800-763-1963 Canada/US).*

★ **Province House** – *Main entrance on Hollis St. Open daily Jul–Aug Mon–Fri 9am–5pm, weekends 10am–4pm. Rest of the year Mon–Fri 9am–4pm.* ☎902-424-4661. Completed in 1819 this Georgian sandstone structure houses the Legislative Assembly of Nova Scotia, an institution that has existed since 1758.

The **Red Chamber**, where the Legislative Council used to meet, can be visited. Note the portraits of King George III and Queen Charlotte at the head of the room. In the **assembly chamber** visitors might witness some spirited debates when the body is in session. Once housing the provincial Supreme Court, the **legislative library** was the site, in 1835, of the self-defence of journalist **Joseph Howe** against a charge of criminal libel. His acquittal marked the beginning of a free press in Nova Scotia. Later he entered politics and led a fight against Confederation but eventually joined the Dominion (now more commonly called federal) government in Ottawa.

★ **Art Gallery of Nova Scotia** – *1741 Hollis St. across from Province House. Open Jun–Sept Tue–Fri 10am–5pm (Thu 9pm), weekends noon–5pm. Rest of the year Tue–Fri 10am–5pm, weekends noon–5pm. $2.50.* ☎902-424-7542. Housed in the stately Dominion Building, this modern museum has four floors of artwork. Nova Scotia artists from the first half of the 20C and other 20C painters are featured on the first floor. Canadian art, including paintings of the well-known **Group of Seven**, occupies the second floor along with British and European works. The mezzanine features regional **folk art**—painting, sculptures, paper and textiles—and a small but excellent collection of **Inuit art**. The lower level is reserved for temporary exhibits.

Grand Parade – Bordered by **City Hall** at one end and **St. Paul's Anglican Church** at the other, this pleasant square has been the centre of Halifax since its founding. Here the militia mustered, the town crier proclaimed the news, and city dwellers hired sedan chairs. Built in 1750 the small timber-framed church is the oldest Protestant church in Canada.

★ **Museum of Natural History**– *1747 Summer St. Open Jun–mid-Oct Mon–Sat 9:30am–5:30pm (Wed 8pm), Sun 1–5:30pm. Rest of the year Tue–Sat 9:30am–5pm (Wed 8pm), Sun 1–5pm. Closed Jan 1, Good Friday, Dec 25. $3 (free in winter).* ☐ ☎902-424-7353. This museum offers a comprehensive picture of Nova Scotia by covering its geology, history, society, and flora and fauna. Micmac displays, natural-history dioramas, and marine life, especially whales and sharks, can be seen.

★ **Public Gardens** – *Main entrance at corner of Spring Garden Rd. and South Park St. Open May–Nov daily dawn–dusk.* Opened to the public in 1867, this 7ha/17acre park is a fine example of an immense Victorian garden, complete with weeping trees, ponds, fountains, statues, formal plantings and an ornate bandstand. Note the massive wrought-iron entrance gate.

★ **Point Pleasant Park** – *Closed to traffic; parking on Point Pleasant Dr. at Tower Rd. and near container terminal. Open year-round daily 6am–midnight.* ✕ *(May–Oct).* ☎*902-421-6519.* Situated at the southernmost point of the peninsula, this lovely 75ha/185 acre park has excellent **views★★** of the harbour and the North West Arm. For many years the park was dominated by the military, who filled it with batteries and forts, the remains of which can still be seen.

Prince of Wales Martello Tower – ⊙ *Open Jul–Labour Day daily 10am–6pm. Grounds open year-round.* ☎*902-426-5080.* The prototype of what came to be called a **Martello tower**, this circular stone structure was the first of its kind in North America. Prince Edward ordered its construction in 1797, naming the tower for his brother—the future George IV. Its design was adapted from a tower on Mortella Point in Corsica that had proved almost impregnable. Such towers were built later in Canada and England to counter invasion by Napoleon's troops.
Exhibits portray the tower's history, architectural features and importance as a defensive structure.

EXCURSIONS

★ **McNab's Island** – *Access by ferry from Halifax harbourfront. For schedules contact tourist office, Halifax* ☎*902-421-8736.* Located in Halifax harbour, east of Point Pleasant Park, the island has beaches, walking trails, good views and the remains of military fortifications.

Sir Sandford Fleming Park – *5.5km/3mi by Cogswell St., Quinpool Rd. and Purcell's Cove Rd. (Rte. 253). Open year-round daily dawn–dusk. Walking trails, swimming, boating, picnic area.* ▣. A peaceful haven in a residential suburb of Halifax, this park is a tribute to **Sir Sandford Fleming** (1827-1915), a prominent engineer from Scotland. Instrumental in the construction of Canada's first continental railway system, he also designed the nation's first postage stamp and urged the adoption of international standard time.
The long stretch of North West Arm can be seen from **Dingle Tower** *(open Jun–Labour Day daily).*

★ **York Redoubt** – ⊙ *11km/7mi by Cogswell St., Quinpool Rd. and Purcell's Cove Rd. (Rte. 253). Open mid-Jun–Labour Day daily 9am–6pm. Rest of the year daily 9am–5pm.* ▣ ☎*902-426-5080.* Located on the bluffs above Halifax harbour, this coastal fort played an integral role in the city's defensive and warning systems.
First constructed in 1793, the defences were strengthened by Prince Edward, who named the redoubt for his brother, the Duke of York. The Martello tower Edward erected in 1798 was part of his signal communication system. During World War II, the redoubt became the centre for coordinating defence of the harbour and city against German attack.
At the north end, the remains of the stone tower can be seen. Aligned along the top of the bluff, a series of gun emplacements face the harbour approach. At the south end, the **command post** contains displays on the defences, and from it *(weather permitting)* there are good **views★** of the harbour.

★ **Dartmouth** – *Pop. 67,798. Map p 239.* Site of a large naval dockyard and research centre, Halifax's twin city on the other side of the inlet has a pleasant waterfront with several shop-lined streets descending to it. Connected to Halifax by two bridges, Dartmouth is serviced by **ferry**, from which the views of both cities are expensive *(departs from Lower Water St. in Halifax Jun–Sept Mon–Sat 6:45am–11:45pm, Sun 12:15pm–5:45pm; rest of the year Mon–Sat 6:45am–11:45pm; holidays 7:45am–11:45pm; no service Jan 1, Good Friday, Easter Sunday & Dec 25. $1.10;* ♿ ☎*902-421-6600).*

Quaker House – *59 Ochterloney St. Visit by guided tour (20min) only, mid-May–Labour Day daily 10am–4pm. Contribution requested.* ☎*902-464-2300.* This house is the sole survivor of 22 dwellings built for a group of Quaker whalers who moved to the province from New England in 1785. Its shingled exterior with paned windows is typical of the houses constructed along the coast from Massachusetts to Nova Scotia in the 18C. Note the framed walls, off-centre front door, exposed beams and narrow winding staircase.

Black Cultural Centre for Nova Scotia – *In Westphal. Rte 7 at Cherrybrook Road. Visit by guided tour (1hr) only, year-round daily 10am–4pm. $2. Reservations required.* ♿ ☎*902-434-6223.* This sizeable museum, library and meeting hall opened in 1983 to foster the province's black history and culture. Exhibits cover early migration and settlement, military service, religion and community. There is a memorial to naval hero **William Hall** (1827-1904), the first Nova Scotian and first black to be awarded the Victoria Cross, the Commonwealth's military medal for exceptional courage.

★ **Uniacke Estate Museum Park** – *Map p 239. In Mt. Uniacke, 40km/25mi northwest by Rtes. 7 and 1. Grounds open year-round daily dawn–dusk. House open Jun–mid-Oct Mon–Sat 9:30am–5:30pm, Sun 1–5:30pm.* ☎902-866-0032. This fine example of plantation-style colonial architecture, with its wide portico rising the two storeys of the house, stands on a peaceful lakeshore estate. Completed in 1815, it was the country home of Richard Uniacke, Attorney General of Nova Scotia from 1797 to 1830.

The interior looks today as it did in 1815 with the original furnishings of the Uniacke family, including several mahogany pieces crafted by George Adams of London.

★★ **Peggy's Cove** – *43km/27mi. Description p 263.*

The beaver symbol 🦫 *indicates that the point of interest described has been designated a national park or national historic site.*

LOUISBOURG FORTRESS★★★
Map p 239

Guarding the entrance of the St. Lawrence River, the approach to Quebec, Louisbourg was once the great 18C fortress of New France, manned by the largest garrison in North America. The $25 million restoration project is the most expensive preservation ever undertaken by the Canadian government.

Historical Notes

A Bleak Beginning – The French had long planned a fortress in Nova Scotia, even considering Halifax as a possible site. When they lost the mainland in 1713 *(p 240)*, they chose the eastern peninsula of Île Royale (now Cape Breton) and commenced construction of a fortified town in 1719.

Following fortification designs elaborated by French military engineers, the plan called for a citadel, six bastions and detached batteries. The considerable expense was still less than the cost of a French warship's six-month patrol of the Atlantic waters to guard the lucrative French fishery. Nonetheless, this massive undertaking was riddled with problems: a harsh climate, a boggy site where the mortar sometimes crumbled, scarce building materials and a few corrupt French officials who lined their pockets at royal expense. Difficult living conditions and lack of discipline among the common soldiers contributed to a mutiny in 1744.

A Not-So-Impregnable Fortress – In 1745, prior to completion, 4,000 New Englanders attacked the "impregnable" fortress. Less than two months later the French surrendered. In 1748 the British agreed to return the fort to the island colony of King **Louis XV**. The following year the French reoccupied the stronghold, while the British founded Halifax as a counter-fortress *(p 271)*. Ten years later Louisbourg was under siege again, this time by British regulars. **James Wolfe**, the second in command, managed to land his forces, and the fortress had to be surrendered a second time. Wolfe went on to capture Quebec City in 1759 *(p 196)*. To prevent further threat to British interests, Louisbourg was destroyed in 1760.

Since 1961 one-quarter of the fortress has been rebuilt according to the original plans and historical records. Furnishings are either original or reproductions.

Access – *37km/23mi south of Sydney by Rte. 22, southwest of town of Louisbourg.*

VISIT *Allow minimum 1/2 day*

🦫 *Open May–Jun daily 9:30am–5pm. Jul–Aug daily 9am–6pm. Sept–Oct daily 9:30am–5pm. $7.50.* ✗ ♿ ☎902-733-2280. *Note: Be prepared for cool temperatures, rain and fog. Comfortable walking shoes recommended.* Models of the fortress and displays on the history of Louisbourg provide orientation in the **visitor centre** *(departure point for bus to fortress; on-board commentary serves as preview of visit).*

Visitors cross a drawbridge to enter the walled town through the elaborate **Dauphine Gate**, manned by a sentry. Over 50 buildings *(most open to the public)* are constructed of wood or roughcast masonry, some furnished to their 1740s appearance, others containing themed exhibits. In the summer season, costumed staff portray 18C French society's leisure, propertied and working classes. Popular attractions include a **bakery**, where visitors can buy bread similar to the kind King Louis' troops lined up for in 1744. Three **period restaurants** serve 18C meals on earthenware and pewter. Along the quay stands the high wooden **Frédéric Gate**, the entrance through which important visitors to this once-bustling port were ushered from the harbour. The rich furnishings on the ground floor of the **ordonnateur's residence** include a harpsichord of the period. Archaeological artifacts recovered during reconstruction are on display at various locations.

★★ **King's Bastion** – Once one of the largest in North America, this military stronghold has become the symbol of reconstructed Louisbourg. Quarters for the garrison provide insight into the lives of the privileged and impoverished in Old World society. The **governor's apartments** consist of ten elegant rooms, lavishly furnished. Not as comfortable but well accommodated are the **officers' quarters**. Drafty and spartan, the **soldiers' barracks** are not at all conducive to a long stay. The **prison** and a **chapel** that once served as the town's parish church can also be visited.

MAITLAND★

Map p 239

Overlooking Cobequid Bay in the Minas Basin, Maitland was once an important shipbuilding centre. The town is best known as the site of the construction of the largest wooden ship built in Canada, the **William D. Lawrence**. Today Maitland's fine houses attest to the wealth created by the former industry.

SIGHT

★ **Lawrence House Museum** – *On Hwy. 15. Open Jun–mid-Oct Mon–Sat 9:30am–5:30pm, Sun 1–5:30pm.* ☎*902-261-2628.* Surrounded by elm trees, this 2.5-storey house is a splendid example of the grand residences of Nova Scotia's shipbuilders and sea captains. The entrance portico with its double, curved staircase is reminiscent of a ship's bridge.

William Dawson Lawrence built this house (c.1870) to overlook his shipyard on the Shubenacadie River at the point where it joins Cobequid Bay. Believing he could double a ship's size without doubling its operating costs, Lawrence constructed an 80m/262ft ship, which weighed 2,459 tons and had three masts, the highest being over 60m/200ft. To complete the vessel, he had to mortgage his house, but the investment proved to be profitable. Launched in 1874, the ship sailed all over the world with many varied cargoes.

The house contains most of its original furnishings, including shipbuilding artifacts, pictures of 19C ships and a 2m/7ft model of the *William D. Lawrence*. A lookout area across the road from the house affords visitors a good **view**★ of the tidal flats.

SHERBROOKE★

Map p 239

This village occupies a pretty **site** on the St. Mary's River, once the location of a French fort (1655). After capture by the English in 1669, the settlement was abandoned until people were attracted by the rich timberlands in 1800. During the early 19C, sawmills sprang up and wooden ships were built. Gold was discovered in 1861, and for about 20 years, the town flourished. The gold did not last, but Sherbrooke survived as a lumber town. Today it is a peaceful rural community and a centre for sports fishing and tourism.

SIGHT

★★ **Sherbrooke Village** – Restored beginning in 1969, this historic village is actually an extension of the town of Sherbrooke. Streets have been closed to traffic, and only a few houses within the village are private residences.

Visit – *Open Jun–mid-Oct daily 9:30am–5:30pm. Rest of the year Mon–Fri 8:30am–4:pm. Closed Dec 25. $4.* ✗ ☎*902-522-2400.* Renovated to reflect the period, the buildings were constructed between 1860 and 1870. A church, schoolhouse, post office, blacksmith shop and several homes can be visited. Built in 1862 with separate downstairs and upstairs cells for men and women, the **jail** occupied half the jailer's house. Of particular interest is the **boatbuilding shop** where wooden boats are still constructed. Above Cumminger Brothers' general store, visitors can don 19C costumes and be photographed in the **ambrotype photography studio**. The process of producing a picture from a negative on dark surfaced glass was used until c.1900. Furnished to the period, **Greenwood Cottage** is an example of a spacious house of the well-to-do, while **McMillan House** reflects the humble status of a village weaver *(spinning demonstrations)*. The hotel serves 1880s fare such as cottage pudding and gingerbread *(copies of recipes upon request)*. The telephone exchange is still operable, and the courthouse is in use today.

Removed from the village is **McDonald Brothers' Mill★** *(.4km/.3mi)*, an operational water-powered sawmill capable of full production. A short walk away *(3min)* through woodlands, a reconstructed **lumber camp** of the 19C shows the living conditions of loggers.

SPRINGHILL★★

Pop. 4,373
Map p 239
Tourist Office ☎902-597-8614

Located inland on the "arm" of the peninsula, east of the Isthmus of Chignecto, this town is famous as a coal-mining centre that has suffered more disasters than any other place of its size in Canada.

In 1891 an enormous blast in one of the mines tore out a vast area. When a subsequent flame swept through the mine workings, 125 men died. Then, in 1916, a subterranean fire filled the galleries. No one was killed, but much damage was done. An explosion and fire in 1956 caused 39 deaths. The next year a fire wiped out most of the business district of the town. Finally, in 1958, an underground upheaval or "bump" caused the deaths of 76 men. All the mines closed after this final disaster, the death knell of an industry already doomed by conversion to oil and gas as heating fuels.

SIGHT

★★ **Miners' Museum** – *On Black River Rd. Follow signs along Rte. 2 (Parrsboro direction). Visit by guided tour (45min) only, mid-May–mid-Oct daily 9am–5pm. $4.50.* ☎*902-597-8614.* This museum commemorates the tragedy of the disasters and the bravery of the rescuers through displays such as newspaper clippings and mining equipment. The interesting **mine tour** is conducted by retired miners. Equipped with hard hats, rubber coats and boots, visitors descend about 270m/900ft into the old Syndicate Mine via a tunnel of regular height, rather than those the miners had to crawl along. Both old and new mining methods are demonstrated *(coal souvenirs can be removed by pick-axe)*.

TRURO

Pop. 11,683
Map p 239
Tourist Office ☎902-895-6328

Set on the Salmon River near its mouth, this city experiences the high tides of the Bay of Fundy and the tidal bore *(p 249)*. Site of a thriving Acadian community called Cobequid before the Deportation, Truro was later settled by people from Northern Ireland and New Hampshire. Today this manufacturing centre is home to the Nova Scotia Agricultural College.

SIGHT

★ **Tidal Bore** – *Viewpoint: leave Hwy. 102 at Exit 14 and take Tidal Bore Rd. (left on Robie and left again on Tidal Bore Rd., if coming from Halifax). Parking area beside Palliser restaurant; contact tourist office for time of next bore* ☎*902-893-2922 (summer season); arrive 15min prior and if possible, stay 1hr to see high tide.* Twice a day the tide rushes up the Salmon River from the Bay of Fundy, causing a wave that may vary from a ripple to several feet in height. What is more interesting than this tidal wave is the tremendous inrush of water and the rapid rise in water level immediately following it. In fact, high tide is reached just over an hour after the arrival of the bore.

The birthplace of Canadian Confederation, and Canada's smallest province, this crescent-shaped island is only 225km/140mi long; a deeply indented coastline varies its width. Separated from Newfoundland by the Gulf of St. Lawrence, the island is just 14km/9mi from New Brunswick and 22km/14mi from Nova Scotia across the **Northumberland Strait**. Iron oxides give the soil its characteristic brick red colour, and on fine summer days, the rolling landscape presents a stunning kaleidoscope of green fields, blue sea and sky, red soil and puffy white clouds.

Historical Notes

Île-St.-Jean and the Acadian Deportation – Jacques Cartier *(p 238)* claimed the island for France in 1534, naming it Île-St.-Jean. Concerted efforts at colonization did not occur until the early 18C when French settlers founded **Port la Joye**, near the present site of Charlottetown, as a dependency of Île Royale, today Cape Breton Island in Nova Scotia *(p 266)*. France's plan to strengthen its claims in the New World brought Acadian farmers to Île-St.-Jean in 1720. In 1755 the British demanded an oath of fealty from Acadians on British territory. Several thousand Acadians chose instead to resettle on Île-St.-Jean. In 1758 England captured Île-St.-Jean, removing the Acadians under the Deportation Order *(p 240)*. About 30 families went into hiding—the ancestors of many of today's island Acadians.

PRACTICAL INFORMATION

Getting There

By Air – Service from Halifax, NS is provided by Air Canada affiliates ☎902-429-7111, or 800-776-3000 (US) to the Charlottetown airport (less than 5km/3mi from downtown) ☎902-566-7997. Taxis and major car rental agencies at the airport.

By Boat – Until completion of the new bridge in 1997*(p 279)*, **ferry** service will continue to be provided by Marine Atlantic between Borden and Cape Tormentine, NB *(departs year-round daily; one-way 45min; $19.50/car, $8/passenger; ☎902-794-5700, or from the US 800-341-7981)*. Northumberland Ferries connects the eastern part of the island at Wood Islands with Caribou, NS *(departs May–mid-Dec daily 6am–8:30pm; no service mid-Dec–Apr; one-way 1hr 15min; $29.75/car, $9.25/passenger; ☎902-566-3838 or 800-565-0201, in Canada)*. From Souris a ferry crosses to the Magdalen Islands, PQ *(p 211)*.

General Information

Accommodations and Visitor Information – The official tourist office publishes the annual *Visitors Guide* giving information on history, attractions, festivals, sports, vacation packages and accommodations. A highway map is included. For a free copy contact **Tourism Prince Edward Island**, PO Box 940, Charlottetown, PE, C1A 7M5 ☎800-463-4734 (Canada/US).

Road Regulations – *(Driver's license and insurance requirements p 314.)* Main roads are paved, particularly along the coasts; some roads are either dirt or gravel surface. Speed limits, unless otherwise posted, are 90km/h (55mph) or 80km/h (50mph) on highways and 50km/h (30mph) in urban districts. **Seat belt** use is mandatory. **Canadian Automobile Assn. (CAA)**, Charlottetown ☎902-892-1612.

Time Zone – PEI is on Atlantic Standard Time. Daylight Saving Time is observed from the first Sunday in April to the last Sunday in October.

Taxes – The national GST of 7% *(rebate information p 318)*, and a provincial sales tax of 10% are levied.

Liquor Laws – The legal drinking age is 19. Liquor is sold in government stores. **Recreation** – *p 242*.

Principal Festivals

Jun–Sept	Charlottetown Festival	*Charlottetown*
Jun	Highland Gathering	*Summerside*
	Old Home Week Provincial Exhibition	*Charlottetown*
Jul	Summerside Lobster Carnival	*Summerside*
Aug	International Hydroplane Regatta	*Summerside*
Sept	PEI Festival of the Arts	*Province-wide*

St. John's Island and the British Regime – Renamed St. John's Island under British rule, the island was annexed to Nova Scotia. The land was granted to wealthy Englishmen and military officers, who petitioned the British government to recognize the territory as a separate colony. In 1769 a new administration was established; and in 1799 the colony was renamed Prince Edward Island in honour of the son of King George III of England.
The island was the site of the historic **Charlottetown Conference** in September 1864, the first of several meetings that led to Canadian Confederation in 1867.

The Island Today – Principal industries today are agriculture, tourism and fishing. Agricultural and aquacultural processing forms the backbone of manufacturing on the island, renowned for its dairy products, lobsters and shellfish, and more than 50 varieties of **potatoes**. Annually over 700,000 visitors are drawn to the unhurried pace of life; **farm vacations** are popular, and **lobster suppers**, held during the summer in church and community halls, provide a sampling of fresh regional seafood and abundant garden produce. A 13km/8mi-long **bridge** *(toll)* over Northumberland Strait, scheduled for completion in 1997, will link Borden, PEI with Jourimain Island, New Brunswick, replacing the existing Borden-Cape Tormentine ferry service.

Visiting the Island – Three scenic drives established by the provincial government are a good approach to touring the island. Organized as circuits of the three counties (Prince, Queens and Kings), the routes provide a leisurely, in-depth means of experiencing splendid scenery, charming community life, historical attractions and recreational activities. The main **tourist office** for the island is located at 178 Water Street in Charlottetown *(open May–early Jun daily 8:30am–6pm; mid-Jun–Aug daily 8am–10pm; Sept–mid-Oct Mon–Fri 8am–6pm; rest of the year Mon–Fri 9am–5pm; ☎902-368-5540)*.

CHARLOTTETOWN★★

Pop. 15,396
Map p 280
Tourist Office ☎902-368-4444

Located near the confluence of the West, North and Hillsborough Rivers at Northumberland Strait, this gracious provincial capital is also a thriving commercial centre, its port serving as a funnel for the region's agricultural bounty. Named for the wife of King George III, the city was founded in 1768.

SIGHTS   *1/2 day*

Attractively situated along the water's edge, **Victoria Park** is home to the regal, white Neoclassical **Government House**, designed by Isaac Smith as the lieutenant-governor's official residence *(not open to the public)*. From the shore, expansive **views★** extend across the harbour to the site of Fort Amherst *(p 281)*.

★★ **Province House** – ☞ *At the top of Great George St. Open Jun daily 9am–5pm. Jul–Aug daily 9am–8pm. Sept–mid-Oct daily 9am–5pm. Rest of the year Mon–Fri 9am–5pm. Closed national holidays.* ☞ ☎902-566-7626. A native of Yorkshire, England, Isaac Smith designed this 3-storey sandstone building (1847) in the Georgian style with Neoclassical details. The **Confederation Chamber**, site of the Charlottetown Conference *(above)*, is restored to its 19C appearance with many of the original furnishings. The provincial legislature still meets in the legislative chamber.

★ **Confederation Centre of the Arts** – *Grafton St., adjacent to Province House. Open Jun–Sept Mon–Sat 9am–9pm. Rest of the year Mon–Sat noon–5pm.* ☒ ☞ ☎902-566-1267. Commemorating the centennial of the 1864 Charlottetown Conference, this national memorial arts centre (1964) houses theatres, the provincial archives, display areas and a restaurant. Temporary exhibits in the **art gallery** feature selections from a large collection of works by Canadian artists, and the main theatre hosts the annual **Charlottetown Festival** musical production, *Anne of Green Gables*.

St. Dunstan's Basilica – *Great George St. Open year-round daily 8am–4pm.* ☞ ☎902-894-3486. The twin 61m/200ft spires of this Gothic edifice (1917) gracefully punctuate Charlottetown's skyline. Interior features include fan vaulting, streaked marble, and a stunning rose window from Munich, Germany. The contemporary stained-glass windows in the facade were designed by island native Henry Purdy.

BLUE HERON DRIVE★★

Map below

Encircling most of Queens County and central Prince Edward Island, this scenic drive encompasses the stunning white beaches of the north coast; charming Acadian fishing villages; sights related to *Anne of Green Gables*; and the red cliffs of the southern coast, bordered by Northumberland Strait.

DRIVING TOUR 1 day
90km/118mi circuit indicated by blue and white signs depicting a blue heron. Visitor centre in Charlottetown (p 278).

★ **Prince Edward Island National Park** – ❂ *In Cavendish, 24km/15mi northwest of Charlottetown. Open year-round. Visitor centre at intersection of Rtes 6 and 13; open Jun daily 9am–5pm, Jul–Aug daily 9am–9pm, Sept–mid-Oct daily 9am–5pm. $3. △ ☎902-672-6350.* One of Canada's smallest but most popular national parks stretches for about 40km/25mi along the north shore of the island, fringing the Gulf of St. Lawrence. Interspersed with boardwalks and paths to the water's edge, the **Gulf Shore Parkway** offers displays on shoreline ecology and views of some of eastern Canada's loveliest **beaches**, sand dunes, sandstone cliffs, salt marshes and freshwater ponds. Picnic sites are scattered throughout seaside and woodland areas, and a variety of interpretation programs are available.

Near the park's eastern entrance, a glance to the south reveals **Dalvay-by-the-Sea**, an elegant Victorian structure (1896), formerly the summer home of Standard Oil magnate, Alexander MacDonald, and now a hotel. The lobby features beautiful woodwork and an enormous fireplace with a hearth of local sandstone.

★ **Green Gables House** – *In Cavendish. Rte. 6 west of Rte. 13, in PEI National Park. Open early May–mid-Jun daily 9am–5pm. Late Jun–Aug 30 daily 9am–8pm. Aug 31–Nov 1 daily 9am–5pm. $2.50. ✗ & ☎902-672-6350.* This small green and white farmhouse belonged to relatives of **Lucy Maud Montgomery**, author of *Anne of Green Gables*. During her childhood years in Cavendish, she visited here frequently and used the house as a setting for the novel, which tells the story of an irrepressible orphan girl adopted by a strict but kindly brother and sister living at "Green Gables" farm. Once described by Mark Twain as the "sweetest creation of child life ever written," this story has become popular in 18 languages, and draws summer visitors to the island from as far away as Japan.

Today the refurbished house re-creates scenes from the novel, including Anne's gable bedroom. In the downstairs hallway, Montgomery's typewriter and several family photographs are displayed.

Anne of Green Gables Museum at Silverbush – *In Park Corner, Rte. 20. Open Jun daily 9am–6pm. Jul–Aug daily 9am–8pm. Sept–Oct daily 9am–6pm. $2.50. ✗ & ☎902-436-7329.* Throughout her life, author L. M. Montgomery visited relatives

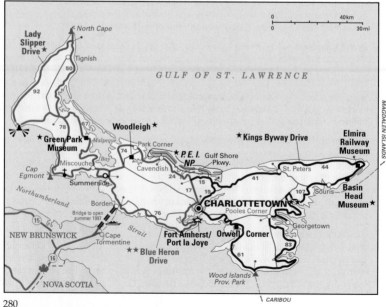

at this spacious house; her 1911 wedding was held in the drawing room. The dwelling and its surroundings appear as settings in the *Anne of Green Gables* series. First editions of the author's books, personal correspondence and family heirlooms are displayed throughout the house.

Malak, Ottawa

Prince Edward Island Coastline

★ **Woodleigh** – *In Burlington, Rte. 234 northeast of Kensington. Open mid-Jun–mid-Oct daily 9am–5pm. $6.50.* ✗ ᨞ ☎*902-836-3401.* Scattered about a pleasant, tree-shaded site are some 17 large-scale replicas of historic British structures. Highlights include an 8m/26ft replica of York Minster Cathedral, complete with 145 glass windows; St. Paul's Cathedral in London; and Scotland's Dunvegan Castle. *Video presentation available on request in the theatre adjacent to the gift shop.*

Fort Amherst/Port la Joye – ᨞ *In Rocky Point, on Blockhouse Point Rd. off Rte. 19. Open mid-Jun–Labour Day daily 10am–6pm. $2.25.* ᨞ ☎*902-675-2220.* The first permanent European settlement on the island was established here by the French in 1720. The British, who captured the area in 1758, erected Fort Amherst, a series of defenses on the site of the original French garrison, and occupied the post until 1768. Today only the earthworks remain—rolling, grass-covered mounds from which sweeping **views**★★ of Charlottetown harbour extend. In the **visitor centre**, displays and a video presentation *(15min)* offer an introduction to the site's history.

KINGS BYWAY DRIVE★

Map p 280

Wandering along the deeply indented bays and harbours of the island's eastern coast, this drive offers a close look at Kings County's vibrant fishing industry. Side roads lead through lush forests past small communities with names such as Cardigan, Greenfield and Glenmartin, that harken to the province's British heritage.

DRIVING TOUR   *1 day*
375km/233mi circuit indicated by purple and white signs depicting a royal crown. Visitor centre at junction of Rtes. 3 and 4 in Pooles Corner.

Orwell Corner Historic Village – *In Orwell, 30km/19mi east of Charlottetown on the Trans-Can Hwy. Open early–mid-Jun Mon–Fri 10am–3pm. Late Jun–Labour Day Tue–Sun 9am–5pm. Early Sept–Oct Mon–Fri 10am–3pm. $3.* ✗ ☎*902-651-2013.* This superbly restored crossroads village, settled in the early 19C by pioneers from Scotland and Ireland, retains the atmosphere and flavour of the island's agricultural origins. Visitors can tour the 1864 **farmhouse**, which also served as post office, general store and dressmaker's shop, along with a church, school, community hall, blacksmith's shop, shingle mill and animal barns. Fiddle music and step dancing are features of the traditional *ceilidh* (KAY-lee) *(Jun–Sept every Wed 8pm).*

★ **Basin Head Fisheries Museum** – *In Basin Head, 10 km/6mi east of Souris on Rte. 16. Open Jun Tue–Fri & Sun 10am–3pm. Jul–Labour Day daily 9am–5pm. Rest of Sept Tue–Fri & Sun 10am–3pm. $3.* ✗ ⟡ ☎902-357-2966. This museum occupies a fine site overlooking the mouth of Northumberland Strait. Boats, nets, hooks, photographs and dioramas illustrate the life and work of an inshore fisherman. Outside, small wooden buildings house a small craft exhibit.

Elmira Railway Museum – *In Elmira, 16km/10mi east of Souris on Rte. 16A. Open Jun Tue–Fri & Sun 10am–3pm. Jul–Labour Day daily 9am–5pm. Rest of Sept Tue–Fri & Sun 10am–3pm. $2.* ⟡ ☎902-357-2481. Formerly the eastern terminus of a railway system linking the island with the continent, this charming station has been transformed into a museum that recounts the railway's 19C–early-20C development. Features include a photographic display highlighting architectural differences among island rail stations, a 1911 station log and still-operational telegraph equipment.

LADY SLIPPER DRIVE★

Map p 280

The picturesque landscape of western Prince Edward Island is fringed with capes and beaches. Named for the province's official flower, this scenic circuit introduces the visitor to shipbuilding at Green Park; the Malpeque Bay, famed for its fine oysters; and fox farming, a major island industry from 1890 to 1939.

DRIVING TOUR *1 day*
288km/179mi circuit indicated by red and white signs depicting a Lady Slipper blossom. Visitor centre on Rte 1A in Wilmot, 2km east of Summerside.

Acadian Museum of Prince Edward Island – *In Miscouche, 8km/5mi west of Summerside, on Rte. 2. Open late Jun–Labour Day Mon–Sat 9:30am–5pm, Sun 1–5pm. Rest of the year Mon–Fri 9:30am–5pm. $2.75.* ⟡ ☎902-436-6237. Erected in 1991, this modern facility for the preservation of Acadian heritage combines an historical museum with a documentation centre for genealogical research. Main gallery dioramas and texts present Acadian history after 1720, incorporating objects from an extensive collection of artifacts, photographs, textiles and journals donated by area families. Audio-visual presentations in the theatre introduce topics such as religion, education and economy. An adjacent gallery presents temporary thematic exhibits of Acadian culture and heritage.

★ **Green Park Shipbuilding Museum** – *In Port Hill, 34km/21mi west of Summerside on Rte. 12. Open Jun Tue–Fri & Sun 10am–3pm. Jul–Labour Day daily 9am–5pm. Rest of Sept Tue–Fri & Sun 10am–3pm. $3.* ☎902-831-2206. Formerly the grounds of an active shipyard, Green Park is today a provincial heritage site commemorating the shipbuilding industry, the island's principal economic activity during the 19C. Erected by the shipyard's owner, **Yeo House** (1865) is a large, steeply gabled Victorian structure restored to reflect the lifestyle of a prominent family of the period. Maps, photographs and tools on display in the **visitor centre** present the art and science of shipbuilding during the industry's 19C heyday.

West Point Lighthouse – *In Cedar Dunes Provincial Park, Rte. 14. Open mid-May–mid-Jun daily 8am–8pm (weekends 9pm). Late Jun–Labour Day daily 8am–9:30pm. Early–late Sept daily 8am–8pm (weekends 9pm). $2.50 (for museum).* ☎902-859-3605. This distinctive 30m/85ft striped lighthouse (1875) was automated by electricity in 1963. A narrow stairway rises past photographs and displays documenting the history of island lighthouses. The tower itself contains numerous examples of lighthouse lenses and lanterns. From the observation platform at the summit, **views** stretch across the shoreline's dark red dunes.

Our Lady of Mont-Carmel Acadian Church – *In Mont-Carmel, on Rte. 11, east of Rte. 124.* Overlooking Northumberland Strait just east of Cap-Egmont, this twin-steepled brick church (1896) replaces two earlier wooden structures, the first of which was built in 1820 as a mission church for the Acadian community of Mont-Carmel. The church's symmetrical facade and rounded interior vaults are reminiscent of religious architecture in France's Poitou region, original home of most of the island's first Acadian settlers.

Newfoundland

Map below

The largest of the Atlantic provinces, Newfoundland consists of a rocky island of the same name and the mountainous mainland of Labrador, with a combined landmass of 405,720sq km/156,648sq mi. The remote shores and wilderness interior of Canada's easternmost province appeal particularly to nature lovers in search of adventure.

Geographical Notes

The Island – Called "The Rock" for its craggy profile, the island of the province has a 9,650km/6,000mi beautiful, deeply indented coastline, studded with bays, coves and islands. In the north and west, the coast is grandiose with towering cliffs and deep fjords *(pp 287 and 288)*. From the heights of the **Long Range Mountains** in the west, a continuation of the Appalachians, the land slopes east and northeast. Parts of the interior are heavily forested; others are expanses of rocky barrens and boggy peatlands, a legacy of glaciers, as are the multitude of lakes and rivers.

Labrador – A rugged land of high mountains (Cirque Mountain, in the **Torngats** of the north, reaches 1,676m/5,500ft), Labrador also possesses coastal settlements nestling under high cliffs, and inland, a barren, largely treeless terrain. Unlike the island, it forms part of the Canadian Shield *(p 16)*. Labrador's 30,000 people reside primarily along the coast and around the mines in its rich iron-ore belt.

The Banks – In Newfoundland "banks" are not money-lending institutions but vast areas of shallow water in the Atlantic to the south and east of the province—usually less than 100m/328ft deep extensions of the continental shelf. For 500 years these waters have attracted fishermen to the fish-breeding grounds. The largest and richest of the grounds is the **Grand Banks**, an area of approximately 282,500sq km/109,073sq mi where the cold Labrador Current meets the warmer Gulf Stream. Sinking below the warmer one, the cold current stirs up plankton on the sea bed. The plankton rises to the surface, attracting great schools of fish.

PRACTICAL INFORMATION

Getting There

By Air – Newfoundland and Labrador are serviced by major domestic and international air carriers such as Air Canada and Canadian Airlines International through Toronto, Montreal and other hubs. Affiliate airlines Air Nova (☎800-4-CANADA, ☎800-776-3000 US), Air Atlantic (☎800-426-7000, Canada/US) and Air Labrador (☎709-753-5593) provide regular connections within the province.

By Boat – Passenger & car ferry service is available from North Sydney, NS to Channel-Port aux Basques *(departs year-round daily; one-way 6hrs 30min, 5hrs in summer; connecting bus service to inland destinations DHL Coachlines ☎709-738-8088)* and to Argentia *(late Jun–Aug Mon, Wed & Fri 7am; Sept 1–13 twice weekly; one-way 14hrs)*. From Lewisporte, NF to GooseBay, Labrador *(departs mid-Jun–Sept twice weekly; one-way 35hrs)*. Passenger service from St. Anthony, NF to Nain, Labrador *(departs weekly)*. For schedules & reservations contact Marine Atlantic, North Sydney, NS ☎902-794-5254 or 800-341-7981 (Canada/US).
The southern coast of Labrador is accessible by ferry from St. Barbe, NF via Blanc-Sablon, PQ *(departs Jul–Aug twice daily; May–Jun & Sept–Oct one-to-two departures daily; Nov–early Jan once daily; no service Jan 3–Apr; one-way 1hr 30min; $17.25/car, $8.50/passenger; Northern Cruiser Ltd., St. John's, NF ☎709-931-2309)*.
Note: Advance reservations are suggested for all ferry services. Fuel tanks must be no more than three-quarters full. For ferry service to **Saint-Pierre and Miquelon** *see p 296.*

General Information

Accommodations and Visitor Information – The government tourist office publishes an annually updated travel guide giving detailed information about attractions and activities, calendar of events, boat and adventure tours, and a listing of accommodations including hospitality homes (private homes that accept paying guests). A copy of this guide, a road map and other useful information are available free of charge from **Department of Tourism, Culture & Recreation**, PO Box 8730, St. John's, NF, A1B 4K2 ☎709-729-2830 or 800-563-6353 (Canada/US).

Road Regulations – *(Driver's license and insurance requirements p 314.)* The Trans-Canada Highway Rte. 1 *(910km/565mi)*, which traverses Newfoundland from Channel-Port aux Basques to St. John's, and most secondary highways are paved. The condition of gravel roads varies according to traffic and weather. Main roads are passable during winter, but it is advisable to check with local authorities before departure (☎709-729-2381, Dec–Mar). **Seat belt** use is compulsory. Speed limits, unless otherwise posted, are: 100km/h (60mph) on four-lane divided highways, 80km/h (50mph) on secondary and 50km/h (30mph) on gravel roads.

Time Zones – Labrador observes Atlantic Standard Time. Newfoundland Standard Time is 30min ahead of Atlantic Standard Time and 1hr 30min ahead of Eastern Standard Time. Daylight Saving Time is observed from the first Sunday in April to the last Sunday in October.

Taxes – In addition to the national 7% GST *(rebate information p 318)*, the province levies a 12% sales tax for which non-residents can request a rebate by contacting: Tax Administration Branch, Department of Finance, PO Box 8720, St. John's, NF, A1B 4K1 ☎709-729-3831.

Liquor Laws – Liquor and wine are available only from government stores except in remote areas where local stores are licensed. Beer is available in most convenience stores. The legal drinking age is 19.

Provincial Holiday *(National Holidays p 319)*

The Queen's Birthday	Monday nearest May 24

Recreation – *p 242.*

Principal Festivals

mid-Feb	**Corner Brook Winter Carnival**	*Corner Brook*
Jul–early-Aug	**Stephenville Festival**	*Stephenville*
Aug	**Royal St. John's Regatta** *(p 292)*	*St. John's*
	Annual Newfoundland and Labrador Folk Festival	*St. John's*
mid-Aug	**Labrador Straits Bakeapple Folk Festival**	*Point Amour*

Newfoundland Today

Fishing Industry – Though herring is also found, **cod** is the traditional catch in the Grand Banks. In recent years, because of depleted stocks, the Canadian government ordered a ban on cod fishing *(p 241)*. Newfoundlanders have always talked about "fishing the banks" however, and the boats they used were called "bankers."

Inshore Fishing – In early summer, the **caplin** "run": these small fish swim ashore to spawn, bringing with them their main predator, the cod. Using large square traps made of netting, a fisherman traditionally earned most of his livelihood during the few weeks of the run. **Cod jigging**, slow and inefficient, is used to a limited extent at other times during the year: shiny lead "jiggers" or baited hooks on small lines attached to a trawl line attract the cod. The use of trawl lines payed out from a boat is known as **longlining**. The method of weighting nets and keeping them vertical with floats is called **gill netting**, a more recent practice. Larger boats called **longliners**, which can stay at sea several days to pursue schools of fish, use either method. Squid, lobster, salmon and caplin (once used only as bait) are taken in as well.

Offshore Fishing – Traditionally, large schooners left the province's ports to fish the banks for months at a time. When schools of fish were located, actual fishing was done from **dories**, small flat-bottomed open craft carried on deck. The catch was either salted on the schooner's deck and stored in the hold ("wet" fishery) or taken ashore and dried on land on wooden racks known as **flakes** ("dry" fishery). The trend since 1945 has been to use draggers, trawlers and longliners instead of schooners and dories because fish can be caught en masse. Filleting plants have replaced flakes, and refrigeration has supplanted salting.

Offshore Oil – Scheduled for completion in 1997, the **Hibernia oil platform**, under construction at Bull Arm, will be the heaviest offshore oil rig manufactured to date. When secured to its drill site some 315km/200mi out in the Grand Banks, the platform will weigh over 1.2 million tonnes/1.3 million tons, heavy enough, it is projected, to withstand collision with the giant icebergs common in these waters. The controversial project, funded both privately and publicly, is estimated to cost nearly $6 billion. Anticipated output when at full production is 125,000 barrels of oil a day—about six percent of the country's total oil production over the next 20 years.

Lifestyle and Customs – Functional rather than fancy characterizes the lives of many Newfoundlanders. About one-quarter of the island's population of 538,349 resides in the capital city of ST. JOHN'S; the remainder live mainly in coastal fishing villages known as **outports**. Traditionally, an outport was any community outside St. John's, but today, with the rise of industrial centres such as Corner Brook, the term is applied to tiny coastal settlements with moored dories and trap skiffs, weather-beaten fishing **stages** (wooden platforms perched on poles above the water for drying fish) and colourful 2-storey "box" houses. In some outports a small "museum" preserves each community's past. Housed in historic homes or commercial buildings (often with a craft shop annexed), these collections of donated artifacts are primarily of local interest. Short on flamboyance, the articles are largely practical, reflective of the modest, hardy lives of the outport inhabitants.

Oral Traditions – Hard times have repeated themselves over the generations of these sea-dependent people, ebbing and flowing with the size of each catch. There's rarely a depression of the human spirit, however. Reserved exuberance abounds. Visitors to Newfoundland are captivated by the wealth of unusual idioms and wonderful accents of its inhabitants. Centuries of isolation have chiselled a character that is independent, individualistic and humourous. Where else are there settlements named Stinking Cove, Useless Bay, Jerry's Nose, Cuckold Cove, Come by Chance and Happy Adventure, or local terms like *tickle* (a narrow waterway)? English is the first language of 98 percent of the islanders, but remarkably varied dialects enrich the provincial tongue. Some have definite Irish overtones; others are reminiscent of England's West Country (Dorset, Devon, Cornwall). Local expressions such as "to have a noggin to scrape" (a very hard task), "to be all mops and brooms" (to have untidy hair) and "long may your big jib draw" (good luck for the future) add colour and humour to every-day conversations.

Rich in tradition, Newfoundlanders possess a wealth of legend, weather lore, folk dances and songs, which attest to their wry perspective on life. Often parodies of British creations, sea shanties such as *Squid-Jiggin' Ground*, *Let Me Fish off Cape St. Mary's*, *Jack Was Every Inch a Sailor* record island character and yearnings with relish, melancholy or humour.

Seafood Specialities – Not surprisingly, cod—eaten fresh, dried or salted—has traditionally been the staple of the provincial diet. **Fish and brewis**, a mixture of boiled salt cod and hardtack (a hard, dry biscuit) soaked overnight, is a traditional dish. Of greater fame is **fried cod tongues**, a dish that should be prepared only with fish caught the same day. Arctic char, salmon, shrimp and halibut are other favourites.

BURIN PENINSULA

Map p 283

The doorstep to a vast offshore fishing industry in the **Grand Banks** *(p 283)*, this barren peninsula of isolated mountain plateaus juts down like a boot into the Atlantic Ocean from the southern coast of Newfoundland between Placentia and Fortune Bays. Just off the "toe" are the island remnants of France's once-great empire in North America: SAINT-PIERRE AND MIQUELON.

DRIVING TOUR

Allow 3 hrs. 203km/126mi south of Trans-Can Hwy. by Hwy. 210 to Fortune.

The drive on Highway 210 is long and deserted until **Marystown** (pop. 6,660), situated on Little Bay. Its huge shipyard *(inaccessible to the public)*, where the trawlers used off Newfoundland's shores are built, is the largest in the province. South of Marystown, Route 210 crosses the peninsula and descends to Fortune Bay, providing views of the southern coast of Newfoundland. Just before entering Grand Bank, there is a view of the south coast and Brunette Island. To the west the coast of the French island of Miquelon is just visible, weather permitting.

Grand Bank – Pop. 3,528. *199km/123mi south of Trans-Can Hwy. by Hwy. 210.* An important fishing centre, this community was once the home of the famous "bankers" *(p 285)*. Some of the houses from that era are examples of the Queen Anne style with their widow's walks or small open rooftop galleries from which women could watch for the return of their men from the sea.

★ **Southern Newfoundland Seamen's Museum** – *Marine Dr. Open Jun–Aug Mon–Fri 9am–4:30pm, weekends 10am–6pm. Rest of the year Mon–Fri 9am–5pm, weekends 12:30–5pm. Closed national holidays.* & ☎709-832-1484. Housed in the former Yugoslavian Pavilion of Montreal's Expo '67, this branch of the Newfoundland Museum network features displays on the history of the Banks fishing industry. Of particular interest are the photographs of ships and fishing, and **models** of the types of ships used. A large glass-encased relief model of Newfoundland shows the banks and the depths of the Atlantic.

Highway 210 continues to **Fortune** (pop. 2,370), another fishing community with an artificial harbour, and the departure point for ferries to the French islands of Saint-Pierre and Miquelon *(p 296).*

THE CAPE SHORE★★

Map p 283

Perhaps Newfoundland's most dramatic coastline, the southwest arm of the Avalon Peninsula from Placentia to St. Bride's delights visitors with its natural wonders and historic sites. Magnificent ocean views and remnants of Europe's territorial struggles await those who travel this isolated shore.

SIGHTS

★ **Castle Hill** – 🐾 *In Placentia, 44km/27mi south of Trans-Can Hwy. by Rte. 100. About 8km/5 mi from Argentia ferry. Open Jun–Labour Day daily 8am–9pm. Rest of the year daily 8:30am–4:30pm. $2.25.* & ☎709-227-2401. This park contains the remains of Fort Royal, built by the French at the turn of the 17C, and rebuilt and renamed Castle Hill by the British. Renowned for its commanding position overlooking the small town of **Placentia** (pop. 1,954), the site affords a **panorama★★** of the city itself, Placentia Bay and **The Gut**—a small channel that separates the bay from two long, deep inlets.

As early as 1500, Placentia's harbour, plentiful fresh water and beaches (where cod could be dried) attracted European fishermen, especially the Basques. To protect their interests in the Newfoundland fishery, the French established a small colony called Plaisance in 1662, building fortifications at sea level and in the hills. After the **Treaty of Utrecht** in 1713 confirmed Newfoundland as British territory, the British kept a small garrison at Placentia until 1811, when it was moved to ST. JOHN'S. Placentia settled down to a prosperous life of fishing and shipbuilding. When the era of wooden ships ended, the shipbuilding industry died, but fishing remains important today. During World War II, construction of a large American base at nearby **Argentia** brought major changes to Placentia. The centre of anti-submarine patrol during the war, Argentia was the site of the famous 1941 off-shore meeting between Churchill and Roosevelt that produced the **Atlantic Charter**, a statement of peace goals adopted in 1942 by the United Nations.

Visit – An interesting **visitor centre** with dioramas, models and panels describes the French and English presence in the area *(open mid-May–Oct only, same hours as the park)*. Visitors walk uphill to the cannons and scant remains of the fort. A pleasant pathway through evergreen forests *(10min walk)* past dry stone walls leads to **Le Gaillardin**, a redoubt built by the French in 1692.

★★ **Cape Shore Drive** – *46km/29mi from Placentia to St. Bride's on Rte. 100. Fuel and food available infrequently. Fog may hamper visibility.* Traversing a straggly, hilly coast, Route 100 is a spectacular ocean drive, providing numerous **views** of beautiful coves, crashing surf and windswept pines. Sparsely populated communities such as picturesque **Gooseberry Cove** *(25km/16mi south of Placentia)* dot the wide inlets of this curving coastline. Colourful flat-topped houses, wool-laden sheep by the roadside and an occasional fishing boat anchored offshore are common scenes until the road turns inland at St. Bride's. The landscape then changes to isolated flatlands and pale-green hillocks, extending to the horizon.

★ **Cape St. Mary's Ecological Reserve** – *Approximately 14km/9mi east of St. Bride's. Leave St. Bride's via Rte 100. Turn right on unpaved road (turn-off for reserve is clearly marked) and continue 8km/5mi. Open year-round. Mid-Jun to mid-Aug is best season to view birds.* Located at the southwest end of the cape, this site has been an official sanctuary for sea birds since 1964 and is one of the largest nesting grounds in North America for **gannets**, relatives of the pelican family. Atop a dramatic shore-line alive with the sights and sounds of an active bird population, its pastoral **setting**★★ is unique.

What is especially thrilling about this preserve is that visitors can get within a few feet of the birds. Providing spectacular **views**★ of the rugged coast, a trail *(25min)* from the lighthouse and visitor centre over short-grass hills reminiscent of moors and often covered with grazing sheep and goats, leads to **Bird Rock**, the precarious domain of hundreds of gannets. Surrounding cliffs attract throngs of noisy black-legged kittiwakes, common murres and razorbills.

GROS MORNE NATIONAL PARK★★

Map p 283

Covering 1,805sq km/697sq mi along the west coast of the province's **Great Northern Peninsula**, this vast, pristine park includes some of the most spectacular scenery in eastern Canada. Designated a UNESCO World Heritage Site in 1987, the park contains geological features that have become a magnet for international scientific research. Consisting of rock 1,250 million years old, the flat-topped **Long Range Mountains** are the northernmost part of the Appalachians. Between them and the coast lies a poorly drained plain, sometimes high above the sea, with a variety of cliffs, sandy shores and little fishing communities.

Access – *44km/27mi northwest of Deer Lake. Take Rte. 430 from Deer Lake to Wiltondale, then Rte. 431 to park, 13km/8mi.*

VISIT *2 days. Map p 288.*
☞ *Open year-round. Hiking, cross-country skiing. $3.* ⌂ *Contact visitor centre (open mid-Jun–Labour Day daily 9am–10pm; rest of the year daily 9am–4pm; closed national holidays & Dec 20–Jan 4; & ☎709-458-2417) near Rocky Harbour for guided boat tours and trail information. Accommodations available throughout local communities.*

★★ **Bonne Bay Area** – *Take Rte. 431 from Wiltondale 50km/31mi to Trout River (food, fuel).* This is a beautiful drive along a deep fjord—a glacial trough whose several arms are surrounded by the squat peaks of the Long Range Mountains. The road travels westward along the **South Arm** from Glenburnie, offering gorgeous **views**★★ of the bay. Fishing boats and small houses are set against the dark blue waters of the arm with the flat-topped mountains rising all around.

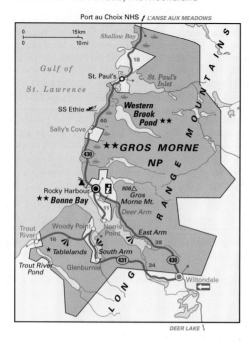

Port au Choix NHS / L'ANSE AUX MEADOWS

DEER LAKE \

From Woody Point, as Route 431 ascends to the west, the red-brown rubble of a desert-like area known as the **Tablelands★** is abruptly visible, a jarring contrast to the lush green vegetation of the rest of the park. These mountains consist of rock that was once part of the earth's mantle—a magnesium and iron layer surrounding the planet's core—and are evidence of plate tectonics, the shifting of the plates within the earth's crust. For a closer look at the Tablelands, stop at the turnoff *(4.5km/2.8 mi from Woody Point)* where a **panel display** describes the geological history of this unique natural feature. This vantage point offers a striking **view** of the barren expanse. A foot path leads from the parking area into the heart of the Tablelands *(for information on guided hikes, contact the visitor centre).* Beyond the little fishing village of Trout River is the long finger lake called **Trout River Pond** *(tour boats depart mid-Jun–mid-Sept daily 9:30am–4pm; round-trip 2hrs 30min; commentary; reservations required; $23; & Tableland Boat Tours ☎709-451-2101).*

Dominating the return drive to Woody Point is the vast bulk of **Gros Morne Mountain** (806m/2,644ft) to the north, the highest point in the park and the park's namesake. *Ferry service from Woody Point to Norris Point may be available; otherwise, visitors must retrace the route to Wiltondale.* From Wiltondale Route 430 travels northeast along **East Arm**, a vantage point for lovely **views★★** of Bonne Bay, and along Deer Arm. For an in-depth preview of the park's unique geology, stop at the **visitor centre** near Rocky Harbour. There videos, talks, literature, photographs and rock displays are provided as well as a telescope for eyeing nearby Gros Morne Mountain *(to reach the summit, take the James Callaghan Trail, 3km/1.8mi south of visitor centre; 6-8hrs round-trip).*

★ From Rocky Harbour to St. Paul's – *40km/25mi by Rte. 430. Fuel and food available in settlements along the way.* Overlooking a wide inlet of Bonne Bay, the small coastal community of **Rocky Harbour** (pop. 1,138) functions as a service and accommodation centre for park visitors.
On a promontory just north of Rocky Harbour, **Lobster Cove Head lighthouse** *(open daily in summer)* provides expansive **views★★** of the town, Gros Morne Mountain, the mouth of the bay and the Gulf of St. Lawrence.
Built on a narrow plain between the sea and the Long Range Mountains, the road affords a pretty drive up the coast past Sally's Cove, one of several little fishing communities along this coastal route. Sometimes the road is at sea level, sometimes higher above a rocky coast, but all along, the Long Range Mountains, just inland, appear like a gigantic step up from the sea because of their cropped tops. Before the turnoff to Western Brook Pond's trailhead, the rusty remains of the **SS Ethie** shipwreck can be seen on the beach. A small panel describes the fate of the ship's 1919 voyage.

★★ Western Brook Pond – *29km/18mi from Rocky Harbour.* Western Brook runs through a spectacular gorge (which, in typical Newfoundland understatement, is called a "pond") in the Long Range Mountains before it crosses the narrow coastal plain and reaches the sea. The pond is flanked by almost vertical cliffs that rise to a desolate boulder-strewn alpine plateau where snow remains in crevices, even in August. Resembling a fjord because of these towering cliffs, this gorge is not a true fjord because it does not extend to the sea; the pond is fresh water. Bonne Bay,

St. Paul's Inlet, Parson's Pond (just north of the park) and the large Bay of Islands *(map p 283)* are fjords. Whether "pond" or "fjord," all of these bodies of water are the result of glacial gouging in the last Ice Age.

A trail leads across the boggy coastal plain *(boardwalks over marshy areas)* to the edge of the pond *(4km/2.5mi walk to boat dock; allow 40min one way)*. Gradually the deep gorge and truncated mountains become clearly visible, weather permitting. The only way to see the interior of Western Brook Pond is to take the **boat trip** *(departs Jun 1–Jun 19 daily 1pm; Jun 20–Sept 6 daily 10am, 1 & 4pm; rest of Sept–mid-Oct daily 1pm; round-trip 2hrs 15min; commentary; reservations required; $23. Norock Assn.* ☎ *709-458-2730; jacket recommended year-round)*. By viewing the varied shapes and exposed surfaces of the cliffs from the vantage point of the boat, at pond level, visitors can sense the geological uniqueness of this ancient glacial valley. The sheer granite cliffs (600m/2,000ft) and the depth of the water (approaching 200m/600ft) can be appreciated. Impressive waterfalls spill over the towering peaks to the cliff bases below.

After Western Brook Pond, the road follows along the coast with views of the mountains, spotted with seasonal snow caught in crevices, and of the shore covered with rocks, boulders and driftwood. The road continues to **St. Paul's**, a small fishing settlement clustered at the mouth of a deep fjord against a backdrop of mountains.

Designated "The Viking Trail," Route 430 exits the park above Shallow Bay and continues north along the coast for another 300km/200mi to L'Anse aux Meadows *(p 290)*, with similar sea views but less dramatic mountain views, since the Long Range peaks are smaller and farther inland. Several native burial grounds are located at the archaeological site in **Port au Choix National Historic Site** *(135km/84mi north of St. Paul's)*.

Western Book Pond

Gros Morne National Park

HEART'S CONTENT Cable Station ★

Map p 283

A little town founded about 1650 on Trinity Bay, Heart's Content is the site of the first successful landing, in 1866, of the **transatlantic telegraph cable**. North America's major relay site for nearly 100 years, the now obsolete station has been converted into a museum by the provincial government.

The landing was the result of years of work by the New York, Newfoundland and London Telegraph Co., led by American financier Cyrus W. Field. The first attempt to lay a cable in 1858 failed after inaugural messages were sent between Queen Victoria and US President James Buchanan. A second attempt in 1865 also failed. Finally in the following year, Field successfully used the ocean liner *Great Eastern* to lay the cable between Valencia, Ireland and Heart's Content, where it joined a cable to New York. Messages initially cost $5 a word, and the station handled 3,000 messages a day. Improved communications technology led to the station's eventual closing in 1965.

VISIT *1.5hrs*

58km/36mi north of Trans-Can Hwy. by Rte. 80, Avalon Peninsula. Open mid-Jun–mid-Oct daily 10am–5:30pm. Rest of the year Mon–Fri 9am–4:30pm. ☎*709-729-0592 or 709-583-2160.* Displays tell the story of communications with special emphasis on the cable's impact on communications. There is a **film** *(20min)* and special section on the laying of the transatlantic cables, the part played by the *Great Eastern* and the importance of Heart's Content. Costumed guides are on site for tours of the replica of the first cable office (1866) and operating room. The original equipment can be compared to the complex equipment in use at the station's closing in 1965.

L'ANSE AUX MEADOWS★★

Map p 283

On a grassy ledge facing Epaves Bay at the northernmost tip of Newfoundland's Great Northern Peninsula, the remains of what is the oldest European settlement in North America authenticated to date are preserved for posterity. This remote site has been included on UNESCO's World Heritage List as a property of universal value.

Historical Notes

The Vikings Explore – By AD 900 the Vikings (also known as the Norse) from present-day Scandinavia had settled in Iceland, and from there explored Greenland, Baffin Island and beyond. The account of a land sighting by a Greenland-destined ship blown off course inspired **Leif Ericsson**, then residing in Greenland, to go exploring. About AD 1000 Ericsson landed at a fertile spot and built a settlement for the winter. He named the location "Vinland" for the wild grapes his crew is said to have found there. This story is preserved in two Norse tales: the *Saga of the Greenlanders* and the *Saga of Eric the Red*, which were communicated by word of mouth for hundreds of years before being recorded.

In Search of Vinland – Though many scholars have tried to find Vinland, its location is unknown. Generally thought to be on the southeastern coast of the US because of the grapes, this location was, however, too far for ships to have sailed in the time suggested by the sagas. Then in 1960, **Helge Ingstad**, a Norwegian explorer and writer, and his archaeologist wife, **Anne Stine**, began a systematic search of the coast from New England northward. Led to a group of overgrown mounds near L'Anse aux Meadows by a local resident, they excavated them from 1961 to 1968. Foundations of eight sod buildings of the type the Norse built in Iceland were uncovered and several artifacts undeniably Norse in origin were found. Evidence of iron working—an art unknown to the North American Indian—was unearthed. Samples of bone, turf and charcoal were carbon dated to around AD 1000.

L'Anse aux Meadows

Though impossible to prove it is the elusive Vinland (no one can envisage grapes growing in Newfoundland), L'Anse aux Meadows is certainly a Norse settlement, and the only one ever discovered to date in North America. Experts believe the settlement was a base of encampment for further exploration, especially trips south in search of timber and trading goods. Occupied by about 100 men and women, the camp was probably deserted after five or ten years. Newfoundland's harsh conditions, coupled with the growing accessibility to southern European markets, most likely led to its abandonment.

Access – *453km/281mi north of Trans-Can Hwy. by Rtes. 430 and 436.*

VISIT   *3hrs*

☞ *Open mid-Jun–Labour Day daily 9am–8pm. Early Sept–last Fri in Sept daily 9am–5pm; phone in advance to confirm Sept hours.* ♿ ☎709-623-2608. In the **visitor centre** displays depict the Norse way of life and what a settlement might have looked like, but the highlight is the collection of artifacts found on-site. A stirring **film** *(28min)* on the Ingstads' search provides an enlightening introduction to the visit. Completely excavated, the site has been preserved as grassy borders that outline the foundations of the original structures. The layout of the dwellings, work buildings and a smithy (the location of the earliest-known iron smelting in North America) can be clearly distinguished. Nearby, three **sod buildings**—a long house, a building and a workshed—have been faithfully reconstructed.

Inside, wooden platforms that served as beds line the walls. Firepits are placed at intervals in the middle of the earthen floors. A few animals skins and iron cooking utensils suggest the spartan existence of the inhabitants.

At the end of "The Viking Trail," **St. Anthony** (pop. 3,164), a large service centre, is the nearest city *(food, accommodations and air service)* to L'Anse aux Meadows. At the turn of the century, a British doctor, **Sir Wilfred Grenfell** (1865-1940), began his medical missionary work in the area, including Labrador. He became world renowned in his time, and today St. Anthony preserves his memory through the hospital he established, a cooperative craft shop and the house local residents built for him. Now called the **Grenfell House Museum** *(open May–Sept daily 9am–7pm; rest of the year by appointment only; $2;* ☎709-454-8596*),* the home contains displays about his social involvement in the province, his medical practice and his personal life.

ST. JOHN'S★★

Pop. 95,770
Map p 283
Tourist Office ☎709-729-2830

One of the oldest cities in North America, the capital of Newfoundland sits on the northeast arm of the Avalon Peninsula, facing the expansive Atlantic Ocean. This historic sea port owes its founding to a fine natural harbour that now services an international shipping trade.

Historical Notes

Early Years – According to tradition **John Cabot** entered the harbour on Saint John's day in 1497. Whether this claim is true or not, it has been established that, by the turn of the century, ships from several European countries were using the harbour as a fishing base. Under charter from Elizabeth I of England, **Sir Humphrey Gilbert** (c.1537-83) sailed to North America, arriving in St. John's harbour in 1583. Finding the crews of several countries assembled in one place, he seized the opportunity to declare Her Majesty's sovereignty, and thus is credited with giving England its first possession in the New World. Before his death at sea, Gilbert reputedly joined in the customary celebrations in St. John's of "fishing admiral" elections. Determined to maintain their fishing monopolies, England's West Country merchants *(p 238)* opposed settlement of Newfoundland, aided by the captains of their ships—the fishing admirals whose often harsh and abusive rule discouraged prospective settlers. From 1675 to 1677 a formal ban on settlement was in effect. But gradually people associated with the growing fishing industry began to take up year-round residence.

The Anglo-French Wars – Fear of French expansion changed the attitude of the British government toward permanent settlement. The French had established fortifications at Placentia in 1662 and proceeded to mount attacks on British harbours, especially St. John's. When a French force from Placentia destroyed St. John's in 1696, the British realized they must have more settlers—permanent residents—to defend their territory. St. John's fell twice again to the French, with the final battle in 1762 at the end of the Seven Years' War, though the city was recaptured soon afterwards. These attacks prompted the British to fortify the harbour entrance and Signal Hill (*p 293*), a strategic promontory between the sea and the city, but St. John's was never again threatened.

Devastating Fires – In the 19C the capital suffered five fires that virtually wiped out the entire community each time. The first in 1816 was followed by others in 1817, 1819, 1846, and the most extensive of all in 1892. A photo taken by Sir Wilfred Grenfell (*p 291*) at the time shows the twin towers of the Basilica of St. John the Baptist, one of the few structures still partially standing amid the devastation. Each time, the city was rebuilt, primarily in prevailing architectural styles such as Gothic Revival and, after the 1892 fire, Second Empire, styles still evident in the historic structures of the city today. The rapid expansion of St. John's as a commercial centre during the 19C was reversed each time by the fires.

Confederation and the 20C – St. John's was a wealthy city in the early 20C and during World War II when it served as a base for North American convoys. After the war the Dominion of Newfoundland's decision to enter Confederation (*p 240*) resulted in a decline in the city's economy, despite a substantial infusion of federal funds. Its industries collapsed as cheaper Canadian manufactured goods entered Newfoundland. Port activity suffered and St. John's importance as a fish-exporting centre was reduced as major firms abandoned the salt-fish trade for growing wholesale consumer markets.

Today the city's harbour serves as a supply and repair depot for international and local shipping. Over 1,000 commercial vessels of approximately 22 nationalities annually visit this major refueling station. Further resurgence is anticipated as a result of the discovery of offshore oil reserves in recent years.

Regatta Day – Each year **Quidi Vidi** (KID-dy VID-dy) **Lake** is the site of St. John's Regatta, the oldest continuing sporting event in North America (since 1826). Held on the first Wednesday in August (or the first fine day thereafter), the regatta is probably the only civic holiday decided that morning. The local population waits for the cry, "The races are on!" and then crowds the lakeshore to watch competitors row the 2.6km/1.6mi course, the major event of the all-day carnival.

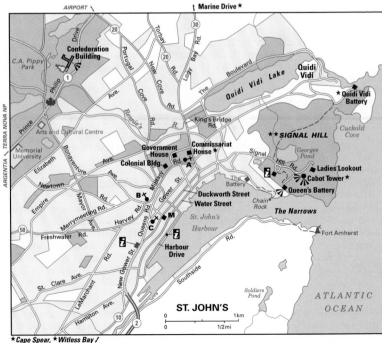

★Cape Spear, ★Witless Bay /

★★ HARBOUR AND OLD CITY *1 day. Map p 292.*

The city's **site**★ borders a harbour almost landlocked except for a slim passage to the ocean known as **The Narrows**. Only about 207m/680ft wide, this channel is flanked by 150m/500ft cliffs rising on the north side to form Signal Hill. For about 1.6km/1mi, the harbour widens to nearly 800m/.5mi, surrounded by the steep slopes on which the city is built. Parallel to the water, **Harbour Drive** skirts the busy dock where ships from Portugal, Spain, Poland, Russia and Japan as well as Canadian ships are often berthed. Narrow streets lined with brightly painted wooden houses, topped with flat or mansard roofs, ascend the hills. Perpendicular to them, the main thoroughfares of the old city, **Water** and **Duckworth Streets**, contain restaurants, shops and banks. Especially colourful, **George Street** is home to several pubs and eateries.

★ **Newfoundland Museum [M]** – *Duckworth St. Open Jul–Aug Mon–Fri 9am–5pm, weekends 10am–6pm. Rest of the year Mon–Fri 9am–5pm, weekends 12:30–5pm. Closed national holidays.* ☎709-729-2329. Offering an insightful introduction to the province, this small museum is devoted to Newfoundland's history and prehistory. The ground-floor gallery permits a behind-the-scene's view of the museum through its natural history collection. The second floor features displays on native cultures, notably those of the Beothuk Indians and Labrador Inuit. On the third floor re-created rooms and reconstructions such as a fishing "stage" with its flakes, ropes and nets depict the life of European settlers from the 18C onward. Replicas of a schoolroom and grocery store of the late 19C are particularly noteworthy.

★ **Commissariat House** – *King's Bridge Rd. Open mid-Jun–mid-Oct daily 10am–5:30pm. Rest of the year by appointment (☎709-729-0592).* ▣ ☎709-729-6730. Dating from 1821 this large clapboard house with its tall chimneys was one of the few buildings to escape the 19C fires. Used for many years by the Commissariat—the department responsible for supplying the military post of St. John's with non-military provisions—the house also served as the local government pay office. After 1871 it became the rectory for adjacent **Church of St. Thomas [A]**, an elegantly simple edifice (1836) of painted wood.

Restored to reflect the 1830 period, the house contains the commissariat offices and kitchen *(ground floor)*, entertaining rooms and bedrooms *(second floor)*. Reconstructed on the grounds, a **coach house** lodges an exhibit on the restoration process.

Within walking distance *(Military Rd.)* stand two other historic structures: the residence of the lieutenant-governor called **Government House**, a Georgian stone building (1830) surrounded by pleasant grounds *(only the grounds can be visited without appointment; for house tour,* ☎709-729-4494*)* and the former seat of the provincial assembly, the **Colonial Building** *(open year-round Mon–Fri 9am–4:15pm & Wed 6:30–9:45pm; open first Tue of each month 2–4:15pm only;* &▣ ☎709-729-3065*)*, a limestone structure with a Neoclassical portico (1850), which now houses the provincial archives *(access weekdays only; no guided tours)*.

Basilica of St. John the Baptist [B] – *Corner Harvey Rd., Military Rd. and Bonaventure Ave. Open year-round Mon–Fri 8am–4:30pm (Wed 8pm), Sat 8am–6:30pm, Sun 8:30am–12:30pm. Closed national holidays except for mass.* ▣& ☎709-754-2170. Situated on the highest point of the ridge above the city, this twin-towered Roman Catholic church has become a landmark, clearly distinguishable from the harbour, Signal Hill and other vantage points. Opened for worship in 1850, the basilica has an ornate interior with statuary and altar carving.

Cathedral of St. John the Baptist [C] – *Gower St. between Church Hill and Cathedral Rd. Open Jul–Aug Mon–Sat 10am–5pm & for services. Rest of the year by appointment.* ✗ *(Jul–Aug weekdays 2–5pm)* ☎709-726-5677. This imposing stone structure was originally designed in 1843 by noted British architect **Sir George Gilbert Scott** (1811–78). Destroyed by fire in 1892, the Anglican church was reconstructed only in this century, a good example of Gothic Revival architecture with a finely sculpted interior, wooden vaulted ceilings and **reredos**, an ornamental stone or wooden partition behind an altar.

★★ **Signal Hill** – Topped by Cabot Tower, Signal Hill is formed of cliffs rising steeply at the mouth of the harbour. A natural lookout commanding the sea approach, the hill permits splendid views of the city and environs by day and night.
Despite its obvious strategic value, Signal Hill was not strongly fortified until the Napoleonic Wars (1803–15). Traditionally used as a signal station to warn of enemy ships, the hill acted in later years as a means to alert merchants to the

arrival of their fleets. In 1901 **Guglielmo Marconi** chose the site for an experiment to prove that radio signals could be transmitted long distances by electromagnetic waves. When he received the letter "S" in Morse code from Poldhu in Cornwall, England—a distance of 2,700km/1,700mi—he made history.

Visit – ☞ *Open mid-May–early Jun daily 8:30am– 4:30pm. Mid-Jun–Labour Day daily 8:30am–8pm. Early Sept–mid-Oct daily 8:30am– 4:30pm. $2.25.* ⅃ ▣ ☎*709-772-5367.* The **visitor centre** contains artifacts, dioramas, audiovisuals and panels on the history of Newfoundland, emphasizing the development of St. John's.

Completed in 1898 to memorialize the quadcentenary of John Cabot's visit to Newfoundland, **Cabot Tower★** also commemorates the diamond jubilee of Queen Victoria's accession. Inside, displays on Signal Hill are complemented by information on communications, including a section about Marconi. The summit of the tower affords a **panorama★★★** of the city, the harbour and the coastline as far as Cape Spear, the most easterly point in North America *(p 295)*.

A path leads to **Ladies Lookout**, the crown of the hill (160m/525ft) and a vantage point offering views of the surroundings. From **Queen's Battery**—the fortification (1833) that dominates the Narrows—there is a good **view★** of the harbour.

St. John's

Below is Chain Rock—a white pillar in the Narrows from which a chain was stretched across the harbour entrance in the 18C to keep enemy vessels out. On the other side of the Narrows stand the remains of Fort Amherst (1763) now housing a lighthouse.

From mid-July through August, students in the 19C uniforms of the Royal Newfoundland Regiment perform a **military tattoo** *(Wed, Thu, Sat, Sun weather permitting; 45min)* consisting of fife and drum corps and military drill near the Queen's Battery. Derived from a Dutch word, *tattoo* is a bugle or drum signal to call soldiers to quarters at night.

ADDITIONAL SIGHTS *Map p 292*

★ **Quidi Vidi Battery** – *Take King's Bridge Rd. Turn right on Forest Rd. When road becomes Quidi Vidi Village Rd., drive 2km/1.2mi to Cuckhold's Cove Rd. Turn right. Open mid-Jun–mid-Oct daily 10am–5:30pm. Rest of the year by appointment (*☎*709-729-0592).* ▣ ☎*709-729-2977.* Built by the French during their occupation of St. John's in 1762, this emplacement, with a colonial-style wooden house at its centre, stands above the community. In the early 19C the British tried to move fishermen away from the inlet and block the channel since it provided a means of attacking St. John's from the rear. The fishermen refused to budge, so the plan was abandoned and the battery strengthened. Restored to the early-19C period, the house re-creates the living quarters of soldiers stationed there.

Below is the tiny fishing community of **Quidi Vidi**, which has a narrow channel connecting to the larger Quidi Vidi Lake, site of the annual St. John's Regatta (*p 292*).

Confederation Building – *Prince Philip Dr. Open year-round Mon–Fri 8:30am–4:30pm. Closed national holidays. Information office on ground floor.* ✕ ♿ 🅿 ☎709-729-2300. Newfoundland's Parliament and some provincial government offices are housed in this imposing building. Constructed in 1960 and expanded in 1985, the edifice stands high above the city, providing a good **view** from its front entrance of the harbour and Signal Hill. When in session the **legislative assembly** can be observed (*sessions Feb–May Mon–Fri, third floor Visitors' Gallery*). Note that the government benches are to the left of the Speaker's chair. Accepted practice elsewhere is for the government to sit on the right. When the Newfoundland Assembly met in the Colonial Building (*p 293*), there was only one fireplace—to the left of the Speaker. The governing body exercised their prerogative and sat by the fire. The tradition remains.

EXCURSIONS

★ **Cape Spear** – 🖝 *Map p 283. About 11km/7mi south; follow Water St. to Leslie St. Turn left at Leslie St. Go over bridge, continue straight after stop sign, following the road (Hwy. 11). Grounds open year-round. Visitor centre open mid-May–Sept daily 10am–5:45pm.* ☎709-722-4210 or 709-722-5367. At longitude 52°37'24", Cape Spear is North America's most easterly point. On clear days there are marvelous **views**★ of the coast and of the entrance to St. John's harbour. Whales can usually be seen in the waters off the cape seasonally (*Jun–Sept*).
Walkways from the parking lot lead to the actual point, the visitor centre, an operational lighthouse (*not open to the public*) and the World War II battery where gun emplacements and bunkers remain. The visitor centre features a small display on the function and evolution of lighthouses. Restored to evoke the life of a lighthouse keeper in the 1840s, the domed, square **1835 lighthouse**★ (*visit by 30min guided tour only, mid-May–Sept daily 10am–5:45pm*) is the province's oldest lighthouse.
The return trip to St. John's (*30km/19mi*) can be made via the villages of Maddox Cove and **Petty Harbour** (pop. 974), the latter a pleasant fishing village with fishing shacks and flakes—wooden racks used to dry the fish.

★ **Witless Bay Ecological Reserve** – *Map p 283. Disembarkation on the islands is not permitted. They can be viewed only by boat. Embarkation from town of Bay Bulls, 30km/19mi south of St. John's via Rte. 10. Then watch for directional signs of your chosen boat tour company to the dock. (Shuttle service to Bay Bulls available from major hotels in St. John's.) Departs May–Oct daily 9:30am–6:30pm; round-trip 2hrs 30min; commentary; reservations required; $30; ✕ ♿ Bird Island Charters* ☎709-753-4850. *Departs mid-May–mid-Oct daily 10am–6:30pm; round-trip 2hr 30min; commentary; $28; Gatherall's* ☎709-334-2887. As feeding and nesting sites, the fish-filled waters and shore islands of Witless Bay attract thousands of sea birds annually. Three barren islets house the bird population: Great, Green and Gull Islands. In summer common murres, greater black-backed gulls, black guillemots and blacked-legged kittiwakes are plentiful. The **Atlantic puffin** colony here is reputedly the largest on the east coast of North America. Tour boats get as close as possible to two of the rocky isles where hundreds of sea birds skim the water, dive, circle overhead or light in the crevices and crannies of the rocks.
An additional highlight of the cruise is **whale watching**★★ (*late spring and summer*). The reserve is a seasonal feeding area for humpback, minke, pothead and fin whales, particularly in summer. Good opportunities to view icebergs at close range may also occur (*late spring and early summer*).

★ **Marine Drive** – *12km/8mi north on Hwys. 30 and 20. Leave St. John's on Logy Bay Rd. (Rte. 30). After 5.5 km/3mi, turn right to Marine Dr.* A pleasant drive up the coast through residential areas north of St. John's, the road ascends and descends, affording endless views of the sea, headlands, cliffs, beaches, boats and fields. The **view**★ from **Outer Cove** is especially lovely. At **Middle Cove** there is an accessible beach, good for strolling along the shore.

SAINT-PIERRE AND MIQUELON*

(France)
Pop. 6,392
Map p 283
Tourist Office ☎508-41-23-84

Few people realize that part of France lies off the coast of North America on tiny islands 48km/30mi by boat from Newfoundland. The two principal islands—Saint-Pierre, and the larger Miquelon, connected by a long sand bar to what was once a third island, Langlade—are home to a French-speaking population. A decidedly Continental flavour pervades these rocky and remote shores.

Historical Notes – Cod fishing is the reason for settlement on these islands. From the early 16C, the archipelago was used as a base for Basque and Breton fishermen working the Grand Banks. By the Treaty of Paris in 1763, it became official French territory, but ownership changed repeatedly as France and England fought for hegemony on the continent. Although France was the loser in this battle, she retained these islands as a *pied à terre* for her fishing fleets.

During US prohibition (1920-33), the islands experienced brief prosperity as a "rum-running" centre. Today only tourism adds to income from the fishing industry. Until 1976 the islands were an overseas French territory. Now they are a *collectivité territoriale* of France, sending a *député* to the French Parliament and a member to the Senate.

VISIT *2 days*

Passenger ferry from Fortune to Saint-Pierre island: departs from Fortune May 1–Sept 30 daily 2:45pm. Next day departs 1pm from Saint-Pierre. One-way 1hr 10min. Commentary. Reservations required. Round-trip $59.95. & Lake's Travel Inc. in Fortune ☎709-832-2006. Warning: the sea crossing can be rough.

Regular flights from St. John's by Provincial Airlines Ltd. ☎709-576-1800. Fog can delay flights. Air service from Sydney and Halifax, NS and Montreal, PQ provided by Air Saint-Pierre. For information & reservations Air Saint-Pierre ☎508-41-47-18 in Saint-Pierre, or Canadian Airlines International ☎800-665-1177 (Canada), ☎800-426-7000 (US).

English is not commonly spoken on the islands. Telephone operators and tourist office staffs are bilingual, however. For accommodations, contact the **Regional Tourist Agency Saint-Pierre**, *C.P. 4274 Place de General de Gaulle, 97500 Saint-Pierre & Miquelon, Amérique du Nord,* ☎011-508-41-23-84.

★ **Saint-Pierre** – From the sea Saint-Pierre appears to be a desolate island of stunted trees and low plants. Upon arrival in the harbour of the island's capital and administrative centre, also named Saint-Pierre, visitors can sense a striking cultural difference from the rest of North America. Lining the waterfront, tall stone buildings house pastry shops, fine restaurants and boutiques stocked with imported goods; the streets are narrow and full of French cars.

At the entrance to the harbour sits the picturesque islet of **Ile-aux-Marins**★ *(accessible from Saint-Pierre by 10min ferry ride)*, once a community of over 800 inhabitants active in cod fishing. Villagers progressively abandoned the site for Saint-Pierre whose fishing industry continued to modernize.

Today the few remaining houses on Ile-aux-Marins are primarily vacation homes for Saint-Pierre residents. Centered in the old schoolhouse, the **museum** contains a highly poetic presentation of isle history through artifacts and memorabilia *(open May–Sept daily 2–5pm; 20FF;* ☎508-41-30-35). The treeless terrain permits good **views** of Saint-Pierre and the remains of one of the more than 600 shipwrecks that have occurred in the archipelago.

Miquelon and Langlade – *Boat departures to Miquelon and Langlade available from Saint-Pierre. In summer, daily ferry to Langlade. Transportation by shuttle van to the village of Miquelon may be arranged (contact Tourist Agency Saint-Pierre above).* Except for the small working town (pop. 709) of the same name, the northern island of Miquelon is untouched moorland of soft hills and long beaches. Along the unpaved road from Miquelon to Langlade (25km/16mi), herds of shaggy wild horses may be spotted roaming the deserted meadows. At low tide seals can be seen lying on the rocks of **Grand Barachois** and a variety of sea birds frequenting the shores. The road crosses the isthmus known as the Dune of Langlade, a sand bar formed in part by debris from the numerous shipwrecks that have occurred since 1800. Situated at the southern end is the "island" of Langlade, largely uninhabited except for a tiny settlement in the hills above the ferry landing. Along the east side of the dune, a wide beach stretches out in the vicinity of Anse du Gouvernement.

TERRA NOVA NATIONAL PARK★

Map p 283

Scarred by glaciers of the past, this 396sq km/153sq mi area on the shores of Bonavista Bay is a combination of rolling country and indented coastline. Deep fjords or "sounds" reach inland, and in early summer these coastal waters are dotted with icebergs that float down with the Labrador Current. The Trans-Canada Highway bisects the park with some good views of the sounds, but visitors must leave the highway to truly appreciate its natural beauty.

Access – *On Trans-Can Hwy. 58km/36mi from Gander, or 210km/130mi from St. John's.*

VISIT *1 day*
◈ *Open year-round. $3/day use fee. Visitor centre open mid-May–early Jun daily 9am–5pm. Mid-Jun–Labour Day daily 8am–8pm. Early Sept–mid-Oct daily 9am–5pm.*
⚠ ♿ ☎*709-533-2801.*

★★ **Bluehill Pond Lookout** – *7km/5mi from park's north entrance. Turn onto gravel road and continue approximately 2km/1mi to the observatory platform.* From the lookout platform there is a **panorama**★★ of the whole park—deep inlets, cliffs, rocks, lakes, forest, bog and hills. To the south Newman Sound and the ocean, scattered with icebergs *(in season),* can clearly be seen in good weather.

★ **Newman Sound** – *12km/8mi from park's north entrance, take road to the visitor centre and Newman Sound. About 1.5km/1mi to the trail.* The beauty of this sound—a deep inlet with a sandy beach—can be appreciated by taking the walking trail along its wooded shore. Seasonal wildflowers and tiny seashells complement the setting.

Ochre Lookout – *18km/11mi from park's north entrance; take gravel road to the tower, about 3km/2mi. Observation deck.* From this lookout tower, another **panorama**★ allows visitors to comprehend the vastness of the park. At this height, Clode and Newman Sounds are clearly visible, weather permitting.

TRINITY★★

Pop. 326
Map p 283

Situated on a hilly peninsula jutting into Trinity Bay, this charming seaside community has a lovely **setting**★ with **views** of the sea, rocks, fields and the small protected harbour. One of the oldest settlements in Newfoundland, the village evokes a feeling of a bygone era with its narrow streets, tiny gardens and colourful "box" houses.

Sufficiently established in 1615, the town became the site of the first Admiralty Court in Canada's history. Sir Richard Whitbourne was sent from Britain to settle disputes between the resident fishermen and those who crossed the Atlantic just for the season. In time, Trinity rivaled St. John's in socio-economic standing, but receded in importance when the latter became the provincial capital. Today a

Cape Bonavista Lighthouse

W. Sturge/Government of Newfoundland

small fishing industry and tourism are its mainstays. It is a popular area for **whale watching** *(departures Jun–Labour Day daily 6am–6pm, weather permitting; minimum 6 people; round-trip 3hrs; commentary; reservations required; $44; Ocean Contact Ltd.* ☎*709-464-3269).*

Access – *74km/46mi northeast of Trans-Can Hwy. by Rte. 230. Turn off Rte. 230 for 5km/3mi.*

VISIT *1 day*

Located in a restored house overlooking the harbour, the **visitor centre** *(open mid-Jun–mid-Oct daily 10am–5:30pm;* ☎*709-464-2042)* has displays presenting the community's history. They chronicle Trinity's rise to prominence from the mid-18C to the early 19C as a center of commerce and society, only to be eclipsed by St. John's in the 1850s. Housed in a seven-room "salt box" dating to the 1880s, the **Trinity Museum and Archives** *(open mid-Jun–mid-Sept daily 11am–8pm)* contains local artifacts and historical documents.

The **Hiscock House** *(open mid-Jun–mid-Oct daily 10am–5:30pm;* ☎*709-464-2042)* has been restored to its early-1900s appearance and contains some original furnishings of the Hiscock family for whom the home was built in 1881.

In a pastoral setting with the sea in the background, **St. Paul's Anglican Church** (1892) stands as a distinctive village landmark. The 31m/102ft clock spire of this large wooden house of worship towers above the town, visible from all vantage points. A small graveyard adjoins the property.

In use for over 150 years, the **Holy Trinity Roman Catholic Church** is distinguished by its detached belfry as well as the clean simplicity of its elegant tower.

EXCURSION TO CAPE BONAVISTA

From Trinity, Route 230 northbound continues inland and returns to the sea at Port Union (pop. 638) and Catalina (pop. 1,205), two fishing communities set along the shore. At Catalina Route 237 crosses the peninsula, ending at Amherst Cove, where Route 235 continues northward to the cape town of Bonavista *(52km/ 31mi north of Trinity).*

Bonavista – Pop. 4,597. This large seaside town is another fishing community with houses set around an outer harbour protected by a breakwater and a shel-tered inner harbour for small boats.

Throughout the 16C, European fishing fleets used the harbour. By about 1600 the area had become a British settlement and remained so, despite several attempts by the French to capture it in the 18C.

Situated by the sea toward the capeside of town, the .6ha/1.5 acre **Mockbeggar Property** *(open mid-Jun–mid-Oct daily 10am–5:30pm;* ☎*709-468-7300)* features a barn, a storage building and the Bradley House. Restored to the 1930s period, the house contains the personal belongings of prosperous local businessman and senator, Frederick Gordon Bradley.

From the town drive about 5km/3mi on Rte. 235, which becomes Church St. Continue past town hall over bridge and bear right at fork.

★ **Cape Bonavista** – Supposedly named Bonavista ("good view") by explorer John Cabot in 1497, the cape is a superb setting with pounding waves, a clear blue sea and interesting rock formations.

A drive through fields with **views** of the sea leads to the remote tip of the cape. A **statue** of Cabot commemorates his first North American landing, though recent research has cast doubt on the authenticity of this claim. Although he sailed under British colours, Cabot was Italian by birth. Completed in 1843 the **lighthouse★** *(open mid-Jun–mid-Oct daily 10am–5:30pm;* ☎*709-468-7444)* has been restored by the provincial government to portray a lightkeeper's living quarters in the 1870s. Exhibits include the construction and restoration of the lighthouse, the operation of the lamps and the lightkeeper's duties. There are sweeping **views** of the rocky coast from the lighthouse itself.

Times given in this guide are approximate. When given with the distance, times allow the visitor to enjoy the scenery; when given for sightseeing, times are intended to provide an idea of the possible length of a visit.

298

Northwest Territories

Dan Heringa/ED&T/GNWT

ontrary to the misconception that the Canadian North is a frozen wilderness, this spectacular continental rooftop abounds in varied landscape: Arctic coastline, myriad lakes, meandering rivers, massive glaciers and polar expanses, all transformed by the light of the midnight sun. A vast region encompassing over a third of Canada, the Territories sustain less than one percent of the country's population. Except for the capital city of YELLOWKNIFE, few large settlements exist in this otherwise frontier wilderness, best suited for lovers of adventure, nature and indigenous cultures. Its planned partitioning before the turn of the century will result in native administration of ancestral lands (*Nunavut p 302*).

Geographical Notes

Landscape – Comprising lands above the 60th parallel (except parts of Quebec and Labrador), the Territories stretch from Hudson Bay to the Yukon. They include the Arctic archipelago between the mainland and the North Pole, and the Hudson and James Bay islands south of the parallel. Even larger prior to 1905, the Territories also encompassed most of Alberta, Saskatchewan, Manitoba, northern Ontario and Quebec.

Mountains border this immense northland on two sides. In the east stand the glacier-strewn peaks of Baffin, Bylot, Devon and Ellesmere Islands. In the west rise the Mackenzie, Selwyn and Richardson Ranges—part of the rugged western backbone of North America. East of the Mackenzie Mountains is a tongue of lowlands, an extension of the plains of central Canada. Down this tongue runs the great Mackenzie River. East of the lowlands lies the scarred face of the Canadian Shield, pitted with lakes. Glaciers that retreated from this region 10,000 years ago scoured and gouged the ancient rocks, leaving behind an intricate pattern of lakes and deep coastal fjords that still exists today. Glacial debris—huge boulders, piles of moraine, **eskers** (narrow ridges of sand and gravel) and **drumlins** (elliptical-shaped hills inclining in the direction of the glacier's retreat)—bear witness to the region's geological history.

Permafrost – After the last Ice Age, a layer of permanently frozen earth developed in all regions where the ground remains at or below 0°C/32°F for two or more years (at least 40 percent of Canada). Permafrost, as it is known, generally starts about 0.3m/1ft or more below the surface and can be very shallow or as much as 370m/1,200ft deep, as at Resolute on Cornwallis Island.

Vegetation – The tree line crosses the Territories diagonally northwest to southeast from the MACKENZIE DELTA to Hudson Bay at the Manitoba border. South and west of this line extends the **boreal forest** of spruce, poplar, tamarack and jack pine. To the north and east is the **tundra**, sometimes called "the barren lands" for its bleak look in winter and lack of trees. In summer dwarf shrubs, tiny flowers of all hues and lichens—flat, rootless growths, part fungus, part algae that survive where no other plant could possibly grow—thrive in the surface ground above the permafrost. The latter prevents moisture from draining away. Known as **muskeg**, this surface ground is sometimes very boggy because it cannot drain.

Climate – Annual precipitation over much of the Territories is so low (Yellowknife 254mm/10in, Inuvik 276mm/11in, Baker Lake 208mm/8in, Iqaluit 409mm/16in) that a great part of the region would be desert if the permafrost did not cradle what moisture there is on the surface. Generally the winters are long, cold and dark and the summers surprisingly warm and sunny, with long hours of daylight. The southern part has 20 hours of daylight, while north, in the Arctic Circle, it never gets dark. The mean daily maximum temperatures for July are 21°C/70°F in Yellowknife, 19°C/66°F in Inuvik, 15°C/59°F in Baker Lake and 12°C/53°F in Iqaluit. The highest recorded temperature in July was 36°C/97°F in Fort Simpson; the lowest was –3°C/26°F in Holman, Victoria Island.

Aurora Borealis – Also known as the Northern Lights, this amazing phenomenon can usually be viewed in fall and winter. The sky "dissolves" into folded curtains of elusive, dancing lights, sometimes many coloured, other times black and white. They seem to occur when electrically charged particles, emitted by the sun, collide with atoms and molecules in the earth's outer atmosphere, causing the latter to emit radiation, sometimes in the form of visible light. Research on these displays is conducted at CHURCHILL, Manitoba.

©Pekka Paviainen/Dembinski Photo Assoc.

Aurora Borealis

Historical Notes

Earliest Settlement – The first inhabitants of North America came from Asia some 15,000–20,000 years ago, across the land bridge that is now the Bering Strait. They settled south of the ice cap that covered the continent. As it retreated, some moved north. Today these people form two distinct groups.

The Inuit – The life of the aboriginal people of the Arctic Coast revolved largely around hunting sea mammals—especially seal and whale—as a source of food; blubber for heat and light; skins for clothing, shelter and boats; and bone or ivory for the blades of their harpoons or other tools. The smaller sea mammals were hunted from **kayaks** (one-person canoes); whales were hunted from **umiaks**, which held up to 12 men. In winter animals were sought at openings in the ice. The occasional excursion south was made by **dogsled** to hunt caribou, the skins of which were used for clothing or bedding.

The Inuit were nomadic—several families living and moving together. In winter they constructed **igloos**, dome-shaped snow houses made of blocks of ice, and entered by a tunnel. For insulation, the interior was lined with skins. In summer they lived in tents made of skins. Time not spent hunting or making clothes—especially their famous parkas—was devoted to carving bone and soapstone, a craft for which they are famous today.

Since the arrival of Europeans their lifestyle has changed drastically: a nomadic way of life is practically nonexistent, and igloos and dogsleds are no longer commonplace. Many still live by hunting, however, supplemented by income from arts and crafts. On the whole they retain more of their traditional lifestyle than North America's other native cultures. The world's total Inuit population is estimated at 115,000. Over 6,700 of them inhabit their Quebec homeland of Nunavik *(see Michelin Green Guide to Quebec)*, a socio-cultural region established through grassroots referendum in 1986 and officially recognized by the provincial government. The creation of a homeland in the Northwest Territories *(Nunavut p 302)* should result in greater autonomy in the 21C for the Inuit of northern Canada.

The Dene – The Athapaskan-speaking peoples of the sub-Arctic lived a difficult life in a meagre environment. Travelling by canoe in summer and toboggan in winter, they hunted caribou and fished, constantly on the move to find food. Home was a conical-shaped lodge similar to the teepees of the Plains Indians *(p 22)*. Today some of these people have preserved a fairly traditional lifestyle based on hunting and fishing, but many live on the fringe of contemporary society.

The Northwest Passage – A sea route between the Atlantic and Pacific Oceans around the north of the American continent was the quest of explorers for centuries after it became obvious that America was a continent and not an adjunct of Asia. The first Europeans to visit this vast region came in search of a trade route to the Orient around the north of the continent. British sailor **Martin Frobisher** made the first attempt in 1576. His voyages were followed by those of **John Davis**, **Henry Hudson** and **William Baffin**, all of whom have left their names on the map, and Sir John Franklin's in 1845. Their reports of ice-filled seas somewhat dampened enthusiasm for the passage. Except for exploration at the western end, no more attempts were made until the early 19C.

Fur Traders – At the same time, other explorers were penetrating the interior of the Territories for skins of abundant fur-bearing animals. **Samuel Hearne** of the Hudson's Bay Company traversed much of the region, especially during his famous 1770-72 trip from CHURCHILL to Great Slave Lake, and later down the Coppermine River to the Beaufort Sea. Not long afterwards in 1789, **Alexander Mackenzie** of the rival North West Company travelled the river that bears his name. He named it the "river of disappointment": it led to the Arctic, not the Pacific Ocean, as he had hoped. After the two fur companies joined in 1821, several trading posts were established in the Territories, some of which remain to this day.

Naval Explorers – Mackenzie's voyage sparked new interest in a northwest passage. The first half of the 19C saw the British Navy equipping expeditions to find a navigable route. **John Franklin** made two overland trips to the western end, sailing a third time, in 1845, to locate the connecting channel from the east. Years passed with no word from him. Eventually a series of expeditions, 38 in all, were sent to discover his fate. It was established that he and his entire crew had perished after years of being marooned in the frozen waters. One effect of this tragedy was the exploration by his would-be rescuers of a large part of the Territories. Finally a passable route of the passage was found between the Canadian mainland and the

Arctic islands, but not successfully navigated until Norwegian **Roald Amundsen** did so between 1903 and 1906. Since then many ships have followed the hazardous route, among them the schooner *St. Roch (p 78)*.

20C Development – In the late 19C and early 20C, the Geological Survey of Canada mounted expeditions under such men as Joseph Burr Tyrrell, Sir William Logan (after whom Mt. Logan is named), George Mercer Dawson (of Dawson City fame) and Vilhjalmar Stefansson to explore and map the Territories. By this time both Anglican and Roman Catholic missionaries were established in the region. In the 1930s a new breed of explorer arrived—the prospector. Several major mineral finds *(below)* encouraged more outsiders to come to the Territories. Mineral as well as oil exploration has continued to attract investment.

Goods are transported to and from the Territories by the Mackenzie and Dempster Highways. Huge strings of barges float up and down the Mackenzie River all summer. Between November and April, winter roads crisscross the frozen land, giving heavy transport access to places reachable only by air the rest of the year.

Partitioning of the Territories – In 1992 the residents of the Northwest Territories voted to divide their land by creating a new territory in the eastern portion. Stretching 2,000,156sq km/772,260sq mi nearly to Greenland from the Manitoba/Saskatchewan border, this homeland has been designated **Nunavut** meaning "our land" in the native language, Inuktitut. After a seven-year transition period, Nunavut is to be administered by its Inuit inhabitants.

Population – Of the 57,649 inhabitants in the Northwest Territories, 59 percent claim aboriginal origin. Of these, about 21,000 are Inuit. (The well-known name *eskimo*, meaning "eaters of raw meat," was given to the Inuit by the Indians of the south. *Inuit* means "the people" in Inuktitut.) Another 9,800 are Dene or Athapaskan-speaking Indians. The rest are Métis and non-native residents.

Resources and Industries

Mining – Since the 1930s the basis of the economy has been mining. Fur trapping, forestry, fishing, tourism and the sale of native arts and crafts also contribute, but to a much lesser extent. Deposits of pitchblende—a source of uranium—and silver were discovered on the shores of the Great Bear Lake in 1930, arousing interest in the mineral possibilities of other regions, and leading to the great gold discoveries at YELLOWKNIFE. Today gold is still mined at Yellowknife, and at Indin Lake and at Contwoyto Lake farther north.

In 1964 the vast zinc and lead deposits at Pine Point on Great Slave Lake were found. These minerals are being mined at Nanisivik near Arctic Bay in the north of Baffin Island and on Little Cornwallis Island. The search for diamonds has become the principal focus of mineral exploration since their discovery in 1991 in the Lac de Gras area.

Oil and Gas – Near Fort Liard, there is a small natural gas extraction and processing plant, and producing oil wells and a refinery at Norman Wells on the Mackenzie. The 1968 discovery of major oil and gas fields in northern Alaska spurred the search for such resources in northern Canada. Two potentially rich areas were identified: the Mackenzie Delta–Beaufort Sea region, and the high Arctic islands. Most oil exploration has been confined to the MACKENZIE DELTA. Limited production and seasonal shipping continue from Bent Horn, the northernmost oil field in the high Arctic islands. Since 1985 lower oil prices have curtailed exploration and development. Recently, however, interest in oil and gas exploration north of the 60th parallel has revived since the lifting of a 25-year moratorium on issuing rights in the Mackenzie Valley.

Handicrafts – The arts and crafts of the native inhabitants as well as the natural beauty and abundant wildlife of the Territories are mainstays of its growing tourism. Largely because of their expressiveness and depiction of a disappearing lifestyle, the distinctive works produced by the aboriginal peoples have long been popular among collectors and connoisseurs. Most famous are the **sculptures** of the Inuit. The grey or green soapstone can easily be worked with chisels and files before being polished to give it a distinctive finish.

Delicate carvings are fashioned from walrus tusks, caribou antlers or whalebone. Wall hangings and prints are also produced. Cape Dorset on Baffin Island is especially famous for the latter. Clothing suited to this climate, particularly Inuit *parkas* and Indian *mukluks* decorated with beautiful beadwork, has become popular farther south.

PRACTICAL INFORMATION
Getting There

By Air – Regular service to Yellowknife is provided by Canadian Airlines International and its affiliates from major Canadian gateway cities ☎800-426-7000 (Canada/US). Scheduled and chartered service in the Northwest Territories is offered by First Air ☎613-839-3340, or 800-267-1247 (US), and NWT Air ☎403-920-2500.

General Information

Accommodations and Visitor Information – Every year the government of the Northwest Territories publishes the *Explorers' Guide*, which lists hotels, motels, lodges, camps and outfitters. For a free copy and road map, contact **Department of Economic Development & Tourism**, Box 1320, Yellowknife, NT, X1A 2L9 ☎403-873-7200 or 800-661-0788 (Canada/US).

Driving in the North – *(Driver's license and insurance requirements p 314.)* Roads have all-weather gravel surfaces and are well maintained. Motorists are cautioned to pass other vehicles slowly to prevent flying rocks or skidding. Unless otherwise posted, the speed limit is 100km/h (60mph). **Seat belt** use is mandatory. Distances between gasoline stations can be great; it is advisable to fill up frequently. It is recommended that motorists carry at least one spare tire, water, first-aid kit, emergency flares and, in winter, snow shovel, parka, warm clothes, and a sleeping bag for each person in the vehicle.

Government **ferry** service (free) is provided along the Mackenzie, Dempster and Liard Highways; for information ☎800-661-0751 (Canada). To access Yellowknife, the **Mackenzie Highway** crosses the river at Fort Providence. The **Dempster Highway** crosses the Mackenzie River at Arctic Red River and the Peel River to reach Fort McPherson. Near Fort Simpson the **Liard Highway**, which connects with the Alaska Highway, crosses the Liard River. There are ice bridges across these rivers in winter. During the three- to six-week freeze-up and thaw periods *(Nov & May)*, the rivers cannot be crossed.

Time Zones – The Northwest Territories span three time zones: Eastern Standard north of Quebec and Ontario, Central Standard north of Manitoba, and Mountain Standard north of Alberta, Saskatchewan and British Columbia. Daylight Saving Time is observed from the first Sunday in April to the last Sunday in October.

Taxes – There is no provincial sales tax, but the 7% GST *(rebate information p 318)* applies.

Liquor Laws – The legal drinking age is 19. Liquor, wine and beer are sold in government liquor stores in the larger communities. Some communities have voted for restrictions on liquor including prohibition of possession.

Provincial Holiday *(National Holidays p 319)*

Civic Holiday	1st Monday in August

Recreation – The Northwest Territories are a wonderland for outdoor enthusiasts. Charter planes transport hikers, fishermen and **canoeists** (with their canoes) to remote regions. The northern summer with its 20 or more hours of daylight makes a visit to this area a unique experience. Outfitters organize and equip wilderness travel year-round. One of the world's great canoe trips is down the **South Nahanni River** *(p 307)*, but other routes of varying degrees of difficulty are available. There are also opportunities for hiking, although this activity is less popular than canoeing in this land of rivers and lakes, with the exception of **Auyuittuq National Park Reserve** *(p 305)*. All wilderness travellers (including boaters, canoeists and hikers) are asked to register with the Royal Canadian Mounted Police detachment nearest their point of departure, and to notify the police when their trip is completed. Warm clothing, a sleeping bag and, beyond the tree line, a stove and fuel should be carried.

Wood Buffalo National Park *(map p 3)* harbours a large free-roaming herd of bison and is the last natural breeding habitat for the rare whooping crane. Owing to four North American flyways that pass through the park, the Peace-Athabasca Delta is well known for its abundance of geese, duck and other waterfowl. The park is open year-round; camping is available at Pine Lake. For details contact the Superintendent, Box 750, Fort Smith, NT, X0E 0P0 ☎403-872-7900.

Lodges are scattered on remote lakes and coasts from the Mackenzie Mountains to the fjords of Baffin Island, where **fishing** is superb (Arctic char, Arctic grayling, great northern pike among others). All non-resident hunters of big game (wolf, moose, caribou, Dall sheep, grizzly, black and polar bears) must be accompanied by a licensed outfitter. Details regarding seasons, package tours, accommodations, outfitters, wilderness excursions as well as hunting and fishing regulations can be obtained from the Department of Economic Development & Tourism *(p 303)*.

Special Excursions – Located 48km/30mi north of the Arctic Circle, **Bathurst Inlet Lodge** offers rafting and canoeing on Arctic rivers, fishing, guided hikes and outdoor natural-history interpretations mid-May–mid-Aug. Seven-day packages include air transportation from Yellowknife, accommodations, meals and guided excursions. For more information, schedules & reservations contact Bathurst Inlet Lodge, PO Box 820, Yellowknife, NT, X1A 2N6 ☎403-873-2595.

In 1986 a national park reserve was created in the northern corner of **Ellesmere Island**, accessible from Resolute Bay. Covering nearly 40,000sq km/15,000sq mi of mountains, glaciers, valleys and fjords, this reserve is the world's northernmost park (latitude 82°N). For information contact the Superintendent, Eastern Arctic District National Parks, Pangnirtung, NT X0A 0R0 ☎819-473-8828.

Principal Festivals

Mar	**Caribou Carnival**	*Yellowknife*
Jun	**Canadian North Yellowknife Midnight Classic**	*Yellowknife*
Jun/Jul	**Annual Midnight Sun Sea-Plane Fly-In**	*Yellowknife*
Jul	**Folk on the Rocks**	*Yellowknife*
	Annual Great Northern Arts Festival	*Inuvik*

Provincial abbreviations used in this guide, such as AB (Alberta), NS (Nova Scotia), PQ (Province of Quebec) and NT (Northwest Territories) are the official Canadian postal designations. A complete listing may be found on p 323.

BAFFIN ISLAND★★★

Pop. 11,385
Map of Principal Sights p 4

Named for British sailor **William Baffin**, who explored coastal waters between 1615 and 1616, the island is the largest, most inhabited and scenically spectacular in the Arctic archipelago. Its mountains rise more than 2,100m/7,000ft with numerous glaciers; its coasts are deeply indented with fjords. About two-thirds of the island lies north of the Arctic Circle (66.5°N) and in the continuous daylight of summer, the tundra blooms with an infinite variety of tiny, colourful flowers.

Most inhabitants are Inuit living in small settlements along the coasts. In some

Dan Heringa/ED&T/GNWT

respects their lifestyle remains traditional *(p 301)*, although they have adopted certain 20C ways (dress, housing, etc.). Their soapstone carvings, prints and lithographs are internationally renowned, especially those from **Cape Dorset**, a settlement on the west coast. The administrative centre and largest community is **Iqaluit** (eh-CALL-oo-it) (pop. 3,552)—formerly called Frobisher Bay—where most non-natives live.

Access – *Daily scheduled flights between Ottawa or Montreal and Iqaluit by First Air ☎800-267-1247 (Canada, US) and Air Inuit ☎514-636-9445; between Toronto and Iqaluit by Air Canada ☎800-661-0789 (Canada), 800-776-3000 (US); regular service between Iqaluit and other communities. Accommodations in Cape Dorset, Iqaluit, Pangnirtung and Pond Inlet.*

Inukshuk

SIGHTS

★★ **Pangnirtung** – Pop. 1,135. Dominated by the snow-capped mountains surrounding the Penny Ice Cap in Auyuittuq National Park Reserve, this little village occupies a spectacular **site★★** on the fjord of the same name. Situated just south of the Arctic Circle, Pangnirtung is an ideal spot for viewing the midnight "light" in summer (there is no sun at midnight, but it never gets dark). It is also a good place to study the tundra landscape and wildlife (small mammals, and some large sea mammals in Cumberland Sound) and to purchase locally woven goods, soapstone carvings and other specialities at the Inuit cooperative.

Even if a visit to the park itself is not planned, the **trip★** down the fjord to the park entrance by boat when the ice has melted *(Jul–Sept; one-way 1hr 30min; $75, if same-day return; warm clothing essential)* or by snowmobile the rest of the year is impressive. *Outfitters' services offered year-round; for information & reservations contact Angmarlik Centre in Pangnirtung;* ☎*819-473-8737.*

★★ **Auyuittuq National Park Reserve** – ✈ *Park headquarters are located in Pangnirtung. Park open year-round. Visitor centre open mid-May–Sept Mon–Fri 8:30am–9pm, weekends 8:30am–5pm. Rest of the year Mon–Fri 8:30am–5pm. Closed national holidays & weekends in winter. $15/day use fee.* ♿ ☎*819-473-8828.* A stark landscape of perpetual ice, jagged peaks of 2,000m/7,000ft and glacier-scarred valleys that become deep fjords along a coast of sheer cliffs (up to 900m/3,000ft high), *Auyuittuq* (ow-you-EE-took) means "land that never melts" in Inuktitut—an appropriate name

Auyuittuq National Park Reserve

for Canada's first national park north of the Arctic Circle. Fully one quarter of its 21,470sq km/8,290sq mi is covered by the **Penny Ice Cap**. Only lichens grow on rocks bared by the ice, but in the valleys, moss heath and a few dwarf shrubs thrive during the long hours of the Arctic summer.

Since its creation in 1972, the park has drawn climbers from all over the world to scale its rugged peaks. Backpackers and campers also come for the challenge of surviving this remote, yet breathtakingly grand landscape. The most visited region is **Pangnirtung Pass,** a huge U-shaped trench that stretches 96km/60mi across the peninsula and rises to 390m/1,280ft. By early July the pass is usually free of ice at the south entrance of Pangnirtung Fjord, and by late July, at North Pangnirtung Fjord, although some years the ice never melts. It can be crossed by properly equipped hikers accustomed to rough mountain terrain and prepared to ford frequent streams of glacial meltwater. There is constant wind, little shelter, and most of the route is on glacial moraine *(on average, 3km/2mi an hour maximum can be covered per day).* However, this is a spectacular trip for those willing to make the effort.

Pond Inlet – Pop. 974. Situated in the northern part of the island, this community overlooks the mountains of Bylot Island—summer home of thousands of snow geese—across the inlet of the same name. Soapstone and whalebone carvings as well as Inuit parkas and footwear can be purchased in the community.

MACKENZIE DELTA★★

Map of Principal Sights p 2

A labyrinth of channels among thousands of lakes 160km/100mi from the mouth of the Beaufort Sea, the 100km/70mi wide delta—one of the world's largest—fractures the northwest edge of the Territories' mainland. It is the estuary of the vast and fast-moving Mackenzie River, and the terminus of its 1,800km/1,100mi journey from the interior's Great Slave Lake.

One of the most prolific areas for wildlife in Canada's Arctic, the delta supports innumerable muskrats, beaver, mink, marten, fox, bear, moose, caribou and smaller mammals. Its channels and lakes abound with fish. Beluga whales calve in the warm waters, and migratory birds congregate here in the spring.

The livelihood of many of the inhabitants of the delta communities—Arctic Red River, Inuvik, Aklavik, Fort McPherson and Tuktoyaktuk—depends on trapping, hunting and fishing. However huge reserves of oil and gas discovered under the Beaufort Sea have impacted the area's economy in more recent times.

Access – *Dempster Highway from the Yukon (Dawson City to Inuvik 798km/496mi) open all year except during freeze-up and thaw periods, p 303). Few services on road. Motorists should be outfitted for emergencies (p 303). Also accessible by air from Edmonton via Yellowknife, and from Whitehorse, Yukon. The best way to appreciate the delta is to fly over it; charters can be arranged in Inuvik.*

VISIT

The Delta – Viewed from the air, this delta is an amazing place. The tangle of muddy arteries belonging to the Mackenzie and the Peel Rivers, which join at this point, can be distinguished from the lakes by their colour. The western edge is clearly marked by the frequently snow-capped **Richardson Mountains**, the eastern edge by the low, humped **Caribou Hills**. Heading north, the land seemingly gives way as the areas of water become greater, until the vast Beaufort Sea is reached and the land disappears completely from view.

Except for areas of tundra along the coast, the land is covered with low scrubs (dwarf willow and juniper) that turn bright yellow with the first frost (usually late August), a most attractive array. The tundra itself is full of lakes, and many colourful, multihued mosses, lichens and flowers bloom in the short but light (24 hours of daylight) Arctic summer.

Inuvik – Pop. 3,206. *On Dempster Hwy.; airport; accommodations.* Meaning "place of man" in Inuktitut, this outpost lies on a large stretch of flat land beside the east channel of the Mackenzie. A thriving community, Inuvik is an administrative centre of the territorial government.

In 1954 the government moved their administrative facilities here from Aklavik, which was frequently flooded. A model northern community was built and opened in 1959. Over the entire delta, the permafrost is only a few inches from the surface, causing problems for house building. The heat from a dwelling soon melts the ice, and residents find themselves living in a swamp. As a result, the houses were constructed on pilings, steamed into the permafrost before construction. Water, sewage and heating ducts are housed together in above-ground **utilidors**, or covered corridors, to keep them from freezing.

The **Roman Catholic Church** is built in the shape of an igloo. It features a marvellously expressive **interior★** with paintings of the Stations of the Cross done in 1960 by Mona Thrasher, then a young Inuit girl.

★ **Tuktoyaktuk** – Pop. 918. *Daily flights from Inuvik; ice road in winter; accommodations.* A former centre for oil and gas exploration in the region, this pleasant little community on the shores of the Beaufort Sea is known simply as "Tuk" to northerners. It is best known for one of nature's most curious phenomena: **pingos**, or huge moss- and turf-covered mounds of solid ice pushed out of the otherwise flat tundra by permafrost action. From the air, they resemble giant boils. Of the thousands in the Canadian North, the vast majority are located on the Tuktoyaktuk peninsula. At the **Fur Garment Shop**, visitors can observe Inuit women making parkas and other items of clothing.

"If some countries have too much history, we have too much geography."
William Lyon Mackenzie King, 1936

A wild, remote and staggeringly beautiful place in the southwest corner of the Territories, this park, extending over 4,700sq km/1,815sq mi, covers a large section of the South Nahanni River, which flows through the Selwyn, Mackenzie and Franklin Mountains before ultimately adding its waters to the Liard River, a tributary of the mighty Mackenzie. In 1978 UNESCO recognized the universal value of this reserve by designating it a World Heritage Site.

Historical Notes – Early in the 20C, tales of placer gold lured prospectors to the valley of the South Nahanni. In 1908 the headless bodies of two adventurers were found. Other men disappeared without trace. Stories of fierce native inhabitants and of mythical mountain men were spread abroad, and the South Nahanni became known as a place to avoid. The mystery remains and the legends are recalled by names in the park such as Deadmen Valley, Headless Range, Broken Skull River and Funeral Range. The park's very inaccessibility is part of its beauty. Unlike other national parks, it will probably never have roads and tourist facilities. But for those willing to make the effort, one of the world's great natural glories awaits.

Access by Road and Air – *From British Columbia: take Alaska Highway to Fort Nelson (p 37), Liard Highway to Fort Liard. From the Yukon: take Alaska Highway to Watson Lake (p 38). In the Northwest Territories: take Mackenzie Highway to Fort Simpson, or Liard Highway to Fort Liard. Air transportation available from Yellowknife, with NWT Air (☎403-920-2500) and Ptarmigan Airways (☎403-873-4461).*

Access by Water – *Various outfitters offer trips descending the river by rubber raft or canoe (equipment is flown in first). Intermediate white-water specialists can descend the river in their own canoe; permission must be obtained from the park first. For details contact the park (p 321) or the Economic Development & Tourism, Yellowknife, NWT (p 303).*

VISIT

☞ *Park open year-round. $10/day use fee (higher fees for overnight). Advance reservations required. For reservations and for details about fees, activities & outfitters contact Park Superintendent, Nahanni National Park Reserve, Box 348, Fort Simpson, NWT, X0E 0N0 ☎403-695-2310.*

★★★ **South Nahanni River** – For more than 320km/198mi, this serpentine waterway coils through the park, entering majestic canyons, cascading over a precipice twice the height of Niagara and passing a series of hot mineral springs that create surrounding vegetation unusual at this latitude (61°–62°N). Each year, this magnificent river attracts countless canoeists and raft-riders to its adventurous waters and wilderness beauty.

Nahanni National Park Reserve

Virginia Falls

The following describes highlights of a descent of the river. The 200km/125mi excursion downriver from Virginia Falls to Nahanni Butte is one of the world's great wilderness trips. Over this distance the river drops more than 120m/400ft (which is why canoeists generally prefer to descend it).

The jewel of the park and one of the North's most spectacular sights is **Virginia Falls★★★** *(illustration p 307)*. Parted by a central pointed rock at the precipice, volumes of water plunge 90m/294ft to the gorge below. The Albert Faille Portage can be followed around the falls *(1.6km/1mi)*. From it, a trail leads to the brink of the cataract where the river can be seen in spectacular rapids, just before it cascades over the rocks. Fourth Canyon is the first of four awesome canyons with immense cliffs and depths as great as 1,200m/3,900ft. Then come the surging waves of Figure of Eight Rapids. The river makes a 90-degree turn known as The Gate, guarded by mighty Pulpit Rock. Third Canyon is followed by the 34km/21mi stretch of Second Canyon. **Deadman Valley**, where headless bodies were found, separates Second Canyon from First Canyon, a twisting 27km/17mi channel. The river passes close to a hot spring where pools of water, at nearly 37°C/98°F, have caused ferns, chokecherries, rose bushes and flowering parsnip plants to proliferate. Before reaching Nahanni Butte, the river divides into a series of channels known as the **Splits**.

"I don't even know what street Canada is on."
Al Capone, 1931

YELLOWKNIFE★

Pop. 15,179
Map of Principal Sights p 2
Tourist Office ☎403-873-4262

The administrative capital of the Northwest Territories lies beside Yellowknife Bay on the northern shore of the Great Slave Lake. Almost completely surrounded by water, the city has a pretty site, set on pink granite, glacier-scarred rocks topped by small trees. A pleasant "old town" (c.1934) co-exists with a modern "new town," where most of the population lives, shops and works.

Historical Notes

Foundation of Gold – Named not for the colour of metal underlying it, but for the copper knives traded by local Indians, Yellowknife is a recent settlement. Its site was visited by Samuel Hearne in 1771, Alexander Mackenzie on his epic journey to the mouth of the river that bears his name, and John Franklin, all of whom were too preoccupied with their travels to notice the gold. Prospectors en route for the Klondike at the end of the 19C did record some sightings, but without pursuit. Not until the discovery of pitchblende in 1930 on the shores of the Great Bear Lake was there interest in the rest of the region. In 1934 exposed gold was found beside the bay and a boom town sprang up overnight.

The boom did not last, however, and the place was almost a ghost town in 1945 when new discoveries were made. The city is still thriving from this second boom. The mining and separating process is very expensive at the two operating mines, but the price of the yellow metal makes them economically viable. When the city became the territorial capital in 1967, Yellowknife's importance was finally acknowledged.

Midnight Twilight – The city lies just north of latitude 62° and thus in summer, experiences nearly 24 hours of daylight. Every year a golf tournament is held on the weekend closest to June 21. The tee-off commences at midnight. Among other hazards on a golf course that is largely sand are the enormous black ravens (depicted on the city's emblem) that delight in making off with the balls.

Yellowknife is also a good centre for boating, canoeing, fishing and camping. Its stores carry a fine selection of Dene and Inuit art and handicrafts.

Access – *By Rte. 3 and Mackenzie River ferry (free) in summer; "ice road" in winter. No road access during freeze-up and thaw periods (p 303). Also accessible by air from Edmonton, Winnipeg, Ottawa and Iqaluit.*

SIGHTS *1 day*

★★ **Prince of Wales Northern Heritage Centre** – *Entrance off Ingraham Trail. Open Jun–Aug Mon–Fri 10:30am–5:30pm, weekends noon–5pm. Rest of the year Tue–Fri 10:30am–5pm, weekends noon–5pm. Closed Jan 1 & Dec 25.* ✗ ⚐ ☎403-873-7551. Overlooking Frame Lake, this attractive museum is an important archaeological and ethnological research centre. It houses displays on the history of settlement of the Territories and a fine collection of Inuit sculpture. The ways of life of Dene and Inuit peoples are described, as are the reasons European settlers came to the North.

★ **Bush Pilots' Monument** – *Steps from Ingraham Dr. in Old Town.* Set on a rock that is the highest point in Yellowknife, this memorial honours the men who opened up the North. From this spot there is a splendid **panorama**★ of the city, the surrounding waters and rocky site. The red-topped tower of the Cominco gold mine dominates the skyline.

A hive of activity, the bay ripples with numerous small float planes arriving from the mining camps or departing with supplies for oil and gas exploration teams. Large black ravens can frequently be seen on the rocks.

From the old town, a causeway crosses to **Latham Island**, where houses perch on rocks and stilts. Here, a Dogrib Indian settlement and views of the Giant and Con gold mines can be seen.

Boat Trips – *Dinner cruises on Yellowknife Bay depart from Government Dock in Old Town first 3 weeks in Jun; round-trip 4 hrs; reservations required; $45. Also cruises (5–12 days) on the Mackenzie River (Jul) and Great Slave Lake (Aug); reservations required;* ✗ *Norweta Cruises* ☎403-873-2489. *For other excursions contact Northern Frontier Visitors Assn.* ☎403-873-4262. These cruises enable visitors to see portions of this enormous lake (28,930sq km/11,170sq mi), which is part of the Mackenzie River system and an important fishing area.

EXCURSIONS

Detah and the Ingraham Trail – These excursions by vehicle in the vicinity of the capital allow the visitor to see the landscape in this transitional area between boreal forest and tundra. The drive to Detah provides views of Yellowknife and its bay.

Detah – *Pop. 150. 25km/16mi.* This Dogrib Indian settlement has a fine **site**★ on flat rocks overlooking the Great Slave Lake.

Ingraham Trail – *64km/40mi to Reid Lake.* This all-weather road northwest of Yellowknife skirts five lakes—a paradise for campers and canoeists.

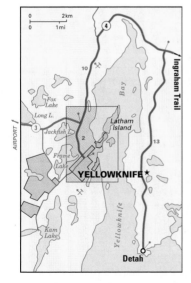

Watson Lake Signposts / Earl L. Brown

Practical Information

> The contents of this section pertain to the country as a whole. Practical information specific to Canada's **provinces** may be found in the regional introductions.
>
> Consult the pages shown for detailed information about:
>
> Queen Charlotte Islands *(p 52)*, Rocky Mountain Parks *(p 56)*, and the cities of **Montreal** *(p 213)*, **Toronto** *(p 174)*, **Vancouver** *(p 73)*.

Planning Your Trip

Tourist Offices – Official government tourist offices operated by provincial, municipal and regional agencies distribute road maps and brochures that give information on attractions, seasonal events, accommodations, adventure travel, sports and recreational activities. All publications are available free of charge *(see regional introductions for addresses)*. Information centres are indicated on the maps by the symbol **冏**.

Outside Canada – If unable to obtain tourist information from the above offices, foreign visitors can request tourist information from the Canadian Embassy or Consulate in their country of residence. For locations in the US and in other countries, contact the Tourist Department at the nearest Canadian Embassy, High Commission or Consulate or at those shown below.
Embassies of other countries are located in Canada's capital, Ottawa. Most foreign countries maintain **consulates** in Canada's regional capitals.

US	One CNN Center, South Tower, Atlanta, GA 30303	☎404-577-6810
	1251 Avenue of the Americas, New York, NY 10020	☎212-768-2400
	550 South Hope St., 9th floor, Los Angeles, CA 90071	☎213-346-2700
Australia	Quay West, 111 Harrington St., Sydney NSW 2000	☎2-364-3000
Germany	Prinz-Georg-Straße 126, Düsseldorf 40479	☎211-172170
United Kingdom	Canada House, Trafalgar Square, London SW1Y 5BJ	☎1-71-258-6346

Foreign Visitors – Citizens of the US visiting Canada need proof of citizenship (a valid **passport**, *or* a driver's license together with a birth certificate or a voter's registration card). Naturalized US citizens should carry their US naturalization certificate. Permanent residents of the US are advised to carry their Alien Registration Cards (US Form I-151 or Form I-551). Persons under 18 who are not accompanied by an adult should carry a letter from a parent or guardian stating name and duration of travel in Canada. Students should carry their ID.
All other visitors to Canada must have a valid passport and, in some cases, a **visa**. No vaccinations are necessary. For **entry into Canada via the US**, all persons other than US citizens or legal residents are required to present a valid passport. It is advisable to ask the Canadian Embassy, High Commission or Consulate in your home country about entry regulations and proper travel documents. Visitors who wish to return to the US after staying in Canada should check with the US Immigration and Naturalization Service.

Health Insurance – Before travelling, visitors should check with their insurance company to see if they have coverage for emergency **medical benefits** for doctor's visits, medication and hospitalization in Canada; otherwise supplementary insurance may be necessary. Liberty Health offers reimbursement for expenses as a result of emergencies under their *Visitors to Canada Plan*. The plan must be purchased before arrival, or within five days of arrival, in Canada. For details contact Liberty Health, 3500 Steeles Ave. East, Markham, ON, L3R 0X4 ☎800-268-3763 (Canada/US).

Canada Customs – Non-residents may import personal luggage temporarily without payment of duties. Persons of legal age as prescribed by the province or territory *(see regional introductions)* may bring into Canada duty-free 200 cigarettes, 50 cigars and some other forms of **tobacco** (contact Revenue Canada at address below). **Alcohol** is limited to 1.14 litres (40 imperial ounces) of wine or spirits, or 24 bottles (355ml or 12 ounces) of beer or ale. All **prescription drugs** should be clearly labelled and for personal use only; it is recommended that visitors carry a copy of the prescription.
Canada has stringent legislation on **firearms**. A firearm cannot be brought into the country for personal protection while travelling. Only long guns (no permit required) may be imported by visitors 18 years or older for hunting or sporting purposes. Certain firearms are prohibited entry; restricted firearms, which include

handguns, may only be imported with a permit by a person attending an approved shooting competition. For more information telephone the Automated Customs Information Service ☎416-973-8022 (Toronto) or 604-666-0545 (Vancouver) or write Revenue Canada, Customs and Excise, Ottawa, ON, K1A 0L5.

Most animals, except domesticated dogs and cats, must be issued a Canadian import permit prior to entry into Canada. **Pets** must be accompanied by an official certificate of vaccination against rabies from the country of origin. Payment of an inspection fee may be necessary. For details, contact Agriculture and Agri-Food Canada, Animal Health Division, Ottawa, ON, K1A 0Y9 ☎613-952-8000.

Disabled Travellers – *Wheelchair access is indicated in this guide by ♿ symbol.* Most public buildings and many attractions, restaurants and hotels provide wheelchair access. Disabled parking is provided and the law is strictly enforced. For details contact the provincial tourist office *(see regional introductions).*

To obtain a guide for travel planning entitled *Handi-Travel,* write to Easter Seals/ March of Dimes, Suite 511, 90 Eglinton Ave. East, Toronto, ON, M4P 2Y3 ☎416-932-8382. Prepayment of $12.95 plus $3 postage is required for all orders.

Currency Exchange – *See "Money" p 318.*

When to Go

Climate – Climatic conditions vary greatly throughout Canada *(for climate information see regional introductions).* Daily weather reports by Environment Canada are available through television, radio and newspapers.

Seasons – From mid-March to mid-May, visitors can enjoy comfortable daytime temperatures but chilly nights in the **spring**; in some areas, spring skiing is still possible. Ontario, Quebec and New Brunswick celebrate the harvest of maple syrup with sugaring-off parties.

Most visitors go to Canada during the **summer** season, extending from the last weekend in May (Victoria Day) to the first weekend in September (Labour Day). July and August are considered peak season and are ideal for outdoor activities such as sailing, kayaking, canoeing or hiking. Hot and often humid days with temperatures ranging from 22°-32°C/70°-90°F can be enjoyed in most provinces. May and September are pleasant months with warm days but cool evenings. However, many tourist attractions have curtailed visiting hours, and it is advisable to phone ahead. The southern regions along the Canada/US border offer spectacular displays of **fall** colours from mid-September until early October.

For the sports enthusiast, the Canadian **winter**, generally from mid-November to mid-March, offers excellent opportunities to enjoy numerous winter activities such as downhill skiing, cross-country skiing and snowmobiling. Most provinces experience heavy snowfall. Main highways are snowploughed, but vehicles should be winterized and snow tires are recommended.

Note: The extreme northern regions of Canada are most accessible during July and August since the temperature rises above 0°C/32°F for only a few months each year.

Mia et Klaus/Tourisme Québec

Getting There

From the US – American carriers offer **air** service to Canada's major airports. Air Canada ☎800-776-3000 (US) and Canadian Airlines International ☎800-426-7000 (Canada/US) fly from larger US cities. Amtrak offers daily **rail** service to Montreal from Washington DC and New York City, as well as from New York City to Toronto. Aside from these direct routes, connections are offered from many major US cities. For schedules in the US ☎800-872-7245. **Bus** travel from the US is offered by Greyhound. For information and schedules call the local US bus terminal. It is advisable to book well in advance when travelling during peak season.

From Overseas – Major airports in Canada serviced by international airlines are: Calgary, Edmonton, Halifax, Montreal, Ottawa, St. John's, Toronto, Vancouver and Winnipeg. Air Canada and Canadian Airlines International offer service to all major European cities, Latin America and the Middle East. Vancouver is the gateway city offering connections to Australia, New Zealand and the Far East.

Getting Around

Given Canada's enormous size, it is impossible to cover all of the country during one visit. *See regional driving tours (pp 6-13) for several two- to three-week itineraries.*

By Air – Domestic air service is offered by Canada's two national airlines: **Air Canada** (consult the local telephone directory in Canada; the US ☎800-776-3000) and **Canadian Airlines International** (☎800-426-7000 Canada/US) as well as affiliated regional airlines. Air service to remote areas is provided by many charter companies. Contact the provincial tourist office *(see regional introductions).*

By Train – **VIA Rail**, Canada's extensive rail network, traverses the country with 18 major routes from coast to coast. First-class, coach and sleeping accommodations are available on transcontinental, regional and intercity trains. Amenities offered are dome cars, dining cars and lounges, baggage handling (including bicycles), reservation of medical equipment, wheelchairs and preboarding aid with 24hr minimum notice. Unlimited train travel for 12 to 15 days within a 30-day period is available systemwide through **Canrailpass** (mid-May to mid-Oct, 12 days $535, 15 days $676; off-season, 12 days $365, 15 days $455). Special rates are offered for advance purchase, youth and senior citizens.

Reservations should be made well in advance, especially during summer months and on popular routes like Edmonton to Vancouver. Canada's legendary cross-country train, *The Canadian,* travels the almost 4,467km/2,700mi from Toronto to Vancouver in four days (one-way $488 plus sleeping accommodation surcharge). For information and schedules in Canada contact the nearest VIA Rail office. In the US call VIA Rail ☎ 800-561-3949.

VIA Rail general sales agents abroad are:		☎
Australia	Walshes World, 92 Pitt St., Sydney	2-232-7499
Germany	Canada Reisedienst, Rathausplatz 2, Ahrensburg	4102-51167
United Kingdom	Long-Haul Leisurail, Peterborough	1733-335599

By Bus – Long-distance buses reach almost every corner of Canada. Greyhound Canada Transportation Corp., 877 Greyhound Way SW, Calgary, AB, T3C 3V8 operates the only trans-Canadian service and offers **Canada Travel Passes**, which are sold internationally. Unlimited travel from 7 days up to 30 days is available. Peak season rates range from $197 to $329 (reduced rates during off-season and for senior citizens). For fares and schedules call Greyhound ☎800-661-8747 *(Canada only)*; in the US, call the local bus terminal. Voyageur Colonial services most of western Quebec and eastern Ontario and offers a 15-day **Rout-Pass** for travel from May 1–October 31 ($195) ☎416-393-7911 or 514-842-2281. Other regional companies supplement Canada's extensive motorcoach service *(see the yellow pages of local telephone directories).*

By Car – Canada has an extensive system of well-maintained major roads. In the northern regions and off main arteries, however, many roads are gravel or even dirt. Extreme caution should be taken when travelling these roads.

Foreign **driver's licenses** are valid for varying time periods depending on the province. Drivers must carry vehicle **registration** information and/or rental contract at all times. Vehicle **insurance** is compulsory in all provinces (minimum liability is $200,000, except $50,000 in Quebec). US visitors should obtain a Canadian

Non-Resident Inter-Province Motor Vehicle Insurance Liability Card (**yellow card**), available from US insurance companies. For additional information contact the Insurance Bureau of Canada, 181 University Ave., Toronto, ON, M5H 3M7 ☎416-362-2031.

Gasoline is sold by the litre (1 gallon = 3.78 litres); prices vary from province to province. All distances and speed limits are posted in kilometres (1mile =1.6 kilometre). During winter it is advisable to check road conditions before setting out. **Snow tires** and an **emergency kit** are imperative. Studded tires are permitted without seasonal limitations in Alberta, Saskatchewan, Yukon and the Northwest Territories, and are allowed in winter in some provinces.

Road Regulations – The **speed limit** on divided highways, unless otherwise posted, is 100km/h (60mph). The speed limit on rural highways is 80km/h (50mph) to 90km/h (55mph); in urban areas 50km/h (30mph). Service stations that are open 24 hours can be found in large cities and along major highways. The use of **seat belts** is mandatory for all drivers and passengers. On Yukon highways, driving with headlights on at all times is required by law. Most provinces prohibit **radar detection devices** in vehicles. Traffic in both directions must stop (except on divided roads) for a yellow school bus when signals are flashing. In all provinces except Quebec, **right turns on red** are allowed after coming to a complete stop. Information on highway conditions in each province can be obtained by contacting the regional Ministry of Transportation *(check the blue pages in the local telephone directories)*.

In Case of Accident – If you are involved in an accident resulting in property damage and/or personal injury, you must notify the local police and remain at the scene until dismissed by investigating officers. For assistance contact the local Government Insurance Corporation. First aid stations are clearly designated along highways.

Canadian Automobile Association (CAA) – This national motor club (1145 Hunt Club Rd., Ottawa, ON, K1V 0Y3 ☎613-247-0117) offers, through the offices of its member clubs, services such as travel information, maps and tour books, accommodation reservations, insurance, technical and legal advice, road and weather conditions. These benefits are extended to members of the American Automobile Association (AAA), clubs of the Commonwealth Motoring Conference (CMC), Alliance Internationale de Tourisme (AIT), Fédération Internationale de l'Automobile (FIA), the Federation of Interamerican Touring and Automobile Clubs (FITAC) and other affiliated clubs. Proof of membership must be presented. The CAA maintains for its members a 24hr emergency road service ☎800-222-HELP *(see regional introductions for CAA listings)*.

Rental Cars – Most major rental car agencies have offices at airports and in large cities in Canada. Minimum age for rental is usually 25. To avoid a large cash deposit, payment by credit card is recommended. More favourable rates can sometimes be obtained by making a reservation before arriving in Canada, but be aware of drop-off charges.

Avis	☎800-331-1212	Hertz	☎800-654-3131
Budget	☎800-527-0700	Tilden	☎800-227-7368

By Ferry – Canada maintains an extensive ferry-boat system. Contact the regional tourist offices for information and schedules *(see regional introductions for details)*.

Precautions

▲ Although Canada experiences severe winters, many regions are afflicted by hordes of biting insects in the summer. Late May to June is black-fly season and in July the mosquitoes arrive. For outdoor activities, insect repellent is a must.

▲ Sturdy footwear with nonslip soles is recommended for hiking.

▲ To protect against surprise storms or cool mountain evenings, carry raingear and warm clothing.

Accommodations

Canada offers accommodation suited to every taste and pocketbook from luxury hotels in major cities, roadside motels, quaint B&Bs in the countryside, hunting and fishing lodges in remote wilderness areas, farm and country vacation houses to campsites and resorts. Many resorts operate year-round offering tennis, golf and water-sports facilities; winter activities include downhill skiing, cross-country skiing and snowmobiling.

Government tourist offices supply listings (free) that give locations, phone numbers, types of service, amenities, prices and other details (*see regional introductions for addresses*). Canada is a vast country, and in less populated regions it may be difficult to find accommodations at the end of a long day's drive. Advance reservations are recommended especially during the tourist season (Victoria Day to Labour Day). During the off-season, establishments outside urban centers may be closed; it is therefore advisable to telephone ahead. Guaranteeing reservations with a credit card is recommended. However, in remote areas, credit cards may not be accepted.

Hotels – Major hotel chains with locations throughout Canada are:

	☎ in Canada	☎ in the US
Canadian Pacific Hotels & Resorts	800-441-1414	800-828-7447
Delta Hotels	800-268-1133	800-877-1133
Four Seasons Hotels	800-268-6282	800-332-3442
Hilton	800-445-8667	800-445-8667
Holiday Inn	800-465-4329	800-465-4329
Radisson International	800-333-3333	800-333-3333
Sheraton Hotels	800-325-3535	800-325-3535
Ramada International	800-228-2828	800-228-2828
Hotel Novotel	800-221-4542	800-221-4542
Best Western International	800-528-1234	800-528-1234
Westin Hotels	800-228-3000	800-228-3000

The above-listed hotels, mostly located in large urban areas, offer a full range of facilities and amenities designed for business people as well as for vacationers. Prices are higher during the summer months. In resort areas, the ski season is also considered high season. Expect to pay more in large cities and resorts. However, many hotels offer packages and weekend specials that are worth investigating.

Motels – Along major highways or close to urban areas motels such as Comfort Inn (☎ 800-221-2222), Relax Inns (☎ 800-667-3529), Days Inn (☎ 800-325-2525) and Choice Hotels (☎800-668-4200) offer accommodations at moderate prices ($67-$115), depending upon the location. Amenities include television, restaurants and swimming pools. Family-owned establishments and small, independent guest houses that offer basic comfort can be found all across Canada.

Bed & Breakfasts and Country Inns – B&Bs and country inns can be found in cities as well as in the countryside. Most are privately owned and can be housed in an an elegant Georgian mansion, a Victorian homestead, an old mill, a restored farmhouse, a country estate or a cozy cottage by the sea. A continental breakfast is usually included in the room rate. A private bath is not always offered. Some have restaurants. Room rates vary according to the location and amenities offered ($25-$150). Some accept major credit cards, but it is advisable to check at the time the reservation is placed (*see regional introductions for reservation services*).

Hostels – Hostelling International-Canada, affiliated with the International Youth Hostel Federation, offers a network of budget accommodations from coast to coast. Hostels provide basic accommodations such as separate dormitory-style rooms (blankets and pillows are provided), shared bath, social areas, laundry facilities and self-service kitchens for $9-$22.50/night per person. Many hostels provide private room facilities as well. In some resort areas outdoor saunas, swimming pools, interpretive programs, theatre workshops and other amenities are offered.

Advance booking is advisable during peak travel times; walk-ins are welcome. Membership is $25/year, but nonmembers are also admitted. To obtain an application or further information, contact Hostelling International-Canada, 205 Catherine St. Suite 400, Ottawa, ON K2P 1C3 ☎613-237-7884.

Universities and Colleges – Most universities make their dormitory space available to travellers during summer vacation (May–August). Rates average $20-$35/day per person. Reservations are accepted. For more information contact the local tourist office or the university directly.

Tourisme Québec

Farm Vacations/Guest Ranches – Farm and ranch lodgings are rustic and especially suited for families with children. The visitor is a paying guest on a working farm, and participation in daily activities depends on the host's preference. Meals are included and are taken with the host family. Guest ranches may be located in rugged country but holiday packages usually include comfortable accommodations and hearty meals. A variety of activities such as hiking, trail riding and campfire gatherings can be enjoyed by the whole family.

Camping – Canada has excellent campgrounds that are operated privately or by the federal and provincial governments. Government sites are located in the many national and provincial parks. Fees are nominal. These campgrounds are well equipped and fill up quickly *(for description of national park campgrounds see p 320)*. Commercially operated campgrounds, often located adjacent to national parks and provincial parks, are more costly but offer amenities such as electrical and water hookups, bathrooms with showers, restaurants, recreational facilities, grocery stores and gas stations. For a list of campgrounds contact the provincial tourist office *(see regional introductions for addresses)*.

Fishing Camps, Fly-in Lodges and Wilderness Camps – Canada offers the experienced angler or the outdoor enthusiast a variety of fishing lodges and camps, some of which are so remote, they can only be reached by private boat or plane. Outfitters offer packages that include transportation, accommodations, meals, supplies, equipment and expeditions led by experienced guides.
Wilderness camps located in Canada's northern regions offer all-inclusive hunting packages. Non-residents must be accompanied by licensed guides. Permits can be obtained through the outfitter, who can also assist with game registration (required by law).
These packages are costly and the number of spaces is usually limited. It is advisable to make reservations well in advance. For information on fishing and hunting regulations and license fees, as well as listings of outfitters, contact the provincial tourist office *(see regional introductions)*.

Tourisme Québec

General Information

Business Hours – Business hours are Monday to Friday 9am–5pm. In general, retail stores are open Monday to Friday 9am–6pm (until 9pm Thursday and Friday), and Saturday 9am–5pm. However, depending on local laws, many neighbourhood stores that sell groceries, small personal items and newspapers remain open in the evenings and on Sundays.

Electricity – 110 volts, 60 cycles. Most small American appliances can be used. European appliances require an electrical transformer, available at electric supply stores.

Language – Canada practises institutional bilingualism: English and French are the official languages for all federal and judicial bodies, federally mandated administrative agencies and crown corporations. The practice has spread to provincial governments and some parts of the private sector. However, in Quebec province the official language is French.

Liquor Laws – Each province abides by different liquor laws, which are strictly enforced *(see regional introductions)*. The legal blood alcohol limit is 0.08%.

Mail – Post offices across Canada are generally open Monday to Friday 8am–5:30pm; extended hours are often available in cities with large populations. Sample rates for first-class mail are: letter (up to 30 grams) or postcard within Canada 45 cents, to the US (up to 30 grams) 52 cents; international mail (up to 20 grams) 90 cents. Visitors can receive mail c/o "General Delivery" addressed to Main Post Office, City, Province and Postal Code. Mail will be held for 15 days and has to be picked up by the addressee. Post offices have fax services and international courier service.

Metric System – Canada has partially adopted the International System of weights and measures. Weather temperatures are given in Celsius (C°), milk and wine are sold by millilitres and litres, and grocery items are measured in grams. All distances and speed limits are posted in kilometres (to obtain the equivalent in miles, multiply by .6). Some examples of metric conversions are:

1 kilometre (km)	=	0.6 miles
1 metre (m)	=	3.3 feet
1 kilogram (kg)	=	2.2 pounds
1 litre (L)	=	33.8 fluid ounces = 0.26 gallons
		(1 US quart = 32 fluid ounces)

Money – Canadian currency is based on the decimal system (100 cents to the dollar). Bills are issued in $5, $10, $20, $50, $100, $500 and $1,000 denominations; coins are minted in 1 cent, 5 cents (nickel), 10 cents (dime), 25 cents (quarter), 50 cents (half a dollar), $1 and $2. It is recommended that visitors exchange money at banking institutions to receive the most favourable exchange rate.

Banks – Banking institutions are generally open Monday to Friday 9am–5pm. Some banks are open on Saturday morning. Banks at large airports have foreign exchange counters and extended hours. Traveller's cheques in Canadian or American currency are accepted universally. Some institutions may charge a small fee for cashing traveller's cheques. Most principal bank cards are honored at affiliated Canadian banks.

Credit Cards – The following major credit cards are accepted in Canada: American Express, Carte Blanche, Discover, Diners Club, MasterCard/Eurocard and Visa.

Currency Exchange – Although US dollars are usually accepted in Canada, visitors should exchange their money for Canadian currency. The most favourable exchange rate can usually be obtained at branch offices of a national bank or other financial institution. Some banks charge a small fee for this transaction. Private exchange companies generally charge higher fees. Airports and visitor centres in large cities may have exchange outlets as do some hotels; however, it is advisable to first check the prevailing rate at local banks. The Canadian dollar fluctuates with the international money market. At press time, $1.33 Canadian equalled US $1.

Exchange facilities tend to be limited in rural and remote areas. If arriving in Canada late in the day or on a weekend, visitors may wish to exchange some funds prior to arrival (a few banks are open on Saturday mornings in major cities, however).

Taxes and Tips – Canada levies a 7% Goods and Services Tax (GST) on most goods and services. Foreign visitors can request a cash **rebate** of up to $500 for short-term accommodations and, for most consumer goods taken out of Canada, by submitting original receipts and identification to any participating Canadian Duty Free Shop or by mail. Rebate claims above $500 must be mailed with an application and original receipts. Provincial sales taxes vary, and are refundable in some provinces (*see regional introductions*). For additional information and rebate forms contact: Revenue Canada, Visitor Rebate Program, 275 Pope Rd., Summerside, PEI C1N 6C6, ☎800-668-4748 (in Canada) or 902-432-5608.

Tips or service charges are not normally added to a bill in Canada. However, it is customary to give 10-15% of the total amount.

National Holidays – *For provincial holidays see regional introductions.* The following holidays are observed throughout Canada. Most banks, government offices and schools are closed:

New Year's Day	January 1
Good Friday	Friday before Easter Sunday
Easter Monday	Monday after Easter Sunday
Victoria Day	3rd Monday in May
Canada Day	July 1
Labour Day	1st Monday in September
Thanksgiving	2nd Monday in October
Remembrance Day	2nd Wednesday in November
Christmas Day	December 25
Boxing Day	December 26

Telephones – To call long distance within Canada and to the US, dial 1+ Area Code +number. For overseas calls, dial "0" for operator assistance. All operators speak English and French. Collect calls and credit card calls can be made from public pay phones. For local directory assistance, check the white pages of the phone directory; outside the local area code dial 1+ Area Code + 555-1212. Most 800 numbers are toll-free. A local call costs 25 cents. Visitors should be aware that many hotels place a surcharge on all calls.

Emergency Numbers – **911** service is operative in many major cities; otherwise dial "0" for the operator and ask for the police. In most provinces a Tourist Alert Program is operated by the Royal Canadian Mounted Police from June until September. If you see your name in the newspaper or hear it on the radio, contact the nearest RCMP office immediately.

Time Zones – Canada spans six time zones, but the coast-to-coast time difference is only 4hrs 30min because Newfoundland time is 30min in advance of the Maritime provinces, which are on Atlantic Time. Daylight Saving Time (clocks are advanced 1 hour) is in effect from the first Sunday in April to the last Sunday in October (*see regional introductions for details*).

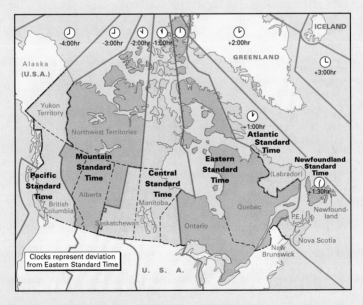

National Parks and Reserves

Since the creation of the first national park in Banff in 1885, the amount of protected land overseen by Parks Canada has grown to 208,126sq km/80,357sq mi. Canada's 30 national parks and 7 national park reserves offer the visitor spectacular scenery, a wealth of wildlife and fauna, as well as unlimited recreational opportunities.

More than 15 million people visit the parks each year. Most points of interest are in the southern national parks, accessible by car. Well-marked hiking trails permit outdoor enthusiasts and novices alike to enjoy the backcountry. Parks are open year-round; however, some roads may be closed during the winter. Daily **entry fees** range from $2.50-$5 per adult. Discounts are offered at some parks to senior citizens (25%) and children (50%). Fees are charged for camping, fishing and guided programs.

Visitor centres (open daily late May–Labour Day; reduced hours the rest of the year) are usually located at park entrances. Staff are available to help visitors plan activities. Trail maps and literature on park facilities, hiking trails, nature programs, camping and in-park accommodations are available on-site free of charge. Interpretation programs, guided hikes, exhibits and self-guided trails introduce the visitor to each park's history, geology and habitats. *For a listing of in-park activities see the appropriate section within each province.*

Activities and Facilities – All **hikers** are required to register at the park office before setting out and to deregister upon completion of the trip. It is a good idea to ask park officials about trail conditions, weather forecasts and safety precautions. Trail distances are given from trailhead to destination, not round-trip, unless otherwise posted. Topographic maps and a compass are indispensable for backcountry hiking. To obtain topographic maps contact Canada Map Office, 615 Booth St., Ottawa, ON, K1A 0E9 ☎800-465-6277 (Canada/US).

Licenses are required for **fishing** and can be obtained from the park office, sporting goods stores or other retail businesses. Some parks offer boat and canoe rentals. Hunting is not permitted within the national parks.

Most park **campgrounds** are open mid-May through Labour Day, and operate on a first-come, first-served basis. Dates are subject to change, and it is recommended that visitors check with the park superintendent for rates and maximum length of stay. Some parks offer reservation services and some offer winter camping. Usually campsites include a level tent pad, picnic table, fireplace or fire grill with firewood, and parking space close to a water source. Most have toilet buildings and kitchen shelters. Some campgrounds are for tents only, while others allow recreational vehicles. Most campgrounds do not have trailer hookups, but many have sewage disposal stations. Many accommodate persons with disabilities. In some locations, certain equipment restrictions apply. Primitive campgrounds, located near hiking trails in the backcountry, can be reached only on foot.

Contact the headquarters of Parks Canada, Department of Canadian Heritage, Hull, PQ, K1A 0M5 ☎819-997-0055 or the individual park *(see listing below)* to obtain additional information and descriptive brochures on services, including outfitters and activities.

Black Bear

A word of caution – Bears and other large animals may be present in many of Canada's national parks. Human encounters with them may result in serious injury. Visitors are asked to respect **wildlife** and observe park rules: don't hike alone; do not take along a dog; stay in open areas wherever possible; never go near a bear or bear cub; keep campsites clean; and store food away from tent or in the trunk of your car. Avoid **hypothermia**. Beware of wind, dampness and exhaustion in regions where weather changes rapidly; carry weatherproof clothing, plastic sheeting and nylon twine for emergency shelter; and eat high-calorie foods.

National Parks and Reserves   ☎

Alberta Regional Office
Box 2989, 220 Fourth Ave. SE, Calgary, AB, T2G 4X3 — 403-292-4401
Banff (*p 57*)
Box 900, Banff, AB, T0L 0C0 — 403-762-1500
Elk Island
Site 4, RR1, Fort Saskatchewan, AB, T8L 2N7 — 403-992-2950
Jasper (*p 65*)
Box 10, Jasper, AB, T0E 1E0 — 403-852-6161
Waterton Lakes (*p 89*)
Waterton, AB, T0K 2M0 — 403-859-2224

Pacific and Yukon Regional Office
300 West Georgia St., Suite 300, Vancouver, BC V6B 6C6 — 604-666-0176
Glacier (*p 49*)
Box 350, Revelstoke, BC, V0E 2S0 — 250-837-7500
Gwaii Haanas (*p 54*)
Box 37, Queen Charlotte, BC, V0T 1S0 — 250-559-8818
Ivvavik
Box 1840, Inuvik, NT, X0E 0T0 — 403-979-3248
Kluane (*p 96*)
Box 5495, Haines Junction, YT, Y0B 1L0 — 403-634-7250
Kootenay (*p 68*)
Box 220, Radium Hot Springs, BC, V0A 1M0 — 250-347-9615
Mount Revelstoke (*p 48*)
Box 350, Revelstoke, BC, V0E 2S0 — 250-837-7500
Pacific Rim (*p 83*)
Box 280, Ucluelet, BC, V0R 3A0 — 250-726-7721
Yoho (*p 61*)
Box 99, Field, BC, V0A 1G0 — 250-343-6324

Prairies and Northwest Territories Regional Office
457 Main St. 9th Floor, Winnipeg, MB, R3B 3G7 — 204-983-3601
Aulavik (Banks Island)
General Delivery, Sachs Harbour, NT, X0T 0T0 — 403-979-3248
Auyuittuq (*p 305*)
PO Box 353, Pangnirtung, NT, X0A 0R0 — 819-473-8828
Ellesmere Island (*p 304*)
PO Box 353, Pangnirtung, NT, X0A 0R0 — 819-473-8828
Grasslands
PO Box 150, Val Marie, SK, S0N 2T0 — 306-298-2257
Nahanni (*p 307*)
Postal Bag 300, Fort Simpson, NT, X0E 0N0 — 403-695-3151
Prince Albert (*p 117*)
PO Box 100, Waskesiu Lake, SK, S0J 2Y0 — 306-663-5322
Riding Mountain (*p 120*)
Wasagaming, MB, R0J 2H0 — 204-848-7275
Wood Buffalo (*p 303*)
PO Box 750, Fort Smith, NT, X0E 0P0 — 403-872-2349

Ontario Regional Office
5160 Yonge St., Suite 500, North York, ON, M2N 6L9 — 800-839-8221
Bruce Peninsula (*p 140*)
PO Box 189, Tobermory, ON, N0H 2R0 — 519-596-2233
Fathom Five National Marine Park (*p 140*)
PO Box 189, Tobermory, ON N0H 2R0 — 519-596-2233

Georgian Bay Islands *(p 140)*
PO Box 28, Honey Harbour, ON, P0E 1E0 705-756-2415
Point Pelee *(p 165)*
RR No. 1, Leamington, ON, N8H 3V4 519-322-2365
Pukaskwa *(p 135)*
PO Box 39, Heron Bay, ON, P0T 1R0 807-229-0801
St. Lawrence Islands *(p 146)*
Box 469, Mallorytown Landing, ON, K0E 1R0 613-923-5261

Quebec Regional Office
3 Buade St., Haute Ville, Quebec, PQ, G1R 4V7 418-648-4177
Forillon *(p 207)*
CP 1220, Gaspé, PQ, G0C 1R0 418-368-5505
Mauricie *(p 234)*
Box 758, Shawinigan, PQ, G9N 6V9 819-536-2638
Mingan Archipelago *(p 203)*
CP 1180, Havre-Saint-Pierre, PQ, G0G 1P0 418-538-3331
Saguenay–St. Lawrence Marine Park
Box 220, Tadoussac, PQ, G0T 2A0 418-235-4703

Atlantic Regional Office
Upper Water St., Halifax, NS, B3J 1S9 902-426-3436
Cape Breton Highlands *(p 268)*
Ingonish Beach, NS, B0C 1L0 902-285-2270
Fundy *(p 248)*
PO Box 40, Alma, NB, E0A 1B0 506-887-6000
Gros Morne *(p 287)*
PO Box 130, Rocky Harbour, NF, A0K 4N0 709-458-2417
Kejimkujik *(p 260)*
PO Box 236, Annapolis, NS, B0T 1B0 902-242-2772
Kouchibouguac *(p 242)*
Kouchibouguac, Kent County, NB, E0A 2A0 506-876-2443
Prince Edward Island *(p 280)*
2 Palmers Lane, Charlottetown, PE, C1A 5V6 902-672-6370
Terra Nova *(p 297)*
Glovertown, NF, A0G 2L0 709-533-2801

Good references for planning a visit to Canada's national parks are: **The Outdoor Traveller's Guide Canada** by David Dunbar *(Stewart, Tabori & Chang, 1991).*

In addition to the national parks, there are over 600 **provincial parks** to explore. More than 100 **national historic sites**, such as the French fortress of Louisbourg *(p 275),* the site of one of the oldest European settlements in Canada *(p 260)* and homes of several Canadian prime ministers, can be found from coast to coast. Designed for daytime visit only, most sites are open from Victoria Day to Labour Day, with reduced hours in the early spring and fall. Some charge a nominal admission fee. At many of these sites interpretation centres and costumed guides provide insight into Canada's history and cultural heritage. For more information contact the appropriate regional office of the Parks Canada.

Barren-ground Caribou

Index

The principal sights in Montreal, Toronto and Vancouver are listed separately as are National Parks and Provincial Parks. Place names appear with the following abbreviations: AB Alberta, BC British Columbia, MB Manitoba, NB New Brunswick, NF Newfoundland, NS Nova Scotia, NT Northwest Territories, ON Ontario, PE Prince Edward Island, PQ Quebec, QCI Queen Charlotte Islands, SK Saskatchewan, YT Yukon Territory. **Maps** are listed on page 13.